ARCHITECTURAL CONSERVATION IN ASIA

At a time when organized heritage protection in Asia is developing at a rapid pace, *Architectural Conservation in Asia* provides the first comprehensive overview of architectural conservation practice from Afghanistan to the Philippines. The country-by-country analysis adopted by the book draws out local insights, experiences, best practice and solutions for effective cultural heritage management that will inform study and practice both in Asia and beyond.

Whereas architectural conservation in much of the Western world has been extensively documented, this book brings together coverage of many regions where architectural conservation has been understudied. Following on from the highly influential companion volumes on global architectural conservation and architectural conservation in Europe and the Americas, with this book the authors extend their pioneering global examination to the dynamic and evolving field of architectural conservation in Asia.

Throughout the book, the authors and regional experts provide local case studies and profile topics that bring depth and insight to this ambitious study. As architectural conservation becomes increasingly global in practice, this book will be of considerable assistance to architectural conservation practitioners, site managers and students of architecture, planning, archaeology and heritage studies worldwide.

John H. Stubbs is Christovich Senior Professor of Architectural Preservation Practice and Director of the Master of Preservation Studies program in the School of Architecture, Tulane University, New Orleans, Louisiana USA. Formerly Vice President for Field Projects for the World Monuments Fund, he is an international architectural conservation consultant.

Robert G. Thomson is trained as a historical archaeologist and preservation planner. He is currently the Acting Federal Preservation Officer for the Presidio Trust, San Francisco, California, USA.

"*Architectural Conservation in Asia* is remarkable in that it is the first book of its kind that provides a systematic and comprehensive overview of architectural conservation not only across geographical and political boundaries, but also across traditional and contemporary built heritage in Asia. In this regard, it is an invaluable reference for students and enthusiasts of architectural conservation, and it provides the necessary foundation for deeper understanding of the topic."

– Ho-Yin Lee, Head of Division of Architectural Conservation Programmes, The University of Hong Kong

"The built heritage of Asia is among the oldest, most widespread, and most diverse in the world. But it is also the most endangered. Wars, rapid urbanization, explosive population growth, antiquities thieves, climate change and other challenges are putting at great risk this heritage which belongs not just to Asia, but to humankind. This new book by Stubbs and Thomson is both timely and critical to generate an international demand for the protection of these irreplaceable assets."

– Donovan Rypkema, President, Heritage Strategies International

"This latest contribution on the histories and current challenges of built heritage conservation by John Stubbs, this time partnering with Robert Thomson, is an important contribution to correcting the overemphasis on Europe, which has shaped how we understand conservation and world history in the modern era. A highly ambitious book, *Architectural Conservation in Asia* provides a unique overview of how the conservation of built heritage has evolved across the region, tackling debates about the materialities of uncomfortable histories, or how 'Asian approaches' to conservation intersect with nineteenth-century colonial practices. I am particularly heartened to see chapters on Central Asia, a long overlooked, yet historically significant, region. This is essential reading for anyone interested in both the global and Asian history of conservation."

– Tim Winter, Research Chair in Cultural Heritage, Deakin University, Melbourne, Australia

"A remarkable achievement. A magnificent guided tour through Asia's architectural conservation. Following the success of *Time Honored: A Global View of Architectural Conservation* and *Architectural Conservation in Europe and the Americas*, this book continues to offer readers an exceptionally wide and valuable perspective, as well as insights into the diverse practices of architectural conservation in Asia. It has achieved this challenging task with confidence and aptitude. This is a go-to book for anyone who wishes to have an overview of Asia's architectural conservation history."

– Yeo Kang Shua, Singapore University of Technology and Design

ARCHITECTURAL CONSERVATION IN ASIA

National experiences and practice

John H. Stubbs and Robert G. Thomson

Foreword by A. G. Krishna Menon

Taylor & Francis Group

LONDON AND NEW YORK

First published 2017
by Routledge
2 Park Square, Milton Park, Abingdon, Oxon OX14 4RN

and by Routledge
605 Third Avenue, New York, NY 10017

First issued in paperback 2021

Routledge is an imprint of the Taylor & Francis Group, an informa business

© 2017 John H. Stubbs and Robert G. Thomson

The right of John H. Stubbs and Robert G. Thomson to be identified as authors of this work has been asserted by them in accordance with sections 77 and 78 of the Copyright, Designs and Patents Act 1988.

All rights reserved. No part of this book may be reprinted or reproduced or utilized in any form or by any electronic, mechanical, or other means, now known or hereafter invented, including photocopying and recording, or in any information storage or retrieval system, without permission in writing from the publishers.

Trademark notice: Product or corporate names may be trademarks or registered trademarks, and are used only for identification and explanation without intent to infringe.

Publisher's Note
The publisher has gone to great lengths to ensure the quality of this reprint but points out that some imperfections in the original copies may be apparent.

British Library Cataloguing-in-Publication Data
A catalogue record for this book is available from the British Library

Library of Congress Cataloging-in-Publication Data
Names: Stubbs, John H., author. | Thomson, Robert G. (Robert Garland), author.
Title: Architectural conservation in Asia : national experiences and practice
/ John H. Stubbs and Robert G. Thomson.
Description: New York : Routledge, 2017. | Includes bibliographical
references and index.
Identifiers: LCCN 2016010194 | ISBN 9781138926103 (hb : alk. paper) | ISBN 9781315683447 (ebook)
Subjects: LCSH: Architecture--Conservation and restoration--Asia. | Cultural property--Protection--Asia.
Classification: LCC NA109.A78 S78 2017 | DDC 720.95--dc23
LC record available at https://lccn.loc.gov/2016010194

Typeset in Bembo and ITC Stone Sans
by Saxon Graphics Ltd, Derby

Companion website: www.conservebuiltworld.com

ISBN 13: 978-1-03-209756-5 (pbk)
ISBN 13: 978-1-138-92610-3 (hbk)

CONTENTS

Foreword by A. G. Krishna Menon — xi
Preface — xv
Acknowledgments — xvii

General introduction — 1
The Asian built environment 1
Influences on Asia's built environment 1
Aims of architectural conservation 3
Asian traditions in heritage conservation 4
Local, national and international operations 6
    INTERNATIONAL INSTITUTIONS WORKING IN ASIAN ARCHITECTURAL CONSERVATION 7
Challenges faced in Asian conservation practice 12
    DISASTER RISKS AND PREVENTATIVE ARCHITECTURAL CONSERVATION, BY CHRISTOPHER MARRION 13
Meeting the challenge 15
    THE POWER OF EXAMPLE: UNESCO ASIA-PACIFIC HERITAGE AWARDS PROGRAM 16
    ARCHITECTURAL CONSERVATION TRAINING IN ASIA, BY WILLIAM CHAPMAN 18
East meets West in conservation practice 23
Influences of Asian conservation abroad 24
    CHARTERS AND OTHER INSTRUMENTS RELATIVE TO ASIAN ARCHITECTURAL CONSERVATION, BY JAMES REAP 25
The high stakes of conservation 27

PART I
EAST ASIA   32

   Introduction   33

1 Japan   39
   A legacy of building, re-building and preservation 41
      RESTORATION OF FIRE-DAMAGED WALL MURALS AT HŌRYŪ-JI TEMPLE 43
      THE NARA DOCUMENT ON AUTHENTICITY 46
   Preservation in a modernizing Japan 47
      MACHIYA AND PROSPECTS FOR THEIR PRESERVATION 49
   The rise of contemporary practice 52
      PRESERVING JAPAN'S LIVING HERITAGE, A SEMINAL IDEA IN THE CONSERVATION
         OF INTANGIBLE HERITAGE 55
      LESSONS IN DAMAGE MITIGATION TO CULTURAL HERITAGE FROM THE GREAT
         EAST JAPAN EARTHQUAKE AND TSUNAMI, BY WESLEY CHEEK 59

2 The People's Republic of China   67
      CHINA'S LOST PAST AND LEGISLATIVE RESPONSE – OVERVIEW 68
      DEVELOPMENT AND CHARACTERISTICS OF CHINESE ARCHITECTURE 71
   Foreign intervention: a historic threat to Chinese heritage 78
   Twentieth- and twenty-first-century Chinese heritage conservation policy 79
      EARLY LEADERSHIP IN ARCHITECTURAL CONSERVATION: LIANG SICHENG 80
      THE CHINA PRINCIPLES 83
   Urban conservation: Beijing, Shanghai, Hong Kong and Macau 84
      REPURPOSING INDUSTRIAL SPACES FOR THE CONTEMPORARY ARTS: BEIJING,
         SHANGHAI AND HONG KONG, BY BENJAMIN CLAVAN 94
   *Regional conservation initiatives: Tibet, Three Gorges, the Great Wall and Heritage
   Towns in Southern China* 101
      LIJIANG AND SHAXI: DUAL APPROACHES TO CONSERVING URBAN VERNACULAR
         ARCHITECTURE 107

3 Taiwan (Republic of China)   123
      THE DEFINING ROLE OF TAIWAN'S MUSEUM COLLECTIONS 125
      TAIWAN'S JAPANESE COLONIAL INDUSTRIAL HERITAGE 127
      ON THE IMPORTANCE OF THE ORDINARY, BY LAKE DOUGLAS 129

4 South and North Korea   135
      TRADITIONAL KOREAN ARCHITECTURE: A NEARLY LOST HERITAGE 136
   Architectural conservation in North Korea 138
   Architectural conservation in South Korea 140
   Challenges of urban conservation in South Korea 142
      SOUTH KOREA'S INTANGIBLE HERITAGE LIST 146
      NEW DESIGN IN HERITAGE CONTEXTS, BY WILLIAM CHAPMAN 146

5 Mongolia   153
      CONSERVATION AND REVIVAL OF BUDDHIST MONASTERIES 155
      HERITAGE CONSERVATION AND NATION BUILDING, BY ALEXANDRA CLEWORTH 157
   Organized cultural heritage protection 159
      CONSERVING IMPERMANENT DOMESTIC STRUCTURES: GERS AND SOVIET-ERA
         HOUSING 163

   Conclusion to Part I   167

PART II
SOUTHEAST ASIA MAINLAND COUNTRIES **168**

Introduction 169

6 Myanmar (Burma) 173
Colonial and post-colonial architectural conservation 176
  CONSERVING MYANMAR'S HISTORIC WOODEN STRUCTURES 179
  CONSERVING YANGON'S COLONIAL HERITAGE 182

7 Laos 189
  CULTURAL SURVIVAL AND REVIVAL IN UNESCO'S THE BUDDHIST SANGHA PROGRAM 192

8 Cambodia 201
  CULTURAL HERITAGE LEGISLATION: THE MATTER OF LOOTING, BY TESS DAVIS 206
Angkor's "re-discovery" and early conservation 209
  CULTURAL HERITAGE MANAGEMENT LEGISLATION 213
The post-civil war years 214
  HERITAGE EDUCATION INITIATIVES AT ANGKOR 215
  THE WORLD MONUMENTS FUND AND THE ANGKOR CONSERVATION COMMUNITY 216
  DIGITAL DOCUMENTATION IN ARCHITECTURAL CONSERVATION, BY OLSEN JEAN-JULIEN 218
Conservation in Cambodia beyond Angkor 222
  THE FRENCH COLONIAL ARCHITECTURAL LEGACY 223
  CONTESTED HERITAGE: THE CASE OF PREAH VIHEAR 225

9 Thailand 231
Royal patronage for architectural heritage protection 234
Towards formalized heritage conservation administration 237
Historical Park planning and conservation 238
Urban conservation initiatives 242
Recent commitment in heritage conservation 243

10 Vietnam 251
  MODERN FOREIGN INTERVENTION AND HERITAGE PROTECTION INTERESTS 252
Conserving architectural ensembles: Hue, Mỹ Sớn, Hanoi and Hội An 256
  PRESERVING HANOI'S URBAN VERNACULAR ARCHITECTURAL HERITAGE 262
  PAINFUL CULTURAL HERITAGE, BY WILLIAM LOGAN 264
  THE HISTORIC URBAN LANDSCAPE (HUL): A PARADIGM SHIFT, BY KEN TAYLOR 266

Conclusion to Part II 275

PART III
SOUTHEAST ASIA ISLAND COUNTRIES — 278

Introduction — 279

11 Singapore — 283
From colony to independent state 283
- THE SUSTAINABLE SHOPHOUSE, BY ANDREW M. LILES 288
- WATERFRONT REVITALIZATION THROUGH ADAPTIVE RE-USE 292

12 Malaysia — 297
- LONGHOUSES OF SABAH AND SARAWAK 299
- THE CONTROL OF RENT ACT'S EFFECT ON MALAYSIAN HERITAGE CONSERVATION 302
- URBAN CONSERVATION AND SOCIAL INCLUSION, BY NILSON ARIEL ESPINO 306

13 Brunei — 311

14 Indonesia — 317
Colonial years 317
- CONSERVATION OF THE BOROBODUR TEMPLE COMPLEX 318

Conservation activity in an independent nation 321
Risk management for heritage sites 323
Bali 323
- COMMUNITY PARTICIPATION IN HERITAGE CONSERVATION: THE CHALLENGES OF BALI'S *SUBAK* SYSTEM 324
- TOURISM DEVELOPMENT VERSUS CONSERVATION IN BALI 325

Timor-Leste (East Timor) 327
Irian Jaya (West Papua) 329

15 The Philippines — 335
- WORLD WAR II DESTRUCTION: ITS LEGACY IN THE PACIFIC 342

Conclusion to Part III — 347

PART IV
SOUTH ASIA — 350

Introduction — 351

16 India — 355
- INDIAN ARCHITECTURAL TRADITIONS: A CHRONOLOGICAL SUMMARY 357

Religious origins of restoration and conservation in India 360
Conservation principles and practice in the colonial era 360
Architectural conservation in modern India 364
- CONSERVING INDIA'S CAVE SITES: BALANCING VISITATION, PROTECTION AND LIVING HERITAGE 366
- COMPLEMENTARY CONSERVATION: INTACH'S UNIQUELY INDIAN APPROACH 370

Indian conservation in practice 372
- CONSERVATION CHALLENGES AND SOLUTIONS IN URBAN AREAS OF INDIA: EXAMPLES FROM MUMBAI 377

Contents **ix**

    BUILDING BRIDGES AT HAMPI: THE IMPORTANCE OF STAKEHOLDER
        COMMUNICATION IN THE MANAGEMENT OF WORLD HERITAGE SITES 379
  Conservation of cultural landscapes 381
    INVENTING CULTURAL SIGNIFICANCE, BY RAHUL MEHROTRA 382
    CONSERVING COLONIAL INDIA 384
    EFFECTS OF THE CASTE SYSTEM ON TRADITIONAL BUILDING AND CONSERVATION
        IN INDIA 388

17 Sri Lanka and Maldives   399
  Sri Lanka 399
    A BRIEF HISTORY OF SRI LANKA 400
  The Cultural Triangle Project and the Central Cultural Fund 405
  Balancing tourism and conservation at Sigiriya 407
  Challenges to the ongoing conservation of Kandy 409
  Maldives 415
  The Maldives islands and Sri Lanka, a shared heritage 416

18 Pakistan   427
    SUMMARY HISTORICAL CONTEXT 429
    THE ROLE OF ISLAM IN ARCHITECTURAL CONSERVATION PRACTICE 431
  Pakistani institutions, legislation, organizations and initiatives supporting conservation 432
  Karachi 435
  Conservation projects in Pakistan 436
    CONSERVATION OF A DISPUTED TERRITORY: KASHMIR AND PAKISTAN'S
        NORTHERN AREAS 439

19 Bangladesh   449
  A brief architectural history of Bangladesh 450
  Conservation in modern Bangladesh 451
  Architectural conservation policy and practice in Bangladesh 452
    CLIMATE CHANGE AND CULTURAL HERITAGE IN SOUTH ASIA, BY NATHAN
        LOTT 454
  Contemporary examples of architectural conservation 457
    CONSERVATION OF MODERN ARCHITECTURE 458

20 Bhutan   467
  Summary history of Bhutan and its architectural heritage 469
  Architectural conservation in Bhutan 470

21 Nepal   481
  Early conservation practice 482
    INTERNATIONAL COLLABORATION IN THE CONSERVATION OF NEPAL'S HERITAGE
        SITES: COOPERATION AND DIFFERENCES 484
    EARTHQUAKE DISASTER IN NEPAL 488
  Conservation beyond Kathmandu 491

Conclusion to Part IV   494

PART V
CENTRAL ASIA   496

Introduction   497

22 Afghanistan   501
Millennia of cultural accomplishment and loss 501
Facing Afghanistan's rebuilding and recovery 505
    RECONSTRUCTION AND COMMEMORATION IN BAMIYAN: CONTROVERSY AROUND THE TREATMENT OF THE BUDDHAS 509
Conservation efforts at the urban scale 510
    SAFEGUARDING AFGHANISTAN'S URBAN HERITAGE: PERSPECTIVES FROM THE FIELD, BY JOLYON LESLIE 514
Threats to rural cultural landscapes 515

23 Kazakhstan, Kyrgyzstan, Tajikistan, Turkmenistan and Uzbekistan   523
    CONSERVATION IN CENTRAL ASIA DURING THE SOVIET ERA 525
Kazakhstan 526
Kyrgyzstan 529
    FEATURING HERITAGE ALONG CENTRAL ASIA'S ANCIENT TRADE ROUTES 530
Tajikistan 531
Turkmenistan 533
    ARCHITECTURAL RECONSTRUCTION IN THE CENTRAL ASIAN CONTEXT: ROOM FOR DEBATE 536
Uzbekistan 536
    THE ARAL SEA: AT THE INTERSECTION OF ECOLOGICAL AND CULTURAL HERITAGE CONSERVATION 538

Conclusion to Part V   547

Looking Forward   549

Glossary   551
General and additional references   559
Image credits   571
Index   581

FOREWORD

One of the interesting consequences of globalization has been that even as it tended to homogenize architectural conservation practices, it threw light on and gave voices to hitherto elided indigenous practices from around the world. The gospel according to the mainstream is that heritage is "universal." As a sentiment this can be an inspiring proposition, but when translated into disciplinary catechism it considers other, particularly non-Western, constructs of architectural heritage conservation as apostasy. It propounds "universal" conservation theology as defined by international charters. These charters evolved out of the Western experience of heritage conservation and established benchmarks which are used to define "correct" practice in dealing with heritage all over the world. As John Stubbs perceptively pointed out in his earlier book, *Time Honored: A Global View of Architectural Conservation*, a foreign perspective may save sites in other cultures, but it can also create incomplete and unsatisfactory results: what is considered important in Eurocentric cultures may not necessarily be valued in the same way by others. Such criticisms are not common in conservation literature and they represent a refreshing acceptance of cultural diversity. But the diverse voices are seldom documented in a systematic manner, thus allowing them to be heard and evaluated.

The present book, *Architectural Conservation in Asia: National Experiences and Practice* by John H. Stubbs and Robert G. Thomson, redresses that lacuna. It follows a tradition in and of itself, albeit a new one, as it is the third in a series that endeavors to document architectural conservation practice in most parts of the world. A research project begun in the late 1990s, John Stubbs's *Time Honored: A Global View of Architectural Conservation – Theory, Parameters and Evolution of an Ethos* (2009) portrays the fundamentals of the field, its history and the general state of architectural heritage protection in our time. Volume II in the series, *Architectural Conservation in Europe and the Americas: National Experiences and Practice*, co-authored with Emily Makaš, built upon the predecessor title addressing the stories of architectural conservation in some sixty-seven countries of the so-called Old and New Worlds, laying out remarkable similarities and some major differences in conservation practice of continents that were an ocean apart. *Architectural Conservation in Asia* complements the earlier works with the critically important story of the Asian experience.

This was a long due disciplinary exercise because there is a certain irony that Asia, a region of the world that has one of the longest histories of architecture, built settlements, and architectural conservation, is among the least known in terms of the conservation practices used to protect local heritage buildings. Home to some of humankind's earliest traces of existence, the civilizations of Asia have developed over the millennia to become the rich and varied melange of cultures that host and define things "Asian" in today's world. The book does an impressive job in defining the merits of conservation through profiling the stories of architectural heritage protection in the thirty countries that comprise the geographical scope of the book, from Afghanistan to the Philippines.

Using principally a historiographical approach the authors guide the reader through Asian heritage conservation in our time. In doing so, Stubbs and Thomson lay out the ample histories of both lay and official conservation efforts in each country in a respectful way that defines the evolution of awareness for the subject in those nations. Not surprisingly, some of the oldest countries such as China and India have some of the longest stories of cultural heritage protection, with notable examples dating to the first millennium and before. More recent efforts from countries such as Uzbekistan and Cambodia have also been valuable contributions; all have stories to tell, with lessons and solutions that should be more widely known and appreciated.

How the cultural heritage of Central, South, East and Southeast Asia evolved is essential to the story of human civilization, and evidences of the story are best viewed and understood in terms of surviving vestiges of the historic built environment. Included in the scope of architectural heritage are the allied interests and accomplishments of human-shaped landscapes, buildings of all scales and sizes, and arrangements of buildings from the individual structure to town, city and mega-city. Also part of the story are the associated topics of craft traditions, interior decor, the arts, the socio-economic forces that have shaped historic environments, and reference to the lifeways of those who lived, and continue to live, in such places. The built environment is the single most telling reflection of a place and its values and ambitions; thus, its utilization, maintenance and perpetuation of its sustaining traditions are complex and important matters.

The vicissitudes of time notwithstanding – and it is well known how the history of Asia is a tumultuous one – the ample accomplishments of many of Asia's civilizations have left widespread legacies in architectural heritage, if only as ruins in some instances. Nonetheless, the distinct architectural heritage of Asia, both real and perceived, is not only a key image of the region, it defines the built environment of Asia's nations. As such it defines our orientation, our sense of place and our uniqueness. No other part of the world is growing faster and changing more rapidly than Asia. Thus, the stakes in architectural conservation practice are high – quite high – in terms of the importance of the endeavor.

The increasingly robust field of organized and planned cultural heritage protection is a product of modern times, and as such Asia is particularly well positioned to lead the way in its accomplishments. Having evolved from the individualized efforts of nations involved in heritage protection scarcely a century ago, East Asia, along with most other parts of the world, has impressively risen to the challenge of cultural heritage protection. Many reasons have been offered for why this is the case, chief among them being the "good sense" of it all. The growing literature in the field – itself a definer of today's growing field of heritage conservation practice – makes this abundantly clear, and enumerates the myriad positive reasons "Why architectural conservation?"

Herein the authors explain in a clear, balanced and easily understood way the similarities and differences in heritage practice in a part of the world that has used distinctly different approaches to heritage conservation from that of the West in a number of ways. Interestingly, as of the past few decades a hallmark of contemporary heritage conservation practice across much of the world is that Eastern concepts and practices in heritage conservation are noticeably influencing practices in the West, and for the better.

The book's abundant illustrations and detailed index enhance its readability and usefulness and its extensive endnotes, further readings and bibliography support the authors' principle aim of it being a "gateway" to further information. It successfully offers an overarching view while avoiding duplication of material. It importantly stresses *solutions* and *best practices* in heritage conservation that reflect its authors' key interests.

Architectural Conservation in Asia is a prodigious enterprise. In my view the authors John Stubbs and Rob Thomson are very much up to the task of such an ambitious work, having extensive combined experience in architectural conservation research and practice in the region. I have known them both for over twenty years, having met them through Stubbs's work for two decades of his serving as Vice President for Field Projects at the New York-based World Monuments Fund. John and I did not know each other while attending Columbia University's Graduate School of Architecture, Planning and Preservation at the start of our careers but since the mid-1990s it has been a pleasure working with him on specific projects at gatherings in Kathmandu and Delhi. Thomson is a trained archaeologist, preservation planner and product of the same Columbia program and I know him to be a similarly indefatigable explorer of Asian heritage.

As the Acknowledgments and Table of Contents of the book testify, this herculean work effort, some ten years in the making, has entailed the help of many others. As Stubbs explained to me in his kind invitation to me to write this Foreword, this is an "all hands on deck" operation with contacts and favors called from scores of friends and colleagues over twenty-five years of international practice. It is my pleasure to have been among those called upon, to introduce this volume as a valuable contribution of newly assembled knowledge on the growing field of heritage conservation in Asia.

A. G. Krishna Menon,
Architect, Urban Planner and Academic,
Convenor, Delhi Chapter,
Indian National Trust for Art and Cultural Heritage,
New Delhi
January 2016

PREFACE

This book is intended to portray traditions, contemporary practices and accomplishments in architectural conservation in Eastern Asia as a component of a broader effort that has previously addressed these topics in other parts of the world. It is written for professionals, students and others interested in cultural heritage management efforts in Asia. In particular, this book hopes to serve all those native to these culturally diverse and dynamic regions who fully appreciate its special qualities in their daily lives.

Preserving cultural heritage in all its forms is a long-standing concern in Asia, in some cases dating back millennia. The present volume examines the evolution of awareness of conserving architecture from its first consciousness to its multi-faceted professional practice of today. *Architectural Conservation in Asia* endeavors to outline the stories of preserving historic buildings and sites by examining the background and contemporary practice of deliberate architectural conservation on a country-by-country and regional basis, as well as mapping trends and citing prospects for the field in general.

Real issues and accomplishments in the field are stressed here based on the experiences, observations and research of its authors and contributors. Particular attention has been paid to reporting on solutions and positive accomplishments in the field. Highlighted essays on more specialized topics, with several contributed by noted specialists, appear throughout the book.

For purposes of this book, Asia refers to the eastern half of the continent comprising the countries of Central Asia to the Southeast Asian island nations. Eastern Russia, the northern border of Asia, is addressed in a predecessor volume in this series by John H. Stubbs and Emily G. Makaš. This geographical scope was selected due to the predominant historic cultural affinities of Eastern Asia, as well as the distinct nature of its architecture and related traditions. While Eastern and Western Asia share many building styles and cultural traditions, the authors concluded that the latter region would be better addressed along with North Africa, perhaps in a future volume. Furthermore, given the current period of turbulent and tragically destructive change underway in parts of Western Asia, attempts to characterize the state of architectural conservation in the region may benefit from the passage of time.

It is not the aim of this book to provide detailed histories or portrayals of the countries and cultures being discussed, nor is it meant to provide detailed architectural histories. For histories of Asian architecture, *The Historic Monuments of Asia* by C. Tagell, and/or the *Global History of Architecture* by F. Ching, M. Jarzombek and V. Prakash are recommended. This book does not focus in detail on conservation technology and techniques that tend to be more easily found on the Web. However, the General and Further Reading sections cite titles of both a more technical and a more global nature.

Architectural Conservation in Asia is the third in a series that endeavors to document architectural heritage conservation practices in most countries of the world. It follows *Time Honored: A Global View of Architectural Conservation – Theory, Parameters and Evolution of an Ethos* (Wiley, 2009) and *Architectural Conservation in Europe and the Americas: National Experiences and Practice* (Wiley, 2011).

John H. Stubbs
Robert G. Thomson

ACKNOWLEDGMENTS

The authors of *Architectural Conservation in Asia*, John Howell Stubbs and Robert Garland Thomson, have had immense help from other individuals, institutions and supporters in relation to the research, writing and compilation of this book that has been developed intermittently for over a decade.

We foremost thank Sharon Genin for her determination and hard work as the project's primary production assistant, who compiled and sorted all text material and images, the index and gave editorial help of all kinds throughout the project. We thank Laura Nusbaum and Jerelyn Ryan Stubbs for their help with copyedit work and image research, respectively. We likewise thank Liz Phul, cartographer, for her designs of the book's maps and Leonardo Leiva Rivera for his revision of the website of the Time Honored Architectural Conservation Documentation project that accompanies the book.

Special thanks are extended to A.G. Krishna Menon for writing the Foreword and for his encouragement and friendship of many years.

We are also especially grateful to the contributors of essays presented as sidebars in the book who volunteered their time and effort: William Chapman, Wesley Cheek, Benjamin Clavan, Alexandra Cleworth, Tess Davis, Lake Douglas, Nilson Ariel Espino, Erin Guerra, Olsen Jean-Julien, Jolyon Leslie, Andrew Liles, William Logan, Nathan Lott, Christopher Marrion, Rahul Mehrotra, A.G. Krishna Menon, Marilyn Novell, James Reap, Ken Taylor and the UNESCO Asia-Pacific office.

Sincere gratitude for additional collegial help from readers, advisers and others who otherwise helped shape the book's contents is extended to: Susanne Annen, Amita Baig, Jeff Cody, Nilan Cooray, Tenzing Chadotsang, Liu Chang, Jeff Chieh-fu Cheng, In-hwa Choi, Marie Chinappi, Frederick Stephen Ellis, Richard Englehardt, Shahnaj Husne Jahan, Rohit Jigyasu, Junne Kikata, Jihong Kim, Ross James King, Chester Liebs, William Logan, Richard Look, John Miksic, Kathy Mu, Robert Murowchick, Anila Naeem, Henda Witarana Saman Priyantha, William Remsen, Hae Un Rii, Shalin Ronald, John Sanday, Michael Shoriak, S. Frederick Starr, Laura Tedesco, Augusto Villalon, Karma Wangchuk, John Weeks and Julian Wheatley.

Such a project could only have been born of institutional support, and here too, there are several to thank. While the book is an independent work of its authors it was informed and enabled by nearly two decades of travel to Asia by John Stubbs as a staff member of the World Monuments Fund, for which we thank the trustees and staff of the World Monuments Fund (New York), especially colleagues Bonnie Burnham, Lisa Ackerman and Margot Note who were particularly helpful. We also thank the scores of other friends, colleagues and teachers met in our Asian pursuits for what we learned and experienced in relation to this project.

Funding for supplemental field research in Japan, Laos and Thailand was provided to John Stubbs in 2012 by the Asian Cultural Council (New York). Robert Thomson received travel funding for his research on heritage education in Asia through a William Kinne Fellows Traveling Prize (Columbia University) and while serving as a Graduate Intern at the Getty Conservation Institute in 2005–2006.

Institutional support from Tulane University in the form of John Stubbs's Favrot and Christovich Professorships were of valuable help, as was research conducted in relation to his being a guest professor in World Heritage Studies in the Architectural Heritage Management and Tourism Program at Silpakorn University, Bangkok.

Libraries that were especially helpful include the Getty Conservation Institute Information Center and the enthusiastic help of its staff Valerie Greathouse and Cameron Trowbridge, the libraries of SPAFA SEAMEO Center for Archaeology and Fine Arts, UNESCO Asia Pacific (Bangkok), ICCROM (Rome), Avery Library at Columbia University and the Asian collections at the University of Hawaii (Manoa).

Finally, the authors wish to thank our editors at Routledge, Taylor and Francis UK, Helena Hurd, Sade Lee, Christina O'Brien, and in the New York office, Wendy Fuller and Trudy Varcianna for their guidance and support in seeing this book through to its realization. The authors would also wish to thank the copyeditor, Kate Reeves and project manager Dave Wright at Saxon Graphics Ltd.

GENERAL INTRODUCTION

The Asian built environment

Asia's rich historic built environment reflects the region's position as the origin of some of the world's most ancient civilizations, cultures and religions.[1] For more than two millennia Asian cultures overlapped and interconnected as they expanded and developed through long-distance trade and communication, activities that eventually introduced followers of Hinduism, Buddhism and the philosophy of Confucianism to Islam, Shintoism and other beliefs.

Built heritage developed accordingly, often melding novel concepts with traditional design. Today the region's works of architecture are among its most distinct examples of cultural heritage, varying in scale from villages to several of the world's most populous megacities. Whether viewing the conservation of Asia's architectural heritage in terms of the distant or recent past, as individual buildings or within arrangements, or as urban or rural cultural landscapes, the range of Asia's built heritage considered "worth preserving" is both vast and ever growing.

A hallmark of contemporary Asian life is constant and rapid change. Thus, defining the current state of Asian architectural heritage and the practice of conserving it in precise, static terms is challenging. In addition to the varied and ever-changing contexts of the Asian built environment, elements of intangible heritage including spiritual beliefs, aesthetic principles and the talent of individuals are ever present. Even the most humble of structures may have subtle layered significances that are important to those who use it, but which remain hidden to outsiders.

For the purposes of this volume, the authors have defined Asia as thirty modern countries, the national borders of which bear the heavy stamp of the colonial period, and frequently have little to do with traditional cultural connections. For example, the former protectorate of French Indochina was dissolved in the mid-twentieth century into Laos, Vietnam and Cambodia. Historically, these modern nations were split between the powerful Khmer and Cham Empires, great rivals of the twelfth through the fourteenth centuries. Nevertheless, today's borders, governments and national institutions do provide an informative basis for discussing the progress of heritage conservation practice on a per-country basis. Such a division also lends itself well to discussing patterns of development on a sub-regional, regional and international basis that is an important part of this endeavor.

Influences on Asia's built environment

Any list of the forces that shape architecture must start with climate and geography, followed by the availability and type of building materials. When these elements blend with creative – as well as destructive – human forces, a historic built environment evolves. By reflecting on these interactions one can appreciate how Asia's built environment developed the way it did and how it survives to the present time.

The authors have defined "East Asia" for the purposes of this volume as the subset of the continent that is south of Russia, north of Australia, east of Iran and west (inclusive) of Japan.[2] Asia's geographic spread is vast and includes almost every climate type, from the sub-equatorial tropics at 8.87°S at East Timor to northern-most China's sub-arctic region at 53.33°N latitude. The architecture of its tropical regions reflects the needs of its population by incorporating interior openness, steep and overhanging roof designs, a variety of shading devices, wall densities, and their varying capacities of durability. In the northern regions, climatic adaptations include the *ondol* system of radiant floor heating, in use for centuries on the Korean peninsula. As elsewhere, function determined the nature of a building's construction: the most durable, monumental, carefully designed and detailed structures were used for religious buildings and state architecture, from administrative buildings to grand palaces. Less permanent building materials, designs and construction techniques tended to be used for housing and work-related facilities.

A multitude of extrinsic historical forces have shaped Asia's traditional built environment as well. For thousands of years, Asia has been an active player in the phenomenon of "globalization." Long-distance trade throughout the past two millennia traces its origins to Antiquity when both land and sea routes first connected Asia with Africa, the Arabian peninsula and Europe, carrying with them commodities, ideas and religion. It was trade, above all else, that was responsible for the cross-cultural blending of populations and cultures across Asia. Land routes traversed the great deserts, steppe and mountains of central Asia, while contemporaneous sea routes connected the continent's coastlines from the north Pacific across the Indian Ocean to the Arabian peninsula and beyond to Southern Africa. Military exploits in Asia, of which there were many, also assured cultural blending, contributing to the presence (or absence) of much of the built environment across the continent.[3] Thus, discussions on the disposition of cultural heritage and its conservation are best seen in terms of these historical patterns and geography, resulting in the varying situations of the modern nations of Asia.

Some of the world's greatest architectural achievements are Asian: Angkor Wat is considered to be the largest religious structure on Earth. Also of enormous size are Borobudur in Indonesia, Wat Phou in Laos, the "mega-stupas" of Sri Lanka and the Hindu temple complexes at Sri Ranganathaswamy, southwest India. Monumental religious architecture of a different kind is exemplified by Japan's Todai-ji temple, one of the largest wooden buildings in the world. The local religious programs and ambitions that generated each of these examples evidently justified their enormity, as did the level of organization and material resources brought to bear by their builders. Asia is also home to a wealth of smaller scale religious buildings: community temples, pagodas, stupas, shrines and spirit houses, equal to the grand monuments in their cultural significance if not scale. Finely built mosques, churches, synagogues, tombs and memorials are common throughout Asia, even in many modest communities. As elsewhere in the world all such buildings are, or were, imbued with special meaning and purpose, and all were built with particular attention and care, often in accordance with ancient traditions and texts.

In terms of civic architecture, the Forbidden City imperial palace complex in Beijing remains unsurpassed in vision and complexity, but numerous other sites in this category exhibit the same level of ambition, grace and quality, notably the great Mughal tombs and garden complexes, and the hybridized Asian-European buildings of the former British colonial capitals. Asia excels, too, in its cave architecture: Elephanta, Ajanta, Ellora and Dambulla in South Asia and the extensive Buddhist cave systems of Dunhuang in western China are among the most impressive to be found anywhere. In terms of engineering ingenuity some of Asia's military fortifications are unparalleled. Sophisticated examples include the elaborate Joseon period Korean and Sengoku period Japanese castle forts, the Great Wall of China (begun in the Qin dynasty), and the walled cities of Rajasthan. Other historic engineering marvels include the pleasure garden irrigation systems of Lahore, Pakistan and Sigirya, Sri Lanka, the large-scale hydrological systems of Angkor and the Grand Canal in China. Human ingenuity is even more evident when one considers Asia's historic domestic architecture, and how well buildings were adapted to their environment. Examples range from earthen architecture in the deserts of Central Asia to the shophouses of Southeast Asia, from rural farmsteads and communal settlements to towns and small cities that, taken together, comprise the region's broad array of cultural landscapes.

From the dawn of the sixteenth century onward, the presence of European colonial interests was a significant factor in the evolution of Asia's built environment and its current political landscape. Cultural exchange associated with these centuries of complex interactions had innumerable influences upon Asia and the colonizing nations alike, whether profound, as in matters of international trade relations, or nuanced, as in the melding of socio-economic systems, technologies and cultural activities.[4] The meeting of East and West occurred in myriad ways that became more complex as the modern world developed. (See below.)

Civilizational developments related to trade and conquests were also very much intra-Asian. Notable were the spread of Buddhism and Hinduism outward from the Indian subcontinent, Khmer conquests in mainland Southeast Asia, the expansion of Islam throughout the region, and the scores of Chinese military exploits from the Emperors Period of the Longshan in c.2500 BCE through the last imperial Qing dynasty in the early twentieth century. Some of these military campaigns resulted in altering the world stage, in particular the expansion of the Mongol Empire under Ghenghis (Chinggis) Khan and his descendants during the thirteenth and fourteenth centuries. These in turn paved the way for their successor empire builders in Central and South Asia: Timur, Babur and Mahmoud of Ghazni, among others. Significant expansionist efforts within Asia occurred throughout recorded history, including the Burmese, Thai, Indian and Japanese exploits through the mid-twentieth century.

In the past century the most ambitious attempt at cultural globalization in the Asia-Pacific region was the Japanese imperial expansion that ended with World War II and the dawn of the atomic age. Several newly independent countries resulted from this conflict, with many adopting new systems of governance.[5] The de-colonization of South Asia resulted in the modern states of India, Pakistan, Bangladesh, Sri Lanka and Myanmar, each emerging from this episode with legitimate grievances about this process, which continue to echo today. Post-war Asia slowly recovered economically as Cold War allegiances formed and re-formed with the competing superpowers of the USSR and the United States. Many countries of Asia, in particular Vietnam, China and Korea, developed through difficult decades of continued pressures and conflicts, notably in response to American intervention in Vietnam and Korea in the 1950s and 1960s in its efforts to stem communism.

During the past seventy years of relatively peaceful conditions, Asian economies have steadily rebuilt from their wartime losses and have caught up with, and in some cases surpassed, the progress and development of their counterparts in the West. India, Japan, South Korea, China, Thailand, Singapore and Malaysia have led the way in the region. Most of these initiatives have been intra-continental, as Chinese, Korean, Thai and Singaporean investment capital supports new development in the less prosperous countries of Cambodia, Myanmar, Vietnam and Laos. Other development schemes recall imperial times, such as China's involvement with infrastructure improvements in neighboring countries, whether in the form of "friendship highways" as in the one to and through Tibet on to Nepal, or technical and financial support for hydroelectric dams along the Mekong and other rivers originating in the Himalayas. Some of the development plans are among the world's largest and most ambitious, such as China's One Belt–One Road initiative that aims to install new transportation systems roughly along the ancient Silk Road trade routes throughout Central Asia, or the Kunming–Bangkok Expressway, a 1,900 km (1,200 mile) highway from Kunming China through Laos to Bangkok at the head of the Bay of Thailand that opened in 2008.

Such transportation and regional development schemes often include cultural heritage protection programs aimed at documenting affected cultural heritage in most of its forms. This can mitigate the circumstances of major social and environmental change, though it is impossible to fully manage change of this scale and magnitude. In such schemes, "cultural diplomacy" has played an increasingly significant role, with long-term effects that will only be understood in the decades to come.[6]

Aims of architectural conservation

Architectural conservation is a central subject in cultural resource management (CRM) due to the built environment's ubiquitous physicality and importance in sustaining our lives. Because the ultimate goal of CRM is the perpetuation – and sometimes enhancement – of a cultural resource, its practitioners frequently must address the valorization of their actions in terms of economic, cultural or societal considerations. One measure of these actions is how a conserved resource will generate a sufficient level of economic return in order to justify its preservation and ongoing maintenance. Another is how a conserved site will (or will not) enhance the social well being of its constituent community. Yet another is the degree to which the cultural meaning of a conserved object changes after having been protected and presented as, for instance, a national symbol. All these considerations are especially true of sites considered to be tourist destinations; however, only a small portion of CRM approaches address tourism issues, focusing on the more tangible issues related to urban and rural neighborhoods, workplaces and so on instead.[7]

Understanding people's motives for conserving the past is an important part of understanding the overall rationale for the endeavor. These reasons can include preserving familiar places for the historical value and sense of orientation (sense of place) they provide, preserving things for their "age value," for reasons of cultural or religious respect, aesthetic appreciation, nostalgia, fear of change and for practical reasons.[8]

While the aims of architectural conservation and CRM include a relatively consistent set of methods, problems and concerns, the field itself is evolving. An earlier emphasis in heritage protection on the techniques of "How to conserve?" has evolved to include the deeper questions of "What to conserve?" and "For whom?" In the past, the conservation architect, conservator and project coordinator may have been solely responsible for material or logistical decisions, whereas today these responsibilities more often include incorporating the active participation of a range of stakeholders. The participatory and consultative nature of CRM today reveals additional values and meanings associated with the historic resource that should be taken into consideration; this approach can also instill a wider understanding and greater sense of "ownership" within a broader range of stakeholders that can prove vital to long-term protection.

In the twenty-first century, cultural heritage is increasingly viewed as a useful resource that can shape the effects of development, by making it more culturally and environmentally sensitive, or halt it altogether. In order to be most effective in this role, cultural heritage in Asia, and indeed worldwide, is best conceptualized by reference to people at various levels, including the individual, familial, communal, national and international.[9] The protection of architectural heritage works best when it is in harmony with this approach. Successful conservation projects are frequently not static but rather highly dynamic and accessible to various stakeholders, carrying associations with our traditions, beliefs, rituals, memory, knowledge and skills, identity, pride, memorialization and many other aspects of everyday life. They are also scalable, creating opportunities to amplify the merits of "saving" a particular building or place in order to maximize the positive benefits reaped by its constituents.

A thorough exploration of traditions in cultural heritage conservation practice, from the past through to today, is an effective way to identify new trends, challenges and opportunities that may influence the practice going forward. Similarly, studying threats to built heritage and the various responses is one of the means for effectively guiding solutions going forward. Such is the aim of this book, following the approach established by its predecessor volumes, *Time Honored: A Global View of Architectural Conservation* and *Architectural Conservation in Europe and the Americas*, here taking on the enormously important topic of architectural conservation in Asia.

Asian traditions in heritage conservation

The topic of Asian traditions in conserving cultural heritage is a long and complex story that is addressed in greater detail in the subsequent chapters. The earliest specific examples are lost to history, but as elsewhere in the world, it likely involved the veneration of religious sites, or preserving buildings for sheer practicality. What differentiates Asia is the additional motive of traditionalism, which involves adherence to ancient doctrines, manuals or practices, especially pertaining to religion, a cultural characteristic in Asia instilled primarily through the spiritual beliefs of its indigenous faiths, and the continuity of such religious practices. Confucian, Buddhist, Hindu and Shinto beliefs nurtured a traditionalism that has long supported respectful attitudes towards the past. Add to this the aims of many Asian leaders who wished to maintain the achievements of their ancestors in order to garner merit, honor and assurance in the afterlife, and one readily sees a matrix of incentives for preserving both physical heritage and traditional lifeways.

Challenges to the status quo and traditional lifeways occurred with some frequency throughout Asia's history. Despite some episodes resulting in radically new directions and revised attitudes towards the past, to a remarkable degree the trajectory of Asian history includes lengthy periods of unbroken continuity, which in some cases continued uninterrupted until modern times. As a result, in many parts of Asia, particularly rural and remote areas, one may find contemporary lifeways that are obvious continua of centuries past. In such circumstances, it is clear that the act of architectural conservation necessarily includes protecting and fostering the livelihoods and cultures of the people who give these buildings, structures and other cultural expressions life.

As for the perceptions of history and architectural conservation, here too it is different in some important respects, depending on one's perspective. Many Asians deeply relate to their surrounding environment through their beliefs and enactment of various traditions in relation to the cultural landscape.[10] There are additional concerns regarding the spiritual and natural context of sites and the religious role that many such sites play: most sites represent continuity of use, and call for wider appreciation of the associated intangible values of heritage sites, including traditional know-how pertaining to their conservation.[11] Working within this context we are reminded that heritage is a living "thing" – just like people.[12] Thus immediately the task of conservation is larger than one might initially expect since *living heritage*, through continuity of lifeways including simple practical responses, is in contrast to the expert-derived notions of heritage.

There is remarkable harmony and pluralism amidst the richly diverse universe of Asian cultural heritage. Asian societies, for the most part, acknowledge cultural pluralism and the co-existence of multi-cultural heritage.[13] Examples of this are evident, such as with the deeply Muslim nation of Indonesia's active promotion of the Buddhist site of Borobudur (see Chapter 14) and the Hindu complex of Prambanan (both in Central Java) as primary exemplars of its heritage. The Taj Mahal, Mohenjo-Daro and the Great Wall of China each represent distant histories to their surrounding contemporary cultures yet they fulfill the aims of universally shared heritage that warrants their inclusion on the World Heritage List.

The UNESCO World Heritage program, which presently lists over 1,050 cultural and natural sites possessing "outstanding universal value," has been actively embraced in Asia since the Kathmandu Valley of Nepal joined the list in 1979.[14] The countries of China and India have been particularly active in putting forward nominations, with China having listed forty-eight sites since 1987 (second only to Italy) and India successfully nominating thirty-two sites since 1983. Nearly all the other countries of Asia have participated, many of them also keeping a Tentative List of Sites for nomination to the UNESCO World Heritage List. The reasons for this participation are the same as elsewhere, including national pride and expectation of increased tourism revenues.

Importantly, the UNESCO Convention's efforts to more equitably balance the World Heritage List since 1994 have resulted in additional Asian nations nominating sites, including previously underrepresented countries such as Mongolia, Bhutan, Myanmar and North Korea. These initiatives have not only focused attention on the topic of equitable distribution of sites, but also raised levels of concern in areas that were relatively behind in attending to their cultural heritage responsibilities.[15] The formulation of Tentative Lists had similarly prioritized sites, with the result that contenders received attention they might not have had otherwise. UNESCO's concerns related to the limited capacity for managing World Heritage Sites has triggered the creation of institutions for serving such sites, once listed. Other initiatives of UNESCO such as its Historic Urban Landscapes (HUL) approach, improving access to information about listed sites and contenders, and expanding educational components of sites have also had their positive effects, not only on World Heritage related sites but other heritage sites throughout Asia. (See On the Importance of the Ordinary in Chapter 3.)

Cultural heritage protection in Asia is trending towards *democratization of heritage*, meaning heritage is being shared and is benefitting more people than ever. However, there are certain areas where public accessibility is not always complete, as in India where the Hindu caste system prohibits members of lower castes from engaging in certain temple activities. (See Effects of the Caste System on Traditional Building and Conservation in India in Chapter 16.) In other cases there may be exclusive events held at sites for tourists at the exclusion of locals. As such, aspects of cultural heritage and its conservation become grounds over which *human rights* or *social justice* issues emerge. On the other hand, many Asian countries facilitate regular and even priority admission to national heritage sites for their own populations, often at no cost or greatly reduced cost in comparison to what is charged for foreigners.

The seminal book *Asian Heritage Management* (Kapila D. Silva and Neel Kamal Chapagain, eds.) sums up well the questions of Asian heritage values and practice:

> Pluralism is not just the acknowledgement of diversity but active and meaningful engagement with this diversity. There cannot be one universal approach based on a single, overarching value system; heritage management must be contextualized to the needs and beliefs of each Asian cultural context.[16]

Local, national and international operations

During the nineteenth century government commitments to architectural conservation did much to help establish national identities, as in the initiatives during the Meiji period in Japan, and the Chakri Dynasty in the Kingdom of Thailand. They willingly embraced Western precepts, namely Western European and some American, of organized heritage protection, and successively built upon them in increasingly sophisticated ways to become the robust cultural heritage protections systems currently in place. China and Korea later did so in the early twentieth century although both were certainly influenced by developments in architectural heritage management in other parts of the world, namely Europe, North America and Australia.

In Asian countries that were subjected to colonial rule, such as India, Vietnam, Cambodia and Indonesia, state-level heritage protection was instituted directly by the colonizing governments. These institutions endured until the post-World War II independence era, after which extant systems were either abandoned or evolved into active present-day institutions. In nearly all cases, this process entailed updating legislation, training and assignment of all-national administrative staffs and workers, and incorporation of the old departments within new governmental structures (frequently under the Ministries of Culture). Unfortunate as colonial rule proved to be in most of the countries of Asia, the foundational work in cultural resources management laid by colonial powers should not be undervalued, as it is responsible for much of the Western-style scholarship, documentation and conservation of architectural heritage in many countries today. The scholarly institutions established during colonial rule such as the École française d'Extrême-Orient (EFEO) and the Royal Asiatic Society were very influential as well as seats of research, repositories of information and venues for documentation, publication and dissemination of the histories of Asia's countries and regions, then little known to the West.

During the nineteenth century, conservation professionals developed a wide range of special research methodologies that both addressed the tasks at hand and also became contributions to the larger field. Included among them was some groundbreaking work in epigraphic studies, archaeological method and conservation methodologies. The physical work expended toward accessing, clearing, documenting, conserving and presenting numerous sites under colonial rule is incalculable, and at certain sites such as Angkor, one marvels at how such feats might have been accomplished under the conditions at the time.

At the same time there was also passionate local interest, with every country having its national heroes in cultural heritage protection, such as R. Soekmono (Indonesia), Liang Sicheng (China), Senarath Paranavithana (Sri Lanka), among many others. Great credit is due to the efforts of other local interests in cultural heritage protection ranging from volunteers and museum staff, to architects, archaeologists and cultural advocates who became engaged and led the way. Some rose through the ranks, and others in allied professions were placed in the position by default. For instance, the Khmer modernist architect H.E. Vann Molyvann was appointed as first head of the APSARA Authority, having purview over Angkor, an entity established as a condition of its placement on the World Heritage List in 1992.

A major driver of the need for enhanced responsibly in the conservation of cultural heritage sites is meeting the demands of growing tourist economies. For long distance Western travelers of the late nineteenth and early twentieth centuries, a tour of the Far East was analogous to the Grand Tours of Europe, with there being some more or less established routes that one could take depending on time and interest. As international travel became easier and less expensive in the twentieth century, the more famous sites became popular tourist destinations that were often proudly marketed both locally and internationally. Once foreign visitation to heritage sites became more commonplace, concern emerged at all levels of the conservation community regarding the protection and display of archaeological, architectural and other historical resources. With more discoveries and access to new sites, and exciting news about them, there was more demand to experience heritage sites as travel destinations. Along with this came the necessity of improved local accommodations and infrastructure to receive growing numbers of visitors. An examination of the history of tourist economies of the key heritage sites of Asia bears this out, be it Angkor, Borobudur, the Taj Mahal or others.

Traditional modes of experiencing the cultural heritage sites of Asia have today been joined by additional travel interests, such as environmental tourism, and more specialized forms of leisure tourism, with all being on offer in abundance in recent years. It is the combination of these forms of tourism, offered at competitive prices, that lure international travelers to the "exotic" destinations of Asia, with nearly a quarter of the world's one billion-plus annual tourists visiting Asia.[17] In this equation heritage protection is crucial.

All Asian countries have national governmental departments in charge of cultural heritage in its various forms. Ministries of Culture or their equivalents are generally divided into two branches: Museums administering the movable heritage and Monuments overseeing the immovable heritage (buildings and archaeological sites). To this have been added divisions in charge of landscapes and sites of natural beauty and most recently, branches that may be in charge of intangible heritage. Recreation and tourism are frequently considered allied government responsibilities, all of which may fall under the purview of ministries of culture, and/or ministries of environment. Whatever these divisions, and however they are organized, the one commonality is that all have the imprimatur of national governments behind them, signaling the vital roles national governments have universally assumed for cultural heritage management.

As the cultural heritage conservation ethos has further developed over the past half century the involvement of both private and public participation, and the role of national and international NGOs has grown exponentially. Regional cooperative efforts in heritage management such as SEAMEO SPAFA and the regional branches of ICOMOS, along with various other multi-national cooperative agreements showcase this growth. Leading in this effort is the UNESCO Asia Pacific office with its regional office in Bangkok, having developed region-specific initiatives such as its influential Asia-Pacific Awards program.

As important are the private international NGOs that provide support, technical expertise and financing toward heritage conservation in Asia. Some have been deeply involved with long-standing on-site programs such as the World Monuments Fund and the Aga Khan Trust for Culture, and others offer help in a more targeted way reflective of their missions, such as the Getty Conservation Institute that is devoted to generation and dissemination of conservation science, educational best practices and advanced research methods.

International institutions working in Asian architectural conservation

Aga Khan Trust for Culture (AKTC)

The Aga Khan Trust for Culture (AKTC) is a philanthropic foundation and cultural arm of the Aga Khan Development Network (AKDN), an assortment of institutions involved in the development of economic, social and cultural activities in developing communities around the world, though largely focused in Asia and Africa. Headquartered in Geneva, Switzerland, the Trust was founded in 1988 and has since established or maintained programs focusing on the preservation of Islamic architecture, the revitalization of historic cities, and the promotion of Central Asian music, among others. The Trust also supports seminars and conferences concentrated on the education and understanding of Islamic societies and produces various publications that illustrate its multi-faceted, but highly collaborative, international work. Its various programs include the Aga Khan Award for Architecture, the Aga Khan Program for Islamic Architecture at Harvard University and the Massachusetts Institute of Technology and the Aga Khan Historic Cities Programme. http://www.akdn.org/aktc.asp

Asian Bank for Reconstruction and Development (Asian Development Bank)

Since its establishment in December 1966 under the United Nations organization now named the Economic and Social Commission for Asia and the Pacific (ESCAP), the Asian Development Bank (ADB) has been dedicated to social and economic development in Asia and the Pacific. The initial group of thirty-one regional members has expanded to sixty-seven. The ADB is an international participant in the advancement of poverty-stricken countries through financial aid in the form of loans, grants and investments, categorized as "hard" or "soft," contingent on the borrowing country's income levels. A push to merge the Bank's Asian Development Fund (ADF) and ordinary capital resources (OCR) in May 2015 greatly broadened its effectiveness. Among its several programs is aid for recovery after natural disasters. http://www.adb.org/about/overview

Association of Southeast Asian Nations (ASEAN)

The Association of Southeast Asian Nations (ASEAN) currently consists of ten member states that work to maintain and improve economic prosperity and political stability in the Southeast Asian region. Citing the growing influence of communism, the founding countries – Indonesia, Malaysia, the Philippines, Singapore and Thailand – convened in Bangkok on August 8, 1967 to sign the ASEAN Declaration and establish the organization, also known as the Bangkok Declaration. As the Association grew in size, the end of the Vietnam and Cold War conflicts further prompted its advancement as an entity dealing in regional trade and security matters. ASEAN's committees on finance, agriculture, industry, trade and transportation as well as the expertise of specialists and private-sector organizations has proven advantageous as ASEAN continues to achieve its objective in nourishing a successful and harmonious relationship between Southeast Asian nations. The organization has provided occasional support for cultural heritage studies and advocacy. http://www.asean.org/asean/about-asean

DOCOMOMO (International Working Party for Documentation and Conservation of Buildings, Sites and Neighborhoods of the Modern Movement)

DOCOMOMO is a non-governmental organization that documents and advocates conservation of important architecture and sites dating from the Modern era. It was founded in the Netherlands in 1998 with its principal objectives being contained in its 1990 Manifesto of Eindhoven. It is a membership organization based in Paris and is increasingly involved with advocating the conservation of modernism in Asia through meetings and its *DOCOMOMO Journal*. http://www.docomomo.com

Getty Conservation Institute

The Getty Conservation Institute, the art, architecture and archaeological subset of The J. Paul Getty Trust, is internationally renowned in the heritage conservation field and has worked worldwide since its founding in 1985. The program's influential scientific research, education, training, field projects and publications have made it a leading voice amongst cultural heritage conservation professionals. The GCI's early involvement in Southeast Asia included a five-day Symposium on the Conservation of Cultural Property in Asia and the Pacific (1991, later published as *Cultural Heritage in Asia and the Pacific: Conservation and Policy*), and an international conference organized with the Asia Society and the Siam Society in Thailand (1995, *The Future of Asia's Past*). It later initiated its Built Heritage in Southeast Asia Conservation Education and Training Initiative (2004–2009) with a current project being its Urban Conservation Planning in Southeast Asia (under the Historic Cities and Urban Settlements Initiative). The GCI served as convenor and principal coordinator of the *Principles for the Conservation of Heritage Sites in China* (*China Principles*) document begun in 2000 and most recently revised in 2015. The technical arm of the Institute has undertaken specialized work such as the workshop "Recent Advances in Characterizing Asian Lacquer" (RAdICAL, 2012), the Asian Organic Colorants project (2006–2010), and ongoing wall painting conservation at the Mogao Grottoes, China. http://www.getty.edu

Global Heritage Fund

Since its establishment in 2002, Global Heritage Fund (GHF) has served developing countries in the preservation and protection of their endangered World Heritage Sites. It has granted support directly to professionals working to restore these threatened structures and provides restoration training and jobs to the local populations, thereby ensuring a revived knowledge of culturally based building practices while contributing to a more sustainable source of revenue for these communities. GHF's "Preservation by Design" process comprises planning, conservation science, community development and partnerships as well as thorough reviews and conditions of applicability and feasibility. Projects in Asia in which GHF has participated include Foguang Temple and Lijiang Ancient Town in China, Mỹ Sơn Sanctuary temples, Vietnam, Banteay Chhmar, Cambodia, and Hampi, India. http://globalheritagefund.org/

Hirayama Trust (Japan)

Ikuo Hirayama (1930–2009) was a prominent Japanese painter, art collector and conservationist. After narrowly surviving the Hiroshima bombings as a teenager during World War II, Hirayama went on to study at the Tokyo School of Art (now Tokyo University of the Arts) and frequently incorporated his harrowing experience into the themes of his paintings, eventually delving into Buddhism and images of the Silk Road. He increasingly worked in the conservation of Japanese culture and became a leading proponent of culling government and private entities for Japanese art preservation in Western collections, leading to the establishment of the Joint Council for the Conservation and Restoration of Ancient Japanese Art Works in Foreign Collections (1991). Hirayama's considerable contributions to the preservation field include the establishment of the International Caravanserai of Culture (Center for the Study of the Silk Road) in Tashkent, Uzbekistan and the Hirayama Ikuo Silk Road Museum in Yamanashi Prefecture, Japan, which houses his original works alongside his personal collections of Silk Road art. http://www.silkroad-museum.jp/english/

International Centre for the Study of the Preservation and Restoration of Cultural Property (ICCROM)

UNESCO established ICCROM in 1956 to promote the conservation of world cultural heritage resources by focusing broadly on training, research and public advocacy. Its educational mission includes convening specialized meetings, conducting short courses and in-field training programs and maintaining one of the world's largest reference libraries on cultural heritage conservation. Its CollAsia program aims to conserve heritage collections through conservation and research training, towards sustainable conservation actions for the Asia-Pacific region. http://www.iccrom.org

International Council on Monuments and Sites (ICOMOS)

The International Council on Monuments and Sites (ICOMOS) is consistently involved in international architectural preservation projects, yet one of the organization's most influential contributions was their compelling 1987–1993 survey of World Heritage Sites. This study revealed the disproportionate nature of the List, which was largely focused on Europe's "historic towns, religious monuments, Christianity, historical periods and elitist architecture" and lacked inclusion of living, traditional cultures and vernacular architecture. Since then, ICOMOS has advanced this research while UNESCO has broadened its scope of cultural significance and enacted numerous related initiatives. ICOMOS has continued to develop its presence in Asian countries through various symposia that have resulted in significant preservation initiatives in the region, such as the Hội An Declaration on Conservation of Historic Districts of Asia (2003), the Seoul Declaration on Tourism in Asia's Historic Towns and Areas (2005), and the Xi'an Declaration on the Conservation of the Setting of Heritage Structures, Sites and Areas (2005). The latter prompted the foundation of the ICOMOS International Conservation Center – Xi'an, an international center in Shaanxi Province, China focused on the advancement of conservation in the Asia-Pacific region through projects, research, and training. http://www.icomos.org

International Institute for Conservation of Historic and Architectural Works (IIC)

For over fifty years, IIC has promoted the knowledge, methods and working standards needed to protect and preserve historic and artistic works across the world via publications, conferences and national groups. It helps conservation scientists, architects, educators and students, as well as collections managers, curators, art historians and other cultural heritage professionals remain aware of technical advances in their fields through its quarterly journal *Studies in Conservation* and annual *Reviews in Conservation*. In 2015 it established the IIC Training Centre for Conservation in Beijing. http://www.iiconservation.org

Japan International Cooperation Agency (JICA)

Succeeding the circa-1974 semi-governmental organization of the same name, the current form of the Japan International Cooperation Agency (JICA) was established on October 1, 2003 and officially launched in October 2008. The Agency acts as an intermediary of the Official Development Assistance (ODA) program for Japan's government, which was developed by the Development Assistance Committee (DAC) of the Organization for Economic Co-operation and Development (OECD) to track international aid flow and loans. Through technical training projects, ODA loans, grant aid, public–private partnerships, disaster relief and voluntary participation, JICA has maintained significant involvement in a wide range of issues consisting of agricultural and rural development, urban and regional development, and natural environment and cultural heritage conservation. Some cultural heritage projects of JICA are conducted in cooperation with the National Research Institute for Cultural Properties, Tokyo. http://www.jica.go.jp

League of Historical Cities

Comprised of 102 cities from sixty-one countries, the League of Historical Cities was established in 1987 in Kyoto, Japan. It aims to strengthen affiliations between historic cities to exchange knowledge and experience and ultimately, world peace by deepening mutual understanding and building on the common foundation of historical cities to strengthen affiliations between them. The League works in affiliation with the United Nations Settlements Programme, ICOMOS and the Organization of World Heritage Cities primarily through its biennial World Conference of Historical Cities. http://www.city.kyoto.jp/somu/kokusai/lhcs

Lerici Foundation (Fondazione Ing. Carlo Maurillo Lerici)

The Fondazione Ing. Carlo Maurillo Lerici, more commonly referred to as the Lerici Foundation, was founded at the University Polytechnic of Milan in 1947 as an institute focused on geophysics that eventually led to its application in the field of archaeology. The "Archaeological Exploration" division of the organization is now headquartered in Rome, Italy and has become a leading voice in the application of non-invasive excavation techniques at significant heritage sites. The Foundation is also involved in the publications *Journal of Applied Geophysics* and *Archaeological Exploration*, as well as the dissemination of their own research and projects. The Lerici Foundation has provided much assistance to preservation and restoration projects in several Asian countries. Current undertakings include the Research and Restoration Project in Wat Phou-Champasak, Laos (Nandin Hall Restoration Project), a partnership with UNESCO for the Mỹ Sơn Conservation Project, Vietnam, and a research project at Sri Ksetra, Myanmar. http://www.lerici.polimi.it/

Patrimoine sans Frontières

Founded in 1992 with the support of the French Ministry of Culture and Communication, Patrimoine sans Frontières is an NGO dedicated to preserving endangered or neglected cultural heritage sites worldwide. Its activities include identifying endangered or neglected cultural sites and issues, raising public awareness, fundraising, mobilizing a network of partners to support a particular project, providing advice to other heritage conservation bodies, organizing exhibitions and co-editing publications. http://www.patrimsf.org

Southeast Asian Ministers of Education Organization Project in Archaeology in Fine Arts (SEAMEO SPAFA)

Initially named the Applied Research Centre for Archaeology and Fine Arts (ARCAFA), established in Phnom Penh, Cambodia in 1971, SPAFA was launched in 1978 to continue the organization's efforts to preserve the cultural heritage of Southeast Asia. SPAFA was officially approved in 1981 and was later re-established as the SEAMEO Regional Centre for Archaeology and Fine Arts in 1985, located in Bangkok, Thailand. The Centre focuses its attention on three flagship programs: Advancing Southeast Asian Archaeology, Sacred Universe and Conservation in the Tropics. A key objective of SEAMEO has been to serve as an authority on Southeast Asian archaeology. The organization has become a leader in underwater archaeology and has since 1981, with other Southeast Asian countries and institutions, developed the Southeast Asian Collaboration Programme on Underwater Archaeology. http://www.seameo-spafa.org

United Nations Educational and Scientific Organization (UNESCO)

Significant sites and culture of Southeast Asia are represented in UNESCO's World Heritage Sites list, Intangible Cultural Heritage Register, Memories of the World Register (Memory of the World Programme), and World Network of Biosphere Reserves (Man and the Biosphere Programme). To promote further cohesion in the region, the Asia/Pacific Cultural Centre for UNESCO was established as a non-profit organization in April 1971 and is headquartered in Tokyo. An early endeavor was to develop and disseminate materials for better cultural understanding while education efforts include international exchange programs supported by UNESCO. The World Heritage Institute of Training and Research for the Asia and Pacific Region (WHITRAP), first considered in July 2004 and implemented in October 2007, was developed under UNESCO since its inception. Housed at Tongji University in Shanghai, China, the organization works to reinforce the guidelines outlined by the World Heritage Convention in the Asia and Pacific region and has been a prominent resource in the evolution of the Historic Urban Landscape (HUL) protocol that has launched several pilot projects in cities throughout China. http://en.unesco.org

World Bank

The World Bank consists of the International Bank for Reconstruction and Development (IBRD) and the International Development Association (IDA), together working to provide financial assistance to developing countries worldwide. The Bank is concerned with poverty reduction and implements strategies to manage public spending while boosting productivity amid the social change. While providing public assistance, the Bank also supports conservation projects like the Jiayuguan Pass along the Great Wall of China and others pertaining to cultural and natural heritage protection in Gansu Province, China. The World Bank supports environmental conservation efforts and natural disaster relief as well. http://www.worldbank.org

World Monuments Fund (WMF)

The World Monuments Fund is a private non-profit organization dedicated to the preservation of endangered architectural and cultural sites around the world. WMF's work spans a range of sites and it has program areas that reflect the evolving needs of the field: architectural conservation, capacity building, training and education, advocacy and disaster recovery. The World Monuments Watch program produces a biennial list of endangered sites in need of immediate attention. WMF is active in the conservation of Southeast Asia having helped at scores of sites in most of the region's countries. Among them are four large temple conservation projects at Angkor, Cambodia, pilot conservation projects in the Forbidden City, Beijing and recent assistance to Yangon Historic City Center, Myanmar. https://www.wmf.org

Some of the greatest influences on heritage protection are the major philanthropic and banking institutions such as the World Bank with its International Bank for Reconstruction and Development, the Asian Development Bank and the network of Tata family trusts (based in India and the UK). These organizations quickly engaged with heritage management projects, expanding their commitment concurrent with specializations regarding particular themes and issues. Along with increased international involvement came the experiences of institutions in other parts of the world that could be applied to their projects in Asia. Lessons learned in infrastructure replacement in Morocco were used in similar circumstances at Jaisalmer in Rajasthan, India and modalities for post-disaster recovery in Lijiang, China after its earthquake of 1996 were informed by the World Bank's experiences in disaster recovery elsewhere.

The New York-based, private World Monuments Fund (established 1965) has applied its experiences gained worldwide to a wide range of heritage conservation projects in Asia. Large-scale financial operations like the World Bank, and at the opposite end of the scale, small subject-specific not-for-profit organizations like the World Monuments Fund, have served as examples for others: in 2002 the Global Heritage Fund was founded and in 2015 China established the Asian Infrastructure Investment Bank (AIIB). As these organizations and others develop to meet the ever increasing demand for new models of sustainable development and heritage protection, their work may lead to enhanced interest in and support of of conserving Asia's historic built environments.

Since its founding UNESCO has played an important role in defining, advocating for, listing and protecting cultural heritage. To this it brings a unique global perspective on the intersections of cultural heritage and global issues, including concerns about the loss of cultural identity and diversity, poverty and sustainable development. Agencies within the umbrella of the United Nations such as the United Nations Development Programme (UNDP), UN Environment Programme (UNEP) and the UN's various peacekeeping missions exemplify "soft power" toward their objectives of helping poorer countries to develop and modernize. Individual nations use World Heritage listing as a form of soft power as well, a means of communicating their cultural, social and even environmental credentials to the world. This dynamic ties directly to tourism and to marketing heritage sites as national "commodities." Sophia Labadi and Colin Long say it best: "Tourism is a form of globalization *par excellence*," capable of bringing foreign earnings and development that is attractive to foreign investors.[18] At the local level, tourism is an effective provider of low-skill jobs and is relatively labor intensive.

The UN's various social and cultural programs within these divisions and the good they have provided toward international peace, cooperation and understanding is incalculable. In this regard the Convention Concerning the Protection of the World Cultural and Natural Heritage (the World Heritage Convention) has been enthusiastically supported by UN member states, with 195 of them having acceded to it since its adoption by UNESCO in 1972. This makes it one of the most popular of the UN's various programs. World Heritage listed sites especially play multiple roles as effective symbols of cultural vibrancy that help to create a certain image of a place or region.[19] "In this sense it is important to acknowledge that the international heritage movement with UNESCO at its pinnacle does not stand outside or counter to the processes of globalization; it is inherently implicated with them."[20]

The mission of UNESCO's World Heritage List for all its aims and accomplishments has not been without its issues in Asia and elsewhere. Take for instance the imbalance of sites on the List, which it has been attempting to address for over two decades now. Its problems emerged out of the Eurocentric origins of the World Heritage Convention that were later addressed in the 1994 *Global Strategy for a Balanced, Credible and Representative World Heritage List*. Progress has been made on this front to the direct benefit of regions like Asia, and the program is more popular than ever. The approach is not without its flaws, with critics such as Marc Askew noting that "countries use the alleged universalism of the World Heritage Convention for their own nationalistic ends."[21] Then there are the problems of the politicization of heritage conservation: the practices of realpolitik can come into play during the nomination and selection process as member states weigh the diplomatic and monetary advantages of supporting heritage proposals of other states, all behind a "de-politicized veneer."[22]

It is fair to say, however, that for any oversights of the various foreign attempts to assist with heritage protection projects in Asia, there were likely far more advantages to their involvement than disadvantages. Borobudur was a jumbled heap of stones before the Dutch and later the UNESCO-led team of specialists sifted through its remains and largely reconstructed the monument to be the object of enormous national pride it is today. At the time, the necessary fundraising for the project's work could only have been done as an international cooperative effort. Similarly, were it not for the internationalized, collaborative approach, the Angkor archaeological park would have almost certainly been handled more inefficiently, with out of control tourism far worse than its current situation. Instead, the process of preserving and presenting Angkor derived from planning and incremental action per the recommendation of a master plan required as a condition of its listing on the World Heritage List in 1992.

Yet for the various unexpected negative consequences the actions of these international players sometimes bring, far more good has occurred when one examines the traceable benefits from their involvements. The policies, charters, conventions and project experiences all stand as examples that can be said to have afterlife, both at specific sites where they are born, and at other places where such lessons are applied. (See below Charters and other Instruments Relative to Asian Architectural Conservation.)

Challenges faced in Asian conservation practice

Much of the second half of the twentieth century in Asia was marked by recovery from conflict, struggles towards autonomy after colonial rule, re-establishment of national identities and headlong strides toward modernization. Since the 1950s the speed and scale of change has likely been as great or greater in Asia than in any other part of the world during the past half-century, in part due to its perceived need for "catching up" to the "modern" West. After the trials of World War II, the establishment of culturally and politically cohesive societies often entailed reflection upon or reconsideration of the past, of which architecture stood as the most physical manifestation. Other priorities across the board prevailed, however, and Asian cultural heritage suffered from inadequate maintenance and underutilization on the one hand, or outright hostility from ideological foes on the other. These conditions signaled problems and questions about what should be saved, how and for whom. A *de facto* triage situation was constantly faced during post-war rebuilding in most of the afflicted countries of Asia. In the process the more "charismatic" or impressive heritage sites were eventually addressed due to their cultural status and as reinforcement of national identity. (See Heritage Conservation and Nation Building in Chapter 4.)

Despite the extensive loss to the region's built heritage through conflict and industrialization, what remains still represents a vast amount of accumulated cultural heritage. In recent decades most of Asia's traditional architecture has come under significant strain from economic pressures, physical expansion, accelerated urbanization and from enormous population increases. Between 1950 and 2014, Asia's urban population has grown from 15 to 50 percent as a percentage of the total population.[23] Economic and physical development in the region is currently proceeding at a greater pace than ever before, with the economies of China, Japan and Korea growing at exceptional rates in the post-war period. As a result, the historic urban and rural cultural landscapes of the region are in constant flux.[24] Unprecedented as well are the new realities of transnational economic policies and changing cultural paradigms driven by global civil society.

As cited in *The Disappearing Asian City* (2002), South East Asian cities such as Phnom Penh, Hanoi and Hong Kong are transforming at extraordinary, dramatic and bewildering rates, causing great concern for those interested in maintaining continuities between past and present. Wholesale movements of communities in and out of urban landscapes, together with dramatic changes brought on by the immense tech markets in both the manufacturing and financial arenas, may be seen as deeply confounding, imposing disorientation on residents. The conservation of social, spiritual and material heritage of Asia's fast changing towns, cities and cultural landscapes pose vexing challenges for heritage managers going forward.

Key issues facing cultural heritage protection today also include natural sources of change, including the effects of earthquakes, storms, floods, weathering and climate change. As noted earlier, the geographical range of Asia is vast and its attendant climatic and natural characteristics represent extremes from serious bio-deterioration and harsh sun exposure in its tropical climates to issues of equally harsh freeze–thaw cycles in its northern climates. Should global temperatures change to the degree predicted by some scientists, expectations will need to change regarding how old buildings will perform under new circumstances.

Natural disasters are particularly effective at demonstrating the fragility of the built environment, and the lives and lifeways that occupy it. Indeed, the greatest and most alarming example of a blend of human and natural threats may emerge as the primary environmental crisis of our time: climate change. (See Climate Change and Cultural Heritage in South Asia in Chapter 19.) It is not only a danger to numerous heritage sites but it also represents a profound threat to the continuity of intangible practices, knowledge systems and even entire societies.[25]

The lists of human-made threats to the historic built environment are equally deleterious, or more so, with the principal one in Asia being uncontrolled development pressures, closely followed by environmental pollution. Illustrations of this are seen in the actions of aggressive and capable entities such as the international development arms of the governments of Japan, Korea and China, who bring their own values and approaches in heritage protection to foreign projects that may not be compatible with local interests. In the domain of energy production alone, the damming of rivers in Asia has profoundly affected the environments and lifeways of millions each year.

Disaster risks and preventative architectural conservation, by Christopher Marrion

The adverse impact from natural and man-made disasters on cultural heritage is increasing on a global basis.[26] Natural hazards posing some of the greater danger to cultural heritage sites and structures include earthquakes, tsunamis, floods, volcanoes, wildfires, structural fires and changes in water level. The impacts of disasters in Asia are quite significant compared with the rest of the world: over the last twenty years, four of the five countries hit by the highest number of natural disasters are in Asia: China, India, the Philippines and Indonesia. Climatological disasters threaten the region as well, affecting vast areas throughout Asia, often in locales where rapid response is very difficult.[27]

Sites, structures and artifacts of cultural significance, intangible heritage, as well as cultural tourism and the related financial resources these sites introduce to local communities all suffer when disasters strike. An appreciable percentage of some countries' Gross Domestic Product (GDP) is from travel and tourism, such as Nepal at approximately 8.9 percent in 2014.[28] With seven of their ten World Heritage Sites damaged from the 2015 earthquakes, it is not difficult to imagine the hardships placed upon not only sites but the surrounding local economies they support, in addition to the shattering loss of lives. (See Lessons in Damage Mitigation to Cultural Heritage from the Great East Japan Earthquake and Tsunami in Chapter 1.)

Man-made hazards are not only those produced by acts of war, but also include: urbanization; mass tourism; changes in functionality or ownership; reduction/loss in care and maintenance; pollution/acid rain; fracking and mining; desertification; alterations to land and water use; and climate change.

Most natural hazards cannot be prevented. However, focusing on disaster risk reduction prior to events can help limit spending significantly larger sums of money in post-disaster recovery.[29] Disaster risk management involves several steps including to help understand goals/objectives, identify hazards including natural and man-made hazards, understand vulnerabilities, assess risks, and develop prevention and mitigation measures to effectively address these risks, and that are architecturally sensitive to the sites/structures. Measures are also typically developed to address not only the prevention/mitigation phase, but the response and recovery phases as well.[30]

Globally, the world has been moving to align with this viewpoint. Examples include the recent adoption of the Sendai Framework for Disaster Risk Reduction 2015–2030 for addressing disasters globally, which replaced the Hyogo Framework for Action 2005–2015, as well as the recent adoption of the Sustainable Development Goals. These documents have not only further expanded the literature for disaster management, but have highlighted and greatly enhanced the importance of ensuring cultural heritage is prominently included in disaster risk management strategies and community resilience. Prevention and mitigation measures exist on many levels: scientific research and engineering analyses can assist with developing effective technical solutions; educational programs can be developed to promote awareness among governing authorities, owners, occupants and users; community based support can be increased to help understand and protect cultural heritage; and international efforts can continue to offer technical and financial support. Effective government policies and international treaties need to continue to be developed and enforced to help in preventing or mitigating the consequences of armed conflicts and civil strife on our cultural heritage. Evaluating the feasibility of preventative and mitigation measures for all forms of hazards should include a measure of their effectiveness to mitigate the relevant hazards, as well as architectural compatibility.

We can learn a significant amount from traditional knowledge that can be incorporated into prevention, mitigation and response measures. Two excellent examples of the technical knowledge gained over centuries are the construction of the temples in Japan and their ability to resist earthquakes and the construction techniques of numerous mosques in Indonesia that were some of the only structures to have consistently resisted the impacts of the Great Indian Ocean Earthquake and Tsunami. With regards to fire, there is important traditional knowledge in Japan related to the protection of the temples, including the development of redundant water supplies fed by gravity, resilient piping and automatic suppression systems within and surrounding sacred sites to function during a fire, or even for fires that develop as a direct result of an earthquake.

Traditional knowledge also offers key information related to floods. It provides a thorough understanding of the original development of Ayutthaya in Thailand: when the city was built centuries ago, flooding was understood to be a natural, re-occurring event. Hence the city was built in the middle of rivers with mitigation measures including canals throughout the city to help manage water flow, as well as walls around the city with retractable gates at each canal opening to the rivers to help manage the floods. Over time, due to various reasons, these water management systems were of limited effectiveness, a situation compounded by the urbanization of the surrounding areas. This situation increased water run-off and limited the ability for the local lands to absorb the water, adding to the water management challenges of the recent floods.

Cultural heritage sites and structures around the world do not typically enjoy adequate protection from the range of hazards and risks that threaten them. Astute hazard and vulnerability assessments, understanding local capabilities, engaging the community, incorporating applicable prevention/mitigation measures and the development and enforcement of appropriate regulations, can either prevent or limit hazards or at least stop them from turning into disasters. Protecting tangible and intangible heritage in advance from the hazards they may face is extremely important as it protects the unique and irreplaceable value they hold for us all.

Other serious threats to Asia's built heritage include lack of financial and technical capacity, inadequate coordination among stakeholders and insufficient site management systems. More nuanced threats include insensitivity at the local level to the importance of heritage protection, over-aggressive tourism management and the illicit trafficking of antiquities, particularly in conflict zones.[31]

Within the socio-economic context of heritage protection there are numerous concerns related to the health, welfare and economic prospects of the inhabitants of Asia's historic cities, towns and historic places. In most of the countries of Asia there are critical needs for improved living conditions, health systems, reduction in pollution and more efficient and balanced planning for both cultural and natural resources. In many countries efforts to raise the quality of governance itself eclipses heritage protection activities. As one measure of this need, fifteen of the thirty countries addressed in this book are ranked in the bottom half of Transparency International's Corruption Perceptions Index.[32]

Many Asian countries struggle with the challenge of raising awareness and appreciation of local or regional histories, and promoting the places worthy of conservation. Serious problems can be attributed to apathy, commodification of heritage and the shortcomings of the heritage tourism economy. In many communities the understandable desire for economic advancement and acquisition of new, modern amenities outstrips communal interest in retaining the traditional trappings of society, including buildings. Even in countries like Bhutan, where promotion of traditional culture has been a key objective of the national government for decades, the pull away from the traditional and toward the global is increasingly strong. In more development-oriented countries like China, Maldives and Singapore, a singular drive toward economic expansion and modernization has come at great cost to traditional societies and environments, to the point where these nations have actively reconsidered their priorities and begun to change direction. There remains great need and opportunity to better teach and share the benefits of sustainable cultural resource management to local communities.

In most cases the elevation of the status of a heritage site improves its situation; however, it is obvious in some cases that over-celebrated sites have been spoiled by excess visitation and commercial exploitation. In any case most sites are not being interpreted for all they are worth as witnesses of their existence across time. As such there remains tremendous potential for more effective heritage site interpretation in Asia.

If conservation of physical materials is one dimension of heritage protection, then preserving its accompanying "intangible heritage" is the other principal component. Intangible heritage encompasses the behavioral aspects (performing arts, rituals, social practices) and symbolic or conceptual aspects (knowledge systems, treatises on building, values and meanings, stories, myths, social structures, memories) that make cultures distinctive from one another. Optimally, the conservation of tangible heritage should go hand in hand with the conservation of its associated intangible heritage. That the two are interdependent should be assumed at the outset of any project, and expertise should be engaged to address both throughout. The need for effective strategies in this regard may be broadly addressed by new pleas for the conservation of intangible heritage, several of which have come out of Asian professional circles. The 2003 UNESCO *Convention for the Safeguarding of the Intangible Cultural Heritage*, while officially adopted in the Paris convention of that year, has received a great deal of support from Asian countries – particularly Japan, China, Korea and Vietnam – on its way to securing 168 ratifying states.

Challenges that lie ahead in CRM include the safeguarding of heritage and heritage sites in light of unprecedented national and international development schemes. Some are enormous in size, such as the Three Gorges Dam on the Yangtze River, completed in 2003, after having displaced 1.2 million people and 116 communities, and labeled by some as an "environmental catastrophe."[33] Other more modest projects, such as the Karakoram Highway, built during the 1970s between Islamabad (Pakistan) and Kashgar (China) can prove highly disruptive to traditional communities by the sudden introduction of new commercial and cultural forces into previously long-isolated communities.

In the face of these many challenges, a pressing need exists for innovative, interdisciplinary approaches to CRM going forward. Heritage education stands out as one of the most promising means for building discourse around engagement and inclusiveness regarding all histories. Similarly, the management and protection of contextual (e.g., non-monumental) heritage offers great promise in Asian communities.[34] In this context, improvements to heritage education always pose challenges. A broad, multivalent approach to conservation, that includes vernacular and more ordinary buildings as well as key historic buildings, is of vital importance as well as accommodating and understanding different views on different cultural heritage conservation practices as a whole.

Meeting the challenge

The professional practice of architectural conservation in Asia has made significant progress from its nineteenth century origins, especially in the past half century. Through this period many countries in Asia have developed serious and capable institutions and professional cadres on par with other global leaders in heritage conservation practice. Attitudinal changes about the past shifted as well, as dramatically evidenced in the People's Republic of China since its Cultural Revolution (1966–1976), and in Myanmar since its opening to the wider world accelerated following elections in 2010.

Given the enormity of the undertaking, since Asian nations began to commit to architectural conservation as a government-supported activity, the effort posed huge financial, logistical and often technical challenges. However, by the mid-twentieth century, nearly every country had begun to set about the organizational task of enhancing their administrative and technical capacity to address the protection of monuments based on considered priorities. In effect, a triage approach was understandably used, which also took into account the symbolic and tourism value of heritage sites. Now, decades on, the cultural resource management systems in most countries have architectural heritage protection ensconced among their national priorities, with the main, and not unusual, limitations being funding and technical capacity.

An integral part of the evolution of the heritage conservation ethos in Asia has been in the strengthening and updating of its heritage protection laws. It has been argued that the onset of legislation for heritage protection in a country is the mark of its commitment and the start of serious, professional attention to the matter. Some heritage protection laws in Asia date to the mid-nineteenth century, as in Japan and Thailand, with some having principles and rules for heritage protection dating to centuries earlier, such as those of the kings of Anuradhapura and Angkor. All such laws in Asia have been updated in recent decades, and many are in active states of reconsideration, updating, expansion and modernization. (See also Cultural Heritage Legislation: The Matter of Looting in Chapter 8.)

Conserving and presenting built heritage in a way that is sustainable – in a way that pays for itself – has always been the goal in most architectural conservation projects as a matter of common sense. Currently, however, there is more reliance than ever on making heritage conservation projects self-supporting. Such outcomes depend on thorough planning that considers alternatives and their feasibility. Funding heritage towards returns on investment, whether direct or indirect, is now commonplace, especially with regard to projects involving adaptive use of buildings and projects done in an urban context. Noteworthy examples in Asia include the renovation of the nineteenth century Central Market in Siem Reap, Cambodia or the commercial developments of early waterfront warehouses Clarke and Boat Quays in Singapore. In other instances, government or other institutional funding can attract supplemental contributions from the private and NGO sectors based on the rationale that conservation projects often benefit existing, or provide new, civic amenities. Otherwise, as the field has matured, increasingly sophisticated schemes of fundraising such as challenge funding, in-kind contributions, tax incentives, fundraising events and public appeals have gained traction. In this connection, effective publicity for endangered sites has proven to work well, with several cause-related advocacy organizations, such as the Anglo-Indian Jaisalmer in Jeopardy campaign, making progress in saving local, national and international heritage sites.

Meeting the challenges in heritage protection has been uneven in the nations of Asia for a variety of reasons, however governmental and institutional support for heritage management and its allied field of cultural tourism have expanded, and the training of new generations of professionals and craftspeople represent real advancements. Encouraging commitment and offering assistance in improving technical and organizational capacity have been goals of UNESCO's heritage sector from its inception. In so doing it realized that celebrating accomplishments is an important form of encouragement. One of UNESCO's most effective tools for honoring progress in architectural conservation is the Awards program of its Bangkok-based Asia-Pacific office.

The power of example: UNESCO Asia-Pacific Heritage Awards program[35]

Throughout Asia and the Pacific, cultural heritage sites are under threat. While national monuments are typically afforded some level of protection, it is the heritage properties in the hands of everyday people that are most vulnerable – from neglect, inappropriate alterations, renewal or even wholesale demolition. And yet it is these properties that tend to be most closely intertwined with the living heritage of a place, and thus their protection is imperative not only as a means of conserving heritage buildings *per se*, but also as a means of safeguarding the culture of a place in a more inclusive sense. Preserving heritage properties thus needs to be a concern for all – not only the state, but also private owners, residents and users.

In a sense, the program now reflects the strides taken in the heritage profession, which has seen the introduction and the adoption of new normative instruments in the culture sphere at the international, regional and national levels, notably the 2001 Convention on the Protection of the Underwater Cultural Heritage and the 2003 Convention for the Safeguarding of the Intangible Cultural Heritage.

The UNESCO Asia-Pacific Heritage Awards recognize excellence in three main areas of achievement: understanding the place, technical achievement, and social and policy impact.

Demonstrating an understanding of the place is the fundamental prerequisite for undertaking conservation work. With the shift towards values-based approaches to conserving heritage that has been engendered by the World Heritage Convention and other seminal documents, it is now widely recognized that conservation decisions must be underpinned by a profound and multivalent understanding of the values of heritage places. These values are not limited purely to aesthetic and architectural values, but encompass cultural, social and historical dimensions as well. The submitted projects are therefore judged by the extent to which the conservation work articulates and interprets these heritage values in an insightful manner. As the use or adaptation of heritage properties has a large bearing on its spirit of place, the issue of appropriate use or adaptation is also considered. Given that heritage values are seen in different light by various constituents and stakeholders of each heritage place, the identification and articulation of the values of a heritage place emerges through a process of reflection and consultation. The achievement of these criteria is thus not just seen in the end product of the restored building, but also reflects the sensitivity of the process as well.

The Jury Commendation for Innovation considers whether the project has an outstanding design concept that demonstrates critical thinking in articulating an innovative response to the specific historic context. The jury looks into how well the new structure helps to reveal the qualities of a place, including its historical, architectural, cultural and social significance. This takes into account the compatibility and appropriateness of the new structure's program and function in its context and how well the new structure integrates with the existing built and natural context. How the new intervention fits with the existing context in terms of typology, siting, massing, form, scale, character, color and texture is key. Projects must also justify the selection of materials and building techniques. Similarly to the conservation category, the Jury Commendation projects also need to demonstrate impact. This includes the manner in which the process and the final product extend the local community's cultural and social continuum and the influence of the project on architectural practice and design policy locally, nationally, regionally or internationally.

The winning projects have often generated even greater catalytic impact after recognition by UNESCO through the Heritage Awards program. The technical methodologies and techniques developed and applied at the winning projects have been disseminated and emulated, not only within national confines, but sometimes in other countries. Winning projects have often become case studies used in teaching heritage conservation in university courses and professional training programs. The building contractors, craftspersons and specialists who have contributed to the successful projects have generally seen an increased demand for their expertise and have been able to apply their experience at other projects, thus building upon and refining their knowledge and skills. A great number of projects have become significant engines of economic growth, enhancing livelihoods and well being within the local community through tourism or revived local cultural industries that include traditional construction trades, which had previously been in decline.

Winning projects have become important advocacy tools, enhancing public awareness of conserving heritage, especially for long forgotten or widely overlooked heritage such as vernacular buildings or modern architecture. In some cases, institutions and knowledge systems have been reinforced, with the renaissance of traditional guilds and cultural practices associated with sustaining heritage places both physically, socially and spiritually. Others have had major educational benefits, both within the building profession or heritage practitioners and among society at large, particularly among youth. Many projects have reported a strengthened sense of ownership in caring for the heritage properties, from local residents as well as authorities at the local and state level. By bolstering a sense of pride within the local community, the recognition from UNESCO for the outstanding conservation efforts has frequently led to greater levels of participation in other conservation projects, thus creating a multiplier effect. They are frequently singled out as exemplars by authorities and local leaders, and in this way, help to inform policy making and mobilize investment and resources. At the highest levels of national policy, the winning projects have called attention to the need for reassessing heritage legislation to safeguard a broader spectrum of heritage. (See also New Design in Heritage Contexts, by William Chapman in Chapter 4.)

Acquiring technical capacity for heritage protection is a function of the commitment of governments, educators, financial support and the prospects of long term work in the field. Another hallmark of the field is the proliferation of educational offerings in CRM: there is now an array of higher education opportunities in the subject in nearly all the countries of Asia. The fostering of traditional architectural crafts training is also found in most countries where it is delivered in institutionalized, apprentice-based or project-specific contexts. Leaders in fostering higher education include experienced national professionals and their protégés at universities and other institutions within countries such as Thailand, India, China and Japan. In a number of circumstances significant funding and instructional assistance have been offered by the international community through the initiatives of organizations such as ICOMOS, UNESCO, Patrimoine sans Frontières, the World Monuments Fund, Japan (JICA) and the Aga Khan Trust for Culture, among others. Foreign assistance in architectural conservation education has also been offered in the form of exchange programs, and the establishment of research centers such as ICOMOS Asia Regional Centre in Xi'an.

Along with improved technical and funding capacity the field of cultural resources management has been steadily expanding within all dimensions of the field, generating previously unimagined specialties and subspecialties. Many have been aided by influential technical developments made possible by recent quantum leaps in digital documentation, telecommunication and data management systems. The age-old techniques of hand-drawn graphic recordation of heritage sites are fast giving way to digital documentation technologies that offer vastly more possibilities for documentation, analysis and dissemination of information.

Importantly, different types of heritage have been addressed in current years, such as the treatment of urban and rural vernacular architecture as cultural landscapes, rather than individual structures. In this way the less obvious sites, objects, features and "connective tissue" may be conserved for their contextual value, along with their more famous, monumental heritage counterparts. These values found a secure home in Asia, with cities such as Hội An in Vietnam serving as early and important exemplars of this type of thinking. (See On the Importance of the Ordinary in Chapter 3 and The HUL: A Paradigm Shift in Chapter 10.) Other perspectives, such as the histories of minority populations, the oppressed, sites where change occurred and sites associated with "pain" and "shame," (sometimes called "dark heritage" or "sites of conscience") resulting from incidents of war and civil unrest or adherence to belief systems based on intolerance, racial discrimination or ethnic hostilities are also now being addressed. (See Painful Cultural Heritage in Chapter 10.)

As the physical and conceptual parameters of the field expand on all fronts one may expect more people, more interest, more access and more demands falling on heritage sites as greater affluence, increased mobility, and the further proliferation of cultural tourism expand the physical and conceptual parameters of the field on all fronts. All of these developments are stimulating both the democratization and commodification of heritage in Asia.

Scholars in the social sciences are increasingly playing a role in cultural heritage management, who recognize its humanizing effects and societal values. Unlike most traditional architectural conservation professionals, sociologists and cultural anthropologists are frequently in a better position to access what communities want and expect in heritage protection, and how to present relevant stories of history and its importance at heritage sites. They are better qualified to measure and analyze differences in the meanings and values that communities and individuals associate with cultural heritage sites and they are increasingly making meaningful contributions to cultural conservation dialogs.[36]

Architectural conservation training in Asia, by William Chapman

Asian countries have been slow to develop capacity in architectural conservation education. Much of this has to do with economic development. China was in the midst first of a massive rebuilding in the 1950s and 1960s; in the 1970s it was caught up in the iconoclastic Cultural Revolution, which had little tolerance for anything remaining of the past. Japan and South Korea similarly focused on industrial and economic development during the post-war era. Thailand, Indonesia and Malaysia were even slower to enter the modern age, a step hindered by a long period of political uncertainty during the same time.

The long war in Vietnam further interrupted any heritage efforts that might have been under way in much of Southeast Asia during this time. While nearly all newly emergent governments expressed an interest in protecting national treasures and heritage, none had the means to underwrite restoration or conservation efforts. The Vietnamese leader Ho Chi Minh, in fact, signed a proclamation calling for the protection of heritage sites as early as 1945, an intention put into law by the revolutionary government in 1957. Other Asian governments made similar gestures, with Indonesian specialists taking over from their Dutch mentors by the late 1950s and newly created Malaysia taking on responsibility for monumental archaeological sites and historic buildings by the late 1970s (as British scholars vacated university and museum posts that dealt with architectural conservation).

Cambodia, Laos and Vietnam all suffered from a dependency on French expertise and the long course of the various Indochina conflicts of the 1960s and 1970s. Cambodia, after 1973, had no national program and no training in conservation. In the late 1980s, the country – still under Vietnamese control – invited in the Archaeological Survey of India (ASI) to undertake repairs at Angkor, Cambodia's principal repository of monumental heritage sites. Vietnam relied on Polish expertise in the work on Cham and other archaeological sites, until later inviting in Italian- and US-led teams. Laos eventually relied on the EFEO and UNESCO in its efforts to restore and develop the picturesque city of Luang Prabang. In each case training played only a small part of these efforts, the exception being the steps taken by the US-based World Monuments Fund to train Cambodian nationals at its designated site in Angkor, Preah Khan.

Other countries also struggled in the wake of independence. India and Pakistan were joint heirs to the British-initiated ASI, begun in 1861. With an emphasis, again, on monumental archaeological sites, the ASI settled into a relatively standardized set of procedures for the stabilization of historic monuments. This system extended to colonial Burma, and, again, continued with little interruption following independence in India, Pakistan (and later Bangladesh), Ceylon (Sri Lanka, after 1972) and Burma (Myanmar, since 1989). Although college and university architecture programs in each of these countries continued to offer some training in history and treatments of historic buildings, much of the staff for the ASI and its equivalents in other former British colonies in Asia tended to be recruited from the field of archaeology, with the work typically carried out by local departments of public works.

Japan would in many ways become a leader in architectural conservation approaches in the 1970s. At the forefront of Japan's contribution were the Tokyo and Nara Research Institutes for Cultural Properties, since 2001 combined to form the National Research Institute for Cultural Properties. Beginning in 1932 and 1952, respectively, the two institutes became training grounds for conservation research and also served as important forums for ideas. The Tokyo branch, known as the Tobunken, began its department of Restoration Techniques in 1973 and expanded the institute's scope in the mid-1990s through its Division of International Cooperation for Conservation. Nara similarly became a center for the study and treatment of historic architecture, offering courses for Japanese architects and archaeologists and also reaching out to other organizations. Although much of the work of both branches of the National Research Institute concentrated on national treasures, Japan's expertise became noteworthy in the Asian context. Japanese experts also became the most outspoken proponents of the idea that Asian approaches to conservation might well differ from those of the West.

China's architectural conservation training lagged significantly behind Japan's. There were no formal architectural programs specializing in conservation before the late 1990s. Expertise generally focused on archaeological sites, with Peking University's Beijing Centre as the key institute for conservation research and training. Although a number of architects and urban planners were exposed to conservation ideals while studying aboard, it was not until 1995 that China began to assert itself as a setting for new conservation thought. Notably drawing upon the guidance of the Los Angeles-based Getty Conservation Institute, Chinese experts representing China-ICOMOS formulated what came to be titled the China Principles (*Principles for the Conservation of Heritage Sites in China*, 2000). Thereafter, specifically Chinese approaches began to be incorporated into university curricula as new architectural programs developed in the late 1990s and early 2000s.

Nearly all, if not all, Asian countries have signed onto international agreements intended to guide conservation practice. These begin with the UNESCO Convention for the Protection of Cultural Property in the Event of Armed Conflict (the Hague Convention, 1954) through the International Charter for the Conservation and Restoration of Monuments and Sites (the Venice Charter, 1964) to the Charter on the Built Vernacular Heritage (Mexico City, 1999). The first note of regional discord was the Nara Document on Authenticity (1994), which suggested that some cultural approaches – notably the tradition of rebuilding in time-honored techniques as is sometimes expressed in Japan and other Asian and Pacific countries – are at odds with the Western ideals set out in the Venice Charter. From that point, it came to be recognized that "authenticity," in the form of continuing craft skills, needed to be considered as an alternative to simply preserving the tangible artifact – a concept increasingly part of any conservation training and practice in the region.

For most of the twentieth century and much of the present time, Asian architectural students have depended on international training abroad for conservation skills. Universities such as Harvard, Cornell, MIT and the University of California at Berkeley historically turned out graduates with some exposure to architectural conservation. With the emergence of specialized historic preservation programs beginning with that at Columbia University in 1968, an increasing number of Asian students obtained training abroad. In the USA, Columbia, Cornell and the University of Pennsylvania provided the specialized training required. The Architectural Association in London and the University of York's Institute for Advanced Architectural Studies, founded in 1962, also filled an important niche.

Eventually, Asian students received their training in a wide range of international programs. These included a number of French universities, as well as architectural degree courses in Australia and New Zealand. New advanced training programs emerged in Japan as well, notably the Graduate School of Conservation at the Tokyo University of the Arts; the Department of Urban Engineering at the University of Tokyo; the School of Architecture in the Faculty of Engineering at Kyoto University; and the Architecture and Environmental Design faculty at Nagaoka Institute of Design. In more recent years, Kyushu University now has architectural conservation training, as does the Jesuit Sophia University and the University of Tsukuba, the latter of which has developed a program focused on World Heritage Sites. Many students from Southeast Asian countries have taken advantage of scholarship opportunities to obtain advanced degrees from these institutions.

Other international organizations and universities have played an equally important part in architectural conservation training in Asia. Many senior officials had an opportunity to attend one or more of the courses of the International Centre for the Study of the Preservation and Restoration of Cultural Properties in Rome (ICCROM), an offspring of UNESCO. Inaugurating its specialized programs in the early 1960s, including a much-respected six-month course on architectural conservation, ICCROM also partnered with regional training organizations, beginning in the 1980s. Australian universities have also played an increasingly significant role in conservation training in the region. The universities of Sydney and Melbourne both offer specialized courses and/or degrees in architectural conservation, reaching out both to East Asia and Southeast Asia – and with faculty strengths in both areas beginning in the 1990s. Deakin University's Cultural Heritage and Museum Studies program has been particularly active in the region, forming a partnership with Silpakorn University in Bangkok for the delivery of specialized architectural training in 2001.

Further afield, the École Nationale Supérieure d'Architecture de Paris-Belleville has had a long relationship with Cambodia, sending its own students (under the direction of Professor Pierre Clément) to work on collaborative projects with their Khmer counterparts as early as 1991. Similarly, the University of Hawai'i at Mānoa initiated an architectural training program for students at the Royal University of Fine Arts (RUFA) in Phnom Penh in 1996; this continued in Thailand from 1997 through 2002, with funding from the Asian Cultural Council and Japan Foundation, attracting students from throughout Southeast Asia.

Most Asian countries have now established their own university training programs. China currently has architectural conservation programs and/or courses at the Chinese University of Hong Kong, at Xi'an University (previously called the Xi'an Institute of Metallurgy and Building), and at the South East University in Nanjing (formerly the Nanjing Institute of Technology). There are also modest programs at Hangzhou University and Zhejiang University, both with ties to urban planning and geography. In addition to the Heritage Research Centre at the University of Peking, Beijing also provides training in historic architecture at the Beijing University of Civil Engineering and Tsinghua University, the latter of which offers a specialized M. Arch degree in architectural conservation. Another center of conservation training is Tongji University in Shanghai, especially through the research interests of Professor Chang Qing and Professor Dai Shibing, Director of the Architecture Conservation Laboratory.

The most international Chinese program is that at the Hong Kong University, begun by Professor David Lung in 2000. Aimed at students both within and outside China – courses are taught in English – the Architectural Conservation Programme (ACP) offers both a PDip (Diploma) and MSc in Conservation, as well as a Bachelor of Arts degree in Conservation (beginning in 2012) and opportunities for graduate-level research degrees. In 2010, the ACP also opened an Architectural Conservation Laboratory to further the university's research interests.

China's advances have been repeated elsewhere in the region. Thailand now has several university programs dealing with aspects of architectural conservation. In the late 1990s, Professor Pinraj Khanjanusthiti introduced an architectural conservation concentration in Chulalongkorn University's MArch program. Other universities have a more general focus. Silpakorn University's graduate degree in Architectural Heritage Management and Tourism, begun in 2001 by former university president Trungjai Buranasomphob, brings together architects, historians, archaeologists and tourism specialists, as do several "Cultural Management" degrees offered by other Thai universities. Several of these are "international programs," with lectures in English (though most students are Thai nationals).

Growth of both specialized architectural training and generalized heritage management programs have been slow to materialize elsewhere in Southeast Asia. The University of Malaysia's Institute of Graduate Studies lists several PhD dissertations on heritage related subjects. The Universiti Teknologi MARA (UiTM) offers a Master's degree in Heritage and Conservation management. The National University of Singapore has no formal degree in architectural conservation, but students in the Architectural Studies Program can specialize in aspects of heritage conservation, as can M Arch, MA, and PhD students. Similarly, the Department of Architecture and Faculty of Engineering at the Univeristas Indonesia provides training in conservation in the context of courses in History and Urban Housing and Development, as does Gadja Mada University in Yogyakarta (which supports a Centre for Heritage Conservation). There are comparable offerings as well at Diponegoro University, Burapha University, and Padjadjaran University. The Institut Teknologi Bandung (ITB) also offers courses in conservation in the School of Architecture, Planning and Policy Development.

Tertiary opportunities for conservation studies in other Southeast Asian countries are only at a beginning stage. There is minimal training at the Royal University of Fine Arts (RUFA) and at the University of Phnom Penh in Cambodia. The same is true at the National University of Laos in Vientiane, and at several universities in Vietnam. The latter include the Hanoi Architectural University and the Ho Chi Minh University of Architecture in Ho Chi Minh City, along with a number of government-backed centers, including the National Center for the Design and Restoration of Cultural Constructions and the Hanoi-based National Center for Monuments Conservation.

By this point, most architectural programs elsewhere in Asia have some level of conservation training. In India, these include the Sir J.J. School of Architecture in Mumbai, the Indian Institute of Technology at Kharagpur, the University of Baroda, the Centre for Environmental Planning and Technology University (CEPT University) at Ahmedabad, the Government College of Architecture in Lucknow, and the MBS School of Planning and Architecture in New Delhi. Pakistan has architectural conservation offerings at the University of Gujrat, the National University of Science and Technology in Islamabad, the Indus Valley School of Art and Architecture in Karachi, and the Beaconhouse National University and the Imperial University in Lahore. The National College of Arts, also in Lahore, has a separate Centre for Cultural Heritage, offering advanced degrees in heritage management. Bangladesh has the Bangladesh University of Engineering and Technology in Dhaka and the Rajshahi University of Engineering and Technology in Rajshahi, both with some training in heritage issues.

Elsewhere training depends largely on interested faculty members. Seoul National University and Sungkyunkwan University in South Korea both have courses but no full-blown programs. (Seoul National University does have an Architectural History Laboratory and a second lab focused on "Architectural Culture," though no specific curriculum on architectural conservation.) The University of the Philippines-Diliman, one of the nation's top architecture schools, provides opportunity for projects focused on historic buildings, as do the Roman Catholic universities of Santo Tomas and Saint Louis. The University of the Philippines has one studio in History, Theory and Criticism that includes some emphasis on historic buildings. There is also a Building Science Studio Lab, although this course focuses more on modern materials and technologies.

Although universities have taken on much of the burden of conservation training, there is a continuing presence of international organizations in the region – a presence going back nearly half a century. In 1971, the Southeast Asian Ministers of Education Organization (SEAMEO) launched a new Applied Research Center for Archaeology and Fine Arts (ARCAFA) in Phnom Penh to address the needs for training both in archaeology and the conservation of monuments. With the expansion of the Vietnamese War, the center transferred to Bangkok in 1973, with an accompanying name change to the SEAMEO Project in Archaeology and Fine Arts, or SPAFA. With only three active members – Thailand, Indonesia and the Philippines – the new center expanded its scope, obtaining a new building in 1985 and reaching out to other Southeast Asian countries. Since re-titled the SEAMEO Regional Centre for Archaeology and Fine Arts, the center retained the SPAFA acronym.

In 1978, Indonesia's Borobudur site became an official sub-center for training in conservation techniques. Between then and 1982, the Borobudur facility held eight training programs for students from Thailand, the

Philippines, Malaysia and Indonesia, issuing certificates of completion for students in the eight-month program. Shortened in subsequent years, the SPAFA program ended in 1992, to be replaced by shorter course offerings, conducted mostly in Bangkok. Around this time SPAFA entered into the first of several cooperative arrangements with the Rome-based ICCROM program. In 1998, this arrangement resulted in a significant training program in Siem Reap, Cambodia, working with Cambodia's APSARA authority, the ruling body for the conservation work at Angkor. The program combined architecture, engineering and archaeology students in a five-month annual training workshop, led by stone conservator Simon Warrack. Known as the Ta Nei project, this program lasted four years, but provided the model for subsequent workshops, including those held by the Getty Conservation Institute (GCI) in 2008–2009.

Similar training programs have been part of most of the international programs in Angkor. Beginning with the World Monuments Fund's program at Preah Khan, other organizations have consistently built training of Cambodian students into their overall conservation projects. In 1998, the International Committee on Conservation (ICC) recommended that fully 1 percent of all project monies be spent on training. The Japanese Government Team for Safeguarding Angkor (JSA), the German Apsara Conservation Project (GACP) and other organizations made good on this promise, providing on-site training for younger architecture and archaeology students as part of their broader mission. At the same time, UNESCO, using funds from the Japan and Toyota Foundations, supported international lecturers for classroom instruction at the Royal University of Fine Arts (RUFA), a program that lasted from 1993 to 2002.

From the 1980s, ICCROM also became increasingly involved in the region. Responding to a massive earthquake that affected the monuments in Pagan (Bagan), Myanmar, ICCROM sent noted mural conservators Paolo Pagnin and Rodolfo Lujan to provide on-site training for both professionals and technicians. This program ran from 1982 to 1988 and laid the groundwork for professional expertise in the country. While UNESCO continued to support work at the site, the Myanmar government disengaged from international cooperation in the late 1990s, ending both training and UNESCO guidance at the site.

In 2002, ICCROM program director Herb Stovel and UNESCO Regional Advisor for Culture in Asia and the Pacific Richard Engelhardt initiated a new ICCROM–UNESCO partnership in Asia, to be called the Asian Academy for Heritage Management (AAHM). Envisioned as an interdisciplinary consortium of expertise in the region, original members included the Australian National University, Deakin University and the University of Melbourne; Hong Kong University, South East University in Nanjing and Tsinghua University in Beijing; the Indira Gandhi National Centre for the Arts in New Delhi; the Gadja Mada University in Yogyakarta; the Showa Women's University and Tokyo Institute of Technology; the Universiti Teknologi Malaysia; Tribhuvan University in Nepal; the University of Santo Tomas in Manila; the University of Kelaniya and University of Moratuwa in Sri Lanka; Chulalongkorn and Silpakorn Universities in Thailand; and the Hanoi Architectural University. With its secretariat in Bangkok (and more recently Hong Kong), the Asian Academy would go on to sponsor a series of workshops on architectural conservation and other aspects of heritage. It also publishes a quarterly newsletter covering conservation issues and events throughout Asia and the Pacific.

A persistent theme of the Asian Academy and other training vehicles in Asia the need remains for continuing attention to craft skills as part of the overall conservation process. A key criterion in UNESCO's Asia-Pacific Awards for Heritage Conservation, a program created in 2000, has been the incorporation of artisanship and crafts training into projects considered for awards. The several winning projects undertaken by the Aga Khan Foundation's Aga Khan Trust for Culture (AKTC) have placed particular emphasis on skills training. The same is increasingly true for Chinese and Indian projects, all of which recognize that conservation practice needs to be cognizant not only of larger issues but of the preservation of traditional techniques as well. In Asia, perhaps more than any other region, artisanship still forms the core of conservation practice.

Various spinoffs from the Asian Academy and other international training initiatives continue to flourish in the overall region. These include programs on architecture, materials conservation, tourism, historic and cultural landscapes, and archaeology (including underwater archaeology). One example among many is the Traditional Architecture Conservation Union of World Heritage Institute Training and Research in the Asia and Pacific Region under the auspices of UNESCO (with the far more felicitous acronym WHITRAP) founded in Suzhou in 2012. Created to assist "scholars, institutes and entrepreneurs on the conservation, research and restoration of traditional architectures in the Asia-Pacific region," WHITRAP joins a succession of international initiatives for training in Asia – initiatives that should continue to promote training in conservation and provide opportunities for practitioners and for the newer generation of architects and other specialists.

East meets West in conservation practice

Musings about oriental and occidental lifeways date back to the late Middle Ages in Europe, if not earlier.[37] From the onset of the fifteenth century, the world's globalizing tendencies resulted in the first circumnavigation of the globe. Chronicles from the Magellan–Elcano expedition (1519–1522) recorded European perceptions of the differences between East and West and signaled the advance of increasing levels of trade relationships and intercultural influences between the two groups.

The protection of Asian heritage using European and New World conservation practices dates from the eighteenth century. While these were imagined as scholarly and benevolent, they were also undoubtedly carried out in support of and consistent with the ambitions of various European colonial powers. (See Meeting the Challenge section above.) The conservation projects and institutions that developed in the following century by European antiquarians or civil servants sought to apply nineteenth century European conservation methods to historic sites in places like India and French Indochina. Accommodation for local field conditions was required and the steps for involvement were similar to what is known today: inventory, research, documentation, planning and implementation of stabilization, repair and even restoration measures. Consideration had to be given towards utilizing local experience and talent to address preservation challenges, and to selecting skilled workers and mobilizing materials. Priorities had to be considered, funding and logistical support garnered, and project oversight arranged for, and a certain amount of on-site learning and training made available to everyone involved in the process. These actions were rudimentary compared to today's architectural conservation processes; however, the basic steps for doing such work were, and are, unavoidable. These are time-tested steps for whole project development, recognized by all concerned parties including government decision-makers. The histories of restoration and preservation in India, Vietnam, Cambodia and Indonesia (Chapters 16, 10, 8 and 14) outline the evolution of modern conservation practice in those countries. Similar patterns were carried out elsewhere, sometimes enhancing traditional methods by the importation of additionally useful foreign methodologies and technologies.

Modern research by Europeans on Eastern architectural history began in the eighteenth century and has grown steadily ever since.[38] Western-style modern research on architectural history originating in Asia dates from the 1930s writings made by the noted historian, architect and preservationist Liang Sicheng, notably in his *Pictorial History of Chinese Architecture*.

In general, the overall aims of architectural conservation in Asia and in the West have far more commonalities than differences. Fostering protected heritage, be it conserving and presenting a famous palace complex, a historic district or an individual building of some historical or architectural distinction, is the goal of each. The end result of rehabilitating a stupa at Bagan, Burma or a castle in Osaka, Japan, entails essentially the same thinking and process as one would experience in a comparable project anywhere else in the world. Similarly, the later practice of preserving traditional neighborhood dwellings and their settings such as the shophouses in Malaysia, or *machiya* in Japan, or tube houses of Old Hanoi are remarkably similar in their aims and outcomes as to what is used in other places during the past half century.

The differences mainly have to do with traditional construction techniques, the role of ancient treatises concerning the relationship between design and spirituality, and conservation approaches. Western conservation traditions have tended to be based on research, documentation, analysis and precedents. Eastern Asia's experiences in conserving traditional architecture, especially wooden structures, may use essentially the same approaches, though the additional practical consideration of replicating buildings "in-kind" plays a more central role in the decision-making process. Age-old techniques and practical considerations have shaped customs of replicating missing elements, or indeed entire historic structures; this practice is something that should be respected by those involved. Such an approach does, however, have the potential to conflict with the tenets of most Western practice, and reconciliation of the two approaches has been sought for nearly half a century. Interestingly, there is consensus that the European and American styles of architecture that spread to Asia from the early seventeenth century onwards are probably best conserved using Western conservation methods. This very approach has been codified, in fact, by the INTACH Charter for the Conservation of Unprotected Architectural Heritage of India (2004).

Key differences in Eastern approaches to architectural conservation are imbued in the religious and philosophical beliefs. As explained in Chapters 16, 17 and 18 the ancient Hindu, Buddhist and Islamic views on restoring and protecting sacred buildings continue to exert significant influence on conservation practice involving similar types of religious buildings.[39] Other differences include an objective to preserve the design integrity (but not necessarily the material authenticity) of buildings during the conservation process, along with matters related to siting, symbolism and principles of construction.

As Neel Kamal Chapagain succinctly states:

> As much as Asian heritage is rooted in its own traditions, it is currently also under the influence of globalization, particularly through institutions like UNESCO, the World Heritage and the Intangible Cultural Heritage listing process, through economic consequences such as tourism and urban migration, as well as conflicts arising from national and international geo-political scenarios.[40]

Thus the contexts of concern in Asian heritage conservation are local, national, regional and international, each with differing levels of participation, interest and commitment.[41] In the end, all architectural conservation is local while some has national and international notice and participation as well.

The expression "heritage diplomacy" refers to the soft power of international aid for heritage conservation practice. It is a growing field of study being addressed mainly by experts in the social sciences and financial institutions involved with international affairs.[42] There are numerous instances in which foreign assistance for heritage related projects has also paved the way for allied interests that may not be heritage-related at all. For example, financial aid used for conserving Angkor's temples paved the way for some foreign trade and industrial interests of the nation making the offer. Stone temple conservation work thereby becomes a part of the diplomatic efforts tied to bridge and road building, rail transportation projects and similar projects. In any case, donor nations must work with host governments for such programs to be realized. Inevitably, one positive outcome is the resulting improvements in technology and work capacity for the host nation. More often than not there is substantial local involvement in both the decision-making and the implementation in such foreign supported projects.

Within this context there are now ample examples of "best practices" in international cooperative conservation projects, including, for instance, the policy that applications for projects must be vetted and approved by the Ministries of Culture that requested the foreign financial and technical assistance. Most modern international governments, QUANGOs and NGOs currently working in the field are keenly sensitive to both best practices and peer reviews of their work. After all, all such involvements entail an invitation by government to participate, and that may be seen as an honor as well as an international relations opportunity.

In an overarching sense, one might categorize the first experiences in deliberate cultural heritage protection as being expansions upon indigenous practices in maintenance and building repair that were already in place, enhanced by borrowings or impositions of useful international practices that were introduced by a variety of means, including some of sufficient cost and technical complexity as to preclude any other choice. The best single place to see such examples is at Angkor where the Royal Kingdom of Cambodia and its convening APSARA Authority has garnered scores of international relief efforts towards stabilizing, partially reconstructing, preserving and presenting the ruins of Angkor. Work at Borobudur, Wat Phu, Mohenjodaro, Mỹ Sơn, Merv, Hội An and scores of other sites in the region have been handled similarly. As the Asian heritage conservation field matures, and due perhaps to the global recession of the first decade of the twenty-first century, there appears to be a trend for international agencies to gradually pull back as local, national and regional initiatives take over.

Influences of Asian conservation abroad

One of the biggest news items in international architectural conservation practice in the past decade or so has been the growing presence and influence of Asian conservation practice on the rest of the world. Until the mid-1990s there was awareness among relatively few professionals, governments and international organizations that Asian cultural heritage conservation was unique. The general sense was that there was a different appreciation for conserving the authenticity of building materials in the conservation process and that it did not seem to matter to its stakeholders if parts of, or indeed, an entire building was replicated either "in kind" or in modern materials, even with less attention to detail. This countered the tenets of the Venice Charter of 1964 and subsequent related declarations. That there may have been different philosophies of conservation in the East and the West was not of great concern to most until the late 1980s when the UNESCO World Heritage program was fully and strongly operational.

As an increasing number of World Heritage Site nominations from Asia were received by UNESCO, qualifications regarding site authenticity (as defined under the Venice Charter) became an acute issue both for the nominators and for ICOMOS, which had the role of vetting the nominations before they were proposed for official listing. The problem called for an international gathering to discuss the differences in Eastern and Western architectural conservation theory. The 1994 meeting in the ancient Japanese capital resulted in the Nara Document on Authenticity, since known as the Nara Document. In sum, the relatively brief document highlights a need for greater recognition of cultural and procedural diversity in conservation practice, and that the cultural values by which resources are evaluated should not be fixed, but rather specific to their context. While not all the conclusions of the Nara conference were recognized as affecting the criteria for World Heritage Listing, the Document did serve as a milestone among Asian accomplishments in the field. The seminal Australian Burra Charter dating from 1979, which called for more regionally specific considerations and criteria for heritage conservation, influenced the thinking associated with the Nara Document. Subsequently, the Nara Document was augmented by meetings and declarations in Asia such as Hội An Protocols for Best Practice in Asia (2005) that spelled out special considerations specific to Asia for preserving authenticity of heritage sites and resources. Experiences in Asian conservation and attendant literature in the field that boldly questioned Western standards of conservation being imposed upon East Asian practitioners underscored concern over the subject, drawing polite polemical responses on both sides.

The topic was further addressed by the Principles for the Conservation of Heritage Sites in China (China Principles, 2000, revised in 2015) an effort that was guided by a consortium of American and Australian advisors to China's State Administration for Cultural Heritage and ICOMOS China. Modeled primarily after the Australian Burra Charter, but customized to suit Chinese architectural traditions and institutions, the Principles serve as a model approach for countries adopting their own heritage conservation standards.[43] With the China Principles and its predecessor agreements, it seems clear that recent experiences in Asian architectural conservation have been broadly acknowledged by the field, and moreover have directly influenced conservation principles in other parts of the world, much in the same way as the earlier, Western-oriented guidance. (See also Chapter 2 on the China Principles and Chapter 16 on the INTACH Charter.)

Charters and other instruments relative to Asian architectural conservation, by James Reap

Within the past fifty years there has been a significant effort in the field of heritage conservation to answer the questions, "What is conservation?," "Why do we do it?" and "How should it be done?" Although the search for these answers had begun more than 100 years prior to the adoption of the World Heritage Convention by UNESCO in 1972, the UNESCO document provided a new global focus. Standards for the protection and management of cultural heritage have been adopted by governmental entities at international, regional and national levels and by a variety of non-governmental organizations and institutions for well over a half century. Perhaps foremost in the governmental arena has been UNESCO itself, and in the professional sphere, the International Council on Monuments and Sites (ICOMOS), identified in the World Heritage Convention as a source of expertise in cultural heritage management. These institutions and organizations provide guidance to governments and professional practitioners through consensus documents identifying best practices in a range of formats and titles that include conventions, recommendations, charters, declarations, resolutions and policies. Arguably the seminal guidance document of the twentieth century was the International Charter for the Conservation and Restoration of Monuments and Sites of 1964, commonly known as the Venice Charter. Adopted by ICOMOS in 1966, it has served as a reference point for the further evolution of conservation theory and practice. Often disparaged in some quarters as having primarily a Western focus, its adoption has been uneven in some regions of the world, including Asia. Although international principles and guidelines have been important in elevating the professional standing of heritage management in Asia, its regional heritage professionals have resisted the imposition of Western precepts that do not comport with their cultural traditions. In Asia, the spiritual view of heritage values, including its intangible aspects, are viewed as crucial elements of cultural policy and practice. While elements of earlier international charters remain important in Asia, new instruments have been adopted by a number of countries and international organizations with an expanded scope to address regional concerns and provide more diverse, culture-specific approaches to common conservation issues. Among the instruments that contain important concepts for the region are:

UNESCO conventions

1972: *Convention concerning the Protection of the World Cultural and Natural Heritage* ("World Heritage Convention") / UNESCO

2003: *Convention for the Safeguarding of the Intangible Cultural Heritage* / UNESCO

ICOMOS charters and documents

1964: *International Charter for the Conservation and Restoration of Monuments and Sites* (The Venice Charter) / ICOMOS

1990: *Charter for the Protection and Management of the Archaeological Heritage* (Lausanne Charter) / ICOMOS

1994: *Nara Document on Authenticity* / ICOMOS

1999: *International Cultural Tourism Charter – Managing Tourism at Places of Heritage Significance* / ICOMOS

1999: *Charter on the Built Vernacular Heritage* / ICOMOS

2003: *Indonesia Charter for Heritage Conservation* / ICOMOS Indonesia and others

2005: *Kyoto Declaration on Protection of Cultural Properties, Historic Areas and their Settings from Loss in Disasters* / ICOMOS Japan

2005: *Seoul Declaration on Tourism in Asia's Historic Towns and Areas* / ICOMOS regional conference, Seoul, South Korea

2008: *ICOMOS Charter on the Interpretation and Presentation of Cultural Heritage Sites* / ICOMOS

2010: *ICOMOS New Zealand Charter for the Conservation of Places of Historic Cultural Value* ("Aotearoa Charter") (Previous editions 1993 and 1995) / ICOMOS New Zealand

2011: *The Valletta Principles for the Safeguarding and Management of Historic Cities, Towns and Urban Areas* / ICOMOS

2013: *Australia ICOMOS Charter for Places of Cultural Significance* ("Burra Charter") (First adopted 1979, with subsequent revisions) / ICOMOS Australia

2015: *Principles for the Conservation of Heritage Sites in China* (Previous editions 2002, 2004) / ICOMOS China

Other regional instruments

1998: *Suzhou Declaration of International Co-operation for the Safeguarding and Development of Historic Cities* / UNESCO

2000: *ASEAN Declaration on Cultural Heritage* / Association of Southeast Asian Nations (ASEAN)

2004: *Charter for the Conservation of Unprotected Architectural Heritage Sites in India* / INTACH

2004: *Yamato Declaration on Integrated Approaches for Safeguarding Tangible and Intangible Cultural Heritage* / Japanese Agency for Cultural Affairs and UNESCO

2005: *Hội An Protocols for Best Conservation Practice in Asia* / UNESCO workshop

2012: *Taipei Declaration for Asian Industrial Heritage* / The International Committee for the Conservation of the Industrial Heritage (TICCIH)

2015: *Recommendations of the International Expert Meeting on Cultural Heritage and Disaster Resilient Communities* (Tokyo, Japan) / UNESCO, ICCROM, ICOMOS-ICORP, ICOM and others

A more complete list of ICOMOS charters and other doctrinal texts may be found at: http://www.icomos.org/en/charters-and-texts

Another example of an Asian contribution is the leading effort from South Korea, Japan and China to international thinking and doctrine regarding conservation of intangible heritage. References to living heritage date to 1950 in Japan and 1962 in South Korea, each of which informed UNESCO's global initiative driven by the Convention for the Safeguarding of the Intangible Cultural Heritage (2003). The concerns of these efforts to preserve living traditions exemplify the expanding dimensions of the cultural heritage conservation field as it concerns matters of *what* to protect.

The above-mentioned special considerations for protecting Asian heritage included recognition of the natural context of Asia (e.g. maintain respect for natural surroundings) and its architectural and related spiritual considerations (e.g. *feng shui* and other astronomical, astrological considerations). It has been argued that many of these Asian precepts for architectural planning are not unique to Asia; however it can be said that their importance is greater and more widespread in Asia than in other parts of the world.[44] In any case such holistic thinking in heritage conservation is an important trend that the field is increasingly taking going forward.

The high stakes of conservation

The historiographical approach of this volume aims to systematically examine each country in Asia with the purpose of characterizing the state of architectural conservation practice and to identify trends. The purpose of this exercise is to help make the conservation of historic resources in Asia as successful an endeavor as possible, and to aid the people interested in contributing to this goal. Thus, the high stakes come in: if the essential mission of architectural conservation is to preserve, protect and promote built heritage deemed worthy of such treatment, then by necessity the failure of this endeavor involves profound loss. This is not a purely academic exercise; one needn't look very far to find examples of regret and remorse over lost heritage resources. Large-scale destruction has occurred due to warfare, as Old Tokyo, the Intramuros of Manila and the Royal Palace of Mandalay – all lost – can attest. But a great deal more has vanished not by incendiary bombs and ground combat, but by intentional demolition due to a failure of the argument for conservation to prevail. The walls of Beijing, the old commercial district of Singapore and many of the *havelis* of Ahmedabad are gone, their absence regretted by many, and their destruction wholly avoidable.

As a matter of merit, the Asian built environment deserves the best argument for conservation that the field can offer. The prevailing influence of thousands of years of religious tradition, coupled with remarkable cultural continuity in countries such as China, has resulted in landscapes that are deep in both spiritual and human capital. Asia's more socially tumultuous areas, such as northern India, offer a stunning showcase of layered history, a testament to the ambitions of competing empires and ideologies. The availability of resources has naturally influenced building practices, and the ephemeral nature of wood and earthen architecture in Asia has directly contributed to maintaining its built cultural assets and their material integrity. Asia's high degree of connection during antiquity via land and sea routes, across the continent and throughout the Indian Ocean basin facilitated the flow of ideas and architectural inspirations across thousands of miles – we can trace the path of the pagoda from Sri Lanka to Japan.

Every heritage conservation exercise involves an evaluation of different – sometimes competing – values. These can include monetary, place-based, traditional, practical, aesthetic, age or the simple value of continuity. These values differ according to the stakeholders consulted and traditions followed in identifying them. Among the most significant of many problems with the colonial construct in Asia and elsewhere was the imposition of Western values on an environment that found them difficult to relate to, alien or even directly in conflict with local values. This dynamic was front and center during the early years of conservation activity by Europeans in Asia; practitioners realized this following the First War of Indian Independence in 1857, after which they actively retreated from any involvement in conserving religious sites for fear of sparking another revolt. Present-day interactions between Western and Eastern practitioners still must navigate these challenging considerations, underscoring the importance of dialogue and mutual understanding in determining the best course forward for a particular conservation project.

Architectual heritage conservation is an ancient practice, and like so much else in Asia it is tied to deep traditions and active belief systems practiced by a constituent community. This type of "living heritage" is a key concept in terms of nurturing and sustaining the vitality of a place, and the importance of infusing it with new purpose or uses. There has been much discussion in the field on the relativity of authenticity in the Asian context, especially as it relates to material integrity. In contrast with Western approaches that place a high value on original materials in restoring old buildings, the Asian view is often connected to a notion of cyclic renewal that involves a process of decline, decay and replacement. Today, with a wider acceptance of both Western and Eastern approaches, this discussion is arguably at prime, in that practitioners in Asia and elsewhere can choose from the best available conservation tools depending on the circumstances, stakeholders or heritage values present.

Like everywhere, conservation in Asia is an intensely local practice. With the advent of dozens of new nations springing from the foundations of ancient cultures during the independence era, conservation also became increasingly national in interest and scope. New countries have used heritage sites and objects to define themselves and underscore differences between their new nationhood and that of their neighbors. One example of this point of view is the presence today of the silhouette of Angkor Wat on the national flag of Cambodia, a practice that dates to its period as a French protectorate, but was perpetuated upon independence in 1953. Similar dynamics exist around the globe, but it holds a special appeal in the context of twentieth-century Asian nationalism, where historic architecture connected contemporary people to the glories of a pre-colonial past. The approach to World Heritage listings is in line with this form of valorization – more is viewed as better.

Threats to the historic Asian built environment involve powerful, pernicious forces that are both within and well outside the realm of conservators' control. Urbanization, inclusive of large-scale emigration due to economic shifts from agrarian to industrial, is among the most prevalent. The rapid growth of Asian cities has resulted in a competition for space and intense development pressure on historic urban districts from Lahore to Shanghai. Natural and human-driven disasters present threats for which we can only prepare appropriate response and recovery plans. A lack of appreciation for and awareness of non-monumental architectural heritage – the contextual, vernacular and small scale – frequently results in loss, since these resources do not garner attention and thus protection. A lack of interest can also translate into a dearth of locally available trained professionals who want or can afford to work with challenging old buildings. The process of globalization, which has brought prosperity and economic growth to many of Asia's poorest regions, has also disrupted the traditional trades and building skills needed not only to create new but properly maintain old architectural resources.

Most Asian countries are still reacting to, if not recovering from, their past encounters with the West, which reached their zenith in the early twentieth century either through direct colonization or a high level of interference in state affairs. Contemporary international organizations, many of which are based in the West, have walked the line between perpetuating these relationships and guarding against them. For its part, UNESCO and its sibling organization ICOMOS has largely succeeded, if for nothing more than providing a platform for the codification, validation and promotion of Asian approaches to heritage management as equivalent to those in the West. This watershed development has benefitted all involved not just in the service of inclusivity, but also in the practical application of a range of acceptable approaches to challenging problems.

An essential premise of this book is that each country has a heritage conservation story to tell, from China to Maldives, and that there are lessons to be learned from each nation's institutions, projects and practitioners. It is a remarkable fact that heritage management is a universally practiced state-level discipline in Asia, albeit at different levels of success and commitment. This is quite an accomplishment: the blend of the disciplines of architecture, archaeology, planning, law and science did not exist a century ago. This status is reinforced by the international organizations that help coordinate the exchange of resources and professional expertise, while also identifying and attempting to resolve issues on a site-specific and regional basis.

Notes

1   For purposes of this book, the authors have defined "Asia" as the sub-set of the continent that is south of Russia, north of Australia, east of Iran and west (inclusive) of Japan. This geographical scope was selected due to the predominant historic cultural affinities of East Asia as well as the distinct nature of East Asian

architecture and its related traditions. "Asia" heretofore will refer to the thirty modern countries covered in this volume, not the traditional geographic definition of the continent.

2. The geographic boundaries used for this volume are related to cultural connections, which by no means follow lines on a map, and the overall approach to this volume and its predecessors. The aim is to logically organize the world and its modern countries into regions and sub-regions that can be studied and described according to commonalities in cultural and architectural traditions, in addition to shared experiences in architectural conservation. Accordingly, Asian Russia and Turkey are discussed in *Architectural Conservation in Europe and the Americas*, whereas western Asia, including the Arabian peninsula and the Middle East, may be addressed in a future volume.

3. The twelfth century Mongolian conquests of the Chinggis Khan dynasty conquered lands from the Mediterranean to the Sea of Japan, forming an empire so large that it has yet to be exceeded in size.

4. Sophia Labadi and Colin Long in *Heritage and Globalisation: Key Issues in Cultural Heritage* (London: Routledge, 2010), 1–15, outline the influences of capitalism and centrally controlled economies.

5. Taiwan broke away from the People's Republic of China in 1949. Bangladesh became independent from Pakistan in 1971, which had itself partitioned from India in 1947; South and North Korea divided in 1948, while South and North Vietnam divided in 1945 and were reunited in 1975. Several of these areas remain on a war footing, including Pakistan and India (the Kashmir region), and North and South Korea.

6. Coined in the past decade, the term "cultural diplomacy" refers to when one country aids another in the name of international government relations. The motives can range from the purely altruistic, as in disaster relief efforts, to overt economic development schemes such as the Chinese technical, financial and logistical support for the Kunming–Bangkok Expressway. See Natsuko Akagawa, *Heritage Conservation in Japan's Cultural Diplomacy: Heritage, National Identity and National Interest* (London: Routledge, 2015).

7. John N. Miksic, Geok Yian Goh and Sue O'Connor (eds.). *Rethinking Cultural Resource Management in Southeast Asia: Preservation Development and Neglect*. Anthem Southeast Asian Studies (London: Anthem Press, 2011). *Sustainability* as it relates to architectural conservation for purposes of tourism is defined as a situation which enables, supports or seeks to ensure that core aspects of culture are packaged for tourism in such a way that they are not altered by commodification and continue to provide both income and psychological sustenance for their bearers until such time as those cultural practices are no longer seen as relevant by the descendants of the people who originally created them.

8. Chapter 4 "Why Conserve Buildings and Sites?" in J.H. Stubbs. *Time Honored: A Global View of Architectural Conservation – Parameters, Theory & Evolution of an Ethos* (Hoboken, NJ: Wiley, 2009) explains rationales and aims of architectural conservation.

9. Neel Chapagain, "Introduction," in Kapila D. Silva and Neel Kamal Chapagain (eds.), *Asian Heritage Management: Contexts, Concerns and Prospects*. (New York: Routledge, 2013), 4.

10. Chapagain, 3.

11. Seung-Jin Chung, "East Asian Values in Historic Conservation," *Journal of Building Conservation* 1 (March 2005), 55–70.

12. Chapagain, 2.

13. Chapagain, 9.

14. The Operational Guidelines of the World Heritage Convention define Outstanding Universal Value (OUV) as "cultural and/or natural significance that is so exceptional as to transcend national boundaries and to be of common importance for present and future generations of all humanity. As such, the permanent protection of this heritage is of the highest importance to the international community as a whole" (Section II. A. paragraph 49).

15. These lapses were sometimes with understandable reasons, as in the case of Cambodia and Bangladesh where war and social upheaval interrupted normal operations.

16. Chapagain, 9.

17. United Nations World Tourism Organization. *World Tourism Barometer*. Volume 13, December 2015, 4.

18. Labadi and Long, 6. This takes into account that "both natural and cultural heritage represent important 'free' resources (in that they already exist, even though they must be maintained at some cost, rather than requiring substantial capital to establish)."

19. Ibid. 8.

20. Ibid.

21. Askew in Silva and Chapagain, 6, 347. See also Marc Askew. "The Magic List of Global Status: UNESCO, World Heritage and the Agendas of States," in Labadi and Long, 19–44.

22. Marc Askew in Silva and Chapagain, 9.

23. United Nations. *World Urbanization Prospects*. (New York: UN, 2014), 8.

24. Miksic et al., xv.

25 C. Long and A. Smith. "Cultural Heritage and the Global Environmental Crisis," in Labadi and Long, 173–191.
26 For the ten-year period from 2004 through 2013, the Centre for Research on the Epidemiology of Disasters (CRED) reports that there were an average of 384 natural disaster events (floods, earthquakes, tsunamis, volcanoes etc.), resulting in 99,820 deaths and 199.2 million people adversely impacted. The report further notes the annual economic damage from natural disasters was an average of US$162.5 billion.
27 These numbers continue to increase. The CRED report additionally notes that during 2014, climatological disasters increased in Asia by 20 percent, while these climatological damages during 2014 were three times their 2004–2013 average.
28 World Travel & Tourism Council. *Travel & Tourism: Economic Impact 2015, Nepal.* 2015. Web. www.wttc.org/-/media/files/reports/economic%20impact%20research/countries%202015/nepal2015.pdf. Accessed June 20, 2016.
29 Christopher Marrion. "Promoting a Culture of Prevention versus Recovery: Reducing Risks to Cultural Heritage from Natural and Human-Caused Disasters." ICOMOS Conference Proceedings, Beijing, China, October 2012.
30 The United Nations International Strategy for Disaster Reduction (UNISDR) summarized the need to move from a culture of response/recovery to a culture of prevention/mitigation as follows:
> Through these initiatives, the UN recognizes that disaster response and humanitarian relief efforts alone will not suffice. Unless the root causes of disaster impacts are recognized and addressed, adaptation is improved, and public awareness is elevated, the risks will impact beyond all possible humanitarian response and resources. Raising disaster risk awareness, promoting a culture of prevention and mobilizing adequate resources to build resilience are both an imperative and an investment in the future, with substantial returns for all.

31 Tourism also has its downside. For all its benefits and the revenues and jobs, in some cases uncontrolled tourism has resulted in the spoliation of sites, imbalances in access including marketing to high spending tourists only, and practices that spoil the character of sites, including the "visitor experience," that render them unsustainable.
32 Transparency International ranks countries on perceived corruption on a scale of 0 (very corrupt) to 100 (very clean). A lower score means a more corrupt government. Source: Transparency International. *Corruption Perceptions Index: 2014 Results.* Web. www.transparency.orgcpi2014/results. Accessed January 15, 2016.
33 Mara Hvistendahl. "China's Three Gorges Dam: An Environmental Catastrophe?" *Scientific American.* March 25, 2008. Web. www.scientificamerican.com/article/chinas-three-gorges-dam-disaster/. Accessed January 12, 2016.
34 Chapagain, 2.
35 Description of the UNESCO Asia-Pacific Awards program is based on the program's official description, and is provided here with permission from the UNESCO Asia-Pacific office, Bangkok.
36 An example of this is found at Phnom Bakeng (Cambodia), where villagers still worship at shrines that were likely built by their ancestors 1,000 years prior. This type of research brought the village and Buddhist community leaders closer to the World Monuments Fund-supported conservation project at Phnom Bakheng (2004–2011).
37 The travels of Venetian merchant Marco Polo through Asia in the late thirteenth century were chronicled in *The Travels of Marco Polo*, ca. 1300. He was not the first European to travel there but was the first to chronicle his twenty-four-year journey, which raised the interest of many in the subject, including Christopher Columbus.
38 J.B. Fischer von Erlach's *Project for a History of Architecture* (1721) is considered the first attempt at an illustrated world history of architecture.
39 For a detailed discussion on Eastern versus Western conservation methodologies see: Kecia L. Fong et al. "Same but Different?: A Roundtable Discussion on the Philosophies, Methodologies, and Practicalities of Conserving Cultural Heritage in Asia," in Patrick Daly and Tim Winter (eds.), *Routledge Handbook of Heritage in Asia* (London: Routledge, 2012), 39–54.
40 Chapagain, 3.
41 For definitions and discussion of differing notions of heritage see Chapter 5, "Who Owns the Past," in J.H. Stubbs, *Time Honored*, and *The Past is a Foreign Country* (Cambridge, Cambridge University Press, 1985) by David Lowenthal.
42 See N. Akagawa, *Heritage Conservation in Japan's Cultural Diplomacy* (New York: Routledge, 2015) and the Association of Critical Heritage Studies (ACHS), directed by Tim Winter. Web. www.integratedheritage.org. Accessed June 20, 2016. There is considerable precedent for the concept of 'cultural diplomacy' in Asia,

one being the largely failed attempts of Western Christian missionaries at religious conversions in the sixteenth and seventeenth centuries. Since the nineteenth century the adoption of Western technological achievements, and its trappings, proved far more influential on Asian economies and life ways.

43 The China Principles dating from 2000 and most recently revised in 2015 were additionally informed by the experiences of other countries that formulated their own principles and procedures, namely the US Secretary of the Interior's Standards and Guidelines for Historic Preservation (1976), the Indian National Trust for Cultural Heritage (INTACH) Charter for the Listing of Non-Listed Cultural Heritage (2004) and others.

44 Neils Gutchow. "The Japanese Practice: Translocation and Reconstruction," in Wim Denslagen and Neils Gutschow (eds.), *Architectural Imitations: Reproductions and Pastiches in East and West* (Maastricht: Shaker Publishing, 2005), 77–97.

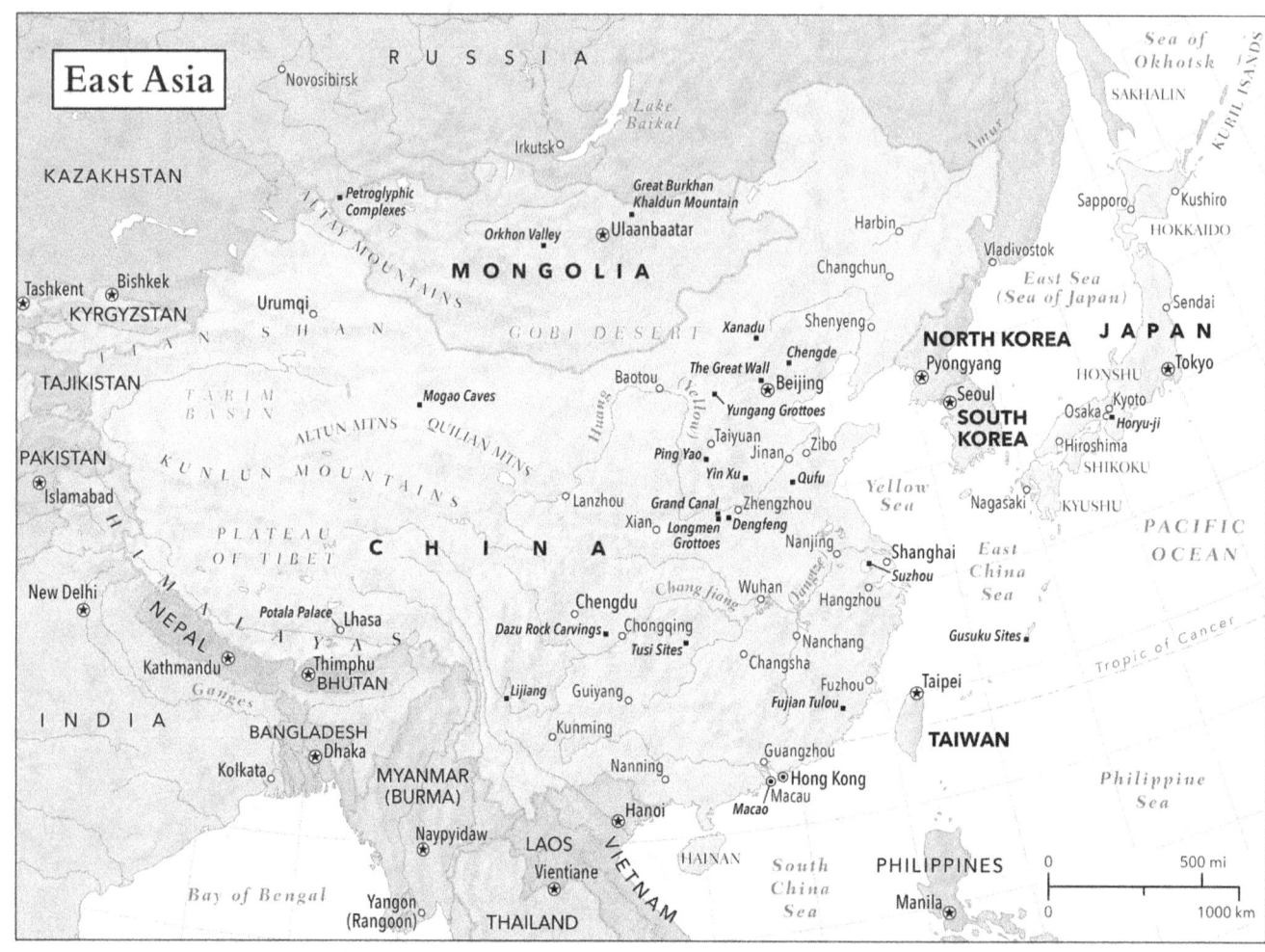

PART I

East Asia

Introduction

Japan, The People's Republic of China, Taiwan, South and North Korea, Mongolia

The far eastern portion of continental Asia that includes the modern nations of China, Mongolia, Japan, Taiwan and the Koreas, is as highly varied as it is vast, encompassing a range of geographic features ranging from the high desert plateaus of China's Xinjiang Autonomous Region to the tropical forests of southern Taiwan. Primarily a temperate zone, much of East Asia is climatically well suited to wet rice cultivation, the practice of which has functioned as an engine for the architectural and engineering innovation for which the region has been known for millennia. Due to its position at the edge of the Eurasian Plate, the region is highly susceptible to seismic and volcanic activity, particularly along its coastal and island portions. This geologic reality, along with the region's large forested areas, has contributed in part to a long tradition of building with wood.

Mainland China developed in relation to its principal river systems, the Yellow (Huang He) and Yangtze, both of which originate in the Tibetan plateau and together drain most of modern China, west to east. The generally parallel path of these rivers created a need for one of the world's great engineering feats, the 2,000 kilometer-long (1,200 mile) Grand Canal, which was completed in the seventh century under the Sui Dynasty.[1] The natural defenses of the Japanese archipelago, Korean peninsula and Taiwan afforded each protection from some of the forces of change that affected the mainland. In contrast, China was relatively vulnerable, in particular to the invasions of Chinggis Khan during the thirteenth century (which originated in Mongolia) and their antecedents. This fluidity famously gave birth to China's Great Wall, but also to the cultural and economic connections that came about due to the two thousand year legacy of the great Asian trade routes. These geographic factors tended to give Japan and Korea a heightened level of control over their relationship with the outside world, and by the nineteenth century both were fiercely resistant to the overtures of the West in particular. Furthermore, Japan's relationship with the rest of Asia during the nineteenth and twentieth centuries is partly attributable to its own relative scarcity of natural resources, which fed its imperial ambitions that began with the nearby resource-rich Korean peninsula.[2]

The present-day nations of East Asia share a cultural cohesion based on common origins that scholars trace back to the third century BCE, under the Xianyang-based Qin Dynasty. Comparable to the cultural commonalities shared by today's Western European countries, the products of this relationship remain in the Chinese writing system, Confucianism and branches of Buddhism, along with traditional systems of government.[3] Today, East Asia constitutes one of the most populous and economically vigorous regions on Earth, with more than 20 percent of the world's people and three of the four largest Asian economies.[4] The cities of East Asia are among the largest and most architecturally distinguished anywhere, and its landscapes bear the imprint of the region's centuries of planning and engineering accomplishments.

East Asia is one of the most active areas for architectural conservation practice in the world, largely by virtue of the post-war contributions of Japanese organizations and institutions, but increasingly due to contributions from China and the Republic of Korea (ROK or South Korea). Each country in the region supports an ICOMOS national committee, and each has successfully nominated multiple sites to the World Heritage List. China has the second-highest number of World Heritage Sites of any nation (behind Italy); even the Democratic People's Republic of Korea (DPR or North Korea), which typically does not participate in international institutions, has two sites on the List.[5] In many ways East Asia's position in the field represents an astonishing turn of events given the tumult of the twentieth century, which negatively impacted the architectural heritage of each nation in the region through wartime destruction, large-scale ideological revolution, or both.

Despite residual antipathy from the Chinese Communist Revolution, the Japanese imperial period and World War II, strong cultural and artistic ties among the East Asian countries that have existed for thousands of years remain strong to this day, largely to the benefit of architectural conservation efforts. With Japan's role as a global leader in the field, China's increasing level of activity both domestically and internationally, a robust system of cultural heritage management in place in the ROK, and a strong regional economy, East Asia is an important focal point for heritage management practice. After a period of violent hostility toward its traditional institutions and their buildings in the 1930s, Mongolia has since begun to embrace its unique cultural landscapes, nomadic heritage and monastery complexes. Taiwan (also known as the Republic of China) remains outside the UNESCO family due to ongoing disagreements with the People's Republic of China, but nevertheless maintains a national conservation infrastructure, and a system for identifying and protecting heritage sites on the island nation.[6] Though the DPR Korea remains obscured behind a repressive and insular regime, recent moves by UNESCO to recognize its cultural heritage indicate progress towards greater visibility into one of the world's most opaque countries.

The great Asian trade routes contributed to the introduction of Buddhism to China from India, and with it came new architectural forms that resulted in hybridized building types, such as the characteristic East Asian *pagoda* – a blend of a traditional Chinese tower (*que*) and a Buddhist *stupa*.[7] Numerous great cities developed on the basis of these ideas, such as Xi'an and Beijing, the latter of which was hailed in the mid-twentieth century as "possibly the greatest single work of man on the face of the earth."[8] The ancient Japanese imperial capital of Nara is home to some of the world's oldest surviving wood buildings, many of which have been restored using techniques developed over the centuries that involve selective replacement of wooden architectural members to perform repairs or maintenance.[9] European entrepôts established as early as the sixteenth century flourished in particular during the nineteenth century, resulting in today's global cities of Shanghai, Hong Kong and Guangzhou (formerly Canton). Numerous ingenious architectural forms have emerged from the region over the centuries, ranging from the uniquely solid defensive domestic complexes of the Tulou circular communal houses of southeast China's Fujian province, to the highly mobile *gers* (tents, or yurts) of Mongolia.

As is the case elsewhere on the continent, many long-standing traditions in the conservation of these distinctive forms of East Asian architecture are tied to religious beliefs, including respect for traditional building practices, philosophies and relationships between the human, spiritual, natural and built worlds. The Chinese concept of *feng shui* entails the importance of harmony between the built and natural worlds, and includes the long-standing use of color as a signifier of function. Another East Asian concept related to the traditional care of buildings and objects is the Japanese of *wabi-sabi*, which roughly translates to an appreciation for the flawed and impermanent. These two examples point to the deeply ingrained approach to management of the built world in East Asia, and the presence of a particular approach to conservation practice that emerged on the international scene during the second half of the twentieth century.

The East Asian notion of authenticity as a fluid, multi-dimensional concept relies on an emphasis on craft, design, and spiritual and cosmological traditions over original material. This perspective is partially based on the influence of Buddhism and Confucianism, but is also tied to the practical limitations of the region's principal building material – wood – along with respect for traditional use and craftsmanship. Among the most famous manifestations of this attitude occurs at the Ise Grand Shrine in Japan every twenty years, whereby several structures on the site are ritually deconstructed and reconstructed on an adjacent site, a practice that dates from 1,400 years ago. Another illustrative case is the Confucius Temple Complex at Qufu in Shandong Province in northeast China, which has been restored no fewer than thirty-seven times by subsequent regimes, due to its significance as a link to Confucius himself, along with his final resting place. Numerous smaller scale restorations and reconstructions occur regularly as part of the maintenance regimes for wooden buildings throughout the region.

Despite an exceptionally tumultuous twentieth century, the conservation legacy of East Asia runs long and deep, with many individual buildings, districts, cities and cultural practices maintained over the centuries. East Asia was not subject to the kind of widespread, direct Western colonization as occurred in South and most of Southeast Asia, therefore conservation measures and organizations were largely developed within their local context, rather than imported by Europeans. The region was not, however, wholly immune from the disruptive activities of Western interests, which manifest in the form of large-scale removal of moveable cultural heritage in the nineteenth and early twentieth centuries from China in particular. The punitive destruction of the Qing Dynasty Yuanmingyuan (Old Summer Palace) outside Beijing by British and French troops in 1860 stands out as a particularly egregious act that in part informed the Chinese approach to heritage protection in the twentieth century. Reaction against foreign attempts to assert themselves in the region during the nineteenth and twentieth centuries led to prevailing attitudes and defensive positioning relative to cultural heritage in China, Japan and on the Korean peninsula.

The countries and kingdoms of East Asia have a tradition of issuing legislation and decrees that presage modern movements toward architectural conservation. The Meiji Restoration era of Japan (1868–1912) witnessed some of the earliest modern legislation for heritage conservation, adopted in 1871 (*Plan for the Preservation of Ancient Artifacts*), which was followed by other legislative efforts to the end of the nineteenth century. Legislation that focused on the conservation of districts also emerged from Japan, such as the *Law for Special Measures for the Preservation of Historic Atmosphere (Ambience) in Ancient Capitals* (or, the Ancient Capitals Preservation Law of 1966). A strong network of grassroots organizations in Japan supported post-war conservation movements in the country, such as the *Zenkoku Machinami Hozon Renmei* (Association for Township Preservation, 1974) complemented by robust training opportunities for professional conservators – such as a multi-year certification course – keeps the field active within the country's shorelines.

The East Asian position on conservation is also informed by loss. For instance, on the Korean peninsula, the widespread loss of traditional homes, palaces and government complexes is attributed to the period of Japanese occupation (1910–1945), the Korean War (1950–1953) and the post-war development programs of the latter twentieth century. For all the devastation wrought by Imperial Japan upon other countries during World War II, the loss brought upon its own cities, towns and populace due to aerial bombardments during the war are immeasurable. In China, the new communist regime's hostility to conservation was signaled after 1949 by a shift from architect and scholar Liang Sicheng's vision of "preserving or restoring to the original condition" in the late 1940s to the new ruling party's approach of "constructing the new, demolishing the old" by the 1950s.[10] Liang's proposal, known as the *Alternative Plan*, to place all new development outside of Beijing's historic core stands out as one of the twentieth century's great missed opportunities for urban conservation planning; instead, the Forbidden City remains as a relatively rare intact fragment of old Beijing after the trials of the Cultural Revolution (1966–1976) and more than a half century of large-scale redevelopment. Mongolia's extreme rejection of its traditional culture and architecture following its independence from Qing and then the Republic of China (1921) control, and the country's falling into the Soviet sphere under the leadership of Khorloogiin Choibalsan, led to the destruction of many monasteries and temples in a bout of Stalinist purges within the landlocked country.

Taiwan's experience with loss – in its case, the loss of a homeland and an ideological struggle – has led to its role as a keeper of a substantial collection of objects originating on mainland China, from where they were moved upon the evacuation to Taiwan by the Republic of China government in 1949. Taiwan also retains examples of its own early period of occupation by Japan, in the form of industrial heritage including railways and resource extraction infrastructure left over from the Japanese period. The biggest blow to the integrity of the East Asian built environment, however, is modernization itself, which has resulted in the creation of the world's second and third largest economies (China and Japan). This phenomenon occurred only within the last half-century at an astonishing pace, from the ashes of World War II and revolution, and at a great cost to the historic built environment.

Among the most important developments attributable to conservation of heritage resources in East Asia is the codified notion of identifying and protecting intangible heritage that grew out of this region. The Japanese *Law for the Protection of Cultural Properties* (1950), which established a system for recognizing "Living National Treasures," and the *Korean Cultural Heritage Protection Law* (1962) were early pieces of national legislation that identified folklore, crafts skills, performing arts and other forms of intangible heritage as assets worthy of protection. This critical development expanded in subsequent decades, culminating in a major landmark in conservation theory and practice in the late twentieth century: the 1994 *Nara Document on Authenticity*.

The *Nara Document* was the first international charter to codify a non-Western approach to conservation, offering an alternative approach to the previous decades of Euro-centric conservation philosophy. The Nara Document describes authenticity as a social construct, and puts forward the idea that tangible and intangible heritage are equally valuable, and that there are multiple sources for cultural values. The Document's approach has proven especially enduring, and is arguably today a widely accepted standard among both Eastern and Western practitioners. The *Japanese Funds-in-Trust for the Preservation and Promotion of the Intangible Cultural Heritage* program with UNESCO in 1993, led to the adoption of the *Safeguarding of the Intangible Cultural Heritage Convention* adopted at the UNESCO General Conference in 2003, which has now been ratified by 163 member states around the globe.[11] The support of intangible heritage has become a hallmark of regional practice; in 2014 the government of the ROK opened a National Intangible Heritage Center in Jeonju, which is designed to showcase, celebrate and perpetuate Korean and international forms of intangible heritage.

Another highly consequential step in managing East Asian heritage is the *Principles for the Conservation of Heritage Sites in China* (also known as the China Principles). Adopted by China ICOMOS in 2000 after three years of successful collaboration between that organization, the Getty Conservation Institute (USA) and the Australian Heritage Commission, the China Principles constitute an important "bridge" between traditional Chinese practices of conservation and international standards, particularly the Venice Charter.[12] In 2015 China ICOMOS adopted a revision of the China Principles after a five-year study of the original document's successes and shortcomings. Revisions include an expansion of the types of heritage covered to include industrial, cultural routes and cultural landscapes; provisions regarding limits on site carrying capacity; and provisions for greater stakeholder involvement and more equitable public use of heritage sites.[13]

Japan's leadership role throughout Asia in architectural conservation collaboration stands out as a regional theme, with aid through the Japanese Trust Fund, which is among the largest contributors to UNESCO's World Heritage Fund, and thus makes much of that organization's work possible. The Japan Foundation operates a Cultural Properties Specialists' Dispatch Program through which professional experience can be shared across the region. Japan has also not missed an opportunity to look ahead at the complex task of conserving architecture connected to Modernism, supporting a national committee for DOCOMOMO (Documentation and Conservation of Buildings, Sites and Neighborhoods of the Modern Movement), along with China, ROK and Taiwan.

Despite the efforts in Japan and elsewhere in the region, professional capacity in the traditional building trades remains an issue of concern in East Asia. As everywhere, natural disasters threaten the region's communities and built environment as they have from time immemorial, but earthquakes, tsunamis and fire pose particular threats. Population growth and urban expansion have placed pressures on the historic cities of East Asia, since at least the post-war recovery effort, with large areas of traditional buildings – Chinese *hutong*, Japanese *machiya*, Korean *hanok*-style buildings – lost in a relentless charge to modernize. In particular, programs to build new roads, freeways, high-speed train lines and other transportation infrastructure have changed the face of China, which since 2010 has been the world's largest auto market.[14]

In the decades since the 1970s, China's rapid development has thrust the country into the position of being the second largest economy in the world. However, much of the wealth is concentrated in the large eastern cities, with the rural areas of west and central China remaining largely underdeveloped. Cultural homogenization within China in particular is an issue, with the government actively promoting emigration from the eastern, Han dominated region to the culturally distinctive areas of Tibet and Xinjiang, where appreciation by the newcomers for the traditional architecture of those regions is not necessarily shared. In general, there has been a diminished appreciation for historic built heritage due to losses during the Cultural Revolution and after, which is an issue in China, but also in Mongolia and Korea. International "mega-events" designed in no small part to exhibit this economic prosperity and pride, such as the 2008 Beijing Olympics and the 2010 Shanghai World Expo have had the effect of accelerating the loss of traditional neighborhoods in these cities, such as the *hutong* districts of Beijing and the *shikumen* neighborhoods of Shanghai. Educational practices in China do not tend to emphasize an appreciation for heritage values, and top-down decision-making leads to ordinary citizens feeling left out of the process for deciding what should or should not be saved.[15]

East Asia supports a number of effective organizations that operate regionally to assist in architectural conservation goals. The World Heritage Institute of Training and Research for Asia and the Pacific Region (WHITRAP) in China, and the Research Centre for Disaster Mitigation of Urban Cultural Heritage – Ritsumeikan University in Japan, are examples of regional conservation training centers that are focused on issues specific to the region.[16] Increasingly, public–private partnerships are playing a role in conservation financing, in addition to the more common government or NGO-funded projects. Mercedes-Benz of China, for example, partnered with the government of China to support a select group of World Heritage properties in China for the period 2007–2013, while Seoul-based Asiana Airlines made a similar arrangement to support World Heritage properties in Korea and Vietnam in 2012–2013.[17] The Japan Consortium for International Cooperation in Cultural Heritage, the foreign aid arm of the Japanese government, over the decades has contributed to over 1,500 projects all over the globe,[18] while the Nara National Research Institute for Cultural Properties since 1952 has supported a series of international exchanges involving archaeologists and researchers studying the development of ancient capitals.[19]

A major shift during the post-war period has occurred between Asia and the West relative to architectural conservation. Rather than a one-way street (West to East), the development of universally acceptable conservation approaches has become much more of a back-and-forth. The result is a more pluralistic approach within the field, but also a broadening of heritage management approaches that can only aid conservationists. For conservation practice in Asia this has been a vitally important development, and will continue to be going forward as East Asian countries continue to engage meaningfully in the field near and far.

Notes

1 UNESCO World Heritage Centre. "The Grand Canal." 2015. Web. http://whc.unesco.org/en/list/1443. Accessed January 13, 2016.
2 Asia for Educators (Columbia University). "Geography of East Asia." 2015. Web. http://afe.easia.columbia.edu/main_pop/kpct/kp_geo.htm. Accessed January 13, 2016.
3 Charles Holcombe. *A History of East Asia: From the Origins of Civilization to the Twenty-First Century*. (Cambridge: Cambridge University Press, 2011), 3–5.
4 The World Bank. "Gross Domestic Product Ranking." 2015. Web. http://data.worldbank.org/datacatalog/GDP-ranking-table. Accessed January 13, 2016.
5 The People's Republic of China has fifty natural and cultural World Heritage Sites listed; North Korea's two are the Complex of Koguryo Tombs (2004) and Historic Monuments and Sites in Kaesong (2013). Source: UNESCO World Heritage Centre. 2015. Web. www.whc.unesco.org/en/statesparties. Accessed January 13, 2016.

6   The PRC has historically opposed the membership of the ROC in the UN and its affiliated organizations (including UNESCO) on the grounds that the PRC does not consider the ROC to be a sovereign state. For more on this issue see: Sigrid Winkler. "Taiwan's UN Dilemma: To Be or Not To Be." The Brookings Institute. June 2012. Web. www.brookings.edu/research/opinions/2012/06/20-taiwan-un-winkler. Accessed January 18, 2016.
7   Nancy Shatzman Steinhardt and Xinian Fu. *Chinese Architecture* (New Haven, CT: Yale University Press, 2002), 85.
8   Quote attributed to Edmund Bacon, the renowned Philadelphia city planner, in the *Design of Cities* (1967). Anthony Tung. *Preserving the World's Great Cities* (New York: Three Rivers Press, 2001), 131.
9   Portions of the Hōryū-ji temple complex are thought to date to the seventh or eighth century CE. Source: UNESCO World Heritage Centre. "Buddhist Monuments in the Hōryū-ji Area." 2015. Web. http://whc.unesco.org/en/list/660. Accessed January 18, 2016.
10 Guolong Lai, Martha Demas and Neville Agnew. "Valuing the Past in China: The Seminal Influence of Liang Sicheng on Heritage Conservation." *Orientations* 35(2) (March 2004), 86.
11 UNESCO. "The States Parties to the Convention for the Safeguarding of the Intangible Cultural Heritage (2003)." Web. www.unesco.org/culture/ich/en/states-parties-00024. Accessed June 20, 2016.
12 Illustrated Principles for the Conservation of Heritage Sites in China followed. Source: Lu Zhou. "Evolution of Cultural Heritage Conservation Philosophy through the Lens of the Revised China Principles," in *International Principles and Local Practices of Cultural Heritage Conservation Conference Proceedings* (National Heritage Center of Tsinghua University and ICOMOS China, 2014), 9.
13 Lu Zhou, 9, and Neville Agnew, Martha Demas and Sharon Sullivan. "The Development of the China Principles: A Review to Date," in *International Principles and Local Practices of Cultural Heritage Conservation Conference Proceedings* (National Heritage Center of Tsinghua University and ICOMOS China, 2014), 25.
14 Angelo Young. "China Extends Lead as World's Largest Car Market by Sales," *International Business Times*. July 7, 2014. Web. www.ibtimes.com/china-extends-lead-worlds-largest-car-market-sales-gm-ford-china-deliveries-double-1621254. Accessed January 13, 2016.
15 Lisa Bixenstine Safford. "Cultural Heritage Preservation in Modern China: Problems, Perspectives, and Potentials." *ASIANetwork Exchange* 21(1) (Fall 2013), 3.
16 *Understanding World Heritage in Asia and the Pacific: The Second Cycle of Periodic Reporting 2010–2012* (Paris: UNESCO, 2012), 46.
17 Ibid., 53.
18 Japan Consortium for International Cooperation in Cultural Heritage. *Japan's International Cooperation in Heritage Conservation* (Tokyo: JCIC, March 2013), 3.
19 Nara National Research Institute for Cultural Properties. "About Us." 2015. Web. www.nabunken.go.jp/english/. Accessed January 13, 2016.

1
JAPAN

With a remarkably rich tradition of architecture and building craftsmanship, Japan has established itself as a global leader in the scholarship and practice of cultural heritage protection during the second half of the twentieth century. The Japanese government has developed a robust system for identifying and documenting cultural assets, both movable and immovable. Through this framework the country prioritizes and protects its considerable cultural resources. Japan's long tradition of appreciating quality and rarity in the arts strongly continues today, as is indicated by annual declarations of highly accomplished artisans and craftspeople. Japan's most significant buildings and works of art are designated as National Treasures; its best architectural craftsmen are honored as being holders of important intangible cultural heritage, and are commonly cited as Living National Treasures.[1]

Despite the widespread destruction that Japanese cultural heritage sustained during World War II, as well as because of modern development throughout the twentieth century, Japan remains unusually rich with examples of architectural heritage. For example, in the historic capital of Kyoto alone there exists an astonishing 1,600 Buddhist temples, 400 Shinto shrines, a trio of palaces and several museums. Seventeen of its historic sites – temples, shrines, monasteries, convents and imperial villas – were specifically cited when Kyoto was placed on the UNESCO World Heritage List. Countless vernacular urban buildings including *machiya* (traditional shophouses) situated within its historic districts add to Kyoto's claim of possessing some 20 percent of Japan's architectural patrimony, making the former imperial capital one of the world's most culturally rich cities, according to the United Nations.

Having the world's third largest economy in tandem with a deeply ingrained respect for cultural traditions have strongly contributed to Japan's active leadership in the heritage conservation field. This role includes financing projects in, and providing technical assistance to, other countries. Japan has also been active in incorporating techniques, ideas and legal frameworks from abroad and adapting them for use in their own conservation efforts.

While maintaining interaction with the international heritage conservation movement, Japan also maintains ways of thinking about architectural restoration and preservation that are distinctive. This includes a tendency towards reconstruction and often a decreased emphasis on conserving material authenticity. In large part this can be attributed to the country's age-old tradition of primarily building in the ephemeral material of wood. In Japan, notions of preserving authenticity have centered on fostering and protecting various craft and artistic traditions, especially the building and restoration craft traditions. As a result, the Japanese have been instrumental in inspiring and informing several groundbreaking international charters, such as the Nara Document on Authenticity of 1994 (ICOMOS) and the Safeguarding of the Intangible Cultural Heritage Convention adopted at the UNESCO General Conference in 2003.

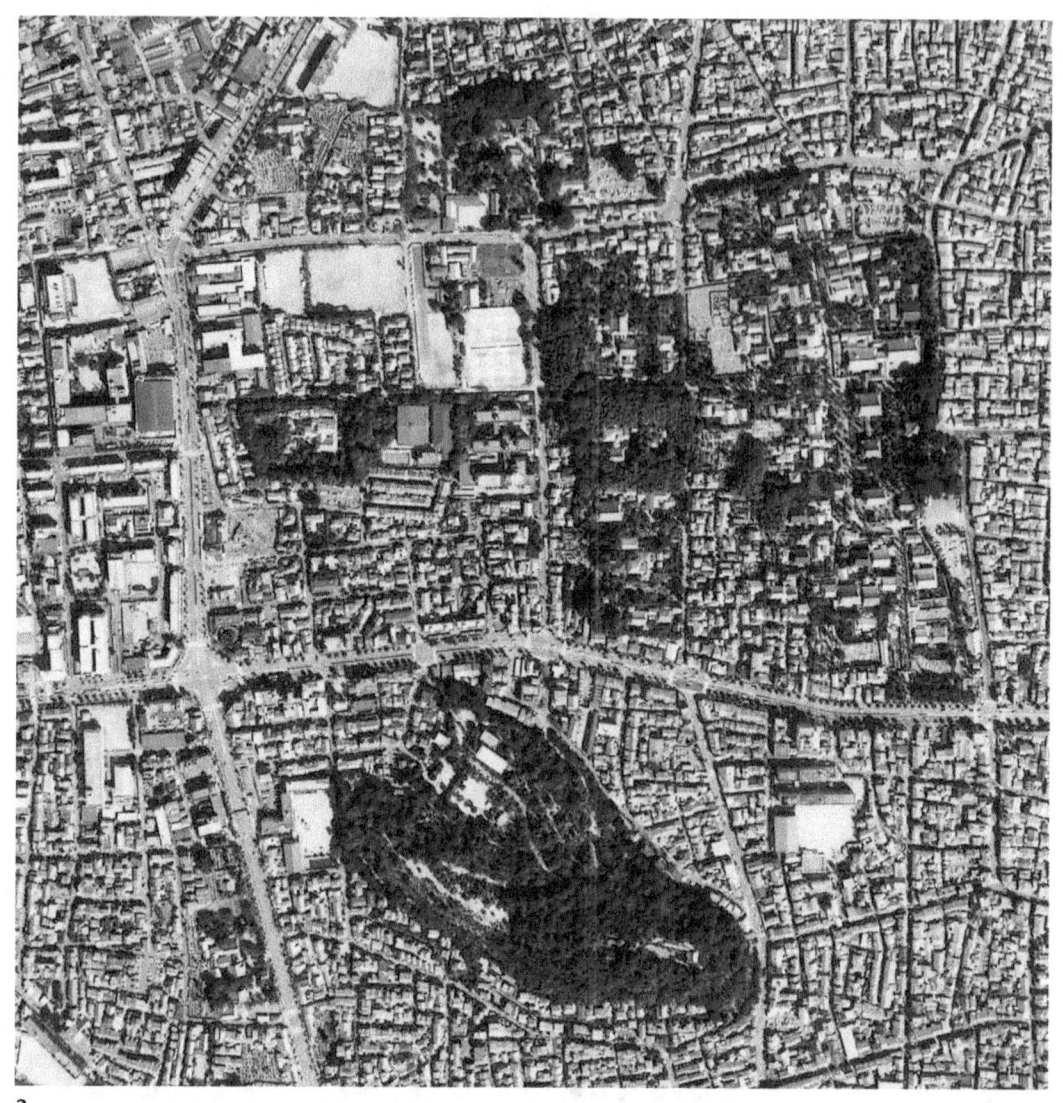

a
b

c

FIGURE 1.1a, b and c Aerial view of the Mt. Funaoka Daitokuji Temple in Kyoto (a), Japan's capital from 794 CE until 1868. Wooded areas in the image generally mark the locations of Kyoto's 198 noted historic buildings and gardens, thirty-eight of which are designated National Treasures and 160 are Important Cultural Properties. The seventeenth century imperial convent of Reikanji (b) represents one of Kyoto's several Buddhist monastic structures and the Kinkakuji (Temple of the Golden Pavilion) (c) represents a secular structure. Clad in gold leaf, the Kinkakuji originally dating from the 1390s as a retirement villa for Shogun Ashikaga Yoshimitsu. Destroyed by fire in 1950 and it was faithfully reconstructed in 1955. Its gold leaf exterior finishes were restored in 1987.

A legacy of building, re-building and preservation

Architecture on a monumental scale first appeared in Japan with the construction of earthworks and religious buildings, during the early first millennium CE. The Kofun period (250 to 538 CE) and the Asuka period (592 to 710 CE) witnessed the construction of hundreds of large earthworks. The key-shaped burial mounds (*kofun*) can be found almost everywhere in Japan, especially on its western coast, and are famous particularly in the Osaka and Nara areas, where they symbolize the Yamato court. This tradition disappeared with the arrival of Buddhism and the reorganization of the Yamato court in Nara in the mid-seventh century CE. This period saw greater contact with China and incorporation into Japanese building styles of the architectural vocabulary of stupas and temples.

The early imperial court in Japan relocated after the death of each successive emperor, meaning that there was not one permanent site on which a multi-generational capital could be constructed. However in 710 CE, influenced by contact with the Chinese court in Chang'an, the imperial court began constructing a palace complex in what is now Nara. Nara contains a number of buildings that have survived from this time, the Asuka period, including the Hōryū-ji temple complex that houses possibly the world's oldest surviving wooden structures likely dating from 670 CE.[2]

After a brief stop in Nagaoka-kyō, the imperial court moved to Heian-kyō (present day Kyoto) in 794 CE. Kyoto would be the seat of imperial power for over 1,000 years, until 1869.[3] Japan's greatest periods of artistic fruition occurred during the Muromachi period (1336–1573 CE) and the Muroyama period (1576–1600 CE). During the latter, considered the "Japanese Renaissance," there was a vogue for building palaces and castles on a flamboyant scale, resulting in impressive examples such as Osaka Castle,[4] and the extraordinary Ninomaru Palace in Kyoto's Nijō Castle.

A long tradition of moving buildings exists in Japan, as can be seen in the practice of an emperor or member of his family donating parts of their palace for integration into a monastery or convent. The inherent capacity of wooden architecture to be easily dismantled and rebuilt made moving and rebuilding structures commonplace.[5] Wood has constituted the primary construction material for most Japanese buildings throughout the country's history,[6] and the specific requirements of maintenance through repair and rebuilding of wooden artifacts have heavily informed the specialized heritage conservation ethos in Japan.

To some extent, the prevailing conservation attitudes in Japan have set it apart from the larger global architectural conservation community. For instance, Japan did not adopt the ICOMOS Venice Charter in 1964 for several reasons. While the charter was recognized and most of its tenets have been respected, it was perceived by Japan and some other non-European countries from the onset that the "monuments-centric" assumptions of the Venice Charter could not readily be applied to building typologies such as wooden religious buildings and the country's less durable wooden vernacular buildings. Such buildings require more frequent maintenance and repair, including occasional replacement of whole parts, a type of conservation intervention that counters notions of conserving material authenticity. This practical reality plus the fact that Japan has maintained a continuity of traditional building skills and methods has helped distinguish Japanese architectural conservation as being in a category of its own.[7] Of importance as well is the other practical reality that the Venice Charter was not an international convention that could be adopted at the intergovernmental level. Thus it could never have been more than only acknowledged, respected and complied with as much as possible. Preserving the historic building fabric comprising many of Japan's monumental structures in honor of its age, patina and authenticity is practiced, in spite of the relative impermanence of traditional Japanese building materials. This is especially true of elaborate wood joinery, fine temple fittings, furnishings and statuary, as seen in some of Japan's earliest temples, shrines and museum collections at heritage sites in Kyoto, Nara and elsewhere. Thus, generalizations about Japanese architectural restorers and preservationists never caring about preserving authenticity are not well founded.

FIGURE 1.2 The Hōryū-ji temple complex at Nara, erected between the mid-sixth and early eighth centuries CE, contains Japan's oldest surviving wooden structure. It has been extensively repaired and reconstructed over time. The two-storey, 17 m high Kondō (Main Hall in left of image) at the western end of the complex was extensively restored in 1954 using funds raised through a public subscription campaign after an accidental fire five years earlier.

Restoration of fire-damaged wall murals at Hōryū-ji temple

Most Japanese works of fine art are made of relatively fragile materials such as paper, wood, lacquer and silk, and are often integral to the design of a flammable wood building. They demand great care in their repair and conservation. Avoiding the risk of fire during that process has always been of great concern.

This situation was tragically illustrated by the accidental burning of the Kondō (Main Hall) of the seventh century Hōryū-ji temple, considered to be the oldest complete wooden structure in Japan, if not in the entire world. On January 26, 1949 a fire broke out in the hall during the process of restoring its famous murals. The damage to the murals was deemed irreparable, although color photo documentation had taken place beforehand.

The damaged architectural elements were rebuilt in 1954, but the walls where the murals were stood bare until years later when faithful reproductions of them were made by one of Japan's foremost mural painters.[8] Thus, the present state of Hōryū-ji depends on centuries of repairs and restorations executed by many people, from seventh century builders to twentieth century archaeologists, historians and government officials.[9]

The work was completed in February, 1968. It was funded by contributions totaling one hundred million yen (US$2,176,000) donated by interested organizations and private individuals. The reconstruction of this invaluable cultural relic is notable as well for being the first national landmark restoration to be funded by a public appeal in Japan.[11]

The differences between dominant Western thought regarding authenticity in historic buildings and Japanese practice in the reconstruction of historic buildings are essential to point out. However, if understood in context, these differences point to a mutual recognition of the importance of cultural heritage. The prevalence of wood in Japanese construction meant that when buildings were lost due to fire, there was often very little original material left from which to rebuild. In spite of the lack of original material, Japanese reconstruction derived authenticity from the tradition of craftsmanship applied to the building process and the element of ritual purpose that the building often embodied. This deliberate process of ceremonial deconstruction and reconstruction is what noted German architectural historian Niels Gutschow has referred to as a "para-religious performance."[10] Even in cases where the reconstruction was not due to catastrophic loss of a structure, it is still possible to observe the emphasis on process and technique over original materials.

Prior to the Meiji period (1868–1912 CE), wooden buildings requiring repair and restoration were customarily dismantled either partially or completely in the restoration process. Though this is considered highly invasive by the standards of most Western conservation practice, this approach could hardly be avoided for practical reasons. It allowed for the replacement of damaged wooden members into the reassembled structure and facilitated adding on to structures during the rebuilding process. For example, during the 1972–1975 CE rebuilding of the Hōryū-ji temple, architectural historian Masaru Sekino found that the temple had been extensively restored on seven occasions. While three of these reconstructions had involved the complete dismantlement and rebuilding, over half of the original members still existed.[12]

The most notable example of this practice involves the periodic reconstruction (called *shikinen sengū*) of the Ise Naikū and Gekū Shinto shrines at the Ise Grand Shrine (Jingū) complex at Ise in Mie prefecture.[13] Multiple wooden buildings within each shrine are carefully disassembled and rebuilt on adjacent sites, on a regular basis every twenty years, a tradition that has been chronicled since 690 CE for the inner shrine (*Naikū*) and since 692 CE for the outer shrine (*Gekū*).[14] An elaborate transferal procession and ceremony takes place at Naikū and Gekū. Every detail is prescribed by tradition, and as the old building is dismantled its wooden parts are carefully replicated for inclusion in the new structure. The most recent reconstruction at Naikū and Gekū occurred in 2013.

Originating in the seventh century, this practice represents a merit-gaining act of devotion, a form of spiritual renewal and, in recent times, a matter of national pride.[15] Prior to the Meiji Restoration of 1868 the Ise Grand Shrine had been more open to the public and its rituals had been somewhat less formalized. For centuries it had been a popular stop for pilgrims traveling to religious sites within Japan. Within the precincts of these shrine complexes Buddhist iconography was commonly found

a

b

FIGURE 1.3a, b and c The Shintō shrine complexes of Naikū (a) and Gekū (b) located in Ise's ancient cypress forests are faithfully reconstructed on an alternating basis at their respective sites every twenty years due to the fragility of its materials and central Japan's harsh climate, and tradition. Both buildings were ceremonially commemorated for the sixty-second time in 2013 after being reconstructed under controlled environmental conditions (c).

and often not distinguished from Shinto objects of worship. After the Meiji Restoration in 1868 the Ise Grand Shrine became central to the new government's reemphasis of the emperor as a central part of a native Japanese religion. The connection of the rituals at Ise and the imperial court were critical to affirming this narrative.[16]

In addition to the spiritual and societal meanings of the venerated shrines at Ise practical considerations also come into play. Replacement of wooden members is a natural response to the material's rapid rate of deterioration in central Japan's damp climate. Similarly, wooden elements and thatch roofs are susceptible to fire damage, although they are resistant to most other prevalent forces of nature, such as frequent seismic activity.

Throughout Japan, traditional craft techniques have been reinforced through the rebuilding tradition, with Ise shrine complex being the most famous example, maintaining a level of continuity of building traditions unrivaled in other parts of the world. In the case of the Ise shrine buildings, the timing of the reconstructions also considers the average life spans of those who protect and maintain the properties. Each carpenter has an opportunity to take part in the reconstruction exercise at least twice during his career, thereby ensuring an adherence to the strict rules for rebuilding, including preservation of its layout and prescribed carpentry techniques.[17]

Despite the Japanese reconstruction tradition and emphasis on the new in contemporary life, an appreciation also exists for the notion of *sabi*, or patina, in craft objects and architectural components.[18] New sculpture is sometimes intentionally weathered in order to acquire this quality. Imperfections, or broken and repaired pieces of old pottery, may be highly revered. Notoriously difficult to translate, *wabi-sabi* attempts to bring out Buddhist aesthetics of the flawed, rustic and impermanent in material objects. *Wabi-sabi* is another consideration in Japanese preservation thought and an important part of the Japanese contribution to valuing and conserving the past.[19]

The Nara Document on Authenticity

One of the most significant developments in the field of world architectural heritage conservation was the adoption of the Nara Document on Authenticity. Proposed by an international team of forty-five conservation experts during the 1994 UNESCO-sponsored Nara Conference on Authenticity in Relation to the World Heritage Convention, the Nara Document outlined, described and codified one of the first non-Western approaches to conservation practice. Foremost, the Nara Document stressed the importance of promoting cultural heritage diversity in all its forms, including the tangible and intangible, and a respect for the heritage of all stakeholders when values may conflict. It also acknowledged that cultural values could be determined from a variety of sources, and that a thorough understanding of all sources and how they have changed over time was required.

A critical element of the debate offered by the Nara Document on Authenticity is the idea that authenticity is a social construct. That is to say that there is no one true measure of what is authentic. Each society strives to construct its own definitions of what it regards as being authentic, but even inside of that definition resides conflict within societies whereby different communities and stakeholders hold conflicting views on the subject. Through this reconceptualization authenticity has been reframed as not only a matter of materials, but of techniques, purpose, craftsmanship and setting.

It has been offered that Western ideas of preservation have their basis in post-Renaissance Europe and therefore are a direct reflection of that social milieu. It is understandable that in this particular setting great attention was paid to buildings as material objects and preservation emphasized conservation of materials. In the wake of World War II these ideas were reaffirmed as much of Europe, and indeed much of Asia, were left with whole cities in ruin. This produced an effort to preserve the historic cities that remained. The Nara Document did not dispute these efforts. What it did do was bring to light that this European conception of preservation was the product of a certain historical moment and social values, not the final word on what was truly authentic.

Most significantly, however, the Nara Document challenged the system by which values and authenticity could be judged by fixed criteria. This position directly contrasted the views promulgated by the Venice and Athens charters, and expanded upon them, by asserting that a variety of factors – tangible or spiritual, fixed or fluctuating – can contribute to a site's significance and that all should be thoroughly understood and respected in the process of research, conservation, maintenance and presentation of a historic property.

The Nara Document paved the way for similar culturally expansive heritage conservation charters, such as the China Principles. Alongside the Australian Burra Charter, the Nara Document, in its totality, probably best portrays the most widely accepted understanding of conservation theory and practice today, especially in Asia.

FIGURE 1.4a and b Time honored craft and building traditions in Japan have characterized Japan's historic architecture. Illustrations from the *Far East Quarterly* (London), 1871 illustrated the carpenter (a) and the sawyer (b). Surviving masters of these and related trades today are considered Living National Treasures.

The complex set of values embodied in the merits of reconstruction and honoring natural processes and patina has informed Japanese legal approaches to architectural conservation, which stands as among the first in the world to be codified into heritage protection legislation. When Emperor Meiji opened Japan to the outside world in 1868, a rapid period of Westernization, modernization and rejection of traditional Japanese culture followed. The changes touched upon all aspects of traditional Japanese life, even including a proposal to adopt the English alphabet for the written Japanese language. Conversely the Meiji Restoration also brought with it a separation of Buddhism from the native folk religions and celebrations of Japan. It is from this period that we begin to regard Buddhism and Shinto as essentially different religions. While Japan was rapidly modernizing, it was also making an appeal to its ancient past.

Preservation in a modernizing Japan

The period immediately following the Meiji Restoration, the early twentieth century, unfortunately witnessed the loss of much cultural patrimony in Japan through modernization. From the Nara period until the Meiji Restoration, responsibility for the construction and repairs of buildings and temples was in the hands of religious institutions and governing authorities. Master craftsmen affiliated with these institutions restored and rebuilt extant buildings for continued use.

After the Meiji Restoration, the Japanese adopted the European concept of restoration and protection of historic buildings for additional cultural reasons, including the practice of inventorying the country's most valuable heritage sites. The national government began to distance itself from its historical Chinese influence, devaluing Buddhist contributions to culture while bringing to the forefront indigenous folkways now labeled as Shinto. At the same time, tradition and native crafts began to be neglected, and Buddhist institutions, which had long been patronized by the state, lost much of their financial standing and innumerable valuable art objects. Some of these cultural artifacts were exported for profit; others were destroyed in the religious and sectarian violence that plagued this period of revolution and turmoil. Both traditional buildings and architectural craftsmanship suffered.[20]

In 1871, a special administrative measure was formulated to protect antiquities. For the first time, temples, shrines and private persons were required to present inventories of cultural properties in their possession to heritage protection authorities. This was followed in 1880 by the granting of government funds for the maintenance of precincts containing Buddhist temples and Shinto shrines.

A young American named Ernest Francisco Fenollosa played a significant role in influencing Japanese attitudes towards the country's history during the tumultuous last three decades of the nineteenth century. In 1878 Fenollosa arrived in Japan to teach at the newly founded Tokyo University. An ardent art lover, he witnessed the crisis of an increasing loss of Japanese cultural patrimony. Along with Japanese art historian Tenshin Okakura, Fenollosa conducted extensive field surveys and studies during the 1880s, ultimately evaluating over 210,000 movable and immovable objects. The large-scale, detailed inventory of cultural properties ushered in a new generation of professionals, such as Chūta Itō and Tadashi Sekino, two Japanese architectural historians who had participated in the Fenollosa-initiated countrywide inventorying of cultural properties and began to develop a new Japanese style based on the traditional models.

This first generation of historians, architects and enthusiasts included master builder Kiyoyoshi Kigo and architect Chūta Itō, who is credited with founding architectural history as a discipline in Japan. These scholars advanced Japanese architectural history in the light of international styles. Kigo and Itō wrote the first comprehensive architectural history of a specific site, "Essay on the Architecture of Hōryū-ji" (1893), and their work on restoration at Hōryū-ji formed the scholarly basis for conservation principles and practice that would be codified in the Law for the Preservation of Ancient Shrines and Temples in 1897.[21]

As was the case in many other countries, art historians and architects who were also architectural historians launched Japan's first experiences in architectural preservation as a special discipline. Their call for the return of an appreciation of traditional values, instead of its rejection, coincided with a growing popular appreciation of all things occidental, and early conservation efforts as at Hōryū-ji served as influential exemplars.

In response to the earlier period of cultural turmoil and growing interest in the study of Japanese architecture the first legislation related to the protection of cultural properties was enacted in 1879. The Law for the Preservation of Ancient Shrines and Temples (*Koshaji Hozonhō*) established architectural preservation as an organized, nationwide project. That it remained in effect until the National Treasures Preservation Act of 1929 reflected the maturation of Japanese preservation thought and practice.[22] This legislation and an accompanying increased awareness of the need for state-organized heritage protection measures led to several landmark publications on Japanese architectural history and the inclusion of Japanese architectural history in university curricula.

A major conservation challenge presented itself by the end of the nineteenth century in the need to restore the Great Buddha Hall (*Daibutsuden*) of Tōdaiji in Nara. The largest religious building in Japan, it had twice been entirely rebuilt to differing designs, once in 1190 and again in 1709 CE. Attempts at fundraising and repair had begun in 1880, but the national government did not offer support until 1891.[23]

By 1899 surveys and a restoration plan were completed in a collaborative effort by Yorinaka Tsumaki, Chūta Itō and Tadashi Sekino. Restoration work was finally begun in 1904.[24] The first threat to the Buddha Hall was that its enormous roof structure was failing due to extreme roof loads distorting the structural frame in general. The second threat was that due to wood deterioration its towering interior wooden columns were in danger of buckling. Because the Great Hall had been listed a "specially protected building" in 1897 a major objective was to make all changes to it appear to be minimal.

Faced with a decision about repairing rather than replacing large portions of the Buddha Hall the project leadership ultimately decided on a hybrid system of repairs, discretely inserting steel members to supplement the existing wood truss system supporting the roof and installing steel belts and bracing at vulnerable points of the Hall's columns. The team approach towards conserving the Great Buddha Hall of Tōdaiji reflected a contemporary approach, with a philosophy towards restoration being remarkably consistent with Western tenets of conservation. The decision to repair rather than replace maintained authenticity while utilizing discretely discernable interventions that are reversible.

The 1897 Law was augmented in 1919 by the Law for the Preservation of Historical Sites, Places of Beauty and Natural Monuments. Then in 1929, the 1897 law was replaced by the Law for the Preservation

a

b

FIGURE 1.5a and b The Great Buddha Hall of Tōdaiji (a) suffered a combination of failures in its enormous wood framed enclosure including the distortion of its framing in the roof area and threats to the stability of its towering wood columns. Discretely inserted new steel trusses were added to the roof system and collars and stiffeners were added to its massive columns (b).

Machiya and prospects for their preservation

Machiya, historic urban townhouses with courtyards, characterize many cities throughout Japan but their centuries-long presence has become highly vulnerable to modernization. Widely associated with Kyoto (*kyo-machiya*) this domestic town architecture formed much of the country's city centers, serving as commercial and residential spaces that often housed the merchant and craftsmen class. As such, *machiya* played an important part of the urban cultural landscapes of Japan. Of the countless numbers that existed relatively few survive today. Those not lost in aerial bombardments of one hundred and fifteen Japanese cities in World War II have fallen to modern pressures of replacement due to high land values, costly upkeep, and high tax rates on inheritance. Diminishing knowledge of traditional construction trades and present-day safety codes have added to the challenges faced in preserving these buildings. Those still standing often maintain their traditional form but historic wooden and tile features are regularly covered or replaced with modern materials.

A single structure is seemingly unimposing, yet city blocks made up of machiya reveal the complexity and subtlety of their design. These streetscapes of multiple machiya are referred to as *machinami*. This indicates that it is more than just a single structure but a repetition, a vibrant city life that is complex in its construction. A narrow front façade and deep interior allowed inclusion of traditional spatial elements while an interconnected arrangement supported lively, close-knit communities. The inherent architectural qualities in machiya, and the lifeways they accommodated, formed smaller, livable cities within the larger urban context. As a result, machiya played a significant role in the structure of Japanese society. The basic organizational block of Japanese urban life, the *cho*, is based off of blocks of machiya. Many of these *cho* were based around a single type of business, such as the production of *tatami* mats, *sake* breweries, or *kimono* makers, creating distinct districts whose names remain part of the Japanese urban fabric even today.

An expansion of Japan's conservation legislation in 1975 allowed historic designation for groups of buildings and spurred interest in the conservation of these neighborhoods. The Great Hanshin earthquake of 1995, which destroyed countless historic structures in and around Kobe, encouraged further legislation and the Law for the Protection of Cultural Properties was amended to include tangible cultural properties in the Official Register. The Kyoto Center for Community Collaboration and its Machiya Machizukuri Fund, established in 2005, provided financial support for restoring some representative machiya that resulted in many properties being admitted to The Landscape Act's "Structures of Landscape Importance" list.

Still, the rate at which machiya are continuously being destroyed has warranted concern by international heritage protection interests. In 2005, the World Monuments Fund supported the Kyomachiya Revitalization Project and the establishment of the Kyomachiya Council, which conducted a survey of surviving *kyo-machiya* in the city's central districts. A national symposium in 2008 focused on the state of machiya conservation in Kyoto that led to the organization's nomination of the city's surviving machiya to the 2010 World Monuments Watch. The Kamanza Cho-ie revitalization project followed soon after and successfully integrated workshops that highlighted community involvement in the restoration of a single, traditional machiya. Subsequent inclusion on the 2012 Watch focused on continued efforts and implementation on a larger, urban scale, during which a machiya constructed in 1932 was rehabilitated into the Kyomachiya Museum-Furaibou and opened to the public in May 2012.

The efforts of Japan's growing interests in conserving machiya have halted further destruction of some for high-rise developments, highways and street widening projects, urging instead the benefits of preserving small-scale, pedestrian-friendly machiya and the local community living within them. In the process of safeguarding these vernacular structures across the country, important elements of Japan's cultural identity are preserved for future generations.

Further reading

"A City Under Siege: Saving Kyoto's Machiya from Destruction." Web. www.japansociety.org/resources/content/2/0/5/4/documents/machiyasymposium.pdf. Accessed June 1, 2016.

Kojima, Fusae. "An Overview of the Kyomachiya Revitalization Project." *World Monuments Fund Journal* (March 6, 2013). Web. www.wmf.org/journal/overview-kyomachiya-revitalization-project. Accessed June 1, 2016.

Löfgren, Karin. 2003. "Machiya: History and Architecture of the Kyoto Town House." KTH Royal Institute of Technology.

Suiko Shoin, Mitsumura. 2008. *Machiya Revival in Kyoto*. Edited by Kyoto Center for Community Collaboration. Kyoto, Japan: Mitsumura Suiko Shoin Publishing Co.

World Monuments Fund. "Completion of Second Phase of Machiya Revitalization Project Celebrated in Kyoto: Restored Townhouse Becomes Machiya Museum." Web. www.wmf.org/sites/default/files/press_releases/Furaibou%20Restoration%20Release.pdf. Accessed June 1, 2016.

of National Treasures, which extended the national inventory list to include cultural properties in the possession of governments, local public bodies and individuals.[25] In 1933 a measure to address the illegal export of Japanese movable cultural heritage items went into effect, and in 1950, after the tragic fire at the Hōryū-ji temple, the present Law for the Protection of Cultural Properties was enacted, superseding all previous legislation. Since then, Japan's Law for the Protection of Cultural Properties has been augmented several times, and now includes categories such as intangible cultural resources, Western-style buildings, rural vernacular residential architecture, and other folk building traditions.[26] Included among these are groups of historic buildings in urban settings termed *machiya*, or shophouses.

In the midst of this period of legislative development came the widespread and unprecedented destruction of World War II. Beginning in 1943, when American air raids were intensified on the Japanese home islands, Japanese authorities began to move cultural properties from museums, temples and important private collections to the countryside. Unfortunately, in the later stages of the war, factories and other war infrastructure were also moved to the countryside. This made rural areas more susceptible to attack than they would have been otherwise. Although Kyoto and Nara were famously spared aerial attacks, elsewhere throughout the country incendiary bombs destroyed thousands of cultural properties, including castles, temples, shrines and other historic buildings. One hundred and fifteen Japanese cities were targeted in conventional bomb raids and Hiroshima and Nagasaki were almost completely obliterated by atomic bombs.[27] Upon the surrender of Japanese forces on August 15, 1945 the country had to rebuild itself with scant resources for anything, let alone cultural heritage concerns. As a result, a period of further loss of both built and movable heritage continued well into the post-war era in Japan, some seven decades later.[28] (See also World War II Destruction: Its Legacy in the Pacific in Chapter 15.)

Completed in 1612, Nagoya Castle, the seat of the descendants of Japan's first Tokugawa shogun, served as a strategic stronghold along the Tokaidō Highway. It was one of several castles destroyed during American air raids during 1945. Nagoya Castle has since been extensively and accurately rebuilt in reinforced concrete. Its donjon, three turrets and three gates were restored with traditional materials "in kind." Salvageable elements were reused where possible in reconstructed areas, although modern amenities were added, such as an extensive new double stairway system that serves several new exhibition galleries spread over several floors and lookout positions at the top of the central tower.

As explained by the noted restoration architect Masaru Sekino in "The Preservation of Wooden Monuments in Japan" (a chapter within UNESCO's *Museums and Monuments* series entitled as early as 1972):

> Nagoya Castle and several other castles destroyed during the Second World War were reconstructed in reinforced concrete which is cheaper as well as being fire-proof and not subject to biological attack, but this practice has been limited to castles which, in view of their original role as fortresses, have some justification for being rebuilt in concrete.[29]

With respect to Sekino's acknowledgment that clearly such an approach sacrifices authenticity, these examples of reconstruction in different materials are understandable, if for practical reasons only. In pointing out the complex choices one faces in restoring or reconstructing traditional Japanese architecture, Sekino helpfully cites the possible range of intervention: *Dismantling and Reassembly* to effectively replace deteriorated or distorted wooden members, *Sheltering* by placing all or part of a building in a museum enclosure, *Periodical Reconstruction* (done for religious and practical purposes).[30] Despite occasional material failure such as cracks and spalling in new plastered exterior finishes, such examples illustrate the architectural conservation dilemmas faced in Japan since the Meiji period: whether to restore "in kind" favoring material authenticity or reconstruct using substitute modern materials.

It was under these circumstances that, five years after the end of World War II in 1950, the Law for the Protection of Cultural Properties (*Bunkazai Hogohō*) came into effect, replacing the National Treasure Law of 1929. It covered works of fine art, historic architecture, archaeological sites, tangible cultural property and cultural landscapes and places of natural beauty. In 1975 the category of groups of traditional buildings was added by amendment and in 2004 protection of cultural landscapes was also added as an amendment.

FIGURE 1.6a and b Reconstruction of Nagoya Castle after complete destruction by aerial bombing in World War II (a). A concrete framed structure supports the replacement building (b).

The next legislative milepost for Japanese conservation efforts was the Law for Special Measures for the Preservation of Historic Atmosphere (Ambience) in Ancient Capitals (or, the Ancient Capitals Preservation Law of 1966). This measure was enacted to safeguard the historic buildings and districts of Japan's cultural capitals of Nara, Kyoto and Kamakura. For the first time, legislation incorporated the first measures covering the designation and conservation of large areas of historic buildings, as opposed to spot designations of a single site. This measure's success led to the 1975 amendment of the Cultural Properties Protection Law to include provisions for "area conservation" in cities, towns and rural areas outside of the ancient capitals. The 1975 amendment also authorizes local governments to designate conservation areas, a small number of which may also be elevated to national status.[31] This allows the overall national approach of the Japanese government to be modular and exportable, thereby including structures that may not be protected by national preservation laws to be recognized by local governments.

As these legal standards regarding conservation of cultural assets were moving forward, Japan was transforming itself into an economic superpower. While not mutually exclusive, these two advancements in Japanese society did not always move in synchronicity. Many vernacular landscapes were subsumed as urban areas rapidly increased in size. At the same time many rural temples, shrines and other historic buildings fell into neglect due to decreasing population, patronage and interest. The national government of Japan walked a delicate balance, powering its way forward economically by means of giant public works projects and urban modernization, while at the same time utilizing the country's rich cultural heritage to maintain national ideas of uniqueness. Also complicating matters was the new Constitution of Japan, written in 1946 by the American government, which contained strong provisions for the separation of church and state. Religious sites throughout Japan soon found funding hard to come by and their constituents relocating to the cities where the new economy was booming.

Another issue that presented architectural conservation in Japan with a complex dilemma is the relativeness of what is considered historic. For many, the Meiji period with its Western style buildings and masonry constructions did not seem to fit the ideals of historic Japan. Adding to this situation was the importation of international experts who brought with them new styles of building, uses of materials and sensibilities towards architecture in general. This new dynamic of foreign styles and modern methods led, in some cases, to buildings constructed during and after the Meiji period being more difficult to protect and preserve under a system of preservation law that was aimed more at traditional, often religious, structures. Another byproduct of Japan's pre-Meiji relationship with Western powers are small pockets of Western style buildings that are concentrated in a few port towns that were open to foreign trade while the rest of Japan remained closed. Areas such as these in Nagasaki and Kobe prove to be a real test for the widespread applicability of Japanese architectural conservation law. Fortunately the modularity of the Japanese approach that allows for local designation of buildings and landscapes that might not fit into the national legal framework and has made possible cooperation between different levels of government to work to preserve these unique structures.

Local citizen participation, or grassroots action groups, had been instrumental to the passage of the Ancient Capitals Preservation Law in the mid-1960s, and continued to grow in organizational and institutional support over the next several decades. National groups like the Zenkoku Rekishiteki Fūdo Hozon Renmei (Federation for the Preservation of Historic Landscapes), established in 1970, and the Zenkoku Machinami Hozon Renmei (Association for the Township Preservation) (1974), helped to generate additional historic building surveys and impressed upon the national government the level of community support for conservation activities. From 1996 through April 2014 some 9,423 buildings were registered. Registration of historic buildings initiates increased recognition, added protection, and engenders local pride in heritage conservation. The success of these organizations at both local and national levels continues to the present, resulting in Japan still having a powerful and important level of grassroots support for architectural heritage protection.[32]

The rise of contemporary practice

In the 1960s and 1970s, administrative reorganization also accompanied a productive period of Japanese heritage stewardship. In 1968 the National Commission for the Protection of Cultural Properties and the Cultural Affairs Bureau of the Ministry of Education were merged to become the Agency for Cultural Affairs (ACA). The ACA stands today as the primary organization for cultural heritage administration in Japan, carrying the responsibility for executing state administrative tasks concerning cultural and religious properties. Within it are two departments: the Department of Culture, which mainly deals with modern art, and the Department of Cultural Properties. This department's four divisions (Fine Arts, Monuments and Sites, Traditional Culture, and Architecture) deal with the protection of cultural properties.

By law, in 1975 cultural properties were divided into five categories: tangible cultural properties, intangible cultural properties, folk cultural properties (which were separated from intangible cultural properties in 1954 by an amendment to the Cultural Properties Protection Law), monuments and groups of historic buildings. This latter category was created in 1975 by an amendment of the Cultural Properties Protection Law. Japanese cultural properties are categorized as "tangible" if they are buildings or other structures or monuments if they are historic sites such as shell mounds, ancient tombs, sites of palaces, forts or castles, or monumental dwellings. This classification can also include groups of historic buildings, historic cities, towns and villages, including castle towns, post-station towns, towns built around shrines and temples and other areas of historic importance.[33] Since 2004 the Cultural Properties Protection Law covers cultural landscapes as a category of cultural property although there have been certain arguments over the legal definitions of "cultural landscape," mainly on the difference between Japanese domestic law and UNESCO related provisions.

At the prefectural and municipal levels, local governments are responsible for the protection of cultural properties within their domain. They are in charge of their protection and have the authority to designate additional historic properties other than those already listed by the national government.

The ACA's Cultural Properties Protection Department administers the conservation and utilization of nationally significant sites. The Council for the Protection of Cultural Properties, an advisory body serving the Minister of Education and the Minister of Cultural Affairs, also oversees many conservation activities, including the licensing of specially trained architectural conservators. Architects can qualify for the required license for conserving listed historic buildings granted by the ACA by training as assistants to conservation architects on two or three projects while taking approximately seven years of obligatory coursework.[34] Graduate level training in architectural and urban conservation today in Japan is offered mainly at the Graduate School of Conservation at the Tokyo University of the Arts, the Urban Planning and Conservation program at the University of Tokyo, and the Architectural History and Conservation Graduate Program at Waseda University. Since 2011 Waseda has also hosted a UNESCO World Heritage Institute. Additionally, Japan's Tsukuba University is home to a Master's Program in World Heritage Studies. Ritsumeikan University, located in Kyoto, is home to the Institute for the Disaster Mitigation of Urban Cultural Heritage, which works with national, prefectural and municipal governments to assist in lessening the damage to cultural assets in the event of a disaster.

The eight-year restoration project that began in 2009 at the eighth-century East Pagoda of Yakushiji in the ancient capital of Heijō-kyō (present day Nara) illustrates Japan's contemporary approach to conserving its ancient wooden buildings. Conservators are dismantling the pagoda, conserving as much of the building's fabric as possible, and replicating irretrievably deteriorated or missing parts as necessary. Careful documentation and materials analysis preceded plans for restoring the three-storey structure, and ongoing conservation work is conveniently accessed within a spacious all-weather enclosed scaffolding system that permits work on all six stages of the pagoda to occur at nearby work areas. As of 2015, decisions had not been made about restoring the predominant red colored finishes and gold trim on the pagoda's exterior. One view called for an approximation of its original painted appearance to honor its original design aesthetic. A second, less intrusive approach that was also being considered was to clean and stabilize its exterior wooden elements, blending newly added wooden elements visually sympathetic with the old, and generally leaving the building with its present timeworn appearance.

The East Pagoda at Yakushiji also reflects Japan's long history of architectural restoration. It was repaired after suffering damage from an earthquake in 1361 as well as several other calamities, including fire and storms as well as settlement problems that were addressed between 1898 and 1900. Following meticulous graphic documentation of the structure, the pagoda's second and third stages were disassembled and extensively reconstructed and its base pedestal was expanded. During a 1950–1952 restoration the building was re-roofed and the bronze pagoda *sōrin* (finial) was restored.

Sixty years later, the Nara Division of the Independent Administrative Institution of the National Institute is carrying out the current work for Cultural Heritage of Japan. The Japanese Association for the Conservation of Architectural Monuments (JCAM) is conducting the technical part of the project.

Despite the rigorous requirements brought about by robust laws, one of the greatest challenges in building conservation faced in Japan continues to be a paucity of competent craftsmen and the diminishing knowledge of traditional construction techniques. In recognition of these issues, in 1975 the Japanese government included a new chapter in the Law for Protection of Traditional Techniques for Conservation of Cultural Properties through which the ACA may declare individuals or groups as "Individual or Organizational Holders of Traditional Conservation Techniques," a designation that acknowledges the importance of skills training and continuity in Japanese conservation practice.[35]

The ACA actively promotes and trains in traditional conservation techniques through documentation and the granting of annual contributions to the organizations who arrange training courses. The use of historic tools and techniques in restoration and preservation has been recognized as being important in Japan for over a half century and is one of the main tenets of the country's heritage conservation work.[36] The National Committee for the Protection of Cultural Properties subsidizes the continued practice of these skills and techniques and takes measures to ensure the training of successors of its "Living National Treasures."

While discontinuity in traditional skills training has become a more recent phenomenon, the ancient twin enemies of architecture in Japan, earthquakes and fire, still constantly threaten the country's historic buildings and sites and require vigilance on the part of building owners and policy makers alike. In a more abstract, but no less threatening, manner, the ongoing process of modernization also undermines the historic functions and uses of Japan's historic buildings and often overlooks adaptive reuse possibilities. Finally, as in other densely populated, geographically restricted parts of the developed world, urban real estate prices have put major pressures on both the built and natural heritage of the country.

a

FIGURE 1.7a, b and c The East Pagoda of the Yakushiji temple complex in the ancient capital of Heijō-kyō near Nara has undergone several restorations since its construction in the eighth century. Its most complete restoration began in 2009 and has entailed disassembly and reconstruction of the 34 m (111 ft) high pagoda within an extensive scaffolding enclosure enabling repair work to occur at the level of each of the pagoda's six stages topped by a bronze *sōrin* (a, b). The scaffolding also permits viewing of the work in progress by visitors to the site, an important aspect of fundraising for this large and expensive project (c).

Preserving Japan's living heritage, a seminal idea in the conservation of intangible heritage

Unlike material building stock, intangible cultural heritage is comprised of metaphysical histories, such as performance, rituals, languages, craftsmanship and so on, that are verbally passed down through generations. Japan has been diligent in ensuring the continuation of its intangible heritage (*mukei-bunkazai*) and included procedures for designation in the earliest edition of the Cultural Properties Protection Law in 1950. To date there are 104 items listed as Important Intangible Cultural Properties on Japan's National Register, managed by the government's Agency for Cultural Affairs, including *kiku-jutsu* (traditional building crafts), *washi* (craftsmanship of hand-made paper), *yamaboko* (elaborate floats made for the annual Gion Festival in Kyoto), and *kumiodori* (musical theater developed on the Okinawa islands). Japan's leadership in intangible heritage conservation practice is affirmed by its being the founder of (under the aegis of UNESCO in 2010) and home to the International Research Centre for Intangible Cultural Heritage (IRCI) in the Asia-Pacific Region in Sakai City, Osaka.

Similar early programs that have been put in place outside of Japan for the protection of intangible heritage are the Cultural Properties Protection Act No. 961 in South Korea (enacted on January 10, 1962) and multiple efforts to develop folklore study programs in China that were initiated as early as the 1910s and 1950s. These influenced the China National and Folk Culture Protection Project in 2003, a national intangible cultural heritage survey from 2005 to 2009, and the establishment of the International Training Center for Intangible Cultural Heritage Protection in the Asia-Pacific Region at the China National Academy of Arts in 2010. Similarly, in 2004 the Charter for the Conservation of Unprotected Architectural Heritage and Sites in India, which was organized by the Indian National Trust for Art and Cultural Heritage (INTACH), recognized that architectural heritage also included historic ways of building.

Globalization and the threat of losing cultural identity and diversity spurred UNESCO to take action, which culminated in a partnership with and formation of the Japanese Funds-in-Trust for the Preservation and Promotion of the Intangible Cultural Heritage in 1993. The Trust financed various documentation projects and disseminated its findings to the public, work that contributed greatly to the enactment of the Convention for the Safeguarding of the Intangible Cultural Heritage in

2003 at the 14th General Assembly of UNESCO in Victoria Falls, Zimbabwe. The Convention came into full effect in 2006, with Japan acting as a State Member of the Intangible Cultural Heritage of Humanity Committee, and by 2016 had grown to include 168 countries.

State Parties are urged to identify and inventory intangible heritage in their jurisdiction while the Committee is charged with assembling the Representative and Urgent Safeguarding Lists, funding for which is derived from UNESCO's International Assistance and Intangible Cultural Heritage Fund. Japan's initiative in the protection of their individual heritage and its strong influence over other countries has paved the way for an important, new growing dimension of the heritage protection practice – the conservation of outstanding intangible values.

Further reading

Falser, Michael (ed.). 2015. *Cultural Heritage as Civilizing Mission: From Decay to Recovery*. Heidelberg, Germany: Springer International Publishing Switzerland, 76.

Intangible Cultural Heritage: An International Dialogue. Symposium organized by Smithsonian Center for Folklife and Cultural Heritage. Washington, DC, June 30, 2014.

Smith, Laurajane and Akagawa, Natsuko (eds.). 2009. *Intangible Heritage*. Abingdon, UK: Routledge.

The Agency for Cultural Affairs. "Important Intangible Cultural Property." Web. http://kunishitei.bunka.go.jp/bsys/searchlist.asp. Accessed August 20, 2015.

UNESCO. "A Living Human Treasure System." "UNESCO/Japan Funds-in-Trust for Intangible Cultural Heritage." "Japan Funds-in-Trust for the Safeguarding of the Intangible Cultural Heritage." "What is Intangible Cultural Heritage?" Web. www.unesco.org. Accessed August 20, 2015.

Ye, Peng and Yao-lin Zhou. 2013. "The Development and Trends of China's Intangible Cultural Heritage Representative List." Paper presented at the 2nd International Conference on Science and Social Research (ICSSR).

Several non-governmental or quasi-governmental initiatives characterize the heritage protection movement in Japan today. These groups share the objectives of promoting awareness and interest in Japanese cultural heritage. They include the Kyoto Mitate International, the Zenkoku Machinami Hozon Renmei (Association for Township Preservation), the Japan National Trust for Cultural and Natural Heritage Conservation, and the Japan Society for the Conservation of Cultural Property.

Kyoto Mitate International is a non-profit organization established in 2000 to conserve the architectural, cultural and natural heritage of Kyoto. The Japan National Trust for Cultural and Natural Heritage Conservation, recognized as a specific public-benefit improvement corporation in 1984, conducts research on important or threatened historic and natural places and carries out conservation projects while engaging the public in conservation activities. The Japanese Association for the Conservation of Cultural Property (JACAM), established in 1971, provides technical oversight of all government-listed historic buildings in Japan. JACAM ensures the quality of conservation work, educates in, and promotes, conservation science and technology, and is a general advocate for architectural heritage protection. It has branch offices in Tokyo, Fukuoka, Hiroshima and Osaka.

Like many other countries across the world, Japan is increasingly confronted with the task of conserving its modern architectural heritage. The restoration and adaptive use of the 1897 Neoclassical Tokyo Station Marunouchi Building began in 2007 and was completed in 2012. Project work entailed façade restoration and installation of a new station hotel in one of its wings. A precursor to this large rehabilitation of a modern complex was the rescue, relocation and restoration of Frank Lloyd Wright's Myonichikan, the old Geidai Music Hall now in Ueno Park, and the forecourt and central portion of the American master's Imperial Hotel, which is now located in the Meiji-Mura Museum near Nagoya.

The loss of significant modern buildings to redevelopment spurred the establishment of DOCOMOMO Japan in 1988. DOCOMOMO Japan advocates preserving significant examples of architectural modernism. Its publication *Japan DOCOMOMO: 100 Selections* (2005) has proved helpful in raising popular awareness for this especially challenging issue in architectural conservation. Other international attention to conserving Japan's wealth of modern architecture has also helped raise the profile of the issue. For instance, the winner of the 2012 World Monuments Fund/Knoll Modernism Prize for conserving modern architecture is the Hizuchi High School in Yawatahama City, Ehime prefecture, on Shikoku Island, which was carefully restored following a two-year debate about how to treat modern buildings after the school was damaged by Typhoon Nida in 2004.

FIGURE 1.8a and b The Second Imperial Hotel, designed by American architect Frank Lloyd Wright, was a prestige Tokyo address from 1923 through the 1950s. Built in elaborately sculpted lava rock it survived the Great Kanto Earthquake in 1923 but due to damage caused by subway construction it was mostly demolished in 1968. The preserved and relocated Entrance Hall, Lobby and front pool area (a) of The Imperial Hotel, along with numerous furnishings and fittings (b) were relocated and are preserved at the outdoor Meiji-Mura architectural museum near Nagoya. The Meiji-Mura features a total of sixty-seven mostly Western-styled structures largely dating from the Meiji period (1868–1912) within an elaborately landscaped setting; it exemplifies the concept of "museifying" historic buildings on a grand scale.

However, the triumphs of conserving modern architectural landmarks seem to be outweighed by the losses, some stories of which have been covered by the international press. The more distinctive portion of Tokyo's elegant 1964 Hotel Okura, a masterpiece of Japanese mid-century modern by Yoshiro Taniguchi, was demolished in September 2015 for replacement by a thirty-eight-storey tower, part hotel and part offices, in anticipation of the 2020 Olympics. American architect and international advocate for the preservation of architectural modernism, Toshiko Mori, cites an additional obstacle to waging a preservation campaign to save the Okura: "It's not as if people are standing up and speaking out. Japan is not an activist culture. There's some sense there's nothing we can do."[37]

Japan is active on the international architectural conservation scene as well and it institutionalized its commitment to international heritage protection by the passage in 2006 of the Law on the Promotion of International Cooperation for the Protection of Cultural Heritage Abroad. Indeed, Japan has been involved in international heritage protection aid-related projects dating from the 1960s, as in its financial aid to Egypt for the rescue of Nubian monuments, and subsequent support for conservation projects in Venice and Florence. It is consistently one of the largest contributors to UNESCO's World Heritage Fund. The Japanese Trust Fund for the Preservation of World Cultural Heritage was established within UNESCO by the Japanese government to conserve historic buildings and sites of outstanding value throughout the world. The Fund supports conservation work through the allocation of financing, equipment and technical expertise, and all manner of related research and documentation work. Angkor in Cambodia has benefited from the Japanese Trust Fund, receiving US$8.75 million between 1997 and 2000 for a multi-phase, long-term project involving the restoration of the Library of Bayon, among other structures.[38] In addition to this support to Cambodia, Japanese conservators have been active elsewhere in Asia including major engagements in Mongolia, Vietnam, Indonesia, India, Nepal, Kazakhstan and Afghanistan. The relatively new and growing discipline of examining the cultural, diplomatic and economic ramifications of international financial and technical assistance in heritage conservation are well portrayed in *Heritage Conservation in Japan's Cultural Diplomacy: Heritage National Identity and National Interest* (2015) by Natsuko Akagawa.

In tandem with this effort is a professional skills training exchange program known as the Cultural Properties Specialists' Dispatch Program. Established in 1990 by the Japan Foundation, the program in its first five years dispatched over forty professionals trained in documentation, museum management, architectural conservation, archaeology and wall painting conservation to projects in numerous foreign countries. In addition, organizations such as the Tokyo National Research Institute of Cultural Properties and the Nara National Cultural Properties Research Institute have hosted on-site training sessions ranging from the conservation of Japanese art and artifacts to advanced building conservation techniques.[39] Although challenges exist in this type of cross-cultural educational exchange, the effort on the part of the Japanese to share expertise and resources represents a significant effort in disseminating professional information on a global scale.

A robust professional network of specialists and advanced training in architectural conservation has existed in Japan concurrent with those of other leader nations in architectural conservation. The Japanese Association for Conservation of Architectural Monuments (JCAM), established in 1971, is affiliated with the Japanese Agency for Cultural Affairs. Its purposes are to restore listed National Treasures and important cultural properties, to educate architectural conservators and research historic architectural techniques and conservation methods, and disseminate information to a wider audience on architectural conservation. Headquartered in Tokyo with branch offices in four other prefectures, JCAM leads in guiding best practices in architectural conservation in Japan. The nation's leading facility for conservation science and technology is the Nara National Research Institute for Cultural Properties that has extensive state-of-the-art laboratories addressing conservation issues of all kinds on all traditional building materials. In 2001 the Nara Institute took in the National Research Institute for Cultural Properties in Tokyo to become one institution.

The long concern for conserving cultural patrimony in Japan is attributable above all else to its appreciation of tradition and cultural continuity. Japan's great buildings such as Hōryū-ji, Tōdaiji, Nagoya Castle and thousands of other individually listed buildings and sites are widely valued and specially protected. In addition, the country's urban and rural vernacular architecture and intangible heritage are also highly respected, whether the item is listed as officially protected heritage or not.

Lessons in damage mitigation to cultural heritage from The Great East Japan Earthquake and Tsunami, by Wesley Cheek

On March 11, 2011 at 2:46 pm a magnitude 9.0 earthquake occurred off the coast of northeastern Japan. This earthquake spawned a series of massive tsunamis that devastated hundreds of miles of coastline. Now referred to as The Great East Japan Earthquake and Tsunami, or the Tōhoku Earthquake, this widespread and complicated disaster has spurred reconsideration across academic disciplines in how to understand and deal with catastrophes of this scale. For those involved in cultural heritage management The Great East Japan Earthquake presented a complex question: what role does the discipline play in times of disaster?

In the wake of the 2004 Indian Ocean Earthquake and Tsunami some rebuilding efforts foundered as they failed to address local cultures and vernacular architecture. For example, a fishing village in Sri Lanka was rebuilt without incorporating traditional methods and neglecting traditional uses. New concrete buildings were erected that lacked porches where fishermen could work on their nets while the groves of trees that provided shade were torn down during the construction process.[40] This situation was partially caused by an influx of non-governmental organizations that were international in scope, but with little local knowledge or experience in the design and function of traditional structures. However, the Sri Lankan government was also guilty of similar oversights. The government requirements for new post-tsunami housing specified indoor kitchens with inadequate ventilation for biomass cooking as well as living areas that were not large enough to incorporate traditional multi-generation families.[41]

Similarly the Indonesian Development Planning Agency constructed a new city for residents of Banda Aceh that was located one and a half miles away from the ocean. This was in accord with new laws that were designed to protect citizens from disasters; however, it did not consider the traditional lifestyles and building patterns of the villagers. The new, safer housing that had been constructed at a tsunami-proof distance from the ocean was quickly rejected and the coastal communities relocated themselves to seaside areas where they could continue their traditional fishing lifestyles.[42]

With those lessons in mind many researchers and practitioners working in the affected areas in Japan are striving to avoid stumbling blocks that have been encountered after other disasters. The importance of local historic structures and ritual sites in the immediate aftermath of disasters has been observed. In the city of Ishinomaki neighborhood shrines and temples were utilized as emergency shelters following the disaster.[43] Shrines and temples had moved locations in response to previous tsunamis and were therefore well positioned to be out of danger and of use immediately after the tsunami destroyed a large percentage of the housing stock.[44] This phenomenon was also recorded in the Shizugawa area of Minamisanriku where pillows and fabric from the Kaminoyama Hachimangu shrine, which had been used in Shinto rituals, were distributed to local residents as temporary bedding.

Murasaki shrine in Kesennuma was also used as a refuge after the tsunami. As the port area of Kesennuma was known to be in danger in the event of a tsunami, people in the area were well practiced in evacuation procedures. Tsunami evacuation paths were well marked with signs reading, "If there is an earthquake, there will be a tsunami." As shrines and temples were generally located on high ground, these evacuation routes often lead to historic buildings and ritual sites. The semi-public nature of Murasaki shrine coupled with local residents' familiarity with its location contributed to a successful evacuation and the shrine's use as a temporary shelter. As with Kaminoyama Hachimangu, ritual supplies stored at Murasaki shrine were also used following the disaster.

As many temples and shrines survived the earthquake due to their flexible timber construction and weathered the ensuing tsunami owing to previous generations' foresight in relocating structures to safe locations, some of these historic structures have become centers for community life and active in the reconstruction process. Kaminoyama Hachimangu has become central as an organizing location for Shizugawa residents who are attempting to prevent, or at least alter plans to construct a 10-meter sea wall between the village and the ocean.

Out of the examination of the Tohoku Earthquake and the reconstruction process that is continuing, the World Bank published *Learning from Megadisasters*. This study calls for what it terms "non-structural measures" as a part of the reconstruction and further mitigation process.[45] What these measures are is not spelled out in detail, but it can be understood that matters of cultural heritage, traditional practices and rituals and festivals can fall into the category of "non-structural." What the World Bank, and many other organizations involved in disaster research have come to understand is that engineering processes alone will not bring back damaged areas, or insure them against further disasters. It will take an understanding of cultural concerns to properly go about the task of reconstruction.

In March of 2015 international experts in disaster mitigation assembled in Sendai, Japan to finalize the

Sendai Framework for Disaster Risk Reduction. This conference was significant both in that it was a major world conference held in the area directly affected by the Great East Japan Earthquake and Tsunami and that it established the world's disaster mitigation framework through the year 2030 (the successor to the Hyogo Framework for Action, which was ratified in 2005 in Kobe, Japan). The Sendai Framework states explicitly that cultural resilience is a necessary component of disaster risk reduction. To that end, the protection of cultural assets is called for in the guiding principles of the document.

In addition to these goals and principles, the Sendai Framework instructs nations and localities to assess and inventory cultural assets and heritage sites so as to be able to better understand the scale of a disaster, and also as preparation for recovery after a disaster. The imperative that the United Nations and the other stakeholders involved in drafting the Sendai Framework are placing on cultural assets and heritage sites is born out of a careful examination of multiple disasters, up to and including the Great East Japan Earthquake. What we have come to understand through this examination is that the material objects, buildings included, involved in the everyday life of people are of critical importance to the fabric of a society and therefore fundamentally linked to the success of rebuilding efforts.

The story of historic cultural sites in the aftermath of disasters is not a perfect one. Disasters are complicated and tragic. However, the involvement of those with an understanding of architectural conservation and cultural heritage in the aftermath of the Great East Japan Earthquake are making significant contributions to post-disaster reconstruction and future mitigation efforts.

Further reading

Aquilino, Marie Jeannine. 2011. *Beyond Shelter: Architecture and Human Dignity*. New York: Metropolis Books. Available through D.A.P./Distributed Art Publishers.

Hayashi, Michiko, Kaori Yamazaki and Takayuki Ōkubo. 2012. "The Temporary Evacuation Shelter Management Organization at Shrines and Temples Located in Ishinomaki, after the Great East Japan Earthquake," *Historical City Planning Disaster Prevention Journal* 6 (July): 149–156.

Kawabe, Satoshi, Michiko Hayashi and Takayuki Ōkubo. 2012. "A Study on Potency of Local Shrines and Temples as a Tsunami Shelter from the Viewpoint of Evacuation Time in East Japan Earthquake," *Historical City Planning Disaster Prevention Journal* 6 (July): 157–164.

Ranghieri, Federica, and Mikio Ishiwatari. 2014. *Learning from Megadisasters: Lessons from the Great East Japan Earthquake*. Washington, DC: World Bank, June 26.

FIGURE 1.9a, b and c More than two weeks after the tsunami the rural area between Kesennuma and Minamisanriku lies in ruin. On March 29, 2011 nine-year-old Koyo Okoshi helps locate bottles of sake from her father's business (a). Looking out from Kaminoyama Hachimangu shrine, the village of Shizugawa has been devastated (b). Three years after the tsunami, the village of Shizugawa celebrates the Kagaribi Festival at Kaminoyama Hachimangu (c).

As such, Japan's cultural heritage has a sense of timelessness and a special relevance to the present. With well over a century and a half of experience in nationally organized and supported heritage protection, Japan's holistic heritage conservation approach is one of the most enlightened and effective cultural heritage management systems in the world.

Japan's contribution to international architectural conservation practice extends beyond its sharing of experiences, technical expertise and financial support. It has made contributions to specialized aspects of architectural conservation theory, thanks in large part to the 1995 Nara Document. A vibrant cultural and professional exchange exists between Japanese professionals and many of their international counterparts resulting in collaborative studies and educational programs. For its many good efforts and accomplishments in architectural heritage conservation both at home and abroad, Japan's example is a model for other countries to follow.

Notes

1. Japan's system of saluting and fostering certain craft traditions was adopted in South Korea in 1993 and also helped inspire the UNESCO Convention for the Safeguarding of Intangible Cultural Heritage, which was adopted at the UNESCO General Conference in 2003. Japan has played a key role in promoting and developing the procedures of this convention and as of 2016 has twenty two intangible cultural properties listed.
2. There has been disagreement based on a determination made in 1905 as to the founding date of Hōryū-ji temple. Excavations made in 1939 suggests it likely replaced the Ikaruga-dera temple that is believed to have been completed in 607 CE and destroyed by fire in 670.
3. Japan has had fifteen capitals throughout its history, with some being replaced at or near the same location, such as Nagaoka-kyō (784–794 CE), that preceded Kyoto (794–1869 CE).
4. Osaka Castle's existing donjon was reconstructed in 1931 with reinforced concrete.
5. Around Kyoto several monasteries contain wooden ceilings made from the floorboards of Fushimi castle, where an important precursor to the battle of Sekigahara took place in 1600 CE. Hundreds of Samurai took their own lives or were killed and their blood stained the wood. The temples that contain these recycled floorboards are Yogen-in, Genko-an and Hosen-in.
6. The Meiji Restoration in 1868 introduced modern construction techniques from abroad.
7. Knut Einar Larsen. *Architectural Preservation in Japan*. ICOMOS International Committee. (Trondheim: Tapir Publishers, 1994), 3.
8. The damaged elements were removed and re-erected in a nearby warehouse, creating a counterpart presentation of the newly reconstructed hall, which was built *in situ* with a mix of old and new members. See Don Choi, "Meiji Restorations: Defining Preservation, Education and Architecture for Modern Japan," *NCPE Preservation Education and Research* 2 (2009), 91.
9. Ibid.
10. "The Japanese Practice: Translocation and Reconstruction," in W.F. Denslagen and Niels Gutschow (eds.), *Architectural Imitations: Reproductions and Pastiches in East and West*. (Maastricht: Shaker Publishing, 2005).
11. A similar though internationally inspired effort at fundraising for some of Japan's most special architectural heritage occurred between 2001 and 2004 through the efforts of the World Monuments Fund in cooperation with the Abbess of the imperial temple-convents (*manzeki amadera*) of Hōkyōji in west-central Kyoto, mostly dating from 1788 with its origins dating to the thirteenth century. Its imperial chapel was dismantled and donated to the convent on the order of Emperor Ninko in 1846. In 2003 it was chosen as a pilot conservation project by the Institute of Medieval Japanese Studies at Columbia University (New York) and the World Monuments Fund. The process entailed dismantling and removal to the Oka Bokkōdō Studio, Ltd. in Kyoto, one of Japan's premier conservation facilities. With the patronage of Her Majesty Empress Michiko, and funding from artist Ikuo Hirayama and his Foundation for Cultural Heritage, with matching funding from the US-based Freeman Foundation and WMF's Robert W. Wilson Challenge to Conserve Our Heritage, specialists from Japan and the United States developed a conservation strategy for the convents. This pilot project was meant to inspire similar action in thirteen similar temple-convents in Kyoto and Nara. See Barbara Ruch. "A Place of Their Own: Piety and Patronage in Japan's Imperial Buddhist Convents," *ICON*, World Monuments Fund (Fall, 2003), 1–3.
12. Cristoph Hendrichsen, "Historical Outline of Conservation Legislation in Japan," in Siegfried R.C.T. Enders and Niels Gutschow (eds.), *Hozon: Architectural and Urban Conservation in Japan*. (Stuttgart/London: Edition Axel Menges, 1998), 12. With the Hōryū-ji temple complex in Nara including Japan's oldest surviving wooden architecture, the Daibutsuden structure housing the Great Buddha at nearby Tōdai-ji

temple is considered the largest historic wooden structure in the world. It measures 48 m (160 ft) tall, 57 m (187 ft) long, and 50 m (165 ft) wide. It was reconstructed following a fire in 1709 based on its original eighth century form with the present building said to be two-thirds its original size.

13 *Shikinen sengū* is the periodic reconstruction of Shinto shrines having associations with spiritual renewal. *Kaitai shūri* is the modern preservation practice of disassembly, repair and reconstruction based on techniques used on other structures by early Master Builders.

14 These chronicles, compiled in the imperial court beginning in 712 CE, combine myth, legend and history to glorify the dynasty. They variously claim that Naikū and Gekū were established in the third century CE, with other sources suggesting even earlier dates.

15 Ise has, since medieval times, represented a stronghold of national myths and its main shrine contains as many as 10,000 Shinto sanctuaries. The Ise Grand Shrine, according to one ancient text, is considered a place where the spirit of supreme deity Amaterasu-ōmikami, considered to be the ancestor of Japan's royal family, could be enshrined forever.

16 John Breen and Mark Teeuwen. *A New History of Shinto* (Chichester: Wiley-Blackwell, 2009).

17 Larsen, 35.

18 This concept comes from tea ceremony culture and the pottery associated with it. An early (mid-1500s) key personage associated with *wabi-sabi* was the connoisseur court figure Sen no Rikyū, who was based at the Daitoku-ji temple complex in Kyoto.

19 Larsen, 40–41. Some contend that the concept of *wabi-sabi* originated in Korea.

20 Larsen, 12. Throughout the Meiji period the government attempted to separate Buddhism and Shinto, suppressing the former and refashioning the latter as Japan's principle religion.

21 Choi, 7.

22 Ibid. Earlier regulations in 1897 called the Application Regulations for Preservation Funds for Ancient Shrines and Temples (*Koshaji Hononkin Shutsugan Kisoku*) covered not only buildings but also stone monuments, religious artifacts and everyday utensils. Importantly, seven criteria for the listing of objects and buildings were articulated as part of these regulations.

23 Choi, 8.

24 Masafumi Yamasaki (ed). *Kyoto: Its Cityscape Traditions and Heritage* (Tokyo: Tokyo Process Architecture Publishing, 1995), 199, 391. Architect Yorinaka Tsumaki wrote his thesis at Cornell University on Japanese architectural history.

25 Despite the repeal of the 1897 Act, the 1919 Act remained in place until 1950.

26 Larsen, 13.

27 It has been cited often that Kyoto avoided the United States' atomic bomb target list largely due to Secretary of War Henry Stimson's personal admiration for its ancient architectural heritage. Recent scholarship suggests that this is apocryphal and that Kyoto was one of several cities saved as a test of the atomic bomb so damage could be accurately measured in comparative terms. In any case, the psychological impact of bombing sites other than military targets such as Hiroshima and Nagasaki were a consideration since a total of 115 Japanese cities were bombed.

28 Olwen Beazley. "Politics and Power: The Hiroshima Peace Memorial (Genbaku Dome) as World Heritage," in Sophia Labadi and Colin Long (eds.), *Heritage and Globalization* (Abingdon, UK: Routledge), 9. Beazley uses the example of the Hiroshima Peace Memorial (Genbaku Dome), a leading example of a site with a difficult or traumatic heritage, delving into political and contested terrain of heritage narratives at international, national, and local levels.

29 Masaru Sekino. 1972. UNESCO *Museum and Monuments* series XIV, Paris, 9, 207.

30 Ibid., 210.

31 Junko Gunto and Arnold R. Alanen. "The Conservation of Historic and Cultural Resources in Rural Japan." *Landscape Journal* 6(1) (1987), 42–61.

32 Ibid., 45.

33 Agency for Cultural Affairs. "Important Intangible Cultural Property." Web. http://kunishitei.bunka.go.jp/bsys/searchlist.asp. Accessed August 20, 2015.

34 Larsen, 9.

35 Knut Einar Larsen and Nils Marstein. *Conservation of Historic Timber Structures: An Ecological Approach* (Oxford: Butterworth Heinemann, 2000), 55.

36 Siegfried R.C.T. Enders. 1998. "Organization and Management of Conservation Projects in Japan," in Siegfried R.C.T. Enders and Niels Gutschow (eds.), *Hozon: Architectural and Urban Conservation in Japan* (Stuttgart: Edition Axel Menges), 22.

37 Christopher Bonanos. "Sayonara Syndrome," *Town and Country* magazine, New York (April 2015), 174.

38 *Report on the Conservation and Restoration Work of the North Library of Bayon, Angkor* (Tokyo: UNESCO and the Japanese Trust for Preservation of World Cultural Heritage, 2000).
39 Nagajiro Miyamoto. "Technological Problems in the International Cooperative Activity for Conservation in Japan." Unpublished paper delivered at the Fifth Seminar on the Conservation of Asian Cultural Heritage, October 17–19, 1995, Nara, Japan.
40 Marie Jeannine Aquilino. 2011. *Beyond Shelter: Architecture and Human Dignity*. (New York: Metropolis Books). Available through D.A.P./Distributed Art Publishers, 37.
41 Shaw, Judith, Iftakar Ahmed et al. *Lessons from the Tsunami Recovery in Sri Lanka and India*. 27 August, 2010. Monash Institute. Australian Policy Online. http://apo.org.au/resource/lessons-tsunami-recovery-sri-lanka-and-india. Accessed November 22, 2015.
42 Aquilino, 39.
43 Michiko Hayashi, Kaori Yamazaki and Takayuki Okubo. 2012. "The Temporary Evacuation Shelter Management Organization at Shrines and Temples Located in Ishinomaki, after the Great East Japan Earthquake." *Historical City Planning Disaster Prevention Journal* 6 (July): 149–156.
44 Satoshi Kawabe, Michiko Hayashi and Takayuki Okubo. 2012. "A Study on Potency of Local Shrines and Temples as a Tsunami Shelter from the Viewpoint of Evacuation Time in East Japan Earthquake." *Historical City Planning Disaster Prevention Journal* 6 (July): 157–164.
45 Federica Ranghieri, and Mikio Ishiwatari. 2014. *Learning from Megadisasters: Lessons from the Great East Japan Earthquake*. (Washington, DC: World Bank, June 26).

Further reading

The Agency for Cultural Affairs. 2011. *Cultural Properties for Future Generations: Outline of the Cultural Administration of Japan*. Booklet. Tokyo: Cultural Properties Dept., Agency for Cultural Affairs.
The Agency for Cultural Affairs (Japan). N.d. "Important Intangible Cultural Property." Web. http://kunishitei.bunka.go.jp/bsys/searchlist.asp.
Akagawa, Natsuko. 2015. *Heritage Conservation and Japan's Cultural Diplomacy: Heritage, National Identity and National Interest*. Abingdon, UK: Routledge.
Albert, Marie-Theres and Birgitta Ringbeck. 2015. *40 Years World Heritage Convention: Popularizing the Protection of Cultural and Natural Heritage*. Berlin: Walter de Gruyter GmbH, 153–173.
Beazley, Olwen. 2010. "Politics and Power: The Hiroshima Peace Memorial (Genbaku Dome) as World Heritage," in Sophia Labadi and Colin Long (eds.), *Heritage and Globalization*. Abingdon, UK: Routledge, 45–65.
Bonanos, Christopher. 2015. "Sayonara Syndrome," *Town and Country* magazine (April), New York, 174.
Carver, Norman F., Jr. 1984. *Japanese Folkhouses*. Kalamazoo, MI: Documan Press.
Choi, Don. 2009. "Meiji Restorations: Defining Preservation, Education and Architecture for Modern Japan," *NCPE Preservation Education and Research* 2: 91.
Clancey, Gregory. 2005. "Modernity and Carpenters: *Daiku* Technique and Meiji Technocracy," in Morris Law (ed.), *Bridging a Modern Japan*. New York: Palgrave, 183–206.
Denslagen, Wim and Niels Gutschow (eds). 2005. *Architectural Imitations: Reproductions and Pastiches in East and West*. Maastricht: Shaker Publishing B.V.
DOCOMOMO Japan. 2005. *100 Selections*. Tokyo: Shinkenchiku-sha Co.
Enders, Siegfried R.C.T. 1998. "Organization and Management of Conservation Projects in Japan," in Siegfried R.C.T Enders, and Niels Gutschow (eds.), *Hozon: Architectural and Urban Conservation in Japan*. Stuttgart: Edition Axel Menges.
Enders, Siegfried R.C.T. and Niels Gutchow (eds.). 1998. *Hozon: Architectural and Urban Conservation in Japan*. Stuttgart: Edition Axel Menges.
Falser, Michael (ed). 2015. *Cultural Heritage as Civilizing Mission: From Decay to Recovery*. Heidelberg: Springer International Publishing, 76.
Gunto, Junko and Arnold R. Alanen. 1987. "The Conservation of Historic and Cultural Resources in Rural Japan," *Landscape Journal* 6(1): 42–61.
Hendrichsen, Cristoph. 1998. "Historical Outline of Conservation Legislation in Japan," in Siegfried R.C.T. Enders and Niels Gutschow (eds.), *Hozon: Architectural and Urban Conservation in Japan*. Stuttgart: Edition Axel Menges, 12.
Ibler, Marianne. 2003. *Modern Japanese Architecture: Masters and Mannerists in the 1950s–60s*. Aalborg, Denmark: Aalborg University Press.
Isozaki, Arata. 2006. *Japan-ness in Architecture*. Translated by Sabu Kohso. Cambridge, MA: The MIT Press.
JACAM (The Japanese Association for Conservation of Architectural Monuments). N.d. Booklet. *Protecting, Handing Down and Revitalizing our Architectural Heritage*. Tokyo: JACAM.

Japan Center for International Cooperation in Conservation. 2011. *Seminar on Implementation of International Conservation Training Program*, Tokyo: National Research Institute for Cultural Properties.

Japan Society. "A City Under Siege: Saving Kyoto's Machiya from Destruction." Web. www.japansociety.org/resources/content/2/0/5/4/documents/machiyasymposium.pdf. Accessed May 17, 2016.

Kinoshita, Ryōichi. 2003. "Preservation and Revitalization of *Machiya* in Kyoto," in Nicolas Fiévé and Paul Waley (eds.), *Japanese Capitals in Historical Perspective: Place, Power and Memory in Kyoto, Edo and Tokyo*. London: Routledge Curzon, 367–383.

Kojima, Fusae. 2013. "An Overview of the Kyomachiya Revitalization Project." *World Monuments Fund Journal*, March 6, 2013. Web. www.wmf.org/blog/overview-kyomachiya-revitalization-project. Accessed September 15, 2016.

Kyoto Center for Community Collaboration. 2008. *Machiya Revival in Kyoto*. Kyoto: Mitsumura Suiko Shoin Publishing Co.

Larsen, Knut Einar. 1994. *Architectural Preservation in Japan*. ICOMOS International Committee, Trondheim: Tapir Publishers.

Larsen, Knut Einar, et al. (eds). 1995. *Nara Conference on Authenticity in Relation to the World Heritage Convention*. Paris: ICOMOS; Rome: UNESCO; and Tokyo: ICCROM and Agency for Cultural Affairs.

Larsen, Knut Einar and Nils Marstein. 2000. *Conservation of Historic Timber Structures: An Ecological Approach*. Oxford: Butterworth Heinemann, 55.

Löfgren, Karin. 2003. "Machiya: History and Architecture of the Kyoto Town House." Stockholm: KTH Royal Institute of Technology.

Meiji-mura Foundation. 2004. *Museum Meiji-mura*. Aichi: Meitetsu Impress Co.

Miyamoto, Nagajiro. 1995. "Technological Problems in the International Cooperative Activity for Conservation in Japan." Unpublished paper delivered at the Fifth Seminar on the Conservation of Asian Cultural Heritage, October 17–19, 1995, Nara, Japan.

Nakagawa, Tadeshi. 2005. *The Japanese House In Space, Memory and Language*. Translated by Geraldine Harcourt. Originally published in 2002 by TOTO Shuppan under the title *Nihon no ie: kukan, koiku, kotoba*. Tokyo: International House of Japan.

Nute, Kevin. 2004. *Place, Time and Being in Japanese Architecture*. New York: Routledge.

Seike, Kiyosi. 1977. *The Art of Japanese Joinery*. Translated by Yuriko Yobuko and Rebecca M. Davis. New York: Weatherhill; Tokyo: Tankosha.

Sekino, Masaru. 1970. "National Protection of the Monuments and Sites in Japan," in *Proceedings of the Symposium on Preservation and Development of Historic Quarters in Urban Programs, in Kyoto and Nara, September 7–13, 1970*. Kyoto: UNESCO Japan.

——. 1972. "The Preservation and Restoration of Wooden Monuments in Japan" 9, UNESCO *Museum and Monuments* XIV. Paris: UNESCO, 207.

——. 1972. "The Scientific and Technical Research for the Preservation of Cultural Property," in *Proceedings of the ASPAC Experts Meeting on the Preservation of Cultural Heritage, May 31–June 4, 1971, Tokyo*. Seoul: Centre for the Asian and Pacific Region, 136–145.

——. 1975. "Conservation of Small Historic Towns in Japan." Paper presented at the ICOMOS Symposium on the Conservation of Smaller Historic Towns, at the 4th General Assembly of ICOMOS, held May 25–30, 1975. Paris: ICOMOS.

——. 1977. "Principles of Conservation and Restoration Regarding Wooden Buildings in Japan," in *Proceedings of the International Symposium on the Conservation and Restoration of Cultural Property: Conservation of Wood. Tokyo, Nara and Kyoto, November 24–28, 1977*. Tokyo: NRICP, 127–142.

Siegenthaler, Peter David. 2004. "Looking to the Past, Looking to the Future: The Localization of Japanese Historic Preservation, 1950–1975." PhD dissertation, University of Texas, Austin (USA).

Smith, Laurajane and Akagawa, Natsuko (eds.). 2009. *Intangible Heritage*. Abingdon, UK: Routledge.

Smithsonian Center for Folklife and Cultural Heritage. 2014. *Intangible Cultural Heritage: An International Dialogue*. Symposium organized by Smithsonian Center for Folklife and Cultural Heritage. Washington, DC, June 30.

Starrs, Roy (ed.). 2014. *When the Tsunami Came to Shore: Culture and Disaster in Japan*. Leiden: Global Oriental.

Suiko Shoin, Mitsumura. 2008. *Machiya Revival in Kyoto*. Edited by Kyoto Center for Community Collaboration. Kyoto, Japan: Mitsumura Suiko Shoin Publishing Co.

Suwa, Sachiko. 2006. "The Preservation of *Kyo-machiya*: A Survey of Past History, Future Plans and Current Attitudes Regarding the Unique Vernacular Architecture of Kyoto." Master's thesis, Kyoto Notre Dame University.

Tze, May Loo. 2014. *Heritage Politics: Shuri Castle and Okinawa's Incorporation into Modern Japan, 1879–2000*. New York: Lexington Books.

Ueda, Atsushi. 1987. "Historical Cities and Post-Modern Architecture. The Rebirth of Machiya in Kyoto: From Moneyland to Loveland," in *Old Cultures in New Worlds. 8th ICOMOS General Assembly and International Symposium. Programme Report – Compte rendu*. Washington: US/ICOMOS, 815–820.

UNESCO. 1950. "Law for the Protection of Cultural Property." May 30, 1950. Last amended March 30, 2007. Web. www.unesco.org/culture/natlaws/media/pdf/japan/japan_lawprotectionculturalproperty_engtof.pdf. Accessed May 17, 2016.

———. 2000. *Report on the Conservation and Restoration Work of the North Library of Bayon, Angkor*. Tokyo: UNESCO and the Japanese Trust for Preservation of World Cultural Heritage.

———. N.d. "A Living Human Treasure System," "Japan Funds-in-Trust for Intangible Cultural Heritage," "Japan Funds-in-Trust for the Safeguarding of the Intangible Cultural Heritage," "What is Intangible Cultural Heritage?" Web. www.unesco.org/culture. Accessed May 17, 2016.

Weiler, Katharina and Niels Gutchow (eds). 2017. *Authenticity in Architectural Heritage Conservation*. Switzerland: Springer International.

World Monuments Fund. "Completion of Second Phase of Machiya Revitalization Project Celebrated in Kyoto: Restored Townhouse Becomes Machiya Museum." Web. www.wmf.org/sites/default/files/press_releases/Furaibou%20Restoration%20Release.pdf. Accessed May 17, 2016.

Yamasaki, Masafumi (ed.). 1995. *Kyoto: Its Cityscape Traditions and Heritage*. Tokyo: Tokyo Process Architecture Publishing Co.

Ye, Peng and Yao-lin Zhou. 2013. "The Development and Trends of China's Intangible Cultural Heritage Representative List." A paper presented at the 2nd International Conference on Science and Social Research (ICSSR).

Zhang, Juwen. 2013. "Folklore Studies in China and the China Folklore Society: A Brief Introduction." Web. www.afsnet.org/news/113754/Folklore-Studies-in-China-and-the-China-Folklore-Society-A-Brief-Introduction.htm. Accessed May 17, 2016.

Ornamented portal, Yunnan Province, PRC.

2

THE PEOPLE'S REPUBLIC OF CHINA

Few, if any, modern nations share the wealth of cultural heritage paired with centuries of relative cultural continuity as does the People's Republic of China (PRC). China boasts an impressive roster of global superlatives: the largest population, the fastest growing economy, one of the world's largest consumer markets, home to some of the world's largest cities, and one of the world's oldest cultures in terms of language and geographic unity. All of these distinctions amount to a body of built cultural heritage matched by few. Twinned with this position is the enormous responsibility for managing and caring for such places and items. And with this responsibility comes the fact that perhaps no other country today has as much to gain – or lose – through the management of cultural heritage over the next several decades as does China. This is largely due to a rapid and unremitting pace of change being experienced in most, if not all, facets of Chinese life today and by recent changes in cultural heritage protection policy.

As the nation continues to open its borders and thinking to the global community of conservation professionals and organizations, and as international bodies further embrace some of China's distinctively unusual positions on heritage protection, the line between gain and loss becomes increasingly stark. It is important to recognize, however, that most evaluations by the international community of specific successes achieved and overall progress made in Chinese cultural heritage management contain a certain measure of Western bias. It could be argued that the Chinese over the course of their history carry an enviable record of conservation of their built fabric, given the amount of centuries-old built heritage that remains extant due to continuous use, care and upkeep. As compared to the West's long legacy of massive cultural, political and religious upheavals, most of which have profoundly affected the built environment, China, at least until the Taiping Rebellion (1850–1864), has maintained a remarkably strong tradition of maintaining its built heritage.

Because many of the tenets of modern cultural heritage management and policy were codified in the West, the Chinese for much of the twentieth century were perceived as lagging behind and being beyond the mainstream of modern standards of conservation professionalism. This perception has been aggravated by the tremendous cultural and political changes China itself experienced in the twentieth century as unexpected and violent political movements overturned thousands of years of history, including preservation efforts, within a few decades.

Since 1990 cultural heritage protection has become a national priority with new government backing. As one scholar explains, the ruling Chinese Communist Party consciously created narratives of China's cultural traditions to emphasize "the 'refined' beliefs, customs and values that manifest in Chinese history."[1] Add to this an exceptional scale and pace of economic development, as modern

China's lost past and legislative response – overview

The long-recorded history of the Chinese court, its foreign affairs and internal conflicts includes countless examples of tumult, shift and upheaval. For instance, one particularly fierce period of persecution of Buddhism in the mid-ninth century CE resulted in the destruction of 4,600 temples and 4,000 shrines.[2] Throughout modern history Westerners have extracted Chinese relics in abundance, in a manner typical of colonizing powers throughout the world, since time immemorial. However, the plundering experienced in China has been particularly egregious, with perpetrators coming from varied lands and social strata. In 1860 both British and French forces sacked the Summer Palace (Yuanming Yuan) outside Beijing, and added to their holdings in 1911 after the Republican revolution. In Dunhuang, a remote oasis in the Taklamakan desert many days' journey from the capital, explorer Sir Marc Aurel Stein removed an estimated 500,000 Song and Tang dynasty manuscripts and paintings during expeditions made in the early years of the twentieth century. More recently, in the face of Japanese encroachment Chinese Nationalists removed hundreds of thousands of imperial treasures from Beijing's Palace Museum to Taiwan in 1948–1949, which loss was followed two decades later by the broad cultural destruction undertaken in the name of the 1966 Cultural Revolution. To these instances of stolen cultural patrimony must be added tens of thousands of cases where tomb robbers and smugglers benefit from the clandestine selling of millions of cultural artifacts abroad through sophisticated networks.[3]

Along with such violation of China's cultural heritage came the predictable hazards of modernization. Especially hazardous for heritage have been the country's massive infrastructure and capital development projects. Over the past thirty years, new dams, roads and railways cut through a rapidly modernizing countryside with unprecedented speed. The problems inherent in such works were recognized by authorities and have been dealt with in a variety of ways, including improved protective legislation and enforcement. Nevertheless, it appears that there is no end in sight of illicit trafficking of antiquities. A lesson for our purposes here is that in typical causal fashion these losses have heightened awareness both within China and internationally. More than ever before there is a global recognition of what is at stake and the importance of finding effective ways to combat the problem as soon as possible.

Present Chinese conservation policies are rooted in ancient regulations on cultural heritage protection. Three main laws issued in 1982, 1992 and 2002 do much towards defining Chinese attitudes toward the legal protection of cultural relics and sites.[4] The 1982 Law of the PRC for the Protection of Cultural Heritage was passed in reaction to destruction caused by the Cultural Revolution. This law's broad definition of cultural relics includes historic buildings, sites and important remains that are related to historical events, and outlines the methodology for having them placed on an official list of protected national heritage. It may be considered the launch of modern scientific policy on heritage conservation issues in China.

In 1992 the PRC Executive Regulation for the Implementation of the Conservation of Cultural Property strengthened the 1982 legislation in various ways, including improving its administrative implementation. It was also the year the PRC ratified the UNESCO World Heritage Convention, after which time Chinese conservators could, for the first time, share heritage conservation efforts with international partners.

A subsequent law passed in 2002, the Law of the People's Republic of China for the Safeguard of Cultural Property, was even more groundbreaking because it acknowledged both Chinese traditional perspectives and international modern conservation approaches. Three of its most important tenets were that: a distinction between movable and immovable heritage was formally introduced, cultural heritage was recognized as "not renewable resources," and the "principle of keeping the former condition" of a cultural artifact, be it an object or a building, was formally mentioned as an objective of conservation methodology.[5]

infrastructure that is needed to support over a billion people is superimposed over a centrally controlled market economy and an extraordinarily complex landscape for cultural heritage conservation policy emerges.

Western-style architectural conservation professionalism in China has grown considerably over the past three decades, along with the nation's cooperation and integration into the global community of cultural heritage management. At the same time, the international community has engaged in the valuable process of modifying some of its own requirements in order to accommodate particularities of Chinese culture and tradition in conservation practice.

Following numerous professional exchanges, conferences and collaborations, the Conservation and Management Principles of Cultural Heritage Sites in China (hereafter, the "China Principles") were ratified in 2000 by the Chinese international committee of ICOMOS and were also adopted by the State Administration for Cultural Heritage (SACH), China's highest regulatory body for heritage protection. These events marked a significant milestone not only for Chinese cultural heritage professionals, but also for all international conservation organizations that can now stand with their Chinese peers, as colleagues and partners that share a global heritage protection policy.

It is significant that the multi-national teams that drafted the China Principles were ultimately successful in producing an acceptable document, given the dissimilar core definitions of architectural restoration and preservation that for centuries have been the credo of Western and Eastern practitioners. A full appreciation of the history, practice, theory and profession of Chinese architectural conservation first requires a clear understanding of how it differs from the same standards that guide Western professional heritage conservation practice. That goal is today more difficult than it would have been in the mid-twentieth century, because over the past several decades there has been a newfound appreciation for Eastern approaches. These have influenced, and are being embodied in, the latest elements of some internationally recognized professional principles and procedures, particularly since 1979 when the Australian Burra Charter was ratified.

Further gains in creating a less Western approach to conservation were made in 1994 with the publication of the Nara Document on Authenticity, which incorporates many Asian concepts about how a modern society relates to both its tangible and intangible cultural heritage. Frameworks such as these provide a better and more appropriate context for the understanding of the Chinese approach to heritage conservation than do either the Athens (1931) or the Venice (1964) charters.

Perhaps the biggest difference between the Eastern and Western approaches is that Western architectural conservation efforts tend to focus on questions of authenticity, maintenance of original built fabric, and conservation of all periods of a historic structure's use, rather than on a continuity of spirit. The Eastern approach to conservation, on the other hand, follows some of these same tenets,

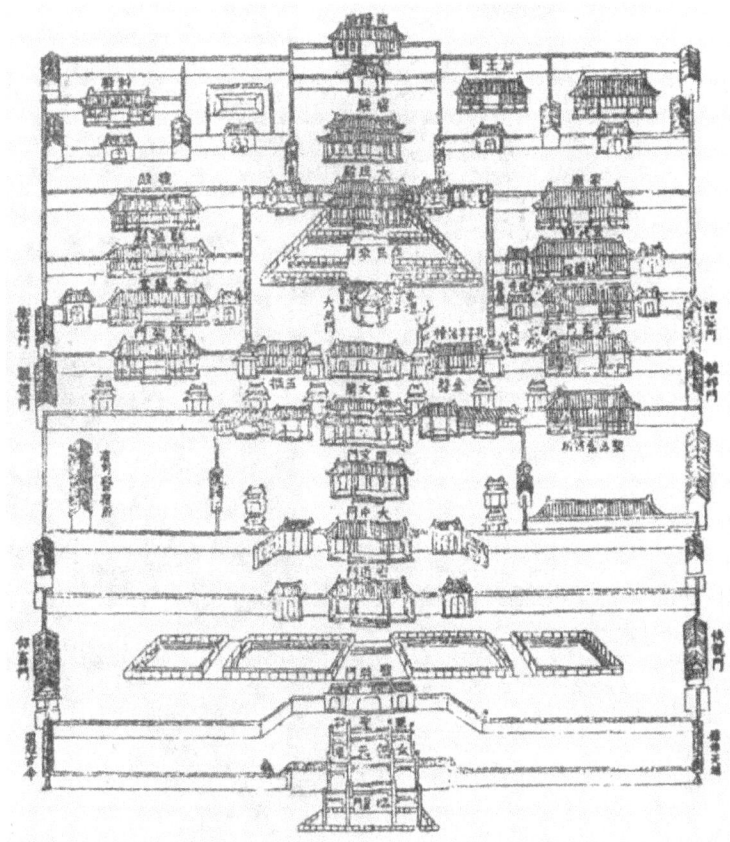

a   PLAN OF THE TEMPLE OF CONFUCIUS, AT CHÜ-FOU

b

c

FIGURE 2.1a, b and c The Temple of Confucius at Qufu, Shandong province was consecrated as a temple in 205 BCE. The long-revered house of Confucius has subsequently been restored, remodeled and expanded nearly forty times. Its plan image from 1912 (a) and a recent aerial image (b) show a large complex resembling the Forbidden City in Beijing. However, the spirit of the Confucius Temple at Qufu and its associated history has been maintained for nearly 2,500 years. The Lingxing entrance gate to the first of nine court areas (c), containing numerous stone stele commemorating visits by Chinese emperors, attest to the historic character and significance of the complex.

but places a greater emphasis on the spirit of a place or object over the particular architectural details of one era over another. Much of this approach – which is embodied in Chinese conservation but is present in Japanese and Korean efforts as well – is informed by the relative cultural, political and religious continuity experienced in China for much of the past 2,500 years, particularly since the death of Confucius in the fifth century BCE.[6] In Europe, where Western heritage conservation ideals are rooted and were first formally codified, that same period of time was turbulent. The European population witnessed the fall of several distinct empires, and experienced substantial cultural and military invasions from the East and South, major religious shifts and the steady progression of dominant, frequently contradictory political philosophies.[7]

One example of this uniquely Eastern approach to conservation is the Confucius Temple complex at Qufu, originally constructed in 478 BCE, shortly after the death of the philosopher whose teachings and writings still dominate much of Chinese cultural dictates. Expanded, renovated or rebuilt thirty-seven times over the past 2,500 years, the Temple complex, which also contains a nearby cemetery where Confucius and many of his descendants were buried, stands today as a tangible record of several dynastic architectural styles. These include those favored by the country's recent government, which conducted its own restorations shortly after the Communist Revolution in 1949.

By no means an intact, wholly authentic monument to Confucius or fifth-century BCE Chinese architecture, the Temple complex nevertheless still represents the ideals of the philosopher as interpreted by successive constituents, governments and building technologies. An emphasis on the *genus loci*, or original spirit of the place, has informed Chinese conservation techniques and philosophy since Confucian times, and continues to do so today. The contrast between an Eastern focus on continuity of meaning and place over the Western protection and codification of objective reality delineates the differences between the opposing conservation ethoses, which in turn affects how the professions operate today. It also, and perhaps most importantly, calls into question the claim of "universality" carried by many of the prevailing conservation principles and guidelines of the past century.[8]

Development and characteristics of Chinese architecture

A summarization of the progress and some key aspects of 3,000 years of Chinese architectural achievement is necessary in order to appreciate the role that architectural heritage protection plays in modern Chinese life. The story is vast: chronologically, spatially – with China being one of the largest and oldest civilizations in Asia – and in cultural sophistication. Built heritage types range from archaeological sites and cultural landscapes comprising both urban and rural vernacular architecture and craft traditions to historic towns and some of the world's largest and most impressive works of architecture and engineering.

Especially in the case of China, where cultural continuity has been essentially the rule until the late nineteenth century, the repair, restoration and maintenance of buildings has changed relatively little over that period of time. Another remarkable feature of Chinese history that is pertinent to its conservation practice is the degree to which restoration activities have been recorded, which provides an invaluable databank of information for professionals wishing to conduct necessary documentation research prior to beginning a modern conservation project. Few other areas of the world present these circumstances to the conservation professional, marking yet another important attribute of the historic built environment of China. Traditions in antiquarianism that valued documentation of inscriptions and history, collection and cataloging of antiquities, and that considered scholarship virtuous have characterized much of Chinese history as well. This has especially been the case from the Song dynasty in the tenth century CE to the present day.[9]

At the center of Chinese spatial, social and ideological beliefs is the concept of *feng shui*. While its prehistoric origins remain unclear, feng shui had become established by about 1000 BCE, a time frame that also saw the development of generally held beliefs of animism, ancestor worship, balance and hierarchies of most material and spiritual things.[10] While a comprehensive discussion of feng shui's complex principles and reasoning is outside of the scope of this chapter, it deserves to be mentioned because its importance to Chinese architecture cannot be overstated. Nearly all of Chinese architecture was – and still is – built according to feng shui principles.

Feng shui specifically applies to the relationship buildings have with their natural environment. A complex series of rules guides the physical positioning of a new structure; considerations include the location of hills, bodies of water and the four cardinal directions. Application of feng shui principles ensure that the structure will be in harmony with nature, and is an important consideration for Chinese conservators, both in a functional sense (i.e., for restoration projects, moving of historic structures or adaptive reuse) and in a cultural sense (i.e., understanding the meaning of particular buildings in relationship to their surroundings).[11]

Also central to Chinese architectural composition and the conservation thereof is color and the spatial relationships among buildings. Particular shades of colors such as red, white and yellow connote very specific uses and associations for particular buildings, materials and structural components. This relationship, of course, must be taken into account when restoring ancient buildings: its original chromatic composition, but also historic continuity expressed in built fabric. Spatial components also come into play when analyzing how buildings have changed over time since that often takes place in regular, predictable patterns that have been rationalized by modern Chinese and ancients alike.[12]

According to Chinese history, these factors – feng shui and color – manifested themselves in the built environment as far back as the Shang dynasty, the dominant state in the North China Plain from about 1600 to 1100 BCE. Excavations in the 1920s and 1930s at the last Shang capital Yin, near present-day Anyang in northern Henan province, unearthed a wealth of elite artifacts and archaeological evidence of buildings.[13] The Shang constructed their palaces and other ritual and administrative buildings on rammed earth platforms with wooden columns and framing capped with a thatched roof. Little else remains of this dynasty in terms of architecture, although they left an impressive legacy of bronze casting, ceramics, and carvings in jade and other stones, as well as what some consider the earliest implementation of town planning: a series of concentric squares, a pattern that is still used today.[14]

Following the Shang were the Zhou (1100–256 BCE), who initially ruled from their capital near the modern city of Xi'an, later moving their capital city about 400 km east under pressure from non-Zhou tribes. Zhou holdings were essentially comprised of numerous vassal states that increasingly vyed for supremacy for several centuries before finally being united under the military rule of the self-proclaimed First Emperor, Shihuangdi, of the state of Qin in 221 BCE.

In addition to receiving credit for standardizing many aspects of Chinese life (such as the system of measurements, writing, coinage and roads), Qin Shihuangdi also launched the Great Wall protective barrier system by ordering the consolidation of several existing portions of rammed earth walls into a single system of defense. Although restored and expanded many times since, the Great Wall remains one of the crowning achievements of human engineering and construction, with the preservation and protection of its remaining 21,196 km (13,170 mile) span representing an almost unimaginable conservation challenge.

The later Zhou dynasty also encompassed the life of China's most notable thinker, Confucius, who died in 479 BCE. Confucianism extolled the values of antiquity and learning from the past while emphasizing the importance of passing on lessons and values from one generation to another, and therefore lie at the heart of Chinese cultural continuity. Calligraphy and painting since the time of Confucius have been the most valued of Chinese art forms, far exceeding architecture or design. Calligraphy in particular was learned through the process of copying great works of the past, a process known as *linmo*. Architectural stylistic development evolved in much the same way, with basic, distinct architectural forms (such as temples, gardens, palaces or houses) passed on from one successive dynasty to another with little change aside from scale and level of ambition.

The Confucian work most relevant to architectural historians and conservationists is the *Zhou Li*, a text dictating principles for spatial relationships in building. The most remarkable architectural achievements of this period, Qin Shihuangdi's Great Wall and necropolis, interestingly, is thought to have led to the Zhou dynasty's demise due to the financial and human resources these huge projects must have consumed in their creation.

Qin Shihuangdi gained international notice in 1974, when farmers digging a well in the rural farmlands east of Xi'an, Shaanxi province, made one of the greatest archaeological discoveries of all time: his massive tomb complex, which contained thousands of life-sized terracotta warriors and horses, in formation. In 2016 excavation work was still ongoing at the site, which now encompasses about 600 pits spread over 22 square miles.

The tomb was said to have been built by 700,000 forced laborers. Unfortunately, while the treasures in his mausoleum complex attest to an ability to create opulent palaces and furnishings, very little tangible evidence from his reign outside of the tomb remains today. Of the several palaces in and around Xi'an that were associated with his rule, none survive today except as archaeological sites.[15] Shortly after Qin Shihuangdi's death, peasant uprisings in response to his forced labor programs resulted in the end of his short dynasty and in all likelihood included the destruction of his tomb and palaces.[16]

A period of civil war followed the collapse of the Zhou and Qin dynasties. Thereafter, several centuries of relative peace and prosperity began in 206 BCE under the Han, which, significantly, is the name taken by the dominant ethnic group in China today.

The Han dynasty, like the Zhou and Qin before them, maintained their capital of Chang'an near present-day Xi'an, developing the city into an impressively planned series of concentric squares, with streets and massive walls delineating its boundaries. Within the city, the Han built numerous large-scale structures, including palaces and residential districts, none of which remain today. Nevertheless, architectural features from the Han dynasty can be seen in several monumental Han tombs and other structures that have been discovered either in caves or buried around Xi'an.

The development of the city also coincided with the formation of the ideas of *yin* and *yang*, or areas of physical balance that can apply to many other areas of the physical and built world. Also, at the end of the second century BCE, the Han established the first noticeable trading routes to the far west. It was this Silk Road, more than sea routes, that first introduced Chinese goods and products to overseas markets.

As China's export goods moved west, Buddhist monks traveled east on the Silk Road. After the collapse of the Han dynasty that was considered one of China's "golden ages" in the third century CE, the centuries-later Tang dynasty introduced new forms.[17]

The Tang dynasty (618–907 CE) entailed a period prolific with impressive architectural examples and engineering projects, many of which are still extant. In their impressive capital, Chang'an, streets and walls were aligned with the cardinal directions (as prescribed in feng shui principles), encircling palaces contained within a sophisticated street grid. Not to be outdone by preceding dynasties' engineering achievements, the Tang were also responsible for constructing the first Grand Canal, linking the Yangtze and Yellow rivers and facilitating movement and trade on a north–south axis between the two east–west waterways of China.[18]

FIGURE 2.2a and b Plan of the necropolis of Qin Shihuangdi, First Emperor of China (a), and its famed collection of approximately 8,000 terracotta soldiers, horses and myriad other artifacts (b), near modern day Xi'an, Shaanxi province.

Interestingly, some of the best examples of Tang city design can be found today in Japan, where many of the principles of urban organization were copied from this period. Tang emperors also built a number of structures at the Huaqing hot springs, east of Chang'an, the foundations of which have been excavated beneath later dynastic pavilions and housing complexes.[19]

The Tang were also the first to embrace Buddhism, resulting in the introduction of the prototypical pagoda form, which is essentially a hybridized adaptation of Indian *stupa* and Han multi-storied watchtowers. One of the most impressive monuments of ancient Buddhist China survives from this period in the caves of Dunhuang, where centuries of murals, statuary and other wall paintings have been preserved because of its remote and dry desert location. It was also during this period that Islam first entered China, resulting in distinctively styled Chinese mosques such as the Great Mosque of Xi'an and the Beacon Tower mosque in Guangzhou.

From 960 to 1279 CE, the Tang's successors, the Song dynasty, dominated China. They left behind an extraordinary legacy of decorative arts and imperial court bureaucracy, but little in the way of architecture. The Song were forced to abandon their capital Bianliang (modern day Kaifeng) in the north in the twelfth century, and re-established their capital at Hangzhou, in the far south, for about 150 years as the Southern Song dynasty.

The Song dynasty produced the highly influential *Yingzao fashi*, a technical construction guide that survives to this day.[20] Although little remains of Song dynasty architecture in Kaifeng, we have highly detailed paintings such as the famous *Qingming Shanghetu*, perhaps the most famous painting in all of Chinese history. Painted in the early twelfth century CE, most scholars believe that it depicts Bianliang during the Northern Song period. However, the combination of relocation to the south and several questionable alliances positioned the Song dynasty for trouble. They led to the successful invasion of Mongol hordes from the north, permanently shifting the balance of power to northeastern China, a dynamic that remains to the present day.

The Yuan, who were essentially sinicized Mongols, established their capital on the site of present-day Beijing, which had until then served as a regional capital for previous dynasties. From 1279 to 1368 CE, Chinggis Khan and his grandson Kublai ruled China – along with most of

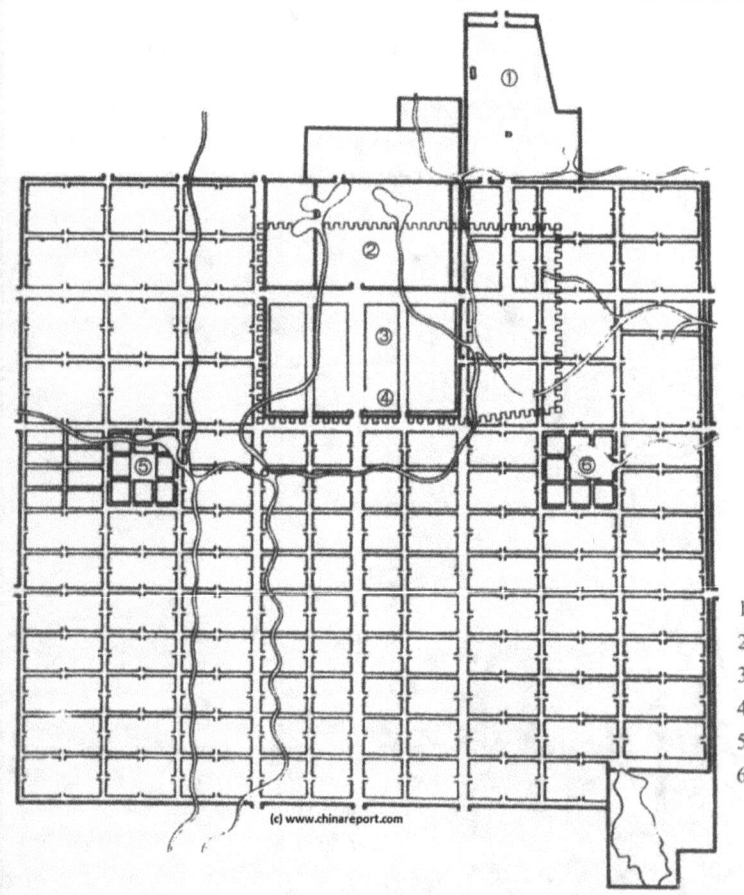

1. Daming Palace
2. Inner Court
3. Imperial City
4. Red Oriole Gate
5. West Market
6. East Market

FIGURE 2.3 Schematic plan of Chang'an during the Tang period, located near present day Xi'an in Shaanxi province.

FIGURE 2.4a and b Mogao Caves (a) and wall painting from Cave 57 (b) from the Mogao Caves. Preservation, restoration, re-working and over-painting of hundreds of the 492 Buddhist cave-temples in Mogao in Dunhuang represent a localized "conservation ethos" that extended from the fifth to the thirteenth centuries CE.

Asia – even extending their dominion into Eastern Europe and the Mediterranean. They ruled first from Mongolia itself but later from Beijing. It was during Kublai Khan's reign that Marco Polo made his famous visit to China during the thirteenth century CE, carrying stories back home to Venice of the powerful, sophisticated world he observed there.

After Kublai Khan's death, a series of weak rulers and an overextended empire eventually allowed Chinese home rule to re-emerge under the Ming dynasty, which is considered by history to be the last ethnic Chinese dynasty. Ming architecture along with that of the later Qing dynasty comprises the primary body of extant dynastic-era structures in modern China.

Having learned from the previous century about foreign rule, the Ming constructed massive fortifications around their major cities, most notably Beijing and Xi'an, of which the former survived until the 1950s and the latter survives today. Ruling a newly sovereign China from 1368–1644 CE, the Ming in many ways comprise the Western vision of typical Chinese art, architecture, monuments and civilization. The Ming rulers first established their capital at Nanjing, but later moved back to Beijing in 1402 CE, where the emperor Yongle began construction of a massive imperial residential compound. His Forbidden City, one of imperial China's most impressive heritage sites, is today referred to as the *Gugong* or Palace Museum.

Beijing, like Xi'an and Nanjing, was conceived from the outset as a giant, artistically integrated urban design, made possible by the wealth of the Yuan, Ming and Qing empires and the need for a capital city of grand ceremonial significance. Such a need had been recommended in the Confucian classic, *Zhou Li*, which detailed the requirements for that place on earth where the emperor "exercised the mandate of heaven," performing vital seasonal ceremonies that established harmony with the forces of nature.[21] During the Ming period, imposing walls enclosed the Inner City. In 1533, Beijing was expanded to the south and a second fortified enclosure was built to enclose it that came to be called the Outer City. A third monumental wall, the innermost, surrounded the Forbidden City.[22] All of these walls incorporated moats and were crossed by wide bridges with ornate balustrades, which led to entrance roads that defined the street plans of adjacent areas.

Consisting of an intricate series of gates, bridges, courtyards, and over 1,000 residential and ceremonial pavilions, grand halls and support structures, the Forbidden City remains one of imperial China's most impressive architectural legacies. Although modified by the succeeding Qing dynasty, it represents the most monumental architectural achievement of the Ming. Other notable Ming heritage sites

FIGURE 2.5 The Temple of Heaven, Beijing, originally completed in 1420 CE during the Ming dynasty by the Emperor Yongle, was last renovated and expanded by the Qing Emperor Qianlong during the mid-eighteenth century.

include Beijing's Temple of Heaven complex, elaborate imperial tombs, and exceptional religious structures such as the 262 ft tall Buddhist "Porcelain Pagoda" or Bao'ensi (Temple of Gratitude) in Nanjing that was extensively restored in 2010, and a monumental extension and improvement of the Great Wall.

The design principles and considerations used in the Forbidden City and its official ritual sites such as the Temples of Heaven and Agriculture reflect the pinnacle of imperial architectural planning. Numerous and important issues were an integral part of a Ming architect's pre-construction work: geomancy, feng shui, hierarchical planning, protection, religious beliefs, court ritual, symbolism, circulation and the highest quality of construction forming a complete city in terms of its functions.

As their three-tiered system of defensive walls makes obvious, a cornerstone of Ming urban design was protection from invasion. So it is surprising to note that the Ming dynasty was also responsible for permitting permanent contacts with European powers.

The Ming dynasty, which ruled for nearly three centuries, left an impressive record of technological advancements and architectural achievements. In addition to their fortifications and city building, the Ming constructed grand tombs, particularly outside Beijing, a tradition carried on by their Qing successors. Ultimately, in 1644 CE, political strife and unwise alliances with the northern Manchu led to the Ming dynasty's demise, ushering in the last, and best known Chinese dynasty architecturally and culturally, the Qing.

The Qing came from the northeastern corner of modern China and established themselves in Beijing, assimilating successfully into their new homeland and occupied territory. This talent for assimilation manifested itself in the architectural record as the Qing's glorification, enhancement, preservation and continued use of the previous dynasty's key architectural achievements. Qing emperors occupied the same palaces as the Ming, and much of the vernacular, religious and urban built fabric remained unchanged during this period, despite the insurgent nature of its leaders. Indeed, among the Qing's greatest legacies are its attempts – and eventual failure – to preserve China's isolation from increasingly assertive Western powers, who were intent on gaining prominence in the massive Chinese marketplace.[23]

The Qing period grandly built upon the precedents left by the Ming. Among the most well-known Qing contributions are three imperial summer palaces that were built outside Beijing: Yuanming Yuan (Old Summer Palace, destroyed in 1860), Yihe Yuan (The Summer Palace) and the Summer Palace in Chengde, the latter two of which have survived mostly intact.[24] The Forbidden City and the Summer Palaces possessed the finest furnishings, amenities and services available.

Emperors of the Qing dynasty, notably Emperor Qianlong, replicated regionally styled buildings, bringing refinements from other areas of China as design elements to their palaces in Beijing. This can be seen at Qianlong's Ningshou Gong (Palace of Tranquility and Longevity), which was completed in 1776 in the Forbidden City, and the creation of a replica historic village at the Summer Palace of shophouses along an artificial waterway copied from those at Suzhou and Nanjing.[25] Such a tradition of repetition, imitation and perpetuity profoundly informs the modern Chinese approach to maintenance, restoration and conservation of historic structures, monuments and built areas.[26]

Importantly, although the Qing were considered Manchu barbarians by their Ming predecessors, it was during the Qing dynasty that a defined antiquarianism took place. This sensibility was much more refined than what had existed some 600 years earlier during the Song dynasty. A key person in this process was Huang Yi (1744–1802), a late eighteenth-century calligrapher, seal carver and collector of rubbings. His antiquarian scholarship documentation and dissemination of research data from his travels in exploration of Chinese history, archaeology and architecture, and advocacy for preserving architecture, both engaged others and began to stir wider interests.

One of Huang Yi's more sensational discoveries was the Wu family shrine and cemetery in Shandong province where important carvings were found. He led the effort to erect a preservation hall and exhibition gallery for the stele that contained the carvings. Along with Huang Yi's own paintings that offered historic context to the stele, we have here the ingredients of an identified "heritage site" in the modern sense – an antiquarian museum and deliberate conservation. Historians of heritage protection in China have proposed that Huang Yi's finding and preservation of the Wu family carvings are among the most important events in Chinese archaeology, because they represented the beginning of planned excavations and public archaeological museums in China.[27]

Subsequent exciting archaeological discoveries and growing antiquarianism resulted in what one author described as the Archaeological Movement of the 1920s where Chinese archaeology began to be approached as a science. Its story – including archaeology's contributions to Chinese cultural relics (movable heritage) protection legislation and museums through to the current time – is well chronicled in J. David Murphy's *Plunder and Preservation*.[28]

The turn of the twentieth century ushered in a long period of internal cultural strife and foreign aggression. Such stress destroyed large portions of China's built environment, and eventually led to the collapse of the imperial system in 1911. This century also set the stage for yet another, even more destructive era, one that witnessed large-scale foreign occupation of Chinese cities, invasion by the Japanese, civil war, the Communist Revolution and the Cultural Revolution. Their cumulative effect was a loss of much of China's 3,000-plus year legacy of material heritage.

Just as the previous dynasties informed the Chinese legacy of cultural heritage conservation practices, so too did these more recent tumultuous events. The burden of cultural heritage conservation rests now, of course, on the present-day leaders and citizens of modern China, just as it did during the dynastic period. But unlike during imperial times, China's modern private citizens can be, and are, involved in heritage issues. The practice and meaning of heritage conservation for its multi-ethnic contemporary populace draws directly from their awareness of, and relationships with, these ancestral political organizations. In this way the Chinese are especially fortunate, as they are in many aspects of the field, to possess such a rich connection with the past, a sense that derives from recorded history and a more spiritual connection with *place* that is, far more so than in the West, often imparted upon their built heritage.

Foreign intervention: a historic threat to Chinese heritage

Myriad possibilities resulting from natural processes and from human action threaten any built cultural heritage. But in China, the intervention and presence of foreigners since the Mongol invasions has always posed an extraordinary threat to the country's cultural heritage.

The centuries of concern in China for the creation and maintenance of a physical barrier against foreign invaders from the north – the Great Wall – were not unfounded, as evidenced by six incursions by Mongol invaders over a period of six decades in the thirteenth century. With conquest, expansion and pillaging as their objectives, great destruction was caused to China's cities, with Beijing being destroyed in a devastating siege and war from 1213 to 1215. Four centuries later the Ming dynasty relinquished Beijing in the Manchu conquest of China in 1618 followed by Qing dynasty control from 1644. Through these turbulent centuries and others cities throughout China suffered related losses, largely to be rebuilt in the manner of the old by succeeding dynasties.

Beginning in 1840, with the advent of the first Opium War against the British, traditional Chinese cultural continuity began to erode, a process that continued steadily until 1911, when the last Qing emperor was forced from his throne. Within this seventy-year period of conflict, foreign imposition and colonization, a nascent movement to preserve Chinese cultural heritage from invading alien economic and military forces was born.

This effort needed to become active on many varied fronts simultaneously. The Treaty of Nanjing in 1846, under which Hong Kong was annexed to Great Britain, permitted the victors to open five major Chinese ports to foreign trade. In 1860 a combined Anglo-French force sacked the imperial Summer Palace of Yuanming Yuan, which since the early eighteenth century had been built and embellished by a number of Chinese and European architects and designers. The foreign armies looted, burned and toppled nearly all the palace's wooden and stone buildings, shipping many of the valuable paintings, movable works of art and other valuables to their home countries. Although the palace was partially rebuilt after 1860, what remained was leveled yet again by another wave of plundering foreign armies in 1900.[29]

With the arrival and assertive presence of foreigners in China at the dawn of the twentieth century came a period during which looting of architectural, monastic and cave sites became commonplace by the newcomers. As a result, Chinese cultural treasures were spread all over the Western world, a situation that continued largely unabated until the 1949 Communist Revolution. This is a highly sensitive memory for today's Chinese cultural heritage managers and engaged citizens, because it symbolizes not only lost cultural heritage but also is a reminder of a historic period of national helplessness against exploitative foreigners.

Throughout the twentieth century but particularly during the Cultural Revolution of the late 1960s, Chinese attitudes toward cultural heritage remained mixed. Nevertheless, the pillaging that took place during the early decades of the twentieth century in large part has informed the development of cultural heritage management policy during its latter years. Much as the architectural conservation movement took root in the West based on popular reactions against unbridled change, industrialization and urban renewal, the modern Chinese conservation consciousness arose out of this period of colonial violation and cultural upheaval.

Twentieth- and twenty-first-century Chinese heritage conservation policy

As a direct response to such systematic plunder by foreigners, in 1909 the waning Qing dynasty imposed the first modern legislation protecting cultural heritage in China. The *Measures for the Protection of Ancient Sites* represented a small, and perhaps solely reactionary, step towards the formulation of a modern system for heritage management, but nevertheless is a significant one.[30]

Architectural conservation work that ensued was informed by the country's early modern scholars of architectural history and restorers, including a Deputy Premier of the former government, Zhu Qiqian (1871–1964). In 1919 he re-issued a thirteenth-century book entitled *The Construction Methods of Building* (*Yingzao Fashi*) that stimulated interest in the history of building methods and systems. Also a former Minister of Public Works, Zhu Qiqian was involved with early conservation efforts in the Forbidden City from 1910 to 1920. In 1929 he founded the Society for the Study of Chinese Architecture in Beijing, and invited two young professors, Liu Dunzhen (1897–1968) and Liang Sicheng (1901–1972), to be Deputy Directors of the Society. From its founding, the Society concerned itself with not only architecture but also the material arts, painting and sculpture, as these subjects are used in decoration, silk, lacquer, metal work, and earthenware and other works. Zhu Qiqian also argued that having a broader scope of work (including concern for intangible culture, such as traditions, beliefs, rituals, music and dance) would help the Society in conducting and explaining its research.[31] The Society's holistic view of heritage conservation is a hallmark of professional conservation practice today in China that is similarly practiced in Japan and Korea.

In the midst of the politically seismic events of the early twentieth century, another early modern conservation dictate was passed in 1930, the *Law for the Preservation of Ancient Objects*.

In 1960, the Communist State Council ratified the *Provision of Regulations on the Protection and Administration of Cultural Heritage*, which defined and called for the protection of all movable and immovable cultural artifacts. At the same time, the *First List of National Key-point Historic Sites*, consisting of 184 nationally important historic buildings and sites, was compiled. These two pieces of legislation became the basis of Chinese cultural heritage management into the 1980s, and ultimately influenced the laws that protect the country's heritage today.[32]

The climate that created the 1960s legislation also encouraged citizens to help preserve key historic buildings out of patriotic loyalty and national unity, but little professional capacity came with the effort. What resulted instead were shoddy patches, concrete consolidations, new coats of paint and modern support materials inflicted upon hundreds of Chinese cultural monuments in the early 1960s. Although this period caused more harm than good in many cases, it pales in comparison to the decade that followed Mao Zedong's attempt to re-consolidate his power. Starting in 1966, the Great Proletarian Cultural Revolution wrought wholesale and unprecedented damage upon China's built and artistic heritage.[33]

The Cultural Revolution ultimately had less to do with ridding China of its ancient feudalist shackles as it did with restoring Mao Zedong's dominance within the national party and distracting the Chinese people from the economic problems brought on by his policies. Caught up in revolutionary demagoguery, gangs of students and soldiers comprising the Red Guard swept through the country, seeking to eliminate anything and anyone with associations to the past. Targeted were the "Four Olds": Old Customs, Old Culture, Old Habits and Old Ideas. In a very literal attempt to "beat down the capitalist past" and "build up a communist present" temples, manuscripts, books, artwork and historic structures were defaced or destroyed, while conservation professionals such as Liang were persecuted, imprisoned or killed.

During these tumultuous times there were heroic interventions made to save heritage, such as the directive given to an army battalion by Premier Zhou Enlai to guard the Forbidden City. From 1966 to 1971 the gates of the Forbidden City were sealed, which saved it from destruction.[34]

Early leadership in architectural conservation: Liang Sicheng

In 1930, as the government moved towards enacting a modern approach to heritage management, the "father of modern Chinese architectural conservation," architect and historian Liang Sicheng, accompanied by a small group of colleagues with similar interests, took an even bolder step forward by founding the Society for the Study of Chinese Architecture. The Society's activities included analyzing Song and Qing construction handbooks and documenting key historic buildings in order to record ancient structures and their construction techniques. Liang and his team of architectural surveyors continued their work through the end of the Sino-Japanese War in 1945, ultimately documenting thousands of buildings and contributing immeasurably to the canon of Chinese architectural history we know today. After the Communist Revolution in 1949, Liang worked to preserve ancient Beijing, but government authorities largely dismissed his efforts. Ultimately accused of treachery against the government during the Cultural Revolution, Liang died in prison in 1972, a tragic end to an admirable life and important career.[35]

During his professional career, Liang also did much to reinforce contemporary Western heritage conservation theory and practice in China. Though contrary to traditional beliefs and methods for conservation, Liang spoke in reaction to insensitive attempts by the government at restoring and reconstructing ancient monuments, instead advocating for research, documentation, authenticity of materials, the maintenance of historic patina and appropriateness of use. Interestingly, given the course of architectural conservation in the Western vs. Eastern worlds, Liang, speaking in the 1960s, was in line, if not ahead, of most contemporary practitioners both at home and abroad.[36] His beliefs in repairing rather than replacing damaged building fabric and honoring changes over time were fundamental Western restoration and conservation tenets as well.

Liang's architectural training in the United States undoubtedly informed much of his thinking, as did his innate ability to combine the traditional with the modern in Chinese architecture.[37] One of the first Chinese scholars to employ the Song-era *Yingzao fashi* building manual, Liang leveraged Western architectural documentation, academic study of other relatively new disciplines such as archaeology and architectural history and conservation against an understanding of traditional building techniques to effectively read and record Chinese buildings. With this understanding came a critical take on both current and traditional modes of handling historic built heritage in China.

During the mid-1930s Liang became a vocal advocate for the government's role in cultural heritage protection, as well as a practitioner of varying degrees of conservation intervention, depending on the conditions and circumstances around a particular site. His aversion to the more traditional approaches, which focused on the repair of, and elaboration on, ancient monuments, continued well into his later career, and he increasingly became a supporter of stabilization and maintenance of historic fabric and patina.

According to one scholar Liang was aware of the Athens Charter, having translated it in 1949. Through his long interest in architectural preservation his actions bolstered the practices that they advocated.[38] Liang's career, which bridged many of the gaps between East and West, did much to set the foundation for later developments in architectural conservation, and presaged the advances in the field that have taken place in the early part of the twenty-first century.[39]

The decision in June 2009 by the head of the Cultural Relics Bureau to preserve Liang Sicheng's courtyard home in a Beijing hutong slated for demolition is a fortunate example of China's re-conceptualizing the value of Beijing's urban cultural heritage in the past two decades. Such successes, if only symbolic, have multiplied since.[40]

The assault on China's past lasted until Mao's death in 1976, after which his successor, Deng Xiaoping instituted many of the open door reforms Mao had hoped to suppress by instigating the Cultural Revolution.[41] A new era of modernization lay ahead, with its attendant different negative impacts on China's historic built environment.

Much as the post-World War II urban renewal assault on Western historic built environments crystallized conservation-minded developments, so too did the Cultural Revolution in China. In 1982 the Provisional Regulations were revised, strengthened and re-named. The newly termed *Law on the Protection of Cultural Relics* created multiple levels of historic and protective designation and decentralized management for historic properties at the national, provincial and municipality levels. That law was itself again re-drafted in 1992, when it emerged as the *Detailed Rules for the Implementation of the Law of the People's Republic of China on the Protection of Cultural Relics*.[42]

Conservation professionals in China have debated for some time the validity of "authenticity" as defined by the Athens and Venice charters, although most have conceded their relevance in the European context and for conserving their own historic stone buildings. But as in Japan, because many important historic structures in China are composed of less permanent materials, particularly wood, concerns for maintaining authenticity are severely challenged. Additionally, considering the relative continuity of Chinese culture and history, cultural sites that have been modified, restored or rebuilt over many centuries of continued use begin to carry their own "validity," regardless of the age and appearance of their materials.[43]

Fortunately, the building craft traditions, albeit much reduced, have survived through this process, which proves to be a priceless cultural asset when reconstruction is without doubt merited. Such was the case in the reconstruction of the 1742 *Jianfu gong*, the Palace of Established Happiness and its gardens, which is located in the northwest corner of the Forbidden City. The palace was destroyed in a fire in 1923 and was painstakingly reconstructed between 1999 and 2008 by the Hong Kong-based China Heritage Fund.[44]

This distinction underscores the importance of ensuring continued use by means of occasional extensive repairs or rebuilding versus conserving the authenticity of as much historic building fabric as possible. In the minds of most present-day stakeholders, Chinese or otherwise, the functional relevancy (viability) and sustainability of a building supersede its material authenticity. Under these conditions, alterations using contemporary materials and methods might be permitted, perhaps to the extent of allowing reconstructions (in-kind or otherwise) as well as new additions. This approach still carries heavy risks however, in that use, if poorly managed, can drift into over-use, particularly when pressing economic and/or tourism factors enter into the picture.[45]

China joined UNESCO in 1985, and within two years had successfully gotten six heritage sites listed on its World Heritage List. By 2016 that list had grown to fifty cultural and natural World Heritage Sites, making China second only to Italy in terms of numbers of sites on the World Heritage List.[46]

The 1994 Nara Conference was held to discuss the differing notions of authenticity in cultural heritage conservation between the Western and Eastern countries. During the session, it was noted

FIGURE 2.6 For most of Chinese history architectural "craftsmanship continuity" superseded conserving authenticity of material and even place. One example is the Huang He Lou (Yellow Crane Tower) on the south bank of the Yangtze River in Wuhan (Hubei), which was originally built in 223 CE. Long a symbol of Wuhan with literary associations, in the Ming and Qing dynasties alone the pagoda-style tower was destroyed seven times and rebuilt and repaired ten times. After its last reconstruction during the Qing dynasty in 1868 it was destroyed in 1884. The tower's site was later occupied by Wuhan Yangtze River Bridge in 1957. In 1981 the Wuhan City Government decided to rebuild it at a new location 1 km from the original historical site. The latest Yellow Crane Tower only approximates its earlier design: it is constructed of steel and concrete, and includes an elevator.

FIGURE 2.7 Fujian Tulou in southwest Fujian province consists of forty-six buildings constructed since the fifteenth century CE. Situated among rice, tea and tobacco fields, the Tulou are circular or square earthen houses that face inwards, originally for defense purposes. They house family clans of up to 800 people. Fujian Tulou is described on the UNESCO World Heritage List as "exceptional examples of a building tradition and function exemplifying a particular type of communal living and defensive organization, and in terms of their harmonious relationship with their environment, an outstanding example of human settlement."

that the task of adequately managing China's vast immovable cultural heritage holdings was almost overwhelming given the huge size of that inventory and the small size of its current roster of conservation professionals. (See also Nara Conference, page 46.) At that time, over 350,000 significant historic buildings and sites had been identified in China, but only a few thousand professionals and technicians were devoted to their care and management. Conservation education and professionalism still lagged behind most other nations, particularly given China's population and wealth of cultural heritage.[47]

By the late 1990s, the situation had improved as nearly all levels of Chinese government, including its autonomous regions, provinces and individual municipalities took up cultural heritage administration and management responsibilities. This level of increased professional, governmental and international participation in architectural conservation activities against the backdrop of debate over the relevancy of Western policies led to discussions of a need for establishing a distinct new set of architectural conservation regulations for China. This thinking culminated in the project to establish the "China Principles," a task that was initiated in 1997 with the technical assistance of ICOMOS, and Australian and American professionals. The China Principles were signed by the Chinese delegation to ICOMOS in 2003.

The China Principles

The People's Republic of China entered the twenty-first century on a positive, proactive note with the completion of a three-year, internationally cooperative project to establish and ratify a new set of principles governing the management of its cultural heritage. The Conservation and Management Principles of Cultural Heritage Sites in China, or, more simply, the China Principles, represent a substantial effort on the part of the Getty Conservation Institute (GCI), the Australian Heritage Commission, ICOMOS International, ICOMOS China, and the Chinese State Administration for Cultural Heritage (SACH), the governmental entity responsible for cultural heritage management in China.

The process began in 1997, when the GCI, SACH and the Australian Heritage Commission joined with a group of Chinese architects, historians, archaeologists, conservationists, planners and managers to discuss and draft a set of principles for cultural heritage conservation practice and site management in China. Consisting of two parts, the first of which lists thirty-eight formal articles, while the second discusses concepts and processes, the China Principles are designed to work in conjunction with existing conservation legislation and traditional site and monument maintenance practices to guide a consistent approach to conservation in China. An English–Chinese glossary is included.

The Principles were further refined through a series of conferences held in China, Australia and the United States that culminated in 2000 with the ratification of the guidelines by China's international committee of ICOMOS.[48] A third section was added in 2005. Called the *Illustrated Principles for the Conservation of Heritage Sites in China*, it outlines illustrated examples of best practice, in a format similar to the *Secretary of the Interior's Standards for the Treatment of Historic Properties* function in the USA.[49]

The primary thrusts of the China Principles, which debuted at a conference held at Chengde in September 2000, pertain to the management, planning, interpretation and emphasis of the values of place rather than just physical intervention. Managing China's existing body of over 760,000 documented historic sites (as of 2004) – over 4,296 of which qualify for National Priority Protected Sites – the China Principles seek to standardize professional practice within this vast and varied range of heritage resources.[50] Drawing upon the Burra Charter, itself an amended approach to the earlier Athens and Venice charters prepared to better represent Australian cultural heritage, the China Principles specifically discuss general conservation principles, process and interventions within the Chinese cultural framework.[51]

Implementation of the Principles was tested on several sites, beginning with Dunhuang's Mogao grottoes in 1999 followed by the Chengde Mountain Resort and Outlying Temples World Heritage Sites in 2001. The work at Chengde focused on applying the "values-based" integrated and holistic management approach promulgated by the China Principles at Shuxiang, the family temple of the Qianlong emperor. It squarely faced the conservation approach favored and promoted since the 1930s by Liang Sicheng versus the period restoration approach that had evolved in China by the 1920s that has persisted until recently.[52]

The Chengde conservation planning process and pilot project at the Shuxiang Temple site tested the viability and acceptability of the Chinese versions of the conservation versus restoration schools of thought led by John Ruskin and Eugène Emmanuelle Viollet-le-Duc in Europe since the mid-nineteenth century.[53] The work at Mogao sought to validate the China Principles by drawing up a master site management plan, including conservation and visitor issues.

A conference was held in August 2003, hosted by the GCI and the Dunhuang Research Academy to mark the completed restoration of Cave 85, and to review the implementation progress of the China Principles. Rounding out its integration with the global conservation community, China hosted the 2005 international congress of ICOMOS in Beijing, itself the nexus of the Chinese challenge of preserving its urban spaces in its current economic climate.

In 2014 a conference hosted by China ICOMOS and the National Heritage Center of Tsinghua University reviewed ten years' application of the China Principles and studied their future direction. Frank appraisals of the first decade of the application of the China Principles were given by national and international experts. In sum, it was agreed that the creation of the China Principles so far had been a sizable, impressive and helpful achievement. Recommendations made at the conference regarding textual modifications and improvements served as a basis for a revised set of China Principles in 2015.[54]

The process for establishing and ratifying the Chinese Principles has been a model of cooperation of expertise from three continents. It is hoped that such interaction will become a successful model for devising a new set of values-based guidelines for non-Western countries interested in conserving their cultural heritage according to baseline international standards.

FIGURE 2.8 Cover of *Principles for the Conservation of Heritage Sites in China* (2015).

Urban conservation: Beijing, Shanghai, Hong Kong and Macau

Though the countryside has been traditionally idealized for centuries, China's heart remains in its cities, where architecture, education, imperial administration and – perhaps most of all – commerce have thrived for centuries. Today, urban China is growing faster than ever, each day absorbing thousands of new rural migrants seeking housing and work, with amenities such as new roadways keeping pace. Considering how the historic built environments of four of China's key cities – Beijing, Shanghai, Hong Kong and Macau – are faring under such pressures is instructive.

In 2014 the population of Beijing was 21.52 million with 368,000 new residents added; and the population of Shanghai was 24.25 million with 970,000 new residents added. Both cities are expected to have populations of over 50 million by 2050. Hong Kong's limited land area of 1,104 sq. km accommodated 7.23 million in 2014 including about 220,000 non-established residents.[55] Macau's population stood at nearly 575,000 in late 2015.[56] Such population pressures in China's cities combined with ambitious government and local population-driven mandates toward modernization and industrial output pose extreme pressures on the older, less densely planned buildings and their sites, with historic unprotected buildings and neighborhoods frequently losing out to redevelopment. Different patterns of land development occur in the immediate peripheries of cities and in countryside locations but have the same effects on China's rural cultural landscapes. Concomitant with rapid population expansion and rising affluence is increased traffic growth. In 2014, automobile sales in China surpassed 20 million, up 14 percent from the prior year, extending China's lead as the world's largest car market.[57] Vehicular traffic pressures on China's historic town and city street systems and demands for widened existing and new thoroughfares is likely to have even greater effects on the country's urban and rural cultural landscapes.

In the late 1940s and early 1950s, Beijing's highly refined, long established plan began to change radically as the Cold War began. Financial aid and teams of experts arrived from Russia, and with their help, a decidedly anti-conservation plan for the future of Beijing was adopted. The party that had come to power had a similar anti-urban bias and so in 1953, the first master plan for the capital, as well as the first centrally controlled five-year plan for the country as a whole, were unveiled.

The Draft on Reconstructing and Expanding Beijing Municipality called for re-making Beijing into a major industrial hub and warned "the foremost danger is an extreme respect for old architecture, such that it constricts our perspective of development."[58] A few Chinese professionals – educated architects who could speak with authority at the time – advanced an alternative plan that recommended that the industrial expansion of Beijing should occur outside the city, in order to allow its core to be preserved as an irreplaceable artifact of Chinese civilization.[59] Liang Sicheng, who once described Beijing as an "unparalleled masterpiece of urban planning," led the effort to preserve the ancient capital by placing all new development at its periphery. American architect and preservation planner Anthony Tung claimed in *Preserving the World's Great Cities* that Liang's Alternative Plan was the "best unrealized idea in urban planning of the twentieth century."[60]

After three decades, the Soviet-style planning and urban renewal projects that were insensitive to heritage protection ended in China, but their effects lingered for several years. This fact was established at a large international conference held in Beijing in July 2000 sponsored by the World Bank, SACH and UNESCO, along with several other Chinese heritage and planning agencies.[61] Since then, a variety of urban conservation approaches have been tried. These range from wholesale replacement of urban areas (as seen especially in Beijing in the years approaching China's hosting the 2008 Summer Olympics) to diligent conservation efforts in surviving historic districts in cities such as Shanghai (its conserved *shikumen* district and suburb of Zhujiajiao) and the West Lake area of Hangzhou as well as in several entire historic towns comprised of distinct architecture. These include Wuzhen (Zhejiang province), Pingyao (Shanxi), Suzhou (Jiangsu), Shaxi (Yunnan) and Tulou (Fujian). UNESCO's noted Historic Urban Landscapes (HUL) methodology has been applied at the Hangzhou and Zhujiajiao examples to good and promising effect.[62]

China's growing international presence and the maturation of its architectural historical scholarship, along with the expanding capacities of the SACH, have facilitated a global appreciation for the riches of China's vast range of architectural heritage. Points of interest include religious architecture reflecting Buddhist, Islamic, Jewish and Christian sites and vernacular built heritage constructed by minority groups living in Tibet, Inner Mongolia and Xinjiang. When modern China's European Colonial architecture and buildings with appropriated Western styles, Chinese and Western blended styles, Moderne through to the International Styles of the present day are added to that list, it is fair to say that China may have more historic architecture to show for its history than practically any other nation.

New approaches to heritage protection in China are increasingly joined by the voices of experts in the social sciences who argue that future work should include criteria for heritage values that might even be re-envisioned and defined differently. In the years to come, integrated architectural conservation and development approaches should be done in a manner that could help professionals, politicians and the public alike to clearly understand how values are directly connected to the development potential and conservation concerns in the city, and how values integrate the two together.[63] A proponent of this approach, conservation architect Kapila D. Silva argues "A way forward is to re-conceptualize values of a historic urban area under the rubric of 'city sense', the unique place attribute that captures the quintessential experience of the historic city."[64]

Beijing

Beijing is situated on the northern edge of the North China Plain, abutting the Yanshan Mountains to the north and the Taihang Mountains to the west. For 3,000 years, its location has linked north and south travel routes. Except for two short interludes in the fourteenth and the twentieth centuries, from 1279 CE until today Beijing has served as the country's capital.

The city's focal point is the enormous Forbidden City, a 72 hectare (178 acre) complex consisting of ninety palaces and courtyards, 980 buildings and 8,704 rooms. This imperial residential complex sits on a north–south axis running from Yongding Gate marking its south terminus to the Drum and Bell Towers, its counterpoints to the north. It was once encircled by an extensive and massive wall system; today only its principal wall, a series of precinct walls, and moat system remain.

Beijing's old city is laid out according to an organizational schema of temples, palaces, markets and residences that date from the Spring and Autumn Period (approximately 771–476 BCE). The Beijing city of the Ming–Qing period was the outstanding example of ancient Chinese cities. Edmund Bacon, the American architect and planner, noted in his book *Design of Cities* (1967) that perhaps the greatest piece of architectural work on earth was the city of Beijing, "which was designed as the emperor's seat of power, with aspirations to become the center of the world … that in terms of design, it was gloriously splendid and provided a wealth of ideas for the development of today's cities."[65]

Throughout its long history, Beijing was rebuilt along the same lines using time-honored construction materials and methods. Ancient as Beijing's design precepts may be, since the 1930s it has grown extensively in every direction, development that has allowed it to serve as the modern capital of the world's most populous nation. This expansion has frequently come at the expense of Beijing's ancient organization and urban landscape, which daily falls to the persistent demands for modern housing, transportation and commercial development.

The master plan for the development of Beijing that was adopted by the country's new Communist government in the 1950s called for the retention of the city's north–south axis and some of the old city's street grid, garden and water system, and designated over 1,000 cultural landmarks for protection. While many of these significant historic buildings and sites, including portions of the nearby Great Wall, several important city gates and towers, and the Forbidden City were rehabilitated and preserved after the 1949 Revolution, the government also pushed forward a number of modernization projects, including road widening and other infrastructure improvements. In the 1960s, a subway was added to the city, along with a system of modern highways. These encircling ring roads greatly improved Beijing's traffic flow but at a high cost: their construction resulted in one of the greatest losses associated with twentieth century urban development in China – the nearly complete destruction of Beijing's 600-year-old Ming dynasty walls.[66]

In addition to its role as the political and cultural capital of modern China, Beijing also ranks high in the nation's economic, industrial and commercial growth. Experiencing economic expansion of 10 percent or more each year since market reforms took hold in 1978 not only marks an astounding rate of growth, but also posed a serious threat to the city's key historic buildings and urban vernacular architecture. There is real irony here in that Beijing is one of the oldest cities in the world and its post-Yuan dynasty period appearance was essentially intact at the turn of the twentieth century. But today, Beijing bustles with traffic, heavy pollution and large-scale residential and commercial development that has replaced most of its historic buildings and urban plan. The problems with conservation and maintenance of its scant remaining historic urban landscape remain vast, and are also representative of many problems experienced in other large Chinese cities.[67]

Beijing's role as the nation's capital has made it a magnet for large-scale political gestures in architecture, but also endows it with a natural leadership role in the management of China's built cultural resources. The nature of ancient Chinese urban planning, particularly in the centuries-old imperial capital of Beijing and the country's other large historic cities, lends significance to the relationship of historic buildings and sites, their urban settings and the populations they serve. This set of circumstances lends Beijing much of its importance as an example of urban development, but also poses challenges to planners in a modern, industrial capital where ancient cosmic truths give way to economic development. For a world capital of Beijing's status only the most rigorous conservation standards should be applied, a situation with which its leaders have only recently begun to grapple. In many cases the awareness has come too late.[68]

The series of misfortunes inflicted upon Beijing from a cultural heritage standpoint during the early Communist years culminated in the destruction of its Ming dynasty city walls. Beginning in the 1950s, in the name of urban renewal and progress, most of this ancient fortification system was razed. For years, Soviet planners and architects had impressed upon Chinese officials the importance of discarding constrictive historic nostalgia in favor of unbridled progress through ideological purity. Faced with a distinct shortage of professional expertise, the Chinese yielded to the Soviets, despite the aforementioned presence of alternative plans that would have preserved the historic city center by shifting development elsewhere. A rash of road construction assaulted the carefully formed plan of Beijing, plowing through ancient gates, over bridges and through walls, shattering the physical and spiritual relationships between urban areas.[69]

FIGURE 2.9a and b
A panoramic view of the hutong district northeast of Drum Tower, Beijing (a), and a typical subdivided hutong courtyard residence (b).

In 1993, planners on the Beijing State Council adopted the Beijing General Development Plan, a long-term conservation plan that was scheduled to remain in effect until 2010. The Plan was informed by a multi-phased prototypical conservation plan and project, the Ju'er Hutong project that addressed the myriad issues related to conserving Beijing's historical urban residential architecture and showed the possibilities for their retention.[70]

The Ju'er Hutong project called for the conservation of the city's *hutong* districts, areas of traditional residential courtyard housing that comprise much of the city's historic core, as well as the general geometric pattern of city street grids and relationships between built areas. As is the case in many rapidly developing urban areas, however, the difference between the plan on paper and in practice has proven to be great. Political and regulatory complexities pose a significant problem in implementing any kind of conservation plan for Beijing, as do complicated land ownership arrangements in which private, governmental and intra-governmental entities grapple for control and profits from land uses.[71] As of 2015 the conservation aspects of the Beijing General Development Plan/Ju'er Hutong recommendations are an ideal yet to be recognized. Therefore, having them serve as a goal for all surviving hutongs is likely unrealistic.

Beijing's built cultural heritage is managed by the city's office of the State Administration for Cultural Heritage (SACH), formerly the Cultural Relics Bureau. SACH can designate protected areas or structures under district, county or city jurisdiction, and has the power to inspect and halt construction excavation at sites where historic built remains are uncovered. This oversight has helped conserve some significant structures, in addition to demarcating zones where known historic resources lie buried. For example, in 2002, an effort to rebuild a three-quarter kilometer section of the wall for a Ming dynasty cultural park spurred interest in the city's imperial past when citizens were encouraged to round up original wall bricks and donate them to the site.[72] Nevertheless, visitors to Beijing today will note that large precincts of hutong neighborhoods, prime examples of distinctive urban vernacular domestic architecture, have recently been or are in the process of being completely razed. At the same time newer popular shopping areas include heavily renovated and even completely new hutong-like neighborhoods. Two examples of extensive "new–old" architectural enclaves are Liulichang Antiques Street and Qianmen Street pedestrian mall in central Beijing. A few of the remaining authentic hutong districts have been designated at the local and national levels, but the fate of the remainder appears headed in the direction of the former Ming city walls.[73]

The rush towards modernization, which has vastly accelerated in the past decade, has altered the skyline and historic character of the whole of Beijing, except for a few protected areas that are mainly associated with monumental structures or sites. These include the Forbidden City area and other palatial sites, the Drum and Bell Towers (Gulou and Zhonglou), several religious heritage sites including the Temples of Heaven and Agriculture, and a few remaining gates.

Efforts have been made to stave off new residential and commercial development, shift industrial structures out of the old town and mitigate the need for transportation improvements, but ultimately to little avail. In particular, maintenance of the old city's characteristic spatial layout has risen to the top of the priority list of local heritage conservationists, the city government and its Capital Planning and Construction Commission. However, Beijing's original low-rise character has largely given way to new high-rise developments that have compromised former historic vistas and circulation systems. The decisions to keep only the grandest and most highly valued architectural heritage and only a few token historic hutong districts in the capital not only reflects city planning and heritage protection during the present era but also serves as an example for numerous other cities in China.[74]

Chinese architectural conservationists are by no means alone when fighting to retain historic low-rise areas in their cities. The forces against their preservation are many and complex, and are well summarized in books such as Anthony M. Tung's *Preserving the World's Great Cities* (2001), *The Disappearing "Asian" City* (2002) edited by William S. Logan, and *Asian Cities: Cultural Heritage and the Interplay Between Nation Building and Internationalism*, by Tim Winter and William Logan (2014).

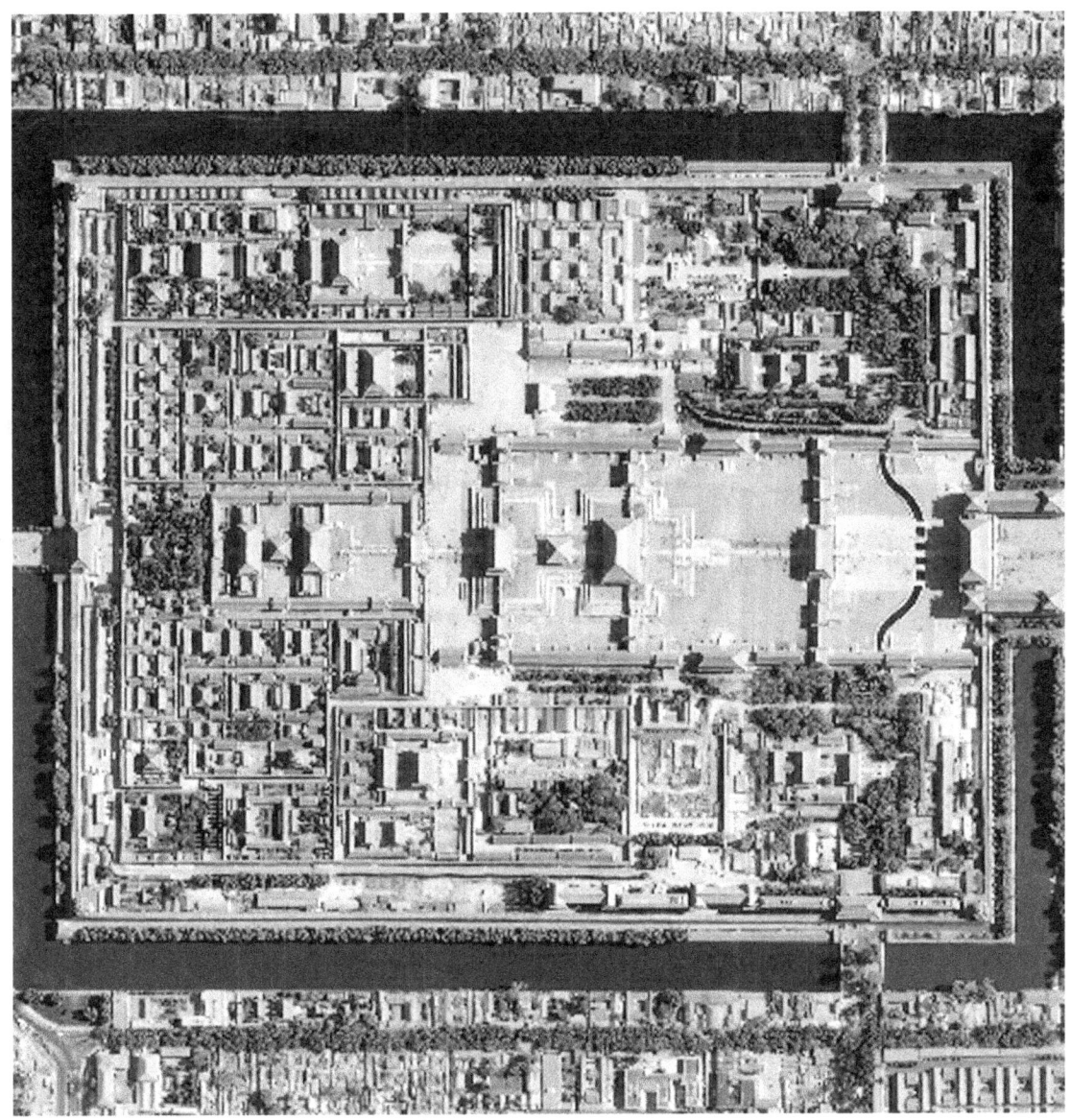

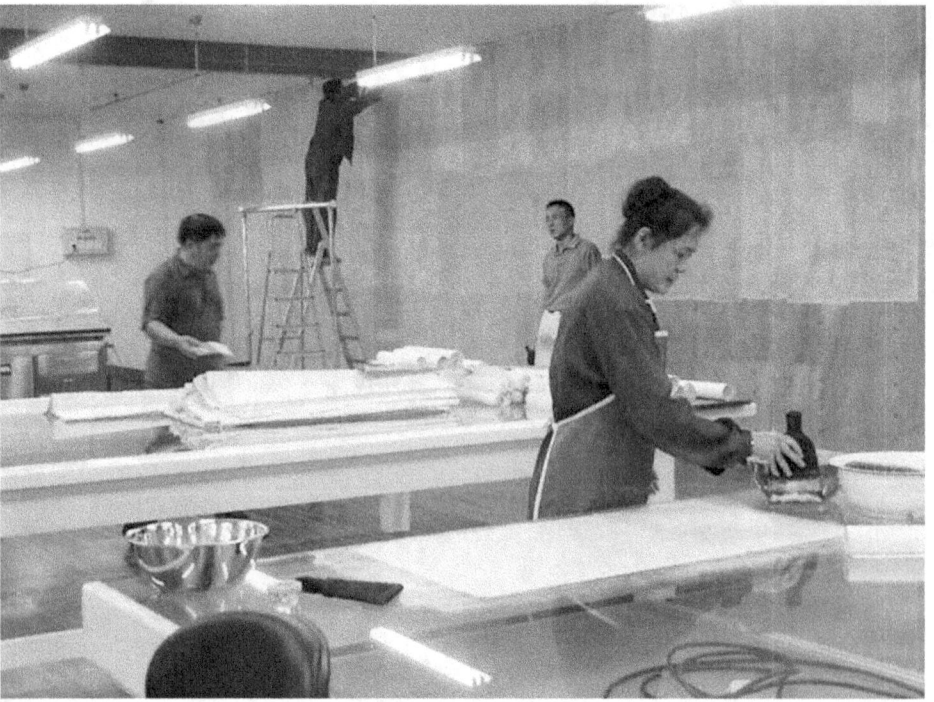

FIGURE 2.10a, b, c and d The vastness of the Forbidden City has posed daunting preservation challenges since the end of the Chinese Empire in 1911 (a). Some hundred years on the Palace Museum conservation department is busy using state-of-the-art documentation and conservation technologies for preserving building exteriors, interiors and their furnishings. Such holistic approaches are an important hallmark of the Chinese approach to heritage conservation. Two key international conservation technical exchange programs centering on important buildings where conservation techniques were further advanced were launched in the late 1990s, with one being the reconstructed Jianfu Gong (Palace of Established Happiness) (b) taken on by the China Heritage Fund (Hong Kong) and the Juanqinzhai (the Studio of Exhaustion from Diligent Service) in the Qianlong Garden taken on by the World Monuments Fund (New York), both in partnership with the Palace Museum Architectural and Collections Conservation Departments. The WMF project mainly entailed restoration and conservation of fine interior finishes and built-in furnishings (c), which required construction of a conservation laboratory (d).

Shanghai

In 2014, Shanghai, China's financial center, was the country's most populous city, with just under 24 million inhabitants, but its prominent position is relatively new. Little more than a modest fishing settlement during most of early Chinese history, Shanghai emerged as an important port near the mouth of the Yangtze River only in the mid-seventeenth century CE, at the end of the Ming dynasty.[75] It did not hold nearly the importance it does today until after the first Opium War (1839–1842 CE), when it became one of five "treaty ports" opened to Western-dominated foreign trade. French, English, German, American and Italian companies claimed land leases that eventually totaled nearly twelve square miles. These lease holdings were known as Concessions and formed the heart of the new city. With extraterritorial status, these colonial enclaves were exempt from Chinese law, and so flourished socially, economically and architecturally until the 1937 Japanese invasion.

The most significant architectural relic from this period of Western occupation is the Bund, a grand boulevard running along the mile-long embankment of the Huangpu River. Used since the late nineteenth century by Western interests for commercial endeavors such as stores, offices, hotels, banks and apartments, the Bund served as the hub of Shanghai's infamous pre-war social scene, which has lent a romantic air to the structures in Western history. The Chinese do not share these romanticized memories of the Bund, however, and by the late 1980s, it had faded considerably, due to neglect, misuse and alterations during and after the Cultural Revolution. At the same time, however, the Chinese government began a two-phase plan to revitalize the Bund and develop the area on the opposite side of the river, a former industrial zone called Pudong.

After US$3 billion in infrastructure investment, Pudong became a new city in its own right, with numerous skyscrapers and landmark buildings of its own built during the 1990s.[76] Today Pudong is home to some of the tallest buildings in the world including the Shanghai World Financial Center (2008) at 492 m (1,614 ft) and the Shanghai Tower (2015) at 632 m (2,073 ft) the tallest building in China and second tallest building in the world after Dubai's Burj Khalifa.[77] Building to such heights and scales in Pudong today represents one of Asia's best displays of ambitions to "modernize" with supersized Western-style buildings and office parks.

The restoration and rehabilitation of the Bund's mostly neo-Classical European buildings, which mainly date from between 1920 and 1930, became a major priority in the city's economic revitalization, an initiative that began after Mao Zedong's death in 1976. An initial plan designating 250 Western-style buildings in Shanghai, including apartment houses and residential estates, as well as all those on the Bund, was increased to 389 in 1999. At last estimate, over 1,000 Western-style buildings, mostly residential structures, dating from between 1842 and 1949, still survive.

As was the case in many major Chinese cities, Shanghai's population boomed in the years immediately following the 1949 Communist Revolution, with many new arrivals finding housing in the 3,000+ new high-rise buildings that were constructed between 1950 and 2000 alone. The unrelenting pressure such development places on any location's historic fabric is very difficult, if not impossible, to sustain, even when a country has put in place a system for designating and placing plaques on select historic buildings, as has China. Across the country, both Western-styled and traditional Chinese buildings alike perpetually risk demolition to make way for new construction, but in some cases, Western buildings with Communist Party associations have been spared as patriotic landmarks. In Shanghai's French Concession the former homes of famous revolutionary leaders, such as Sun Yat-sen and Zhou Enlai have been preserved, along with the building in which the Chinese Communist Party was formed in 1921.[78]

Restoration of the Bund was completed in 1993, work that included a widening of the road and installation of a retaining wall and promenade along the riverfront. The Chinese government, which owned all of the Bund buildings, invited many of their old occupants to return, restore and re-occupy the old buildings. Conservation efforts on the Bund buildings have ranged from comprehensive to merely façade restorations, but for the most part the buildings there reflect the Chinese government's evolving conservation ethos. Several villas and Concession neighborhoods have also been renovated or restored to accommodate new businesses, residences, galleries and restaurants. In many cases, the restorations are completed not for nostalgic reasons, given local sensitivity about the colonial era, but for pragmatic economic reasons, including for their tourism value. However, despite such

FIGURE 2.11a and b
View of the Bund, Huangpu district, Shanghai in 1928 (a), and in 2015 (b).

heritage-supportive benefits, Shanghai's historic fabric remains under constant threat from a large-scale, rapid development that continues with few signs of abatement.[79]

Nevertheless, one project begun in the late 1990s elected to reuse a historic neighborhood: the privately funded Xintiandi development, which invested US$141 million in Shanghai's Luwan district in the former French Concession. Two blocks of nineteenth century brick residential and courtyard structures were redeveloped with shops, restaurants and galleries targeting tourist revenue. Some of the original buildings have been carefully restored, while others were demolished in order to accomplish the overall site plan.

Xintiandi was meant to be Phase One of a larger revitalization project that would eventually expand into the Taipingqiao district. That second phase aimed in particular to preserve the traditional nineteenth century Shanghainese shikumen houses, with their unusual layout, building materials and orientation patterns combining Western and Chinese elements.[80]

Much like what is happening to Beijing's hutong neighborhoods, as the development of Shanghai accelerates the surviving shikumen and similarly indigenous *lilongs* (communities centered on lanes) are being lost each year due to the practicalities of denser new commercial and residential development.[81] Development pressures have increased since 2002 when plans were announced for the 2010 World Expo, an international trade fair that opened in May 2010. A large variety of new development and infrastructure improvements commenced that considered the city's historic architecture.

In 2004 the Shanghai government created twelve preservation zones, giving historic neighborhoods limited protection. Included were the Wujiang Road area; the Zhexingli neighborhood, where more than 300 buildings from the 1920s and 1930s have survived; the former Jewish Ghetto area and its centerpiece the Ohel Rachel synagogue; the former British-designed estate of Zhang Shule where one shikumen survives; and Holy Trinity Cathedral. Built in 1869 to designs by George Gilbert Scott, during the Cultural Revolution the cathedral suffered neglect including the loss of its steeple. It was restored and re-opened in conjunction with the Expo.[82] Local advocacy groups including the Ruan Yisan Heritage Foundation, the Shanghai Discovery and Documentation Society, and the Royal Asiatic Society Shanghai joined the government in these restorations and conservation endeavors, revealing the effectiveness and potential of such partnerships.

As with the more monumental historic buildings along the Bund, only the most versatile and resilient of Shanghai's newer buildings are likely to endure. The result will be new, glass-clad, high-density architecture harking to China's future juxtaposed with its predecessor European colonial counterparts.

Hong Kong

This former colonial seat of power – with Hong Kong island wrested from the Chinese in 1841 and the mainland section known as Kowloon in 1860 during the two Opium Wars – blossomed economically and architecturally for much of the past century as a British protectorate. For 156 years it was their key trading capital in Asia. Upon the island-city's return to the PRC in 1997, its free market system has essentially continued unabated, often at the cost of its historic colonial buildings on the densely packed urban island.

Hong Kong's colonial government regulated historic buildings through the Antiquities & Monuments Office (AMO) that served as an advisory board to the colonial government on historic designations. The AMO began a comprehensive survey of historic buildings in Hong Kong beginning in 1995, which it completed in 1997 before the territory was handed back to the Chinese government.

Aside from using its "declaration" as a means for conservation, the AMO frequently resorted to developing new, commercially viable uses for historic buildings. For example, the Western Market, a 1906 meat market building, was saved in this way in 1989 by a remodeling of its interior, restoring the façade and opening the old building to new upscale shops. In other cases historic buildings have been employed to house restaurants, retail and office space, often at the cost of their authenticity and historic context.[83]

Similar struggles to deal with Hong Kong's historic built environment arise among the city's large network of governmental agencies. Although the AMO regulates territorial conservation activity, various competing bodies, all operating under similar, overlapping mandates, often contradict each other. Movements to expand the powers of the AMO, to designate districts and neighborhoods rather than just individual landmarks, and completion of a heritage charter have all been proposed to improve the framework of Hong Kong's cultural heritage management system. Various leaders from within the AMO and from the University of Hong Kong, particularly Professor David Lung, professor and chair of the Antiquities Advisory Board for over a decade, have advocated for these reforms. Unfortunately, such battles are often waged uphill against developers and government officials alike.[84]

In 1997, when control of Hong Kong was returned to the PRC, the Architectural Services Department (ASD) became the AMO's partner in controlling its heritage management. Since then, the ASD has initiated conservation studies for a number of historically significant colonial-era buildings, including the Yau Ma Tei Theatre, the Wanchai's Stone Nullah Lane and Bethanie Hall at the University of Hong Kong.

Rehabilitation of Western buildings in several Chinese cities, including Hong Kong, has become an effective means for attracting Western business and investment. Many foreign businesses seek a prestigious location for their Chinese office, and so cities without available European or American architecture often have difficulty competing for foreign investment. In most cases, however, the pace of development exceeds that of historic building surveys, so architectural heritage is sometimes lost before it is even documented. Some tax burdens have been placed on speculative real estate ventures in an effort to slow down and regulate the system in Hong Kong, but the effects have been limited.[85]

Non-governmental organizations such as the Chinese Modern Architectural History Society, established in 1986, have taken it upon themselves to conduct architectural surveys of particular styles of buildings in Hong Kong before they are razed for new development. While this type of activity remains encouraging, grassroots citizen action in China seldom scores victories, particularly when they face governmental inaction or plans against the conservation of significant structures.

A trend towards new Western-style homes on the outskirts of Chinese cities built by the new middle and upper classes reveals an affinity for "new traditional"-style buildings, which are often convincing in the historical accuracy of their details. Another nostalgic trend in Chinese development is the advent of historical-themed amusement parks, where historic townscapes and building styles are replicated and reconstructed. "Splendid China," an amusement park in Shenzhen, along with others elsewhere in the country replicate on a smaller scale many of China's most famous cultural monuments, along with examples from the West. This trend in historic fantasy suggests an increasingly Westernized attitude towards cultural heritage in China, which has both its up and downsides. If Hong Kong's municipal government, business interests and citizens can work with the Chinese government in Beijing, some of this appetite for nostalgia could be channeled into conserving surviving actual heritage sites. But, as in New York City, another densely built world capital surrounded by water, successful conservation programs in Hong Kong will rely on vigilance, government efficiency, strict enforcement and rigid rules.[86]

Repurposing industrial spaces for the contemporary arts: Beijing, Shanghai and Hong Kong, by Benjamin Clavan

In Beijing, a former multi-building electronic components factory enclave built in 1957 in association with East Germany, whose representatives brought Bauhaus building principles along with their construction expertise, is transformed into China's premier 798 Art Zone, also known as the Dashanzi Art district. In Shanghai, a light bulb factory originally built in 1897 that was transformed into a power plant in 1955, to which a 165 m-high smokestack was added in 1985, and that was then renovated into a World Expo pavilion in 2010, is yet again repurposed in 2012 into the Shanghai Contemporary Art Museum, known more popularly as the Power Station of Art. In Hong Kong, a project initiated by the Hong Kong government in partnership with the Hong Kong Arts Development Council, but underwritten by the philanthropic Hong Kong Jockey Club, transforms a 1977 multi-storey, multi-unit, small-scale manufacturing building into the Jockey Club Creative Arts Center (JCCAC).

It is reported that China had only twenty-five museums when the Communist Party took control of the country in 1949. Today, depending on whom you ask and how you define *museum*, the country probably has over 4,000 formal art venues. In 2012 alone, 451 new museums opened in China according to the vice-president of the China Museums Association.[87] Part of the reason for this breakneck growth is the declaration of the 2009 State Council that upgraded culture to the level of a strategic industry for the nation. As a consequence of this decision, the country is striving, almost overnight, to increase the per capita number of museums in the short term to one per 250,000 people.[88]

Another reason for the dynamic growth in museum building is the approximately two million new dollar millionaires and 152 new billionaires that China has produced since it (re-)opened its economy to entrepreneurship. Supporting a wide range of arts for the status it confers, not to mention the investment potential, has led a number of the newly wealthy to join the museum building binge.[89]

Setting aside the difficult, if not impossible, task of filling all of the new spaces with art,[90] finding trained staff to curate both the permanent and the temporary exhibitions, managing and operating the facilities, and finding a steady audience or *any* audience – all of the venues require a physical shell. Building new facilities from

FIGURE 2.12a Beijing: the 798 Art Zone. The name derives from *Sub-factory 798* which was the largest of a number of buildings in the Joint Factory 718 complex that produced both military and civilian electronics equipment.

the ground up, of which there are also plenty of examples in China, is both time-consuming and typically more expensive than renovating existing structures.

Why target industrial spaces? Artists traditionally have gravitated to large loft-type studios and living spaces, first for the wide-open and high spaces such venues provide for large-scale art and also for the relatively inexpensive rents such spaces normally offer. The gritty ambience of industrial buildings has also supported and helps foster the traditional freedom of expression to which most artists aspire. Art galleries began to follow the artists to these spaces, not only to be closer to the artists themselves, but to showcase their art in non-typical, non-museum-like settings ... and also to benefit from lower rents. Gradually, and now more rapidly, it is the museums themselves that are attempting to replicate this bohemian environment.

In China, government authorities, institutions (for-profit and non-profit alike), and private individuals are all simultaneously fighting for the most visible and "hippest" locations and structures. These are few and far between in what most agree is the uniformly anonymous built environment that up until very recently has characterized the urban landscape of all of post-1949 China. Anything old – even ten or twenty years young – is ripe for the picking.

Aside from 798, Beijing has another significant repurposed art zone, the 22 International Art Plaza. This has as its focus the first non-governmental and non-profit art museum in China, the Today Art Museum. Partially housed in the renovated boiler room of a former brewery, the Today was founded in 2002 and renovated by architect and professor Wang Hui as a venue specifically to foster the development of contemporary Chinese art.

Shanghai has several examples of industrial zones being repurposed for the arts. M50 Creative Park (or 50 Moganshan Road) has always been seen as a stepchild of Beijing's 798 arts enclave. M50 is a smaller district, with fewer buildings, none with the pedigree of 798 and with very few of the new architectural interventions now prevalent at 798. M50 is located on the grounds of the Chunming Slub Mill, a former textile factory and warehouses located near Suzhou Creek. What it has that the Beijing district no longer does is more of an *ad hoc* feeling. Cars and trucks still traverse the narrow roads throughout the site and park in any available open area; some of the buildings that form the district still sport dingy corridors with galleries shoe-horned into whatever spaces are available.

FIGURE 2.12b and c Shanghai: Power Station of Art. Original Design Studio, Shanghai was the architect for this latest repurposing of the original Shanghai Nanshi light bulb factory.

In 2005, a steel factory complex in Shanghai was transformed into the Redtown Cultural and Art Community that includes the Shanghai Sculpture Space, the private Minsheng Art Museum,[91] a large outdoor sculpture park and privately owned gallery spaces. The Sculpture Space is located inside the almost intact main foundry building of the No. 10 Steel Factory dating from 1956. A contemporary two-storey office block has been inserted down the center of the huge, shed-like structure providing a series of more intimate gallery spaces on the first level and creative spaces for rent to architects, designers and so on on the second. The still wide and high-ceiling spaces along the remaining edges allow for over-scale installations. This multi-purpose use creates a constant flow of people wandering through a sculpture wonderland.

The West Bund area of Shanghai, bordering the Xuhui riverside, is being transformed into a cultural precinct that incorporates its industrial heritage. There, at the privately owned Long Museum West Bund, China-based architect Studio Deshaus have very visibly integrated remnants of a coal-conveying platform from the 1950s and an underground parking garage from the first decade of the twenty-first century to create a new industrial-*style* art venue. In the same precinct is the Yuz Museum, another privately owned contemporary art museum, completed in 2014, that incorporates historic massive airplane hangars from the now closed Longhua Airport.

Hong Kong's repurposing story is a little more complex. In this jammed city, there are few free manufacturing buildings to provide a platform for art. Instead, redundant public buildings and semi-public spaces are being transformed. For instance, the renovation of the 1951 Police Married Quarters into the PMQ Art Hub has helped to reinvigorate the trendy hillside SoHo district on Hong Kong Island. The 2014 development labels itself as a center of "creative industries" and strives to have artisans on-site creating works for sale. Architect Billy Tam, a director at Hong Kong's Thomas Chow Architects, added a glass cube, museum-like exhibition space that now ties together the two formerly separated residential wings of the structure. In the wings now are 130 studio workshops, along with shops, restaurants, a library, a rooftop garden and outdoor gathering areas. The project has become an overwhelming destination success, so much so that the hoped-for artisan base is already being pushed aside in favor of higher-rent-paying retail establishments.

The art community is holding out hope for a more sustainable enclave at the historic Central Police Station Compound (CPS). Sponsored again by the philanthropic Jockey Club, and slated to open in 2018, is the renovation and additions to a grouping that includes the historic police station, a Headquarters block and Victoria Prison. The oldest building was constructed in 1864; other additions were added in 1905 and between 1910 and 1925. It is probably the largest group of colonial-era

FIGURE 2.12d Shanghai: Shanghai Sculpture Space. Opened in 2006, Architects BAU (Brearley Architects + Urbanists of Victoria, Australia and Shanghai, China) have created two major spaces in the former steel plant: the "mixed use" commercial offices and gallery hall and an exhibition hall.

FIGURE 2.12e Hong Kong: PMQ Art Hub.

FIGURE 2.12f Hong Kong Jockey Club Creative Arts Centre. The Shek Kip Mei Flatted Factory Building was transformed by P&T Architects and Engineers Limited and Meta4 Design Forum Limited and re-opened in 2008. It is run by the Hong Kong Baptist University and programmed and managed by the Hong Kong Arts Centre.

buildings remaining in Hong Kong. The entire project, including the addition of two new buildings, is being promoted as a center for "heritage, arts and leisure."

The conservation of both historically important and work-a-day industrial buildings in China is both admirable and important for preserving the social and cultural history of a country that is undergoing unprecedented physical transformations of its built environment. Cities throughout the world can look to the array of types of buildings in China that have been repurposed for art and begin to eye their own varied resources. They can also look to the drama that has been added to some of these venues by contemporary architectural additions and renovations, and at the strengthening of the urban fabric that such transformations provide. At the same time, the true test of the success of these efforts is the vitality and independence of the art that these buildings showcase. This is a long-term issue for every country – and notably for China – that no rush of building, however special or significant, is ever going to eclipse.

Further reading

He, Jinliao 2014. *Creative Industry Districts: An Analysis of Dynamics, Networks and Implications on Creative Clusters in Shanghai*. Part of series: Advances in Asian Human-Environmental Research. Switzerland: Springer International Publishing.

Jacobson, C. 2013. *New Museums in China*. Princeton, NJ: Princeton Architectural Press.

Johnson, J. 2013. "Boom: The Future of the Museum in China," *Symposium*, Columbia University Graduate School of Architecture, Planning and Preservation, April 1. Published on YouTube.com, April 5: Web. www.youtube.com/watch?v=xaCYw2O3s5Q. Accessed June 1, 2016.

Rowe, P.G. 2011. *Emergent Architectural Territories in East Asian Cities*. Basel, Switzerland: Birkhäuser.

Varutti, M. 2014. *Museums in China: The Politics of Representation After Mao*. New York: Boydell & Brewer.

Macau

Macau exemplifies the struggles that heritage conservation faces to remain viable in the midst of an explosion of development. In Macau, the challenge is how to strike a balance between preserving its Portuguese and Chinese cultural heritage, as acknowledged by its designation as a UNESCO World Heritage Site, and supporting a lucrative gambling industry driven by the easing of restrictions since its return to Chinese jurisdiction.

Macau, a port of strategic importance in the development of international trade, was under Portuguese administration from the mid-sixteenth century until December 20, 1999, when sovereignty was transferred to China. With the handover, Macau, like Hong Kong two years earlier, was designated a Special Administrative Region (SAR). The implementation of China's "one country, two systems" principle granted Macau a high degree of autonomy that led directly to the expansion of Macau's gambling industry.[92]

From the late 1980s until the transfer to the PRC in 1999, the historic center of Macau benefited from generous financial and technical support from the Lisbon-based Calouste Gulbenkian Foundation in support of its aims to conserve Portuguese heritage abroad. Several of its European Baroque and nineteenth-century buildings, streetscapes and plazas, with some reflecting regional syncretism, were restored under this program including the prominent façade of seventeenth-century St. Paul's church, destroyed by fire in 1835.

The problem in Macau is partially a matter of scale: the relatively small area of the historic city core and its individual resources seem dwarfed by the nearby mega casinos. Macau's urban fabric is thus represented by two incongruent landscapes: a compact, 450-year-old historic center and a booming casino industry that has become the world's largest.[93] As early as the eighteenth century, Macau's government promoted gambling in an effort to generate revenue when the colony's robust trade moved to the new British colony of Hong Kong.[94] In 1962, gambling came under the control of the Sociedade de Turismo e Diversões de Macau (STDM), which held a monopoly on gaming in Macau for forty years. The gambling industry was maintained at a relatively modest scale during these years, with casinos primarily offering Chinese-style games.[95]

After the handover, the decision in 2002 by the PRC to let the local STDM gaming monopoly expire ushered in the arrival of American and Australian casino operators. These experienced operators developed enormous Las Vegas-style, "clean" casinos with family-oriented activities and brought with

FIGURE 2.13 The ruins of St. Paul's church, destroyed by fire in 1835. The remaining façade of the seventeenth-century church, with representations of Portuguese, Chinese and nautical motifs, is among the most popular sites in the historic center of the city.

them major investments in related services.[96] Concurrent deregulation of building heights, developer-friendly policies, and the easing of travel restrictions for mainland visitors brought an influx of tourists and opened Macau to unprecedented development and the exponential growth of Macau's gross domestic product (GDP).[97] With concomitant infrastructure development, and ongoing land reclamation projects that have physically joined the former Coloane and Taipa islands, creating a new landfill area called Cotai to accommodate new casinos, the growth of the gambling industry in Macau appears unstoppable.

In July 2005, Macau was inscribed as a World Heritage Site. Macau immediately moved to capitalize on the honor by leveraging its status to promote tourism and attract ancillary services such as hotels and shopping centers.[98] Despite the economic benefits, the branding of a heritage city can also

FIGURE 2.14 The view from Guia Fortress, constructed in the seventeenth century to hold off Dutch invasion. Land reclamation and subsequent high-rise casino construction, such as the 261 m Grand Lisboa tower shown here, have isolated the fortress from its once strategic position near the sea.

contribute to its perception as a theme park. The designation of Macau's Historic Center as a World Heritage Site, when paired with the recent development of Las Vegas-style casinos such as The Venetian Macau, which conspicuously fabricate history with emulations of recognizable world sites, has had mixed results. Continuing the trend toward fantasy landscapes such as those for which Las Vegas is known, casinos currently under construction, such as the Sands' Parisian Macao including a half-scale Eiffel Tower, contribute to a complex landscape in which some critics claim it has become increasingly difficult to distinguish the authentic heritage buildings from the pseudo-historical ones.[99]

Today, the range of pressures brought on by Macau's World Heritage status suggests that cautions cited by UNESCO in the World Heritage nomination, such as insufficient urban planning, growing population, increased vehicle traffic and the high numbers of tourists, should not be viewed as merely abstract concerns. The economic dependency of the government on gambling revenue has led to recent development beyond levels unimagined only a few years ago. Although zones have been defined to protect the "natural or built up setting of classified monument, complex and sites,"[100] these protections are sometimes circumvented through manipulations of local ordinances.[101] Ironically, the designation of Macau as a World Heritage Site has also prompted the demolition of older buildings as developers race to replace these structures before they become protected resources.[102]

The World Heritage Committee recommended that Macao "make every effort to develop the management system so as to retain the existing structure and visual integrity, and to maintain the principal sightlines of the nominated area within its contemporary setting."[103] However, recent developments have already affected the visual integrity of the Historic Center.[104] Development adjacent to the historic Guia Lighthouse is a case in point.

The most prominent of Macau's World Heritage Sites is the complex encompassing the Guia Lighthouse and Fortress atop Guia Hill, the highest point in Macau. The fortress was constructed to defend against Dutch invaders in the seventeenth century. The lighthouse, erected in 1865, was said to be the first Western-style lighthouse along the Chinese coast and represents a particularly visible symbol of Macau's Portuguese past. In 2006, controversial high-rise projects near the hill were proposed, triggering alarms that the new construction would diminish views to and from the fortress. With extensive land reclamation at the base of the hill and throughout Macau already physically separating the lighthouse from the water, conservationists were concerned that the projects, which would be higher than Guia Hill itself, would further "sever the bond between the lighthouse and the ocean, thereby destroying the spatial relationship symbolizing the maritime and trading port culture on which Macau's cultural significance is founded."[105]

In fact, there had been a 20.5 m height limit set for nearby development, intended to preserve visual connections for Guia Hill. However, the protective legislation was repealed in 2006 by Chief Executive Order 248/2006, which states that because of changing conditions, including the scarcity of available land for development, the regulations were no longer able to "ensure systematic and rational land use."[106] Moreover, the order stated that the change was required to implement the "development needs of the gaming sector, one of Macau's economic pillars."[107] This legislation appears to go against stated policies regarding the importance of maintaining sightlines of designated monuments, as the World Heritage Committee recommended for Macau.[108] Eventually, a 90 m height restriction was established for buildings near Guia Hill and the 91 m Guia Lighthouse.[109]

Regional conservation initiatives: Tibet, Three Gorges, the Great Wall and Heritage Towns in Southern China

Three examples of heritage conservation projects outside of China's major urban areas provide an overview of some of the larger conservation management issues that exist in China's vast rural regions. Although the examples listed below of heritage protection considerations in Tibet, the Three Gorges Dam and the Great Wall are large scale, internationally renowned projects and sites, the issues that they highlight, including pressures of economic development, provision of tourism infrastructure and management, and challenges to cultural continuity apply to many of the lesser-known sites as well.

Tibet

Tibet has formally been a semi-autonomous region of the PRC since 1950, a status similar to the semi-autonomous region of Inner Mongolia. It stands out as a distinctive region due to its rich architectural traditions, strong religious identity and particular conservation issues.

Modern transportation and communication methods ensure that Tibet is no longer as remote as before, and Tibet today struggles to defend its distinct cultural, artistic and spiritual identity against Beijing's dominant central government. Subject to widespread purges and destruction of cultural monuments during the Cultural Revolution, Tibet – particularly its capital of Lhasa – still experiences forceful government policies. Today, a steady stream of Han immigrants threatens to overwhelm the native population. These political factors combine to create difficult heritage management challenges for the region's significant buildings, especially when added to the more typical hazards of a harsh, alpine climate, occasional earthquakes and limited funding for conservation activities.

Historically a highly spiritual people, Tibetans traditionally built each settlement around a Buddhist temple or a monastery. Considered the center of communities, these buildings were the focal point of all activities, secular and religious alike. As in Nepal and Mongolia, the clergy functioned as patrons of the arts and the crafts, as revealed by intricate mural paintings and woodcarvings found in nearly all temples and monasteries. Though interrupted over the course of the past century, these maintenance and craft traditions still persist in some areas of Tibet, although that approach may entail total re-construction of an old temple with new materials and technology rather than repairing it. Such action may be justified on religious grounds based on Buddhist religious beliefs regarding the temporariness of all things and gaining merit by building anew. (See also: Religious Origins of Restoration and Preservation in Chapter 16.)

Established around the seventh century CE as the center for Tibetan Buddhist studies and culture, Lhasa – along with the rest of Tibet – was annexed into the PRC in 1950 after a brief period of independence from China. The capital city contains several important monuments to its cultural development, including the World Heritage-designated Potala Palace, Jokhang Temple Monastery and Norbulinka Palace. Today, all serve as focal points for Tibetan nationalist fervor and the region's aspirations for autonomy. Following the destruction of numerous Tibetan monasteries during the Cultural Revolution, the Chinese Communist government attempted to reconcile with, and simultaneously tighten its control over, the Tibetans by funding the restoration of many razed temples and complexes. But after limited success in winning the hearts and minds of dissatisfied Tibetans through restoration, the Beijing government reversed course, taking on a new approach of forced assimilation and undermining of Tibetan built heritage.[110]

After decades of international isolation imposed by geography and by the Chinese government, the Tibetan plateau was finally opened to the outside world in the late 1980s. For the first time, its cultural treasures were brought into the full view of the international community. However, due to the restrictive policies of the Chinese government, international agencies have yet to play a significant permanent role in Tibet. This situation, coupled with its long isolation, distant geographical location and unique construction technology, has created difficult conditions for engaging international professionals equipped to deal with Tibetan buildings, not to mention calling upon local conservationists, making the task of conserving Tibet's many significant buildings all the more daunting.

Lhasa, Tibet's political and traditional capital, stands out as an interesting case study in the treatment of culturally marginalized people and their attendant built environment. It has entailed manipulation and control through the selective demolition or conservation of important cultural monuments while also being a case in which the central government applies differing standards to select nationally significant bodies of heritage for protection. Nevertheless, with some difficulty, several international campaigns have successfully shed light on the plight of Lhasa's built heritage. One such group, the Tibet Heritage Fund (THF), led by German conservationist Andre Alexander, worked until 2000 on restoring and protecting the region's unique architectural treasures. Beginning in 1996, the THF restored and conserved dozens of individual buildings that had been destroyed through neglect or improper alterations, largely with the financial backing of high profile sponsors, such as the German government and the Prince of Wales.

The THF extensively documented the historic city of Lhasa and took responsibility for protecting its historic properties, many of which were slated for demolition. Although Lhasa is technically one of the PRC's "protected" cities, it has recently undergone dramatic changes due to the massive immigration of ethnic Han Chinese. Between 1950 and 2000 Lhasa's population increased more than tenfold, from 30,000 to 400,000 persons. While the population skyrocketed, the number of historic buildings declined, from over 1,000 documented in 1950, to only about 180 in 2000.[111]

The THF was instrumental in acquiring several properties, and also framed a conservation plan for the area around the Jokhang temple, including the protection of the inner city as a living historic area and halting the ongoing demolition of traditional contextual residences.[112] Uncomfortable with the negative attention generated by the THF's activities, the Chinese government in 2000 deported several of the fund's foreign managers and ordered their Lhasa offices closed.[113]

Other international organizations at work in Tibet include the Kham Aid Foundation, which was founded by American Tibetan scholar Pamela Logan.[114] It conducts extensive educational outreach programs along with conservation projects of art and architecture in the eastern reaches of the region. Other organizations involved in conservation projects in Tibet include the Shalu Association, based in France, and the New York-based World Monuments Fund. The Shalu Association has had some success at nearly a dozen important monuments, including Shalu, Yemar, Gongkar, Drathang and Drongkhar temples in Central Tibet along with the Namseling Manor.

In addition to work in Tibet's urban areas, other foreign-led efforts have documented and studied religious architecture and prehistoric monuments outside Lhasa. Italian scholar Roberto Vitali has

FIGURE 2.15a and b Distant and courtyard views of Potala Palace, Lhasa.

104 East Asia

conducted extensive documentation of monasteries in western Tibet, including Tholing, one of the oldest monasteries in the region. Combining ancient documents with oral history and visual documentation, Vitali proposes a visual and textual reconstruction of how the complex may have appeared prior to its destruction.[115] American archaeologist John Bellezza has traveled extensively around the Tibetan Plateau, documenting pre-Buddhist sites including rock art, ruins, tombs and megaliths.[116] The efforts of both these individuals provide an important foundation of knowledge to inform future physical heritage conservation interventions by trained Tibetan professionals.

The approach to architectural conservation in Tibet, as elsewhere, is evolving towards the incorporation of larger collections of buildings and cultural landscapes. Many important scenographic views and much

FIGURE 2.16a and b Rural vernacular housing along "Arniko Highway," southwest Tibet (a), and communal participation in roof tamping in Lhasa (b).

contextual heritage of the region's individual sites are marred by recent development, which detracts from the protective designation of a site. As Tibet, along with the rest of China, undergoes widespread change in terms of large-scale development and an ever-increasing population, cultural heritage protection will only become more important as a means toward retaining the region's distinctive cultural character.

In the name of modernization, the Chinese government has compromised many historic built environments, including those in Tibet and in other regions. However, this type of assertion of authority may be giving way to more empathetic support. With the ratification of the nationwide China Principles, top-down planning may yield more in favor of more amenable heritage protection practices that involve more local participation and negotiations and the conservation of a wider selection of architectural heritage types.

Three Gorges

Until 2006, an unprecedented blend of cultural and ecological marvels were situated along the mighty Yangtze River, as it flowed through the burgeoning metropolis of Chongqing on its way to the Pacific. When the US$26 billion Three Gorges Dam project was completed on the river, an estimated 1.3 million people were displaced.[117] The waters rose over five hundred feet in some areas, inundating thousands of cities, towns, villages, temples, tombs and archaeological sites. Alongside concerns for the loss of cultural heritage were the ecological concerns of silt and pollutant accumulation in the new lake, and even climatic change due to the new 1,084 square kilometer surface area of water that was now exposed.[118]

Although many of the most significant cultural objects were relocated to higher ground (much as was done prior to the completion of Egypt's High Dam project at Aswan in the 1960s), untold losses were suffered due to the disappearance of ancient villages and townscapes and their context, undiscovered or "less significant" sites and population displacement. As of 2016, the verdict remains undecided on whether the Three Gorges Dam was beneficial or not for south-central China's environmental and architectural heritage, since its benefits are touted as vast, in terms of the hydroelectric power that it is meant to produce and assistance given in controlling the flood-prone Yangtze.

Damming the Yangtze River had been first envisioned nearly a century earlier: it was originally proposed by Sun Yat-sen in 1919. Two other schemes involving Japanese and American engineers were planned in 1939 and 1944 respectively. The present accomplishment, a Chinese design, was approved by the National People's Congress in 1992 and stands today as the largest operating hydroelectric facility in the world.

Planning for such projects has its attendant considerations of displacement and often loss to cultural heritage along river routes. While efforts were made to document and mitigate loss in the case of the Yangtze project, rigorous research on alternative solutions in the manner of environmental impact studies made in other nations was not an influential part of this project. The case was made for the cost-efficiency of hydroelectric power and how it prevents greenhouse emissions that are created by fossil fuel power generation. Nonetheless, there are lessons to be learned for the future as China considers dams in other regions. These include damming the upper reaches of the Mekong River in Yunnan province, which may have downstream impacts on lives and heritage sites in other countries.[119]

The Great Wall

Only recently have conservation considerations been given to China's most famous landmark, the 8,850 km (5,500 mile)-long Great Wall. Built in successive phases of stone, brick and rammed earth from the Zhou to the Ming dynasties (from the fifth century BCE to 1644 CE), the Wall has been variably maintained in some way by every dynasty, government and individuals along its route over the course of its long existence. But as a prime tourist attraction in modern times, particularly the sections close to urban centers, the Wall has been subject to a number of interventions that undermine its integrity as one of human history's premier engineering and construction achievements.

This massive and largely unregulated built structure has suffered from a variety of problems from a conservation perspective: from neglect and natural deterioration to intentional destruction. Nearly every large heritage site management challenge is found somewhere along the Wall's length, including

FIGURE 2.17a and b Section of the Great Wall near Badaling before restoration in 1907 and a contemporary photograph of the restored Wall at Jianshanling.

insensitive economic development of local constituents, accessibility and safety issues, and control of the Wall's approximately 11 million annual visitors.[120]

Management of the Wall will for some time remain a significant challenge to all concerned with its protection due to its size, its construction, its value as a "must-see" heritage site and jurisdictional control as it passes through nine provinces. Until the late 1990s China's central government had no thorough documentation of the Wall and its condition nor any specific plans for its protection and presentation except in the fully restored sections at Badaling and Mutianyu north of Beijing. Despite this, national and international interest in the Wall changed in 1984 when Deng Xiaoping's open door and reform policy was put into place and sections of the Wall began to be restored. The listing of the Great Wall in its entirety as a UNESCO World Heritage Site in 1987 spotlighted its importance but did not focus on issues related to its conservation.[121] Deteriorating conditions of the Wall and modern threats to it were first respectfully elucidated by the international Friends of the Great Wall in 2001. Further attention to condition problems at the Wall was also drawn when the World Monuments Fund placed the Great Wall on WMF's Watch List of most endangered sites in 2002.

In 2002 a team of government conservation experts from the State Administration for Cultural Heritage, in cooperation with the all-Chinese China Great Wall Society, Beijing, conducted a survey of 101 areas along the Wall and noticed numerous threats to structural stability and integrity. The survey resulted in an increased level of awareness at the national governmental level and support for the Wall's improved conservation, a focus that was further encouraged by NGOs such as the China Great Wall Society. In 2003 a state law was passed to protect the entire Great Wall. Among other things, it established a 500 m buffer zone on either side that would prohibit damaging activities such as mining and quarrying.[122] Until then, penalties for defacing or even demolishing sections of the Wall were weak and seldom enforced, but that later changed both on the regional and national levels.[123]

In 2007 SACH and the Bureau of Surveying and Mapping carried out a general survey using infrared and GPS technologies that helped locate some areas concealed over time by sandstorms.[124] As of 2016, still to be done is a large-scale conditions survey and conservation master plan prepared and implemented in order to effectively maintain its stability and regulate its use and as a vast linear cultural landscape. Such a survey including documentation of its immediate hinterland would be unprecedented, with the exception of recent surveys of Silk Road heritage routes (see Chapter 23). Oversight of the project should fall under the scope of the Chinese national government that is well known for rallying support for projects of national interest, involving local stakeholders along its route, and supplying national and international expertise as required.

Heritage Towns in South China

Lijiang and Shaxi: dual approaches to conserving urban vernacular architecture

In 2000 the Chinese government announced the discovery of "Shangri-La," located within its borders just north of Burma, straddling Tibet, Yunnan and Sichuan provinces. The area was so named following confirmation of an eight-year US$9.6 billion investment to promote the region's beauty to foreign tourists seeking an authentic, historic, mystical land in harmony with natural beauty and to improve the region's infrastructural ability to cope with the anticipated crowds.[125] Such beauty does exist in the area's foothills, snowcapped mountains and historic villages such as Lijiang, seat of the ethnic Naxi culture.

Lijiang is situated on a historic managed waterway system lined with paved streets and lanes, serving a meandering plan of urban vernacular architecture. Much of it was extensively damaged in an earthquake on February 3, 1996, but city planners ensured that the entire old village was rebuilt using traditional techniques and materials. The old town was declared a World Heritage Site in 1997, and has since become a popular tourist destination.

The massive planned investment program for Lijiang and its immediate region focused on models of cooperation of stakeholders in tourism and conservation and informing locals, especially the Naxi chiefs, of the merits of joining the ranks of world heritage. However, the project did not take several factors into account that would be needed if Lijiang was to maintain its sense of authenticity as the home of the Naxi community. Through major effort and investment Lijiang was rehabilitated, retaining what could be preserved and rebuilding the rest with traditional methods. In doing so the tenuous balance between conservation and

FIGURE 2.18a and b Lijiang (Yunnan province): Conservation work that tends towards over-restoration.

development, and conserving the authenticity – or not – of China's historic towns was squarely faced. New infrastructure installed with significant funding from a World Bank disaster assistance loan allowed the historic center of the town to be essentially rebuilt with underground services, new paving, canal containment systems and parking. The urban architecture, primarily houses and shophouses, were restored and a range of new commercial buildings were designed in the manner of old ones to frame a sizable new open market area.

Today, in both authentic and newly constructed buildings, merchants – including a number of Naxi dressed in their traditional garb – serve a population that now consists mostly of tourists. Considering the "sameness" of the merchandise in many of Lijiang's shops the whole visitor experience of the place, while interesting in some ways, gives the impression that this fabled historic town is anything but authentic. This is not for a lack of trying to preserve Lijiang's old town. The Old Town Protection Plan for Lijiang, which was created in 1988, and a subsequent Country Master Plan had ensured that new buildings would be constructed beyond the Old City.[126]

In 1997, concerned with potential problems of uncontrolled tourism and other development projects being carried out in historic Lijiang, the World Heritage Committee warned there could be negative impact on heritage values and "requested the State Party to review the current comprehensive Management Plan of the property."[127] In response, Lijiang's municipal government passed the "Protection and Management Regulations for Lijiang, Historical and Cultural City of Yunnan Province, 1994." This legislation established three cultural heritage protection zones in the Old City, and penalized non-compliance. For instance, in Zone I there is an absolute ban on all development; in Zone II, original buildings must be retained but reconstruction may be allowed if designs are compatible with the surroundings; and in Zone III, there are strict controls on the height and appearance of new development in order to create a protection or buffer zone around Zones I and II.[128]

Despite all the planning for urban conservation and efforts at rehabilitation that has occurred in Lijiang, there were problems. Less than optimal coordination between the national and local government levels and local constituencies, and some ineffective oversight of enforcement of the regulations, continues to affect the project.

Before the Lijiang revitalization effort was completed an alternate approach to preserving a representative historic Yunnanese town was proposed by a consortium of NGOs working in cooperation with the Chinese government at the national, regional and local levels in the historic town of Shaxi. Shaxi, a remarkably intact Ming period town about 100 km south of Lijiang, is situated on the Horse Tea Route to Tibet. Wealthy in its day, Shaxi remains well-endowed with fine town architecture including its Xiangjiao Temple building (now a museum) and a large town square defined by the distinctive Sideng Theatre building at its center.

The Shaxi Rehabilitation Project (SRP), which combined local government talent with Zurich's Swiss Federal Institute of Technology of Zurich, was conceived by Swiss architect and planner Jacques Finer in 1999. Finer's conservation approach was based on careful documentation and conservation planning for all aspects of the poor and underutilized town, with a special aim to engage locals in all aspects of the process. The careful documentation, analysis and conservation planning for Shaxi's architecture and urban features proved vital to successful fundraising and for gaining local, regional and national approval for the project. Finer wisely engaged interested foreign supporters including the American Express Philanthropic program and the Robert W. Wilson Challenge grant administered by the World Monuments Fund. He also nominated Shaxi to the World Monuments Fund's Watch List in 2002, which also helpfully raised the project's profile.

SRP's initial task was to install new infrastructure. After underground utilities and paved surfaces were restored, landscaping was done to coordinate with an extensive building conservation phase that followed.

An important hallmark of the SRP project was its commitment to conserve Shaxi's surviving temples, public and commercial buildings, and houses, using a light touch in their interventions, even preserving time-worn finishes and similar special features of the town's architecture. The project opened to great fanfare in June 2005 and, as intended, serves well as a demonstration project of its kind, showing the merits of both public–private partnerships and how international technical and financial support can aid an essentially local project.[129]

The Lijiang and Shaxi examples were noticed at the time as being exemplars of their differing approaches, one being more successful than the other. In June 2005 The Xi'an Declaration on the Conservation of the Setting of Heritage Structures, Sites and Areas was passed at the 15th General Assembly of ICOMOS in Xi'an, which was hosted by China ICOMOS. In part, it states:

> Heritage structures, sites and areas of various scales, including individual buildings or designed spaces, historic cities or urban landscapes, landscapes, seascapes, cultural routes and archaeological sites, derive their significance and distinctive character from their

perceived social and spiritual, historic, artistic, aesthetic, natural, scientific or other cultural values. They also derive their significance and distinctive character from their meaningful relationships with their physical, visual, spiritual and other cultural context and settings.[130]

Much is at stake here, beginning with the careful handling of all aspects of urban fabric that connects individual historic buildings and sites in historic urban settings through the guarding against adjacent high-rise structures within their view. Then the difficulties of gaining consensus on such matters and implementing the principles of the Xi'an Declaration and similar doctrine become apparent, and stand as one of the key challenges in historic urban conservation in the future.

The Lijiang and Shaxi experiences (see Sidebar), plus heightened concerns about effective planning of urban–rural integration in China, have led to new thinking in urban landscape conservation. An early attempt to address the matter on a region-wide scale was made in September 1999 at the Leadership Conference on Conservancy and Development. This conference, sponsored by the Yunnan Provincial Association of Cultural Exchanges with Foreign Countries, was a forum where ideas for effective conservation and integration of Yunnan's rich natural and urban ecologies on a province-wide basis were solicited.

Several years later, a regional approach was exemplified in Chengdu, Sichuan province, when both before and after its disastrous May 2008 earthquake NGOs and environmental advocates urged holistic conservation of the characteristic forest-basin geographic feature of the Chengdu Plain, including its hundreds of villages. Despite such popular action, however, post-disaster recovery priorities that entailed the government's massive program to consolidate and rebuild villages proved to be a greater priority. Nonetheless, Chengdu today is implementing some of the most important policies in urban–rural integration in China.[131] In their measured successes all such endeavors point up the exponentially greater difficulties of controlling and implementing urban landscape conservation at all scales in China and elsewhere.

The stakes are high for doing better in this realm, especially where conserving vulnerable vernacular architecture is concerned. Ye Rutang, President of the Architectural Society of China, in his preface to Wang Qijun's *Vernacular Dwellings (Ancient Chinese Architecture)*, eloquently outlined the architectural heritage to be considered:

> In China's extensive and profound cultural treasury, ancient architecture is one of the important components, and is, in a sense, of a symbolic nature. The beauty and elegance of ancient Chinese architecture has a uniqueness of its own in the world architectural system. The strict formality of the city layouts, the lively arrangement of village settlements, the grouping of buildings round courtyards, the comprehensive building code for wood structures, the great variety of colour and architectural form, the perfect harmony of the decorative and structural functions of building elements, the integration of furniture, interior decoration, painting, sculpture and calligraphy into a comprehensive art of architecture all go to manifest the distinctive characteristics of the traditional Chinese culture.
> … When one comes to study China's ancient architecture, he will have a deeper comprehension of the oriental philosophy of the "oneness of nature and man" inherent in the architectural forms, as well as of the Chinese people's respect for Confucianism, the expression of their philosophical meditation on time and space through material forms, and their all-embracing aesthetic tastes.[132]

The recent level of engagement between Chinese heritage officials and professionals and their Western counterparts and others represents a significant step forward for architectural heritage protection in China since it has both expanded the purview of best practices and takes into account other forms and scales of cultural heritage. While the past century has been an especially tumultuous time for China's cultural heritage much good work has been accomplished and vast amounts of cultural heritage remains. For years to come buildings, cultural landscapes and art comprising China's tangible cultural heritage are likely to be further identified, documented and conserved through more supportive heritage management policies.

a

b

c

FIGURE 2.19a, b and c The ancient villages of Xidi and Hongcun in southern Anhui province are a pair of traditional villages organized along intersecting systems of streets and waterways that bear witness to the lifeways of many such villages in the region that once existed. A view of Xidi shows this special vernacular architecture (a). Hongcun is an example of a waterfront village (b). At a different scale the carefully conceived Classical Gardens of Suzhou in Jiangsu province dating from the eleventh to the nineteenth centuries seek to re-create natural landscapes in miniature (c). The former reflects practical aesthetic considerations in a rural town's layout and the latter reflects at a more intimate scale the profound metaphysical importance of natural beauty in Chinese culture. Both are protected UNESCO World Heritage Sites.

Although heritage protection policies were ignored during the mid-century years of the Cultural Revolution, it is important to remember when evaluating the state of Chinese cultural heritage affairs that both the nation and people have been participating in conservation-minded activities for most of its collective history. The formation and conservation of collections of artworks and objects is part of the ancient Chinese tradition of valuing material culture – both movable and immovable. Throughout much of China's history, its emperors have had a serious antiquarian interest, amassing collections of ancient art, manuscripts and architectural examples. The scope of imperial collecting is legendary, especially during China's final Qing dynasty. As, or more, important has been the essentially unbroken tradition in Chinese culture of respect for the past and for traditional ways, a view that adds to China's having one of the world's most accomplished and sustained cultures.

Western heritage conservation perspectives focus on maintaining material connections to the past through specific tangible cultural expressions. This is especially the case for buildings and sites. In comparison, Asian heritage conservationists put a greater emphasis on "place," its meaning and continuity of use. This discrepancy in attitude towards material conservation is often explained in the country's preferred choice of building material: wood. This extremely versatile building material is often all that's needed for purposes ranging from structure to décor. The prevalent use of wood, which requires periodic replacement and maintenance, speaks to the Chinese faith in both the continuity of culture and the sustainability of cultural values inherent in a particular site chosen for historically significant or monumental structures.

The Chinese are legendary throughout history for rallying to the causes of their leaders quickly, efficiently and thoroughly. From the massive construction projects of antiquity to the pace of economic development in the twenty-first century, a spirit of communalism and working together permeates Chinese history, even when projects are initiated under duress.

If the past century is viewed in comparison to the balance of Chinese history, the ravages set upon its built heritage seem small in comparison to the long periods of care and respectful concern for the country's distinctive cultural heritage. With this perspective in mind, China's new era of leadership and energy for cultural heritage protection is an especially promising initiative, in addition to being a vital part of international heritage conservation practice.

Notes

1 Jaiwen Ai. "Selecting the Refined and Discarding the Dross: The Post-1990 Chinese Leadership's Attitude Towards Cultural Tradition," in Patrick Daly and Tim Winter (eds.) *Routledge Handbook of Heritage in Asia*. (London: Routledge, 2010), 136.
2 J. David Murphy. *Plunder and Preservation Cultural Property Law and Practice in the People's Republic of China*. (Oxford: Oxford University Press, 1995), 44.
3 Ibid., 52–61.
4 Ibid., Appendix II, "Annotated Chronological Index of Selected People's Republic of China Statutory and Other Materials Relating to Cultural Property," 183–197.
5 Anna Dal Maso. "Chinese Policies on Cultural Heritage Preservation: A Way to Understand the Peculiar Approach to Conservation in China." *Research Conference Proceedings on Asian Approaches to Conservation* (2006), Asian Academy for Heritage Management, UNESCO and ICCROM, 44–45. In her discussion of "keeping the former condition" in Chinese conservation practice Dal Maso helpfully compares the evolution of thought and practice on the subject to Cesare Brandi's *Teoria del Restauro* (Torino: Piccola Biblioteca Einaudi, 2000, 1st edition 1963). She also cites leading Chinese counterpart thinker Guo Hong's "Discussion on the Substance and Importance of the 'Principle of Keeping the Former Condition' and the Intersection of Arts and Science in Conservation," *Wenwu baohu yu kaogu kexue*, Beijing, 16(1) (February 2004), 60–64 and Li Xiaodong, *Outlines of Chinese Laws for Protection of Cultural Relics* (Beijing: Xueyuan chubanshe, 2002).
6 Although recent historic analyses of China since the time of Confucius have revealed a more dynamic trajectory, marked by many abrupt changes, relative to Europe's ebb and flow of empires since the fifth century BCE, China's cultural continuity has remained comparatively constant.
7 Chen Wei and Andreas Aass. "Heritage Conservation: East and West," *ICOMOS Information* 3 (1989), 3–8.
8 Li-Hsin Chang. *Chinese Attitudes Toward the Past: Tracing the Development of Historic Preservation in China*. Unpublished graduate thesis, Columbia University, February 2003. See also Wei and Aass.
9 Just as important was the existence of a social class with both the means and the motivations to study and collect.
10 The Yangshao and Hongshan cultures (c. 5000–3000 BCE) are considered the source of feng shui's establishment.
11 Milton Meyer. *China: A Concise History*. (London: Rowman & Littlefield Publishers, 1994), 59.
12 Ibid., 102.
13 Bamber Gascoigne. *A Brief History of the Dynasties of China*. (London: Constable & Robinson, 2003), 16.
14 Meyer, 103.
15 Gascoigne, 51.
16 Archaeological excavations revealing charred roof timbers have tended to confirm the account in *Shiji* (Historical Records) that Xiang Ju, a rebel in the Qin dynasty, burned Shihuangdi's palace and tomb in 206 BCE.
17 Gascoigne, 86.
18 Ibid., 88.
19 Meyer, 106.

20 Ibid.
21 Anthony Tung. "Erasing Beijing; A Conservation Tragedy," *ICON*, WMF (Fall 2003), 41.
22 Beijing's population at this time is estimated to have been one million people.
23 Gascoigne, 198.
24 Meyer, 108. Occupying a land area of 290 ha, the Old Summer Palace or Yuanming Yuan is located in northwest Beijing, surrounding Kunming Lake. It was built in 1750 during the sixty year reign of Emperor Qianlong and has been restored three times, most recently in the 1950s. Qianlong was inspired by garden and building designs noticed during six trips he made south of the Yangtze. Chinese garden art reached it pinnacle during his reign and is best expressed in the Summer Palaces of Beijing and Chengde as well as in parts of the Forbidden City, in particular the Ningshou Garden.
25 The shop-lined Suzhou-like waterway in the Back Hill and Back Lake areas of the Summer Palace, built purely for effect and amusement, originally dates from the mid-eighteenth century. It is roughly contemporaneous with counterpart ideas of precisely replicated rural vernacular buildings that formed Marie Antoinette's *hameau* (1783) at Versailles and the artificial farmstead at Chantilly (1774), both in LeNôtre designed settings.
26 Li-Hsin Chang, 7.
27 Hung Wu. "Internalizing Ruins," *A Story of Ruins: Presence and Absence in Chinese Art and Visual Culture*. (London: Reaktion Books, 2012), 79. Of perhaps equal significance in terms of influence was the work of foreign archaeologists working in China in the 1920s.
28 Murphy, 35–37. An additional comprehensive portrayal of Chinese cultural heritage protection laws, including architectural heritage protection, is found in Jocelyn Fresnais, *La Protection du Patrimoine en Républic Populaire de Chine, 1949–1999*. (Paris: Éditions du C.T.H.S., 2001).
29 See Liu Chang, *Shenxiu Siyong: Form Study of Yuanming Yuan Interior Design*. (Beijing: Tsingua University Press, 2004), for extensive research, analysis and reconstruction drawings of the former Yuanming Yuan Palace.
30 Neville Agnew, Martha Demas and Guolong Lai. "Valuing the Past in China: The Seminal Influence of Liang Sicheng on Heritage Conservation," *Orientations* 35(2) (March, 2004): 82–89.
31 Guangya Zhu. "China's Architectural Heritage Conservation Movement," *Frontiers of Architectural Research* 1(1) (2012): 10–22.
32 Murphy, 82.
33 Li-Hsin Chang, 37.
34 Xie Yinming and Qu Wanlin. "Shei baohule Gugong? (Who Protected the Forbidden City?)" *Dang de wenxian (Communist Party of China Documents)* 5 (2006), 70–75 (in Chinese) *People Net*, July 25, 2007.
35 Lin Zhu. *A Brief History of Chinese Construction Society*. (Taipei: Architecture & Culture Publisher, 1997), 124.
36 Liang Sicheng. *Liang Sicheng Quan Ji*. [The Complete Works of Liang Sicheng] Volumes I–VII. (Beijing: Chinese Architecture and Industry Publisher, 2001), 442–443.
37 Liang Sicheng and his wife Lin Huiyin both studied architecture at the University of Pennsylvania from 1924 to 1928. They were well traveled in Europe and had visited many of its numerous famous historic buildings and sites.
38 Sidney Wong. "Research Notes: Lin Huiyin and Liang Sicheng as Architectural Students at the University of Pennsylvania (1924–27)," *Planning and Development* 23(1) (2008), 75–93. See p. 87, last line.
39 Agnew, Demas and Lai, 86.
40 Journalist for the Xinhua News Agency Wang Jun had engaged authorities in a debate on the wisdom of saving Liang Sicheng's personal home, a symbolic preservation victory at the time. See Thomas Hahn in Wang Jun. *Beijing Record: A Physical and Political History of Planning in Modern Beijing*. (Hackensack, NJ:World Scientific Publishing, 2011), Foreword, 3.
41 Kuttan Mahadevan. *Society and Development in China and India*. (New Delhi: B.R. Publishing, 1994), 47–79.
42 SACH (State Administration of Cultural Heritage) 2009. "Chinese Law Protecting Natural and Cultural Heritage." "Planning for Sustainable Tourism," in *The Conservation of Cultural Heritage in 60 Years*. Beijing: Beijing Cultural Relics Press, 40.
43 Guo Zhan. "The Particularity of 'Authenticity' in the Conservation of Cultural Property in China," in *Proceedings from the Nara Conference on Authenticity*. (Tokyo: Agency for Cultural Affairs, 1995), 324.
44 May Holdsworth. *The Palace of Established Happiness: Restoring a Garden in the Forbidden City*. (Beijing: Forbidden City Publishing House, 2008), 100–177.
45 Zhan, 325.

46 UNESCO World Heritage List. Web. www.whc.unesco.org/heritage.htm. Accessed July 15, 2015. Nineteen World Heritage Sites in China were listed between 2004 and 2015, making the current total forty-eight.
47 Zhan, 324.
48 Neville Agnew and Martha Demas. "The China Principles," *Conservation: The GCI Newsletter* 13(1) (1998), 1.
49 Zhang Bai. "On the Development of the Principles for the Conservation of Heritage Sites in China," in *Principles for the Conservation of Heritage Sites in China*. (Los Angeles: The Getty Conservation Institute, 2002), viii. The Illustrated China Principles issued by ICOMOS China produced in 2005 was created under the leadership of Lu Zhou, Cultural Heritage Conservation Institute, Urban Planning and Design Institute of Tsinghua University, Beijing.
50 China Principles. Getty Conservation Institute, 50. Web. www.getty.edu/conservation/our projects/field projects/china/. Accessed July 20, 2016.
51 Zhang, ix.
52 Martha Demas, Lori Wong, Neville Agnew, Linli Li, Dong Chen and Qing Chen. "Facing the Past in China: Contemporary Challenges of Architectural Conservation," in Contributions to the Hong Kong Congress September 22–26, 2014: An Unbroken History: Conserving East Asian Art and Heritage, Austin Nevin, Joyce H. Townsend, Shayne Rivers and Barry Knight (eds.), *Studies in Conservation* 59 (Supp.1), S32–S35. London: International Institute for Conservation of Historic and Artistic Works (IIC).
53 At Shuxiang Temple the China Principles were mostly applied to the prevalent problem of flaking *caihua* (architectural decorative painting). From 1997 to 2001 field representatives of the World Monuments Fund were testing the same premise for conserving versus restoring Qing period *caihua* at its pilot conservation work at buildings comprising Xiannongtan (Temple of Agriculture) outside Beijing.
54 "Review of Ten Years' Application of the China Principles and Study of its Future Directions." Conference Proceedings, in *International Principles and Local Practice of Cultural Heritage Conservation* (Beijing: National Heritage Center of Tsinghua University and ICOMOS China, 2014).
55 Web. http://worldpopulationreview.com/world-cities. Accessed August 13, 2015.
56 Web. http://countrymeters.info/en/Macau. Accessed September 2, 2015.
57 Web. www.businessinsider.com/china-car-market-up-14-percent-20-million-sales-2014-1. Accessed August 13, 2015.
58 Tung, 43.
59 Ibid.
60 Tung, 42. Interestingly, although much of the destruction of Beijing's urban fabric has taken place in the twentieth century, as China emerged from centuries of isolationism, occupation and political upheaval as a world power, several plans for its conservation had been proposed and rejected during that time. The Japanese, while preparing for occupation of China during the late 1930s, proposed a solution, one that during the 1950s, was later advocated for in vain by leading Chinese conservationist Liang Sicheng: construct a new, modern capital to the west of the old city. After the Communist Revolution, however, anti-feudal and anti-traditionalist attitudes led to the wholesale neglect – in some cases, outright assault – of Beijing's ancient urban fabric. This rapidly led to its deterioration as modern industrial development infiltrated the city's historic core.
61 Cultural Heritage Management and Urban Development: Challenges and Opportunities. A World Bank and UNESCO-sponsored conference held in Beijing from July 5–7, 2000.
62 Ken Taylor. "Cultural Heritage and Urbanization in China." 2013. Web. www.thechinastory.org/2013/cultural-and-urbanisation-in-china/. Accessed August 15, 2015.
63 Kapila D. Silva. "Conserving Asian Urban Heritage; The Need for Re-Conceptualizing the Value-based Management Approach," in Siriwan Silpacharanan and Jeffrey Campbell (eds.) *Research Conference Proceedings on Asian Approaches to Conservation*. (Bangkok: Asian Academy of Heritage Management. Chulalongkorn University, 2006), 16.
64 Ibid. Importantly, procedures for effective urban conservation are being documented for wider dissemination. One such publication is Ye Yumin, *Coordinating Urban and Rural Development in China: Learning from Chengdu* (Northampton, MA: Edward Elgar Publishers, 2013).
65 Cai Yanxin and Lu Bingjie. *Chinese Architecture*. (Beijing: China Foto Press, 2007), 12; and, Edmund N. Bacon, *Design of Cities*. (New York: Viking Press, 1967), 244.
66 Huanzhang Ke. "Preservation and Development of Beijing," *Building in China* 4(4) (December 1991).
67 Sen-Dou Chang. "Beijing: Perspectives on Preservation, Environment and Development," *Cities* 15(1) (1998), 13–25.
68 Ibid., 15.
69 Tung.

70 Wu Liangyong. *Rehabilitating the Old City of Beijing; A Project in the Ju'er Hutong Neighborhood*. (Vancouver: Urbanization in Asia, University of British Columbia Press, 1999), xviii.
71 Sen-Dou Chang, 17.
72 Erik Eckholm. "Restoring an Ancient City's Glory Brick by Brick," *The New York Times*. September 30, 2002.
73 Tung, 164. See also Daniel Abramson, "Beijing's Preservation Policy and the Fate of Siheyuan," *Traditional Design and Settlements Review* 13(1) (2001).
74 See Daniel Benjamin Abramson. "The Aesthetics of City-Scale Preservation Policy in Beijing," *Planning Perspectives* 22(2) (2007).
75 The region around Shanghai dates from as early as 770 BCE, the Spring and Autumn era of Chinese history. Most authorities agree that the current location of Shanghai was established in the Song dynasty (1227–1279 CE).
76 S. Streshinsky. "Shanghai Sees the Light," *Preservation, National Trust for Historic Preservation*, Washington, DC 35 (September/October, 2000).
77 The American firm Kohn Pederson Fox were architects for the Shanghai World Financial Center (2008). Jun Xia (Gensler) is architect for the Shanghai Tower (2015).
78 Streshinsky, 37. These house museums and other Communist Party heritage sites and their interpretive centers are heavily visited, with recent limits being a reported 80,000 visitors a day.
79 Streshinsky, 38. See also: Edward Denison and Guang Yu Ren. *Building Shanghai; The Story of China's Gateway*. (Hoboken, NJ: John Wiley & Sons, 2006), 214–239.
80 You-Ren Yang and Chih-hui Chang. "An Urban Regeneration Regime in China: A Case Study of Urban Redevelopment in Shanghai's Taipinqiao Area," *Urban Studies* 44(9) (August 2007) 1819.
81 Adolfo F.L. Baratta and Nicoletta Setola. "Preservation and Requalification of the Shanghai Urban Heritage; The Case Study of the JingAn Villa District," in *Asian Cultural Heritage. Proceedings of ICOMOS Thailand International Conference, 2011*. October 15–17, Phuket, Thailand, 241–253.
82 Dan Levin. "In Shanghai, Preservation Takes Work," *The New York Times*, May 2, 2010, 22–23.
83 Jeff Cody. "In the Shadow of Skyscrapers: Hong Kong's Colonial Buildings Await New Custodians," *CRM Bulletin* 19(3) (1996), 23.
84 "Interview with Professor David Lung: Now and Then." *Heritage Hong Kong* 4(2) (2003), 4–9.
85 Cody, 23.
86 See Jeff Cody. "Heads or Tails? The Preservation of Western-style Buildings in China," *CRM Bulletin* 19(3) (1996), 22–28.
87 The Economist.com. "Mad About Museums," December 21, 2013. Web. www.economist.com/news/special-report/21591710-china-building-thousands-new-museums-how-will-it-fill-them-mad-about-museums. Accessed May 18, 2016.
88 S. Gaskin. "China's Aggressive Museum Growth Brings Architectural Wonders." CNN.com, April 30, 2014. Web. www.cnn.com/2014/04/29/world/asia/china-museums/. Accessed May 18, 2016. In comparison, the United States counted approximately five art museums per 250,000 people in 2014, and nearly nine museums of all types per the same number of people. (Extrapolated from Institute of Museum and Library Services. "Government Doubles Official Estimate: There Are 35,000 Active Museums in the United States," IMLS.gov. May 19, 2014. Web. www.imls.gov/government_doubles_official_estimate.aspx. Accessed May 18, 2016.)
89 See, D. Alberge, "China's Wealthy Building New Museums to Display the Country's Treasures," FT.com (*Financial Times*), June 27, 2014. Web. www.ft.com/intl/cms/s/0/5002360a-f632-11e3-a038-00144feabdc0.html#axzz3j8UGYIuw. Accessed May 18, 2016.
90 F. Langfit. "China Builds Museums, but Filling Them is Another Story." NPR.org, May 21, 2013. Web. www.npr.org/sections/parallels/2013/05/21/185776432/china-builds-museums-but-will-the-visitors-come. Accessed May 18, 2016.
91 The Minsheng Art Museum is one of two museums owned and run by the Chinese banking giant Minsheng in Shanghai. The other is the Shanghai 21st Century Minsheng Art Museum (known as M21) located in the renovated French Pavilion from the 2010 World Expo. In Beijing, the private institution has also recently opened the Minsheng Contemporary Art Museum, reportedly the country's largest public contemporary art space, inside a renovated 1980s electronics factory. See also, Peggy Yuan. "New Beijing Collection Joins Rising Ranks of China's Private Art Museums." SCMP.com (*South China Morning Post*), July 23, 2014. Web. www.scmp.com/news/china/money-wealth/article/1842954/rise-chinas-private-art-museums. Accessed May 18, 2016.

92 T. Chung. "Valuing Heritage in Macau: On Contexts and Processes of Urban Conservation," in T. Chung and H. Tieben (eds.), *Macau Ten Years after the Handover* (Special Issue), *Journal of Current Chinese Affairs* 38(1) (2009), 129–160.
93 C.L. Chu. "Spectacular Macau: Visioning Futures for a World Heritage City," *Geoforum* 65 (2015), 440–450. Web. http://dx.doi.org/10.1016/j.geoforum.2015.06.009. Accessed May 18, 2016.
94 Philippe Pons. *Macao*. (Hong Kong: Hong Kong University Press, 2002), 109–120.
95 Hendrik Tieben. "Urban Image Construction in Macau in the First Decade after the Handover, 1999–2008," in T. Chung and H. Tieben (eds.), *Macau Ten Years after the Handover* (Special Issue), *Journal of Current Chinese Affairs* 38(1) (2009), 52.
96 T. Chung, 143.
97 Tieben, 49.
98 T. Chung, 141.
99 J. Porter, 2009. "The Past is Present: The Construction of Macau's Historical Legacy," *History & Memory* 21(1) (2009), 66, 84–90; see also C.L. Chu, "Spectacular Macau: Visioning Futures for a World Heritage City," *Geoforum* 65 (October 2015), 440–450.
100 Macao Decree Law no. 56/84/M 1984: Article 14, June 30, 1984. Web. www.macauheritage.net/en/Decree/law5684m.aspx. Accessed August 1, 2015.
101 T. Chung, 149–151.
102 Chu, 2.
103 World Heritage Nomination: The Historic Centre of Macao, International Council on Monuments and Sites (ICOMOS) recommendations with respect to inscription, p. 62.
104 Sharif Shams Imon. "Managing Change in the Historic City of Macao," *Historic Environment* 21 (2006): 19.
105 T. Chung, 149.
106 MOG 34/2006 (2006), Chief executive order 248/2006 (Macau SAR Government, Official Gazette). Boletim Oficial da Região Administrativa Especial De Macau, I Série, Suplemento, 15, 16 April, 2008, 1062–1063; in T. Chung.
107 MOG 34/2006 (2006).
108 World Heritage Nomination, 62.
109 T. Chung, 147–152.
110 UNESCO World Heritage List. March 1, 2004. Web. www.whc.unesco.org/heritage.htm. Accessed May 18, 2016.
111 Heather Stoddard. "The Lhasa Valley and Tibetan Architecture." Paper presented at the conference *The Lhasa Valley: History, Conservation and Modernization in Tibetan Architecture*. (Meudon: CNRS, UPR), 299.
112 K. Larsen. *The Lhasa Atlas: Traditional Tibetan Architecture and Townscape* (Boston, MA: Shambhala, 2001).
113 Jonathan Napack. "The Destruction of Lhasa," *The Art Newspaper* (December 2000), 26.
114 The China Exploration and Research Society and the Kham Aid foundation were responsible for the conservation efforts at the Palpung Monastery, one of the pilot projects of conservation in eastern Tibet. In 1996 the World Monuments Fund recognized the monastery as an endangered site on its 1996 World Monuments Watch® List.
115 Roberto Vitali. *Records of Tholing: A Literary and Visual Reconstruction of the "Mother" Monastery in Guge* (Dharamshala: Amye Machen, 1999).
116 John Bellezza. "Pre-Buddhist Archaeological Sites in Northern Tibet: An Introductory Report on the Types of Monuments and Related Literary and Oral Historical Sources," *Kailash* 17(1) (2000).
117 The Yangtze River dam was completed in 2006, and its turbines were operational in 2012.
118 Erik Eckholm. "As Dam on Yangtze Closes, Chinese Tally Gain and Loss," *The New York Times*. June 9, 2003, A1.
119 Present ecosystems including important cultural heritage areas in Laos, Thailand and Cambodia, in particular, are at risk from plans to control natural flooding upstream on the Mekong River.
120 In 2014, 10,720,000 people visited the fully restored Badaling and Mutianyu areas combined. Six other sections along the Wall's length have been restored. Tourism figures: National Tourism Administration of the People's Republic of China and China Odyssey Tours, 2014.
121 Plans for featuring the Badaling section of the Great Wall began in 1953 that involved repairs with period bricks and modern mortar.
122 William Lindesay. *Images of Asia: The Great Wall*. (Oxford: Oxford University Press, 2003), 87.
123 Elizabeth Rosenthal. "Vandalism and 'Improvements' Mar Great Wall," *The New York Times*. June 12, 2003, A3.
124 BBC World News. "Great Wall Even Longer," April 20, 2009. Web. http://news.bbc.co.uk/2/hi/asia-pacific/8008108.stm. Accessed July 15, 2015.

125 Ted Anthony. "China Finds Shangri-La Exactly where Tourists Want it," *San Francisco Chronicle*. July 26, 2002, A15.
126 Katrinka Ebbe and Donald Hankey. *Case Study: Lijiang, China Earthquake Reconstruction and Heritage Conservation*. (Washington DC: The World Bank, 2000), 14.
127 WCC-07/31.COM/7B.69.
128 Ebbe and Hankey, 12–13.
129 For a wider comparison of heritage management systems in Southern China, all in the Pearl River Delta, where the cities of Guangzhou, Hong Kong and Macau have differing political-administrative systems as a result of their distinctive recent histories, see Frederick Lee and Hilary Du Cros, "A Comparative Analysis of Three Heritage Management Approaches in Southern China: Guangzhou, Hong Kong, and Macau" in Kapila D. Silva and Neel Kamal Chapagain (eds.), *Asian Heritage Management, Context, Concerns and Prospects*. (London; Routledge, 2013), 105–121.
130 ICOMOS and ICOMOS China. Xi'an Declaration on the Conservation of the Setting of Heritage Structures, Sites and Areas (2005) Art. 2.
131 Daniel Benjamin Abramson and Yu Qi, "'Urban–Rural Integration' in the Earthquake Zone: Sichuan's Post-Disaster Reconstruction and the Expansion of the Chengdu Metropole," *Pacific Affairs* 84(3) (2011).
132 Rutang Ye. Preface in Wang Qijun. *Vernacular Dwellings (Ancient Chinese Architecture)*, English edition (New York: Springer, 2000), 495–523.

Further reading

Abramson, Daniel Benjamin. 2001. "Beijing's Preservation Policy and the Fate of Siheyuan," *Traditional Design and Settlements Review* 13(1).

———. 2014. "Conservation on the Edge: Periurban Settlement Heritage in China," in *Change Over Time*, an international Journal of Conservation and the Built Environment, University of Pennsylvania (Spring): 92–113.

Agnew, Neville (ed.). 2010. *Conservation of Ancient Sites on the Silk Road*. Proceedings of the Second International Conference on the Conservation of Grotto Sites, Mogao Grottoes, Dunhuang, People's Republic of China, June 28–July 3, 2004. Los Angeles: Getty Conservation Institute.

Agnew, Neville and Martha Demas. 1998. "The China Principles," *Conservation: the GCI Newsletter* 13(1).

Agnew, Neville and Martha Demas (eds). 2015. *Principles for the Conservation of Heritage in China*. Los Angeles: Getty Conservation Institute.

Agnew, Neville, Martha Demas and Guolong Lai. 2004. "Valuing the Past in China: The Seminal Influence of Liang Sicheng on Heritage Conservation," *Orientations* 35(2): 82–89.

Agnew, Neville, Martha Demas, and Sharon Sullivan. "The Development of the China Principles: A Review to Date," in *International Principles and Local Practice of Cultural Heritage Conservation: Conference Proceedings*. Beijing: National Heritage Center of Tsinghua University, ICOMOS China, 11–30.

Ai, Jiawen. 2012. "Selecting the Refined and Discarding the Dross: The Post-1990 Chinese Leadership's Attitude Towards Cultural Tradition," in P. Daly and T. Winter (eds.), *Routledge Handbook of Heritage in Asia*. London: Routledge, 129–138.

Allan, Sarah (ed.). 2005. *The Formation of Chinese Civilization: An Archaeological Perspective*. New Haven: Yale University Press.

Anthony, Ted. 2002. "China Finds Shangri-La Exactly where Tourists Want it," *San Francisco Chronicle*, July 26, 2002.

Balachandran, Sanchita. 2007. "Object Lessons: The Politics of Preservation and Museum Building in Western China in the Early Twentieth Century," *IJCP* 14: 1–32.

Bandarin, Francesco and Ron Van Oers. 2012. *The Historic Urban Landscape. Managing Cities in an Urban Century*. Oxford: Wiley Blackwell.

Baratta, Adolfo F.L. and Nicoletta Setola. 2011. "Preservation and Requalification of the Shanghai Urban Heritage; The Case Study of the JingAn Villa District," in *Asian Cultural Heritage: Proceedings of ICOMOS Thailand International Conference*, Paris: ICOMOS, October 15–17, 2011, Phuket, Thailand.

Beckwith, Christopher J. 2009. *Empires of the Silk Road*. Princeton, NJ: Princeton University Press.

Bellezza, John Vincent. 2014. *The Dawn of Tibet: The Ancient Civilization on the Roof of the World*. Lanham, MD: Rowman & Littlefield.

Berliner, Nancy and Brian Hotchkiss (eds.). 2008. *Juanqinzhai in the Qianlong Garden, The Forbidden City, Beijing*. London: Scala Publishers.

Blumenthal, Tami and Helaine Silverman. 2013. *Cultural Heritage Politics in China*. New York: Springer.

Bosker, Bianca. 2013. *Original Copies: Architectural Mimicry in Contemporary China*. Honolulu: University of Hawai'i Press.

Boyd, Andrew. 1962. *Chinese Architecture and Town Planning: 1500 B.C.–A.D. 1911.* New York: Transatlantic Arts.
Cai, Yanxin and Bingjie Lu. 2007. *Chinese Architecture.* Cultural China Series. Translated into English by Andrea Lee and Selina Lim. Beijing: CICC.
Campanella, Thomas J. 2008. *The Concrete Dragon: China's Urban Revolution and What it Means for the World.* New York: Princeton Architectural Press.
Cao, C.Z. 2009. "The Development of the Conservation of China's Historical and Cultural Heritage," *China's Ancient Cities* (6): 4–9. In Chinese.
Chan, Selina Ching. 2005. "Temple-building and Heritage in China," *Ethnology* 44(1): 65–70.
Chang, Li-Hsin. 2003. *Chinese Attitudes Toward the Past: Tracing the Development of Historic Preservation in China.* Unpublished graduate thesis, Columbia University, February 2003.
Chang, Li-Sheng 1996. "The National Palace Museum: A History of the Collection," in Wen Fong and James C.Y. Watt (eds.), *Possessing the Past.* New York: The Metropolitan Museum of Art, 3–25.
Chang, Sen-Dou. 1998. "Beijing: Perspectives on Preservation, Environment and Development," *Cities* 15(1): 13–25.
Cheng, Lei and Zhu Qi (eds.). 2008. *Beijing 798 – Now: Changing Arts, Architecture and Society in China.* Beijing: Timezone 8.
Cheung, Sidney C.H. 2003. "Remembering through Space: The Politics of Heritage in Hong Kong," *International Journal of Heritage Studies* 9(1): 7–26.
Chu, Cecilia L. In press. "Spectacular Macau: Visioning Futures for a World Heritage City," *Geoforum*; available at: http://dx.doi.org/10.1016/j.geoforum.2015.06.009.
Chu, Cecilia and Kylie Uebergang. 2002. *Saving Hong Kong's Cultural Heritage.* Hong Kong: Civic Exchange.
Chung, Thomas. 2009. "Valuing Heritage in Macau: On Contexts and Processes of Urban Conservation," in Thomas Chung and Hendrik Tieben (eds.), *Macau Ten Years after the Handover* (Special Issue), *Journal of Current Chinese Affairs* 1 (China Aktuell 1): 129–160.
Cody, Jeff. 1996a. "Heads or Tails? The Preservation of Western-style Buildings in China," *CRM Bulletin* 19(3): 23.
——. 1996b. "In the Shadow of Skyscrapers: Hong Kong's Colonial Buildings Await New Custodians," *CRM Bulletin* 19(3): 24–28.
Dal Maso, Anna. 2006. "Chinese Policies on Cultural Heritage Preservation: A Way to Understand the Peculiar Approach to Conservation in China," in *Research Conference Proceedings on Asian Approaches to Conservation* (2006), Asian Academy for Heritage Management, UNESCO and ICCROM, 44–45.
Demas, Margaret, Neville Agnew and Fan Jinshi. 2015. *Strategies for Sustainable Tourism at the Mogao Grottoes of Dunhuang, China.* New York: Springer.
Denison, Edward and Guang Yu Ren. 2006. *Building Shanghai: The Story of China's Gateway.* Chichester: John Wiley & Sons.
du Cros, H. and Y.S.F. Lee (eds.). 2007. *Cultural Heritage Management in China: Preserving the Cities of the Pearl River Delta.* London: Routledge.
Eakin, Hugh. 2004. "The Future of China's Past," *ARTNews* (December): 126–135.
Ebbe, Katrinka and Donald Hankey. 2000. *Case Study: Lijiang, China. Earthquake Reconstruction and Heritage Conservation.* Washington, DC: The World Bank.
Eckholm, Erik. 2001. "Restoring an Ancient City's Glory Brick by Brick," *The New York Times*, September 30, 2002.
——. 2003. "As Dam on Yangtze Closes, Chinese Tally Gain and Loss," *The New York Times*, June 9, 2003.
Elliott, Jeannette Shambaugh. 2005. *The Odyssey of China's Imperial Art Treasures.* Edited by David Shambaugh. Seattle: University of Washington Press.
Fan, Jinshi. 2010. *The Caves of Dunhuang.* Edited and translated by Susan Whitfield. Hong Kong: London Editions (HK).
Feng, Han. 2012. "Cultural Landscape: A Chinese Way of Seeing Nature," Chapter 5 in Ken Taylor and Jane Lennon (eds.), *Managing Cultural Landscapes* (Abingdon, Oxon: Routledge), 105.
Fresnais, Jocelyne. *La protection du patrimoine en République populaire de Chine 1949–1999.* In French. Paris: Edition du Comité et des travaux historiques et scientifiques.
Gascoigne, Bamber. 2003. *A Brief History of the Dynasties of China.* London: Constable & Robinson.
Getty Conservation Institute. 1993. "Conservation of Ancient Sites on the Silk Road," in *Proceedings of the International Conference on the Conservation of Grotto Sites, Mogao Grottoes, Dunhuang, People's Republic of China, October 3–8, 1993.* Marina del Rey: Getty Conservation Institute.
Getty Conservation Institute. n.d. "China Principles." Web. www.getty.edu/conservation/our projects/field projects/china/. Accessed July 20, 2015.
Gruber, S. 2007. "Protecting China's Cultural Heritage Sites in Times of Rapid Change: Current Developments, Practice and Law," *Asia Pacific Journal of Environmental Law* 10 (3&4): 255–301.

Guo, Hong. 2004. "Discussion on the Substance and Importance of the 'Principle of Keeping the Former Condition' and the Intersection of Arts and Science in Conservation," *Wenwu baohu yu kaogu kexue* 16(1) (February): 60–64 (in Chinese).

Hong Kong Antiquities and Monuments Office. 2003. "Interview with Professor David Lung: Now and Then," in *Heritage Hong Kong* 4(2).

Hsu, Pen-Shang and Shang-chia Chiou. 2009. "A Study of Traditional Carpentry Tool Skills Applied in Restoration of Historical Monuments in Taiwan," paper presented to the International Association of Societies of Design Research, Seoul.

ICOMOS. World Heritage Nomination: The Historic Centre of Macao, ICOMOS recommendations with respect to inscription, 62. Web. http://whc.unesco.org/uploads/nominations/1110.pdf. Accessed June 1, 2016.

ICOMOS China. 2005. *The Illustrated Principles for the Conservation of Heritage Sites in China*. In Chinese. Beijing: ICOMOS China.

Imon, Sharif Shams. 2008. "Managing Change in the Historic City of Macao," *Historic Environment* 21(3): 16–21.

Jiang, Lan. 2007. *Disappearing Architecture of China*. Translated into English by Chen Fuming. Singapore: Marshall Cavendish Editions.

Ke, Huanzhang. 1991. "Preservation and Development of Beijing," *Building in China* 4(4) (December), 2–10.

Kirkby, R.J.K. 1985. *Urbanization in China: Town and Country in a Developing Economy 1949–2000 AD*. New York: Columbia University Press.

Knapp, Ronald G. (ed.). 1986. *China's Traditional Rural Architecture: A Cultural Geography of the Common House*. Honolulu: University of Hawai'i Press.

——. 2001. *China's Vernacular Architecture*. Honolulu: University of Hawai'i Press.

Lai, Guolong, Martha Demas, and Neville Agnew. 2004. "Valuing the Past in China: The Seminal Influence of Liang Sicheng on Heritage Conservation," *Orientations* 35(2) (March): 82–89.

Larsen, Knud and Amund Sinding-Larsen. 2001. *The Lhasa Atlas*. Boston: Shambhala.

Lee, Leo Ou-fan. 1999. *Shanghai Modern: The Flowering of a New Urban Culture in China, 1930–1945*. Cambridge, MA: Harvard University Press.

Li Xiaodong. 2002. *Outlines of Chinese Laws for Protection of Cultural Relics*. Beijing: Xueyuan Chubanshe.

Liang Sicheng. 1984. *A Pictorial History of Chinese Architecture: A Study of the Development of Its Structural System and the Evolution of Its Types*. Edited by Wilma Fairbank. Cambridge, MA: MIT Press.

——. 1986. *Liang Sicheng Wenji (The Collected Papers of Liang Sicheng)*, volume 4. Beijing: Zhongguo Jianzhu Gongye Chubanshe (China Construction Industry Publishing House).

——. 2001. *Liang Sicheng Quan Ji*, volumes I–VII. Beijing: Chinese Architecture and Industry Publisher.

Liang, Z.H. 2009. "A Review of the Research of the Theory and Practice of Cultural Heritage Conservation in China," *Journal of Guizhou Normal University (Social Science)* 6: 55–61. In Chinese.

Lin, James C.S. (ed.). 2012. *The Search for Immortality: Tomb Treasures of Han China*. Cambridge: Cambridge University Press.

Lindesay, William. 2008. *The Great Wall Revisited: From the Jade Gate to Old Dragon's Head*. Cambridge, MA: Harvard University Press.

Liu, Chang. 2004. *Shenxiu Siyong: From Study on Yuanming Yuan Interior Design to Design Practice for the Beijing Chateau*. Beijing: Tsinghua University Press.

Liu, Dunzhen. 1993. *Chinese Classical Gardens of Suzhou*. Translated by Chen Lixian. New York: McGraw-Hill. Previously published in Chinese by Chinese Architecture and Building Press.

Lu, Xin. 2008. *Western Architects and City Planners in China*. Translated by Lisa Gardiner and Hester Robinson. Ostfildern, Germany: Hatje Cantz Verlag.

Lung, David. 1999. "The Heritage of Hong Kong Architecture," in Norman Owen et al., *The Heritage of Hong Kong*. Hong Kong: FormAsia, 30–57.

Macau Heritage. 1984. Macao Decree Law no. 56/84/M 1984: Article 14, June 30, 1984. Web. www.macauheritage.net/en/Decree/law5684m.aspx. Accessed August 1, 2015.

Macau SAR Government. 2006. MOG 34/2006 (2006), Chief executive order 248/2006 (Macau SAR Government, Official Gazette). Boletim Oficial da Região Administrativa Especial De Macau, I Série, Suplemento, 15, 16 April 2008, 1062–1063.

Mahadevan, Kuttan. 1994. *Society and Development in China and India*. New Delhi: B.R. Publishing.

Meyer, Michael. 2008. *The Last Days of Old Beijing: Life in the Vanishing Backstreets of a City Transformed*. New York: Walker & Co.

Meyer, Milton. 1994. *China: A Concise History*. London: Rowman & Littlefield Publishers.

Murphy, J. David. 1995. *Plunder and Preservation: Cultural Property Law and Practice in the People's Republic of China*. Hong Kong: Oxford University Press.

Napack, Jonathan. 2000. "The Destruction of Lhasa," *The Art Newspaper* (December).

Owen, Norman et al. 1999. *The Heritage of Hong Kong: Its History, Architecture and Culture*. Hong Kong: FormAsia Books.

Paludan, Ann. 1991. *Images of Asia: The Ming Tombs*. Hong Kong: Oxford University Press.
Pons, Philippe. 2002. *Macao*. Hong Kong: Hong Kong University Press.
Porter, J., 2009. "The Past is Present: The Construction of Macau's Historical Legacy," *History & Memory* 21(1), 66: 84–90.
Qian, Fengqi. 2007. "China's Burra Charter: The Formation and Implementation of the China Principles," *International Journal of Heritage Studies* 13(3): 255–264.
Rosenthal, Elizabeth. 2003. "Vandalism and 'Improvements' Mar Great Wall," *The New York Times*, June 12.
SACH (State Administration of Cultural Heritage) 2009. "Sixty Years of Conservation of Immovable Cultural Heritage," in *The Conservation of Cultural Heritage in China in 60 Years*. Beijing: Beijing Cultural Relics Press; State Administration of Cultural Heritage, 28–44. In Chinese.
Stapleton, Kristin. 2000. *Civilizing Chengdu: Chinese Urban Reform, 1895–1937*. Cambridge, MA: Harvard University Asia Center.
Steinhardt, Nancy S. 1990. *Chinese Imperial City Planning*. Honolulu: University of Hawai'i Press.
Stoddard, Heather. 1997. "The Lhasa Valley and Tibetan Architecture." Paper presented at the conference *The Lhasa Valley: History, Conservation and Modernization in Tibetan Architecture*, November 27–29, 1997, Paris. Meudon, France: CNRS.
Sun, Dazhang. 2002. *Ancient Chinese Architecture: Ritual and Ceremonial Buildings*. Vienna: Springer-Verlag. Previously published in Chinese by China Architecture & Building Press.
Tieben, Hendrik. 2009. "Urban Image Construction in Macau in the First Decade after the Handover, 1999–2008," in T. Chung and H. Tieben (eds.), *Macau Ten Years after the Handover* (Special Issue), *Journal of Current Chinese Affairs* 38(1): 49–72.
Tung, Anthony. 2001. *Preserving the World's Great Cities*. New York: Clarkson Potter.
——. 2003. "Erasing Old Beijing; A Conservation Tragedy," *ICON*, WMF (Fall): 38–43.
UNESCO. 2000. *Proceedings of the Conference "China – Cultural Heritage Management and Urban Development: Challenge and Opportunity," July 5–7 2000, Beijing*. Beijing: UNESCO.
UNESCO. N.d. World Heritage List. Web. www.whc.unesco.org/heritage.htm. Accessed July 15, 2015.
Van Oers, Ron and Francesco Bandarin. 2010. "Managing Cities and the Historic Urban Landscape Initiative – An Introduction," in Ron Van Oers and Sachiko Haraguchi (eds.), *UNESCO World Heritage Papers 27 Managing Historic Cities*. Paris: UNESCO World Heritage Centre.
Vitali, Roberto. 1999. *Records of Tholing: A Literary and Visual Reconstruction of the "Mother" Monastery in Guge*. Dharamshala: Amye Machen.
Wang, J.H. et al. (eds.). 1999. *The Theory and Planning of the Conservation of Historic and Cultural Cities*. Shanghai: Tongji University Press. In Chinese.
Wang, Jun. 2011. *Beijing Record: A Physical and Political History of Planning in Modern Beijing*. Hackensack, NJ: World Scientific Publishing.
Wang, Qijun. 2000. *Vernacular Dwellings (Ancient Chinese Architecture)*. Vienna: Springer-Verlag.
Warr, Anne. 2014. "Shanghai: City of Multiple Viewpoints," *Historic Environment* 26(3): 98–105. Ringwood, Victoria: ICOMOS Australia.
Wei, Chen and Andreas Aass. 1989. "Heritage Conservation: East and West," *ICOMOS Information* 3: 3–8.
Wong, Lori and Neville Agnew (eds.). 2013. *The Conservation of Cave 85 at the Mogao Grottoes, Dunhuang*. Los Angeles: Getty Conservation Institute.
Wong, Yong-tsu. 2001. *A Paradise Lost: The Imperial Garden Yuanming Yuan*. Honolulu: University of Hawai'i Press.
Wood, Frances. 2005. *The Forbidden City*. London: The British Museum Press.
Wright, Arthur F. 1958. "The Cosmology of the Chinese City," in G.W. Skinner (ed.), *The City in Late Imperial China*. Stanford: Stanford University Press.
Wu, Hung. 2013. *A Story of Ruins: Presence and Absence in Chinese Art and Visual Culture*. London: Reaktion Books.
Wu, Liangyong. 1999. *Rehabilitating the Old City of Beijing: A Project in the Ju'er Hutong Neighborhood*. Vancouver, BC: UBC Press.
Xu, Yinong. 2000. *The Chinese City in Space and Time: The Development of Urban Form in Suzhou*. Honolulu: University of Hawai'i Press.
Yang, Xiaoneng (ed.). 1999. *The Golden Age of Chinese Archaeology*. New Haven: Yale University Press.
Yuchen, Enbo. 2000. *The Forbidden City – Former Imperial Palace*. Beijing: People's China Publishing House.
Yunnan (China) Provincial Association for Cultural Exchanges with Foreign Countries. 1999. Leadership Conference on Conservancy and Development. *Collected Works*. Twenty-four booklets. In Chinese.
Zhan, Guo. 1995. "The Particularity of 'Authenticity' in the Conservation of Cultural Property in China," in *Proceedings from the Nara Conference on Authenticity*. Tokyo: Agency for Cultural Affairs, 323–325.
Zhang, Bai. 2002. "On the Development of the Principles for the Conservation of Heritage Sites in China," in *Principles for the Conservation of Heritage Sites in China*. Los Angeles: The Getty Conservation Institute.

Zhang, Donia. 2013. *Courtyard Housing and Cultural Sustainability: Theory, Practice and Product*. Guildford, UK: Ashgate.

Zhang, S. 2008. *An Introduction to Integrated Conservation: A Way for the Protection of Culture Heritage and Historic Environment*, 2nd edition. Shanghai: Tongji University Press. In Chinese.

Zheng, Xiaoxie. 1983. "The Protection of the Characteristics of Historic Chinese Cities," *Jianzhu Xuebao (Architectural Journal)* 12: 4–7.

Zhu, Guangya. 2012. "China's Architectural Heritage Conservation Movement," *Frontiers of Architectural Research* 1(1): 10–22.

Zhu, Lin. 1997. *A Brief History of Chinese Construction Society*. Taipei: Architecture & Culture Publisher.

3

TAIWAN (REPUBLIC OF CHINA)

A number of factors, political and historical, affect the unusual cultural heritage management environment in Taiwan, officially known as the Republic of China (ROC). Many of these relate to the island nation's contentious relationship with its mainland neighbor, the People's Republic of China (PRC). Three classifications of physical heritage make up Taiwan's material culture: indigenous and pre-ROC archaeological sites and structures, European colonial buildings, and its large collection of Imperial Chinese works of art and literature. This collection was moved from the mainland to Taiwan in 1949, at which time the retreating Chinese nationalist party, the Kuomintang, set up their opposition government on the island, formerly known as Formosa.[1] Taiwan's exclusion from the United Nations is mainly due to efforts by the PRC, which still regards the island as a renegade province. This has left the island largely outside the scope of UNESCO, the world's largest heritage conservation organization. Although UNESCO has increasingly been involved in Taiwan through the promotion of cultural programs and helping identify possible World Heritage Sites, the island's marginal status among the world's nations has acted as an isolating factor.

Also specific to Taiwan's peculiar political situation has been its unrelenting drive toward economic development and growth, often at the expense of historic buildings. Unlike Mainland China, Taiwan lacks an extensive history in the form of centuries-old buildings, sites and cities, with most of the development on the island dating to within the last 300 years. Furthermore, because so much of Taiwan's population arrived in a mass political exodus from the mainland, it has been regarded as a temporary home by many of the newcomers who similarly lack personal or cultural connections to the island's inherent cultural heritage. Although these attitudes have been changing in recent years, they initially informed many of the early policy decisions regarding cultural heritage management and, in some ways, stunted the growth of the field into the late twentieth century.[2]

In the context of its complex relationship with the PRC, Taiwan has seen itself not only as a manager of the island's existing built heritage, but as caretaker *in absentia* of the cultural patrimony of Chinese civilization, chiefly from two specific past threats. The first threat was the Japanese war of aggression that began on the mainland in 1938 and the second was the widespread destruction of cultural heritage during the early years of Communism in the PRC, especially later in the 1960s during the Cultural Revolution.

FIGURE 3.1a and b Showing Taiwan's current interest in preserving architecture of all periods, Taipei City's Department of Cultural Affairs restored the Japanese-built, Kishu An Cuisine House dating from 1917, built next to the river in the Guting district of Taipei. The restoration of this Municipal Historical Site entailed saving one of three original buildings, the other two of which were destroyed by fire, and adding a new structure to create a literary center and park, "The Kishu-An Forest of Literature." The project involved multiple community organizations and honors noted modern Taiwanese literary figures, one of whom lived in the structure after World War II.

The defining role of Taiwan's museum collections

The story of modern cultural heritage conservation in Taiwan largely revolves around the dramatic account of the removal of thousands of works of fine Chinese art, furniture and literature from Mainland China to the island, brought by retreating nationalist forces led by General Chiang Kai-shek at the end of World War II. Since that time, the Taiwanese government has lent its considerable resources to the conservation and presentation of these items, most prominently at the Palace Museum in the capital, Taipei. Partly due to the singular focus of these efforts, conservation of existing buildings, sites and other historical materials in Taiwan somewhat lagged until legislation and other organizational frameworks were established in the last two decades of the twentieth century.

The preservation of China's cultural heritage from the political upheavals of the mid-twentieth century by moving it from place to place in hundreds of crates is one of the most remarkable efforts at rescuing cultural heritage in the history of the field. The complexity of the operation even exceeds the cultural heritage rescue efforts in Russia during World War II. In order to accomplish this remarkable feat, the government of the Republic of China, as represented by the Academia Sinica (which today serves as Taiwan's foremost academic institution), the Palace Museum in Beijing, the Central Museum of Nanking, and the Central Library and the Provincial Museum of Honan collected and crated artifacts ranging from the Yin and Chou dynasties (1401–219 BCE) to the collections of the Manchu emperors in the Palace Museum. The collections remained on the move, first to Nanking and then to Shanghai, throughout the 1930s. When the Marco Polo Bridge Incident ignited war with Japan in 1937, these items, together with the collections of the Academia Sinica and the Provincial Museum of Honan, were shipped again to Sichuan. After the war, as Chinese Communists took over Mainland China, all items were shipped by order of Chiang Kai-shek to the Central Museum in Taipei, and they form the core of its famous collection today. Approximately 65,000 items from the Central Museum and the Palace Museum in Beijing alone were removed to Taiwan, with tens of thousands of items of all kinds taken from other museums. A still untold number of items also left the Mainland in the hands of private collectors.[3]

This dramatic sequence of events still affects cultural heritage management in Taiwan, placing an unusual emphasis on museums as the primary drivers of Taiwanese identification with their heritage. Taiwan's first museums in a modern sense date to 1868, and by 1936, one year before Japan started its war of aggression, there were seventy-seven museums, fifty-six art galleries and forty-two other depositories.[4] Since the establishment of the ROC, various museums and institutions have worked diligently to acquire, document, preserve and present Chinese cultural heritage from all periods in the new nation of Taiwan.

During the 1950s a number of museums opened in Taipei to receive and display various collections that were once housed on the Mainland. In 1966, in response to the Cultural Revolution on the Mainland, the Taiwanese government initiated a program of "Chinese Renaissance," which celebrated traditional culture and culminated in the opening of the new National Palace Museum in Taipei that same year. The new building is modeled after the Imperial Palace in Beijing, a situation consistent with the Taiwanese government's quest to reclaim the lost heritage of the Mainland.[5]

Despite the emphasis on the display of objects in museums, significant efforts have been made in Taiwan to preserve architectural heritage sites, such as colonial buildings, the cultural center of Tainan and early examples of Taiwanese vernacular architecture. Among the best examples of colonial architecture in Taiwan are Dutch, Spanish and British colonial military and administrative buildings at Tamsui (New Taipei City) dating from the sixteenth century through the late nineteenth centuries. One of the largest Neolithic archaeological sites in the Pacific Rim, the 2,000 to 5,000-year-old Peinan Culture Site, exhibits the artwork and monoliths of the aboriginal peoples in Taiwan. Of more recent genesis, the island of Kinmen, with its massive military infrastructure of tunnels and bunkers along with traditional clan villages, exhibits one of the earliest defensive strongholds set up by the newly established ROC against assaults from the Mainland. Other historic structures from the period of Japanese colonization beginning in the late nineteenth century include such feats of engineering as mountain railways and the establishment of Chinkuashih, a massive mining community in northeast Taiwan, abandoned in 1971.[6]

FIGURE 3.2 The herculean effort to remove thousands of historic works of art, furniture and literature from the People's Republic of China by retreating nationalist Kuomintang to the Republic of China (Taiwan) was perhaps the largest art repatriation effort of all time. This image of some of the 2,972 crates of artifacts being transported in the late 1930s shows part of the circuitous shipping effort by road, rail and water via Nanjing and Hong Kong across the Taiwan Strait arrived on three ships in 1948.

Taiwan has ample legislation for the protection of its cultural heritage, though most of it is aimed at the protection of objects. Early conservation laws dating from 1909 and 1930, when the island was still part of Mainland China, form the basis for protective legislation in the ROC. The Measures for the Protection of Ancient Sites and Law for the Preservation of Ancient Objects (1909) established definitions of and protections for historic sites and objects and proposed an early organization of institutes charged with the preservation of cultural patrimony.[7]

In the early twenty-first century, Taiwan took significant steps towards shoring up a national framework for legislative protection and management of all kinds of cultural heritage. The Cultural Heritage Act, updated in 2002 from an earlier version, allocates jurisdiction for Historic Site designation, requirements for listing, and management guidelines for the ongoing care of historic buildings and sites. The Taiwanese Department of the Interior handles the registration of historic sites and structures, and along with local authorities, classifies them at the national, special-municipality, county or city level. Privately owned designated structures are eligible for up to a 50 percent reduction in land-value or building taxes under this law, providing some incentive for owners to cooperate or actively seek listing for their properties.[8]

Once designated, historic structures fall under the jurisdiction of the Council for Cultural Affairs, which together with the Department of the Interior, Ministry of Education, Ministry of Economic Affairs and local authorities puts together a conservation management plan. Designated historic sites remain under the control of the Ministry of the Interior. The Ministry of Education assigns permits for archaeological excavations and manages the process by which artifacts and other objects are registered, documented and presented.[9]

The Commission of Cultural Affairs, which is headed by a cabinet-level official that reports directly to the Prime Minister, leads heritage preservation activities in Taiwan. Since its creation in 2002 the National Center for Research and Preservation of Cultural Properties has handled project planning and implementation, documentation, training and research programs from its offices in Tainan City.

FIGURE 3.3 Fort Santo Domingo in Tamsui overlooking the Taiwan Strait was originally erected by the Spanish as a wooden fort in 1629. After their expulsion by the Dutch East India Company it was rebuilt as San Antonio in 1644. From 1683 to 1867 it operated under Qing dynasty Chinese rule but has changed hands several times since. It was most recently used by the British until 1972. In 2005 the fort was reopened after rehabilitation of the Victorian-era residential portion of the site now referred to as the Former British Consular Residence. Items on display at the fort and residence present the shared heritage of Taiwan.

Taiwan's Japanese colonial industrial heritage

At the conclusion of the Sino-Japanese War in 1895, the island of Taiwan was ceded to the Imperial government of Japan, which remained in control until after World War II. This occupation coincided with a steep spike in the industrialization of the Japanese economy, making timber- and mineral-rich Taiwan an important center for mining and logging in the early twentieth century. Much physical evidence of this period still exists in Taiwan, including monumental rail systems and large-scale mining communities. Although timber harvesting and mining continued after the establishment of the ROC, market forces and environmental concerns largely closed the industries in the 1970s and 1980s, but architectural remnants of the era still remain.

Taiwanese conservation authorities have recently begun to document, preserve and promote these industrial heritage sites towards further developing the country's tourist economy. The Alishan Mountain and Old Mountain Line Railways, both former timber trains built by the Japanese on the steep slopes of Taiwan's highlands, have been identified as potential World Heritage Sites based on their innovative engineering, historic significance and scenic surroundings. Similarly, the old mining community of Chinkuashih in northern Taiwan, abandoned since the 1970s, contains workers' housing, heavy machinery and mine shafts from nearly eighty years of copper and gold extraction by the Chinese, Japanese and Taiwanese. In 2001, a plan to re-interpret the area as a tourist attraction, museum of the mining industry, and center for geological studies was implemented by local authorities in an effort to preserve the singular industrial legacy of early twentieth-century Taiwan.[10]

FIGURE 3.4a and b The establishment of Chinkuashih mining town in Jueifang Township after the discovery of gold in the region in 1889 is an engineering marvel that today is interpreted by the Taipei County's Cultural Affairs Bureau as Gold Ecological Park. One of the most productive sources of gold, copper and other precious metals in the world, the site was mined by tens of thousands of workers until it was closed in 1987. Now a popular attraction, with its interpretative display allowing visitors to touch a 220 kg pure gold ingot extracted from the site, Chinkuashih is also a site of conscience having associations among the Taiwanese of ethnic divisions and antipathies experienced there under Japanese colonial rule. During World War II 400 to 500 British and Commonwealth prisoners of war worked and died there under forced labor conditions.

The establishment of the Center marks a strong level of commitment on the part of the Taiwanese federal government to preserve significant historic buildings and sites of various periods and types throughout the island.[11]

At the local level, Taiwan's cities, towns and villages have made numerous efforts toward preserving some of the characteristic communities on the island. For example, in 1987 the Lukang Cultural Preservation & Local Development Promotion Center conducted a study focusing on the architectural and handicraft heritage of this mid-sized central west-coast city. Once a vibrant trading port and artisan community, Lukang rose in prominence during the eighteenth century, only to decline in the late nineteenth because of harbor silting and the disinterested Japanese colonial administration. In an effort to foster awareness of this brief moment of importance, and of the city's distinctive architecture and urban development pattern, the Lukang Preservation Center studied the historic architecture and recommended dozens of its courtyard residences, temples and narrow mercantile streets for conservation or reconstruction. Concurrently, the handicraft tradition of Lukang was revived, contributing to a tourist economy and heritage awareness advocacy within the community.[12]

On the importance of the ordinary, by Lake Douglas

Much attention in academic, political and social spheres has been given over the last century or so to the value of architectural and cultural preservation, its relevance to contemporary life and its importance to the human experience. We identify structures and places of cultural relevance and we mark them, document them and celebrate their contributions to a collective past, even though it is not always clear *whose* past it is we're celebrating. We mount campaigns to "save" iconic structures from demolition, sometimes with creative, contemporary uses in mind and sometimes not, and we mourn when structures are "lost" by pressures of economic development, benign neglect or, most recently, acts of "cultural terrorism." Indeed, those who seek international political attention have only to obliterate an ancient pile of stones as at Palmyra – already, in fact, a fragmentary ruin of a former existence – to cause an immediate uproar and subsequent condemnation.

Regardless of culture or geographic location, quite often the collective histories and people chosen for commemoration are those who commanded the most resources, who distinguished themselves in their professions (or on the fields of battle), and who set in motion acts that changed the course of history, whether architectural, cultural, political, economic or social. Often it is an association of historical figures with artifacts (including structures) that creates an appreciation of the importance – and therefore survival – of built works, thereby enabling preservation over time through patronage and widespread public acceptance of these artifacts as objects worthy of study: "George Washington slept here" (allegedly) and therefore the structure in which he stayed is enshrined on the US National Register of Historic Places.

Without much thought, we ascribe value, represented by historical importance and cultural relevance, to the biographies and built works of the rich and powerful few but we routinely neglect consideration of the unknown many who facilitated the creation of the artifacts or events we study. Perhaps it is human nature to seek out the best and celebrate the prime examples of periods and artistic movements, creating "icons" that are frozen in time, enclosed in gilt frames, and separated from their cultural context, physical surroundings and the often unknown hands that made them. Philosopher Michel Foucault astutely observed that power controls discourse, and in the case of cultural conversations in general (and particularly in my field of garden history) the discourse has been more about the artifact (a designed garden or landscape) as an object, independent of its context, rather than about the artifact as an expression of its time and place, as an object reflecting society, nature, economics, material culture and numerous other influences.

When considering cultural conservation and how we should approach ascribing value, we must remember that places and objects of cultural significance are not just those associated with power or those connected to our personal heritage. Nineteenth-century colonial binary social constructs and implied value systems of "West" (Occident) vs. "East" (Orient) and "us" vs. "them" will not work in twenty-first century multi-cultural global social, political and cultural economies. Alternative approaches to the culture of place, proposed by twentieth century philosophers and historians of the French Annales School (Emanuel Le Roy Ladurie), American cultural geographers (John Brinckerhoff Jackson), international post-colonial theorists (Edward Said), and even novelists (Paul Scott) offer important clues to how we might better understand and appreciate cultures and civilizations different from our own. These alternative perspectives have relevance for all interested in the culture – and preservation – of place and avenues for fruitful explorations and discussions.

The challenge for all interested in cultural preservation, regardless of our origins, backgrounds or particular areas of historical or thematic interest, is to look under the surface, behind the façade and beyond the powerful, thereby gaining an understanding and deeper appreciation of "the other." Where are, for instance, the Chinese and Cambodian equivalents of Ladurie's *The Peasants of Languedoc* and how would they inform our understanding of the evolution of Asian culture? What about the appreciations of Jackson's "truck stops and bus stations" (the name undergrads gave his seminar at Harvard) in Thailand and Indonesia, and their impacts on contemporary life and social systems in those countries? How can we apply geographer Derek Gregory's observations about America's involvement in Afghanistan and the Middle East, post-September 11, 2001, rooted firmly in Said's writings? And what can we learn from Paul Scott's *The Raj Quartet* about cultural transitions from colonial to post-colonial societies that can inform how we approach cultural preservation in newly industrializing countries and expanding global economies?

Clearly we must become literate in multiple approaches to cultural preservation. We must extend our appreciation of what is studied and valued beyond that with which we are already acquainted, and we must redefine our research agendas outside the accomplishments and people already established in traditional readings of history. We must consider that there may be more to appreciate in the quotidian than in the iconic, the celebrated and the famous. With the explosion of multinational corporations and the cookie-cutter outlets now populating the world, we must study – and celebrate – the everyday (and, perhaps at first glance, insignificant) fabric of life. Characteristic uses of colors and materials, calligraphic gestures and graffiti, foodways and social systems, spatial typologies, vernacular eccentricities (both architectural and landscape), and linguistic patterns define indigenous cultures, record human existence, and fill in the blanks between the icons of history. It is these details that separate one place from another.

As responsible citizens of today's international community and students and stewards of cultural expressions, we have two tasks: first, we certainly should continue to study and learn from the iconic and the unique, but we must also acknowledge that there is equal significance in the ordinary, everyday details of human expression. And second, we must become acquainted with the lives and cultural contributions of "the other," learning *about* them and *from* them. And in so doing, we record and preserve culture, thereby enabling "them" to become part of "us."

Further reading

Gregory, Derek: *The Colonial Present: Afghanistan, Palestine and Iraq* (2004).
Jackson, John Brinckerhoff: *Landscapes* (1970); *The Necessity for Ruins* (1980); *Discovering the Vernacular Landscape* (1984).
Ladurie, Emanuel Le Roy. *The Peasants of Languedoc* (1974); *Montaillou: Cathars and Catholics in a French Village, 1294–1324* (1978).
Said, Edward: *Orientalism* (1978).
Scott, Paul: *The Raj Quartet* (1974).

Recent efforts to revive and preserve Taiwanese handicraft traditions have been joined by a focus on the indigenous heritage of the island. Before the arrival of Chinese from the Mainland in the fifteenth century, Taiwan was largely populated with Austronesian peoples who may have migrated there as early as 6,000 years ago. The Tao, another Austronesian group that arrived from Philippine Batan Island several centuries ago, has successfully maintained many cultural traditions, such as boat building, ritual ceremonies, folklore and residential architecture styles. The Tao community is concentrated on Orchid Island, about seven kilometers off the southwestern Taiwanese coast, and the regional cultural heritage authority is working with the community to record and preserve its traditions. Orchid Island has also been identified as a potential World Heritage Site, should Taiwan join the United Nations in the future.[13]

The perpetually sensitive question of Taiwan's relationship to the Mainland has also resulted in some distinctive contributions to the nation's historic structures. The former military enclave of Kinmen Island, which lies just 2 km off the Mainland coast, is home to numerous military installations, traditional villages and a system of underground tunnels constructed to shelter defensive command centers. After cross-Strait tensions eased in the mid-1990s, Kinmen opened up as a national park and tourist attraction, preserving and exhibiting its once off-limits military infrastructure and traditional residential communities. Although the product of a legacy of sometimes-violent conflict between the two nations, Kinmen nevertheless stands as an important architectural site significant to the histories of both countries.[14]

In recent years, Taiwan's government has begun to take an extraordinary leadership role in conserving cultural patrimony and engaging the public. Although a nationalist sentiment and an effort to validate the causes and existence of the breakaway republic motivates these efforts, so too does a genuine desire to preserve the island's own cultural attributes. As Taiwan and Mainland China continue to work toward a permanent solution to the question of their relationship, cultural heritage will continue to factor into the equation, just as it did in the establishment of the ROC in 1949. To some extent, these circumstances have led to a superior level of care and management of all forms of physical cultural heritage under the protection of the government of Taiwan. By directing the resources of an increasingly prosperous national economy to organizations such as the National Center for Research and Preservation of Cultural Properties and the National Palace Museum, the government of Taiwan is moving toward a more promising future for conservation of all its cultural heritage, despite the uncertain political realities.

FIGURE 3.5a and b Taiwan's Orchid Island was settled by the Tao, an ethnic minority group who migrated from the Batan Archipelago 800 years ago. The traditional lifeways of the Tao changed little until restrictions to the island's access were lifted in 1967 and modernization began to have its effects. It remains an example of living heritage and has been identified as a potential World Heritage Site, should Taiwan join the United Nations in the future.

Notes

1 The large number of Imperial Chinese objects brought to Taiwan by the Chinese Nationalist Party has been put forth by the present government of Taiwan as a legitimizing factor supporting its claim that it is the keeper of the real heritage of China, waiting to reclaim the Mainland from its alleged illegitimate Communist government.
2 Ellen Lapidus. "Taiwan Warms to Preservation." *Preservation News* 27(1) (February 1987), 6.
3 Eugene Y.C. Wang. *Preservation of Cultural Heritage in the Asia and Pacific Region*. Proceedings of the first ASPAC Seminar on the Promotion of Cultural and Social Co-operation in the Asian and Pacific Region (Seoul, May 19, 1969), Cultural and Social Centre for the Asian and Pacific Region. (Seoul: Hollym Corp. Publishers, 1971), 106.
4 Ibid., 90.
5 Jane Ju. "The National Palace Museum, Taipei." Paper delivered at a symposium on Conservation Issues in China and Taiwan, Columbia University, New York, April 2, 2004.
6 International Organization of Folk Art. "World Heritage Days." 2002. Web. www.iov.org.tw/english/event_2002/event200209.htm. Accessed September 2, 2004.
7 Lin Zhu. *A Brief History of Chinese Construction Society*. (Taipei: Architecture & Culture Publisher, 1997), 124.
8 Government of the Republic of China. "Cultural Heritage Act." 2002. Web. http://wh.cca.gov.tw/en/documents/documents_1.asp?documents_id=1. Accessed September 2, 2004.
9 Ibid.
10 International Organization of Folk Art. "Legend of the Gold City." 2002. Web. www.iov.org.tw/english/event_2002/photo2002_09/event200209b.htm. Accessed September 2, 2004.
11 National Center for Research and Preservation of Cultural Properties. "About the NCRPCP." 2002. Web. www.ncrpcp.gov.tw/ncrpcp13.htm. Accessed September 2, 2004.
12 Han Pao-Teh. *Lukang, Taiwan: Its Background, Architecture and Handicrafts*. (Taipei: Lukang Cultural Preservation & Local Development Promotion Committee and the Asia Foundation, 1987), 84–91.
13 International Organization of Folk Art. "Orchid Island." 2002. Web. www.iov.org.tw/english/event_2002/photo2002_09/event200209c8.htm. Accessed September 2, 2004.
14 International Organization of Folk Art. "Kinmen: Taiwan's Front Gate." 2002. Web.www.iov.org.tw/english/event_2002/photo2002_09/event200209c10.htm. Accessed September 2, 2004.

Further reading

Chen, K.-T. 2004. "Excavated Ceramics of Taiwan: Some Issues," *Field Archaeology of Taiwan* 9 (1/2): 137–165.
Chuang, Fang-jung, Huang Su-chuan, and Wu Shu-ying. 1987. *Historical Sites of the First Rank in Taiwan and Kinmen*. Taiwan: Council for Cultural Planning and Development.
Council for Cultural Affairs, Republic of China. 2009. *Encyclopedia of Taiwan*. Web. http://taiwanpedia.culture.tw/en/knowledgetree. Accessed July 12, 2012.
Cultural Affairs Council of the Ministry of Culture, Republic of China. 2005. Cultural Heritage Preservation Act. Taipei: R.O.C. Laws and Regulations Database. Amended November 9, 2011. Web. http://law.moj.gov.tw/Eng/LawClass/LawAll.aspx?PCode=H0170001. Accessed May 18, 2016.
Dawdy, S.L. 2010. "Clockpunk Anthropology and the Ruins of Modernity," *Current Anthropology* 51(6): 761–793.
Gonzalez-Ruibal, A. 2008. "Time to Destroy: An Archaeology of Supermodernity," *Current Anthropology* 49(2): 247–279.
Government of the Republic of China. 2002. "Cultural Heritage Act." Web. http://wh.cca.gov.tw/en/documents/documents_1.asp?documents_id=1. Accessed September 2, 2004.
Gross, M. 2006. "Going to Taipei," *The New York Times*. Web. http://travel.nytimes.com/2006/02/12/travel/12going.html. Accessed February 12, 2006.
Ju, Jane. 2004. "The National Palace Museum, Taipei." Paper delivered at a symposium on Conservation Issues in China and Taiwan, Columbia University, New York. April 2, 2004.
Lapidus, Ellen. 1987. "Taiwan Warms to Preservation," *Preservation News* 27(1) (February 1987): 6.
Lee, I.-C. 2007. "The Formation of Military Dependent's Village Culture and Mainlanders' Identities: The Study on Renher-village in Tainan County (1950–2007)." Master's thesis, Department of History, National Cheng Kung University, Tainan, Taiwan.
Lucas, G. 2004. "Modern Disturbances: On the Ambiguities of Archaeology," *Modernism/modernity* 11(1): 109–120.
——. 2005. *The Archaeology of Time*. London: Routledge.

Luo, Y.-L. 1991. "Chuan-ts' (Military Dependent Villages): Definition and Redefinition of the Spatial Meaning." Thesis, Graduate Institute of Building and Planning, Taiwan University, Taipei.

National Center for Research and Preservation of Cultural Properties (Taiwan). 2002. "About the NCRPCP." Web. www.ncrpcp.gov.tw/ncrpcp13.htm. Accessed September 2, 2004.

Taipei Tang-Bu Cultural Association. 2002. "What is TangBu?" Web. www.ttbca.org.tw/english/index.htm. Accessed August 18, 2012.

Tang, Y.-H. 2004. "The Culture and Ethnic Identity Changes of Shui-Jiao Military-dependent Villagers." Thesis, Graduate Institute of Taiwan Culture, National University of Tainan, Taiwan.

Wang, Eugene Y.C. 1969. *Preservation of Cultural Heritage in the Asia and Pacific Region*. Proceedings of the first ASPAC Seminar on the Promotion of Cultural and Social Co-operation in the Asian and Pacific Region (Seoul, May 19, 1969), Cultural and Social Centre for the Asian and Pacific Region. Seoul: Hollym Corp. Publishers (1971), 106.

Zhong, X. 2009. *Project of Restoration and Reuse of the Historical Building of Hukou Military Dependents' (Second) Village in HsingChu County*. HsingChu County: HsingChu County Government.

Zhu, Lin. 1997. *A Brief History of Chinese Construction Society*. Taipei: Architecture & Culture Publisher.

Restored Building Eave, Danyang, South Korea.

4

SOUTH AND NORTH KOREA

As is the case in neighboring China and Japan, Confucian and Buddhist traditions and holding ancestors in high esteem drives the architectural conservation ethic on the Korean peninsula. From the early Three Kingdoms period (57 BCE–668 CE) onwards, regulations pertaining to the protection and restoration of Buddhist temples existed, alongside efforts to conserve ancestor-related objects of worship.[1]

Outside forces have since ancient times factored significantly in the development of the peninsula's built environment. Invaded over the centuries by Chinese, Mongol and Japanese military forces, the Korean peninsula's cultural heritage reflects numerous foreign influences, in addition to its indigenous architectural styles, traditions and innovations. The twentieth century in particular involved multiple foreign interventions, including the Japanese occupation from 1910 until 1945, partition into North and South Korea, and a multi-national war involving Chinese, Russian and American forces that still weighs heavily on the region to this day.[2]

FIGURE 4.1 The elegantly proportioned, fifteenth century Deoksugung Palace in Seoul is representative of palace complex architecture of the Joseon dynasty (1392–1897) that uses the *pungsu* principles of integrated landscape, architectural and geographical design.

Traditional Korean architecture: a nearly lost heritage

The Korean peninsula's earliest traces of architecture are found in Paleolithic dwellings of rock shelters, caves and portable shelters that may date to as early as 30,000 BCE. Among the earliest surviving constructed buildings are the Koguryo tombs in the Pyongyang region that date from the third century BCE to the seventh century CE, a timeframe that includes the Three Kingdoms period. The rich tradition in Korean architecture dates to this era and was consistent in terms of design concepts, style, quality and ambition with that of neighboring China. Since this period, Korean design principles have been informed by Chinese Confucianism and *feng shui* (known as *pungsu* in Korean), although there were regional refinements that distinguish it. These include distinctive aesthetics in roof designs and the uniquely Korean ways of heating residential and communal buildings by radiant floor heating utilizing *ondol*, an underfloor heating system.[3] Other distinctively characteristic traditional Korean architectural precepts include soundly built, well-proportioned buildings having subtly curved roof edges, intricate interior designs, and efficient town planning designs that are especially mindful of the relationships between built forms and natural features.

Royal properties such as palaces and administrative buildings are among the most finely designed and richly appointed architecture on the peninsula, in addition to its noteworthy array of elaborate military fortresses. Religious temples and shrines, such as the thirteenth century Geukrakjeon temple in Andong, South Korea, were designed and constructed with great care, helping them to last for centuries.

Despite the Korean peninsula's remarkably long and varied history, relatively little of its traditional architectural heritage remains today, mainly due to three tumultuous periods, which since the early twentieth century have affected the country's built environment: the period of Japanese occupation from 1910 to 1945, the Korean War years from 1950 to 1953 and the subsequent post-war years, during which time widespread urban modernization and economic expansion was achieved at considerable cost to its traditional built heritage.

During the era of Japanese occupation Korea's royal palaces, Joseon royal family tombs, estates, government buildings and fortresses were especially targeted for removal or major alteration and re-purposing. For instance, the fourteenth century Gyeongbokgung Palace in Seoul, South Korea, which is the largest Joseon dynasty palace, was partly dismantled and relocated by the Japanese imperial government, and its General Building was constructed in front of the main sector of the Palace.

Other monumental structures were extensively remodeled such as the seventeenth century Gyeonghuigung Palace, also in Seoul, which was used as a middle school and primary school for Japanese students in the early twentieth century. According to Peter Bartholomew, president of the Royal Asiatic Society and a board member of the National Trust in Korea, of all the lesser royal palaces that existed between 1518 and 1945 there were only a few left by 2013.[4] Under the Japanese, new and replacement architecture was mainly built in European styles, frequently at the expense of traditional Korean architecture. These buildings still elicit negative associations for some in North and South Korea to this day, with many having been removed, and major reconstruction campaigns launched to undo the damage of the occupation period.

The Korean War entailed widespread damage, both intended and collateral, throughout the affected regions of North and South Korea. As was the case during World War II, modern warfare methods destroyed large swathes of the peninsula's towns, villages and settlements. Approximately five million soldiers and civilians lost their lives in a conflict that remains highly divisive on the Korean peninsula and in the larger geopolitical context beyond.

Following the partition, development and modernization in the Republic of Korea (South Korea) began in earnest. Since the early 1960s, losses to its surviving built heritage have been both extensive and thorough. Over the relatively short period of thirty years, conservation advocate Peter Bartholomew estimates that the number of traditional Korean homes has shrunk from 800,000 to 7,000 today.[5] For instance, a 2013 survey found that the total numbers of *hanoks* (traditional residential buildings) in Seoul decreased from around 130,000 in 1960 to 12,594 in 2013. Many losses are attributable to recent activity, with the number of hanoks reduced by approximately half between 2002 and 2013.[6] Another ardent advocate for preserving traditional Korean architecture is British expatriate David Kilburn who has been particularly concerned with hanoks in Seoul. In 2005, Mr. Kilburn launched a website to chronicle demolitions in the city of Seoul's designated hanok protection zones. According to his estimation, by 2010 the number of hanoks had fallen to fewer than 900 from about 1,600 in 1985.[7]

Throughout the rest of South Korea, of an estimated 350 walled towns and villages that had existed, only a handful remain.[8] Bartholomew estimates that 97 percent of historic traditional buildings have been lost and that 99 percent of all the country's palaces have been destroyed, with nearly all of Korea's earlier government centers now gone.⁹ Almost more worrisome than these statistics, according to Bartholomew, is the fact that deleterious effects of war, occupation and foreign influence during most of the twentieth century broke cultural traditions such as the passage of design and construction techniques down through generations.

As great as the loss of Korea's traditional architecture has been, there has been since the early 1990s a growing interest and commitment on the part of government and architectural conservationists to retain and conserve what can still be saved of Korea's architectural past. Local concern and notice of contemporaneous developments in heritage conservation in other parts of Asia, mainly China, has had an effect. Many remedies often lie in reconstruction, entailing disassembly and reassembly either *in situ* or *ex situ* or reconstruction *de novo*. As discussed elsewhere in this volume, reconstruction has long been practiced in East Asia with the blessings of heritage agencies and conservation professionals alike; in many cases on the Korean peninsula there exist few alternatives if vanished examples of the country's architectural history are to be experienced, studied and celebrated.

Noted writings from Korean architectural conservationists have called for a need to re-evaluate the importance of authenticity in restoration, reconstruction and other conservation projects. In an article titled "East Asian Values in Historic Conservation" in the British *Journal of Architectural Conservation*, Seung-Jin Chung, a professor in the Department of Architectural Engineering at Hyupsung University in Hwaseong, South Korea, writes that in contrast to some of the tenets of the Venice Charter of 1964 that are fundamentally based on European values and attitudes, East Asian conservation principles reflect the spiritual and naturalistic sensibilities of their culture and architecture.¹⁰ In questioning the Western conservation philosophy that stresses the aesthetics and authenticity of monuments Chung argues that while this is recognized as well in Eastern conservation philosophy more should be taken into account. Issues to also consider include the social and environmental context, in particular, building in harmony with nature, spiritual "messages" and meanings associated with the site, and a recognition that some historic Asian architecture is planned from the standpoint of a world (cosmological) conception and includes considerations for royal hierarchical planning, belief systems of Confucianism and Taoism, I Ching philosophy, astronomical determinations and the yin–yang principle.¹¹ He cites as proof of the viability (and acceptability) of reconstruction retaining all prior values the Throne Hall of Gyeongbokgung Palace in Seoul, built in 1395, destroyed in 1592–1598 Japanese invasions, and reconstructed in 1867 where in addition to the reconstruction returning all the physical and spiritual values of the building, its building siting relationships were re-instated.¹² This example points to the powerful appeal of reconstructing important lost examples of the past and also the longevity of the concern for doing so.

Chung summarizes by saying there is a case for a new charter that takes as its starting point the principle of conveyance of spiritual messages, the principle of conservation applied to settings within the natural environment, and the principle of conservation applied to complexes of buildings.¹³ His idea, in the light of other leaders in Asian conservation theory, had constructive effects on global views of architectural conservation practice. (See also the Nara Principles, China Principles and the ICOMOS Xi'an Declaration in Chapters 1 and 2.)

This tumultuous recent history has influenced the practice of architectural conservation on the Korean peninsula in several ways. Perhaps most significant has been the division of North and South Korea in 1945, with the former entering the twenty-first century governed by an isolationist, autocratic regime that restricts its population's access to foreign information and influence. North Korea's long period of isolation and steady economic decline have resulted in a minimally developed modern heritage conservation infrastructure, with only limited scholarship concerning its important sites. In contrast, over the past seventy years South Korea's modern, Westernized market economy has developed along lines similar to that of Japan. South Korean architectural conservation practitioners are part of a global community, and encounter many of the same opportunities and challenges as are presented to other developed countries such as Taiwan, Singapore and Japan.

Despite the stark differences of their present-day approach to heritage conservation, the two Koreas share the same legislative roots. The first conservation legislation for Chōsen (the Japanese name for the Korean peninsula) was written by the Japanese in the early twentieth century. An early initiative to document and conserve Korean cultural heritage was begun immediately prior to the Japanese occupation, and lasted from 1902 to the last days of the Joseon dynasty in 1910.¹⁴ Japanese officials

FIGURE 4.2
Reconstruction in 1867 of the Throne Hall of Gyeongbokgung Palace, originally built in 1395 and destroyed in the 1590s, continues the intentions, techniques and spirit of its original builders. A subsequent restoration campaign spanned 2000–2003.

hired to help with the effort remained in place during the initial years of their occupation, at first acting under the 1916 Rules on Ancient Sites and Relics Preservation, which addressed only individual sites and movable heritage artifacts.[15] The aims of the Act were to regulate archaeological and art historical research; provide funding for conducting scientific excavations, the systematic collection of Korean art, the building of museums, the restoration of relics and monuments; enforcement of customs laws governing the export of Korean antiquities; and the establishment of academic committees, research institutions, and municipal offices responsible for the identification, protection, transportation and promotion of Korean art and culture.

In 1933, the Preservation of Korean National Treasure, Historic Sites and Natural Monuments Act replaced the earlier legislation that prescribed certain repair practices and incorporated important natural sites. This period remains highly controversial today due in particular to concerns that inventories established under the law led to illegal excavations and the export of cultural treasures out of Korea to Japan during this period.[16]

Architectural conservation in North Korea

Since the withdrawal of Japanese colonial forces and subsequent occupation by the Chinese Army in 1945, the architectural conservation movement in northern Korea (known after 1948 as the Democratic People's Republic of Korea, or North Korea) has taken its own course. Following more than sixty years of militarization, collectivization and isolationist dictatorial rule, few practices and processes for conserving significant cultural heritage have developed above the 38th parallel, the national boundary that separates North and South Korea. The Democratic People's Republic of Korea Law on the Protection of Cultural Property (1994) and its Regulations (2009) govern heritage protection at the national level, which are administered by the National Bureau for Cultural Property Conservation (NBCPB). Despite North Korea having the Korean Cultural Preservation Centre and a system of nationally designated monuments, little scholarship conducted within the country has been externally distributed and few international exchanges of advanced heritage protection knowledge have taken place.

FIGURE 4.3 The UNESCO World Heritage listed tomb of King Tongmyong (58–19 BCE), located 20 km (12 miles) south of Pyongyang, North Korea, is one of sixty-three individual tombs believed to belong to the ancient Goguryeo Kingdom.

The situation changed in 2004, however, when the South Korean Cultural Heritage Administration, in conjunction with UNESCO, announced plans to assist in a conservation project focusing on a complex of ancient Koguryŏ (Goguryeo) tombs located in Pyongyang, North Korea, and its surrounding provinces, which had been designated as World Heritage Sites earlier that year. Italian, Japanese, Chinese and South Korean experts all contributed to the effort to conserve the tombs and their 1,500-year-old wall paintings, a project that indicated the North Korean government was becoming more receptive to allowing international participation in their system of cultural heritage management. Similarly, UNESCO's emphasis on recognizing diverse world heritage, including lesser-known sites such as the North Korean tomb complexes, hoped to connect the isolated government to current conservation practice, technology and peer exchange. In 2013 the historic monuments and sites of Kaesong, twelve separate components that testify to the history and culture of the Koryo dynasty from the tenth to the fourteenth centuries CE, were inscribed on the World Heritage List. Laid out using principles of geomancy (the auspicious arrangements of buildings on a site), the former capital city of Kaesong, including remains of its palaces, administrative buildings, tomb complex and defensive walls and gates, embody the cultural, political and spiritual values of a crucial era in the region's history.[17]

Given its joining the World Heritage Convention in 1998, with two sites listed on the UNESCO World Heritage List by 2013 and five others having been proposed on the Tentative List, it is clear that the Democratic People's Republic of Korea is taking increasingly serious steps toward conserving at least its most noteworthy architectural heritage, as illustrations of the Korean peninsula's distinguished cultural past and for the prestige it brings the country.

Architectural conservation in South Korea

After World War II, the military government of the US occupational forces guided the management structure for South Korea's cultural heritage. The Former Royal Household Affairs Office was initially set up to manage the Joseon dynasty's movable and immovable cultural heritage, a collection of resources that represented the bulk of documented Korean cultural patrimony. In 1961, eight years after the end of the Korean War, that office was folded into the newly established Bureau of Cultural Properties, which itself was part of the South Korean Ministry of Education. The following year, a new Cultural Property Protection Act went into effect. Along with the National Museum (established in 1908) the Bureau of Cultural Properties took up the task of managing and conserving South Korea's heritage.[18]

Despite the administrative overlap between South Korea's Bureau of Cultural Properties and the Museum administrative systems, the 1962 legislation was surprisingly inclusive in its designated areas of protection. Its amended tenets form the basis for the present-day legislation called the Cultural Heritage Protection Act (*Munhwajae Bohobeop/Daehan Minguk Munhwa Jaecheong:* Cultural Heritage Administration) that was last updated in 2015. Administered by the Cultural Heritage Administration (CHA) based in Daejeon, the Act describes several types of heritage: nationally designated, locally or provincially designated, movable objects (treasures), heritage sites (scenic, natural and historic), intangible heritage and folklore material. The legislation also provides protection for "undesignated cultural heritage," defined as resources determined as worthy of protection but not yet formally listed. South Korea places a strong emphasis on the preservation of intangible cultural heritage, which includes activities such as traditional crafts, dance, music and cuisine. The designation of "living national treasures" is an important function of the legislation, and underscores the importance placed upon recognizing, celebrating and perpetuating traditional skills and practices in South Korea.[19] Although the legislation's protective provisions extend from buildings to dramatic productions, and from traditional clothing to *pansori*, a form of music, the Cultural Property Protection Act nevertheless had its limitations. For instance, the Act set the cut-off for age designation at prior to the period of Japanese occupation (1910–1945), a decision that left many early Western-style buildings out of the range of protection. Also, no provision existed in the law for protecting contextual buildings, cultural landscapes, historic vistas or historic districts.

In order to address these shortcomings, the Traditional Building Preservation Act was enacted in 1984 to direct an expanded focus towards the larger built environment. Its scope encompassed vernacular and contextual architecture, architectural districts and measures for building surveys and documentation standards.[20] This revision responded not only to the limitations of the 1962 legislation, but also to the widespread destruction of built heritage that coincided with South Korea's modernization boom that began in the 1960s. Although surveys taken after the Korean War (1950–1953) indicated that the majority of individual sites were protected under government ownership, contextual and vernacular buildings were being lost at a rapid pace, as was the case in much of the world during the economic expansion of the 1960s. The government of South Korea repealed the Traditional Building Preservation Act in 1999, and undertook a series of revisions, the most recent of which dates to 2012.

The 1990s were notable for another series of administrative shifts in South Korea's heritage management infrastructure, as well as for the creation of additional categories of protected structures and conservation incentives. The Cultural Properties Administration was briefly transferred to the Ministry of Culture, Sports and Tourism, then in 1999 elevated to the status of an independent agency, the Cultural Heritage Administration.[21] The reorganization also emphasized a two-tiered system of management, under which cultural properties were divided into nationally or locally designated cultural properties. South Korea's central government established a system of tax breaks and subsidies for the owners of designated properties.[22] Along with the subsidies, a system of technical assistance through the central government is also provided for nationally designated structures, while the responsibility for maintaining locally designated properties rests with local governments.

The current organization of the CHA reflects a broad and sophisticated view of heritage management and its associated disciplines, as well as South Korea's unique heritage types and regional histories. The CHA oversees three bureaus, each focused on heritage policy, conservation and promotion, and under which are various divisions that concern topics including intangible cultural heritage, historic cities, and the management of royal palaces and tombs. The CHA also manages a number of heritage management institutions, including the Korea National University of Cultural Heritage, which aims to bring a knowledgeable and skillful workforce to the field, as well as the National Research Institute of Maritime Cultural Heritage, the National Palace Museum, the National Intangible Heritage Center, and the National Research Institute of Cultural Heritage (NRICH).[23] The NRICH, for its part, consists of administrative divisions dealing with archaeology, natural, artistic and cultural heritage, as well as conservation science. Five national research institutes concentrating on regional heritage fall under the NRICH, along with the country's Cultural Heritage Conservation Science Center.[24]

A network of non-governmental organizations (NGOs) complements the CHA and its various activities, including the National Trust of Korea, a membership organization that conducts heritage advocacy programs and raises funds to purchase, preserve and present cultural and natural heritage properties. Founded in 2000 and modeled after the British National Trust, the Korean Trust has acquired seven properties ranging from individual traditional residential buildings to endangered plant and animal habitats. The Trust aims to secure twenty properties by 2020 as a means of expanding its scope of protection and participation in the national conservation movement.[15]

Despite the expansion of the South Korean governmental and NGO heritage conservation infrastructure during the 1990s, advocates and professionals alike have criticized the field for a bias against buildings constructed during and after the period of Japanese occupation. In 1999, the destruction of the Gookdo Theater, built in 1936 and was one of the architectural treasures of the Early Western building style, galvanized this issue, and triggered the creation in 2001 of a designation category for Early Modern Buildings by the Cultural Heritage Administration. This development also signaled the growing role of various local NGOs that were advocating for the conservation of local landmarks and significant buildings left out of the government system. In one watershed case, a group of local activists rallied to the defense of a collection of 1950s missionary houses located near the Hannam University in Daejeon. The buildings, which represented a transitional architectural style that blended traditional Korean building techniques and Western interior plans, had been neglected by government heritage protection organizations. The group ultimately succeeded in convincing the university to purchase the buildings' site for use as a public park. This organizational success transitioned in 2007 into a nationwide organization known as the Green Trust devoted to environmental conservation and sustainability that supports projects through its Green Climate Trust Fund.

FIGURE 4.4 Conservation of a collection of 1950s missionary houses located near the Hannam University in Daejeon, which reflect a blend of Korean traditional crafted exteriors and Western, in particular American, style interiors.

A story with perhaps wider implications in the balance between development plans, public opinion and architectural conservation involves a 1990 government plan to construct a high-speed train route linking Seoul, the South Korean capital, with Pusan, the country's largest port and its second largest city. As originally planned, the train route ran through the center of the ancient Silla Kingdom[26] city of Gyeongju, a city of 300,000, that is home to thirty-two state-level designated historic monuments and twenty-three historic sites, including a World Heritage Site: the eighth-century Seokguram Buddhist Grotto and Temple of Bulguksa complex. After five years of negotiations with public opposition groups, scholars and Ministry of Culture officials, the train was re-routed around Gyeongju at great expense to the financiers. The decision underscored the compromises involved between economic expansion and architectural conservation in Korea, which is increasingly coming into balance following the late twentieth century development boom, as well as the heightened organizational heft of public opposition groups in favor of conservation measures.[27]

Challenges of urban conservation in South Korea

Urban conservation in South Korean cities has nevertheless remained a difficult task, owing to the traditional morphologies of the urban environment, increased real estate pressures and conflicts with planning and development needs. Like Beijing's *hutong* neighborhoods, many traditional South Korean city and townscapes consist of densely packed, one-storey courtyard homes on irregular lots separated by narrow lanes in hanok districts. The primarily wood and masonry buildings that comprise this urban vernacular architecture do not easily lend themselves to modern adaptations or the incorporation of amenities or utilities, and as a result, there is a dearth of urban conservation districts consisting of hanoks in South Korea. Protected built heritage of cities and towns more often occurs on an individual building or site-specific basis.

One notable case involves South Korea's capital and largest city, Seoul. In 1976, the city government designated a traditional hanok residential sector known as Bukchon (North Village) as a traditional landscape district. Originally an aristocratic neighborhood with buildings dating to the late Joseon period, many of the residences had been inadequately maintained, subdivided, removed in favor of larger modern structures or abandoned. In a situation familiar to urban conservation efforts the world over, the hanok district had become undesirable due to a combination of public perception that the buildings were inadequate and substandard, and local government planning decisions that incentivized the creation of new, more dense buildings at the expense of retaining the historic, low-scale neighborhood.[28]

In response to this unfortunate situation, beginning in 2000 a grassroots citizens movement partnered with the municipal government to pilot a conservation program for the Bukchon district, focusing on a program to directly incentivize residents to undertake conservation measures on their own properties. The program included subsidies such as loans and grants for repairs to traditional buildings that have averaged 25 percent of the total cost of rehabilitation. Between 2001 and 2011, building owners registered 501 hanoks with the program and completed restoration on 342 buildings, with over US$9.5 million in subsidies dispersed.[29] Additionally, the city purchased properties from owners who wished to sell their houses and then rents them to individuals and groups for use as museums, traditional inns or studios. The program succeeded in thoroughly revitalizing the Bukchon district and its hanoks, making it a prime tourist destination in Seoul and earning recognition in 2009 by UNESCO Bangkok's Asia-Pacific Awards for Cultural Heritage Conservation program. A subsequent master plan for Seoul dating from 2004 recognized several surviving pockets of traditional urban residential buildings, however, little protection is afforded and plans were made for redevelopment known as *jaegaebal*. A few hanoks have been saved since though Korean urban preservationists still face challenges buttressed by developers and property owners that older buildings are outdated, inconvenient, expensive to maintain and in the way of making the higher profits afforded by replacement buildings.[30]

Despite ongoing challenges, the years of advocating for the preservation of remaining hanok districts has begun to generate results. The success of the Bukchon conservation program has spawned similar incentive programs for traditional property owners in villages, such as Hahoe and Yangdong, located in Andong, North Gyeongsang province. The successful rehabilitations of the old homes have revived interest in hanoks and other traditional forms of architecture in Seoul and beyond. Sensitively rehabilitated hanoks can be rented at noticeably higher prices, although the struggle to save such elements in the urban cultural landscapes of Seoul and other Korean towns having the same opportunities may be almost too late with demolition remaining a likelihood in the light of increasing development and economic pressures. (See also sections on *hutong* and *shikumen* conservation in Beijing and Shanghai, Chapter 2.)

Against the background of Korea having lost so much of its built heritage through wars and modernization since the early twentieth century, there remain the difficulties of safeguarding landmarks against accidents, vandalism and other more prosaic yet no less destructive threats. The fourteenth-century Namdaemun Gate, officially called Sungnyemun (the Gate of Exalted Ceremonies), and among the most revered architectural sites in the country, might have survived its arson attack on November 10, 2008 had there been fire alarms, sprinklers, a security system or guards, all of which were apparently lacking.[31] In December 2010 fire also destroyed the 1,300-year-old Cheonwangmun, a major wooden structure at Busan's Beomeo Temple. Hwaseong Fortress, a World Heritage Site, has also been damaged by fire. In addition there is the usual list of other threats to architectural heritage, with some, such as vandalism, being new, that also warrant taking precautions, especially for the nation's most valued treasures.

c

FIGURE 4.5a, b and c Views of Cheonggyecheon, a creek flowing through downtown Seoul, in 1961 (a) and in 2005 (b). The rehabilitated stream was opened to the public following completion of a major urban renewal initiative along its bank. The project entailed removal of an elevated highway and restoration of two historic bridges. The fifteenth-century Supyo stone or Water Mark Bridge was relocated in 1958 and again in 1965 to its present location in a restored landscape setting over the Cheonggyecheon (c).

FIGURE 4.6a and b The 550-year-old Namdaemun Gate (a) was restored between 2010 and 2013, work that was required as a result of an act of arson in 2008 (b).

South Korea's intangible heritage list

The Korean 961 Law of 1962 covers folklore considered to be national cultural heritage and was amended in 1970 to include individuals (*ingan munhwajae*) deemed to be human or living cultural heritage. Between 1961 and 1968 Go Sangnyeol, then-director of the Cultural Heritage Administration, surveyed South Korea for intangible cultural properties and interviewed old master craftsmen. The first items to be inscribed on the intangible heritage list were taken from these initial surveys, and later others were added based on the opinions of researchers and also those of winners of the annual folk tradition competitions. The recommendation of local administrations was also sought.[32]

Major stakeholders of the intangible heritage program are designated as "living national treasures" or officially, "holders" (*boyuja*), individuals who possess knowledge or skills essential for preserving Korean culture. Some of these "holders" have obtained significant national exposure or fame. For example, Han Bongnyeo, a holder for the Korean royal court cuisine, supervises the authentic presentation of Joseon dynasty food in historical movies and television series.[33]

The UNESCO Convention for the Safeguarding of the Intangible Cultural Heritage was established in 2003 and South Korea joined the program a year later. In 2005 China declared about 1,200 properties as intangible cultural heritage, including sixteen items belonging to a Korean minority living in that country. These included the traditional wedding ceremony, *Arirang* (a folk song) and *nolttwigi* (a traditional seesaw game). The CHA decided that they also would benefit from broadening the scope of intangible heritage to properties that do not have any designated "holders," like *kimchi*, *hangul* (since the fifteenth century the official alphabet of South and North Korea) or Goryeo ginseng (Korea's prominent ginseng).[34] In 2011 the CHA opened its National Intangible Heritage Center (NIHC) in Jeonju, which hosts performances and promotes education along with the perpetuation of both Korean and international intangible heritage. The large facility (59,930 square meters or 645,100 square feet), which was constructed at a cost of US$66 million, represents a significant commitment to the promotion and protection of intangible heritage that stands out both within Asia and in the world beyond.[35] (See also Conserving Intangible Heritage in Chapters 1 and 2 on Japan and China.)

New design in heritage contexts, by William Chapman

Appropriate new design in heritage contexts has always been problematic. This applies to new buildings in historic streetscapes or placed in vernacular landscapes, additions to historic buildings, protective and interpretive features at monumental archaeological sites, and insertions into older structures. There is no universal agreement on the best approach to these problems. Some designers opt for the "conservative approach," selecting architectural features that mimic historic surroundings. Others choose contrast: new architectural designs that somehow complement existing forms and historical and/or visual contexts. Both approaches, of course, have their pitfalls. Historicist designs have a way of cheapening the historic buildings they are meant to balance. Overtly modern architecture can overpower what is around it. Often too, new architecture – both imitative and contemporary – can cause irreparable damage both to individual structures and sites.

A new building or design's scale has much to do with the appropriateness of the intervention. A small, simple addition to a small vernacular building almost invites a traditional design. A massive new wing for a large commercial or institutional building seems always to call for greater creativity, probably on a scale comparable to the level of design intent of the original structure. The relative sophistication of the new design has much to do with the quality of the final product. So too does the budget: nothing succeeds less well than a cheap addition to a grand historic building.

Asia is relatively new to the idea of contextual design. Residents of older towns and villages typically followed precedent, gradually substituting new materials as they became available such as the use of galvanized metal or concrete tile, to replace thatch or ceramics, concrete instead of mud brick for walls, and so on. Much new construction over the past half century has been concentrated in Asia's rapidly expanding cities. There new, multi-storey buildings pushed aside older shops and courtyard houses, the latter the basic building block of much of China.

Traditional design, nonetheless, continues to hold sway among religious buildings. Chinese temples, Thai, Laotian and Cambodian monasteries, Hindu temples, and the region's many mosques all retain elements recognizable to the populace. Only the materials have changed: substitute porcelain tiles now serve as floors; sheet metal roofs and aluminum doors enclose now air-conditioned spaces; concrete, instead of brick, forms the supporting outer walls.

In the context of repair and maintenance age-old designs have often remained in favor. Thus the continued use of embedded porcelain for Chinese temples, both in China and throughout Southeast Asia, or the renewal of paint coverings for Indian temples. These practices are so prevalent, in fact, that even the heritage establishment, in the guise of UNESCO and other international arbiters of heritage practice, accepts duplication and/or renewal as an appropriate treatment for historic preservation projects. (This is noticed in the UNESCO Asia-Pacific Awards for Cultural Heritage Conservation, a program in place since 2000. Among the early winners are several Chinese temples that required complete resurfacing to restore their original appearance. See also The Power of Example: UNESCO Asia-Pacific Heritage Awards program in the Introduction.)

Official restrictions on design practice are not generally favored in Asia. Most large cities, with the exception of Singapore, and more recently Penang and Melaka (Malacca), do not support design review. Residents of Thailand see architectural choice as a constituent of democratic freedom. The same is true in many other Asian countries, including China, India, Pakistan and most of Southeast Asia as well. Patina, so appreciated in Western tradition, often means simply mold and poor maintenance in much of Asia. Nuances of texture, surface character and materials are unappreciated as they might be in the West; clean and neat is typically the byword for attractive.

Concrete has become the predominant building material in most of the region. Traditional materials, such as the mud brick common in much of South Asia, from India to Afghanistan, has fallen from use with the proliferation of concrete masonry units (CMU). Safety, at least in earthquake-prone areas, is also an issue; mud brick often performs very badly in seismic events, reinforcing the idea that concrete is a superior material. In urban contexts, concrete has quickly won out over materials such as wood and stone, both for its cheapness and the fact that it is readily available.

In addition, few Asian architects have been exposed to ideas of context in design. There are important exceptions, especially at the high end of design. Charles Correa, Geoffrey Bawa, I.M. Pei and other Asian architects have certainly infused aspects of culture and some overriding reference to place and history into their architecture. The same was true of Cambodia's best-known modern architect, Vann Molyvann, whose work of the 1950s and 1960s has received increasing attention in recent years. However, the average locally trained architect in China, India, Pakistan or Indonesia usually has more practical matters to consider. "Heritage context," to use a high-minded concept, is rarely one of these.

Many heritage-type projects have tended to fall back on replicative design, whether undertaken by Asian or international architects. The several additions to the Raffles group properties, including the Raffles Hotel in Singapore and the Royale in Phnom Penh, Cambodia, are frank celebrations of historicism. The Singapore hotel even includes a two-storey shopping arcade with features inspired directly by the late nineteenth century hotel, all part of its US$160 million redevelopment under Architects 61 and Bent Severin and Associates in 1989–1991. A similar nostalgia is integral to other historic hotel developments in the region. The early twentieth century Railway Hotel in the beach resort of Hua Hin, Thailand, also received a new wing undistinguishable from the old one during its redevelopment in 1989, a project overseen by US-trained Thai architect Bundit Chulasai.

An alternative to historicism has been a kind of cultural architecture that attempts to honor tradition and culture. The Angkor National Museum in Siem Reap, constructed by the Thai-owned Vilailuck International Holdings company in 2007, cites the towers and arcades of Angkor Wat as its predominate design motifs. Criticized by Cambodians for its relatively steep entry fee, the museum is little distinguishable from the many heritage-inspired hotels that have proliferated in the provincial town since the reopening of the Angkor Archaeological Park in the 1990s. (Images of the face of the Bayon temple and other ancient Khmer references are common in house and modest guesthouse and restaurant design as well, reinforcing the forced historicism of much design at the site.)

In other contexts, more direct evocations of the past have been attempted. Chiang Mai, Thailand's Dhara Dhevi Hotel, a property of the Mandarin Oriental Group and developed in 2005 by Thai entrepreneur Suchet Suwanmongkol, shocked many for its direct evocation of temple and palace architecture, both long considered sacred to Thais. Designed by architect Rachen Intawong, the Dhara Dhevi includes a bar in a temple *mondop*, towers based on designs for northern Thai and Burmese monasteries, and a resident population of grounds-keepers dressed in traditional costume.

The many newer hotels at the World Heritage city of Luang Prabang, Laos, similarly draw their design inspiration from traditional buildings. Following guidance offered through UNESCO's Maison Du Patrimoine (Heritage House), hotel developers have replicated the plaster-covered masonry of traditional Lao-Vietnamese shophouses, inserting culturally inspired wood fretwork to further the illusion of history. At the recently opened Hotel de la Paix, a project built within the footprint of the historic Ban Mano Prison, the developer surgically removed evidence of the old facility's architectural evolution to create a version of traditional Laotian culture, with accompanying arcaded pavilions and reflecting pools.

Such designs are examples of a long-standing tradition of romanticism in the region, a predilection engendered in part by foreign visitors and residents. Post-war expatriate and silk merchant Jim Thompson (1906–1977) helped initiate an appreciation for Thai culture through his late 1950s reassembly of older wood houses for his canal-side Bangkok dwelling. This practice continues throughout Asia as other foreign residents seek out historic buildings, converting them to residences and shops, in ways often perplexing to local people. Scholar Darryl Collins has recently completed a complex of Cambodian houses in Siem Reap, moving derelict properties to a single site for a new purpose. Other important examples include recent interventions in Pondicherry on India's southeast coast and Fort Galle in Sri Lanka, where foreigners and local residents share in the revitalization of the historic site for enjoyment and tourism development.

It is likely that what might be called "scenography" will continue to prevail in Asia's heritage efforts, especially those aimed at the tourism market. From re-workings of Shikumen (Stone Warehouse Gate) housing in Shanghai for luxury retail outlets to new "Indo-chic" hostelries in the French colonial hill-town of Dalat in Vietnam, contrived versions of the past answer to important cultural and economic motives. These kinds of architectural evocations of the past are not purely for foreign consumption. Asiatique, a 2012 riverfront development in Bangkok that houses some 1,500 shops and forty restaurants facing the Chao Phraya, suggests a historic warehouse district, much like a festival marketplace in Boston or Baltimore. Although occupying the site of the former East Asiatic Company pier, nearly all of the development is new, combining ersatz and authentic in ways that are confusing to the average visitor. Notably, it is as popular with Thai urbanites as it is with foreign visitors.

A significant window into trends in Asian design and attitudes to the past is found in the results of the UNESCO Asia-Pacific Heritage Awards program. Initiated by the Bangkok regional office in 2000 to encourage better-quality design and conservation practice in the region, the Asia-Pacific Awards give emphasis to reuse and restoration. But there are also examples of new design in the form of additions and insertions, and, after 2005, a separate "Jury Award" for innovative new design in heritage contexts.

Much of the new design reflects additions for new functions. Elevators, alternative entrances and provisions for accessibility are typical new elements. Few projects, however, include substantial new additions. A 2002 Award of Merit was the CHIJMES, a reuse project in Singapore incorporating the chapel and ancillary structures of the former Convent of the Holy Infant Jesus. To accommodate new retail space and parking needs the project architects, Ong & Ong Architects and Didier Repellin Architects, created a sunken courtyard and hidden parking structure. The substantial renovation of the Catholic Church of the Immaculate Conception in Hong Kong (a Honourable Mention awardee in 2003), by project architect Anna Kwam and others, involved the significant insertion of new lighting and sound systems, with little change to historic fabric. Similar conservatism was evident in the rehabilitation of the Suzhou River Warehouse in Shanghai (Honourable Mention 2004), a project requiring the judicious removal of timber floors and the introduction of new stairs and skylights. Supervised by owner and architect Teng Kun-Yen the intervention aimed to demonstrate the reuse potential of industrial buildings in a city that had up to then ignored them.

The Jury Awards provide perhaps better insights into the direction of architectural practice. The first was awarded in 2005 to the Meridian Gate Exhibition at the Palace Museum (known popularly as the Forbidden City) in Beijing. Designed by a team led by architect Lang Hongyang, the project consisted of the insertion of a high-tech steel and glass cube within the highly ornamented southern entrance to the palace. A second commendation went to the Yuhu Primary School, a restrained wood and stone primary school located in a picturesque southwestern Chinese village. Designed by Li Xiaodong, in cooperation with the National University of Singapore, the design was meant to complement and not compete with traditional village structures.

A high-tech infill design at the Whitfield barracks in Hong Kong won the Jury Commendation in 2007. Its new facilities overseen by the Architectural Services Department for the Special Administrative Region of Hong Kong, the early twentieth century Whitfield barracks now hosts a Heritage Discovery Center. A two-storey, transparent block provides a minimalist enclosure for gallery spaces and new circulation. In 2008, the Jury awarded its commendation to a contemporary steel and glass addition to a privately owned Singapore bungalow. The award citation recognized the sensitivity of the architects, Eng Yew Hoon and Ang Gin Wah, to historic materials and the careful attention the siting, noting that the "sensitively designed extensions provide a counterfoil to the original, classically inspired building."

Subsequent awards have reinforced these themes. The Maosi Ecological Demonstration Primary School (a 2009 awardee), situated in a vernacular rock-cut village in northwest China, showed sensitivity to material and siting. In 2011, the commendation was shared by a reconstructed communal house in a round (circular)-building village in Sichuan, China and an educational center spanning an archaeological site in Sydney Harbour, Australia. The year 2012 awarded a reading room for the Portuguese School of Macau, a simple pavilion inserted into the space of the original building.

In 2014, the UNESCO award program changed the title of the new design projects from the "Jury Commendation of Innovation" to "New Design in Heritage Contexts." UNESCO's aim is to strengthen the award category and to better define the program's intentions and thereby increase the number of entries. It is evident too, that the program wants to consider both additions to existing buildings and architecture and design that promote a sense of cultural context in the broadest sense.

Contextual design does occur in Asia but often not in the framework of explicit heritage efforts. Vietnamese architect Yo Trang Nghia's bamboo structures evoke traditional rural architecture in profoundly poetic ways. His "WNW bar" (water and wind bar) in Binh Duong Province, Vietnam of 2009 suggests a village hall but serves a commercial purpose. Chinese architect Wang Shu's design for the Ningbo Museum of Contemporary Art (2001–2005) recalls a waterfront warehouse, connecting visitors to movement of waters and riverine commerce. A second project, the Xiangshan campus of the China Academy of Art in Hangzhou (2002–2004), relies on traditional materials and forms. He thoughtfully situates the campus buildings into the hilly landscape, employing water features suggestive of an ancient Chinese garden. His Ningbo History Museum (2003–2008) evokes an archaeological site, the stratigraphy of its outer brick and stone walls simulating layers of time.

Dissident architect Ai Weiwei similarly evokes a sense of place in his designs for artists' studios in Caochandi (2004–2006). Utilizing the dark gray brick of Beijing, he instills a timeless urban quality in his simple block-like buildings and courtyards. Although he eventually stepped away from the project, Ai provided the initial inspiration for the Beijing Olympics' National Stadium (2007–2008), the birds-nest design that spoke of China to many.

Probably no other contemporary designer better understands the idea of cultural and historic context than Japanese architect Kengo Kuma. His Bato Hiroshige Museum in Nakagawa (2009) embraces traditional Japanese ideas of structure and tectonics, while conveying a sense of timeless simplicity. His Great (Bamboo) Wall House near Beijing (2002) provides a visual and tactile contrast to the nearby Great Wall. In his Asakusa Culture Center he educes the essence of historic shops, stacked one above the other. With the Yusuhara Marche, a small hotel and market, Kuma employs thatch panels as awnings, recalling rural farm dwellings and small-town shop fronts. And on Korea's Jeju Island, he has created an artful complex of resort residences clad in wood and capped by roofs of volcano stone.

The work of Kuma and other contemporary architects demonstrates that contextual design is alive in Asia. The challenge is to bring this sensitivity more directly into the closer orbit of heritage efforts. UNESCO has done much to call attention to special places. It is now time for Asian architects and others working in the region to better integrate new design into places of special historic and cultural value.

The Republic of Korea (South Korea)'s strong federal system of cultural heritage management helps mitigate development pressures on local governments, although administrative overlap and bureaucratic inefficiencies affect the national system. At the same time, a weak local-level architectural conservation infrastructure compromises the efficient management of historic resources, since most decisions still need to go through a central government office. The scope of activities undertaken by the CHA remains substantial, however, and South Korea's dedication to supporting its own, along with global, intangible heritage is noteworthy and an admirable contribution to the field. As a signatory to various international charters and conventions, home to twelve World Heritage Sites, and possessor of a robust governmental system for cultural heritage protection, growing economy and activist population, South Korea is well poised to improve management of its architectural heritage and in step with the regional leaders in architectural conservation.[36]

FIGURE 4.7a and b The work of Kengo Kuma at Lotte Jeju Resort on Jeju Island exemplifies the rich potential of new architectural designs in the manner and context of other traditional buildings. He is one of several architects who contributed designs to the Lotte Jeju Resort housing development that is comprised of mostly organic forms and materials.

Notes

1. Kyoung-ho Chang. "Cultural Property Preservation and the Effects of Preserving Traditional Buildings as a District," *Architecture and Environment* 57 (May 1998), 72–75.
2. The Korean War (1950–1953) was an especially violent and destructive conflict involving United Nations forces led by the United States of America aiming to combat perceived threats resulting from the spread of Communism. The USA fought alongside South Korea, while China, assisted by the Soviet Union, fought with North Korea, resulting in a July 1953 truce that partitioned the peninsula at the 38th parallel. As of 2016, political differences between North and South Korea remain unresolved.

3 The *ondol* radiant floor heating practice dates to at least 698 CE, during the Baekjae Dynasty, as borne out by archaeological evidence. Recent excavations show early types of ondol that date to the third–second century BCE in North Okjeo, a tribal state located in the northern Korean peninsula. For more information, see Robert Bean and Kwang Woo Kim, "Part 1: History of Radiant Heating & Cooling Systems," *ASHRAE Journal* 52(1) (2010), 40; Kiho Song, *Ancient Heatng System Kang of Northern Okjeo, Goguryeo and Balhae*. (Seoul: Seoul National University Press, 2006).
4 Peter Bartholomew, "Catastrophic Losses to Korea's Architectural Heritage," lecture given at the Royal Asiatic Society, Korean Branch, 2013.
5 Larisa Epatko, "Saving History: South Korea's Preservation Dilemma," *PBS News Hour Blog*, January 21, 2011. Web. www.pbs.org/newshour/rundown/south-korea-preservation/. Accessed October 26, 2015.
6 Yongchan Kwon, Saehoon Kim and Bonghee Jeon, "Unraveling the Factors Determining the Redevelopment of Seoul's Historic Hanoks," *Habitat International* 41 (October 2013), 280–289.
7 John M. Glionna. "A Foreigner's Battle to Preserve South Korea's Hanok Houses," *Los Angeles Times*, October 17, 2010.
8 Ibid.; Bartholomew.
9 Glionna; Bartholomew.
10 Seung-Jin Chung. "East Asian Values in Historic Conservation," *Journal of Architectural Conservation* 1 (March 2005), 55.
11 Ibid. 62, 64.
12 Chung also cites as an early example of reconstruction the rebuilding of Kyeonghoe-ru pavilion at the Gyeongbokgung Palace dating from 1492 on its original site in 1867, p. 61.
13 Ibid. 69.
14 Japanese rule of Korea as a protectorate in1905 and its annexation in 1910 was the culmination of a process that began with the Japan–Korea Treaty of 1876. The Joseon dynasty began in 1392.
15 Kang Woobang, "Managing Cultural Heritage of Korea and its Measures," *Proceedings of the Tenth Seminar of the Conservation of Asian Cultural Heritage*. Tokyo: National Research Institute for Cultural Properties (2003), 19.
16 Shin Bum Shik. "Korea," in Mario T. Gatbonton (ed.), *Preservation of Cultural Heritage*. (Seoul: Hollym, 1971), 130.
17 Historic Monuments and Sites of Kaesong, World Heritage List Inscription, July 2012. Web. http://whc.unesco.org/en/list/1278. Accessed October 17, 2015.
18 Kang, 21. The legal framework of cultural heritage preservation is based on the number 961 Law of 1962 (Munhwajae Bohobeop), which in turn is based on the similar Japanese Act of 1950. The Korean Act is broader in scope, also extending to folklore. The act was amended in 1970 to include individuals (*ingan munhwajae*) considered to be "human cultural heritage."
19 Cultural Heritage Administration of Korea. "Regarding the Administration of Cultural Heritage." 2015. Web. http://jikimi.cha.go.kr/english/qa/faq_02_01.jsp?mc=EN_08_01. Accessed February 23, 2016.
20 Sohyun Park Lee. "A Proposal for the Preservation of Early Western Architecture in Seoul, Korea." Master's thesis, University of Oregon, 1990.
21 Cultural Heritage Administration of Korea. "About the CHA: History." 2015. Web. http://english.cha.go.kr/english/about_new/history.jsp?mc=EN_02_05. Accessed February 20, 2016.
22 Under the Special Local Taxation Act, property tax on real estate designated as cultural heritage shall be exempted. Property tax on registered cultural heritage assets shall be reduced by 50 percent.
23 Cultural Heritage Administration of Korea. "Organization." 2015. Web. http://jikimi.cha.go.kr/english/about_new/organization.jsp?mc=EN_02_06. Accessed February 20, 2016.
24 The regional branches of the National Research Institutes of Cultural Heritage concern the cultures and ancient kingdoms of the Buyeo, Gaya, Naju, Jungwon and Gyeongju. National Research Institute of Cultural Heritage. "Organization." 2015. Web. www.nrich.go.kr/english_new/nrich/organization.jsp. Accessed February 20, 2016.
25 The National Trust of Korea. 2015. www.nationaltrust.or.kr/eng/sub_01.asp. Accessed February 20, 2016.
26 The Silla dynasty ruled the Korean peninsula from 57 BCE until 935 CE.
27 Kim Young Hoon. "The Conflicting Logic of Development and Conservation: A Korean Experience." *Proceedings from the Seventh Seminar on the Conservation of Asian Cultural Heritage* (Tokyo: Tokyo National Research Institute of Cultural Properties, 1998).
28 Project Profile: 2009 Award of Distinction, Hanok Regeneration in Bukchon. UNESCO Bangkok Asia-Pacific Awards for Cultural Heritage Conservation. 2009. Web. www.unescobkk.org/culture/wh/asia-pacific-heritage-awards/previous-heritage-awards-2000-2013/2009/award-winners/2009dt2/. Accessed February 20, 2016.

29 Indera Syahrul Mat Radzuan, Yahaya Ahmad and Song Inho. "A Rethink of the Incentives Programme in the Conservation of South Korea's Historic Villages," *Journal of Cultural Heritage Management and Sustainable Development* 5(2) (2015), 183.
30 Ibid.; Bartholomew. According to Bartholomew, as of 2012 90 percent of Seoul's hanoks have been destroyed since the 1960s.
31 Kim Rhan. "Poor Security Blamed for Gate Burnout." *The Korea Times*. February 11, 2008. Web. www.koreatimes.co.kr/www/news/nation/2008/02/117_18720.html. Accessed February 20, 2016.
32 Suh Heun-gang and Ahn Hong-beom. "Fifty Years of Endeavors for Preservation and Transmission," *Koreana*. Web. www.koreana.or.kr/months/news_view.asp?b_idx=2243&lang=en&page_type=list. Accessed October 10, 2015.
33 The Cultural Heritage Administration. "Heritage Conservation in South Korea." Web. https://en.wikipedia.org/wiki/Heritage preservation in South Korea. Accessed October 26, 2015.
34 Ibid.
35 Ibid.
36 As of 2016, South Korea has twelve cultural and one natural World Heritage Sites, with fifteen sites added to the tentative list, and eighteen items have been registered as UNESCO intangible cultural heritage.

Further reading

Barnes, Gina L. 1993. *China, Korea and Japan: The Rise of Civilization in East Asia*. London: Thames and Hudson.
Chang, Kyoung-ho. 1998. "Cultural Property Preservation and the Effects of Preserving Traditional Buildings as a District," *Architecture and Environment* 57 (May): 72–75.
Chung, Seung-Jin. 2005. "East Asian Values in Historic Conservation," *Journal of Architectural Conservation* 11(1) (March), 555–570.
Gatbonton, Mario T. (ed.). 1971. *Preservation of Cultural Heritage: Australia, China, Japan, Korea, Malaysia, New Zealand, Philippines, Thailand, Vietnam*. Seoul: Hollym.
Han, Sang Woo. 2001. *Cultural Heritage Management in South Korea*. Unpublished PhD thesis, University of Minnesota.
Kang, Woobang. 2003. "Managing Cultural Heritage of Korea and its Measures," in *Proceedings of the Tenth Seminar of the Conservation of Asian Cultural Heritage*. Tokyo: National Research Institute for Cultural Properties, 19.
Kim, Kwang-Joong. 2001. "Realities of Urban Conservation in Korea," *Urban Morphology* 5(2) (2001): 118–119.
Kim, S.S. et al. 2007. "Assessing the Economic Value of a World Heritage Site and Willingness-to-Pay Determinants: A Case of Changdeok Palace," *Tourism Management* 28(1) (2007): 317–322.
Kim, Young Hoon. 1998. "The Conflicting Logic of Development and Conservation: A Korean Experience," in *Proceedings from the Seventh Seminar on the Conservation of Asian Cultural Heritage*. Tokyo: Tokyo National Research Institute of Cultural Properties.
Korean Overseas Information Service. 2004. "Symposium on Preservation of Goguryeo Tombs due October 25–28." Web. http://www.korea.net/pda/newsView.asp?serial_no=20041022018&part=106. Accessed November 1, 2004.
Lee, Sohyun Park. 1990. "A Proposal for the Preservation of Early Western Architecture in Seoul, Korea." Unpublished Master's thesis, University of Oregon.
North Village Preservation Office of Seoul City. 2000. Web. http://Hanok.seoul.go.kr/. Accessed November 1, 2004.
Rii, H.U. 2002. "Seoul, Republic of Korea: Removing the Reminders of Colonialism," in William Logan (ed.), *The Disappearing "Asian" City: Protecting Asia's Urban Heritage in a Globalizing World*. Hong Kong: OUP China, 74–87.
Seth, Michael J. 2011. *A History of Korea: From Antiquity to the Present*. New York: Rowman & Littlefield Publishers.
Shik, Shin Bum. 1971. "Korea," in Mario Gatbonton (ed.), *Preservation of Cultural Heritage*. Seoul: Hollym, 130.

5

MONGOLIA

Mongolia, a vast, sparsely populated nation, occupies a strategic landlocked position between China and Russia.[1] It has relatively few permanently settled areas and is one of the last countries in the world with a substantial and vibrant nomadic population and culture. Once a dominant power on the Asian – and indeed global – stage during the age of Chinggis (Genghis) Khan and the Yuan and the Qing dynasties, Mongolia has more recently been subject to the influences of its more powerful neighbors. The country suffered particularly turbulent times during a brutal period of cultural repression from 1936 until 1938 under Marshal Khorloghiyin Choibalsan, the leader of the Mongolian People's Republic, and again in the 1950s under his successor President Yumjaagiin Tsedenbal. During these periods, and particularly in 1937, much of the built religious heritage of Mongolia was destroyed and its traditional culture was persecuted.[2]

Despite its recent hardships, Mongolia has profoundly influenced the history of Inner Asia over the centuries. Various confederations of Turkic and other pastoral people banded together to govern the Mongolian steppe through the first millennium CE, until the Mongols rose to power in the twelfth century and established a dominant regional presence. The great Chinggis Khan conquered all of Mongolia by 1206 CE, establishing a feudal system of military governance that ultimately facilitated his conquest of most of Asia and eastern most Europe later in the thirteenth century. After the death of Chinggis Khan, his grandson Kublai Khan overran China in the late thirteenth century CE, becoming the first ruler of the Yuan dynasty.[3]

During the rule of Kublai Khan, the historical connections of Buddhist communities in both Tibet and Mongolia were strengthened, facilitating the transfer of building and artistic traditions to east Central Asia. It was at a later period, however, during the seventeenth century CE that Mongolian art and culture reached its zenith. The first Bogd Khan (a spiritual leader for the Mongolian people), Zanabazar, was a celebrated monk and statesman, as well as one of the great artists of Mongolia. One of his successors, the eighth Bogd Khan (1911–1924), built the Bogd Khan Palace Complex in what is now the capital Ulaanbaatar; he became a theocratic ruler under the Manchu domination of Mongolia. Today, it is a museum housing collections of items that belonged to the Bogd Khans. After alternating conflicts between China and Russia in the early twentieth century, the reign of the last Bogd Khan ended and a new government was created, modeled as a Stalinist communist dictatorship. During this period heavy traditional cultural and architectural losses were sustained.[4]

Despite the Soviet era's cultural destruction, approximately seven hundred temples in varying conditions exist today, and a number of internationally led efforts have been launched to document and restore many of them. These noble efforts to conserve what is left are cause for optimism, although

FIGURE 5.1 Destruction of the eighteenth century Buddhist Togchin Temple in Zuunmod in the vicinity of Ulaanbaatar was emblematic of the similar loss of scores of other religious heritage sites in Mongolia in the 1930s under Soviet rule.

Mongolia's difficult transition from a planned economy to a free market economy has complicated ongoing efforts. In a similar vein, the Mongolian government and its heritage protection agencies face the daunting task of preserving a traditional culture strongly identified with its nomadic attributes, while simultaneously attempting to modernize the long-isolated nation. In response, the government is actively seeking external help in promoting its national culture, while internally supporting culture-based enterprises and developing its tourism potential in a way that will protect Mongolia's cultural heritage. These developments strongly suggest a promising trend in which the government invests in its cultural heritage, including its architectural heritage, in order to develop a culturally enlightened, self-sufficient and sustainable Mongolian nation.

In contrast to the preservation of cultural heritage, the conservation of natural resources was commonplace in Mongolia for well over a millennium. The Huns, who were among the earliest civilizations in the region, held mountains, rivers and wild animals sacred, thus affording protection for these natural resources. Chinggis Khan himself regulated land use and treatment of built resources in his famous thirteenth century *Ikh Zasag* legal decrees.[5] Today, the government of Mongolia has begun to adopt legislation and professional guidelines for the regulation and treatment of its temples, carved stone stelae, ruined towns, archaeological sites, and, in particular, the culture and mobile architecture of its semi-nomadic people.[6]

Mongolia has recently placed two cultural landscapes sites that have special historical, geographical and spiritual associations on the UNESCO World Heritage List. The first, listed in 2011, the

Conservation and revival of Buddhist monasteries

Though the first modern regulation about the protection of ancient cultural heritage was written in 1924 as the Rule of Preserving Ancient Monuments, the subsequent years under the communist regime witnessed the destruction of hundreds of monasteries, monuments and temples.[7] After this intense period of anti-cultural, anti-spiritual violence, limited early modern conservation took place beginning in 1944, when a number of cultural edifices were restored and some of the larger monasteries were placed under state protection.[8]

In 1973, the Historical and Cultural Heritage Restoration Organization developed projects that restored over thirty architectural heritage sites throughout Mongolia. The restoration work was concentrated at the Erdene Zuu, Amarbayasgalant and Gandantegchinlen monasteries, buildings that represent the most distinguished cultural landmarks of their type in Mongolia. In 1979, UNESCO supported conservation of architectural heritage in Mongolia when it contributed to the restoration of the Amarbayasgalant Monastery. This restoration project continued until it stalled in 1993 due to lack of funds, but was later re-started and completed with additional funding and support organized by an elderly Buddhist monk.[9]

Fortunately, Mongolia's re-emergence onto the global stage, which began during the 1990s, happened at a time when its exotic architecture and traditions were considered to be attractive areas for foreign investment and assistance. In particular, the revival of Buddhist community activities, many of which involve temple maintenance, drew assistance from distant religious organizations. In one such case, the US-based Foundation for the Preservation of the Mahayana Tradition contributed to the restoration of remaining structures at the Manchu-era Dara Ekh Monastery in southeast Ulaanbaatar, which had been heavily damaged during the country's communist era.[10] This restoration work, completed in 2003, enabled an innovative addition to Mongolia's Buddhist traditions: the creation of the Dolma Ling Nunnery, the first residential nunnery in Mongolia.

Additionally, new programs such as the Cultural Restoration Tourism Project (CRTP) organized an effort in which foreign visitors worked with Mongolian communities to restore a neglected monastery once famous for its library. The eighteenth century Baldan Baraivan Monastery in Khentii Aimag has been partially restored via a project that began in 1999 with the assistance of the CRTP, whose volunteer foreign visitors partially funded and conducted the work.[11] The project

FIGURE 5.2 Restoration of the Amarbayasgalant Monastery in Selenge Aimag began in 1979 under the aegis of UNESCO. This restoration continued for over ten years and the project was later completed with funding raised by the Monastery.

did not succeed after 2006 due to a disagreement with local authorities over project management responsibilities. Nonetheless, building techniques used at Baldan Baraivan remain worthy of proper restoration because they show strong influence but not strict adherence to the Tibetan style and its use of local materials. Early rehabilitation work made use of the same local materials found in the original construction, an admirable approach that is consistent with the idea of sustainable conservation.

Drawing support from numerous international and domestic sources through innovative programs has become a hallmark of Mongolia's cultural heritage conservation infrastructure. Due to its traditional nomadic culture and a long period of isolation, the field of architectural conservation is relatively new to Mongolia, although repair and maintenance of Buddhist religious buildings has existed there for centuries.

FIGURE 5.3a and b
Rehabilitation and new construction materials at the Tibetan-style Baldan Baraivan Monastery used locally available materials, a common and sustainable approach.

FIGURE 5.4 The Petroglyphic Complexes of the Mongolian Altai dating from the Late Pleistocene Period represent the most complete and best-preserved visual record of human prehistory and early history of a region at the intersection of Central and North Asia over a period of 11,000 years. In 2011 it became the country's fourth site to be placed on the UNESCO World Heritage List.

Petroglyphic Complexes of the western Mongolian Altai dating from the Late Pleistocene Period, represent the most complete and best-preserved visual record of human prehistory and early history of a region at the intersection of Central and North Asia over an 11,000-year period. The second, the Great Burkhan Khaldun Mountain and its surrounding sacred landscape, was listed in 2015. Situated in the northeast of the country in the central part of the Khentii mountain chain where the vast Central Asian steppe meets the forests of the Siberian taiga, Burkhan Khaldun is associated with the worship of sacred mountains, rivers and *ovoos* (shamanic rock cairns), in which ceremonies have been shaped by a fusion of ancient shamanic and Buddhist practices. The site is also believed to be the place of Chinggis Khan's birth and burial.

Heritage conservation and nation building, by Alexandra Cleworth

Developing countries struggling to emerge into the world economy, particularly those with only nascent democratic regimes, frequently look to the promotion of significant cultural heritage sites to achieve four goals: to reclaim a past history, to generate revenue, to foster national pride, and in some cases to provide legitimacy for a new government. These sites have important ramifications for the national economy: while many aspects of cultural heritage can be exported to attract foreign interest (museum exhibits, music and dance ensembles, etc.), the permanent nature of architectural structures precludes this as an option. Instead, they bring international attention home: inviting tourism revenue and additional foreign investment, both specifically for individual sites and for related infrastructure in general. Historic structures, carefully conserved and managed, offer a glimpse into hidden, half-forgotten history, inviting us to step into the past to better understand the present.

The past century played out in brutal fashion for Mongolia: caught between Chinese warlords and the Russian Revolution, it survived political and religious purges during a repressive communist regime, only to finally emerge as a democratic nation right as the harsh economic realities of the post-Cold War geopolitical world offered reduced aid. By supporting heritage conservation, the international community also supports the political stability of a country recently celebrating its twenty-fifth year of democracy.

Mongolia is an archaeologist's dream: stunning scenery, a unique culture, and an opportunity to shed new light on a place and history still unknown for much of the world. For those interested in cultural resource management, Mongolia is a veritable showcase of the latest techniques, some tough challenges, and the most rewarding outcomes. With each new exciting discovery comes the responsibility of protection. The Gobi Desert's Flaming Cliffs presented the world with the first dinosaur eggs, discovered by paleontologist Roy Chapman Andrews in the 1920s; subsequent dinosaur skeleton finds had to be fiercely guarded, and teams of cultural heritage specialists have worked together to enforce the return of these finds to Mongolia.

The joint Mongolian–Smithsonian Deer Stone Project employs portable hand-held laser scanners, providing highly accurate digital files that can then create high-resolution 3D models. This technology is an important resource for the documentation and future protection of these graceful, mysterious stelae, located in the northern grassy steppes, vulnerable to extreme weather and vandalism. Finds like the deer stones unite Mongolian cultural artifacts with those of Siberia and beyond. Excavation work at Kharkhorum could confirm literary records of life at the palace of a great khan, a window into the sedentary style of a culture known for life on horseback. As each new artifact comes to the surface, a plan is needed not just for conservation of the object, but to protect against looting. Safeguarding cultural patrimony is even more challenging in a country with the lowest population per square kilometer in the world.

The conservator faces the enormous task of restoring delicate artwork from Bronze Age cave paintings to nineteenth century painted exteriors of temples, requiring precise attention to detail in both execution and materials, which can be difficult to source. Questions on how the spread of Tibetan Buddhism, specifically the Mahayana sect, covered a land known for one of history's greatest warriors remain: one intriguing topic is why certain features of Tibetan monastic architecture were adopted and not others. By viewing the architectural information across the greater Asian landmass, individual structures are given a fresh perspective. Archaeology and cultural resource management play an especially important role in Mongolia, as well as other parts of Asia that have suffered similar destruction of sites under authoritarian regimes. Because these sites were expressly demolished or radically altered for political purposes, with the aim of obliterating any vestiges of a previous culture (including destroyed historical records and a decimated population in many cases), it is only through the archaeological record and analysis of structural remains that scholars can provide supporting evidence to the, at times, shocking oral witness to history.

The restoration of these precious resources presents yet another challenge: throughout Asia there is a tradition of reuse of buildings, and it is often the case that the landscape itself is the truly sacred area; perspectives on authenticity greatly differ from many Western traditions. After Gandantegchinlen Khiid, the capital's main monastery, Amarbayasgalant Khiid is considered to be one of the country's most intact architectural complexes, and a site of rare beauty. Built between 1726 and 1737 by Enkh-Amgalan Khan, it lost roughly one-third of its monastery grounds during the communist purges. An astonishing amount of restoration work has been done, but there are its detractors. One difference of opinion is in its use of materials: are they authentic representations of the original monastery bricks, tiles and paint? This raises the question of who controls heritage sites: does the present serve the past? Should authenticity be the primary goal, even if the result is a slower restoration process that risks increased site deterioration? If the restoration techniques and furnishings need to be of museum quality, does that imply that the site needs to be a cultural museum, instead of a living, breathing religious cultural entity? How is it decided which sites will be restored as museums and which sites are reconstructed as contemporary, evolving entities that sustain continued "living heritage"? Volunteers from around the world have contributed to various restoration projects in Mongolia and perhaps this communal bond serves a greater purpose overall than strict adherence to one vision of restoration; the complexities of this issue ensure an ongoing debate.

The Mongolian people have paid a high price for choosing a free and open society. Gone are many of the state-supported education and health benefits, and the safety nets for their most vulnerable populations. But they cherish their past, and recognition from the outside world of the importance of preserving this unique and fascinating cultural legacy that has endured and persevered despite a century of hardship, spurs them on to take increased action on both a legislative and a budgetary scale to protect these heritage sites, and guard these resources as part of our shared global cultural heritage.

Organized cultural heritage protection

After the collapse of the Soviet Union in the 1990s, Mongolia emerged from a long period of isolation, at which time much of the country's history and cultural heritage was exposed to the outside world for the first time in generations. In 1992 the Mongolian population adopted the present national constitution that placed all forms of cultural heritage under state protection and care. Heritage protection falls under the auspices of the Ministry of Education, Culture and Science with an officer in charge of the nation's cultural properties including the state and provincial museums. In 1998 an inventory of the country's historic buildings and sites was completed, resulting in national protection of 119 sites and provincial-level protection of 233 additional sites. In response to growing concern for cultural heritage protection in Mongolia, the Law of Historical and Cultural Values was modified in 2001. Since referred to as the Law of Protection of Cultural Heritage, the legislation regulates conservation of both tangible and intangible cultural heritage. It also deals with the identification, classification, registration, conservation and presentation of different forms of cultural heritage and also addresses the rights of the owners of listed historic buildings.[12]

In July 2004, UNESCO and the World Heritage Committee added the Orkhon Valley to the list of World Heritage Sites, constituting Mongolia's first listed cultural heritage site. This cultural landscape is traditionally regarded as the cradle of Mongolian civilization and includes the historic city of Kharkhorum (a legendary seat of the vast empire of the Mongols), Erdene Zuu Monastery (one of the most important monasteries in the country), the Tuvkhun Monastery, stone edicts to Bilge Khan, and painted petroglyphs dating to the Neolithic period, among other important historic features. The nomination succeeded after the German World Heritage Foundation provided financial and professional assistance to Mongolian authorities in assembling a management plan for the vast site.[13]

Between 2000 and 2005, the Institute of Archaeology, Mongolian Academy of Sciences, and the Department of Pre- and Early Historical Archaeology, University of Bonn, Germany conducted

FIGURE 5.5 The Orkhon Valley cultural landscape consisting of Kharkhorum, seat of Chinggis Khan's empire, Erdene Zuu and other monasteries, stone stelae, Neolithic petroglyphs, and its natural setting were listed as Mongolia's first UNESCO World Heritage Site.

in-depth archaeological research at Kharkhorum and located the remains of the palace of Ögödei Khan, son of Chinggis Khan, and determined other aspects of the then-seat of the Mongol Empire. The team investigated part of a craftsmen quarter and other sites in Kharkhorum to determine the settlement's founding date and duration.[14]

Listed three times on the World Monuments Fund Watch List of Most Endangered Sites (in 1996, 1998 and 2000), the Bogd Khan Winter Palace Museum complex at the northern edge of Ulaanbaatar near the Tull River received much-needed support from WMF between 2002 and 2005. Mongolia's Ministry of Education, Culture and Science nominated the Winter Palace, built for the eighth Bogd Khan, Javzandamba Khutagt, to the Watch List due to funding needs and the international attention it would garner. Conservation work at the site included providing technical and financial assistance in the restoration of its richly painted Imperial Chinese-style arrangement of courtyard buildings and towards restoration of the greater complex.[15]

a

b

FIGURE 5.6a and b
Archaeological research between 1994 and 2004 was conducted at Kharkhorum, the longest enduring seat of Chinggis Khan's empire, that yielded a variety of trade artifacts, evidence of iron and pottery production, and possibly the remains of a dragon kiln.

After its re-listing in 1998 and 2000, technical and financial support was extended to the site under a pilot project to conserve the Library building that formed one side of the site's prominent south courtyard complex. In 2002 similar support was furnished for the adjacent Naidan Temple that had significant exterior wall paintings. In 1999 the National Administration for Cultural Heritage (NACH) in the People's Republic of China conducted similar pilot conservation work at the ceremonial entrance gate to the Palace complex. Following its successful completion an accord was signed for the NACH team to assist in the restoration of five structures at the Bogd Khan Palace Museum complex and in 2004 four additional buildings were restored. The Japan International Cooperation Agency (JICA) has also been active in the cultural heritage protection field in Mongolia, primarily by providing financial assistance for the purchase of equipment needed for the photographic documentation and preservation of objects in museums.[16]

Mongolia faces a severe shortage of trained conservation personnel working in the field of architectural conservation. A School of Civil Engineering and Architecture at the Mongolian University of Science and Technology in Ulaanbaatar exists, but instruction that addresses restoration and preservation of built heritage is limited. Similarly, few native craftsmen skilled in the traditional building trades remain after the break in continuity of traditional arts training during the 1930s and 1950s. Fortunately, this is beginning to change. Conservation projects done in partnership with knowledgeable foreign heritage protection groups transfer know-how and technology. Today's radically improved technologies for documentation, data management and conservation science are being used increasingly in Mongolia's cultural heritage management efforts.

Mongolia stands as one of the last countries in Asia to reorganize and modernize its cultural heritage management systems and to commit to training a new generation of architectural heritage protection experts and craftspeople. There are real pressures on the country's built and natural environments including those related to land development – especially mining operations – and requirements of tourism. Such pressures have stirred heightened interest in preserving and presenting the country's architectural and other cultural heritage, with a positive result being the formation of a more effective heritage management system that currently references and often utilizes international best practices in heritage conservation. Perhaps most important is the intense pride of Mongolia's citizens in the country's glorious past, which will ensure continued support for the protection of its cultural heritage.

a

b

c

FIGURE 5.7a, b, c and d
The Bogd Khan Palace in Ulaanbaatar was built between 1893 and 1903. Designed in the Chinese Imperial style with a series of four courtyards it is entered by elaborate gateway buildings and temples that led to the principal palace structure. Beginning in 1999 the World Monuments Fund supported restoration of the Library (a) including its exterior painted finishes (b, c), a pilot conservation project that was followed by the larger, more complex restoration of the Naidan Temple structure. WMF's work inspired separate funding and restoration of the complex's principle entrance gate, which was undertaken by the National Administration for Cultural Heritage of the People's Republic of China (d). The NACH team subsequently expanded its scope to include four additional structures.

d

Conserving impermanent domestic structures: gers and Soviet-era housing

The principal form of traditional Mongolian domestic architecture, the *ger*, or *yurt*, is a mobile circular tent that dates to the first millennium BCE. Images of gers, remaining virtually unchanged in design, have been seen on cave paintings dating back to the Bronze Age. As such it may be the oldest continuously used architectural form in the world.

The ger is made up of layers of canvas that are insulated with sections of felt and can be assembled and dismantled in a matter of a few hours. It remains a common form of housing in Mongolia today, with groups of gers, called *khoroos*, established in and on the outskirts of the capital and its smaller towns.[17] The traditional and present-day nomadic way of life of many Mongolians extends to their handicrafts and other cultural expressions as well. With the regional towns of Mongolia serving as seats for trading and the provision of modern amenities, most artistic endeavors have been directed to the creation of portable works, such as saddles, personal jewelry, leatherwork and embroidery.[18]

During the country's rule as a satellite state of the Soviet Union as the Mongolian People's Republic from 1924 to 1992 many Russian lifeways were adopted, including governance, education, and economic and military institutions. This is well evidenced by the capital's Soviet-era architectural town planning and architectural principles. One example is the superimposition of the present-day government palace and public square atop the oldest section of Ulaanbaatar on land once occupied by the monastery and temple complex of Ikh Khuree. The new center of government was named Sükhbaatar Square with Saaral Ordon (Government Palace) at its center. The square's center was prominently marked by a mausoleum and equestrian statue of Damidin Sükhbaatar, one of the leaders of Mongolia's 1921 Revolution. The Sükhbaatar mausoleum was removed and the square was renamed Chinggis Khaan Square in 2013, now increasingly surrounded by modern buildings. Notable buildings from the Russian period include the building of the Radio and Postal Communications Committee (since demolished), the Mongoliatrans company headquarters, and the Military Club reflecting the Constructivist style. Impressive remaining architecture in the Classical idiom from the Soviet era includes the Drama Theatre and the Ministry of Foreign Affairs. Both were built as scaled-down versions of Imperial Russian architecture in Moscow and Leningrad (St. Petersburg), a style that was revived in the twentieth century, and re-labeled by some historians as Stalinist architecture.

The Stalinist-era "Russification" of Mongolia brought with it characteristic collectivized housing in the form of steel, concrete and masonry framed multi-storey buildings in a variety of block arrangements.[19] As at countless other locations across the former Soviet Union and its satellite partners, from Vladivostok to Havana, there has since arisen the question of how such architecture could be saved for purposes of maintaining a sense of historical stratigraphy, or at least to retain their more durable components in their rehabilitation to more modern standards.

a

164 East Asia

FIGURE 5.8a and b The classic transportable Mongolian *ger* is structurally stable in part due to the lattice of wood concealed between its felt wall sheathing (a). Approximately eighty-seven *khoroos*, or neighborhoods of gers in and around Ulaanbaatar represent semi-permanent settlements that house over half of the capital's residents (b). Services such as power and water supply are scarce. While not monumental in character this age-old domestic form and the lifeways it supports could certainly be termed "living heritage."

b

FIGURE 5.9 A deteriorated housing block in Ulaanbaatar's western sector, before extensive architectural renovation brought it up to more modern standards and aesthetics.

Notes

1 The area of what is now Mongolia has been ruled since the late first millennium CE by empires including the Xiongnu state, Xianbei state, the Turkic Khagnate and others. The Hannu Empire, founded in 209 BCE, was the first empire of nomadic people in the region of present-day Mongolia and is considered to be the cultural source of the Mongol Empire. The Khitan people founded a state known as the Liao dynasty (907–1125 CE) in Central Asia and ruled Mongolia and northern parts of China, Korea and parts of the Russian Far East. In 1206 Chinggis Khan famously forged the then-divided tribal groups of the region and beyond into the largest contiguous empire in world history, which succeeded his reign until the collapse of the Mongol-led Yuan dynasty in 1368. At the end of the seventeenth century a region of the Manchu-led Qing dynasty controlled what is now Mongolia until its demise in 1911. During an array of political changes over the next eighty years Outer Mongolia, as opposed to Inner Mongolia that remained a Chinese province, survived as a *de facto* independent nation experiencing varying Soviet influences until full independence was finally achieved with its Revolution in 1990. The country's constitution of 1992 established its current multi-party system that supports its growing market economy.
2 Jasper Becker. *Lost Country: Mongolia Revealed*. (London: Hodder & Stoughton, 1992). The second religious persecution that resulted in the loss of Buddhist and other Mongolian heritage in the Inner Mongolian region of the People's Republic of China occurred during the Chinese Cultural Revolution (1966–1976).
3 Larry Moses and Stephen A. Halkovic. *Introduction to Mongolian History and Culture*. (Bloomington, Indiana: Research Institute for Inner Asian Studies, 1985), 52–65.
4 Ibid., 141–153.
5 Z. Oyumbileg. "Achievement Report on Cultural Heritage Protection." Report to the Ministry of Education, Science, and Culture, Mongolia. Unpublished. In 2000, Z. Oyumbileg was the sole ministerial official responsible for Mongolia's cultural properties. Her duties also included supervising all museums. The earlier Ministry of Culture has been merged into the Ministry of Education, Science and Culture.
6 In 2013 the Mongolian Parliament passed amendments to the Law on Protecting the Cultural Heritage of Mongolia in order to include specific articles concerning management of cultural and natural heritage inscribed on the World Heritage List and the National Tentative List.
7 The origins of Mongolia's national heritage protection legislation date from August 7, 1924 with "The Rule of Preserving Ancient Monuments" that importantly set the framework for the examination, study and preservation of ancient historical and cultural values. Ancient monuments were defined as grave markers, stone markers, documents, sacred poles, stone mounds, ruins of ancient cities, sacrificial objects and related decorations.
8 Per the report made to the first mission of the World Monuments Fund to Mongolia on June 2, 1999 of Z. Oyumbileg, heritage division director, Ministry of Education, Science, and Culture, Mongolia.
9 Ibid.
10 Foundation for the Preservation of the Mahayana Tradition. "Dolma Ling Nunnery: A New Chance for a Brave Group of Women." 2002. Web. www.fpmt.org/mongolia/nunnery.html. Accessed September 2, 2004.
11 Cultural Restoration Tourism Project. Baldan Baraivan Project. 2000. Web. http://baldanbaraivan.org/. Web. Accessed September 2, 2004.
12 Ibid. Building upon The Rule of Preserving Ancient Monuments (1924), in 1970 The Law on the Protection of Cultural Properties of the Mongolian People's Republic was enacted. It regulated a wide range of activities including the classification, protection, utilization, study and promotion of cultural heritage and its enforcement. This legislation enabled the Department of the Restoration of Historical and Cultural Heritage and the Bureau for the Study of Historical and Cultural Properties, in a way that had positive effects. In 1994 and in 2001 the Law was amended with further provisions strengthening its purview over additional matters such as exportation of antiquities and protection of cultural and intangible heritage. The Ministry of Education, Culture and Science is in charge of the protection of Mongolian cultural heritage. Within the Ministry, the Department of Culture and Art is solely responsible for issuing regulations and policies to protect cultural heritage. The protection of tangible cultural heritage is supervised by three organizations: the Institute of Archaeology, Mongolian Academy of Sciences; the Cabinet of Archaeology-Anthropology, National University of Mongolia; and the Mongolian National Historical Museum. Source: B. Gunchinsuren, Jeffrey H. Altschul and John W. Olsen. *Protecting the Past, Preserving the Present; Report on Phase 1 Activities of the Oyr Tolgoi Cultural Heritage Program Design for Ömnögovi Aimag*. Sustainability East Asia LLC, February 2011, 225–232.
13 German World Heritage Foundation. Orkhon Valley Cultural Landscape. 2004. Web. www.welterbestiftung.org/orkhon_valley.htm. Accessed September 2, 2004.
14 Ernst Pohl, et al. *Production Sites in Karakorum and Its Environment: A New Archaeological Project in the Orkhon Valley, Mongolia*. Web. www.silkroadfoundation.org/newsletter/vol10/SilkRoad_10_2012_pohl.pdf. Accessed 10 October, 2015.

15 World Monuments Fund. "Bogd Khan Palace: WMF Restores an Early Twentieth Century Buddhist Masterpiece," *Icon* (Winter 2002–03), 44–45.
16 Ministry of Foreign Affairs of Japan. "Cultural Grant in Aid to Mongolia for the Cultural Heritage Centre of Mongolia." 1999. Web. http://www.mofa.go.jp/announce/announce/1999/7/710-3.html. Accessed September 2, 2004. A number of projects in Mongolia are funded by the Ministry of Foreign Affairs of Japan through JICA (cultural grants in aid).
17 Beginning in 2012, Ulaanbaatar's neighborhoods of gers (in districts called khoroos) were mapped in a project of The Asia Foundation in support of its Urban Services Project for Ger Districts of Ulaanbaatar. The project was created in partnership with the Australian Agency for International Development (AusAID). Web. http://asiafoundation.org/in-asia/2013/10/23/mapping-ulaanbaatars-ger-districts/. Accessed October 10, 2015.
18 The Asian Art Museum (San Francisco). "Mongolia: The Legacy of Chinggis Khan." Exhibit held from July 19 to October 15, 1995. Web. www.asianart.com/mongolia/intro.html. Accessed September 2, 2004. This was the first such exhibition on Mongolian art since the country emerged from Soviet control and was an eye opener for the outside world on the arts of Mongolia. Many of the exhibited works had been highly influenced by both Tibetan art and religion, which are similar to Mongolia's.
19 In the 1950s relations between the Mongolian People's Republic and the People's Republic of China improved and China supplied considerable aid in the form of building new industries and housing. This included the "120 myangat" district that consisted of hurriedly and mostly poorly constructed *paneletki* structures with prefabricated walls. Most were in failing condition by the time the Soviet Union collapsed in 1991.

Further reading

Amitai, Reuven and Michal Biran (eds.). 2004. *Mongols, Turks, and Others: Eurasian Nomads and the Sedentary World*. Leiden: Brill's Inner Asian Library.
Bawden, C.R. 2002. *The Modern History of Mongolia*. London: Routledge.
Becker, Jasper. 1992. *The Lost Country: Mongolia Revealed*. London: Hodder and Stoughton.
Brumfield, William. 2004. *History of Russian Architecture*. Seattle, Washington: University of Washington Press.
de Rachewiltz, Igor. 2006. Translated condensed version of the anonymously written *The Secret History of the Mongols c. 1250* based on surviving transcriptions or translations into Chinese characters dating from the end of the fourteenth century. Leiden: Brill Academic Publishing.
German World Heritage Foundation. 2004. "Orkhon Valley Cultural Landscape." Web. www.welterbestiftung.de/home/die-projekte/orkhon-tal/. (In German). Accessed May 17, 2016.
Gunchinsuren, B., Jeffrey H. Altschul and John W. Olsen. 2011. *Protecting the Past, Preserving the Present: Report on Phase 1 Activities of the Oyr Tolgoi Cultural Heritage Program Design for Ömnögovi Aimag*. Ulaanbaatar: Sustainability East Asia.
Hugo-Brunt, Michael. 1974. *Bibliography of Architecture, Planning and Landscape in China: Including Materials on Hong Kong, Korea, Manchuria, Mongolia and Tibet*. Monticello, Illinois: Council of Planning Librarians.
——. 1976. *Architecture and Planning in China, Mongolia and Korea*. Monticello, Illinois: Council of Planning Librarians.
Japan International Cooperation Agency. 2002. *Survey Report of the Study of the Living Environment of the Ger Area in Ulaanbaatar, Mongolia*. Ulaanbaatar: Japan International Cooperation Agency of Mongolia, Research, Construction & Architecture Corporation.
Ministry of Foreign Affairs of Japan. 1999. "Cultural Grant in Aid to Mongolia for the Cultural Heritage Centre of Mongolia." Web. www.mofa.go.jp/announce/announce/1999/7/710-3.html. Accessed May 17, 2016.
Moses, Larry and Stephen A. Halkovic. 1985. *Introduction to Mongolian History and Culture*. Bloomington, Indiana: Research Institute for Inner Asian Studies.
Office of Architecture Planning. 1990. *Plan for Year 2010 for Ulaanbaatar*. Ulaanbaatar: Office of Architecture Planning.
Peissel, Michael. 2005 *Tibetan Pilgrimage: Architecture of the Sacred Land*. New York: Harry Abrams.
Pohl, Ernst, et al. *Production Sites in Kharkhorum and Its Environment: A New Archaeological Project in the Orkhon Valley, Mongolia*. Web. www.silkroadfoundation.org/newsletter/vol10/SilkRoad_10_2012_pohl.pdf. Accessed May 17, 2016.
Tsultem, N. 1988. *Mongolian Architecture*. Translated by D. Bayarsaikan. Ulaanbaatar: State Publishing House.
UNESCO. "Amarbayasgalant Monastery and its Surrounding Sacred Cultural Landscape." Web. http://whc.unesco.org/en/tentativelists/5947/. Accessed May 17, 2016.
——. "Orkhon Valley Cultural Landscape." Web. http://whc.unesco.org/en/list/1081. Accessed May 17, 2016.
——. "Petroglyphic Complexes of Mongolian Altai." Web. http://whc.unesco.org/uploads/nominations/1382.pdf. Accessed May 17, 2016.
Weatherford, Jack. 2004. *Genghis Khan and the Making of the Modern World*. New York: Random House.

CONCLUSION TO PART I

Despite lingering grievances from the Japanese imperial ambitions of the early twentieth century, an evolving diplomatic relationship between China and Taiwan, and political tension on the Korean peninsula, an increased level of partnership among the East Asian countries is emerging, joining the considerable resources of its nations together for the conservation of their shared and unique cultural heritage. At the same time, inter-government cooperative schemes and an increasing number of regional NGO initiatives for heritage conservation are asserting their influence in ways that add to a more harmonized and systematic view of East Asian cultural heritage and its protection.

The region has made great contributions to the field of architectural conservation in Asia, through an emphasis on intangible heritage, successful country-specific conservation principles, collaborative and generous national aid organizations, and ready engagement with global heritage management bodies. This situation was by no means preordained, as the social, political and military upheavals of the first half of the twentieth century left the nations of East Asia in turmoil, and in the midst of a great period of loss of traditional buildings, cities and practices. While this rate of change has continued, unfortunately with continued losses to the historic built environment through the various processes of modernization, it has achieved a greater level of balance in recent decades, thanks to the positive contributions of East Asian nations and their institutions.

In 2013 China launched an ambitious economic development strategy known as the "One Belt, One Road" program, which aims to develop infrastructure along overland and maritime commercial routes that would improve connections between China and the rest of Asia, and beyond. The nation has put an initial US$50 billion investment into its Asian Infrastructure Investment Bank, and another $40 billion in direct infrastructure investment, which will undoubtedly have a long-term effect on the relationships between the people of East Asia and their neighbors to the west.[1] Just as the original Asian trading routes did over 2,000 years ago, these new connections will lead to change and new ideas that no one today can predict. The effect this will have on the architectural heritage of East Asia is a particularly open question, and will rely on continued collaboration and vigilance on the part of practitioners across the continent.

Note

1   "Where all Silk Roads Lead." *The Economist*. April 11, 2015. Web. www.economist.com/news/china/21648039-through-fog-hazy-slogans-contours-chinas-vision-asia-emerge-where-all-silk-roads. Accessed January 13, 2016.

PART II

Southeast Asia mainland countries

Introduction

Myanmar (Burma), Laos, Cambodia, Thailand, Vietnam

The great north–south rivers of Mainland Southeast Asia – the Mekong, Irrawaddy, Chao Phraya and Song Koi – along with their associated floodplains and deltas, are vital geographical features of this vibrant region of Asia. These waterways have historically provided modes of transport and commercial corridors to the coastal ports, passing through extensive forest tracts that for millennia have provided plentiful sources of architectural timber to the region's great builder civilizations. The mountains that frame the river valleys provide a variety of stone sources that have contributed to the renowned carving and dry stone construction traditions evidenced at Angkor and Wat Phou. A cycle of dry and wet seasons in the region has made the development of sophisticated water management strategies an essential component of its successful civilizations. From the *baray* (reservoirs) and irrigation systems of ancient Khmer cities, to the harvesting of the Tonlé Sap fisheries, and the extensive rice cultivation by the kings of Burmese and Champa civilizations, the people of Mainland Southeast Asia have long been adept at controlling their resource-rich environment.[1]

For centuries the region has maintained direct artistic, cultural and religious connections to both South Asia and China, making it a center of Theravada Buddhism and Hinduism, in addition to Confucianism and Taoism. Ancient regional cultures including the Chenla, Pyu and Mon developed to later become the Khmer, Burmese and Vietnamese dynastic kingdoms through centuries of conquest and assimilation, giving rise to the contemporary political landscape of Mainland Southeast Asia. The rise of colonial cities such as Rangoon (Yangon) and Saigon (Ho Chi Minh City) through the twentieth century alongside the traditional urban centers of Bangkok, Hanoi, Mandalay and Phnom Penh define this growing region today as the legacies of colonialism and a tumultuous twentieth century gave way to the fast-growing and generally prosperous region.

The principle of gaining religious merit for the conservation of important buildings runs through Southeast Asia's spiritual and architectural traditions, as evidenced by numerous examples of later Khmer, Burmese and other rulers preserving and renovating their predecessors' temples and memorials. Due to the continuity of many of these cultural traditions, this approach continues to inform conservation practice in the region today, with the Thai monarchy in particular remaining active participants in the practice of heritage promotion and management. Like the neighboring Southeast Asian island nations, competing colonial interests shaped the contours of the region's modern nations. In the nineteenth and early twentieth centuries, the British established a sphere of colonial influence in the west (Burma), and the French in the east (French Indochina) while the independent Kingdom of Siam (Thailand) dexterously maintained its autonomy inbetween.

The post-colonial experience in each of the five countries has varied considerably, but for the most part it has been difficult, including the communist/Marxist revolutions in Vietnam, Laos and Cambodia and the isolationist military dictatorship in Myanmar. Thailand's present system of constitutional monarchy came to pass in 1932 and, while it has largely remained a bastion of stability in the region, the early twenty-first century has witnessed some signs of strain. The extraordinarily destructive Vietnam War era and the genocidal Khmer Rouge regime represent some of the worst post-colonial episodes anywhere in Asia, with millions killed, countless communities disrupted and thousands of heritage resources destroyed, damaged or pillaged due to lawless conditions. A legacy of this era that remains today is the unexploded ordnance that continues to pose a very real threat to those who live and work in areas yet to be cleared of mines and other hazards.

Although the tradition of maintaining religious buildings through duties of their caretakers and donors wishing to accumulate spiritual merit dates back thousands of years, Europeans largely introduced modern historical research and architectural conservation methods to the region, beginning with surveys of monumental sites as early as the eighteenth century. These small-scale ventures eventually blossomed into major scholarly institutional undertakings, in particular with the establishment of the École française d'Extrême Orient in Hanoi in 1898. The EFEO diligently continued its work through the twilight of the colonial era and into the post-independence tumult that engulfed much of the region after World War II. The work of EFEO and its counterparts in Burma and Indonesia established institutional and heritage conservation frameworks, including legislation that would be built upon by the independent governments and Southeast Asian professionals in subsequent decades. Locally, the Thai monarchy's role in promoting museums and architectural heritage protection as a national priority and the establishment of Thai Fine Arts and Archaeology departments (established in 1912 and 1924, respectively) were among the first contemporary-style conservation organizations established by the non-European governments of Asia.

The history of architectural conservation in Mainland Southeast Asia is strongly tied to its important monumental sites such as Angkor, Mỹ Són and Bagan, where European and local professionals together developed innovative and resourceful approaches to protecting the region's architectural heritage in the face of many challenges. Angkor stands out as one of the largest, longest and arguably most successful international conservation campaigns in Asia. Due to the scale, majesty and fame of places like Angkor, Sukhothai, Luang Prabang, Hue and other architectural marvels of Southeast Asia, the region became and remains a focal point for conservation practice, drawing professionals from all over the world. The enormous amount of work to preserve, present and celebrate the architectural heritage of the region has resulted in their impressive preservation today, the establishment of cultural resource management systems in each country and, importantly, national pride and a sense of nationhood in each country.

Due in part to the efforts of these institutions, along with global organizations such as UNESCO, ICOMOS, ICCROM, the World Monuments Fund and many others, and an increasing number of East Asian government and non-government cooperative initiatives, Southeast Asia enjoys a relatively high degree of professionalism and training in architectural conservation, particularly in Thailand but increasingly in Vietnam and Cambodia as well. All of these factors combine to produce a dynamic field of conservation practice, international collaboration, and regional and local heritage conservation advocacy.

Today, a high level of regional cooperation and exchange follows an example established by the early European colonial architectural conservationists, who during the course of their own missions to the region traveled between the Cham sites of Vietnam, Borobudur on Java and Angkor in Cambodia to compare research and share effective techniques. While Angkor and Bagan rank among the world's best known ancient cities, hundreds of lesser-known sites and structures now receive conservation attention thanks to increasing levels of professional engagement, cause-specific NGO activity, and public engagement. In recent decades, however, the increasingly influential tourism industry has played a growing role in making conservation and presentation of certain sites major national priorities, in addition to providing important sources of revenue. For countries like Thailand, Cambodia and

Vietnam, cultural heritage tourism ranks among their primary economic contributors, with visitation numbers at places such as Angkor, Chiang Mai and Hội An growing exponentially year-to-year.[2] Less-developed countries, such as Laos and Myanmar, have taken notice and are in pursuit of their neighbors' market share. Future heritage conservation efforts in the region will have to factor in the opportunities and challenges that accompany large-scale tourist visitation, as Southeast Asia continues to be a preferred destination.

These circumstances have led to a highly varied experience in cultural heritage management, ranging from the long-isolated (Myanmar) to the deeply engaged (Thailand), and episodes of crisis response (Vietnam and Cambodia and, to a lesser degree, Laos). The cessation of conflict following the collapse of the Khmer Rouge in 1979 led to a renaissance in conservation activities at Angkor beginning a decade later, while the powerful wave of modernization in Thailand following World War II revived its long-standing conservation ethic. Similarly, urban conservation in Hanoi in the 1980s and 1990s came about largely because of the economic reforms of that period that led to previously unknown economic expansion and development. In Myanmar, the government's response following the devastating 1975 earthquake at Bagan resulted in some destructive interventions that raised the level of concern and elicited international offers to assist from UNESCO, ICCROM and other international organizations.

The ongoing international effort to save Angkor beginning in the early 1990s remains a crucial touchstone in the story of Asian architectural conservation. Initially working under extremely difficult circumstances in terms of safety, the teams that ventured into the forests around Siem Reap to protect what remained after more than a decade of neglect and war, fostered an ongoing spirit of collaboration and shared purpose that has resulted in a dynamic, productive environment for conservation activity and exchange. The APSARA Authority, established 1993, and its International Coordinating Committee, fosters a noteworthy global laboratory for conservation methods and strategies in one place, and a unique forum for sharing these among conservation professionals in a peer review-style forum.

The Bangkok Charter (1985) foreshadowed the later Nara Document on Authenticity (1994) and the Principles for the Conservation of Heritage Sites in China (the China Principles, 2000, revised 2015) by incorporating Asian perspectives on authenticity and continuity into Western-style conservation guidelines. Advocacy and funding organizations such as the Yangon Heritage Trust have raised the profile both locally and internationally of the endangered colonial heritage in the former British capital of Yangon (Rangoon). The UNESCO Convention on the Protection of Underwater Cultural Heritage (2001) came about following the discovery of a major shipwreck off the central Vietnamese coastal port town of Hội An, and has since been leveraged to extend protection to underwater resources throughout the world. Pioneering work in cultural landscape conservation in the 1980s began in Vietnam among the characteristic streets and shophouses that comprise the urban landscape of the former imperial capital of Hue. In Laos, the integrated conservation planning strategies such as the *Plan de Sauvegarde et de Mise en Valeur* (PSMV, or Safeguarding and Enhancement Plan) and the *Maison du Patrimoine* (or Heritage House/Heritage Department), along with the UNESCO Buddhist Sangha program have done much to support traditional building arts training and conservation advocacy in Luang Prabang, Lao PDR. The use of satellite imaging of vast archaeological landscapes traces its origins to a collaboration between the World Monuments Fund, the Royal Angkor Foundation and NASA in 1994, both presaging the widespread use of LIDAR today and pioneering other forms of digital documentation.

Just as is seen in South Asia, conservation of the extensive built legacy of Southeast Asia's colonial period remains a complex and frequently fraught challenge, associated with painful memories, or obsolete functions, in some cases in poor structural conditions due to long-term neglect following episodes of conflict or uncertain ownership. Problematic issues such as restoring buildings for religious merit without proper conservation advice, the use of incompatible materials, and the loss of original character have been most acute at Bagan, where hundreds of historic structures have received such treatments, creating a long-term need to correct these interventions where possible. Similarly, addressing the problematic aftereffects of early twentieth century conservation approaches, such as the improper use of modern concrete, harsh chemical cleaning of fragile stone surfaces, and use of ferrous metals in reconstructed masonry and stonework, will remain a major task in the decades to come. The looting of unprotected sites is a tragic legacy that goes back to the colonial era, and movable sculpture and statues appear with missing or dubious provenance in auction houses and museums abroad. Addressing this scourge may presage solutions to the current and emerging illicit antiquities trade from Afghanistan, Iraq and Syria. Development pressures associated with rapid expansion of the tourism economy such as airports and hotels at Luang Prabang and the massive expansion of the Angkor–Siem Reap area have created needs for urban planning at a large scale. Resource extraction (such as mining and deforestation) that began during the colonial period and accelerated in the independence era, affects traditional lifeways of historically isolated minority populations, and alters the fragile environments that once supported the great builder civilizations of Mainland Southeast Asia.

The Association of Southeast Asian Nations (ASEAN), established in Bangkok in 1968, promotes cooperation among all ten countries of Mainland and Insular (Maritime) Southeast Asia, from Myanmar to the Philippines, on cultural heritage management issues and through a Cultural Heritage Fund. Also based in Bangkok, the Southeast Asian Ministers of Education Organization Center for Archaeology and Fine Arts (SEAMEO-SPAFA) promotes cultural heritage projects through training and coordination, emphasizing cooperation, collaboration and resource sharing among member countries since 1987. The role of Angkor as an exemplar of conservation practice cannot be overstated, with international teams from Japan, India, France, the USA and China among many others arriving each field season to work, publish and collaborate on the shared mission of conserving and presenting the spectacular site. Organizations like the Siam Heritage Trust and the Center for Khmer Studies in Siem Reap have contributed cultural heritage-related scholarship to regional efforts in conservation. The Getty Conservation Institute, in collaboration with local conservation agencies and SEAMEO SPAFA, organized a regional training program for mid-career conservation professionals from the region between 2004 and 2009, at Wat Phou, Siem Reap and Chiang Saen (Thailand), focusing on conservation issues common to the mainland countries, including archaeological site management, academic program development and conservation planning for urban development.[3] Alongside support from internationally based organizations, these institutional efforts have served to bolster an already active community of national professionals within the region that are well poised to conserve and maintain the region's spectacular architectural heritage.

Notes

1 Mark Cleary. "Historical Geography of Mainland Southeast Asia," in Keat Gin Ooi (ed.), *Southeast Asia: A Historical Encyclopedia, from Angkor Wat to East Timor*, Volume 1. (Santa Barbara, CA: ABC-CLIO, 2004), 594–595.

2 This spectacular growth is illustrated by visitor patterns at Angkor, which was welcoming 200 tourists per year in the early twentieth century, and was virtually inaccessible during the Khmer Rouge period (1975–1979). In 2014 the APSARA Authority reported that 2.059 million international tourists visited Angkor, generating US$59 million in entry ticket revenue. Sources: Tim Winter. *Post-Conflict Heritage, Postcolonial Tourism: Tourism, Politics and Development at Angkor*. (London: Routledge, 2007), 30; and "Press Release: Statistics of International Tourist Visits to Angkor and Revenue of Angkor Ticket Sales, 2014." APSARA Authority. 2014. Web. http://apsaraauthority.gov.kh/imgs/documents/135/2014_en.pdf. Accessed January 8, 2016.

3 "Built Heritage in Southeast Asia: Education and Training Initiative (2004–2009)." The Getty Conservation Institute. 2012. Web. www.getty.edu/conservation/our_projects/education/sea/. Accessed January 9, 2016.

6
MYANMAR (BURMA)

Politically isolated and the subject of comparatively little involvement or research by the world beyond its borders, the Republic of the Union of Myanmar (called Burma from 1835 to 1989, during British rule)[1] is fast evolving from its former shadowy presence on the international heritage conservation landscape, with its vast cultural riches and world-renowned sites. Home to several indigenous imperial capitals, most notably Mandalay and Bagan (formerly Pagan), and their

FIGURE 6.1 Dhammayangyi Temple (1170 CE) is the largest temple in Bagan and exemplifies a "four-face" temple design.

colonial counterpart of Yangon (formerly Rangoon), Myanmar's predominantly Buddhist culture has influenced its deep legacy of architectural, aesthetic and cultural traditions. Due to the country's decades of insularity and pariah status within the global community, many of the international conservation agencies and donor countries have been limited in their ability to participate in Myanmar's efforts to conserve its built heritage. As a result, the country's military dictatorship has been largely left to its own devices and has made some unwise decisions that compromised the authenticity and integrity of some of Myanmar's architectural treasures. Particularly widely criticized has been the heavy-handed interventions made in Bagan. Beginning in 2008, however, political reforms and a new spirit of openness have begun to alter the cultural and conservation landscape in Myanmar, creating the potential for a new era of collaboration with the international heritage community.

FIGURE 6.2 Shwedagon Pagoda in Yangon is one of Myanmar's most sacred temples and one of the region's most important Buddhist heritage sites. Originally built in 1485 CE its present form dates from 1769 CE. It is the principal architectural landmark of Yangon (with maintenance work visible here) and represents a continuity of design in Buddhist architecture.

Myanmar's early history was influenced by competition among its various ethnic groups, in particular the southern Mon (who established the kingdoms of Thaton and Bago beginning in the ninth century CE), the northern Pyu (who established the first century BCE capital of Sri Ksetra), and, later, the Burmese (who arrived by the ninth century CE).[2] The Burmese kings traditionally were dedicated patrons of architectural projects, as evidenced by the sheer number of elaborate temples, pagodas and *zedi* constructed during their periods of dominance. The ongoing wars of the early years helped to supply the Burmese monarchs with the workforce required to construct huge collections of temples and other religious structures at sites like Bagan, as well as sophisticated infrastructure projects to support agricultural cultivation.

Myanmar's first empire, established in 849 CE, located its capital, Bagan, at a strategic location on the Irrawaddy River, the region's central geographical feature. In 1057, King Anawrahta supposedly conquered the Mon capital of Thaton, and returned to Bagan with captive Mon craftsmen and builders who were highly skilled in building and the decorative arts. The Mon proceeded to influence Bagan's cultural life for the next century, leaving a lasting impression on thousands of temples, pagodas and shrines in the capital and elsewhere, their stylistic influences mixing with then-established Pyu and Brahmanic Indian motifs. In addition to the craftspeople, Theravada Buddhist monks also returned to Bagan with the King, ultimately leading him to convert to the ascetic sect. This had a twofold influence on Myanmar's development: first, it established a cultural link to Sri Lanka (the center of Theravada Buddhism) and, second, it instilled a tradition of constructing and maintaining religious structures in order to gain spiritual merit, a concept that continues to affect both new religious buildings and conservation activity in the country to this day.[3]

After Anawrahta's death the Burmese Empire continued to expand, and by the twelfth century, Bagan was known throughout the region for its extraordinary quantity of intricately decorated pagodas, stupas and shrines. There are differing theories as to what caused Bagan's demise, the most prominent being that the city's ostentatious wealth proved irresistible to the neighboring Mongols, leading to a series of invasions in the late thirteenth century. Kublai Khan's Yuan dynasty finally sacked the city in 1287 CE, after which replacement seats of the kingdom grew up around Mandalay and Inwa (formerly Ava). The Mon kingdom, meanwhile, prospered via trading networks with connections to India and Malaysia, and continued to contribute to the collective national aesthetic sensibility through religious architecture.

FIGURE 6.3 Panorama of Bagan, looking north from Shwesandaw Phaya, one of the tallest of the ancient city's over 2,500 temples, pagodas and shrines. It is estimated that over 4,000 such buildings existed at Bagan at the pinnacle of the empire's power, before it was forced to relocate to Ava, south of the modern Mandalay area, where the new capital was founded by 1364 CE.

Colonial and post-colonial architectural conservation

From the early nineteenth century, European colonizers increasingly became entrenched in neighboring India, the Dutch East Indies and French Indochina. Beginning in 1819, the British gradually took control of Myanmar through a complex series of wars and treaties, culminating with the exile of the last Burmese king in 1886.

As a province of the British Indian Empire, Myanmar's early conservation activity was administered by the Archaeological Survey of India (ASI), although numerous surveys and scholarly descriptions of important national sites (in particular, in Bagan) had taken place earlier under the aegis of the Archaeological Survey of Burma (ASB). British Viceroy Lord Curzon visited the province in 1901 and promptly recommended the protection and study of Bagan and the royal palace at Mandalay. This recommendation led to a heightened role for Myanmar's new Archaeology Department, which had been established within the Epigraphy Office only two years earlier.[4]

The ASI introduced India-based John Marshall's seminal conservation manual to Myanmar, thereby exposing its monumental sites to Western scholarly research, formal documentation, methodical restoration and conservation interventions for the first time. (See also Chapter 16 – India, pages 363–4.) Special protection status was granted to forty-eight significant ancient historic buildings in the province based on the requirements of the British system. Directed by the French ancient languages expert Charles Duroiselle, during the early twentieth century the ASI began to decipher inscriptions and identify other sites, piecing together Myanmar's early history while also working to implement Marshall's conservation principles – though sparingly – at Bagan.[5]

During the same period, Bagan – along with Angkor and Borobudur – became a locus of architectural conservation information exchange among the region's Dutch, French and British colonial officials and the focus of considerable study by local and foreign institutions alike. This situation continued until the Japanese invasion of 1942 and World War II, during which time conservation activity effectively ceased. With the Japanese withdrawal in 1945 and full independence gained in 1948, Myanmar experienced a period of major political upheavals that resulted in an isolationist military government and a precarious situation for the country's important historic buildings and sites.

By 1952 a Ministry of Culture had been established in Myanmar, within which a Directorate of Archaeology assumed responsibility for national heritage conservation. Further protection was formalized in 1957, when the government implemented the Antiquities Preservation Act to delineate the Directorate's activities and priorities. However, five years later General Ne Win's socialist government seized power, and soon implemented its own series of radical social and governmental reconfigurations, including the nationalization of all cultural property and industry. Over the next decade only sporadic survey work and historical research were accomplished.

In 1972 the Directorate was reorganized into a new Department of Archaeology, consisting of three divisions: research and training; cultural heritage preservation; and administration and finance.[6] That same year, an updated inventory of 680 culturally significant sites was published, of which 378 were located in Bagan.[7]

The importance that survey document placed on Bagan made the news of a massive earthquake at the site on July 8, 1975 all the more alarming. Although the international community's response to the government's call for assistance was swift and thorough, the earthquake signaled a long period of unfortunate events at Bagan. Of the more than 2,500 inventoried monuments there, over 100 were severely damaged, with as many as 300 harmed in some way.[8] For its own part, the Myanmar government appointed an Advisory Committee for the Restoration of Bagan, which assessed damage, identified emergency interventions and initiated some repairs.[9]

Following the earthquake, UNESCO led a mission comprising a diverse group of international experts to Bagan, sending a technical staff to assist with evaluations, set priorities for future actions, and coordinate fundraising for repairs. The International Centre for the Restoration and Conservation of Cultural Property (ICCROM) was part of the effort, sending a team led by Guatemalan conservator Rodolfo Lujan to attend to damaged murals.[10] The Institute of Earthquake Engineering and Engineering Seismology (IZIIS), based in Skopje, Macedonia (then Yugoslavia), also contributed by evaluating the structural stability of damaged buildings and recommending how best to protect the structures against future seismic harm.[11]

FIGURE 6.4 Restorations of ancient buildings at Bagan are varied in their method, need and quality. Modestly sized buildings that represent this can be seen at the Zan-Ti Group. There, a series of almost identical shrines have been restored (minus their stucco finishes) with their donorship prominently credited on nearby markers. Their contrast with nearby unrestored structures clearly illustrates the extent of the rebuilding of Bagan's damaged shrines in recent years. Since 1975, approximately 1,200 religious monuments have been restored or rebuilt.

These positive developments continued through 1992, when British conservation architect John Sanday drew up a master plan proposal for the site per the recommendations of UNESCO, and a second phase of repairs had been completed under the supervision of Pierre Pichard of the École française d'Extrême-Orient (EFEO). Furthermore, in 1993, Myanmar's new government, then known as the State Peace and Development Council,[12] formed a group called the Myanmar Cultural Heritage Protection Central Committee to guide the Ministry of Culture and the Department of Archaeology on issues regarding cultural heritage protection policy.

By 1995, more than 250 monuments in Bagan had been either restored or repaired through the combined efforts of the international community and governmental authorities.[13] During the post-earthquake period, the Department of Archaeology also initiated a large number of repairs at a variety of structures. The joint efforts of the government and private donors resulted in the renovation of 1,175 ancient religious monuments and 689 brick mounds at Bagan during the ten-year period of 1995 to 2005. With a recent inventory of 3,122 ancient religious monuments recorded at the site, this flurry of renovation activity accounts for restorative intervention at nearly 40 percent of Bagan's extant religious monuments.[14]

Despite the attention and resources brought to bear at Bagan, the large-scale government interventions also had an unfortunate side. In 1990, officials forcibly removed the inhabitants of the Bagan site proper for resettlement outside the archaeological zone. Aside from the trauma it caused the local population – some of whom claimed descent from ancient Bagan's last inhabitants – it removed daily life from within the site, thereby creating a static archaeological park.

Perhaps most troubling to the global conservation community, however, has been the Myanmar government's lack of action on UNESCO's master plan proposal and its insistence on establishing its own development scheme, one that favors the patronage of various government profit-making operations rather than focusing attention on protecting the buildings.[15] This development approach can be seen in prominent new construction: the Aureum Palace Hotel's Nan Myint Viewing Tower at the east end of Bagan's central plain and the 2008 Golden Palace museum, which stand incongruously on the otherwise temple-silhouetted plain.

Individuals both within, and influenced by, the government have taken an outsized role in the restoration of individual structures at Bagan, motivated by their duty to the system and by an opportunity to earn spiritual merit. These interests also continue to develop the site purely for its tourism draw, with little regard for the complex cultural landscape and with little archaeological sensitivity.

While the national Department of Archaeology has purview over the whole area, local pagoda councils have organized a number of restorations, but unfortunately the quality of their interventions has been quite uneven. Insensitive and frequently inaccurate interventions now plague Bagan as the funding of such works continues, sometimes sourced from private individuals living outside of

FIGURE 6.5a and b Several initiatives taken since the late 1990s to present Bagan to visitors have drawn criticism from international archaeologists, historians and heritage protection professionals. Most notably is the erection of a 198-foot viewing tower with hotel rooms in its massive shaft and a large, ornate site museum that could have been more discreetly placed.

Myanmar.[16] In many cases, the restoration of these structures has included inexpert workmanship, conjecture, liberal replacement of old materials with new, stucco removal and the remodeling of some historic structures. Instances of over-engineered structural repairs using reinforced concrete, which proved to be too heavy and rigid, have caused further damage during subsequent earth tremors.

Another unaddressed, chronic problem involves erosion caused by the Irrawaddy River. Over the centuries, the river has cut away as much as a kilometer of part of the city's western edge, which has resulted in the loss of nearly a third of Bagan's original buildings. Although this erosion process is almost imperceptible, landslides continue to occur each year. While the government has taken such protective measures as the establishment of protected archaeological districts (within which no hotel or commercial development can take place), its decision-making process has been largely isolated from the international community. This has resulted in a rejection of standard conventions and appropriate techniques of conservation, insensitive planning, and a collective loss of authenticity at this hugely significant site.

In addition to the management of its ancient capitals, the architectural conservation community in Myanmar confronts another challenge: the restoration and adaptive reuse of the nation's wealth of surviving British colonial buildings in the country's key cities. The greatest concentration exists in Yangon, in the form of public, commercial and residential buildings.

The Yangon Heritage Trust (YHT), an influential advocacy group established by Dr. Thant Myint-U (a historian and the grandson of former UN Secretary-General U Thant), identified a number of such examples in its important 2012 publication *30 Heritage Buildings of Yangon*.[17] The volume grew out of an international conference of experts held in June 2012 that also discussed new

Conserving Myanmar's historic wooden structures

Though the dramatic stone and brick masonry of Bagan stands as archetypal Burmese structures, many of the nation's important historic buildings are, or were, constructed of wood. Mandalay – completed only in the late nineteenth century to serve as the last royal capital of the Burmese dynasty – still contains many of these wooden vernacular, religious and royal structures, though a number of them have been lost in recent years during civil conflicts or due to insufficient upkeep. Elsewhere in the country, wooden monasteries comprise a significant number of important historic buildings, yet no comprehensive plan exists on the part of the government for attending to their maintenance needs.

A carefully planned city founded in 1857 by King Mindon, Mandalay remained the capital of the country until the British shifted their administration south to Yangon in 1862. With the notable exception of the Kuthodaw Pagoda, most of the city was constructed of wood, including buildings designed by French and Italian architects commissioned by the King.[18] After the transfer of the capital, the majestic Royal Palace was converted to residences for British soldiers. In 1945 the mostly wooden palace complex went up in flames along with other important buildings in Mandalay, under the assault of Allied aerial bombardments aimed at expelling the occupying Japanese forces.

In 1989, the government began rebuilding the Royal Palace based on original plans and drawings. Out of a total of 114 buildings extant in 1886, eighty-nine buildings were rebuilt, with the majority of work completed by 1996. The restoration also included the removal of certain additions made by the British, such as the railway built across the palace moat. Rather than timber, the government opted to reconstruct Mandalay Palace and the surrounding moat with concrete and sheet metal roofs. This decision, and the use of forced local labor, have been severely criticized.[19]

In 1998 as part of the "Visit Myanmar" year, many old buildings were demolished to widen roads in Mandalay in an attempt to "improve" the city. During this modernization effort the popular Italian-designed Zeigyo wooden market building was razed and was replaced by a concrete facsimile, which does not possess ventilating qualities and so remains damp after rains.

While a few of the wooden monasteries throughout the country have been restored, many stand vulnerable to decay due to environmental factors, neglect, a lack of available conservation expertise, and a limited capacity on the part of the government or resident monks to maintain them. Approximately seventy wooden monasteries have been documented by local and international efforts, but no comprehensive plan for their conservation has yet been forthcoming.

FIGURE 6.6a and b One type of Myanmar's outstanding cultural assets – its wooden Buddhist monasteries and temples – is illustrated by Mandalay's Shwe Nandaw Kyaung monastery. Despite their vulnerability to fire and natural deterioration, many survive. This important landmark was saved due to its fortunate relocation during the 1930s from the grounds of the former national palace (destroyed in World War II) to its present location.

possibilities and methods for conserving such structures in Myanmar's future. Among the report's conclusions was that for nearly twenty years, central Yangon's commercial buildings, along with colonial-era houses located throughout the city (including the traditional, environmentally compatible wood bungalows commonly known as Bengali Houses), have been gradually demolished. These are often replaced with inferior new structures, some already at risk of collapse. As of 2015, at least half are gone and the pace of decline is accelerating. Judging by this trend, Yangon may meet the fate of other Asian cities that realized too late the value of their lost heritage.

Negative memories associated with British colonial rule do not seem to play a major role in decisions about the conservation of its related built heritage. Rather, the chief threat is neglect paired with a lack of initiatives for imaginative reuse. This is unfortunate, because most, if not all, of British colonial Asian architecture was well adapted to Myanmar's tropical setting. The issue was amplified in 2005, when many government ministries relocated from colonial buildings in Yangon to the new upcountry capital, Naypyidaw. In addition, the usual promise of real estate gains that would be realized by replacing historic structures with larger, often internationally financed new buildings, is an increasing threat to the country's built heritage. The stakes are especially high in Yangon given the confluence of events involving the capital's relocation, the country's re-opening to outside investment, the emergence of influential local groups such as the YHT, and the return of the international architectural conservation community after decades of isolation.

FIGURE 6.7 The former Rowe and Company Department Store (more recently the Immigration Department Building) built in 1910 in Yangon is an example of a former British colonial commercial building awaiting imaginative adaptive re-use. The sensitive restoration and repurposing of such structures will serve as both cultural and commercial assets and help distinguish the former capital's distinctive urban character.

Recently, YHT has been making notable progress in advocating for architectural heritage conservation among Yangon's government, commercial and private sectors. Several insensitive new construction projects recently proposed for Yangon have been halted or modified as a result of its efforts. Despite this, there are daunting challenges remaining to be addressed, such as opaque or questionable ownership of structures or parts thereof and soaring land values. According to Dr. Thant Myint-U, an important next task is to demonstrate how century-old large structures can be smartly and efficiently adaptively used.[20] These interests and forces will collectively affect the future of the city's impressive inventory of architecturally majestic, yet highly vulnerable, buildings.

As Myanmar gradually accelerates its efforts to join its region's modern pace of development, new cultural heritage initiatives in more remote parts of the country are under way. In 2013, archaeological research began in northwest Myanmar aimed at understanding and interpreting the site of Dhanyawadi, one of the ancient Arakanese capitals that thrived from the sixth century BCE to the eighth century CE. Nearby Mrauk U, a successor capital of the Arakan state from the fifteenth to the eighteenth century, resembles Bagan in its collection of stupas and temples spread over a vast plain. In the case of both sites, however, remote locations and a lack of infrastructure connecting them to the rest of Myanmar and to neighboring Bangladesh have inhibited their conservation but also helped safeguard them from human harm.

Conserving Yangon's colonial heritage

As Myanmar's political and economic restrictions ease, cities like Yangon have directly benefitted from a growing economy and increased development. A hub of colonial architecture within not just the nation but the greater region of Southeast Asia, a few of Yangon's notable historic buildings from that era represent some of the country's best opportunities to embrace its newfound liberalization without sacrificing the richly built heritage of its past.

The seat of power during British Imperial rule was the Ministers' Building historically known as the Secretariat. This massive brick complex was constructed in a grand Victorian style shortly after the turn of the twentieth century. Covering nearly sixteen acres in the heart of Yangon, the Ministers' Office is one of the most famous colonial buildings in the nation. This is not only due to its architectural grandeur but also for its role as witness to sensitive moments in the country's history, perhaps most notably as the site of General Aung San's assassination in 1947. Off-limits to the public since the military's assumption of power in 1962, the building's interiors and side galleries have remained largely abandoned and empty.[21] In 2012, the government leased the property to the Anawmar Art Group, a locally based private entity that has tentative plans to develop it as a museum and cultural center, with additional space for compatible commercial enterprises.[22]

Another important cultural heritage landmark, the ca. 1877 Ministry of Railways building, housed the former headquarters of the Burma Railway Company. As of 2015, the structure was slated for redevelopment as a luxury boutique hotel, part of a larger mixed-use development plan. Led by a local developer backed by international investors, the multi-million dollar project may represent a new and promising interest in re-using Yangon's larger heritage buildings.[23]

Other icons of colonial architecture face more tenuous situations. The Pegu Club was once the most exclusive British gentlemen's club in the nation, with oppressive membership rules to ensure its prestige among the ruling elite. Derelict and in poor condition since the end of World War II, this two-storey ca. 1882 teak building is among the oldest of British construction in the nation. Nevertheless, it is not on the Yangon City Development Committee's key list of protected sites. Its future remains uncertain.[24]

Economic stagnation and political isolation may have inadvertently saved Yangon's spectacular colonial buildings from demolition, but their fate today is threatened by the rapidly emerging climate of modernization in the absence of established planning and building regulations. If the city's colonial buildings are to be preserved through adaptive reuse and development, local authorities must exercise discretion such that these distinctive structures are sensitively protected while their functions remain relevant to Yangon's modern population.

a

b

c

FIGURE 6.8a, b, c and d Among the gems of Yangon's colonial building stock, the massive complex known as the Secretariat (a) has been largely untouched during the last fifty years, including its historic interior (b). Dating to 1877, the former headquarters of the Burma Railway Company (c) has recently been scheduled for redevelopment as a boutique hotel, while the famous Pegu Club (d) currently languishes without a definite conservation plan on the horizon.

UNESCO has included Mrauk U on its list of tentative World Heritage Sites since 1996, but the site remains at risk due to many of the same forces that have challenged Bagan since the 1970s: insensitive development, overzealous restoration and the absence of an effective management plan. In 2012, the US-based Global Heritage Fund added Mrauk U to its list of ten Asian sites "in peril," due in part to a regional railroad development that has pushed through the site, and unchecked development pressures aimed at capitalizing on a nascent tourism industry.[25]

If the health of a national conservation program can be measured by the status of a country's most important site, the situation in Myanmar remains precarious. Criticized by many as a national reconsolidation effort reflective of the values and aspirations of the military regime rather than of those of the culturally diverse Burmese people, Myanmar's recent architectural conservation projects have continued to frustrate and worry international heritage protection advocates. Aside from denying the multi-cultural reality of historical and contemporary Myanmar, the restoration projects at Mandalay and Bagan in particular have eliminated critical historical evidence in favor of contemporary conjecture and preference. While other points of concern at Bagan include control of new construction, site management, sensitive planning, heritage education and the need for additional archaeological mapping, the frequently irreversible interventions are the most problematic.

Recent shifts by Myanmar's national government toward operating in a more inclusive and internationally cooperative manner are encouraging signs that could indicate an objective reassessment of conservation work today, and a re-prioritization toward using more current techniques in architectural heritage protection. The international response to such shifts has been immediate and impressive, with Italy stepping forward in 2011 to fund a €400,000 (approximately US$500,000) UNESCO-led program to begin rebuilding professional capacity in site management and conservation skills, in collaboration with Myanmar's Department of Archaeology and National Museum.[26] In 2012, the Australian Foreign Ministry announced a multi-faceted aid program aimed at bringing planners and other officials from Myanmar to Australia to tour successful conservation projects, while also

FIGURE 6.9 Exposure and conservation of original murals depicting Buddhist scriptures in the Ananda Temple (1090–1105 CE) at Bagan, part of an extensive restoration funded by the Archaeological Survey of India begun in 2012.

providing direct financial and professional support to the Yangon Heritage Trust in its efforts to document and reuse the former capital's architectural treasures.[27] The Archaeological Survey of India, in a renewed effort to help at Bagan, also pledged US$22 million for the restoration of the well-proportioned and remarkably intact 170 ft-high Ananda Temple that contains four 31 ft standing Buddha statues. These fresh, new approaches may reactivate the spirit of international cooperation that briefly existed after the 1975 earthquake and set the country on a positive path towards preserving and presenting its remarkable array of cultural heritage.

Notes

1. The country was called Burma from 1835 to 1948 during British rule and the name was also used until 1989 when the military regime changed the country's name from Burma to the Union of Myanmar, along with most site and city names. Several foreign governments, including the United States, did not recognize the current regime until the country declared itself as being open to democratic reforms in 2012. Thus, adoption of the new country name Myanmar and the new city names since 1989 has been inconsistent, although contemporary names are used herewith.
2. Russell L. Ciochon and Jamie James. "The Power of Pagan," *Archaeology* 45(5) (September–October 1992), 37. Archaeological evidence reveals that *Homo sapiens* lived in the region now known as Burma around 11,000 BCE and that their predecessors *Homo erectus* were present as early as 750,000 years ago.
3. Ibid.
4. Paul Strachan. *Imperial Pagan: Art and Architecture of Old Burma.* (Honolulu: University of Hawai'i Press, 1990), 4.
5. Ibid.
6. AusHeritage and ASEAN. Cultural Heritage Management Profile: Myanmar. COCI Development of an ASEAN Regional Policy and Strategy for Cultural Heritage Management.
7. Pierre Pichard. *The Pentagonal Monuments of Pagan* (Bangkok: White Lotus Co., 1995), 24.

8 Miguel A. Corzo (ed.). *The Future of Asia's Past: Preservation of the Architectural Heritage of Asia*. (Los Angeles: The Getty Conservation Institute, 1995), 14.
9 U Nyunt Han, 1989: 95.
10 Ciochon, 40.
11 Pedrag Gavrilovič. *Burma: Conservation of Cultural Heritage of Selected Sites: The Restoration of Monuments in Pagan* (Paris: UNESCO, 1987).
12 The State Peace and Development Council (SPDC) served as the country's cabinet; it initially assumed power in September 1988 as the State Law and Order Restoration Council (SLORC) and changed its name in November 1997. It was officially dissolved in March 2011.
13 Pichard, *The Pentagonal Monuments of Pagan*, 44.
14 A stone inscription at the entrance to the Bagan Museum records the renovated ancient religious monuments in the archaeological zone, Bagan. Inscribed December 31, 2005.
15 Joe Cummings and Michael Clark. *Lonely Planet: Myanmar (Burma)*, 7th ed. (London: Hawthorne, 2002), 292–293.
16 Richard Covington. "Sacred and Profaned," *Smithsonian Magazine* (December 2002). On 24 August, 2016 a 6.8 magnitude earthquake in Central Myanmar damaged scores of buildings at Bagan, in particular several that had been inadequately 'restored' during the past decade.
17 Through February 2014 the Yangon Heritage Trust inventoried approximately 4,000 historic buildings in Yangon.
18 Jacques Dumarçay and Michael Smithies. *Cultural Sites of Myanmar, Thailand and Cambodia*. (Kuala Lumpur: Oxford University Press, 1995), 31.
19 Web. www.myanmar.com/ACOCI/CULTURE/2000/Mandalay.htm. Accessed May 17, 2016.
20 Thant Myint-U. Information within Dr. Myint-U's Mellon Lecture entitled "Saving Yangon's Historic City Center" hosted by the World Monuments Fund, New York, February 24, 2014.
21 Association of Myanmar Architects. *30 Heritage Buildings of Yangon: Inside the City That Captured Time* (Chicago: Serindia Publications, 2012).
22 "Restoring Rangoon." 101 East – Al Jazeera English, May 22, 2013. Web. www.aljazeera.com/programmes/101east/2013/05/20135229324313702.html. Accessed February 11, 2014.
23 Ibid.
24 Association of Myanmar Architects, 142–144.
25 Global Heritage Fund. *Asia's Heritage In Peril*. Report published May 2012. Web. www.globalheritagefund.org/images/uploads/docs/GHFAsiaHeritageinPeril050112_lowres.pdf . Accessed February 14, 2014.
26 UNESCO World Heritage Centre. "Italy Announces Support to UNESCO for Safeguarding Cultural Heritage in Myanmar." December 14, 2011. Web. http://whc.unesco.org/en/news/825/. Accessed February 14, 2014.
27 Australian Minister for Foreign Affairs. "Australia Supports Preservation of Yangon's Urban Heritage." Media Release, June 6, 2012. Web. http://foreignminister.gov.au/releases/2012/bc_mr_120606a.html. Accessed February 15, 2014.

Further reading

Association of Myanmar Architects. 2012. *30 Heritage Buildings of Yangon: Inside the City that Captured Time*. Chicago: Serindia Publications.
Aung-Thwin, Michael. 1985. *Pagan: The Origins of Modern Burma*. Honolulu: University of Hawai'i Press.
AusHeritage and ASEAN-COCI (eds.). 2001. "Cultural Management Profile, Myanmar," in *ASEAN-Australia Project: Development of an ASEAN Regional Policy and Strategy for Cultural Heritage Management*. Melbourne: Cultural Heritage Center for Asia and the Pacific.
Chapman, William. 2010. "The British in Burma: Pagan and Other Sites during the Colonial Era, 1852–1942," *Na Jua: Journal of the Faculty of Architecture, Silpakorn University* 24 (2009–2010): 183–203.
Charney, Michael. 2009. *A History of Modern Burma*. Cambridge: Cambridge University Press.
Ciochon, Russell L. and Jamie James. 1992. "The Power of Pagan," *Archaeology* 45(5) (September–October): 34–41.
Covington, Richard. 2002. "Sacred and Profane: Misguided Restorations of the Exquisite Buddhist Shrines of Pagan in Burma May Do More Harm Than Good," *Smithsonian* 33(9) (December 2002). Web. www.smithsonianmag.com/people-places/sacred-and-profaned-72955322/. Accessed June 1, 2016.
Dumarçay, Jacques and Michael Smithies. 1995. *Cultural Sites of Myanmar, Thailand and Cambodia*. Kuala Lumpur: Oxford University Press.
Engelhardt, Richard A. 1998. *Mission Report for Yangon and Bagan, Myanmar, 14–16 January 1998*. Bangkok: UNESCO.

Falconer, John, et al. 2001. *Burmese Design and Architecture*. Singapore: Periplus.
Fraser-Lu, Sylvia. 2002. *Splendour in Wood: The Buddhist Monasteries of Burma*. Bangkok: Orchid Press.
Gavrilovič, Predrag. 1987. *The Restoration of Monuments in Pagan: Application for Repair and Strengthening of Monuments in Pagan-Burma*. Technical report. Paris: UNESCO.
——. 1992. *Repair and Strengthening of Selected Monuments in Pagan: Myanmar*. Assignment report. Bangkok: UNESCO.
Giantomassi, Carlo, et al. 1993. *Conservation of Mural Paintings, External Stuccoes and Stone Buildings: Myanmar*. Paris: UNESCO.
Guillon, Emmanuel. 1999. *The Mons: A Civilization of Southeast Asia*. Translated by James V. DeCrocco. Bangkok: Siam Society.
Gutman, Pamela. 2001. *Burma's Lost Kingdoms: Splendours of Arakan*. Bangkok: Orchid Press.
Harvey, Godfrey. 1992. *British Rule in Burma, 1824–1942*. London: Ams Press.
Hudson, Bob. 2008. "Restoration and Reconstruction of Monuments at Bagan (Pagan), Myanmar (Burma)," *World Archaeology* 40(4): 553–571.
ICCROM. 2000. "Myanmar," in *ICCROM, A World Heritage Strategy for Southeast Asia*. Rome: ICCROM.
Luce, Gordon Hannington. 1932. "Burma's Debt to Pagan," *Journal of the Burma Research Society* 22(2): 120–127.
——. 1949. "A Century of Progress in Burmese History and Archaeology," *Journal of the Burma Research Society* 32: 79–94.
Ma, Thanegi and Barry Michael Broman. 2005. *Myanmar Architecture: Cities of Gold*. Singapore: Times Editions, Marshall Cavendish.
Moore, Elizabeth. 2007. *Early Landscapes of Myanmar*. Bangkok: River Books.
Moore, Elizabeth H., Hansjorg Mayer and U Win Pe. 1999. *Shwedagon: Golden Pagoda of Myanmar*. London: Thames & Hudson.
Nwe, T.T. and J. Philp. 2002. "Yangon, Myanmar: The Re-invention of Heritage," in W.S. Logan (ed.), *The Disappearing "Asian" City*. New York: Oxford University Press, 147–165.
Nyunt Han, U. 1989. Assistant Director, National Project. National Project Ministry of approval on 6 December of a *Report within Project MYA/86/019, Annex 1: Diary of the Mission*, was carried out under "Conservation of Cultural Heritage at Selected Sites in Myanmar", 4–30 August, 1994. Web. http://unesdoc.unesco.org/images/0009/000999/099997eo.pdf. Accessed February 16, 2014.
Nyunt Han, U. 2013. "A Retrospective and Prospective Review on the Conservation of Ancient Monuments in Pagan," in Y. Ishizawa and K. Kono (eds.), *Cultural Heritage in Asia 4*. Tokyo: Institute of Asian Cultures, Sophia University, 91–99.
Pagnin, Paolo. 1994. *Conservation of Stone, Pagan, Union of Myanmar*. Mission progress report, UNESCO and UNDP, December 20, 1993–January 31, 1994. Venice: UNESCO.
Peleggi, Maurizio. 2012. "The Unbearable Impermanence of Things: Reflections on Buddhism, Cultural Memory and Heritage Conservation," in Patrick Daly and Tim Winter (eds.), *Routledge Handbook of Heritage in Asia*. London: Routledge, 55–69.
Pichard, Pierre. 1976. *Burma: The Restoration of Pagan*. Paris: UNESCO.
——. 1992–2000. *Inventory of Monuments at Pagan*. 8 volumes. Gartmore, Stirlingshire, Scotland: Kiscadale; Paris: UNESCO.
——. 1994. *Conservation of Monuments in Pagan*. Assignment report. Paris: UNESCO.
——. 1995. *The Pentagonal Monuments of Pagan*. Bangkok: White Lotus Co.
Sanday, John. 1992. "Myanmar: Guidelines for a Masterplan for the Conservation and Preservation of the Historic District of Pagan." Unpublished report for UNESCO, Bangkok.
Singer, Noel F. 1993. *Burmah: A Photographic Journey, 1855–1925*. Gartmore, Stirlingshire, Scotland: Strachan-Kiscadale.
Stadtner, Donald M. 2005. *Ancient Pagan: Buddhist Plain of Merit*. Bangkok: River Books.
——. 2011. *Sacred Sites of Burma: Myth and Folklore in an Evolving Spiritual Realm*. Bangkok: River Books.
Stargardt, Janice. 1990. *The Ancient Pyu of Burma*. Volume 1 of *Early Pyu Cities in a Man-Made Landscape*. Cambridge: PACSEA.
Strachan, Paul. 1989. *Pagan: Art and Architecture of Old Burma*. Gartmore, Stirlingshire, Scotland: Kiscadale.
——. 1990. *Imperial Pagan: Art and Architecture of Old Burma*. Honolulu: University of Hawai'i Press.
Taw Sein Ko. 1907. *Report of the Superintendent, Archaeological Survey, Burma, for the Year Ending 31st March 1907*. Rangoon: Superintendent of Government Printing.
Thaw, Aung. 1972. *Historical Sites in Burma*. Yangon: Beikman Press.
Ueno, Kunikazu. 1998. *Burma: Conservation of Cultural Heritage at Selected Sites in Burma Project: Findings and Recommendations*. Paris: UNESCO.
Yarmola, Jean-Claude Ivan. 1992. *Restauration: Reinforcement of the Selected Historic Brick in Pagan (Myanmar)*. Report for the United Nations Development Fund, Mission 4. Paris: UNDP.
Zari, Donatella, et al. 1987. *Conservation of Mural Paintings in Pagan: Burma*. Assignment report. Paris: UNESCO.

Laotian ornamental corbel.

7

LAOS

Bordered by China, Vietnam, Cambodia, Thailand and Myanmar, the People's Democratic Republic of Laos (the Lao PDR) is comprised of mountainous regions, lowlands and a vast river network, including the mighty Mekong. Its modern history has been relatively turbulent: since the early nineteenth century it has been at war with nearly all of its neighbors, been colonized by the French, and due to its geography, became entangled in the Second Indochina, or American War (the Vietnam War) during the 1960s and 1970s. Nevertheless, Laos retains an extraordinary natural and cultural heritage, much of which has been subject to heritage protection measures only since the early 1990s.

These circumstances have resulted in a relatively underdeveloped architectural conservation environment, albeit one that has developed substantially in recent decades. Like its neighbors Cambodia and Myanmar, Laos has a rapidly growing tourist industry that is driven by its natural and cultural heritage sites, and has increasingly become a target for international investment by its more economically developed neighbors, Thailand and China.

Since 1990 the number of foreign visitors to the Lao PDR has risen from 14,000 per year to over 3.5 million in 2014. These numbers are even more striking when one considers that Laos' population is today only 6.5 million citizens. Tourism revenue has rapidly become a major income source, and now constitutes the second largest economic engine in the country (after mining).[1] But unlike the other former French colonies of Vietnam and Cambodia, the modern nation of Laos lacks a unifying national identity forged by a single dominant ethnic group. Today, non-Lao ethnic "minorities" comprise 40 percent of its population.[2] This situation – largely a remnant of the colonial legacy – complicates issues related to local "ownership" of nationally significant sites, and places undue pressure of national identity-building on the country's major heritage sites, including Luang Prabang, the Champasak Cultural Landscape and the Plain of Jars.

The varied geography of Laos has resulted in a diverse landscape of architectural typologies and associated conservation considerations. In the northern mountainous region of the country the generally well-preserved vernacular architecture of ethnic minority peoples distinctly reflects environmental, social and religious influences, as seen especially in temple, pagoda and shrine forms. Distinctive land settlement patterns, rural domestic architecture and traditional agricultural practices also persist throughout Laos. Colonial-hybrid architecture constitutes the urban areas of Luang Prabang and smaller towns such as Savannakhet and Pakse, and, to a lesser extent, the modern capital of Vientiane. Ruins of Hindu and Buddhist temples from the Khmer Empire are found across southern and central Laos, with the most outstanding example being the Wat Phou temple complex, dating from the fifth to fifteenth centuries CE.

FIGURE 7.1 The Wat Xieng Thong in Luang Prabang, dating from 1560 CE, is considered to be the most important symbol of the country's Buddhist religious heritage. It is notable for the colored-glass mosaics that adorn the exteriors of several of the main buildings within the complex.

Located in the Champasak Province in the southwestern corner of the country, Wat Phou is the largest temple complex in the Lao PDR. Since the nineteenth century, it has received considerable conservation attention from the French. Today, Wat Phou benefits from a multi-national program involving a revived French effort, as well as teams from Italy, India and the United States. It is Luang Prabang, however, that represents the most active architectural conservation effort in the country to date. It is also the site that embodies many of the field's successes and risks in the region.

Located in north-central Laos on a promontory at the confluence of the Mekong and Nam Khan rivers, Luang Prabang served as the capital of the Lane Xang kingdom from the fourteenth through sixteenth centuries CE, before it was relocated to the more defensible location of Vientiane, some 300 km to the south. When the Lane Xang kingdom split apart in the seventeenth century CE, Luang Prabang once again became a seat of royal power until the French moved the capital to Vientiane in 1946, where it remains today.

Though affected by wars in past centuries, and largely destroyed in the nineteenth century by regional fighting, Luang Prabang was either rebuilt or survived as a remarkable blend of religious, domestic and civic buildings.[3] French urban planners, architects and restoration experts working under the École française d'Extrême Orient (EFEO) were active at Luang Prabang in the nineteenth century, as well as at several other locations in Laos including early Khmer sites and at Wat Phou. Documentation of these sites and some temple restorations were carried out, though they generally received less attention than those in neighboring Cambodia and Vietnam.[4]

The urban composition of Luang Prabang includes modest vernacular residences of wooden and tile-roofed buildings, religious structures (wats and monasteries), an array of European colonial structures, and hybrid buildings such as Chinese-style shophouses. Over the past quarter century various forms of modern architecture, usually government and commercial buildings, have been added to the mix, with some degree of sensitivity to Luang Prabang's historic context, though this has been much less the case in the country's other cities and towns.

By virtue of its mixture of French and traditional Lao architecture and its highly intact urban fabric, Luang Prabang was added to the World Heritage List in 1995. However, since then development pressures and its status as the country's pre-eminent tourist destination have periodically threatened its distinctive character. In the decades since its listing, UNESCO, along with its local and national partners, has collaborated to identify and address threats to Luang Prabang's character. Many challenges remain, particularly with regard to ongoing development pressures.

The national Ministry of Information, Culture and Tourism, in cooperation with the provincial authorities, oversees a comprehensive system for management and heritage conservation in Luang Prabang's historic center. Since 2000 these efforts have been supported in large part by a detailed management plan known as the Plan de Sauvegarde et de Mise en Valeur (PSMV – or Safeguarding and Enhancement Plan). The PSMV defines land uses within the old town as protected, safeguarded or monastery zones and the surrounding area as natural and landscape zones, including large swaths of land on the opposite side of the Mekong River.[5]

At the local level, conservation and heritage planning activities are coordinated through a cooperative institution originally known as the Maison du Patrimoine (or Heritage House, restructured in 2009 as the Heritage Department). As a function of the provincial Department of Culture, the Heritage Department carries out the PSMV, work that includes reviewing and approving all building permits within the World Heritage Site boundaries. Staffed by a team of Lao architects, Heritage Department employees engage in on-site conservation awareness and assistance for Luang Prabang's building owners, while helping in the implementation of the various internationally led conservation projects.[6]

Today, many monumental brick structures exist in Luang Prabang, including colonial buildings and Lao temples, but most of the buildings that define the character of the historic city consist of bamboo, clay, lime mortar and timber. Most usual is wood frame construction covered by a woven bamboo and plaster wall finish referred to as *torchis*, a composition that decays rapidly in a tropical climate.[7] In addition to the potential fragility of many of the city's buildings, the work of the Heritage Department is complicated because much of Luang Prabang's large quantity of historically significant vernacular construction is privately owned and is widely scattered throughout the city. The Heritage Department, along with various other European and Lao partners, addresses this challenge by providing property owners with appropriate maintenance and repair assistance via a series of fascicule (manuals) that cover topics such as traditional lime mortar recipes, timber framing and torchis replacement.[8]

FIGURE 7.2 French colonial era shophouses in Luang Prabang.

Cultural survival and revival in UNESCO's Buddhist sangha program

In 2000, UNESCO, in partnership with the Luang Prabang Department of Culture and Information and the local Buddhist monk community (sangha), launched a three-year pilot program focused on traditional craft training and certification. Based in Wat Xieng Mouane, the program focuses on the training and certification of young Buddhist monks in traditional methods of temple design and maintenance within the context of Buddhism itself. Historically, younger monks learned building, sculpture and painting techniques from their elders, but in the 1970s this ancient system broke down due to an anti-religious political climate and the closure of temples throughout the Lao PDR.

The pilot program initially trained thirty monks in the design and creation of architectural bronze, stone, wood and painted works of art, as well as in the fundamentals of building conservation. Participants received certification at one of three levels: apprentice, artisan or master, depending on the time and training commitment undertaken. Initially, instructors were drawn from the faculty of the Luang Prabang School of Fine Arts, but ultimately the program expects to be able to train sufficient master craftsmen within the monastic community so that the program can be as self-sufficient as possible.

A key objective of the program is to tap into the Buddhist concept of "merit," whereby spiritual enhancement can be gained from the restoration and conservation of existing buildings and works of art. Phase II of the program, which ran from 2004 until 2007, witnessed the expansion to Theravada and Vajrayana monastic communities in ten countries, from Mongolia to Sri Lanka, thus greatly expanding the reach and benefits of this innovative program.[9]

a

b

FIGURE 7.3a and b The UNESCO Buddhist sangha program in Luang Prabang fosters the restoration crafts among young monks.

With the sustained assistance of UNESCO, the French and other foreign governments and its active local conservation infrastructure, Luang Prabang has come to represent one of the true success stories in cultural heritage protection in Southeast Asia. However, its achievements have not been without challenges.

Development pressures are both local and national, such as those created by the construction of two high-rise hotels within Luang Prabang's 12,500 hectare buffer zone, the expansion of its international airport, and a proposed dam 60 km upstream on the Mekong River. Each of these has raised serious concerns within the World Heritage Committee, triggering several UNESCO monitoring missions and the drafting of specific recommendations to remedy the situation. In a demonstration of effective collaboration between the World Heritage Committee and local management frameworks, each issue has to date been addressed satisfactorily, so that the site has been able to avoid being added to UNESCO's List of World Heritage in Danger.[10]

The experience, institutional capacity and connections with the foreign conservation community gained at Luang Prabang since its World Heritage listing in 1995 have undoubtedly been key to improvements made in the Laotian heritage management infrastructure. Over two decades of involvement, a national framework for heritage conservation has been developed in consultation with UNESCO, one that today is supported at the highest levels of government. Presently, the Department of National Museums, Historic Buildings and Archaeology within the Ministry of Information, Culture and Tourism manages this authority, although the system still relies heavily on outside support.[11] Nevertheless, significant heritage protection measures have been put in place throughout the country and have led to the development of conservation projects outside of Luang Prabang, most notably in Vientiane and at Wat Phou.

Rapidly modernizing Vientiane, the political hub of Laos, shares many of the conservation burdens shouldered by capital cities elsewhere in the developing world: population pressures, infrastructure development and minimally controlled growth. The Lao situation is aggravated by the introduction of incompatible new architectural styles and materials, and the government's determination to craft a new, unified Lao identity from the remains of a colonial and ethnically diverse history.

The issue of identity as it relates to heritage conservation has become increasingly complicated in recent years as Laos becomes less and less isolated from the rest of the world, only to find itself subject to unwanted external cultural influences, the unrelenting presence of foreign tourists and increased scrutiny of its political systems.[12] Added to all this, there exists a national perception that Vientiane suffers as a result of Luang Prabang's being a potent symbol of the former kingdom, with the former serving as the resource-strapped country's "modern" capital, while the latter fills the role as its "cultural" hub. This combination of challenges presents an unclear vision of the future for Vientiane, at least in terms of how it is modernizing itself to be a more appealing urban environment.

The Chenla and Khmer ruins of Champasak, which include the monumental Wat Phou temple complex and its associated cultural landscape, were listed as a World Heritage Site in 2001. First documented during the Mekong Expedition of the 1860s, the four-hectare, axially oriented temple complex is comprised of a series of buildings, shrines and *baray*.[13] It was revisited by French archaeologists in the 1980s, including teams from Angkor, and has been the subject of multi-national conservation efforts since the early 1990s. Wat Phou in particular has become an active training center for Lao conservation professionals thanks to successful collaborations with international teams from the United States and Italy.

With UNESCO support, the Champasak Heritage Management Plan was adopted in 1998, delineating management zones and regulations for the entire 39,000 hectare site within which Wat Phou occupies four hectares. The challenges inherent in protecting this large site, significant due to its intact collection of dispersed landscape features and archaeological zones, is underscored by concerns raised by UNESCO in 2012. These include the construction of a new road within the site's boundaries, an incompatibly designed project center, and a proposed 25 m high water tank located outside of but visible from within the site's boundaries.[14]

In order to address the Champasak site's immediate and long-term needs, the international heritage community has implemented a multi-faceted conservation program similar in concept (if not scale) to efforts at Angkor in Cambodia, which focus on documentation, stabilization of key structures and

FIGURE 7.4a and b Built under royal patronage in 1818, Wat Sis Saket, is the oldest *wat* in Vientiane because it was spared destruction during the Siamese invasion of 1828. The authenticity of the temple site, including its impressive surrounding cloister containing approximately 2,000 Buddha images and the rare surviving cycle of wall paintings within the *sim* (central building), makes Wat Sis Saket a highly valued heritage destination today among Lao and foreign visitors alike. In the French colonial era the ornate exterior woodwork adorning temples, which in former times had been laboriously hand carved, was often replaced with cast cement replicas. The replication of Haw Pha Kaew (now a museum) and Wat Si Muang are two current examples.

professional capacity building. In addition to the EFEO, among the longest running international programs at Wat Phou is the Milan-based Lerici Foundation. Since 1990 their work has included archaeological investigations, documentation and training for local professionals. In further support of capacity building in Laos and the wider region, the US-based Getty Conservation Institute (GCI) initiated a multi-year program at Wat Phou in 2008 that brought twenty-five mid-career professionals from the five Mekong River countries (Myanmar, Cambodia, Vietnam, Thailand and Laos). Participants received on-site training in international conservation standards and best management practices for site conditions common throughout the region. The effort, which was co-supported by the Lerici Foundation, the Lao government and Thailand's SEAMEO-SPAFA, continues today as a regionally focused education initiative by the GCI that addresses shared issues in architectural conservation, including urban heritage preservation, risk assessment and community engagement.[15] The US-based Global Heritage Fund has also contributed to building stabilization efforts at Wat Phou since 2006, using many of the same successful conservation practices developed in the 1990s and 2000s at Angkor, including anastylosis and improvements to on-site water management.[16]

FIGURE 7.5a, b and c
Architectural conservation at the grandly planned ancient Khmer site of Wat Phou in southern Laos (a) has been conducted by teams of architects, engineers and conservators from France (EFEO), Italy (The Lerici Foundation), India (The Archaeological Survey of India) and the United States (Global Heritage Fund and the Getty Conservation Institute). Here technicians supported by the Archaeological Survey of India are reinstating the west cornerstone of the principal entrance to the Southern Palace of the complex (b, c).

Another site that was subject to early twentieth century study and documentation, only to be interrupted by the American war in Vietnam of the 1960s and 1970s, is the picturesque yet mysterious Plain of Jars. Located in northeast Laos among the gently rolling plains of Hua Phan Province, this fifth century BCE site is comprised of thousands of monumental limestone, granite and sandstone, urn-shaped "jars" scattered over an area of more than 5,000 square kilometers. It was first documented and studied in the 1930s by the EFEO's noted French archaeologist Madeleine Colani and is now understood to consist of more than eighty individual sites thought to be associated with ancient local burial practices.

During the Vietnam War, the area was extensively bombed by the United States military, which left behind a horrible legacy of unexploded ordnance (UXO) that limits study and access to the site to this day. Efforts to clear the area of UXO and restart archaeological work began in the 1990s, and in 1993 the Plain of Jars sites were added to the Lao PDR national heritage list.[17]

Challenges to the ongoing conservation of the Plain of Jars sites abound, from continued UXO remediation, to visitor management and interpretation, to documentation and research of a vast, little-understood site dating from the distant past. Since 1998 UNESCO Bangkok has led a multi-phased program aimed at protecting the Plain of Jars, including furthering research, the development of a locally based tourist infrastructure, and the conservation of the monuments themselves. These efforts are intended to culminate in the generation of a site management plan, and in the preparation of a World Heritage Site nomination dossier, so that the Plain of Jars might soon join Luang Prabang and the Champasak cultural landscape on UNESCO's World Heritage List.[18]

Since the 1990s, Laos has been transformed from a rarely visited country with a collection of heritage sites that had remained largely unstudied for half a century, to a regional hub of international heritage collaboration and burgeoning tourist destination. This transformation has been nothing short of remarkable, and offers numerous lessons about the potency of World Heritage listing and the potential it can bring to countries.

FIGURE 7.6 View of the Plain of Jars.

FIGURE 7.7 Unusual examples of architectural heritage in Laos are found near the Vietnam border where various village and farm buildings are partially constructed of remnants of Vietnam War materiel, (here cluster bomb casings) – advertised by local tour companies as "Warchitecture."

The Lao experience also underscores the pitfalls of increased visitation and development pressure that can come to bear on even the most protected heritage sites. Great gains in professional capacity development have been realized in Laos in recent decades, notably multi-national training efforts and the restoration of traditional monastic maintenance practices. But among the most challenging obstacles to realizing an effective, integrated cultural heritage management system remains the continuing shortage of locally based practitioners and the need for consistent national support for heritage management infrastructure that is appropriate for large-scale international tourism and investment.[19] To this end, the international community has set the foundation for effective heritage management through its engagement in Laos, but increased self-sufficiency remains a goal in the long term.

Notes

1 *The Nation.* "Tourism is Laos' Second Highest Income Earner." May 14, 2013. Web. www.nationmultimedia.com/aec/Tourism-is-Laos-second-highest-income-earner-30206071.html. Accessed June 23, 2014.
2 Lao PDR today is one of the most ethnically diverse countries in Asia. Its population consists of three principle ethnic groups, the Hmong, the Kmu and the Lao, and forty-nine officially recognized sub-groups.
3 Boun Nhang Phongphicit. "Planning for the Future of Luang Prabang." Paper delivered at *The Economics of Heritage: UNESCO Conference on Adaptive Re-use of Historic Properties in Asia and the Pacific*, May. (Paris: UNESCO, 1999).
4 Emmanuel Guillon. *Cham Art.* (London: Thames & Hudson, 2001), 11.
5 Giovanni Boccardi and William Logan. *Mission Report: Reactive Monitoring Mission to the Town of Luang Prabang World Heritage Property, Lao People's Democratic Republic, 22–28 November 2007* (Paris: UNESCO, 2008).
6 Phongphicit, 3.
7 UNESCO Bangkok. *Impact: The Effects of Tourism on Culture and the Environment in Asia and the Pacific.* Tourism and Heritage Site Management – Luang Prabang, Lao PDR. (Bangkok: UNESCO, 2004), 27–28.
8 Lynne Dearborn and John Stallmeyer. *Inconvenient Heritage: Erasure and Global Tourism in Luang Prabang* (Walnut Creek, CA: Left Coast Press, 2010), 88–89.
9 UNESCO Bangkok. "Cultural Survival and Revival in the Buddhist Sangha." Web. www.unescobkk.org/culture/ich/cultural-survival-and-revival-in-the-buddhist-sangha/phase-i-pilot-project-in-luang-prabang/. Accessed June 21, 2014.
10 UNESCO World Heritage Centre. *State of Conservation – Town of Luang Prabang, Laos.* Web. http://whc.unesco.org/en/soc/2818. Accessed June 21, 2014. See also François Greck. "Luang Prabang, Laos," in *The Future of Asia's Past: Preservation of the Built Heritage of Asia.* Proceedings from the International Conference held in Chiang Mai, Thailand, January 1995 (Los Angeles: Getty Conservation Institute, 1995).
11 Phongphicit, 6.
12 William S. Logan, Colin Long and Roz Hansen. "Vientiane, Laos: Lane Xang's Capital in the Age of Modernization and Globalization," in *The Disappearing "Asian" City.* (Hong Kong: Oxford University Press, 2002), 51–69.
13 A *baray* is an artificial body of water that is often part of large scale Khmer architectural settings.
14 UNESCO Mission Report: Vat Phou and Associated Ancient Settlements within the Champasak Cultural Landscape (N481)/Vat Phou et les anciens établissements associés du paysage culturel de Champassak. (République démocratique populaire lao) (N 481), February 15–21, 2012.
15 Getty Conservation Institute. "From Risk Assessment to Conservation: Safeguarding Archaeological Complexes in the Mekong Region Vat Phou, Lao PDR, 2008." Web. www.getty.edu/conservation/our_projects/education/sea/sea_component1.html. Accessed June 23, 2014.
16 Global Heritage Fund. "Wat Phou Project Overview." Web. http://globalheritagefund.org/what_we_do/overview/completed_projects/wat_phu_laos. Accessed June 23, 2014.
17 Lia Genovese. "The Plain of Jars: Mysterious and Imperiled." 2012. Web. http://ghn.globalheritagefund.com/uploads/documents/document_2006.pdf . Accessed June 23, 2014.
18 UNESCO Bangkok. "Safeguarding the Plain of Jars." Web. www.unescobkk.org/unit-archive-folders/clt-archive-folder/heritage/world-heritage-and-immovable-heritage/the-plain-of-jars-important-but-imperiled/phase-iv/main-activities/world-heritage-nomination/. Accessed June 23, 2014.
19 Keophilavanh Aphaylath, "Country Brief: Lao PDR," in *Culture and Sustainable Development: East Asia and Pacific Working Group Proceedings*, from the conference Culture Counts: Financing, Resources and the Economics of Culture in Sustainable Development, held in Florence, Italy (October 1999). (Washington, DC: The World Bank, 1999).

Further reading

Aphaylath, Keophilavanh. 1999. "Country Brief: Lao PDR," in *Culture and Sustainable Development: East Asia and Pacific Working Group Proceedings*, from the conference Culture Counts: Financing, Resources and the Economics of Culture in Sustainable Development, held in Florence, Italy. Washington, DC: The World Bank.

Askew, Marc, William Logan and Colin Long. 2006. *Vientiane: Transformations of a Lao Landscape*. Routledge Studies in Asia's Transformations. London: Routledge.

Ateliers de la Peninsule Co. 2004. *Luang Phabang: An Architectural Journey*. Vientiane: Ateliers de la Peninsule.

AusHeritage and ASEAN-COCI (eds.). 2001. "Cultural Management Profile, Laos," in *ASEAN–Australia Project: Development of an ASEAN Regional Policy and Strategy for Cultural Heritage Management*. Melbourne: Cultural Heritage Center for Asia and the Pacific.

Boccardi, Giovanni and William Logan. 2007. *Mission Report: Reactive Monitoring Mission to the Town of Luang Prabang World Heritage Property, Lao People's Democratic Republic, 22–28 November 2007*. Paris: UNESCO.

Box, Paul. 1996. *Final Report: GIS Training Program for Wat Phou GIS Team, Laos and Vietnam, August 1996*. Bangkok: UNESCO.

———. 1997. *Lao People's Democratic Republic: Capacity Building in Heritage Management and Archaeological Master Plan Definition of Wat Phou and Associated Sites*. Bangkok: UNESCO.

Brocheux, Pierre and Daniel Hémery. 2010. *Indochina: An Ambiguous Colonization, 1858–1954*. Berkeley: University of California Press.

Dearborn, Lynne and John Stallmeyer. 2010. *Inconvenient Heritage: Erasure and Global Tourism in Luang Prabang*. Walnut Creek, CA: Left Coast Press.

Genovese, Lia. 2012. "The Plain of Jars: Mysterious and Imperiled." Web. http://ghn.globalheritagefund.com/uploads/documents/document_2006.pdf. Accessed June 23, 2014.

Getty Conservation Institute. 2008. "From Risk Assessment to Conservation: Safeguarding Archaeological Complexes in the Mekong Region Vat Phou, Lao PDR." Web. www.getty.edu/conservation/our_projects/education/sea/sea_component1.html. Accessed June 23, 2014.

Global Heritage Fund. "Wat Phou Project Overview." Web. http://globalheritagefund.org/what_we_do/overview/completed_projects/wat_phu_laos. Accessed June 23, 2014.

Greck, François. 1995. "Luang Prabang, Laos," in Miguel A. Corzo (ed.), *The Future of Asia's Past: Preservation of the Built Heritage of Asia*. Proceedings from the International Conference held in Chiang Mai, Thailand, January, 1995. Los Angeles: Getty Conservation Institute (1995), 4–5.

Heywood, Louise. 2006. *Ancient Luang Prabang*. Bangkok: River Books.

The Laotian National Inter-Ministerial Co-ordinating Committee for Vat Phou. 1999. *Chompasak Heritage Management Plan*, 3 parts. Vientiane: Government of the Lao People's Democratic Republic, Ministry of Information and Culture.

Lerici Foundation. 1999. *Conservation Recovery of the Khmer Monumental Complex of Vat Phou (Laos): Hydraulic Engineering Work to Stabilize the Slopes and Consolidate the Shorelines*. Draft report. Milan: Politecnico di Milano.

Logan, William S., Colin Long and Roz Hansen. 2002. "Vientiane, Laos: Lane Xang's Capital in the Age of Modernization and Globalization," in *The Disappearing "Asian" City*. Hong Kong: Oxford University Press.

The Nation. 2013. "Tourism is Laos' Second Highest Income Earner," May 14, 2013. Web. http://www.nationmultimedia.com/aec/Tourism-is-Laos-second-highest-income-earner-30206071.html. Accessed June 23, 2014.

Phongphicit, Boun Nhang. 1999. "Planning for the Future of Luang Prabang." Paper delivered at *The Economics of Heritage: UNESCO Conference on Adaptive Re-use of Historic Properties in Asia and the Pacific*, May. Paris: UNESCO.

Pichard, Pierre. 1997. *The Conservation of Vat Phu Temple*. FIT/536/LA0/70. Bangkok: UNESCO.

Rattanavong, H., et al. 2000. *Treasures of Luang Prabang*. Translated by Mike Callaghan. Vientiane: Institute of Cultural Research, Cultural Association of the Silk Routes.

Schipani, S. 2008. *IMPACT: The Effects of Tourism on Culture and the Environment in Asia and the Pacific: Alleviating Poverty and Protecting Cultural and Natural Heritage through Community-based Eco-tourism in Luang Namtha, Lao PDR*. Bangkok: UNESCO.

Stuart-Fox, Martin. 1997. *A History of Laos*. Cambridge: Cambridge University Press.

UNESCO Bangkok. 2004. *Impact: The Effects of Tourism on Culture and the Environment in Asia and the Pacific. Tourism and Heritage Site Management - Luang Prabang, Lao PDR*; and *Impact: Tourism and Heritage Site Management in the World Heritage Town of Luang Prabang, Lao PDR*. Bangkok: UNESCO.

———. "Cultural Survival and Revival in the Buddhist Sangha." Web. www.unescobkk.org/culture/ich/cultural-survival-and-revival-in-the-buddhist-sangha/phase-i-pilot-project-in-luang-prabang/. Accessed June 21, 2014.

Central tower of Angkor Wat, Cambodia.

8

CAMBODIA

The Khmer people and their predecessors have occupied the Mekong River basin for at least the past four thousand years. While debate surrounds the nature and extent of the predecessor third through eighth century cultures of Funan and Chenla, by the ninth century CE, the Khmer kingdom had become a powerful civilization. Beginning with King Jayavarman II (802 CE) a succession of rulers expanded their empire across much of modern-day Thailand, Laos and Vietnam. Building from earlier lingual, cultural and religious influences imported from India, the Khmer at their peak established a complex and sophisticated hierarchical society that produced one of the greatest architectural achievements of the ancient world: the multi-centered historic city of Angkor.

Located in today's north-central Cambodia, the ancient Khmer kingdom expanded gradually, reaching its apex during the reign of Jayavarman VII (1181–ca.1220 CE). Beginning in the thirteenth century, the southwesterly expansion of the Thai state began to erode Khmer dominance, ultimately resulting in the decline of Angkor. By the middle of the fifteenth century, the capital stood largely abandoned, and the tropical forests gradually engulfed the majority of its elaborately carved stone monuments. Inscriptions and historical accounts indicate that the site was visited intermittently thereafter, including two attempts at re-occupation by the Khmer court. In all likelihood, much of Angkor was never completely abandoned, and at least its principal temple complex, Angkor Wat, probably remained in partial use until 1863, when the French colonial period began.

In the mid-fifteenth century Phnom Penh supplanted Angkor as the country's political and economic seat. This position endures into the present day, chiefly due to Phnom Penh's access to Mekong River trade routes. When the capital was relocated, the Cham, a people located to the east in what is today central Vietnam, periodically pressured the borders of Cambodia (then known as Kampuchea). Khmer supremacy was also at times threatened by the Kingdom of Siam, to the northwest in present-day Thailand. Since the decline of the Angkorian Empire, Kampuchea existed as an independent state, but one that was subordinate to its larger and more powerful neighbors. Consequently, over the years Kampuchea's territory was progressively diminished, to the benefit of both the Cham and the Siam Kingdom. The establishment of Cambodia (or "Cambodge") as a French protectorate in 1863 prevented further apportionment by its neighbors despite recurring aggression from Thailand, the French maintained control of Cambodia until its independence was declared in 1953.[1]

Under the leadership of Prince Norodom Sihanouk, independent Cambodia flourished as a modern Southeast Asian nation until 1970, when it was drawn into the conflict between neighboring North and South Vietnam. Between April 1975 and January 1979, every aspect of Cambodian life was

FIGURE 8.1 Angkor Wat (ca. 1120–1150), one of four temples built by King Suryavarman I, is considered to be the largest religious building in the world. It is one of over sixty monumental structures in the Angkor Archaeological Park. This UNESCO World Heritage Site and protected historic cultural landscape covers the core area of Angkor, approximately 160 square kilometers, the greater Angkorian region.

FIGURE 8.2 Like many of its other key historic buildings, the Royal Palace at Phnom Penh and the city's modern street plan date from 1863, when Cambodia became a French protectorate.

radically altered under Khmer Rouge leader Pol Pot's Marxist agrarian reform policies. Monks were killed or deported, religious shrines and sculptures violated, and ultimately an estimated 1.7 million Cambodians died under the regime's murderous rule.

Despite the atrocities directed at religious parties in general and at Cambodia's educated population in particular, a few survivors from the educated citizenry and others have returned since 1979 to rebuild the nation, focusing their efforts on the religious institutions, temples, shrines and infrastructure that were destroyed during the Pol Pot regime. Since then, Angkor has been the focus of one of the largest organized heritage protection and conservation efforts in Asia, involving multiple long-term international efforts that have simultaneously trained a new generation of Cambodian conservators.

The story of the making of the archaeological park at Angkor from the late nineteenth century onwards reflects both the history of the country and the evolution of the field of architectural conservation in general. From the first widespread realization of its existence following its discovery by European explorers in the mid-nineteenth century, the ruins of Angkor have remained a richly enchanting destination for both researchers and tourists. It is today one of the most actively studied and visited cultural heritage sites in the world. Throughout the twentieth century, Angkor has attracted legions of scholars specializing in history, archaeology and conservation, eventually becoming, in the words of American architectural preservation educator William Chapman, "the single largest laboratory for observing contemporary heritage conservation practice in the world."[2]

The greater Angkorian region (with the Angkor Wat temple complex at its core) occupies approximately 1,000 square kilometers, including its immediately surrounding villages and farmlands. The large Tonlé Sap Lake, which is located at greater Angkor's southern edge, historically ensured an abundant food supply for the local population. Angkor's situation on a gently sloping and well-watered

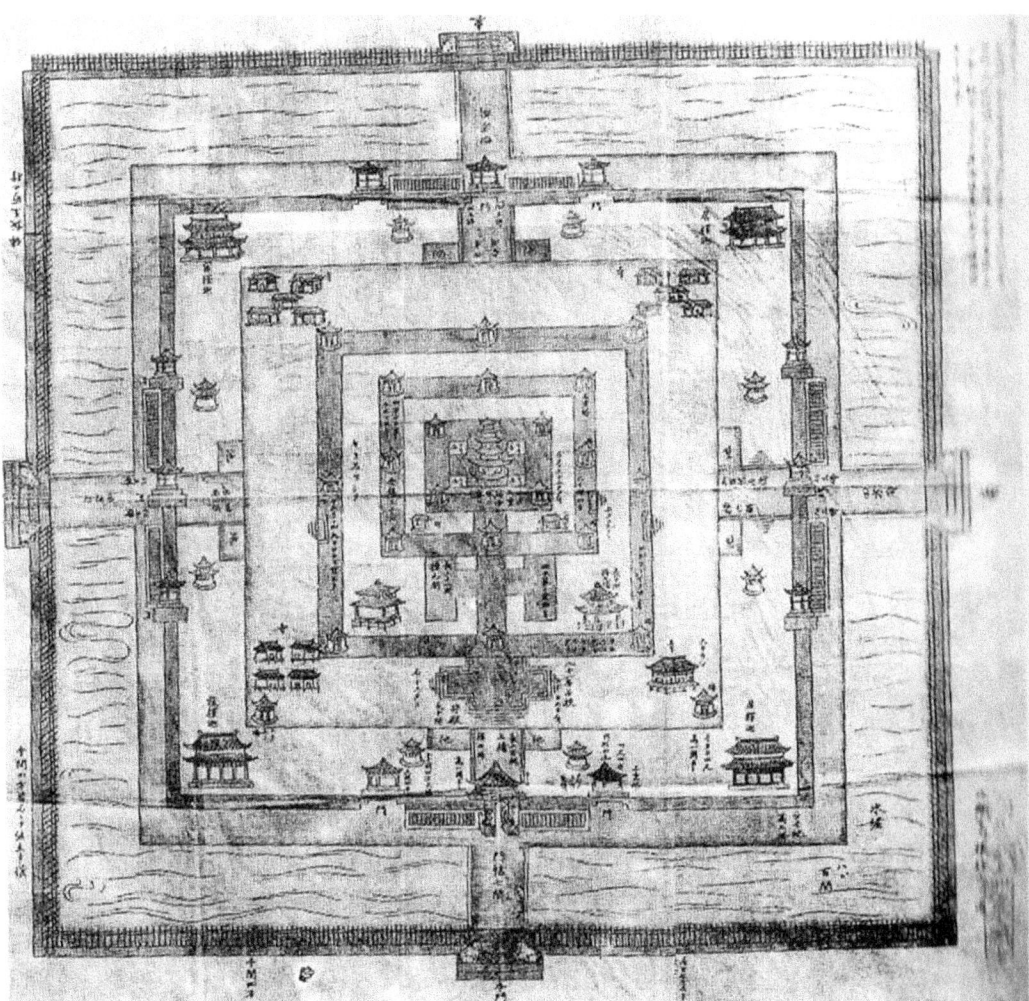

FIGURE 8.3 Plan recorded by a Japanese traveler of the ancient megalopolis of Angkor at its peak development in the early seventeenth century CE.

alluvial plain allowed for the creation of an extensive system of reservoirs, waterways and agricultural systems. Between the ninth and twelfth centuries, Khmer kings constructed five cities and scores of individual architectural and engineering works throughout the greater Angkor area and at strategic locations beyond. At least sixty-four significant architectural sites exist at Angkor today, and an estimated 1,000 other settlements and monuments from the ancient Khmer period are located elsewhere within present-day Cambodia's borders. Impressive Khmer temples and other building remains can be found in neighboring Thailand and Laos as well.

From the time of their construction, the monuments of Angkor have been under stress due to heavy use, a tropical environment, and the region's history of ideological and military conflict-related destruction and looting. In a city that may at its peak have supported as many as a million people, its significant monuments (the stone structures, which outlasted countless other less durable buildings that once existed) were likely frequently used for both religious and secular purposes.

During the thirteenth century, a wave of religious iconoclasm swept the city when a Hindu resurgence in Khmer culture prevailed, supplanting Buddhism in religious importance and resulting in the destruction of thousands of Buddhist images throughout Angkor.[3] Historical accounts and archaeological evidence reveal that two invasions occurred there, first from 1177 to 1178 CE by the Cham and again in 1431 CE by the Siamese. Each series of raids entailed heavy plundering and some destruction to buildings, and eventually Angkor was abandoned as the seat of the Khmer kingdom. During the four centuries that followed until Angkor's re-discovery in 1860, most of the ancient city became progressively covered by a thick overlay of jungle, which widely resulted in stone displacement and building collapses caused by the growth of uncontrolled vegetation, particularly by root damage.

In a sense, the great efforts to partially restore and present Angkor's significant historic buildings over the last century and a half have been no less stressful on the surviving architectural fabric of the ancient capital. The extant brick, sandstone and laterite structures of Angkor that French researchers and scholars found in the late nineteenth century usually required thorough *dégagement* (disentangling from jungle overgrowth), structural consolidation and occasional extensive reconstruction. The most suitable approach for undertaking this enormous task was utilizing the method of *anastylosis*, the re-assembling of collapsed stone building elements.

From the 1930s until recently, reinforced concrete was widely used to restore Angkor's masonry buildings, a treatment that sometimes had unfortunate consequences. Although cast-in-place reinforced concrete props have saved numerous structures from further collapse, concrete used as a fill or in patching often creates problems related to material incompatibility, most notably differences in strength and porosity. One unanticipated issue related to the use of concrete was that salts leached from the new repairs onto original carved sandstone elements, resulting in efflorescence and stone spalling.

The removal of exquisitely detailed sculpture adorning Angkor's buildings was first seen as a matter of practicality and national pride. Since Cambodia was then a French Protectorate, the finer pieces of sculpture were publicly displayed in the National Museum in Phnom Penh, or exported to France to be displayed in Paris at the Musée Indochinois (now the Musée Guimet). During the peak years of Cambodia's devastating civil war, the widespread damage to Khmer stone sculpture at temple sites throughout the country, along with looting and willful neglect, tragically went on unchecked.[4] Yet more valuable sculpture removals, including some dramatic episodes of looting, occurred through the mid-1990s despite efforts by international agencies led by UNESCO. Such vandalism remains a pressing issue in the more remote areas of the country today.

Despite Kampuchea's turbulent history, there are remarkably few examples of succeeding Khmer kings at Angkor desecrating the work created by their predecessors. On the contrary, there are today numerous extant examples of temples having been renovated and expanded. Angkor Wat was "restored" by King Ang Chan during the sixteenth century and the Bayon was extensively remodeled at the turn of the twelfth century by Jayavarman VII to its current famous appearance. As a result, the ancient capital area became a place where a visitor could easily view evidence of the successive reigns of former rulers.

The construction of the principal buildings and highly sophisticated hydraulic management features at Angkor represented an immense technological achievement. While many of the world's great cities grew out of established agricultural bases Angkor was conceived to create its own prosperous

a

FIGURE 8.4a and b Built from 1917 to 1920 and expanded in 1924, the National Museum in Phnom Penh is a blending of Western European and ancient Khmer design principles and motifs (a). The museum houses representative stone and bronze sculpture and presents other artifacts from all periods of Khmer history in a way that is practical from a conservation standpoint while also offering visitors a didactic display (b). A second, larger exhibit of ancient Khmer art and sculpture was installed at the Angkor National Museum in Siem Reap in 2007.

Cultural heritage legislation: the matter of looting, by Tess Davis

On April 4, 2012, the United States filed suit against Sotheby's in New York, demanding the auction house forfeit a statue of a mythical Hindu warrior valued at US$3 million that had been "illicitly removed" from remote jungle ruins in Cambodia. This was an *in rem* action[5] brought against the property itself, which resulted in the somewhat whimsical case name of *U.S. v. 10th Century Cambodian Sandstone Sculpture*. It relied on a series of Cambodian codes dating back to at least 1900 CE that recognized that French Indochina's ancient art was part of the "national domain" and "reserved" to the state. The complaint revealed that the expert Sotheby's hired to review the 1,000-year-old masterpiece warned it was "definitely stolen" and suggested returning it to Cambodia to "save everyone some embarrassment." Additional evidence soon came to light that the warrior statue had been pillaged in 1972, during the chaos heralding the Killing Fields, the genocide in which almost two million Cambodians lost their lives.

The *New York Times* and *Los Angeles Times* then identified another five "blood antiquities" that had been looted from the same site during the same conflict, but were nonetheless on display at American museums. The resulting scandal eventually revealed a major trafficking network that stretched from the Southeast Asian kingdom to the heights of the global art market, implicating not only Sotheby's, but some of the world's top collectors, galleries and museums. In doing so it also launched an international, and ongoing, effort to bring home the Cambodian people's plundered past.

At the time of this writing in late 2015, Cambodia has now recovered not only the Sotheby's warrior (the auction house settled the action in December 2013), but another statue from Christie's, two from the Metropolitan Museum of Art, and one each from the Norton Simon, Cleveland and Denver museums. Negotiations still continue for others. With the exception of Sotheby's, all of these institutions have acted, and are acting, voluntarily, without involvement from the courts.

Cambodia is to be congratulated for this well-deserved success. But these pieces are just a few of the thousands, perhaps tens of thousands, remaining. The looting and trafficking of conflict antiquities, along with that of gems and timber, became an organized industry during the civil war, financing some of history's worst murderers. Nor is this a historical problem: Cambodia's tragedy is being repeated again and again today, especially in the Middle East and North Africa.

While four decades ago the global hotspot was Indochina, that is Vietnam, Laos and indeed Cambodia, today it is what was once Mesopotamia, and is now the target of the so-called Islamic State of Iraq and Syria. Experts warn that ISIS is earning "tens of millions" by looting the region's ancient sites and selling its buried treasures to the highest bidder. And ISIS is not alone. This plunder has become a multi-billion dollar illegal enterprise that funds criminals, rebel armies and terrorists around the globe. No country with a past worth protecting has been spared. The illicit antiquities trade stretches from Afghanistan, to China, to the United States, and everywhere inbetween.

Given the reach and scale of this destruction, it is no wonder that court dockets are increasingly full of repatriation claims, brought by countries fighting to recover their national treasures. With the chaos raging in the Middle East, North Africa, Afghanistan and beyond, such litigation will likely only increase in the years to come. It is thus important for anyone interested in cultural heritage preservation to have a basic understanding of these cases.

This is a relatively new and complicated area of the law, incorporating elements of preservation law, but also administrative, criminal, property and trade law. Additionally, given the growing role of violent extremists like ISIS in looting and trafficking, even terrorist financing laws may be applicable (indeed the US Federal Bureau of Investigation recently warned the art market that such laws may be used against those who buy or sell conflict antiquities from Iraq and Syria). However, *U.S. v. Cambodian Sculpture* illustrates many of the relevant concepts, and thus can serve as a case study.

Like many such repatriation cases, *U.S. v. Cambodian Sculpture* hinged on whether the warrior was stolen property, and whether Cambodia was its legal owner. Sotheby's alleged that no crime had been committed when the piece was hacked from its pedestal in the 1970s, despite the colonial laws put forward by prosecutors, claiming that Cambodia's ancient ruins did not become state property until a 1992 law. Interestingly, this defense had been used before, and was equally unsuccessful.

In the 1920s, Frenchman André Malraux was arrested and tried for pillaging the Cambodian temple of Banteay Srei, in a scandal that made international headlines. Malraux too argued that the country's ruins were abandoned property with no legal owner. However, Cambodia's ownership of its archaeological heritage was confirmed first by the trial court in Phnom Penh, and then by the appellate court in Saigon, based on the very same laws at issue in *U.S. v. Cambodian Sculpture*. Given that Malraux went on to become his country's first Minister of Culture, and one of its most acclaimed novelists, this segment of Cambodian history has become a treasured chapter in the Indochina canon.

We will never know if an American court would have also upheld Cambodia's codes because Sotheby's settled the case before it reached trial, but the US Attorney, the Cambodian government and UNESCO all believed them to be valid. Such ownership laws do frequently determine whether looted objects can be repatriated. This is because courts in the USA and United Kingdom, two of the world's major destinations for antiquities both licit and illicit, often require them to return art to its country of origin. In simplest terms, these patrimony laws are what make looted antiquities "stolen property," as well as national governments the rightful owners.

They are not unique to Cambodia, but actually part of a wider legal regime that dates back to eighteenth-century France, and still reaches throughout the Francophone world and beyond. In fact the origin of the now universal idea that "artistic, historical, scientific monuments" are part of a national cultural heritage, which is both the property and responsibility of the state, came about during the French Revolution. The storming of the Bastille in Paris on July 14, 1789 and the chaos that followed did not spare, and in fact targeted, artworks and historic buildings. And the backlash to this, as well as the revolution's own goals, led to some of the world's first preservationist laws and policies.

These included creating a national register and classification system of cultural heritage, which many countries around the world still practice today, and in much the same way. Once thus categorized, objects and sites were legally protected as state property, under an increasing number of decrees. France continued to flesh out these legal protections throughout the 1790s and first decades of the 1800s. By the height of its colonial empire, they were well established, and thus made their way into the laws of Cambodia, but also the rest of Indochina, and even North African countries such as Algeria, Morocco and Tunisia.

The 1900 Cambodian decree is fairly typical of these others, recognizing that art and archaeology, "above and below ground," was part of the "national domain." It additionally declared that movables and immovables, whose conservation was in the public interest from a historical or artistic perspective, "shall be classified." Once classified, they benefited from the many additional legal protections, which prohibited their unauthorized alteration, movement, sale, export, destruction and even restoration. Furthermore, such property was "inalienable" and "imprescriptible," under penalty of any sale's nullification.

During this same time period, in addition to the French civil law, other legal systems also began to enact similar legislation. In the late nineteenth and early twentieth centuries, the Ottoman Empire, which governed until after World War I, issued a series of decrees protecting its art and antiquities. Greece, Italy and even El Salvador enacted patrimony laws during this time. And as the map was redrawn in the post-war years, many of the newly independent governments followed in their footsteps. This momentum has continued to the present day, with UNESCO now recognizing ownership laws as a "best practice," and issuing model provisions to aid in their drafting.

Legal drafters in the eighteenth century could not have envisioned today's post-colonial world, where nations like Cambodia, Egypt and Mexico are passionately pursuing legal claims against collectors, auction houses, museums and governments in the West. Even by the 1970 UNESCO Convention, which remains the leading international agreement on the illicit antiquities trade, many in the art market actively fought against criminalizing antiquities looting and trafficking. Repatriation cases were even more novel.

However, they are important today, not only to deter an illegal industry that puts billions into the hands of criminals and worse, but to right some of the world's past wrongs. These old laws are being used to meet new needs. When all other options have failed (and litigation should always be a last resort) they have thus become an important tool for both lawyers and heritage conservationists.

agriculture. Angkor's five large *barays*, or reservoirs, were built to store water, maintain water levels in its moats and canals, and probably also to irrigate the fields beyond. From these great reservoirs, navigable canals channeled water to moats encircling the temple complexes, providing a mode of transportation for people and goods. Water flowed south primarily from the Kulen Hills region 30 km northeast of Angkor through a series of small rivers and canals, with remnants flowing further southward into the seasonally fluctuating Tonlé Sap lake. These irrigated tracts provided fertile rice cultivation and farmlands where several crops were grown each year, supporting the strength and prosperity of the Khmer Empire.

Today, Angkor's vast hydrological system sits largely disused and its original system of operation remains a matter of debate despite extensive scholarly research. Teams from the University of Sydney, Australia have recently led efforts to identify the history and roles of key human-made features throughout the wider Angkor region in its Greater Angkor Project (GAP), conducting a state of the art remote sensing survey verified by archaeological investigations. The vast expanse of the greater Angkor area, which is generously graced with a rich variety of remarkably well-preserved architectural forms representing nearly 500 years of stylistic evolutions, gives credence to its description by historian Arnold J. Toynbee: "Angkor is not orchestral; it is monumental."[6] Given today's perspectives on cultural heritage, it's actually both.

An inscription at the intermediate gallery of Angkor Wat temple's east entrance provides evidence of the extensive restoration done during the sixteenth century by King Ang Chan of the key temple sites of Angkor Wat and at Phnom Bakheng, the state temple of the nearby earlier capital Yasodharapura that was built by Yasovarman I. Touchingly, it was dedicated by his mother in the seventeenth century: "[He] restored the holy city of Yasodharapura, long deserted, and rendered it superb and charming ... ornamented with shining gold, palaces glittering with precious stones, like the palace of Indra on earth."[7] Historical evidence of this initiative can be seen today in the restorations of portals in the upper reaches of Angkor Wat and in the sixteenth century restorations of a statue of Vishnu in Angkor Wat's west *gopura* (entrance building), which is currently considered to be the most famous statue in Khmer art.[8]

FIGURE 8.5 Restorations of destroyed portals in the upper reaches of the Angkor Wat temple date from an attempted revival of Angkor under King Ang Chan in the sixteenth century CE. Note the two recycled rounded sandstone columns that once lined the western causeway, one now used as a lintel to support a decorated fronton.

Angkor's "re-discovery" and early conservation

Efforts to understand the history and extent of Angkor date from its "re-discovery" in 1860 by French naturalist Henri Mouhot, who explored the area with support from the London-based Royal Geographical Society.[9] While other foreign travelers preceded Mouhot to Angkor, it was his enthusiastic account that was received with greatest interest in France and the Western world. Over the next half-century, the jungle-enveloped ruins were intermittently cleared of vegetation and mapped, inscriptions were noted, and the city's buildings and waterways slowly came to light once more.

The extensive research activities at Angkor beginning in 1898 by the École française d'Extrême-Orient (EFEO) resulted in the subsequent establishment of the Conservation d'Angkor, a site management and research facility based in the nearby town of Siem Reap, in 1908.[10] From that time through the early 1960s, conservation work at Angkor commenced in earnest, although work was interrupted by Cambodia's occupation by Japanese forces during World War II. A cadre of mostly French historians, epigraphers, archaeologists, architects and others in related professions worked to research, restore, preserve and present the monumental ruins of Angkor and its environs as representations of the Khmer Empire and its role in Southeast Asia. The initial projects undertaken were archaeological in scope, but from the early 1920s, work increasingly focused on restoration and conservation of the buildings themselves.

By the 1960s staffing at the Conservation d'Angkor facility had grown to approximately 1,100 people, with positions ranging from scholars and administrators to craftsmen and maintenance crews, all working to document, research, conserve and present the archaeological park.[11] After completing the construction of access roads – and while clearing thousands of hectares of jungle overgrowth – an array of conservation interventions began, ranging from on-site stabilization and repairs of partially collapsed and damaged building elements to complete building reconstructions, often using anastylosis.

a

b

FIGURE 8.6a, b and c The first use of anastylosis in the reconstruction of a temple in Cambodia was at Banteay Srei in the early 1930s. The seated hanuman figures are cast stone replicas of the originals, stolen from the temple in 1924, that are now in the National Museum in Phnom Penh (a). The most recent uses of anastylosis on a grand scale have been when it was implemented by the EFEO at the Baphuon (b) and by the World Monuments Fund at Phnom Bakheng (c).

French architect Henri Marchal first used the anastylosis technique at the Banteay Srei temple. Marchal reconstructed Banteay Srei's five shrines, dismembered by tree growth and a scandalous attempt at looting in 1924,[12] between 1931 and 1936.[13] Prior to the Banteay Srei project, Marchal had traveled to Java to observe anastylosis techniques implemented at the ninth century CE Buddhist site Borobudur, work being done under the direction of his Dutch colleague, Theodoor van Erp.[14] Conducted under difficult conditions, Marchal's bold approach was made easier by Banteay Srei's relatively diminutive size and the richness of its carvings, which left more clues for re-assembly than would normally be the case for a Khmer temple.

Marchal's use of anastylosis at Banteay Srei validated the approach, and ever since it has been used to varying degrees in repairing and reconstructing ancient Khmer architecture. By far the boldest example of its use has been EFEO's recent reconstruction of the Baphuon in Angkor Thom, a project that has involved the removal and replacement of approximately 350,000 sandstone blocks.[15]

In contrast to anastylosis reconstruction, the EFEO also employed an alternate approach of preserving Khmer ruins in their jungle settings, essentially, leaving them "as-found." Such an approach is important from the standpoint of conservation philosophy in that it represents a more authentic picture of the collapse patterns and appearances of ancient buildings.

In accordance with this approach, the twelfth century CE temple of Ta Prohm has largely been spared major restoration interventions since the 1930s. However, beginning in 2004 the Archaeological Survey of India (ASI) has undertaken survey and stabilization work at Ta Prohm, work that includes extensive reconstruction of several key buildings, along with improvements in visitor circulation through the ruins.

By virtue of its appearances in several recent movies and its picturesque setting (several massive *ficus* and *bok* trees grow on and amidst its towers, shrines, courtyards and galleries) Ta Prohm is one of

FIGURE 8.7 Numerous films have been made at Angkor during the past century, ranging from several that were locally produced by King Norodom Sihanouk in the 1950s and 1960s to the globally popular *Lara Croft: Tomb Raider* in 2001.

Angkor's most visited sites. The ASI had initially proposed extensive removal of the trees in order to structurally stabilize the buildings, which would have undone the French concept of presenting Ta Prohm in its near as-found state. Instead, at the behest of Japanese, French and American conservation teams, the scope of the Indian proposal was modified to include only the cleaning of the temple site and introduction of timber walkways, along with the retention of several of the trees in question.[16]

Research, restoration and stabilization work, improved access, and presentation of the historic city of Angkor, progressed under French leadership from the mid-1950s until about 1970. During this time, French archaeologist Bernard Philippe Groslier directed conservation efforts at Angkor, introducing modern scientific rigor such as photography, surveying and assiduous documentation along with the use of improved construction equipment and modern building materials. Groslier's era came to a close in 1972, when political unrest led to the departure of most EFEO personnel. A reduced Khmer staff continued site maintenance activities until the Khmer Rouge takeover in 1975.[17] During Cambodia's civil war, the country's most important archaeological sites were largely spared from vandalism and destruction, though Cambodians associated with the state and foreign-supported heritage protection activities were not so fortunate. Of the approximately 1,100 inhabitants of Siem Reap province who oversaw and maintained the Angkor Archaeological Park, less than a dozen survived the tragic Khmer Rouge years.[18]

Cultural heritage management legislation

From the colonial era through the turbulent period of independent regimes, Vietnamese occupation, and into the present day, numerous legislative decrees have been implemented in attempts to conserve Cambodia's extensive cultural heritage. Currently, the architectural heritage of the greater Angkor region falls under the purview of the Autorité pour la Protection du Site et l'Aménagement de la Région d'Angkor (APSARA Authority), with all other cultural heritage sites remaining under the responsibility of the Ministry of Culture. The protective legislation and operational guidelines of both have been largely shaped by the adoption of Western European concepts for heritage protection adapted to Cambodia's physical circumstances. The APSARA Authority's oversight of Angkor is enriched by the presence of several international organizations that work there, each having both reporting responsibilities as well as the right to review and comment on work being carried out by other conservation teams. As such, additional principles and procedures reflecting today's international charters and agreements (such as the Venice Charter) are recognized in Cambodia.

The first French colonial law to specifically address built heritage conservation in Cambodia was a 1900 decree calling for the classification, protection and preservation of all buildings within the Indochina colonies by the EFEO. Royal ordinances of 1923 and 1931 reinforced the earlier legislation, calling for the imposition of fines for those who do not report artifacts they have discovered. This legislation was likely the result of an internationally sensational case of looting, when the young French writer André Malraux and his wife were apprehended with hundreds of kilograms of architectural sculpture clandestinely removed from Banteay Srei temple.[19]

The 1990s witnessed the next wave of legislative action following the United Nations' establishment of control after the brutal Khmer Rouge era came to an end. In the early 1990s, amendments to the national penal code included sanctions against the destruction, theft and illicit trafficking of cultural property. In 1991, King Norodom Sihanouk signed the Hague Convention for the Protection of Cultural Property in the Event of Armed Conflict (1954), the Convention on the Means of Prohibiting and Preventing the Illicit Import, Export and Transfer of Cultural Property (1970) and the World Heritage Convention (1972), thereby enabling the inclusion of Cambodian sites on UNESCO's World Heritage List.[20]

The then-interim government, with international assistance, drafted a set of laws on heritage management that established the National Heritage Protection Authority for Cambodia (NHPAC) in 1992. The next year, however, a newly elected government created the Supreme Council on National Culture to assume NHPAC's responsibilities.

The 1993 Constitution of the Kingdom of Cambodia was redrafted to include several articles regarding the preservation and promotion of "national culture" and the obligations of the state in protecting cultural resources. Significantly, Article 71 of the Constitution designated all national and World Heritage Sites as neutral zones where military activity was not permitted.[21] This move, in all likelihood, came in direct response to the use of conservation facilities and ruins as military installations during the conflicts of the 1970s.

In May 1994, following the establishment of the APSARA Authority in charge of heritage management at Angkor, a Royal Decree on Siem Reap Angkor Region Identification and Management was established. This decree defined the perimeter of protection in Siem Reap and designated five areas for protection in accordance with the Zoning and Environmental Management Project (ZEMP). The ZEMP served solely as the operational Master Plan for Angkor until 2012 when it was supplemented by the Tourism Management Plan initiated by the Technical Advisory Committee of APSARA.

During the late 1990s, various regulations were instated to control tourist development in the Angkor region. In January 1996, a new Law on the Protection of Cultural Heritage was passed, expanding the definition of "heritage site" by eliminating age and size requirements. The twentieth century closed with the passage of additional legislation that both clarified and secured the role of the APSARA Authority and further regulated land use and construction in Siem Reap and Angkor. In the early 2000s Cambodia adopted legislation and entered into bilateral agreements with Thailand and the United States that were aimed at curtailing the exportation and sale of looted cultural property. This active period through today of institutional and organizational capacity building in Cambodia has in part made up for the tumultuous governmental situation over the prior several decades and has ushered in a new, promising era of international collaboration and necessary regulation.

The post-civil war years

An uneasy peace returned to the Angkor region in 1979. That August, the Ministry of Culture began to re-establish the function of Conservation d'Angkor with the assistance of various international organizations that were again working on-site. Groups from across the world – including those from Australia, Poland, the USSR, Sweden and India – offered to help restart conservation efforts at Angkor during the late 1980s. The ASI eventually initiated a controversial conservation program at Angkor Wat that included extensive interventions utilizing concrete and chemical washes on stone façades and relief detailing. Although the ASI's work in completing abandoned prior projects helped considerably, coverage of the team's approach in the global media brought concern for the monument back into a public forum, which heralded a new era of international involvement at the site.

Since initiating the recovery of Cambodia's modern society and infrastructure in the late 1980s, the country's leaders have recognized the importance of revitalizing Angkor as the primary symbol of Cambodia, and as a means of boosting its economy through tourism.

In 1993, Cambodia adopted its current national flag, placing an image of an Angkor temple at the center. It thus became the only country whose flag proudly incorporates an image of its built heritage, underscoring the importance of the site to the country's new identity.

After King Norodom Sihanouk signed the Hague Convention for the Protection of Cultural Property in the Event of Armed Conflict (1954), the Convention on the Means of Prohibiting and Preventing the Illicit Import, Export and Transfer of Cultural Property (1970), and the World Heritage Convention (1972) in 1991, UNESCO took the lead in producing the Zoning and Environmental Master Plan (ZEMP) for Angkor. Its creation was a condition of listing Cambodian heritage sites on the World Heritage List in 1992. Subsequently, in 1996 the King signed cornerstone legislation for safeguarding heritage in Cambodia: the Law on the Protection of Cultural Heritage, which clearly defines cultural property, assigns responsibility for management, establishes rules regarding the import/export of movable heritage and outlines procedures for inventorying properties.

The process of producing the ZEMP did much to spur state-of-the-art research on a variety of topics, ranging from documentation of the accomplishments of the French over the past century to existing land use studies and formulation of new heritage protection laws and systems. The master plan also included a population study of Siem Reap province, and detailed how local villagers used the archaeological park. The ZEMP was based on a then-new, computerized Geographic Information System (GIS) and Global Positioning System (GPS) as provided by the Government of Hungary.[22]

A landmark in the history of the effort to conserve Angkor occurred in August 1993 with the creation of the Autorité pour la Protection du Site et l'Aménagement de la Région d'Angkor (APSARA Authority), an independent governmental organization charged with revitalizing the Angkor Archaeological Park through conservation and presentation of its many sites. A significant component of the APSARA Authority's system of operations is the International Coordinating Committee for the Safeguard and Development of the Historic Site at Angkor (ICC), which oversees the multiple international efforts on-site, enforces standards of practice, and holds regular meetings where the various Angkor conservation parties present their work for review and discussion among the professional teams.[23]

The APSARA Authority's International Coordinating Committee is chaired by representatives from France and Japan, with UNESCO serving as its acting Secretariat. Some thirty national and organizational members regularly attend its administrative and technical meetings. Internally, its administrative board is comprised of the heads of relevant Cambodian ministries and offices, all presided over by the Prime Minister.

Since its creation, the APSARA Authority has accomplished much at Angkor through its efforts of simplifying communications via regular meetings, harmonizing application and reporting procedures, and raising standards for conservation practice.[24] The main participants in the conservation efforts there thus far have been the EFEO, Sophia University, the University of Sydney's Department of Archaeology, the Japanese Team for Safeguarding Angkor (JSA), the German Apsara Conservation Project (GACP), the World Monuments Fund (WMF), the Archaeologial Survey of India (ASI), the Royal Angkor Foundation, the Chinese Government Team for Safeguarding Angkor and the Swiss Banteay Srei Conservation project, supplemented by several others.

Heritage education initiatives at Angkor

During the Khmer Rouge's disastrous rule most of Angkor's caretakers perished along with as much as a third of the country's population – approximately two million persons. When foreign conservation organizations such as the World Monuments Fund (WMF) began work at Angkor in 1989, fewer than a dozen Cambodian archaeologists, architects or conservators remained. From the beginning of their work in Cambodia, the WMF and others such as Japan's Sophia University involved teachers from the University of Fine Arts in Phnom Penh and students from that school's first graduating class since the 1960s.

Along with other conservation and education organizations, the WMF established the Center for Khmer Studies in Siem Reap in 1999 to provide a meeting ground in Cambodia for scholars and students of Khmer culture. The Center supports a scholars-in-residence program, partners with universities in Phnom Penh as well as abroad, and oversees research programs in the social sciences, including archaeology, linguistics and studies of vernacular architecture. The EFEO and two Japanese missions to Angkor have instituted similar graduate-level training opportunities for a burgeoning number of students who wish to pursue careers in heritage conservation management.

Today, many projects at Angkor are staffed and managed by Cambodian architects, archaeologists and technicians who oversee a variety of specialized tasks. While architectural conservators are actively at work on the structures, they are also developing a new generation of Cambodian conservators. The recent architectural conservation education effort fits firmly within the tradition of conservation pedagogy, and greatly promotes the survival of the site and the professional community in Cambodia.[25] (See also Architectural Conservation Training in Asia, by William Chapman in General Introduction.) Such heritage conservation efforts aid not just the famed historic buildings of Angkor but the country as a whole. Its growing economy relies heavily on tourism, and heritage conservation groups working in Cambodia help ensure the best utilization of this valuable resource.

Since the 1970s, the looting of fine sculpture and historic artifacts from Angkor has been a constant concern and better heritage education is considered part of the solution. Countless pieces have been smuggled out of the country in recent years, possibly destined for wealthy private collectors, a fact that would make their eventual repatriation difficult if not highly unlikely. In 2003 the government of Cambodia joined the "Convention on the Means of Prohibiting and Preventing the Illicit Import, Export and Transfer of Ownership of Cultural Property," a 1970 UNESCO decree that establishes means for cooperation between party countries to curtail the illegal import, export and sale of looted cultural materials. Cambodia's participation has already led to a reduction in the market for stolen antiquities.[26] Today, through better security, local level involvement in site maintenance, and the cooperation of governments and international NGOs, the situation is much improved.[27] (See above: Cultural Heritage Legislation: the Matter of Looting, by Tess Davis.)

Heritage conservation advocacy and training have been key in the above positive developments.

Faced with the vast amount of conservation and other work needed to maintain, interpret and manage Angkor, beginning in the late 1980s the Ministry of Culture and the APSARA Authority (its successor at Angkor), granted responsibility for conserving specific historic monuments to qualified foreign organizations. Each works along the lines of typical archaeological research concessions found in other countries, with specific work protocols, reporting procedures, and training and technical exchange responsibilities.

In spite of the limited range of materials and construction techniques utilized in ancient Khmer architecture, the scope of conservation approaches applied by the various foreign organizations varies fairly widely. These variations are mainly due to slight differences in conservation philosophies and technologies practiced by the disparate organizations, making Angkor a major center for international exchange among conservation professionals.

Accordingly, the conservation approaches over the years have ranged from massive interventions, such as the dismantling and re-assembly of whole galleries at Angkor Wat and at Baphuon temple (done by the EFEO in the 1960s and 1970s as well as during the past two decades) to the far less radical *in situ* conservation work undertaken since 1997 at the German APSARA Conservation Project at Angkor Wat, and since 1992 by WMF at Preah Khan and Ta Som. One of the greatest achievements of the APSARA Authority has been to provide an effective peer review forum for the scrutiny of both proposed and ongoing conservation projects. This practice has ultimately served to reduce mistakes and has enhanced coordination between the conservation teams, much to the benefit of the site and level of professional performance at Angkor.

FIGURE 8.8 Developed in close cooperation with UNESCO since 1993, the APSARA Authority – whose purview includes the Angkor Archaeological Park and its surrounding area – fosters and exemplifies contemporary heritage conservation practice in Cambodia. In 2016, the Authority, headquartered in Siem Reap, consisted of fifteen departments and more than five hundred personnel.

The World Monuments Fund and the Angkor conservation community

Since 1989, the New York-based World Monuments Fund (WMF) has been one of the most active organizations working with the Royal Cambodian Government to facilitate international cooperation and project management at Angkor.[28] At the same time, the WMF has operated within the administrative framework of the numerous other international organizations involved at Angkor, organizing conferences, sponsoring educational programs, and supporting documentation and restoration programs. Working closely with organizations such as Sophia University, the Royal Angkor Foundation (Hungary), the German APSARA Conservation Project, EFEO and UNESCO, all under the aegis of the APSARA Authority, WMF continues at the forefront of efforts to preserve and present the monumental remains of Angkor.

From training Cambodian architecture and archaeology students to initiating space-borne radar imaging of Angkor, WMF remains committed to building mutual trust and cooperation with all those who work to conserve Cambodia's architectural heritage. WMF has assisted the Royal Cambodian government in efforts to develop sustainable conservation projects in and around Angkor through its flagship project at Preah Khan (which began in 1991) among other efforts. The APSARA Authority in turn has supported the WMF's work by providing professional staff, site security and cooperative training initiatives.

In a groundbreaking project, WMF has collaborated with the Budapest-based Royal Angkor Foundation to obtain the Cambodian government's approval for the NASA spaceborne radar imaging of Angkor acquired by the space shuttle *Endeavor* in November 1994. This data proved to be an invaluable resource to archaeologists, historians, geographers, planners, ecologists and others who were studying the origins of Angkor, its hydrology, its relationship to the Tonlé Sap, and modern development in the region. Subsequent over-flights of Angkor at lower altitudes and the use of additional survey technologies have done much for drawing attention to the importance of viewing Angkor not as individual sites, but as an enormous cultural landscape.

The Greater Angkor Project (GAP) led by University of Sydney's Professor Roland Fletcher and Dr. Damian Evans commenced in 1997 and has accomplished probably more than any other single research initiative at Angkor. In 2007 it completed its mapping survey of the greater Angkor region combining previously existing ground surveys, aerial surveys and radar remote-sensing data provided by NASA. In 2012 the University of Sydney GAP team conducted an aerial light detection and ranging (LIDAR) survey of Angkor Wat and its surrounding areas.[29] Astounding new discoveries have been made through the GAP project on how the land management system of Angkor and its hinterland settlements operated and recent LIDAR images have transformed perceptions of the extent and arrangement of Angkor's cultural landscape across time. (See figure 8.10b below.)

Since the APSARA Authority's inaugural meeting in March 1994, WMF has participated in nearly every session of the Technical Committee of the International Coordinating Committee on the Safeguarding and Development of the Historic City of Angkor (ICC) and has attended its annual plenary sessions. During its first decade of work in Cambodia WMF developed a close relationship with the architecture faculty at the Royal University of Fine Arts in Phnom Penh. After training in site documentation and conservation techniques with WMF, several members of the university's Khmer staff shared their experience in architectural conservation and site management with other young Cambodian professionals. WMF has also conducted and participated in an assortment of training programs and workshops over the years including the APSARA Authority and ICCROM's Ta Nei Cultural Resource Management Workshops, which were conducted in 2000 and 2001. Several of its participants entered successful careers in cultural heritage management and are now working in various organizations in and around Angkor.

WMF's main achievements in architectural conservation at Angkor have been the completion of two signature projects: restoration of the Churning of the Sea of Milk Gallery at Angkor Wat (2012), and of the temple of Ta Som (2006). As of mid-2016, it remains active in two other large and long-running projects: Preah Khan and Phnom Bakheng.

Within the many diverse and impressively coordinated international efforts undertaken to safeguard Angkor, a number of developments have occurred in the areas of documentation, conservation science and fieldwork techniques, each of which constitute significant contributions to the general field of architectural conservation. The use of computer assisted drawings (CAD), laser measuring, non-destructive structural analyses, computerized inventories of stone conditions and pathologies, and remote sensing documentation have helped heritage conservation managers cope with the enormous scale of the site as well as the data it generates. The use of LIDAR has revolutionized archaeological research methods at Angkor and has opened whole new perspectives on its history.[30] On a more micro level, experimentation with environmentally sensitive biocides, *in situ* epoxy and non-ferrous steel structural repair techniques, along with stone filling, patching and consolidation methods have assisted at every stage of conservation projects, from stabilizing structures to cleaning surfaces.

a

FIGURE 8.9a, b and c The WMF project entailing the disassembly and rebuilding of the corbelled stone vaults (a) protecting the Churning of the Sea of Milk bas-relief (b) in the east gallery of Angkor Wat (c) from 2002 until 2012 represents a major technical accomplishment in architectural conservation. Two earlier attempts since the 1950's had failed making the recent campaign a good example of "re-restoration".

Digital documentation in architectural conservation, by Olsen Jean-Julien

Documentation in architectural conservation is the process of capturing information to describe the physical configuration, condition and use of monuments, groups of buildings and sites.[31]

From the aforementioned GIS based ZEMP for Angkor started in 1992 to a scanning project for Egyptian pyramids launched in November 2015, a vast array of digital documentation techniques is being used, from digital photogrammetry to geographic information systems, 3D modeling, archiving and communication.

Such data collection and management techniques are reputed to be more accurate and more economically produced than those obtained from surveys using traditional techniques. Data collected are easily converted to Computer Aided Design (CAD) programs for conservation, management, restoration works, education and information dissemination.[32]

This unprecedented capacity to produce, access and manipulate cultural contents conveys many hopes but also many challenges.[33] Looking back in the history of architectural documentation, this text is an outline of the road we have taken going from simply recording physical configuration of buildings to the actual promises and controversies regarding interpretation and presentation of cultural information to worldwide audiences.

Antecedents to digital documentation in architectural conservation

Documentation of architecture is a very old practice. The reproduction of patterns in traditional architecture supposes a mental reconstruction of the built forms and their decorative elements. Archaeological investigation of complex architecture and cities in ancient civilizations, such as Chinese temples and Aztec, Mayan and Egyptian pyramids, revealed the existence of planning processes where documentation played important roles.[34]

However, the modern and systematic documentation of architecture is associated with the use of geometry to design buildings and to understand the values of architecture. For Vitruvius (80–15 BCE), a building is beautiful "when the appearance of the work is pleasing and in good taste, and when its members are in due proportion according to correct principles of symmetry."[35]

The works of the Renaissance architects Filippo Brunelleschi and Leon Alberti established principles for accurate representations of buildings using linear perspectives in geometry.[36] By the eighteenth century, the mastering of linear perspectives had led to mechanical reproduction techniques aiming to capture and disseminate information about architecture in new ways. The Italian architect Giovanni Battista Piranesi was made famous for his series of perspectival etchings documenting the city of Rome between 1745 and 1774.[37]

The invention of photographic techniques in the first half of the nineteenth century improved the use of linear perspectives by providing more realistic representations. Throughout the nineteenth century, photographers and painters were included in scientific or exploratory missions to document architecture and landscape as a part of the exploration process. An example is the work of Louis Delaporte who published engraved images of Angkor Wat in 1880 having been a member of the French Mekong Expedition 1866–1868.

But it was the idea to use a photographic camera as a measuring instrument that truly transformed the practice of documenting architecture and landscape. With this idea, the first steps had been taken into what we now call Photogrammetry and Remote Sensing, that is to say "the art, science, and technology of obtaining reliable information from noncontact imaging and other sensor systems about the Earth and its environment, and other physical objects and processes through recording, measuring, analyzing and representation."[38]

From 1867, when the German engineer Albrecht Meydenbauer first used the term *photogrammetry*[39] to the invention of the first computer hardware in the 1940s, various experimental techniques have produced more accurate maps and more contextualized data about natural sites, buildings, social environments and cultural practices.

The advent of digital documentation

In 1963, Ivan Sutherland designed the *Sketchpad* as a man–machine graphical communication system to enable users to interpret information drawn directly on a computer display.[40] This invention marked the emergence

FIGURE 8.10a
Engraving of Angkor Wat façade by Louis Delaporte (1880).

of computer graphics and Graphic User Interface technologies, which led to the creation of interactive virtual environments with computers, and thus initiated a whole new digital world.

Fifty years later, cultural heritage professionals from a wide range of disciplines in sciences and humanities have fully embraced the digital world. A first step was the use of existing computer technologies for the digitalization, representation, archiving, preservation and communication of cultural heritage. Now, a new sub-field in computer sciences, known as Cultural Heritage Informatics, is emerging with the objective of developing tools, applications and digital user experiences suited to the study of cultural heritage.[41]

As a part this process, digital documentation for architectural conservation is concerned with four series of activities: digital data acquisition; digital reconstruction, modeling, visualization and interpretation; data management, archiving and preservation; and finally, representation and communication.

Digital data acquisition

Data acquisition is a fundamental part of the documentation process. Building on photogrammetric and remote sensing techniques developed since the early twentieth century, many 2D and 3D data collection and data processing methodologies are now available to capture information related to sites, buildings and landscapes. Aerial photogrammetry is combined with close-range photogrammetry using techniques like laser scanning and drone surveys.

Light detection and ranging (LIDAR) techniques are being used to determine the distance to an object by transmitting a laser beam. LIDAR is useful in creating building models and topographical maps. Its ability to map the ground in tree-covered areas, like the Angkor Park in Cambodia, has proven particularly effective for archaeologists.[42] Different scales of a digital model provide precise geographic information as well as physical dimensions of buildings that allow for better interpretations of the significance of World Heritage Sites.[43]

But non-contact data acquisition goes beyond the external physical configuration of buildings and sites. Cameras equipped with thermal sensors are now being used to identify cavities, rooms, hallways and material differences in the Egyptian pyramids. As all materials emit an energy radiation as a function of their temperature, differences in emissivity allow verification of stone characteristics and what lies behind them.[44]

Digital reconstructions, modeling, visualization and interpretation

Digital reconstructions and three-dimensional modeling (3D Modeling) using CAD and finite element methods (FEM) to analyze and rule out errors in models are

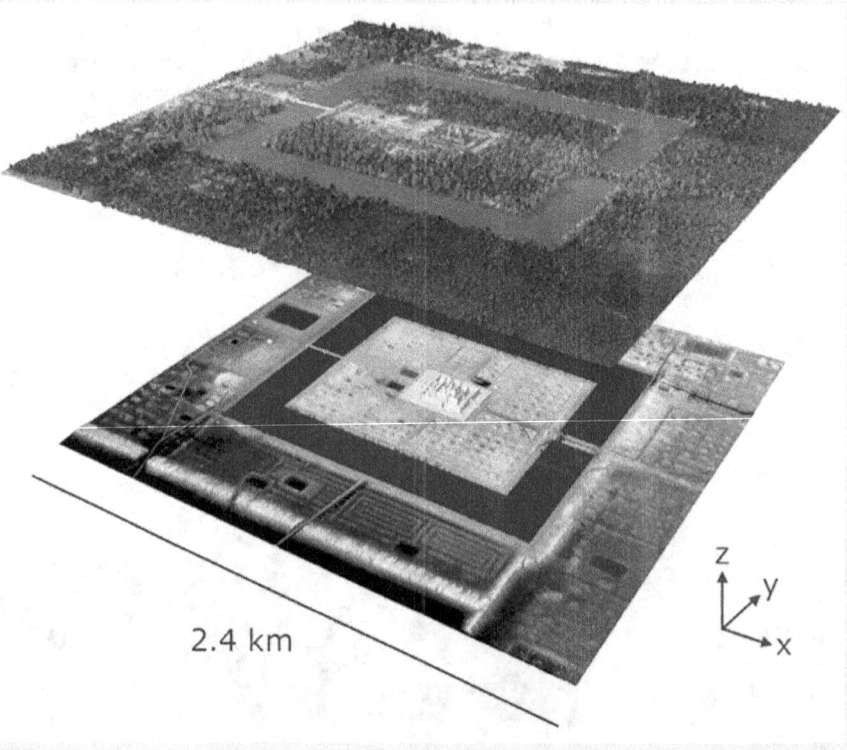

FIGURE 8.10b Angkor Wat showing conventional view (top) compared to a digital terrain model derived from LIDAR ground returns (bottom).

standard practices in architectural documentation today. Various reproduction and prototyping techniques are available, providing accurate models of buildings and heritage sites. Computer animation technologies and graphic user interface design have improved the immersion techniques and attempts are being made to insert those models in interactive virtual environments.

Data management, archiving and preservation

An important challenge of digital documentation is the ability to manage and preserve the data collected. Relational database management systems (RDBMS) and geographic information systems (GIS) developed in the 1990s made systematic digital inventories possible.

Now digital inventories are able to index large-scale multi-media and multi-lingual data. They facilitate the addition of special categories, providing detailed information on topics such as nuances of colors and textures, historical development, original materials and techniques, use and condition, with the inclusion of sounds, pictures and videos.

Beyond the classic database management systems, the new systems can help in documenting and interpreting both tangible and intangible aspects of buildings and sites. Storytelling, music and even semiotic systems in spoken languages can be part of the database.

However, as Robin Letellier puts it, the challenges to regularly update digital inventories, train new human resources, and acquire new hardware and software imply long-term financial commitment that many countries simply cannot afford. Database management systems need active maintenance, consisting of the periodical backup and migration of digital data to new software and hardware, to help prevent the risk of computer-based documentation becoming obsolete or lost because it can no longer be accessed.[45]

Representation and communication

The main purpose of documentation is to provide contents for the representation and interpretation of the past and to communicate values and meaning between different social groups and different generations. The digital era comes with a variety of tools that make this possible. From the internet to digital libraries and documentation centers, from tablets to virtual presentation tools located in classrooms, heritage sites and visitor's centers, from movies to museums, contents related to heritage buildings and sites are accessible virtually anywhere.

New information and communication technologies help us understand geographic contexts of the objects or places under consideration. The representation of heritage sites, including architectural configurations and details, is

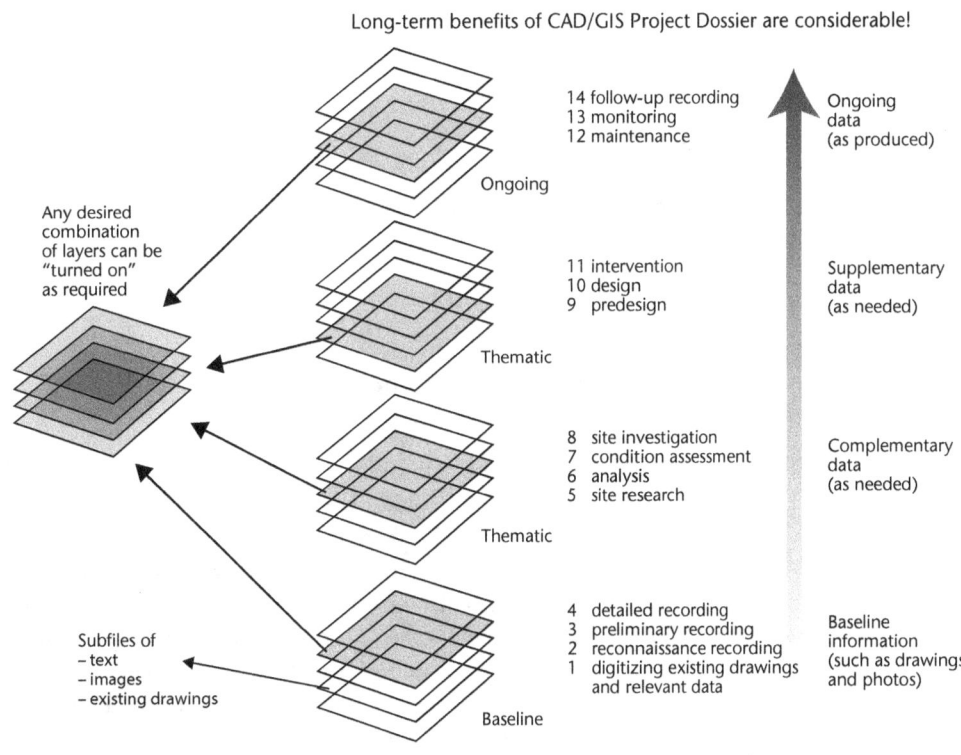

FIGURE 8.10c Shematic example of a GIS graphic database.

the result of multi-disciplinary efforts to organize and visualize huge amounts of data and to include the participation of stakeholders in the interpretation process.[46] There is then little question that the digital documentation of heritage buildings and sites can be of great value.[47]

But as Alfred Schutz puts it, the representation of a thing is quite different than the thing itself.[48] Even with the participation of stakeholders, the representation of the past is not the past itself. The accelerated rhythm of changes in the digital era and the facility to create new data also introduce new management problems and increase the possibility of confusion in the interpretation of heritage's values.

With the possibilities of digital documentation, conservation professionals become more aware of their interpretive responsibility. In 2008, the ICOMOS General Assembly recognized that "every act of heritage conservation is by its nature a communicative act."

There are a growing number of applications of digital documentation such as the work since 2003 of the CyArk organization that conducts laser scanning of whole buildings towards creating a free, 3D online library of the world's cultural heritage sites. New portable documentation systems such as digital tablets offer more possibilities for documentation, analysis and presentation purposes. The act of documentation allows us to more fully understand the history and composition of our environment so that we can then make the best decisions for its conservation.

Now, the challenge is how this new communicative rationality and action can better serve sustainable management of heritage sites. With the great power of digital documentation and communication, there is a great responsibility to conceive interpretive programs that can provide equitable and sustainable economic, social and cultural benefits to all stakeholders through education, training and employment opportunities at heritage sites.[49]

References and further reading

Barton, J. 2010. "Terrestrial LiDAR (3D Laser Scanning) Digital Preservation Technologies." Web. http://www.cyark.org/education/terrestrial-lidar-3d-laser-scanning. Accessed May 17, 2016.

Cambodian Archaeological Lidar Initiative (CALI). 2015. Web. http://angkorlidar.org/. Accessed May 17, 2016.

Cultural Heritage Informatics Initiative – Michigan State University (CHI). 2015. Web. http://chi.anthropology.msu.edu. Accessed May 17, 2016.

Grimm, A.K. 1980. "The Origin of the Term Photogrammetry." Revised and completed article earlier published under the title "Der Ursprung des Wortes PHOTOGRAMMETRIE" at the 1980 Hamburg ISPRS-Congress. Web. http://www.isprs.org/society/history/Grimm-The-Origin-of-the-Term-Photogrammetry.pdf. Accessed May 17, 2016.

International Society for Photogrammetry and Remote Sensing (ISPRS). 2015. "The International Society for Photogrammetry and Remote Sensing – Historical Background." Web. http://www.isprs.org/society/history.aspx. Accessed May 17, 2016.

Jean-Julien, O. 2003. *Digital Revolution, Documentation and Redefinition of the Historic Preservation Discipline. The National Historic Park of Haiti: From Management to Re-appropriation.* New York: Columbia University.

Kalay, Y.E., T. Kvan and J. Afflek. 2008. *New Heritage: New Media and Cultural Heritage.* London: Routledge.

Letellier, R., W. Schmid and F. LeBlanc. 2007. *Recording, Documentation, and Information Management for the Conservation of Heritage Places: Guiding Principles.* Los Angeles: The Getty Conservation Institute.

Sutherland, I.E. 1963. "Sketchpad: A Man-Machine Graphical Communication System." Paper presented at the AFIPS Spring Joint Computer Conference, Detroit, Michigan, May 21–23, 1963.

Conservation in Cambodia beyond Angkor

As Cambodia rapidly modernizes several new conservation challenges stand out: namely how to best protect the country's wealth of vernacular architectural forms especially those found in rural towns and villages, and a rich legacy of architecture from the French colonial period, constructed between the 1850s and the early 1950s. Furthermore, recent years have seen growing interest in preserving Cambodian post-independence modernist architecture, especially in Phnom Penh.

Cambodian rural vernacular forms, found along the waterways and in myriad farming villages throughout the country, reflect ways of life that are essentially unchanged over centuries. In fact, some of the same rural domestic buildings in existence today correspond with the houses carved in the famous twelfth century CE bas-reliefs of the Bayon at Angkor Thom. These well-tempered traditional forms usually consist of a raised wood frame construction with two, three or four rooms that are protected by simple pitched roofs. The raised floor affords protection from flooding, insects and vermin, and provides optimum ventilation and storage for farm implements and animals. Traditional Cambodian rural dwellings situated along roadways often incorporate an excavated open water collection pond in the front and agricultural plots to the rear.

While such vernacular forms today house a significant portion of Cambodia's population, traditional living patterns are giving way to the attractions of urban life and modern amenities that are especially appealing to the country's youth. Despite their relatively obscure status in relation to the country's grand temples, Cambodian vernacular buildings have recently been the subject of research and documentation by the Center for Khmer Studies and other international research efforts.[50]

The French colonial architectural legacy

The legacy of French colonial architecture and urban infrastructure still defines the character of Cambodia's capital and provincial centers. The century-long period of colonial occupation, which began in the 1850s, resulted in hybrid styles of then-contemporary French designs that were adapted to Cambodia's tropical climate. As a result, a plethora of amalgamations of popular French domestic and urban architectural styles from the late nineteenth and early twentieth centuries were applied to the needs of a modernizing Cambodia. The predominant urban building type, however, remained the traditional two- and three-storey shophouse form. After the 1920s, construction of this building type increasingly included materials and details found in early European Modern architecture. All were designed to provide maximum comfort in Cambodia's hot and rainy climate, and today they serve as useful examples of environmental compatibility and energy efficiency for modern architects and builders. (See also The Sustainable Shophouse in Chapter 11.)

With its generous boulevards, living quarters, public spaces and low vertical silhouette, the plan of Phnom Penh's historic urban center was until recently one of the best surviving examples of European colonial architecture in Southeast Asia. After achieving independence in 1953, the Cambodian government strove to forge its own identity, and architecture was considered an important vehicle for this process. An expansion on precedents in ferro-cement designs rapidly developed for commercial, residential and public buildings.

One of the foremost Khmer architects of this period is Vann Molyvann, who served as an apprentice to Le Corbusier. A first-generation leader of the International Style, Molyvann blended traditional Cambodian design motifs and bold modernist principles in a burst of new nationalist architecture erected in Phnom Penh. Molyvann likewise used Western-inspired urban development plans that respected local environmental factors found in the capital and other cities in the growing country. Unfortunately, the historical value of much architecture from this period remains under-appreciated. Even Molyvann's masterpiece, the National Olympic Sports Stadium, faces an uncertain future at the present time.

While the Cambodian constitution and a 1997 law on Cultural Heritage Preservation provide protection for historic sites, more specific legislation (and enforcement) for areas such as the historic center of Phnom Penh is still greatly needed. Fortunately, many of the grander colonial structures have been rehabilitated as embassies, offices, market buildings and restaurants, and are thus well positioned to serve as exemplars for others. The countless more modest buildings such as residences and shophouses comprising the capital's urban cultural landscape are not faring so well due to constant development pressures.

Although many post-independence buildings have survived and some have been restored, other landmarks have been severely altered in their renovation. Protecting significant examples of Cambodia's early modern architecture, and instilling an appreciation for it among the populace, remains a challenge in modernizing Cambodia.

FIGURE 8.11a and b Preservation of Phnom Penh's modernist National Olympic Stadium building (1963–1964), which was designed by the prominent Cambodian architect Vann Molyvann, has been an ongoing struggle due to increasing land values, development interests and an under appreciation of early modern architecture.

Contested heritage: the case of Preah Vihear

The temple of Preah Vihear was built between the eleventh and twelfth centuries CE during the height of the Khmer Empire. Until recently, it was the focal point of a six-decade-long boundary dispute between Thailand and Cambodia, a disagreement that started in the mid-twentieth century and culminated in a three-year armed conflict that began when the site received UNESCO World Heritage designation in 2008. Since then Preah Vihear has stood as an unfortunate exemplar of contested architectural heritage.

Modern territorial ambiguity between Thailand and Cambodia is linked to Cambodia's colonial past. Cambodia, a French protectorate since 1863, gained national sovereignty only in 1953, a year before French Indochina was dissolved. At that time, in 1954, Thailand seized the site, claiming that Preah Vihear was located within its Si Saket Province. The matter was brought to the International Court of Justice, and in 1962 the ICJ, after consulting a Franco-Siamese map from 1907,[51] ruled that the temple was in fact within Cambodian borders. However, the ICJ did not make any specific resolutions regarding the area surrounding the temple.

The listing of Preah Vihear as a Cambodian UNESCO World Heritage Site stirred some age-old enmity between Thailand and Cambodia and resulted in the militarization of the area surrounding the temple. This escalated to an armed conflict that was finally resolved in 2011 after Cambodia requested the ICJ to re-interpret the 1962 judgment based on the 1907 boundary map. In November 2013 the ICJ ruled that Cambodia has sovereignty over the area surrounding the temple and as a result Thai troops were withdrawn from the area. The three years of tension resulted in approximately twenty deaths and thousands of displaced civilians, and minor damage to the temple. As of late 2015, distrust between both countries remains and Cambodian military personnel continue to patrol the area.

International accords to protect heritage sites such as UNESCO's Convention Concerning the Protection of the World Cultural and Natural Heritage (1962), and the Convention for the Protection of Cultural Property in the Event of Armed Conflict (The Hague, May 14, 1954) present significant opportunities to safeguard cultural heritage. Alternatively, as in the case of Preah Vihear, ownership over architectural heritage can trigger unfortunate situations for the countries involved as well as for the cultural patrimony in question. Regional governmental collaborations that promote economic and political progress, such as the Association of Southeast Asian Nations (ASEAN), may help stem such problems by promoting cooperation and integration among its participating neighbors.

The territorial dispute over ownership of Preah Vihear illustrates the power of cultural patrimony in some instances, be it a matter such as national pride, honor or economic interest.

Since 1990 the Cambodian Ministry of Culture, the Royal Government and the APSARA Authority have developed a robust cadre of trained heritage protection and tourism personnel to preserve and present Cambodia's cultural heritage. Nevertheless, there remain challenges in the implementation of heritage conservation plans and enforcement of the country's legal regulations.

As was widely predicted by tourism experts and others working to help modernize the country, Cambodia has again become a very popular tourist destination, having fulfilled Prime Minister Hun Sen's 2005 declaration "Angkor will be the locomotive that pulls the country into modernity."[52] With an estimated 90 percent Cambodia's foreign visitors going to Angkor, jumping from 1,055,000 in 2000 to 4,502,000 in 2014, it is imperative that the country establish and enforce stronger legislation to protect its significant historic buildings from encroaching development as well as uncontrolled tourism and related problems. A sizable number of people live in the archaeological park, many of whom subsist on collecting forest products, with some tracing their family and heritage back to the times of Angkor's builders.[53] Those deriving physical and economic sustenance from the area now face issues related not to neglect, but rather to growing tourism and development.

Angkor is central to the ecological, economic and cultural health of Cambodia and symbolizes the country's rich cultural patrimony. Effective cultural heritage conservation is crucial for stability and prosperity in this country that has suffered so much in recent decades. Despite its many challenges, Cambodia's efforts at protecting its cultural patrimony provide some inspiring examples of international heritage protection policy and operation, in particular those of international cooperation and financing, education, tourism management and architectural conservation practice.

Notes

1 David P. Chandler. *A History of Cambodia*. (Boulder, CO: Westview Press, 1993).
2 John H. Stubbs. *Time Honored: A Global View of Architectural Conservation* (Hoboken, NJ: John Wiley & Sons, 2009), 282.
3 Varying forms of Hinduism and Buddhism have coexisted and sometimes conflicted in Cambodia's past. Since 1847 the national religion has been Theravada Buddhism, the faith of the majority of the nation's populace.
4 Choulean Ang, Eric Thompson and Ashley Thompson (eds.) 1998. *Angkor: A Manual for the Past, Present and the Future*. (Paris: UNESCO), 106.
5 As defined by thefreedictionary.com, an "in rem" lawsuit (Latin for "in the thing itself") is filed "*against an item of property, not against a person (in personam)*." The proceeding takes no notice of the owner of the property but determines rights in the property that are conclusive against all the world.
6 Arnold J. Toynbee. *East to West: A Journey Round the World* (New York: Oxford, 1958).
7 Inscription at the east entrance to the main perimeter gallery of Angkor Wat that cites its restoration in the sixteenth century. *Journal of the Asiatic Society of Bengal* 36(1) (1900), 76.
8 Per the presentation of conservator Simon Warrack of the German APSARA Conservation Project, at the biannual APSARA Meeting on October 21, 2003.
9 Dawn Rooney. *Angkor: Cambodia's Wondrous Khmer Temples* (Hong Kong: Odyssey, 2011), 47.
10 The École française d'Extrême-Orient (EFEO) was established in Hanoi in 1898 as the Mission Archéologique d'Indochine through the efforts of the French Academy of Inscriptions and Belles-Lettres. (See also Chapter 10, Vietnam.)
11 Emmanuel Guillon. *Cham Art* (London: Thames & Hudson, 2001).
12 French writer André Malraux, his wife Clara and accomplices looted 600 kg of sculpture and lintels from Banteay Srei in 1923, but were apprehended and placed under house arrest in Phnom Penh and Saigon pending recovery of the stolen materials. This event served to highlight attention on conservation and restoration of the temple, which proceeded in 1924. Later as a literary figure, Malraux came to be an outspoken critic of the French colonial system. Malraux later fictionalized his Cambodian experience in his novel *The Royal Way* and served as the Minister of Culture in President Charles de Gaulle's cabinet.
13 Marchal's use of the anastylosis method was inspired by its recent successful application in Java and in Greece. Having perfected the method at Banteay Srei by 1931, the technique was used at the temples of Neak Pean, Banteay Samre, the Baphoun, and the north and south gates of Angkor Thom.
14 William Chapman. *A Heritage of Ruins: The Ancient Sites of Southeast Asia and Their Conservation* (Honolulu: University of Hawai'i Press, 2013), 76.
15 Bruno Dagens. *Angkor: Heart of an Asian Empire* (New York: Abrams, 1995). Interrupted by the Khmer Rouge years the Baphoun conservation project was resumed in 1994 and completed as a partial reconstruction in 2013 by EFEO architect Pascal Royer.
16 Chapman, 94.
17 Ang et al., 103.
18 World Monuments Fund, *Considerations for the Conservation and Presentation of the Historic City of Angkor*, Siem Reap, Cambodia, WMF Angkor series Vol. I, September 1992, 3.
19 Rooney, 328.
20 Ang et al., 104. Norodom Sihanouk was elected chair of the Cambodia's Supreme National Council in 1991 and was officially reinstated as King in 1993.
21 The full text of Article 71 of the Cambodian Constitution (1993) reads: "The perimeter of the national heritage sites as well as heritage that has been classified as world heritage, shall be considered neutral zones where there shall be no military activity."
22 Chapman, 98.
23 Ang et al., 103.
24 Ibid.
25 Robert G. Thomson. "On-site Conservation Training in Cambodia: A Critical Survey of Activities at Angkor," *Built Environment* 33(3) (November 5, 2007), 371.
26 Jane Perlez. "A Cruel Race to Loot the Splendor That Was Angkor," *The New York Times*. March 1, 2005. Web. www.nytimes.com/2005/03/21/international/asia/21cambodia.html?pagewanted=2&_r=0. Accessed June 25, 2014.
27 Public education efforts by UNESCO, border guard facilities, cooperation with Interpol, various intergovernmental accords and advocacy organizations such as Saving Antiquities for Everyone (SAFE) have begun to address this difficult task.

28 For a detailed account of the World Monuments Fund's twenty-year project at Preah Kahn, see Michael D. Coe and John H. Stubbs (eds.), *Preah Khan Monastic Complex*. (London: World Monuments Fund, Scala, 2011).
29 Damian Evans, et al. "Uncovering Archaeological Landscapes at Angkor Using LIDAR," *Proceedings of the National Academy of Sciences*. Web. http://www.pnas,org/cgi/10.1073.pnas.13065539110. Accessed 25 July 2013.
30 Ibid. New discoveries determined by LIDAR are revealed in headlines such as Research May Alter Accepted History of Cambodia's End. *The Cambodia Daily*, June 13, 2016. https://cambodiadaily.com and Revealed: Cambodia's Vast Medieval Cities Hidden Beneath Jungle. World News. June 10, 2016. *The Guardian* https://theguardian.com/world/2016/jun/11/lost-city-medievel-discovered-hidden-beneath-cambodian-jungle
31 ICOMOS, 1996. Principles for the recording of monuments, groups of buildings and sites. Ratified by the 11th ICOMOS General Assembly in Sofia, October 1996. International Council on Monuments and Sites. www.icomos.org.
32 Barton. "Terrestrial LiDAR (3D Laser Scanning) Digital Preservation Technologies." 2010. Web. www.cyark.org/education/terrestrial-lidar-3d-laser-scanning. Accessed May 17, 2016.
33 Y.E. Kalay, T. Kvan and J. Afflek. *New Heritage: New Media and Cultural Heritage* (London: Routledge, 2008).
34 Z. Hawass. *The Treasures of the Pyramids* (Cairo: American University in Cairo Press, 2003).
35 Vitruvius. *The Ten Books on Architecture*. Translated by M.M. Hicky. New edition (New York: Dover – Kindle Edition).
36 L.B. Alberti. *Della Pintura / On painting*. Original 1436 text translated by J.R. Spencer (New Haven: Yale University Press, 1956).
37 A.M. Hind. *Giovanni Battista Piranesi: A Critical Study* (London: Holland Press, 1978).
38 International Society for Photogrammetry and Remote Sensing (ISPRS). "The International Society for Photogrammetry and Remote Sensing – Historical Background." 2015. Web. www.isprs.org/society/history.aspx. Accessed May 17, 2016.
39 A.K. Grimm. "The Origin of the Term Photogrammetry." Revised and completed article earlier published under the title "Der Ursprung des Wortes PHOTOGRAMMETRIE" at the 1980 Hamburg ISPRS-Congress. Web. www.isprs.org/society/history/Grimm-The-Origin-of-the-Term-Photogrammetry.pdf. Accessed May 17, 2016.
40 I.E. Sutherland. "Sketchpad: A Man-Machine Graphical Communication System." Paper presented at the AFIPS Spring Joint Computer Conference, Detroit, Michigan, May 21–23, 1963.
41 Cultural Heritage Informatics Initiative – Michigan State University (CHI). 2015. Web. http://chi.anthropology.msu.edu. Accessed May 17, 2016.
42 E. Gregersen, "Light Detecting and Ranging (LIDAR)." *Encyclopedia Britannica*. Web. www.britannica.com/technology/lidar. Accessed May 17, 2016.
43 Cambodian Archaeological LIDAR Initiative (CALI). 2015. Web. http://angkorlidar.org/. Accessed May 17, 2016.
44 Web. www.Scanpyramids.org. Accessed May 17, 2016.
45 R. Letellier, W. Schmid and F. LeBlanc. *Recording, Documentation, and Information Management for the Conservation of Heritage Places: Guiding Principles* (Los Angeles: The Getty Conservation Institute, 2007).
46 O. Jean-Julien, *Digital Revolution, Documentation and Redefinition of the Historic Preservation Discipline. The National Historic Park of Haiti: From Management to Re-appropriation* (New York: Columbia University, 2003).
47 Kalay et al., 2008.
48 A. Schutz. *The phenomenology of the social world / Alfred Schutz* (Evanston, Illinois: North-western University Press, 1967).
49 ICOMOS, 2008. The ICOMOS Charter for the Interpretation and Presentation of Cultural Heritage Sites – ratified by the 16th General Assembly of ICOMOS, Québec (Canada), on October 4, 2008 – International Council on Monuments and Sites. Web. www.icomos.org. Accessed May 17, 2016.
50 In 1998 Professor William Chapman of the University of Hawai'i conducted a typological analysis of the rural dwellings of the Siem Reap region.
51 The long running debate about the jurisdiction of Preah Vihear and other matters of historical context can be found at https://en.m.wikipedia/org/wiki/PreahVihear Temple.
52 From HE Hun Sen's letter to the December 2005 meeting of APSARA in Siem Reap.
53 Keiko Mura. "The People of Angkor: Living With a World Heritage Site," *Siksacakr Newsletter* 2 (October 2000), Center for Khmer Studies, Siem Reap, 9.

Further reading

Ang Choulean, Eric Prenowitz and Ashley Thompson. 1998. *Angkor: A Manual for Past, Present and Future.* 2nd edition. Phnom Penh: APSARA/UNESCO.

Bhandari, C.M. 1995. *Saving Angkor.* Bangkok: White Orchid Press.

Brand, Michael and Chuch Phoeurn. 1992. *The Age of Angkor: Treasures from the National Museum of Cambodia.* Studies in Asian Art, no. 1. Canberra: Australian National Gallery.

Briggs, Lawrence Palmer. 1999. *The Ancient Khmer Empire.* Originally published 1951. Bangkok: White Lotus Press.

Brocheux, Pierre and Daniel Hémery. 2010. *Indochina: An Ambiguous Colonization, 1858–1954.* Berkeley: University of California Press.

Chandler, David. 2008. *A History of Cambodia.* 4th edition. Boulder, CO: Westview Press.

Chapman, William. 2013a. "Angkor on the World Stage: Conservation in the Colonial and Postcolonial Eras," in Kapila D. Silva and Neel Kamal Chapagain (eds.), *Asian Heritage Management.* London: Routledge, 215–235.

——. 2013b. *A Heritage of Ruins: The Ancient Sites of Southeast Asia and Their Conservation.* Honolulu: University of Hawai'i Press.

Chou Ta-kuan [Zhou Daguan]. 1998. *The Customs of Cambodia.* 3rd edition. Translated from the French by Paul Pelliot and from the Chinese by J. Gilman d'Arcy Paul. Bangkok: Siam Society.

Clark, Joyce (ed.). 2007. *Bayon: New Perspectives.* Bangkok: River Books.

Coe, Michael D. 2003. *Angkor and the Khmer Civilization. Ancient Peoples and Cultures.* London: Thames & Hudson.

Coe, Michael D. and John H. Stubbs (eds.). 2011. *Preah Khan Monastic Complex: Angkor, Cambodia.* London: Scala.

Cunin, Olivier. 2007. "The Bayon: An Archaeological and Architectural Study," in Joyce Clark, *Bayon: New Perspectives.* Bangkok: River Books, 136–224.

Dumarçay, Jacques, et al. 2001. *Cambodian Architecture, Eighth to Thirteenth Century.* Leiden: Brill.

Edwards, Penny. 2007. *Cambodge: The Cultivation of a Nation, 1860–1945.* Honolulu: University of Hawai'i Press.

Evans, Damian, et al. 2013. "Uncovering Archaeological Landscapes at Angkor Using LIDAR," Proceedings of the National Academy of Sciences. July 2013. Web. www.pnas,org/cgi/10.1073.pnas.13065539110. Accessed July 25, 2013.

Fletcher, Roland, et al. 2008. "The Water Management Network of Angkor, Cambodia," *Antiquity* 82(317) (2008): 658–670.

Freeman, Michael and Claude Jacques. 1999. *Ancient Angkor.* London: Thames & Hudson.

Grant Ross, Helen, and Darryl Leon Collins. 2006. *Building Cambodia: New Khmer Architecture, 1953–1970.* Bangkok: Key.

Groslier, Bernard P. 1966. *Angkor: Art and Civilization.* Translated by E.E. Smith. New York: Praeger.

ICC Angkor. 2009. *Fifteen Years of International Cooperation for Conservation and Sustainable Development.* Phnom Penh: UNESCO.

Jacques, Claude and Philippe Lafond. 2007. *The Khmer Empire: Cities and Sanctuaries from the 5th to the 13th Century.* Translated by Tom White. Bangkok: River Books.

Jessup. Helen Ibbitson. 2004. *Art and Architecture of Cambodia.* World of Art. London: Thames & Hudson.

JSA (Japanese Team for Safeguarding Angkor). 1996–2010. *Annual Reports of the Technical Survey of Angkor Monuments.* Siem Reap: Japan International Cooperation Center.

Lafont, Masha. 2004. *Pillaging Cambodia: The Illicit Traffic in Khmer Art.* Jefferson, NC: McFarland.

Langlois, Walter G. 1966. *Andre Malraux: The Indochina Adventure.* New York: Praeger.

Leisen, Hans, Jaroslav Poncar and Simon Warrack. 2000. *German APSARA Conservation Project, Angkor Wat.* Cologne: APSARA Conservation Project.

Mannikka, Eleanor. 1996. *Angkor Wat: Time, Space, and Kingship.* Honolulu: University of Hawai'i Press.

Miura, Keiko. 2004. "Contested Heritage: People of Angkor." PhD dissertation, University of London.

Molyvann, Vann. 1995. "Angkor: A Recent Past of Destruction, Future Prospects of Preservation." Paper presented to the international conference *The Future of Asia's Past: Preservation of the Architectural Heritage of Asia,* Chiang Mai, January 11–14, 1995.

——. 2003. *Modern Khmer Cities.* Phnom Penh: Reyum Publishing.

Moore, Elizabeth. 2007. "Spaceborne and Airborne Radar at Angkor: Introducing New Technology to the Ancient Site," in James Wiseman and Farouk El-Baz (eds.), *Remote Sensing in Archaeology.* New York: Springer, 185–216.

O'Reilly, Dougald. 2007. "Shifting Trends of Heritage Destruction in Cambodia: From Temples to Tombs," *Historic Environment* 20(2): 12–16.

Osborne, Milton. 1969. *The French Presence in Cochin China and Cambodia.* Ithaca: Cornell University Press.

Prenowitz, Eric and Ashley Thompson (eds.). 1998. *Angkor: A Manual for the Past, Present and the Future.* Paris: UNESCO.

Rooney, Dawn. 2006. *Angkor: Cambodia's Wondrous Khmer Temples.* 5th edition. Hong Kong: Odyssey.

Roveda, Vittorio. 1998. *Khmer Mythology: Secrets of Angkor.* New York: Weatherhill.

Sharrock, Peter D. 2015. *Banteay Chhmar: Garrison-temple of the Khmer Empire.* Bangkok: River Books.

Snellgrove, David. 2004. *Angkor: Before and After: A Cultural History of the Khmers.* Bangkok: Orchid Press.

Stubbs, John H. and Katherine L.R. McKee. 2007. "Applications of Remote Sensing to the Understanding and Management of Cultural Heritage Sites," in James Wiseman and Farouk El–Baz (eds.), *Remote Sensing in Archaeology.* London: Springer, 515–540.

Toynbee, Arnold J. 1958. *East to West: A Journey Round the World.* New York: Oxford.

Ueno, Kunikazu. 1994. *Zoning and Environmental Management Plan for Angkor.* Bangkok: UNESCO.

Warrack, Simon. 2007. "Involving the Local Community in the Decision-Making Process: The German Apsara Project at Angkor Wat," in Rosalia Varoli-Piazza (ed.), *Sharing Conservation Decisions: Lessons learnt from an ICCROM Course.* Rome: ICCROM, 92–96.

——. 2011. "Learning from Local Leaders: Working Together Toward the Conservation of Living Heritage at Angkor Wat, Cambodia," *Changes Over Time,* 1(1) (Spring): 34–51.

Winter, Tim. 2007. *Post-Conflict Heritage, Postcolonial Tourism: Culture, Politics and Development at Angkor.* London: Routledge.

The Chao Praya River and Bangkok from Wat Arun.

9

THAILAND

Known for most of its history as the Kingdom of Siam (its current name was officially adopted only in 1947), Thailand's leadership has long been invested in conserving its important historic architectural and other cultural assets. Thailand's experience in protecting and restoring its monuments is based in the tradition-oriented nature of the Thai people and their deep respect for the authority of the reigning Chakri dynasty, which has reigned since 1782 and has been a driving force in heritage conservation, especially over the past century. Tenets of the country's predominant religion, Buddhism, have also incentivized a conservation mentality, because it is believed that donors gain spiritual merit whenever their actions advance the religion (for example, by constructing or improving a religious structure, sculpture or image). Taken together, these two strong forces have helped Thailand maintain its wealth of built heritage, despite the deleterious effects of its tropical, flood prone environment.

Perhaps the most important of Thailand's many great national achievements over its long history has been its agility in largely avoiding the great cultural calamities that affected its region during the past 500 years. Notably, it was able to insulate itself from European colonialism and the post-colonial strife that so plagued its neighbors during the late twentieth century. This fact and the steady presence of Thailand's constitutional monarchy, buffered by the tenacious national pride of the Thai people, has enabled this country to emerge as one of modern Southeast Asia's economic leaders. It is today a pillar of stability in the region, one that is well equipped to maintain a sophisticated, effective heritage conservation program.

Thailand's long-standing and robust tourism economy is also a major influence on its modern policy towards heritage protection. At the same time, however, the country's rich cultural and environmental heritage has been subject to the tremendous pressures of modernization in the latter half of the twentieth century. This is especially the case in its urban areas and tourism hubs. Ethnically distinct populations are still able to carry on lifestyles little changed by time in several scattered rural areas, but the situation is vastly different for ethnic Thais, who predominantly populate the country's rapidly developing major cities. The capital mega-city of Bangkok, along with provincial seats such as Chiang Mai and Chang Rai in the north, and the popular seaside destinations of Phuket, Pattaya and Koh Samui to the south, have been transformed over the past century – in particular since the 1960s. The exponential rate of growth of new construction and road systems was slowed only briefly by the Asian economic crisis of the late 1990s.

Until the 1990s, architectural conservation efforts were primarily concentrated on relatively few major sites in Bangkok, Chiang Mai, Chiang Rai and the cultural landscapes, parks and reserves

c

FIGURE 9.1a, b and c Dating from 1888 Wat Pongsanuk (a) in Lampang Province in north central Thailand received the UNESCO Asia-Pacific Award for Cultural Heritage Conservation in 2008. The centerpiece of a larger monastic complex in the Pongsanuk community, its principal structure is the Viharn Prh Chao Pun Ong, which represents a blend of Burmese and Thai styles, cruciform in plan with a three-tiered roof (b), that is considered a masterpiece of Mahayana Buddhist architecture from the Lana Kingdom that once occupied most of northern Thailand. It suffered damage during World War II and subsequent abandonment, a process that was slowly reversed beginning in 1957, with a more effective restoration starting in 2004 with the help of experts from Chiang Mai University joined by conservation experts, a carefully chosen team of craftsmen and community helpers. Its missing elements and interior finishes were restored as faithfully as possible (c) and the project was completed in 2007.

surrounding the former capitals of Sukhothai and Ayutthaya. However, the Thai government's success in developing a pool of talented specialists and a robust system of park lands has resulted in an ability to expand their scope to additional sites, including Phuket, Pattani, Lopburi and Petchaburi.

Thai history is frequently divided into two primary periods, each comprised of five epochs. The first period, which dates from the sixth to thirteenth centuries CE, reflects the time when the region was dominated first by Mon-speaking peoples from southern China during the Dvaravati kingdom, and later by the neighboring Khmer. It was during this period that the concept of gaining religious merit by financially supporting architectural projects became a means to promote conservation.[1] Those who worked to promote the Buddhist religion by erecting images of Buddha and founding monasteries hoped to further their personal progress in achieving Nirvana.[2] This practice is widely credited as the basis of early preservation practices and is still perpetuated to this day. The rewards to be received in a donor's next life were directly dependent not only on the result – for example, a newly built or restored shrine – but on how well the work was executed, and what materials were used.[3] Modifying or making additions to existing parts of the Buddhist wat to fulfill the needs of the monks or to update the design to the trends of the time was widely accepted. (See also Religious Origins of Preservation in India, p. 360.)

The expulsion of the Khmer in the thirteenth century CE marks the beginning of the second era, known as the Sukhothai period. This era lasted for only another 100 years, yet generated the first instances of distinctly Thai art and culture. Following the end of the Sukhothai period were the U-Thong period in central Thailand (thirteenth–fifteenth centuries CE), and the Ayutthaya period (1350–1767 CE). During this latter period, its namesake city served as the seat of the Thai kingdom, which thrived as a culturally coherent and politically powerful entity.[4]

FIGURE 9.2 The nineteenth-century town of Phuket in the far south of Thailand has been the subject of architectural surveys and integrated conservation planning measures. In addition to it being a major tourist destination, Phuket has a vibrant conservation movement that preserves and features its Peranakan Chinese-Malay heritage, which dates from the prosperous tin mining era of the late nineteenth through the early twentieth centuries.

Royal patronage for architectural heritage protection

The first widespread act of conservation, one that was solidly rooted in the idea of obtaining religious merit, occurred in 1638, when King Prasat Thong of Ayutthaya proclaimed that:

> he would be the renewer of everything, and that the people by building and repairing many new temples, had to serve the gods, so that everybody might receive rewards for his good deeds from the gods. In such a way the king sought to change everything spiritually. In view of this the king has had all the principal temples in the entire country and even in uninhabited places, repaired.[5]

The scope of this ambitious undertaking was tempered somewhat by the fact that at the time, the concept of preservation usually meant that the monument would be extensively renovated or possibly deconstructed and rebuilt.[6] As was the case in neighboring Cambodia, successor kings continued with this practice, using auspicious occasions to implement an ambitious reconstruction project, one often designed to outdo work done by a predecessor.

Burmese attacks violently ended the Ayutthaya period in 1767, but the kingdom's populations regrouped on the west bank of the Chao Praya River, establishing the new capital of Thon Buri. King Chao Phraya Chakri (also known as Rama I) reigned from 1782 until 1809. Thon Buri was a short-lived capital: it lasted only a few years before King Rama I established the present capital of Bangkok across the river in 1782.[7]

It was under Rama's Chakri dynasty, which continues to the present time, that the Kingdom of Siam famously evaded the spread of European colonial influence that engulfed its neighbors. This came about due to a series of savvy diplomatic moves on the part of the Thai monarchs, including treaties and trade agreements with the British in particular, but also through modernization reforms designed in part to manage foreign involvement in Thai affairs while simultaneously strengthening the Thai national identity. Meanwhile, the Thai monarchs leveraged the British and French desire to retain an independent "buffer state" between their Indian and Indochinese colonial holdings, although the Kingdom relinquished territorial holdings in present-day Cambodia, Laos and Malaysia in the process.[8]

An important part of the process of national identity building has been the development of Thailand's capital city. Bangkok has grown from a small fishing village in the mid-eighteenth century to one of Asia's principal metropolises in the twenty-first. The Chakri dynasty's original design for the new capital entailed two significant heritage-minded actions. The first was that survivors of the destruction of the former capital of Ayutthaya were sought out for their memories of its physical appearance so that Bangkok's design could incorporate Ayutthaya's most outstanding features as closely as possible. In this task even surviving architectural materials from the former capital were used in the re-building of the new. The second was the reconstruction from memory of the kingdom's written laws, policies, religious texts and similar institutional documents that were lost when Ayutthaya was destroyed in 1767.

Another example of recycling and rebuilding occurred after the accession of King Nangklao (Rama III, who reigned from 1824 until 1851). In 1824, the King oversaw the construction of Bangkok's famous Wat Pho, including the installation of nearly 400 seated Buddhas, murals and relief sculptures that had been salvaged from Ayutthaya. The temple served as one of the country's earliest institutions of medical and scientific study; today it is one of Thailand's most visited and revered places of worship.[9]

King Mongkut, Rama IV, who reigned from 1851 until 1868, initiated a Westernization trend in Thai culture during his reign. He also instilled a European approach to cultural heritage protection, partly breaking from the traditional Buddhist cycle of decay and renewal, and emphasizing a linear understanding of history and stylistic development.[10] In relation to this Mongkut focused on restorations of monuments from previous dynastic reigns and very few new buildings were erected during his reign.

King Mongkut's son and successor King Chulalongkorn, Rama V, who reigned from 1868 to 1910, was the first Thai sovereign to tour Europe, and his visions for his modern capital were largely inspired by his travels abroad and his subsequent study of Western language, culture and architecture. Many new buildings constructed during his reign incorporated Western design elements and materials, such as imported marble, creating a style known today as Thai Baroque.

Although these architectural flourishes were novel, foreign influences have always been integral to Thai craft and design.[11] Over the years, various foreign styles have been incorporated into what is today called "Thai architecture," however, the theme also applies to other adaptations of Thai culture. King Mongkut's and King Chulalongkorn's international approach created the basis for Thailand's Western-styled government and economic models, which rapidly brought the country to the forefront of regional influence in Southeast Asia, a position it holds today.

Both King Mongkut and King Chulalongkorn also promoted European-style heritage conservation during their reigns, establishing these practices as important state-sponsored activities and setting the stage for twentieth century government policy. King Mongkut famously restored the Wat Phra Pathom stupa in Nakhon Pathom, located west of Bangkok in Thailand's central plains. It was a site he had visited as a young monk, shortly after his ascension to the throne.[12] King Mongkut supported the clearing of debris and vegetation from ruins at Ayutthaya and his Royal Proclamation of 1854 ordered local officials to prosecute looters at heritage sites.[13] The Proclamation altered the concept of built heritage conservation in Thailand and effectively secularized the commitment to preserving the country's glorious history. In 1859, King Mongkut constructed Prapaspipithapan Hall within the Royal Palace grounds in Bangkok in order to exhibit important relics of Thai culture thereby associating culture and heritage conservation as elements of state-sponsored nationalism. Through preservation of historic monuments and artifacts, the monarchy encouraged successive generations to have a unified vision of their past culture on a local and national level.[14] His son, King Chulalongkorn, opened the Hall to the Thai public upon taking the throne, and carried on his father's restoration efforts at Ayutthaya through to his own death in 1910.[15]

FIGURE 9.3 The clearing of debris and vegetation from chedi Phukhao Thong at Ayutthaya in the 1850s stands as an early example in Southeast Asia of heritage site conservation and presentation.

King Mongkut's views that built heritage conservation could promote nationalism found further support in 1904 when the Siam Society was founded.[16] The organization's mission is to research Thai history for the purpose of educating Thailand's population about their past and instilling a sense of nationalism.[17] Three years later, in 1907, King Chulalongkorn established the Antiquarian Society to research Thai history.[18] Each in their own way, these organizations sought to better understand the past so as to promote a more viable future.

The 1883 publication of Camilo Boito's *Prima Carta del Restauro* (Charter of Restoration) changed the face of Thai conservation.[19] In this text, Italian restoration specialist Boito promoted the importance of maintaining and respecting the integrity of original materials, views that were adopted by King Chulalongkorn. In turn, the King advised the restorers of Thailand's historic monuments to follow the original design of the monument or building, using as much of the original material as possible. All work on historic buildings needed the King's approval, and aspects that needed repair were not to be made to look new. This was a revolutionary conservation approach at the time and was advanced compared to many of the conservation approaches taking place around the world.

The royal family remained actively interested in the protection of Thailand's cultural patrimony for much of the first half of the twentieth century, as princes and kings – along with several outsiders – conducted scholarly research and launched several institutions for the purposes of conserving historic Thai artifacts, buildings and sites. However, despite royal patronage and the country's more sensitive approach to preservation, at the turn of the twentieth century Thailand's national antiquities and monuments were being threatened by a powerful force: modernization. Crown Prince Maha Vajiravudh (later King Rama VI, who reigned from 1910 until 1925) was the first to conclude that progress can be a destructive aspect in the preservation of one's culture. The Crown Prince is attributed as having said:

> If we are forced to choose between progress or preservation of antiquities, it is normal to think of progress first, so that we have to sacrifice antiquities for the sake of progress. In our country, how many bricks from the buildings of Ayutthaya went into the making of railway embankments? My only hope is that there will not be too many occasions when we will have to barter antiquities for progress.[20]

He recognized that while progress is inevitable, it does not necessarily have to be at the expense of a nation's iconic and historic structures. Prior planning that incorporated insights from knowledgeable urban planners and architects could ensure that all possible alternatives are considered before action is taken to permit progress. Also, if the location is in proximity to a historic structure, it is important to ensure that the new structure's design is sensitive to the surrounding historic architectural context. The Crown Prince's conclusion on progress was a revolutionary theory at the time yet holds true to this day.[21]

Towards formalized heritage conservation administration

King Vajiravudh improved centralized oversight of heritage in 1912 when he established the Fine Arts Department (*Krom Silpakorn*), a new heritage management administrative entity that was created through the merger of the Department of Court Craftsmen and the Royal Museum. He incorporated the Museum Department within the Ministry of Public Works (which originally was solely in charge of preservation responsibilities) to create the Department of Art and Crafts, and also established the kingdom's first Archaeology Department in 1924, following the example of neighboring colonial governments in British Burma and French Indochina. Responsibilities of the Fine Arts Department and Department of Art and Crafts included the restoration of temples and producing images of Buddha, and their establishment made the act of protecting national heritage a state responsibility.

Early in his reign, King Vajiravudh's brother, King Prajadhipok (Rama VII, who reigned from 1925 until 1935), established a national museum system for Thailand and established the Royal Institute by decree in 1926. This decision, which gave the Royal Institute governance oversight of the Fine Arts Department, the Museum Department and the Archaeological Department, consolidated several cultural institutions under a single umbrella organization.[22]

Like his brother, King Prajadhipok was interested in preserving Thailand's antiquities for the purpose of fostering national pride. He appointed Prince Damrong Rajanubhab to be in charge of the Royal Institute. In 1930 the Prince issued a series of considerations that were to be followed when antiquities were being preserved. First: restorations must keep to the original design and should not have their form and decoration altered. Second: monuments or historic buildings could not be damaged or destroyed in order to make a new building. And third: any new building had to be kept a certain distance from the original building so as to avoid compromising its integrity.[23] These rules shifted the Royal Institute's task away from restoring historic buildings to an earlier appearance to conserving them complete with their changes over time.[24]

In addition to issuing domestic decisions regarding heritage, King Prajadhipok initiated cross-border scholarly exchange among colonial governments when he invited French scholars from the École française d'Extrême Orient (EFEO) in Hanoi to the kingdom for the purposes of studying Thai architecture and art. In 1932 the king was deposed in a coup d'etat, and the absolute monarchy was replaced by a constitutional monarchy. Politics temporarily interrupted the royal family's prominent role in Thai cultural heritage management, but fortunately, the scholarly documentation and research initiatives continued to evolve under the tumultuous military rule of Field Marshall Phibun Songkhram. In 1935 the Royal Institute became a research center and lost responsibility for the Fine Arts Department. In turn the Fine Arts Department, now overseen by the Ministry of Education, was put in charge of archaeology, conservation and overseeing museums. Further administrative shifts occurred in 1952, when the Division of Culture, the branch of the government that oversaw the Fine Arts Department, became the Ministry of Culture and was given broader administrative responsibilities. The Ministry now also oversaw the Departments of Publicity, Fine Arts, Religious Affairs and Culture.[25]

Despite the Thai government's numerous shifts in power from the 1932 coup d'etat until 1979, when stability under the monarchy was restored, that period was marked by both legislative action and the commencement of specific projects involving architectural restoration and conservation. The Conservation Act of 1934, for example, established a system for a national inventory and refocused attention on the former capitals of Ayutthaya and Sukhothai. During the Japanese occupation during World War II most conservation activity came to a halt, but after the war, restoration projects resumed at several sites around the country. Through the early 1950s, much of the activity tended towards reconstruction, rather than conservation.[26]

In 1957, the Ministry of Culture was disassembled and the Fine Arts Department fell under the jurisdiction of the Ministry of Education. During the 1960s, the national conservation approach was changed: less intensive interventions were done, and more conservation guidelines were put in place. During this time, there was also a move to publicize the importance of preservation due to the massive amount of destruction that was taking place as Thailand was being modernized.

In 1961 the government passed the Act on Monuments, Antiquities, Objects of Art and National Museums. Among other issues, this legislation reinforced the position of the Fine Arts Department as the chief agency for conservation activity, by requiring that any work to be done on a national monument required the approval of, and a permit from, the Department. During the 1960s much additional progress was made in heritage administration matters: a National Register of heritage sites was launched to update a nationwide inventory begun in 1934, and UNESCO was invited to help develop a plan for maintaining Sukhothai as an archaeological and historic park with a focus on attracting tourism.[27]

During the 1970s, the Education Department was restructured once again, and the Fine Arts Department was given authorization not just to preserve historical sites, but also to designate them as well. Through the 1980s, the Fine Arts Department issued even more restrictions on new developments that were in close proximity to ancient monuments. It went so far as to stop all new development by the state and by private developers in Bangkok's historic section (Krung Rattanakosin). Thai ideas of conservation evolved so as to more closely mirror international conventions, with the Fine Arts Department stating that the conservation of monuments was not only for the basis of scholarship, but also that historical monuments needed to be part of local communities.

As of 2016, the Fine Arts Department is the governmental department that oversees state-funded preservation projects, and remains a driving force for the conservation of Thailand's historical heritage. The Department of Religious Affairs also plays an active role in establishing budgets and maintenance plans for important temples. The temples that receive the most investment and are prioritized for repair are the royal temples.[28] Unfortunately, many temples, while historic, do not hold royal status and usually have to wait longer for repairs to take place. Many temples do not receive funding from the Fine Arts Department: all maintenance and repair costs fall on the general public. But while this situation would be a major concern elsewhere, Thailand's strong Buddhist traditions ensure that temple upkeep is generally adequately funded by private donations made by the surrounding community.[29]

Historical Park planning and conservation

Beginning in the 1980s the Thai government launched a new initiative to conserve the country's key historic buildings and sites in order to tap into an economic opportunity that would come to define the nation for the next several decades: tourism.

The National Historical Park System, today a network of ten sites, is the centerpiece of the Thai system of cultural heritage conservation and promotion.[30] Fine Arts Department staff, many of whom had been involved with the UNESCO-led conservation effort in Indonesia at Borobudur, the Regional Centre for Archaeology and Fine Arts (SPAFA), and the Southeast Asian Ministers of Education Organization (SEAMEO), conducted much of the work performed at these sites during the late 1970s and early 1980s. Despite this international pedigree, some members of the broader conservation community have since criticized the work performed at Sukhothai and Ayutthaya as having been too heavy-handed and insensitive to the site's authenticity.[31] Nevertheless, ongoing projects at these sites and at the other Historical Parks represent a high point of Thai conservation activity, and remain active environments for international exchange and the application of professional standards.

FIGURE 9.4 The ancient Sukhothai Historical Park consists of the stabilized and restored remains of over 150 stupas, temples, shrines and associated support buildings, including Wat Mahathat, located within a seventy square kilometer cultural landscape.

Among the most remarkable complexes of monumental architecture in the world, Sukhothai reached its zenith from the thirteenth through the fifteenth centuries CE, during which time it developed its distinctive architectural style. High towers, or *chedis*[32](stupas) surmounted by lotus-bud domes, were originally reliquaries; Khmer and Sinhalese influences can be seen in the intricate stucco-sculpted walls and detailed engraved ceilings. Sukhothai's princes were prolific builders, and today, this carefully planned city consists of the ruins of more than 150 significant structures, along with innumerable Buddha figures, which are the most characteristic of Sukhothai art forms.[32]

The seventy square kilometer Sukhothai Historical Park currently incorporates the archaeological site, its surrounding plain and backdrop of hills, and a collection of monumental structures into a unified cultural landscape. Work began at the site in the 1960s and in 1982 a master plan was completed. The plan included the assignment of land use zones, plans for the phased restoration of architectural monuments, archaeological investigations, landscape improvements, and accommodations for tourism. Plans to restore the character of the site's general appearance, including establishment of orchards and other tree clusters, were derived from accounts of the city's appearance found in ancient inscriptions at the site.

The Sukhothai master plan also included the relocation or "redevelopment" of as many as 600 homes located within the park's boundaries.[33] Although the conservation work addressed the condition of the monuments and greatly advanced scholarly understanding of the site – ultimately contributing to its World Heritage listing in 1991 – the issue of the relocated families underscores the challenges of conserving large-scale sites that are home to pre-existing resident communities. Similarly, the overall treatment of the property received some criticism both internally and internationally due to its overly park-like qualities, which were considered to be incompatible with the site's historic character.[34]

Based in part on the work performed at Sukhothai – and in response to Western-oriented conventions such as the Venice Charter – Thai conservation professionals established the Bangkok Charter in 1985. This approach foreshadowed the later Nara Document on Authenticity (1994) and

Principles for the Conservation of Heritage Sites in China (2002) by accommodating non-Western approaches to conservation and authenticity, and allowing for a greater degree of reconstruction – particularly of religious heritage such as Buddha images.[35] Despite the criticism regarding certain conservation techniques, the Thai approach to managing and presenting Sukhothai represents a watershed event for the development of a distinctly Thai cultural heritage policy.

In addition to Sukhothai, a second historical park that has received substantial conservation attention is Ayutthaya, Thailand's second capital. It was established in 1350 CE at the convergence of the Chao Phraya, Lopburi and Pa Sak rivers, which created a strategic location 80 km north of Bangkok in Thailand's central plains. The ancient city, surrounded on all sides by the rivers and a natural floodplain, had a technologically advanced approach of using this water as protection, transportation, drainage and irrigation. However, despite its naturally strategic barrier against enemies, the Burmese invaded it in 1767. The city was destroyed, the national capital moved to Bangkok, and Ayutthaya was largely abandoned for centuries and gradually fell into ruins.

In the 1960s, legislation protecting the site as an ancient monument was enacted in tandem with early conservation projects. A 1964 study examined historical maps so that Ayutthaya's original city plan could be replicated.[36] Plans for the Ayutthaya Historical Park were adopted in 1967 and were implemented in 1976, launching the site's revival as a heritage site.[37] However, much looting and neglect continued into the late 1980s despite the Fine Arts Department's early conservation efforts.

In the 1990s, approximately 200 families were relocated outside of the park boundaries,[38] and UNESCO declared a portion of the historical park as a UNESCO World Heritage Site. The designated sites received enhanced protection and maintenance as a result, and Ayutthaya' visibility on the world stage increased immensely.[39] However, some of the monuments that do not have World Heritage designation are underfunded and receive less conservation work by comparison.

In 1994, the Fine Arts Department began to revise the Ayutthaya Historical Park's master plan reorganizing conservation efforts under a new plan finalized in 1996.[40] In addition to work by the Fine Arts Department, other groups that have also contributed to the protection of Ayutthaya's temples and shrines include the World Monuments Fund, the American Express Foundation, The Asian Development Bank and the US Ambassador's Fund for Cultural Preservation.[41]

In 1995, a flood submerged substantial parts of the Ayutthaya site for over two months. While its island location has always been susceptible to flooding, in recent years inundations have become more regular and severe due to the province's land management practices, which include deforestation and filling in of river marshland. In response to these calamities, in 1996 the World Monuments Fund placed Ayutthaya on its Watch List of 100 most endangered sites, a move that drew global attention to the site's increasingly severe flood-related challenges. After another inundation at the seventeenth century Wat Chaiwatthanaram at Ayutthaya in 2011, the WMF partnered with the Fine Arts Department to leverage financial support from the US Ambassador's Fund for Cultural Preservation. As a result, a multi-year project aimed at documentation, materials testing, emergency conservation and a monitoring program to assist in future flood responses at the site was launched.[42]

The challenges at the Wat Chaiwatthanaram complex highlight an overall national need for combining micro-level conservation practices such as conserving the centuries-old masonry structures, with macro issues like regional water management practices and ecological protections.[43] Unfortunately, despite the international conservation aid, it is likely that Wat Chaiwatthanaram will continue to suffer the cumulative effects of flooding and associated material deterioration until a comprehensive ecological plan and larger site protection can be formulated and implemented.[44]

In addition to its work at Sukhothai and Ayutthaya, two principal sites of early Thai heritage, the Fine Arts Department has also engaged in conserving and presenting architectural remains that represent other periods of the nation's history. Professional conservation work on the formidable stone structures at the ancient Khmer sites of Prasat Phimai and Prasat Phnom Rung began in the nineteenth century with documentation efforts by French teams, including Henri Parmentier, renowned for his work at Cham and Khmer sites in the region. Through the EFEO, Angkor conservator Bernard-Philippe Groslier advised on the reconstruction of both sites, relying upon the technique of anastylosis to stabilize the building foundations of these predecessors to Angkor Wat.[45] Similar disassembly for foundation stabilization purposes has subsequently been used at individual temples and other historic buildings throughout Thailand, including in densely occupied Bangkok.

FIGURE 9.5a, b and c Ayutthaya, the capital of Siam from 1350 until 1767, has been the subject of heritage protection measures since the 1960s. Recently it has faced an increasing number of conservation challenges, especially flooding (a), due to its low elevation at the confluence of three rivers. Integrated conservation planning measures for many of the site's temples, shrines and enclosures have assumed periodic replacement of the more vulnerable lower masonry and stucco surfaces of affected buildings. Deteriorated Wat Mai Chairichit (b) was restored in 1997 (c).

Urban conservation initiatives

Over the past fifty years, Bangkok, along with the northern provincial cities of Chiang Mai and Chiang Rai, have been comprehensively transformed by unremitting programs of building construction and infrastructure development. In the 1930s, the pinnacles of chedis and temples were still Bangkok's tallest structures. But after World War II, rapid high-rise construction elongated the city's urban silhouette as concurrent alterations to its extensive *klong* (canal) network paved the way for future mass transit systems.

At the close of World War II, Bangkok's population stood at just over 1 million; as of 2014 its metro area supports 14 million residents. Huge swaths of the city have been completely redeveloped, and as a result many of Bangkok's historic sites today sit isolated among newer residential, commercial and public buildings. Due to its twentieth-century growth Bangkok is no longer a low-scale, traditional Southeast Asian city reflective of its strategic regional location and nineteenth-century prosperity, but has instead become an overwhelming and teeming metropolis struggling with several of modernity's worst problems: overpopulation, traffic congestion and pollution.

While much historic fabric has been lost over the past century, portions of Bangkok's ancient klong network and select districts of traditional buildings still exist. Beginning in the 1970s, national and grassroots efforts emerged to advocate for their preservation. Subsequent decades of urban conservation activity in the city have highlighted the long-standing tension between top-down planning and local priorities, a common theme in modern Thai public policy. Urban conservation efforts in Bangkok and Thailand's other cities also struggle against a nationwide focus on historic temples, archaeological sites and traditional steep-gabled stilt houses, which are being maintained at the expense of most other forms of urban architectural fabric.[46]

FIGURE 9.6 The Old Customs House on the Chao Praya River in central Bangkok is a reminder of the city's late nineteenth-century character and scale. Strong protective legislation is the only way that historic buildings of this size can successfully compete against the financial returns that are being realized from larger new commercial structures in the city, especially those located close to the river.

FIGURE 9.7 Restoration and preservation of traditional Thai houses is increasingly in vogue, however, it takes commitments of resources and maintenance. Located in the Khaosaming district, this house reveals their practicality and distinct character.

The Fourth National Social and Economic Development Plan (1977), one in a series of centralized planning efforts, called for, among other things, the preservation of Bangkok's Rattanakosin Island. Located within the historic core of the city, the island houses one of a relatively few remaining collections of traditional Thai residences, shophouses, stupas, palaces and fortifications.[47] The master plan called for conservation of traditional religious structures and buildings associated with the ruling elite, along with the creation of large plazas and other landscaped areas emphasizing views of these buildings. Over the next several decades, implementation of the plan has been questioned for its insufficient public consultation, and its bias towards the "heritage of high culture" at the expense of the full scope of urban fabric and traditional Thai urban architecture.[48] As in much of Southeast Asia, the movement to preserve the less monumental aspects of the urban cultural landscape remains a challenge, but one with great opportunities for improvement within the Thai heritage conservation field.

Recent commitment in heritage conservation

Bangkok's status as a regional hub, national capital and cosmopolitan city accounts for its role as a center for conservation activity. Headquartered there is the Office of Archaeology and National Museums (OANM), Thailand's national bureau for cultural heritage management, which operates out of the Fine Arts Department and is responsible for project development along with on-site management of conservation projects. Each of OANM's two divisions has offices at the regional level that manage local historical parks. One division is responsible for architectural projects while the other oversees archaeological projects.[49]

Bangkok is also home to several non-governmental organizations (NGOs) and government-affiliated enterprises, such as the Tourism Authority of Thailand, which complement national legislative heritage protection efforts. The coordinating body for NGO activities is the government's Office of the National

Culture Commission (ONCC), which also interfaces with the many advocacy organizations working privately against uncontrolled urban development. The Fine Arts Commission of the Association of Siamese Architects, and the Siam Society, established in 1904 under the royal patronage of King Rama V's eldest son, are among the most notable. Additionally, the Siam Society successfully promotes the preservation of Thailand's built heritage, as well as appreciation for its culture, art and natural environment, through a series of lectures, exhibitions, study tours and publications.[50]

Another important Bangkok-based regional NGO is SPAFA, which since 1987 has promoted ASEAN cultural and educational exchanges via its SEAMEO Center for Archaeology and Fine Arts. The opportunities created by its workshops, training programs and seminars have done much to promote the professional development of regional talent, and have helped create a professional network of historic conservation professionals in Thailand and the region. Additionally, UNESCO's Pacific Regional Office in Bangkok remains highly active in disseminating expert advice, project support and program development for the growing ranks of heritage conservation professionals in Thailand and its surrounding region.[51]

At the university level, initiatives advocating sensitive new development and architectural conservation are being led by the Silpakorn University's Departments of Architecture and Archaeology, and by both the Department of Architecture and the Institute of Thai Study at Chulalongkorn University. Graduate and Doctoral level degrees in architectural conservation are offered at both universities. Most OANM staff members have attained such degrees, or comparable ones received at foreign institutions of higher education.[52]

Thailand's multi-faceted commitment to heritage protection is also reflected in its government's efforts to participate in global conservation initiatives. As of 2016 the Thai Ministry of Culture was moving forward with the process of joining the 2003 UNESCO Convention on the Safeguarding of the Intangible Cultural Heritage, a group of 168 nations that have agreed to list intangible cultural heritage practices or customs and establish means for their support, documentation and perpetuation.[53] The process for becoming a member state to the Convention involves the creation of a national inventory of intangible cultural heritage, in which Thailand may include traditional poetry recitations (known as *sae-pa*), Thai massage and musical theater performances (*Likay Hulu*).[54] Adoption of the Convention and passage of associated national legislation would place Thailand in the company of Cambodia, Laos, Vietnam, Philippines and Malaysia, five of the ten ASEAN nations that currently participate in this important and emerging field of heritage preservation.

To commemorate the eighty-fourth Royal Birthday Anniversary of His Majesty King Bhumibol Adulyadej, the Patron of the Siam Society and protector of fine arts and cultural heritage of Thailand, in 2011 the Council of the Society launched the Siamese Heritage Protection Program. The Program serves the central activity of the Siamese Heritage Trust. Through a series of public events, associated lectures, tours and media opinion pieces, the Program highlights issues and problems in the management of the cultural heritage of Thailand, both tangible and intangible, with the aim of contributing to heritage conservation, generating ideas on how heritage management can be improved, and raising the visibility of cultural heritage management as a national issue of general public interest.[55] Established by the Siam Society, the Siamese Heritage Trust is modeled on English Heritage, the UK National Trust and other national trusts elsewhere in Southeast Asia, such as Badan Warisan Malaysia. The purpose is specifically to mobilize the Thai private sector to support conservation activities. The Society's 2003 publication *Protecting Siam's Heritage*, edited by Chris Baker, originated as the centenary edition of the *Journal of the Siam Society*, one of Asia's oldest and most prestigious cultural journals. The book features a collection of nineteen essays concerning cultural heritage conservation in Thailand reflecting on the state of practice, effective case studies and emerging trends.

In the opening years of the twenty-first century through 2015 the tourism sector accounted for nearly 10 percent of Thailand's gross domestic product, or national income, among the highest percentages of any Asian country.[56] While such revenue can underpin a large amount of economic growth, it also makes the Thai economy overly reliant on income that is driven by factors it cannot control, such as a fluctuation in tourism numbers due to political or health-related crises.

Though much work remains to be done, there exists a growing understanding within government circles that heritage conservation and tourism planning need to work closely together to ensure that

FIGURE 9.8a and b Preservation work done at the Grand Palace in Bangkok (a) likely represents the highest possible standard of architectural conservation in Thailand. Restoration of mirror mosaic and roof repair work in the west gable of the Amerindra Winitchai Hall (b).

the goal of safeguarding the national built heritage is not lost in a rush to earn revenue through tourism. In the tradition of their ancestors, Thailand's current royal family continues to strongly support King Rama V's commitment to conserving the country's rich heritage by sponsoring numerous programs that promote Thailand's built and natural heritage, as well as its artistic and musical traditions. As Queen Sirikit's representative noted in a speech to heritage conservation professionals in 1996 in Chiang Mai: "economic growth today could lead to cultural poverty tomorrow."[57] With so much to lose – or gain – from effective heritage management policy and practice, Thailand remains in a strong position to continue to develop its own effective heritage management practices, and reinforce its position as a regional leader in the field.

Notes

1. Samuel Beal. *Buddhist Records of the Western World*. Translated from the Chinese of Hiuen Tsiang, 629 CE. (Delhi: Munshiram Manoharlal, 1969), 146–147.
2. Peter Skilling. "For Merit and Nirvana: The Production of Art in the Bangkok Peroid," *Art Asiatiques* 62 (2007), 78.
3. Stone construction provided the most amount of merit due to its ability to last. Brick, also used for temple construction, was considered less meritorious than stone. Wood, being far less durable, obtained the lowest level of merit. It was used for secondary buildings, such as the kitchens or monks' dormitories. Wood was not used for long term temple buildings until the nineteenth century.
4. Keith Mundy. *Thailand*. (Singapore: MPH Publications, 1992), 182.
5. Jeremias Van Vliet. "Description of the Kingdom of Siam," *Journal of the Siam Society* 7 (1910), 74–75.
6. Chris Baker, *Protecting Siam's Heritage* (Chiang Mai: Siam Society, 2013), 21.
7. World Monuments Fund/US ICOMOS. "Thailand: A Heritage of Moveable Buddhist Kingdoms," in *Trails to Tropical Treasures: A Tour of ASEAN's Cultural Heritage*. (New York: World Monuments Fund, 1992), 41.
8. D.R. Sar Desai. *Southeast Asia: Past & Present*. (Chiang Mai: Silkworm Books, 1981), 133–139.
9. Trudy Ring, Robert M. Salkin and Sharon La Boda (eds.). *International Dictionary of Historic Places 5 – Asia & Oceania*. (New York: Routledge, 1996), 98. The task of reconstructing Siam's lost written records was not completed until 1805.
10. Maurizio Peleggi. "Politics of Ruins and the Business of Nostalgia," in *Studies in Contemporary Thailand* 10 (Bangkok: White Lotus Press, 2002).
11. Foreign influences that inspired the Thai Baroque style include Indian, Pyu, Mon, Khmer, Ceylonese, Persian and Chinese design motifs and styles of architecture, the latter especially during the first three reigns of the Chakri dynasty, as the family was of Chinese origin.
12. WMF/US ICOMOS, 39.
13. King Mongkut's Royal Proclamation of 1854 advanced a creative way to help protect temples against vandalism and looting. It announced that everyone living within approximately 500 feet from a monastery was responsible for the safekeeping of that monastery, and must report thievery or damage to the appropriate authority within one month of the occurrence. If a non-local noticed and reported the damage first, the responsible residents were required to pay for the repair to this "ornament of the Thai Kingdom." Source: *Prachum Prakat Ratchakam Tee*, volume 1 (1984), first published 1960. (Bangkok: Rongpim Guru Sapha Ladprao, 1984): 71–72.
14. Peleggi, 31.
15. David K. Wyatt. *Thailand: a Short History*. (New Haven, CT: Yale University Press, 1984). Later King Chulalongkorn transformed the former Wang Na Palace, located not far from the Grand Palace grounds, into the National Museum, thus opening the private collections of King Mongkut to the public.
16. The Siam Society was established under the patronage of Crown Prince Vajiravudh (to be Rama VI) in direct emulation of the Royal Asiatic Society.
17. Siam Society. Web. http://www.siam-society.org/. Accessed October 27, 2015.
18. Piriya Krairiksh. 2013. "A Brief History of Heritage Protection in Thailand", in Chris Baker (ed), *Protecting Siam's Heritage* (Chiang Mai: Silkworm Books, 2013), 22.
19. Nikom Musigakama (ed.). *Tidsadee Lae Naew Thang Patibat Karn Anurak Anusorn-satan Lae Laeng Borankadee*. Document No.1/2532 [1989]. (Bangkok: Kong Borankhadi, 1990), 89.
20. Maha Vajiravudh, HRH Crown Prince. *Tieo Muang Phra Ruang Rattanakosin Sok 126*. (RS 127/BE 2451). (Bangkok: Rongpim Bamrung Nukullkit, 1908), 241.

21 It was under King Vajiravudh's order that the city walls and moat of Chiang Mai were preserved, an act that marked the first time in Thailand that urban infrastructure (as opposed to religious monuments) were officially cited for conservation.
22 WMF/US ICOMOS, 41.
23 Damrong Rajanubhab, Somdet Phrachao Boromwong Thoe Krom Phraya. *Pathakata Roeng Sa-nguan Raksa Kong Boran*. Published for the cremation of Nai Lek Na Songkhla at Wat Mongkut Kasat Triyaram, April 27. (Bangkok: Krom Silpakorn, 1973), 12–13.
24 Musigakama, 94.
25 Krasuang Watthanaatham. *Article 2546* (Bangkok: Rungsil Karn Pim, 2003), 19–21.
26 Peleggi, 39.
27 Thailand Fine Arts Department. *Sukhothai Historical Park Development Project: Master Plan.* (Bangkok: Fine Arts Department, 1977), 5.
28 Royal temples, which are partially funded by the royal family, tend to receive preferential treatment by the government. They were among the first to be rebuilt after the flooding of 2011.
29 Merit-based donations are the driving force behind the preservation of Thailand's main historic architecture, the Buddhist wat.
30 The ten parks are: Ayutthaya, Kamphaeng Phet, Mueang Sing, Phanom Rung, Phimai, Phra Nakhon Khiri, Phu Phrabaht, Si Satchanalai, Si Thep and Sukhothai.
31 Peleggi, 41.
32 UNESCO. *Sukhothai and Ancient Thai Civilization: A Lesson in Harmony* (Paris: UNESCO, 1984).
33 Fine Arts Department. *Sukhothai Historical Park Development Project* (Bangkok: Fine Arts Department & Ministry of Education, Government of Thailand, 1982), 177–180.
34 William A. Chapman. *A Heritage of Ruins: The Ancient Sites of Southeast Asia and their Conservation.* (Honolulu: University of Hawai'i Press, 2013), 148–149.
35 Denis Byrne. "Chartering Heritage in Asia's Postmodern World," *Getty Conservation Institute Newsletter* 19(2) (Summer 2004). Web. http://www.getty.edu/conservation/publications_resources/newsletters/19_2/news_in_cons1.htm. Accessed June 26, 2014.
36 This research, featured in the Siam Society's 1970 publication *In Memoriam Phya Anuman Rajdhon*, became the basis for the zoning of the Ayutthaya Historical Park.
37 Krairiksh, 42–43.
38 Sunait Chutintaranond. *Ayutthaya: The Portraits of the Living Legends* (Bangkok: Plan Motif Publishers, 1996).
39 UNESCO World Heritage Center. "Historic City of Ayutthaya." Web. http://whc.unesco.org/en/list/576. Accessed November 7, 2015.
40 Krairiksh, 51.
41 Pakamas Jaichalard. "U.S. Grants Bt34 Million Fund for Wat Chai's Restoration," *The Nation*. January 8, 2014. Web. www.nationmultimedia.com/national/US-Grants-Bt34-Million-Fund-for-Wat-Chais-Restorat-30223746.html. Accessed November 7, 2015.
42 *Art Daily*. "New US State Department Award for Work in Ayutthaya," January 10, 2014. Web. http://artdaily.com/news/67366/New-US-State-Department-award-for-work-in-Ayutthaya--Thailand#.U6xGnxzeW1Y. Accessed June 26, 2014.
43 Fine Arts Department of Thailand & National Research Institute for Cultural Properties, Tokyo, Japan. *Conservation of Monuments in Thailand IV. Seminar Proceedings*, September 4–5, 2008, Bangkok, Thailand. (Tokyo: NRICP, 2008).
44 Colin Amery. *Vanishing Histories: 100 Endangered Sites from the World Monuments Watch.* (New York: Harry N. Abrams and the World Monuments Fund, 2001), 108.
45 Chapman, 152–153.
46 Worrasit Tantinipankul. "Thailand's Neglected Urban Heritage: Challenges for Preserving the Cultural Landscape of Provincial Towns of Thailand." Paper delivered at the Association of Critical Heritage Studies Conference, Gothenburg, Sweden, June 5–8, 2012. Web. http://criticalheritagestudies.org.preview.binero.se/sites/default/files/1367079_p191-tantinipankul-thailand-s-neglected-urban-heritage.pdf. Accessed July 4, 2014.
47 Marc Askew. "Bangkok: Transformation of the Thai City," in Marc Askew and William S. Logan (eds), *Cultural Identity and Urban Change in Southeast Asia – Interpretive Essays.* (Geelong: Deakin University Press, 1994), 87.
48 Chatri Prakitnonthakan. "Rattanakosin Charter: The Thai Cultural Charter for Conservation," *Journal of the Siam Society* 100 (2012), 117.
49 Chapman, 153–155.
50 WMF/US ICOMOS, 43.

51 UNESCO Bangkok office supports a remarkable array of programs and activities in support of architectural conservation throughout the ASEAN region. Their web presence is an extremely helpful resource for reports, program summaries and discussion of issues affecting heritage conservation in Thailand and the region. Web. www.unescobkk.org/culture/protecting-our-heritage/wh/.

52 Despite the present capacity to train architects at Thailand's leading universities in the principles of traditional design, that is, geometry, mathematics, proportion and symbolism, there was recently a call to do more in "Preserving the Vanishing Thai Architectural Identity Following the Identity of ASEAN Economic Development Community" by Prof. Vacharee Svamivastu, Faculty of Architecture, KMITL, Bangkok, April 22–24, 2014. Web. http://sydney.edu.au/southeast-asia-centre/documents/pdf/svamivastu-vacharee.pdf. Accessed December 9, 2015.

53 UNESCO Bangkok. "Thailand to Ratify the UNESCO Convention for the Safeguarding of the Intangible Cultural Heritage." February 24, 2012. Web. www.unescobkk.org/en/news/article/thailand-to-ratify-the-unesco-convention-for-the-safeguarding-of-the-intangible-cultural-heritage/. Accessed June 26, 2014.

54 *Bangkok Post*. "Thailand Hurries to List Cultural Icons." March 12, 2013. Web. www.bangkokpost.com/lite/topstories/340110/thailand-hurries-to-bag-cultural-icons. Accessed June 26, 2014.

55 The Siamese Heritage Trust program as described on its website: www.siamese-heritage.org. Accessed December 28, 2015.

56 Michael S. Arnold. "Thailand's Political Unrest Deals a Blow to Key Tourism Sector," *The Wall Street Journal*. May 22, 2014. Web. http://blogs.wsj.com/economics/2014/05/22/thailands-political-unrest-deals-a-blow-to-key-tourism-sector/. Accessed June 26, 2014.

57 Miguel A. Corzo (ed.). *The Future of Asia's Past*. (Los Angeles: The Getty Conservation Institute), iv.

Further reading

Aasen, Clarence. 1998. *Architecture of Siam: A Cultural History Interpretation*. New York: Oxford University Press.

Aranyanark, Chiraporn. 1984. "Conservation of Sukhothai Monuments," *SPAFA Digest* 5(1): 31–32.

——. 1999. "Major Problems in Conservation of Monuments in Thailand," in *Conservation of Monuments in Thailand [I]*, Fine Arts Department and National Research Institute of Cultural Properties, 29–42.

Arnold, Michael S. 2014. "Thailand's Political Unrest Deals a Blow to Key Tourism Sector," *The Wall Street Journal*. May 22, 2014. Web. http://blogs.wsj.com/economics/2014/05/22/thailands-political-unrest-deals-a-blow-to-key-tourism-sector/. Accessed June 26, 2014.

Askew, Marc. 1994. "Bangkok: Transformation of the Thai City," in Marc Askew and William S. Logan (eds.), *Cultural Identity and Urban Change in Southeast Asia – Interpretive Essays*. (Geelong: Deakin University Press), 105–106.

——. 2002. *Bangkok: Place, Practice and Representation*. London: Routledge.

Baker, Chris (ed.). 2013. *Protecting Siam's Heritage*. Chiang Mai: Silkworm Books.

Bangkok Post. "Thailand Hurries to List Cultural Icons." March 12, 2013. Web. www.bangkokpost.com/lite/topstories/340110/thailand-hurries-to-bag-cultural-icons. Accessed June 26, 2014.

Byrne, Denis. 2004. "Chartering Heritage in Asia's Postmodern World," *Getty Conservation Institute Newsletter* 19(2) (Summer). Web. www.getty.edu/conservation/publications_resources/newsletters/19_2/news_in_cons1.html. Accessed June 26, 2014.

Chapman, William A. 2013. *A Heritage of Ruins: The Ancient Sites of Southeast Asia and their Conservation*. Honolulu: University of Hawai'i Press.

Chatkul Na Ayudhaya, Wongchat. 1999. "Brick Architecture: A Case Study of Restoration of the Chedi of Wat Parsat," in Fine Arts Department and National Research Institute of Cultural Properties, *Conservation of Monuments in Thailand (1)*: 118–123.

Chotikavanit, Somkid. 1995. "The Conservation of Ayutthaya Historical City." Paper presented to the international conference *The Future of Asia's Past: Preservation of the Architectural Heritage of Asia*, Chiang Mai, January 11–14, 1995. Summarized in Corzo, *Future of Asia's Past*, 30–31.

Chutintaranond, Sunait. 1996. *Ayutthaya: The Portraits of the Living Legends*. Bangkok: Plan Motif Publishers.

Corzo, Miguel Angel (ed.). 1995. *The Future of Asia's Past: Preservation of the Architectural Heritage of Asia: Summary of an International Conference Held in Chiang Mai, Thailand, January 11–14, 1995*. Los Angeles: The Getty Conservation Institute.

Diskul, M.C. Subhadradis. 1995. "Architectural Preservation Policy in Thailand." Paper presented to the international conference *The Future of Asia's Past: Preservation of the Architectural Heritage of Asia*, Chiang Mai, January 11–14, 1995. Summarized in Corzo, *Future of Asia's Past*, 6–9.

Engelhardt, Richard, Montira Horayangura Unakul and Julia Davies. 2013. "Lessons from the UNESCO Asia-Pacific Awards for Cultural Heritage Conservation: International Best Practices in Thailand," in Chris Baker (ed.), *Protecting Siam's Heritage*. Chiang Mai: Silkworm Books, 335–350.

Fine Arts Department.1968. *Palaces and Ancient Temples in Ayutthaya*. Bangkok: Fine Arts Department.
———. 1988. *Sukhothai Historical Park*. Bangkok: Fine Arts Department.
Fine Arts Department and Ministry of Education, Government of Thailand. 1982. *Sukhothai: Historical Park Development Proiect: Master Plan*. Bangkok: Fine Arts Department.
Harrison, Rachel V. and Peter A. Jackson. 2010. *The Ambiguous Allure of the West: Traces of Colonialism in Thailand*. Hong Kong: Hong Kong University Press.
Higham, Charles and Rachanie Thosarat. 1998. *Prehistoric Thailand: From Early Settlement to Sukhothai*. Bangkok: River Books.
ICOMOS Thailand. 2009. Proceedings of ICOMOS Thailand International Conference, *Conservation and Management of Sacred Places*, Bangkok, February 7–9. Bangkok: ICOMOS.
———. 2011. Proceedings of ICOMOS Thailand International Conference 2011, *Asian Urban Heritage*, Phuket, October 15–17. Bangkok: ICOMOS.
Jumsai, Sumet. 2013. "A Record of Historical Conservation, 1964–2012," in Chris Baker (ed.), *Protecting Siam's Heritage*. Chiang Mai: Silkworm Books, 41–54.
Kammeier, H. Detlaf. 2013. "Heritage Conservation in Asia: Shifts and Developments, 1972–2012," in Chris Baker (ed.), *Protecting Siam's Heritage*. Chiang Mai: Silkworm Books, 281–294.
Kasetsiri, Charnvit. 1976. *The Rise of Ayudhya: A History of Siam in the Fourteenth and Fifteenth Centuries*. Kuala Lumpur: Oxford University Press.
Krairiksh, Piriya. 2013. "A Brief History of Heritage Protection in Thailand", in Chris Baker (ed.), *Protecting Siam's Heritage*. Chiang Mai: Silkworm Books, 15–40.
Leksukhum, Santi. 2008. *Ruins and Reconstructed World Heritage Sukhothai, Si Satchanalai and Kamphaeng Phet*. Translated by Jittipol Sutinsak. Bangkok: Thaweewat Press.
Mundy, Keith. 1992. *Thailand*. Singapore: MPH Publications.
Peleggi, Maurizio. 2002. "The Politics of Ruins and the Business of Nostalgia," in *Studies in Contemporary Thailand* 10. Bangkok: White Lotus Press.
Prakitnonthakan, Chatri. 2012. "Rattanakosin Charter: The Thai Cultural Charter for Conservation," *Journal of the Siam Society* 100: 123–148.
———. 2013. "The Thai Cultural Charter for Conservation," in Chris Baker (ed.), *Protecting Siam's Heritage*. Chiang Mai: Silkworm Books, 123–148.
Rojpojchanarat, Vira. 1987. "The Conservation of Monuments in Thailand," in SPAFA, *Final Report: Workshop on Community-Based Conservation and Maintenance of Historic Buildings/Living Monuments, Bangkok, Thailand, August 23–30, 1987*. Bangkok: SPAFA, 39–49.
SarDesai, D.R. 1981. *Southeast Asia: Past & Present*. Chiang Mai: Silkworm Books.
SEAMEO SPAFA Regional Centre for Archaeology and Fine Arts. 2011. *Houses That Speak to Us. Community-Based Architectural Heritage Preservation in Phrae, Thailand*. Bangkok: SEAMEO SPAFA.
Sekler, Eduard F. 1985. *Sukhothai Historical Park: Development of an Inventory: Thailand*. Technical report. Paris: UNESCO.
Siribhadra, Smitthi, Elizabeth Moore and Michael Freeman. 2001. *Palaces of the Gods: Khmer Art and Architecture in Thailand*. Bangkok: River Books.
Skilling, Peter. "For Merit and Nirvana: The Production of Art in the Bangkok Period," *Art Asiatiques* 62 (2007): 76–94.
Stent, James. 2013. "Siam's Threatened Cultural Heritage," in Chris Baker (ed), *Protecting Siam's Heritage*. Chiang Mai: Silkworm Books, 1–14.
Suksri, Naengnoi. 1999. *The Grand Palace Bangkok*. London: Thames & Hudson.
Taitakoo, Doosadee. 1994. "The Market Study of Sukhothai Historical Park," in Sadao Watanabe and Yukio Nishimura (eds.), *Regional Planning for Historic Site Conservation in Northern Thailand*. Bangkok: UNESCO, 117–144.
Tantinipankul, Worrasit. 2012. "Thailand's Neglected Urban Heritage: Challenges for Preserving the Cultural Landscape of Provincial Towns of Thailand." Paper delivered at the Association of Critical Heritage Studies Conference, Gothenburg, Sweden, June 5–8. Web. http://criticalheritagestudies.org.preview.binero.se/sites/default/files/1367079_p191-tantinipankul-thailand-s-neglected-urban-heritage.pdf. Accessed July 4, 2014.
UNESCO. 1982. *Sukhothai Historical Park Development Project Master Plan*. Paris: UNESCO.
UNESCO Bangkok. 2012. "Thailand to Ratify the UNESCO Convention for the Safeguarding of the Intangible Cultural Heritage." February 24, 2012. Web. www.unescobkk.org/en/news/article/thailand-to-ratify-the-unesco-convention-for-the-safeguarding-of-the-intangible-cultural-heritage/. Accessed June 26, 2014.
Van Beek, Steve. 1984. *Sukhothai and Ancient Thai Civilization: a Lesson in Harmony*. Paris: UNESCO.
———. 1999. *Bangkok Then and Now*. Nonthaburi: AB Publications.
Van Vliet, Jeremias. 1910. "Description of the Kingdom of Siam" *Journal of the Siam Society* 7: 1–108.
World Monuments Fund/US ICOMOS. 1992. "Thailand: A Heritage of Moveable Buddhist Kingdoms," in *Trails to Tropical Treasures: A Tour of ASEAN's Cultural Heritage*. New York: World Monuments Fund.
Wyatt, David K. 1984. *Thailand: a Short History*. New Haven, CT: Yale University Press.

Secondary entrance portal, Temple of Literature, Hanoi, Vietnam.

10

VIETNAM

One of the oldest cultures and nations in Southeast Asia, Vietnam traces its origins to the Bronze Age Dong Son period (500 BCE–200 CE).[1] Vietnam's rich and varied cultural heritage is largely due to its location as the extensive edge of mainland Southeast Asia, which exposed its inhabitants to South China Sea trade routes. Culturally, Vietnam has been significantly influenced for over two millennia by the imperial dynasties of China to its north, and to a lesser extent by the kingdoms of Cambodia and Thailand to its west, and by other Pacific Asian cultures, notably Indonesia and Malaysia.

The native Champa ruled the area that is now central Vietnam from the fifth to the thirteenth centuries CE, with intermittent foreign rule by the Angkor-based Khmer between the ninth and fourteenth centuries. Earlier, though, for nearly one thousand years until the tenth century CE, northern Vietnam was dominated by the Han Chinese, whose presence left behind strong cultural and architectural legacies that continued to influence portions of the country into the nineteenth century.

The Dai Viet (Great Vietnam) period from 1054 to 1400 CE is the basis for Vietnam's modern society that includes the Kinh, Tay, Tai, Hoa, Muong and other ethnic minorities.[2] A more local ruling presence was realized in the Nguyen emperors who ruled from their capital at Hue in the eighteenth and nineteenth centuries. Key influences on Vietnam during the modern period included growing French involvement since the seventeenth century that culminated in its control under French colonial rule in 1887.[3] Along with the Kingdom of Cambodia, this formed the original French Protectorate of Indochina. The federation was expanded by the addition of Laos after the Franco-Siamese War in 1893. French colonization ended in the first Indochina War (1946–1954) and that was followed by military involvement of the United States from 1954 until 1975, known as the Second Indochina War, the Resistance War Against America, or simply the American War.

The cultural traditions and present state of development of Vietnam's complex history are well reflected in the country's architecture and urban planning. From the country's capital in Hanoi to the 'south capital' of Ho Chi Minh City, and in its sizable other towns such as Da Nang and Hue are found Chinese- and French-influenced street plans, citadels, palaces and lesser domestic buildings; Hindu, Buddhist and Confucian temples and shrines; and a range of commercial building types. Over a century of French colonial influence is also reflected in what remains of distinct Western colonial architectural styles ranging from French provincial styles to early twentieth century *architecture moderne*, all adapted to tropical conditions. Adaptations such as ample fenestration, generous balconies, roof overhangs and *portes-cochère*, and well-ventilated rooms and courtyards served their inhabitants well as comfortable living environments. During this period Hanoi was a center of historical research and architectural conservation activity from the late nineteenth century, as home to the École française d'Extrême-Orient (EFEO). From its headquarters, the EFEO conducted scholarly research and assisted in architectural restoration and conservation efforts at some of Vietnam's most important sites, and several beyond its borders.[4]

Modern foreign intervention and heritage protection interests

Vietnam's French colonial era was characterized by moderate to harsh exploitation with its colonizers viewing their task as one of civilizing and modernizing the nation while establishing a productive East Asian trade source. Similar aims were apparent in adjacent Cambodia and Laos, countries that also were part of French Indochina. European colonization of the period customarily entailed inventories of resources of all kinds, the establishment of infrastructure including transportation routes, ports, and other assets supportive of commerce. Great expenditures were made to establish administrative seats, defense systems, and commercial, religious and educational institutions, and to provide lifestyle amenities for the legations and sizable expatriate community who led colonial operations.

When Hanoi was selected to be Indochina's administrative seat, plans and investments were made in Vietnam's development according modern planning precepts that included major re-planning and building interventions in the country's key cities and towns. Due to their size and proximities to the Red and Mekong rivers respectively, Hanoi in north central Vietnam and the port city of Saigon in the south received special attention as regional seats of administration. Thus the French colonial architectural legacies in the historic centers of these cities are readily noticeable due to their urban infrastructure, especially in street plans and surviving historic architecture. Ports, harbors, road systems and the Saigon–Hanoi railway were part of the early industrialization and modernization process. Less tangible legacies of the French colonial eras include vestiges of French-based legislation, educational systems and government organization.

From the late nineteenth century until the advent of World War II, Vietnam served as a hub of Asian cultural heritage research and conservation activity due to the presence of the École française d'Extrême-Orient (EFEO) that was established in Hanoi in 1898. Under the leadership of the noted French archaeologist Henri Parmentier, the EFEO launched extensive studies of the ancient Cham capital of Mỹ Sơn in central Vietnam beginning that same year, followed by work commencing in 1901 at Angkor, seat of the Khmer Empire, in north-central Cambodia. Both projects continued for the next four decades, greatly enhancing the Western world's knowledge of the histories, languages and cultural expressions, including art and architecture, of these countries. Documentation and conservation were aspects of such research with some of its methodologies such as inventories, epigraphic studies and a few conservation methods, namely anastylosis, that are still in use today.

Parmentier himself worked extensively at Mỹ Sơn, publishing some of the earliest reports on its buildings and archaeological remains, as well as at Bang An, to the south and Po Nagar in Nha Trang.[5] Although documentation and analysis of the sites continued for years, the focus remained primarily on classifying and protecting Mỹ Sơn's extraordinary Cham sculpture, rather than on its buildings.[6] Parmentier established an impressive museum in Da Nang in 1915 in order to display Cham artifacts, and the office continued to publish research on the ancient cultures of Vietnam until the outbreak of World War II, when conservation work across the region ceased.[7] It followed the establishment in 1910 of the National Museum of Vietnamese History in Hanoi (formerly the Musée Albert Finot) that was later modified to serve as EFEO headquarters.

In 1945 following the Japanese overthrow of the Vichy French government, Ho Chi Minh, the founder of the Indochina Communist Party, led an armed insurrection first against the Japanese occupiers and, when the French returned later that year, against the long-time colonial power. Following a prolonged conflict known as the First Indochina War, the French concluded their colonial era in Vietnam in 1954 following their defeat at the Battle of Dien Bien Phu in 1954 and the defeat of the French Union in 1954. The adoption of the Geneva Accords of 1954 led to the partition of the country, with Ho Chi Minh's Communist-ruled Democratic Republic of Vietnam in control of the north and the Republic of Vietnam in the south. In 1957, EFEO withdrew its resources and the researchers who had returned to Hanoi following the Allied victory in World War II.

Beginning in the early 1950s a three decade-long period of conflict began that exacted a heavy toll on the Vietnamese people and their cultural heritage. Concerned with the spread of communism in the region, the United States began covert support of the French through its strategy of containment during the Cold War. This led to wide-scale war in 1965 and after much destruction,

FIGURE 10.1 The Museum of Cham Sculpture in Da Nang built in 1915 is a landmark in Vietnam's efforts at cultural heritage protection and interpretation. The design of the enveloping entrance wings of the museum features monumental Cham sculpture in partially enclosed galleries with views to garden areas beyond. The smaller and more fragile artifacts are featured in galleries within in the main block of the museum with support spaces to the rear of the facility.

disruption and loss of life in Vietnam and neighboring areas of Cambodia and Laos the Americans and the South Vietnamese army were defeated by the Viet Cong (southern communist troops) at the storming of the Presidential Palace in Saigon on April 30, 1975. North and South Vietnam were reunified the following year. On July 2, 1976 the National Assembly of the Unified Vietnam re-named the country The Socialist Republic of Vietnam.

A Cambodian Khmer Rouge incursion in Tay Ninh Province in November, 1977 slowed hopes of a new start and led to Vietnam being in a near-constant state of conflict on that front for another eleven years. Another costly border clash with the Chinese broke out on the China–Vietnam border in 1979. Its resolution later that year marked the end of over a century of struggle for peace and independence and the onset of Vietnam's long and impressive recovery.

During the early post-war years Vietnam's government cautiously embraced an open-door policy that allowed for foreign assistance to help with economic development and the management of cultural resources. From the 1980s onward French, Chinese and American interests returned to Vietnam, slowly re-establishing cooperative bilateral relationships. Noting Thailand's remarkable success in promoting heritage tourism since the 1980s, Vietnam has increasingly worked closely with UNESCO, Bangkok's Southeast Asian Regional Centre for Archaeology and Fine Arts (SEAMEO SPAFA) and other overseas organizations to conserve four principal heritage resources: the former capital city of Hue, the former Cham religious center of Mỹ Són, the historic harbor town of Hội An, and the historic center of Hanoi. The sites of the Ho Citadel and Tràng An are also priorities by virtue of the World Heritage listing. Concurrently, as peace and collaboration supplanted war and isolation, international partnerships, professional capacity building, and conservation policy-making efforts increased, especially for projects that support the country's tourism economy. All of these projects were internationally assisted conservation ventures, with UNESCO coordinating international technical and financial assistance at Hue, and the Polish Ateliers for Conservation of Cultural Properties (PKZ) organization working at Mỹ Són during its first period of restoration.

From the early 1990s technical and financial support provided by the Japan International Cooperation Agency (JICA) at Hue, Hội An, Mỹ Sơn, Hanoi and Ho Chi Minh City, and technical assistance, such as that provided by the Deakin University in Australia with urban conservation planning in Hanoi occurred with positive results. Other nations including France, Canada and Austria helped in diverse ways to address conservation challenges in Hanoi. The French Ministry of Foreign Affairs and architects and planners from the City of Toulouse began assistance to Old Hanoi in 1996, and the US-based World Monuments Fund assisted in conservation at the Temple of Literature in Hanoi in 1995, and later supported conservation at the royal tombs of Minh Mang and Ta Tung Tu outside Hue.

Today, Vietnam is one of Southeast Asia's economic leaders. The protection and display of the nation's cultural heritage is a major part of the Ministry of Culture, Sports and Tourism's mandate. Cultural heritage protection has a prominent position in Vietnam's political agenda as evidenced in the words of leader Le Kha Phieu, General Secretary of the Communist Party (1997–2001): "Historic tradition, culture and revolution are sources of energy for the population. One should not forget national history at the risk of forgetting oneself."[8]

The after-effects of nineteenth and twentieth century colonial rule combined with years of war resulted in sizable losses of both population and property in Vietnam, including historically significant buildings and other cultural heritage. After the American War the country's leadership was under considerable pressure to rebuild its infrastructure, institutions and public amenities, a need that could finally be addressed during peaceful conditions and after the end of the US-led economic embargo in 1994. During this process a flood of international influences poured in, bringing with them new styles of architecture and large development plans that launched a new period of urban growth and modernization. As a country that had changed little since World War II, Vietnam's leadership approached the task of modernization in a logical and methodical way. Naturally, at times this goal came up against interests in preserving what it could of the country's cultural patrimony, including its architectural heritage of all periods and kinds, and so the task would understandably prove difficult.

In 1957, Ho Chi Minh's government enacted the Decree on the Management, Classification and Methods to Organize the Protection and Restoration of the Historical and Cultural Monuments. This law built upon earlier French legislation he had authorized in the north of the country in 1945 and set the foundation for national conservation efforts later in the century. These were able to begin following the end of the American War in 1973 and the country's reunification in 1975. In 1984, Vietnam's newly formed national government ratified the Ordinance on the Protection of Historical Cultural Relics and Scenic Sites, and signed the World Heritage Convention three years later.[9]

In 2001 Vietnam introduced new comprehensive national legislation in its Law on Cultural Heritage (No. 28/2001/QH10 of June 29, 2001), which recognizes and affords protection to recognized tangible and intangible heritage including archaeological sites and artifacts, famous landscapes and beauty locations, architectural heritage of all kinds, cultural historical collections and even accurate duplicates of precious historic objects or parts thereof.[10] Its seventy-four articles detail its coverage and procedures and today serve as a model of modern national heritage legislation in Asia.

One notable recent international protocol for heritage protection is associated with Vietnam: the UNESCO Convention on the Protection of Underwater Cultural Heritage (2001). This legislation resulted from the discovery off the coast of Hội An of a late fifteenth century shipwreck laden with some 250,000 mostly ceramic artifacts, and is aimed at protecting innumerable other historic shipwrecks.[11]

At present the Ministry of Culture, Sports and Tourism is Vietnam's primary government ministry for heritage management.[12] The lead government agencies involved in conserving the country's important and complex architectural heritage are the Institute on the Conservation of Monuments and the Department of Cultural Heritage, both of which report to the Ministry of Culture, Sports and Tourism.[13] These organizations operate within a framework of national departments, institutes and national centers, along with local offices located at major heritage sites such as Hội An and Hue. The system of national centers and institutes focuses on topics such as archaeology, Southeast Asian studies, social sciences and the humanities.[14] Architectural conservation activity falls under the Department of Preservation and Museology, which also maintains the national inventory of historic sites and regulates archaeological work.

FIGURE 10.2 The Buddhist One Pillar Pagoda in Hanoi (ca. 1049 CE) and its adjacent communal house are examples of long-standing institutions preserved by perpetual care and use. The temple, destroyed before the withdrawal of the French Union forces in 1954, has been completely reconstructed. Raised on a single pillar of stone the legend-laden building was designed to resemble a lotus blossom. A replica of it was built in the Thú Dúrc district of Saigon in the early 1960s.

Repair, restoration and preservation of individual works of architecture in Vietnam have a long history and reflect many of the same approaches to building protection as is found in both China and Japan. Concern for protecting royal property and civic structures dates back to at least the 1500s when ruling dynasties promulgated laws concerning the protection of ramparts, religious buildings and monuments erected by the royal families.[15] Despite the extensive rebuilding necessitated by war damage and urban redevelopment in cities such as Hanoi, Da Nang and Ho Chi Minh City, numerous monumental structures such as walls and gates or significant heritage buildings such as temples and pagodas, communal houses, and patriotic monuments have been preserved to high conservation standards. The historically rich 1,000-year-old capital city of Hanoi was practically undamaged by the American War and has played a lead role in valuing and planning for the conservation of its urban cultural landscape. Such broad thinking in cultural heritage management, coupled with strict and strictly controlled laws for heritage protection and sound present capacity among architects and conservators to implement work has resulted in Vietnam having not only the vision but also the capacity to conserve its built heritage in impressive ways.

FIGURE 10.3 Ho Chi Minh's summer residence, built only a half century ago, is a simple two-storey wood structure erected on stilts in the botanical garden behind the Presidential (former Governor's) Palace in Hanoi. Scrupulously preserved and presented as a furnished house museum and "patriotic monument," it is a popular destination for those wishing to observe the home and workspace of Vietnam's most important twentieth century political figure.

Conserving architectural ensembles: Hue, Mỹ Són, Hanoi and Hội An

Vietnam was one of the first Asian countries to recognize the value of conserving cultural landscapes, irrespective of whether they were large archaeological sites, expansive palatial settings, most or all of a historical town, or urban cultural landscapes ranging in size from a few city blocks to large sectors of a city. This type of heritage protection is more complicated than the conservation of an individual site due to the increased physical scale and the inclusion of infrastructure and landscape features that also must be maintained. Typically conservation covering whole districts or urban cultural landscapes involves more stakeholders and participants, and thus more variables, which demands larger and more methodical systems of management.

One of several prominent urban cultural landscape conservation projects initiated in the 1990s has been the reconstruction, restoration and conservation of the royal capital in Hue, the seat of the Nguyen dynasty, which dates from the nineteenth and early twentieth centuries. Since 1994, over one hundred individual structures have been fully or partially reconstructed within the site's boundaries.[16] Frequently, work done by the Hue Monuments Conservation Centre's staff of over 700 persons is executed in collaboration with international teams, projects that include conducting research, traditional crafts training and promotion of performing arts. The Centre receives funding from a combination of admission fees to monuments in Hue and direct funding from the national government and various international parties.[17]

FIGURE 10.4a, b and c The Ngo Mon (Moon Gate), principle entranceway to the former Imperial Palace of Hue, before (a) and after (b) restoration of damages sustained in 1968 during the twenty-six-day Battle for Hue. The restoration was completed in 1992 and was funded primarily by the Japanese Funds in Trust for Preserving World Heritage. The An Dinh Palace (c) was restored in two phases beginning in 2008 in a cooperative venture between the Hue Monuments Conservation Centre and the German Conservation, Restoration and Education Project (GCREP).

The UNESCO effort at Hue was launched in 1981, and aimed to restore significant structures and building complexes in the former imperial city while also addressing issues related to environmental degradation. It also focused on rekindling traditional crafts industries, which had been undermined by decades of conflict. Although the Imperial Palace complex had lost many buildings during military struggles, numerous structures have since been restored, including the early nineteenth century Ngo Mon (Moon Gate) through funds provided by the UNESCO Japanese Trust for Preserving World Heritage in 1992.[18] The prominent An Dinh Palace was restored in two phases beginning in 2008 in a cooperative venture between the Hue Monuments Conservation Centre and the German Conservation, Restoration and Education Project (GCREP), which used mortar compositions and painting methods based on traditional building techniques.

Conservation activity at sites associated with Hue extends beyond its World Heritage Site boundaries to the royal tomb complexes of the Nguyen kings, which are situated outside of the royal city and comprise their own distinctive architectural assemblies. The first Nguyen ruler, Gia Long, established Hue as his capital in 1802, and the city thrived under his successors until king Bảo Đại abdicated in 1945. The carefully planned fortified complex of palaces, temples and support buildings was added to the World Heritage List in 1993, and has since then been subject to ongoing restoration and conservation work under the auspices of the Hue Monuments Conservation Centre, a branch of the Ministry of Culture, Sports and Tourism's National Cultural Heritage Department.

A joint project between the World Monuments Fund and the Hue Monuments Conservation Centre has contributed to the revival of the Minh Mang Tomb, a landscaped complex containing forty structures that were built between 1840 and 1843 as the resting place of the second Nguyen king. It is situated on the west bank of the Perfume River 12 km south of Hue City. Seeking to remedy decades of neglect and damage suffered after its abandonment in 1945 and subsequent war damage, the project included structural stabilization, moisture proofing and conservation of decorative finishes at several of the deteriorated buildings in phases of work that began in 1997 and continued through 2012. The newly conserved tomb complex, a sophisticated cultural landscape inclusive of walks, bridges, water

FIGURE 10.5a, b and c Restoration of the east entrance shrine of the Tomb of Minh Mang on the west bank of the Perfume River south of Hue (a) involved conservation of painted finishes in 2004 (b, c), a project of the Hue Monuments Conservation Centre partially funded by the World Monuments Fund.

features and buildings, has regained a significant role in the local and tourist realms, attracting nearly 500,000 mostly Vietnamese visitors annually.[19]

At Mỹ Són, religious center of the ancient Cham kingdom, the Polish State Laboratory for the Conservation of Historic Monuments (Pracownie Konserwacji Zabytków, or PKZ), led by architect Kazimierz Kwiatkowski, worked between 1981 and 1991 to addressed damage sustained during the American War. It also focused on general stabilization and conservation of the long-neglected monuments, as well as training local technicians on archaeological and documentation techniques.[20] Later work was carried out at other Cham sites throughout Vietnam by many of these same workers, who often employed anastylosis techniques they had used at Mỹ Són to repair and reconstruct masonry components of collapsed towers or brick façades.[21]

During the 1990s, as many of these projects were still ongoing, Vietnam was granted its first three cultural World Heritage designations: Hue, listed in 1993, along with Mỹ Són and Hội An, which were both listed in 1999. At Mỹ Són, UNESCO arranged a three-way project team consisting of the Italian government, the Italian Lerici Foundation (based at Milan's Polytechnic University) and Vietnamese authorities, to establish a master plan and perform extensive restorations at the site beginning in 1999. As part of the program, the Lerici Foundation staff has conducted survey and documentation phases at the site, concentrating on the impacts of flooding and bomb damage, and the status of the 1980s Polish-led interventions.

The Italian–Vietnamese Mỹ Són conservation program continued for over a decade, and was completed in 2013. Among its many accomplishments were digital Geographic Information Survey (GIS) mapping of the area, improvements of site access and facilities for visitors, and the stabilization and partial restoration of multiple monuments in the early twelfth century "Group G" complex, a *quincunx* of shrines (five structures in a square, with one at each corner and the center) and their associated enclosure wall. The long-range achievements generated by the project include the development of standardized guidelines for restoring and conserving Cham sites in Vietnam and elsewhere in the region and the development of specialized, compatible masonry and mortar restoration techniques that emulate original construction techniques. Additionally, the joint program trained twenty site management specialists and more than fifty field technicians, creating a cadre of locally based craftspeople and their managers who can employ the Mỹ Són conservation project methodology at other Cham sites.[22]

FIGURE 10.6 The monumental remains of Mỹ Són, seat of the Cham kingdom that ruled from the fifth through the thirteenth centuries is located 54 km west of Da Nang in central Vietnam. Under the French École française d'Extrême-Orient (EFEO), conservation work at this site concentrated on sculpture. From 1980 until 1989 an international assistance effort led by the Polish State Laboratory (Ateliers) for Conservation of Cultural Properties (PKZ) stabilized and partially restored Mỹ Són's distinctive brick shrines.

Among the best-publicized heritage conservation efforts in Vietnam has been the protection and restoration of Hanoi's Old Sector, which was once the city's administrative and commercial center. It consists of the Thang Long-Hanoi citadel area, the Area of the 36 Commercial Streets (or Pho Co or market town) and the French Quarter. The French Quarter has two parts. The first, south of the market town and including Hoan Kiem Lake, has a Parisian-style layout of broad tree-lined streets flanked by villas and public buildings. Its historic residential areas from all eras, and its religious buildings and street patterns that accommodate French-style boulevards and lakes contribute to Hanoi's distinctly special surviving historic urban character. The other is to the north of the citadel and has an irregular pattern of both wide and narrow roads. Due to minimal development since Vietnam's independence in 1954 and the country's subsequent focus on its war-related struggles and general recovery through the 1980s, much of this area's traditional Vietnamese and late nineteenth and early twentieth century colonial fabric remained intact. Hanoi's historic center is today the economically vital heart of an ever-expanding national capital.

Situated strategically near the confluence of the Red River, the To Lich River and the Kim Nguu River, Hanoi's predecessor settlements date to the fifth century CE during Chinese rule. Since the Vietnamese takeover from the Chinese during the Ly Dynasty (1009–1225 CE) the settlement's protective walls, citadels, palaces and domestic buildings, as well as its location, allowed it to thrive as a regional trading destination. Confirming this were the first Western traders, the Dutch and English, who arrived in the seventeenth century. After the capital was established in Hue in the late eighteenth century the city was declared a provincial city and took the name Bac Thanh (Northern Citadel). In 1831 it was renamed Hanoi, meaning "the city in the bend of the river." In 1848 the Emperor Tu Duc ordered Hanoi's palaces destroyed and their riches removed to Hue, after which time the Hanoi citadel fell into ruin. Nevertheless, the city's center for craft production and trade continued to thrive and expand.

In 1873 the French attacked Hanoi, but it was nine years before they would establish control over the city. Reconstruction of Hanoi, especially of its battle-damaged areas, began in 1882. It was at this time that a distinct colonial European appearance began to emerge, not only in Hanoi but also in other cities of importance to the French. New infrastructure and planning based on Western technologies and urban design precepts were implemented, destroying most, but not all, indigenous Vietnamese buildings in the process. Emerging from the makeover of Hanoi were a new French Concession area, the erection of St. Joseph's Cathedral (a building that replaced the venerated Buddhist Bao Thien pagoda, which dated to the foundation of the city) and the removal of many of the citadel's walls and gate buildings.

In 1894 a second European quarter began that entailed installation of a bridge over the Red River, and rail lines and tramways in the city. Impressive civic buildings were erected including the neoclassical French Governor General's Palace and the Opera House, a modest copy of the Palais Garnier opera house in Paris. In his book *Hanoi: Biography of a City*, Australian heritage planner William Logan credits the creation of the Palace and the modernization of central Hanoi in general to the then-governor general Paul Dourmer's "overwhelming passion to construct a colonial capital that would reflect the glory of France."[23] This period of urbanization was followed by new urban master plans in 1921 and later in 1943 that further rationalized and beautified the principal streets of Hanoi and planned for an expansion at the city's periphery.[24] The main changes planned during the French period were completed by 1945, the year of the revolution led by Ho Chi Minh.

Among the most distinctive and famous of Vietnam's urban developments is the "36 Streets and Guilds" Quarter. Historically this area has also been called the commoner or merchant city, where merchants and craftsmen made and sold their goods on streets organized by some thirty-six different trades or guilds. The large district's mostly meandering street pattern includes approximately seventy streets bordered by the To Lich River to the north, the Red River to the east, and the Lake of the Returned Sword to the south. Dating back to the Ly dynasty this famed merchant area included on-site manufacture of paper, textiles, pottery and trades including dyeing, bronze casting and blacksmithing. Every commercial product was offered there, from clothes, medicines, leather and baskets to boats, armaments and sedan chairs. The hundreds of shophouses that form the architectural context of the 36 Streets Quarter were distinctive as well, usually being long linear structures called "tube houses," originally more than two storeys high (per building code restrictions), organized around light sources and courtyards, which accommodated an artisan's extended family. Building styles in the Old Quarter ranged from simple "classic" wood framed indigenous shophouses to more durable stuccoed masonry buildings that reflect a mix of Asian and European styles, especially in their ornamentation. Shrines, temples, market areas, and a few remaining signs of the guilds of the district are evident today in this extremely popular "eternal soul of the city."

Preserving Hanoi's urban vernacular architectural heritage

Irrespective of the unique elements within the 36 Streets Guild District and other similar shophouse districts in Hanoi, these historic commercial and residential areas have, since the late 1980s, been faced with almost overwhelming pressures to modernize. In such an environment, only the most strictly protected were likely to survive. The problem began in the 1950s when the French departed, creating a loss of planning control, and continued through the next two decades due to social change and densification during the war years. By the 1970s, Hanoi was impoverished due to wartime conditions, and renovations made to support higher occupancies led to inferior construction expansions at front areas of set-back buildings and on rooftops.

Since the return of peaceful conditions land values have increased, and building renovations are occurring with increasing frequency, often incorporating insensitive rehabilitation such as all-new glass and metal "modern" façades. Much of this work was evidently done unofficially, after hours and behind tarps obscuring the work from public view and inspection. The gradual degradation of the authentic variety of historic districts is a problem in Vietnam as it is around the world. Preserving the historic character of historic districts is often beyond the control of its residents, since problems may stem from apathy, ignorance, greed and corruption. Official regulation of rehabilitation work, reasonable guidelines for modifications and new design, and diligent enforcement of historic district preservation guidelines are the best hope for successful preservation results. Otherwise, the authenticity, the variety and the overall historic character of the district that earlier drew interest will be lost.

The implementation of the *đổi mới* economic liberalization policies beginning in 1986 spurred the Hanoi metropolitan area's rapid population growth and development.[25] This sudden boom in population demanded changes to the sector's infrastructure requiring new construction, which in several cases undermined Hanoi's traditional built environment.[26] In the late 1980s, planners in the Vietnamese Ministry of Culture, Sports and Tourism began efforts to protect Hanoi's Old Sector. They were helped in this task in 1990, when UNESCO issued a series of planning and conservation recommendations within a program that emphasized documentation, policy development, public outreach and training of local technicians in conservation skills.[27] Since then, a number of individual buildings have been restored as part of the effort to preserve Hanoi's historic core. Work on several of them was executed through a partnership with the French city of Toulouse, which since 1996 has supported a

a

b

FIGURE 10.7a, b and c Plan of the Old Sector of Hanoi from 1885 showing the Thang Long Citadel to its west (a), Contemporaneous postcard view of Rue Paul Bert in the French concession (b), unrestored colonial buildings within the 36 Streets District (c). While there have been losses, much of the district has been rehabilitated.

program of professional exchanges and a series of pilot projects that demonstrate best practices for sensitively modernizing historic residential areas and buildings.[28] The Toulouse partnership has been expanded, and today includes support from Brussels and the European Commission for a project called "Hanoi 2010: Heritage and Cultural Identity." Between 2003 and 2006, Hanoi 2010 strengthened enforcement of heritage regulations in the Old Sector, while also building capacity for planning and conservation management through training and delivery in GIS systems (computer generated geo-referenced information) to local planners.[29]

Other notable conservation projects in post-*đổi mới* Hanoi have included the revival of the Hotel Metropole, which opened in 1901 and is located in the center of the business district. In 1987, the hotel was among the first buildings to undergo major renovations in anticipation of the country's developing tourism economy. Upgrades increased its capacity from 109 rooms to 390 rooms, and improvements were made in the surrounding neighborhood's electricity network, water supply and telephone system.[30] In 1994 the American Express Corporation through the World Monuments Fund underwrote the rehabilitation of shelters that protected the commemorative stele at the Temple of Literature, a Temple of Confucius, at Vietnam's national university, the Imperial Academy. A post-colonial rehabilitation and museum project of a different kind occurred between 1995 and 1997 with the rehabilitation of the French-built Maison Centrale, which was built in 1899. Also known as Hỏa Lò Prison, the building housed numerous political prisoners during the Vietnamese campaign for independence. The prison now serves as a museum honoring the independence movement and the lives of those who were jailed in its service, as well as presenting to visitors information about the country's colonial-era justice system and the building's role during the American War.[31] Like Robben Island in South Africa and the Tuol Sleng Genocide Museum in Phnom Penh, the Hỏa Lò Prison serves as a site of "difficult" or "painful" heritage, leveraging its architecture, authenticity and associations to sustain the memories of injustice that are invariably part of history.[32]

Painful cultural heritage, by William Logan

The inscription of Gorée Island, a slave trade depot off the coast of Senegal, on UNESCO's World Heritage List in 1978 and of Auschwitz-Birkenau in 1979 marked a major shift in the way we think about cultural heritage. Instead of listing places of which humanity is proud, we now also seek to protect places we want to remember because of the dreadful lessons they teach us about humanity's capacity for evil. Later in the century, the Hiroshima Peace Park (Genbaku Dome) was inscribed in 1996 and Robben Island, where Nelson Mandela had been imprisoned by South Africa's apartheid regime, in 1999. These places exemplified the resilience sometimes shown by the victims of extreme acts of willful harm and inhumanity – a transcendence that shames the perpetrators but, most importantly, offers the hope of securing a peaceful future.

The principles and practices at the World Heritage level are not developed in isolation from national and local heritage systems. Many ideas filter down to national and local heritage systems, just as some concepts and practices that have developed at a local level are taken up by the global system. This reciprocity can be seen with the notion of regarding significant places of pain and shame as heritage. This began locally, as in Senegal, Japan and South Africa, moved into and was publicized through the global system and then was taken up by other countries and local areas. Of course, most societies have their scars of history and there is no shortage of sites to choose from. A vast range of places, sites and institutions represent the legacy of these painful periods: massacre and genocide sites, places related to prisoners of war, civil and political prisons, and places of "benevolent" internment such as leper colonies and lunatic asylums.

In Asia many such sites are related to colonial oppression, the struggle for independence and civil wars between groups with opposing political ideologies. In some countries the time is not yet ripe to confront highly painful episodes in their past. In Vietnam, for instance, the civil war that raged in the two decades up to 1975 has not yet been met with full reconciliation between the two sides or historical justice for those who suffered on the South Vietnam side (Logan and Witcomb 2013). While the northern soldiers are buried in official war cemeteries and their sacrifice extolled in ceremonies and the media, the cemeteries of dead southern soldiers were destroyed by order of the victorious Hanoi government and memorials to them continue to be forbidden. In other cases, governments choose to completely forget painful and shameful events, such as the 1965 Suharto coup in Indonesia or the successive coups in Thailand.

These places of pain and shame are difficult to manage, not only for the usual reasons of conserving the historic fabric but also because tensions often still exist. The very fact that they are being conserved may even re-ignite past tensions. Very sensitive interpretation of the sites is required. In 2015 Japan nominated for World Heritage listing a serial site nomination of twenty-three places reflecting the country's Meiji industrial revolution. This inflamed the South Koreans because several of the sites had operated using forced Korean labor. Several of the sites already had interpretation panels indicating this, and the conflict at the 2015 World Heritage Committee session in Bonn was only resolved by Japan promising to provide similar interpretation at other sites, notably at Hashima Island. Memorial sites constructed after the event can also prolong tensions. The Nanjing Massacre Memorial honors those Chinese lives lost in 1937 but also serves a Chinese nation-building function and does little to ease Sino-Japanese tensions.

This ability to exacerbate international and inter-community tensions is a long way from UNESCO's constitutional goal of building peace in the minds of men. The matter was taken up in the sustainability policy adopted by the General Assembly of States Parties to the World Heritage Convention in November 2015 (UNESCO 2015). The policy calls on States Parties when implementing the Convention to consider the three dimensions of sustainable development – environmental sustainability, inclusive social development and inclusive economic development – together with the fostering of peace and security. It asks for an inclusive approach to be used in identifying, conserving and managing World Heritage properties that promote consensus and celebrate cultural diversity, as well as the understanding of and respect for heritage belonging to others, particularly neighboring States Parties. It encourages nominations that have potential to generate fruitful dialogue between States Parties and different cultural communities, and expects that cross-culturally sensitive approaches will be applied in the interpretation of World Heritage Sites.

This policy initiative taken at center will now influence practice at the local level, although at different speeds from one country to another. As one might expect, heritage site managers and other practitioners are often torn between following the official line and reflecting community attitudes towards past events. The policy should provide them with a basis for arguing against the protection of places connected with the perpetrators of evil, such as the house of Ta Mok, the "Butcher" in Pol Pot's regime, that is now a museum and becoming a cult worship place in Anlong Veng, Cambodia (Long and

Reeves 2009). The policy may also challenge the recent trend at national and World Heritage levels of nominating places associated with international wars.

References

Logan, William and Keir Reeves (eds.). 2009. *Places of Pain and Shame: Dealing with "Difficult Heritage"*. London: Routledge.

Logan, William and Andrea Witcomb. 2013. "Messages from Long Tan, Vietnam: Memorialization, Reconciliation and Historical Justice," *Critical Asian Studies* 45(2): 255–278.

Long, Colin and Keir Reeves. 2009. "'Dig a Hole and Bury the Past in It': Reconciliation and the Heritage of Genocide in Cambodia," in William Logan and Keir Reeves (eds.), *Places of Pain and Shame: Dealing with "Difficult Heritage"*. London: Routledge, 68–81.

UNESCO. 2015. *Policy for the Integration of a Sustainable Development Perspective*. WHC-15/20.GA/INF.13. Paris, November. Web. http://whc.unesco.org/archive/2015/whc15-20ga-inf13-en.pdf. Accessed November 13, 2015.

FIGURE 10.8 The French colonial Maison Centrale in Hanoi, Vietnam, now restored and re-used as the Hỏa Lò Museum (Source: William Logan).

International technical assistance for heritage conservation has concentrated more in Hanoi than any other site in Vietnam due to the complexity of urban conservation in such a dynamic setting as the capital and the nature of work at the 36 Streets precinct. The roster of nations that have helped in one form or another include Australia, Belgium, Canada, France, Germany, Japan and the United States.[33]

The town of Hội An on the coast of the South China Sea in Quảng Nam Province of Vietnam's South Central Coast region is an exceptionally well-preserved trading port dating from the fifteenth to the nineteenth centuries. Its buildings and street plan reflect a mix of both indigenous and foreign influences that have combined to result in a unique heritage site. In 1999 Hội An was placed on the UNESCO World Heritage List. During the first millennium CE it was the largest harbor in Southeast Asia, controlled by the Cham for its strategic importance in the spice trade. Its location on the estuary of the Bon River made it an important Vietnamese trading port in the sixteenth and seventeenth centuries for Chinese, Japanese, Dutch and Indian traders. Each left traces of their involvement, with one notable remaining building being the "Japanese Bridge," a unique covered structure with a Buddhist temple integrated into one side.

The Historic Urban Landscape (HUL): a paradigm shift, by Ken Taylor

Current urbanization policies often ignore the importance of cultural heritage preservation and promotion and the great potential of creativity in addressing social, environmental and economic urbanization challenges. How does culture weigh in addressing urbanization challenges today?[34]

The later 1980s and early 1990s were particularly fruitful for the conservation discipline in terms of critical debate and understanding of the concept of heritage, in which a comprehensive definition with an operational framework for "Cultural Landscapes" was elaborated. Next to guiding the conservation of physical elements under this new heritage category, it also proved to be of great significance as a driver to re-think other heritage categories and their conservation principles that were established in earlier periods.

One field of major impact has been urban conservation and the associated development of the Historic Urban Landscape (HUL) approach to urban conservation. The HUL idea essentially espouses recognition of the layering of significances and values in historic cities, deposited over time by different communities under different contexts.[35] It is an approach that relates closely to the cultural landscape concept (cities may therefore be categorized as a type of cultural landscape)[36] and contrasts markedly with a focus of urban conservation that has historically been on architectural fabric and planning ensembles with an emphasis all too often on famous buildings or monuments.

The growth of Asian cities is reflective of what is occurring throughout the developing world overall. In a chapter within *Designing Sustainable Cities in a Developing World*, R. Zetter and G.W. Watson note that globalization has dramatically impacted on city design with two particular negative outcomes. One is the accelerating destruction of the patrimony of indigenously designed and developed urban places and spaces, with culturally rooted built environments eroding. The other is that pressures are commodifying the place-identity of historic urban places, detaching them from their local, spatial and temporal continuity, while still representing them as preserved authentic artifacts for global cultural consumption.[37] It is this dilemma that HUL is intended to address while accepting that the notion of drawing a tight boundary around historic urban places and preserving them unchanged is not feasible. A critical factor is addressing acceptable levels of change involving values of local communities as well as catering for other stakeholders such as government agencies and tourism. It is an understanding of the significance of built urban heritage as places where people live their everyday lives, where social values and sense of place are manifest. An example is Hội An in Vietnam where, in spite of changes brought about by tourism for example, there is a sense of social continuity.

The HUL paradigm was first set out at a UNESCO conference in Vienna, May 2005,[38] and was advocated for in the *Vienna Memorandum on World Heritage and Contemporary Architecture – Managing the Historic Urban Landscape*. It followed concern by the World Heritage Committee about the impacts of modern developments on historic urban areas and compatibility with the protection of their heritage values. This was particularly so with its proposition of the Historic Urban Landscape (HUL) notion as a tool to reinterpret the values of urban heritage, and its indication of the need to identify new approaches and new tools for urban conservation.

FIGURE 10.9a and b Views of the harbor side and in-town fish market in Hội An.

The culmination of thinking on new international approaches to urban conservation came in 2011 with the UNESCO *General Conference Recommendation on Historic Urban Landscape [HUL]*.[39] This instrument recognized the layering of significances and values in historic cities deposited over time by different communities under different contexts. Dr. Ron van Oers[40] summarized the thinking on HUL as follows:

> Historic Urban Landscape is a mindset, an understanding of the city, or parts of the city, as an outcome of natural, cultural and socio-economic processes that construct it spatially, temporally, and experientially. It is as much about buildings and spaces, as about rituals and values that people bring into the city. This concept encompasses layers of symbolic significance, intangible heritage, perception of values, and interconnections between the composite elements of the historic urban landscape, as well as local knowledge including building practices and management of natural resources. Its usefulness resides in the notion that it incorporates a capacity for change.

Historic urban communities such as Hội An and numerous others in Asia are therefore representative treasures, not only of living regional landscape culture, but of world culture and deserve to be recognised and celebrated as such. (See also Urban Conservation Initiatives in Chapter 9, Thailand.)

Further reading

Bandarin, F. 2012. "From Paradox to Paradigm? Historic Urban Landscape as an Urban Conservation Approach," in K. Taylor and J.L. Lennon (eds.), *Managing Cultural Landscapes*. Routledge Key Issues in Cultural Heritage Series. London: Routledge, 213–232.

Bracken, G. (ed.). 2012. *Aspects of Urbanization in China: Shanghai, Hong Kong and Guangzhou*. Amsterdam: University of Amsterdam Press, International Institute for Asian Studies.

Greffe, X. 2009. "Urban Cultural Landscapes: An Economic Approach," in *Working Paper No1/2010*, Department of Economics, International Centre for Research on the Economics of Culture, Institutions and Creativity, University of Turin. Web. http://www.cssebla.it/wp-content/uploads/1_WP_Ebla_CSS-2.pdf. Accessed May 18, 2016.

Licciardi, G. and R. Amirtahmasebi, (eds.). 2012. *The Economics of Uniqueness. Investing in Historic City Cores and Cultural Heritage Assets for Sustainable Development*. Washington DC: World Bank.

Taylor, K. 2012. "Landscape and Meaning: Context for a Global Discourse on Cultural Landscape Values," in K. Taylor and J.L. Lennon (eds.) *Managing Cultural Landscapes*. Routledge Key Issues in Cultural Heritage Series. London: Routledge, 21–44.

van Oers, R. and Rogers A. Pereira. 2012. "Historic Cities as Models of Sustainability," *Journal of Cultural Heritage Management and Sustainable Development* 2(1): 1–10.

van Oers, R. and K. Taylor. 2015. "Asian Theoretical and Best-Practice Framework for the Historic Urban Landscape: Heritage for the Future," in K. Taylor, N. Mitchell and A. St Clair (eds.), *Conserving Cultural Landscapes: Challenges and New Directions*, New York: Routledge, Chapter 12.

Interests and efforts in preserving craft traditions and intangible cultural heritage date to the 1980s in Vietnam. Since then, its government has encouraged and supported diverse traditional performing arts and craft traditions, including traditional building arts. Along with the similar early initiatives of China, Korea and Japan, Vietnam's experiences in conserving living and intangible heritage inspired and informed the 2003 UNESCO Convention on Safeguarding of the Intangible Cultural Heritage. In 2003 Vietnam was a signatory of the Convention and has since hosted workshops on the subject while fulfilling a number of its goals. The effort was joined in 2012 by the World Monuments Fund by its placement of the fishing villages in Ha Long Bay (Quàng Ninh Province) on its World Monuments Watch List as an example of living heritage threatened by an influx of tourists and associated onshore development. As a result, extra attention has been given to controlling tourist-related development in the area.

At a workshop to review Vietnam's decade-long membership in the UNESCO convention, Pham Cao Phong, Secretary General of the Vietnam UNESCO National Committee, said:

> Intangible cultural heritage constitutes an important part of Vietnamese culture. Among them, seven have been inscribed by UNESCO, reflecting our rich culture full of national characteristics. It means that Vietnam is actively contributing to the global inventory of heritage, diversifying humanity's spiritual life.[41]

FIGURE 10.10 The dramatic setting of rock formations in the deep blue waters of Ha Long Bay on Vietnam's northeastern sea coast is home to three traditional fishing villages that represent special Vietnamese lifeways dating to the early nineteenth century. Some four hundred households live on boats and floating wooden houses that are inextricably linked to their settings, forming an integrated cultural landscape and living tradition. Listed with government approval on the World Monuments Fund's Watch List in 2012, Ha Long Bay represents an example of Vietnam's commitment to protecting such fragile cultural heritage.

Since the economic and governmental reforms of the 1980s – which included ratifying the World Heritage Convention in 1987 – the Vietnamese government has substantially developed its cultural heritage management system. Significant sites are far better protected than they had been previously, and – perhaps more significantly – are better positioned to participate in the global tourist economy. The progress made during the subsequent decades is nothing short of amazing, given the condition of the country after a long struggle for independence and years of destructive war and embargo. The Vietnamese Communist Party's emphasis on cultural promotion as both an official state activity and an assertion of national pride has reinforced programs and agencies tasked with the care of the country's significant historic buildings and other heritage protection programs.

With eight designated World Heritage Sites,[42] open borders for visitors, a comparatively liberalized economy and a number of high-profile, internationally sponsored conservation projects under way, Vietnam has become a magnet for foreign tourism and is a regional leader in conservation activity.[43] While the difficulties of enforcing existing heritage protection legislation and development pressures in Vietnam's rapidly growing cities continue to threaten conservation goals, progress made during the last three decades indicates that Vietnam is today in a promising era of cultural heritage management.

Notes

1. Peter N. Peregrine and Melvin Ember. *Encyclopedia of Prehistory: Volume 3; East Asia and Oceania.* (New York: Springer, 2001), 170.
2. As of 2015, an approximate breakdown of ethnic groups shows Kinh (Viet) at 86.2 percent, and other groups at about 2 percent each. The ethnic groups of Vietnam's Central Highlands are collectively called Degar, and were referred to in colonial times as Montagnard or "mountain people."
3. French involvement in Vietnam dates to as early as 1620 when Jesuit father Alexandre de Rhodes wrote the first Vietnamese Catechism. The spread of Roman Catholicism in Vietnam increased despite Emperor Minh Mang's issuance of an edict in 1825 prohibiting foreign missionaries: "These missionaries make the people's hearts crooked, thus destroying our beautiful customs. Truly this is a great disaster for our land." Minh Mang, Edict Against Christianity (in Mark W. McLeod, *The Vietnamese Response to French Intervention, 1862–1874.* Westport, CT: Greenwood Publishing Group, 1991, 27). Concomitant trade interests of the French East India Company led to military collaboration with the Nguyen family in the south. This culminated in complex diplomatic and trade relations, with military force occasionally exerted, until 1864 when all French territories in southern Vietnam were declared to be the new colony of Cochinchina. Subsequent conquest of Annam and Tonkin in 1883–1885 expanded French control that was followed by the Sino-French War (1884–1885), which forced Chinese disengagement from Vietnam. The former French possessions of Cochinchina, Annam and Tonkin form modern Vietnam.
4. The Hanoi-based EFEO conducted scholarly research projects at Borobudur in Indonesia, Wat Phou (Laos) and at Angkor in Cambodia. The French colonial administration conducted urban development, modernization and conservation work in the former royal capital of Luang Prabang and the current capital of Vientiane and in Phnom Penh and Siem Reap in Cambodia. Smaller towns like Siem Reap and Battambang in Cambodia and Da Nang in Vietnam were similarly modernized.
5. The Cham believed in a blend of the Hindu, Mahayana Buddhist and Islamic faiths that is expressed in sculpture that adorned its brick and stone temples and shrines.
6. Ky Phuong Tran. *Unique Vestiges of Cham Civilization.* (Hanoi: Gioi Publishers, 2000), 32.
7. Emmanuel Guillon. *Cham Art.* (London: Thames & Hudson, 2001), 11. The Cham Museum in Da Nang featured the monumental stone sculpture of Champa in a covered fresh air setting with its smaller and more fragile artifacts enclosed within internal spaces. The museum's enveloping entrance wings and entrance block are elevated and open on the sides to garden areas. Galleries and museum support spaces to the rear are designed to be enclosed more securely. The typology of French colonial museums in Indochina is a genre in and of itself, with another outstanding example being the National Museum in Phnom Penh that also blends French neoclassical civic architectural planning principles of the time with local traditional design motifs.
8. Le Kha Phieu, extract from an address to the people of Kinh Bac, given during his visit to Dinh Do (Do Temple) in Dinh Bang village in Bac Ninh province, March 15, 1998.
9. Quoc Binh Truong. "Country Brief: Vietnam," in *Culture and Sustainable Development: East Asia and Pacific Working Group Proceedings.* (Washington, DC: The World Bank, 1999), 32.
10. Legislation, The National Assembly, Socialist Republic of Vietnam, No. 28/2001/QH10 of 29 June 2001, Article 4, 1–12.
11. Cu Lao Cham. *Hội An Shipwreck*, April 21, 2014. University of Glasgow. Web. http://traffickingculture.org/encyclopedia/case-stutied/hoi-an-shipwreck. Accessed September 18, 2015.
12. UNESCO. *Situation and Trends in Cultural Policy in Member States of Asia and the Pacific: Socialist Republic of Viet Nam.* World Conference on Cultural Policies, Mexico City, July 26–August 6, 1982. (Paris: UNESCO, 1982), 78–79. Other agencies overseen by the Department of Culture are the Fine Arts Museum, the Department of Fine Arts, the Institute of Research into the History of Art, the Institute of Fine Arts Research, the Viet Nam Film Division, the Documentary Film Company, the Film Slides Studio, the Vietnamese Circus Union, the Vietnamese Dance School and the Ministry of Culture's College for the Cultural Professions.
13. UNESCO, 64.
14. William Chapman. *A Heritage of Ruins: The Ancient Sites of Southeast Asia and their Conservation.* (Honolulu: University of Hawai'i Press, 2013), 118.
15. Ministry of Construction, Research Institute on Architecture. *Preserving Hanoi's Architectural and Landscape Heritage.* (Hanoi: Construction Publishing House, 1999), 49.
16. An excellent book on this is Natsuko Akagawa's *Heritage Conservation and Japan's Cultural Diplomacy: Heritage, National Identity and National Interest* (London: Routledge, 2014). Natsuko uses Hue as her main case study.
17. Hue Monuments Conservation Centre. "About Us." 2014. Web. www.hueworldheritage.org.vn/TTBTDTCDH.aspx?KenhID=148&TieuDeID=76&l=en. Accessed August 7, 2014.

18 UNESCO. "Monuments of Hue City, Vietnam." 2001. Web. www.unesco.org/culture/japan-fit/html_eng/vietnam.shtml. Accessed December 1, 2004.
19 World Monuments Fund. "Minh Mang Tomb." 2011. Web. www.wmf.org/project/minh-mang-tomb. Accessed August 7, 2014.
20 UNESCO Bangkok. "My Son Sanctuary World Heritage Site, Vietnam." 2012. Web. www.unescobkk.org/culture/wh/ap-sites/myson/. Accessed July 17, 2014.
21 Dao Kinh Hoang. "Cultural Monuments Maintenance and Strategy in Vietnam." Unpublished paper delivered at the UNESCO Conference *Conserving the Past: An Asian Perspective of Authenticity in the Consolidation, Restoration and Reconstruction of Historic Monuments and Sites* held in Hội An, Vietnam, February 25–March 3, 2001.
22 UNESCO. *Safeguarding of My Son World Heritage Site – Project Completion Report (2003–2013)*. (Hanoi: UNESCO Office in Vietnam, 2013), 14. Web. http://unesdoc.unesco.org/images/0022/002264/226433e.pdf. Accessed May 18, 2016.
23 William Stewart Logan. *Hanoi: Biography of a City*. (Kensington, Australia: New South Wales University Press, 2000), 86.
24 Hanoi's 1921 master plan was developed by the architect–town planner Ernest Hebrard. The 1943 plan that called for development of the city towards the south was developed by Louis-Gorges Pineau. Source: *Preserving Hanoi's Architectural and Landscape Heritage*, 10.
25 Đổi mới is the name given to the economic reforms initiated in Vietnam in 1986 with the goal of creating a "socialist-oriented market economy."
26 Fergus T. Mclaren. *Building Transformation in Hanoi's French Colonial Quarter: Can the Past Survive?* CSAME Working Paper, Heritage in Asia Series. (Victoria, Australia: Deakin University, 1996), 3.
27 William S. Logan. "Heritage Planning in post-Đổi mới Hanoi: The National and International Contributions," *APA Journal* 61(3) (1995), 328–344.
28 Ha Noi Heritage & Identity: Cooperation between the Cities of Hanoi and Toulouse for the Safeguard of the Old Quarter. "Co-Operation Initiatives." 2011. Web. www.toulouse-hanoi.org/english/co-operation-initiatives/history-of-co-operation/. Accessed August 7, 2014.
29 Hanoi 2010. "The European Project: The European Asia URBS Programme." 2010. Web. www.hanoi2010.org/uk/pagesEditos.asp?IDPAGE=68&sX_Menu_selectedID=m1_94597121. Accessed August 7, 2014.
30 Mclaren, 11.
31 The prison was colloquially known in the United States as the "Hanoi Hilton" due to its role in housing prisoners of war during the American War.
32 William Logan. "Hoa Lo Museum, Hanoi: Changing Attitudes to a Vietnamese Place of Pain and Shame," in William Logan and Keir Reeves (eds.), *Places of Pain and Shame: Dealing with "Difficult Heritage"*. (London: Routledge, 2008), 182.
33 The highest contribution in terms of financial support, as well as technical support, has been from Japan at the Citadel of Hue and the Hội An restoration and conservation projects via its foreign aid for heritage conservation programs.
34 United Nations Conference on Trade & Development (UNCTAD). "Culture Vital for Development Progress, Deputy Secretary-General Tells Meeting." Web. http://unctad.org/es/paginas/newsdetails.aspx?OriginalVersionID=501. Accessed May 17, 2016.
35 F. Bandarain and R. van Oers. *The Historic Urban Landscape. Managing Heritage in an Urban Century*. (Chichester, UK: Wiley Blackwell, 2012).
36 Ken Taylor. "Cities as Cultural Landscapes," in F. Bandarin and R. Van Oers (eds.), *Reconnecting the City* (Chichester, UK: Wiley Blackwell, 2014).
37 R. Zetter and G.W. Watson. "Designing Sustainable Cities," in R. Zetter and G.W. Watson, *Designing Sustainable Cities in the Developing World*. (Aldershot, UK: Ashgate, 2006), 3–18.
38 UNESCO, 2005. International conference on "World Heritage and Contemporary Architecture – Managing the Historic Urban Landscape," UNESCO World Heritage Centre in cooperation with ICOMOS and the City of Vienna at the request of the World Heritage Committee, adopted at its 27th session in 2003.
39 UNESCO 2011.
40 R. Van Oers. "Managing Cities and the Historic Urban Landscape Initiative – an Introduction," in R. Van Oers and S. Haraguchi (eds.), *UNESCO World Heritage Papers 27 Managing Historic Cities*. (Paris: UNESCO World Heritage Centre, 2010), 7–17, 14.
41 Le Fuong. "Vietnam Proactively Protects UNESCO Intangible Heritage," VoV World Service, July 5, 2013. Web. http://vovworld.vn/en-US/Culture/Vietnam-proactively-protects-UNESCO-intangible-cultural-heritage/165019.vov. Accessed September 20, 2015.

42 Vietnam's listed World Heritage Sites include two natural sites and six cultural ones, including the Trang An Landscape Complex (2014), a combined cultural/natural property.
43 Since joining ASEAN in 1995, Vietnam has participated in regional efforts in heritage conservation, and is actively involved in other international organizations such as ICOMOS and ICCROM as well as UNESCO's ever-evolving initiatives.

Further reading

AusHeritage and ASEAN-COCI (eds.). 2001. "Cultural Management Profile, Vietnam," in *ASEAN-Australia Project: Development of an ASEAN Regional Policy and Strategy for Cultural Heritage Management*. Melbourne: Cultural Heritage Center for Asia and the Pacific.

Bandarin, F. 2012. "From Paradox to Paradigm? Historic Urban Landscape as an Urban Conservation Approach," in K. Taylor and J.L. Lennon (eds.), *Managing Cultural Landscapes*. Routledge Key Issues in Cultural Heritage Series. London: Routledge, 213–232.

Baptiste, Pierre. 2009. "The Archaeology of Ancient Champa: The French Excavations," in A. Hardy, M. Cucarzi and P. Zolese (eds.), *Champa and the Archaeology of Mỹ Sơn*. Singapore: NUS Press, 14–25.

Bouillevaux, Charles-Emile. 1858. *Voyage dans l'Indochine, 1848–1856*. In French. Paris: Palme.

Box, Paul. 1996. *Final Report: GIS Training Program for Wat Phu GIS Team, Laos and Vietnam, August 1996*. Bangkok: UNESCO.

Bracken G. (ed.). 2012. *Aspects of Urbanization in China: Shanghai, Hong Kong and Guangzhou*. Amsterdam: University of Amsterdam Press, International Institute for Asian Studies.

Brocheux, Pierre and Daniel Hémery. 2010. *Indochina: An Ambiguous Colonization, 1858–1954*. Berkeley: University of California Press.

Chapman, William. 2013. *A Heritage of Ruins: The Ancient Sites of Southeast Asia and their Conservation*. Honolulu: University of Hawai'i Press.

Cherry, Haydon. 2009. "Digging up the Past: Prehistory and the Weight of the Present in Vietnam," *Journal of Vietnamese Studies* 4(1) (Winter): 84–144.

Cucarzi, Mauro. 2000. *Investigation, Zoning and Management of Mỹ Sơn Monument and Archaeological Site*. Technical report. Milan: Lerici Foundation.

Engelhardt, Richard and P.R. Rogers. 2009. *Hội An Protocols for Best Conservation Practice in Asia: Professional Guidelines for Assuring and Preserving the Authenticity of Heritage Sites in the Context of the Cultures of Asia*. Bangkok: UNESCO Bangkok.

Gatbonton, Mario T. (ed.). 1971. *Preservation of Cultural Heritage: Australia, China, Japan, Korea, Malaysia, New Zealand, Philippines, Thailand, Vietnam*. Seoul: Hollym Corporation.

Glover, I.C. and M. Yamagata. 1995. "The Origins of Cham Civilization: Indigenous, Chinese and Indian Influences in Central Vietnam as Revealed by Excavations at Tra Kieu, Vietnam, 1990 and 1993," in C.T. Yeung and W.I. Li (eds.), *Archaeology in Southeast Asia*. Hong Kong: University Museum of Art and Archaeology, 145–169.

Greffe, X. 2009. "Urban Cultural Landscapes: An Economic Approach," *Working Paper No1/2010*, Department of Economics, International Centre for Research on the Economics of Culture, Institutions and Creativity, University of Turin. Web. www.css-ebla.it/wp-content/uploads/1_WP_Ebla_CSS-2.pdf. Accessed May 18, 2016.

Guillon, Emmanuel. 2001. *Cham Art*. London: Thames & Hudson.

Hanoi 2010. 2010. "The European Project: The European Asia URBS Programme." Web. www.hanoi2010.org/uk/pagesEditos.asp?IDPAGE=68&sX_Menu_selectedID=m1_94597121. Accessed August 7, 2014.

Hardy, Andrew, Mauro Cucarzi and Patrizia Zolese (eds.). 2009. *Champa and the Archaeology of Mỹ Sơn (Vietnam)*. Singapore: NUS Press.

Hoàng-Dạo Kinh. 2001 "Cultural Monuments Maintenance and Restoration in Vietnam: Choosing a Strategy." Unpublished paper presented to the UNESCO conference "Conserving the Past: An Asian Perspective of Authenticity in the Consolidation, Restoration and Reconstruction of Historic Monuments and Sites" held in Hội An, Vietnam, February 25–March 3, 2001.

——. 2009. "Champa: The Vietnam-Poland Conservation," in A. Hardy, M. Cucarzi and P. Zolese (eds.), *Champa and the Archaeology of Mỹ Sơn*. Singapore: NUS Press, 26–32.

Hue Monuments Conservation Centre. 2014. "About Us." Web. www.hueworldheritage.org.vn/TTBTDTCDH.aspx?KenhID=148&TieuDeID=76&l=en. Accessed August 7, 2014.

ICCROM. 2000. *A Global Heritage Training Strategy for Cultural Heritage to Improve Implementation of the World Heritage List. Southeast Asia*. Prepared for the World Heritage Committee, Rome. Web. http://cif.icomos.org/pdf_docs/Documents%20on%20line/ICCROM%20Global%20Training%20Strategy%202000.pdf. Accessed May 18, 2016.

Intarapasan, Budsakayt. 2010. "Cultural Heritage across Borders: Inclusive Tourism and Barrier-Free Design in the Greater Mekong Sub-region." PhD dissertation, Silpakorn University.
Karnow, Stanley. 1983. *Vietnam: A History: The First Complete Account of Vietnam at War*. New York: Viking Press.
Langlois, Walter G. 1966. *Andre Malraux: The Indochina Adventure*. New York: Praeger.
Le Bonheur, Albert. 1998. "The Art of Champa," in M. Girard-Geslan et al., *Art of Southeast Asia*. Translated by J.A. Underwood. New York: Abrams, 251–308.
Licciardi, G. and R. Amirtahmasebi (eds.). 2012. *The Economics of Uniqueness. Investing in Historic City Cores and Cultural Heritage Assets for Sustainable Development*. Washington DC: World Bank.
Logan, William S. 1995. "Heritage Planning in Post đổi mới Hanoi: The National and International Contributions," *APA Journal* 61(3), 328–344.
——. 2000. *Hanoi: Biography of a City*. Sydney: University of New South Wales Press.
——. 2008. "Hỏa Lò Museum, Hanoi: Changing Attitudes to a Vietnamese Place of Pain and Shame," in William Logan and Keir Reeves (eds.), *Places of Pain and Shame: Dealing with "Difficult Heritage"*. London: Routledge, 182.
——. 2014. "Making the Most of Heritage in Hanoi, Vietnam," *Historic Environment* 26(3): 62–71.
Logan, William S. and K. Reeves (eds.). 2009. *Places of Pain and Shame: Dealing with "Difficult Heritage"*. London: Routledge (see, especially, the Introduction, 1–14).
Mclaren, Fergus T. 1996. "Building Transformation in Hanoi's French Colonial Quarter: Can the Past Survive?" CSAME Working Paper, *Heritage in Asia Series*. Victoria, Australia: Deakin University, 3.
Nguyen, Kim-chi. 1999. *Preserving Hanoi's Architectural and Landscape Heritage*. Hanoi: Construction Publishing House.
Pavie, Auguste. 1898–1919. *Mission Pavie Indo-Chine, 1879–1895*. 10 volumes. Paris: Leroux. Translated by Walter E.J. Tips as *Pavie Mission Indochina Papers, 1879–1895*. 6 volumes. Bangkok: White Lotus Press.
Research Institute on Architecture, Ministry of Construction. 1999. *Preserving Hanoi's Architectural and Landscape Heritage*. Hanoi: Construction Publishing House.
Taylor, K. 2012. "Landscape and Meaning: Context for a Global Discourse on Cultural Landscape Values," in K. Taylor and J.L. Lennon (eds.), *Managing Cultural Landscapes*. Routledge Key Issues in Cultural Heritage Series. London: Routledge, 21–44.
Toulouse Hanoi Organization. 2011. Ha Noi Heritage & Identity: Cooperation between the Cities of Hanoi and Toulouse for the Safeguard of the Old Quarter. "Co-Operation Initiatives." Web. the www.toulouse-hanoi.org/english/co-operation-initiatives/history-of-co-operation/. Accessed August 7, 2014.
Tran Ky Phuong. 2001. *Unique Vestiges of Cham Civilization*. Hanoi: Gioi Publishers.
Trán Thi Thúy Diém. 2001. "History of the Museum: From Henri Parmentier to the Museum of Cham Sculpture," in Emmanuel Guillon (ed.), *Cham Art: Treasures from the Da Nang Museum, Vietnam*. Translated by Tom White. Bangkok: River Books, 10–12.
Trúóng Quóc Binh. 1999. "Country Brief: Vietnam." *Culture and Sustainable Development: East Asia and Pacific Working Group Proceedings*. Washington, DC: The World Bank, 32.
——. 2001. "*Current Situation of Activities for Cultural Protection in Vietnam.*" Paper presented to the UNESCO conference "Conserving the Past: An Asian Perspective of Authenticity," held at Hội An, February 25, 2001.
UNESCO. 1982. "Situation and Trends in Cultural Policy in Member States of Asia and the Pacific: Socialist Republic of Viet Nam." Proceedings of the World Conference on Cultural Policies, Mexico City, July 26–August 6, 1982. Paris, UNESCO, 78–79.
——. 2001. "Monuments of Hue City, Vietnam." Web. www.unesco.org/culture/japan-fit/html_eng/vietnam.shtml. Accessed December 1, 2004.
——. 2008. "Cultural Tourism and Heritage Management in the World Heritage Site of the Ancient Town of Hội An, Viet Nam," in Hội An Centre for Monuments Management and Preservation, *Impact: The Effects of Tourism on Culture and the Environment in Asia and the Pacific*. Bangkok: UNESCO.
UNESCO Bangkok. 2012. "Mỹ Són Sanctuary World Heritage Site, Vietnam." Web. www.unescobkk.org/culture/wh/ap-sites/myson/. Accessed July 17, 2014.
UNESCO Hanoi. 2013. "Safeguarding of Mỹ Són World Heritage Site – Project Completion Report (2003–2013)." Hanoi: UNESCO Office in Vietnam. Web. http://unesdoc.unesco.org/images/0022/002264/226433e.pdf. Accessed May 18, 2016.
van Oers, R. and Rogers A. Pereira. 2012. "Historic Cities as Model of Sustainability," *Journal of Cultural Heritage Management and Sustainable Development* 2(1): 1–10.
van Oers, R. and K. Taylor. 2015. "Asian Theoretical and Best-Practice Framework for the Historic Urban Landscape: Heritage for the Future," in K. Taylor, N. St Clair-Harvey, and A. Mitchell (eds.), *Conserving Cultural Landscapes: Challenges and New Directions*. New York: Routledge, Chapter 12.
Vickery, Michael. 2009. "A Short History of Champa," in A. Hardy, M. Cucarzi and P. Zolese (eds.), *Champa and the Archaeology of Mỹ Són*. Singapore: NUS Press, 45–60.
World Monuments Fund. 2011. "Minh Mang Tomb." Web. www.wmf.org/project/minh-mang-tomb. Accessed August 7, 2014.

Scaffolded wooden monastery tower, Mandalay, Myanmar.

CONCLUSION TO PART II

The mainland countries of Southeast Asia offer multiple lessons in the benefits of collaboration in architectural conservation activities, from the offices of Bangkok-based international institutions to the temple complexes of Angkor. The legacy of colonialism and its aftermath still hangs over Mainland Southeast Asia, from the scars of the Vietnam War, to Myanmar's decades of isolation, to Cambodia's ongoing recovery from a despotic regime. In recent decades, however, Mainland Southeast Asia has returned to the fore of the field, regaining the place it held at the beginning of the twentieth century when it was a vibrant area of research, discovery and conservation.

Thailand retains a leadership role, with its successful national Historical Parks system, heritage programs supported by a proud and enduring monarchy, and national institutions like the Fine Arts Department that are approaching a century of experience in conservation practice. The UNESCO Asia-Pacific Office in Bangkok is a nucleus of activity, positively influencing the region and beyond with programs such as Heritage Awards and other regional initiatives that promote best practices, share expertise and raise awareness around critical issues. SEAMEO SPAFA offers another example of a high-functioning regional heritage promotion organization organized around cooperation, a model that would serve other regions, such as South and Central Asia, quite well.

Of the new approaches in conservation practice that have originated in this region, the Hội An Protocols for Best Conservation Practice in Asia (adopted 2005), and the 2001 UNESCO Convention on the Protection of the Underwater Cultural Heritage stand out. Each has sought to address issues particular to the Asian context, and have since offered strategies for practitioners both within Southeast Asia and beyond. The perpetuation of traditional crafts is also a focus here, as elsewhere in Asia, and has found particular success in partnerships with religious communities such as Cultural Survival and Revival in the Buddhist Sangha program, which began as a pilot project in Luang Prabang, Laos in 2000.

Owing to a relatively stable contemporary political environment, along with Thailand's role as a long-standing popular destination, heritage tourism in the region has been a well-established phenomenon since at least the 1980s. With Angkor now one of the world's top tourist destinations, the region functions as a real-time case study in how tourism can both positively and negatively influence heritage resources. While the economic benefits of the industry are clear, less clear are the implications of the practice on a large scale, raising questions not only of authenticity and management, but also heritage values, interpretation and ownership. What remains to be seen are the effects of mass tourism on the role that heritage sites play in the lives of their constituent communities, and how these relationships can be responsibly managed with the help (or hindrance) of the conservation community.

Angkor will undoubtedly continue as a nexus for conservation practice, activity, innovation and challenges in the years to come. After decades of dedicated work by thousands of foreign and Cambodian professionals representing more than a dozen national teams, it seems certain that Angkor has been, for now, "saved." The challenging questions that follow, however, remain unanswered: For whom has it been saved? How can its long-term security be assured? How can lessons learned at Angkor be exported to other sites in the region? The questions pertaining to what comes next for Angkor are vexing, yet critical in forming an actionable understanding of how the site will fare in the years to come.

In all likelihood, the proving ground where the next phase of challenges in the field of architectural conservation will be tackled is Myanmar. Barring an unforeseen change of course, the government reforms that started to accelerate in 2010 appear irreversible, meaning that the people of Myanmar will continue their reintegration into the regional and international community after a long period of isolation, with ramifications that no one can readily predict. Inevitably, the changes that Myanmar will experience in the first half of the twenty-first century will implicate its built environment in one way or another. The analogies from the last century are apparent: Yangon resembles Singapore of the 1950s in many ways, and the physical characteristics of Bagan echo Angkor prior to the latter's emergence as a major tourist destination in the 2000s. Decisions made in Myanmar by its new leadership, its citizens and the participating conservation professionals will either repeat some of the twentieth century's mistakes, or reflect some of the many positive outcomes of architectural heritage conservation practice that are to be found throughout Southeast Asia.

Buddha within stupa base, Borobodur, Indonesia.

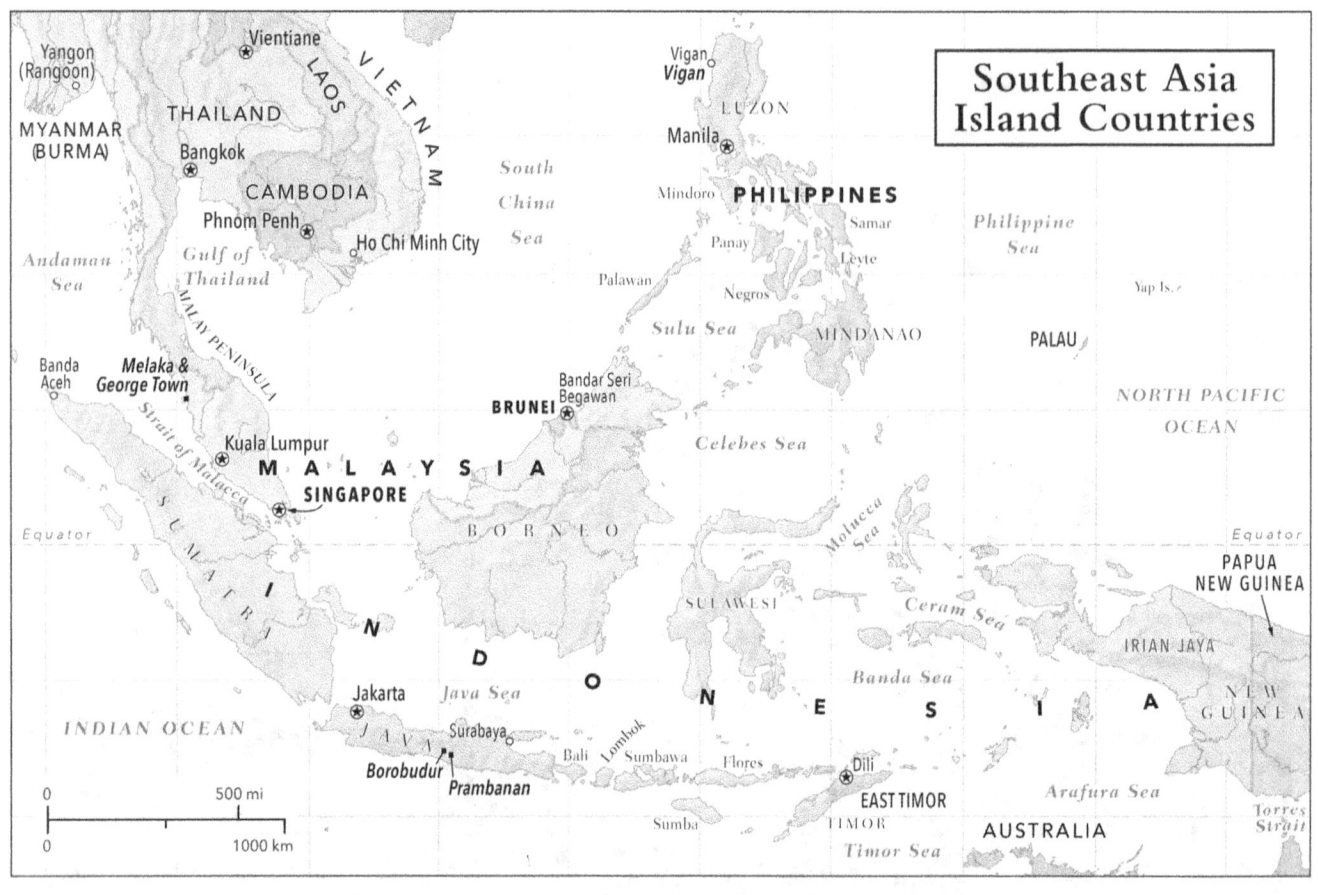

PART III

Southeast Asia island countries

Introduction

Singapore, Malaysia, Brunei, Indonesia, Timor-Leste, the Philippines

Maritime (or Insular) Southeast Asia comprises a series of island and peninsular nations spreading across the chain of seas connecting the Indian and Pacific oceans, and constitutes a hugely diverse collection of cultures spanning tens of thousands of islands stretched along the equator. Climatically defined by the equatorial monsoon weather cycle, and frequently impacted by the volcanic activity that is responsible for the islands' origins, the region for centuries has fostered commercial and cultural exchange. The agricultural commodities of Maritime Southeast Asia, which have historically included tea, rubber, coffee, tobacco and most of all spices, have long drawn long-distance visitors to its ports via the ancient Indian Ocean trade routes. As a result, the region has been connected to the Muslim world in the west since the earliest days of Islam, as well as to China and points north.[1]

Today, while the six nations of Maritime Southeast Asia are together experiencing significant population and economic expansion, their level of development varies considerably. Singapore, Brunei and Malaysia are among the most developed countries in Asia; Timor-Leste is one of the least developed. Indonesia is the region's largest market, and the Philippines is less fully developed. Of these last two countries' capitals, Jakarta and Manila are poised to sustain the greatest levels of population growth in the decades to come along with associated urban expansion, while Kuala Lumpur and Singapore are already burgeoning, global metropolises. Despite the countries' differing economic conditions at present, they nearly all share a strong connection to the Muslim world. With over 200 million faithful, Indonesia is the world's largest Muslim country by population; Malaysia and Brunei are also predominantly (Sunni) Muslim, whereas the majority of Filipinos practice Roman Catholicism and Singapore's population is a mixture of religious beliefs including Buddhism, Taoism and Christianity.[2]

Dutch traders arrived at the port city of Banten (northwest Java) in 1596 and ultimately came to dominate most of Maritime Southeast Asia during the colonial period through the establishment of the *Vereenigde Oost-Indische Compagnie* (VOC, or Dutch East India Company), and later a colonial government across most of what is now Indonesia. The British ultimately challenged the Dutch position from present-day Malaysia, in particular from their regional commercial hub of Singapore. The Spanish colonial relationship with the Philippines began even earlier (1542) and was followed by an American colonial period that ended after World War II.

The shared colonial experience of the Maritime nations has influenced their built environment as well as their modern conservation framework, despite the absence of a single dominant foreign interest (such as the British in South Asia). The Dutch-administered *Oudheidkundige Dienst van Nederlandsch-Indie* (Archaeological Service of the Dutch Indies), established in 1913, was a prominent, early conservation organization in the region. Under the Dutch, the site of Borobudur (located in central Java) became a hub of conservation training and innovation from the late nineteenth century forward, a position it continues to hold under the current Indonesian administration. Singapore, which has been referred to as the regional economic "miracle" due to its fiscal successes, also offers one of the field's most compelling case studies, illustrating the power of reversing course from single-minded development to an embrace of architectural conservation. Due in part to the experiences of these countries' institutions, along with steady support from global organizations, the region enjoys a relatively high degree of professionalism and training in architectural conservation, particularly in Indonesia.

Dutch innovations in architectural conservation included a remarkable spirit of professional camaraderie between colonial powers on the islands and mainland. The most consequential occurred between Dutch civil service engineer Theodore van Erp and French architect Henri Marchal in the 1930s because it led to the introduction of the anastylosis method of reconstructing monumental stone structures to Angkor, where it has been extensively utilized since. World War II played a major disruptive role in the region, affecting the Philippines and Singapore in particular, and resulting in the cessation of all conservation activity for the duration of the conflict. The war also marked the transition between the colonial era and that of the independent states. The legacy of the war still burdens places like Manila's colonial-era Intramuros neighborhood, which never fully recovered from the destruction wrought by fighting between the Japanese and Allied forces. Practitioners trained under the colonial entities, such as Indonesia's R. Soekmono and the landscape architect I.P. Santos of the Philippines, maintained prominent roles in the field long after the Europeans' departure.

The region's distinctive architectural typologies offer many interesting challenges and opportunities for conservation. These include the characteristic shophouses, the massive longhouses of Borneo, Malay stilt houses and Brunei water cities (Kampong Ayer), hybrid colonial–indigenous trading communities (Georgetown, Malacca), agrarian communities manifest as cultural landscapes (Bali's Subak system and the Rice Terraces of the Philippine Cordilleras), and the sixteenth to eighteenth century Philippine Baroque Roman Catholic cathedrals.

As is the case on the mainland, the Maritime countries' rich ecological environments are under pressure from development, industry and extractive practices, creating a nexus of interest in cultural and natural heritage conservation. This is particularly acute in the case of the region's disappearing rainforests and threatened traditional cultures such as Dani of Irian Jaya (in Indonesia's West Papua province). The monumental architecture of the kind found farther to the north in the mainland is largely absent in the Maritime countries (with the notable exceptions of Borobudur, Padang Lawas and the Prambanan temple complex); instead, heritage resources generally consist of smaller scale, contextual and vernacular resources, along with archaeological sites.

The Save Borobudur campaign, a joint program between UNESCO and the Indonesian government, initially ran from 1972 to 1983, and stands as one of the watershed achievements of architectural conservation in Asia, largely serving as an inspiration for the most recent phase of conservation at Angkor that began in the 1990s. The development of architectural conservation in Indonesia and indeed much of the region follows this project, thanks in no small part to the sustained, regionally focused training efforts that accompanied the conservation work. The Borobudur training program, run in collaboration with SEAMEO SPAFA since 1971, was a highly effective training model that for more than a decade supplied well-trained professionals across Indonesia's vast archipelago, as well as to the mainland.

Singapore's heritage conservation renaissance, which began after a 1983 Tourism Task Force Report concluded that unbridled development was actually costing the city-state money in lost tourism revenues, is another milestone event in the story of Asian heritage conservation.[3] The country's turnaround has resulted in a highly effective conservation planning entity in the Urban Redevelopment

Authority (URA), and Singapore's famous "3 Rs" approach to conservation (maximum Retention, sensitive Replacement and careful Repair).[4]

Maritime Southeast Asia is also home to a number of successful conservation trusts and Non-Governmental Organizations (NGOs). The Badan Warisan Malaysia (Heritage of Malaysia Trust), a private citizens' group founded in 1983, is largely responsible for protecting the historic core of Malacca and advocating for conservation goals.[5] Vigan, Philippines, a sixteenth century Spanish colonial town on Luzon island, deserves praise for its effective management program that has included the development of conservation design guidelines, robust stakeholder participation and practical tools for building owners such as maintenance schedules. Maritime Southeast Asia's distinctive landscapes and traditional patterns of development have resulted in "living cultural landscapes"; the Rice Terraces of the Philippine Cordilleras on Luzon island are notable for being the first designated as such by UNESCO in 1995.

The dispersed geography of Maritime Southeast Asia creates challenges for efficiently implementing conservation projects at remote sites: Indonesia consists of 18,000 islands spread over nearly 2 million square kilometers, while the Philippines is comprised of 7,000 islands over 300,000 square kilometers. Risk preparedness for protecting heritage assets against frequent earthquakes, volcanic eruptions, tsunamis and typhoons is a crucial if gradually addressed issue, with the Indonesian National Board for Disaster Management (BNBP) and the Indonesia Disaster Fund (IDF) taking leading roles in this area. Climate change will undoubtedly affect the risk preparedness equation in the Maritime countries, all of which have major coastal communities, cities and heritage sites that could be affected by sea level rise and increased storm severity.

Changes to traditional lifeways due to development, urbanization and new opportunities threaten sites linked to their agricultural practices, such as rice terraces and other cultural landscapes. The Rice Terraces of the Philippine Cordilleras site was on the UNESCO list of World Heritage in Danger due to these shifts from 2001 to 2012, and was only removed following a sustained, multi-year effort to stabilize the social and environmental threats to the site. It will be crucial to effectively manage a rapidly growing commercial tourism industry in places like Indonesia, where cultural heritage tourism constitutes a significant and growing economic contributor, with visitation numbers at places like Borobudur approaching levels that have become detrimental to the sites. Urban areas around the world grapple with competition for space, but the issue is especially acute in places like Singapore and parts of Malaysia, which are severely land-constrained, a condition that contributes to housing shortages for growing populations in places where historic districts and individual buildings already exist.

The Maritime Southeast Asian countries share the benefits of a highly collaborative region with their neighbors on the mainland, with well-formed cultural heritage programs under ASEAN and SEAMEO SPAFA present on the islands as well. The Java-based Centre for Borobudur Studies has also contributed to the dissemination of historic, conservation and regionally applicable information since the advent of the campaign in the 1970s. The Aga Khan Trust for Culture has engaged in the region owing to the shared Islamic heritage there, participating in projects focused on master planning, capacity building and project implementation at George Town (Malaysia).[6] With a range of conservation successes to point to across the region, and a long history of institutional cooperation, Maritime Southeast Asia appears poised to remain a center of activity and innovation in the field for decades to come.

Notes

1. Mark Cleary. "Historical Geography of Insular Southeast Asia," in Keat Gin Ooi (ed.), *Southeast Asia: A Historical Encyclopedia, from Angkor Wat to East Timor, Volume 1.* (Santa Barbara, CA: ABC-CLIO 2004), 591–592.
2. BBC News. "Indonesia Country Profile." 2015. Web. http://www.bbc.com/news/world-asia-pacific-14921238. Accessed January 10, 2016.
3. Russell A. Smith. "The Role of Tourism in Urban Conservation: The Case of Singapore," *Cities* 5(3) (1988), 251.
4. Yew Lih Chan. "Conservation and Change – A Singapore Case of Urban Conservation and Development." Paper delivered at the ICOMOS 2005 Xian Conference.

5 Elizabeth Cardoza. "Heritage Stewardship in Malaysia: The Role of the NGO." Unpublished paper delivered at the World Monuments Fund Conference on Conservation in South and Southeast Asia, July 28–31, 2004.
6 Aga Khan Trust for Culture. "AKTC Signs Agreement for further Collaboration on Regeneration of Penang's George Town World Heritage Site." October 16, 2015. Web. www.akdn.org/Content/1360. Accessed January 6, 2016.

11

SINGAPORE

As one of the world's few remaining city-states, Singapore offers a compact, well-defined case study in the complex relationship between urban development, heritage tourism and architectural conservation. Possessing one of Asia's most successful economies, and a relatively brief yet distinctive historic architectural legacy, Singapore's post-colonial history has unfolded mostly under one powerful, long-term leader, resulting in a host of unusual circumstances that differentiate the island nation from its Southeast Asian neighbors.

Perhaps more than anywhere else in Asia, Singapore's recent history has demonstrated the power a heritage tourism economy holds over the field of architectural conservation. During the 1980s, the country's leadership underwent a wholesale attitude reversal towards architectural conservation at the national level, albeit only after much of the country's singular, multi-cultural architectural heritage had already been lost. Due to this shift, Singapore now boasts well-funded museums, thriving historic districts, and many successful interpretations of the country's distinctive cultural heritage. But the move to embrace conservation as a national priority has not been fully realized; practices such as façadism, wherein a building's exterior is allowed to remain unchanged while its interior is gutted, are still common. Today, Singapore's leaders also grapple with several issues that actively challenge architectural conservation activities, including rapid population growth, real estate development pressures and post-colonial identity conflicts.[1]

From colony to independent state

The Republic of Singapore is a modern nation, without a long-standing built heritage or unified cultural identity predating the nineteenth century. The Englishman Sir Thomas Stamford Raffles established a British East India Company trading outpost in Singapore in 1819. Although this location had served as a regional trading hub on and off for at least six centuries it only became a major international commercial site after the arrival of the British.[2] Due to its strategic location near the Straits of Malacca at the tip of the Malay peninsula, Singapore rapidly expanded during the nearly 150 years of British rule. In 1965, it became an independent state headed by Lee Kuan Yew, whose strong and long-standing leadership was the catalyst for its relatively rapid economic development.

By the late twentieth century this small island on the equator was home to over five million people, primarily of Chinese, Malay and Indian descent. Within little more than fifty years it had developed the infrastructure necessary to support its position as a major global economic center that contains the

FIGURE 11.1a and b Collyer Quay circa 1950 (a) and in 2009 (b).

busiest container trans-shipment port in the world. Today many of the world's major financial and corporate firms call Singapore home, with regional headquarters established in modern new skyscrapers adjacent to an architecturally vibrant commercial district. While it fiercely guards its independence from Malaysia and Indonesia, Singapore remains closely intertwined with its neighbors, with whom a strong cultural and historical identity is shared.

By the 1880s, many vernacular housing structures constructed in the local style from raffia, *atap* (palm leaf) and timber were joined by more modern structures to provide permanent housing for Singapore's growing expatriate business community. Architectural styles from British India were also imported from South Asia to the growing city in response to Singapore's hot and humid tropical climate. European architects borrowed many ideas from Malay architectural styles, and included wide verandas, fretted eaves, delicately carved ventilation openings and *pintu pagar*, swinging doors that enhanced sun protection and air circulation in their constructions. French colonial-inspired louvered window shutters permitted breezy shade while protecting against frequent rain. Chinese architectural contributions included half-moon shaped air vents and jack roofs (vented rooftop additions). Ceramic balusters, tiles and roof treatments on the crowded, interconnected shophouses[3] and terrace houses of Singapore helped guard against the ever-present threat of fire while providing a decorative counterpoint.[4] Throughout the nineteenth and well into the twentieth centuries, intermingled Eastern and Western architectural elements and styles rapidly evolved into a cityscape of unusual diversity.

Many of Singapore's most substantial colonial buildings were constructed in the European Classical Revival style by indentured Indian workers and convicts. To achieve the look of polished marble in a country that had none, workers applied an exterior coat of Madras *chunam* over a base of lime concrete or imported brick.[5] Notable examples of these fine finishes today can be seen at Saint Andrew's Cathedral, at the Sri Mariamman temple, and at the Istana, home of the country's president.[6] These stately structures are among the best examples of the country's well-managed architectural patrimony, and are important reminders of its distinctive building traditions. But the rapid decay rate of natural building materials in Singapore's tropical climate, combined with the zeal with which the new nation strove to modernize and house a burgeoning population, contributed to the loss of swaths of traditional urban fabric during the mid-twentieth century era of urban renewal.

At the beginning of the twenty-first century, Singapore's reputation is that of an active manager and promoter of its distinct cultural heritage. This posture is far from that held in the mid-century decades following independence. After World War II, Singapore was devastated by years of occupation and possessed few resources other than an available workforce. Upon achieving independence from the Federation of Malaysia in 1965, the autocratic Singaporean government, headed by its influential first Prime Minister, Lee Kuan Yew, wasted little time in modernizing the island to attract foreign investment. During the 1960s and 1970s, huge swaths of the city were razed by the government in the name of modernization, housing and economic development. Lost built heritage included much of the distinctive government and commercial districts that comprised the heart of the old downtown.[7]

In response to chronic housing shortages, the government stimulated construction of high-rise housing to replace the population's traditional housing stock of single- or two-storey traditional shophouses and modest *kampong* (village) homes. At the same time, modern, air-conditioned, multi-storey office buildings, hotels and shopping centers began to replace low-rise neighborhood business districts. Land reclamation, which began in the nineteenth century, remains a key strategy for managing growth in Singapore. Since 1819, the land area of Singapore has expanded by nearly 25 percent due to land reclamation, from 578 square kilometers (359 square miles) to 718 square kilometers (446 square miles).[8]

Singapore's success in the rapid creation of a world-class business center is universally regarded as nothing short of astonishing. Within less than forty years, the island has become the home of many of the world's most important international companies, which were attracted by its modern technological infrastructure, political stability, and a highly educated and internationally minded workforce. But in the successful quest for this economic prosperity, a high cost was paid by Singaporeans: the disappearance

FIGURE 11.2 The Sri Mariamman temple, built in 1827, was renovated in 1903, 1923 and in the 1960s. Due to its local significance and relative monumentality, the South Indian Dravidian-style Hindu temple complex has been conserved as an example of Singapore's early religious architecture.

of many irreplaceable buildings, and the sanitization of its traditional environment and multi-cultural architectural vocabulary.

The loss of historic architectural patrimony might have gone on unimpeded were it not for another economic force that attracted the government's attention in the early 1980s: a precipitous drop-off in tourism, which had previously been a major financial contributor to the country's revenue stream. In their rush to modernize, Singapore's leaders were inadvertently eliminating an element that attracted most visitors: its historic physical character. Once this problematic issue had been identified, the government declared a moratorium on further development projects, and created a government-sponsored Tourism Task Force to explain what went wrong, and how to fix it. Their findings, presented in 1983, translated into a 180-degree shift in government policy towards its historic buildings, and set the stage for what has today become a model for Asia's conservation efforts.

The Tourism Task Force report identified three main problems: foreign protectionism; Singapore's high cost of living; and the loss of tourism attractions. "(I)n our effort to build up a modern metropolis, we have removed aspects of our Oriental mystique and charm which are best symbolized in old buildings, traditional activities and bustling roadside activities" the report succinctly and famously stated.[9] It recommended the preservation of Chinatown and other historical neighborhoods, and targeted several problem issues to be addressed – most importantly, the 1953 Control of Rent Act, which, like in neighboring Malaysia, was seen as an obstacle to conservation since it discouraged building investment and maintenance as it prohibited rental increases and evictions for tenants in buildings constructed prior to 1947.[10]

The first areas targeted for conservation were those originally laid out by Raffles in his development plan of 1828, which delineated riverside mercantile and government districts, as well as ethnic housing

FIGURE 11.3 Shophouses from two periods converted in 1992 to pedestrianized Bussorah Mall in Kampong Glam with Sultan Mosque in the background.

quarters. After addressing Chinatown (the country's top cultural tourist attraction), the report recommended focusing on Little India and two predominantly Malay areas, Geylang Serai and Kampong Glam. Additionally, several other historically or culturally significant areas were mentioned: Boat Quay (the island's original business center) and Fort Canning, a colonial military site. Haw Par Villa, a family home since turned into a popular recreational park, was also listed.[11]

Following the release of the Tourism Task Force report, the Singapore Tourist Promotion Board (STPB) commissioned a study on tourism development from Pannell, Kerr, Forster, a well-known regional consulting group, to assist them in developing an appropriate tourism development plan. The study clearly underscores the importance of architectural conservation to tourist development, stating:

> Conservation for conservation's sake is not in itself a viable endeavor. Conservation to enhance the image of a product can improve its economic viability and therefore be beneficial. Likewise, conservation to restore or maintain something that will result in national pride is also beneficial ... As important as conservation is to tourism, its major goals should provide a sense of place to the local population, a different and entertaining place that is socially clean. The local acceptance is vital to the tourism aspect as interchange among local residents and visitors are necessary for its ultimate success.[12]

This last point stands out in particular: creation of contrived or artificial places that do not appeal to the local residents will not be interesting to tourists, and will likely fail. But while Singapore has sustained criticism as an overregulated, sanitized environment, it has successfully promoted various sectors of its tourist economy that access its authenticity, including its thriving *pasar malams* (night markets), which sell many types of items but are particularly known for their distinctive food courts, along with small-scale boutique hotels and shopping areas in colorful neighborhoods.[13]

In October 1986, the Singaporean government released its initial five-year Tourism Product Development Plan, following the recommendations of the Tourism Task Force report.[14] With the release of this plan, the government's planning vehicle, the Urban Redevelopment Agency (URA), effectively became the country's premier architectural conservation agency, a position formalized in 1989. Its initial conservation efforts were fivefold: revitalizing Chinatown, Little India, Kampong Glam and the Singapore River area; creating a Heritage Link for all colonial buildings; upgrading the colonial-era Raffles Hotel (notable due to its private ownership); redeveloping Haw Par Villa and Fort Canning; and re-creating the recently demolished Bugis Street area in Kampong Glam. In order to engage as much of the Singaporean public as possible with their plans, the URA detailed its activities through a public exhibit that described the values and benefits associated with the plan.[15]

The sustainable shophouse, by Andrew M. Liles

The generally recognized definition of sustainability is living in a manner that advocates the health and welfare of future generations. This interest is both long-standing and widespread. For instance, sustainability is at the core of the fifteenth century Seventh Generation rule of the Native American Iroquois Confederacy that assumes one's actions will serve seven generations hence. Sustainability is also the central concern of the 1987 *Our Common Future: Report on the United Nations World Commission on the Environment* (also known as the *Brundtland Report*).[16]

Traditional vernacular architecture pre-dating the advent of modern air conditioning systems notably responds to environmental forces in ways that offer an inherent resiliency for their continued use by future generations. Built in a time when designing for optimum light, ventilation, and the capture or retention of coolness or warmth directly related to thermal comfort, the shophouse typology of tropical Asia is a model of efficiency, economy and flexibility. The preservation of the means and systems by which past generations operated buildings pre-dating the era of mechanical air conditioning is the purest and most sustainable way of both preserving historic buildings and ensuring minimal energy consumption for their present and future users.

The Southeast Asian shophouse typology dates to at least the mid-1800s in Indonesia, Vietnam, Cambodia and Singapore. Single shophouses are generally the width of one room and span in length from a front veranda to a rear courtyard or access way. The width of shophouses was usually derived from the capacities of building resources of the time, as well as possible building norms and regulations. For instance, the spans of timber beams and an early façade tax based on building widths gave shape to Singapore's early shophouses.[17] The linearity of shophouses permits natural light and ventilation via the front and rear window and openings. Intermediate windows and vents may open to interior courtyard areas.

Typically two-to-four storeys in height, shophouses support both a mixed-use function and create a considerable urban density. Ground floors function as commercial space while the upper floors often house the proprietor's family. Serving as both shelter and a filter to the outside, the façade area way and upper balconies provide spaces for public interaction. The shophouse's linear open plan allows a diversity of uses whether home, store or office. The inherent flexibility and sustainability of the shophouse format exemplifies the moniker "long life, loose fit," building for both longevity and the potential for adaptation.[18]

The core benefit of the shophouse lay in its potential for aggregation. Common walls with adjacent units allow for an economy of materials usage. In arrangement with other shophouses, front verandas combine to become a commercial arcade that may possess a distinct vitality and character. In numbers they form a "bazaar."[19] The covered arcade, sometimes referred to as the "five foot" way, also accommodates commercial activities and public exchange protected from the harsh tropical climate.[20] Considering their mixed residential and commercial functions, blocks of shophouses represent successful urban neighborhoods, which were described by the American urban activist Jane Jacobs as having clearly demarcated public and private realms, with inherent security provided by their "natural proprietors" and a constant pedestrian presence.[21]

The mixed-use urban condition afforded by shophouses is equally valuable, if not more so, from a cultural standpoint. Family businesses within shophouses solidify community identity, or sense of place, through small-scale economic activity. From an urban development perspective, street fronts composed of shophouses can easily and economically accommodate varying terrains, including hillsides and frontage on waterways.

Hanoi is rich with examples of shophouses and their stylistic evolution. The indigenous "tube houses" of the Old Quarter offer variations on the standard form, usually being narrow and longer in plan. A repeating pattern of rooms and courtyards may be an entire block in length. Often housing generations of families, the Vietnamese tube house may rise upwards of four storeys. Vietnamese shophouses dating from the French colonial era expanded upon indigenous forms of architecture that also capitalized on passive light and thermal comfort strategies, though with stylistic developments. They were constructed with high ceilings and cross ventilation in varying styles ranging from nineteenth century French provincial architecture to modern styles with shade-producing cast concrete balconies and *brise-soleil*.[22]

In 2014 a United Nations report noted that "fifty-four per cent of the world's population lives in urban areas, a proportion that is expected to increase to sixty-six per cent by 2050."[23] Three decades prior, Singapore had modernized in a manner entailing replacement of its urban vernacular architecture to the point that the report of the Tourism Task Force of 1984 claimed its tourist economy had suffered directly from the loss of the country's built heritage. Singapore risked completely losing its "Oriental mystique and charm best symbolized in old buildings, traditional activities and bustling road activities."[24] The report referred specifically to the traditional shophouse districts of Singapore, that while not modern and in vogue at the time, were supporting vibrant commercial and social functions that the country's visitors desired to experience. The usefulness and economic viability of the shophouse typology was re-evaluated, and policies for preserving and even re-creating them were implemented. This experience has stood as an example that other Asian cities have noted: the vitality and sustainability of historic cities can be fostered by preserving traditional urban structures such as the shophouse. (See also page 262.)

The Plan commenced successfully in late 1987, as real estate developers, drawn by competitive prices for shophouse districts and weakened rent control regulations, poured development monies into conservation projects in the targeted areas.[25] Today, Chinatown, Little India, Kampong Glam and their environs are thriving tourist destinations as well as popular entertainment spots for the local population. Districts of hotels, restaurants and cafés operating in rehabilitated shophouses have thrived, in some cases expunging an area's former unsavory activities raising concerns around gentrification in the process. The memory of what might have been, however, is not far away, as HDB estates[26] and business skyscrapers closely encircle these first conservation districts.

Ongoing conservation efforts are supported today by a variety of governmental organizations, including the aforementioned URA, the Preservation of Monuments Board (PMB) and the National Heritage Board (NHB). All were established in the 1970s and 1980s and all are today active in the now-institutionalized task of cultural heritage management. The URA is officially charged with all aspects of urban planning as well as a broad range of conservation-related tasks, including identification and recommendation of buildings for conservation; providing a legal framework to facilitate private sector involvement in conservation; and maintaining an active public relations role in keeping the importance of conservation at the forefront of public awareness. From an inventory of 3,200 buildings in ten conservation areas in 1989, as of 2011 the URA has granted conservation status to over 7,000 buildings located in 100 areas throughout the country.[27] Because the URA's role includes development proposals in addition to architectural conservation, the agency is tasked with striking a balance between extremely limited developable land and maintaining a heritage list that is representative of Singapore's diverse ethnic composition.

The National Heritage Board (NHB) and its Preservation of Sites and Monuments (PSM) division help to augment the URA's planning and conservation duties at the national level. While the NHB manages heritage institutions and policy (including the national museums, collections and promotion of heritage programs) under the Ministry of Culture, Community and Youth, the PSM division oversees research and publication, conservation support, public awareness and advising the government on issues related to national monuments and sites.[28] Originally known as the Preservation of Monuments Board, the PSM provides technical assistance to property owners, including administration of a National Monuments Fund, which was established in 2008 to provides up to US$1 million each year in grants to address pressing maintenance needs for one of twenty-nine qualifying (non-profit, non-commercial) national monuments.[29] In 2014, National Monuments Fund grants were gained to repaint and repair spalling at the Sultan Mosque (a current Saracenic-style structure built in 1928), fix humidity damage at the ca. 1830 Nagore Dargah Indian Heritage Center and begin structural repairs at the nineteenth century Hindu Sri Mariamman temple. The S$1.09 million (US$763,000) grant given to the Sultan Mosque was the second largest in NMF's history.[30]

FIGURE 11.4a, b and c Two preserved ranges of shop houses on a major shopping street in the Tanjong Pagar historic district (a,b) are well-suited for both residential and commercial purposes. Five-foot arcaded ways in front of the connected buildings allow for ease of foot traffic and protection from the elements. This design element is shared with the highly decorated Peranakan shophouses that are located on Chinatown's Neil Road (c).

FIGURE 11.5 The Sultan Mosque was among the Singaporean landmarks restored with funding from the National Monuments Fund in 2014.

The evolution of Singapore's professional framework for heritage conservation, combined with the realities of the country's highly constrained geography, have contributed to the development of several distinctly Singaporean methods of practice. The URA encourages conservation practice based on the "3 Rs": maximum Retention, sensitive Replacement and careful Repair. Intensification of use through expansions to an existing building's envelope, or the addition of subsidiary wings, is a commonly used tactic for retaining the economic viability of a conserved property. Owners of shophouses located in heritage areas are permitted to expand upward and to the rear based on design guidelines and standard dimensions.

Adaptive reuse, which is employed throughout the world as a conservation tactic, is particularly attractive to property owners/investors in Singapore where the economic performance of one's real estate holdings is of paramount importance. Examples include the conversion of the Convent of the Holy Infant Jesus school, a convent and orphanage complex that was built between 1840 and 1904, into a popular retail, restaurant and event space now billed as CHIJMES. Contextual preservation, whereby new buildings in the proximity of traditional districts or individual monuments are expected to respond to the older structures, is less frequently emphasized in Singapore. Therefore, it is not unusual to see tall buildings constructed directly adjacent to low-rise traditional structures.[31]

In contrast to its regional neighbors – and to the vibrant architectural conservation field in general – relatively little archaeological activity occurs in Singapore. One exception is the work being done at Fort Canning, where ten separate fourteenth century sites are being studied. The work is progressing largely without government support, although there is a permanent archaeological site on display at Fort Canning Park. As of late 2015, archaeology in Singapore remains a discipline largely lacking in government support.[32]

Waterfront revitalization through adaptive re-use

The island of Singapore has been an important regional trading hub since time immemorial, due to its strategic location near the Straits of Malacca. The Singapore River, its major inland trade route, flows into the harbor at the island's southern end, facilitating both upcountry imports and vessel trans-shipments by a variety of trading partners. During the period of British colonization under Sir Thomas Raffles, Chinese, Malay and British trading houses, among others, successfully plied their trade thanks in part to Singapore's favorable geography.

As the British colony expanded upriver during the nineteenth century, industrialization advanced at a rapid pace. The introduction of steam-powered ships in the early 1800s, the opening of Egypt's Suez Canal in 1869, and the development of cargo containerization in the 1970s further advanced Singapore's status as a worldwide trade center. Today the island is one of the world's most active container ports, regularly vying with Hong Kong for the global #1 position in annual tonnage handled.

As commercial activity flourished the local population grew rapidly, straining the city's infrastructure. Waste pollution in the Singapore River rose to a level that compromised its navigability.[33] By the mid-twentieth century, the river had become an undesirable representation of the city, one that many officials did not wish to uphold as the city-state matured into a modern, independent nation. Prime Minister Lee Kuan Yew acknowledged citywide pollution and its effects on the river and initiated programs to stimulate its revitalization, culminating in a nationwide cleanup challenge issued in February 1977.[34] Overseen by the Ministry of the Environment, the decade-long initiative was vast, comprehensive, and included the construction of new sewerage systems, the cleaning and dredging of waterways, and the relocation of farms, squatters, hawkers, lighter barges and unauthorized workshops. The cleanup effort also entailed the development of regulated factories, new housing and proper infrastructure for the relocated workers who would operate out of new food market centers.

In 1985, before the river cleanup operation was fully realized, the Urban Redevelopment Authority (URA) released a master plan for the rehabilitation of three defined urban areas along the Singapore River waterfront: Boat Quay, Clarke Quay and Robertson Quay. Each had different characteristics: Boat Quay consisted mainly of historic shophouses, Clarke Quay was comprised of warehouses (*godowns*) and Robertson Quay had large factory warehouses and newer hotel structures. The URA studied successful approaches applied elsewhere, as at the Paseo del Rio in San Antonio, Texas, and incorporated commercial properties along new, landscaped promenades. By integrating existing bridges, this master plan linked the three designated districts with pathways and provided numerous leisure spaces along both banks of the Singapore River. The nearby Kallang River Basin was also cleaned of its polluting elements and redeveloped in 1987, though its predominantly industrial and rural architecture was replaced by new recreational buildings such as Singapore Sports Hub and Singapore National Stadium.

The environmental improvements made to and along the river resulted in formal architectural preservation efforts, beginning with "conservation area" designations of Boat Quay and Clarke Quay in 1989. Within a few years, over 100 historic shophouses in Boat Quay, some dating to the 1820s, had been restored and rehabilitated while fifty larger godowns in Clarke Quay had been consolidated into a pedestrian zone comprised of culinary and entertainment spots. Robertson Quay was listed as a protected historic district in 2014 and today serves as an arts hub.

The Singapore River master plan also encouraged mixed-use buildings, utilizing ground floors to create a lively street life while the allotted residential units in and around the riverside areas maintained the flow of activity. Further guidelines and legislation that limit building floor area ratios and provide height restrictions have aided Singapore in retaining its distinct architectural character, an all-encompassing feat that transformed a deteriorated industrial thoroughfare into a highly celebrated natural attraction.

Today, the banks of the Singapore River no longer pulse with activity as trading goods are loaded and off-loaded from boats docked on its shores, but the riverfront still surges with life. Boat Quay, Clarke Quay and Robertson Quay encompass some of Singapore's most important commercial and visitor attractions. All of them – especially Boat Quay, which is located close to the city's Central Business District – are popular venues for leisure time, and are enjoyed by both local professionals and tourists alike.

Further reading

Belle, Iris, Uta Hassler and Wiepke van Aaken. "From Godown to Downtown: The Evolutions of Singapore's Port-Related Building Stock." *BDC* (12)(1) (2012), 500–507. Web. www.idb.arch.ethz.ch/files/hasslerbellevanaaken_2012_from_godown_to_downtown.pdf. Accessed May 18, 2016.

Dobbs, Stephen. *The Singapore River: A Social History, 1819–2002* (Singapore: Singapore University Press, 2003).

Hong, Tan Chung. "Planning for the Development of Singapore's Urban Waterfront," in L.S. Chia and L.N. Chou (eds.), *Urban Coastal Area Management: The Experience of Singapore: Proceedings of the Singapore National Workshop on Urban Coastal Area Management,*

Republic of Singapore, 9–10 November 1989. (Singapore: ICLARM, 1991), 53–58.

Miksic, John. "Singapore," in John N. Miksic and Geok Yian Goh (eds.), *Rethinking Cultural Resource Management in Southeast Asia* (London: Anthem Press, 2011).

——. *Singapore and the Silk Road of the Sea* (Singapore: National University of Singapore, 2013).

Tortajada, Cecilia, Yugal Joshi and Asit K. Biswas. *The Singapore Water Story: Sustainable Development in an Urban City State* (Oxford: Routledge, 2013).

Urban Redevelopment Authority. "Urban Design (UD) Plans and Guidelines for Developments Within Singapore River Planning Area." Web. www.ura.gov.sg/uol/circulars/2013/nov/dc13-17.aspx. Accessed May 18, 2016.

Wong, Tai-Chee, Belinda K.P. Yuen and Charles Goldblum (eds.). *Spatial Planning for a Sustainable Singapore* (Dordrecht: Springer Science + Business Media, 2008).

Yuan, Lim Lan. "Singapore's Experience in Housing and Urban Development," in Darshini Mahadevia (ed.), *Inside the Transforming Urban Asia: Processes, Policies, and Public Actions.* (New Delhi: Concept Publishing Company, 2008), 532–546.

FIGURE 11.6
Rehabilitation of former warehouses serving aquatic trade along Boat Quay on the Singapore River as a public and tourist leisure zone featuring waterside bars and restaurants adjacent to the city's commercial and banking district.

FIGURE 11.7
This aerial view of the Singapore Civic District includes the modern Supreme Court building (center left, with roof disc), the domed 1930s era Old Supreme Court building, and Parliament (to the right). Visible in the background are central business district skyscrapers and the three towered futuristic Marina Bay Sands hotel, which rises up from land recently reclaimed from the sea. This juxtaposition of historic and modern architecture cwell represents Singapore's sense of place and ambitions for the future.

In this major regional business hub, economic success speaks loudly to Singapore's populace and government. The private investors that have supported the government's conservation priorities since the early 1980s have also reinforced their own economic well-being through the revitalization and protection of Chinatown, Boat Quay, Little India and Kampong Glam, all of which have become successful real estate ventures. Government support and incentives, coupled with small and large-scale private investment, have demonstrated the economic case for built heritage conservation in Singapore. Therefore, since the government altered its position towards conservation in the mid-1980s, there has been a growing interest in Singapore's built heritage, accompanied by public reaction against the rapid changes and the loss of familiar landmarks that so defined the first two decades of independence.

But despite its success to date, Singapore's heritage conservation program is at a crossroads. If its population, as predicted, continues to grow at its current pace, it will become nearly impossible for the government to maintain the status quo of its conservation areas.[35] Adequate housing for an increasingly prosperous population remains a national priority, along with the maintenance of the country's high quality of life via adequate recreation areas and infrastructure improvements. Due to these continued pressures, it is presently unclear what the government of Singapore's future commitment will be towards architectural conservation.

Based on experience to date, the long-term success of maintaining Singapore's historic architecture rests on the integration of a comprehensive cultural management program with the country's economic development goals. Only time will tell which of these factors will dominate the future direction of governmental policy. However, it seems likely that as the conservation ethos both in Singapore and in the region becomes entrenched, there will be no going back to the days of clearing historic areas with little concern for the long-term ramifications of such action.

Notes

1 John Miksic, correspondence with the authors, November 26, 2015. Singapore's tourism industry is mainly focused on the MICE sector (meetings, incentives, conventions, exhibitions), rather than heritage tourism per se. Nevertheless, the country offers several unique experiences to the visitor and resident alike, such as whimsical Tiger Balm Garden (1937), which would benefit from additional conservation attention.
2 World Monuments Fund/US ICOMOS. "Singapore: From Fishing Village to City-State." *Trails to Tropical Treasures: A Tour of ASEAN's Cultural Heritage*. (New York: World Monuments Fund, 1992), 33.
3 Shophouses are Singapore's primary regional urban residential/commercial form.
4 Anthony Tung. *Preserving the World's Great Cities: The Destruction and Renewal of the Historic Metropolis*. (New York: Clarkson Potter, 2001), 175.
5 Chunam, a plaster made from egg white, *jaggery* (coarse sugar) and shell lime, is traditionally mixed with coconut husks and water to create a building's final surface and intricate moldings. After the chunam paste has hardened, it is given a final polishing, for a look similar to white marble.
6 Kip Lin Lee. *The Singapore House 1818–1942*. (Singapore: Times Editions, Preservation of Monuments Board, 1988), 73.
7 Tung, 182.
8 National University of Singapore: Department of Biological Sciences. "The Natural Heritage of Singapore: Land Area of Singapore." Web. www.dbs.nus.edu.sg/staff/details/hugh_tan/Ch4%20Waste-%20and%20Reclaimed%20Land%20p.%2078.pdf. Accessed January 20, 2015.
9 Russell A. Smith. "The Role of Tourism in Urban Conservation: The Case of Singapore," *Cities* 5(3) (1988), 251.
10 Ole Johan Dale. "Sustainable City Centre Development: The Singapore City Centre in the Context of Sustainable Development," in Tai-Chee Wong, Belinda K.P. Yuen and Charles Goldblum (eds), *Spatial Planning for a Sustainable Singapore*. (New York: Springer Science & Business Media, 2008), 44.
11 Pannell, Kerr, Forster. *Tourism Development in Singapore*. (Singapore: Singapore Tourist Promotion Board, 1986), 1–3.
12 Ibid.
13 T.C. Chang. "Heritage as a Tourism Commodity: Traversing the Tourist–Local Divide," *Singapore Journal of Tropical Geography* 18(1) (June 1997), 46–68.
14 Smith, 252.
15 Urban Redevelopment Authority of Singapore. "Conservation of Built Heritage." 2014. Web. www.ura.gov.sg/uol/about-us/our-people/groups-departments.aspx. Accessed January 31, 2015.

16 The seminal 1987 *Report on the World Commission on Environment and Development: Our Common Future* is a summarization of all known considerations for environmental sustainability to be recognized multilaterally by the world's nations. Web. www.un-documents.net/our-common-future.pdf. Accessed May 18, 2016.
17 Julian Davison. *Singapore Shophouse*. (Singapore: Laurence King Publishing, 2011), 16.
18 The phrase *long life, loose fit* was championed by the Welsh architect Alex Gordon at the height of a major British recession in the late twentieth century. It is now recognized as a core criterion of sustainable design by the American Institute of Architects Committee on the Environment.
19 Patricia Tusa Fels. "Penang, Malaysia – Penang's Shophouse Culture," *Places*, 9(1) (1994), 54. Web. https://placesjournal.org/article/penangs-shophouse-culture/. Accessed May 18, 2016. Adjacent buildings can be combined to accommodate larger programs such as warehouses and multi-residential use.
20 Ibid., 48.
21 Jane Jacobs. *The Death and Life of Great American Cities*. (New York: Random House, 1961), 35.
22 A *brise-soleil* (in French, literally: "sun breaker") is an architectural feature that deflects sunlight in order to reduce heat gain, such as an overhang on a building's southern façade.
23 United Nations Department of Economic and Social Affairs, Population Division. *United Nations World Urbanization Prospects*. Revised 2014.
24 K.C. Wong, et al. *Report of the Tourism Task Force*. (Singapore: Ministry of Trade and Industry, 1984).
25 Singapore's Control of Rent Act was ultimately abolished in 2001.
26 Housing Development Board public housing estates provide housing for Singaporeans within a defined economic strata.
27 Urban Redevelopment Authority. "A Brief History of Conservation." 2011. Web. www.ura.gov.sg/uol/conservation/vision-and-principles/brief-history.aspx. Accessed January 30, 2015.
28 National Heritage Board. "About Preservation of Sites & Monuments." 2013. Web. www.nhb.gov.sg/NHBPortal/faces/oracle/webcenter/portalapp/pagehierarchy/Page779.jspx?_afrLoop=1035616603636041&_afrWindowMode=0&_afrWindowId=14ztqnuv9r_58#%40%3F_afrWindowId%3D14ztqnuv9r_58%26_afrLoop%3D1035616603636041%26_afrWindowMode%3D0%26_adf.ctrl-state%3D14ztqnuv9r_114 Accessed January 30, 2015.
29 Preservation of Monuments Board. "National Monuments Fund." 2010. Web. www.nhb.gov.sg/NHBPortal/Places/Sites&Monuments/UsefulInformationforMonumentOwners/NationalMonumentsFund?_afrLoop=1092215022322943&_afrWindowMode=0&_afrWindowId=null#%40%3F_afrWindowId%3Dnull%26_afrLoop%3D1092215022322943%26_afrWindowMode%3D0%26_adf.ctrl-state%3D160o0pxn4g_4. Accessed January 30, 2015.
30 Melody Zaccheus. "$1.1M Aid for Restoration of 3 National Monuments." October 15, 2014. Web. http://news.asiaone.com/news/singapore/11m-aid-restoration-3-national-monuments#sthash.6Bbjnxae.dpuf http://news.asiaone.com/news/singapore/11m-aid-restoration-3-national-monuments. Accessed January 30, 2015.
31 Yew Lih Chan. "Conservation and Change – A Singapore Case of Urban Conservation and Development." Paper delivered at the ICOMOS 2005 Xi'an Conference.
32 WMF/US ICOMOS, 37.
33 The formation of the Singapore River Commission in 1898 and its expansive report on the condition of the river revealed the astounding amount of ship traffic and goods traveling through the waterway. To ensure future opportunities for growth the Commission proposed modifications to the river and its environs, but these along with plans by a government-appointed committee in 1905, an analysis by the Legislative Council in 1919, and the establishment of the Singapore River Working Committee in 1954 and its 1955 report of recommendations were never realized. The river's role in Singapore's growing economy – though no longer as crucial – made any closures financially detrimental and a United Nations' 1963 survey found such a project at the river to be impractical. Stephen Dobbs. *The Singapore River: A Social History, 1819–2002*. (Singapore: Singapore University Press, 2003), 12–14.
34 Wong et al., 81.
35 The Urban Redevelopment Authority, in its 2013 Population White Paper, expects the population of Singapore to grow from 5.3 million in 2013 to as much as 6.9 million by 2030.

Further reading

Alexander, James. 2006. *Malaysia, Brunei and Singapore*. Singapore: New Holland.
Chan, Yew Lih. 2005. "Conservation and Change – A Singapore Case of Urban Conservation and Development." Paper delivered at the ICOMOS 2005 Xi'an Conference.

Chang, T.C. 1997. "Heritage as a Tourism Commodity: Traversing the Tourist–Local Divide," *Singapore Journal of Tropical Geography* 18(1) (June 1997): 46–68.

Dale, Ole Johan. 1999. *Urban Planning in Singapore: The Transformation of a City*. London: Oxford University Press.

——. 2008. "Sustainable City Centre Development: The Singapore City Centre in the Context of Sustainable Development," in Tai-Chee Wong, Belinda K. P. Yuen, Charles Goldblum (eds.), *Spatial Planning for a Sustainable Singapore*. New York: Springer Science & Business Media, 31–57.

Kong, Lily. 2011. *Conserving the Past, Creating the Future: Urban Heritage in Singapore*. Singapore: Urban Redevelopment Agency.

Lee, Kip Lin. 1988. *The Singapore House 1818–1942*. Singapore: Times Editions, Preservation of Monuments Board.

Mileto, C., et al. 2014. *Vernacular Architecture: Towards a Sustainable Future*. London: CRC Press/Balkema/Taylor & Francis Group.

National Heritage Board (Singapore). 2013. "About Preservation of Sites & Monuments." Web. www.nhb.gov.sg/NHBPortal/faces/oracle/webcenter/portalapp/pagehierarchy/Page779.jspx?_afrLoop=1035616603636041&_afrWindowMode=0&_afrWindowId=14ztqnuv9r_58#%40%3F_afrWindowId%3D14ztqnuv9r_58%26_afrLoop%3D1035616603636041%26_afrWindowMode%3D0%26_adf.ctrl-state%3D14ztqnuv9r_114. Accessed January 30, 2015.

National University of Singapore: Department of Biological Sciences. "The Natural Heritage of Singapore: Land Area of Singapore." Web. www.dbs.nus.edu.sg/staff/details/hugh_tan/Ch4%20Waste-%20and%20Reclaimed%20Land%20p.%2078.pdf. Accessed January 20, 2015.

Pannell, Kerr, Forster. 1986. *Tourism Development in Singapore*. Singapore: Singapore Tourist Promotion Board.

Preservation of Monuments Board. 2010. "National Monuments Fund." Web. www.nhb.gov.sg/NHBPortal/Places/Sites&Monuments/UsefulInformationforMonumentOwners/NationalMonumentsFund?_afrLoop=1092215022322943&_afrWindowMode=0&_afrWindowId=null#%40%3F_afrWindowId%3Dnull%26_afrLoop%3D1092215022322943%26_afrWindowMode%3D0%26_adf.ctrl-state%3D160o0pxn4g_4. Accessed January 30, 2015.

Smith, Russell A. 1988. "The Role of Tourism in Urban Conservation: The Case of Singapore," *Cities* 5(3): 245–259.

Tung, Anthony. 2001. *Preserving the World's Great Cities: The Destruction and Renewal of the Historic Metropolis*. New York: Clarkson Potter.

Urban Redevelopment Authority and Preservation of Monuments Board (Singapore). 1993. *Objectives, Principles and Standards for Preservation and Conservation*. Singapore.

——. 1994. "Our Heritage is in Our Hands: A Public-Private Partnership in Conservation." Exhibition booklet: *Exhibition on our Built Heritage: Working Towards Quality Restoration*, April 5–11, 1994. Singapore: Urban Redevelopment Authority.

——. 2011. "A Brief History of Conservation." Web. www.ura.gov.sg/uol/conservation/vision-and-principles/brief-history.aspx. Accessed January 30, 2015.

——. 2014. "Conservation of Built Heritage." Urban Redevelopment Authority of Singapore. Web. www.ura.gov.sg/uol/about-us/our-people/groups-departments.aspx. Accessed January 31, 2015.

Wong, Tai-Chee, Belinda K.P. Yuen and Charles Goldblum (eds.). 2008. *Spatial Planning for a Sustainable Singapore*. New York: Springer Science & Business Media.

World Monuments Fund/US ICOMOS. 1992. "Singapore: From Fishing Village to City-State." *Trails to Tropical Treasures: A Tour of ASEAN's Cultural Heritage*. New York: World Monuments Fund.

Zaccheus, Melody. 2014. "$1.1M Aid for Restoration of 3 National Monuments." *The Straits Times*. Wednesday, October 15, 2014. Web. http://news.asiaone.com/news/singapore/11m-aid-restoration-3-national-monuments#sthash.6Bbjnxae.dpufhttp://news.asiaone.com/news/singapore/11m-aid-restoration-3-national-monuments. Accessed January 30, 2015.

12

MALAYSIA

The multi-ethnic Federation of Malaysia is comprised of thirteen states located at the southern end of the Malay peninsula and along the northern coastline of Borneo. Its strategic position halfway along the India-to-China sea trade route has exposed the indigenous population to a steady stream of influences from the outside world – particularly the Islamic religion – but the arrival of the Portuguese in 1511 marked a crucial point in Malaysia's history as they became the first of three successive European colonial powers to occupy the country. Today, extant built heritage in the historically significant port of Malacca clearly reflects Arab, Portuguese and Dutch architectural styles while British design influences can be seen in the buildings of George Town, Malacca's late eighteenth century counterpart and the capital of Penang.

Since gaining independence from Great Britain in 1957, Malaysia transformed from an agriculturally driven nation into one of Asia's strongest developing economies. Due to its fiscal successes, Malaysia's ambitious government brought peace and stability to its multi-cultural population and has been able to support museums, academic institutions, non-governmental organizations and conservation activities. In addition to its participation in global heritage organizations, such as UNESCO and ICOMOS, the Malay peninsula's 500-year legacy as a predominantly Muslim society has created deep connections to the larger Islamic world and its heritage infrastructure, notably with organizations like the Aga Khan Trust for Culture.

Since the 1990s, several highly publicized "Visit Malaysia" campaigns have raised the country's international profile and strengthened its foreign exchange holdings. By the 2010s, the tourism industry had become a critical factor in the country's economic profile, generating 25 million visitors in 2012 and comprising the seventh largest financial driver of the Malaysian economy.[1]

But while promoters of Malaysia's scenic natural riches have capitalized on overseas interest in its beaches and jungles, financial contributions from the government to conserve colonial-era buildings have only recently emerged. Internal biases of ethnic Malays reluctant to acknowledge the value of other groups' heritage sites, powerful local developers and a history of complicated urban planning regulations are among the major challenges for the country's still developing heritage conservation community.[2]

When compared to several of its Southeast Asian neighbors, Malaysia's list of monumental heritage sites such as Angkor, Borobudur or Bagan is more limited.[3] Instead, the development of architectural conservation in Malaysia is largely linked to the heterogeneous trading settlements situated along the Strait of Malacca – most notably, George Town and Malacca – and, to a lesser extent, its prehistoric and pre-European archaeological record, which includes some small-scale shrines and landscape features.

FIGURE 12.1 Aerial view of historic George Town in Penang.

Malaysian built heritage can be organized into three major types: vernacular residential structures common to other parts of Southeast Asia; unique blends of southern Chinese and indigenous architectural styles; and nineteenth century British administrative buildings and town plans.[4] Stilted Malay vernacular homes were constructed for climatic comfort and feature pitched roofs, high ceilings, well-shaded verandas and numerous carved openings to encourage natural cross- and stack-ventilation. Many regional modifications in the size and shape of these homes were made due to influences from local peoples, particularly Thai, Javanese, Indian and Arab.[5] Because they were made from traditional, natural building materials – timber for structure, rattan and tree roots for securing joints, bamboo and leaves for floors and walls – few old homes exist today, although some made with "new" European technologies, such as zinc and clay roof tiles, glass windows, brick and cement columns are still extant.[6]

Within recent centuries, the influx of southern Chinese laborers to the Malay peninsula produced a rich array of residential, commercial and religious architectural styles, such as terrace homes, shophouses, Buddhist temples and clan association buildings. These were typically constructed of more durable materials than local Malay architecture and often included clay roof tiles and plaster detailing.[7] Chinese intermarriage with Malays resulted in a melded culture known as *Peranakan Cina*, an economically prosperous landowning class that favored the addition of ornate plaster carvings, glazed tiles and flamboyant colors to traditional architectural forms. In the 1980s, Kuala Lumpur's rapid urbanization accelerated the loss of Peranakan architecture and prompted a formal architectural conservation movement in the capital.[8] But while local perception that these buildings are foreign in origin often inhibits efforts to restore and protect them, many impressive examples can today be found, notably in Melaka and in George Town, Penang, as well as in neighboring Singapore.

Longhouses of Sabah and Sarawak

Structures referred to as "longhouses" have existed in many indigenous cultures worldwide but those found in the river villages of Sabah and Sarawak, on the island of Borneo, are highly distinctive. The relatively secluded nature of Malaysian Borneo has allowed numerous longhouses to stand and remain in use for centuries, retaining the culture cultivated in these communities and providing a strong basis for their inclusion in architectural protection policies.

The most recognizable feature of Malaysian longhouses is their extraordinary length and capacity to house scores of families. A typical structure consists of a veranda on its river-facing façade that precedes a shallow depth of living quarters. Interior spatial arrangements differ from tribe to tribe but a general social hierarchy affecting individual accommodation size and location within the building exists in most of these rural communities. Still, much of the longhouse is utilized for communal food preparation, storage and shared daily tasks. To adapt to the climate and resist outside attacks, longhouses were raised on thick pillars, made of hand-sawn ironwood, and strategically constructed to hold inhabitants under one large, thatched roof.[9] Building materials, like timber, bamboo, tree bark, rattan and palm leaves, were acquired from surroundings or salvaged from previous structures, ensuring a long tradition of construction trade skills and a strong continuation of this vernacular form.

The architecture and society of longhouses became more widely known by the mid-nineteenth century after Spenser St. John, the British Consul-General to the Sultan of Brunei, sailed the Baram River to the great site he called "Longusin." Here he witnessed a community of approximately five hundred families (population estimated at 2,500),[10] an experience he later described in *Life in the Forests of the Far East* (1862). The states of Sabah and Sarawak were also acknowledged for their great natural beauty in the early years of foreign settlement and in 1891 the so-called White Rajah Charles Brooke established *Muzium Sarawak* (Sarawak Museum) to exhibit tribal artifacts of indigenous cultures, and native vegetation and animal life of the regions. After Malaysian Borneo's annexation into the Federation of Malaysia in 1963, and the subsequent authority of government-sponsored organizations, Muzium Sarawak remained focused on showcasing local tribal cultures.

By the 1960s the state government had recognized foreigners' interest in longhouses and sought to capitalize on their economic benefits, but visiting multiple sites across the large states proved difficult. As a solution, the government later constructed a living museum nearby to Kuching, the capital city of Sarawak, which displays various housing structures found within Malaysian Borneo. The 17 acre Sarawak Cultural Village (*Kampung Budaya Sarawak*) in Kuching includes longhouse models of the Bidayuh, Iban, Orang Ulu and Melanau tribes. Constructions of a Penan jungle settlement, a Malay townhouse, a Chinese farmhouse and pagoda, and re-enactments by staff members in traditional dress reinforce the museum's function as a microcosm of the country's vernacular architecture and cultural legacy.

Though Malaysian Borneo evaded early modernization while under the British colonial government of the Brooke dynasty, recent developments to the island, such as paved roads, have decreased local river traffic and altered the function of longhouses. The migration of younger generations to bigger cities has also greatly reduced the number of longhouse occupants and shifted the social makeup of longhouse residences. While the forest environment where Malaysian tribes traditionally settled is continuously destroyed, government and tourism organizations are promoting its natural beauty as an attraction for ecotourism. The tourism industry is largely centered on traditional native life and many longhouses throughout Sabah and Sarawak are now visited by tour groups or have been rehabilitated into guesthouses and visitor lodges.

Despite the growth and threat of tourism, advances in longhouse preservation are developing. Sarawak Heritage Society formed in 2006 and has worked to increase awareness of the state's unique local heritage and the value of its preservation. The organization's involvement includes advocacy, documentation, community engagement programs, exhibitions and training. In late 2014, the Ministry of Housing officially supported longhouse architecture and cultural preservation efforts by implementing a loan program to aid residents in the reparation, reconstruction and maintenance of their homes.[11] Though this regulatory system deviates from the organic development of historic longhouses it strongly encourages the longevity of these remarkable structures.

Further reading

Bahauddin, Azizi, Aldrin Abdullah and Nor Zarifah Maliki. 2015. "The Rungus Longhouse of Sabah, Malaysian Borneo – A Dying Architecture." EDP Sciences. Web. www.shs-conferences.org/articles/shsconf/pdf/2015/05/shsconf_icolass2014_02002.pdf. Accessed June 2, 2016.

Chin, Lucas. 1980. *Cultural Heritage of Sarawak*. Sarawak: Sarawak Museum.

Metcalf, Peter. 2009. *The Life of the Longhouse: An Archaeology of Ethnicity*. New York: Cambridge University Press.

"State Govt Dedicated to Preserving Longhouses." *The Borneo Post*, October 30, 2014. Web. www.theborneopost.com/2014/10/30/state-govt-dedicated-to-preserving-longhouses/. Accessed May 19, 2016.

Ting, John. 2005. "The Egalitarian Architecture of the Iban Longhouse," in A. Leach and G. Matthewson (eds.), *Celebration – Proceedings of the 22nd Annual Conference of the Society of Architectural Historians, Australia and New Zealand*. Napier, New Zealand: SAHANZ, n.p.

FIGURE 12.2 Peranakan shophouse in Terengganau showing Chinese design influence and the random variety of a typical Malaysian historic urban streetscape.

FIGURE 12.3 A typical multi-family Dayak longhouse in Borneo.

Malaysia **301**

The arrival and establishment of a vibrant British expatriate community in the mid-1800s created a demand for new housing plans. Westernized bungalows styled after Anglo-Indian designs became popular with both Westerners and Peranakans alike. Concurrently, British administrative buildings, often conceived in a hybrid style inspired by classical, Gothic, Tudor and Moorish detailing, were constructed with more permanent materials such as stone and brick. Many of these structures share design characteristics with their contemporary counterparts in England.[12]

Colonial-era documentation and conservation of sites in Malaysia did not nearly approach that seen in neighboring countries.[13] After independence the Malaysian government passed the Town and Country Planning Act of 1976, which established development regulations. The Antiquities Act, passed in the same year, authorized the designation of historic sites for government protection. Though the Ministry of Culture, Arts and Tourism and the Museum and Antiquities Department have both been active in the intervening years, little coordination exists between these two laws so penalties have been weak and loosely enforced.[14] The following sidebar explains the strict limits on evictions and teardowns by landlords as dictated by the Control of Rent Act, which, until 1997, had protected many historic residential buildings and indirectly contributed to conservation efforts in Malaysia.

A substantial portion of Malaysia's historically significant public buildings have been in constant use and consequently well kept. Mosques have fared well through regular maintenance and support from

FIGURE 12.4a and b The *Astana* in Kuching, Sarawak. It was built in 1870 by the second White Rajah, Charles Vyner Brooke, as a wedding present for his new wife (a). It is today used by the Governor of Sarawak (b).

the country's predominantly Muslim population while *istanas*, state palaces originally built for many royal families, have most often remained in familial possession. Privately owned homes have been less fortunate and presently rank among the most threatened constructions across Malaysia, though a promising trend has recently begun. Young professionals are purchasing and rehabilitating these homes, which are now considered status symbols. Offsetting this, though, has been the growing use of abandoned buildings as birdhouses for swifts. Their edible nests comprise the main ingredient in birds' nest soup and have become an expensive local delicacy.[15]

The importance of conserving the vestiges of a colonial past began to develop in Malaysia during the 1970s when early conservation planning policies and protected zones were first implemented in Malacca and George Town, two of the best examples of colonial trading towns in all of Southeast Asia.[16] As is often the case in many newly autonomous developing countries, the prestige of using imported plans, updated techniques and materials to create modern buildings is far more important to the country's image than the conservation of older building stock. It is a considerable source of pride that the Petronas Twin Towers, the holder of the world's tallest building title until 2004, are located in the capital, Kuala Lumpur. While Malaysia's planners are certainly aware that Singapore's clean-slate planning strategies were not economically beneficial in the long term, the negative effect of urban development on the country's built heritage was perceived to be relatively minimal in comparison since Malay tourism relies far more heavily on its natural, rather than architectural, attractions.

Due to government inaction and insufficient policies, a robust grassroots advocacy network has grown in Malaysia. The development was led by the country's first independent conservation entity, Heritage of Malaysia Trust (*Badan Warisan Malaysia*), a private citizens' group that formed in 1983. Initially the Trust focused its efforts on peninsular Malaysia but eventually broadened its scope to cover the country's two states located on the island of Borneo, Sabah and Sarawak.

By the mid-1980s, the Trust began to see several conservation victories. It successfully blocked the proposed demolitions of the colonial-era Loke Hall (1907), the nineteenth century Gedung Raja Abdullah tin warehouse, and Kuala Lumpur's historic wholesale market. Since then, it has initiated numerous conservation campaigns while actively advising the government ministries on legislation, decision-making and policy. Throughout its first two decades, the Trust has coordinated activities related to the conservation of the Kampong Cina historic district in Kuala Terengganu and the historic core of Malacca.[17]

The Control of Rent Act's effect on Malaysian heritage conservation

The Control of Rent Repeal Act of 1997 highlighted an arduous phase in Malaysia's efforts to fairly house its citizens while preserving an active historic community. The issue was particularly acute in George Town, where thousands of buildings and households were affected by the change. At issue was the 1966 freeze placed on rent increases and evictions in all buildings constructed before 1948, which had for decades enabled many poor families to live in increasingly desirable historic buildings and districts throughout Malaysia. Poor communication between the government and tenants, aggravated by distrust between landlords and tenants, resulted in the worst possible of outcomes: people left without homes and historic buildings left without legal protection.

The government's desire to fashion George Town into a cultural tourism destination placed many residents – the lifeblood of the area's built fabric – in the uncomfortable position of constraining their landlord's desire and eligibility for government subsidies and tourist income.

Most attempts to remedy the situation including negotiations between a local residents group, a housing developers association, the Penang Heritage Trust and local and national leaders, were unsuccessful. A once promising system devised to offer loans and subsidies to developers involved in property restoration and organized to reduce rents to existing tenants stalled due to lack of promotion and participation. The situation illustrates the delicate balances involved in conserving both resident communities and the built heritage that sustains them, the dual edged sword that heritage tourism offers municipalities.[18]

With George Town and Malacca now inscribed on the World Heritage List, and the Malaysian government's increasing responsiveness to the conservation issues of these historic towns, the period of greatest threat may indeed be receding. Continued vigilance will be required, particularly since tourism development has become a key sector of the Malay economy.

FIGURE 12.5 The waterside Kampong Cina district adjacent to Malacca's commercial center has been preserved by the Heritage of Malaysia Trust through local advocacy efforts that began in the late 1990s. In 2004, citizen action resulted in the passage of a more supportive Cultural Properties Act.

By 1995, a sister group, Friends of the Heritage of Malaysia Trust (*Sahabat Warisan Malaysia*) had been absorbed into the Heritage of Malaysia Trust and strengthened its operational capacity.[19] Following the 1997 decision to repeal the Control of Rent – an action carried out in 2000 – the Heritage of Malaysia Trust has intensely lobbied the government for the creation of a new national strategy for heritage management and legislation to support its activities. Similarly suited for such challenges, the Penang Heritage Trust, Malacca Heritage Trust, Perak Heritage Society, and other local and regional groups represent additional assets in the grassroots effort to solicit government and citizen assistance in conservation.[20]

Despite this infrastructure, private and religious ownership issues, development pressures, conflicting interests among Malaysia's diverse populations and government inaction undermine both international and local grassroots organizational efforts to conserve Malaysia's historic towns and cities. In George Town, matters are further complicated because many of the city's nearly 5,000 pre-World War II shops, mosques, temples and shrines are located on *waqf* land, which has been donated in trust for use by Muslim community organizations.[21] The Asian economic slowdown of the late 1990s offered a temporary window for reconciliation of these conflicting issues, however the repeal of the Control of Rent Act necessitated leadership from the government, grassroots campaigns and international communities to set George Town back on course, an effort that continues.[22]

In response to these phenomena, the World Monuments Fund (WMF) placed George Town's densely packed historic core on its 2000 and 2002 Watch List. As part of this awareness effort, the WMF initiated a pilot project in 2005 to rehabilitate a nineteenth century shophouse to serve as the headquarters for the Penang Heritage Trust. The program illustrated best practices for the conservation of George Town's historic buildings and involved the training of local craftspeople in traditional building trades and the installation of didactic resources.[23] Other private sector successes recently achieved in George Town, including the restoration of the nineteenth century Cheong Fatt Tze mansion, have led to the strengthening of local conservation regulations and have encouraged the practice of adaptive reuse elsewhere in the city.[24]

FIGURE 12.6 A poster created by the Heritage of Malaysia Trust advocating for architectural heritage protection in Kuala Lumpur.

In 2008, UNESCO inscribed "Melaka and George Town, Historic Cities of the Straits of Malacca" as Malaysia's first cultural site on the World Heritage List,[25] marking a significant achievement for the still at-risk cities. Since then, the Malaysian UNESCO State Party has regularly reported on its efforts to develop conservation guidelines for each city, enforce management plans and evaluate the impact of certain types of development on heritage resources. The latter activity led to the decision to remove swiftlet nest farming from the World Heritage property and buffer zones by the end of 2013, addressing the industry's negative impact on structures within the historic townscapes.[26]

In 2005, the Malaysian government adopted the National Heritage Act (NHA), which updated previous laws and made the Ministry of Information, Communications and Culture responsible for protecting built, natural, intangible and other cultural heritage. A new position, Commissioner for Heritage, was created with the responsibility to nominate new heritage sites, maintain a register of designated sites, and advise local planning councils on matters related to conservation and protection of heritage resources. The Commissioner and the Ministry are both advised by a National Heritage Council, a body that is comprised of the Directors-General of the Museums and Antiquities Department and Town and Country Planning and the Secretaries-General of the Ministry of Culture, Arts and Heritage and the Ministry of Tourism, among others. Listing on the national Registry does not confer explicit legal protection – only honorary status – which has led to calls for revisions to strengthen safeguards, improve the role of public participation and generally bring Malaysian law into alignment with international policy guidelines.[27]

Legislative maneuvering within recent decades, such as the government's repeal of the national Control of Rent Act and its continued focus on modernization and large-scale tourism, has intensified pressure on Malaysia's historic resources. And yet, updated legislation, increased awareness of responsible heritage tourism practices, a strong NGO community and stable political environment, and the refined management of threatened historic cities like Malacca and Penang suggest that Malaysia is poised to assume a regional leadership role in heritage management. A concerted effort by the country's heritage protection groups to sensitize the nation to the benefits of conservation is being implemented via various educational programs and community-based activities.

FIGURE 12.7a and b A George Town streetscape illustrating the historic urban character valued by inhabitants and visitors to Malaysia, but seen as under-built sites by real estate developers (a). Intact historic residential districts do more than provide urban character, they are time-tested habitats that support lower-income populations that are vital to the modern city (b).

Urban conservation and social inclusion, by Nilson Ariel Espino

Incorporating social inclusion policies into urban historic preservation efforts offers unique advantages to both social and conservation agendas. Including affordable housing programs in historic neighborhoods under renovation, for example, or helping informal businesses improve their conditions and stay in the area, can bring numerous win–win situations to low-income populations and authorities seeking to preserve urban heritage.[28]

On the social front, historic neighborhoods often present central locations that contrast radically with the peripheral zones that low-income families typically have to occupy in the Global South, often in self-built settlements lacking basic services. Low-income households living in centrally located older zones spend less time commuting to their jobs, and can enjoy access to standard urban services. They can also take advantage of high foot traffic in their surroundings for their small businesses, many of which can be run from their homes. Educational opportunities tend also to be more available in central urban areas, where many key public and private institutions are located. In general, strong social programs in urban historic preservation can address quite effectively the challenges of urban social segregation in general, one the most pervasive and intractable problems cities face today.[29]

On the conservation front, the advantages of social inclusion policies are equally compelling. The renovation of historic neighborhoods often changes dramatically their functional and social character, and not necessarily for the better, even when the buildings are competently restored and effectively saved from destruction. Areas that had a mix of residences and businesses can be turned into an open-air mall, catering mostly to tourists. Permanent residents that had a real neighborhood life are replaced with wealthier and much smaller households, who use the living units as seasonal housing. Schools close for lack of students, and temples or churches for lack of worshippers. The effect can be strikingly deadening. Incorporating affordable housing programs for the local population can avoid these kinds of negative wholesale transformations, and keep the neighborhood grounded in the local culture and social dynamics. These programs can work as an effective counterweight to the unavoidable (and also necessary) tourist investments, and help strike a good working balance that guarantees that the area can be both a successful tourist magnet and a real local neighborhood within the city.

Social inclusion programs have to be incorporated into conservation plans from the very beginning, and they have to be an intrinsic part of the renovation philosophy and approach. They cannot be an afterthought, or a sort of bonus. Regardless of whether the programs are implemented by the historic conservation agencies themselves (which has many advantages) or by other more specialized institutions working in close coordination, they have to be present from the very beginning, and be carried out in parallel. Conservation agencies cannot simply assume that social issues are someone else's business. Agencies dedicated to historic preservation frequently believe that their responsibility is solely with the preservation of buildings – their typology, materials, authenticity, and so on – and not with the activities that take place there, and even less with the interests of the current occupants and users, especially if they are low-income. These issues are assumed to be the responsibility of other institutions of the government, say, those that cover the sectors of housing or employment. What usually happens is that the social impacts of conservation efforts, such as displacements of housing and jobs, are not addressed by anyone, and the problems of the original low-income communities, such as crime, unemployment, sub-standard housing or lack of education, are simply transferred to another part of the city. The city loses the opportunity to finally address the needs of the neighborhood's population, and of harnessing the process for the benefit of the historic center.

Incorporating social programs to urban historic conservation involves funds beyond those normally allocated to preservation work. This should not be seen as an added expense, but rather as an investment in the future of the place; specifically, as a strategy in defense of socio-cultural authenticity. On the other hand, these social funds appear less onerous when one realizes the costs that displacement and urban exile imposes on low-income households (and on society in general) in terms of reduced employment and educational opportunities, increased commuting times, or destruction of community networks. Finally, the presence of social inclusion programs only stresses the need for a socially responsible approach on the part of conservation programs.[30] After all, the process of rehabilitating historic neighborhoods cannot be exempt from the concerns of social policy that apply to any other large-scale urban project.

Further reading

Espino, N. Ariel. 2008. "Heritage Preservation, Tourism, and Inclusive Development in Panama City's Casco Antiguo," *Land Lines* (October 2008): 14–17.
——. 2015. *Building the Inclusive City. Theory and Practice for Confronting Urban Segregation.* London: Routledge.
UNESCO. 2008. *Historic Districts for All. A Social and Human Approach for Sustainable Revitalization.* Paris: UNESCO.

As in most multi-ethnic countries with complex indigenous and colonial legacies, encouraging community participation in heritage conservation efforts is a difficult task. The deleterious effects of Malaysia's tropical climate on its built heritage are relentless and hasten the rate of architectural loss. Unless Malaysia's architectural conservationists can accelerate their inroads in governmental circles and encourage public cooperation, natural deterioration of historic fabric will continue and the allure of modern skylines may prevail.

Notes

1 Bernama. "Nazri Aziz: Malaysia to reap RM168bil from tourism by 2020." *The Star* (Malaysia). October 9, 2013. www.thestar.com.my/News/Nation/2013/10/09/nazri-aziz-tourism/. Accessed August 4, 2014.
2 Lorien Holland. "Whose Heritage?," *Far Eastern Economic Review* 164 (May 3, 2001), 56–58.
3 The most notable of Malaysia's early monuments include the Bujang Valley sites of Hindu and Buddhist temples from the fifth to eleventh centuries CE, and the Johor Lama fort and capital site of the sixteenth century. The site of Pengkalan Kempas in Negeri Sembilan is another important pre-colonial monument.
4 World Monuments Fund/US ICOMOS. "Malaysia: Land of Sultans and Strategic Ports." *Trails to Tropical Treasures: A Tour of ASEAN's Cultural Heritage*. (New York: World Monuments Fund, 1992), 22–25.
5 A. Ghafar Ahmad. "Malay Vernacular Architecture." School of Housing, Building & Planning, Universiti Sains Malaysia. 2004. Web. www.hbp.usm.my/conservation/. Accessed May 19, 2016.
6 Ibid.
7 A. Ghafar Ahmad. "Southern Chinese Architecture." School of Housing, Building & Planning, Universiti Sains Malaysia. 2004. Web. www.hbp.usm.my/conservation/. Accessed May 19, 2016.
8 A. Ghafar Ahmad. "The Architectural Styles of the Peranakan Cina." Unpublished paper presented at *Minggu Warisan Baba dan Nyonya*, Universiti Sains Malaysia, December 3, 1994.
9 In areas where the terrain did not allow for one long structure, the community was made up of multiple smaller longhouses. The open-air space beneath the longhouse also protected the structure from river flooding and provided covered areas for animals, such as pigs and chickens, to live.
10 Peter Metcalf. *The Life of the Longhouse: An Archaeology of Ethnicity*. (New York: Cambridge University Press, 2009), 33.
11 *Pakej Pinjaman Perumahan Rumah Panjang Mesra Rakyat* or "People-Friendly Longhouse Housing Loan Package."
12 A. Ghafar Ahmad. *British Colonial Architecture in Malaysia* (Kuala Lumpur: Museums Association of Malaysia, 1997).
13 William Chapman. *A Heritage of Ruins: The Ancient Sites of Southeast Asia and their Conservation*. (Honolulu: University of Hawai'i Press, 2013), 190. Early twentieth century archaeological work was limited but took place at sites like Lembah Bujang, a complex thought to have served as the center of a Hindu-Buddhist community from the third to twelfth century CE. Many of the buildings on site, ancient Hindu temples or *candi*, have been reconstructed or relocated and preserved at the Bujang Valley Archaeology Museum. Despite ongoing conservation efforts, initiated in the 1960s and 1970s, the archaeological area continues to be invaded by modern development and many candi have been demolished to make way for new constructions.
14 Elizabeth Cardoza. "Heritage Stewardship in Malaysia: The Role of the NGO." Unpublished paper delivered at the World Monuments Fund Conference on Conservation in South and Southeast Asia, July 28–31, 2004.
15 Heritage of Malaysia Trust (Badan Warisan Malaysia). "Conserving our Heritage," 2004. Web. www.badanwarisan.org.my. Accessed May 19, 2016.
16 UNESCO. "Melaka and George Town, Historic Cities of the Straits of Malacca." 2008. Web. http://whc.unesco.org/en/list/1223. Accessed August 10, 2014.
17 Cardoza, 7.
18 Khoo Salma Nasution and Gwynn Jenkins. "Georgetown, Pulau Pinang, Malaysia: Development Strategies and Community Realities," in William S. Logan (ed.), *The Disappearing "Asian" City*. (Oxford: Oxford University Press, 2002), 216–217.
19 WMF/US ICOMOS, 23.
20 Cardoza, 5.
21 Holland, 2; and Nor Asiah Mohamad, Sharifah Zubaidah Syed Abdul Kader and Zuraidah Ali. 2012. "Waqf Lands and Challenges from the Legal Perspectives in Malaysia." *Sustainable Built Environment: Lesson Learned from Malaysia and Japan*. IIUM-Toyo Joint Symposium 2012.

22　Nasution and Jenkins.
23　World Monuments Fund. "George Town Historic Enclave." 2005. Web. www.wmf.org/project/george-town-historic-enclave. Accessed August 21, 2014.
24　Jonathan Kandell. "Cheong Fatt Tze Mansion: A Singular Obsession Drives a Penang Landmark's Transformation," *Architectural Digest* 60(8) (2003), 100.
25　In 2012 a second Malaysian site was added to the World Heritage List: the Archaeological Heritage of the Lenggong Valley, a collection of Paleolithic, Neolithic and Metal-Age archaeological sites.
26　UNESCO. "State of Conservation (SOC) Melaka and George Town, Historic Cities of the Straits of Malacca." 2013. Web. http://whc.unesco.org/en/soc/1984. Accessed August 21, 2014.
27　Nurulhuda Adabiah Mustafa and Nuraisyah Chua Abdullah. "Preservation of Cultural Heritage in Malaysia: An Insight of the National Heritage Act 2005." Proceedings of International Conference on Tourism Development, February 2013, George Town, Malaysia.
28　N. Ariel Espino. "Heritage Preservation, Tourism, and Inclusive Development in Panama City's Casco Antiguo," *Land Lines* (October 2008), 14–17.
29　Nilson Ariel Espino. *Building the Inclusive City. Theory and Practice for Confronting Urban Segregation*. (London: Routledge, 2005), 3–4, 125–131.
30　UNESCO. *Historic Districts for All. A Social and Human Approach for Sustainable Revitalization* (Paris: UNESCO, 2008).

Further reading

Ahmad, A. Ghafar. 1994. "The Architectural Styles of the Pernakan Cina." Unpublished paper presented at *Minggu Warisan Baba dan Nyonya*, Universiti Sains Malaysia, December 3, 1994.

——. 1997. *British Colonial Architecture in Malaysia*. Kuala Lumpur: Museums Association of Malaysia.

——. 2004. "Malay Vernacular Architecture," "Southern Chinese Architecture," School of Housing Building & Planning, Universiti Sains Malaysia. Web. www.hbp.usm.my/conservation/. Accessed May 19, 2016.

Alexander, James. 2006. *Malaysia, Brunei and Singapore*. Singapore: New Holland.

Andaya, Barbara Watson and Leonard Andaya. 1982. *History of Malaysia*. London: Macmillan.

Ariffin, Syed Iskandar. 2013. "Islamic Perspectives and Malay Notions of Heritage Conservation," in Kapila D. Silva and Neel Kamal Chapagain (eds.), *Asian Heritage Management*. London: Routledge, 65–86.

AusHeritage and ASEAN-COCI (eds.). 2001. "Cultural Management Profile, Malaysia," *ASEAN-Australia Project: Development of an ASEAN Regional Policy and Strategy for Cultural Heritage Management*. Melbourne: Cultural Heritage Center for Asia and the Pacific.

Bernama. 2013. "Nazri Aziz: Malaysia to Reap RM168bil from Tourism by 2020." *The Star* (Malaysia). October 9, 2013. Web. www.thestar.com.my/News/Nation/2013/10/09/nazri-aziz-tourism/. Accessed August 4, 2014.

Cardoza, Elizabeth. 2004. "Heritage Stewardship in Malaysia: The Role of the NGO." Unpublished paper delivered at the World Monuments Fund Conference on Conservation in South and Southeast Asia, July 28–31, 2004.

Chapman, William. 2013. *A Heritage of Ruins: The Ancient Sites of Southeast Asia and their Conservation*. Honolulu: University of Hawai'i Press, 190.

Gatbonton, Mario T. (ed.). 1971. *Preservation of Cultural Heritage: Australia, China, Japan, Korea, Malaysia, New Zealand, Philippines, Thailand, Vietnam*. Seoul: HollyM Corporation.

Heritage of Malaysia Trust (Badan Warisan Malaysia). 2004. "Conserving our Heritage." Web. www.badanwarisan.org.my. Accessed May 19, 2016.

Holland, Lorien. 2001. "Whose Heritage?," *Far Eastern Economic Review* 164 (May 3): 56–58.

ICOMOS. 2008. *Melaka as a World Heritage City*. Melaka, Malaysia: The Melaka State Government and Melaka Historic City Council.

Kandell, Jonathan. 2003. "Cheong Fatt Tze Mansion: A Singular Obsession Drives a Penang Landmark's Transformation," *Architectural Digest* 60(8): 100.

Loo, Yat Ming. 2013. *Architecture and Urban Form in Kuala Lumpur: Race and Chinese Space in a Postcolonial City*. Burlington, VT: Ashgate Publishing.

Miller, Harry. 1966. *A Short History of Malaysia*. New York: Praeger.

Mohamad, Nor Asiah, Sharifah Zubaidah Syed Abdul Kader, and Zuraidah Ali. 2012. "Waqf Lands and Challenges from the Legal Perspectives in Malaysia." *Sustainable Built Environment: Lesson Learned from Malaysia and Japan*. IIUM-Toyo Joint Symposium.

Nasution, Khoo Salma. 2014. "George Town: The Discreet Charm of Rejuvenated Heritage," *Historic Environment* 26(3): 40–49.

Nasution, Khoo Salma and Gwynn Jenkins. 2002. "George Town, Pulau Pinang, Malaysia: Development Strategies and Community Realities," in William S. Logan (ed.), *The Disappearing "Asian" City*. Oxford: Oxford University Press, 208–228.

Nin, Khoo Su. 1993. *Streets of George Town, Penang: An Illustrated Guide*. Penang: Aracea Books.

UNESCO. 2008. "Melaka and George Town, Historic Cities of the Straits of Malacca." Web. http://whc.unesco.org/en/list/1223. Accessed August 10, 2014.

Winzeler, Robert L. 1998. *Indigenous Architecture in Borneo: Traditional Patterns and New Developments – Including Papers from the Fourth Biennial International Conference on the Borneo Research Council, Bandar Seri Begawan, Brunei Darussalam*. Borneo Research Council.

World Monuments Fund. 2005. "George Town Historic Enclave." Web. www.wmf.org/project/george-town-historic-enclave. Accessed August 21, 2014.

——. 2013. *State of Conservation (SOC) Melaka and George Town, Historic Cities of the Straits of Malacca*. Web. http://whc.unesco.org/en/soc/1984. Accessed August 21, 2014.

World Monuments Fund/US ICOMOS. 1992. "Malaysia: Land of Sultans and Strategic Ports." *Trails to Tropical Treasures: A Tour of ASEAN's Cultural Heritage*. New York: World Monuments Fund, 22–25.

Yeoh, Seng Guan et al. (eds). 2002. *Penang and its Region: The Story of an Asian Empire*. Singapore: NUS Press.

Zuraini, Ali. 2015. *Mubin Sheppard and Pioneering Works in Architectural Conservation in Malaysia, 1950–1994*. Kuala Lumpur: University of Malaysia.

Domes and minarets of Omar Ali Saifuddin Mosque (The Golden Mosque), Brunei.

13

BRUNEI

Oil-rich Brunei, formally known as Brunei Darussalam or "the Abode of Peace," is a compact and prosperous Muslim sultanate on the northern coast of Borneo. Without the monumental ancient architecture found elsewhere in Southeast Asia, it has to date had little opportunity to play a significant role in regional architectural conservation. A strong centralized government, popular wealth and a comparatively harmonious relationship with its British colonial past might bring to mind comparisons to nearby Singapore, but there are important differences. Brunei's population is small, its architectural patrimony is relatively young, and it is much less internationally engaged.

The Islamic Sultanate of Brunei was formally established in the late fourteenth century CE, and at its apex reigned over an area that encompassed most of the island of modern-day Borneo and portions of what are now the Philippines. The sultans of Brunei were an important regional trading power, ruling from their ancient capital, Kota Batu. Unfortunately, very little is known of this period of the country's history and little remains of the former capital today. After more than a century of decline, Great Britain assumed full control over the much-diminished territory in 1888. With the support of the sultans British rule extended for nearly a century, until full independence was granted on January 1, 1984.

Brunei's modern capital, Bandar Seri Begawan, constitutes the only major urban area in the country, much of which remains covered in jungle, including several important nature reserves. The country's cultural heritage consists primarily of the densely built villages (or *kampongs*), several Islamic-era royal tombs, the archaeological remains of Kota Batu, pre-independence industrial mining sites, and mid-twentieth century monuments celebrating the nation's Islamic identity, such as the Omar Ali Saifuddin mosque (completed in 1958).[1]

Following the adoption of a national constitution in 1959, the newly formed government of Brunei established a Museums Department to manage the sultanate's cultural heritage. Shortly thereafter a small Archaeology Section within the Department began excavations at Kota Batu, which had been abandoned since the seventeenth century. The work revealed evidence of the city's monumental architecture as well as artifacts indicating trade connections throughout Southeast and mainland Asia.

In 1967 the government passed the Antiquities and Treasure Trove Enactment, which remains the chief mechanism for managing cultural heritage in Brunei.[2] Since then, excavations have continued at Kota Batu while the Museums Department's supervisory agency, the Ministry of Culture, Youth and Sport, has taken up the task of promoting Brunei's cultural heritage and conservation programs within the country.[3] The Museums Department also oversees a variety of facilities, including the Brunei Arts and Handicraft Training Center, the National Archives and the "House of Twelve Roofs" (*Bubungan*

FIGURE 13.1 The Omar Ali Saifuddin mosque in Bandar Seri Begawan opened in 1958 is a relatively new structure built in the manner of traditional grand mosques.

Dua Belas), the former home of British Residents and High Commissioners. The hybrid colonial-Malay wooden residence, which was built in 1906, is one of the oldest buildings in the sultanate, and today houses a collection of photographs honoring the legacy of Britain and Brunei's historical relationship.[4]

To date, the sultanate's cultural heritage management efforts have focused more on traditional crafts skills such as the woodcarving, weaving and metalworking supported by government-run institutions including the Brunei Handicrafts and Training Centre, than they have on architectural conservation.[5] But while the country is a relative novice in the field of formal heritage management and conservation, it is an active one. In 2011 it became party to UNESCO's cultural heritage charters, although it has not yet had any of its heritage sites listed on the World Heritage roster. However, with its participation in the wider field now established, distinctive forms of Bruneian heritage such as its water villages are emerging as subjects of conservation discussion both at home and abroad.

Brunei's traditional urban centers, its water villages, remain among the most distinctive – and most threatened – architectural features in the country. These unique communities consist of vernacular-style wooden houses resting on stilts over water that are interconnected by a series of bridges and walkways. The largest and oldest collection of these villages, collectively known as *Kampong Ayer* (literally, "water village"), traces its origins to the ninth century BCE, and today consists of over 3,000 buildings connected by more than 35 km of walkways and connecting structures. The kampong's

FIGURE 13.2 Archaeological excavations at Kota Batu.

location at the mouth of the Brunei River, across the water from the land-based capital, Bandar Seri Begawan, results in a vivid contrast between the modern and traditional ways of life offered by each.

The majority of the sultanate's population lived in water villages until the early twentieth century, when the British helped establish the present-day capital on land, thereby initiating a gradual shift away from these traditional communities. In the decades following independence, the government of Brunei has conducted a series of programs aimed at relocating residents out of the kampong and into new land-based settlements. These programs continued until the 1980s, when the government shifted direction and instead began to rehouse the population in a modern kampong. *Kampong Bolkiah* was completed in 1994, and by the turn of the twenty-first century, was home to over 30,000 persons, or nearly 10 percent of the nation's population. Today the kampong functions as a critical reservoir of middle to lower-income housing in the prosperous capital city.

Issues threatening the traditional character of Kampong Ayer include a declining population, the substitution of concrete and sheet metal for traditional building materials, limitations around modern infrastructure such as electricity, fresh water, communications, sewage and trash collection, and threats from fire. While the government of Brunei has worked to address these deficiencies and maintain the civic health of the kampong, it has done so less in the spirit of Western-style urban conservation, and more with a focus on the health and welfare of the district's residents.[6]

In 2011 Brunei ratified UNESCO's World Heritage Convention and the Convention for the Safeguarding of the Intangible Cultural Heritage (2003), removing itself from the very small list of United Nations member states that had not done so.[7] Two years later, the sultanate followed this move by submitting a tentative list of four sites to the World Heritage Committee: two natural sites, Tasek Merimbun Park in Tutong and the Abana Rocks Coral Reef Formation; and two cultural sites, one along the Brunei River, and an area called Industrial Heritage of Colliery.[8] The Brunei River site includes Kampong Ayer and its environs, while the Colliery site encompasses a former coal mining area in Serasa at the northernmost tip of Brunei. Active from 1883 until 1924 CE, the coal mines served as an important economic engine for the country prior to the discovery of its valuable oil reserves in 1929.[9] Its nomination would be a first for industrial heritage sites in Southeast Asia, following the lead of other similar properties in Europe and North America, such as the Wallonia Mining Sites of Belgium and Germany's Zollverein Coal Mine Industrial Complex.

FIGURE 13.3 A view of a water village (Kampong Ayer) that reflects the character of prevalent lifeways throughout much of Brunei's history.

FIGURE 13.4 The Colliery Industrial Heritage Site in Serasa.

Brunei's entry into the international heritage management community introduces the possibility that it could play a larger role in architectural conservation efforts among the ASEAN nations, or even within the larger Muslim world. Far from alone in confronting the challenge of supporting traditional communities such as the kampong in a rapidly modernizing world, Brunei's emphasis on improving the infrastructure and livability of these communities may offer lessons in the preservation of similarly fragile urban districts in the region. With its centralized government and a need to diversify its economy beyond the petroleum sector, Brunei could follow the example of Singapore by turning to heritage conservation and promotion as an economic development opportunity, or decide to leverage its wealth and role as a regional economic leader to support architectural conservation projects both within and outside its borders. While the story of architectural conservation policy and practice in Brunei has just recently begun, the country's potential to play a larger role in the region and beyond remains profound.

Notes

1 World Monuments Fund/US ICOMOS. 1992. "Brunei Darussalam: The Abode of Peace," in *Trails to Tropical Treasures: A Tour of ASEAN's Cultural Heritage*. (New York: World Monuments Fund), 9–13.
2 This law was updated in 1984 and in 1991.
3 World Monuments Fund/US ICOMOS, 11.
4 Rozan Yunos. "Guarding Brunei's Treasures," *The Brunei Times*. June 28, 2009. Web. www.bt.com.bn/golden_legacy/2009/06/28/guarding_bruneis_treasures. Accessed February 2, 2015.
5 Government of Brunei Darussalam. "Brunei Museums Department." 2004. Web. www.museums.gov.bn/rujukan.htm. Accessed December 1, 2004.
6 Andrew Jones. "Urban Conservation Issues in Brunei Darussalam: The Case of Brunei's Water Villages," *Planning Perspectives* 12(4) (1997): 457–475.
7 UNESCO Bangkok. "Brunei Darussalam Has Ratified World Heritage and Intangible Cultural Heritage Conventions." August 30, 2011. Web. www.unescobkk.org/en/news/article/brunei-darussalam-has-ratified-world-heritage-and-intangible-cultural-heritage-conventions/. Accessed February 2, 2015.
8 *Borneo Bulletin*. "Brunei's Nominations for World Heritage Sites." March 12, 2013. Web. http://bruneiresources.blogspot.com/2013/03/bruneis-nominations-for-world-heritage.html?m=1. Accessed February 2, 2015.
9 Rozan Yunos. "Before the Oil, it was Coal: The History of Brooketon Coalmine in Muara," *The Brunei Times*. April 14, 2007. Web. www.bruneiresources.com/goldenlegacy/tgl_before_the_oil.html. Accessed February 2, 2015.

Further reading

Alexander, James. 2006. *Malaysia, Brunei and Singapore*. Singapore: New Holland.
Borneo Bulletin. 2013. "Brunei's Nominations for World Heritage Sites," March 12. Web. http://bruneiresources.blogspot.com/2013/03/bruneis-nominations-for-world-heritage.html?m=1. Accessed February 2, 2015.
Government of Brunei Darussalam. 2004. "Brunei Museums Department." December 1. Web. www.museums.gov.bn/rujukan.htm. Accessed December 1, 2004.
Jones, Andrew. 1997. "Urban Conservation Issues in Brunei Darussalam: The Case of Brunei's Water Villages," *Planning Perspectives* 12(4): 457–475.
UNESCO Bangkok. 2011. "Brunei Darussalam Has Ratified World Heritage and Intangible Cultural Heritage Conventions." August 30. Web. www.unescobkk.org/en/news/article/brunei-darussalam-has-ratified-world-heritage-and-intangible-cultural-heritage-conventions/. Accessed February 2, 2015.
World Monuments Fund/US ICOMOS. 1992. "Brunei Darussalam: The Abode of Peace," in *Trails to Tropical Treasures: A Tour of ASEAN's Cultural Heritage*. New York: World Monuments Fund, 9–13.
Yunos, Rozan. 2007. "Before the Oil, it was Coal: The History of Brooketon Coalmine in Muara," *The Brunei Times*. April 14. Web. www.bruneiresources.com/goldenlegacy/tgl_before_the_oil.html. Accessed February 2, 2015.
——. 2009. "Guarding Brunei's Treasures," *The Brunei Times*. June 28. Web. www.bt.com.bn/golden_legacy/2009/06/28/guarding_bruneis_treasures. Accessed February 2, 2015.

Balinese stonework detail.

14

INDONESIA

Modern Indonesia, a vast archipelago of nearly 18,000 islands that stretches for over 6,000 km along the equator, encompasses a broad range of cultural heritage, including early hominid fossils, massive Buddhist structures, wooden mosques, Hindu temples and a wide variety of vernacular buildings. According to fossil dating, hominids inhabited what is now the island of Java nearly two million years ago, which places the region among the world's earliest in the development of fundamental cultural trends.

By the fourth century CE, influences from the Indian subcontinent were evident on the Indonesian islands, including Sanskrit text, Buddhism, Hinduism and associated architectural styles. This exchange led to the construction of the Buddhist Borobudur and Hindu Prambanan in the eighth and ninth centuries and peaked with the establishment of the Hindu Majapahit Empire in eastern Java in the thirteenth century. Islamization of the islands began in the late thirteenth century, which, along with infighting among the islands' various kingdoms, eventually helped to end the Majapahit Empire in the sixteenth century, just as Europeans were beginning to make inroads into the region.[1]

Indonesia is the most populous predominantly Muslim country in the world[2] but is also home to a patrimony that vividly reflects the successive tides of regional influence that was active in the eastern Indian Ocean basin for many years. During the Dutch colonial period, European–Asian hybrid architecture developed in several cities, including Jakarta, Semarang and Surabaya, as did conservation programs, legislation and scholarship.

Several of Indonesia's more famous heritage sites have been the focus of conservation work for over a century, but the country's historic urban centers have only recently been addressed as they become increasingly threatened by population expansion and economic development. Fortunately, due to a long tradition of international collaboration with some of the best conservators in the field and the availability of myriad professional training opportunities, local heritage conservationists are able to confront the challenges that rapid modernization poses to Indonesia's patrimony. Because of lessons learned at sites like Borobudur, Indonesia remains well poised for ongoing success as one of the region's leaders in architectural heritage conservation practice and policy.

Colonial years

The colonial governments of the Portuguese, Dutch, British and, to a lesser extent, the French influenced the development of early heritage conservation practices on the islands that today comprise modern Indonesia. Forays onto the Malay peninsula gave the Portuguese an early claim to the region in the mid-sixteenth century and the Dutch gradually assumed control from their foothold in Melaka

FIGURE 14.1 A late nineteenth century photograph of Borobudur.

in the early nineteenth century. Their dominance was largely due to the strong local presence of the Batavia (Jakarta)-based Dutch East India Company. Although the British briefly took control during the Napoleonic Wars (1811–1815),[3] Indonesia was known as the Dutch East Indies until 1949, when the Netherlands relinquished its colonial claim and the new nation was born.[4]

As was the case in nearby Cambodia, the development of Indonesia's heritage policy closely followed work on its largest monument – Borobudur – which was the focus of numerous conservation and documentation projects throughout the nineteenth and early twentieth centuries.

Conservation of the Borobudur temple complex

Borobudur ranks among Asia's greatest heritage conservation success stories of the twentieth century. Built in the eighth and ninth centuries during the height of the Sailendra dynasty, the temple compound stands as the world's largest Buddhist monument and serves as a historical marker for the introduction of Mahayana Buddhism into Indonesia.

For still unknown reasons the great site, and the rest of the monuments of central Java, were abandoned after ca. 910 CE. Borobudur was subsequently covered by volcanic ash deposits and vegetation took over further concealing the complex. It wasn't until the early nineteenth century, when British Lieutenant Governor of Java Sir Thomas Stamford Raffles set out to locate the temple grounds and its treasures, that Borobudur began its recovery.[5] Since then, a number of European amateur and professional architectural conservationists have worked at Borobudur. Important connections between those working at other sites in the region, especially at Angkor in Cambodia, resulted in beneficial information exchanges.

Dutch army officer and engineer Theodore van Erp was among the most active early conservationists in Indonesia and oversaw the first restoration efforts at Borobudur from 1907 to 1911. Van Erp identified several pressing issues within the structure's 10,000 square meter footprint, including differential settling in the foundation and earthquake and rainwater damage in the core of the temple mountain, which was caused by seepage from joints on the flat surfaces and through porous volcanic stone building blocks. Van Erp and his team addressed these problems by applying cement and paving stones to the surfaces that had allowed water into the structure and by reconstructing other failing structural and decorative elements. In the course of his work, van Erp and his assistant, J.J. de Vink, are thought to have introduced the process of anastylosis to Southeast Asia. This method, which had only recently been pioneered in Europe, was employed by van Erp to assist in the reassembly of Borobudur's dislocated temple construction materials.[6] While touring the site in the 1930s, French archaeologist Henri Marchal observed the results and later applied the same practice to his own restoration work at Angkor. The technique is still being widely used there.[7]

As happened elsewhere in the region, World War II and Japanese occupation halted most conservation projects in Indonesia. At Borobudur, the very limited work that continued consisted mostly of vegetation clearing. Indonesia's independence was realized after Japan's defeat and the country's status as a focal point for conservation activity in the region was reinstated. In the 1950s, the Indonesian Archaeological Institute requested UNESCO's help in evaluating conservation needs at both Borobudur and its neighboring ninth century Hindu temple complex, Prambanan. After a series of preliminary evaluations, the advisory relationship was renewed in 1967 after it was determined that water percolation, penetration, seepage and consequent erosion of the temple's oil foundation, and leaning walls at Borobudur were cause for immediate concern about the structure's stability.[8] The UNESCO panel, along with their Indonesian counterparts, quickly determined that the temple's problems were legion: an unstable earthen core, degraded sculptural detail due to lichen infestation, water infiltration and collapsed structural stone components. A large-scale intervention was proposed and included the massive task of disassembling, cleaning, reassembling and stabilizing hundreds of thousands of stones, efforts that ultimately took another decade to complete.[9]

Because the scope of work needed to stabilize Borobudur entailed a greater financial cost than could be met solely by national financial resources, a "Save Borobudur" program was officially launched in 1972 with the support of the Indonesian government and an international team of experts organized by UNESCO. By the end of the restoration project in 1983, numerous countries had contributed to the program, US$25 million had been spent, and hundreds of Indonesian craftsmen and conservators had been involved in the precedent-setting effort. One million building stones were removed, cleaned, repaired and reassembled using the carefully administered numbering system necessary for the herculean task.[10] Restoration efforts also included improved drainage infrastructure and the installation of concrete slabs under essential points of the monument to stabilize its slopes. A pre-stressed "belt" of concrete was also added around its base to protect its foundations from seismic shifts and to limit the centuries-old issue of the monument settling and spreading.[11] Additional, less-dramatic interventions took place in 1985, including epoxy resin injections into some joints and the implementation of measures for the long-term care and management of the site. Lead sheets, araldite tar and an internal drainage system were some of the major materials added.[12]

FIGURE 14.2 Theodore van Erp, who introduced the anastylosis method of ruins reconstruction, at Borobudur in 1902.

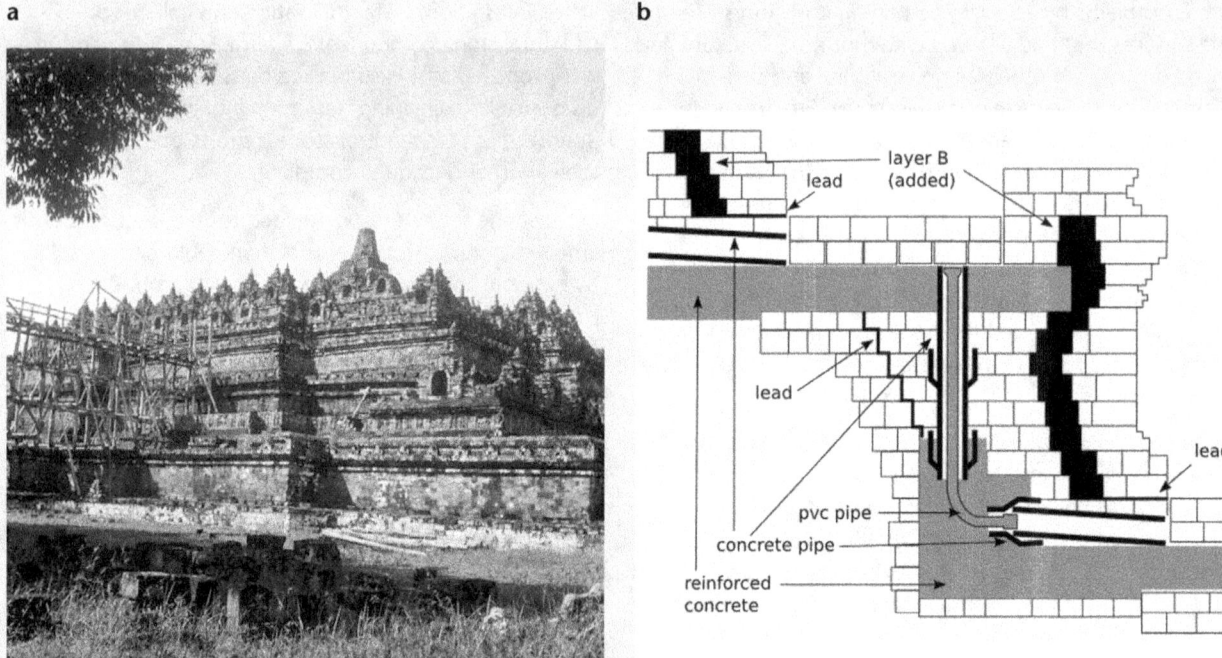

FIGURE 14.3a and b Conservation work at Borobodur was carried out during the UNESCO-led international campaign to conserve Borobudur between 1960 and 1980 (a). The main challenge entailed providing improved water drainage methods (b).

Inspired, in part, by the scarcity of original documents from the van Erp-era restorations (a deficiency that complicated some of the earlier phases of project planning), the Centre for Borobudur Studies was established in 1970 as a project archive and research institution. The Centre today houses archival materials from the restoration work itself, as well as general references on Buddhism, civilizations of ancient Indonesia and conservation studies.[13] Beyond a restored monument and a new class of trained professionals, the Borobudur project still exhibits an institutional and management legacy decades after its 1983 completion. Although relatively minor problems with site circulation and maintenance still persist in 2015, the level of international, governmental and professional coordination involved in Borobudur's restoration since the late 1950s is worthy of considerable praise. Over one million local tourists, almost all of whom are Muslims, visit the site annually. There was one incident of terrorist bombing in the 1980s, but no significant vandalism has occurred to date.

In 1901, as interest in Borobudur and the East Indies' other architectural marvels grew, the Dutch government established the Commission in the Netherlands Indies for Archaeological Research in Java and Madura. Among the Commission's first activities was the generation of research and publications on Tjandi Djago, a Buddhist terraced shrine, and Tjandi Singosari, a Siva tower, both of which are located in eastern Java. When Dr. Nicolas Johannes Krom became Commission head in 1910,[14] he set about reorganizing the group to more closely resemble the Archaeological Survey of India and the École française d'Extrême Orient, of which he had direct experience due to his travels throughout the region. Krom also initiated the first survey program of ancient structures in the Dutch East Indies and encouraged guidelines for moderate interventions as part of any restoration effort. Dr. F.D.K. Bosch, who succeeded Krom in 1915, oversaw ongoing restoration projects at the major Javanese monuments for the next two decades, as well as the expansion of the Archaeological Service's activities to include research into prehistoric sites and the Islamic history of the East Indies.[15]

The Dutch first deployed protective legislation in Indonesia with the passage of the Ordinance on Monuments in 1931, which established a systematic approach to documenting historic properties and setting forth professional guidelines for conservation activities.[16] However, like elsewhere in the region, World War II and Japanese occupation halted most projects in Indonesia.

Conservation activity in an independent nation

The period after independence has been marked by several episodes of political turmoil and numerous ethnic and religious clashes. Nevertheless, a substantial level of awareness and professional support for cultural heritage management has emerged since the early twentieth century.

The withdrawal of the Dutch in 1945 ushered in a new era of governmental organization and, as such, the Archaeological Service was reconstituted as the Indonesian Archaeological Service in 1951. A.J. Bernet Kempers, the Dutch head of the former organization, assisted in transitioning leadership to the new generation of freshly trained Indonesian professionals. These included R. Soekmono, who went on to direct the organization for the next twenty-five years, and Satyawati Suleiman, one of the few women active in national conservation projects in Southeast Asia at that time.[17] Since then, many women have occupied important positions in official Indonesian heritage organizations, such at the National Museum, which has had several female departmental directors.

The post-independence era in Indonesian conservation practice is defined by an enormous and sustained effort to restore, manage and train students at Borobudur. Work accomplished there has not only succeeded in addressing the site's most pressing problems but has established a solid infrastructure for conservation activity there and at other significant sites in Indonesia. In addition to the tangible results of cleaned stones, stabilized walls and poured concrete, the nearly twenty-five year period of training and management programs following the launch of the "Save Borobudur" program accomplished the invaluable task of firmly reinforcing a conservation ethic while establishing a multi-generational professional network of practitioners in the country. Due to the enormous scale of the project and the relative unavailability of trained professionals, the ramping up of professional capacity occurred simultaneously with the conservation of the monument.

The first step taken in 1971 was the institution of a three-year series that consisted of on-site training courses geared at creating a new class of conservation professionals. Once the conservation project was under way, Borobudur was selected to be one of Bangkok-based SEAMEO SPAFA's[18] three regional training centers. Between 1978 and 1981, SEAMEO SPAFA ran a series of courses at Borobudur for Southeast Asian students on the subjects of architecture, chemistry, documentation and the techniques of monument conservation. For its part, Indonesia's Directorate for Protection and Development of Historical and Archaeological Heritage (DPDHAH) capitalized on this level of activity and on the presence of international experts by instituting a training program for its own staff. During the four-month DPDHAH courses, offered from 1977 through 1986, staff responsible for other heritage sites in Indonesia convened at Borobudur while the Borobudur site staff spread to other sites across the country and shared their knowledge with colleagues.[19] Due to the sustained emphasis on conservation training at Borobudur, the government agencies responsible for implementing work there and at other important sites across Indonesia share a high level of professionalism that is often recognized as one of the best in Southeast Asia.

DPDHAH's work is supported through a partner organization, the National Research Center for Archaeology (NRCA), also part of the Ministry of Education and Culture. The NRCA operates through regional offices distributed across the country and has structured its operations according to three chronological periods in Indonesia's history: prehistory; the classical period of Buddhist and Hindu kingdoms; and the Islamic period, which covers the years of post-European contact. For its part, the DPDHAH is divided into four operational clusters: conservation and preservation, restoration, documentation, and protection. Within this organizational framework, Indonesian researchers and conservators have maintained a reputation for sophisticated application of up-to-date conservation standards, including reversibility of work, minimal interventions, respect for multiple eras of historic significance and preservation of historic patina.[20] These approaches all stem from the Borobudur project experience and the high level of international interaction that occurred throughout the 1970s and 1980s and serve as a model system for both nationwide policy and regional practice.

After several bureaucratic reorganizations, responsibility for the massive Borobudur restoration effort of the 1970s and 1980s fell to the Directorate for Protection and Development of Historical and Archaeological Heritage.[21] As part of the long-term management effort, the DPDHAH established a multi-zonal framework that recognized the totality of the site, its scenery and its broad archaeological "footprint," an approach that later became a model for similar UNESCO-led management efforts at

Angkor and Wat Phou.²² Today, the site is overseen by the Borobudur Heritage and Conservation Institute (BHCI), a governmental organization established in 1991 to provide ongoing maintenance, monitoring and research on the monument along with professional training and the development of best practices for conservation work at similar structures all across Indonesia.

By the early 2000s, Borobudur had become the country's top tourist destination and was receiving as many as 2.5 million visitors annually.²³ As Borobudur's popularity among tourists increased, the number of people economically dependent upon it grew to over 30,000 people – both directly (as site staff and caretakers) and indirectly (in the regional tourist economy).²⁴ Expectations that the site can function as a broad-based economic engine are high. However, recent studies have indicated that tourist numbers have supplemented state tax revenue and infrastructure but the economic benefits have not been shared with the largely agrarian local communities.²⁵

In 1992, to manage increasing tourist pressure on the site, the government instituted a system of zoned areas immediately around Borobudur. PT Taman, a state-run corporation, was established to manage tourist shops and to collect admission fees, as well as to oversee the utilization of the site for religious ceremonies and educational activities. The monument zone itself is managed by the BHCI. This segmented approach to management, both at the economic level through the corporation and at the conservation level by the governmental institute, has been successful, though criticism has arisen around a lack of shared objectives between the managing parties and the absence of local voices in decision-making at the site.²⁶

While Borobudur dominated conservation activity throughout Indonesia in the post-independence era, other significant projects were being undertaken at nearby Prambanan (a massive ninth century CE Hindu temple complex originally consisting of 232 shrines, which was probably completed just after

FIGURE 14.4a and b Many of the temples and shrines at the immense Hindu complex of Prambanan have benefited from ruins conservation experiences at Borobudur. Restoration and reconstruction at the site by Dutch conservators commenced in 1918 and was extensive at the main Shiva temple at the center of the complex. Anastylosis was used where possible, although due to the disappearance of many of its ornamental stones a considerable amount of conjectural restoration was required. The temple's appearance 1897 (a), since its completion in 1953 (b), and the fact that conservation continues today at the complex is evidence of the enormity of the task.

Borobudur), at Padang Lawas (an eleventh century CE Hindu–Buddhist temple complex in Sumatra), and at Tanah Lot (the sixteenth century CE Hindu–Balinese temple on Bali).

Although Indonesian conservationists have recently begun to address a broader scope of sites, the majority of conservation work remains concentrated on Java. However, since the worst of the Asian economic crisis that affected the region in the late 1990s has passed and a greater degree of political stability has been established, a new focus has started to develop in Indonesia's conservation-based NGOs and public interest group communities. These factors, along with the professional conservation establishment, work together to counteract the powerful forces of unplanned growth and demands of the tourist industry on the country's fragile historic sites and structures.

Risk management for heritage sites

Indonesia owes its geographic existence, and near-constant danger from natural catastrophe, to its region's highly volatile seismic zone. For millennia, the archipelago's population and architectural heritage has suffered the effects of earthquakes, volcanic eruptions and tsunamis. Ancient earthquakes were blamed, in part, for the condition of Borobudur and Prambanan when the major conservation programs of the twentieth century were initiated. The 2004 Indian Ocean earthquake and tsunami that struck Banda Aceh in north Sumatra killed 221,000 people and leveled huge swaths of the city, a place that had served as a sultanate capital and has for centuries been a traditional embarkation port for pilgrims making the *hajj* to Mecca. Another earthquake hit in March of the following year, causing further damage. On Java, the 2006 Yogyakarta earthquake severely damaged multiple buildings at Prambanan – some of which will be under restoration until at least 2015 while others may never be rebuilt.[27] Mt. Merapi, Indonesia's most active volcano, erupted in October 2010, killed over 300 people and displaced 130,000. Since the volcano is located only 30 km from Borobudur, volcanic ash from Mt. Merapi rained down on the monument and caused corrosive damage that clogged its vital drainage system and temporarily necessitated closing the park to visitors. Park staff undertook emergency measures to clean the structures and restore its systems in order to minimize both the damage to the ancient stone surfaces as well as the economic injury caused by the closure.[28] This level of care extended to even wrapping the monument in plastic sheets. Global warming has also been blamed for accelerated deterioration of Borobudur's delicate relief carvings as higher temperatures contribute to an increase in lichen and fungus growth.[29] These experiences underscore the need for an effective and efficient disaster response infrastructure in Indonesia, for both the country at large and its individual heritage sites.

A 2009 earthquake in western Sumatra significantly damaged the old town of Padang, a seventeenth century trading city with over 250 registered heritage buildings. In response to the event, and in recognition of the larger issue of disaster preparedness for Indonesian heritage sites, the World Monuments Fund collaborated with the Indonesian Heritage Trust and the Dutch Prince Claus Fund for Culture and Development to assemble the *Guidelines for Managing Post-Disaster Conservation of Heritage Buildings, Case Study: Padang*. The document details best practices in the preparedness, emergency response and post-disaster phases of heritage protection and recovery. It also makes recommendations for strengthening civil institutions in order to better protect heritage resources in disaster prone areas.[30]

Coupled with the 2008 establishment of the National Agency for Disaster Management (BNPB) and the Indonesia Disaster Fund (IDF), Indonesia stands in a strong position to respond to its next disaster and to offer other nations the tools for the preparation of their own institutions to face a catastrophe.[31]

Bali

East of Java lies the culturally rich island of Bali, which has served as a major tourist destination since the 1960s. Bali is rife with examples of how tourism and heritage management can simultaneously cooperate and conflict. In addition to its remarkable environmental assets of verdant, hilly terrain, ample seashores and comfortable climate, the island's attraction rests on its religious traditions and folkways, many of which are displayed in the island's architecture, landscape and craft traditions.

As Bali strives to compete for tourist dollars, its hurried mission to develop its economy has resulted in unplanned growth, inferior construction, inadequate infrastructure and development threats to its cultural resources. The island's capital city, Denpasar, particularly struggles with this type of growth along with substandard infrastructure, as do the major tourist towns of Kuta and Ubud. In some cases, hotel construction and other tourist-related accommodations in these communities have compounded the problems by threatening the integrity of Bali's historic sites and traditional culture.

Community participation in heritage conservation: the challenge of Bali's *subak* system

In 2012, Indonesia's fourth cultural site – the "Cultural Landscape of Bali Province: the Subak System as a Manifestation of the Tri Hita Karana Philosophy" – was inscribed onto the UNESCO World Heritage List. This distinctive 19,500-hectare cultural landscape derives its outstanding universal value (OUV) from its collection of rice terraces, temple structures, 1,100-year-old water management systems and 2,000-year-old organizational philosophy that is spiritually connected to distant India. The rice farming practices generated by this system have been among the most successful in the region, an indication that the OUV of the subak system has the literal value of having supported Bali's dense population for centuries. Identified in the nomination, and a continued challenge to this day, are the development and societal pressures that threaten the landscape itself, its setting, and the complex economic forces at play in contemporary Bali.[32]

In 2012 the Balinese provincial government adopted a plan that envisioned a Governing Assembly, with representatives from government agencies and the subak community, which was authorized to make decisions about the site's management. Financial subsidies to lend support to traditional lifeways were also part of the management plan, presumably to help the practitioners resist the opportunity to sell their contributing agricultural land for tourism or other development. Two years after the adoption of this plan, the full function of the Assembly and supporting infrastructure remains unrealized, evidently leading some members of the subak community to give up on the proposal and sell their land.[33] While it is certainly too soon to judge the fate of the subak community and its lands following its World Heritage listing, the situation illustrates the challenges inherent in the engagement of distinctive communities in the preservation of their own heritage.

FIGURE 14.5
Land development in Denpasar, Bali's capital city, has created serious pressures on the city's infrastructure and urban character and has expanded its periphery.

As in many other parts of the developing world, conflict between heritage planning and economic development exists in Indonesia. Beginning in the 1960s, the World Bank began to underwrite economic development projects that focused on tourism and infrastructure development in parts of Indonesia, especially on Bali. The introduction of the automobile also played a significant role in the rapid change of Indonesian cities and townscapes. In places like Bali, where tourist infrastructure places stringent demands on civic leaders, the omnipresent automobile clogs nearly all but the most remote streets and roads.[34]

The Cultural Office of the Province of Bali has started to address this issue through a World Bank-funded, comprehensive cultural heritage conservation program based on expanded inventories of diverse heritage types. This ambitious program includes several pilot conservation projects that address Bali's heritage by type: archaeological heritage (such as the Neolithic Cekik site); monumental architecture (like the Taman Ujung Palace, an early twentieth century residence of local kings); and religious structures (such as Pura Besakih, the island's principal Hindu temple complex). The program also includes the maintenance of living traditions, like weaving, and the archival work and conservation of ancient manuscripts.[35]

The government of Indonesia, with the support of the international architectural conservation community and numerous advocacy groups, has recently begun raising awareness levels across the country and focusing on renewed educational initiatives with the launch of Indonesia Heritage Decade (2004–2013) and the declaration of 2003 as "Indonesia Heritage Year." With a program developed to create a traveling exhibit highlighting significant Indonesian cultural heritage, forge connections between conservation-focused citizen groups and organizations, and publish a book on heritage sites in Indonesia, the initial stages of the effort indicate a strong drive towards greater conservation activity. In 2003, Indonesia ICOMOS, the Ministry of Education and Culture, and the Indonesian Network for Heritage Conservation put forth an Indonesian Charter for Heritage Conservation, a document that outlines the above goals and details the significance of heritage in specifically Indonesian terms.[36] Among these is the concept of *saujana*, the intertwining of natural and cultural heritage, which the charter seeks to emphasize in an effort to maintain the full spectrum of Indonesia's significant culture.[37]

Tourism development versus conservation in Bali

The construction of Le Meridien Hotel along the south-central shore of Bali exemplifies the dilemma between local traditions and foreign investment in Bali. The upscale, European-style hotel was built adjacent to the fifteenth century site of Tanah Lot, one of Bali's three most important temples and the seat of Hindu religious activity along the island's south-central coast.

The temple's position on a small island just offshore had served it well over the centuries. Unfortunately, this location also attracted the attention of developers seeking to build a large, international-style hotel away from the other tourist areas in the Nusa Dua area. In the 1980s, developers succeeded in constructing the Le Meridien Hotel and its eighteen-hole golf course, a fairway now considered among the best in Asia. Important spaces and vistas of the development are organized around the historic site.

Other interventions at Tanah Lot have been similarly problematic. The installation of approximately 100 concrete tetrapods, as part of a World Bank-funded project to protect the island from ocean wave action, has introduced some unwanted changes, including siltation of the area between the island and the mainland that has limited the traditional means of access between the beach and the bluff. Similarly, white-and-black-banded sacred snakes, which previously inhabited the mainland bluff, have greatly diminished due to the large number of visitors and the altered landscape around the temple site. Popular tourist facilities around the hotel, consisting of shops, restaurants, and cafés that offer sunset views of Tanah Lot, also clutter the north and east areas of the site.

Numerous citizens' groups expressed outrage over the hotel's construction plans and had cited concerns with the development's encroachment on the temple site. Although developers ultimately succeeded, the episode created awareness regarding the delicate balance between the tourism economy and integrity of cultural sites in Bali. The hotel stands as a bold example of the global trend of tourist-based infrastructure that threatens this balance and as a reminder to Indonesians of the risks in protecting their cultural interests, even in the face of economic pressures.

FIGURE 14.6a and b Indonesia's easternmost Hindu temple, Tanah Lot (a) on Bali's south-central coast, has been subject to both nearby development pressures (b) and natural threats.

In 2004, a group led by conservation professionals and students established the Indonesian Heritage Trust (*Badan Pelestarian Pusaka Indonesia*, or BPPI), which aims to support the government's efforts to promote heritage conservation in the country. As an organization, the BPPI strives toward enhanced integration of conservation efforts between government, the private sector and communities in an effort to strengthen the process and include a wider range of constituents. With a ten-year government effort under way, a freshly minted Indonesian Charter for Heritage Conservation, and a new batch of organizations to support it, Indonesia has signaled several strong moves toward a healthy conservation infrastructure. However, given the government's efforts and its role as a regional tourist hub, Indonesia has a parallel opportunity to establish a leadership position in responsible and well-managed heritage tourism, as well as in disaster preparedness and response. In order to do so, communities – such as the island of Bali and the area around Borobudur – must effectively balance respect for their fragile heritage resources with effective management tactics and economic demands. This formula must become a by-product of the Indonesian Heritage Decade, or any future effort on the part of the conservation community in Indonesia, in order to maintain the nation's strong legacy of effective heritage planning.

Timor-Leste (East Timor)

A former Portuguese colony established in 1769, Timor-Leste (East Timor) occupies the eastern half of Timor, a 30,777 square kilometer island located in the south-central Indonesian archipelago, 600 km north of Australia. One of Asia's youngest countries, Timor-Leste's path to self-determination has proven exceptionally difficult, with a high cost to its populace and heritage resources. Within days of the Portuguese departure in 1975, the Indonesian government began a violent period of suppressing the Timor-Leste independence claim, resulting in a destructive twenty-four-year occupation.[38] Full independence was finally recognized in 2002, but only after communal fighting had claimed an estimated 70 percent of its residential and public buildings, including cultural artifacts and public archives.[39]

FIGURE 14.7 The *uma lulik* (sacred houses), Timor-Leste's most distinctive architecture, are a preservation priority as symbols of its indigenous culture.

With the western half of the remaining part of Indonesia, and more than 300 years of Portuguese influence, the small new nation has focused on its distinctive hybrid culture as a means for renewal, self-definition and recovery.[40] Among the architectural types in the mostly rural country are the indigenous wood and palm thatch *uma lulik* (sacred houses), and Portuguese-period institutional buildings reflecting European architectural styles.

The Ministry of Tourism within the State Secretariat for Art and Culture oversees state-level conservation activity through its departments of Architectural Heritage, and Archaeological and Ethnographic Heritage.[41] In collaboration with the UNESCO Jakarta office the government has created a series of strategy documents that focus on the development of cultural institutions in the country, including the creation of five Regional Cultural centers, a National Library and National Museum.[42] At least two of the cultural centers entail adaptive reuse of historic buildings: the Uma Fukun Cultural Center, which is currently housed in a nineteenth century former Portuguese military barracks in the capital, Dili, and a new cultural center planned for the 1933 Municipal Market in Timor-Leste's second city of Baucau.[43] The government also aims to aid in the reconstruction or restoration of uma lulik in rural communities throughout the country, a process that will aid in the perpetuation of this distinctive form of spiritual architecture.[44]

Active partnership agreements with various cultural institutions in nearby Australia have focused in particular on museums, collections and traditional crafts.[45] Foreign governments, including the United States, contributed to the effort to rebuild uma lulik in 2010.[46] In this, one of Asia's poorest countries, capacity building in support of heritage conservation remains a critical task in Timor-Leste's sustained revival from a dark period of the region's history.

FIGURE 14.8 Plans for the rehabilitation of the deteriorated 1933 Municipal Market in Baucau to become a cultural center reflects the State Secretariat for Art and Culture's interest in conserving Timor-Leste's Portuguese colonial heritage.

Irian Jaya (West Papua)

The western half of the island of New Guinea, formerly called Irian Jaya, is comprised of Indonesia's easternmost provinces, Papua and West Papua. Its fertile lands that host a rich biodiversity and numerous indigenous cultures that remained relatively isolated from modern development and lifestyles until the early twentieth century. Europeans – the Portuguese, Spanish and Dutch – have been present on the island since the early 1500s, yet these settlements were concentrated on the island's coastline. The interior highlands, consisting of steep, densely forested mountains, were thought to be inhabitable, but when American zoologist Richard Archbold flew over Irian Jaya in 1938 – then a part of Dutch New Guinea – he witnessed signs of human settlement. This "discovery" began the contact between the Dani people of the Baliem Valley and the modern world, an ongoing development that has since provided a basis for cultural heritage tourism in the region.[47]

Conservation efforts have been largely focused on the natural landscapes of Irian Jaya. After the Netherlands' complete withdrawal from West New Guinea in 1963 and the following annexation into Indonesia in 1969, the region's natural resources were exploited for oil, timber, and gold and copper mining. The World Wide Fund for Nature (WWF), the International Union for Conservation of Nature (IUCN), and the Indonesian Government's Directorate General of Forest Protection and Nature Conservation initiated conservation strategies in 1980 and have since cultivated a network of international assistance that has worked to protect the unique natural environment and biological composition of the area.[48] Lorentz National Park in the Province of Papua was listed as a national park in 1997, was added to the World Heritage List as a natural site in 1999, and is now the largest conservation area in Southeast Asia.[49]

FIGURE 14.9 Indigenous buildings such as those of Yalis village of Serkasi, Papua province, have been threatened by incursions of modernity since discovery by the wider world in the 1930s.

However, the mediation between indigenous cultures, tourism and modern developmental forces continuously threatens native traditions. The influx of Christian missionaries in 1954,[50] Japanese, Australian and US troops during World War II, and Javanese Indonesians during multiple government-initiated transmigration programs has slowly diluted the indigenous population and weakened their political representation.[51] Eagerness for independence has existed within native Papuans since their adoption into Indonesia[52] a situation that escalated into the Papuan Spring, a period between 1998 and 2000 in which numerous pro-independence activists formed a wider and more connected movement.[53] The struggle for an amicable solution and the implications of such remain to be seen, yet the Dani culture has mostly persisted.

In 1963, filmmaker Robert Gardner produced *Dead Birds*, an anthropological documentary centered on the Dani people, and published a book, *Gardens of War* (1977), comprised of the photographs he took during his visit. Aside from this film, a statue of a Dani warrior in the capital city of Wamena,[54] and the handicrafts sold in tourist markets, little historic documentation of this traditional culture and its architecture exists today.

The vastness of Indonesia likely contains the longest and most varied evidence of human history in Asia. Ironically, Indonesia's situation along the earthquake- and volcano-prone Pacific Ring of Fire has also posed threats to its inhabitants probably longer than any other place on Earth. And such geological threats persist from the northwestern tip of the country to its easternmost point, as was evidenced by the devastation of Banda Aceh in Sumatra due to the Indian Ocean tsunami in January 2004 and threats posed by the eruption of Mt. Umsini and associated earthquakes in Irian Jaya in September 2015. In addition, the usual threats to Indonesia's cultural patrimony in the form of natural and human actions have also had their negative effects. Despite this and due to the work of heritage conservationists, the rich cultural heritage of Indonesia continues to thrive, with its rich surviving and conserved architectural heritage being testament to its endurance.

Notes

1. World Monuments Fund/US ICOMOS. "Indonesia: Crossroads of Civilizations, Since the Beginning of Man." *Trails to Tropical Treasures: A Tour of ASEAN's Cultural Heritage* (New York: World Monuments Fund, 1992), 15–19.
2. As of 2013, Indonesia's population was just under 250 million persons.
3. This brief period of British rule allowed Thomas Stamford Raffles to conduct some of the earliest surveys of the Borobudur ruins in eastern Java.
4. Phil Grabsky. *The Lost Temple of Java* (London: Seven Dials, 2000), 62.
5. *National Geographic*. "Borobudur Temple Compounds." Web. http://travel.nationalgeographic.com/travel/world-heritage/borobudur-temple/. Accessed May 19, 2016.
6. William Chapman. *A Heritage of Ruins: The Ancient Sites of Southeast Asia and their Conservation* (Honolulu: University of Hawai'i Press, 2013), 48.
7. Bruno Dagens. *Angkor: The Heart of an Asian Empire* (New York: Abrams, 1989), 108.
8. R. Soekmono. *New Light on Some Borobudur Problems* (Jakarta: Archaeological Institute of the Republic of Indonesia, 1969), 3.
9. UNESCO. *The Restoration of Borobudur* (Paris: UNESCO, 2005).
10. Chapman, 52–53.
11. UNESCO, 201.
12. Daigor Chihara. *Hindu-Buddhist Architecture in Southeast Asia* (New York: E.J. Brill, 1996).
13. UNESCO, 206.
14. He succeeded the first head of the Commission, J.L.A. Brandes.
15. R. Soekmono. "Archaeological Research in Indonesia: A Historical Survey," *Asian Perspectives: A Journal of Archaeology and Prehistory of Asia and the Pacific* 12 (1969): 94–96.
16. During the remainder of the twentieth century over 3,000 sites were documented and around 1,600 were restored, constituting a considerably successful period for conservation activity. World Monuments Fund/US ICOMOS, 17.
17. Chapman, 51.
18. Ibid., 54.
19. UNESCO, 204–205.

20 Edi Sedyawati, in Miguel Angel Corzo (ed.), *The Future of Asia's Past: Preservation of the Architectural Heritage of Asia: Summary of an International Conference Held in Chiang Mai, Thailand, January 11–14, 1995* (Marina del Rey, CA: Getty Conservation Institute, 1995).

21 Haryati Soebadio. *Cultural Policy in Indonesia.* (Paris: UNESCO, 1985), 16.

22 The Southeast Asian Ministers of Education Organization Regional Centre for Archaeology and Fine Arts, established in 1978 and hosted by the Government of Thailand.

23 Up to 90 percent of Borobudur's tourists are domestic visitors.

24 Wiendu Nuryanti. "Heritage Conservation: New Alliances for Past, Present and Future." Unpublished paper delivered at the World Monuments Fund conference on Heritage Conservation in South and Southeast Asia, Colombo, Sri Lanka, July 28–30, 2004.

25 Devi Rosa Kausar. "Tracing the Relevance of Borobudur for Socio-Economic Development through Tourism" in Jamie Kaminski, Angela M. Benson and David Arnold (eds.), *Contemporary Issues in Cultural Heritage Tourism.* (London: Routledge, 2013), 208.

26 Kausar, 210.

27 Chapman, 66–67.

28 Kausar, 211.

29 Sugita Katyal and Adhityani Arga. "Global Warming Threatens Indonesia's Borobudur Temple." Reuters. September 6, 2007. Web. http://uk.reuters.com/article/2007/09/06/global-warming-indonesia-idUKNOA63591320070906. Accessed August 22, 2014.

30 Indonesian Heritage Trust. *Guidelines for Managing Post-Disaster Conservation of Heritage Buildings, Case Study: Padang* (Jakarta: Indonesian Heritage Trust, 2011).

31 The World Bank. "Indonesia: A Reconstruction Chapter Ends Eight Years after the Tsunami." December 26, 2012. Web. www.worldbank.org/en/news/feature/2012/12/26/indonesia-reconstruction-chapter-ends-eight-years-after-the-tsunami. Accessed August 22, 2014.

32 UNESCO. "Cultural Landscape of Bali Province: The Subak System as a Manifestation of the Tri Hita Karana Philosophy." 2012. Web. http://whc.unesco.org/en/list/1194. Accessed August 22, 2014.

33 UNESCO. "State of Conservation Report: Cultural Landscape of Bali Province: The Subak System as a Manifestation of the Tri Hita Karana Philosophy." 2014. Web. http://whc.unesco.org/en/soc/2815. Accessed August 22, 2014.

34 Shasha Deng. "Bali Tourism Association Urges to Address Traffic Congestion." Xinhua News Global Edition. December 13, 2011. Web. http://news.xinhuanet.com/english/world/2011-12/13/c_131303721.htm. Accessed August 22, 2014.

35 L. Harper and E. Pangdjaja (eds.). "IBA Brief: Bali, Indonesia." Proceedings of the Culture Counts conference held in Florence, Italy, October 1999. (Washington, DC: World Bank, 1999), 19–20.

36 The full text of the Charter is online here: www.international.icomos.org/charters/indonesia-charter.pdf.

37 Laretna T. Adishakti. "Building Alliances in Indonesia." Unpublished paper delivered at the World Monuments Fund conference on Heritage Conservation in South and Southeast Asia, Colombo, Sri Lanka, July 28–30, 2004.

38 By some accounts, 200,000 East Timorians – as much as 25 percent of the population – perished during the Indonesian occupation due to violence or famine. BBC News. "East Timor Country Profile." 2015. Web. www.bbc.com/news/world-asia-pacific-14919009. Accessed January 6, 2016.

39 The UN administered Timor-Leste for two years following the withdrawal of the Indonesian forces. UNESCO. *Timor-Leste – UNESCO Country Programming Document, 2009–2013.* (Jakarta: UNESCO Jakarta Office, 2009), 7.

40 The population of 1.2 million traces its origins to the indigenous Melanesian and Malayo-Polynesian people, along with mainland Asian, European and Arabic roots from its centuries as part of the Southeast Asian trade network.

41 State Secretariat of Art and Culture. Web. www.cultura.gov.tl/en/institution/team. Accessed May 19, 2016.

42 UNESCO, 17. Web. http://www.unesco.org/new/en/jakarta/about-this-office/regional-networks Accessed 5 January 2016.

43 Funding from UNESCO and Trust Fund for East Timor. "Uma Fukun Timor – East Timor Cultural Center, Dili, East Timor." *Australian Institute for the Conservation of Cultural Material* 86 (March 2003), 1. Web. https://aiccm.org.au/sites/default/files/NationalNewsletter_86_Mar2003_0.pdf. Accessed January 6, 2016.

44 State Secretariat for Arts and Culture – Timor-Leste. "Projects." 2015. Web. www.cultura.gov.tl/en/institution/projects. Accessed January 6, 2016.

45 Cecilia Assis and Robyn Sloggett. "Developing Museum to Museum Cultural Engagement between Australia and Timor-Leste." Web. www.tlstudies.org/pdfs/TLSA%20Conf%202011/chp_21.pdf. Accessed June 2, 2016.

46 David Hicks. *Rhetoric and the Decolonization and Recolonization of East Timor*. (London: Routledge, 2014), 15.
47 Dutchmen Hendrikus Albertus Lorentz and Captain Van Overeem encountered the Dani in 1909 and 1921, respectively, but the meetings with Archbold and his subsequent write-up in a 1941 issue of *National Geographic* exposed the Dani to a worldwide audience. "The 11 Things that Have Changed the Dani Tribe of Papua." WowShack. February 14, 2015. Web. www.wowshack.com/the-11-things-that-have-changed-the-dani-tribe-of-papua/. Accessed December 24, 2015.
48 Ronald G. Petocz. *Conservation and Development in Irian Jaya: A Strategy for Rational Resource Utilization*. (The Netherlands: E.J. Brill, 1989), 117–121.
49 UNESCO. "Lorentz National Park." Web. http://whc.unesco.org/en/list/955. Accessed December 24, 2015.
50 Andrew Buckser and Stephen D. Glazier. *The Anthropology of Religious Conversion*. (Lanham, MD: Rowman & Littlefield, 2003), 55–68.
51 Paul Sillitoe. *Social Change in Melanesia: Development and History*. (Cambridge: Cambridge University Press, 2000), 235–236.
52 The years between 1963 and 1969 were planned as a transitional period from Dutch to Indonesian rule over the region. In 1969, the government held a vote among the Papuan people for or against assimilation into Indonesia, known as the "Act of Free Choice." Many have accused the government of using forceful tactics to gain votes against Papuan independence, which has become the basis of the liberationist movement in the region. Conditions have become more severe and the area is currently held under heavy military control. Richard Chauvel, *Constructing Papuan Nationalism: History, Ethnicity, and Adaptation*. (Washington, DC: East-West Center Washington, 2005); and Gemima Harvey, "The Human Tragedy of West Papua." *The Diplomat*. January 15, 2014. Web. http://thediplomat.com/2014/01/the-human-tragedy-of-west-papua/. Accessed May 19, 2016.
53 Alexander Zaitchik. "Illusions of Grandeur." *Foreign Policy*. Web. http://foreignpolicy.com/2015/05/15/illusions-of-grandeur-john-anari-tom-bleming-west-papua/. Accessed December 24, 2015.
54 The statue displays the warrior in a traditional *koteka*, or penis sheath. As part of *Operasi Koteka*, the Indonesian government provided modern-day clothing to the Dani intending to separate them from their traditional clothing. Younger generations typically dress in contemporary fashions. Larry L. Naylor. *Culture and Change: An Introduction*. (Westport, CT: Greenwood Publishing, 1996), 116.

Further reading

Adishakti, Laretna T. 2004. "Building Alliances in Indonesia." Unpublished paper delivered at the World Monuments Fund conference on Heritage Conservation in South and Southeast Asia, Colombo, Sri Lanka, July 28–30, 2004.

Affandy, Frances B. and Ahmad Rida Soemardi (eds.). 1999. *Monuments and Sites: Indonesia*. Report of the Indonesian National Committee of the International Council on Monuments and Sites. Bandung: ICOMOS Indonesia/Bandung Society for Heritage Conservation.

Anom, I. Gusti Ngurah, and Samidi. 1995. "Preservation and Presentation Management of Borobudur." Paper presented to the international conference *The Future of Asia's Past: Preservation of the Architectural Heritage of Asia*, Chiang Mai, Thailand, January 11–14, 1995. Summarized in Corzo, *Future of Asia's Past*, 11–14.

Atmadi, Parmono. 1999. "The Conservation Projects of Borobudur and Prambanan Temples," in Frances B. Affandy and Ahmad Rida Soemardi (eds.), *Monuments and Sites: Indonesia*. Report of the Indonesian National Committee of the International Council on Monuments and Sites. Bandung: ICOMOS Indonesia/Bandung Society for Heritage Conservation, 27–31.

AusHeritage and ASEAN-COCI (eds.). 2001. "Cultural Management Profile, Indonesia," in *ASEAN-Australia Project: Development of an ASEAN Regional Policy and Strategy for Cultural Heritage Management*. Melbourne: Cultural Heritage Center for Asia and the Pacific.

Chapman, William. 2013. *A Heritage of Ruins: The Ancient Sites of Southeast Asia and Their Conservation*. Honolulu: University of Hawai'i Press.

Chihara, Daigor. 1996. *Hindu-Buddhist Architecture in Southeast Asia*. New York: E.J. Brill.

Codrington, Stephen. 2005. *Planet Geography*. Sydney: Solid Star Press, 725–748.

Corzo, Miguel Angel (ed.). 1995. *The Future of Asia's Past: Preservation of the Architectural Heritage of Asia: Summary of an International Conference Held in Chiang Mai, Thailand, January 11–14, 1995*. Marina del Rey, CA: Getty Conservation Institute.

Cribb, Robert. 2000. *Historical Atlas of Indonesia*. London: Routledge Curzon.

Deng, Shasha. 2011. "Bali Tourism Association Urges to Address Traffic Congestion." Xinhua News Global Edition. December 13. Web. http://news.xinhuanet.com/english/world/2011-12/13/c_131303721.htm. Accessed August 22, 2014.

Dumarçay, Jacques. 1983. *Borobudur*. 3rd edition. Translated by Michael Smithies. Kuala Lumpur: Oxford University Press.

———. 1991. *The Temples of Java*. 2nd edition. Translated and edited by Michael Smithies. Singapore: Oxford University Press.

Friend, Theodore. 2003. *Indonesian Destinies*. Cambridge, MA: Harvard University Press.

Gallop. 1995. *Early Views of Indonesia: Drawings from the British Library = Pemandangan Indonesia di Masa Lampau: Seni Gambar dari British Library*. In English and Indonesian. Honolulu: University of Hawai'i Press.

Gomez, Luis O. and Hiram W. Woodward (eds.). 1981. *Barabudur: History and Significance of a Buddhist Monument*. Berkeley Buddhist Studies 2. Berkeley: University of California Press.

Grabsky, Phil. 2000. *The Lost Temple of Java*. London: Seven Dials.

Harper, L. and E. Pangdjaja (eds.). 1999. "IBA Brief: Bali, Indonesia." Proceedings from Culture Counts conference held in Florence, Italy, October 1999. Washington, DC: World Bank, 19–20.

ICCROM. 2000. "Indonesia," in ICCROM, *A World Heritage Strategy for Southeast Asia*.

Indonesian Heritage Trust. 2011. *Guidelines for Managing Post-Disaster Conservation of Heritage Buildings, Case Study: Padang*. Jakarta: Indonesian Heritage Trust.

Katyal, Sugita and Adhityani Arga. 2007. "Global Warming Threatens Indonesia's Borobudur Temple." Reuters. September 6. Web. http://uk.reuters.com/article/2007/09/06/global-warming-indonesia-idUKNOA635913 20070906. Accessed August 22, 2014.

Kausar, Devi Rosa. 2013. "Tracing the Relevance of Borobudur for Socio-Economic Development through Tourism," in Jamie Kaminski, Angela M. Benson and David Arnold (eds.), *Contemporary Issues in Cultural Heritage Tourism*. London: Routledge, 200–216.

Kempers, A.J. Bernet. 1976. *Ageless Borobudur: Buddhist Mystery in Stone, Decay and Restoration, Mendut and Pawon, Folklife in Ancient Java*. Wassenaar, Netherlands: Servire.

———. 1991. *Monumental Bali: Introduction to Balinese Archeology and Guide to the Monuments*. Hong Kong: Periplus.

Miksic, John N. 1980. "Classical Archaeology in Sumatra," *Indonesia* 30 (October): 42–66.

———. 2004. *Borobudur: Golden Tales of the Buddhas*. Hong Kong: Periplus.

Ministry of Culture and Tourism (Indonesia) and UNESCO. 2007. *Action Plan for the Rehabilitation of Earthquake-Affected Prambanan World Heritage Site (Including Prambanan and Sewu Temples), May 2007*. Jakarta: Ministry of Culture and Tourism/UNESCO.

Munoz, Paul Michel. 2006. *Early Kingdoms of the Indonesian Archipelago and the Malay Peninsula*. Singapore: Editions Didier Millet.

Nas, Peter J.M. (ed.). 1986. *The Indonesian City: Studies in Urban Development and Planning*. Dordrecht, Holland: Foris Publications.

———. (ed.). 2007. *The Past in the Present: Architecture in Indonesia*. Leiden: KITLV Press.

Ricklefs, M.C. 2008. *A History of Modern Indonesia since c. 1200*. 4th edition. Palo Alto, CA: Stanford University Press.

Rojpojchanarat, Vira. 1983. "Supplementary Report of Thailand for SPAFA Consultative Workshop on Restoration of Ancient Monuments," in SPAFA, *Final Report: Consultative Workshop on Restoration of Ancient Monuments, Yogyakarta, Indonesia, August 2–7, 1983*. Bangkok: SPAFA, 97–109.

Samidi. 1989. "Conservation of Historical and Archaeological Sites in Indonesia," *SPAFA Digest* 5(1): 23–30.

Schefold, Reimar, et al. (eds.). 2003. *Indonesian Houses. Volume 1: Tradition and Transformation in Vernacular Architecture*. Leiden: KITLV Press.

Schnitger, F.M. 1989. *Forgotten Kingdoms in Sumatra*. London: Oxford University Press.

Sedyawati, Edi. 1995. "Monuments Management in Indonesia." Paper presented to the international conference *The Future of Asia's Past: Preservation of the Architectural Heritage of Asia*, Chiang Mai, January 11–14, 1995. Summarized in Corzo, *Future of Asia's Past*, 11–14.

———. 1997. "Potential Challenges of Tourism: Managing the National Heritage of Indonesia," in Wiendu Nuryanti (ed.), *Tourism and Heritage Management*. Yogyakarta, Indonesia: Gadjah Mada University Press, 25–35.

Simanjuntak, Truman, et al. (eds.). 2006. *Archaeology: Indonesian Perspective: R.P. Soejono's Festschrift*. Jakarta: LIPI.

Soebadio, Haryati. 1985. *Cultural Policy in Indonesia*. Paris: UNESCO.

Soekmono, R. 1969a. *New Light on Some Borobudur Problems*. Jakarta: Archaeological Institute of the Republic of Indonesia.

———. 1969b. "Archaeological Research in Indonesia: A Historical Survey," *Asian Perspectives: A Journal of Archaeology and Prehistory of Asia and the Pacific* 12: 94–96.

SPAFA. 1985. *Final Report: Consultative Workshop on Archaeological and Environmental Studies on Srivijaya, Jakarta. Padang, Prapat and Medan, Indonesia. September 16–30, 1985*. Bangkok: SPAFA.

Sutaba, Made. 1998. "Preservation of Living Monuments in Bali," *SPAFA Journal* 8(2) (May–August): 5–9.

Taylor, Jean Gelman. 2003. *Indonesia: Peoples and Histories*. New Haven, CT: Yale University Press.

Titin, Fatimah, Kiyoko Kanki and Lareina T. Adishakti. 2005. "Borobudur: Recent History of Its Cultural Landscape: Toward the Sustainable Rural Development as the Landscape Rehabilitation." Paper presented to the international seminar *Cultural Landscapes in the 21st Century*, Newcastle-upon-Tyne, UK, April 11–16, 2005.

Tjahjono, Gunawan. 1999. *Indonesian Heritage Series 6: Architecture*. Singapore: Archipelago Press.

Tjandrasasmita, Uka. 1980. "Restoration of Historical Monuments in Indonesia," in SPAFA, *Final Report: Workshop on Techniques of Monument Restoration, October 6–19, 1980, Yogyakarta, Indonesia*. Bangkok: SPAFA, Appendix 5c.

——. 1983. "Restoration and Conservation of Ancient Monuments in Indonesia," in SPAFA, *Final Report: Consultative Workshop on Restoration of Ancient Monuments, Yogyakarta, Indonesia, August 2–7, 1983*. Bangkok: SPAFA, 73–96.

——. 1989. "Borobudur Conservation Laboratory," in SPAFA, *Final Report: SPAFAICCROM Seminar on Conservation Standards in Southeast Asia, Bangkok, Thailand, December 11–16, 1989*. Bangkok: SPAFA, 31–36.

UNESCO. 2005. *The Restoration of Borobudur*. Paris: UNESCO.

——. 2012. "Cultural Landscape of Bali Province: The Subak System as a Manifestation of the Tri Hita Karana Philosophy." Web. http://whc.unesco.org/en/list/1194. Accessed August 22, 2014.

——. 2014. "State of Conservation Report: Cultural Landscape of Bali Province: The Subak System as a Manifestation of the Tri Hita Karana Philosophy." Web. http://whc.unesco.org/en/soc/2815. Accessed August 22, 2014.

Van Dullemen, C.J. 2010. *Tropical Modernity: Life and Work of C.P. Wolff Schoenmaker*. Amsterdam: Martien de Vletter SUN.

Voûte, Caeser and Mark Long. 2008. *Borobudur: Pyramid of the Cosmic Buddha*. New Delhi: O.K. Printworld.

Wijaya, Made. 2002. *Architecture of Bali: A Source Book of Traditional and Modern Forms*. Honolulu: University of Hawai'i Press.

The World Bank. 2012. "Indonesia: A Reconstruction Chapter Ends Eight Years after the Tsunami." December 26. Web. www.worldbank.org/en/news/feature/2012/12/26/indonesia-reconstruction-chapter-ends-eight-years-after-the-tsunami. Accessed August 22, 2014.

World Monuments Fund/US ICOMOS. 1992. "Indonesia: Crossroads of Civilizations, Since the Beginning of Man." *Trails to Tropical Treasures: A Tour of ASEAN's Cultural Heritage*. New York: World Monuments Fund, 15–19.

15

THE PHILIPPINES

The Philippines consists of more than 7,000 islands, geographically separated from the rest of Southeast Asia by the South China and Celebes seas. It was thus largely left to develop on its own for centuries, removed from the Hindu, Buddhist and Islamic influences that affected its neighbors to the west. As such, the islands largely lack the ancient indigenous monumental architecture found on the Asian mainland and on the Indonesian archipelago.

Despite its relative isolation, the outside world eventually arrived, first Arab and Chinese traders in the ninth to twelfth centuries CE, and eventually the Spanish in 1521. Today's Philippines society is a complex blend of seventy ethnic groups that speak eighty different languages and dialects.[1]

FIGURE 15.1 The Tabon cave complex in Palawan, found in 1962, contains human remains dating to ca. 22,000 BCE. Its discovery raised awareness of the long prehistory of the Philippines and the responsibilities of heritage conservation in general.

The famed Portuguese navigator Ferdinand Magellan did not survive his encounter with the Philippines, but perished in the service of Charles I of Spain on the island of Mactan in 1521. Nevertheless, the archipelago became part of the Spanish Empire by the end of the sixteenth century. Iberian influence and subsequent missionary activity resulted in the conversion of many Filipinos to Roman Catholicism, and to the construction of numerous monumental churches, which reached its apex between the sixteenth and eighteenth centuries.

With administrative connections to Mexico, the Spanish padres brought church construction styles from the Americas and Europe, resulting in a hybrid style known today as Philippine Baroque. Nearly four centuries of Spanish colonization has resulted in a rich array of forts, churches and administrative buildings, many of which survive despite widespread destruction due to fierce fighting throughout the islands during World War II. With the Treaty of Paris and conclusion of the Spanish-American War in 1898, the Philippines' ruling power shifted from Spain to the United States, ushering in a new era of colonialism and heritage management.

The first notable step toward heritage protection taken by the Philippines' colonial government was made in 1933, when it established the Philippine Historical Research and Markers Committee (PHRMC), which ultimately took charge of identifying and purchasing significant sites and objects. The PHRMC was succeeded by the Philippine Historical Committee in 1937. The PHC's activities were assumed by the Japanese administration of the Philippines until the PHC was restored in 1947.[2]

Due to its deep indigenous prehistory, much of the early heritage conservation effort in the Philippines took place within the sphere of archaeology. Americans Henry Otley Beyer and Robert Bradley Fox worked throughout the Philippines in the twentieth century on various prehistoric archaeological surveys as well as on the development of the National Museum and archaeology program at the University of the Philippines. Beyer's work on the Rizal-Bulacan Archaeological Survey in the 1920s and 1930s and Fox's efforts at the Tabon caves complex in the 1950s and 1960s enhanced awareness around, and scholarship of, the Philippines' cultural heritage.[3] As a result of these projects and a subsequent increase in illegal artifact sales and export, the first cultural heritage legislation, the Cultural Properties Preservation and Protection Act, went into effect in 1966.[4] Due to the damage sustained to historic buildings and urban areas during World War II, especially those in Manila, and growing concerns for the protection of surviving historic buildings and heritage areas throughout the country, legal protection of the nation's historic buildings and sites was also an aim of the initial heritage protection legislation.

The National Historical Commission (NHC) replaced the PHC in 1965. Throughout the late 1960s and early 1970s the NHC was very active. It established a modern heritage conservation framework for the Philippines, including a series of specialized centers that among other things focused on materials conservation and architectural conservation; a National Registry of Historic Structures; and a system of house museums. During the Ferdinand Marcos administration, in 1971, the NHC was supplanted by the National Historical Institute (NHI), which carried on the NHC's cultural promotion and maintenance duties, from architecture to dance, folk art, music and drama.

The end of the Marcos years in the late 1980s and political turmoil of the early 1990s created an uncertain period for heritage management activity, but in 1992 President Corazon Aquino signed a law to consolidate all legislation under one heading. Republic Act No. 7356 also created a National Endowment Fund for Culture and the Arts (NEFCA) and the National Commission for Culture and the Arts (NCCA).[5] The NCCA was created as the umbrella organization to administer funds for the NEFCA and to oversee the operations of the National Museum, the NHC, the Cultural Center for the Philippines, the National Library and the National Archives of the Philippines.[6]

In 2010 the NHC was reorganized into the National Historical Commission of the Philippines (NHCP), which is presently one of three government agencies mandated to oversee architectural conservation, heritage studies and promotion in the Philippines. The NHCP is organized into five divisions (Finance & Administrative, Historic Preservation, Historic Sites & Education, Research, Publications & Heraldry, and Materials Research Conservation), several of which were established under the earlier NHI.[7] The Historic Preservation Division maintains a registry of over 500 historic resources, including heritage zones and individual sites, structures, caves, landscapes and memorial shrines. The HPD also plans and executes architectural conservation projects in the Philippines, publishes best-practice standards and guidelines, and provides technical assistance to other government entities dealing with heritage sites or research.[8]

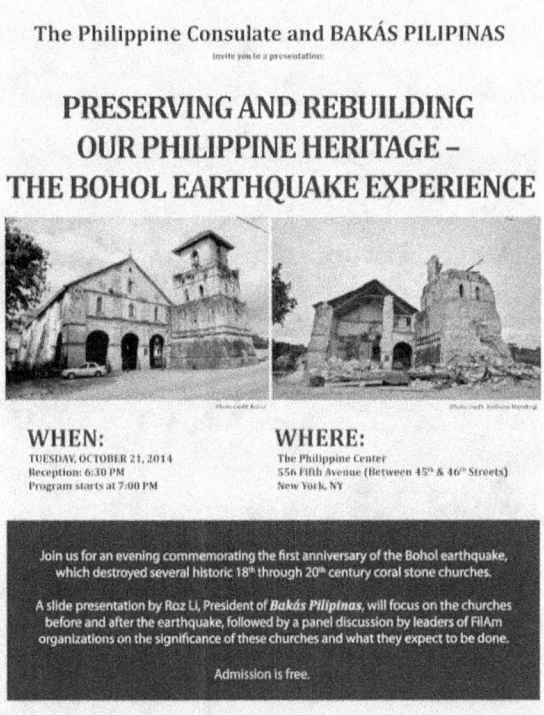

FIGURE 15.2 Establishment of the National Historical Commission in 1965 and later its Materials Conservation Center in Manila introduced effective national capacity to conserve the physical heritage of the Philippines. Since 2010 the National Historical Commission of the Philippines has been the country's lead agency for architectural conservation, heritage studies and heritage advocacy. It is overseeing restoration of coral stone Baclayon Church (1596) in Bohol after the Bohol Earthquake in October 2013 in partnership with the national heritage advocacy group Bakás Pilipinas. A call for international technical assistance and funding assistance was promoted by Bakás Pilipinas in New York City on the first anniversary of the event.

Despite the robust system for heritage management at the national level, historic sites ranging from rock shelters to the teeming streets of Manila struggle with a wide variety of challenges. Population density and major pressure for economic development continue to hamper conservation-sensitive planning in this country of nearly 100 million people. Manila itself is often cited as a case study in unplanned, uncontrolled growth and subsequent urban blight, which includes the widespread loss of considerable historic cultural assets. Although precise conservation regulations exist across the Philippines, enforcement frequently falls by the wayside in places like Manila, due in part to a lack of law enforcement, limited public awareness and support, and political conflicts of interest.[9]

The tale of conservation efforts in Manila sadly includes the near total destruction of the city during US air raids and ground combat in order to drive out Japanese forces during World War II. Nearly all of the city's colonial core, known as the Intramuros, was damaged or destroyed, including most of its sixteenth-century fortifications and many of the cross-cultural hybrid architecture that had developed there due to the presence of its Chinese, Spanish, Mexican and indigenous residents.

Centuries before the American colonial period (1898–1946) the Intramuros thrived as a regional trading hub, governmental and religious center. Its decline began in 1904 when American architect and planner Daniel Burnham helped establish a new urban center, the Extramuros, outside the Spanish walls. The Extramuros eventually drew residents and businesses out of the traditional narrow, grid street plans and into the grand avenues and axes of the City Beautiful- style suburbs.[10] After the catastrophe of World War II many squatters moved into the ruined historic center, a phenomenon that still troubles the city today.[11]

Although in the post-war years Manila itself has expanded to more than twice its pre-war area, the Intramuros was never rebuilt. As of 1979, the year before it was declared a national heritage area, 40 percent of Manila's historic core was still unrestored or underdeveloped, with the remaining area having been taken over by light industry and warehousing. In the late 1990s, over 1,500 squatter families still lived in the compact Intramuros district, frequently occupying available plots of vacant land, taking advantage of the government's slow pace in rebuilding or revitalizing parts of the area.[12]

During the 1980s a large-scale government effort to rebuild and revitalize the Intramuros was launched with the establishment of the Intramuros Administration, a special planning organization that spearheaded efforts to issue new building codes, and design guidelines and plans for aligning

FIGURE 15.3a, b and c The Gate of Santiago at Intramuros in Manila as it appeared ca. 1900 (a), during World War II (b) and after subsequent restoration (c).

FIGURE 15.4 Urban rehabilitation projects accomplished by the Intramuros Administration in the Intramuros historic center of Manila have entailed a variety of approaches to architectural conservation including the addition of new upper storeys to damaged earlier structures.

conservation activities with long-term planning objectives. The Administration, today an arm of the Department of Tourism, actively encourages the rebuilding of Spanish colonial-style structures. It provides historic plans and construction assistance for property owners, and restricts insensitive development in an attempt to fulfill the district's reputation as Manila's heritage center.

The Intramuros Administration's top-down planning approach eventually failed, largely due to a lack of participation on the part of landowners and residents and an inability on its part to effectively communicate the benefits associated with historically minded development.[13] As a result, the Intramuros remains largely underused, a painful symbol of the challenges facing urban rehabilitation and heritage awareness in the Philippines.

While the attempts at revitalizing Manila's historic core remain unfulfilled, the Philippines did successfully nominate three cultural World Heritage Sites in the 1990s: the Baroque Churches of the Philippines (which includes the Church of San Agustin in the Intramuros), the 2,000-year-old Rice Terraces of the Cordilleras, and the Spanish colonial town of Vigan.

Located approximately 450 km from Manila on the northern end of Luzon, the country's largest island, Vigan is recognized as one of the best-preserved Spanish colonial towns in Asia, due to a largely intact sixteenth century street grid and broad collection of contributing buildings. In addition to the strong Spanish architectural influence, the city exhibits elements of the town planning decreed by the Spanish Empire in its Law of the Indies, in that it has two main central plazas, Plaza Salcedo and Plaza Burgos, facing its cathedral. Prior to the arrival of the Spanish, a predecessor coastal settlement had been an active regional trading port due to its strategic location on the western coast of North Luzon facing the South China Sea. Thus, Vigan's architectural heritage reflects an infusion of Chinese and indigenous Ilocano building designs.

In 2012 UNESCO officially recognized Vigan as a model of best practice for World Heritage Site management, noting its consistently enforced local and national legislation, the development and use of design guidelines and maintenance schedules for the historic town, and – most significantly – the local community's success in developing stakeholder participation in conservation activities.[14]

FIGURE 15.5 The historic town of Vigan contains the most intact Spanish colonial town in the Philippines in part due to its location in the north, which insulated it from World War II damage. Its success as a well-conserved historic town is also due its administrators engaging local stakeholders in their conservation efforts and leading development through conservation-based policies.

One of the most unusual examples of Spanish colonial church building that occurred in the Philippines over a period of nearly three centuries is one of its latest, the minor basilica of San Sebastián in Manila. Before its construction in 1891, four previous basilicas had stood on its location before each was destroyed by fire and earthquakes. Intent, therefore, on designing this basilica for durability Spanish architect Genaro Palacios built a fire- and earthquake-resistant structure made entirely of steel, using Burgos Cathedral in Burgos, Spain, for his design inspiration.

San Sebastián's Gothic revival-style wall surfaces and most of its ornaments are thus made entirely of cast iron and steel. Prefabricated in Binche, Belgium and transported in eight separate shipments, its walls were designed to be filled with a sand, cement and stone mixture. The finishing touches, mostly in *tromp l'oeil*, were done by local artisans including installation of its stained glass windows that were imported from Germany.[15]

Despite the durability of its latest design, by the 1990s San Sebastián was showing material failure due to corrosion. Since 2010 it has been the subject of an international appeal to restore it, using state-of-the-art architectural conservation techniques. The US-based not-for-profit *Bakás Pilipinas*, the Philippine Historic Preservation Society, has led the charge in this technically complicated effort that remains in process. The Society also responded as an international convener to help garner technical assistance and funding to restore several coral stone historic churches affected by the Bohol Earthquake of October 15, 2013, with the 1596 Baclayon Church, the second oldest in the Philippines, serving as a symbol of the project.

The Rice Terraces of the Philippine Cordilleras are notable as the first "living cultural landscape" named to the World Heritage List due to the unique overlay of human agricultural practices and natural forms that developed over nearly 2,000 years and that are still in use today. Five clusters of actively cultivated rice terraces comprising some 4,000 square miles (10,360 square kilometers) are distributed across four municipalities on the island of Luzon, presenting challenges for implementation of a management plan, maintenance of site boundaries and protection of the frequently fragile agricultural economies upon which the farming communities depend.

For millennia, Cordilleras' traditional cultivation techniques and practices have been passed on generation to generation. However, in recent times the decline in agricultural profits has led farmers to seek city jobs, a trend that has contributed to the deterioration of the terraces. This combination of challenges led to the Philippine government's request that the rice terraces be placed on UNESCO's 2001 List of World Heritage in Danger; the World Monuments Fund also supported the call for action by adding the site to its 2000 World Monuments Watch list.[16]

Over a decade of intensive support from the local Cordillera community, who were not supported by the national government despite international community assistance, has resulted in the removal of the site from the UNESCO World Heritage in Danger list in 2012, due to improvements in its management practices, establishment of a technical exchange and cooperation program with the World Heritage Site of Cinque Terre (Italy) and the allocation of US$70,000 annually from a multinational hydroelectric facility for maintenance of the terraces.[17] Although the site's recovery is cause for celebration, it continues to be threatened by typhoons, changes in the availability of water for irrigation and rural and urban migration patterns that threaten to disrupt the traditional farming practices that have been passed along through the millennia.

FIGURE 15.6 The stone and earthen rice terraces of Banaue in Ifugao province in the northern central Philippine Cordilleras are marvels of agricultural practices that date back two millennia. The draw of higher paying jobs in the cities in recent years has decreased the usage and maintenance of these systems of terraces that demand cooperation among farmers. An international consortium of power companies, called e8, involved with construction of a hydroelectric dam downstream on the Ambangal River has shown corporate responsibility towards helping with the preservation of these distinct cultural heritage landscapes.

World War II destruction: its legacy in the Pacific

The war in the Pacific Theater lasted from December 7, 1941 to August 14, 1945. It was a tremendously destructive period for the people and cultural heritage sites in the greater Pacific Rim, from the Aleutian and Hawai'ian islands, to the southwest Pacific Islands, and in nearly all east and southeast Asian nations. If one includes the early imperial Japanese army invasions of Manchuria and eastern China, the War in the Pacific can be said to have started ten years earlier, in 1931. Modes of destruction ranged from conventional aerial and naval attacks of Pearl Harbor by the Japanese on December 7, 1941 to the nuclear bombings of Hiroshima and Nagasaki by the American forces on August 6 and 9, 1945. The most heavily contested battle zones were decimated by the unprecedented power of twentieth century weaponry. The estimated loss of life of World War II in the Pacific was 6 million military deaths and 26 million civilian deaths.[18]

While most targets during World War II in the Pacific were considered to be of strategic importance there was widespread "collateral" damage to numerous cities, towns and rural areas that contained buildings and artifacts of historic cultural significance. The city of Manila was largely destroyed in both ground fighting and aerial bombardment over thirty days beginning on February 3, 1945 in what was the Pacific War's first episode of urban combat. Earlier, in China, the cities and rural populations of Chongquing, Guangzhou, Shanghai and Nanking suffered greatly under Japanese invasion.[19]

In the final six months of the war the full brunt of US airpower was felt in Japan's cities. As American forces closed in on Japan from May through August 1945 long-range bombers reduced large sections of nearly seventy cities to rubble through "area bombing." According to Japanese police statistics there were sixty-five raids on Tokyo between December 6, 1944 and August 13, 1945, which resulted in 137,582 casualties with 787,145 homes and buildings destroyed and 2,625,279 people displaced.[20] The nighttime incendiary bombing of Tokyo on March 9–10 was particularly destructive, affecting 84.7 percent of the area of the city according to the US Strategic Bombing Survey.[21] The Bombing Survey concluded, for events prior to August 6, 1945, "probably more persons lost their lives by fire in Tokyo in a six-hour period than at any time in the history of man."[22]

Following the Tokyo offensive of March 9–10, 1945, the firebombing was extended nationwide. In the ten-day period beginning on March 9, 9,373 tons of ordnance destroyed 31 square miles of Tokyo, Nagoya, Osaka and Kobe. Overall bombing strikes destroyed 40 percent of

FIGURE 15.7 Tokyo along the Sumida River after area bombing, March 9–10, 1945.

the sixty-six Japanese cities targeted. Through such raids Tokyo alone eventually lost an area of some 56 square miles.

The final dramatic acts of destruction responsible for ending the war were the bombing of Hiroshima and Nagasaki on August 6 and August 9, 1945, respectively. The roughly circular zone of destruction caused by the atomic weapon used at Hiroshima alone covered some 4.4 square miles (11.4 square kilometers), including 1 square mile (2.6 square kilometers) that was completely decimated except for some concrete framed buildings, with the remainder of the zone lost through the ensuing "fire-wind" that caused an estimated 70–80 thousand deaths, with an equal number of injured.[23] Along with the comparable atomic bombing of Nagasaki three days later, World War II ended on August 14 and 15, 1945 and the Atomic Age began.

Despite its role as the greatest calamity of the twentieth century, there is a relative paucity of World War II commemorative sites focused on the Pacific Theater. There are Pacific War memorials in the cities and towns of several nations and a number of museums and interpretive centers at sites where war-related history occurred, as at Pearl Harbor and Hiroshima. Likewise, there are several museums beyond the Pacific region that memorialize and interpret the war such as the World War II Museum in New Orleans, Louisiana, the Nimitz Museum in Fredericksburg, Texas and the Darwin Military Museum in Australia. There are additionally numerous battle monuments and plaques across the Pacific region. However, it appears that more sites of the Pacific War, and surviving war materiel, could and should be preserved and commemorated before all first-hand memory is gone and the more exposed sites and artifacts are lost to pillaging and natural deterioration. Challenges to such action could be attributed to the relative proximity of World War II to the present time, that it represents a history that some may prefer to forget, and that its sites are spread across such a vast area in sometimes remote places. Nonetheless the opportunity – and the responsibility – exists to do more in the way of protecting heritage of all kinds associated with a war that significantly changed the course of world history.

FIGURE 15.8a, b and c Well-preserved and presented Pacific War heritage includes the Atomdome (a), the Hiroshima Peace Memorial Park (1954) by architect Kenzō Tange and Memorial Cenotaph (1952) (b). Pacific War-damaged buildings yet to be stabilized, restored and preserved include sites in the Intramuros of Manila (see Figures 15.3 and 15.4). Remembrances of war that remain *in situ* include the stabilized and presented ruins of the former barracks at Corregidor in Manila Bay (c).

The Philippines serves as an example of a country that has put in place an appropriate legal and institutional framework for heritage conservation projects, yet one that did not fully embrace the implications or requirements of those demands until the passing of the National Cultural Heritage Act of 2009 (RA10066), which mandated the conservation of cultural heritage and placed the responsibility on two agencies, the National Museum and the National Historical Commission of the Philippines (formerly the National Historical Institute). The law authorizes both agencies to declare and list heritage buildings, sites and monuments as either National Cultural Treasures or Important Cultural Properties. If the property is of historic significance, the responsible agency is the National Historical Commission of the Philippines (NHCP). For properties of artistic significance, the responsible agency is the National Museum. Declared properties are supervised by the appropriate agency, which oversees its state of conservation and is empowered to grant public funds for further conservation. Both the National Museum and NHCP are administratively supervised by the National Commission for Culture and the Arts (NCCA), which is the highest authority in implementing conservation of heritage in the country. RA10066 is improving the awareness of government authorities and the general public towards the necessity of conservation. Most importantly, the legislation gives the NCCA power to issue Cease and Desist Orders that halt demolition of threatened heritage until an appropriate solution can be arrived at for its conservation or adaptation into a new use.

Although the nation's colonial legacy has in some ways complicated the relationship between the modern Filipino population and its historic built environment, the consciousness that has been developed since the passing of RA10066 is evident in the increased public participation towards the protection of cultural heritage. Today the Philippines proudly supports its multi-cultural identity that with a sustained educational and public participation effort could ultimately embrace its similarly multi-faceted heritage.

Notes

1. World Monuments Fund/US ICOMOS. "The Philippines: A New Dialect Every Hundred Islands." *Trails to Tropical Treasures: A Tour of ASEAN's Cultural Heritage* (New York: World Monuments Fund, 1992), 26–31.
2. National Historical Commission of the Philippines. "NHI Through the Years." April 1, 2013. Web. http://nhcp.gov.ph/nhi-through-the-years/. Accessed August 10, 2014.
3. Wilfredo Ronquillo. "Philippines," in Tim Murray (ed.), *Encyclopedia of Archaeology: History and Discoveries* (Santa Barbara, CA: ABC-CLIO, 2001).
4. WMF/US ICOMOS, 29.
5. Ibid., 31.
6. National Commission for Culture and the Arts, Philippines. "About the NCCA." 2011. Web. www.ncca.gov.ph/about-ncca/about-ncca/about-ncca-history-mandate.php. Accessed August 14, 2014.
7. National Historical Commission of the Philippines. "NHI Through the Years." April 1, 2013. Web. http://nhcp.gov.ph/nhi-through-the-years/. Accessed August 10, 2014.
8. National Historical Commission of the Philippines. "Historic Preservation Division." 2013. Web. http://nhcp.gov.ph/historic-preservation-division/. Accessed August 10, 2014.
9. Wilkie B. Delumen. "Cultural Heritage Conservation in the Philippines: A Responsive Approach." Unpublished paper delivered at the World Monuments Fund Conference on Conservation in South and Southeast Asia, July 28–31, 2004.
10. The City Beautiful was a reform philosophy of North American architecture and urban planning during the 1890s and early 1900s with the intent of introducing beautification and monumental grandeur to cities.
11. Fergus T. Maclaren and Augusto Villalon. "Manila's Intramuros: Storming the Walls," in William S. Logan (ed.), *The Disappearing "Asian" City*. (Oxford: Oxford University Press, 2002), 4–20.
12. Ibid., 11.
13. Ibid., 19.
14. UNESCO. "Vigan, Philippines Recognized for Best Practice in World Heritage Site Management." October 25, 2012. Web. http://whc.unesco.org/en/news/948. Accessed August 19, 2014.
15. The stained glass windows were made by Heinrich Oidtmann Company in Germany. Architectural historian Ambeth Ocampo has verified reports that the famous engineer Gustave Eiffel designed the structure of the church that Genaro Palacios designed in a Gothic revival style. Howie Severino. "An Eiffel in Quiapo," *Howie Severino's Sidetrip*, GMA Network, May 5, 2006.

16   UNESCO. "World Heritage Committee Inscribes Two Sites on the List of World Heritage in Danger." December 12, 2001. Web. http://portal.unesco.org/culture/es/ev.php-. Accessed August 19, 2014.
17   World Monuments Fund. "Past Watch Site: Rice Terraces of the Philippine Cordilleras." January 2012. Web. www.wmf.org/project/rice-terraces-philippine-cordilleras. Accessed August 19, 2014. The sustainable energy company e8, which consists of ten electrical companies from G8 countries including Japan, the United States and Germany, donated $1million to create a small hydroelectric plant for Ifugao province, and partially funded a program of the Rice Terraces Conservation Fund for repair and maintenance of the terraces. "Going Green will Help Asia's Stairway to Heaven," *The Art Newspaper* 211 (March 2010), 21.
18   Wikipedia, "War in the Pacific, Casualties and Losses," 3. Web. https://en.m.wikipedia.org/wiki/Pacific War. Accessed September 2, 2015.
19   To this day, relations between China and Japan remain tense, due in part to conflict episodes during the Second Sino-Japanese War (1937–1945), hampering regional cooperation around cultural and economic activities.
20   Mark Selden. "A Forgotten Holocaust: US Bombing Strategy, the Destruction of Japanese Cities and the American Way of War from World War II to Iraq," *The Asia Pacific Journal: Japan Focus* 5(5) (2007), 2. Web. http://apjjf.org/-Mark-Selden/2414/article.html. Accessed August 30, 2015.
21   Ibid., 3.
22   Ibid.
23   "The Effect of Atomic Bombing on Hiroshima and Nagasaki," *The United States Strategic Bombing Survey*, Chapter 2, p. 3. Web. www.ibiblio.org/hyperwar/AAF/USSBS/AtomicEffects/AtomicEffects-2.html. Accessed September 4, 2015.

Further reading

Conejos, Sheila and Detlef Kammeier. 1998. *A Strategic Plan Framework for the Urban Conservation of the Downtown Area of Cebu City, Philippines*. Bangkok: AIT.

Delumen, Wilkie B. 2004. "Cultural Heritage Conservation in the Philippines: A Responsive Approach." Unpublished paper delivered at the World Monuments Fund Conference on Conservation in South and Southeast Asia, July 28–31.

Gatbonton, Mario T. (ed.). 1971. *Preservation of Cultural Heritage: Australia, China, Japan, Korea, Malaysia, New Zealand, Philippines, Thailand, Vietnam*. Seoul: HOLLYM.

Lasafin, Trinidad and Detlef Kammeier. 1993. *Urban Conservation in the Philippines: The Intramuros Project*. Bangkok: Asian Institute of Technology.

Maclaren, Fergus T. and Augusto Villalon. 2002. "Manila's Intramuros: Storming the Walls," in William S. Logan (ed.), *The Disappearing "Asian" City*. Oxford: Oxford University Press, 4–20.

Manahan, Geronimo V. 1994. *Philippine Architecture in the 20th Century*. San Juan, Manila: Kanlungan Foundation.

National Commission for Culture and the Arts, Philippines. "About the NCCA." "Historic Preservation Division." "NHI Through the Years." Web. www.ncca.gov.

Phelan, John Leddy. 1967. *The Hispanization of the Philippines*. Madison: University of Wisconsin Press.

Ronquillo, Wilfredo. 2001. "Philippines," in Tim Murray (ed.), *Encyclopedia of Archaeology: History and Discoveries*. Santa Barbara, CA: ABC-CLIO.

UNESCO. "Vigan, Philippines Recognized for Best Practice in World Heritage Site Management." "World Heritage Committee Inscribes Two Sites on the List of World Heritage in Danger." Web. http://portal.unesco.org.

Villalón, Augusto F. 2001. *Lugar: Essays on Philippine Heritage and Architecture*. Makati City, Philippines: The Bookmark.

——. 2012. "Continuing Living Traditions to Protect the Rice Terraces of the Philippine Cordilleras," in Ken Taylor and J. Lennon (eds.), *Managing Cultural Landscapes*. London: Routledge, 291–307.

Villalón, Augusto F. and Rodrigo D. Perez III. 1996. *Poet of Space: The Architecture of Leandro V. Locsin*. Manila: Cultural Center of the Philippines.

World Monuments Fund/US ICOMOS. 1992. "The Philippines: A New Dialect Every Hundred Islands." *Trails to Tropical Treasures: A Tour of ASEAN's Cultural Heritage*. New York: World Monuments Fund, 26–31.

Modern central Jakarta.

CONCLUSION TO PART III

The Southeast Asian Maritime states have long been a point of interconnectivity, both within Asia and to the wider world beyond. The region's contemporary role as one of the world's centers of Islam places it in an advantageous position to serve as a cultural bridge between Asia, Africa, the Middle East and southeastern Europe. Within Asia, the Maritime countries share much with their counterparts on the Mainland, and each has benefited from the experiences of the other in the field of heritage management. The regions also share experience with the increasing influence of cultural heritage tourism, along with major modernization drives evidenced by cities such as Singapore and Kuala Lumpur, and the forces of globalization. As on the Mainland, the Maritime nations have benefited from the positive influence of regional cooperation through ASEAN and SEAMEO SPAFA, and the initiatives of the UNESCO Asia-Pacific office in Bangkok.

The region's chief contribution to architectural conservation is without a doubt the Save Borobudur effort, which, in the decades that followed its launch, has offered a model for other "safeguarding" campaigns in Asia and beyond. The spirit of collaboration that emerged from the Dutch period of stewardship pointed the way toward numerous effective conservation techniques that have been widely adopted elsewhere in Asia since, particularly the highly effective practice of anastylosis. The Borobudur campaign that began in the 1970s expanded upon its predecessor's approach in order to achieve the site's greatest legacy: the ranks of trained professionals that have contributed to its conservation over the decades, and the experience that has been applied to other sites around the region. Always a testament to a successful conservation, the adoption of some of the approaches used at Borobudur at the still-continuing Angkor conservation effort affirms its high level of efficacy.

Of course, the story of Borobudur's revival is not yet concluded. Its experience as a focal point of conservation attention in the 1970s and 1980s will continue to offer lessons for how other, less well-attended sites across Southeast Asia, such as Mrauk-U in Myanmar and Wat Phou in Laos, might be handled in the twenty-first century. The longevity of the structural interventions and the consequences of its status as a premiere tourist destination in a heavily trafficked region also have yet to be fully revealed.

Similarly, the legacy of Singapore's remarkable transformation from a paradigm of all new development to a bright spot of conservation activity is still unfolding. In addition to the change in policy direction, the city-state's continued innovation in the area of large-scale conservation planning stands out as another lesson to be shared and adapted across the region. On a smaller scale, the grassroots advocacy of the Badan Warisan Malaysia (Heritage of Malaysia Trust) on behalf of George Town and Malacca, and the effective management of the city of Vigan points to effective strategies in stakeholder engagement and the sustained execution of management plans, all lessons that are highly relevant to other small to mid-sized heritage towns throughout Asia.

Sites such as the Rice Terraces of the Philippine Cordilleras demonstrate the fragility and resilience of cultural landscapes as living heritage sites, resources that are highly vulnerable to shifting natural and social factors that can completely undermine conservation management efforts. The experience of these sites in the Southeast Asian Maritime nations are also cause for hope and continued reliance on innovation, as evidenced by the removal of the Rice Terraces site from the list of World Heritage in Danger after more than a decade.

Looking ahead there is much cause for optimism in the region, but there are also some critical questions. How will the Muslim nations of Southeast Asia respond as other parts of the Islamic world increasingly grapple with instability and iconoclasm relative to their multi-cultural heritage? How will heritage tourism influence the future development of unique communities such as Kampong Ayer, and how will the management practices of Borobudur continue to influence the larger conservation dialogue within Asia? These questions underscore the pivotal nature of the region in the field of heritage conservation, one that it will continue to hold into the century ahead.

Stepwell of Chand Baori in Abhaneri, Rajasthan, India.

PART IV

South Asia

Introduction

India, Sri Lanka, Maldives, Pakistan, Bangladesh, Bhutan, Nepal

From the world's highest peaks to the coral atolls of the central Indian Ocean, South Asia's geographic diversity is matched only by the richness of its varied cultures and the majesty of its architectural wonders. The spiritual source of Hinduism and Buddhism, the region is also a major center of Islam, and its worshippers actively sustain an enduring legacy of temples, vihara, mosques and gardens along with other architectural expressions of faith. Cultural exchanges, invasions, and the flow of commodities through the Himalayan passes northward to Tibet and Central Asia have influenced the course of South Asian history for thousands of years. So too have the maritime trade routes connecting the South Asian littoral to the Islamic regions of East Africa and the Arabian peninsula, and to the Buddhist communities of Southeast Asia. The relatively recent legacies of the Mughal and British empires firmly bind the nations of South Asia to this day, but before those came the great kingdoms of antiquity and the middle ages, such as the Mauryan, Gupta, Vijayanagara and Chola among many others. Cultural continuity among the religious communities and their sacred spaces in Pakistan, India, Sri Lanka, Bangladesh, Nepal, Bhutan and Maldives informs the field of cultural heritage management throughout the region, embodying the notion of "living heritage" that is essential to the contemporary field of practice in South Asia today.

Each of the major religions practiced for centuries in South Asia places value on the practice of conservation as an act of faith, expressing it in terms of *jiirnnoddharana, muhafazah* or the earning of merit.[1] In the modern context of architectural conservation practice, most countries in the region trace their institutional and legal origins of heritage protection to their shared experience as part of the British Empire, which directly administered or exercised considerable influence over the entire region from the late eighteenth century to the 1950s. Conservation under the British was a direct instrument of the colonial system, a mixed legacy that continues to inform the field to this day. The institutions and policies from the colonial period endure in a number of modified forms: the Archaeological Survey of India (established 1861); the Ancient Monuments Preservation Act (1904), which forms the basis for conservation legislation in India, Pakistan, Sri Lanka and Bangladesh; and Sir John Marshall's *Conservation Manual* (1923), the recommendations of which remain relevant, if somewhat dated, to contemporary practitioners. Marshall's *Manual*, itself a reflection of the great conservation debates of nineteenth century Europe, advanced minimal treatments, respect for patina, distinction between "living" and "dead" monuments and conservation procedures, some of which are still actively practiced by professionals across the region.

Scholarship during the colonial period flourished and provided a solid foundation for Western and local understanding of the region's history, albeit with a heavy European bias that warrants modern revisions. A colonial-era focus on vast archaeological sites such as Harappa, Mohenjo-Daro, Anaradhapura and the Vihara at Paharpur still colors the field, as does a legacy of focusing on monumental sites at the expense of contextual or vernacular architectural typologies. The early institutions like the ASI, for all their exclusionary practices, did succeed in training the first generation of non-European conservation practitioners, such as Rai Bahadur Daya Ram Sahni of India, A.H. Dani of Pakistan and Senarath Paranavithana of Sri Lanka, who went on to advance the field in their respective countries in the post-independence era. Although not all of these countries were directly annexed into the British Empire, such as the case with Nepal, Bhutan and Maldives, the influence of this period still permeates the geopolitical atmosphere of the region. Partially in response to the dynamics of the colonial era, each of these fiercely independent kingdoms and sultanates remained largely closed to the outside world until as late as the 1970s, creating interesting challenges for integrating with the contemporary world of conservation practice.

In general, South Asia stands out as an extremely dynamic and active region for heritage conservation policy, practice, opportunities and challenges. As of 2001 all countries in the region had ratified the UNESCO World Heritage Convention, and as of 2015 all but Bhutan and Maldives have ICOMOS committees.[2] The International Safeguarding Campaign for Mohenjo-Daro, launched in 1974, was among the first initiatives led by UNESCO, in partnership with Pakistan; Sri Lanka's Cultural Triangle Project began its work in 1980, and the two together marked watershed conservation initiatives that continue to inform projects throughout Asia to this day.[3] India, Sri Lanka and Nepal in particular have taken a leadership role in the region and in Asia as a whole through a variety of initiatives that have inspired success both within and beyond their borders.

The profound societal changes that occurred due to the emigration of millions of people during Partition in 1947 continue to reverberate across the region, not only in geopolitical terms such as the conflict in Kashmir, but also in the stewardship of individual buildings on one side or the other of South Asia's borders. The governments of India, Pakistan and Bangladesh remain largely at odds with one another more than half a century after independence, while Sri Lanka only recently emerged from a near thirty-year civil war that had its roots in the colonial era. These legacies continue to complicate regional cooperation, and imperil some heritage sites due to direct conflict or neglect due to competing national priorities. Nevertheless, each country of South Asia has developed its own national conservation policy and practices that differ from the relative homogeneity of the colonial period. In many cases the current approaches to heritage management are in greater harmony with the dominant religious traditions of each country than they were under the colonial regimes, during which engagement between religious communities and conservation authorities was frequently tense if not altogether avoided.

As in East Asia, rapid population growth, urbanization and a shift from predominantly agrarian to modern industrial economies have profoundly affected the three most populous countries of South Asia (India, Pakistan and Bangladesh), which together constitute more than 20 percent of the world's population.[4] While the Himalayan countries and Indian Ocean island nations have not grown as quickly, the influences of globalization remain powerful, with forces such as mass tourism and (in the case of Maldives, Nepal and Bhutan) emergence onto the global stage unfolding with profound consequences for management of the built world.

A critical concept that runs through cultural heritage management in South Asia is that of "living heritage," which is embodied not only in continuously functioning religious sites such as the 2,000-year-old Buddhist cave shrines at Dambulla, but also in craft traditions, building trades and other forms of intangible heritage with unbroken, deeply historic cultural connections. As the Sri Lankan archaeologist and artist Jagath Weerasinghe aptly points out, "living sacred sites are the most vulnerable of cultural heritage sites" due to the complex relationships between their constituent communities and the conservation "experts" that seek to protect them from harmful change. In recognition of this fragility, efforts have been made by South Asian organizations in the post-independence era to more cleanly integrate these ideas with those of modern conservation practice.[5]

The legacy, record and endurance of the ASI stands out in Asia, if not the world, with a nearly unparalleled institutional history in the region that extends back to the earliest days of the professionalized field. More recently, South Asia has successfully created a newer generation of governmental and non-governmental trusts and foundations, several of which have highly sophisticated fundraising and advocacy operations that serve their constituent communities while also offering examples to be emulated elsewhere. Among these leading organizations are the Indian National Trust for Art and Cultural Heritage (INTACH), the various site-related Sri Lankan heritage foundations, the Kathmandu Valley Preservation Trust and the Heritage Foundation of Pakistan. These have inspired newer efforts such as the Bhutan Trust Fund that is in the early stages of addressing the common regional problem of insufficient governmental capacity to meet the substantial conservation obligations carried by each country carries.

Related to these organizational innovations are a range of charters that have been advanced by groups of professionals as a means to define conservation in the South Asian context, in distinctively South Asian terms. The INTACH *Charter for the Conservation of Unprotected Architectural Heritage and Sites in India* (2004) is a noteworthy example, as is the *Lahore Principles* (1980), which aimed to establish a pan-Islamic heritage approach with aspirations beyond South Asia's boundaries. Regional best practices advocate for community-based conservation projects, an approach that includes addressing larger social needs, aspirations and cultural traditions (including support for master craftspeople, or *raj mistris* as they are known in India), in addition to conservation objectives. These have as a rule generated greater levels of success and sustainability than more traditional top-down approaches.

The Aga Khan Trust for Culture (AKTC) programs in the Gilgit-Baltistan province of Pakistan (formerly known as the Northern Areas), which began in the late 1980s, stand out as groundbreaking efforts in local community revival in the face of dramatic change. These spawned later, similar efforts targeting urban districts such as Lahore Fort and Delhi's Nizamuddin Basti. The Cultural Triangle Project in Sri Lanka and Hanuman Dhoka Conservation Project in Nepal beginning in the 1970s importantly focused on interdisciplinary approaches involving craft training, community participation and the active role of local professionals with the support of international partners. More recently, Bhutan has undertaken a highly consultative approach to government reform including updates to its national heritage management approach that appears headed toward a successful resolution in the very near future.

A number of challenges remain in South Asia for optimizing conservation practice and results. Regionally, there exists a generally low level of infrastructure development and maintenance, which frequently leaves communities and their heritage assets vulnerable to natural disasters such as earthquakes, floods and typhoons. Increasingly, manmade calamities such as environmental degradation and global phenomena such as climate change are having profound effects on the region's heritage assets, from the yellowing of the Taj Mahal's marble cladding to the possible inundation of the entire nation of Maldives within the next century. Many challenges exist around conserving the built heritage of the colonial era, much of which carries complicated cultural legacies in addition to architectural, engineering and historic values. Hill stations, social clubs, churches, administrative buildings and historic railway infrastructure are among the typologies enmeshed in this difficult circumstance.

Like neighboring Central Asia, much of the region remains underdocumented in terms of heritage surveys and inventories that are inclusive of the contextual, vernacular and traditional as well as the monumental. This legacy is due in part to the colonial-era approach to monument conservation, but also to the focus in places like Bhutan on religious structures as the principal emblems of cultural heritage, rather than a mixture of building types.

Enormous population pressures in the historic quarters of cities like Mumbai, Karachi, Delhi, Kolkata, Lahore and Dhaka threaten individual buildings and entire districts. Incompatible modern construction and infrastructure pervasively encroach upon historic buildings and cultural landscapes in many of the region's urban areas, underscoring the challenges associated with enforcing conservation buffer zones. A general lack of appreciation for traditional residential districts, especially in cities, compounds the gaps in heritage inventories and complicates district-wide conservation planning efforts. Reasonably adequate heritage protection legislation exists in most South Asian countries, but in nearly all countries enforcement of existing heritage regulations, policies and protection measures remains uneven, leading to frustration on the part of conservation advocates and the loss of many historic buildings, spaces and districts. Finally, improved general training opportunities across the region would benefit all, with a particular focus on risk preparedness, conservation methods, site interpretation and visitor management.[6] The last need is particularly acute as tourism management and promotion remains a pressing concern for India, Sri Lanka, Nepal, Maldives and, increasingly, Bhutan.

UNESCO has played an active role in the region since the earliest days of the World Heritage Convention in the 1970s, coordinating efforts from its offices in Delhi and Kathmandu. A range of European, American and Australian conservation missions have maintained steady presences throughout the region; the ASI has also participated in conservation projects both inside and outside the region. Various organizations focused on sub-areas of South Asia, such as the American Himalayan Foundation, have contributed to site-specific projects and cultural exchanges aimed at promoting conservation objectives within the region. The AKTC organized a specific Cultural Service for Pakistan to support its three decades of programs there, and has supported sustained conservation programs in Delhi including the World Heritage Site of Humayun's Tomb and its adjacent districts. The South Asian Association for Regional Cooperation (SAARC) maintains a Culture Center in Colombo, where promotion of performing and visual arts, and literature are organized. The organization also selects "cultural capitals" for South Asia every two years (Dhaka will serve this function in 2016–2017). The organization has pledged to work toward collaborating on transnational nominations to the World Heritage List as a means of supporting greater South Asian cultural heritage beyond national boundaries.[7] Another promising regional effort is known as "Project Mausam," spearheaded by the Indian Ministry of Culture and the ASI, which aims to research themes and ultimately submit nominations for World Heritage Sites related to the Indian Ocean trade routes and the cultural connections they spawned between Arabia/East Africa, South Asia and the Southeast Asian archipelagos.[8]

Continued innovation, adaptation and evolution in the field of heritage management are a hallmark of South Asian practice, as evidenced by the above initiatives and the long history of conservation activity in the region. The decades to come will present even more challenges for the region's built heritage, but they will undoubtedly be met with this same spirit.

Notes

1 *Jiirnoddharana* is a Sanskrit term that translates as "deliverance from decay"; *muhafazah* is an Arabic term for "conservation"; the process of earning merit for the conservation of holy sites is integral to the practice of Buddhism.
2 World Heritage Convention reference: Of the South Asian nations, Maldives signed the Convention most recently, in 2001. ICOMOS reference: List of Committees. ICOMOS. 2015. Web. www.icomos.org/en/network/national-committees/mission-and-purposes/list-of-national-committees. Accessed January 5, 2016.
3 Pakistan – International Campaign for the Safeguarding of Moenjodaro. UNESCO World Heritage Center. 2015. Web. http://whc.unesco.org/en/activities/303/. Accessed January 5, 2016.
4 In 2015 there were approximately 1.5 billion people in India, Pakistan and Bangladesh, out of a total population of just over 7 billion worldwide.
5 Jagath Weerasinghe. "Living Sacred Heritage and 'Authenticity' in South Asia," in Helmut K. Anheier and Yudhishthir Raj Istar (eds.), *Cultures and Globalization: Heritage, Memory and Identity*. (London: Sage Press, 2011), 145.
6 *Understanding World Heritage in Asia and the Pacific: The Second Cycle of Periodic Reporting 2010–2012*. (Paris: UNESCO, 2012), 45.
7 The SAARC includes Afghanistan in addition to the countries identified with the South Asian region for this book. Source regarding cultural capital: Anita Joshua. "Bamiyan to be SAARC Cultural Capital for 2015." *The Hindu* (India). September 26, 2014. Web. www.thehindu.com/news/international/south-asia/bamiyan-to-be-saarc-cultural-capital-for-2015/article6446281.ece. Accessed January 5, 2016.
8 "Mausam" is the source of the English word "Monsoon." Program information: "Project Mausam: Maritime Routes and Cultural Landscapes Research Programme 2014 to 2019." Indira Gandhi National Centre for the Arts. 2014. Web. http://ignca.nic.in/mausam.htm. Accessed January 5, 2016.

16
INDIA

Modern India's immense collection of significant historic architectural and artistic works represents the collective achievements of many great civilizations. Its broad roster of heritage sites spans thousands of years, numerous reigning empires and several religious beliefs, including two of the world's most prominent faiths, Buddhism and Hinduism.[1] One of the world's largest and most populous countries,[2] India faces the challenging task of conserving its patrimony in a dynamic, vast and rapidly developing environment. Its 3.3 million square kilometers (1.3 million square miles) contains a large variety of topography, climates, and ethnic and artistic traditions. These factors have produced architectural splendors associated with some of Asia's greatest periods of building, including the Vijayanagara (fourteenth–sixteenth centuries CE) and Mughal empires (sixteenth–nineteenth centuries CE), and represent a vast temporal range, from the cave sites of Bhimbetka (paintings dating to 30,000 years from present) to the twentieth century Indo-Saracenic government buildings of New Delhi. While each geographic region carries its own distinctive local culture and deep historical traditions, each also maintains a connection to India's contemporary national identity, born out of the country's independence from Britain in 1947 and subsequent partition from the modern states of Pakistan and Bangladesh.

The complexity of India's geographic and cultural landscapes has challenged efforts to document and conserve its heritage since the nineteenth century, when Western conservation practices were first introduced to South Asia. Added to this are modern pressures from an expanding population that is increasingly urban, and rapid development in one of the world's largest and fastest-growing economies.[3] Nevertheless, Indian heritage conservationists have risen to meet these challenges in impressive ways. Architectural conservation practice in India today is vibrant and sophisticated, combining modern approaches with an established colonial-era institutional framework and centuries-old traditions of maintaining and caring for venerated places. Contemporary professional practice remains highly active at local, national and international levels, supporting projects that feature some of the most innovative and effective practices in the field today. Since independence, national organizations – chief among them the Archaeological Survey of India (ASI) and the Indian National Trust for Art and Cultural Heritage (INTACH) – have made great strides forward in the conservation of India's heritage while also forging a distinctive approach to architectural conservation practice that has influenced the wider global field in South Asia and beyond.

The richness and diversity of India's architectural heritage also presents one of its chief conservation challenges: the effective identification, management and protection of culturally significant sites, which are spread across a huge, rapidly changing nation. While a number of individual monuments enjoy

FIGURE 16.1 The city of Jaipur (Jaipur state) viewed from its Amber Fort is representative of the extraordinarily rich and varied architectural heritage of India.

UNESCO World Heritage status and the commensurate attention that brings, less than ten thousand heritage sites are recognized by national, regional and local heritage conservation authorities, and countless others remain unrecognized from the standpoint of heritage protection.[4] INTACH has estimated that the number of archaeological monuments that receive formal protection stands at only 1–3 percent of the total number nationwide, and that only 0.025 percent of non-monumental heritage resources – such as historic districts, landscapes or locally significant resources – are listed.[5] The argument advanced by INTACH and others is an essential truism of the field: effective architectural conservation begins with the identification and documentation of what's important to conserve. An improvement of this disparity in recognition and resources depends upon identifying important sites – a process that has been under way since the earliest days of the ASI in the 1860s – while also strengthening the bonds between constituent communities and heritage agencies. To date, steps have been taken to address the situation, most notably the 2004 *Charter for the Conservation of Unprotected Architectural Heritage and Sites in India*, developed by INTACH after a multi-year effort to define the characteristic elements for an Indian Heritage and Conservation Management Charter, discussed in detail later in this chapter.[6] For its part, the ASI released an updated National Policy for Conservation of Ancient Monuments, Archaeological Sites and Remains (NPC-AMASR) in 2014, which aimed to comprehensively update the agency's conservation strategy for the first time since the 1920s, though the document has suffered criticism for failing to adequately address the ASI's monument-centric approach to conservation in India.[7]

Indian architectural traditions: a chronological summary

India is home to some of the most widely recognized cultural heritage sites in the world: the Taj Mahal in Agra, a lasting symbol of beauty and architectural achievement, which the Mughal emperor Shah Jahan had built for his wife in the seventeenth century; the Mahabodhi Temple in Bodh Gaya, where the Buddha attained nirvana and to which pilgrims from across the Buddhist world travel; the intricately carved and elegantly executed Jain and Brahman Khajuraho temple complexes (tenth–eleventh centuries CE); the fortified cities of Rajasthan; and the cave temples at Elephanta, Ellora and Ajanta, essential destinations for Asian art connoisseurs and scholars for centuries, while also remaining active places of worship for millions of people.

In addition to its indigenous achievements, centuries of colonization have imbued India's built environment with a legacy of European architectural traditions, including Christian religious buildings, Victorian-style residences and Classical revival public buildings. Since the sixteenth century CE, the Portuguese, Dutch, French and, most significantly, the British have constructed buildings across South Asia, work that reached its apex with the design and construction of Sir Edwin Lutyens' New Delhi (1912–1930). The fusion of Western architectural styles with indigenous forms and materials generated distinctive designs frequently referred to as "Indo-Saracenic" style, perhaps best exemplified by Frederick William Stevens' 1887 Chhatrapati Shivaji (former Victoria) Terminus in Bombay, and Robert Chisholm's Napier Museum (1880) in Thiruvananthapuram. An exuberant blend of Eastern and Western artistic traditions contributes to modern India's distinctive cultural landscape, and embodies a complex relationship between the ancient and modern worlds, indigenous and foreign influences.

The legacy of innovative architectural and urban design in South Asia stretches back thousands of years, with its origins generally credited to the Harappan civilization, which emerged in the fourth millennium BCE along the Indus River and its tributaries in what is now northern India, eastern Pakistan and parts of Afghanistan.[8] Characterized by highly developed urban centers such as Harappa and Mohenjo-Daro (both in present-day Pakistan), Harappan sites offer evidence of what may be Asia's earliest examples of sophisticated urban planning, including axonometric street grids, organized food production and distribution, elaborate sanitation and drainage systems, and monumental mud brick architecture.[9] A number of important Harappan sites fall within India's modern borders, including Dholavira, Lothal, Bhirrana and Rakhigarhi, the last of which is located approximately 150 km northwest of Delhi in the Indian state of Haryana. Identified by archaeologists as early as 1915, the ASI has conducted extensive excavations since 1997, identifying it as the largest Harappan site discovered to date, and revealing characteristic street grid and drainage systems, residential and defensive structures made of sun dried and fired brick, and ritual structures associated with fire worship.[10] As with many Harappan sites across South Asia, Rakhigarhi is presently threatened by a lack of adequate site conservation, erosion of its mud brick structures, and encroachment by modern development. At Rakhigarhi a joint United States–Indian partnership is working to address these threats through engagement with the local community on economic development potential around the site, alongside a conservation and management plan with Indian authorities and the local university.[11]

The Harappan period had waned by the mid-second millennium BCE, and was followed in northern India by the arrival of Aryans, a group of previously nomadic people that had originated in present-day Iran. Their culture gradually gave rise to the Hindu building traditions that dominated much of the architectural development across South Asia from the third or second century BCE into the modern era.[12] During the Maurya period (fourth–second centuries BCE) much of modern India was united under a series of powerful rulers beginning with its namesake Chandragupta Maurya (340–298 BCE) and his successor, the great Ashoka (304–232 BCE), who marked his empire with columns and, according to legend, some 84,000 Buddhist stupas.[13] While the legacy of the Mauryan empire and its achievements has been profound, little remains of its collective built work, save for a few remnant columns along with the Great Stupa at Sanchi (third century BCE), part of a *vihara* (monastery complex) located in today's Madhya Pradesh state.[14]

Following the dissolution of the Mauryas, various Central Asian, Greco-Bactrian, Buddhist and Hindu kingdoms held sway in the north, while the Satavahana Empire consolidated power across the south and central portions of South Asia. As patrons of Buddhism the Satavahanas contributed to the early phases of construction at the Ajanta caves during their rule (second century BCE–second century CE). Blending new artistic and design techniques from the earlier Buddhist and Jain traditions that had been spread across South Asia by the Mauryas, an early high point of Hindu temple and secular structures (in addition to political unity) is associated with the Gupta period (fourth–sixth centuries CE), as exemplified by the sixth century Dashavatara temple at Deogarh and associated Jain temples located in present-day Madhya Pradesh state.

The Guptas ultimately gave way in the fifth century to a fragmented series of kingdoms including the Buddhist Pala Empire in northeast India, the Hindu Chalukyas in the west and south, and the Hindu Gurjara-Pratihara kingdoms of the northwest. Each of these left behind a legacy of influential buildings, including the finely carved Jain temples at Osian in today's Rajasthan, a series of temples at Aihole (Karnataka), and the monumental towers and multi-tiered porch temples of Gwalior. Another important descendant of the Guptas were the Rashtrakuta kings, who immediately succeeded the Chalukyas, ruling over much of the Deccan Plateau in central and southern India (eighth–tenth centuries). The Rashtrakuta king Krishna I (756–775) ushered in a high point in the architectural development of Hindu temple design: the extraordinary Kailasanatha temple at his capital in Ellora (Maharashtra), an enormous and elaborately decorated building, carved directly out of a rock hillside.[15] The Chandella Dynasty largely succeeded the Gujara-Pratiharas by the tenth century, then held sway over much of central India for several centuries while leaving behind the extraordinary temple complexes at Khajuraho, with their intricately detailed carving and exuberantly clustered tower designs.[16]

The Kalingas and Eastern Gangas based in Odisha (Orissa) during the eighth to thirteenth centuries were also great, early temple builders, using a characteristic style comprised of a sequence of halls punctuated by a pyramidal sanctuary structure, all accented with deep horizontal banding in the stonework. The style is amply on display in the many temples at Bhubaneshwar (largely from the ninth century), and culminates with the richly carved Surya Temple at Konarak (mid-thirteenth century). Further to the northeast, in Bengal, are the temples at Bishnupur built by the long-standing Malla dynasty during the seventeenth century, featuring distinctive roof profiles coupled with terracotta tile decorative elements.[17]

In southern India, meanwhile, a series of smaller Buddhist and Islamic kingdoms, which had maintained maritime trade connections with Arabia and Southeast Asia in the early centuries CE, were gradually replaced by a series of dominant Tamil Hindu rulers by the seventh century, thus leading to the development of influential building traditions that ultimately spread beyond South Asia to the shores of mainland and island Southeast Asia. From the seventh to the twelfth centuries the region was largely dominated by the Chola and Pallava, both Hindu kingdoms that vied for dominance over what is now Kerala, Tamil Nadu, Karnataka and Ahndra Pradesh.[18] This era gave birth to Dravidian style temples, which have come to embody the architectural contributions of the south, with their distinctive pyramidal *gopura* (entrance gates) organized around rectangular enclosures that typically contain a tank, columned halls and porches. The early eleventh-century Brihadeshvara temple at Thanjavur (Tanjore), Tamil Nadu exemplifies the architectural achievements of the Chola period Dravidian temples, with its massive thirteen-storey pyramidal tower.[19]

The arrival of Muslim armies from Central Asia beginning in the tenth century triggered a major shift in the trajectory of Indian architectural traditions, ushering in the highly influential period of Islamic building, first under the Delhi Sultanates (1206–1526) followed by the prolific Mughal period (1526–1857), with its centers in Delhi and Agra. After consolidating power in the north, by the early fourteenth century the armies of the Delhi Sultanate under Ala-ud-din Khalji began to push south, and briefly achieved the formidable task of uniting north and south India under a single throne, that of Muhammed bin Tughlaq, in the mid-fourteenth century.[20] The accomplishment was fleeting, as the Bahmani Sultanate broke off from their Delhi-based rulers shortly thereafter and survived as an independent Muslim entity based in Ahsanabad (present-day Ghulbarga in Karnataka) until 1518, when it splintered into the Deccan Sultanates.[21]

Violently at odds with their Muslim neighbors, the Hindu Vijayanagaras arose concurrently with the Bahmani, establishing a thriving dynasty between the fourteenth and seventeenth centuries, based at its namesake capital, which is adjacent to present-day Hampi (Karnataka). The Vijayanagaras were prolific builders, establishing the vast Shrirangam temple complex, and expanding other important temple-towns such as Madurai (Tamil Nadu). The Vijayanagaras were conquered by the Deccan Sultanates, and then succeeded by the Nayakas (fifteenth–seventeenth centuries) and the Mysore Kingdom, which endured until 1799 when it was overthrown by the army of the British East India Company.

In the northwest, the Rajasthani kingdoms excelled in graciously imposing defensive buildings, temples and *haveli* (courtyard palaces), which reached their pinnacle of design during the fifteenth–nineteenth centuries. Home to fiercely independent maharajas that repelled Muslim invasions from the north for centuries, then kept the Mughals and even British at arm's length, Rajasthan boasts a wealth of elegantly designed cities such as Udaipur, Jodhpur, Bikaner, Jaipur and Chittor. The ambitious architectural programs of Rajasthan's rulers extended well into the twentieth century, culminating in the construction of Umaid Bhawan palace, India's largest royal residence, completed by the Maharaja of Jodhpur in a hybrid Art Deco/Indo-Saracenic style in 1943.

The Mughals stand among the great builder dynasties of Asia, combining indigenous elements of north Indian structures with Central Asian Persian and Turkic designs, resulting in several of India's finest architectural expressions. The great Mughal buildings (sixteenth–nineteenth centuries) are frequently tombs, mosques, forts and *haveli*, but gardens also stand out as a central contribution to the Indian built environment. The Jama Masjid, Red Fort and Humayun's Tomb in Delhi, Akbar's capital at Fatehpur Sikri, and of course the incomparable Taj Mahal stand among the pinnacles of Mughal architectural achievement. The Mughal era came to an end in 1857 when the last emperor, Bahadur Shah II, was exiled to Burma by the British due to his role in the Sepoy Mutiny (also known as India's First War of Independence). The Marathas, one of the last great pre-colonial Indian empires, were partly responsible for the decline of the Mughal Empire in the eighteenth century before falling themselves to the British following the Third Anglo-Maratha War of 1818.

India's nearly 500-year colonial period generated countless architectural works, representing a wide range of styles, building types and ambitions. The colonial cities of Bombay (Mumbai), Calcutta (Kolkata), New Delhi, Pondicherry (Puducherry) and Goa remain among the nation's principal urban areas, in many cases renamed, but all with distinctive building types and neighborhoods, along with complex conservation challenges. Hill stations such as the British "summer capital" at Simla (Shimla) and the extensive railroad networks that shuttled colonists, armies and Indians across the great South Asian expanses remain important features of the contemporary Indian landscape, and a lasting legacy of the late colonial period. British and Indian architectural firms based in South Asia designed Art Deco-style apartments, civic buildings and theaters from the 1920s into the 1960s, many of which remain clustered in urban districts, notably the Back Bay district of Mumbai.[22] Colonial architecture also, of course, bears the indelible stamp of colonialism itself, in all its stark inequities and injustices. This burdened legacy remains difficult for some to bear, leading to rejected calls for conservation by some contemporary stakeholders.

The post-independence era ushered in a prolific period of design and construction across the country, but also a drive to develop a distinctly modern Indian style. While foreign architects contributed to this effort with projects such as Chandigarh, a regional capital (of Punjab and Haryana) with a master plan by Swiss-French architect Charles-Edouard Jeanneret-Gris, "Le Corbusier," and individual buildings such as the US Embassy in New Delhi by American architect Edward Durell Stone, Indian architects working in the post-independence era have produced innovative Modern works that may be expected to move into the conservation spotlight in the years to come. Among these are the work of Habib Rahman, such as the Gandhi Memorial (1949) and the Rabindra Bhavan apartments (1961, both in Delhi) along with Charles Correa, chief architect and planner for Navi (New) Mumbai.

FIGURE 16.2 An architectural symbol of early modern India is the Chhatrapati Shivaji (former Victoria) Terminus in Bombay (1887) designed in the "Indo-Saracenic" style that represents a fusion of Western architectural styles with indigenous forms and materials.

Religious origins of restoration and conservation in India

Home to practitioners of many religions, India is also the cradle of two of the world's most prominent religious faiths – Buddhism and Hinduism – each of which have thrived without interruption for millennia to the present day. The 2,500-year-old Buddhist faith originated in northern India, and later spread across deserts, mountains and oceans to distant points including Mongolia, Japan and Sri Lanka. Today it is present in most countries of the world. The older Hindu faith is practiced by hundreds of millions of people in great concentrations in South and Southeast Asia, primarily from the western Indian state of Gujarat to Bali in eastern Indonesia.[23]

Each of these two systems of belief carries with it strong architectural traditions that are manifest in shrines, temple complexes and other holy sites. Over the centuries, a coda outlining proper treatment for Hindu and Buddhist religious buildings has developed and become interwoven into religious practices. Sanskrit treatises dating to the ancient empires of north and south India, known as *tantras*, *agamas* or *samhitas*, frequently address topics related to the design, construction and restoration of temple buildings according to the principles of Hindu beliefs. Texts focused on building and architecture (*vastu*) were collected after the fourth century CE into the *Vastushastras*, which form a complete digest of building and artistic methodologies based on Hindu beliefs; among the most extensive of these is the *Manasara*, which describes a wide range of topics from building site selection to jewelry making.[24] The *Brithat Samhita*, a Gupta period (fourth–sixth century CE) text written by the court astrologer Varahamihira, describes the connection between temple construction and the acquisition of religious merit, stating "let him who wishes to enter the worlds that are reached by meritorious deeds of piety and charity build a temple to the gods."[25] The *Shilpa Prakasha*, an eleventh century Sanskrit manuscript describing the art and architecture of Hindu temples in the eastern Indian state of Odisha (formerly Orissa), states that patrons of temples might receive fame, if not immortality, because "everything vanishes with time, only a monument lasts forever." To this end, the acts of erecting and maintaining Hindu temples are frequently recorded in carvings or inscriptions, noting the individual's pious deed on the temples themselves.[26]

The Hindu concept of *prasada-purusa* maintains that temples and other prominent buildings, such as those associated with semi-divine rulers, are "living" things that, once built, enter into the cycle of birth, adolescence, maturity, old age and death. Consistent with the wider system of beliefs regarding living things, the cycle does not necessarily end with this last step. Traditional texts such as the *Mayamatam*,[27] an important twelfth century CE treatise on housing, architecture and iconography, describe the renewing process of *jiirnoddharana*, a Sanskrit term that translates as "deliverance from decay" or "the raising up of what is old or decayed." Detailed descriptions of this process touch upon topics familiar to architectural conservationists in the present day, including the maintenance of original architectural forms, selection of appropriate replacement materials, and the proper incorporation of new materials into older construction.[28]

This type of active maintenance is also connected to rituals aimed at protecting the sanctity of temples from unwanted negative forces. Because many temples, cave complexes and even abandoned dynastic capitals remain active places of worship to the present day, they continue to benefit from the same simple acts of building maintenance – such as re-daubing earthen masonry walls or patching roof leaks – that constitute an exercise in "living heritage."[29] Despite the antiquity of these concepts, they remain alive and well among those tasked with managing significant buildings in India today, a line of continuity that underpins the approach to modern conservation practice.

Conservation principles and practice in the colonial era

Architectural conservation practice in the modern sense gained official status during the mid-nineteenth century in India, as British rule across South Asia was ascendant. As such, much of the legislation, policy and practices of the pre-independence years were based on the principle of top-down, exclusionary strictures inherent to colonialism, which by definition excluded Indians from decision-making regarding their own heritage. While the British colonial period, and to a lesser degree that of the French, Dutch and Portuguese, carries a profoundly complicated legacy, the story of its emergence is key to understanding Indian architectural conservation practice in the late twentieth and twenty-first centuries. The conservation infrastructure of the British period remains an indelible influence on Indian professional practice today, with many of the same institutions and legislation still in existence, albeit in modernized forms.

Since commerce was one of the primary motives driving the European presence in South Asia from the moment Vasco da Gama arrived in Calicut (today's Kozhikode in the state of Kerala) in 1498, it is logical that an early task of the colonizers was to inventory the material, cultural and human assets that were on hand in this "new" world. Many, if not most, of the early interactions between European expeditions and South Asian communities were violent episodes of European looting and destruction, aimed more at establishing domination than practicing conservation. But as successive waves of Portuguese, French, Dutch and British arrived over time, and as the scope and ambition of the colonial enterprise developed, so too did efforts to evaluate, quantify, understand and ultimately protect such resources.

An interest in surveying and protecting South Asia's key physical assets, including its historic architectural sites, first developed during the late eighteenth century under the strictly regimented British governance of India.[30] From the mid-nineteenth century British rulers of India viewed conservation of the more famous monuments as an extension of the colonial mission to "civilize" the country where the supposed lack of civilization was evidenced by the deteriorated condition of important buildings.[31]

The British period can be credited for a vast expansion of the West's scholarly understanding of Indian history, architecture, language, art and religions, and many of the early European contributors to Indian architectural conservation practice were passionately engaged in the study of its ancient cultures. One of the earliest mentions of conservation-minded architectural intervention in British India was in 1774, when the British writer Samuel Johnson wrote to Warren Hastings, the first Governor General of Bengal, encouraging him to "survey the remains of the ancient edifices, and trace the vestiges of [India's] ruined cities."[32] A decade later, Sir William Jones founded the Asiatic Society in Calcutta to bring together European scholars interested in the arts, architecture, history, languages and literature of the region.[33]

In 1857, following India's First War of Independence (also known at the time as the Indian Rebellion or the Sepoy Mutiny), the British Crown ended the de facto rule of the East India Company, establishing direct governance over Company territories and protectorates from its capital, Calcutta. This shift from a commerce-based enterprise to full-blown governance under the Raj was profound. The scope and ambitions of Imperial regulation expanded to cover all areas of Indian civic affairs, including management of architectural monuments and sites.

Colonial legislative action on conservation began with the passage of a series of laws regulating the use of culturally significant public buildings. In 1863, the Religious Endowments Act (also known as Act XX) established a system by which historically significant places of worship would be managed by religious trusts, with provisions for the government's intervention in order to influence the maintenance and care of the facilities, among other purposes. The Treasure Trove Act (1874) aimed to protect archaeological or other cultural deposits from looting, while a series of government moves over the remainder of the nineteenth century helped establish a network of local and national heritage management policies under the Raj.[34]

In 1861 the Viceroy Earl Canning appointed a British Army Engineer and scholar, Alexander Cunningham, to conduct the first government-sanctioned survey of archaeological sites. This set the groundwork for what would become in the next decade the Archaeological Survey of India (ASI), the organization that remains a pillar of modern practice in the country to this day. The principal output of the ASI during its early decades consisted of reports documenting Cunningham's tours of important archaeological sites in northern and central India, rather than actual conservation work at the sites themselves. In 1881 a new Viceroy, Lord Lytton, appointed Major H.H. Cole to serve as Curator of Ancient Monuments, and tasked him with surveying sites across India in order to produce a report detailing a national program for architectural conservation work.[35] The ten-volume document, entitled *Preservation of National Monuments in India* (1881–1884), represented a departure from the earlier archaeology- and epigraphy-focused work of Cunningham and others by including a series of recommendations relating specifically to the "repair and restoration" of architecture.[36]

FIGURE 16.3 The Ellora cave complex near Aurangabad, one of the largest rock-hewn monastic temple complexes in the world, dating from the sixth through the twelfth centuries CE, was among the first of several sites in India to receive conservation attention, in the modern sense, with visitor management and stabilization measures through an initiative established under Lord Curzon, British Viceroy in India from 1899 to 1905.

The decades immediately following publication of Cole's report saw little progress in executing its recommendations. The colonial government in Calcutta instead treated the ASI's charge of creating a national inventory of sites as a finite task, and left all conservation work at those sites to local governments or individual efforts.[37] Evolving attitudes toward architectural conservation practice in Europe, coupled with the appointment of Lord George Nathaniel Curzon, himself a noted traveler and writer on Central Asian affairs of the day, marked a significant shift in the approach to conservation in India.

During his relatively brief tenure as the Viceroy (1899–1905), Curzon established a framework for contemporary architectural conservation practice in India, while also closely binding conservation policy to the colonial enterprise.[38] At the time, the Taj Mahal's finer building materials were being pillaged, and the great caves at Ajanta and Ellora were suffering from careless exploration, vandalism and uncontrolled visitation. In response, Curzon bolstered the national government's role in conservation, reorganizing the ASI into a system of regional offices (or Circles) and appointing a Director-General.[39]

In addition to a fivefold increase in the central government's spending on archaeology, the Curzon administration oversaw the 1904 passage of the Ancient Monuments Preservation Act. The Act mirrored legislation of the same name that was passed in Great Britain in 1882 and serves as the basis for later regulation in post-independence India, Pakistan and Bangladesh.[40] The Act was important not only because it prohibited unauthorized excavation and trafficking of archaeological materials, but also for granting the government in Calcutta the authority to identify and protect buildings, tombs and cave painting sites, regulate the types of activities, such as mining, that could occur near significant sites, compel the sale of neglected sites to the government, and levy penalties, including fines and imprisonment, for damaging monuments or otherwise violating terms of the law. Designation or listing of key heritage sites included publicly as well as privately owned structures and sites, and the law granted the government certain rights over significant privately owned listed sites.[41]

The Ancient Monuments Preservation Act notably included specific instructions for buildings actively in use for religious purposes, such as mosques, temples and stupas, treating them differently from non-religious structures. This approach had its roots in the 1863 Religious Endowments Act, which had been passed in a climate of religious discontent that had helped trigger the 1857 First War of Independence; as a result, the colonial government's attempts at the time were to remain neutral in its treatment of various religious groups. The intent of this provision was that the government was to avoid directly intervening in the maintenance of historically significant religious structures, instead relying on religious societies or trusts for the buildings' care. In practice, the policy was unevenly carried out, with various instances of the government's conservation efforts running afoul of religious activities, temple design or ceremonial significance.[42]

Perhaps the most consequential decision Lord Curzon made regarding heritage administration was the appointment in 1902 of British archaeologist John Marshall as the ASI's Director-General, a post he filled until 1928. Marshall instituted Western-style conservation practice in South Asia, introducing a series of principles for conservation work in British India in his *Conservation Manual: A Handbook for the Use of Archaeological Officers and Others Entrusted with the Care of Ancient Monuments*, which was published in 1923. This manual was an expansion of his earlier *Conservation of Ancient Monuments* (1907), a document that spelled out a code of practice for those responsible for the conservation of significant historic buildings and sites in India.

Marshall's *Manual* was divided into two sections: the first dealt with regulations, principles and practices, and the second prescribed specific conservation actions and solutions. This watershed document set forth some basic principles that reflected the outcome of the nineteenth century debates regarding conservation versus restoration, with the former being associated with "dead" monuments (such as ruins), emphasizing requirements for documentation prior to re-erecting fallen elements, and incorporating new elements as inconspicuously as possible. For "living" monuments, such as active religious sites, a greater degree of restoration is permitted under the *Manual*, accounting for the continuity of craft traditions and use patterns for such places.[43]

Marshall was far ahead of his contemporaries in architectural conservation practice, certainly in Asia but also in many parts of the West, by recognizing and respecting the concept of "living heritage," which remains crucial to the management of cultural heritage in the region. He acknowledged the value of historic patina and the wisdom of minimal intervention, noting:

> although there are many buildings whose state of disrepair suggests at first sight a renewal, it should never be forgotten that their *historical value is gone when their authenticity is destroyed*, and that our first duty is not to renew them but to preserve them [emphasis added].

In addition to restrictions and management guidelines, Marshall's *Manual* suggests numerous innovative technical solutions and repair techniques specific to the building materials and architectural expressions of South Asia.[44]

Under Marshall's directorship, the ASI began training Indian practitioners for service in the department, beginning in 1903 with two scholarships for proficiency in Sanskrit and Persian/Arabic, and later expanding to cover the fields of archaeology, chemistry and architecture. The scholarships reflected Marshall's view that the future of conservation in India must depend more and more on the degree of interest taken in it by Indians themselves. The success of this approach was evidenced by the fact that among the first recipients of this scholarship was Rai Bahadur Daya Ram Sahni, who in 1931 became the first Indian appointed to serve as Director-General of the ASI.[45]

Both Marshall and Curzon deserve recognition for advances made in the fields of archaeology, epigraphy and conservation across South Asia. However, it must be acknowledged that their efforts were ultimately in the service of the colonial enterprise, and – particularly in the case of Curzon – designed to support the unjust cause of British rule over millions of Indian subjects. Despite this mixed legacy, the colonial period set the groundwork for contemporary practice across South Asia, its institutions and practices still influencing the way conservation is practiced in India today.

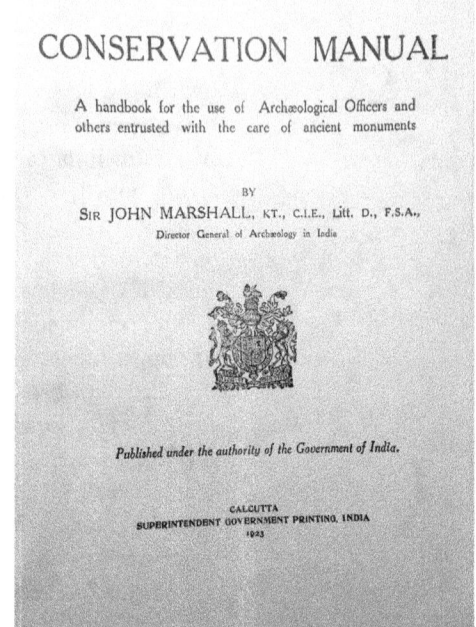

FIGURE 16.4 Cover of *Conservation Manual: A Handbook for the Use of Archaeological Officers and Others Entrusted with the Care of Ancient Monuments* (1923), the source of conservation principles and procedures administered today by the Archaeological Survey of India.

Architectural conservation in modern India

In the decades following its independence on August 15, 1947, the new nation of India experienced two major developments that exerted a lasting influence on the management of its cultural heritage. First was the profound societal and political transformation that came about due to the partition of former British India into the modern states of Pakistan, Bangladesh and India.[46] The decision by the dissolving British Raj and Indian political parties to split India along religious lines resulted in the sudden displacement of an estimated 14 million people, as huge populations violently shifted from one side of the newly created border to the other.[47] Migration on this scale left many important mosques, temples and secular communities damaged or abandoned by their constituents. In the immediate wake of partition, Muslim monuments in places like Delhi were intentionally destroyed, or occupied by military and refugee camps, and priceless collections, such as that of the Lahore Museum and of Mohenjo-Daro (the famous Harappan site now located in Pakistan), were contentiously divided between the two new nations.[48] Partition also set the course for long-term, destructive conflict, including three wars fought between India and Pakistan in the twentieth century, a corrosive stalemate in the contested region of Jammu and Kashmir, and periodic flashpoints such as the 1992 destruction of the sixteenth century Babri Masjid at Ayodhya in a wave of political–religious violence that left 2,000 dead.[49]

The second post-colonial development that substantially influenced contemporary cultural heritage management in India has been the nation's rapid transformation from a predominantly agrarian society to a modern, industrialized nation with a population in excess of one billion. Economic development since 1947 has unquestionably improved the lives of millions in post-independence India: by the opening years of the twenty-first century, life expectancy has doubled, literacy rates more than tripled, and the nation now possesses one of the world's largest economies.[50] However, as in much of the world, this growth has come at the expense of architecturally and culturally significant buildings and places, notably the traditional neighborhoods of its burgeoning cities, including Mumbai (Bombay), Ahmedabad and Delhi, and its fragile ancient structures that are particularly susceptible to pollution and development pressures.

In perhaps the most prominent case, the Taj Mahal – undoubtedly the architectural symbol of India – has suffered for decades due to environmental pollution from scores of nearby factories, vehicle and generator emissions and the adjacent, contaminated Yamuna River. These factors combined have

FIGURE 16.5a, b and c Restoration and conservation of the Taj Mahal date to the 1890s, although the current documentation methodologies and conservation technologies have been used there since the early 1990s under the aegis of the Archaeological Survey of India (a). Responding to concerns over the effects of air pollution, scientific analyses began and various measures to stem the problem, ranging from removing the sources of pollution to conservative stone cleaning, have been implemented (b). Of equal concern are needs to control visitation (tourist wear) to India's most popular architectural heritage site that receives millions of visitors per year (c).

deteriorated the marble edifice and its foundations, triggering a call to action at the highest levels of government and from the international community. In a 1996 decision aimed specifically at protecting the Taj Mahal, along with the nearby Red Fort and Fatehpur Sikri, the Indian Supreme Court created a 10,400 square kilometer (4,000 square mile) protective zone around the monuments (billed the Taj Trapezium Zone, or TTZ, in reference to its shape in plan) within which certain types of industries including iron foundries, lime factories and brick kilns were ordered closed. Further regulations, including the prohibition on vehicular traffic within 500 meters of the Taj, were imposed, and the Agra municipality was ordered to establish a full-time electrical grid so as to curtail diesel generator use in the TTZ.[51] Important as these steps were, the Taj remains under threat by the forces of industrialization in Agra. A joint US/Indian study in 2014 demonstrated that the continued discoloration of the Taj's translucent, white Markana marble surfaces was directly attributable to vehicle emissions, road dust and trash burning, suggesting that the dramatic measures taken in the 1990s were inadequate to address the monument's environmental threats.[52]

In the face of these challenges, architectural conservation practice and policy since independence has continued to develop, with updates and expansion of colonial-era laws, growth in professional capacity, and the emergence of new organizations – notably the 1984 founding of the Indian National Trust for Art and Cultural Heritage – that have greatly contributed to the identification and management of India's vast architectural heritage.

Conserving India's cave sites: balancing visitation, protection and living heritage

Several of India's best-known heritage sites are Buddhist, Jain and Hindu caves – natural and hand-excavated underground spaces for worship and meditation – of a type found throughout South and East Asia. Three of the best known, the World Heritage Site caves of Ajanta, Ellora and Elephanta, hold elaborate carvings, frescoes and other wall paintings that depict religious and secular scenes, created over many centuries by artisans and worshippers. The cave interiors also share common conservation issues, including humidity and physical damage to the delicate wall surfaces from high visitation, degradation of paint layers, water infiltration due to vegetation growth, and infestation by insects and bats. At the surrounding sites, problems such as inadequate visitor facilities, encroachment by commercial development, waste management and inconsistently enforced management plans also threaten the integrity of the caves.

Beginning in the early 1990s the ASI, in partnership with the Maharashtra Tourism Development Corporation, and the Japanese International Cooperation Agency (JICA), developed an initiative to address the common problems that threaten cave sites in India. The initiative sought to improve tourism infrastructure along with the economic development potential for the larger region through a series of collaborations and phased financial loans from the Japanese government to the local development corporation.[53] Focusing on the second century BCE–fifth century CE Ajanta and Ellora caves, located in the western state of Maharashtra, the effort encompassed local infrastructure upgrades, such as road improvements, expansion of the nearby airport and shoring of the electrical grid. In the immediate vicinity of the caves, improvements including fencing, access paths and transit systems were introduced to control the movement of visitors around the sites. The surrounding forests were partly replanted, and drinking water, sewage and drainage systems were upgraded.[54] In order to protect the sensitive environment inside the caves, limitations have been placed on the number of visitors that can access the caves at any one time. In 2013 new visitor centers were inaugurated at each site with services and amenities including interpretation, in addition to scale replicas of several of the most famous cave interiors, so that visitors can experience facsimiles of the originals outside their fragile environment.[55]

In many ways, this program has been successful in its goals: between 2001 and 2010, the number of annual visitors to Ajanta and Ellora roughly doubled to 1.5 million, and US$57 million of development funding has been spent over the course of the project's two phases.[56] However, scholars and observers of the program have questioned the approach to developing religious sites such as India's cave temples as tourist destinations, cautioning that doing so risks undermining the role that the sites have for the religious communities that sustain them. A 2003 study revealed that eight of the top ten domestic tourist destinations in India are pilgrimage sites, and that over 100 million people travel for religious purposes in India each year.[57] With these numbers, pressures on fragile sites such as India's cave temples will only increase, signaling a need for increasingly effective strategies for preserving pilgrimage sites for future worshippers and visitors alike.

FIGURE 16.6a, b and c Conservation of the richly carved and painted caves of Ajanta, Ellora and Elephanta in central India has been a high priority for the Archaeological Survey of India for over a century. Site management efforts at Ajanta (a, b) to help control the site's high volume of annual visitors include a new visitor center (c) that features replicas of the cave interiors.

The ratification of the Indian Constitution in 1950 affirmed the role of heritage in the newly independent state, declaring "It shall be the duty of every citizen of India to value and preserve the rich heritage of our composite culture."[58] With this charge, the ASI in the years immediately following independence faced several major challenges. Among them were realigning a mission that began under the British in the nineteenth century to support Indian rather than colonial priorities. The organization also faced the daunting task of protecting the historic properties entrusted to its care in a new climate of economic expansion, rapid cultural change and strengthening Indian national identity.

The newly formed nation required adjustments to its heritage legislation in order to reflect the central government's relationship with India's individual states and the semi-autonomous princely states that were gradually being absorbed into the Republic. In 1951 the new Indian government passed a revised and expanded version of the 1904 legislation, titled the "Ancient and Historical Monuments and Archaeological Sites and Remains (Declaration of National Importance) Act." The Act re-affirmed the status of previously listed sites of national importance, and augmented the list with an additional 450 resources, mainly drawn from the princely states, such as the Rajasthani forts of Jaisalmer and Chittorgarh.[59] The Act also empowered the states to implement their own heritage protection legislation to deal with sites that had not been declared nationally significant, but nevertheless had local importance. The "Ancient Monument and Archaeological Sites and Remains Act" of 1958 replaced the 1951 legislation, constituting a further, comprehensive revision to the national heritage legislation. This Act and its associated Rules (1959) form the basis of professional and legal practice today, addressing issues such as the regulation of private and/or public ownership of significant properties, management of the process by which conservators and archaeologists work in India, and establishing a threshold age of 100 years for qualification as a site of national significance. The legislation, often known as AMASRA, was amended and validated in 2010 to incorporate new provisions for regulating activities within buffer zones around designated monuments, specify decision-making authority over the types of activities that can occur in such areas, and strengthen penalties for violating conditions of the law. Similarly, in 1972 Indian lawmakers updated the British-era Antiquities Act of 1947 with the Antiquities and Art Treasures Act, which regulates the registration and handling of movable objects including museum collections, and the export trade in artifacts and manuscripts.[60]

While these legislative updates modernized specific aspects of professional practice, India's size, administrative complexity and range of heritage types present a need for an equally vast legal and institutional infrastructure to adequately protect its many important sites. Since the 1960s, advocates around the country, such as the late attorney and conservation advocate Shyam Chainani of the Bombay Environmental Action Group, have lobbied for enhanced levels of heritage protection at the national, state and local levels. Their actions have led to some additional legislative protection for vulnerable resources, notably the passage of targeted regulations designed to protect specific types of heritage properties, including hill stations, military cantonments and historic districts.

These public policy enhancements dovetailed with related efforts to protect India's natural resources, and in some cases, legislation covering ecologically sensitive resources has been effectively applied to protect adjacent, historically significant built areas. For instance, the Coastal Regulation Zone (CRZ) Notification, passed in 1991, regulates demolition and new construction in areas located within 500 meters of the high tide line (inclusive of tidal rivers and marshes) that are classified as having "outstanding natural beauty/historically/heritage," and consequently has been used to protect threatened buildings in Goa and Mumbai, among other places.[61] Similarly, the Environmental Protection Act (1986) allows for the designation of large areas as "Eco Sensitive Zones," which triggers regulations for certain types of industrial activities and/or development within the defined boundary. In addition to the famous example of the Taj Mahal's TTZ area, the Environmental Protection Act has been used to protect hill stations such as Matheran, Mahabaleshwar and Panchgani, located in the ecologically rich Western Ghats of Maharashtra, from insensitive development.[62]

At the local level, cities and urban districts have utilized the designation of heritage precincts and zones as part of their long-term master planning efforts, much like in other countries. In the holy city of Varanasi (also known as Benares), located in Uttar Pradesh, a series of ten-year planning efforts beginning in 1991 identified five heritage zones, encompassing the renowned *ghats* (steps) lining the River Ganga (Ganges), collections of temples and monasteries, in addition to the stupas and archaeological area of Sarnath, where the Buddha gave his first sermon in 528 BCE. Varanasi embodies the Indian version of living heritage, with its thousands of shrines dedicated to numerous faiths, pilgrimage routes, traditional medical care, charitable organizations, music and handicrafts interwoven into the fabric of the ancient city. At the center of it all is the holy Ganga itself, a resource of profound spiritual and ecological value for much of South Asia, but also one that suffers from heavy pollution and decreased volume, conditions that compromise traditional bathing rituals, and threaten the stability of the adjacent architecture. Among the restrictions for the heritage zones incorporated into the planning codes are 200 meter buffer zones whereby new construction and demolition are not permitted.[63] Due to concerns around lax enforcement of the development restrictions, a local heritage advocacy group filed a Public Interest Litigation suit against the Varanasi Development Authority. In 2013 the High Court in Allahabad ordered the VDA to resolve pending cases around illegal construction in the prohibited zones, and follow through with proposed removal of completed buildings in the same.[64] The case underscores the importance of enforcement of existing heritage management provisions, and the vigilance required of interested parties to ensure that local conservation efforts are not undermined by inaction or competing interests.

In 2015, the ASI had jurisdiction over 3,600 designated sites of national importance, which includes a wide range of architectural, archaeological, secular and religious resources. Administratively part of the Ministry of Tourism and Culture, Department of Culture, the ASI is organized geographically into twenty-seven Circles, and two mini-Circles (at Hampi and Ladakh). A range of professional branches covers the fields of archaeology (Excavation and Prehistory Branches, and Underwater Wing) and historic architecture (Building Survey and Temple Survey Projects). It also has branches for epigraphy, conservation science and historic gardens (the latter known as the Horticulture Branch). Complementing the ASI at the local level are State Departments of Archaeology, which are required by the national legislation but are frequently underfunded and understaffed.[65]

FIGURE 16.7 Holistic heritage conservation planning began in 1991 for Varanasi (also known as Benares), located in Uttar Pradesh, encompasses the renowned *ghats* (steps) lining the River Ganga (Ganges) and the area's temples and monasteries, stupas and archaeological areas. Varanasi represents India's living heritage in the truest sense, with its thousands of shrines dedicated to numerous faiths, pilgrimage routes, traditional medical care, charitable organizations, music and handicrafts interwoven into the fabric of the ancient city.

The ASI also undertakes Indian conservation missions abroad. Since independence, this has included a series of high-profile projects at Angkor in Cambodia beginning in the early 1980s, as well as conservation, excavation, survey and collections management assistance in nearly a dozen countries in Africa, the Middle East, South and Southeast Asia. In order to respond to the increasing demands for trained professionals to manage sites under its care, the ASI established the Delhi-based School of Archaeology in 1959. Upgraded to its current status as the Institute of Archaeology in 1985, the program offers a two-year postgraduate course for fifteen students each year in a full range of conservation disciplines, including site management, structural stabilization, conservation science and museology.[66]

Despite its institutional legacy and status as the principal agency for heritage management in India, the ASI has sustained criticism for inadequately maintaining monuments under its protection, and for its focus on monumental sites at the expense of contextual, small-scale or locally significant resources.[67] At a philosophical level, many have expressed concerns over the decades that the agency remains overly centralized and monument-focused, oriented more toward a Western, science-based view of conservation, and less toward a traditional Indian approach that would more effectively connect with its core constituency: the Indian people.[68] The ASI's updated National Conservation Policy (NCP-AMACR of 2014) has attempted to address these limitations by incorporating contemporary aspects of the field, such as encouraging the role of the traditional crafts and constituent communities in conservation projects, and promoting universal accessibility of heritage sites.[69] However, critics have noted that the Policy remains exclusively focused on monuments of national significance, likening its approach "to a project solely to protect the tiger without factoring in the other elements in an ecosystem."[70]

In response, several new institutions have emerged both within and outside the government during the 1970s and 1980s in order to buttress the ASI's operations, along with the larger cause of architectural conservation training and practice. In 1976 the Ministry of Culture created the National Research Laboratory for Conservation of Cultural Property (NRLC) in Lucknow, which was established to support the use of conservation science techniques in museums and departments of archaeology throughout the country. Along with the New Delhi-based National Museum Institute of History of Art, Conservation and Museology (NMI, established in 1989), the NRLC has established collaborative relationships with international organizations including ICCROM, AusHeritage, the University of Applied Arts, Vienna, and the US-based Getty Conservation Institute, in order to expand local professional capacity for the management of collections and archival materials. Architecture schools at six campuses offer advanced degree programs in conservation and several of its sub-disciplines, including materials conservation and historic landscape architecture.[71] This relatively small number of programs, considering India's population and the scale of its field of practice, points to a need for additional training opportunities for conservation professionals. Perhaps the most significant development in this post-independence era of institution building was the establishment of the Indian National Trust for Art and Cultural Heritage (INTACH) in 1984 as a non-governmental organization devoted to conserving the country's artistic traditions and cultural heritage.

Complementary conservation: INTACH's uniquely Indian approach

Modeled in part after the British National Trust and the US National Trust for Historic Preservation, INTACH was founded in 1984 by then-Prime Minister Indira Gandhi and traditional arts activist Pupul Jayakar.[72] The mission of INTACH is to complement the architectural and archaeological conservation work done by the ASI, while also promoting Indian arts and culture, inclusive of the decorative arts and intangible heritage. From its earliest days, INTACH has received support from India's political leadership, with Prime Minister Rajiv Gandhi serving as its first chairman. Its founding leadership included important participants in the field of conservation, such as B.K. Thapar, Amita Baig and Martand Singh. Pupul Jayakar succeed Rajiv Gandhi as chair in 1989 and led INTACH until 1997.

A highly effective, member-driven NGO, INTACH is comprised today of 160 chapters. It has become the largest employer of architectural conservation professionals in the country, filling some of the advocacy and organizational gaps in the Indian system, and has overseen the conservation of hundreds of individual sites.[73] While a core mission of INTACH's has been the systematic, comprehensive documentation of non-monumental sites throughout India, it also supports youth education programs, technical publication, training, intangible and natural heritage initiatives.

Among INTACH's significant contributions to the field of architectural conservation in India and beyond are its publications, which range from nationwide charters to public-focused brochures that cogently describe heritage sites. A notable and ambitious early effort in this vein is Bernard M. Feilden's *Guidelines for Conservation: A Technical Manual* (1989). The *Guidelines* update and enrich Sir John Marshall's canonical *Conservation Manual* with a late-twentieth century perspective, integrating ideas from the Venice and Burra charters, along with a new section on urban management and heritage areas. Another publication, the seminal *Charter for the Conservation of Unprotected Architectural Heritage and Sites in India* (2004) articulates a clear vision for conservation practice in the context of the international charters, with a distinctly Indian perspective aimed at enhancing its relevancy in the country. INTACH has also prepared a series of professional Conservation Briefs or "how-to" guides that cover a range of topics from the use of traditional lime mortars to preparing a historic garden inventory.

The INTACH Charter is especially effective in its emphasis on the value of "living heritage" as something to be simultaneously protected and leveraged to enhance the present-day appreciation for objects of the past. The Charter emphasizes an interdisciplinary approach to conservation, linking the built environment to the natural world, the scientific to the vernacular, and the traditional to the modern. Significantly, the Charter asserts that while the Western ideology of conservation advocates minimal intervention, India's indigenous traditions embrace the opposite. Based on this, the document proposes a binary framework for conservation treatment alternatives:

resources of national significance that are managed by the ASI or State Departments of Archaeology are to be treated according to conventional international standards; all others may employ hybrid strategies, inventively combining indigenous and official practices, especially those that incorporate the contributions of local craftspeople, or *raj mistris*. The focus on maximizing community benefits through conservation activity extends to guidance on tempering the role of the conservation professional, by taking into account the desires and aspirations of the local community and developing approaches that prolong the economic viability of traditional building practice.

The INTACH strategy for listing significant sites downplays the standard 100-year age requirement, instead relying on a fifty-year threshold for its National Register of Historic Properties. Similar to the Japanese practice of recognizing craftspeople as Living National Treasures, the Charter calls for the creation of a Register of Craftspeople so that the link between important buildings and the people that can sustain them may be reinforced. In an example of the Trust's support for traditional craft skills, a seed grant and marketing program was developed for the *tambat* community, coppersmiths that maintain a 400-year-old craft tradition concentrated in a historic district of the Maharashtra city of Pune. The collaboration between the tambat community and INTACH has included the development of contemporary designs for traditional copper vessels, and promotion of the community's crafts in order to create new markets for their sale and use.[74] The program underscores INTACH's distinctly Indian brand of conservation through its combination of public engagement, local crafts promotion, and, by extension, invigoration of the traditional neighborhood that house the tambat community's living and work spaces.

FIGURE 16.8 Founded in 1984 the Indian National Trust for Art and Cultural Heritage (INTACH) has developed a wide array of programs that mainly address those sites in India that are not primarily under the purview of the Archaeological Survey of India (ASI). Among its most active initiatives is its Youth in INTACH program that offers both classroom and hands-on training, internships and workshops in many parts of India, as well as an annual summit. Pictured is the INTACH First Student Heritage Club Excursion, outside the Governor's House, in North Bengal 2007.

Indian conservation in practice

The scale of architectural conservation work in India ranges from sweeping, multi-decade planning efforts involving some of the world's largest cities, to the protection of small-scale sites and structures. The sheer number and diversity of projects across India touch upon a variety of pertinent issues, including urban conservation, development of community-based conservation strategies, cultural landscapes, and novel approaches for encouraging conservation in the Indian context. The following section does not attempt to identify every architectural conservation project in India today, but rather highlight illustrative, geographically diverse examples of the state of the field in the early twenty-first century. It is useful to begin this overview with a discussion of Delhi, the nation's capital and a nexus of conservation policy and practice in South Asia.

Architectural conservation in Delhi is challenged by factors present in many of the world's fast-growing cities, where rapid urbanization increases competition for land and resources, while placing enormous pressures on historic sites and districts. Although India has the largest rural population in the world, census numbers between 2001 and 2011 marked the first time that the rate of urban population growth exceeded that of the rural. Delhi and Mumbai, both cities with large numbers of historic monuments, districts and sites, now rank among the five largest cities in the world, each with populations of over 20 million.[75]

While Mumbai owes its prominence largely to the British period, Delhi stands as one of the world's great ancient metropolises, containing a range of architectural legacies including the Maurya (fourth century BCE), the Delhi Sultanate (1206–1526), the Mughals (1526–1857) and the Raj (in the form of the last British imperial capital, designed by Sir Edwin Lutyens between 1911 and 1931). Over time, its nine administrative districts (including New Delhi) have spread over nearly 1,500 square kilometers, absorbing nearby smaller villages into the urban sprawl. Factors such as the increased commercialization, unrestricted development, and the inability of many authorities to either enforce architectural conservation regulations or provide the infrastructure to meet the requirements of current tenants stand as major impediments to successful urban conservation strategies in Delhi.

Delhi boasts numerous impressive conservation projects, even while the city struggles to define its overall relationship with and commitment to architectural heritage protection. In 1999 the INTACH Delhi Chapter prepared a survey identifying over 1,200 heritage buildings in the city, an increase of over a thousand new sites from the 174 that had been previously listed by the ASI as significant. As a result of this identification effort, INTACH lobbied for new legislation and agreements to ensure that this gap in protection was adequately addressed. Five years later, in 2004, the National Capital Territory Legislative Assembly passed the Delhi Ancient and Historical Monuments and Archaeological Sites and Remains Act (State Archaeology Act). Pursuant to this Act, the Department of Archaeology of the Government of the National Capital Territory of Delhi and INTACH signed a Memorandum of Understanding (MOU) on October 29, 2008, relative to the protection and subsequent conservation of 250 buildings from the INTACH list. Conservation work on fourteen sites, ranging from the 1863 Gothic revival Mutiny Memorial to a series of Mughal-era tombs, was spurred as part of the city-wide preparations for the 2010 Commonwealth Games, the largest international event ever hosted by the municipality. The conservation strategies at each monument included cleaning, infill of missing materials, restoring plaster finishes and installation of architectural lighting to draw attention to the previously neglected structures. This approach went farther than ruin stabilization, which is a more typical approach for similar buildings, and instead included restoration and reconstruction of missing elements using traditional craft skills. The conservation work was coupled with extensive documentation of each project, thereby greatly augmenting available information for the structures, and setting a new standard for historic resource documentation in Delhi.[76]

In addition to individual monuments, neighborhood-wide conservation programs have taken root in select precincts of Delhi, most notably in the Nizamuddin Basti, a dense collection of Mughal-era buildings including Humayun's Tomb, a major monument and World Heritage Site. The Nizamuddin Basti program serves to illustrate the success that can arise from public–private-sector partnerships (or PPP), as well as the larger common good that can result from a well-coordinated, holistic approach to conservation in complex urban environs. Often cited as an architectural precursor to the Taj Mahal, the sixteenth century Humayun's Tomb holds the resting places of Mughal emperor Humayun

(1508–1556), his wife and several family members. Prior to the project's commencement, the structure had suffered significant deterioration from neglect, water damage and prior ineffective conservation interventions. In addition to the architectural and structural deficiencies, its surrounding gardens were inadequately maintained and overgrown.

In 1997, the Aga Khan Trust for Culture initiated an ambitious conservation effort, financing the US$650,000 garden restoration and ultimately partnering with the ASI and the philanthropic organization Sir Dorabji Tata Trust in 2007 to restore the red sandstone structure.[77] The project drew upon the work of 1,500 local and international craftspeople, with a particular focus on the revival of ancient techniques used at the time of the tomb's original construction. Tilework artisans from Samarkand, Uzbekistan (the onetime home to Babur, Humayun's father and the founder of the Mughal dynasty) were brought in to train local craftspeople in the process of restoring the blue, yellow, green and white tile finishes on the building's canopies (or *chhatri*). Additionally, the conservation team removed more than 1 million kilograms of cement from the tomb complex, which had been used in the early twentieth century in a misguided restoration attempt, and subsequently hastened deterioration in portions of the buildings. The project incorporated a number of digital tools to augment the documentation effort, including laser scanning of the buildings, ground penetrating radar to identify underground structures, and global positioning system (GPS) software to map replacement plant species. Conservation of the tomb and the reinstatement of the gardens and landscaped contexts took more than six years, and the site re-opened to the public in 2013.[78]

Building on the successful conservation of Humayun's Tomb, several organizations including the ASI, the Municipal Corporation of Delhi, the Central Public Works Department and the Aga Khan Development Network established an agreement in 2007 to focus conservation efforts on the greater

a

FIGURE 16.9a, b and c The Humayun Tomb complex located in the Nizamuddin Basti district of Delhi has been a focus project of the Aga Khan Trust for Culture from 1997. The project entailed the careful conservation of the Humayun and Isa Khan tombs (a, b), complete with a simplified version of the site's former lushly landscaped gardens (c). The projects entailed the fostering of historic building crafts traditions and involved participation by the Archaeological Survey of India, the Sir Dorabji Tata Trust and the World Monuments Fund.

Nizamuddin Basti neighborhood, beyond Humayun's Tomb, and inclusive of the Sunder Nursery, a former garden now used by the city's public works department to grow street trees. The Nizamuddin Basti area is comprised of a concentration of Mughal and pre-Mughal sites including tombs and shrines of varying scales, clusters of traditional residential buildings, landscaped gardens and small-scale monuments. This public–private-sector collaboration called upon the help of an interdisciplinary team that included 100 members of the community as consultants and collaborators to the project. Earlier conservation planning had identified several distinct needs within the local community, such as improved public sanitation and access to education. To address these needs, the program focused on traditional crafts and job skills training, early childhood education centers and a school for over 600 pupils, and a venue for cultural programs that focused on the life and work of the thirteenth century Sufi poet-composer Hazrat Amir Khusrau Dehlavi.[79] Major utility and infrastructure improvements were also incorporated into the project, including sanitation system upgrades, installation of new public toilets, and façade improvements to buildings across the district.

A centerpiece of the comprehensive conservation effort was the restoration of the district's *baoli* (step well), a heavily used pilgrimage site built in 1322, and located adjacent to the shrine of the neighborhood's namesake, the fourteenth century Sufi saint Hazrat Nizamuddin Auliya.[80] One of the few remaining spring-fed wells left in Delhi, the baoli measures 27 m deep and is surrounded on three sides with buildings contemporary to its construction, and on the fourth side steps to access the well. A partial structural collapse in 2008 along with an accumulation of contaminated water made the baoli unusable, and a potential hazard to the community. Conservation of the well included replacement of the leaking subterranean sewer pipes that had been contaminating the water and the removal of several tons of accumulated debris at the bottom of the well. The collapse was repaired, the masonry repointed, and a lime mortar was used to replace the epoxy coating that had been applied during a previous conservation effort. Now cleaned and structurally sound, the baoli once again serves as a destination for Sufi pilgrims, as well as a public space where neighborhood youth play in the spring-fed holy waters.

The creation of an urban park around the sixteenth century Sunder Nursery has been another major component of the Nizamuddin Basti conservation program. Just over 40 ha in size, the Sunder Nursery includes buildings and pavilions in a traditional Mughal garden setting that functioned historically and currently as a nursery; at present, 8.08 ha have been set aside for Delhi's Central Public Works Department, which is growing plants used in city-wide planting and greening efforts. Ultimately plans call for the restoration of several pavilion structures along with the establishment of an interpretive center highlighting the ecology of the Delhi region.[81]

Re-establishing public open spaces in conjunction with conservation works has become a hallmark of the Aga Khan Trust's approach to its projects. Rather than approach these distinct but important heritage elements in Nizamuddin Basti separately, conservationists implemented a comprehensive neighborhood revitalization strategy that addressed multiple aspects of community functioning. The conservation plans served as vehicles to address both the care of important heritage sites, as well as broader needs within the community. By approaching these needs holistically, conservationists were able to involve the community in their efforts, while also improving quality of life for local residents.

Complementing the Humayun's Tomb and the Nizamuddin Basti neighborhood projects, which emphasized technical and structural improvements to historic buildings, the Delhi Heritage Route Project underscores the value of improving site access, interpretation, amenities and information regarding the city's important heritage sites. The project was conceived with the goal of revealing and connecting the various heritage sites and precincts of the city in order to make them more accessible to citizens and visitors, and to highlight the potential for improvements to Delhi's cityscape. The initiative began with the development of eight heritage routes by INTACH's Delhi Chapter in 2008, under the dynamic leadership of Chapter head A.G. Krishna Menon. This INTACH project, spurred by the approaching Commonwealth Games and linked to a push for UNESCO World Heritage City status, was supported internationally by the American Express Corporation and the World Monuments Fund. The routes included a six-mile stretch from Red Fort to Humayun's Tomb, with numerous lesser-known heritage sites between. The project ultimately offers a strategic vision for improved visitor amenities and landscapes along the route, while also providing increased access to information

 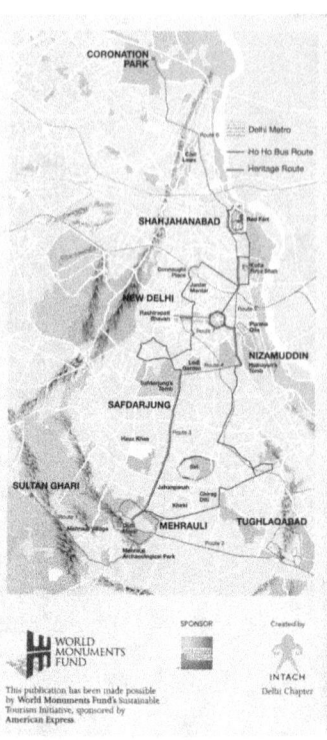

FIGURE 16.10 An urban park was created around the sixteenth century Sunder Nursery in the Nizamuddin Basti neighborhood near Humayun's Tomb in Delhi. A nearby *baoli* (step well) has been transformed from a polluted and dangerous waste pit to a healthy spring-fed urban water amenity for locals and Sufi pilgrims, which was an integral part of the Tomb area rehabilitation project. Additional neighborhood improvements such as building façade improvements and modernized public toilet facilities made this facet of the Humayan Tomb precinct project a model of contextual planning in architectural conservation practice.

FIGURE 16.11 Map of the Delhi Heritage Trail, one of several projects launched in 2008 by INTACH's Delhi Chapter that has the aim of connecting and highlighting the histories of the various heritage sites and precincts of the city in order to make them more accessible to citizens and visitors alike.

about the sites via improved signage and walking tour booklets. Individual tour guides were also trained to give heritage walks along the route. Clean-energy "hop-on, hop-off" buses were also introduced along the route to streamline the flow of visitors and reduce traffic and air pollution.

In 2013, the walks program evolved to include a publishing effort that encompassed twenty booklets and eighteen maps delineating an expanded network of heritage routes across the city, including information about historic buildings and also contemporary features such as restaurants and non-heritage attractions (such as the National Zoo) along the way.[82] The program now serves as a model for other civic improvement projects throughout Delhi, illustrating the effectiveness of a sustained, coordinated public awareness campaign that couples the efforts of government, non-government and community groups to spotlight heritage conservation.[83]

Efforts to promote architectural heritage in Delhi, such as the INTACH survey, neighborhood revitalization efforts and the Heritage Walks project have generated results, but setbacks in the larger movement to conserve the city's historic buildings remain an issue. A complementary approach has been promoted by the Delhi Development Authority (DDA). This government entity, responsible for master planning and setting priorities for development in the capital, dedicated a section of the Master Plan for Delhi 2021 to architectural conservation priorities. The Plan delineates six heritage zones and three archaeological parks, including the Mehrauli neighborhood, home to the Qutub Minar, and Chirag Delhi, a former village featuring Mughal-era tombs and former defensive fortifications.[84]

While promising, the DDA's approach to designating historic districts is not shared across the spectrum, as evidenced by Delhi's recently unsuccessful bid to become a World Heritage City. In 2008, INTACH established a Memorandum of Understanding with the municipal government of Delhi to work toward achieving a World Heritage City designation by 2015, and in 2012, Delhi was placed on the tentative list for this honor. Yet Delhi's bid was abruptly withdrawn from the list in May 2015, amid concerns that having a World Heritage City designation would result in excessive prohibitions on development. Despite the fact that the nomination was based on only 1.5 percent of the city, centered mainly on the Shahjahanabad and the Lutyens Bungalow Zone,[85] officials from the Ministry of Culture reported "reservations from the urban development ministry that if Delhi is declared World Heritage City, there would be lots of restrictions."[86] The decision to withdraw Delhi from the list represented a major setback in the efforts to promote and manage the city's heritage resources and highlights the tension between conservation priorities and new development.

Conservation challenges and solutions in urban areas of India: examples from Mumbai

Delhi's struggle to protect the individual and contextual integrity of its significant historic architecture illustrates a particular challenge faced by Indian conservators in their increasingly diverse and complex urban centers. The size, scope and number of India's metropolises – and the rate at which they are expanding – demands new solutions for conserving built forms ranging from indigenous religious sites to colonial infrastructure. As is the case in China, India's dominant urban trend is a determined drive toward modernization, which competes with conservation planning and restrictions on development designed to protect heritage sites.

Recently, architectural conservationists have begun to work with city planners to introduce community-driven uses for buildings in historic areas to help drive large-scale conservation efforts. One such example in Mumbai involved a grassroots campaign whereby a group of residents petitioned the state government to maintain the Oval Maidan, a nine-hectare, nineteenth century green space adjacent to the city's Churchgate district. The Maidan had become unmaintained and used as an illegal dumping ground, until the Oval Cooperage Residents Association successfully convinced the state government to allow them to clear debris, install a fence and – significantly – build a walking track that reinvigorated the public use of the space. As soon as this new, popular use was introduced into the dilapidated area in 1999, the community group in charge of the space was able to rally public support for the restoration of the Oval's historic features.

Other examples of this trend in the historic Fort area of Mumbai include the designation of a contemporary art gallery district. The Kala Ghoda district contains multiple significant historic buildings including Indo-Saracenic marvels such as the David Sassoon Library, along with contextual fabric dating from the nineteenth century development of the district under the British. Revival of the area began with a survey project by young architects and urban designers that revealed the district housed the largest concentration of contemporary art galleries in India. Consequently, the Urban Design Research Institute (UDRI), a Mumbai-based advocacy group for architecture and urban planning, helped lobby the local government to designate Kala Ghoda as an arts district.[87]

Since 1999 the area has hosted the Kala Ghoda Arts Festival, which has grown to become a major event attracting 150,000 attendees over nine days. The festival and advocacy efforts of the UDRI and others has triggered a revival of public spaces and renewed investment in the historic district, perhaps to a fault. Members of the Kala Ghoda community were surprised to learn of the state tourism development corporation's 2014 plans to promote the area as a cultural hub modeled after Times Square in New York City, including the installation of billboards, electronic signs and a huge Indian flag. The proposal was quickly dropped after encountering stiff resistance from the same organizations that had overseen the organic renewal of the neighborhood over the previous two decades. Citing specific Indian Supreme Court rulings that prohibited large-scale advertisements in heritage districts such as Kala Ghoda, along with state and national laws that create buffer zones around individual heritage sites, the proposal fizzled under pressure from the neighborhood groups.[88] These projects in Mumbai offer potent examples of successful efforts to engage a local population in conservation. They represent an innovative level of experimentation with the rapidly evolving Indian urban developments that could prove essential to future conservation efforts.

Official architectural heritage management in India is comprised of a complex network of governmental and advocacy support organizations that are of particular importance to conservation efforts in the country's urban environments. Municipal Corporations, known also as *Mahanagar Palika* or *Mahanagar Nigam*, are local governmental entities that support various aspects of urban development in cities of more than 500,000 residents; they have played an important role in promoting urban conservation issues in several major Indian cities, including Jaipur, Delhi and Ahmedabad.[89]

In Ahmedabad in northwestern India the Municipal Corporation (AMC) has played a particularly active role in highlighting and advancing local conservation concerns, including efforts to conserve its walled old town and its distinctive built fabric. Built as a fortified city in the fifteenth century, Old Ahmedabad today is comprised of *havelis* (private courtyard mansions) and *pols* (small residential clusters organized around a family, caste or profession). For most of the twentieth century many were at risk of serious deterioration and loss due to a lack of appreciation of traditional architecture, deferred maintenance and real estate development pressures.

In 1985 the AMC initiated a program to address these issues and has since made steady progress. In 1996 the AMC established a designated Heritage Cell tasked with a broad range of activities aimed at significantly increasing governmental participation and public interest in local conservation. As part of its effort to promote conservation through public policy, the AMC initiated a program to pinpoint pressing concerns related to the field, prepare a gazette of historic resources, and propose a comprehensive urban conservation policy. In collaboration with a team of French conservation architects and planners, the AMC conducted a comprehensive survey in 2001 that identified 15,000 local heritage properties, and at the same time it established a partnership with ASI to restore the distinctive walls and gates of the old town. In collaboration with the state government, the AMC also helped to provide owners of eligible historic properties with grants that covered 50 percent of the cost to make building façade improvements.

At the advocacy level, the AMC promoted conservation through public relations and community outreach efforts, calling for conservation approaches through local media outlets, as well as through newsletters, trainings and workshops. In 1997, it launched a unique heritage walk program that

FIGURE 16.12 View along the *Krantidarshan Padyatra*, or Freedom Walk, in central Ahmedabad, a route that includes twenty-eight key historic properties associated with several of India's early advocates for independence.

highlighted the connections between Ahmedabad and India's independence movement. Known as the *Krantidarshan Padyatra*, or Freedom Walk, the route includes twenty-eight key historic properties associated with several of India's early advocates for independence, many of whom have connections to the city.[90]

In 2015 the AMC began overseeing a Transfer of Development Rights (TDR) program whereby properties identified on heritage registers within the old city can sell future development rights to sites elsewhere in Ahmedabad in return for funds to improve their historic building. First employed in Karnataka in 2005, TDR is based on a formula linked to the level of historic property and a property's size (calculated by floor space index, or FSI). Property owners can sell their rights to developers, as long as the proceeds are invested back into their property within three months.[91] The potential for this program to benefit neglected historic structures in Ahmedabad is huge, with estimates as high as US$50 million that might be generated through the 2,500 properties that qualify for the program.[92]

In contrast to difficult episodes at Hampi (see sidebar), successful collaboration between international conservationists and local community-based teams came about in the small community of Basgo, located in the mountainous Ladakh region of Jammu and Kashmir. There, international and local teams worked together on comprehensive, community-driven conservation programs that have included identifying and documenting key historic sites, as well as on technical conservation efforts focused on specific resources.

Building bridges at Hampi: the importance of stakeholder communication in the management of World Heritage Sites

India's famously complex governmental structures, along with its active representative democracy, have in some instances conflicted with the international bodies that participate in heritage management, even at highly visible World Heritage Sites. One complex and tragic example is the ruined site of the fourteenth century Vijayanagara Hindu capital city of Hampi, located in the southwest state of Karnataka. In 1999 local officials initiated construction of two vehicular and a single footbridge crossing the Tungabhadra River adjacent to the site, which consists of a vast composition of over 1,600 structures ranging from the monumental to the sublime.

The World Heritage Committee determined that the bridges would undermine important views of the site's majestic step-pyramid temples, increase vehicular traffic into and through the site and erode its rural setting.[93] UNESCO promptly placed the site on the list of World Heritage in Danger, and began working with the state government of Karnataka to halt construction on the bridges, one of which had been 80 percent completed prior to the intervention. Agreement was ultimately reached to stop work on the partially completed bridges, which had been a priority of the local citizenry in order to shorten travel times between regional hubs (Hospet and Gangavathi), facilitate transport of agricultural products and create a more direct route for tourists visiting the region's various Vijayanagara sites. UNESCO removed Hampi from the Heritage in Danger list in 2006 following a series of concessions on the part of the state government that would allow the completion of the Anegundi Bridge as a temporary crossing that would ultimately be removed, and construction of a bypass around the World Heritage Site.

Work resumed in 2009 only to be halted again, this time by an accidental collapse that tragically killed eight and injured dozens of construction workers.[94] In early 2015, the India State Party reported to UNESCO that the debris from the collapsed bridge was being removed, and that an agreed-upon bridge location would proceed based on a cultural impact assessment study.

The initial bridge episode led to the drafting of an innovative "Integrated Management Plan" in 2006 by the esteemed professor of conservation at the School of Planning and Architecture (Delhi), Nalini Thakur, which focused on treatment of the site as a living cultural landscape that includes twenty-nine villages and tens of thousands of residents, rather than a static collection of monuments. While community involvement and the ability of residential stakeholders to thrive remains an area of focus under the new management plan, protection of the integrity of the site remains a top priority, as evidenced by the state High Court's dramatic decision to relocate nearly 350 families from the Virupaksha Bazaar in 2011, which had been deemed an illegal encroachment on the site.[95] The controversies at Hampi underscore the need for international heritage organizations to work with local political and economic interests to ensure that appropriate heritage site management can occur, while also allowing political leaders to remain responsive to their constituents.

In 2003 the Namgyal Institute for Research on Ladakhi Art and Culture (NIRLAC) partnered with the Basgo Welfare Committee (BWC) in an effort to aid village elders in the task of preserving their villages' common heritage.[96] With support by the US-based Ford Foundation, these efforts resulted in a comprehensive survey of heritage sites in Ladakh that includes locally significant structures such as stupas, monasteries, mosques, palaces and vernacular structures, as well as mountains, lakes and other landscape features. In order to ensure a comprehensive and accurate outcome, as well as establish accountability at the local level, the survey listing process was developed in collaboration with various local village communities and included unique, culturally significant criteria, such as determining the age of a site by the number of generations associated with a particular place, rather than the more typical measurement in years. The BWC efforts to develop a comprehensive list were successful: by 2009, 450 villages had been surveyed, with 4,500 culturally significant sites identified. These results substantially augmented the ASI's survey of sites of national significance in Ladakh, which, in contrast, consisted of only eleven sites.[97]

Once identified, the BWC coordinated the restoration of a complex of three Maitreya (Future Buddha) temples at Basgo dating to the eleventh–fifteenth centuries, which the World Monuments Fund had included on its 2000 Watch List due to their rapidly deteriorating structural condition. Between 2002 and 2004 two of the temples in the trio were conserved (the Chamchung Lhakhang and Chamba Lhakhang), with the third (Serzang Lhakhang) completed in 2006. Each building is constructed of mud brick and timber framing and features ancient wall paintings representing religious scenes associated with the Buddha. Conservation efforts of the temple were led by an international team of Indian and US-based conservators, but were developed and executed in direct consultation with the village community. This collaboration ensured that the site was effectively revived while also meeting important spiritual and cultural standards that would allow the temple to continue to serve the community as an important place of worship.

FIGURE 16.13 Conservation at Chamba Lhakhang (ca. fourteenth century), one of three Maitreya temples at Basgo located in the mountainous Ladakh region of Jammu and Kashmir, entailed roof repairs, earthen wall consolidation and conservation of religious murals. Selected for the type of conservation it represented, local stakeholders and craftsmen were assisted by international experts with the technically difficult task of mural conservation, in a demonstration project that could be replicated at other sites in the region.

Centuries of deterioration and leaking from the timber-framed roof had resulted in damage to paintings on the interior mud brick walls. The damage was so severe, in fact, that by 2002, when conservation of Chamba Lhakhang began, local constituents no longer deemed them suitable for worship. After the paintings were de-consecrated by a senior monk, the teams were able to re-frame and replace the roof in kind while correcting leaks, and stabilizing and conserving the wall paintings. Structural shoring was necessary at the precariously sited buildings due to foundation erosion, much of which was completed using local labor sources. Painting conservators were also able to clean, stabilize and infill lost sections of the paintings, using restoration techniques that were discernable from the original.[98] Executed despite tremendous logistical challenges, such as working at nearly 4,000 m during brief four-month field seasons, the project was nevertheless a widely hailed success, earning the renewed spiritual use and ongoing maintenance of the temples by the local community, in addition to a 2007 UNESCO Asia-Pacific Award for Cultural Heritage Conservation.[99]

Conservation of cultural landscapes

As in much of Asia, cultural landscapes in India are often as significant as individual or collections of buildings, especially when connected to sites of religious pilgrimage. The aforementioned Humayun's Tomb, Delhi Heritage Trail and projects at Basgo in Ladakh are examples that initially focused on the conservation of individual structures; however, all were developed with regard to their physical context as well as in support of their monuments-specific aims. They were versions of the historic landscape conservation approach, which within urban settings has recently also been termed the Historic Urban Landscape (HUL) approach. The optimum HUL approach, however, evenly addresses all cultural assets within a defined area. (For the HUL approach, see also Chapter 10.)

Located in the Braj region of Uttar Pradesh, Govardhan Hill is a quintessential example of a rural cultural landscape and represents a combination of architectural elements and natural features manipulated by people for a specific cultural purpose.[100] Efforts to conserve the significant landscapes of Braj underscore both the importance of cultural landscapes in South Asia and the challenges inherent in maintaining them over time under heavy use.[101]

Govardhan Hill is a Hindu pilgrimage site comprised of a 7 km ridge and *van* (forest groves) along the Yamuna River, in addition to approximately 1,000 *kunds* (ceremonial ponds) distributed across the surrounding area. The ridge is particularly significant for its connection to the story of Indra's defeat at the hands of Lord Krishna. Though it has served as a pilgrimage site for centuries, increased vehicular use by worshippers as well as its proximity to the popular tourist destination of Agra, have greatly facilitated access in recent decades; by the early 2000s pilgrimage visitors to the Braj region were estimated at more than 50 million each year. As the increased site use and the changing modes of access (from walking to driving) has damaged the site's natural elements, they have also challenged traditional ritual activities that were central to worship at the site. For instance, increased use has damaged built and natural markers that guide the way for pilgrims to visit specific worship sites at Govardhan Hill.[102]

The Braj Foundation, a local NGO working since 2005 with substantial support from the private sector, has spearheaded efforts to restore the integrity of the larger cultural landscape, while continuing to facilitate religious visitation. In 2010, the Foundation collaborated with the University of Illinois on conservation planning and design for the site, which identified the loss of many of the kunds and van that were described in the traditional Krishna texts and once found throughout the landscape. In response the organization, which draws much of its funding from the construction industry, helped to implement water management systems and physically reconstructed nearly forty kunds, many of which had silted in or had their water sources diverted. The Foundation has also promoted the replanting of van as part of the effort to restore the traditional landscape and active pilgrimage activity at Govardhan Hill.[103] The situation in Braj points to a need for further development in the management of cultural landscapes in India, particularly those subject to heavy use by tourists or religious pilgrims, since changing use patterns will impact these important sites whether they are planned for or not.

FIGURE 16.14 Govardhan Hill, in the Braj region of Uttar Pradesh, is an important Hindu pilgrimage site comprised of a 7 km ridge and forest groves along the Yamuna River in addition to ceremonial ponds distributed across the surrounding area. Receiving more than 50 million visitors a year, pressures on the land and support facilities have been detrimental to the site and demand improved circulation, conservation of the site's various features, improved circulation and provision of visitor amenities. Since 2005 the Braj Foundation, a local NGO, with wide support and foreign technical assistance has been trying to address the situation.

Inventing cultural significance, by Rahul Mehrotra

The dynamic and rapidly transforming nature of urban India exerts an incredible pressure on our built heritage in cities, both for its sheer survival as well as its integrity. In fact, contemporary Indian cities are fast becoming almost incomprehensible entities, highly pluralistic urban landscapes that are characterized by intense dualities. These cities defeat conventional notions of "the city" and are represented more accurately through the "mutation" of urban space rather than as a largely "static" and stable entity.

Two distinct cities exist in India today – the static city and the kinetic city. They are two completely different worlds that amazingly co-exist in the same urban space. The static city is represented through architecture and its monuments, is unchanging and built in permanent materials. The kinetic city is one that occupies interstitial spaces in the urban system and is a city in motion – the kuchcha city built of temporary material. Processions and festivals form the integral spectacle and memory of the kinetic city where its very expression is temporary in nature and is in constant flux.

In urban India architecture is no longer the spectacle of the city. There now exist numerous other urban spectacles that emerge out of an incredibly prolific production of popular culture. In fact, in this dynamic situation, cultural memory is often an enacted process and not necessarily encoded in architecture but rather in temporal happenings. How then do heritage activists and professionals respond to, or engage in, the act of "conservation" in such a context where the emerging images of our built environment are a complete blur?

The first issue that practitioners of heritage conservation must address and articulate is the notion of change. In fact, one of the major reasons for the failure of the implementation of most urban conservation ideas in India is that these proposals don't account for, or define, change as a notion. The complete negation of the idea of "change" in fact is what usually characterizes (to the public at large) the role of heritage activists. This "nostalgic" approach to conserving urban settings is a self-perpetuating phenomenon captured succinctly in the following passage from Italo Calvino's book *Invisible Cities*: "the traveler is invited to visit the city and, at the same time, to examine some old post cards that show it as it used to be … if the traveler does not wish to disappoint the inhabitants, he must praise the Postcard City and prefer it to the present one, though he must be careful to contain his regret at the changes within definite limits."

Interestingly, people tend to discuss change in terms of the loss of something as opposed to new possibilities – because people tend to perceive any new condition as worse than some magic moment in the past – so they develop a narrative to describe that sense of loss. The English press in India is particularly guilty of this myopic view and writings on heritage issues in most English dailies drip with nostalgia! The question really for heritage activists and professional practitioners is how do you actually identify new typologies and work with them? How do you articulate the idea of the heritage as a dynamic, fluid and evolving entity? How do you deal with the notions of the static and kinetic cities – and recognize the numerous spectacles the kinetic city is constructing as intrinsic to the process of the evolution of our contemporary heritage?

It is here that the notion of "cultural significance" is of importance. Cultural significance as an all-encompassing idea is something that emerged clearly in the conservation debate in the 1980s (with the Burra Charter to be more precise). The Burra Charter defined it as the "aesthetic, historic, scientific or social value for past, present and future generations." Implicit in this definition is the belief that "significance" is static. It is a definition that is "object"-centric (devoid of life) with its roots in the debate propagated by the antiquarians of the Renaissance. What is the validity of such a notion in a highly pluralist society where cultural memory is often an enacted process? What is our cultural reading for the kinetic city that now forms a greater part of our urban reality?

The questions then are: how do you identify the contemporary engines that drive this process of conservation or urban renewal? How do you read cultural significance and the validity or necessity to sometimes invent "cultural significance" to drive this process? When engaging issues in this manner, historic urban centers could be viewed as incredible resources – drained of their iconography or symbolic content! Thus, it is critical to not focus on pure cultural memory in a narrow historical sense but also (in the faltering economy of South Asia) see historic landscapes as resources – accept the dualities evident in the contemporary urban landscape as being simultaneously valid. Heritage activists would then slip back and forth between the role of a planner, the role of a conservationist in the pure sense, and that of a designer who can see the possibilities in the way spaces can be used, and reinterpreted.

Situated on the southwest coast of India, Kochi (formerly Cochin, and also known as Ernakulam) is an important port city that rose to prominence in the fourteenth century as a spice-trading center before becoming one of the earliest European colonies in India by the turn of the sixteenth century. The Portuguese first occupied the city (later moving their principal trading port north to Goa) and were later followed by the Dutch and finally the British. Over the centuries the city developed a remarkably diverse population representative of the Arabian Sea cultures, including Malabar Jews, Saint Thomas Christians, Muslims and Hindus. By the early twenty-first century, historic Kochi was home to the legacies of these diverse origins and a wealth of architecturally unique, but functionally obsolete buildings.

The Kochi-Muziris Biennale provides a compelling example of adaptive reuse of historic buildings in an area that has struggled with finding new uses for its important heritage resources. Contemporary art promoters collaborated with local conservationists to spearhead the Kochi-Muziris Biennale in 2012, creating an international contemporary art exhibition housed within a variety of the city's historic buildings.[104] Many of the event spaces are located nearby to the Jew Town Road Godown, a historically rich section of Kochi that features the magnificent Paradesi Synagogue, founded in 1568.[105]

Although the primary goal of the large-scale arts event is to promote the contemporary art movement in southern India, the Kochi-Muziris Biennale has also served as a catalyst to the successful rehabilitation and creative reuse of several historically significant buildings that had otherwise been neglected. The 1860s Aspinwall House, a spice-trading warehouse, and a seventeenth century Dutch barracks were both used as gallery spaces, while the Pepper House served as an events venue, café, artist residence and

FIGURE 16.15a and b Views of the urban cultural landscape of Kochi (Cochin), Malabar Coast, southwest India. The sixteenth century Paradesi Synagogue (a) and the Jew Town Road neighborhood (b) are conservation efforts that began in the early 1990s.

studio space. The 1850s Durbar Hall was rehabilitated for US$500,000 and served as the festival headquarters and also a year-round exhibit space. In addition to widespread acclaim for the festival's successes, some controversy has been generated by the use of historic buildings to support the program. Organizers have been criticized based on concerns that conservationists did not consult appropriately with the Kerala Archaeology Department in the rehabilitation of the Durbar Hall, and there has been some controversy surrounding the project's use of government funds.[106] A second event was held in 2014, with a third scheduled for 2016, and planners are expecting the attendance to double to an estimated 800,000 visitors. Heritage conservationists must closely monitor the condition of and changes to these buildings and their surrounding area as the Kochi-Muziris Biennale expands in scope and the number of visitors increases over the next several years. Time, along with careful assessment, will reveal more about how these heritage buildings are faring under Kochi's program of renewal and reuse.

Conserving colonial India

Although the colonial era in India can evoke painful memories, and the architectural vestiges of this time stand as physical embodiments of this chapter, the country has nevertheless made a considerable effort to preserve European buildings constructed between the sixteenth and twentieth centuries. Of India's twenty-eight built World Heritage Sites, three represent examples from the colonial era: the Chhatrapati Shivaji (formerly Victoria) Terminus, the Mountain Railways of India and the Churches and Convents of Goa. Local designations include many more sites and structures from the colonial period, which present a range of challenges for conservation professionals in India.[107]

Efforts to conserve railway heritage, including stations, rolling stock, engineering structures and a wealth of documentation, began in the 1970s, with the opening of railway museums in Delhi and Mysore.[108] Railroad resources broadly fall under the category of industrial heritage, which has otherwise not gained much of a foothold in South Asia. Conservation of railroad heritage enjoys support both from within India and from foreign enthusiasts. The Darjeeling Himalayan Railway Society, for instance, receives support from over 800 members in twenty-two countries and was instrumental in lobbying for World Heritage Site status (achieved in 1999) for that property.[109] The designation was expanded to include the

Kalka Shimla route (in 2005) and the Nilgiri Mountain Railway (in 2008) to constitute the Mountain Railways of India World Heritage Site.

The effort to conserve Dalhousie Square in Kolkata (Calcutta), serves as an effective example of conservation practices focused on colonial-era resources, and implemented at the state level. An urban district built when the British Raj administered the colony from Calcutta (prior to moving to New Delhi in 1911), Dalhousie Square is a landscaped two square-kilometer area with a tank (artificial rectangular pool) at its center. Renamed Binoy-Dadal-Dinesh Dag after independence, the square and its surrounding administration buildings had suffered from neglect and disuse for decades, while incompatible development had encroached on the nineteenth-century buildings and landscapes. This trend culminated in its listing on the WMF's list of 100 Most Endangered Sites for 2002–2004. Through the combined efforts of the Heritage Commission of West Bengal, the local chapter of INTACH, and Kolkata-based Centre for Action Research in Conservation of Heritage (ARCH), a local, professionally led advocacy group, the square was designated a local heritage precinct and documented by students from Jadavpur University.

Planned to be the administrative quarters of the British, the symmetrically planned Dalhousie Square has been marred by new construction such as the nondescript modern Telephone Bhavan that replaced the Dalhousie Institute club. The grand Senate Hall of Calcutta on the square was similarly replaced with a nondescript new structure. Such intrusions have pointed up the importance of reconciling the role of thousands of British Colonial buildings that remain in Calcutta and the importance of careful consideration toward their replacement and restoration. Although long-term conservation of the Victorian, Georgian and Classical Revival buildings of Kolkata will require a higher level of cooperation from local merchants, traffic planners and other civic leaders, growing interest in conserving India's European architectural heritage illustrates a promising trend.[110]

Efforts by site or project-specific non-governmental organizations (or NGOs) have emerged as an effective model for leveraging international support in concert with locally based advocacy and professional conservation resources. At Jaisalmer, a twelfth-century fortified city located in the Thar Desert of western Rajasthan, the London-based organization Jaisalmer in Jeopardy has worked in collaboration with INTACH since 1996 to address various issues related to conservation, infrastructure and development in the majestic walled city. Located on the former caravan routes between northern India and Persia, Egypt and points west, Jaisalmer is now one of six locales that constitute the Hill Forts of Rajasthan World Heritage Site.

A case study in the natural and manmade challenges facing conservation efforts in India, the delicately carved yellow sandstone buildings of the citadel and lower town areas of Jaisalmer are threatened primarily by the introduction of a modern water supply system, brought in the early 1990s to support a burgeoning population of 65,000 and a growing tourism industry within the city's medieval walls. The increased consumption of water with inadequate wastewater removal systems has affected Jaisalmer's historic buildings as well as the battered stone walls forming its citadel. The problems are manifest in erosion caused by rising damp at foundation walls that can eventually cause collapse.[111]

The effort to save Jaisalmer faced a wide scope of conservation issues, ranging from the maintenance of finely carved sandstone detailing, to solving the city's large-scale groundwater problems. In addition there have been a number of modernization issues such as the insensitive wiring and lighting of buildings and squares that compromised the historic town's overall appearance. In partnership with INTACH and the World Monuments Fund, Jaisalmer in Jeopardy helped execute conservation projects at representative buildings as demonstrations of compatible ways to install such modern amenities. The collaborative effort also launched an innovative streetscape program that addressed the water management issue while also providing direct benefits to the residents of the ancient fort.[112]

Beginning in 2000, Jaisalmer in Jeopardy and INTACH launched a pilot project focused on two of the fort's primary residential streets, Dhunda Para and Kotri Para, in order to address water and sewage infrastructure, the accumulation of structurally inappropriate cement mortar repairs, and the need for sanitation facilities. Priorities were set based on direct engagement with residents, which recognized a desire for modern amenities. Project leaders then paired these needs with a menu of streetscape improvements, including compatible replacement paving, effective drain systems and more efficient water supply lines, along with installation of new public and private toilets. Residents were briefed on

FIGURE 16.16a and b The conservation of the array of fine British colonial buildings forming Dalhousie Square in Kolkata (Calcutta) has been successful except for a few modern intrusions that serve as reminders of what is at stake in modernizing India's cities. The contrast is seen in comparing the scale and design of the Telephone Bhavan building (ca. 1950) (a) with the nineteenth century St. John's Church that was restored in 2012 (b).

the use of preferred lime mortar repair techniques for historic sandstone masonry construction, as opposed to repointing with hard cement, and public education campaigns were established regarding sanitation and hygiene.[113] Ultimately the Jaisalmer in Jeopardy program installed toilets for 2,500 residents of the old city in addition to a school, many of which were built as additions to existing buildings using compatible sandstone masonry construction. The infrastructure project complemented a series of more traditional, building-focused conservation efforts, including the stabilization of the Har Raj Ji Ka Mahal, a portion of the Maharani's Palace, which was threatening further collapse, to deliver tangible, beneficial results to this unique heritage site.[114]

a

b

FIGURE 16.17a and b Conservation in the well-preserved historic city of Jaisalmer in Rajasthan since 1996 began at the urging of advocacy organizations such as INTACH, Jaisalmer in Jeopardy and the World Monuments Fund. Demonstration conservation projects included application of solutions to the citadel's failing monumental walls (a), infrastructure improvements to representative streets, and restoration of the façade of the Maharani's Palace on the principal town square (b).

Effects of the caste system on traditional building and conservation in India

For millennia, Hindu architectural traditions have been governed by detailed treatises, many of which also describe the intricate web of social structures that are intertwined with the practices of building, particularly structures of religious significance. These practices trace their origins to the Aryan period (as early as 1500 BCE), when collections of Sanskrit poems such as the *Rig Veda* ("Verses of Knowledge") were composed to record religious adulations, as well as aspects of daily life and customs of the period. The hierarchy of social stratification broadly referred to as "caste" (*varna*) likely developed later, though its precise origins are uncertain and remain controversial topics of scholarship.[115]

The traditional caste system organizes Indian society by placing *brahmans* on top, followed by *kshatriya* (warrior class), *vaishya* (merchant class) and *shudras* (laborers and servants). Outside the *varna* system are the *panchama* (also known as untouchables, or Dalit) who were excluded from the traditional social systems and temple life. Within each of these groups were thousands of family-based communities linked to a sect, tribe or traditional occupation (referred to as *jati* or "birth"). Many of these occupations were linked to the building trades, along with other important roles relative to the design, construction, adornment, sanctification, management and repair of religious buildings. The Australian architectural historian George Michell explains this organization in detail his volume *The Hindu Temple* (first published in 1977), summarizing an account that describes the construction of a temple at Konarak (Odisha) from a thirteenth century palm leaf manuscript. Construction projects were organized according to these socially based divisions of labor, encompassing the tasks of preparing sites and quarrying stone (*shudra*) to highly skilled, finished stone carvers and artists (*vaishya*) working in guild-based teams based on generations of specialization, with the financial patronage of the local rulers (*kshatriya*), all under the direction of master builders and religious authorities (*brahman*).[116]

British administrators leveraged caste distinctions as part of the colonial framework of governance until the 1920s, when its policies changed to begin affirmative action programs for the traditionally lower castes. This trend continued after independence, with the Indian Constitution of 1950 prohibiting the practice of "untouchability" and including further measures intended to expand opportunities for lower caste groups. Numerous laws and programs today deal with traditionally disadvantaged "Scheduled Classes and Scheduled Tribes," which reserve positions for lower-caste persons in areas such as education, professional fields and the bureaucracy. While these contemporary practices create beneficial opportunities outside of the ancient caste system, they have also indirectly led to the decline of traditional craftsmanship and the lack of artisans in many communities, particularly in rural areas of India. Because people involved in some craft traditions are still often considered to be of a lower *jati*, traditional discrimination against these groups has sometimes led to the discontinuation of the craft or a migration of these artisans out of the rural areas. Low wages and familial desire for generational advancement also play a role in the decline of traditional crafts professions. This, combined with the introduction of modern materials and technology, has made it even more difficult for traditional crafts to survive.

As a result, architectural conservationists in India frequently find it difficult to execute projects in remote areas where local craft traditions have disappeared. For example, in the Pithoragarh district of northern India (Uttarakhand), an elegant woodcarving tradition is dying out as craftsmen, or *shilpkars*, leave the villages seeking work and better social conditions elsewhere, a phenomenon that is found throughout India. Although not always due to the lingering caste system, the depletion of skilled craftspeople is endemic to most of South Asia, where there has been a steady trend in the past few decades toward the discontinuation of the ancient trades of wood, stone and metal working.[117]

In many ways, India presents a series of contrasts that challenge the field of architectural conservation today: it is at once ordered and chaotic, traditional and dynamic, monumental and fine grained, graceful and sullied. As one of the largest and fastest growing countries in the world, the need for effective conservation policies, practices and institutions in India is perhaps more acute than anywhere else in Asia. Many of the building blocks are already in place, including a multi-faceted legal framework, dynamic public–private partnerships, innovative incentive programs, effective heritage protection institutions, and a wealth of successful projects. At the same time, there remain real questions around the degree to which Indian conservation institutions can effectively prevail over inefficient local, state and national political forces, powerful episodes of destructive nationalism, and as to their capacity to effectively enforce the robust laws that are in place. In some cases, such as the monasteries of Ladakh, that need is being met; in others, such as Hampi and in urban areas across the country, loss is occurring and the ties that bind heritage to its communities are under stress.

India is often hailed as the "world's largest democracy" and, like any democracy the world over, its execution has its flaws and gaps. But the essence of the statement is true: over 800 million people were eligible to vote in the 2014 national elections, and democratically elected governments have been in place with only brief interruptions since 1947, a record that is unmatched in the region, not to mention most of the world.[118] As such, architectural and other forms of cultural heritage conservation, with their roots in democratic and civic engagement, have a natural home in India. This unique status is evident in how conservation projects, both the successes and failures, unfold in India. India's confidence with heritage conservation is also evident in the contributions the country has made to the field thus far, most notably a clear articulation of what it means to practice the field in the country, in the form of the INTACH Charter.

Conservation efforts in the post-independence era, but especially since the government instituted market-oriented economic reforms in the 1970s, point to the need to balance economic expansion, population growth and increasing urbanization with responsible environmental and cultural resource management. Awareness of the importance of conserving historic structures, whether individual structures or enclaves of buildings, is growing, and in recent years the importance of the surrounding landscape to the historic sites is also increasingly recognized. The 2010 Amendment & Validation of the AMASR to prohibit all future development within 100 m of designated monuments, and to regulate development within a 300 m radius, stands as evidence of this trend, and an indication of a paradigm shift in national heritage management towards a more contextualized, less monument-centric, view.

Heritage conservation professionals in the public, private and non-profit sectors are adapting the profession in contemporary India, beyond the country's colonial-era institutions and practices, as India defines its own heritage values and further establishes the Indian approach to heritage management. By ingraining the modern Indian perspective on built heritage and its approach to traditional concepts of renewal, conservationists can ensure greater authenticity, accountability and partnership in the protection and promotion of the country's cultural treasures, thereby enhancing the relevancy of conservation in today's India. Additionally, international and local heritage conservationists should continue to find effective ways to engage the Indian public in conservation efforts. This will further integrate cultural heritage conservation values into everyday life for Indians committed to preserving their country's architectural heritage, creating generations of its advocates for years to come.

Architectural conservation efforts in India also point to the need to "start at the beginning" when approaching ambitious heritage management projects. Thorough preparation achieved through comprehensive surveys that define, identify and map heritage sites with extensive local input, creates a foundation from which subsequent building-specific conservation projects can proceed. India's efforts also underscore the value in integrating architectural conservation fully into the broader cultural context. Integrated heritage management combines architecture, natural and human-made landscapes, along with community benefits and participation; using these tools, conservationists can balance project priorities to ensure that heritage management also addresses current needs of the people it is meant to benefit.

Each conservation success in India underscores the importance of collaboration between organizations, including government, the private sector and advocacy organizations, and the integration of conservation values with Indian life and culture. Identifying innovative ways to promote and integrate heritage conservation practice and enforcement into the existing legal frameworks and development schemes remains a key goal. The recently launched Heritage City Development and Augmentation Yojana[119] (known as HRIDAY), is one such example, whereby the Ministry of Urban Development will establish partnerships with municipal governments and local heritage organizations in twelve cities across the country to implement "heritage linked urban development" that includes a focus on infrastructure improvements, economic growth, inclusive heritage conservation and promotion.[120] The HRIDAY initiative serves as an example of a promising Indian model of what A.G. Krishna Menon has described as "conservation oriented development policy," the idea of which is to embrace the need for change in the built environment in order to encourage the integration of traditional patterns of development. In so doing, Menon argues, the role of traditional buildings and artisans may be supported in an authentically Indian context that recognizes rather than resists the need for renewal, development and change.[121]

This is a highly rational and pragmatic approach, well suited to India's scale and pace of change, and its vast wealth of heritage resources. If India does not achieve this balance, it has much to lose. By integrating heritage management with development initiatives, by solidifying its own culturally coherent approach to heritage management, and by collaborating at the local, regional and international levels, India stands to reinforce its position as a leader, both in the region, and on the global stage of cultural heritage management.

Notes

1 While Buddhism and Hinduism are the two most prominent global faiths that originated in India, other religious communities with great architectural traditions also call India home, notably Jainism and Sikhism. India also has the world's third largest Muslim population (13 percent of total) and large numbers of Christians, as well as practitioners of Judaism, Zoroastrianism and numerous traditional indigenous faiths. Though Hindus account for nearly 80 percent of the total population, the Constitution defines India as a secular state, with freedoms of religious expression inscribed under Article 25. Source: 2011 Census of India. Ministry of Home Affairs. Web. www.censusindia.gov.in/Census_Data_2001/India_at_glance/religion.aspx. Accessed September 5, 2015.

2 India's population exceeded 1 billion persons in 1999. According to the United Nations Department of Social and Economic Affairs, in 2015 India had the world's second largest population (after China), estimated at 1.31 billion. The UN expects India's population to surpass that of China to become the world's largest by 2022. Source: Rick Gladstone. "India Will be Most Populous Country Sooner than Thought, U.N. Says." *The New York Times*. July 29, 2015. Web. www.nytimes.com/2015/07/30/world/asia/india-will-be-most-populous-country-sooner-than-thought-un-says.html?_r=0. Accessed September 29, 2015.

3 In 2015 India had the world's eighth largest economy (by GDP); estimates predict it will grow to become the third largest by 2030, behind only the United States and China. Source: Jeanna Smialek. "These will be the World's 20 Largest Economies in 2030." *Bloomberg News*. April 10, 2015. Web. www.bloomberg.com/news/articles/2015-04-10/the-world-s-20-largest-economies-in-2030. Accessed September 5, 2015.

4 According to Amita Baig, former Director General of the Architectural Heritage Division of INTACH, "there are barely 3,650 [heritage sites] protected by ASI and another 5,000 odd protected by the State Governments ... [leaving] tens of thousands unprotected." Source: personal correspondence, October 2, 2015. In the case of India, "heritage sites" are defined as: buildings, artifacts, structures, areas, streets and precincts of historic or aesthetic or architectural or cultural or environmental significance and natural features of environmental significance or of scenic beauty including but not restricted to sacred groves, scenic points, walks, rides, paths, hills, hillocks, water bodies such as lakes, kayals (and the areas adjoining the same), open areas, wooded areas, etc. Source: Shyam Chainani. *Heritage Conservation: Legislative and Organizational Policies for India*. (New Delhi: INTACH, 2009), 9.

5 These estimates are based on comparing the number of protected resources and relative size of England with that of India. Though a rough and possibly contentious comparison, it nevertheless illustrates the magnitude of the issue as identified by INTACH. Reference: Chainani, 11–12.

6 INTACH. "Introduction," in *Charter for the Conservation of Unprotected Architectural Heritage and Sites in India*. (New Delhi: INTACH, 2004), 2.

7 A.G. Krishna Menon. "Monumentally Limited." *The India Express*. June 12, 2013. Web. http://archive.indianexpress.com/news/monumentally-limited/1127923/. Accessed November 6, 2015.

8 The Harappan civilization has also been known as the Indus Valley, or Indus-Sarasvati civilization. The ASI now uses the term "Harappan" to identify the sites located across a huge area of South Asia including Indian and Pakistani Punjab, Sindh and Baluchistan (Pakistan) along with Gujarat, Maharashtra, Rajasthan and Haryana (India). Source: Amarendra Nath. *Excavations in Rakhigarhi, 1997–98 to 1999–2000*. (New Delhi: Archaeological Survey of India, 2014), 4.

9 Mortimer Wheeler. *Civilizations of the Indus Valley and Beyond*. (New York: McGraw Hill, 1966), 19. See also Mohenjo-Daro and Harappa in Chapter 18 – Pakistan.

10 Nath, 110–114.

11 Global Heritage Fund. "Rakhigarhi, India: Overview." Web. http://globalheritagefund.org/what_we_do/overview/investigations/rakhigarhi_india. 2015. Accessed August 20, 2015.

12 George Michell. *The Hindu Temple: An Introduction to Its Meaning and Form*. (Chicago: University of Chicago Press, 1988), 16–17.

13 Stanley Wolpert. *A New History of India*. (New York: Oxford University Press, 1984), 68.
14 *Vihara* is a Sanskrit term for a Buddhist monastery or quiet place of worship. The Great Stupa is credited as India's oldest surviving stone building, and is part of the Buddhist Monuments at Sanchi World Heritage Site, inscribed in 1989. Source: Buddhist Monuments at Sanchi. UNESCO World Heritage Centre. Web. http://whc.unesco.org/en/list/5242015. Accessed September 29, 2015.
15 Stanley Wolpert. *A New History of India*. (Oxford: Oxford University Press, 1984), 103.
16 Michell, 104–117.
17 Michell, 112-117, 156.
18 Wolpert, 112.
19 Michell, 145–146.
20 While not directly subjected to the destructive overland invasions from Central Asia beginning in the eleventh century, southern India had been in contact with the Islamic world during Mohammed's lifetime due to maritime trade routes across the Arabian Sea. This contact from the earliest days of Islam is evidenced by the Cheraman Juma Masjid and the Palaiya Jumma Palli mosques, located in Kerala and Tamil Nadu, respectively. Both dating from the 620s (and both extensively rebuilt from their original construction) these are the oldest mosques in India and perhaps among the oldest in the world.
21 Wolpert, 113–117.
22 Jon T. Lang. *A Concise History of Modern Architecture in India*. (Delhi: Permanent Black, 2002), 13.
23 "Hindu" and by extension "Hinduism" have historically been terms used by outsiders to describe people living in what is today India (i.e., beyond the Indus River). *Sanatana Dharma* is among the traditional terms used to describe the system of beliefs and way of life that's generally referred to as the "Hindu" faith, the world's third largest after Christianity and Islam. According to the Global Religious Landscape study of the Pew Research Center in 2012 there were an estimated 1 billion Hindus and 500 million Buddhists in the world. Source: Pew Research Center. Web. www.pewforum.org/2012/12/18/global-religious-landscape-exec/. Accessed September 20, 2015.
24 Michell, 78.
25 Michell, 50.
26 Michell, 58.
27 Translated from Sanskrit by French scholar Bruno Dagens and brought to the attention of the architectural conservation field by the Sri Lankan archaeologist Gamini Wijesuriya. Source: *Mayamatam: Treatise of Housing, Architecture and Iconography*. Edited and translated by Bruno Dagens. (Delhi: IGNCA, 2007); and John H. Stubbs, *Time Honored, A Global View of Architectural Conservation*. (Hoboken, NJ: Wiley, 2009), 276.
28 Binumol Tom. "Jiirnnoddarana: The Hindu Philosophy of Conservation," in Kapila D. Silva and Neel Kamal Chapagain (eds.), *Asian Heritage Management: Contexts, Concerns and Prospects*. (London: Routledge, 2013), 37–39.
29 According to UNESCO, "intangible cultural heritage is also known as 'living heritage' or 'living culture'." The terms are defined as: the practices, representations, expressions, knowledge and skills handed down from generation to generation. This heritage provides communities with a sense of identity and is continuously recreated in response to their environment. It is called intangible because its existence and recognition depend mainly on the human will, which is immaterial, and it is transmitted by imitation and living experience. Source: UNESCO. "Safeguarding Communities' Living Heritage." 2012. Web. www.unesco.org/new/en/culture/resources/in-focus-articles/safeguarding-communities-living-heritage/. Accessed June 29, 2015.
30 The India Act of 1784 established the quasi-governmental role of the British East India Company, a framework that remained in place until 1857. The same year, Sir William Jones established the Asiatic Society in Calcutta, which four years later began publishing the *Asiatick Researches* journal to share the research and survey activity of its members. This was not unique to India; there were similar actions inventorying physical and cultural heritage at the time in Dutch-controlled Indonesia and French-controlled Indochina. Source: Archaeological Survey of India. "History of the Archaeological Survey of India." 2011. Web. http://asi.nic.in/asi_aboutus_history.asp. Accessed September 29, 2015.
31 Astrid Swenson. "The Heritage of Empire," in Astrid Swenson and Peter Mandler (eds.), *From Plunder to Preservation: Britain and the Heritage of Empire c. 1800–1940*. (Oxford: Oxford University Press, 2013), 10.
32 B.K. Thapar. "India," in Henry Cleere (ed.), *Approaches to the Archaeological Heritage*. (Cambridge: Cambridge University Press, 1984), 63.
33 Their area of study came to include what is now India, Pakistan, Bangladesh, Sri Lanka and Burma.
34 Archaeological Survey of India. "History of the Archaeological Survey of India." 2011. Web. http://asi.nic.in/asi_aboutus_history.asp. Accessed May 2, 2015.

35 John Marshall. "The Story of the Archaeological Department in India," in John Cumming (ed.), *Revealing India's Past: A Co-operative Report of Archaeological Conservation and Exploration in India and Beyond*. (London: The India Society, 1939), 3–6.
36 Tapati Guha-Thakurta. *Monuments, Objects, Histories: Institutions of Art in Colonial and Postcolonial India*. (New York: Columbia University Press, 2004), 56–58.
37 Marshall, 5.
38 Indra Sengupta. "A Conservation Code for the Colony: John Marshall's Conservation Manual and Monument Preservation Between India and Europe," in M. Falser and M. Juneja (eds.), *"Archaeologizing" Heritage?* (Berlin: Springer-Verlag, 2013).
39 John Kenneth Galbraith. "The Economic and Social Returns of Preservation," in *Preservation: Towards an Ethic in the 1980s*. (Washington, DC: Preservation Press, National Trust for Historic Preservation, 1980), 58.
40 Sengupta, 24.
41 Jagat Pati Joshi. "Regional Overview: India." From *Protecting the Past for the Future* UNESCO conference proceedings. (Canberra: Australian Government Publishing Service, 1983).
42 Indra Sengupta. "Monument Preservation and the Vexing Question of Religious Structures in Colonial India," in Astrid Swenson and Peter Mandler (eds.), *From Plunder to Preservation: Britain and the Heritage of Empire c. 1800–1940*. (Oxford: Oxford University Press, 2013), 174.
43 Jukka Jokilehto. *A History of Architectural Conservation*. (Oxford: Butterworth-Heinemann, 1999), 277.
44 N.L. Batra. *Heritage Conservation: Preservation and Restoration of Monuments*. (Delhi: Aryan Books International, 1996), 6.
45 Marshall, 15.
46 Partition initially separated British India into East and West Pakistan, and India. East Pakistan later became Bangladesh in 1971 following the Bangladesh Liberation War with West Pakistan (the current Pakistan).
47 United Nations High Commissioner on Refugees. "The State of The World's Refugees 2000: Fifty Years of Humanitarian Action." 2000. Web. www.unhcr.org/4a4c754a9.html. Accessed July 10, 2015.
48 Nayanjot Lahiri. "Partitioning the Past: India's Archaeological Heritage after Independence," in Geoffrey Scarre and Robin Cunningham (eds.), *Appropriating the Past: Philosophical Perspectives on the Practice of Archaeology*. (Cambridge: Cambridge University Press, 2012), 308.
49 "The Mosque at Ayodhya: A Destructive Legacy." *The Economist*. November 26, 2009.
50 The World Bank. "India Overview." 2015. Web. www.worldbank.org/en/country/india/overview. Accessed July 20, 2015.
51 Siraj Qureshi. "Taj Mahal Threatened by Pollution." *India Today*. June 2, 2015. Web. http://indiatoday.intoday.in/story/taj-mahal-pollution-supreme-court-order/1/441781.html. Accessed July 15, 2015.
52 "Air Pollution Analyzed at India's Taj Mahal." *Archaeology Magazine*. December 12, 2014. Web. www.archaeology.org/news/2767-141210-india-taj-mahal-pollution. Accessed July 15, 2015.
53 Dev Mehta and Walter Spink. "Ajanta, India," in Miguel Angel Corzo (ed.), *The Future of Asia's Past: Preservation of the Architectural Heritage of Asia, Chiang Mai, Thailand, January 11–14, 1995*. (Los Angeles: Getty Conservation Institute, 1995), 13.
54 Japanese International Cooperation Agency. "Ajanta-Ellora Conservation and Tourism Development Project: Evaluation Report." 2007. Web. www.jica.go.jp/english/our_work/evaluation/oda_loan/post/2007/pdf/project28.pdf. Accessed September 12, 2015.
55 Jayashree Bhosale. "Maharashtra Opens Visitor Centres at Ajanta and Ellora." *The Times of India*. September 20, 2013. Web. http://articles.economictimes.indiatimes.com/2013-09-21/news/42272656_1_maharashtra-tourism-development-corporation-mtdc-tourist-information-centres. Accessed July 20, 2015.
56 Maharashtra Tourism Development Corporation. "Ajanta Ellora Conservation and Tourism Development Project: A Report." 2005. Web. http://aurangabad.nic.in/newsite1/documents/AEDP_Phase_I_and_II(10).pdf. Accessed September 5, 2015. Financial figure from Bhosale's *Times of India* article above.
57 Kiran A. Shinde. "Shifting Pilgrim-Trails and Temple-Towns in India," in Patrick Daly and Tim Winter (eds.), *Routledge Handbook of Heritage in Asia*. (London: Routledge, 2012), 336–337.
58 Article 51 A (f) of the Constitution of India.
59 Archaeological Survey of India: Thrissur Circle. "Legislations." 2011. Web. www.asithrissurcircle.in/Legislations.htm. Accessed August 18, 2015.
60 B.K. Thapar. "India," in Henry Cleere (ed.), *Approaches to the Archaeological Heritage: A Comparative Study of World Cultural Resource Management Systems*. (Cambridge: Cambridge University Press, 1984), 66.
61 In 2003 the legislation was amended to specifically prohibit demolition or reconstruction of buildings of archaeological or historical importance without the permission of the Ministry of Environment & Forests.
62 Shyam Chainani. *Heritage & Environment: An Indian Diary*. (Mumbai: Urban Design Research Institute, 2007), 171, 470–471.

63 Rana P.B. Singh. "Varanasi, India's Cultural Heritage City: Contestation, Conservation & Planning," in Rana P.B. Singh (ed.), *Heritagescapes and Cultural Landscapes*. (New Delhi: Shubhi Publications, 2011), 205–254.

64 The PIL suit was initiated in 2005 by the Kautilya Society, a Varanasi-based advocacy group focused on environmental and heritage protection, and urban development issues. In 2015 the court order was renewed, further calling for development of protection regulations for the ghats. Source: "Finalize Model By-Laws to Protect Varanasi Ghats: HC." *The Times of India*. April 8, 2015. Web. http://timesofindia.indiatimes.com/city/allahabad/Finalise-model-by-laws-to-protect-Varanasi-ghatsHC/articleshow/46855445.cms. Accessed September 14, 2015.

65 B.K. Thapar. "Policies for the Training and Recruitment of Archaeologists in India," in Henry Cleere (ed.), *Archaeological Heritage Management in the Modern World*. (Oxford: Routledge, 2000), 288.

66 The Archaeological Survey of India website provides detailed summaries of its history, organization and activities. Source: http://asi.nic.in/index.asp.

67 At the operational level, these concerns are reflected in a 2013 government audit of the agency's activities, which revealed that inventories of sites and artifact collections were not up to date, staffing shortages existed across the organization, and documentation of excavations and conservation projects were not being sufficiently maintained. Ministry of Culture (India). *Report of the Comptroller and Auditor General of India on Performance Audit of Preservation and Conservation of Monuments and Antiquities*, Report 18 of 2013. (Delhi: Ministry of Culture, 2013), viii–xiii.

68 Patrick Daly and Tim Winter (eds.), *Routledge Handbook of Heritage in Asia*. (London: Routledge, 2012), 46.

69 Tine Trumpp and Frauke Kraas. "Urban Cultural Heritage in Delhi, India. An Asset for the Future or a Neglected Resource?" *ASIEN: The German Journal on Contemporary Asia* 134 (January 2015), 21–22.

70 Shortcomings of the Policy include a failure to promote collaborative strategies with state and local conservation organizations and the private sector and an inadequate focus on professional capacity building. Source: Nachiket Chanchani. "Leaving No Stone Unturned." *The Hindu*. August 17, 2013. Web. www.thehindu.com/opinion/lead/leaving-no-stone-unturned/article5029723.ece. Accessed November 7, 2015.

71 Kamal Jain and Namrata Dalela. "Academic Conservation Training Programmes in India and International Networking," in Gabriela Krist and Tatjana Bayerova (eds.), *Heritage Conservation and Research in India: 60 Years of Indo-Austrian Collaboration*. (Vienna: Bohlag Verlau, 2010), 140–144. The six programs offering training in architectural conservation studies are: the Sir J.J. School of Architecture in Mumbai; the Indian Institute of Technology at Kharagpur; the University of Baroda; the Centre for Environmental Planning and Technology University (CEPT University), Ahmedabad; the Government College of Architecture in Lucknow; and the Department of Architectural Conservation in the School of Planning and Architecture in New Delhi.

72 Seed funding for the Trust came from a bequest from Charles Wallace, a British merchant who died in 1916, leaving half of his vast fortune to the British Treasury and half to the Treasury of British India. A 1968 agreement between the two governments established that the funds would be used for scholarships for academic study and cultural exchange to improve the relationship between the two nations. The Prime Minister decided to put the funds into use in 1982 for a non-governmental trust, which became INTACH two years later. Source: A.G. Krishna Menon. *Indian National Trust for Art and Cultural Heritage: 1984–2009*. (New Delhi: INTACH, 2009), 9.

73 Daly and Winter, 46.

74 "INTACH Helps Rejuvenate 'Tambat' Art." *The Times of India*. March 7, 2012. Web. http://timesofindia.indiatimes.com/city/pune/Intach-helps-rejuvenate-tambat-art/articleshow/12170017.cms. Accessed August 3, 2015.

75 In 2014 the United Nations estimated that India had 857 million rural residents, the most in the world. China was second with 635 million rural residents. Source: United Nations. "World's Population Increasingly Urban with More than Half Living in Urban Areas." July 10, 2014. Web. www.un.org/en/development/desa/news/population/world-urbanization-prospects-2014.html). Accessed August 4, 2015. The urban population in India grew from 27.81 percent in the 2001 Census to 31.16 percent in the 2011 Census. The proportion of rural population declined from 72.19 percent to 68.84 percent. Source: *The Economic Times of India*. "Almost 70% Indians Live in Rural Areas: Census Report." July 15, 2011. Web. http://articles.economictimes.indiatimes.com/2011-07-15/news/29777954_1_rural-areas-urban-areas-census-report. Accessed August 3, 2015.

76 INTACH Delhi Chapter. "Protection & Conservation of Monuments in Delhi." 2010. Web. www.intachdelhichapter.org/protection-conservation-delhi.php. Accessed August 18, 2015.

77 The Sir Dorabji Tata Trust was established in 1932 by the namesake son of Jamsedhji Tata, the prominent Indian industrialist and founder of the Tata Group. It funds educational, humanitarian and healthcare related causes across the country.
78 Vishnu Varma. "As Public Monuments Crumble, Private Aid Seen as Possible Savior." *The New York Times*. October 17, 2013. Web. http://india.blogs.nytimes.com/2013/10/17/as-public-monuments-crumble-private-aid-seen-as-possible-savior/?_r=0). Accessed September 29, 2015.
79 Among the legacies of the project is Insha-e-Noor, a women's art collective that creates traditional crafts like *sanjhi* (hand-cut paper patterns) embroidery and crochet based on design motifs in the tomb's architecture, such as the *jalli* patterns.
80 *Baolis* are traditional water harvesting systems common in the arid regions of the country that are generally rectangular, 'L' or 'T' shaped tanks with a circular well at the bottom. Frequently they are used as community gathering spaces and rest stops due to the cooling effect of the water and associated shelter.
81 Aga Khan Trust for Culture. *Project Brief: Humayun's Tomb – Sundar Nursery – Hazrat Nizamuddin Basti Urban Renewal Initiative, Delhi, India.* (New Delhi: Aga Khan Trust for Culture, 2013).
82 The World Monuments Fund has sponsored the Delhi Heritage Walks program from the beginning, and was instrumental in securing funding for the 2013 publishing effort. Source: Unpublished INTACH Delhi Project Report on the Delhi Heritage Route Project, October 2, 2013. Correspondence with A.G. Krishna Menon, July 11, 2016.
83 INTACH. "Delhi Heritage Route: Humayun's Tomb – Red Fort." Unpublished Heritage Routes Project Report. March 9, 2015.
84 "Conservation of Built Heritage Included in Delhi Master Plan." *The Times of India*. June 22, 2014. Web. http://articles.economictimes.indiatimes.com/2014-06-22/news/50772330_1_dda-delhi-master-plan-delhi-development-authority. Accessed August 18, 2015.
85 Shahjahanabad is the formerly walled portion of Delhi, also known as "Old Delhi," founded by Mughal emperor Shah Jahan in 1639. The Lutyen's Bungalow Zone, designed by its namesake British architect and built in the 1920s–1930s, encompasses the central residential area of New Delhi. The LBZ is especially threatened due to high land prices and low density in an increasingly crowded city.
86 "Delhi Gives Up Bid to Get World Heritage City Tag." *The Hindustan Times*. May 23, 2015. Web. www.hindustantimes.com/newdelhi/delhi-gives-up-bid-to-get-world-heritage-city-tag/article1-1350170.aspx. Accessed August 3, 2015.
87 Rahul Mehrotra. "Planning for Conservation: Looking at Bombay's Historic Fort Area." Paper delivered at the World Monument Fund Conference on Heritage Conservation, Colombo, Sri Lanka. July 28, 2004.
88 Max Bearak. "Plan for a Times Square in Mumbai Stirs Criticism." *The New York Times*. November 4, 2014. Web. www.nytimes.com/2014/11/05/realestate/commercial/Development-of-Kala-Ghoda-in-Mumbai-Stirs-Controversy.html?_r=0. Accessed August 24, 2015.
89 Shri Debashish Nayak. "Creating Opportunities for Strategic Partnerships Toward Urban Conservation." Paper delivered at the World Monuments Fund Conference on Heritage Conservation, Colombo, Sri Lanka. July 28, 2004.
90 Debashish Nayak, "Municipal Initiative in Heritage Education," in *Sharing Good Practice – Heritage Education in Asia*. Asian Regional Cooperation Conference, New Delhi, December 2–4, 2008. (New Delhi: INTACH, 2009), 71–79.
91 India Real Estate Forum. "Transfer of Development Rights." 2014. Web. www.indiarealestateforums.com/news-feed-blogs/26-bangalore/436-transfer-of-development-rights-tdr. Accessed September 13, 2015.
92 "Heritage FSI Trading from August 15." *The Times of India*. August 3, 2015. Web. http://timesofindia.indiatimes.com/city/ahmedabad/Heritage-FSI-trading-from-August-15/articleshow/48322970.cms. Accessed August 24, 2015.
93 ICOMOS. *Heritage at Risk: Hampi*. 2000. Web. www.international.icomos.org/risk/world_report/2000/india_2000.htm. Accessed August 24, 2015.
94 M. Ahiraj. "Rs. 10 Crore Gone with the Hampi Bridge." *The Hindu*. January 28, 2009. Web. www.thehindu.com/todays-paper/tp-national/tp-karnataka/rs-10-crore-gone-with-the-hampi-bridge/article383979.ece. Accessed August 24, 2015.
95 UNESCO State Party of India. *State of Conservation Report by the State Party: Hampi, 2015*. February 2015. Web. http://whc.unesco.org/en/list/241/documents/. Accessed September 13, 2015.
96 NIRLAC was founded in 1985 as a Trust to promote scholarship, documentation and conservation of Ladakh's cultural heritage. Basho Welfare Society was an existing village-level initiative that was extended to include conservation activities in partnership with the NIRLAC and WMF. Organization background source: Personal correspondence with Amita Baig. Project background source: Tara Sharma and Mark

Weber. "Temple Guardians: A Community's Initiative in Conserving its Sacred Heritage," *World Monuments Fund Context* 8(1) (Spring/Summer 2011).
97 Tara Sharma. "A Community-Based Approach to Heritage Management from Ladakh, India," in Kapila D. Silva and Neel Kamal Chapagain (eds.), *Asian Heritage Management: Contexts, Concerns, and Prospects*. (London: Routledge, 2013), 280–281.
98 Sharma and Weber, 82.
99 UNESCO Bangkok. *2007 Pacific-Asia Heritage Awards*. Award of Excellence: Maitreya Temple. 2007. Web. www.unescobkk.org/culture/wh/asia-pacific-heritage-awards/previous-heritage-awards-2000-2013/2007/award-winners/2007ex/. Accessed August 24, 2015.
100 Amita Sinha. "Cultural Heritage and Sacred Landscapes of South Asia," in Kapila D. Silva and Neel Kamal Chapagain (eds.), *Asian Heritage Management: Contexts, Concerns, and Prospects*. (London: Routledge, 2013), 184–187.
101 Braj is not a politically defined region, but rather a culturally defined area within the Agra–Delhi–Jaipur triangle where the classic Sanskrit epic, the *Mahabharata*, is set and the youth of Lord Krishna is recounted.
102 "Govardhan Hill in Braj, India: Imagined, Enacted, Reclaimed." University of Illinois at Urbana-Champaign Department of Landscape Architecture/Braj Foundation Project Report. 2010. Web. www.projects.landarch.illinois.edu/india-projects/govardhan/report/govardhan_report.pdf. Accessed September 29, 2015.
103 The Braj Foundation. 2010. Web. www.brajfoundation.org/index.html. Accessed August 24, 2015.
104 Muziris is the name of an ancient trading port in the vicinity of present-day Kochi. The organizers of the arts festival used the name to evoke the cosmopolitan character of the region that dates back to antiquity.
105 The synagogue clock tower and its clock works were rehabilitated by the World Monument Fund between 1996 and 2006.
106 "Renovation of Durbar Hall Lands in a Controversy." *The New Indian Express*. November 29, 2011. Web. www.newindianexpress.com/cities/kochi/article249864.ece. Accessed August 4, 2015.
107 UNESCO World Heritage Centre. "India." 2015. Web. http://whc.unesco.org/en/statesparties/in. Accessed September 29, 2015.
108 R.R. Bhandari. "Architectural Heritage of Indian Railways," *RITES Journal* (January 2009), 14.3–11.
109 Zeynep Aygen. *International Heritage and Historic Building Conservation: Saving the World's Past*. (London: Routledge, 2013), 159.
110 Manesh Chakraborti. "Reviving the Original City Centre: Second Coming of Dalhousie Square." Paper delivered at the World Monument Fund Conference on Heritage Conservation, Colombo, Sri Lanka. July 28, 2004.
111 World Monuments Fund. *Restoration of Jaisalmer Fort, Rajasthan, India: WMF Second Technical Mission, Assessment of Outer Fort Walls*. (New York: World Monuments Fund, 2000), 9.
112 "Jaisalmer in Jeopardy" promotional pamphlet (London: Jaisalmer in Jeopardy Fund, 2004).
113 UNESCO Bangkok. "Jaisalmer Streetscape Revitalization Project: 2002 Honorable Mention." 2002. Web. www.unescobkk.org/culture/wh/asia-pacific-heritage-awards/previous-heritage-awards-2000-2013/2002/award-winners/2002hm4/. Accessed August 24, 2015.
114 Jaisalmer in Jeopardy: Projects. 2002. Web. www.jaisalmer-in-jeopardy.org/projects.html. Accessed August 24, 2015.
115 Wolpert, 25, 31–32.
116 Michell, 49–51, 55–57.
117 L. Tenzing, Tamrakar U. Raya and S. Garbyal, "Documentation of the Woodcraft in the Chaudas and Byans area of Pithogarh." A socio-economic and cultural report for INTACH. May 1997.
118 "Indian Election 2014: Your Interactive Guide to the World's Biggest Vote." *The Guardian* (UK). April 7, 2014. Web. www.theguardian.com/world/2014/apr/07/-sp-indian-election-2014-interactive-guide-narendra-modi-rahul-gandhi. Accessed August 24, 2015.
119 *Yojana* is an ancient unit of measure, but also means "blueprint" or "plan" in Hindi.
120 Launched in January 2015, the HRIDAY scheme is planned as a twenty-seven-month effort that will funnel US$70 million to twelve Indian heritage cities that had been identified by the Ministry of Culture: Ajmer, Amaravati, Amristar, Badami, Dwarka, Gaya, Kanchipuram, Mathura, Puri, Varanasi, Vellankanni and Warangal. Funds will go towards the goal of "strategic and planned development of heritage cities, aiming at improvement in overall quality of life with specific focus on santiation, security, tourism, heritage revitalization and livelihoods retaining the city's cultural identity." Source: Ministry of Urban Development & National Institute of Urban Affairs. "HRIDAY: Heritage City Development and Augmentation Yojana." 2015. Web. http://hridayindia.in. Accessed November 7, 2015.
121 A.G. Krishna Menon. "Conservation in India: a Search for Direction," *Architecture + Design* (1989), 27.

Further reading

Clements, Jonathan. 2013. *An Armchair Traveller's History of the Silk Road*. London: bookHaus.
Cœdès, George. 1968. *The Indianized States of Southeast Asia*. Edited by Walter F. Vella and translated by Susan Brown Cowing. Honolulu: East-West Center Press.
Coningham, Robin. 2010. *The Ancient Indus*. Cambridge: Cambridge University Press.
Dagens, Bruno. 2000. *Mayamata: Treatise of Housing, Architecture and Iconography*. 2 vols. New Delhi: Indira Gandhi National Centre for the Arts.
Directorate General, Central Public Works Dept. 2013. *Handbook of Conservation of Heritage Buildings*. New Delhi: CPW Dept.
Dossal, Mariam. 1991. *Imperial Designs and Indian Realities: The Planning of Bombay City, 1845–1875*. Delhi: Oxford University Press.
Eaton, Richard M. and Phillip B. Wagoner. 2014. *Power, Memory, Architecture: Contested Sites on India's Deccan Plateau, 1300–1600*. New Delhi: Oxford University Press.
Feilden, Bernard M. 1989. *Guidelines for Conservation: A Technical Manual*. New Delhi: The Indian National Trust for Art and Cultural Heritage.
Fergusson, James. 1876. *History of Indian and Eastern Architecture*. 2 vols. Revised. London: Murray, 1910.
Getty Conservation Institute. 1993. *Conservation of Ancient Sites on the Silk Road*. Proceedings of the International Conference on the Conservation of Grotto Sites, Mogao Grottoes, Dunhuang, People's Republic of China, October 3–8, 1993. Marina del Rey: Getty Conservation Institute.
Gupta, Divay. 2007. *Conservation Briefs: Identification and Documentation of Built Heritage in India: Process for Identification and Documentation of Cultural Heritage*. New Delhi: INTACH (UK) Trust.
Gutschow, Niels. 2006. *Benares: The Sacred Landscape of Varanasi*. Stuttgart: Editions Axel Menges.
Harle, J.C. 1994. *The Art and Architecture of the Indian Subcontinent*. 2nd edition. New Haven, CT: Yale University Press.
Havell, E.B. 1920. *A Handbook of Indian Art*. New York: E.P. Dutton and Company.
Hopkirk, Peter. 1980. *Foreign Devils on the Silk Road: The Search for the Lost Cities and Treasures of Chinese Central Asia*. Amherst: University of Massachusetts Press.
Hosagrahar, Jyoti. 2012. "Heritage and Modernity in India," in Patrick Daly and Tim Winter (eds.), *Routledge Handbook of Heritage in Asia*. London: Routledge, 283–294.
INTACH, Delhi Chapter. N.d. Delhi Heritage Route, Four booklets: *Humayun's Tomb, Purana Qila, Kotla Firoz Shah, Red Fort*. New Delhi: INTACH.
——. N.d. Three booklets: *A Walk around Chandhi Chowk & Jama Masjid, A Walk around Darya Ganj & Sunehri Masjid, A Walk around Nizamuddin*. New Delhi: INTACH.
INTACH Pondicherry Chapter. 2004. *Architectural Heritage of Pondicherry: Tamil and French Precincts*. Pondicherry: INTACH.
Irschick, Eugene F. 2015. *A History of the New India Past and Present*. London: Routledge.
Jain, Kulbhushan. 1989. "Planning for Conservation Project: Fatepur Sikri," in B. Allchin, F.R. Allchin and B.K. Thapar (eds.), *Conservation of the Indian Heritage*. New Delhi: Cosmo Publication, 201–221.
Kalia, Ravi. 1999. *Chandigarh: The Making of an Indian City*. New Delhi: Oxford University Press.
Khan, Ahmad Nabi. 2003. *Islamic Architecture in South Asia: Pakistan–India–Bangladesh*. Oxford: Oxford University Press.
Kidambi, Prashant. 2007. *The Making of an Indian Metropolis: Colonial Governance and Public Culture in Bombay, 1890–1920*. Historical Urban Studies. Hampshire: Ashgate.
Kock, Ebba. 2006. *The Complete Taj Mahal and the Riverfront Gardens of Agra*. London: Thames & Hudson.
Krist, Gabriela and Tatjana Bayerovà. 2010. *Heritage Conservation and Research in India: 60 Years of Indo-Austrian Collaboration*. Vienna: Böhlau Verlag.
Kuriakose, Benny. 2007. *Conserving Timber Structures in India*. Conservation Briefs. New Delhi: INTACH.
Lahiri, Nayanjot. 2006. *Finding Forgotten Cities: How the Indus Civilization was Discovered*. London: Seagull Books.
Livingston, Morna. 2002. *Steps to Water: The Ancient Stepwells of India*. New York: Princeton Architectural Press.
Madsen, Axel. 1989. *Silk Roads: The Asian Adventures of Clara and André Malraux*. New York: Pharos Books.
Mehrotra, Rahul. 2007. "Conservation and Change: Questions for Conservation Education in Urban India," *Built Environment* 33(3): 342–356.
——. 2011. *Architecture in India since 1990*. Mumbai: Pictor Publishing.
Menon, A.G. Krishna. 1994. "Rethinking the Venice Charter: The Indian Experience," *South Asian Studies* 10: 37–44.
——. 2003. "The Case for an Indian Charter." Seminar, 530. Web. www.india-seminar.com/2003/530/530 a.g. krishna memom.htm. Accessed April 1, 2012.
——. 2009. *Indian National Trust for Art and Cultural Heritage 1984–2009*. New Delhi: INTACH.
Michell, George. 1988. *The Hindu Temple: An Introduction to its Meaning and Forms*. 2nd edition. Chicago: University of Chicago Press.

———. 1989. *The Penguin Guide to Monuments of India: Buddhist, Jain, Hindu*. Harmondsworth, UK: Penguin.

———. (ed). 1993. *Temple Towns of Tamil Nadu*. Mumbai: Marg Publications.

———. 2000. *Hindu Art and Architecture*. World of Art. London: Thames & Hudson.

———. (ed). 2008. *Vijayanagara: Splendour in Ruins*. Ahmedabad: Mapin Publishing.

Michell, George and Snehal Shah (eds.). 1988. *Ahmadabad*. Mumbai: Marg Publications.

Nilsson, Sten. 1968. *European Architecture in India 1750–1850*. Translated from the Swedish by Agnes George. London: Faber and Faber.

Pal, Pratapaditya (ed.). 2008. *Sindh: Past Glory, Present Nostalgia*. Mumbai: Marg Publications.

Panter-Downes, Mollie. 1967. *Ooty Preserved: A Victorian Hill Station in India*. New York: Farrar, Straus and Giroux.

Patel, Alka. 2004. *Building Communities in Gujarat: Architecture and Society during the Twelfth through Fourteenth Centuries*. Brill's Indological Library, volume 22. Leiden: Brill.

Prakash, Vikramaditya. 2002. *Chandigarh's Le Corbusier: The Struggle for Modernity in Postcolonial India*. Studies in Modernity and National Identity. Seattle: University of Washington Press.

Pramar, V.S. 2005. *A Social History of Indian Architecture*. Oxford: Oxford University Press.

Rezavi, Syed Ali Nadeem. 2013. *Fathpur Sikri Revisited*. New Delhi: Oxford University Press.

Robinson, Francis (ed.). 1989. *The Cambridge Encyclopedia of India, Pakistan, Bangladesh, Sri Lanka*. Cambridge: Cambridge University Press.

Roy, Sourindranath. 1961. *The Story of Indian Archaeology, 1784–1947*. New Delhi: ASI.

Sachdev, Vibhuti and Giles Tillotson. 2002. *Building Jaipur: The Making of an Indian City*. London: Reaktion Books.

Scrivner, Peter and Vikramaditya Prakash (eds.). 2007. *Colonial Modernities: Building, Dwelling and Architecture in British India and Ceylon*. Abingdon, UK: Routledge.

Shankar, Pratyush. 2014. *Himalayan Cities: Settlement Patterns, Public Places and Architecture*. New Delhi: Niyogi Books.

Sharma, A.K. 1999. *The Departed Harappans of Kalibangan*. New Delhi: Sundeep Prakashan.

Sharma, Tara. 2013. "A Community-Based Approach to Heritage Management from Ladakh, India," in Kapila D. Silva and Neel Kamal Chapagain (eds.), *Asian Heritage Management: Contexts, Concerns, and Prospects*. London: Routledge, 271–284.

Singh, Priyaleen. 2006. *Historic Gardens: Making an Inventory for the Indian Context*. Conservation Briefs. New Delhi: INTACH.

Singh, Upinder. 2004. *Discovery of Ancient India: Early Archaeologists and the Beginnings of Archaeology*. New Delhi: Permanent Black.

Spink, Walter M. N.d. *Ajanta: A Brief History and Guide*. Detroit: University of Michigan.

Subramanian, Lakshmi (ed.). 2008. *Ports Towns Cities: A Historical Tour of the Indian Littoral*. Mumbai: Marg Publications.

Sundaram, P.S.A. 1989. "The Future Shape of Urban Conservation in India," in B. Allchin, F.R. Allchin and B.K. Thapar (eds.), *Conservation of the Indian Heritage*. New Delhi: Cosmo Publication, 259–272.

Tadgell, Christopher. 1990. *The History of Architecture in India: from the Dawn of Civilization to the End of the Raj*. London: Architecture Design and Technology Press.

Thaper, B.K. 1989. "Agencies for the Preservation of Cultural Heritage in India," in B. Allchin, F.R. Allchin and B.K. Thapar (eds.), *Conservation of the Indian Heritage*. New Delhi: Cosmo Publication, 163–168.

Tillotson, G.H.R. 1987. *The Rajput Palaces: The Development of an Architectural Style, 1450–1750*. New Haven, CT: Yale University Press.

Tom, Binumol. 2007. *Traditional Conservation of Timber Architecture: A Case Study of Thai Kottaram, Kerala*. Conservation Briefs. New Delhi: INTACH UK Trust.

Volwahsen, Andreas. *Living Architecture: Islamic Indian*. New York: Grosset and Dunlap.

Wescoat, Jr., James L. and Joachim Wolschke-Bulmahn (eds.). 1996. *Mughal Gardens: Sources, Places, Representations, and Prospects*. Washington DC: Dumbarton Oaks.

Aerial view, lower approach to Sigirya, Sri Lanka.

17

SRI LANKA AND MALDIVES

Sri Lanka

The teardrop-shaped island nation of Sri Lanka (formerly known as Ceylon) has long been a crossroads of religion and culture, owing to its advantageous position off the tip of the Indian peninsula, at the meeting point of the Arabian Sea and the Bay of Bengal.[1] Centuries of sea-based commerce brought missionaries, explorers and traders to Sri Lanka's shores, influencing the development of its architectural and artistic traditions and resulting in a heterogeneous mosaic of cultures, cities and buildings. Theravada Buddhist and Hindu traditions from India arrived early and remain a powerful influence on the modern culture of Sri Lanka, including its contemporary political tensions.[2] Muslim influences from Arabia and South Asia came later, along with elements of Christian culture introduced by Europeans during the nearly 500-year colonial period, which ended with independence in 1948.[3]

Sri Lanka has been an early and active player in the contemporary field of architectural conservation in South Asia, ratifying the World Heritage Convention in 1980 and listing most of its sites during the following decade. The country's rich heritage, combined with its progressive, active professional field, has resulted in the relatively small nation of Sri Lanka possessing a disproportionately high concentration of designated heritage sites. This accomplishment is evidenced by its six cultural World Heritage Sites: the Golden Temple of Dambulla, the Old Town of Galle and its fortifications, and the ancient cities of Polonnaruwa and Sigiriya, and the Sacred Cities of Anuradhapura and Kandy.[4] In addition to internationally recognized sites, thousands of locally designated heritage resources exist on the nation's inventories.[5]

Much of this progress in stewarding its cultural assets was undermined during the three decades following Sri Lanka's ratification of the World Heritage Convention due to the twin tragedies that have inflicted great harm on the Sri Lankan economy, populace and built environment: the country's civil war (1983–2009) and the 2004 Indian Ocean tsunami. Each of these episodes exacted a steep price on several of the country's most prominent heritage resources and their constituent communities; its national tourism economy, which was a substantial factor in Sri Lanka's post-independence prosperity, has been especially hard hit during this period. Despite these setbacks, since 2002 Sri Lanka has stood out as one of the fastest growing economies in South Asia. Cessation of hostilities has created opportunities for the rebuilding of the country – especially in the war-torn east and north – and for reorienting government institutions and the economy that had been defined by the war years.[6] In recent years, the government's focus on intensively developing the tourism sector has placed a strain on the country's infrastructure in general, and its heritage sites in particular, signaling a need for enhanced management strategies to improve the balance between growth and conservation.[7]

FIGURE 17.1 Presentation of the archaeological remains of Anuradhapura (dating to the third century BCE), the first ancient capital of Sri Lanka.

A brief history of Sri Lanka

The story of the myriad groups that influenced the multi-faceted culture of Sri Lanka begins in prehistory, with the presence of Mesolithic and Neolithic cultures from tens of thousands of years before present. Sri Lanka's dominant ethnic group, the Sinhalese, trace their origins to the fifth century BCE when a group of Indo-Aryan migrants from northeastern India arrived.[8] The fifth century CE Indian epic poem, *Ramayana*, includes many episodes that take place in Lanka ("resplendent land" in Sanskrit), including Hanuman's construction of a bridge across the sea, which has been interpreted as referring to the relationship between the mainland and island Sri Lanka in antiquity.[9] Sri Lanka's great chronicle, the *Mahavamsa*, recounts the famous tale of the third century BCE Emperor Ashoka (of the Indian Mauryan dynasty), who had embraced Buddhism after renouncing war in his country, sending his son Thera Mahindra and his only daughter, Sanghamitra, to preach and propogate Theravada Buddhism in Sri Lanka. According to the *Mahavamsa*, there they met King Devanampiyatissa of Anuradhapura, who elected to convert to Buddhism. With the introduction of Buddhism, a major building campaign was launched in the city as the royal family enthusiastically commissioned works of art to express their newfound devotion.[10]

Advances in navigation during the fourth and fifth centuries CE enabled emissaries from Anuradhapura to reach Southeast Asia and beyond, leading to the introduction of Theravada Buddhism to present-day Myanmar, Laos, Vietnam, Thailand and Cambodia. These connections helped establish Sri Lanka as a principal cultural and religious source for much of Southeast Asia, a relationship that endures to this day. Evidence of Sinhalese temple design influencing the architecture of these distant places can be found today across the region, including numerous monuments in Sukhothai such as the fourteenth century Wat Chang Lom.[11] With the arrival of Arab merchants in the seventh century, Islam was introduced to Sri Lanka, and by the eighth century, Muslim Arab traders controlled much of the commerce in the Arabian Sea, helping to spread goods from the island's spice trade to East Africa, Arabia, China and the Eastern Mediterranean.

The reign of the Buddhist kingdoms did not go unchallenged, particularly from across the Palk Strait on the nearby Indian mainland by a series of Chola forces beginning in the second century BCE. In the tenth century Anuradhapura collapsed, setting the stage for the eleventh century CE rise of Polonnaruwa, the second of the great Sinhalese kingdoms of antiquity. That kingdom thrived from the eleventh century under the ruler Parakramabahu I, who oversaw the construction of sophisticated gardens supported by irrigation and water retention systems, in addition to monumental Buddhist places of worship, rock-cut sculptures and palaces.[12] Armies from the Hindu Tamil Pandyan Empire (sixth century BCE–fourteenth century CE) overwhelmed Polonnaruwa in the fourteenth century, bringing its relatively brief but prosperous heyday to a close. The Polonnaruwan rulers were succeeded by several smaller Hindu and Buddhist kingdoms, including the Gampola, who built temple complexes that carried on the traditions of their predecessor builders, exemplified by the Lankatilaka and Gadaladeniya Vihara (fourteenth century) located near Kandy.[13]

The dawn of the sixteenth century marked the beginning of the European presence in Sri Lanka, first with the arrival of the Portuguese explorer Lorenzo de Almeida in 1505, and the establishment of a fort at Colombo in 1517. The Portuguese capture of the coastal Kotte and Jaffna kingdoms left the central highlands kingdom of Kandy as the sole remaining stronghold against European incursions. The Dutch supplanted the Portuguese in the seventeenth century, enhancing or constructing a series of coastal forts, including Galle (in 1640), ultimately establishing control over the entire island except for the central Kingdom of Kandy. By the end of the eighteenth century, the British had ousted the Dutch, and in 1802 they launched an unsuccessful attack against Kandy in a bid to fully occupy the island. An 1815 invasion with the aid of local rulers was different, however, resulting in the taking of the Sinhalese capital by the British army, the exile of King Sri Vikrama Rajashinha, and the entire island falling under the rule of King George III.[14]

Colombo, the present-day capital and largest city in Sri Lanka, rose to prominence in the nineteenth century under the British. Kandy remains the island's cultural and religious center, home to significant temples and palaces. The most important among them is the Sri Dalada Maligawa (Temple of the Tooth). The colonial period also brought about further demographic diversity. Both the Dutch and British periods facilitated the arrival of Javanese and Malaysian Muslims, which further contributed to the island's Islamic culture, and the expansion of its Indian Tamil population, and the establishment of long-standing European-descended communities, such as the Burghers.[15]

As Britain's Imperial period drew to a close, power-sharing arrangements were established with the Sinhalese-run government, and in 1948 Ceylon gained independence as a Dominion under the Commonwealth. The British influence on modern-day Sri Lanka remains strong to this day in its institutions and laws for architectural conservation. A tragic legacy of the transfer of power at independence, however, included aggravated ethnic tensions between the majority Sinhalese and minority Tamils that ultimately ignited a nearly thirty-year-long civil war in 1982.[16]

The war between the government and the separatist organization Liberation Tigers of Tami Eelam (LTTE) had devastating effects on the country and its population, and at times threatened to destabilize the entire region by drawing in India through the use of tactics such as suicide bombings and political assassinations.[17] One of many horrific episodes from this period was the bombing of the Sri Dalada Maligawa in Kandy by the LTTE on January 25, 1998, which damaged the World Heritage Site and killed more than a dozen people. Efforts at peace talks led to a relative calm in the late 1990s and early 2000s, but this was undermined by another tragic event: the December 26, 2004 Indian Ocean tsunami. The tsunami struck without warning, devastating the southern and eastern coastlines and dealing a serious blow to Sri Lanka's economy and fragile political stability. Amid accusations of uneven disaster response between Tamil and Sinhalese areas, the civil war flared anew, producing another chapter of damage and destruction, including assassinations and assaults on infrastructure.[18] In May 2009 government forces initiated an overwhelming, decisive assault on LTTE strongholds in Mullaitivu District that wiped out the separatist leadership, bringing this divisive, destructive chapter of Sri Lanka's history to a close.[19]

Today, Sri Lanka's modern population reflects its diverse historical connections, consisting primarily of Sinhalese, along with substantial populations of Hindu Tamils, Muslims of South Asian and Arabian origin, and Christian groups.[20] Although the cultures have intermingled somewhat, Sinhalese and Tamils tend to maintain their traditional languages, religions and cultures, in geographically separate environments. The country's Tamil populations are concentrated in the north and east, while the largest numbers of Sinhalese are in the center and south of the island, a cultural division that was reinforced by the recent conflict.[21] Vibrant ancient traditions and festivals remain part of Sri Lanka's intangible cultural heritage, such as the Esala Perahera festival, celebrated each summer in Kandy in honor of the Sacred Tooth Relic with a spectacular display of traditional costumes and dances.

FIGURE 17.2 The Esala Perahera festival, held annually in July and August, embodies a long-standing religious cultural celebration in the historic setting of Kandy. This image from 1885 represents a tradition that began in the third century BCE, a ritual enacted to request the gods for rainfall. The ritual later incorporated a celebration of the Sacred Tooth Relic.

As in Pakistan, India and Bangladesh, modern heritage conservation practice in Sri Lanka has its roots in the country's colonial past, as well as ancient traditions connected to its religious practices. Though part of the same imperial system through most of the nineteenth and well into the twentieth centuries, important differences emerged in how conservation was organized and executed between Sri Lanka and its northern neighbors. British explorers, antiquarians and administrators began to study the island's built heritage not long after the fall of Kandy, with the Ceylon Branch of the Royal Asiatic Society performing early documentation and restoration work at Anuradhapura and Sigiriya, each of which had been re-discovered by Europeans in the late nineteenth century.[22] The Society supported the translation of important early Pali and Sinhala texts, including the *Mahavamsa*, and also helped establish several national institutions including the State Archives, the Historical Manuscripts Commission, and the Department of Archaeology. Its *Journal* has been published since 1845, when it initially reported on discoveries such as the Sigiriya frescoes in the 1890s. Today it continues to publish scholarly articles concerning Sri Lankan history, art and literature.[23]

In 1868 the British colonial government commissioned a survey of the island's ancient buildings and sites, work that resulted in the photo documentation of Anuradhapura and Polonnaruwa, and a complete survey of Anuradhapura in the 1870s. Initial work at the two ancient capitals took place in the 1880s under the supervision of Stephen Montagu (S.M.) Burrows, including vegetation clearing and some limited excavation. The Department of Archaeology officially began its work in 1890 under the direction of Henry Charles Purvis (H.C.P.) Bell, an officer with the Ceylon Civil Service, including some early excavations at Sigiriya. In 1897 the murals at Sigiriya and Polonnaruwa were documented, bringing these masterpieces of early Sri Lankan art to the world's attention.[24] Bell made several contributions to the modern field today, but among the most consequential was his decision to shift responsibility for architectural conservation projects away from the engineer-led Public Works

Department, and to a specialized unit within the Department of Archaeology comprised of architects. Unlike in British India and Burma, architects took the lead in conservation projects in Sri Lanka based on a greater level of sensitivity to historic and sacred buildings than that of the engineers. To this day architects continue to lead the Architectural Conservation Division within the Department of Archaeology, and there is a generally high level of participation by licensed architects in conservation projects, due to this distinctive approach within the region.[25]

As was the case elsewhere in the Asian colonial world, Europeans led Sri Lanka's institutions and field projects during the nineteenth and early twentieth centuries. It wasn't until 1940 that the first Sinhalese head of the Archaeology Department, Dr. Senarath Paranavitana, was appointed.[26] Heritage conservation became an increasingly scholarly endeavor through the end of the British period in 1948, after which time professionally trained archaeologists from the Department of Archaeology in the newly independent nation built upon the colonial-era foundations of heritage management.

Because Buddhism still plays a prominent role in the lives of the majority of Sri Lankans, many of the sculptures, *vihara* and stupas that constitute the ruined ancient capitals and significant sites remain active places of worship to this day.[27] The maintenance of key monuments was a practice perpetuated for centuries according to Buddhist traditions of earning spiritual "merit" for such deeds. These acts led to the conservation of important sites in antiquity, in particular those at Anaradhapura. In one such example, a twelfth century inscription from Polonnaruwa recounts how the king had appointed a "Chief Conservator of Monuments" (*Loke Arakmena*), granting him "unlimited wealth" to carry out restoration of the Mirisawetiya stupa and other vihara in the earlier capital.[28]

While the imposition of colonial rule disrupted many traditional practices, the establishment of the Archaeology Department in the late nineteenth century, and the institutionalization of the field that followed, helped to set the stage for state-sponsored conservation of religious sites after independence. The British-era Archaeology Department adopted practices such as hiring a local villager to look after, and periodically perform light maintenance on, isolated monuments (known as a *gramasvaka*), and retained specialized masons and weed-pullers to assist in regular maintenance cycles.[29] In the late nineteenth and early twentieth centuries conflicts arose between the Archaeology Department and "restoration committees" that were focused on reconstructions of Buddhist monuments in particular, frequently without the benefit of documentation.[30] An outcome of this tension was the passage of the Antiquities Ordinance of 1940, which strengthened the role of the Department in regulating conservation projects on both publicly and privately owned resources, including religious monuments.

In the first decades following independence, this framework led to an enhanced role for the national government in funding and overseeing the restoration of Buddhist sites, in some cases undoing earlier conservation campaigns by the restoration societies. During these early years the Department undertook conservation and protection measures for numerous living religious structures, including the Kataragama Kirivehera stupa, which traces its origins to the second century BCE (1960–1970) and Yatala Stupa (1987), the re-erection of standing Buddha images at Maligawela (1991) and Dambegoda (1990), and the construction of a contemporary protective shelter over the famous twelfth century Gal Vihara reclining and seated Buddhas.[31] Conservation of these sites followed the Archaeology Department's principles regarding restoration of religious monuments, which aim to return degraded structures to a form acceptable to their particular religious community, while adhering to international standards regarding documentation, retention of original materials, and minimizing the use of new materials.[32]

Another landmark conservation project from this period involved the complete disassembly, relocation and reconstruction of the Nalanda Gedige on a raised berm, which began in the 1970s in order to avoid inundation by the adjacent Mahaweli River following construction of a hydropower project. Thought to date between the eighth and tenth centuries, the distinctive *gedige* (Buddha image house) features an elegant hybrid Buddhist-Hindu style that has been much admired among scholars, worshippers and laypeople alike for centuries. The noted archaeologist P.L. Paranavitana oversaw the multi-year effort, working with the Department of Archaeology. The project recalled the 1968 relocation of the Abu Simbel temples in Egypt in its approach, but also in terms of the commitment on the part of the national government to conserve architectural heritage alongside modern development.[33]

The colonial-era focus on survey and documentation at the great ruined cities contributed to an archaeology-centric heritage conservation practice and regulations in Sri Lanka during its early independence years. Since then, an increased emphasis on the living, urban and intangible heritage of the country has led to a robust, well-rounded field of practice, which is reflected in the evolution of the nation's heritage protection institutions and legislation. The advent of the multi-disciplinary Cultural Triangle Project (discussed below), initiated just over thirty years after independence, is the chief example of this trend.

The Department of Archaeology remains the principal government agency for conservation and heritage site management and for the enforcement of laws protecting historically significant resources. The Department, which reports to the cabinet-level Ministry of National Heritage, is organized into a wide range of divisions, each with specific responsibilities related to different resource types and activities.[34] Its enabling legislation, the Antiquities Ordinance No. 9 of 1940 and the ordinance's Amendment No. 24 of 1998, serve as the primary legislative tools for identifying and protecting archaeological, architectural and movable cultural resources. Under this legislation, resources in public or private hands may be listed if they demonstrate historical and archaeological value and are over 100 years of age. According to the ordinance, cultural sites fall into one of two categories: archaeological reserves and protected monuments. While "reserves" are owned and maintained by the government and may contain more than a single building, "protected" buildings are privately owned, having national significance and requiring permission from the state for any repairs or alterations. Each affords a designated monument a 400 yard (356 m) buffer zone in which development is regulated, a provision that was added to the legislation due to development pressures in the mid-1900s at designated sites.[35] Due to the island nation's rich maritime history the Antiquities Ordinance also addresses underwater archaeological resources, which are recognized in the legislation as holding particular value to the history of Sri Lanka.[36]

In 2000 the Law was amended to require the preparation of an Archaeological Impact Assessment for a broad array of activities, ranging from infrastructure development to mining activities, to determine if a proposed project would harm culturally significant resources. Following the preparation and review of a report the Director General of Archaeology holds the ultimate authority for releasing projects. Assessments have recently been employed to identify potential cultural resource issues with port development at the sixteenth century Portuguese and Dutch fort at Galle and land reclamation proposals adjacent to the Galle Face Green in central Colombo.[37]

In addition to the Antiquities Ordinance, the Sri Lankan government has several tools available for affecting heritage protection at the local, municipal, district and regional levels through its planning ordinances. These include the Urban Development Act (1978), the Housing and Town Improvement Ordinance (1915), and the Town and Country Planning Ordinance (1946). Each is administered by separate federal agencies, and all are leveraged as useful tools for protecting heritage assets, especially individual monuments and their surrounding context, and historic districts.[38]

Sri Lanka's history of developing new laws, strategies and institutions at the governmental level has been complemented for decades by a strong body of non-governmental organizations focused on heritage management. Established in 2005, the non-profit National Trust for Cultural and Natural Heritage (known as the National Trust – Sri Lanka) represents another component of an already robust framework for national heritage management at all levels of Sri Lankan society. The National Trust's primary activities include publishing books about Sri Lankan art and architecture, organizing lecture series, and having its scientific committees give expert advice on conservation projects.[39] The Trust partnered in 2007 with the Prince Claus Foundation of the Netherlands to address flooding and deterioration of the Malwana Fort, a sixteenth–seventeenth century Portuguese fort located on the Kelani River, 20 km (12 miles) inland from Colombo.[40]

Relatively new institutions such as the National Trust bolster the already-strong presence of highly effective organizations, in particular its national ICOMOS chapter. ICOMOS Sri Lanka, established in 1983 in association with the Cultural Triangle Project (CTP), remains an active and effective participant in the conservation landscape in the island nation. Its institutional vibrancy has been sustained by the involvement of Dr. Roland Silva, the first Asian to hold the office of president of ICOMOS International, and by the hosting of the 10th General Assembly in Colombo in 1993, the first time the meeting was held outside of Europe.[41] ICOMOS Sri Lanka proved its resolve in the aftermath of the 2004 tsunami through its tireless survey and advocacy efforts on behalf of heritage in the recovery process. It was instrumental in making a successful case that the conservation of heritage properties was an essential part of the post-disaster recovery effort in Sri Lanka, in terms of maintaining a sense of place amid great loss, along with the efficiencies and sheer logic of retaining what's useful and meaningful, rather than wiping the slate clean following a disaster.[42]

Development of a national heritage resource inventory has been a major area of activity in the independence years, with tens of thousands of listed heritage sites as of 2014. Maintaining adequate government funding for maintaining and managing this large number of sites, however, has proven a greater challenge.[43] Fortunately, since the 1980s Sri Lanka has remained at the forefront of developing innovative heritage management programs and funding mechanisms. Two hallmark efforts from this period stand out as significant contributions to the field of architectural conservation in Asia in the late twentieth century: the Cultural Triangle Project (CTP) and related Central Cultural Fund (CCF), both of which were inaugurated in 1980.

The Cultural Triangle Project and the Central Cultural Fund

The CTP came about due to a 1978 request from the Sri Lankan Government to UNESCO for assistance in conservation planning and management of several important sites located in the island's interior. The program launched in 1980 and ran until 1997, during which time thousands of professionals contributed to a variety of projects that together constituted the largest conservation program in Sri Lanka's history.[44] Six sites were identified at the outset: two monastery complexes in Anuradhapura, the rock-cut caves of Dambulla, the citadel and gardens of Sigiriya, a monastic complex at Polonnaruva, and a collection of significant buildings in Kandy.[45] Anuradhapura, Polonnaruva and Kandy form the three "triangle points" that together encompass some of the island's best examples of architectural and cultural heritage, including hundreds of stupas, temples, caves, ruins, archaeological areas, and colonial and modern buildings.[46] Dr. Roland Silva, the eminent Sri Lankan archaeologist, played an integral role in the establishment and ongoing success of both the CTP and CCF, and served as the Director General of the latter from 1980 to 1997.[47]

The CTP created a management framework that was tailored to Sri Lanka's institutions, constituencies and heritage sites in order to optimize conservation successes. The program's unique approach created a model for heritage management in a developing country in which local experts led the way in the design and implementation of conservation projects.[48] In order to accomplish its conservation objectives, the CTP brought together government administrators with technical experts, academics and private architectural consultants who worked in cooperation with temple authorities and other local stakeholders. An annual review by the joint UNESCO–Sri Lankan Working Group, which includes participation of international experts, monitored the progress of projects within the CTP, an approach that helped ensure that outside expertise was available when needed, and allowed local professionals to compare their work with international approaches to practice.[49]

The method for funding CTP activities also represented a significant innovation in the evolution of Sri Lanka's architectural conservation field of practice. Originally planned as a ten-year effort, funding was initially set at US$52 million, 60 percent of which was provided by UNESCO and the remaining 40 percent by the Government of Sri Lanka. The UNESCO funds were raised through the creation of an international network of donor institutions in more than six countries.[50] For its part, the Sri Lankan government established the Central Cultural Fund (CCF) to manage the UNESCO donations and national contributions, and to act as the implementing agency for the CTP. The board of directors for the CCF is chaired by the Prime Minister, who is joined by six cabinet ministers along with professionals from the field. Each project site has its own multi-agency, interdisciplinary team assigned to it, which covers the full range of the professional field, from laborers to craftspeople to scientists.[51] Admission fees for foreign visitors to CTP sites provide a significant, ongoing source of funding for the CCF.

The development of professional capacity has also been a key component of the CTP. Academic partnerships have led to the establishment of two advanced degree programs at Sri Lankan universities: the Postgraduate Institute of Archaeology (established in 1986 at the University of Kelaniya in

Colombo) and the Post Graduate Unit of Architectural Conservation of Monuments and Sites (inaugurated in 1983 at the University of Moratuwa, outside of Colombo).[52]

Dambulla, a Buddhist cave and temple complex located in the central Matale District, offers a case study in the successes and challenges of implementing the CTP. Dating to the second or third century BCE, Dambulla consists of a series of natural and cut caves filled with Buddhist murals, statues and shrines, which are set in the context of a vast archaeological zone. The caves and paintings have been subject to continuous maintenance and repeated restorations over the centuries, most substantially during the reign of King Kirti Sri Rajasinha of Kandy (1747–1782). Worshippers have used the site without interruption for over 2,000 years, and it attracts tens of thousands of pilgrims and tourists annually. Though it does not draw the same tourist numbers as nearby Sigiriya, visitation at the caves for religious purposes spikes during the full moon festivals of Poson and Vesak, creating periods of intensive use that can damage the murals.[53]

The CTP effort at Dambulla began in 1982 and was largely complete by 1993, during which time it focused on the management and conservation of the site's diverse resources, as well as on addressing issues common to cave temple sites throughout South Asia. The temple authorities initially embraced CTP's heritage management plan for the site. From the start of the collaboration, the monks indicated a preference for a more contemporary approach to preserving the murals in their current, imperfect state rather than retouching or repainting them, as is commonly practiced at similar wall or cave paintings elsewhere in the Buddhist world. Early efforts at managing the site included the removal of modern commercial stalls around the vihara plaza and the restoration of a traditional bodhi tree shrine at the base of the rock. The CCF constructed remote parking lots, and made allowances for the construction of new modern temples outside of the historic core. The CTP's scope also incorporated research into the composition and physical characteristics of the murals' pigments and plaster beds, preventative and selective conservation of the murals, on-site training and copying the murals for the purposes of off-site study and interpretation.[54]

For all its accomplishments, the program at Dambulla also highlighted the challenges inherent in maintaining adequate funding levels and ongoing collaboration among stakeholder groups following the conclusion of the initial CTP effort in 1997. While universally lauded as a success, and acknowledged as a paradigm shift in the development and deployment of a national safeguarding campaign, the chief

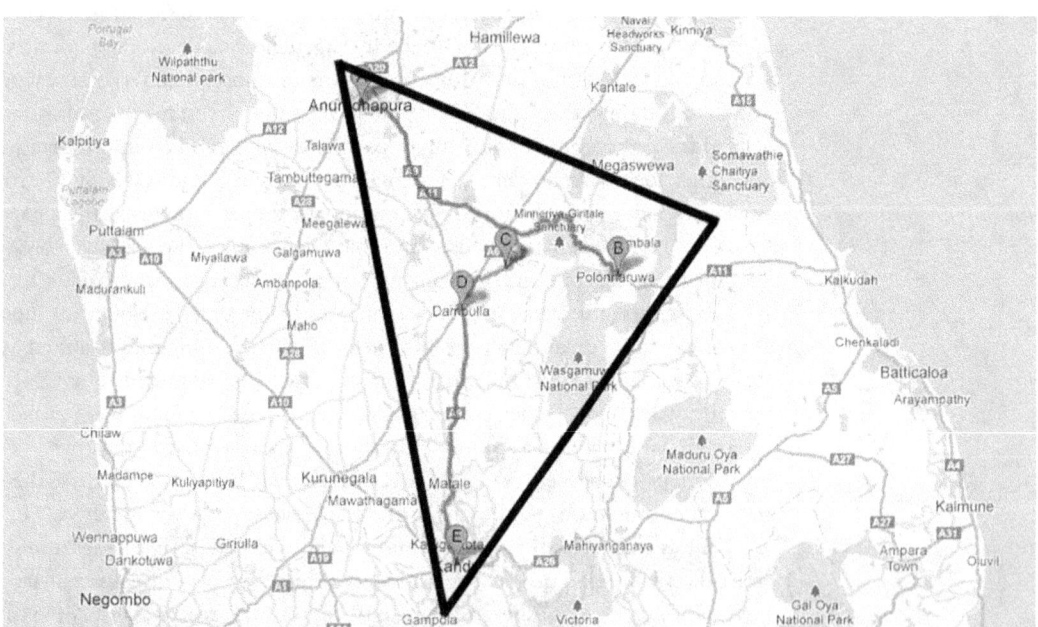

FIGURE 17.3 The designation in 1980 of the Cultural Triangle, a special heritage zone that encompasses five of Sri Lanka's key heritage sites plus scores of smaller sites, was an advanced concept at the time as it allowed both the systematic protection and presentation of numerous heritage sites and in their scenic natural context. Established tour routes with numerous visitor amenities are within this approximately 3,500 square kilometer area.

issue with the CTP appears to be one of sustainability. The Sri Lankan state party to UNESCO successfully added Dambulla to the World Heritage List in 1991, just under a decade after launching the CTP campaign at the site. Beginning in 1993, religious authorities assumed active management of the site, and since then issues have arisen relative to maintenance of the murals, management of the site and cooperation between CCF officials and the monks in charge. New construction within the buffer zone in particular has raised objections from UNESCO, while the opening of facilities meant to support the interpretation and protection of the site languished for years. In a most troubling development, the relationship between the monks that manage the site and CCF personnel deteriorated substantially after 1996, to the point where the chief monk at the site has questioned the value of the World Heritage Site status, and the CCF has publicly raised concerns regarding the monks' ability to adequately conserve the temple's paintings.[55]

In a 2014 State of Conservation Report, UNESCO cited deterioration of the cave murals, an inadequate maintenance program, and several new constructions within the buffer zone, most notably a 100 ft (30 m) Buddha statue erected near the base of the rock (though outside of the view of the caves themselves) as serious concerns.[56] A project aimed at protecting the highly vulnerable murals by reproducing them and placing the replicas on display suffered delays of almost two decades due to disagreements between site personnel and CCF managers.[57] In 2003, the Painting, Conservation & Research Center opened at last, featuring copies of the murals, as well as a facility for research and conservation of traditional wall paintings throughout the country.[58] As of 2015, disagreements around the management of the temple appear as yet unresolved, with the integrity of the murals themselves hanging in the balance, a situation that points to a need to revive the spirit of collaboration and cooperation from the early days of the CTP.

Balancing tourism and conservation at Sigiriya

Sigiriya, a fifth century citadel located less than 15 km (9 miles) from Dambulla, is among Sri Lanka's most visited cultural heritage sites, and another centerpiece of the CTP. The Sinhalese King Kasyapa established the site in 477 CE after seizing the throne at Anuradhapura to serve as both a defensive outpost and beautifully designed landscape in the great tradition of Sri Lankan pleasure gardens.[59] The fortified palace complex, which Kasyapa named *Simha-giri* or Lion Mountain, sits on the summit of a granite outcrop 180 m (590 ft) above a forested plateau. The rock is surrounded by extensive terraced gardens featuring an intricate irrigation network comprised of water retention structures (tanks) and surface and sub-surface hydraulic systems extending for hundreds of meters out from its base.[60] The plan of the ancient site, recognized as one of the most sophisticated and best-preserved ancient landscapes in Asia, measures approximately 15 ha (approximately 25 acres) inside a rectangular wall, with a series of inner fortifications, axially centered on the citadel.[61]

In addition to its impressive architectural, landscape and urban design features, Sigiriya also boasts remarkable examples of early fresco painting and epigraphic inscriptions that document its centuries of use. The much-acclaimed frescoes depicting the *Sigiri landun* (delicately detailed female figures, floating above clouds), contemporary to the citadel and gardens, adorn a niche on the western face of the rock that is accessible only by a recently built spiral staircase. The original work is thought to have contained up to five hundred such figures, which would have completely filled the 140 m long and 40 m high niche.[62]

The royal court abandoned Sigiriya in 495 CE following Kasyapa's death. It was used as a Buddhist monastery until the thirteenth century, when the complex fell into a long period of decline and eventual abandonment. A British army unit rediscovered Sigiriya in 1831 and in 1874 the Royal Asiatic Society of Ceylon undertook documentation of the ruined citadel and surrounding gardens; formal archaeological work began in 1894 under the Archaeological Survey of Ceylon and continued uninterrupted under the Department of Archaeology following independence.[63] Sigiriya was listed as a World Heritage Site in 1982, the same year the interdisciplinary study under the CTP began, addressing topics including epigraphy, art history, landscape design and conservation of the site's remnant architectural features.[64] The CTP program succeeded in improving visitor access and amenities on the site, while also spurring the preparation of a 1989 regional plan under the Urban Development

FIGURE 17.4a and b The fifth century CE ancient city of Sigiriya, situated atop a 200 m stone mountain, was first noticed by antiquarians in the 1830s (a). Its marvels include its carved Lion Gate, a sophisticated water management system and the remains of the settlement atop which is one of the best examples of urban planning of the first millennium. Frescoes protected by rock overhangs that depict "The Maidens of the Clouds" are attractions that have made Sigiriya Sri Lanka's most visited cultural site (b).

Authority[65] that encompasses the 9,400 ha (36 square mile) administrative district around Sigiriya, in order to manage development and protect the site's wider context.[66] Largely considered a success, the regional plan was leveraged to block the proposed construction of a military airfield within 3 km of the site in 2001.[67] In 1998, the government established the Sigiriya Heritage Foundation as a management authority that could leverage public and private funds to protect and promote the site, but as of 2015 the institution has not yet begun its work.

In the current era of greater stability and security, tourism has begun to regain its place as a cornerstone of the Sri Lankan economy, which relies heavily on heritage sites and stunning natural scenery to draw visitors. The numbers of foreign tourists visiting the Cultural Triangle properties increased nearly tenfold between 1988 and 2014. This generated an even more substantial jump in revenue collected from ticket sales at the sites, which in 2014 totaled over US$13 million.[68] In 2011 the Ministry of Economic Development launched an ambitious Tourism Development Strategy that aimed to increase the number of arrivals from 500,000 to 2.5 million by 2016. This will undoubtedly expand economic opportunities in the country, but it also runs the risk of straining the country's infrastructure and capacity for managing heritage sites.[69]

Sigiriya's compelling story and dramatic setting contributes to its status as Sri Lanka's most popular historic site, receiving approximately 700,000 visitors in 2014. With the conclusion of the civil war that number is only poised to grow as the tourism industry recovers and the site becomes more heavily promoted.[70] Crowd control has already become an issue, with reports of visitors walking on the fragile brick walls and a lack of adequate site security to manage the number of tourists.[71] Managing the exponential growth of tourism in Sri Lanka and its impacts on the Cultural Triangle sites and beyond stands out as a critical, ongoing challenge that will require the same level of diligence, planning and consensus building as was required to achieve the successes of the CTP during its initial phase.

Challenges to the ongoing conservation of Kandy

Kandy, Sri Lanka's last pre-colonial capital, remains the primary religious and cultural center for the country's Buddhist population, and is a major pilgrimage site drawing hundreds of thousands of national and international worshippers each year.[72] During its centuries-old Esala Perahera festival, the Sri Dalada Maligawa's (The Temple of the Tooth) most sacred relic – a tooth said to belong to the Buddha himself – is ceremonially carried through the city, accompanied by elephants, dancers and worshippers performing adulations.

The Sri Dalada Maligawa is the most revered place in Sri Lanka and among the holiest in Buddhism, and remains an active, living heritage site within a dynamic, growing urban context. Kandy possesses a characteristic low-scale urban character, comprised of buildings dating principally to the nineteenth century, picturesquely nestled among hills around a lake. The city has confronted two major challenges since 1990 related to conservation of its unique urban form: from development pressures to population growth and tourism, and a direct, iconoclastic assault on its heritage resources during Sri Lanka's civil war.

In 1971 the area surrounding the Sri Dalada Maligawa was set aside under the Town and Country Planning Ordinance (1946) in order to protect its historic buildings from insensitive development that was beginning to affect the city's traditional architecture and character.[73] As part of the CTP effort that began in 1980, a series of planning exercises were undertaken that ultimately led to the designation of the blocks around the temple complex as a "Sacred Area" under the Urban Development Authority.[74] This designation created zoning controls in three areas radiating outward from the temple complex that regulated the height of new construction, restricted incompatible types of development (such as heavy industry), and mandated the use of compatible design and materials for new construction to maintain uniformity within the historic context. Conservation of all buildings within the temple complex was completed under the CTP charge, and a subsequent survey effort identified around four hundred key historic buildings for conservation, which were celebrated with specially designed plaques. World Heritage Site status was bestowed upon the city in 1988.[75]

In 1992 the Kandy Municipal Council established the Kandy World Heritage Committee, which includes roles for the CCF project manager, the Department of Archaeology Assistant Director in Kandy, the UDA and religious authorities for the main temples. Together they prepared a Master Plan, finalized in 1999, which focused on conservation priorities within the old city.[76] Although some progress has been made, such as the establishment of an Association of Heritage Building Owners, sustained, effective conservation planning measures remain somewhat elusive in Kandy. Development pressures have persisted in recent decades, despite efforts to manage them effectively and regulate urban growth.

The Sri Dalada Maligawa was the most high profile among many heritage resources damaged during the prolonged Sri Lankan civil war.[77] On the morning of January 25, 1998 a suicide bomb attack struck, killing sixteen people and heavily damaging several buildings in the temple complex, including fragile sculpture and frescoes.[78] The LTTE had deliberately targeted the temple in an attempt to demoralize the Sinhalese leadership and populace, which historically have revered the complex as a touchstone for authority and the continuity of Sinhalese culture.

In response to the calamity a national fundraising campaign was launched, in which an outpouring of support generated three times the needed funds. The Department of Archaeology staff was promptly tasked with restoring the temple in consultation with the chief monks in charge of the site, with a major priority being the restoration of religious function as quickly and seamlessly as possible.[79] At the insistence of the religious community, carved stone elements and new timber were locally sourced, albeit with difficulty, a decision that ultimately contributed to a revival of Sri Lanka's stone carving industry.[80] In the process of restoration, many elements of the late-seventeenth-century building were created anew, a product of both necessity and of a conservation approach that favored continuity of function and association over material authenticity.[81] Additionally, while the success of this project serves as a clear example of restoration as a means for recovery from a post-conflict episode, the process also served as a prelude to a much larger recovery effort related to the country's built heritage – the aftermath of the 2004 Indian Ocean tsunami.

On December 26, 2004, a powerful, 9.3-magnitude earthquake centered off the coast of Sumatra triggered a tsunami that struck the Sri Lankan coast several hours later with devastating results. Although the area most directly affected included the country's southern and eastern coasts, the tsunami inflicted untold damage on the entire nation through the destruction of transportation infrastructure and coastal communities, economic disruption, loss of property and agricultural assets, as well as the harm inflicted upon movable and immovable heritage.[82] Total damages amounted to US$1.1 billion, with more than 30,000 lives lost, the displacement of half a million people across the country, and 100,000 homes damaged or destroyed.[83] It is frequently noted that, due to the tsunami's scale and scope, not a single Sri Lankan was unaffected by the disaster.[84]

Cultural sites damaged in the country's coastal region included a huge range of structures, from lighthouses to mosques, archaeological collections to historic townscapes. The immediate aftermath of the tsunami witnessed an outpouring of assistance from local and international organizations that appropriately focused on the humanitarian response. Thanks to the vigilance of the local ICOMOS chapter the conditions of affected heritage resources across the country were quickly documented so that they could be considered as part of the long-term recovery effort.[85] The episode exposed vulnerabilities in disaster response strategies in general and in Sri Lanka in particular, but has also revealed opportunities for the revival of affected communities ranging from small coastal villages to the World Heritage Site of Galle.

Galle stands out in the region not only as an exceptionally well-preserved example of colonial-era fortifications and hybridized Dutch, British and Sri Lankan architecture, but also as a complete ensemble comprised of cultural landscapes, urban assemblages and individual buildings. Galle was a thriving commercial port for over one thousand years before the Portuguese captured it in 1587; in turn, the Dutch ousted the Portuguese in 1640 and later constructed Galle's massive ramparts as part of a series of forts along the Sri Lankan coastline.

Galle remained an important commercial port after the British assumed command in 1796 until the early twentieth century when it was supplanted by Colombo, after which it remained a regional administrative center. Efforts to protect the 40 ha (about 100 acre) fort and its distinctive architecture date to its listing under the Antiquities Ordinance in 1940. Development pressures in the 1980s led to the site's inclusion in the CTP effort, in addition to a movement to have Galle listed as a World Heritage Site, a status it achieved in 1988.[86] Because Galle Fort includes a functioning town of more

FIGURE 17.5a and b The distinctive, mostly wooden and tile roofed architecture of Kandy, the penultimate Sri Lankan capital, reflects the city's role as the country's cultural and religious center for over two centuries (a). Controls of the design of new buildings and preservation of Kandy's historic buildings are overseen by the Department of Archaeology. Oversight of the Temple of the Tooth, which was rebuilt in 1998, is managed by the Buddhist community (b).

than 700 private homes, along with businesses, places of worship and government administration buildings, the management of change presents particular challenges calling for specialized organizations and highly functional strategies.[87]

In response to these needs, the government passed legislation to create the Galle Heritage Foundation (GHF) in 1994 as a governmental entity with the authority to acquire and dispose of property, raise and borrow funds to conserve historic buildings, promote the site and its attributes, and coordinate the various stakeholder groups concerned with heritage in Galle.[88] The GHF board includes a wide range of players including national and local government officials, university program directors, and citizen appointees.[89]

A Development Plan prepared by ICOMOS Sri Lanka in 2002 highlighted the types of issues confronting the ancient city, ranging from the social (scant awareness of the significance of the site, a disconnect between the tourism industry and local residents) to the logistical (the lack of effective solid waste disposal, conflicts between vehicles and pedestrians, haphazard utility infrastructure). Proposals offered by the 2002 plan included standards for infill construction, guidelines for owners for appropriately modifying their historic buildings, and identification of priority conservation projects. The GHF was tasked as the implementation authority for the 2002 Development Plan, with support from the CCF, and within its first years accomplished a great deal despite ongoing challenges. These included uneven enforcement of development regulations (particularly regarding the buffer zone) and the prevalence of foreign acquisition of heritage properties in the fort, thereby changing the character of the residential community.[90] A positive outcome of the plan included the enhanced engagement of the residential community regarding the planning process, driven by a greater appreciation for the city's unique heritage and demonstrated by the monitoring of development controls by activist citizens' groups.[91]

The impact of the 2004 tsunami interrupted progress around these promising trends, and introduced new challenges regarding the conservation of Galle and other coastal heritage resources. While Galle's ancient ramparts largely protected the old city from the primary waves, seawater breached the walls in three places while also undermining the ramparts' foundations, damaging the original sewer system, and destroying the Marine Archaeology Lab along with much of its collection.[92] The fortifications did not protect the old city outside the walls, including its commercial district and bus depot, where the waves killed as many as 4,000, decimating the surrounding community and leaving greater Galle as one of most heavily impacted areas in Sri Lanka.[93]

In response to the tsunami, one sweeping measure made by the government was to establish a 100 m buffer zone along the coastline within which development would be tightly regulated.[94] A well-timed appeal to government officials by ICOMOS Sri Lanka within one week of the disaster asked to include heritage resources, along with fishing and tourism-related facilities, as allowable within the newly established zone. This was an essential concept given the importance of setting and context for such sites. ICOMOS Sri Lanka also spearheaded a heroic effort to immediately survey cultural sites nationwide in order to assess damage to and inventory what remained. The national ICOMOS chapter enlisted university students to help with survey efforts, but they were challenged by the lack of capacity and resources and by the difficulty of accessing many disaster-struck areas, especially in the north and east. The National Physical Planning Department, which led the way on recovery planning efforts, included the surveyed sites in their redevelopment plans for the stricken areas; the surveys themselves were based in part on the existing Archaeology Department inventories and a 1989 survey of coastal areas, demonstrating the value of maintaining heritage lists as a disaster preparedness measure.[95]

The years following the tsunami witnessed a mix of positive and negative developments related to the way in which the recovery effort was carried out.[96] On the positive side, the event helped raise global awareness of the value of Sri Lanka's heritage sites, particularly in the case of Galle, although ICOMOS Sri Lanka raised the issue of disproportionate attention paid to the World Heritage property, at the expense of the adjacent old city where most of the damage actually occurred.[97] Inside the fort's walls, a number of individual buildings were rehabilitated as part of the recovery effort, including the seventeenth century Old Dutch Hospital, which underwent a comprehensive stabilization project between 2006 and 2011 and now serves as a mixed-use shopping and dining area.[98]

The recovery effort at Galle also included reconstruction of the picturesque cricket ground, which sits on the Esplanade, a spit of land that connects the fort to the mainland. While the use of the site as for cricket dates to the early twentieth century, the reconstructed facility includes a three-storey spectators' pavilion that partially blocks views of the fort's northern walls. Prior to its completion in 2007 UNESCO formally raised objections to the structure, which lies within the fort's buffer zone, and proposed a series of remedies including the removal of the pavilion and other unauthorized structures. To date, no compromise has been reached, and although the revived cricket ground serves as a signal that the area has recovered from the tsunami's destruction, it also acts as a reminder of the vigilance needed regarding development at the renowned yet highly sensitive location.[99]

In 2015 the Government of Sri Lanka adopted a proposal for an "Integrated Management System" for Galle, which envisions a strengthened role for the Galle Heritage Foundation in the overall management of the World Heritage Site. The system proposes to appoint a series of "task managers" to act as points of contact between the GHF and the various sectors that influence the city's operation and development.[100] Also in 2015 the GHF adopted the Galle Heritage Site Management Plan, a joint effort of the Sri Lankan–Netherlands Cultural Cooperation Program, and the Postgraduate Institute of Archaeology at the University of Kelaniya, filling a long-standing gap in the management structure of the site.[101] These two developments proved useful in guiding the evaluation of complicated projects, such as the recent decision on the part of the Sri Lankan Port Authority to abandon a proposal for a new shipping port in Galle's harbor in favor of a cruise ship- and tourism-focused port. The decision was based in large part on analysis that determined the former would imperil historically significant shipwrecks, would involve blasting that could damage nearby buildings, and would include new construction that would be incompatible with the historic setting of the harbor.[102] These developments demonstrate an ongoing dedication to sustained, innovative conservation strategies for one of Sri Lanka's most significant – and most complex – heritage sites.

With the conclusion of the civil war in 2009, the Sri Lankan central government and local stakeholders now have an opportunity to transition from a period of hostility and internal instability to one more focused on conservation and management of its heritage resources. The civil war produced a climate of tension and sectarianism that generally hampered the ability of the international community to engage in Sri Lankan conservation efforts, and of local institutions to fully flourish. It also effectively partitioned the island, cutting off large areas of the north and east from central government control and funding, thereby leaving the architectural resources in those parts of the country neglected and highly vulnerable. UNESCO, along with the governments of the Netherlands and Japan in particular, have remained active partners in the country's conservation institutions, but the cessation of hostilities and reintegration of these parts of the country will create openings for new and expanded partnerships with the international conservation community. One such opportunity lies with the conservation of the seventeenth century Dutch Fort at Jaffna, located at the island's northern tip, and left in perilous condition due to the decades of fighting and neglect. A joint project between the Department of Archaeology and the Government of the Netherlands launched a multi-phased project in 2009 that aims to repair the fort's ramparts, conserve its buildings, and convert the installation into a museum in order to aid the region's economic recovery.[103]

The revival in tourism, which is heavily promoted by the government and already under way, will place added pressure on the country's heritage managers to accommodate the rush of visitors to the island's most popular cultural sites. But given the funding model in place for the CCF it will also create generate resources for additional conservation programs. Similarly, the tourism economy offers opportunities for creative adaptive reuse projects converting distinctively Sri Lankan buildings into tourist facilities. One such example is the Tea Factory Hotel in central Nuwara Eliya, a 1935 former tea processing facility that was converted into a fifty-seven-room hotel, providing local employment opportunities and earning an Award of Merit from the UNESCO Office in Bangkok's Asia-Pacific Heritage Award program.[104]

A promising recent international partnership is the "Integrated Plan for Conservation, Preservation and Development of Cultural Heritage in the Southern Region," also known as the "Cultural Triangle of the South." Building off a similar approach to the original CTP effort, the Government of the Netherlands partnered with the CCF, Department of Archaeology and other institutions beginning in

FIGURE 17.6a, b and c Galle Fort (a) built by the Portuguese in 1588 and expanded by the Dutch from 1699 is one of the most intact colonial fortifications in the Indian Ocean. The tsunami of 2004 (b) affected the colonial fort of Galle in ways ranging from damage to its waterfront structures to the economic impact of the disaster on the country at large (c). The recovery process has ultimately reinvigorated the development of management plans and strategies for conservation of this unique resource.

2006 to initiate a total of eighteen small-scale projects between Bentota-Galle, Matara and Kataragama-Yala along the southeast coast of the island. The effort focused on a tourism development plan, on work on the ramparts at Galle, and at related Dutch forts at Matara and Katuwana, concentrating on site museums and interpretive installations.[105]

In the near term it is likely that insufficient funding from the central government will remain high on the list of challenges for meeting Sri Lanka's conservation needs and challenges. The CCF offers an effective organizational model, but one that may benefit from continuing evolution to help meet its stated goal "to meet expenses incurred in developing, restoring, and preserving cultural monuments."[106] For instance, the Department of Archaeology is just one of several branches of both the Ministry of National Heritage and Ministry of Cultural and Art Affairs that receive support from the CCF, thus diluting the fund's impact.[107]

Despite its extraordinary challenges, ranging from a protracted civil war to one of the twenty-first century's worst natural disasters to date, Sri Lanka stands out as a deserving leader in the field of architectural conservation in Asia. The small country's historic position as a hub of international trade and as a global center for Buddhism, and its rich cultural and natural resources underpin a strong body of institutions, laws and professional capacity. While enforcement of existing laws and maintaining the momentum of successful projects like the Cultural Triangle Project have proven challenging, practitioners in Sri Lanka have consistently responded to setbacks with new strategies, innovative proposals and reinvigorated organizations. From Galle to Kandy to Sigiriya, efforts to conserve the country's unique properties are constantly being refreshed when new challenges present themselves. This spirit of resiliency is as admirable as it is necessary in a dynamic, rapidly developing country like Sri Lanka.

Maldives

An independent archipelago located 750 km (465 miles) southwest of Colombo, the Maldives islands are comprised of a series of coral atolls, consisting of approximately 1,190 islands, only 198 of which are inhabited. The country's history mirrors that of its larger island neighbor to the north, with an early cultural legacy of Buddhist and Hindu communities, long-standing connections to Indian Ocean trade routes, and periods of Portuguese, Dutch and British occupation followed by a tumultuous independence era beginning in 1965. A major difference between Sri Lanka and Maldives, however, is the dominant religion of its people. Islam has been ensconced as the official state religion of Maldives per its 1997 constitution; national law requires its citizens to be Muslims, and prohibits Maldivians from practicing any other religion.[108] The country of just under 400,000 has a nascent cultural heritage infrastructure with limited governmental support and a small community of advocacy organizations supporting conservation. Maldives ratified the World Heritage Convention in 1986, but as of 2015 has yet to list a World Heritage Site.

Since 2000 Maldives has possessed one of Asia's highest economic growth rates, with tourism, services and fishing as its leading industries.[109] The 1.2 million foreign tourists that traveled to the Maldives in 2014 came largely for its natural scenery, rather than its cultural heritage.[110] The connection between economic growth and the tourism industry has led to a vigilant national approach to protecting the archipelago's beaches and waters advanced by the country's Environmental Protection Act and five-year development plans, and a commitment to sustainable, carbon-neutral development. This commitment comes not only from a desire to protect the tourism industry, but also from an acute awareness among many Maldivians that the country is among the world's most vulnerable to climate change.[111] Maldives is the lowest-lying country on Earth, with more than 80 percent of its land at an elevation of less than 1.6 m (5.24 ft) above sea level. This unique topography leaves the nation highly susceptible to natural disasters – as tragically demonstrated by the 2004 Indian Ocean tsunami – and the more gradual threats of sea level rise, extreme weather patterns and tidal variations. During his time in office, the former Maldivian president Mohamed Nasheed, who led the country from 2008 until 2012, famously assumed a high-profile role in raising awareness of his country's plight, and by extension, to the global threat of climate change.[112] Climate change in the twenty-first century threatens not only the country's low-lying heritage resources, but also the nation's very existence. Some estimates forecast the complete inundation of the islands by 2100.[113]

In late 2015, global leaders convened in Paris under the auspices of the United Nations Conference on Climate Change to negotiate what was hailed as a landmark international accord. The core of the agreement was a pledge by the world's industrialized nations to hold aggregate global temperature increases at a level not to exceed 2° Centigrade (3.6° Farenheit) over current levels. The absence of numerical CO_2 limits disappointed some activists, while delegates conceded that domestic politics (notably those in the United States) made such constraints unattainable.[114] Past international climate negotiations were beset by disagreement between industrialized and developing nations as to who would shoulder responsibility for emission cuts. In Paris, however, the dichotomy shifted, with endangered island and coastal nations pleading for assistance from large emitters in both the West and Asia.[115] That dynamic, alongside growing environmental concerns in China and promises of private sector investment in clean energy, spurred heads of state to commit to the goal and five-year progress reports.

The Maldives islands and Sri Lanka, a shared heritage

The earliest settlers of the coral atolls are thought to have arrived from what is now Sri Lanka and mainland India by approximately 500 BCE. An account in the fifth century Sri Lankan epic poem the *Mahavamsa* identifies the early settlers of the Maldives as passengers on a wayward ship from the party of banished Prince Vijaya, who had been sent from Bengal to Sri Lanka in 500 BCE.[116] Hinduism arrived shortly thereafter, and then during the third century BCE representatives from the court of the Emperor Ashoka introduced Buddhism to the Maldives.[117] Evidence of trade connections with Rome in the first century CE and China during the Song dynasty (tenth century CE) appears in the archaeological record, testifying to the Maldives' long tradition of contact with the distant world, despite its relative isolation.[118] Successive kings from the Hindu Chola dynasty, based in mainland India, brought the Maldives under their sway during the late tenth and early eleventh centuries.[119]

As in Sri Lanka, Buddhism and Hinduism remained dominant for over 1,000 years, as evidenced by archaeological remains of stupas found on several islands across the archipelago. H.C.P. Bell of the Archaeological Survey of Ceylon conducted excavations on Toddu Island in the south Maldives in 1922, discovering the remains of several Buddhist stupas dating to the islands' pre-Islamic period. Arab traders from the distant shores of the Indian Ocean introduced Islam beginning in the tenth century, culminating in the conversion of king Sri Sandaneyka Adeettiya in 1153 CE.[120] The great Berber traveler of the Middle Ages, Ibn Battuta, visited the Maldives in the fourteenth century, famously praising its people for their piety and for their "beautiful mosques and ... edifices made of wood." Battuta noted that the Maldives produced cowrie shells (used as currency) and *coir* (coconut fiber ropes highly valued for their resistance to seawater rot) as their chief trading commodities.[121]

The Portuguese occupied the Maldives for a brief, violent period between 1558 and 1573 that culminated in their expulsion by force by the local population. The Dutch maintained trade and military agreements with the islands' kings during the seventeenth and eighteenth centuries in concert with their activities in Ceylon to the north.[122] Many of the coral stone mosques that stand today as among the best examples of indigenous Maldivian architecture were constructed during the early eighteenth century, toward the twilight of the Dutch period.[123] After they assumed control over Ceylon in 1796, the British adopted the Dutch relationship with the islands until 1887, when the Maldives became a British protectorate under the authority of the Governor General in Colombo.[124] The islands retained this status until full independence in 1965.

Following independence, the country experienced a series of leadership transitions that resulted in the abolition of the sultanate, and the thirty-year regime of Maumoon Abudul Gayoom (1978–2008), under whom the tourism economy expanded rapidly, but political and media freedoms were constrained.[125] The tourist economy has traditionally been based on Kaafu atoll, which includes the country's capital, Malé, and today holds just under half of all tourist resorts in the country. Malé itself occupies an island of just under six square kilometers, with a population of 150,000, making it one of the most densely populated places in the world. Population pressures in Malé have created an enormous demand for buildable space, but have also generated sociological ills that have been attributed to the difficult process of modernization and development in the capital.[126]

FIGURE 17.7a and b Elements of authentic Maldivian vernacular architecture (a) are often incorporated into the design of new tourist resort developments, as can be seen at Maldivian architect Mohammed Shafeeq's Lighthouse at Baros Resort, Maldives (b). Such detail helps create a stylish and luxurious local atmosphere for guests.

As is the case in many island cultures, the people of the Maldives have developed distinctive forms of vernacular architecture that are adapted to their unique environment. These architectural types, which include palm thatch, naturally ventilated spaces, and coral lime plaster finishes, have been incorporated into many of the resort developments as a means of promoting Maldivian built culture and also in practical response to the scarcity of many building materials in the island nation.[127]

While the 2004 tsunami did not result in a high number of casualties in the Maldives relative to other affected countries, the archipelago sustained a crushing economic blow, with an estimated US$400 million in damage (which represented 62 percent of the country's GDP) and one-third of its population displaced or temporarily relocated by the disaster.[128] Political instability has escalated since the 2004 disaster, with several tumultuous changes in leadership, and alarming episodes such as a mob's 2012 attack on the National Museum that resulted in the destruction of thirty pre-Islamic artifacts dating from as early as the sixth century.[129] The National Museum attack points to a troubling rise in iconoclastic attitudes toward heritage in Maldives, but the republic's weak conservation framework has contributed to the loss of ancient Islamic buildings as well. These circumstances have contributed to calls from both inside and outside the government for an overhauled conservation management system in the island nation.

For much of the post-colonial era, the National Center for Linguistics and Historical Research (NCLHR), based in Malé, had been the principal institution for national heritage management. The NCLHR was responsible for partnerships with foreign archaeological missions, the management of the National Museum, and with research and promotion of Dhivehi, the national language of Maldives. Between 2001 and 2006 the National Planning Ministry made a series of recommendations regarding improvements to the country's heritage management system via the country's National Development Plans. The Plans noted that the NCLHR lacked a sufficient number of adequately trained professionals and described its enabling legislation (the Historical and Cultural Property Law of the Republic of Maldives, 1978) as inadequate, vague and lacking in definitions about what constitutes heritage.[130] The studies further noted that the country lacked a national inventory of sites and possessed a highly limited institutional framework for heritage management, which – along with high transportation building material costs – greatly constrained conservation activity in the archipelago.[131] The reports recommended a complete overhaul of conservation institutions, management and professional capacity. As of 2015 this has yet to fully materialize.

In 2010 the government of President Mohamed Nasheed took several steps toward reorganizing the country's conservation infrastructure, discontinuing the work of the National Centre by reallocating the linguistic studies program to the Maldives National University and creating a new Heritage Department, which initially reported to the Ministry of Tourism.[132] As of 2015 the Department of Heritage has been made a part of the Ministry of Education, and a new Maldivian Heritage Protection and Preservation Law is under consideration by parliament.[133]

In 2011 the Maldivian state party signed the UNESCO Convention for the Safeguarding of the Intangible Cultural Heritage, in a bid to support the documentation and preservation of traditional performing arts in particular. In doing so, the government at the time aimed to counter increasingly conservative attitudes toward certain aspects of intangible heritage that were deemed as un-Islamic among more traditional segments of society in Maldives.[134]

In another move to address gaps in the country's heritage management system, a new National Museum opened on July 26, 2010 (the country's Independence Day), creating a permanent home for an institution that had moved four times since its inception in the 1950s. Comprised of two buildings, one of which is part of the old sultan's palace and the other newly designed and financed by the Chinese government, the National Museum houses a collection that represents the full scope of Maldivian history, including a collection of rare pre-Islamic objects and sculpture. These materials were singled out and destroyed during the shocking attack on the facility on February 7, 2012 during an episode of general political unrest that culminated in the resignation of President Nasheed. The destroyed objects included a coral stone Buddha head dating to the sixth or seventh century CE, and fragmentary Hindu statues and other objects dating to the early centuries of the islands' occupation.[135] The incident signaled a troubling reaction to the country's attempts to present its full history in a manner consistent with international museum norms.

In 2013 the Heritage Department submitted a proposal to UNESCO's World Heritage Tentative List consisting of six coral stone mosques, which constitute a distinctive type of Maldivian indigenous architecture. The technique used to carve the live coral stone and construct the mosques represents a hybrid of East African and indigenous craft traditions that are believed to date to the pre-Islamic period. The places of worship, erected between 1658 and 1815, are spread geographically across the archipelago. They include the Ihavandhoo, Meedhoo, Malé and Fenfushi Friday Mosques, and the Malé Eid and Isdhoo Old Mosques. The modestly scaled structures typically consist of a small prayer hall and minaret resting on a coral stone base, topped by a timber framed roof and interior ornamentation consisting of lacquer rendered calligraphy. The mosques often sit within a landscaped compound containing one or more fresh water wells used for ablutions, and often a cemetery featuring finely carved coral stone markers.[136] In 2014 the Heritage Department engaged the Archaeological Survey of India for assistance in developing a conservation strategy for the mosques, a number of which were exhibiting signs of deterioration due to leaks and deferred maintenance.[137] The partnership represents a revival of a previous joint program during 1987 and 1988 with the Indian National Research Laboratory for the Conservation of Cultural Property that worked on the Malé Friday Mosque. The joint program was a promising step towards international engagement on the part of the Maldivian conservation community.[138]

Although mosques like those identified in the World Heritage nomination are revered by many Maldivian citizens and remain active places of worship, their survival is not necessarily ensured without further legislative protection and vigilance on the part of the conservation community. In 2014 the Malé city council approved the demolition of the Fandiyaaru Miskiy (Judge's Mosque), (built ca. 1747) without prior notification to the Heritage Department after a donor financed the construction of a new, four-story mosque in its place. While Heritage Department officials acknowledge the missed opportunity for saving the building, they also concede that no law existed that required their approval prior to the mosque's demolition. REVIVE, an advocacy group established in 2011 by arts students to promote history, liberal arts education and Maldivian culture, threatened legal action over the incident, demonstrating a relatively rare instance of heritage advocacy in Maldives.[139]

Maldives presently sits at a political, ecological and cultural crossroads relative to conservation of its heritage resources. A highly volatile political climate during much of the twenty-first century appears to have slowed several efforts to establish a modern conservation infrastructure that is supported by governmental agencies, comprehensive legislation and activist, academic and professional communities. Conservative religious elements within Maldivian society appear aggravated by the political environment and world events, as evidenced by the National Museum attack and prevailing attitudes toward the country's pre-Islamic heritage. All of this is set against the backdrop of threats to the country's very existence due to an unpredictable global climate crisis in which the experience of Maldives may serve as a prelude for low-lying regions from Karachi to Shanghai. Politicians on both sides of the current government divide appear to acknowledge the need to do more for the country's heritage, both in terms of expanding the tourist economy and by way of supporting the country's unique culture. But the forces aligned against such progress have proven formidable, and will require a truly concerted effort both locally and internationally to overcome.

Notes

1   Ceylon, an Anglicized version of the Portuguese name for the island (Ceilao), was in use from 1815 to 1972, after which the government of Sri Lanka officially changed its name.
2   Buddhism is thought to have arrived in the second century BCE, after which it spread throughout the island, largely at the expense of existing Hindu communities. Hinduism has a deeper history in Sri Lanka, predating the arrival of Buddhism by several centuries. Source: K.M. de Silva. *A History of Sri Lanka*. (Berkeley: University of California Press, 1981), 50.
3   BBC News. "Sri Lanka Country Profile." 2015. Web. www.bbc.com/news/world-south-asia-11999611. Accessed December 21, 2015.
4   By comparison, Thailand has more than three times the population of Sri Lanka (67 million people vs. 20 million), and almost ten times the area (200,000 square miles vs. 25,000), but half the number of cultural World Heritage Sites (three vs. six). As of 2015 Sri Lanka has numerous cultural sites on the tentative World

Heritage Sites list, including the Buddhist shrine of Seruwila Mangala Raja Maha Vihara, comprising a stupa and a collection of other monuments, and the ancient pilgrim route along the Mahaweli River from Seruwila to Sri Pada (Sacred Foot Print Shrine). Source: World Heritage Centre. Sri Lanka. 2015. Web. http://whc.unesco.org/en/tentativelists/?action=listtentative&pattern=sri+lanka&state=&theme=&criteria_restrication=&date_start=&date_end=&order=. Accessed October 14, 2015.

5   In an interview the National Heritage Minister, Jagath Balasuriya, noted that over 250,000 sites have been registered in Sri Lanka. Source: Lahiru Pothmulla. "National Heritage Protected at Minimal Costs: Interview with National Heritage Minister Jagath Balusuriya," *Daily Mirror* (Sri Lanka), October 4, 2014. Web. www.dailymirror.lk/53314/national-heritage-protected-at-minimal-costs. Accessed October 28, 2015.

6   World Bank. "Sri Lanka Country Overview." 2015. Web. www.worldbank.org/en/country/srilanka/overview. Accessed December 5, 2015.

7   The Sri Lankan government has set a goal of welcoming 2.5 million tourists by 2016 up from 600,000 in 2009. "Post Tiger Economy." *The Economist*. February 3, 2014. Web. www.economist.com/blogs/gulliver/2014/02/sri-lankan-tourism. Accessed December 5, 2015.

8   De Silva, 7, 3.

9   Sally Pomme Clayton. "Ramayana Synopsis." The British Library. 2005. Web. www.bl.uk/learning/cult/inside/corner/ramayana/synopsis/html. Accessed October 28, 2015.

10 UNESCO World Heritage Centre. "Sacred City of Anuradhaupura." 2015. Web. www.whc.unesco.org/en/list/200. Accessed December 5, 2015.

11 Peter Reeves (ed.). *The Encyclopedia of the Sri Lankan Diaspora*. (Singapore: EDM, 2013), 49–50.

12 UNESCO World Heritage Centre. "Ancient City of Polonnaruwa." 2015. Web. www.whc.unesco.org/en/list/201. Accessed December 5, 2015.

13 De Silva, 94.

14 De Silva, 225–229.

15 Reeves, 24–29.

16 A series of official moves, such as declaring Sinhalese (rather than English) as the national language in 1956, and the declaration of Buddhism as the state religion in the 1972 constitution served to alienate the Tamil minority in the early decades of the independence era. Source: Lawrence Vale. *Architecture, Power and National Identity*. (London: Routledge, 2014), 229.

17 On May 21, 1991, a suicide bomber presumed to be affiliated with the LTTE assassinated the Prime Minister of India, Rajiv Gandhi, in Tamil Nadu, south India. Gandhi's decision to send an Indian Peacekeeping Force to Sri Lanka from 1987 to 1990 is suspected as a reason for the attack.

18 Sehar Mushtaq. "Identity Conflict in Sri Lanka: A Case of Tamil Tigers." *International Journal of Humanities and Social Science* 2(15) (August 2012), 207.

19 Jon Lee Anderson. "Death of the Tiger: Sri Lanka's Brutal Victory over its Tamil Insurgents." *The New Yorker*. January 17, 2011. Web. www.newyorker.com/magazine/2011/01/17/death-of-the-tiger. Accessed November 30, 2015.

20 Sri Lanka's modern population consists of Sinhalese (approximately 75 percent), Hindu Tamils (15 percent), Muslims (7 percent), and Christians (less than 1 percent). Source: Government of Sri Lanka. "Census of Population and Housing, 2012." 2012. Web. www.statistics.gov.lk/PopHouSat/CPH2011/Pages/Activities/Reports/FinalReport/Population/Table%20A3.pdf. Accessed November 30, 2015.

21 Global IDP (Internally Displaced People) Database. *Profile of Internal Displacement: Sri Lanka. Compilation of the Information Available in the Global IDP Database of the Norwegian Refugee Council*. (Geneva: Norwegian Refugee Council/Global IDP Project, 2005), 13.

22 The Society was formed in 1845, and renamed Royal Asiatic Society of Sri Lanka in 1972.

23 The Royal Asiatic Society of Sri Lanka. "[History of the] Society." 2015. Web. www.royalasiaticsociety.lk/about/. Accessed October 28, 2015.

24 Department of Archaeology (Sri Lanka). "History of the Department of Archaeology." 2015. Web. www.archaeology.gov.lk/web/index.php?option=com_content&view=article&id=54&Itemid=54&lang=en. Accessed October 12, 2015.

25 Gamini Wijesuriya. "Are We Ready to Learn? Lessons from the South Asian Region," in Neville Agnew and Janet Bridgland (eds.), *Of the Past, For the Future, Integrating Archaeology and Conservation*. (Los Angeles: Getty Conservation Institute, 2006), 158; and Personal email correspondence with Nilan Cooray, January 8, 2016.

26 Ibid.

27 Vihara are Buddhist monasteries. Stupa are Buddhist places of worship; in Sri Lanka they are typically masonry half-domes (*gharbaya*) resting on a plinth (*pesavalalu*) and topped with a spire (*koth kerella*).

28 Gamini Wijesuriya. *The Restoration of Buddhist Monuments in Sri Lanka: The Case for an Archaeological Heritage Management Strategy*. (Colombo: ICOMOS, 1993), 12.
29 Gamini Wijesuriya. "Are We Reinventing the Wheel? Archaeological Heritage Management in Sri Lanka under British Colonial Rule," in Susan Lawrence (ed.), *Archaeologies of the British: Explorations of Identity in the United Kingdom* (London: Routledge, 2013).
30 Restoration societies were part of a religious revival movement that was connected to the independence drive in Ceylon. They consisted of a wealthy patron, private citizens and monks, and undertook many stupa and other religious building restorations. Source: Wijesuriya, *Restoration of Buddhist Monuments*, 42.
31 Wijesuriya, *Restoration of Buddhist Monuments*, 45–49, 58–63.
32 Wijesuriya, *Restoration of Buddhist Monuments*, 43.
33 "The Lone Ruin at Nalanda." *Ceylon Today*. October 13, 2013. Web. www.ceylontoday.lk/64-44854-news-detail-the-lone-ruin-at-nalanda.html. Accessed January 8, 2016.
34 The Archaeology Department divisions include: Archaeology Services, Architectural Conservations, Chemical Conservation (Conservation Science), Activities (Exploration and Documentation, Maintenance, Project Monitoring and Evaluation, Public Services), Research (Excavation, Epigraphic and Numismatic) and Facilities (Museums). Source: Department of Archaeology (Sri Lanka) website, www.archaeology.gov.lk/.
35 Pali Wijeratne. "Management of the Cultural Heritage in Galle Fort – Before and After the 26/12 Tsuname Devastation." Paper delivered at the 2005 ICOMOS International Conference, Xian, China. Web. www.icomos.org/xian2005/papers/3-49.pdf. Accessed December 12, 2015.
36 Department of Archaeology (Sri Lanka). "Exploration and Documentation Division." 2015. Web. www.archaeology.gov.lk/web/index.php?option=com_content&view=article&id=75&Itemid=82&lang=en. Accessed October 28, 2015.
37 A. Wijesuriya et al. *Underwater Archaeological Impact Assessment of the Colombo Port City*. (Colombo: University of Kelaniya, 2013). Web. http://repository.kln.lk/handle/123456789/7268?show=full. Accessed December 5, 2015. R. Anderson et al. *Galle Harbor Maritime Archaeological Impact Assessment Report for Sri Lankan Department of Archaeology* (Perth: Government of Western Australia, 2007). Web. http://museum.wa.gov.au/maritime-archaeology-db/maritime-reports/galle-harbour-maritime-archaeological-impact-assessment-report-sri-lankan-departmen. Accessed December 5, 2015.
38 Pali Wijeratne. "Post-Tsunami Redevelopment and the Cultural Sites of the Maritime Provinces in Sri Lanka." ICOMOS Conference Paper. 104. Available via Internet.
39 The Trust's scientific sub-committees resemble those of International ICOMOS, and cover a range of topics, including Monuments and Sites, Moveable Artifacts, Natural Heritage, Intangible Heritage, Paintings, Sculpture and Visual Arts, Architectural Conservation, Cultural Routes and Industrial Heritage. Source: National Trust – Sri Lanka. "2014 Annual Report." Web. www.thenationaltrust.lk/the-trust/downloads/ANNUAL_REPORT_2014_26-Mar-2015.pdf. Accessed December 12, 2015.
40 Owing to disagreements with the landowner the project did not get under way until 2009; the site was listed under the Antiquities Ordinance that same year. National Trust – Sri Lanka. "2014 Annual Report"; and Cultural Heritage Connections. "Restoration of Malwana Fort." 2013. Web. www.culturalheritageconnections.org/wiki/Restoration_of_Malwana_Fort. Accessed December 21, 2015.
41 ICOMOS Sri Lanka. "Institution." 2015. Web. http://icomos.lk/institution. Accessed December 12, 2015.
42 Pali Wijeratne, 108. "Post-Tsunami Redevelopment and the Cultural Sites of the Maritime Provinces in Sri Lanka." ICOMOS Conference Paper. 104. Available via Internet.
43 Pothmulla.
44 Ministry of Internal Affairs, Wayamba Development and Cultural Affairs. "About the World Heritage Sites." 2015. Web. www.cultural.gov.lk/web/index.php?option=com_content&view=article&id=60&Itemid=71&lang=en. Accessed December 5, 2015.
45 The specific sites included in the CTP effort included the following: Jetavana and Abhayagiriya monasteries (third century CE and first century BCE) at Anaradhapura; Alahana Pirivena center of learning (twelfth century CE) at Pollonaruva; Temple of the Tooth Relic, four Hindu *devales* (shrines) and two Buddhist monasteries (sixteenth to eighteenth centuries CE); along with the palace and garden at Sigiriya and caves at Dambulla. Source: Roland Silva. "The Cultural Triangle of Sri Lanka," in Henry Cleere (ed.), *Archaeological Heritage Management in the Modern World* (Routledge: London, 2012).
46 Roland Silva. *Conservation Theory: National and International Contributions*. (Colombo: Director General of Archaeology, 2004), 13–33.
47 Silva stands as one of Sri Lanka's foremost practitioners in the field of architectural conservation. Educated in Europe, Dr. Silva served as Commissioner of Archaeology from 1983 to 1991 and Chancellor of the University of Moratuwa (2008–2013), in addition to his roles with ICOMOS and the CCF.

48 Silva, *Archaeological Heritage Management*, 222.
49 Senake Bandaranayake. "The Dambulla Rock Temple Complex, Sri Lanka: Ten Years of Management, Research and Conservation," in Neville Agnew (ed.), *Conservation of Ancient Sites on the Silk Road: Proceedings of an International Conference on the Conservation of Grotto Sites*. (Los Angeles: Getty Conservation Institute, 1997), 50–54.
50 Donors included the UNDP, the World Food Programme and the governments of Great Britain, France, Egypt, Qatar, Pakistan and Japan. Source: UNESCO. "Address by Mr. Frederico Mayor, Director General of UNESCO, at the Ceremonial Session to Mark the Tenth Anniversary of the International Campaign for the Safeguarding of the Cultural Triangle of Sri Lanka, Colombo, December 11, 1990." Web. http://unesdoc.unesco.org/images/0008/000894/089429eo.pdf. Accessed December 5, 2015.
51 Silva, *Archaeological Heritage Management*, 223.
52 The PGIAR offers one, two and three year courses in archaeology, museology and heritage management. The Department of Architecture at the University of Moratuwa offers a two year postgraduate program in architectural conservation of monuments and sites. P.B. Mandawala. "The Central Cultural Fund and the WH Site Management in Sri Lanka in Comparison to the Indian Case." ICOMOS Sri Lanka. Web. http://portal.unesco.org/geography/en/files/10677/12283839945Prashantha_Mandawala.pdf/Prashantha+Mandawala.pdf. Accessed December 5, 2015.
53 Vesak commemorates the birth, enlightenment and passing of the Lord Buddha; the Poson Festival celebrates the arrival of Buddhism in Sri Lanka. The festivals occur in May and June, respectively, and draw large numbers of devotees to heritage sites like Dambulla. Source: Namini Wijedasa. "Controversy Rocks Historic Dambulla Temple." *The Sunday Times* (Sri Lanka), June 1, 2014. Web. www.sundaytimes.lk/140601/news/Controversy-Rocks-Historic-Dambulla-Temple-101116.html. Accessed December 5, 2015.
54 Bandaranayake, 53–55.
55 Wijedasa.
56 UNESCO. "State of Conservation Report: Golden Temple of Dambulla." UNESCO World Heritage Centre. 2014. Web. http://whc.unesco.org/archive/2014/whc14-38com-7B-Add-en.pdf. Accessed December 5, 2015.
57 Chamintha Thilakarathana. " What Price Conservation?" *The Sunday Times* (Colombo), October 18, 1998.
58 Painting Conservation & Research Center, Painting Museum, Dambulla. Central Cultural Fund. 2015. Web. http://ccf.lk/dabulla.htm. Accessed December 5, 2015.
59 Other examples of such gardens are found at Anaradhapura and Polonnaruva, as well as later examples at Galabadda (eleventh century CE) and culminate with the royal complex at Kandy (nineteenth century). Nilan Cooray. "The Sigiriya Royal Gardens: Analysis of the Landscape Architectonic Composition." Publication info. 2012. 25.
60 UNESCO. "Ancient City of Sigiriya." World Heritage Centre. 2015. Web. http://whc.unesco.org/en/list/202. Accessed September 15, 2015.
61 Cooray, 37, 64.
62 Senake Bandaranayake and Madhyama Saṃskṛtika Aramudala. *Sigiriya: City, Palace, and Royal Gardens* (Colombo: Central Cultural Fund, Ministry of Cultural Affairs, 1999).
63 T.W. Rhys Davis. "Sigiriya, the Lion Rock, near Pulastipura, Ceylon; and the Thirty-Ninth Chapter of the Mahawanza," *Journal of the Royal Asiatic Society* 7(8) (1874); and Cooray, 62.
64 Cooray, 90–100; and D.A. Sharmini Perera, V.G.R. Chandran, D.A.C. Surang Silva and K. Chinna. "Tourist Expectation and Perception of World Heritage Site Sigiriya: Policy and Institutional Implications for Sri Lanka," *Institutions and Economies* 7(2) (2015), 166–184.
65 The UDA was established by an act of parliament in 1978 to serve as the principal urban planning entity for the government of Sri Lanka. Its authority can reinforce conservation objectives for declared areas that include conservation regulations.
66 Cooray, 115.
67 UNESCO. "State of Conservation: Ancient City of Sigiriya." 2001. Web. http://whc.unesco.org/en/soc/2562. Accessed December 12, 2015.
68 A total of 74,062 tourists visited CT sites in 1988, as compared to 627,136 in 2014. Source: Ibid.
69 Sri Lanka Tourism Development Authority. "Developing and Planning the Markets." 2011. Web. www.sltda.lk/developing_markets. Accessed December 12, 2015.
70 The visitors to Sigiriya were evenly split between foreign and domestic. Source: Sri Lanka Tourism Development Authority. "Sri Lanka Tourism Statistical Report 2014." Web. www.sltda.lk/sites/default/files/annual_statistical_report-2014.pdf. Accessed December 12, 2015.
71 "Sigiriya Under Threat." *Daily Mirror* (Sri Lanka). July 7, 2015. Web. http://www.dailymirror.lk/78559/sigiriya-under-threat. December 12, 2015.

72 Gamini Wijesuriya. "The Restoration of the Temple of the Tooth Relic in Sri Lanka: A Post-Conflict Cultural Response to Loss of Identity," in Nicolas Stanley-Price (ed.), *Cultural Heritage in Postwar Recovery: Papers from the ICCROM FORUM, October 4–6, 2005*. (Rome: ICCROM, 2005), 89.

73 The Town & Country Planning Ordinance (1946 revised 2000), has the authority to regulate and promote "integrated planning ... to provide for the protection of buildings of architectural and historic interest" including designation of specially protected areas. Source: Government of Sri Lanka. "Town and Country Planning Ordinance." 2013. Web. www.srilankalaw.lk/volume-VIII/town-and-country-planning-ordinance.html. Accessed December 12, 2015.

74 The designation acts as a zoning control, whereby culturally significant buildings are protected and types of development are limited. Prashantha B. Mandawala. "Buffer Zones in World Cultural Heritage Sites: Sri Lankan Examples in Urban and Natural Setting (Kandy & Sigiriya)." Unpublished paper. 2001. Web. www.academia.edu/5034100/world_heritage_site_of_sigiriya. Accessed December 12, 2015.

75 P.B. Mandawala, "The Central Cultural Fund."

76 *Periodic Reporting Exercise on the Application of the World Heritage Convention: Sacred City of Kandy*. UNESCO. 2003. Web. http://whc.unesco.org/archive/periodicreporting/apa/cycle01/section2/450.pdf. Accessed December 12, 2015.

77 In addition to the bombing of the Sri Dalada Maligawa (Temple of the Tooth Relic) in Kandy in 1998, many sites suffered from neglect and isolation while hostilities kept professional teams and other site stewards away.

78 The temple had been attacked less than a decade earlier, on February 8, 1989, by members of the Janatha Vimukthi Peramuna (JVP), a Communist opposition party that used militancy to achieve its aims against the ruling regime. Damage was minimal as compared to the 1998 attack.

79 Wijesuriya, "The Restoration of the Temple of the Tooth Relic," 89.

80 Ibid., 92.

81 Jagath Weerasinge. "Living Sacred Heritage and 'Authenticity' in South Asia," in Helmut K. Anheier and Yudhishthir Raj Istar (eds.), *Cultures and Globalization: Heritage, Memory and Identity*. (Thousand Oaks, CA: Sage Press, 2011), 145.

82 "Asia: Sri Lanka Profile – Timeline." BBC News. Web. www.bbc.com/news/world-south-asia-12004081. Accessed September 15, 2015.

83 Dumeetha Luthra. "Sri Lanka's Slow Tsunami Response." BBC News. June 25, 2005. Web. http://news.bbc.co.uk/2/hi/south_asia/4618683.stm. Accessed December 12, 2015.

84 Because the affected region included many tourist resorts in Sri Lanka, as well as Indonesia and Thailand, thousands of foreigners from dozens of countries around the world were also killed by the waves, with Sweden and Germany as the hardest hit. Source: "Survivors of 2004 Tsunami Left Horrified." *The Daily Mail* (London). December 25, 2012. Web. www.dailymail.co.uk/news/article-2253133/Boxing-Day-Tsunami-Survivors-2004-tsunami-left-horrified-ambushed-trailer-movie-Boxing-Dat-tragedy.html. Accessed December 12, 2015.

85 Wijeratne, 105. "Post-Tsunami Redevelopment and the Cultural Sites of the Maritime Provinces in Sri Lanka." ICOMOS Conference Paper. 104. Available via Internet.

86 UNESCO World Heritage Centre. Old Town of Galle and its Fortifications. UNESCO. 2015. http://whc.unesco.org/en/list/451. Accessed December 12, 2015.

87 Wijeratne, Xian conference paper.

88 The GHF receives direct appropriations from the federal government to finance its administrative activities. In 2015 its budget amounted to 16 million Sri Lankan rupees (approximately US$110,000). Source: Galle Heritage Foundation and Prashantha B. Mandawala. *Integrated Management System for Galle*. (Colombo: Government of Sri Lanka, 2015), 48.

89 Government of Sri Lanka. Galle Heritage Foundation Act (No. 7 of 1994). 2015. Web. www.commonlii.org/lk/legis/num_act/ghfa7o1994273/s6.html. Accessed December 12, 2015.

90 Although foreign investment in heritage properties within Galle has resulted in the rehabilitation of numerous buildings as hotels, restaurants and private dwellings, it has raised the issue of gentrification and displacement within the fort.

91 Wijeratne, Xian conference paper.

92 UNESCO World Heritage Centre. "State of Conservation: Old Town of Galle and its Fortifications." UNESCO. 2005. Web. http://whc.unesco.org/en/soc/1316. Accessed December 12, 2015.

93 Daniel Breece. "Galle: Good Intentions Melt with the Ocean's Hypnotic and Monetary Power." *The Guardian* (UK). January 27, 2014. Web. http://theguardian.com/cities/2014/jan/27/galle-intentions-tide-power-sri-lanka-tourism. Accessed December 1, 2015.

94 The buffer zone was ultimately revised in many places under considerable pressure from coastal development interests and those whose livelihoods depended on close access to the sea. The zone was shrunk to as little as

25 m in many places. Source: "100 Meter Tsunami 'Buffer Zone' Revised." BBC News. October 14, 2005. Web. www.bbc.com/sinhala/news/story/2005/10/051014_tsunamiban.shtml. Accessed December 21, 2015.

95 Wijeratne, 105. "Post-Tsunami Redevelopment and the Cultural Sites of the Maritime Provinces in Sri Lanka." ICOMOS Conference Paper. 104. Available via Internet.

96 The larger tsunami response effort was subjected to criticism regarding inefficiencies of aid distribution, and politicization of the rebuilding and conservation process; according to Transparency International, nearly half of the US$2.2 billion received in aid was either unaccounted for or spent on unrelated projects. Source: "Tsunami Aid Goes Missing." *The Sydney Morning Herald*. December 28, 2009. Web. www.smh.com.au/world/tsunami-aid-goes-missing-20091227-lgb4.html. Accessed December 12, 2015.

97 P. Wijeratne. "Post-Tsunami Redevelopment and the Cultural Sites of the Maritime Provinces in Sri Lanka," in H. Meier, M. Petzet, and T. Will (eds.), *Heritage at Risk: Cultural Heritage and Natural Disasters*. (Colombo: ICOMOS, 2006), 106.

98 The World Monuments Fund collaborated with ICOMOS on the initial Old Dutch Hospital rehabilitation project. The Urban Development Authority carried out the adaptive reuse project in 2014. Source: World Monuments Fund. "Historic Galle: Historic Healing after the 2004 Tsunami." 2015. Web. www.wmf.org/project/historic-galle. Accessed September 14, 2015.

99 UNESCO World Heritage Centre. "State of Conservation: Old Town of Galle and its Fortifications." 2008. Web. http://whc.unesco.org/en/soc/913. Accessed December 12, 2015.

100 Under the Integrated Management System, the task managers would be assigned to manage the following areas of activity: conservation of listed monuments and inappropriate new construction; adaptive reuse of existing and construction of new buildings; traffic and planning; environmental protection; public advocacy and awareness. Source: Galle Heritage Foundation. "Management Plan: Galle Heritage Site Management Plan Formulated." 2015. Web. www.galleheritage.gov.lk/index.php?option=com_content&view=article&id=66%3Amanagement-plan&catid=6%3Anews&lang=en. Accessed December 12, 2015.

101 Galle Heritage Foundation.

102 Studio Thompson Heritage Consultants. "Heritage Impact Assessment of the Galle Port Development Project on the World Heritage Property of Old Town of Galle and its Fortifications: Preliminary Report." January 2015. Web. http://whc.unesco.org/en/list/451/documents/. Accessed December 12, 2015.

103 Cultural Heritage Connections (Dutch Center for International Heritage Activities, Government of Netherlands). "Conservation of Dutch Fort in Jaffna." 2013. Web. www.culturalheritageconnections.org/wiki/Conservation_of_Dutch_Fort_in_Jaffna. Accessed January 8, 2016.

104 The Tea Factory Hotel has one of five Asia Pacific Heritage Awards for projects in Sri Lanka since the program's inception. UNESCO Bangkok Asia Pacific Heritage Awards. "2001 Award of Merit: Tea Factory Hotel." Web. www.unescobkk.org/culture/wh/asia-pacific-heritage-awards/previous-heritage-awards-2000-2013/2001/award-winners/2001mr3/. Accessed January 8, 2016.

105 Government of the Netherlands. "Integrated Plan for Conservation, Preservation and Development of Cultural Heritage in the Southern Region within a concept 'A Cultural Triangle in the South' under the Netherlands–Sri Lanka Cultural Cooperation Programme 2006/2009." 2013. Web. www.culturalheritageconnections.org/wiki/Integrated_Plan_for_Conservation,_Preservation_and_Development_of_Cultural_Heritage_in_the_Southern_Region_within_a_concept_'A_Cultural_Triangle_in_the_South'_under_the_Netherlands-Sri_Lanka_Cultural_Cooperation_Programme_2006/2009. Accessed December 12, 2015.

106 Central Cultural Fund, Chap. 388, Act No. 57 of 1980, XIV/220-224. Government of Ceylon Legislative Enactments.

107 *Daily Mirror* interview with Jagath Balusuriya.

108 Sri Lanka is primarily a Buddhist nation. Asian Studies Department, Michigan State University: Windows on Asia. "Maldives-Religion." 2015. Web. http://asia.isp.msu.edu/wbwoa/south_asia/maldives/religion.htm. Accessed December 12, 2015.

109 United Nations Development Programme. "About Maldives." 2015. Web. www.mv.undp.org/content/maldives/en/home/countryinfo/. Accessed December 12, 2015.

110 Ministry of Tourism – Republic of Maldives. "2015 Tourism Yearbook." Web. www.tourism.gov.mv/statistics/annual-publications/. Accessed December 12, 2015.

111 Among the commitments undertaken by the government of Maldives include a target for all energy to come from renewable sources by 2020. Source: The World Bank. "Concerted Efforts Needed to Support Maldives Adapt to Climate Change, World Bank Report Findings Indicate." June 19, 2013. Web. www.worldbank.org/en/news/press-release/2013/06/19/concerted-efforts-needed-to-support-maldives-adapt-to-climate-change-world-bank-report-findings-indicate. Accessed December 21, 2015.

112 Tom Ginsburg. "Trouble, Again, in Paradise." *The Huffington Post*. September 4, 2012. Web. www.huffpost.com/us/entry/18-44396. Accessed December 21, 2015.
113 Nimral Gosh. "Shrinking Isles." *The Straits Times* (Singapore). July 5, 2015. Web. www.straitstimes.com/asia/sinking-isles. Accessed December 21, 2015. See also Chapter 19 – Bangladesh for a detailed discussion of the threats of sea level rise to low-lying countries like Bangladesh and Maldives.
114 Suzanne Goldberg. "How US Negotiators Ensured Landmark Paris Climate Deal was Republican-Proof." *The Guardian*. December 13, 2015. Web. www.theguardian.com/us-news/2015/dec/13/climate-change-paris-deal-cop21-obama-administration-congress-republicans-environment. Accessed May 20, 2016.
115 "The Paris Agreement Marks an Unprecedented Political Recognition of the Risks of Climate Change." *The Economist*. December 12, 2015. Web. www.economist.com/news/international/21683990-paris-agreement-climate-change-talks. Accessed May 20, 2016.
116 Husnu Al Suood. *The Maldivian Legal System*. (Malé: Maldives Law Institute, 2014), 3.
117 Naseema Mohamed. "Note on the Early History of the Maldives," *Parcourir les Collections* 70(1) (2005), 9–10.
118 Andrew D.W. Forbes. "A Roman Republican Denarius of c. 90 B.C., from the Maldive Islands, Indian Ocean," *Parcourir les Collections* 28(1) (1984), 53–54 and Mohamed, 12.
119 Mohamed, 10.
120 Al Suood, 6.
121 *The Rehla of Ibn Battuta – India, Maldive Islands and Ceylon*. Translated by Mahdi Husain. (Oriental Institute: Baroda, India, 1976). Web. www.maldivesculture.com/index.php?option=com_content&task=view&id=198&Itemid=61. Accessed December 12, 2015.
122 Al Suood, 13.
123 UNESCO World Heritage Centre. "Coral Stone Mosques of the Maldives." 2013. Web. http://whc.unesco.org/en/tenativelists/5812. Accessed December 12, 2015.
124 Al Suood, 18.
125 "Maldives Country Profile." BBC News. 2015. Web. www.bbc.com/news/world-south-asia-12651486. Accessed December 21, 2015.
126 Sociological issues in Malé include high costs of living, gang violence and increased drug use among un- and underemployed youth. Source: Mohamed Faisal. "Living on a Crowded Island: Urban Transformation in the Maldives." Victoria University of Wellington (New Zealand). Unpublished background to a research in progress (2008). Web. http://devnet.org.nz/sites/default/files/Mohammed%20Faisal.%20Living%20on%20a%20crowded%20island%20Urban%20transformation%20in%20the%20Maldives.pdf. Accessed December 21, 2015.
127 "Looking Back at Historical Architecture of the Maldives." *Builders Maldives*. July 2010.
128 The World Bank. "Maldives Country Assistance Strategy." 2013. Web. http://web.worldbank.org/WBSITE/EXTERNAL/COUNTRIES/SOUTHASIAEXT/0,,contentMDK:21620178~pagePK:146736~piPK:146830~theSitePK:223547,00.html. Accessed December 21, 2015.
129 Vikas Bajaj. "Vandalism at Maldives Museum Stirs Fears of Extremism." *The New York Times*. February 13, 2012.
130 Sixth National Development Plan. Ministry of Planning and National Development: Government of Maldives. 2001. Web. www.planning.gov.mv/en/images/stories/publications/ndp/6th%20ndp/. Accessed December 12, 2015.
131 *Maldives: Poverty Reduction Strategy Paper. Staff Country Reports – International Monetary Fund*. (Washington, DC: IMF, 2008), n.p.
132 "Maldives National Museum, Malé: Reinterpreting the Maldivian Past." *Minivan News* (Maldives). July 24, 2010. Web. www.maldivesculture.com/index.php?option=com_content&task=view&id=235&Itemid=42. Accessed December 21, 2015.
133 "Will Submit Heritage Preservation and Protection Law to Maljis: Minister Maleeh." *VN News* (Maldives). April 22, 2014. Web. http://vnews.mv/19345. Accessed December 12, 2015.
134 "Maldives to Sign UNESCO Convention to Protect Country's Intangible Heritage." *Minivan News* (Maldives). September 14, 2011. Web. http://minivannewsarchive.com/society/maldives-to-sign-unesco-convention-to-protect-countrys-intangible-heritage-25587. Accessed December 21, 2015.
135 Hawwa Lubna. "Mob Storms National Museum, Destroys Buddhist Statues: 'A Significant Part of our Heritage is Lost Now'." *Minivan News* (Maldives). February 9, 2012. Web. http://minivannewsarchive.com/society/mob-storms-national-museum-destroys-buddhist-statues-a-significant-part-of-our-heritage-is-lost-now-31813. Accessed December 21, 2015.
136 UNESCO, "Coral Stone Mosques of the Maldives."
137 Archana Jyoti. "Maldives Seeks India's Help in Conserving Heritage." *The Daily Pioneer* (India). September 4, 2014. Web. www.dailypioneer.com/nation/maldives-seeks-indias-help-in-conserving-heritage.html. Accessed December 21, 2015.

138 UNESCO, "Coral Stone Mosques of the Maldives."
139 "Historical 'Fan'diyaaru' Mosque Demolished." *Minivan News* (Maldives). February 2, 2014. Web. http://minivannewsarchive.com/society/historical-fandiyaaru-mosque-demolished-76671. Accessed December 12, 2015.

Further reading

Bandaranayake, Senake and Madhyama Saṃskṛtika Aramudala. 1999. *Sigiriya: City, Palace, and Royal Gardens*. Colombo: Central Cultural Fund, Ministry of Cultural Affairs.

De Silva, Henda Witarana Saman Priyantha. 2001. *Integration of Cultural Heritage in Post-War Reconstruction Planning: With specific Reference to Sri Lanka*. Master's Thesis, University of York.

Gamburd, Michele Ruth. 2013. *The Golden Wave: Culture and Politics after Sri Lanka's Tsunami Disaster*. Bloomington: Indiana University Press.

Manawadu, Samitha. "Cultural Routes of Sri Lanka as Extensions of International Itineraries: Identification of Their Impacts on Tangible and Intangible Heritage," in 15th ICOMOS General Assembly and International Symposium: *Monuments and Sites in their Setting – Conserving Cultural Heritage in Changing Townscapes and Landscapes*, October 17–21, 2005, Xi'an, China.

Mandawala, P.B. 2015. *The Central Cultural Fund and the WH Site Management in Sri Lanka in Comparison to the Indian Case*. Colombo: ICOMOS Sri Lanka.

Nubin, Walter. 2002. *Sri Lanka: Current Issues and Historical Background*. Hauppauge, NY: Nova Publishers.

Perera, D.A. Sharmini, V.G.R. Chandran, D.A.C. Surang Silva, and K. Chinna. 2015. "Tourist Expectation and Perception of World Heritage Site Sigiriya: Policy and Institutional Implications for Sri Lanka," *Institutions and Economies* 7(2): 166–184.

Reeves, Peter (ed.). 2013. *The Encyclopedia of the Sri Lankan Diaspora*. Singapore: EDM.

Rhys Davis, T.W. 1874. "Sigiriya, the Lion Rock, near Pulastipura, Ceylon, and the Thirty-Ninth Chapter of the Mahawanza," *Journal of the Royal Asiatic Society* 7: xiii.

Robinson, Francis (ed.). 1989. *The Cambridge Encyclopedia of India, Pakistan, Bangladesh, Sri Lanka*. Cambridge: Cambridge University Press.

Scrivner, Peter and Vikramaditya Prakash (eds.). 2007. *Colonial Modernities: Building, Dwelling and Architecture in British India and Ceylon*. Abingdon, UK: Routledge.

Silva, Roland. 2004. *Conservation Theory: National and International Contribution*. Colombo: ICOMOS Sri Lanka.

———. 2012. "The Cultural Triangle of Sri Lanka," in Henry Cleere (ed.), *Archaeological Heritage Management in the Modern World*. Routledge: London.

UNESCO. *The Cultural Triangle of Sri Lanka*. 1993. Paris: UNESCO/Central Cultural Fund, Sri Lanka.

Weerasinghe, S.G.M. 1995. *A History of the Cultural Relations between Sri Lanka and China*. Colombo: Ministry of Cultural Affairs.

Wijeratne, P. 2006. "Post-tsunami Redevelopment and the Cultural Sites of the Maritime Provinces in Sri Lanka," in H. Meier, M. Petzet and T. Will (eds.). *Heritage at Risk: Cultural Heritage and Natural Disasters*. Paris: ICOMOS, 106.

Wijesuriya, Gamini. 1993. *The Restoration of Buddhist Monuments in Sri Lanka: The Case for an Archaeological Heritage Management Strategy*. Supplement to a Symposium held during the 10th General Assembly of the ICOMOS, July 30–August 4. Colombo: ICOMOS Sri Lanka.

———. 2001. "'Pious Vandals': Restoration or Destruction in Sri Lanka?," in R. Layton, P. Stone and J. Thomas (eds.), *Destruction and Conservation of Cultural Property*. London: Routledge, 256–263.

———. 2003. "The Past is in the Present: Perspectives in Caring for Buddhist Heritage Sites in Sri Lanka," in H. Stovel, N. Stanley-Price and R. Killick (eds.) *Conservation of Living Religious Heritage*. ICCROM Conservation Studies No. 3. Papers from the ICCROM 2003 Forum on Living Religious Heritage: Conserving the Sacred, 31–43.

———. n.d. "The Restoration of the Temple of the Tooth Relic in Kandy, Sri Lanka: A Post-Conflict Cultural Response to Loss of Identity," in Nicholas Stanley Price (ed.), *Cultural Heritage in Postwar Recovery*. ICCROM Conservation Studies No. 6. Papers from the ICCROM Forum, October 4–6, 2005.

18
PAKISTAN

Modern Pakistan sits at the geographic and cultural hinge of Central and South Asia, the Iranian Plateau and the Arabian Peninsula beyond. Each of these regions has played a significant role in the development of the mélange of cultures that comprise the contemporary nation. Ethnically and linguistically diverse, with centuries of influence from numerous religious traditions, modern Pakistan was established in 1947 based on a unifying Muslim identity, defined in large part by an opposition to India, its larger colonial-era sibling. Perhaps best known as home to Asia's earliest cities, the Harappan sites of Mohenjo-Daro and Harappa, Pakistan's rich history includes contributions from prominent Buddhist, Hindu, Hellenistic, Jain and Zoroastrian civilizations, as well as those connected to its Islamic heritage.[1]

Pakistan's post-independence political history has been turbulent, marked by shifts between military and civilian rule, by conflicts with neighboring India and its Muslim sister state of Bangladesh, and by violent upheavals in Afghanistan to the north. Political instability both within and around Pakistan has taken a toll on its cultural sites, as well as on the country's ability to support strong architectural conservation practices. This is in spite of the fact that Pakistan possesses an extensive legal framework for conservation policies, and an active network of institutions and professionals devoted to the field. National, provincial and municipal governments throughout the country have adopted heritage protection legislation, but enforcement of existing laws, coordinated programming and sustained conservation efforts remain critical shortcomings.[2] According to Mohammed Rafique Mughal, the former director of the national Department of Archaeology and Museums, Pakistan has to date generally lagged behind other regional players such as China, India and Sri Lanka in following heritage conservation professional best practices, such as the adoption of commonly accepted conservation techniques, procedures and consistent documentation of projects.[3] Further complicating the situation has been the passage of significant constitutional reforms in 2010 that were intended to shift various responsibilities from the federal to the provincial governments in a process known as "devolution," but have, at least in the near term, left hundreds of heritage sites and conservation professionals in limbo.[4]

Pakistan's general lack of infrastructure development has made both its population and the country's historic architecture susceptible to natural disasters, such as the 2005 earthquake that killed 73,000 people in the northeast, and a series of floods in 2010 and 2011 that collectively affected nearly 30 million citizens and caused more than US$10 billion in damage.[5] These factors have complicated efforts to manage and maintain large-scale archaeological properties such as the World Heritage Sites of Mohenjo-Daro, Taxila and Harappa against flooding, erosion, encroachment and looting.

Since 1974, Mohenjo-Daro has been the subject of a series of UNESCO-led International Safeguarding Campaigns, which have directed US$23 million to the site during a period of nearly forty years, to be used for the installation of flood mitigation measures, creation of site management strategies and the overall consolidation of the mud brick structures.[6] But the heavy rains that caused devastating flooding in Punjab in 2010 and 2012 threatened the site due to inundation and water table rise, returning it to a precarious state of conservation, and underscoring the magnitude of its conservation challenges. Illegal trafficking in antiquities is a critical issue in the northern portions of the country, where thin governmental control, a precarious security situation due to the neighboring conflict in Afghanistan, and an illicit market for Gandharan-style sculpture and artifacts have led to widespread looting and destruction of the region's sites.[7] The unresolved conflict over Kashmir remains one of Partition's enduring tragedies, with territorial disputes flaring up between Pakistan, India and China more or less continuously since 1947. These disputes stand out as a major contributor to regional political instability, with wide-reaching implications including those related to conservation.

Population pressures play an active role in the architectural conservation scene in this, the world's sixth most populous country. Since independence, Pakistan has become increasingly urban, with approximately 40 percent of its nearly 200 million citizens living in the major urban centers of Lahore, Karachi and Rawalpindi.[8] Each of these cities contains historic urban cores, but they do not possess sufficient infrastructure to support rapidly expanding populations, nor have adequately enforced legal protections been instituted for their heritage buildings and districts. Underscoring the importance of enforcement, a survey completed by N.E.D. University of Engineering and Technology and the Government of Sindh between 2006 and 2009 revealed that 22 percent of listed heritage buildings in Karachi, Pakistan's largest city, had either been fully or partially demolished by their owners.[9]

Maintaining comprehensive inventories that reflect the true diversity of Pakistani culture remains another key issue in the field of heritage management. Although Pakistan's founding father, Muhammad Ali Jinnah, envisioned the creation of a Muslim homeland, separate from a Hindu India, most historians

FIGURE 18.1 Conservation beginning in 1999 of the Uch Monument Complex (fifteenth–sixteenth centuries CE) west of Lahore, in partnership between the Department of Archaeology and Museums and the World Monuments Fund, have focused on community participation, training and environmental health issues to reconnect communities with their histories.

agree that his vision included a separation between the dominant religion and the state, and equal rights for minority faiths.[10] But in the decades since independence, the idea of a singular Muslim identity unifying Pakistan has not proven as straightforward as its founders had intended. Although the country is 97 percent Muslim, its enormous population speaks over fifty languages in addition to its official language Urdu,[11] and its distinct Baloch, Sindhi, Punjabi, Pashtun and Pathan communities retain strong ethnic identities.[12] National heritage inventories have tended to mirror Pakistan's Muslim identity at the expense of the true diversity of its cultural and built heritage. As of 2013, of the 355 properties listed by the Department of Archaeology as being nationally significant, approximately one-third are archaeological sites. Of the remaining two-thirds, only 10 percent represent non-Islamic properties.[13]

This chapter will highlight significant conservation efforts at the major sites that fall within Pakistan's present-day boundaries, and will discuss the policies and practices that emerged following independence, but it will primarily focus on management of the nation's architectural heritage after 1947.[14]

Summary historical context

North-central Pakistan, including the Potwar (Panjistan) Plateau and the Soan Valley in the north of Punjab, contains Paleolithic archaeological sites that date as far back as two million years.[15] The Early Harappan period, an era that signaled the rise of large, organized urban settlements, is represented by sites such as Rehman Dheri (dating from 4000 BCE), which was studied beginning in the 1960s by the eminent Pakistani archaeologists A.H. Dani of Peshawar University and F.A. Durrani of the Archaeology Department.[16] The great cities of the Harappan (also known as the Indus Valley) civilization emerged around 2500 BCE, and are best represented by two of Pakistan's most important archaeological sites: Mohenjo-Daro ("Mound of the Dead") and Harappa, each of which underwent excavation by the Archaeological Survey of India beginning in the 1920s, and have been subject to intensive conservation campaigns since. Characterized by burnt-mud brick structures organized on an axonometric grid, with a central mound, large-scale buildings, tanks and other sophisticated water management features, Harappan sites are recognized as among the earliest planned cities in Asia.[17]

The decline of the Harappan period by the eighteenth century BCE was followed by the arrival of the Aryans during the sixteenth century BCE and, later, of the Achaemenids in the sixth century BCE; the latter group established long-standing cultural, linguistic and architectural links between today's Pakistan and Persia that remain highly influential. Alexander the Great arrived in 327 BCE, crossing the Indus the following year at Hund (in present-day Khyber Pakhtunkhwa Province) where he was received at Taxila by its ruler, Ahmbi (also known as Taxilis). Alexander ultimately conquered Punjab before reversing course and marching south through Sindh to the coast of the Arabian Sea near modern Karachi.[18]

Alexander's immediate successor state, the Seleucids, fell to Chandragupta Maurya in 305 BCE, bringing the majority of present-day Pakistan into the Mauryan Empire, which at its height encompassed most of South Asia until its fall in the second century BCE. Taxila remained an important Mauryan, Greco-Bactrian, Parthian and Kushan-Sassanian urban center until its sacking in the mid-fifth century CE; it was particularly renowned as a Buddhist center of learning from the fifth century BCE to the second century CE.[19] The Gandharan region, centered on the Swat Valley and modern Peshawar, fostered thriving Buddhist communities at Takhi-i-Bahi and Sahr-i-Bahlol (today a World Heritage Site) in addition to Taxila. The culture of this region is today renowned for their hybrid sculptural style that blends Hellenistic and Eastern influences. The Gandharan period reached its apex under the Kushans from the first through fifth centuries CE, before its decline and ultimate collapse at the hands of invaders from Ghazni (present-day Afghanistan) in the tenth century.[20]

Islam arrived in the region in 711 CE, with the invasion of Sindh (modern day southeastern Pakistan) by Umayyad armies from Western Asia, under the command of their general Muhammad bin Qasim. In the tenth century, forces led first by Sabuktigin, and later by his son Mahmoud of Ghazni, began a series of destructive raids on the region, targeting the Hindu temples of Punjab and Kathiawar, ultimately destabilizing the Umayyad presence and bringing its period of influence to a close. A series of invasions originating in Central Asia followed the pattern set by the Ghaznavids, with Mongol and Timurid incursions ultimately leading to the birth of the Mughal Empire under Babur in 1526. The Mughals reinforced Islam's dominance in the region and hastened the flow of architectural ideas from Arabia, Persia and Central Asia, culminating in the spectacular buildings and gardens of Pakistani cities such as Lahore and Sheikhupura.[21]

FIGURE 18.2a, b and c The ancient site of Taxila (a) in northwestern Pakistan, a Buddhist cultural center dating from the fifth century BCE, is a World Heritage Site due to its fine third century BCE stone carvings in the Gandharan style (b, c), which exhibit Hellenistic influences.

Sikhism, a faith founded in the sixteenth century by Guru Nanak (born near Lahore in 1469), maintained a growing presence in the Punjab, gaining strength following the death of Aurangzeb in 1707, an event that signaled the decline of the Mughal Empire. The growth of Sikh *misls* (sovereign states forming a confederacy) under the spiritual leadership of a series of successor gurus, culminated in the rise of the Sikh Empire in 1799 under Ranjit Singh (1780–1839). Resulting from the Sufi and Bhakti schools of thought, Sikhism constitutes a reform movement in both Hinduism and Islam. *Gurdwaras*, Sikh shrines (meaning "gateway to the guru"), function as places of worship, schools, meeting places and rest stops for travelers, in addition to enshrining the *Granth Sahib*, the Holy book of the Sikhs.[22] Because Sikh rule lasted for almost a century in the Punjab, hundreds of gurdwaras dot the Pakistani landscape today, with sites like Janam Asthan in Nankana Sahib and Panja Sahib among the most culturally significant.[23] The Sikh Empire lasted until 1849 when the Sikh armies were defeated by the British at the Battle of Gujrat, ultimately resulting in the annexation of large portions of modern-day Pakistan into the expanding British territorial holdings.

The Mughal Empire, which briefly had its capital at Lahore between 1585 and 1598, cemented Pakistan's connection to the rest of South Asia. By the turn of the nineteenth century, the British began to usurp Mughal dominance over South Asia, as the former assembled their vast colonial possessions into what would become the Raj (1858–1947). After World War II, leaders in the Muslim League, the (Indian) Congress Party and the withdrawing British administration made a series of decisions, influenced by escalating sectarian violence and a complex political landscape, that led to the partition of Sindh, Baluchistan, the Northwest Frontier Provinces, portions of Punjab and Jammu Kashmir, along with Bengal in the east, from the rest of India.[24] Hence, on August 14, 1947, the modern state of Pakistan was born.[25]

The 1947 partition of British India into West and East Pakistan (later called Pakistan and Bangladesh), India and Burma resulted almost immediately in the displacement of as many as 17 million people. As the principal political parties of the Muslim League and the Indian National Congress moved toward Partition, the 565 princely states of South Asia decided which of the three new states they would join. Hindu, Muslim and Sikh populations in the Bengal and Punjab provinces in particular were forced to abandon their traditional communities, homes and religious buildings in a wave of sectarian-nationalist fervor following the Partition. As a result, thousands of significant religious and secular buildings were abandoned by their constituent populations, in the process sometimes becoming symbolic targets of the hostile environment created by Partition.

Since independence from Britain, Pakistan has struggled with a series of geopolitical conflagrations, the most consequential of which were the Indo-Pakistani Wars of 1947, 1965 and 1999, and the Bangladesh Liberation War of 1971. The last of these resulted in the independence of East Pakistan (Bangladesh) from West Pakistan (Pakistan), drawing India in along the way, and further contributing to ill will among the three countries. The smoldering conflicts between the South Asian neighbors have had profound effects on the cultural resources of the region in general, and on Pakistan in particular. Ongoing tension, much of which centers around the status of disputed Kashmir, has inhibited economic and institutional cooperation among the neighbors, resulting in resources diverted, along with tens of thousands killed or displaced by protracted conflict. Resolution of the Kashmir issue, and the overall normalization of the regional political climate, would generate positive benefits for the cultural heritage of Pakistan and its neighbors, and their populations alike.

The role of Islam in architectural conservation practice

Islam plays a significant role in most aspects of Pakistani culture and society, including architectural conservation. Though it is a democratic parliamentary republic, Pakistan's state religion is Islam. As such, governmental institutions frequently incorporate Islamic principles into their policies, and religious-based practices – such as the *waqf* system described below – are influential forces in the management of land, buildings and other assets. The Arabic term used for conservation is *muhafazah*, which can be defined as the act of "protection, recording, preserving, guarding, keeping and observing." In Islam, humans are viewed as stewards of the earth, responsible for maintaining it in balance. The hierarchy of significant things worthy of conservation starts with the Quran, followed by the *hadith* (verbatim quotes from the Prophet Muhammed himself), then the three holiest sites in Islam: al Masjid al Haram (the Sacred Mosque in Mecca), al Masjid an Nabawi (the Prophets Mosque in Medina), and al Aqsa Mosque (in Jerusalem). The mosques are of particular importance in their service to pilgrims and worshippers. As in other faiths, care and protection of religious buildings such as mosques is viewed as a deed worthy of spiritual merit. But for mosques in particular, preservation of the material form is less important than the perpetuation of the meaning and value of the place.

The last in this hierarchy is the care of the natural environment; care of the four elements together (Quran, hadith, mosque, nature) is thought to shape a virtuous existence.[26]

As defined by *shariah* (Islamic) law, *waqf* (or *auqaf* in Pakistani Urdu) is a permanent and irrevocable religious endowment of a specified, non-perishable property such as a building, land or money. Similar to a trust in the Western world, the beneficiary of a waqf may be either a person or an entity, and is often an institution such as a mosque, *madrassa* (school), or *sabil* (charitable water dispensary). In 1959 under President Muhammed Ayub Khan the Pakistani government nationalized all auqaf holdings, including land, shrines, mosques and charitable facilities, and created the Department of Religious Endowments and the Advisory Council for Islamic Ideology to manage them. These policies were expanded under Ayub Khan's civilian and military successors, and today auqaf departments exist at the provincial level as well. While these changes were undertaken in Pakistan and elsewhere in the Islamic world mainly for political purposes, it had a profound practical effect on heritage management. Under the new legislation, the state assumed ultimate authority over the maintenance, expansion and conservation of historic shrines, mosques and other significant buildings, and religious authorities carrying out this work were made agents of the state.[27] As a result of these legislative changes, the Departments of Auqaf at the federal and provincial levels have become major players in Pakistan's architectural conservation landscape.

That role has contributed to some jurisdictional conflicts between the departments of religious affairs and archaeology at the federal and provincial levels. This is especially the case within large sites or municipalities where religious buildings are managed by one entity and adjacent secular buildings are overseen by another. These circumstances have led to tensions between the entities, frequently to the detriment of the resources, and to accusations of work carried out with little professional conservation oversight. For example, in 2015 the Khyber Pakhtunkhwa provincial Department of Archaeology moved to assume management of over 500 sites in and around Peshawar that were under control of the auqaf department and other government entities, arguing that they had not been properly maintained.[28] In Lahore, the Walled City of Lahore Authority was established in 2012 to coordinate conservation activities in the old city, assuming control of a *hammam* and several mosques from the local auqaf department.[29]

Beyond the federal and provincial departments of auqaf, Islamic ideas have driven conservation initiatives, and influenced conservation practice in Pakistan since independence. The Principles for the Conservation of Islamic Architectural Heritage (also known as the Lahore Principles), were an outgrowth of the International Symposium on Conservation and Restoration of Islamic Architectural Heritage (1980). The Principles recast the Venice Charter (1964) in terms of the conservation of Islamic architecture, and in particular emphasized cooperation among Muslim countries (*ummah*) to conserve common heritage sites, and also to collaborate with non-Muslim conservation entities.[30] The Principles defined particular types of Islamic heritage, including gardens and townscapes in addition to monuments, and emphasized the role of traditional craftspeople in the perpetuation of the common heritage of the Muslim world.[31] These Principles led to an effort to develop a National Charter for Conservation and Preservation of Cultural Property for Pakistan (known as the Lahore Charter, drafted in 1989), but the document was never formally adopted by the government, and therefore had little impact beyond its creation.[32]

In March 1992 the government launched a National Conservation Strategy in an attempt to promote resource conservation and sustainable development as part of its economic growth program. It identified two cultural concepts that should be tapped to drive heritage management in the Islamic republic: *qanaat* ("being content with what one has," a conservation ethic derived from Islamic moral values) and *haquq-ul-abad* ("rights of fellow human beings," fostering community spirit and responsibility).[33] As had been the case with prior efforts to rally a national standard and strategy for meeting conservation challenges, this too failed to leave much impact due to inadequate follow-through on its promising ideas.

Pakistani institutions, legislation, organizations and initiatives supporting conservation

The Ancient Monuments Preservation Act of 1904, adopted when the regions that would become Pakistan[34] were part of British India, initially regulated conservation policy up to and beyond independence in 1947. The Antiquities Export Control Act was adopted upon independence in order to manage movable objects. In 1968 the Antiquities Act usurped both earlier laws, identifying 1857 as the threshold date for ancient monuments, and granting the federal government control of antiquities without owners and monuments in danger.[35]

Parliament revised the 1968 law as the Antiquities Act of 1975, established seventy-five years as the age for qualifying objects or sites, and incorporated measures to ban new construction from within 200 ft (61 m) of a protected site. Although further amendments to the Antiquities Act were made in 1978 and 1992, it otherwise remains Pakistan's primary heritage legislation. As of 2015 its provisions did not yet address key concepts of contemporary practice, such as intangible heritage and cultural landscapes.[36]

The Antiquities Act addresses both movable and immovable (built) heritage, while also noting the importance of urban ensembles, including streets, squares and groups of buildings, in addition to more traditional monuments. Despite this, as is the case in India, local, provincial and national inventories tend to be monument focused. Few examples of conservation districts, ensembles of historically significant buildings or cultural landscapes are on the country's list of heritage resources, which thus overlooks many important heritage properties.[37] Principles and strategies relative to a professional cultural heritage practice also do not appear in any legislation, which results in a key missing piece of the national conservation strategy. While the aforementioned Lahore Charter (1989) codified these, the government's failure to adopt and propagate them as official standards of practice leaves the issue largely unaddressed.[38] The country's Culture Policy (1995, updated in 2008) does address recording, promotion and protection of intangible heritage, but it has been criticized as contributing to the piecemeal approach to heritage management, rather than working as part of an integrated, comprehensive conservation policy that addresses the tangible, intangible, movable, immovable, monumental and vernacular alike.[39]

A satellite network of laws governs provincial-level conservation activities, which have risen in importance since the passage of major constitutional reforms in 2011 shifted significant powers away from the central government and to the provinces. Provincial legislation includes the Punjab Special Premises Ordinance of 1985, North-West Frontier Province (now KPK) Antiquities Ordinance of 1997, the Punjab Heritage Foundation Act 2005, and the Sindh Cultural Heritage Preservation Act of 1994. These laws tend to follow the model of the 1975 Antiquities Act, with minor differences accounting for penalties and date ranges (KPK using 1922 as a threshold date for determining antiquity, for instance), but they do not otherwise substantively expand or identify regional heritage types or approaches. The Sindh legislation stands out due to its inclusion of a provision that relieves owners of property taxes for non-commercial buildings listed under either the provincial or national legislation and enables a board to distribute funds to identify, initiate and finance conservation projects in the province.[40] The governmental system of both central and provincial archaeology departments has led to some management overlaps. Although the amended 1975 Antiquities Act dictates that the federal government has jurisdiction over all World Heritage Sites, 25 percent of the approximately 400 federal-level historic buildings and sites also fall under the control of provincial government bodies.[41]

The federal Department of Archaeology and Museums (DOAM) inherited the mantle of the British-era Archaeological Survey of India, and as of 2015 has remained a consistently important player in the conservation system of Pakistan. Upon independence, DOAM was initially placed under the Department of Education, but since then has been shuffled no fewer than six times as part of a series of ministerial re-organizations. In 1997 it ultimately landed within the (then) newly created national Ministry of Culture.[42] But in April 2010 the 18th amendment to the Pakistani constitution was passed, which profoundly changed the national governmental structure from a strongly centralized federal system to a largely de-centralized system of empowered provincial and local governments. Beginning in 2011, through the controversial process known as "devolution," the portfolios of seventeen federal ministries, ranging from agriculture to sport, were transferred to the provinces.[43]

The Ministry of Culture was among the departments that were dissolved, resulting in a major restructuring of governmental responsibility for managing heritage properties, the allocation of conservation personnel and of applicable legislation. By most accounts, through 2015 the process has not been smooth, instead generating legal quarrels, organizational confusion and suspension of most conservation work at hundreds of sites across the country. Hanging in the balance appear to be the fate of the 409 federally listed heritage sites (including the country's six UNESCO World Heritage Sites), and clarity around whether or not the UNESCO sites and the 800 government staff that manage them were appropriately transferred to the provinces during devolution in 2011.[44] Furthermore, there remains confusion around which government entities bear responsibility for paying staff, and which are responsible for managing ongoing international agreements for site management and conservation projects. Supporters of devolution have pointed to the opportunities that may emerge from a streamlining of bureaucratic layers, and grassroots empowerment that could come from local control of heritage sites. But concerns remain that the transfer was not set up with adequate tools, funding or strategy to guide this outcome. The ongoing dispute over site ownership seems to be a strong indicator that the devolution process has yet to benefit conservation efforts in the country.[45]

As of 2015, with the passage of the 18th amendment several years in the past, the federal DOAM remains within the national Ministry of Information, Broadcasting and National Heritage.[46] Another federal entity with responsibilities for historic buildings and sites that has been subject to uncertainty due to devolution is the Evacuee Trust Properties Board (ETPB). Established in 1975 as a means to manage primarily Hindu and Sikh properties that were essentially abandoned due to post-Partition emigration from Pakistan, the ETPB manages billions of rupees in land and other buildings across the country, but mainly concentrated in Sindh and Punjab. Adoption of the 18th amendment led the governments of Punjab and Sindh to request that the ETPB properties be devolved to the provincial governments, but the federal government refused, citing international treaty obligations that required the board to continue operating at the federal level. As of 2015 the matter remained with the Supreme Court of Pakistan, awaiting resolution, with the fate of these significant heritage assets in the balance.[47]

In 1994, an act of Parliament established the National Fund for Cultural Heritage (NFCH). Created partly to assist in coordination between competing heritage management agencies, the NFCH has also funded publication of research, assisted in coordination with international organizations, acquired leases on historic properties in private hands, and contributed to public awareness campaigns around heritage issues. Financial sources for the Fund are drawn from direct grants from the federal government, donations from the private sector and from income generated by historic buildings owned by or leased to the Fund.[48] Composition of the NFCH board includes the Minister of Information and Broadcasting, the director of the Archaeology Department, university faculty, museum directors and other professionals working in the field.[49] Decision-making by the NFCH has been criticized as opaque, and its level of activity appears to have diminished, particularly following the passage of the 18th amendment and devolution of the Ministry of Culture; as of 2015 the fate of the Fund and its worthy ambitions appears uncertain.[50]

At the provincial level, similar efforts have proved more lasting, such as the Endowment Fund Trust for Preservation of the Heritage of Sindh. Established in 2008 and supported by an initial government grant, the Trust solicits applications from property owners for publicly accessible projects that are significant to the heritage of Sindh. The Trust raises funds from private sources, and has undertaken projects as varied as the restoration of a Jain temple complex at Nagarparkar (ninth through fifteenth century CE) and the proposed rehabilitation of the early nineteenth century Naukot Fort, located at the edge of the Thar Desert, as a museum.[51]

Another leader in Pakistan's non-governmental sector is the Karachi-based Heritage Foundation. Established in 1980 by Yasmeen Lari, Pakistan's first female architect and an accomplished conservation professional, the Heritage Foundation supports a variety of projects, with an emphasis on historic resource documentation, heritage advocacy and management of conservation projects. The Foundation is also a global leader in sustainable development as a strategy for disaster preparedness, generating designs for and leading the construction of tens of thousands of homes in flood prone areas using inexpensive, locally available, resilient materials (e.g. wattle and daub) that are also thoughtfully designed.[52] The organization implemented its distinctive approach to sustainable design following the devastating 2011 floods in Sindh in an effort to promote economic recovery by helping to rebuild housing and develop craft skills training for women in particular.[53]

In addition to its new architectural work, the Heritage Foundation has led documentation and conservation efforts of individual buildings, as well as several historical centers of Pakistan. Beginning in the 1990s, the organization's Heritage Documentation Program has assembled a National Register of Historic Places of Pakistan;[54] since then, the Foundation has published nearly a dozen volumes, organized geographically, that constitute a systematic record of hundreds of buildings and sites across the country. Responding to a frequently cited critique of conservation practice in Pakistan, the Foundation has published a seven-volume series of practical guides aimed at improving conservation practice, covering topics such as masonry cleaning, property owner's handbooks and site documentation. The Foundation's output includes an impressive publishing portfolio, and management of an archive and documentation center for heritage resources, which are available for reference purposes.[55]

The Foundation has undertaken numerous conservation and advocacy projects throughout the country, including protection of the Hindu Gymkhana Club in Karachi,[56] the Quaid-e-Azam House (Flagstaff House) Museum associated with the founder of Pakistan, Mohammed Ali Jinnah, the GPO Building in Lahore and the nineteenth century Sethi House in Peshawar. In partnership with UNESCO, the Foundation has undertaken critical documentation work at the Thatta World Heritage Site and assisted with the 2003–2005 stabilization of the mirrored Shish Mahal ceiling in Lahore Fort World Heritage Site.[57] Through this diverse range of activities, as well as an outreach and advocacy arm known as KaravanPakistan, the Heritage Foundation well-exemplifies the effectiveness of the non-governmental sector of Pakistan's heritage conservation field.

Karachi

Pakistan's largest city, Karachi,[58] located at the intersection of the Indus and the Arabian Sea, possesses some of the country's strongest local conservation regulations. The Indus River has historically served as the backbone for the Sindh – and, by extension, for Pakistan as a whole – supporting earlier capitals (such as Thatta and Hyderabad), and its shifting course has over centuries both given and taken away prosperity.[59] Similar to Mumbai, its Indian sibling to the southeast, Karachi developed into a major urban center under the British, beginning with its annexation from the Talpur Mirs in 1839.[60] Its growth mushroomed following independence, as millions of people displaced by Partition immigrated to the new country's economic center. This pattern of growth, echoed in many cities across the region, has resulted in a large population of newcomers and a booming real estate market, which in turn has resulted in an environment where appreciation for heritage buildings often takes a backseat to other development interests.[61]

Efforts to conserve Karachi's distinctive architectural heritage dates to the decade following independence, with the creation of the Karachi Development Authority in 1957, which created powers for zoning and historic building protection. The Karachi Building and Town Planning Regulations of 2002 serve as a regulatory tool for the Sindh Building Control Authority in the monitoring of Karachi's listed heritage properties.[62] The Regulations include penalties that permanently withhold new permits for a site where unauthorized demolition of a heritage building has occurred – a potentially powerful tool, yet one that is rarely enforced. The regulations also feature a limited provision for transferring development rights, a process that involves the sale of unused floor area from a heritage property plot to other sites where the additional height or area can augment a development project. Unfortunately, subsequent amendments to the regulations have limited the utility of this otherwise attractive incentive.[63]

FIGURE 18.3 Restoration of the Gymkhana Club in Karachi, a club erected during the British Raj for the Hindu commercial elite. Its design was based on the tomb of Itamad-ud-Daulah (1628) in Agra (India). The deteriorated building was slated for demolition in 1984, an outcome that was prevented by an intervention by the Heritage Foundation. It was rehabilitated using government funds and since 2005 houses the National Academy for Performing Arts.

The listing process in Karachi suffers from an unfortunately negative perception by many property owners. Over 1,700 buildings have been listed, yet the prevailing attitude among property owners is that listing is an inconvenient encumbrance.[64] Provisions in the law exist for appealing listings, which owners exercise up to 28 percent of the time. The military and other federal entities have also resisted listing, arguing that the provincial laws do not apply to federal property. Such was the case of an Army-owned colonial period bungalow located in the Karachi Cantonment. In 1997, after submitting an application for delisting that was not approved, the Army proceeded with demolition anyway, arguing that it was not held to provincial regulations regarding heritage buildings.[65]

Conservation projects in Pakistan

Architectural conservation projects in Pakistan range in both scale and context. Among the largest include the decades-long efforts to conserve the Mohenjo-Daro archaeological site, the Walled City of Lahore projects undertaken in part by the World Bank and the Aga Khan Historic Cities Program, and the community-focused programs in Gilgit-Baltistan coordinated by the Aga Khan Cultural Service – Pakistan and other international partners. An examination of these projects, while by no means comprehensive, demonstrates the range of challenges and opportunities faced by conservationists working in Pakistan. They underscore the challenging environment that the profession encounters in Pakistan.

The Punjabi city and former Mughal capital of Lahore has been an important political, commercial and industrial center for centuries, and thus possesses a deep architectural history. Lahore's walled city is a small (2.6 square kilometer) area in the northwestern corner of the modern metropolis' sprawl, but it contains numerous cultural properties including the Fort portion of the World Heritage Site, gateways, residential buildings, palaces, tombs and squares.[66] Lahore's distinctive architectural styles range from the Ghaznavid (eleventh century), Mughal (sixteenth century), Sikh (eighteenth century) and British eras. As is the case in many of Pakistan's historic urban centers, in addition to its architectural heritage the Old City harbors traditional crafts industries and elements of intangible heritage not found elsewhere in the country.

Owing to its profound historical and cultural importance, and its acute needs, from 1983 through 1992 the Government of Pakistan and the World Bank collaborated on an ambitious US$16 million urban development plan that focused on capacity building among municipal institutions and infrastructure improvements within the Walled City. In 1980, prior to the project's launch, it was estimated that 25–30 percent of residents lived in overcrowded, sub-standard conditions with inadequate access to municipal services. Upon completion, the World Bank's Lahore Urban Development Project had improved conditions for 70,000 residents of the Walled City through the replacement of drainage lines, paving, street lighting and solid waste management. The project set the stage for subsequent phases of work focused on the Walled City that targeted its historic resources, as well as the needs of its populace.[67]

Over the course of the 2000s these needs came into sharp focus, as both the Lahore Fort and Shalamar Gardens site were placed on UNESCO's List of World Heritage in Danger in 2000. The major factors for that decision were issues with encroachment, deferred maintenance of the contributing buildings, and the 1999 demolition of a portion of the gardens' Mughal-era hydraulic system during construction for a road expansion project.[68] The population of the Old City itself had declined from 240,000 in the 1950s to 150,000 in 2005 due to deteriorated living conditions within the ancient walls, signaling that the efforts of the prior decade to improve services and infrastructure were needed more than ever.[69]

After more than a decade the Directorate General of Archaeology of Punjab (DGAoP)[70] adequately responded to UNESCO's concerns regarding the Lahore Fort and Shalamar Gardens site by addressing encroachment issues through the relocation of an unauthorized market and bus stand. The Department also strengthened regulations for controlling future encroachments, secured a five-year funding program, and adopted an updated management plan. Consequently, in 2012 UNESCO removed the site from the List of World Heritage in Danger.[71]

In 2006 the World Bank launched the Punjab Municipal Services Improvement Project (2006–2013), a US$55 million project that included a pilot project inside the Walled City. Work focused on

FIGURE 18.4 The poor condition of the early seventeenth century Shalamar Gardens in Lahore prior to the 1970s led to the need for comprehensive conservation of the famed gardens and its contexts. Restoration work included botanical studies, repair of the garden's Mughal hydraulic system, and landscaping.

the Shahi Guzargah (Royal Route) between the Delhi Gate and the Chowk Purani Kotwali, a road used by Mughal nobility to enter the city from Delhi en route to the Lahore Fort.[72] One aim of the project was to connect significant public buildings and spaces between the Delhi Gate and Lahore Fort with a series of infrastructure, streetscape and public space improvements so as to demonstrate the potential of the Old City to residents and visitors alike. Installation and maintenance of infrastructure in the Walled City, which until then had been uncoordinated and ad hoc, resulted in discordant elements such as overhead utility wires, incompatible signs and unauthorized commercial stalls. In 2012, the Government of Punjab established the Walled City of Lahore Authority (WCLA) as a centralized entity charged with overseeing rehabilitation and development inside the city's ancient walls. The WCLA has since worked in partnership with the World Bank, the Aga Khan Trust for Culture and other international and local entities to coordinate the pilot project and its future phases, as well as other conservation efforts within the Old City.[73]

The resulting pilot project consisted of a 0.33 km long route beginning at the Delhi Gate. Utility services were replaced underground, streets were repaved, the façades of over 700 buildings were improved, and twenty-three residences were rehabilitated. Nearly 150 unauthorized shops were relocated, along with residential developments that were obscuring buildings and had encroached upon public space. This delicate task was negotiated through a hands-on consultative approach by municipal staff.[74] A second phase of the project began in 2015 and is scheduled to run until 2018. The scope of the second phase included completing the route to the Lahore Fort; addressing an additional 500 residential and commercial buildings; rehabilitating monuments located along the route including the Akbari Gate, Moti Bazaar and Mariam Zamani Mosque; and restricting automobile traffic along the route.[75]

FIGURE 18.5a and b The condition of the Wazir Khan mosque area (a) and others in Old Lahore could benefit from façade improvements and other urban conservation measures. In other areas restoration has been successful (b).

In addition to its architectural conservation activities, the program sought to refurbish commercial and social gathering places to alleviate population pressure on existing public spaces. But even when both phases have been completed, only 11 percent of the Old City will have been addressed, and there is much more to be done. In response, the Aga Khan Historic Cities Program (AKHCP) has prepared an infrastructure development plan for the entire Old City, implementation of which began in 2010 and will continue on a phased basis over fifteen years.[76] The AKHCP also plans to rehabilitate the seventeenth century Wazir Khan Mosque and its associated Shahi Hammam in order to enhance public space within the Old City.[77]

Conservation of a disputed territory: Kashmir and Pakistan's northern areas

From the moment of India and Pakistan's birth, the affiliation of Kashmir has proven an intractable question, with profound ramifications on the residents and architecture of this topographically spectacular and culturally rich region of South Asia. When faced with the decision of which country to join upon Partition in 1947, the Hindu Maharaja Hari Singh, to the dismay of his majority Muslim subjects, chose neither. Within weeks, Pakistan had invaded, leading the Maharaja to flee to India and agree to join the Republic. War followed, resulting in a UN-negotiated ceasefire that set a "temporary" border, known today as the Line of Control. Under this arrangement the northern third of the region has been controlled by Pakistan and the remainder by India. Two wars later (in 1965 and in 1971) a stalemate ensued, with positions becoming ever more entrenched. Fighting spilled over again in 1989 with pro-independence and pro-Pakistan militias expelling Hindus from the Kashmir Valley, a situation that culminated in the 1999 Kargil conflict, an undeclared war that resulted in further civilian and military casualties and additional ill will between the two nuclear-armed neighbors.[78]

The detrimental effects of a half century-plus of warfare and political uncertainty have fallen squarely upon the populace, economy and built environment of Kashmir. A region that has been celebrated for its singular beauty since Mughal times is now administratively torn between Pakistani Azad Kashmir and Indian Jammu and Kashmir.

Always prone to seismic activity, a terribly destructive earthquake in 2005 centered in the Pakistani-administered region killed almost 90,000 and displaced nearly 3 million persons. This episode underscored the vulnerability of this politically fragile region, and the importance of its traditional systems of earthquake resistant construction. As compared to modern concrete construction, the *taq* (timber laced masonry) and *dhajji dewari* (timber framed masonry infill) systems that are indigenous to Kashmir have evolved to withstand a certain amount of seismic movement, and as such offer compelling alternatives for modern concrete frame with masonry infill.[79]

As is the case in much of the developing world, the traditional form of construction is threatened by the perceived advantages of "modern" building types, which in fact perform poorly in terms of seismic strength, temperature control and durability. Srinagar, the capital of Indian-controlled Jammu and Kashmir, has been particularly susceptible to this phenomenon, with large numbers of traditional residential buildings lost since the 1990s.[80] But more than any single trend in planning or conservation, the historic architecture of Azad Kashmir and Jammu and Kashmir is threatened by the residual effect of one of the world's longest-running territorial disputes. Until the Kashmir question is resolved, the conservation efforts of both nations will be hampered by the lost opportunities for collaboration and the economic drain that the standoff has created.

The vast, abandoned city of Mohenjo-Daro illustrates a completely different set of conservation circumstances from Lahore, in terms of policy, practice and the nature of its threats. Located on the banks of the Indus River approximately 400 km north of Karachi, the 5,000-year-old ruined city is among Asia's earliest urban settlements, and its discovery in the 1920s was one of the great archaeological moments of the twentieth century. Like its contemporary Harappa, it has a complex grid-planned street layout and sophisticated masonry architecture; Harappa, however, was plundered for its material in the mid-nineteenth century by a British-era railway construction project, nearly destroying the majority of the site.[81]

Excavations at the huge mud-brick site[82] began under the Archaeological Survey of India nearly a century ago, and the conservation of the fragile architectural remains has posed a major challenge ever since. But since the 1960s, increasingly intensive irrigation in this fertile agricultural region has caused

FIGURE 18.6 Aerial view of Mohenjo-Daro, Pakistan (ca. 3000 BCE) since its first excavation in the 1920s.

the water table to rise, thus undermining the structural integrity of large areas of standing ruins. Ground salts have permeated the earthen architectural remains via capillary action, breaking apart the ancient bricks from within; wind and rain have also steadily eroded the exposed ancient structures. In 1974 UNESCO, in collaboration with the Government of Pakistan, launched the International Safeguarding Campaign for Mohenjo-Daro. The program ran until 1997, channeling US$11 million into conservation measures, hydrological engineering, and capacity building to improve site management and stability of Mohenjo-Daro's features.[83]

In addition to consolidating and protecting Mohenjo-Daro's architectural remains, site conservation also required planning for the region's climatic conditions, seasonal flooding from the Indus River, and the heavy annual monsoon rains. Various low-impact techniques were implemented, such as capping the brick walls with salt-free mud from the nearby riverbed to protect them from precipitation. A moratorium on new research excavation had been imposed in 1965, preventing the exposure of additional wall footings or other structures to the elements, thus keeping the majority of the site in a stable, buried state, and archaeological activity limited to salvage operations as warranted.[84] Over the course of the Campaign several critical milestones were achieved, including adding Mohenjo-Daro to the World Heritage List (1980), implementation of groundwater control measures, stabilizing structures and constructing an on-site conservation laboratory.[85]

Despite the heavy investment in funds, expertise and engineering, the future of Mohenjo-Daro remains frustratingly in question. During the initial Campaign, the project team constructed hydrological control measures, including a series of tube wells meant to control groundwater levels,[86] and "river training" features, which consist of a series of earthen berms and channels designed to direct river water away from the archaeological site in the event of flooding. Unsustainable costs associated with the pumping systems have rendered them largely ineffective over time, leaving the fragile archaeological features vulnerable to water damage even while under active monitoring.[87] Conservation work at the site since the close of the Safeguarding Campaign has been sporadic, owing to the lack of funding and resources on the part of DOAM, which has meant an inability to comprehensively implement planned conservation measures. A revised master plan was prepared and submitted to the Pakistani government in 2009, and in 2012 the Government of Sindh announced a US$1 million management plan to address the ongoing conservation work, monitoring and mapping of the site under the new provincial administration.[88]

In contrast to Lahore's challenges in reconciling a constituent population with a dense, historic urban environment, the problems at Mohenjo-Daro instead center on the long-term care, management and maintenance of an uninhabited site of no less cultural significance. In 2010, responsibility for the Lahore sites and for Mohenjo-Daro was transferred from DOAM to the Sindh provincial authorities. Control of the site remains an ongoing issue, with the case of thieves audaciously making off with

FIGURE 18.7 Conservation issues at Mohenjo-Daro include problems relating to rising damp and consolidation of its earthen walls and flooring areas. For over half a century numerous studies have been made and recommendations tried toward conserving and presenting this challenging site.

around forty objects from the site museum in 2002, including some of its famous carved seals, still unresolved.[89] Continued deterioration of the mud brick features have led some to call for reburial of the exposed portions of the site as a last-ditch effort to save what remains, indicating the level of despair felt by some at the consistent setbacks in the effort to protect the site. In 2012, the Pakistani archaeologist Dr. Asma Ibrahim signaled the field's pessimism regarding the situation, stating, "if things carry on like this, in my assessment, the site will not last more than twenty years."[90] This grim assessment comes after decades passed and tens of millions of dollars spent on a resource of critical importance, which surely accounts for the frustration that a solution at this premier site is not forthcoming, and so many good intentions have gone unrewarded.

The examples of Lahore's Walled City and Mohenjo-Daro offer stark examples of the opportunities that exist, and the challenges ahead for the field of conservation in Pakistan. While the legislative foundation for effective conservation practice in the country is in place, a critical problem remains: the institutions, political stability and continuity of purpose needed to drive sustained conservation efforts remain uneven. A frequently cited example of the disappointing reality at many heritage sites in Pakistan is the state of Shikarpoor Historic City in northern Sindh, the only city where the entire municipality is protected as a heritage asset.[91] With over 1,200 heritage properties identified, the former hub of trade via the Bolan Pass to Central Asia and Afghanistan reached its apex in the eighteenth and nineteenth centuries, and has been celebrated since for its architectural beauty.[92] The advent of railway transport and demographic shifts following Partition combined to erode the city's traditional social systems; later in the twentieth century a lack of enforcement of heritage regulations, and an insatiable market for decorative architectural elements has resulted in the loss of hundreds of buildings, leading many to conclude that Shikarpoor is all but lost.[93]

Such developments do not bode well for the revival of a vibrant heritage tourism sector in Pakistan, which remains an unexploited opportunity, yet one that seems increasingly out of reach as the regional and national security situation deteriorates. While neighboring countries have thriving heritage tourist sectors that have helped support vulnerable sites, and raised the profile of historic cities and places, Pakistan remains largely off the tourist map. According to the World Bank, in 2012 Pakistan received just over 950,000 foreign tourists as compared to India's 6.5 million; and while India's tourist numbers are on the rise, Pakistan's are discouragingly trending downward.[94]

A fractious political and social environment both internally and regionally is partly to blame for the tenuous nature of Pakistan's conservation efforts. Another vestige of its colonial experience is the national government's framework for supporting conservation activities that is based on the analysis of cultural heritage sites as objects for study or exemplars of heritage, rather than as integral components of a living society.[95] This outdated view contributes to the monument-centric approach that remains a factor in both the national and international approach to heritage management in the country. The profound demographic shifts that took place upon independence – another colonial legacy – are still playing out in terms of growth in Karachi and depopulation in the Walled City of Lahore, and the uncertain fate of Evacuee Trust Property Board holdings following the devolution movement. These wounds have healed with the passage of time, but they are periodically re-opened as conflict over Kashmir, for instance, remains unresolved.

Capacity building for conservation professionals in Pakistan represents an area where potential growth has yet to be fully realized. The country has a dedicated cadre of professionals including a prominent corps of female practitioners, but as of 2015 no degree program in architectural conservation is available. Only elective courses and heritage management and archaeology are offered at two universities; archaeology degree programs are more common, with the University of Peshawar in

FIGURE 18.8 Restoration of Baltit Fort (Karimabad, Hunza), with help of the Aga Khan Trust for Culture's Historic Cities Support Programme, resulted in the adaptive re-use of the site as a museum and cultural complex. This program, which began in the late 1980s, was followed by a series of community-based conservation projects in Gilgit-Baltistan (formerly known as the Northern Areas) that later led to the participation of the AKTC in the Lahore Fort projects. This influential project is a good instance of the "power of example" in architectural heritage conservation.

particular taking a leadership role in both training and fieldwork.⁹⁶ Several Pakistani architectural firms have developed specializations in conservation work through commissions from national, provincial and NGO projects, but the number of formally trained professionals remains small. Institutions such as the Heritage Foundation and Lahore Walled City Authority have demonstrated an aptitude for both partnering with other institutions, and cutting through some of the logistical challenges of effectively operating in Pakistan's complex environment.

The government's capacity to develop reform measures such as the devolution movement indicates that change is possible, and successful pilot projects in places like Gilgit-Baltistan and Lahore point towards successful strategies. Once the complications of devolution have been resolved, the shift to provincial and municipal-led efforts like those occurring in Sindh, Punjab and Karachi show promise and could reflect positively upward to the national level institutions, while also benefiting local communities in the process.⁹⁷ Resolution of internal and external conflicts, enforcement of heritage laws and execution of programs may yet lead to a full realization of the country's promise.

Pakistan's active and productive non-governmental sector, committed conservation professionals, and its astounding diversity of heritage resources stand out as promising components from which to improve upon the state of conservation practice in the country.

Future challenges for heritage conservationists in culturally rich and complex Pakistan are legion, including the difficulty of defining its physical boundaries and interpreting areas of cultural importance. Coming to terms with these challenges will likely involve a greater level of cooperation with its neighbors – in particular with India – via resource, information and professional exchanges. Although political tensions between the two nations remain high, cultural heritage is one area where much is shared, and it could be a fertile common ground on which to nurture future relationships.

Notes

1. The discoveries of Mohenjo-Daro, Taxila and Harappa in particular fueled European scholarly interest and activity during the nineteenth and early twentieth centuries, and set the stage for architectural conservation programs at each site in the post-independence era. Source: Mohammed Rafique Mughal. "Heritage Preservation in Pakistan: From National and International Perspectives." Unpublished article. 2010. Web. www.rafiquemughal.com/MUGHAL_2010_Chapter-on-Heritage-Preser-In-Pakistan.pdf. Accessed November 14, 2015.
2. Anila Naeem. "The Conflict of Ideologies and Ambiguities in Conservation Policy: A Legacy of Shared Built Heritage in Pakistan," in Kapila D. Silva and Neel Kamal Champagain (eds.), *Asian Heritage Management: Contexts, Concerns and Prospects*. (London: Routledge, 2013), 95.
3. Mughal (2010).
4. "Devolution," triggered by a 2010 amendment to the Pakistani constitution, is the process by which federal government authorities are dissolved at the national level and transferred to the provinces. A detailed discussion of this process and its implications for architectural conservation begins on page 433 of this chapter. Jamal Shahid. "Archaeology Department Wants Devolved Sites Back." *Dawn* (Pakistan). December 16, 2012. Web. www.dawn.com/news/771853/archaeology-dept-wants-devolved-sites-back-2. Accessed November 14, 2015.
5. UNESCO Islamabad. *Pakistan: UNESCO Country Programming Document (CPD), 2013–2017*. (Islamabad: UNESCO, 2013), 3–4. Web. http://unesco.org.pk/documents/2013/PAKISTAN_CPD.pdf. Accessed November 7, 2015.
6. UNESCO Islamabad. "Safeguarding Moenjodaro." 2015. Web. http://unesco.org.pk/culture/moenjodaro.html. Accessed November 14, 2015.
7. UNESCO CPD, 21.
8. UNESCO CPD, 6.
9. The survey was a research-based initiative from the Heritage Cell – Department of Architecture and Planning, N.E.D. University of Engineering and Technology (HC-DAPNED), Karachi, in collaboration with the Department of Culture, Government of Sindh. The first phase of this research project was undertaken from 2006 to 2009; while the second and third phases are still ongoing. The official title of this project was "Karachi Heritage Buildings Re-survey Project" (KHBRP). Naeem (2013), 98 and personal email correspondence, January 4, 2016.
10. The question of Jinnah's intentions regarding Islam, the state and the role of religious minorities remains hotly contested in Pakistan today, with various groups claiming different interpretations of his speeches to

justify their views on this controversial topic. Source: A.H. Nayyar. "Stop Distorting Jinnah's Words." *The Express Tribune* (Pakistan). August 13, 203. Web. http://tribune.com.pk/story/58978. Accessed December 5, 2015.

11 Urdu, Pakistan's official language, is closely related to Hindi and Persian. English is also widely spoken in Pakistan.

12 UNESCO CPD, 19.

13 Naeem (2013), 90. While the devolution movement may yet result in a more locally based and thus more representative approach to heritage inventories, a great deal of work remains to be done to compile comprehensive heritage inventories that accurately reflect the country's diverse population.

14 Today's Pakistan was known as West Pakistan until 1971 when East Pakistan – today's Bangladesh – achieved independence. The experience of East Pakistan/Bangladesh is discussed in Chapter 19. A detailed description of architectural conservation under the British Raj is found in Chapter 16 (India). It is worth noting that the early architectural surveys conducted by Alexander Cunningham, James Burgess and H.H. Cole on behalf of the East India Company, and later the British Crown, focused on the regions of British India that now constitute modern Pakistan. The British-era ASI conducted numerous projects in Sindh, the former Northwest Frontier Provinces and present-day Pakistani Punjab, leaving behind a legacy of conservation that reverberates to this day.

15 Jane McIntosh. *The History of Archaeology: An Introduction*. Edited by Paul Bahn. (London: Routledge, 2014), Chapter 6.

16 Mukhtar Ahmed. *Ancient Pakistan: An Archaeological History, Vol. 2*. (Reidsville, NC: Foursome Group, 2014), 53.

17 Sir Mortimer Wheeler. *Civilizations of the Indus Valley and Beyond*. (New York: McGraw Hill, 1966), 14–15.

18 James Wynbrandt. *A Brief History of Pakistan*. (New York: Checkmark Books, 2008), 24–29.

19 UNESCO World Heritage Center. "Taxila." Web. http://whc.unesco.org/en/list/139. Accessed May 20, 2016.

20 Rafi U. Samad. *The Grandeur of Gandhara: The Ancient Buddhist Civilization of the Swat, Peshawar, Kabul and Indus Valleys*. (New York: Algora Publishing, 2011), 1–2.

21 Stanley Wolpert. *A New History of India*. (Oxford: Oxford University Press, 1989), 122–125.

22 Patwant Singh. *The Sikhs* (New York: Crown Publishing Group, 2007).

23 Nankana Sahib is located at the birthplace of Guru Nanak. Important holy sites in Sikhism exist in India as well, with the Harmandir Sahib (Golden Temple) in Amristar (Indian Punjab) serving as the faith's most important building. Hugh Tinker. *South Asia: A Short History*. (London: Macmillan Press, 1989), 77.

24 Christophe Jaffrelot, ed. *A History of Pakistan and its Origins*. (London: Anthem Press, 2004), 1–2.

25 The name "Pakistan" itself is a twentieth century construct, having been proposed in 1933 by Chaudri Rhemat Ali, then a Punjabi Muslim student at Cambridge. It is derived from the first letters of the principal provinces of Punjab, Afghan (Northwest Frontier Province), Kashmir, Sindh and the suffix of Baluchistan. The "i" was added for ease of pronunciation. Source: Jaffrelot, 13.

26 Syed Iskandar Ariffin. "Islamic Perspectives and Malay Notions of Heritage Conservation," in Kapila D. Silva and Neel Kamal Chapagain (eds.), *Asian Heritage Management: Contexts, Concerns and Prospects*. (London: Routledge, 2013), 68, 72–74.

27 Jocelyne Cesari. *The Awakening of Muslim Democracy*. (Cambridge: Cambridge University Press, 2013), 50–51.

28 Hidayat Khan. "Saving History: Archaeology Dept. Seeks Control of City's Historic Sites." *The Express Tribune* (Pakistan). January 30, 2015. Web. http://tribune.com.pk/story/830224/saving-history-archaeology-dept-seeks-control-of-citys-historic-sites/. Accessed November 25, 2015.

29 Asad Kharal. "Conservation and Restoration: Walled City Authority Takes Over Heritage Sites." *The Express Tribune* (Pakistan). April 4, 2013. Web. http://tribune.com.pk/story/530818/conservation-and-restoration-walled-city-authority-takes-over-heritage-sites/. Accessed November 25, 2015.

30 UNESCO. *International Symposium on Conservation and Restoration of Islamic Architectural Heritage: Report and Recommendations*. (Paris: UNESCO, 1983), 21–26. Web. http://unesdoc.unesco.org/images/0005/000578/057821EB.pdf. Accessed May 20, 2016.

31 Mughal (2010), 9.

32 Naeem (2013), 96.

33 Naeem (2013), 89.

34 Modern Pakistan is a federal republic that is administratively divided into four provinces: Balochistan, Punjab, Sindh and Khyber-Pakhtunkhwa (or KPK), which until 2010 was known as the North-West Frontier Province; and four territories (Gilgit-Baltistan, Azad Kashmir, Islamabad Capital Territory, and the Federally Administered Tribal Areas, or FATA).

35   1857 was the year of the First War of Independence (also known as the Sepoy Mutiny), and is generally regarded as the beginning of the Pakistan Movement that by 1947 resulted in independence from Britain and partition from India.
36   Mohammed Rafique Mughal. "Heritage Management and Conservation in Pakistan: The British Legacy and Current Perspective." *Pakistan Heritage* 3 (2011), 123–124.
37   Mughal (2011), 5. As of 2015, of the 355 properties listed by the Department of Archaeology as being nationally significant, approximately one-third are archaeological sites.
38   Naeem (2013), 96.
39   Imrana Tiwana. "Situational Analysis on Culture in the Four Provinces of Pakistan (Report commissioned by UNESCO)" (August 2011), 16. Web. http://unesco.org.pk/culture/documents/situationanalysis/Situational_Analysis_Culture_in_the_Four_Provinces.pdf. Accessed November 7, 2015.
40   Naeem (2013), 96–97.
41   M. Rafique Mughal. "Heritage Legislation in Pakistan." *The World Heritage Newsletter* 16 (April–June, 1998), 2.
42   Tiwana, 28.
43   "Cabinet Approves Devolution of Seven Ministries." *Dawn* (Pakistan). June 28, 2011. Web. www.dawn.com/news/640139/cabinet-approves-devolution-of-seven-ministries. Accessed November 7, 2015.
44   Jamal Shahid. "Heritage Sites Belong to the Federation, not Provinces: Law Ministry." *Dawn* (Pakistan). March 2, 2015. Web. www.dawn.com/news/1166796. Accessed November 7, 2015.
45   Tiwana, 35.
46   Ministry of Information, Broadcasting & National Heritage: Department of Archaeology and Museums. 2015. Web. http://nationalheritage.gov.pk/doam.html. Web. Accessed November 7, 2015. DOAM is comprised of four branches: the Exploration and Excavation Branch; the Antiquity Trade Control Branch; the Preservation, Conservation, Restoration and Presentation Branch; and Museums.
47   United Nations Development Programme in Pakistan. "Analysis: Five Years of the 18th Constitutional Amendment: Federalist Imperatives on Public Policy and Planning." 2015. Web. www.undp.org/content/pakistan/en/home/library/hiv_aids/development-advocate-pakistan--volume-2--issue-1/analysis--five-years-of-the-18th-constitutional-amendment--feder.html. Accessed November 25, 2015.
48   Government of Pakistan. "National Fund for Cultural Heritage Act of 1994." 1994. Web. www.na.gov.pk/uploads/documents/1329798391_972.pdf. Web. Accessed November 25, 2015.
49   Prior to the 2011 devolution process, the chair of the Fund was the Minister of Culture. The National Fund for Cultural Heritage, Pakistan. 2011. Web. http://www.heritage.gov.pk. Accessed November 25, 2015.
50   Naeem (2013), 98.
51   Endowment Fund Trust for Preservation of the Heritage of Sindh. 2015. Web. http://eftsindh.com/#. Accessed November 25, 2015.
52   "Yasmeen Lari: On the Road to Self-Reliance." *Al Jazeera*. August 12, 2014. Web. www.aljazeera.com/programmes/rebelarchitecture/2014/08/yasmeen-lari-road-self-reliance-20148511850548381.html. Accessed November 25, 2015.
53   *Heritage Foundation's DRR-Compliant Sustainable Construction Build Back Safer with Vernacular Methodologies: DRR-Driven Post-Flood Rehabilitation in Sindh* (Heritage Foundation and IRM, December 2011).
54   Ayesha Aga Shah. "New Heritage Properties in Karachi." *Archi Times* (Pakistan). 2012. Web. http://archpresspk.com/new-version/New-heritage-properties-in-Karachi.html. Accessed November 7, 2015.
55   Pakistan Heritage Foundation. "About the Pakistan Heritage Foundation." 2015. Web. www.heritagefoundationpak.org/Page/1307/About-Us--Registration--Mission--Vision--Board-of-Directors-HF-Offices-Registration-Heritage-Foundat. Accessed November 29, 2015.
56   This was a club for the Hindu upper classes who formed a strong commercial elite in Karachi in the years before independence in 1947 and was based on the tomb of Itamad-ud-Daulah (1628) in Agra (India). The buildings had deteriorated over the years and were slated for demolition in 1984. This was prevented by an intervention by the Heritage Foundation, which paved the way for the building's conversion to a cultural center.
57   Pakistan Heritage Foundation. Project summaries linked from the homepage. 2015. Web. http://www.heritagefoundationpak.org/Hf. Accessed November 29, 2015.
58   With an estimated population of nearly 24 million people (2015), Karachi is Pakistan's most populous city, as well as the largest city in the Muslim world and third largest overall. Source: World Population Review. "Karachi Population." 2015. Web. http://worldpopulationreview.com/world-cities/karachi-population. Accessed December 12, 2015.
59   Anila Naeem. "Attempting Typological Classification of Sindh's Historic Urban Landscape." *Proceedings from ICOMOS Thailand International Conference: Asian Urban Heritage, October 15–17, Phuket, Thailand* (Bangkok: ICOMOS Thailand, 2011), 263.

60 Anila Naeem. "Karachi: Losing its Historic Face." *Journal of Research in Architecture and Planning (NED University, Karachi)* 3 (2004 – Conservation and Cultural Heritage), 78.
61 Naeem (2004), 89.
62 In February 2011 the KBCA's jurisdiction was extended from Karachi over the entire province of Sindh, and is now known as the Sindh Building Control Authority (SBCA). Expansion of the Karachi regulations to apply to all of Sindh is currently under consideration. Source: Personal email correspondence with Anila Naeem, January 4, 2016.
63 Naeem (2004), 98.
64 The HC-DAPNED initiative is responsible for a dramatic increase in the numbers of listed properties in Karachi since it began in 1994, from 581 listed properties in 1996, to 1,743 by the end of 2015. Additional surveys are planned for the future. Source: Email correspondence with Anila Naeem, January 4, 2016.
65 Naeem (2004), 89.
66 The World Heritage Site is officially the "Fort and Shalamar Gardens in Lahore," comprised of two separate complexes. The Gardens are located approximately 7 km outside the Fort proper. Source: UNESCO World Heritage Center. "Fort and Shalamar Gardens in Lahore." 2015. Web. http://whc.unesco.org/en/list/171. Accessed January 4, 2016.
67 The World Bank. *Project Completion Report: Lahore Urban Development Project.* (Washington, DC: The World Bank, 1994), 1–10. Web. http://documents.worldbank.org/curated/en/1994/08/734144/pakistan-lahore-urban-development-project. Accessed May 20, 2016.
68 UNESCO. "Better Conservation in Pakistan and the Philippines Allow Committee to Remove Two Sites from World Heritage List in Danger." June 27, 2012. Web. http://whc.unesco.org/en/news/891/. Accessed November 25, 2015.
69 Aga Khan Trust for Culture. "Pakistan: Conservation and Development in Gilgit-Balistan and the Punjab." 2015. Web. www.akdn.org/hcp/pakistan.asp. Accessed November 25, 2015.
70 In 2004 authority over the site was transferred from the DOAM to the DGAoP.
71 UNESCO. *State of Conservation Report: Lahore Fort and Shalamar Garden World Heritage Site.* (Paris: UNESCO, 2012), 3–7. Web. http://whc.unesco.org/en/list/171/documents/. Accessed May 20, 2016.
72 Due to the complexities of working in the Old City, the full scope of the project was not implemented. The World Bank notes that the remainder will be carried out by the provincial government in a Phase II of the program. The World Bank. "Punjab Municipal Services Improvement Project: Project Review Report." June 2, 2015. Web. www-wds.worldbank.org/external/default/WDSContentServer/WDSP/IB/2015/08/13/090224b08306eaa5/1_0/Rendered/PDF/Pakistan000Pun0Improvement0Project0.pdf. Accessed November 25, 2015.
73 Asad Kharal. "Conservation and Restoration: Walled City Authority Takes Over Heritage Sites." *The Express Tribune* (Pakistan). April 4, 2013. Web. http://tribune.com.pk/story/530818/conservation-and-restoration-walled-city-authority-takes-over-heritage-sites/. Accessed November 25, 2015.
74 Asad Zaidi. "In Lahore, Improving Livelihoods and Preserving Heritage go Hand in Hand." The World Bank. October 28, 2013. Web. www.worldbank.org/en/news/feature/2013/10/28/in-lahore-improving-livelihoods-and-preserving-heritage-go-hand-in-hand. Accessed November 25, 2015.
75 Ali Raza. "WCLA Starts Rehabilitation of Buildings." *The International News* (Pakistan). October 2, 2015. Web. www.thenews.com.pk/Todays-News-5-343288-WCLA-starts-rehabilitation-of-buildings. Accessed November 25, 2015.
76 The involvement of AKTC and AKHCP in Lahore came about due to their prior successful projects in Gilgit-Baltistan, which began in 1989.
77 AKTC Pakistan Program Summary. Web. www.akdn.org/our-agencies/aga-khan-trust-culture. Accessed May 20, 2016.
78 "A Brief History of the Kashmir Conflict." *The Telegraph* (UK). September 24, 2001. Web. www.telegraph.co.uk/news/1399992/A-brief-history-of-the-Kashmir-conflict.html. Accessed November 25, 2015.
79 Naseer Ganai. "Kashmir May be Hit by Mega Quake Soon." *India Today.* April 12, 2012. Web. http://indiatoday.intoday.in/story/kashmir-may-be-hit-by-mega-quake-soon-study/1/184173.html. Accessed November 25, 2015.
80 Randolph Langenbach. "The Earthquake Resistant Mud and Brick Architecture of Kashmir." *Adobe 90: Proceedings, International Conference on Earthen Architecture, Las Cruces, New Mexico.* (Los Angeles: Getty Conservation Institute, 1990), 95–97.
81 Wheeler, 28.
82 Mohenjo-Daro covers 600 acres, or about 250 hectares of terrain.
83 Rafique Mughal. "Mohenjo-Daro, Pakistan," in Miguel Angel Corzo (ed.), *The Future of Asia's Past: Preservation of the Architectural Heritage of Asia.* (Los Angeles: The Getty Conservation Institute, 1995), 20.

84　Shereen Ratnagar. "The Conservation of Mohenjo-Daro," *Marg* 50(2) (December 1998), 84–89.
85　UNESCO. "Safeguarding Moenjodaro." 2015. Web. http://unesco.org.pk/culture/moenjodaro.html. Accessed November 25, 2015.
86　Tube wells consist of a metal-lined shaft equipped with a pipe and mechanical pump, designed to lift water out of a sub-surface water table and move it elsewhere (often for the purposes of agricultural irrigation). The tube wells at Mohenjo-Daro were designed to lower groundwater tables so as to limit capillary action that transmitted salts into the ancient mud brick structures.
87　Huma Yusef. "Dancing on the Ruins." *The New York Times*. September 14, 2012. Web. http://latitude.blogs.nytimes.com/2012/09/14/flash-floods-threaten-pakistans-archaeological-heritage/?_r=0. Accessed January 4, 2016.
88　Oversight of Mohenjo-Daro was transferred to the Government of Sindh as part of the 2011 devolution process. Sources: "Rs100M for Mohenjodaro Master Plan." *Dawn* (Pakistan). February 20, 2012. Web. www.dawn.com/news/696939/re100m-for-mohenjodaro-master-plan. Accessed December 5, 2015; and UNESCO. "State of Conservation Report: Moenjodaro, Pakistan." 2011. Web. http://whc.unesco.org/en/list/138/documents/. Accessed November 29, 2015.
89　"Karachi: Plunder of Artifacts Continues Unchecked." *Dawn* (Pakistan). May 16, 2007. Web. http://dawn.com/news/247159/karachi-plunder-of-artefacts-continues-unchecked. Accessed November 29, 2015.
90　Aleem Maqbool. "Mohenjo Daro: Could this Ancient City be Lost Forever?" BBC News. June 27, 2012. Web. www.bbc.com/news/magazine-18491900. Accessed November 29, 2015.
91　Shikarpur remained a significant historic trade center of Sindh because of its strategic location on the caravan trade route linking India, Afghanistan, Khorasan and Central Asian Khanates.
92　The listed heritage properties include 1,163 buildings, twenty-seven urban elements and thirteen open spaces. The Department of Culture, Government of Sindh listed the town in March 2012 under the Sindh Cultural Heritage Preservation Act 1994. Source: Shikarpoor Historic City Campaign (2007–Ongoing). Heritage Cell – Department of Architecture & Planning, NED University of Engineering & Technology, Karachi. 2015. Listing occurred due to the ongoing efforts of the Shikarpoor Heritage Safeguarding Campaign initiated by HC-DAPNED in 2007. Source: www.neduet.edu.pk/arch_planning/Heritage/webpages/SHCC(2007-Ongoing).html. Accessed January 4, 2016.
93　Shameen Khan. "Requiem for a City." *Dawn* (Pakistan). February 28, 2014. Web. http://www.dawn.com/in-depth/requiem-for-a-city/. Accessed November 25, 2015.
94　Although India is four times larger than Pakistan in terms of area, and has five times the population, these statistics represent a meaningful difference. The World Bank. "International Tourism, Number of Arrivals." 2015. Web. http://data.worldbank.org/indicator/ST.INT.ARVL. Accessed November 29, 2015.
95　Yasmin Cheema. "State Intervention and its Limits." Paper delivered at the WMF Conference on Heritage Conservation, Colombo, Sri Lanka. July 28, 2004.
96　Mughal (2010), 126.
97　Naeem (2013), 102.

Further reading

Agnew, Neville (ed.). 2010. *Conservation of Ancient Sites on the Silk Road*. Proceedings of the Second International Conference on the Conservation of Grotto Sites, Mogao Grottoes, Dunhuang, People's Republic of China, June 28–July 3, 2004. Los Angeles: Getty Conservation Institute.
Beckwith, Christopher J. 2009. *Empires of the Silk Road*. Princeton: Princeton University Press.
Bianca, Stefano (ed.). 2005. *Karakoram: Hidden Treasures in the Northern Area of Pakistan*. Torino: U. Allemandi for Aga Khan Trust for Culture.
Cheema, Yasmin. 2007. *The Historical Quarters of Karachi*. London: Oxford University Press.
Clements, Jonathan. 2013. *An Armchair Traveller's History of the Silk Road*. London: bookHaus.
Daechsel, Markus. 2015. *Islamabad and the Politics of International Development in Pakistan*. Cambridge: Cambridge University Press.
Hankey, Donald and The World Bank. 1994. *Lahore, Pakistan: Conservation of the Walled City*. Washington, DC: The World Bank, South Asia Infrastructure Unit.
Kausar, S. 2012. "Shalimar Gardens Lahore: A Lost Paradise," in *The Herald Annual Special Issue "Critical Heritage: The Future of Pakistan's Past"*. Karachi: Dawn Group, 22–23.
Khan, Ahmad Nabi. 2003. *Islamic Architecture in South Asia: Pakistan–India–Bangladesh*. Oxford: Oxford University Press.
Lahore Development Authority. 1981. *The Walled City of Lahore: Strategies for Upgrading, Renewal and Conservation*. Lahore: Metropolitan Development Wing, Lahore Development Authority.
Lari, Suhail Zaheer. 1994. *A History of Sindh*. New York: Oxford University Press.

Mughal, M.R. 1998. *Heritage Legislation in Pakistan*. Paris: UNESCO.
Mumtaz, Kamil Khan. 2002. *Architecture in Pakistan*. Singapore: Concept Media.
Naeem, Anila. 2004. "Karachi: Losing its Historic Face," *NED Journal of Research in Architecture and Planning* 3: 78–91.
——. 2008. "Institutionalizing Conservation Training: South Asian Perspective – Focusing on Pakistan," in Salim Elwazani and Jamal Qawasmi (eds.), *Responsibilities and Opportunities in Architectural Conservation*, Vol 2. The Center for the Study of Architecture, CSAAR, 401–416.
——. 2013. "The Conflict of Ideologies and Ambiguities in Conservation Policy: A Legacy of Shared Built Heritage in Pakistan," in Kapila D. Silva and Neel Kamal Chapagain (eds.), *Asian Heritage Management: Contexts, Concerns and Prospects*. London: Routledge, 87–104.
Robinson, Francis (ed.). 1989. *The Cambridge Encyclopedia of India, Pakistan, Bangladesh, Sri Lanka*. Cambridge: Cambridge University Press.

19

BANGLADESH

Carved out of the traditionally Muslim region of East Bengal, and designated East Pakistan following the Partition of British India in 1947, modern Bangladesh straddles the nexus of four major river systems where they meet the Bay of Bengal. Altogether, the Jamuna-Brahmaputra, the Padma-Ganges (Ganga), the Surma-Meghna and the Padma-Meghna drain 1.6 million square kilometers of the continent, and sustain the livelihoods of up to 400 million South Asians, placing Bangladesh at a critically important geographic crossroads.[1] At just under 150,000 square kilometers (58,000 square miles), Bangladesh is a compact, politically volatile country that is home to 10 percent of the world's population, making it one of the most densely populated nations on Earth. Since independence from Pakistan in 1971 it has also consistently ranked among the poorest, with over 40 percent of its population living beneath the international poverty line.[2] This area's rich ecology has given rise to thriving indigenous cultures over the millennia, while also attracting the attention of conquering empires, beginning with the Maurya in the third century BCE on through the period of British rule that ended in the mid-twentieth century. As a result, modern Bangladesh supports an abundance of significant architectural resources, from the ancient to the modern.

Due to its unique geography, water is an ever-present factor in the lives of the Bangladeshi people, and among the most challenging factors in the conservation of the country's built environment. Each year approximately 64,000 people are displaced by riverbank erosion, a phenomenon that affects livelihoods, infrastructure and the economy, along with the population's homes, mosques, cemeteries and temples.[3] Massive, devastating floods and cyclones are perpetual threats and have killed tens of thousands of people in the twentieth century, most notably in the 1974, 1988, 1998 and 2004 floods, and the cyclones of 1970, 1991 and 2007.[4]

The symbiotic relationship of Bangladesh's lands with its rivers and seas, historically both beneficial and destructive, renders the nation and its heritage resources particularly vulnerable to the threats of climate change. As rising sea levels, extreme weather and accelerated snowmelt subject the area to an intensified risk of water inundation in the future, the role of water management in the protection of the country's built environment will become ever more critical, especially at historic architectural and archaeological sites (see sidebar on p. 454). Even in the absence of water-related natural disasters, day-to-day maintenance issues, such as proper drainage and other protective measures associated with increased moisture and rising water tables, remain critical challenges throughout the country.

Efforts to protect the country's cultural heritage sites are further complicated by a persistently volatile political and economic environment, which has diminished the country's conservation capacity along with its ability to manage heritage sites and develop effective institutions to plan and oversee conservation efforts. Finally, societal factors including poverty, population density, and religious and ethnic tension lingering from Partition and the Bangladesh War of Liberation contribute to an exceptionally challenging environment for architectural and archaeological resource conservation.

A brief architectural history of Bangladesh

The development of permanent human settlements and associated architecture in the great delta region is closely linked to the cultivation of rice, which fostered the emergence of sophisticated trading cities by the fifth century BCE. Major commercial hubs such as Tamralipti (today's Tamluk) and Lakhnauti-Gaur thrived for centuries, but their existence was always subject to the vicissitudes of adjacent rivers. The waterways regularly changed course, flooded or silted, resulting in the periodic abandonment or shifting of population centers. Hinduism, Jainism and Buddhism thrived in the early centuries CE, intermingling with indigenous faiths, and producing pre-Islamic monuments such as the influential *vihara* at Paharpur (eighth–twelfth centuries CE). Powerful Buddhist and Hindu empires, such as the Sena, held sway over the region, ruling from capitals such as the aforementioned Gaur and Navadwip, until Muslim armies from the northwest invaded in the early thirteenth century.[5]

The influence of Islam began to appear along the coast as early as the eighth century CE, a product of the trade routes that connected the delta area to the rising Muslim kingdoms to the west. The forces of the Turkic Mamluk Dynasty, based in Delhi, arrived in the Bengal delta in 1204 under the command of Muhammad bin Bakhtiyar Khilji, which, along with the proselytizing of various Sufi *pirs*, established Islam as the dominant faith in much of Bengal. By the sixteenth century CE the region had become part of the Mughal Empire. During that time, Bengal's connections to the greater world were strengthened by its prodigious export of valuable goods, particularly the ever-important rice, but also textiles such as its world-renowned muslin.[6]

Dhaka, Bangladesh's modern capital, was historically a regional center and major economic engine for the Mughal Empire. Its prosperity attracted traders from around the globe, which by the seventeenth century included Portuguese, Dutch, English and French merchants. In 1690, the British established Calcutta (today Kolkata, in West Bengal, India), a city that ultimately became the capital of British India and the hub from which the Raj expanded its reach over all of South Asia.[7] In 1905, the British viceroy, Lord Curzon, partitioned Bengal into two provinces – Bengal, and East Bengal and Assam – briefly making Dhaka (known under the British as Dacca) the capital of the latter. Political unrest led the British administration to reverse its decision in 1911, the same year that the capital of the Raj shifted to New Delhi. This episode set the stage for the later partition of Bengal that came with the creation of Pakistan and an independent India in 1947, and the difficult political epilogue that followed.[8]

The modern history of Bangladesh follows a complex political and cultural path that continues to unfold today. During the British Raj, Bengal was one of India's largest and most prominent provinces, but its division in 1947 created a Muslim-majority East Bengal, politically aligned with Pakistan and separate from the Hindu-majority West Bengal, which joined India.[9] In 1956 East Bengal was renamed East Pakistan, but cultural differences and perceived neglect from Islamabad (Pakistan's capital after 1960) created popular discontent that culminated in full-scale revolt following the devastating Bhola cyclone of 1970.[10] A brief but violent War of Liberation in 1971 lasted for nine months and resulted in full independence for Bangladesh. This hard-fought war bore a high cost, including the loss of millions of lives and outbreaks of sectarian violence but, as a result, the majority of Bengalis gained full independence for the first time since the eighteenth century. Since 1971 a series of natural and political calamities have roiled Bangladesh, including intermittent struggles between military and civilian rule, sectarian conflict between Muslims and Hindus, and an unremitting series of environmental calamities, including famine, cyclones and flooding.[11]

Bangladesh's extremes of population density and poverty remain widespread despite gradual improvements. In recent years population growth has slowed, democratic leadership has been maintained, and expanding industrial development including manufacturing has added to its traditional agricultural sector, diversifying the country's economic base.[12] But the legacy of Partition, the War of Liberation, its subsequent military dictatorships and a persistently tense political environment leaves many obstacles in the path toward establishing a stable climate where architectural conservation can flourish.

Conservation in modern Bangladesh

As is the case with India and Pakistan, the legacy of Partition also weighs heavily on modern Bangladesh. Millions of Hindus emigrated from East Bengal to India in the decades following Partition, leaving behind important Hindu heritage sites, districts and buildings within its borders.[13] These include the Panam Nagar (Panam City) district of Sonargaon, near Dhaka, a historically Hindu trading community that today is comprised of largely abandoned buildings dating from the Mughal period to the colonial era. The World Monuments Fund Watch List featured Sonargaon-Panam Nagar in 2008 citing the widespread decline of its historic buildings, attributable to deferred maintenance, flooding and abandonment.[14] Even in notoriously crowded Dhaka, traditionally Hindu districts (*mohalla*) such as the Shakhari Bazaar struggle from deterioration and abandonment due to the legacy of Partition. The Shakhari Bazaar is comprised of commercial and residential buildings, along with temples, dating from the sixteenth to the nineteenth centuries. Its resident Hindu community has long been marginalized by Independence War-era discriminatory legislation concerning property inheritance, and has also grappled with the decline of traditional trades, such as conch shell (*shankha*) carving. These conditions have led to the gradual deterioration of the neighborhood, as evidenced by the collapse of a five-storey building in 2004 that killed nineteen persons, and the estimated loss of more than 40 percent of the historic buildings in the densely populated district.[15]

Population pressures, driven by a high demand for arable or non-flooded land, frequently displace historic buildings off the sites they occupy, as they are razed or otherwise degraded in favor of other uses.[16] Since 2008, more than 500 listed historic buildings in Puran Dhaka (Old Dhaka) have been lost to development, despite their local designation as historic resources. In the capital city, the Department of Archaeology came under fierce criticism in 2015 after demolishing a section of the 400-year-old wall of the Mughal-period Lalbagh Fort to create access for a parking lot, in apparent violation of its own rules for protecting heritage sites.[17] The fort was added to UNESCO's Tentative List of World Heritage Sites in 1999 but has not been listed in part due to concerns around inappropriate rehabilitation work.[18] Lacking strong support from the government, preservation organizations find themselves in direct – and even violent – competition with building owners who are seeking to profit from Dhaka's speculative real estate market. A vivid example involves the 200-year-old Rococo-style building known as the Baro Bari, formally listed in 2009 as part of a heritage thoroughfare in Old Dhaka along

FIGURE 19.1 The deteriorating century-old French Rococo-style Baro Bari in Old Dhaka is threatened by development.

with ninety-three other buildings and eight roadways.[19] Notified that the unauthorized demolition of the building was imminent, Taimur Islam, a local architect and founder of the conservation organization the Urban Study Group (USG), rushed to the site to find a team of laborers sleeping in the building, ready to begin demolition early the next morning when government offices would be closed.[20] While demolition was temporarily averted, the episode illustrates the vigilance required even for protected buildings in Dhaka's threatened old city.

Despite these significant challenges, monsoon-driven weather patterns and a near-constant exposure to water – particularly flooding and rising damp – stand as the greatest threats to Bangladesh's built heritage. Along with the typical patterns of aging and wear, nearly all of the country's historic buildings constantly cope with high water tables and rising damp, which by capillary action draws soluble salts into brick foundations and walls, resulting in accelerated decay. Colonial-era building materials, such as wood, cast iron and plaster, that were often added to secular buildings of Bangladeshi origin, tend to fare even worse in the perpetually damp climate. Major Colonial-era sites such as the Indo-Saracenic style Ahsan Manzil palace in Dhaka (completed in 1872 on the banks of the Buriganga River), and the Chummery House, a Georgian-style civil service residence built in 1911, present persistent challenges to heritage conservationists due to their materials' interaction with Bangladesh's climate.[21]

Architectural conservation policy and practice in Bangladesh

European understanding of Bengali history expanded due to the enthusiastic scholarly documentation of ancient cultures by its colonizers during the late nineteenth and early twentieth centuries, particularly through archaeological survey and research. The Asiatic Society, established in Calcutta in 1784, carried out early surveys and archaeological investigations throughout India, including Bengal. In 1861, the Archaeological Survey of India (ASI) embarked on a series of documentation expeditions of northern India, work that also touched what is now Bangladesh.[22] By the late nineteenth century the ASI expanded its ambitions and activities, including recordation and conservation work at both Gaur and the vihara at Pahapur.[23] As a result, some of Bangladesh's most significant archaeological and architectural sites were the subject of professional documentation, research and conservation under the ASI.

The Antiquities Act of 1968, applicable to East and West Pakistan, replaced the British-era Ancient Monuments Preservation Act of 1904, forming the basis for present-day practice and regulations in Bangladesh. The newly formed parliament amended the 1968 legislation (Act No. XIV) in 1976, largely to update the pre-independence legislation to reflect Bangladesh's separation from Pakistan.[24] The 1971 Constitution addresses the need for centralized authority for heritage protection in Article 24, which requires the state to "adopt measures for the protection against disfigurement, damage or removal of all monuments, objects or places of special artistic or historic importance or interest."[25] The Antiquities Act requires the creation of an Advisory Committee comprised of the Director of the Archaeology Department, two members of parliament and three other participants "having special knowledge of antiquities," which is to be consulted in the listing of antiquities, and the resolution of disputes regarding whether or not a property is in fact an antiquity covered under the law. Under the legislation, a resource must be older than 100 years to qualify for listing.[26]

The Department of Archaeology, which sits within the Ministry of Culture, bears responsibility for conservation of monuments listed under the Antiquities Act, an inventory that today amounts to 448 sites located throughout the country.[27] This number has grown threefold since independence in 1971, when only 152 monuments were listed, marking a significant expansion of sites identified for protection under the legislation. However, staffing at the Department of Archaeology has not been expanded commensurate to this growth, and adequate funding for its operations and projects remains a chronic issue. In 2008, the director of the Archaeology Department stated that his organization was running with 28 percent less staff than needed to manage its duties.[28] The Department of Architecture, under the Ministry of Housing and Public Works, also participates in conservation projects in addition to its role in overseeing the Bangladesh National Building Code (Conservation and Rehabilitation of Historical and Cultural Heritage, 2012). While the Department of Archaeology bears primary responsibility for designation of sites under the Antiquities Act, along with excavation projects and management of World Heritage Sites, the Department of Architecture has taken on numerous conservation tasks, including adaptive reuse and reconstruction efforts.[29]

The Antiquities Act is bolstered by Section 3 of the Bangladesh National Building Code, which includes thorough, detailed regulations regarding all aspects of conservation activity, including identification of resources, documentation methods, establishment of buffer zones, public engagement concerning rehabilitation projects, and detailed specifications regarding the use of compatible building materials as part of a conservation undertaking. The Code also contains standards of practice detailing approaches to repair, consolidation and restoration of architectural elements, direction for the transfer of development rights, and guidelines for energy efficiency and sustainability. Altogether the 2012 Code outlines a detailed and forward-looking roadmap for conservation practice in Bangladesh, that is both specific to the country's environment and architectural characteristics, and in line with general best practices at the international level.[30]

While Bangladesh has many of the tools in place to support a national program, enforcement of existing laws, insufficient professional capacity and prioritization of conservation at the national level remain critical issues. Bangladesh inherited its legislation concerning *waqf* (Muslim religious trust) management and administration from its pre-independence period (1962). However, unlike in Pakistan, subsequent regulations have not been adopted in an attempt to coordinate maintenance and alterations of a historic religious property by its waqf authority with national or provincial conservation objectives.[31] In particular, pre-Mughal (1204–1576 CE) and Mughal (1576–1751 CE) mosques are frequently subject to insensitive expansions by their governing committees to meet growing communities of worshippers. In these cases, the problem does not lie in a paucity of funds, but rather in a lack of information on the part of the mosque committees as to appropriate conservation strategies that would allow for retention of portions of their historic places of worship, while also enabling expansion to meet the needs of the religious community.[32]

In spite of these efforts, in Dhaka, many conservation-minded professionals want to see greater community and institutional support of conservation. Frustrated with the lack of action on the part of the government to conserve heritage sites in Dhaka, a coalition of community activists and architects led by

FIGURE 19.2 The Puran Dhaka (Old Dhaka) district of the capital contains many examples of listed historic buildings suffering from the effects of groundwater and flooding.

architect Taimur Islam formed the Urban Study Group (USG) in 2004. In 2010, the organization filed a petition with the Supreme Court to protect 2,500 buildings in Dhaka with heritage status after finding that the century-old district council building in Old Dhaka had been demolished because it was not included on the government's existing list. The Supreme Court heard the USG's petition and in 2013 ordered the authorities concerned, including the city's development authority (known as the *Rajdhani Unnayan Kartripakkha*, or Rajuk) and the Department of Archaeology, to update the list of buildings to include heritage values and to formulate policies for protecting the sites.[33] Following this decision, the USG has continued to pressure the government, aiming to ultimately have these 2,500 buildings of architectural and historic value in Old Dhaka included on the government's official list of heritage sites.[34] As of 2015, the Rajuk began development of a new effort to guide development in Dhaka over the next twenty years, under a Detailed Area Plan (or DAP). Although previous DAPs have included heritage protection zones in Old Dhaka, as advocated for by conservationists, little action has come in the way of enforcing the plans in order to forestall destructive or inappropriate developments.[35]

Climate change and cultural heritage in South Asia, by Nathan Lott

The United Nations report, *Climate Change 2014: Impacts, Adaptation and Vulnerability* highlighted the combined risks of extreme weather, sea-level rise and poverty, prompting newspaper headlines such as: "Why South Asia is so Vulnerable to Climate Change."[36] Indeed, the implications of this global challenge for Asia are particularly acute, and it will reshape historic cities in ways heritage stewards cannot ignore. Experts now agree that significant effects of climate change are unavoidable, even as the international community attempts to curb emissions and avoid the most disastrous outcomes. This recognition has prompted many cities and nations to focus efforts on resiliency – the ability to adapt to change in ways that minimize loss and accelerate recovery from extreme weather events.

Climate change

The UN consortium of scientists known as the Intergovernmental Panel on Climate Change estimates future climatic conditions by synthesizing numerous computer models encompassing ocean currents, glacial melt, atmospheric moisture and other factors. Humanity's understanding of Earth's climate system has improved greatly since the late nineteenth century, when physicists first recognized that carbon dioxide and other heat trapping gases in the atmosphere play a key role in retaining a portion of the sun's warmth. During the same time frame, humanity's output of these climate-altering gases has accelerated greatly with the industrial revolution and, later, the rise of manufacturing in China, India and other Asian nations.

The unintended consequences of those emissions affect Asia in many ways. Warmer ocean waters will expand, contributing to sea-level rise, and produce stronger Pacific cyclones. Indian monsoons, too, will become more intense, as warmer air absorbs more moisture.[37] Between 1980 and 2010, glaciers in Nepal and Bhutan lost nearly one-quarter of their mass.[38] Accelerated melting poses the near-term risk of flooding and the long-term risk of fresh water shortages for China, India and Pakistan. Together, thermal expansion and glacial melt will raise global sea level by nearly a meter in the next 100 years. However, local effects will vary, with erosion and land subsidence aggravating factors in places like the Mekong Delta.[39]

As rising oceans absorb carbon dioxide, they will become more acidic and less hospitable to coral and other marine life. On land, warmer temperatures and extended droughts will threaten crop production. A 2012 report from the World Bank cautions that if global average temperature increases by 4°C, "all tropical islands in the Pacific will see unprecedented extreme temperatures become the new norm in all months of the year."[40]

Storms and floods

All these climatic phenomena will occur in an Asia that is rapidly changing. In many cases, human behaviors and effects on the landscape will determine the extent of climate impacts. Such was the case in Uttarakhand, India, in 2013, where deforestation, mining and dam building exacerbated flooding during a particularly heavy monsoon.[41] The rains accelerated snowmelt and melting at Chorabari Glacier, further contributing to floodwaters. An American Meteorological Society report found humanity's alteration of the climate likely contributed to the timing and severity of the monsoon.[42] However, the loss of life and cultural heritage was exacerbated by the proliferation of homes and hotels along riverbanks, some built to serve Hindu and Sikh pilgrims. Tourism to the Badrinath, Kendarth and other nearby temples had more than doubled since 2000 as economic growth and transportation infrastructure made pilgrimage attainable for more Indians.

While some mountain villages host increasing numbers of tourists, it is the coastal cities of Asia – including many ancient and colonial capitals – that have grown most significantly in recent decades. That growth increases assets at-risk and may compound vulnerability as forests and marsh give way to buildings and pavement. One analysis of 393 cities in thirty-one developing nations found that just ten Asian cities account for half the potential damages from cyclonic storm surges – the phenomenon of flooding that occurs when a tropical storm makes landfall.[43] In fact, Manila, Karachi and Jakarta alone shoulder 40 percent of the risk (another study found that Bangladesh and India currently experience 86 percent of cyclone mortality, reflecting their vulnerable populations).[44]

Historic cities located near river deltas are vulnerable to flooding from both river and sea, and rapid urbanization may increase exposure. Such is the case in Thailand, where the ancient capital of Ayutthaya north of Bangkok was inundated by the Chao Phraya River in 2011.[45] Though Ayutthaya was built well inland from the ocean, subsequent development filled many of the area's historic *klongs*, or canals; this diminished their capacity to channel water to sea or absorb influx at high tide. Nearby settlements also saw flooding in 2013 and 2014, and some areas of the city nearest the coast see recurrent flooding at high tide.[46] Site visits by ICOMOS and ICCROM spurred Thailand's Fine Arts Department to develop a disaster mitigation plan; among the early results is a floodwall for Panan Cherng Wora Wiharn Temple that can be raised or lowered as needed.[47] The flood barrier not only protects a Buddha statue venerated by the local populace but also transforms the temple into a place of refuge. This insightful approach aligns heritage protection with public safety.

Rising seas

Low-lying and laced with rivers, Bangladesh is for many the primary example of climate change's disproportionate impacts on Asia – and on the poor in particular. The World Bank recently warned:

> [T]he impacts of progressive global warming will fall hardest on the poor. Low crop yields and associated income loss from agriculture will continue the trend toward migration from rural to urban centers. In Bangladesh, 40 percent of productive land is projected to be lost in the southern region of Bangladesh for a 65cm sea level rise by the 2080s. About 20 million people in the coastal areas of Bangladesh are already affected by salinity in drinking water.[48]

The Sundarbans natural heritage area in southwestern Bangladesh is particularly vulnerable to sea-level rise, and loss of the surrounding wetlands will leave Dhaka more exposed to storm surge.

However, human migration may constitute the greater risk factor to heritage sites like the Lalmai-Mainamati group of monuments in Bangladesh's Comilla region. Dating to the seventh through twelfth centuries CE, these stonework and earthen ruins dot an 18 km ridge of relatively high ground between Dhaka and Chittagong. They are remnants of the religious center from which Buddhism was carried to Southeast Asia. Protecting these fifty dispersed sites and the wealth of archaeological information they contain will require careful land-use planning and enforcement in the face of climate-driven migration.

A 2014 study examined likely sea-level rise impacts on UNESCO World Heritage Sites and found that an increase in global mean temperature of 2°C would correlate with eventual sea-level rise sufficient to partially inundate the historic mosque city of Bagerhat, Bangladesh; Chhatrapati Shivaji Terminus, the churches and convents of Goa, Elephanta Caves, and monuments at Mahabalipuram in India; and Hội An Ancient Town in Vietnam.[49] Warming of 4°C would threaten additional sites in India, Pakistan, the Philippines, Sri Lanka, Thailand and Vietnam.

The Mekong River passes through six nations on its way from the Tibetan Plateau to the Pacific Ocean, and human activity along its course has profound implications for the delta's resiliency in the face of rising seas. Saltwater intrusion claimed 60 km² of the delta's arable land in 2014.[50] Apparent solutions may aggravate the problem: withdrawing groundwater for drinking, irrigation and industry is causing land subsidence at a rate sufficient to cause the land to sink 0.8 m or more by 2050.[51] Upriver, six Chinese dams built for hydropower – a low-emissions electricity source – have become unintended sediment traps. The dams prevent stones and silt from being carried downstream, stalling the delta's natural land-building system. The rice fields of the Mekong Delta are a cultural landscape fast disappearing. It remains to be seen if the construction of dykes and weirs can stall the retreat.[52]

While the Mekong illustrates the difficulty of managing natural resources across national boundaries, the islands of Maldives – often cited as the flattest nation on the globe – face the challenge of managing overwhelming change in relative isolation. In 2007, the republic issued a climate adaptation plan that called for consolidating population and development, shoreline protection through hard and soft infrastructure, and protecting House Reef.[53] The latter is doubly important because the reef both protects the islands from storm surge and erosion and serves as the centerpiece of its tourism

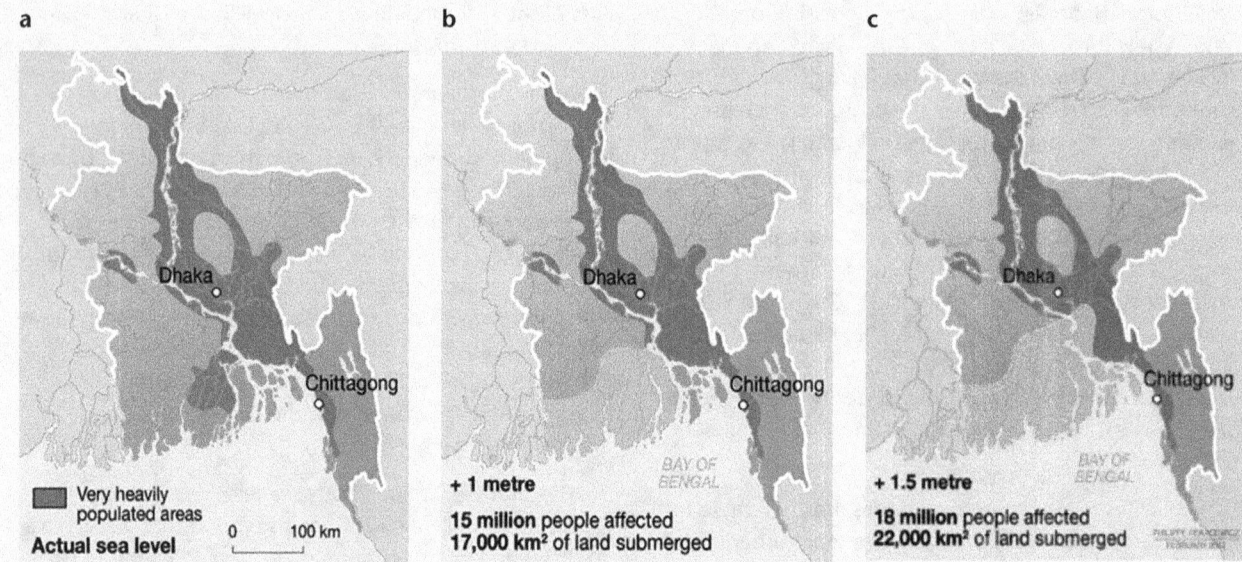

FIGURE 19.3a, b and c Images from the UN Intergovernmental Panel on Climate Change report showing land loss in Bangladesh under sea-level rise scenarios of 1 and 1.5 m.

economy. However, abnormally warm ocean currents have twice bleached the corals (killing off symbiotic algae), and ocean acidification is a long-term threat.[54] The Maldives ca. 1,700 coral stone mosques – made of blocks cut from nearby reefs – are testimony to the interlacing of nature and culture that has characterized the Maldives in the past and will do so in the future.

Rohit Jigyasu, president of ICOMOS India, writing in World Heritage Review No. 74, posits that climate change may adversely affect built heritage, rendering it more vulnerable to non-climate disasters like earthquakes: "higher temperatures, wider temperature fluctuation and relative humidity, are often responsible for the aggravation of underlying risk factors, which increase the vulnerability of heritage properties and contribute to disasters." This underscores the importance of maintenance and repair at historic sites and cities in south Asia, even as nations invest in sustainable development out of harm's way.

For heritage stewards working in twenty-first century Asia, an understanding of climate change and its likely effects on cultural property is essential. Those who find strategies that contribute to societal goals – flood protection, pollution reduction, food security – while protecting historic places can serve as models for deliberate preservation in the midst of change. With the advent of the December 2015 Paris Agreement on climate change, strategies may yet emerge for reversing course, if indeed it is not too late for meaningful action.

Further reading

Coletter, Augustin and Kishore Rao (eds.). "Archaeological Sites" and "Historic Cities and Settlements." *Case Studies on Climate Change and World Heritage.* (Paris: UNESCO, 2007), 54–77. Web. http://whc.unesco.org/en/activities/473. Accessed May 20, 2016.

Jigyasu, Rohit. "Fostering Resilience: Towards Reducing Disaster Risks to World Heritage." *World Heritage Review* 74 (2014), 4–13. Web. http://en.calameo.com/read/00332997281ba181741f8. Accessed May 20, 2016.

Vachani, Sushil and Jaweed Usman (eds.). *Adaptation to Climate Change in Asia.* (Cheltenham, UK: Edward Elgar Publishing, 2014). Web. www.elgaronline.com/view/9781781954720.xml. Accessed May 20, 2016.

Vujicic-Lugassy, Vesna and Laura Frank (eds.). *Managing Disaster Risks for World Heritage.* (Paris: UNESCO, 2010), 1–66.

World Bank. *Turn Down the Heat: Climate Extremes, Regional Impacts and the Case for Resilience.* (Washington DC: International Bank for Reconstruction and Development/The World Bank, 2013), 1–213. Web. www-wds.worldbank.org/external/default/WDSContentServer/WDSP/IB/2013/06/14/000445729_20130614145941/Rendered/PDF/784240WP0Full00D0CONF0to0June19090L.pdf. Accessed May 20, 2016.

Contemporary examples of architectural conservation

The ancient architecture of Bangladesh is characterized by its use of brick, a necessity in an area largely free of suitable building stone and lumber but with abundant supplies of clay. Ironically, the attractiveness of brick and the lack of awareness of the value of heritage conservation in rural communities have threatened some of Bangladesh's archaeological sites, where residents commonly "recycle" historic materials to build housing. In the late twentieth century, the common use of traditional brick has been supplanted by concrete block faced with stucco. Whereas exposed brickwork generally requires minimal upkeep, stucco tends to turn black with biological growth and peel, and requires repeated whitewashing when subjected to monsoon conditions.[55]

A perpetual lack of funds and the frequent use of incompatible new building materials such as concrete, wood and corrugated sheet metal to repair or expand traditionally constructed buildings have led to a number of unsuccessful rehabilitations of important buildings throughout Bangladesh. At the early eighteenth century Star Mosque in Armanitola, for example, an incongruous corrugated metal structure was added to the mosque to accommodate a growing congregation.[56] At the 1905 Old High Court in Dhaka, multiple additions, both interior and exterior, were constructed with materials ranging from concrete to corrugated metal and wood.[57] The seventeenth century Chhoto Katra palace, a Mughal-era administrative complex in Old Dhaka, is in danger of being subsumed by unauthorized constructions, ranging from vendor stalls inside its archways to adjacent multi-storey buildings immediately adjacent.[58] This ad hoc approach to modifying buildings using incongruous materials and features has disfigured the architectural forms and detailing of many significant structures in Bangladesh, diminishing their historic and cultural presence in the built environment.

Conservation of the historic contexts of the country's more important historic sites is seldom emphasized, resulting in isolated architectural landmarks surrounded by intrusive and insensitive development. Old Dhaka constitutes both the historic and commercial core of the city, and hastily built new construction is frequently incompatible and out of scale with the existing urban fabric,

FIGURE 19.4 Completed in 1872, the Ahsan Manzil, the palace and grounds of the Nawabs of Dhaka, was damaged due to neglect and intrusions on its site, including the nearby construction of a shopping center. After seven years of rehabilitation beginning in 1985 the shopping center was removed, the building and riverside site was restored, and the building began to operate under the auspices of the Bangladesh National Museum.

notably with the remaining Mughal-era structures. In addition, over time the river has changed its course and moved away from the Mughal settlements, creating space for new construction that obscures the visibility of historic buildings from the river as well as from other parts of the city.[59]

Despite the challenges, examples of successful conservation and adaptive reuse projects are to be found in Dhaka. An early post-independence conservation project involved the adaptive reuse of the previously mentioned Ahsan Manzil palace and grounds. A tornado badly damaged the palace in 1888, triggering a major rebuilding campaign that resulted in its current Indo-Saracenic design. The graceful two-storey domed structure, oriented toward the river, fell into decline in the early twentieth century. Many years of neglect eventually led to threats of structural collapse, a situation complicated by the large community of squatters and descendants of the Nawab's family that had sub-divided the rooms and occupied the building in the decades following the patriarch's death. The surrounding grounds had also been sub-divided, and a shopping center was constructed at the building's rear.

Because of its prominent location along the Buriganga River in 1985 the government began to restore the palace and convert it to a national museum. Leading up to the extensive restoration, governmental teams documented the building, replaced heavily deteriorated brickwork, and moved to protect it against future dampness and damaging salt by re-grading the site and improving roof drainage. Many missing elements were replaced, including decorative cast-iron work, marble flooring and sandstone details obtained from both local and Indian sources. The multi-storey shopping center was cleared in order to partially restore the original grounds. Rehabilitation was completed in 1992. By 2015, the site had become a key museum in Bangladesh.[60]

Conservation of modern architecture

An issue of particular concern in Bangladesh, and one that is shared with many parts of the developing and developed world, is conservation of the nation's modern architecture. Bangladesh is home to a number of important twentieth-century buildings, chief among them the concrete, marble and brick *Jatiyo Sangsad Bhaban*, the National Assembly building, which was designed by the American architect Louis I. Kahn.

Soon after a second Pakistani capital was established at Dhaka in 1959, Kahn was asked to prepare studies for a National Assembly building to house the government in the east. The design was intended to celebrate the democracy and modernity of the new state while incorporating influences from local architectural styles, especially Islamic pre-Mughal and Mughal architecture. Construction work on the 840-acre complex began in 1966, but ground to a halt during the civil war in 1971 with only three-quarters of the complex completed. After twenty years of construction, Kahn's monumental assembly building opened in 1983, and today sits in the midst of an artificial lake, plazas, landscapes and peripheral hostels for housing legislators that are all part of the original design.[61] Commended for its design, which "drew upon and assimilated both the vernacular and monumental archetypes of the region," the National Assembly received the Aga Khan Award for Architecture in 1989 and is recognized today as a masterwork of modern architecture.[62]

Although he initially met with some resistance in a country that experiences excessive floods and rains, Kahn insisted on water as a motif in the setting of the buildings and in the landscaping for the Assembly grounds. The intention was to demonstrate the importance of the control of water. With the implementation of shallow lakes interconnected with canals that drain water away from the site, the National Assembly building appears to rise out of and float on water.[63]

However, even with modern drainage systems in place, the modern complex of buildings faces threats from water and wind. Kahn had designed the building to respond to regional conditions by using local materials and planning for the exigencies of extreme weather, with deeply recessed windows intended to protect against wind and rain. However, the buildings had to be modified when it became clear that frequent wind-driven rains were so intrusive that it was necessary to cover windows and replace materials. Heavy rainfall had also penetrated some of the brickwork.[64]

Since construction, several additions to the grounds of the assembly complex were made that were not part of Kahn's original design, including residences built by the parliamentary speaker and deputy speaker, and the graves of several prominent Bangladeshi politicians.[65] In 2015, the prime minister directed the Ministry of Housing and Public Works to begin restoring the National Assembly's grounds. Work will include the relocation of the graves of two former presidents and two prime ministers, among others, in a bid to restore elements of Kahn's original design.[66]

Bangladeshi architect Muzharul Islam, whose regional modern style characterized by an open, airy aesthetic was pioneered in the post-independence years, has been instrumental in bringing internationally recognized modern architects including Kahn, Richard Neutra and Paul Rudolph to Bangladesh.[67] Islam's significant works include several buildings on the campus of Dhaka University (1953–1954) and the National Library (1980–1984). Nevertheless, conservation of Islam's important buildings remains a challenge, as exemplified by the insensitive addition of a telephone transmission tower to the main university library building, raising concerns on the part of architects and conservation professionals alike.

a

b

FIGURE 19.5a and b Designed to acknowledge and celebrate the nation's inextricable relationship with water, the National Assembly building in Dhaka, designed by the American architect Louis Kahn, has suffered from dampness and buffeting by monsoon conditions (a, b).

As a relatively young independent nation, Bangladesh has developed a strong sense of cultural identity from its archaeological resources, which lend a special importance to the national Archaeology Department. Much of the work of conserving Bangladeshi built heritage concerns monumental ruins and archaeological sites. Most notably, these include Mahasthangarh (fortified ruins dating from the fourth century BCE through the seventeenth century CE) and Bangladesh's two cultural World Heritage Sites, Paharpur (a Buddhist *vihara* dating to the eighth century CE)[68] and Bagerhat (the fifteenth century capital of Ulugh Khan-i-Jahan). The work at Mahasthangarh has proceeded productively since 1993 under a joint French–Bangladeshi archaeological team, revealing flourishing pre-Islamic eras associated with the Gupta (fourth–sixth centuries CE) and Pala-Sena periods (eighth–twelfth century CE) expanding the local and international visibility of this important era of Bangladesh's history.[69]

Located in the northwestern Naogaon district, the extensive ruins at Paharpur constitute one of the largest and most architecturally influential Buddhist sites in South Asia, and as such stands among the most important pre-Islamic sites in Bangladesh. In use from the eighth through twelfth centuries CE and a World Heritage Site since 1985, the site is in great need of a comprehensive conservation and management plan to address natural deterioration and several misguided conservation interventions that have contributed to its compromised state. For centuries, environmental salinity and plant growth have attacked the masonry and terracotta material used in the temple buildings. In the 1930s the problem was exacerbated by the use of salt-laden bricks and mortar as part of a conservation program. In recent years, vandalism and theft triggered the authorities' removal of the structure's distinctive terracotta plaques for safekeeping.

Beginning in 1984 UNESCO, in collaboration with the Department of Archaeology (then called the Department of Archaeology and Museums), the Norwegian Organization for Development Cooperation (NORAD), and the government of Japan, launched an ambitious "International

FIGURE 19.6 Conservation of the ancient site of Mahasthangarh by the Archaeology Department in cooperation with the French archaeologists of the France–Bangladesh Joint Venture organization has increased the visibility of Bangladesh's cultural heritage.

Campaign to Safeguard the Ancient Monuments and Site of Paharpur Vihara and Those of the Historic Mosque City of Bagerhat." This was carried out over three phases until the program's conclusion in 2002. The focus of the campaign was primarily on capacity building for Department of Archaeology (DOA) staff in particular, but also on skills training in Bangladeshi institutions in general. Staff training efforts sought to provide Bangladeshi professionals with opportunities to study abroad and connect with international colleagues on best practices through on-site conservation activities at the properties themselves. Ultimately, the Campaign's accomplishments included construction of a site museum at each location, land acquisition to secure buffer zones, and integration of information about the sites in Bangladeshi national educational curricula, thereby raising awareness of the country's World Heritage properties and ancient history. Campaign shortcomings included uneven results in its professional development and capacity-building efforts. In particular, according to UNESCO's evaluation of the program, the effort appears to have struggled to reinforce the application of internationally accepted conservation strategies within DOA staff, and to create sustained opportunities for organizational improvement that would fundamentally address the critical issue of providing a well-trained cadre of professionals to manage the country's heritage sites.[70]

In 2009 the World Heritage Committee called for developing a comprehensive management plan at Paharpur, including improvements to the site's drainage system, identification of a well-defined buffer zone, and enhanced staffing, citing the possibility that the site could be added to the List of World Heritage in Danger. The establishment of a protective buffer zone around the site is critical due to nearby coal mining activities that resulted in a series of tunnels beneath the temple complex, and the importance of maintaining visual and contextual relationships between the complex and its natural environment. Due to understaffing in the Department of Archaeology, many key conservation decisions were made in isolation, and the World Heritage Committee recommended refraining from carrying out major conservation work until the complete management plan is in place.[71]

In a promising development aimed at fostering regional cooperation around heritage sites, in 2013 the Asian Development Bank (ADB) initiated a multi-year, US$12 million project in cooperation

FIGURE 19.7 The extensive ruins of the Buddhist vihara at Paharpur, a pre-Islamic temple complex that was used as a monastery in the eighth through twelfth centuries CE, were inscribed on the UNESCO World Heritage List in 1985. Despite multi-phased efforts to conserve and present Paharpur Vihara, in 2009 the World Heritage Committee called for a holistic management plan for the site.

with the Government of Bangladesh to improve tourism infrastructure at Paharpur, Mahasthangarh and Bagerhat, along with Kantaji (an eighteenth century Hindu temple complex in Dinajpur district). Through a series of loans, the bank aims to support enhanced transportation networks between and around the target sites, enhance on-site facilities such as visitor centers, and conduct capacity building among Archaeology Department staff. Activities are coordinated with similar efforts in Nepal and India under the South Asia Tourism Infrastructure Development Project, which aims to create connections between heritage sites and supporting facilities (including airports and utility systems) in the neighboring nations to foster economic development.[72] Although the ADB did not initially place conservation at the center of the program, it has since emerged as a key component. The work in Bangladesh will also produce management plans for the four target sites, in addition to site improvements in a bid to address management and infrastructure in a holistic manner.[73]

Bangladesh is home to many important expressions of traditional South Asian art and architecture, from Mughal-period works to urban districts that date from the British colonial period. Nationalism, spurred by a relatively recent independence movement, and a desire to distinguish itself from its neighbors and former colonial counterparts, India and Pakistan, have encouraged government policies aimed at enhancing the status of Bangladeshi arts and culture, including architecture. To date, international assistance has tended to focus on archaeological sites such as Mahasthangarh, Paharpur and Bagerhat. The limited resources and competing priorities of the national government have complicated efforts by conservationists to counter the forces of nature and development that compromise the nation's significant built heritage, particularly in its urban areas. Despite the existence of conservation regulations, even acknowledged heritage sites are subjected to insensitive or illegal alterations that threaten their eligibility, in some cases on the part of the very agencies that are tasked with protecting them.

Conservation of Bangladesh's rich architectural heritage faces an array of challenging problems, including unresolved conflicts from the eras of partition and independence, high levels of poverty, population density, ongoing political instability, and government corruption and inability to effectively conserve the nation's architectural heritage. But in a country that is recognized as among the world's most vulnerable to climate change, by far the biggest threats to conservation are rising seas and increasing intensity of storms, which will have dire consequences for buildings and sites that already struggle with the effects of water and extreme weather. Without concerted efforts on the part of government agencies, and without rapid improvement of the country's economic conditions, the loss of the country's significant historic sites as well as the deterioration of modern buildings will continue. There are many factors in Bangladesh, such as the presence of local organizations like the Urban Study Group, and a history of sustained international collaboration on conservation projects, that indicate a potential for improvement in architectural conservation, but the challenges remain great and time short.

Notes

1   Guy Arnold. *World Strategic Highways*. (London: Routledge, 2000), 223.
2   The International Poverty Line is defined as one person living on US$1.25 per day in 2005 dollars. Source: UNICEF. "Bangladesh Statistics." 2015. Web. www.unicef.org/infobycountry/bangladesh_bangladesh_statistics.html. Accessed November 16, 2015.
3   *The Economist*. "Bangladesh: The Game of the River." April 19, 2014. Web. www.economist.com/news/asia/21601053-last-bangladesh-starts-tame-mighty-brahmaputra-game-river. Accessed December 12, 2015.
4   BBC News. "Bangladesh Country Profile: Timeline." 2015. Web. www.bbc.com/news/world-south-asia-12651483. Accessed December 12, 2015.
5   Willem van Schendel. *A History of Bangladesh*. (Cambridge: Cambridge University Press, 2009), 11–24.
6   Muslin, a thin cotton fabric, was a cherished commodity produced in Bengal for centuries, and among the earliest drivers of European colonial interest beginning in the sixteenth century. Source: Van Schendel, 24–31.
7   The capital of British India moved from Calcutta to New Delhi in 1911. Dhaka, known under the British as Dacca, was briefly the capital of East Bengal and Assam. The partition of East and West Bengal, which lasted only from 1905 to 1912, set the stage for the later partition of India and East Pakistan in 1947.
8   Joya Chatterji. *The Spoils of Partition: Bengal and India, 1947–1967*. (Cambridge: Cambridge University Press, 2007), 9–10.

9 William Dalrymple. "The Great Divide: The Violent Legacy of Indian Partition," *The New Yorker*, June 29, 2015.
10 The Bhola cyclone is considered one of the worst natural disasters in recorded history, attributable for an estimated 500,000 deaths. The slow relief response on the part of the national government based in West Pakistan led to increased support for the pro-independence Awami League the following year, which escalated into the Bangladesh War of Liberation. Source: Palash Ghosh. "Hurricane Sandy: The Bhola Cyclone in Bangladesh Killed Half-Million in 1970," *International Business Times*. October 29, 2012. Web. www.ibtimes.com/hurricane-sandy-bhola-cyclone-bangladesh-killed-half-million-1970-855356. Accessed December 12, 2015.
11 Ahmed Salahuddin. *Bangladesh: Past and Present*. (New Delhi: APH Publishing. 2004), 1.
12 BBC News. "Bangladesh Country Profile." October 8, 2015. Web. www.bbc.com/news/world-south-asia-12650940. Accessed November 15, 2015.
13 Bangladesh's population today is 86 percent Muslim. Source: Government of Bangladesh. "Bangladesh National Portal: Know Bangladesh." 2015. Web. http://bangladesh.gov.bd/. Accessed November 16, 2015.
14 World Monuments Fund. "Sonargaon-Panam City: 2008 Watch List." 2015. Web. www.wmf.org/project/sonargaon-panam-city. Accessed November 16, 2015.
15 In 1965 the government of Pakistan passed the "Enemy Property Act," which facilitated confiscation of property owned in Pakistan by Hindus who had migrated to India. The Act was revised as the Vested Property Act after the Independence War, but continues to drive displacement in traditionally Hindu communities across Bangladesh. Taimur Islam and Homaira Zaman. "Conservation of a Historic *Mohalla*," *The Daily Star* (Dhaka), April 21, 2006. Web. http://archive.thedailystar.net/magazine/2006/04/03/cover.htm. Accessed November 16, 2015.
16 Saha Alam Zahiruddin. "Bangladesh's Experience in Architectural Conservation: Five Projects," in Abu H. Imamuddin and Karen R. Longeteig (eds.), *Architectural and Urban Conservation in the Islamic World*. (Geneva: The Aga Khan Trust for Culture. 1990), 109.
17 Abid Azad. "Authorities Demolish Lalbagh Fort Wall to Build Car Park," *Dhaka Tribune*, June 28, 2015. Web. http://dhakatribune.com/bangladesh/2015/jun/26/authorities-demolish-lalbagh-fort-wall-build-car-park. Accessed December 12, 2015.
18 Tawfique Ali. "Nothing Done to Protect Heritage Sites," *The Daily Star* (Dhaka). June 15, 2008. Web. http://archive.thedailystar.net/newDesign/story/php?nid=41159. Accessed November 16, 2015.
19 Md Mizanur Rahman Himadri. "Blame Game Bars Preservation," *The Daily Star* (Bangladesh). September 22, 2014. Web. www.thedailystar.net/blame-game-bars-preservtion-42805. Accessed December 12, 2015.
20 Tansy Hoskins. "Old Dhaka in Danger: Young Volunteers Bid to Save Historic City from Developers," *The Guardian*, March 11, 2015. Web. www.theguardian.com/cities/2015/mar/11/old-dhaka-danger-young-volunteers-save-historic-city-developers. Accessed December 12, 2015.
21 Zahiruddin, 103.
22 Chapter 16 (India) contains a detailed discussion of the role of the Archaeological Survey of India in South Asia during the British period. See also: "History" on the Archaeological Survey of India website. http://asi.nic.in/asi_aboutus_history.asp. Accessed November 14, 2015.
23 John Cumming (ed.). *Revealing India's Past: A Cooperative Record of Archaeological Conservation and Exploration in India and Beyond*. (London: The India Society, 1939), 19, 46.
24 Iftikhar-ul-Awwal. "Heritage Management in Bangladesh: An Appraisal," *Bangladesh National Museum Newsletter* 4(4)–5(1) (October–December 2002 and January–March 2003), 8. As of 2015 there is an effort to update the Antiquities Act, with draft legislation having been submitted to parliamentary committee for consideration. Source: Mohiuddin Alamgir. "Draft Antiquities Act 2015: Government to Ban Structure within 250m of Heritage Sites." *New Age* (Bangladesh). June 20, 2015. Web. http://newagebd.net/131169/draft-antiquities-act-2015. Accessed December 12, 2015.
25 UNESCO 2005 Convention on the Protection and Promotion of the Diversity of Cultural Expressions: Quadrennial Report on Measures to Protect and Promote the Diversity of Cultural Expressions. Bangladesh State Party Submittal (April 30, 2013). Web. http://en.unesco.org/creativity/sites/creativity/files/periodic_report/Bangladesh_Report_OwnFormat_EN_2013_0.pdf. Accessed December 12, 2015.
26 Government of Bangladesh. The Antiquities Act, 1968 (with 1976 amendments). 2015. Web. http://bdlaws.minlaw/gov/bd/print_sections_all.php?id=353. Accessed December 12, 2015.
27 Since some listings include multiple buildings, this amounts to over 500 individual structures. Source: Logan UNESCO report.
28 Ali.
29 Zahiruddin, 97.

30 Government of Bangladesh. Bangladesh National Building Code, Chapter 3: "Conservation and Rehabilitation of Historical and Cultural Heritage." 2012. Web. https://law.resource.org/pub/bd/bnbc/2012/gov.bd.bnbc.2012.09.03.pdf. Accessed December 12, 2015.

31 The Waqfs Ordinance (1962). Government of Bangladesh. 2010. Web. http://bdlaws.minlaw.gov.bd/print_sections_all.php?id=326. Accessed December 12, 2015.

32 Fariel Kahn. "Unplanned Modernization May Lead to Threat to Architectural Heritage: A Case of Historic Mosques of Dhaka City," *International Journal of Research in Engineering and Technology* 4(2) (February 2015), 499–517.

33 Himadri.

34 Akram Hosen Mamun. "Architectural Visions to Save Dhaka's Heritage Sites," *The Daily Star*. June 21, 2011. Web. http://architve.thedailystar.net/newDesign/print_news.php?nid=190794. Accessed December 12, 2015.

35 "New Dhaka Master Plan in Making." *The Daily Star* (Bangladesh). September 14, 2015. Web. www.thedailystar.net/city/new-dhaka-master-plan-making-142786. Accessed December 12, 2015.

36 Neal Bhatiya. "Why South Asia is so Vulnerable to Climate Change," *Foreign Policy* (April 22, 2014). Web. http://foreignpolicy.com/2014/04/22/why-south-asia-is-so-vulnerable-to-climate-change/. Accessed November 15, 2015.

37 Andy Turner. "The Indian Monsoon in a Changing Climate." Royal Meteorological Society. 2012. Web. www.rmets.org/weather-and-climate/climate/indian-monsoon-changing-climate. Accessed May 20, 2016.

38 Amy Sellmyer (ed.). *Glacier Status in Nepal and Decadal Change from 1980 to 2010 Based on Landsat Data*. (Kathmandu, Nepal: International Centre for Integrated Mountain Development, 2014).

39 Laura Erban, Steven Gorelick and Howard Zebker. "Groundwater Extraction, Land Subsidence, and Sea-Level Rise in the Mekong Delta, Vietnam." *Environmental Research Letters* 9(15) (August 2014).

40 Potsdam Institute for Climate Impact Research and Climate Analytics. *Turn Down The Heat: Why a 4°C Warmer World Must Be Avoided* (Washington, DC: World Bank. 2012). Web. www-wds.worldbank.org/external/default/WDSContentServer/WDSP/IB/2012/12/20/000356161_20121220072749/Rendered/PDF/NonAsciiFileName0.pdf. Accessed May 20, 2016.

41 Yadavm Narendra and Vivekanand Sahani. "Case Study of Uttarakhand Flood Disaster – 2103." Web. www.slideshare.net/ynarendra/uttrakhand-disaster-flood-2013. Accessed May 20, 2016.

42 Deepti Singh, Daniel E. Horton, Michael Tsiang, Matz Haugen, Moetasim Ashfaq, Rui Mei, Deeksha Rastogi, Nathaniel C. Johnson, Allison Charland, Bala Rajaratnam and Noah S. Diffenbaugh. "Severe Precipitation in Northern India in June 2013: Causes, Historical Context, and Changes in Probability," *Explaining Extreme Events of 2013 from a Climate Perspective: Special Supplement to the Bulletin of the American Meteorological Society* 95(9) (September 2014). Web. www2.ametsoc.org/ams/assets/File/publications/BAMS_EEE_2013_Full_Report.pdf. Accessed May 20, 2016.

43 Henrike Brecht, Susmita Dasgupta, Benoit Laplante, Siobhan Murray and David Wheeler. "Sea-Level Rise and Storm Surges: High Stakes for a Small Number of Developing Countries," *The Journal of Environment and Development* (January 2012). Web. http://jed.sagepub.com/content/early/2012/01/23/1070496511433601.abstract. Accessed May 20, 2016.

44 V. Murray, G. McBean, M. Bhatt, S. Borsch, T.S. Cheong, W.F. Erian, S. Llosa, F. Nadim, M. Nunez, R. Oyun, and A.G. Suarez. "Case Studies," in *Managing the Risks of Extreme Events and Disasters to Advance Climate Change Adaptation. A Special Report of Working Groups I and II of the Intergovernmental Panel on Climate Change* (Cambridge: Cambridge University Press, 2012).

45 Mishka Stuip and Jan Luijendijk. "Flood Risk Assessment Historic Bangkok (Ayutthaya)." Asian Development Bank and UNESCO-IHE Knowledge Partnership. Web. http://adb-knowledge-partnership.unesco-ihe.org/flood-risk-assessment-historic-bangkok-ayutthaya. Accessed May 20, 2016.

46 Somkid Buapeng. "Groundwater Situation and Land Subsidence Mitigation in Bangkok and Its Vicinity." Department of Groundwater Resources, Thailand Ministry of Natural Resources and Environment (ca. 2007). Web. http://siteresources.worldbank.org/INTWRD/Resources/Somkid_Buapeng_Ministry_of_Groundwater_Resources_Thailand_Groundwater_in_Bangkok.pdf. Accessed May 20, 2016.

47 "Thailand: Ayutthaya to Get New Flood Wall," *Dredging Today*, August 29, 2013. Web.www.dredgingtoday.com/2013/08/29/thailand-ayutthaya-to-get-new-flood-wall/. Accessed May 20, 2016.

48 *Turn Down The Heat*.

49 Benjamin Marzeion and Anders Levermann. "Loss of Cultural World Heritage and Currently Inhabited Places to Sea-Level Rise" (supplemental figures). *Environmental Research Letters* (2014).

50 Navin Singh Khadka. "Climate Change: Mekong Delta Heads for Troubled Waters." BBC World Service. October 20, 2015. Web. www.bbc.com/news/science-environment-34407061. Accessed May 20, 2016.

51 Laura Erban, Steven Gorelick and Howard Zebker. "Groundwater Extraction, Land Subsidence, and Sea-level Rise in the Mekong Delta, Vietnam," *Environmental Research Letters* (August 15, 2014), 9. Web. http://iopscience.iop.org/article/10.1088/1748-9326/9/8/084010/pdf. Accessed May 20, 2016.

52 Viet Hoaa, Le Thi, Nguyen Huu Nhanb, Eric Wolanski, Tran Thanh Congb and Haruyama Shigekoa. "The Combined Impact on the Flooding in Vietnam's Mekong River Delta of Local Man-made Structures, Sea Level Rise, and Dams Upstream in the River Catchment," *Estuarine, Coastal and Shelf Science* (October 12, 2006), 71. Web. www.researchgate.net/publication/222428368_The_combined_impact_on_the_flooding_in_Vietnam's_Mekong_River_delta_of_local_man-made_structures_sea_level_rise_and_dams_upstream_in_the_river_catchment. Accessed May 20, 2016.

53 Ministry of Environment, Energy and Water. *National Adaptation Program of Action*. Republic of Maldives. 2007. Web. http://unfccc.int/resource/docs/napa/mdv01.pdf. Accessed May 20, 2016.

54 Jon Bowermaster. "Warming Seas Continue to Plague Coral Reefs in Maldives." *National Geographic*. October 24, 2011. Web. http://voices.nationalgeographic.com/2011/10/24/coral-reefs-in-maldives-hit-by-second-bleaching-event/. Accessed May 20, 2016.

55 "Architecture for Islamic Societies: National Assembly Building, Dhaka, Bangladesh". *Aga Khan Awards for Architecture, 1989*, 131.

56 Zahiruddin, 105.

57 Ibid., 106.

58 Ananta Yusuf. "Chhoto Katra on Verge of Destruction," *The Daily Star* (Bangladesh). October 20, 2015. Web. www.thedailystar.net/city/chhoto-katra-verge-destruction-159964. Accessed December 12, 2015.

59 Mohammad Sazzad Hossain. "Strategies to Integrate the Mughal Settlements in Old Dhaka," *Frontiers of Architectural Research* 2(4) (December 2013), 420–434.

60 Zahiruddin, 99, 102–103.

61 "National Assembly Building of Bangladesh," *Architectuul*. 2015. Web. http://architectuul.com/architecture/national-assembly-building-of-bangladesh. Accessed November 16, 2015.

62 "Architecture for Islamic Societies: National Assembly Building, Dhaka, Bangladesh." *Aga Khan Awards for Architecture, 1989*.

63 Ibid., 131.

64 Ibid., 131–133.

65 Lisa Rochon. "Hands off Arthur Erikson," *The Globe and Mail* (Toronto). June 30, 2004, R1.

66 Media accounts at the time suggest that the bid to restore Kahn's landscape may in fact be another symptom of Bangladesh's caustic political environment, with the relocated graves belonging to members of the ruling government's chief opposition. "Actions Underway to Preserve Louis Kahn's Design of Bangladesh Parliament," *News Next BD*. November 16, 2015. Web. http://newsnextbd.com/actions-underway-to-preserve-louis-kahns-design-of-bangladesh-parliament/. Accessed November 16, 2015.

67 Tawfique Ali. "DU Defies Building Rules and Codes-IV: Defacing the Distinct Features of Architectural Works," *The Daily Star* (Dhaka). November 11, 2007.

68 Vihara is the Sanskrit and Pali term for a Buddhist monastery.

69 France in Bangladesh: Embassy of France in Dhaka. "The Franco Bangladeshi Archaeological Mission." October 7, 2012. Web. www.ambafrance-bd.org/The-Franco-Bangladeshi. Accessed December 12, 2015.

70 William Logan. *Evaluation Report Bangladesh: The International Campaign for the Protection, Preservation, Restoration and Presentation of the Ancient Monuments of Paharpur Vihara and those of the Mosque City of Bagerhat*. UNESCO Report (June 2001). Web. http://unesdoc.unesco.org/images/0014/001448/144842e.pdf. Accessed November 16, 2015.

71 World Heritage Committee. "State of Conservation: The Ruins of the Buddhist Vihara at Paharpur (Bangladesh)." 2009. Web. http://whc/unesco.org/en/soc/669. Accessed November 16, 2015.

72 The Asian Development Bank. "South Asia Tourism Infrastructure Development Project (Bangladesh, India, Nepal): Project Data Sheet." 2015. Web. www.adb.org/projects/39399-013/main?page-2=1&page-3=1#tabs0-1. Accessed December 12, 2015.

73 Email correspondence with Dr. Nilan Cooray, International Heritage Consultant to the Government of Bangladesh, December 17, 2015.

Further reading

Glassie, Henry. 1997. *Art and Life in Bangladesh*. Bloomington: University of Indiana Press.

Imamuddin, Abu H. and Karen R. Longeteig (eds.). 1990. Papers in Progress. Volume One. *Architectural & Urban Conservation in the Islamic World*. A collection of papers based on a workshop sponsored by the Aga Khan Trust for Culture with the Institute of Architects Bangladesh, Bangladesh University of Engineering & Technology and the UNDP, in April 1989. Geneva: The Aga Khan Trust for Culture.

Khan, Ahmad Nabi. 2003. *Islamic Architecture in South Asia: Pakistan–India–Bangladesh*. Oxford: Oxford University Press.

Robinson, Francis (ed.). 1989. *The Cambridge Encyclopedia of India, Pakistan, Bangladesh, Sri Lanka*. Cambridge: Cambridge University Press.

20
BHUTAN

Stretched across the eastern Himalayas, between India and China, the landlocked Kingdom of Bhutan has only recently begun to engage in contemporary architectural conservation practice. Bhutan stands out among the nations of Asia, if not the world, as a country that is especially concerned with protection, promotion and safeguarding of its unique cultural heritage as a matter of not only national pride, but also of national preservation. Vajrayana Buddhism deeply influences all aspects of life in the kingdom today, in particular its architectural and artistic traditions.[1] Bhutan's economy is based primarily on agriculture and the export of hydroelectric power, with tourism playing an increasingly significant role following decades of a highly regulated relationship with the industry, and a deliberate strategy to manage the number and types of tourists that visit. Two-thirds of Bhutan's population is rural, and the country has historically coped with limited infrastructure largely owing to the country's mountainous topography, making movement of people and materials around the country difficult.[2] As the kingdom continues on its modernization path – with a growing, increasingly well-educated urban population and a road network connecting all 205 *gewogs* (counties) – it does so on its own terms, offering a compelling contrast to the typical development patterns of its Asian neighbors, particularly with regards to architectural conservation.

Like neighboring Nepal and the formerly independent regions of Sikkim and Tibet, Bhutan's mountain slopes and forested valleys are punctuated by monasteries and stupas along with timber-framed structures mainly constructed of masonry or rammed earth. The country's fiercely guarded isolation lasted well into the twentieth century, leaving it relatively uninfluenced by outside cultures in the modern era, making Bhutan a unique environment for contemporary architectural conservation practice. As it gradually opens to the outside world, many opportunities exist for effectively managing its distinctive architectural and other cultural resources through local capacity development, novel approaches and effective partnerships with outside organizations.

Since the eighteenth century, Bhutan has been subject to considerable external pressures including the expansive ambitions of the British Raj. Tensions between regional rivals India and China have influenced Bhutan's own internal policies, as has the inexorable influence of globalism. For most of the twentieth century the country responded to this atmosphere by turning inward rather than accommodating these forces, taking a highly protective posture relative to its distinctive culture. Television, mobile phones and Internet access were unavailable until 1999, leaving Bhutan's population of less than a million citizens isolated from media and other external influences to an unusual degree.[3] In terms of cultural heritage conservation this strategy has paid off in many respects, in no small part due to the survival of most of its Bhutanese Buddhist heritage, including architecture. Since the country's moves to modernize that began in the 1970s, it has sought to balance promotion and protection of its traditional culture with other development-related goals.

Famously, the fourth King Jigme Singye Wangchuck in 1972 explained this approach in terms of supporting his country's "Gross National Happiness" (rather than, or at least in addition to, its Gross National Product), and the concept continues to guide the kingdom's development strategy as a key metric. Cultural heritage protection is one of the four "pillars" that supports the idea of Gross National Happiness (often referred to as GNH),[4] and within this pillar there are four key areas of activity: a code of public conduct that includes a requirement for traditional dress in places of worship and government offices (*gho* for men, *kira* for women); the oral transmittal of traditional practices from one generation to the next; a communal support system including participation in festivals and rituals; and the preservation of monuments, traditional arts and crafts.[5]

From the standpoint of architectural conservation, this approach has created an environment where many of the field's values are supported by strong government policy, and especially by the country's influential monarchy. These values include the promotion of traditional building trades such as woodworking and mural painting, the use of traditional architectural styles such as those featured in traditional *dzong* and *lhakhang*, and support for intangible heritage practices that perpetuate the maintenance and use of the country's historic buildings.[6] Bhutan's approach is not without its critics, with some arguing that the focus on GNH belies the country's poverty, imposes cultural homogeneity

FIGURE 20.1 The seventeenth century Paro Taktsang, or "Tiger's Nest" monastery in the Paro Valley of Bhutan is one of the country's holiest, and most architecturally stunning buildings. Following a destructive 1998 fire, the government oversaw the full restoration of the complex, which was completed in 2005.

at the expense of ethnic minorities such as Nepali Hindus, and compromises individual freedoms.[7] These challenges to the country's official policy have become particularly consequential since the pace of government reforms has accelerated in the twenty-first century, most tangibly with the monarchy's 2005 decision to relinquish its absolute power in favor of a representative democracy. In 2010 the government initiated a process to develop new national heritage legislation, signaling that its approach to state-level architectural conservation would continue to evolve alongside larger governmental reforms. The steadily growing tourism industry will undoubtedly play an increasing role in this process as the number of foreign visitors has increased from literally zero prior to 1974 to almost 140,000 in 2014.[8] How Bhutan will continue to adapt to its rapidly changing relationship with the outside world remains an open question, and a highly consequential one relative to its architectural conservation efforts.

Summary history of Bhutan and its architectural heritage

For centuries Buddhism has played a central role in nearly all aspects of traditional Bhutanese culture, including its architectural and artistic traditions. Introduction of the faith into what is now Bhutan began during the reign of the Tibetan King Srongtsen Gampo (r. 627–649, CE) who oversaw the construction of temples in the Paro Valley (western) and at Bumthang (central Bhutan). In 747 CE the Buddhist master Padmasambhava (also known in Bhutan as Guru Rinpoche) arrived from India to preach Mahayana Buddhism, which gradually supplanted animism as the dominant faith in the central Himalayan valleys, evolving over the centuries with periodic influences from neighboring Tibet.[9] The Drukpa sect of Buddhism, which had arrived from Tibet in the twelfth century, became dominant under the leadership of Ngawang Namgyal (b. 1594), who fled Lhasa for Bhutan in 1616. By the time of his death in 1651 much of present-day Bhutan was united under his spiritual and administrative leadership. Many of the *dzong* (administrative forts) that remain in use to this day were constructed throughout Drukyul – the Land of the Thunder Dragon – during this period.[10] The Drukpa sect remains the state religion of Bhutan, and many of the legal, political and administrative practices established during this period formed the basis for the system of governance in the modern-day kingdom.

The period of political unity ushered in by the first *shabdrung*[11] gradually eroded during the seventeenth and early eighteenth centuries amid a series of reciprocal invasions involving neighboring Tibet, Cooch Behar and Sikkim. It was not until the late eighteenth century that the country united again, in this case against the increasingly hostile moves of neighboring British India. Conflict over the British–Bhutanese borderlands of Cooch Behar and the Duars evolved into war in 1772–1773 and 1864–1865, respectively, resulting in territorial losses by the kingdom and increased British influence in its affairs. Due in part to his role in mediating the Anglo-Tibetan Convention of 1904 and the ensuing British patronage, Ugyen Wangchuck succeeded in establishing the country's hereditary monarchy as the first Druk Gyalpo (Dragon King) in 1907. Under the Treaty of Punakha (1910), the monarchy agreed to cede control over its foreign affairs to Britain in exchange for defense against China, shifting the historic weight of influence from Tibet southward, to India.[12]

An independent Republic of India inherited the British relationship with Bhutan after 1947, but the kingdom's continued independence was not necessarily ensured, nor was its security from communist China, which invaded Tibet in 1951. The presence of two powerful and increasingly competitive neighbors has greatly influenced the Bhutanese government's approach to foreign relations and internal policy for much of the twentieth century. Following the incorporation of the previously independent Buddhist kingdom of Sikkim into India in 1975, the newly crowned King Jigme Singye Wangchuck accelerated his predecessor's strategy of cultural promotion as a means of national defense against a similar fate.[13] The desire to present itself as a distinctive culture to the outside world via tourism informed the decision to welcome previously barred foreign tourists in 1974.[14] Bhutan also increased its participation in the international community during this period of reform, including joining the United Nations in 1971, which later set the stage for its ratification of the UNESCO charter in 2001.

In 1998 the king relinquished some powers to the elected national assembly, and a cabinet appointed by the assembly took a greater role in the country's governance. The 2005 announcement by the king that he would abdicate his throne in 2008 in concert with national elections opened the door to the current political arrangement.[15] Today, Bhutan is a multi-party democracy with a prime minister as head of a council of ministers, and the king serving as a largely ceremonial head of state. Its transition to democracy was regarded as relatively smooth and well-organized compared to that of many other countries, with high levels of citizen participation in the drafting of a constitution and gradual engagement in the newly formed political process.[16]

Architectural conservation in Bhutan

Bhutan's mountainous terrain and historically isolated valleys have resulted in distinctive regional and linguistic sub-groups that are reflected in the country's cultural and building traditions.[17] Prominent craft traditions in Bhutan include painting, particularly in association with architecture, and many secular and religious buildings in the country are richly adorned on the interior and exterior with colorful imagery, designs and patterns.

Traditional architecture in Bhutan closely resembles that of neighboring Tibet, with differences in the roof type – Bhutanese buildings generally exhibit a sloped roof rather than flat – and the elaborate nature of Bhutanese architectural woodworking.[18] Common issues affecting traditional architecture in Bhutan include damage from seismic activity, replacement of historic roof materials (wood shingles) with corrugated iron sheeting and associated drainage issues, and deterioration of decorative and structural timber elements and wall paintings.[19]

Most prominent among the distinctive Bhutanese forms of architecture are the country's *dzong*, a highly practical combination of defensive fortification, administrative center and place of worship. At least one dzong is found in each of the country's twenty *dzongkhag* (administrative districts), and nearly all remain living buildings, in some cases with new functions (such as the National Museum at the old watchtower of Paro Dzong), but more often with a continuation of their historic uses. The oldest dzong that was built during the reign of the country's founding shabdrung is the Semtokha Dzong (1629) in the capital of Thimphu. Upon its completion, this complex served as the prototype for the

FIGURE 20.2 Built as a combination of defensive fortification, administrative center and place of worship the *dzong* of Bhutan are a building type distinctive to the mountain kingdom. The Semtokha Dzong dating from 1629 in the capital of Thimphu is among the oldest associated with the country's founder.

country's other dzong, many of which also date to the seventeenth century. A typical complex consists of defensive outer buildings organized around a courtyard, within which sits a tower (*utse*) that houses the temples. The dzong is split between the resident monastic order, and the civil administration of the particular dzongkhag, reflecting the dual nature of religious/secular governance practiced in Bhutan.

Punakha Dzong, built in 1637, is among the most well known in the country due to its richly adorned architecture and sculptures, its forty-four temples, and its association with the country's founder and the current monarchy. The temple (*machen*) housing the embalmed body of the *Shabdrung* inside the Punakha Dzong is the kingdom's most sacred temple. The current government offices are housed in the Trashichho Dzong in Thimphu, the capital city, which has been rebuilt numerous times since the seventeenth century due to fire (a constant threat to historic buildings in Bhutan) and the ascent of new monarchs. Constructed of masonry walls with fastener-free timber framing, most dzong feature richly rendered interior painting concentrated in the temple areas, with less decorative painting in the administrative areas. Conservation measures at the kingdom's dzong are regularly undertaken to address damage from fires or natural disasters such as floods or landslides, deterioration, expansion and adaptive reuse. Due to the "living" nature of the buildings, conservation projects typically emphasize the traditional uses and the perpetuation of craft traditions rather than Western practices relative to use of original materials.[20]

Conservation policy in the kingdom has developed iteratively, with more changes to come as the government continues to evolve its organizational structure, and its approach to cultural issues in particular. The Special Commission for Cultural Affairs was established in 1985 to oversee conservation activities, but was reorganized several times following Bhutan's process of governmental reforms, culminating with the creation of the Department of Culture in 2003.[21] The Department of Culture (presently within the Ministry of Home and Cultural Affairs) oversees the government entity responsible for architectural conservation in Bhutan, the Division for Conservation of Architectural Heritage. The Division maintains inventories of heritage resources, supports the districts in conservation project planning, sets guidelines for new construction of cultural buildings and is tasked with publication and documentation of conservation projects.[22] The Bhutanese government regularly funds up to three conservation-related projects per administrative district during each budget cycle, including construction costs, and funding for the preparation of master plans, with a particular focus on the country's various dzong. The country's 2014/15 budget included funds for the preparation of a master plan and the related execution of conservation work of Trashigang Dzong, construction of a new National Conservation Laboratory, and the renovation of multiple temples.[23]

Another funding mechanism for conservation activity in the kingdom is the Bhutan Cultural Trust Fund, established in 1999 as a non-profit trust funded by donations from the international community as well as individuals, corporations and other entities in Bhutan. Like similar funds in Nepal and Sri Lanka, the Bhutanese entity is intended to provide ongoing funding for promotion of cultural programs and conservation activities in the country.[24] The fund has yet to be applied, however, as it may only be put to use once it reaches the equivalent of US$5 million;[25] as of 2015 it had not yet achieved one-fifth of that goal, demonstrating the challenges of adequately funding conservation efforts in the mountain kingdom.[26]

A growing sector of the economy that could be leveraged to fill this gap is the tourism industry. Tourism remains highly regulated in Bhutan, and though there are no longer quotas limiting the number of visitors each year, the costs of getting to Bhutan and government regulations applicable to tourists have the practical effect of suppressing the number of visitors as compared to neighboring India, Nepal and China. Bhutan has actively managed its tourism sector in order to welcome a low volume of well-funded tourists, as opposed to large numbers of budget travelers. Tourists pay a fee of several hundred US dollars per day to visit Bhutan, and tour operators also pay a royalty directly to the government for each visitor they host.[27] Into the 1990s the quota was kept at just 200 tourists per year, but that number was gradually raised and limits ultimately were dropped. The growth in tourism since it has become more accessible has provided some capital to support conservation projects, but officials point to a perpetual shortage of trained craftspeople to carry out work, and insufficient funds to support the number of projects identified by the department as barriers to their progress.[28]

FIGURE 20.3a and b Within their typology the design variations of Bhutan's *dzong* reflect their natural settings, ambitions of their builders and defensive function. Continued use is what ensured their survival over time. Associated with the country's founder and monarchy, Punakha Dzong, dating from 1637, is richly adorned with forty-four temples and other buildings (a, b).

The World Monuments Fund (WMF) has identified several sites in Bhutan on its biennial Watch List in recent years, including Phajoding (thirteenth century monastery) and the nineteenth century Wangduechhoeling Palace, citing increased development pressures and neglect, respectively, as threats to the buildings' distinctive character.[29] The birthplace of the first king of modern Bhutan, the Wangduechhoeling Palace (built 1856), has been abandoned for decades and suffers from deferred maintenance and neglect. The Watch listing triggered a proposed collaboration between the US/Bhutanese Bhutan Foundation and the Ministry of Home & Cultural Affairs to rehabilitate the building for use as a traditional culture and regional interpretative center for the Bumthang Valley. The scope of work would include protection of its distinctive carved and painted wood elements and the installation of exhibits on the natural heritage of the area and on traditional archery.[30] WMF has also partnered with the Bhutan Foundation and the Prince Claus Foundation (Netherlands) to provide emergency response aid and repair advice to Department of Culture staff following a 2009 earthquake that damaged the seventeenth century Drametse Lhakhang (monastery complex) and the nearby seventeenth century Trashigang Dzong.[31] The response was supplemented by funding from the Government of Bhutan to train trades people in construction techniques for greater seismic resiliency.[32]

As in many other parts of the world, the heritage conservation movement in Bhutan has developed in concert with ecological conservation efforts. Protection and management of the nation's forest and water resources is a particularly important area of government activity, with the National Forest Policy (1974) directing management of the country's forests, water quality and grazing practices. The kingdom banned the export of timber in 1999, and approximately 70 percent of the country is covered in forest.[33] In a remarkable commitment to ecological management, the constitution mandates that 60 percent of the country must remain under forest cover, and 25 percent of the total land area in Bhutan is protected as nature reserves.[34] Yet architectural conservation-focused legislation has lagged somewhat behind environmental protection efforts, with no comprehensive cultural heritage legislation in place, and only the country's dzong, monasteries and stupas listed as protected heritage assets.[35] Because contextual and non-religious buildings do not benefit from protection under national law, they are especially vulnerable to demolition or alteration.[36] The issue has become acute in Thimphu, where many traditional residential buildings have been lost due to a lack of regulations to protect them, and the economic opportunities available to property owners by replacing them with modern apartment buildings.[37]

In order to address this shortcoming, the government of Bhutan began consultation in 2010 on a new Heritage Sites Bill with a variety of stakeholders, including international partners and government ministry officials. The Department of Culture also engaged the World Bank during this process to provide detailed feedback on the bill via a Poverty Social Impact Analysis (PSIA) conducted in 2012–2013. The analysis aimed to describe the potential impacts of the proposed legislation, with a special focus on the economic opportunities it might offer traditional communities, property owners and institutions, as well as recommendations for effective implementation of the bill once adopted.[38]

In its analysis the World Bank found that while the government had dramatically reduced poverty in Bhutan from 23 percent in 2007 to 12–13 percent in 2012, expansion of the country's heritage conservation infrastructure stood out as a key opportunity for continued poverty reduction and economic opportunities in the kingdom.[39] These potential benefits were seen as particularly high for traditional rural communities and for owners of distinctively Bhutanese buildings in the country's capital.[40] The PSIA encouraged the use of financial incentives (as opposed to punitive measures) for property owners and religious authorities to encourage conservation. It also recommended increasing staffing and managing conservation processes at the local and district levels, where current official heritage management capacity remains quite limited.[41]

With regards to international engagement on the formulation of the new legislation, the Department of Culture partnered with UNESCO and the Swiss international development aid organization (Helvetas) in a series of workshops to address two areas that have historically been underrepresented in Bhutanese heritage management: cultural landscapes and archaeology. The Swiss partnership began in 2008 with the excavation of the sixteenth century ruins of Drapham Dzong, located in Bumthang District of central Bhutan.[42] A second phase (2011–2014) involved additional fieldwork, but also

FIGURE 20.4a, b and c An example of international cooperation to assist in the conservation of Bhutan's architectural heritage was the response by the World Monuments Fund in partnership with the Prince Claus Foundation (Netherlands) and the Bhutan Foundation to provide emergency response aid and repair advice to the Department of Culture staff following the 2009 earthquake that damaged the seventeenth century Drametse Lhakhang monastery complex (a, b). Conservation work entailed structural repairs incorporating earthquake resilient features and restoration of finishes (c).

critical capacity building exercises and consultation on measures to incorporate into the new legislation in order to enhance archaeological management in the country.[43] A series of UNESCO workshops on cultural landscapes in Bhutan held in 2014 and 2015 involved briefings to members of the Bhutanese parliament on principles and methods of cultural landscape conservation in anticipation of the passage of the country's upcoming conservation legislation.[44]

Bhutan's unusual experience during the late twentieth and early twenty-first centuries of rapidly moving from complete isolation to international engagement has created a unique environment for architectural conservation practice. With most ecclesiastical structures including its monasteries, temples, stupas and dzong still actively used and maintained by their traditional communities, Bhutan retains an exceptionally high degree of "living heritage."[45] Having largely avoided many of the forces that have heavily affected its neighbors, including colonization, full engagement in the global economy, large-scale tourism, rapid population growth and industrialization, Bhutan now faces a series of critical choices as it continues its process of reform and policy development. According to official statements, its objectives are to strike a deliberate balance between promotion of its traditional culture and economic development in order to moderate the impact of a gradual entry into the global community.

In order to confront these challenges, the kingdom's government initiated a multi-year planning effort in 1999 termed "Bhutan 2020: A Vision for Peace, Prosperity and Happiness." The planning document relies upon the concept of Gross National Happiness and its supporting "pillars," making several specific recommendations relative to cultural heritage conservation that indicate a roadmap for future developments in Bhutan. The ambitious list of recommendations includes adoption of a revised building code that incentivizes the use of traditional building materials and techniques; completion of a survey of significant historic resources;[46] and development of professional capacity in heritage conservation including improving infrastructure for access to remote heritage sites, addressing vandalism and theft at heritage sites, and an increased focus on cultural landscapes as focus of conservation efforts.[47]

Also part of the kingdom's strategy for heritage conservation through craft traditions – including the building arts – is the promotion of its *zorig chusum* (or, Thirteen Traditional Crafts of Bhutan), which factor into many architectural works, including temples, dzong or traditional houses. The trades include: jewelry making, paper making, embroidery, fabric and bamboo weaving, fabrication of wooden cups and bowls, stone and wood carving, ceramics, stone masonry, bronze casting, ironworking and painting. Bhutan directly fosters programs to encourage the perpetuation of these craft traditions through government-sponsored institutes for perpetuation of intangible heritage, and for promotion as part of the tourism sector.[48]

The Heritage Sites Bill, proposed in 2015, should greatly help in accomplishing many of these objectives. If enacted, the legislation would include protection for "heritage villages" in addition to cultural landscapes, both of which are vital to conserving the kingdom's intangible cultural heritage. The Bill would also shift more heritage protection authority and decision-making powers from the central government and to the *dzongkhags* and *thromdes* (district and local governing bodies) that will likely enhance local participation. It would also address protection of archaeological resources, which heretofore has been largely overlooked in the country's heritage management practices.

Few other Asian countries have focused on cultural heritage conservation and promotion as a means of national defense to the degree that Bhutan has done. As stated in the preamble of one of the Kingdom's Five Year Plans, promotion of traditional cultural heritage is "not being taken because of sentimental values or orthodox views to uphold past practices, but that they are crucial steps that must be taken to consolidate and safeguard the sovereignty and security of the nation."[49] In the years to come, Bhutan will be an important proving ground for how other Asian countries might constructively resist the negative aspects of globalization, while also protecting their own heritage in inclusive and sustainable ways.

Notes

1 As many as 75 percent of Bhutanese are Buddhist, with the remainder primarily Hindu of Nepali heritage, and a small population of Muslims. Source: BBC News. "BBC Country Profile: Bhutan." 2015. Web. http://bbc.com/news/world-south-asia-12641778. Accessed December 27, 2015.

FIGURE 20.5a and b An initiative begun in 2008 by the Swiss Helvetas international aid organization in partnership with UNESCO and the Department of Culture involved excavation of the sixteenth century ruins of Drapham Dzong, located in Bumthang District of central Bhutan (a). The project entailed archaeological research (b) that includes a landscape component aimed at enhancing both archaeological site management and cultural landscape conservation capacity in Bhutan.

2 The World Bank. "Bhutan Overview." 2013. Web. www.worldbank.org/en/country/bhutan/overview. Accessed December 27, 2015.
3 BBC Country Profile: Bhutan.
4 The other three pillars are: good governance, sustainable and equitable development, and environmental protection.
5 Bhutan Development Update. World Bank – Poverty Reduction and Economic Management, South Asia Region. April 2014. Web. http://documents.worldbank.org/curated/en/2014/04/19455214/bhutan-development-update. Accessed December 30, 2015.
6 *Dzong* are a distinctive form of Bhutanese architecture that function as administrative centers, defensive forts and places of worship. They are discussed in detail later in this chapter. *Lhakhang* are Tibetan or Bhutanese monastery-temple complexes.
7 *The Economist*. "The Pursuit of Happiness." December 16, 2004. Web. www.economist.com/node/3445119. Accessed December 27, 2015.
8 Bhutan Tourism Council. "Bhutan Tourism Monitor: 2014." 2014. Web. http://tcb.cms.ebizity.net/attachments/tcb_081415_btm-2015---booklet-(web).pdf. Accessed December 30, 2015.
9 Robert L. Worden. "Bhutan," in Andrea Matles Savada (ed.), *Nepal and Bhutan: Country Studies*. (Washington, DC: Library of Congress, 1993), 253.
10 Drukyul remains the kingdom's traditional name, and the one used by its modern-day people; the name *Bhutan* likely has Sanskrit origins and only came into widespread use by foreigners in the nineteenth century. Source: Worden, 256.
11 This honorific, meaning "At Whose Feet One Submits," was taken by Ngawang Namgyal, and used by subsequent Bhutanese rulers until the establishment of the current hereditary monarchy in 1907. Source: Worden, 265, 262.
12 *Public Broadcasting Service*. "Living Edens: Bhutan." 2008. Web. www.pbs.org/edens/bhutan/Bhu_people2.htm. Accessed December 27, 2015.
13 Worden, 266.
14 Marti Ann Reinfeld. "Tourism and the Politics of Cultural Preservation: A Case Study of Bhutan," *Journal of Public and International Affairs* 14 (Spring 2003), 14.
15 The king abdicated two years early, in 2006, handing the throne to his son, Jigme Khesar Namgyel Wangchuck.
16 World Bank, "Bhutan Overview."
17 As many as twenty-three languages in Bhutan are spoken, including English and the national language, Dzongkha. Source: Bhutan: Languages. Ethnologue. 2015. Web. www.ethnologue.com/country/BT/languages. Accessed December 27, 2015.
18 Laura Blake. *Bhutan's Buddhist Architecture*. (Self Published, 2015), 14.
19 Cornielle Jest. *Safeguarding of the Cultural Heritage of Bhutan*. (Paris: UNESCO, 1992), 13. Web. http://unesdoc.unesco.org/images/0009/000941/094150eo.pdf. Accessed December 27, 2015.
20 Dorji Yangki. "Sacred Fortresses of the Himalayas: Dzong Architecture of Bhutan," *Orientations* 39(1) (January/February 2008), 55–61.
21 Government of Bhutan. "Ministry of Culture: Background." 2015. Web. www.mohca.gov.bt/?page_id=5734. Accessed December 27, 2015.
22 Division for Conservation of Architectural Heritage, Department of Culture, Ministry of Home and Cultural Affairs. Bhutan Foundation. 2015. Web. http://www.bhutanfound.org/mohca. Accessed December 27, 2015.
23 Ministry of Finance: Bhutan. "National Budget 2014–2015." June 2014. Web. www.mof.gov.bt/wp-content/uploads/2014/07/BR2014-2015ENG.pdf. Accessed December 27, 2015.
24 Bhutan Foundation. "Bhutan Cultural Trust Fund." 2015. Web. www.bhutanfound.org/?p=907. Accessed December 30, 2015.
25 Government of Bhutan, Gross National Happiness Commission. "Turning Vision into Reality: The Development Challenges Confronting Bhutan (Eleventh Round Table Meeting)." 2011. Web. http://11rtm.gnhc.gov.bt/RTMdoc/RTM_Text_Final15July2011.pdf. Accessed December 30, 2015.
26 National Budget (2014).
27 Reinfeld, 15.
28 Sonam Pelden. "We Don't Have Funds," *Bhutan Observer*. January 19, 2008. Web. http://bhutanobserver.bt/print.aspx?artid=5041. Accessed December 27, 2015.
29 World Monuments Fund. "Projects: Phajoding." 2015. Web. www.wmf.org/project/phajoding. Accessed December 27, 2015.

30 The Bhutan Foundation is a US-based non-profit focused on supporting environmental and cultural conservation, governance and sustainable development in Bhutan. Source: Bhutan Foundation. "Renovation & Rehabilitation of Wangduechhoeling Palace in Bumthang." 2015. Web. www.bhutanfound.org/palace?p=1029. Accessed December 27, 2015.

31 The effort was part of a partnership between WMF and the Prince Claus Fund known as the Cultural Heritage Emergency Response program, whereby US$1 million annually is raised to provide emergency response funds to heritage sites damaged by natural disasters. World Monuments Fund. "Projects: Drametse Lhakhang." 2015. Web. https://www.wmf.org/project/drametse-lhakhang. Accessed December 27, 2015.

32 World Monuments Fund. "Projects: Trashigang Dzong." 2015. Web. www.wmf.org/project/trashigang-dzong. Accessed December 27, 2015.

33 Food and Agriculture Organization of the United Nations. "Bhutan: Global Forest Resource Assessment 2015 – Country Report." 2015. Web. www.fao.org/documents/card/en/c/7c60d643-a8c7-4c1e-b5e5-21ef4bb803b3/. Accessed January 8, 2016.

34 UNESCO. "Application of the World Heritage Convention by the States Parties: Bhutan." 2002. Web. http://whc.unesco.org/archive/periodicreporting/APA/cycle01/section1/bt-summary.pdf. Accessed December 30, 2015.

35 Government of Bhutan, Ministry of Home & Cultural Affairs. "Forward Plan: Heritage Sites Bill of Bhutan." 2014. Web. http://www.cabinet.gov.bt/RIA/forwardplan/heritage.pdf. Accessed December 30, 2015.

36 New construction is governed by the Bhutan Building Rules (2002), which includes use of the "Guidelines on Traditional Architecture" for new construction in order to maintain a distinctively Bhutanese look and feel of new buildings and the greater built environment. Source: Ministry of Communications, Government of Bhutan. Department of Urban Development & Housing. "Bhutan Building Rules." 2002. Web. www.mowhs.gov.bt/wp-content/uploads/2010/11/Bhutan-Building-Rules-2002.pdf. Accessed December 30, 2015.

37 Tashi Dema. "Report Urges Setting a Premium on Traditional Houses." Kuensel (Bhutan). February 25, 2014. Web. http://kuenselonline.com/archive/report-urges-setting-a-premium-on-traditional-houses/. Accessed May 20, 2016.

38 World Bank, "Bhutan Overview," 17–20.

39 The World Bank attributed this reduction largely to the expansion of agricultural markets for Bhutanese farmers.

40 World Bank, "Bhutan Overview," 12.

41 World Bank, "Bhutan Overview," 20.

42 Archaeology. SAARC Cultural Portal: Bhutan. 2014. Web. www.saarcculture.org/old-site/portal/countries/index.php?option=com_content&layout=blog&view=category&id=126&itemId=&mid=3&lid=bh. Accessed December 30, 2015.

43 Helvetas (Swiss Inter-cooperation Agency). "Bhutan-Swiss Archaeological Project." 2015. Web. https://bhutan.helvetas.org/en/activities/projects/archaeological_project_bhutan/. Accessed December 30, 2015.

44 UNESCO. "Bhutan 2015: Workshop and Forum on the Cultural Landscape and Sustaining its Significance." September 7, 2015. Web. http://whc.unesco.org/en/news/1342/. Accessed May 20, 2016.

45 Dasho Sangay Wangchung. "Issues of Sustainable Conservation." Paper delivered at the WMF Conference on Heritage Conservation, Colombo, Sri Lanka. July 28, 2004.

46 The survey has got under way, identifying over 2,000 *lhakhangs* (temples or monasteries), twenty-five *dzongs* and over 10,000 *choetens* (stupas) in order to set conservation priorities.

47 Planning Commission, Government of Bhutan. "Bhutan 2020: A Vision for Peace, Prosperity and Happiness." 2011. Web. www.gnhc.gov.bt/wp-content/uploads/2011/05/Bhutan2020_2.pdf. Accessed December 30, 2015.

48 Tourism Council of Bhutan. "Arts & Crafts." 2015. Web. www.tourism.gov.bt/about-bhutan/Arts-crafts. Accessed January 8, 2016.

49 Cultural Policy of Bhutan. International Information and Networking Centre for Intangible Cultural Heritage in the Asia-Pacific Region under the auspices of UNESCO (ICHCAP). 2010. Web. www.ichcap.org/eng/ek/sub1/pdf_file/south_asia/Bhutan_2010_13_Annex_4_Cultural_Policy_of_BhutanBhutan_2010.pdf. Accessed December 27, 2015.

Further reading

Aris, Michael. 1982. *Views of Medieval Bhutan*. London: John Swain & Son.

Gayleg, Sonam. 2009. *Historic Districts as an Alternative Approach to Preserve the Bhutanese Architectural Heritage*. Master's Thesis, Massachusetts Institute of Technology.

Meyer, Kurt and Pamela Deuel Meyer (eds.). 2005. *In the Shadow of the Himalayas: Tibet, Bhutan, Nepal, Sikkim: A Photographic Record by John Claude White, 1883–1908*. Ahmedabad: Mapin. Distributed in North America by Antique Collectors' Club.

Schickelgruber, Christian and Francoise Pommaret (eds.). 1998. *Bhutan: Mountain Fortress of the Gods*. Boston: Shambhala.

Shankar, Pratyush. 2014. *Himalayan Cities: Settlement Patterns, Public Places and Architecture*. New Delhi: Niyogi Books.

White, J. Claude. 1984. *Sikkim and Bhutan*. New Delhi: Cosmo Publications.

Yangki, Dorji. 1969. "Sacred Fortresses of the Himalayas: Dzong Architecture of Bhutan = Les forteresses sacrées de l'Himalaya: l'architecture Dzong au bhoutan," in *Orientations*.

Carved portal, Patan, Nepal.

21

NEPAL

In recent decades, Nepal's dramatically rugged landscape and ethereal historic wood and masonry religious structures, public buildings and houses have benefited from the sustained attention of foreign architectural heritage protection organizations and participation of local institutions. This trend has led to a surge in conservation activity and traditional building skills in this mountainous nation. But conservation activity in Nepal is not a new phenomenon. The country's rich cultural and architectural heritage, which is rooted in the Hindu and Buddhist faiths, includes many historic accounts of conservation efforts dating back centuries. Throughout the country, inscriptions recount maintenance and reconstruction regimes, ranging from the rebuilding of the Kanakmuni Buddha stupa in Niglihawa in 245 BCE by the Mauryan emperor Ashoka, to the reconstruction of numerous religious structures in Kathmandu, Bhaktapur and Patan by the Shah King Ran Bahadur Shah, of the modern state's founding dynasty, following a devastating earthquake in 1934.[1]

Support for historic built and civic architecture in the principle towns of Kathmandu Valley was sustained by other means as well. Traditionally parcels of agricultural land were set aside to provide revenue for the maintenance and repair of religious buildings in a practice termed the *Guthi* system. In 1962 the concept was institutionalized at the statewide level via large land acquisitions and the creation of the central administrative agency, the *Guthi Sansthan*.[2] The forested mountainsides have historically provided plentiful building material, and a rich culture of wall painting has developed over the centuries, constituting the principal media for traditional design and artistic expression by ethnic groups such as the Newars. The nature of these building and decorative materials, however, compels ongoing maintenance and restoration, circumstances that have necessitated the perpetuation of traditional craft skills through the centuries. This wealth of "living," or continuously used, architectural heritage has propelled Nepal's many conservation projects – led first and foremost by the Institute of Engineering and the Department of Archaeology, the Kathmandu office of UNESCO and the Kathmandu Valley Preservation Trust (KVPT) – to the fore of the regional and international heritage management scene. The work of these groups has attracted the participation of additional foreign and multi-national efforts and financial support since the earliest days of the UNESCO World Heritage Convention.

Geographically, Nepal is divided into three parts: the *Himal*, or the mountainous areas, the *Pahar*, or the hilly regions, and the *Terai*, which consists of the plains. Nepalese have historically migrated from other countries, mainly from Tibet or India, with a portion of the population being indigenous to Kathmandu Valley. The citizenry currently consists of some of sixty caste and/or ethnic groups, over 90 percent of whom are of the Hindu or Buddhist faiths.[3] Major portions of the country lie in hilly areas, with the Kathmandu Valley located in this region. Hindu Brahmin and Newari populate

FIGURE 21.1 The general condition of the Bhairavnath Temple in Bhaktapur in the Kathmandu Valley dating from the seventeenth and eighteenth centuries is testament to the sound construction of many of the key religious buildings of Nepal and commitment to maintenance by rulers and members of the community. Despite the record earthquake of April 25, 2015 considerable amounts of historic architectural fabric of this kind has survived.

the Kathmandu Valley area and ethnic Tibetan and Thakali populate Nepal's mountainous areas along the northern border with China, including the formerly autonomous kingdom of Mustang, which has been a focus of recent conservation activity. Groups including the Tharus, who share cultural and artistic characteristics with their Indian neighbors to the south, populate the *Terai* regions in the southernmost parts of Nepal.[4]

Early conservation practice

Nepal, an insular and independent monarchy under the Shah and Rana kings from 1768 to 2008 CE, was only opened up to the Western world in the 1950s when a limited parliament was established along with the framework for a modern conservation and heritage management institutions. The government formed the Department of Archaeology in 1952, which remains the principal national entity responsible for carrying out cultural heritage programs, maintenance of inventories and coordination with foreign partners. Shortly thereafter, in 1956, after consultation with international cultural agencies, the Ancient Monuments Preservation Act went into effect, setting the stage for a long-standing relationship between Nepalese heritage managers and United Nations cultural experts. During the 1970s, the first historic building surveys were conducted throughout the country, and the extensive Kathmandu Valley Inventory was drawn up over a period of three years and published by Anton Schroll (Vienna) with funding from the US-based JDR III Fund. This culminated in the inscription of seven distinct collections of buildings and sites in the Kathmandu Valley to the World Heritage List in 1979.[5]

A seminal architectural conservation event for Nepal, and indeed for South Asia as a whole, followed shortly thereafter: the Hanuman Dhoka Conservation Project. This project proceeded with technical and financial assistance from UNESCO[6] and constituted the restoration of the Hanuman Dhoka Royal Palace and several associated temples and palaces located within the sixteenth through eighteenth century CE Kathmandu Durbar Square. The restoration, which was led by British conservation architect John Sanday under the direction of the Department of Archaeology, occurred in a series of phases between 1972 and 1980, and resulted in the development of new methods for documenting and conserving buildings in Nepal, including training programs for local artisans and craftsmen in traditional building conservation methods that would inform the next several decades of conservation work in the country.

As a result of its success at Hanuman Dhoka, in 1978 UNESCO published a comprehensive technical handbook entitled *Building Conservation in Nepal: A Handbook of Principles and Techniques*.[7] The *Handbook* provided a template for conservation projects, consisting of structural reinforcement; replacement of deteriorated timber elements; cleaning, consolidation and – when necessary – reproduction of decorative brick, wood and metal details, with the participation of local craftsmen and other religious and government stakeholders throughout. In many ways, the process mirrors the centuries-old building maintenance strategy for a region accustomed to periodic yet devastating earthquakes that necessitate large-scale rebuilding of damaged structures and reuse of salvaged building materials.[8] In the early 1980s, shortly after the completion of the Hanuman Dhoka project, this formula was put to use at the Bramayani Conservation Project, a restoration effort focused on a seventeenth century shrine located in Panauti village southeast of the Kathmandu Valley. It has subsequently spawned other similarly successful projects throughout Nepal.[9]

FIGURE 21.2 Restoration between 1972 and 1980 of the Narayan Temple, the Hanuman Dhoka Palace and the Basantapur Tower in the Kathmandu Durbar Square, former government seat of the Nepalese Kingdom, followed its inclusion on the World Heritage List. UNESCO's involvement was followed by additional international architectural conservation activity in the historic towns of Kathmandu Valley. (In the Malla Period the present Durbar Squares were petty kingdoms that were united by King Prithvi Narayan Shah in 1774.)

International collaboration in the conservation of Nepal's heritage sites: cooperation and differences

Along with places such as Chartres Cathedral, the Ancient City of Damascus and Tikal, Nepal's traditional building complexes and temples were among the first to be recognized by UNESCO as worthy of a World Heritage designation. This recognition triggered a relationship with the greater international heritage community that has since both stimulated and challenged its participants, largely due to the difficulty in reconciling international standards with local practices in Nepal.[10] Nepalese professionals and traditional craftspeople working to conserve Nepalese architecture were joined by outsiders attracted by the astounding beauty and the enchanting built environment and lifeways of the Kathmandu Valley. The majority of these engagements were productive, resulting in the application of additional technical and financial resources to a number of Nepal's heritage sites. An unexpected, and likely undervalued, result at the time was that such international collaborations affected the views of the Western conservators and organizations in ways that would later inform conservation practice in other parts of the world.

Possibly the earliest international initiative of this kind was conducted by the US-based International Fund for Monuments, the predecessor of the World Monuments Fund. Its international support for restoring Gokarna Temple conducted by John Sanday began in 1968. Other early contributions in the late 1960s and early 1970s came from teams originating in Germany, the Netherlands, France, Italy, Japan, the United Kingdom and the United States.[11]

Among the challenges faced in some of these collaborations were differing beliefs by some international experts and local experts, craftspeople and communities about how to reinstate or restore missing building elements. Understandably, local interests would prefer a completed building in the manner of the existing or original, even if the restored elements were based on conjecture. This approach runs contrary to accepted international standards such as the tenets of the Venice and Burra charters and the US Secretary of the Interior's Standards for Rehabilitation. Nevertheless, in Nepal local expectations that images of religious figures or deities would be fully restored tend to prevail, which is an object lesson for international practitioners.

In 1999 the Kathmandu Valley Preservation Trust (KVPT) and leading international experts along with their Nepalese counterparts organized a workshop that attempted to reconcile differences in restoration approaches practiced in the country.[12] The focus topic was how to best restore and conserve the fourteenth century Sulima Temple in Patan Darbar Square, which is a two-tiered Hindu shrine that was in poor condition. Missing structural roof struts presented a challenge in the joint efforts of local conservationists, custodians of the temple, international experts and the KVPT that had undertaken the conservation project. There was no conclusive evidence of the original designs of all of the structure's highly adorned wood elements but there was a good sense of the styles and themes portrayed. So as to be honest about the authenticity of replacement struts a proposal representing the "Western approach" was made to install plain unshaped wood replacements. This idea was rejected by the Nepalese religious community and local users who preferred newly crafted struts with figural carvings that matched the remainder of the temple's decorative schema. The work of Newari master carvers helped convince the foreign collaborators of the wisdom of this approach, which ultimately was carried out. In the end, the foreign teams determined that the international conservation doctrine-driven directives being used in Nepal required adaptation to the local context, when necessary, in order for such projects to be successful – a valuable lesson for Nepal and collaborative efforts elsewhere.[13]

FIGURE 21.3 Cover of the proceedings of an international conference convened in 1999 by the Kathmandu Valley Preservation Trust to squarely confront the issue of conserving authenticity and the roles of restoration, reconstruction and replication in the conservation of key historic buildings in Nepal.

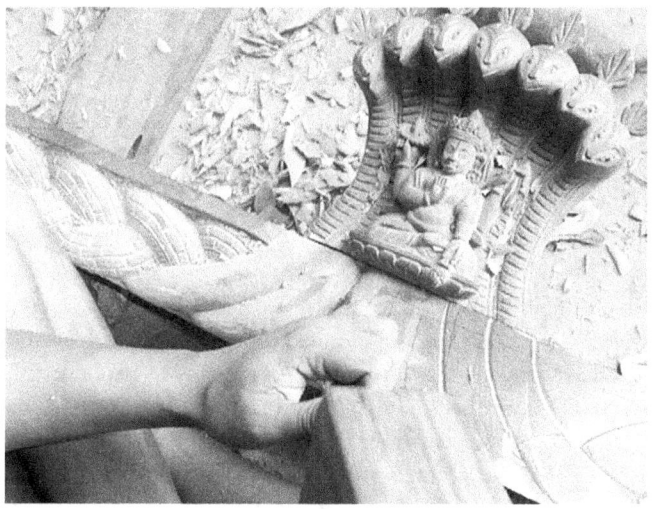

FIGURE 21.4a, b and c Sulima Temple in Patan as it appeared in 1968 (a) and after restoration in 1998 (b). The integration of new architectural fabric where necessary, as in the case of missing or provisionally supported roof struts, was done in a manner consistent with traditional temple repairs using wooden replicas or close approximations. (c) Justification of this was based on careful documentation, the potential of reversibility, preference of users of the temple, and the fostering of traditional wood carving arts.

The Bhaktapur Development Project of the Federal Republic of Germany, in partnership with the Nepalese Department of Industries, launched a similar campaign in 1974 at another World Heritage Site, the fourteenth through eighteenth-century town of Bhaktapur (Bhadgaon), located approximately 13 km east of Kathmandu.[14] As at Hanuman Dhoka, the Bhaktapur Development Project sought to restore an active temple complex while also reviving the ancient and world-renowned Nepalese woodworking tradition, which was largely lost during the Rana period (1846–1951), when such traditions were largely supplanted by modern construction techniques and materials.[15] Engaging the skills of local artisans in Bhaktapur served the dual purpose of restoring the buildings and developing skills in local craftspeople. The program succeeded in initiating a marketable, crafts-based trade that supports the tourist industry, while simultaneously supporting a local workforce available for future conservation projects. Given the rate of deterioration of wooden architectural components, a population of trained craftspeople has been an invaluable asset to ongoing and future restoration efforts at Nepal's urban and remote heritage sites alike.[16]

When Nepal ratified the UNESCO World Heritage Convention in 1978, seven palace and religious buildings and public spaces were declared World Heritage Sites, including three located in urban settings (Kathmandu, Patan and Bhaktapur), two associated with Hindu religious sites (Pashupatinath and Changu Narayan), and two important Buddhist sites (Bauddhanath and Swayambhunath). While the World Heritage designations and subsequent conservation projects have succeeded in raising the profile of the sites and fostering a thriving tourism economy, the development of the infrastructure to

FIGURE 21.5 A 1971 campaign that launched the restoration of the buildings comprising Darbar Square in Bhaktapur near Kathmandu by the Bhaktapur Development Program of the Federal Republic of Germany, in partnership with the Nepalese Department of Industries, addressed the conservation of a historic urban environment.

support this new sector began to negatively affect the architectural context of these structures. New development and the absence of effective conservation planning soon led to intrusions in the form of insensitive new and renovated buildings that surround the World Heritage Sites. At Bauddhanath, Nepal's largest stupa, increased tourist activities in the area resulted in a stupa thought to date to the fifth century now being surrounded by art and craft stores, rather than the traditional residences and workshops of multiple ethnic groups from all over Nepal that once defined the site.[17]

In order to avoid similar encroachments, in 1981 the Nepalese government decided to act on The Kathmandu Valley Masterplan, prepared by an international team of consultants after a mission in 1974 regarding the conservation of the Kathmandu Valley's heritage sites. In 1984 the government requested that UNESCO further commit to the masterplan for the conservation of cultural heritage sites throughout the Kathmandu Valley area, thus launching the Kathmandu Valley Program.[18]

The Kathmandu Valley area, which falls in the *Pahar*, or the hilly regions of the country, contains the majority of Nepal's architectural treasures, and thus has been the focus of the majority of architectural conservation activity in the nation to date. Due in part to the strong artistic tradition of the resident Newari people, the Kathmandu Valley region comprises the arts and crafts center of Nepal. Historically, the Newaris have played a major role in the development of the decorative arts, sculpture and architecture of not just Nepal but also neighboring Tibet and parts of southern China. Over the centuries, the cross-cultural exchanges resulted in a fusion of the original Newari aesthetic combined with Tibetan and Chinese art, forging new decorative styles. The Golden Gate of Bhaktapur, built in 1754 CE, features Tibetan and Chinese motifs inlaid among the periodic designs, and illustrates one example of this style.

In 1990, an alliance of local citizens, joined by a team of mostly American architects and art historians, established the private, non-profit Kathmandu Valley Preservation Trust (KVPT) in order to document and conserve the historic buildings in the valley, promote traditional building trades and foster international collaborations. Since its founding, the KVPT has expanded the scope of its projects from restoring dozens of individual structures to addressing whole enclaves of buildings, including the Patan and Kathmandu Darbars.[19] At the Darbar complexes, the KVPT collaborated with the Government of Nepal and with foreign universities and funds. Such partnerships have allowed the

FIGURE 21.6a, b and c Restoration by the KVPT of the Buddhist monastery of Itum Baha (a) in Patan, a project of Japan's Nippon Institute of Technology, entailed the whole range of possible interventions for such structures, from installation of seismic resistance measures to installation of missing structural members (left unadorned), to stabilization of damaged materials and finishes (b), to the discrete insertion of electrical and plumbing in order to restore the visual integrity of the whole (c).

KVPT to address critical seismic deficiencies in buildings – some dating to the twelfth century – as well as to create adaptive reuse programs and the restoration of historic finishes.

In each project the KVPT has focused on training and education in order to build local capacity for ongoing maintenance and preservation, as well as economic development and job creation. This successful emphasis has built on the early Kathmandu Valley programs initiated under UNESCO in the 1970s in order to extend the reach and sustain the impact of limited-term multi-national assistance programs. In the case of the Patan Darbar project, the KVPT has completed the restoration of several architectural and decorative components that constitute the palace complex, in addition to making seismic upgrades that are essential to the building's survival in the earthquake-prone region. In each, restorations were based on extant historic photographs and/or other illustrations that informed decisions on the removal of later, insensitive paving, partitions or other modern interventions, and the wholesale replacement of severely damaged or lost structural members and decorative elements. In each case, traditional trades were employed including gilding, stonemasonry, wood carving, timber framing and *repousse* (decorative patterns in relief), whereby local tradespeople teamed with conservation specialists and foreign artists in order to collaborate on the finished product.[20] Major international technical and financial assistance was provided to the Keshab Narayan Chowk courtyard in the Museum section of the Palace complex by the Austrian government.

Although in many ways a model program with several great successes, the Kathmandu Valley Project sustained criticism for its emphasis on the monumental and grand buildings that contribute to the heritage complexes, at the expense of the more prosaic, contextual structures. In order to address the issue of conserving Kathmandu's less monumental heritage sites, the KVPT undertook a survey of modest, semi-private Buddhist monasteries and other religious sites in order to repair and advocate for the retention of these lesser-known resources.[21]

All conservation work in Nepal has been guided by the Department of Archaeology since its founding in 1953. It has primary responsibility within Nepal's Ministry of Tourism, Culture & Aviation to establish and monitor its archaeological research and protection of cultural heritage. Its scope of responsibilities include: protection of monuments and archaeological sites, archaeological research and documentation, heritage-related advocacy and publications, oversight of national museums, control of illicit trade in cultural heritage, and technical and financial assistance to local individuals and organizations involved with architectural conservation. The Department's conservation architects, archaeologists, historians, museum directors and other staff represent a continuity of involvement and quality control in cultural heritage protection in Nepal, which is critically important considering the nature of heritage protection in Nepal and the constant pressures upon it. The particularly destructive earthquake of April 25, 2015 has posed the most recent challenge to the Department.

Earthquake disaster in Nepal[22]

The geologically active region of Nepal has suffered earthquakes for centuries, with recorded events dating to 1255 CE and major episodes in the twentieth century alone dating to 1916, 1934, 1966 and 1988.[23] Earthquakes and tremors have been so common across the history of the region that local construction techniques developed to counteract their effects. The predominant use of timber construction on stone foundations and brick masonry wall infill reflects this concern, with such structural systems able to sustain vibrations that may require only relatively minor repair.

As if by ill fate, after so much work and progress in architectural conservation in the Kathmandu region since the 1970s, a series of powerful earthquakes struck Kathmandu Valley in 2015. On April 25 one of 7.8 magnitude struck, with its epicenter between Kathmandu and Pokhara, followed by an aftershock located further east on May 12 having a magnitude of 7.3. Aftershocks continued for the following three months. The devastation to the built environment of the towns and villages that comprise the greater Kathmandu area was extensive, with an estimated loss of life from the series of earthquakes exceeding 8,800 with over 21,000 injuries.

In the Durbar Squares of Hanuman Dhoka in Kathmandu, Patan and Bhaktapur, many buildings collapsed completely, while others sustained major structural damage. Other religious sites, such as Swayambhunath and Baudhanath temple, one of Buddhism's most significant shrines in the Kathmandu Valley, were also damaged. According to the Department of Archaeology throughout the country an estimated 750 monuments were affected by the earthquake.

Of the traditional brick masonry and timber frame structures, those that had not received professional attention in recent years suffered the most.[24] The aftermath of the 2015 earthquake revealed that out of fifty-five buildings restored by KVPT since 1991 in Kathmandu and Patan, only three suffered major or minor structural damage.

The spirit of rebuilding and resilience in Kathmandu since the earthquake is exemplified in the quote in a status report from Nepal by the KVPT in May 2015:

> Concerned as we all are with the scale of the humanitarian crisis in Nepal, now must also be the time to plan for the future, ensuring the protection of the cultural treasures critical to Nepal's revenues and national pride. KVPT is asking all our friends and past partners to start support for the restoration and damage assessment for the temples of Kathmandu and Patan. This architectural heritage is culturally and spiritually important, but also economically for tourism that brings much needed revenue to Nepal.

There was worldwide response to the disasters and an array of relief efforts, with the main ones concerning architectural heritage protection led by the KVPT supported by the World Monuments Fund, ICOMOS, ICCROM, the Smithsonian Institution, the Ambassadors Fund for Cultural Preservation of the U.S. Department of State and several others. A system of triage for conserving damaged buildings was adopted in cooperation with national heritage conservation authorities, after which measures to stabilize structures were implemented based on urgency. The question of resources and priorities with, of course, relief efforts going to survivors being first, had to be taken into account. Around this situation KVPT and their counterparts commenced work on the Itum Baha and several more conservation projects are planned.

a

b

c

FIGURE 21.7a, b and c Geological history repeats itself with the latest devastating earthquake to strike the Kathmandu Valley being in April 2015. It is estimated that some 750 monuments were severely damaged or destroyed (a). Structural stabilization measures installed in the Royal Patan Palace during phases of restoration between 1986 and 1997 ensured against its loss in the earthquake, with it suffering almost no damage (b). Parts of the Hanuman Dhoka and Basantapur Tower, Durbar Square in Kathmandu fared less well (c).

Conservation beyond Kathmandu

As is generally the case with any successful conservation endeavor, the efforts in the Kathmandu Valley have gradually led to related projects and programs focused on other regions of Nepal. One such project at the fifteenth century CE Thubchen Gompa monastery complex in the remote Upper Mustang area of the Himalayas, near the border with Tibetan China, illustrates the logistical challenges associated with access and project coordination in remote, high-altitude sites, combined with highly technical conservation and coordination with local stakeholders. Sponsored by the American Himalayan Foundation and led by conservation architect John Sanday, the project focused on restoring finely executed wall murals that were in various stages of deterioration due to roof failure, water leaks and plaster detachment. Immediate structural interventions were required to stabilize the roof and portions of crumbling exterior wall, followed by cleaning and consolidation of the murals in order to remove centuries of soot generated by the traditional burning of butter lamps, and the re-attachment of decorative plaster finishes to the interior walls.[25]

The nearest airport giving public access to the Upper Mustang area is Jomsom, which is at least a three-day trek to the village of Lo Manthang, the location of the Thubchen Gompa, at an elevation of over 12,000 ft (3,500 m). Structural interventions called for the replacement in-kind of many of the wood structural members, a task that presented an enormous problem due to the local scarcity of suitable timber. Instead, the team had to acquire materials either from the lower regions of Mustang Valley, or from Tibet, 1,000 km away. Both options required labor-intensive efforts and ultimately involved porters carrying the structural timber posts and planks for days across the mountainous terrain. To compound the challenges, the weather conditions in the Upper Mustang only permit a small window of time when work can proceed, thus necessitating annual phasing of project activity.[26] The project, which began in 1996, was ultimately successful in restoring the building to its traditional use and reviving the deteriorated wall paintings. This outcome led to its application at several nearby monasteries, including two at Jamba Gompa in 2001, a site known for its numerous depictions of traditional diagrams of the spiritual cosmos. The performance of religious rituals in Jamba Gompa resulted in both of the temples being revived for religious worship and functions.

Nepal is a global leader in international collaboration on architectural conservation projects and will continue to be fertile ground for experimentation, negotiation and cooperation. Debates on principles and procedures for conserving historic buildings in Nepal traceably informed the Nara Document on Authenticity (1994) and Nepal has since been consistently cited as a proving ground for conservation theory and practice. Conserving Nepal's World Heritage Sites, along with its wide variety of urban and rural vernacular buildings, will require the government and international community alike to focus on the education of constituent communities about the significance of these structures and their proper conservation, probably in the same collaborative spirit that has proven so successful since the 1960s. And as the needs of citizens evolve in a country balancing modernization with tradition, so too will conservation tactics and partnerships change in order to ensure the long-term success of groundbreaking projects and programs that have already been accomplished.

Notes

1. Saphalya Amatya. *Art and Culture of Nepal: An Attempt Towards Preservation.* (New Delhi: Nirala Publications, 1999), 31–33.
2. Niels Gutschow. "Conservation in Nepal: a Review of Practice," in Erich Theophile and Neils Gutschow (eds.), *The Sulima Pagoda: East Meets West in the Restoration of a Nepalese Temple.* (Trumball, CT: Weatherhill, 2003), 11.
3. Nepal Central Bureau of Statistics, *Nepal in Figures 2006.* Kathmandu, 6.
4. UNESCO. "About Nepal." 2004. Web. www.unesco.org/kathmandu/main/aboutnepal.php#top. Accessed September 2, 2004.
5. H.R. Ranjitkar. "Nepal." *Protecting the Past for the Future. Australian National Commission for UNESCO.* (Canberra: UNESCO, 1983), 71.
6. Financial assistance from Japan, Italy and France also contributed to the completion of the project.
7. John Sanday. *The Hanuman Dhoka Royal Palace, Kathmandu: Building Conservation and Local Traditional Crafts.* (London: AARP, 1974).

8   Gutschow, 12.
9   John Sanday. "An Introduction to the Bramayani Conservation Project, Panauti," *Ancient Nepal: Journal of the Department of Archaeology* 76 (June–July 1983), 3–7.
10 Gutschow, 16.
11 Among the many individuals to contribute to these collaborations, British conservation architect John Sanday has been at the fore of architectural conservation efforts in south and southeast Asia for over four decades. A veteran of several projects organized by the World Monuments Fund, the American Himalayan Foundation and others, his firm, John Sanday Associates, Ltd., has become one of the foremost experts on the restoration of both stone and wooden buildings. A critical component to his numerous successful projects has been the involvement and training of local craftspeople in traditional building trades, such as woodworking, stone carving, brickmaking and mural restoration. This formula helped foster establishment of teams of local artisans that continued their careers in conservation work with others or as independent local conservation artisans.
12 The proceedings of the 1999 conference were published as *The Sulima Pagoda, East Meets West in the Restoration of a Nepalese Temple*, edited by Erich Theophile and Niels Gutschow (Trumball, CT: Weatherhill, 2003).
13 Erich Theophile and Rohit Ranjitkar. "The Sulima Strut: A Conservation Design Problem Illustrating Global Issues," in Erich Theophile and Neils Gutschow (eds.), *The Sulima Pagoda: East Meets West in the Restoration of a Nepalese Temple*. (Trumball, CT: Weatherhill, 2003), 51–59.
14 The *darbar* are comprised of distinctive, multi-tiered wood and masonry pagoda-style structures arranged around courtyards that are fronted by galleries and administrative buildings.
15 John Sanday. "Traditional Crafts and Modern Conservation Methods in Nepal." *Appropriate Technologies in the Conservation of Cultural Property*. (Paris: UNESCO, 1981), 9.
16 Shaphalya Amatya. "Architectural Woodwork in Nepal," *Ancient Nepal: Journal of the Department of Archaeology* 109 (December 1987–January 1988), 1–3.
17 Ranjitkar, 71.
18 Ibid.
19 Kathmandu Valley Preservation Trust. "Mission of the Kathmandu Valley Preservation Trust." Web. www.kvptnepal.org/mission.php. Accessed July 2, 2013.
20 Kathmandu Valley Preservation Trust, *The Restoration of the Patan Darbar Palace Complex – Progress Report November 2012* (Kathmandu: KVPT, 2012).
21 Kathmandu Valley Preservation Trust. "Buddhist Kathmandu Campaign." Web. http:www.kvptnepal.org/projects-buddhist.php. Accessed July 2, 2013.
22 Information herein on the status of the April 25, 2015 earthquake with permission from reports by the KVPT/WMF collaborative dated May 18, 2015 in an international appeal. Web. www.wmf.org/blog/update=kathmandu-valley-preservation-trust-patan-royal-palace-complex-after-nepal-earthquake. Web. Accessed 28 December 2015.
23 DPNet-Nepal. "Disaster Preparedness Network Nepal." Web. http://dpnet.org.np/index.php?pageName=earthquake. Accessed December 28, 2015.
24 The Patan Royal Palace Complex was included on the World Monuments Watch in 2006, and since then, WMF and KVPT have worked together to protect the historic complex, which was left almost unscathed by the earthquake. In 2015 the Cultural Heritage Sites of Nepal were again put on the Watch list.
25 World Monuments Fund. "Gompas of Upper Mustang." January 2011. Web. www.wmf.org/project/gompas-upper-mustang. July 2, 2013.
26 American Himalayan Foundation. "Thubchen Gompa: A New Ceiling for the Roof of the World." 1998. Web. www.asianart.com/ahf/index.html. Accessed September 2, 2004.

Further reading

Amatya, Saphalya. 1999. *Art and Culture of Nepal: An Attempt Towards Preservation*. 2nd edition. New Delhi: Nirala Publications.
Banerjee, N.R. 1977. "Principles of the Conservation of Ancient Monuments with Special References to Nepal," *Ancient Nepal* 40: 17–27.
Bhattarai-Upadhyay, Vibha. 2006. "Cultural Heritage Management: How Do the Locals See It? Case Study of the Neighbourhood of Bhaktapur Palace Square," in *Our Modern: Re-appropriating Asia's Urban Heritage*, Proceedings of the 6th mAAN International Conference, Tokyo, Japan, 72–80.

———. 2013. "Traditions Overlooked: Re-thinking Cultural Heritage Conservation in the Kathmandu Valley, Nepal," in Kapila D. Silva and Neel Kamal Chapagain (eds.), *Asian Heritage Management: Contexts, Concerns and Prospects*. (New York: Routledge), 157–175.

Chapagain, Neel Kamal. 2007. "Revisiting Conservation Charters in Context of Lomanthang, Nepal: Need to Acknowledge Local Inhabitants and Changing Contexts," *City & Time* 3(2): 55–64.

Gutschow, Niels. 1997. *The Nepalese Caitya*. Stuttgart: Edition Axel Menges.

———. 2011. *Architecture of the Newars: A History of Building Typologies and Details in Nepal*. 3 vols. Chicago: Serinda Publications.

Hosken, F.P. 1974. *The Kathmandu Valley Towns: A Record of Life and Change in Nepal*. New York: Weatherhill.

Meyer, Kurt and Pamela Deuel Meyer (eds.). 2005. *In the Shadow of the Himalayas: Tibet, Bhutan, Nepal, Sikkim: A Photographic Record by John Claude White, 1883–1908*. Ahmedabad: Mapin. Distributed in North America by Antique Collectors' Club.

Sanday, John. 1999. "The Gateway to Nirvana – Conserving the Temples of Mustang," *Orientations* 30(10): 84–89.

Shankar, Pratyush. 2014. *Himalayan Cities: Settlement Patterns, Public Places and Architecture*. New Delhi: Niyogi Books.

Slusser, Mary Shepherd. 1982. *Nepal Mandala: A Cultural Study of the Kathmandu Valley*. 2 vols. Princeton: Princeton University Press.

Theophile, Erich and Niels Gutschow (eds.). 2003. *The Sulima Pagoda: East Meets West in the Restoration of a Nepalese Temple*. Trumbull, CT: Weatherhill.

Tiwari, S.R. 1987. "Heritage Conservation in Nepal," *Tribhuvan University Journal* 13(2): 13–18.

UNESCO/UNDP. 1981. *Master Plan for the Conservation of the Cultural Heritage in the Kathmandu Valley*. Paris: UNESCO and UNDP.

CONCLUSION TO PART IV

The nations of South Asia share some of the longest and most enduring institutions for modern architectural conservation, as well as centuries-old traditions that guide the care of culturally valued places. Together these have created a foundation for professional practice that, since the independence era, has generated numerous milestone conservation initiatives. Among these efforts are the Cultural Triangle Project in Sri Lanka, the Hanuman Dhoka Conservation Project in Nepal, and the community revitalization projects in the Hunza Baltistan region of Pakistan. Innovative policies have also emerged within the region in recent years, including Bhutan's national program that uses cultural heritage protection as a key government performance metric, a practice that elevates the field in a way seldom found elsewhere in the world. South Asia abounds with examples of "living heritage," and each of its countries is well poised to contribute to this vital aspect of the field in the form of effective management strategies, promotion and best practices.

South Asia is a particularly receptive environment for community-based conservation strategies, which have proven successful in multiple contexts in the region. Opportunities exist for further development of this highly participatory approach, based on projects such as the Hazrat Nizamuddin Basti program in Delhi and at Galle in Sri Lanka, so as to define and share best practices with other Asian communities. Related to community-focused projects is an ongoing effort in the region to recognize and protect small-scale, contextual heritage resources, in addition to prominent architectural monuments. This shift is taking place in the context of moving beyond the conservation practices of the colonial era, and towards a distinctively local perspective on heritage management. Non-governmental organizations such as INTACH have led the way on this more inclusive approach from within India, but other nations in the region have the opportunity to follow that lead within their own borders.

The government agencies working in the field of cultural resource management in South Asia have much to offer, but diligence and enforcement of existing regulations remains an ongoing challenge throughout the region. While effective governmental practices are to be found, such as Sri Lanka's approach to coordinating heritage and land use planning at the national level, more could be done to optimize the performance of this key sector of heritage management.[1] Fortunately, a dynamic and creative NGO community led by organizations such as INTACH and the Heritage Foundation of Pakistan has performed ably in places where government agencies have not. The complementary role of this sector extends to proposals for tackling major national issues, such as INTACH's 2004 Charter for the Conservation of Unprotected Architectural Heritage and Sites in India, which has done much to raise awareness around the issue of vulnerable, undocumented sites that comprise huge areas of South Asia's built environment. Similarly sustained, solution-oriented approaches will be required to address the region's acute ecological fragility, as exemplified by environmental pollution in cities like Delhi and Agra, and the climate change-related threats to the Maldives, Sri Lanka, Bangladesh and other coastal communities.

In a region where urbanization and population expansion remains a driving force, new approaches will be needed to manage growth, support communities and deliver necessary infrastructure improvements, while also conserving heritage assets. India's Heritage City Development and Augmentation Yojana (known by the acronym HRIDAY), launched in early 2015, aims to tackle this notion of "heritage linked urban development" in twelve cities across the country. Once complete, the results of this multi-year plan will be ripe for analysis and possible replication elsewhere in the region. Embodied in approaches like the HRIDAY program is the notion that change is part of the natural functioning of South Asian communities, and that conservation strategies must accommodate – and perhaps even facilitate – these processes in order to remain relevant and effective. The key will be to accommodate the level of change needed and desired for communities to thrive, while also applying sound conservation practices to the heritage assets that are involved. Fortunately, the architectural conservation profession possesses tools to accommodate this need – in particular the practice of "adaptive reuse," whereby old buildings are sensitively altered to serve a new purpose – that are time-tested within the region and elsewhere.

The continued vitality of the field in South Asia will depend in part on whether or not the geopolitical disruptions that accompanied the transition of these nations to full independence can subside rather than inflame. Regional stability and cooperation have the potential to create an environment that will facilitate collaboration and support among nations that already share so much. But the risks involved in not taking up the challenge are as great as the potential for leadership and new ideas in this vital, burgeoning region of Asia.

Note

1 Gamini Wijesuriya. "Are We Ready to Learn? Lessons from the South Asian Region," in Neville Agnew and Janet Bridgland (eds.), *Of the Past, for the Future. Integrating Archaeology and Conservation, Proceedings of the Conservation Theme at the 5th World Archaeological Congress, Washington, D.C., 22–26 June 2003*. (Los Angeles: Getty Conservation Institute, 2006), 160.

PART V

Central Asia

Introduction

Afghanistan, Kazakhstan, Kyrgyzstan, Tajikistan, Turkmenistan and Uzbekistan

The six landlocked nations that constitute Central Asia share a history influenced by fluid exchange, largely attributable to the more than 2,000 year legacy of the great Asian trade routes commonly referred to as the Silk Road.[1] These corridors connected the region to the civilizations of China, Persia and the Eastern Mediterranean, while the equally important "Great Indian Road" south, through Afghanistan to India, completed one of history's most storied cultural crossroads.[2] Though sparsely populated today by Asian standards, the vast region boasts a number of ancient urban settlements, several of which remain major population centers and modern capitals to this day. The region's nomadic people have played hugely influential roles in shaping the culture and contours of history in Central Asia through cycles of conflict and symbiosis with the region's important urban centers. Cities like Samarkand, Herat, Ghazni and Bukhara today struggle to balance modern development with urban conservation, while places like Ai Khanoum, Panjakent, Otrar and Merv (the last of which was thought to have once been the largest city in the world) survive only as vast archaeological sites punctuated by massive, crumbling mud brick edifices.[3] The effective conservation of earthen architecture – the region's principal historic building material – stands above all else as the Central Asia's chief heritage management challenge.

All six countries today share an Islamic heritage that greatly informs the region's contemporary culture. Historically, they also share overlapping influences from antiquity, and later Timurid, Ghaznavid, Mongol, Mughal, Persian to Russian and finally Soviet empires. The legacy of the USSR remains deeply imprinted on the modern nations of Central Asia. Kazakhstan, Kyrgyzstan, Tajikistan, Turkmenistan and Uzbekistan were part of the Soviet Union from the 1920s until 1991, whereas the Soviet invasion of Afghanistan in 1979 contributed to decades of instability that continue to reverberate worldwide. This shared history suggests many opportunities for regional cooperation on cultural heritage management, but to date these have largely gone unfulfilled due to a regional climate of instability and competing governmental priorities within each country. Nevertheless, an accounting of common architectural conservation challenges serves as a steppingstone toward solutions for addressing them, and successful individual projects also represent goals that the neighboring countries might aim to match. The contemporary climate of political volatility, however, hangs heavily over the region, with sectarian and ethnic tensions, along with civil and regional wars that range from simmering (in the case of Kyrgyzstan and Uzbekistan) to full-blown (in the case of Afghanistan and Tajikistan).

Due to these conditions, many heritage resources in the Central Asian countries remain highly vulnerable, despite concerted efforts on the part of the limited local conservation community and international agencies. Direct damage from open conflict and official neglect (including deterioration, improper conservation and looting), conspires with environmental conditions that are especially detrimental to archaeological sites and ancient mud brick structures. The challenges related to conserving mud brick architecture cannot be overstated: erosion due to exposure and age, deterioration caused by water and wind, the presence of soluble salts and a lack of effective maintenance strategies for exposed archaeological resources stand out as the chief reasons for the poor condition of many of the historic buildings of Central Asia.

The Soviet-era practice of reconstructing monumental architecture, vividly exemplified by the almost completely rebuilt fifteenth century Bibi Khanoum mosque in Samarkand, Uzbekistan, persists in the region despite complications associated with the practice. While large-scale reconstructions can result in fully legible buildings that convey the grandeur of their original builder's intentions, the reconstructions are frequently carried out using materials that are physically and sometimes visually incompatible with surviving historic fabric. The projects also frequently involve a degree of conjecture that clashes with most international conservation norms. In contrast, vast ruined cities that exist only as archaeological sites, such as Panjikent, Tajikistan, can be reasonably well-conserved as archaeological sites, but with limited professional capacity for interpretation and presentation these important ancient sites remain largely imperceptible to all but a few visitors and local stakeholders. The proper balance between the two approaches remains a key aspect of developing a successful regional approach to architectural conservation in the region.

Afghanistan ratified the UNESCO World Heritage Convention in 1979 and the former Soviet republics followed suit within a few years of their independence. However, as of 2015 only Kazakhstan, Kyrgyzstan and Tajikistan had ICOMOS national committees, reflecting the relatively limited professional capacity in the region.[4] In the years immediately following the Central Asian republics' independence, UNESCO, bolstered by Funds in Trust donations made principally by the Japanese government, has supported a host of conservation projects in several Central Asian countries, with the arrangement channeling millions of US dollars put toward these efforts.[5] In Afghanistan, Italian teams and the *Délégation Archéologique Française en Afghanistan* (DAFA) were especially active for decades prior to the 1979 Soviet invasion, after which further work became impossible. Since the ousting of the Taliban government in 2001 numerous international teams and aid resources have poured into Afghanistan with substantial amounts of both aid and goodwill, but these responses have not always been coordinated on a regional level with other Central Asian efforts, and in some cases have come under criticism for their level of effectiveness.

As is the case across much of Asia, conservation approaches in the region have frequently involved a focus on monumental heritage. During the Soviet years and into the present day, this approach has often resulted in clearing away contextual buildings in once extremely dense cities in order to "present" the monuments, or to create tourist-oriented plazas for cultural events. Post-independence projects have begun to confront the complex legacy of Soviet conservation methodology, although examples of updated conservation approaches are relatively few. While the Soviet era generated a great deal of scholarship revealing the rich history of the Central Asian republics, much of this material was not widely available outside of the Soviet sphere, and thus can be difficult to access today. An additional complication related to this legacy is that Russian tends to be the preferred language among conservationists in the former Soviet republics, which limits the audience for scholarship and professional networking.[6]

The work of international organizations around Asian trade corridors places the region at the center of an emerging heritage typology – the cultural route – that will likely continue to evolve in the Central Asian context in the decades to come. Similarly, the historic trajectory of the region has made it a natural locus for the study of cultural landscapes; the World Heritage Sulaiman-Too Sacred Mountain in Kyrgyzstan is one such site where a collection of natural, built and prehistoric features combine to tell the story of this great trading hub. Areas associated with the region's distinctive nomadic cultures are additional, promising areas for growth and leadership on the part of the Central Asian countries.

The field of architectural conservation in Central Asia faces profound challenges despite the cultural richness of the region and the many opportunities that exist for effective, collaborative heritage management. Currently, the only two Asian cultural sites on the list of World Heritage in Danger are within the region: the Cultural Landscape and Archaeological Resources of the Bamiyan Valley and the Minaret and Archaeological Remains of Jam, both in Afghanistan.[7] Innumerable lesser-known sites that might have been difficult to address under the best of circumstances have not fared well in recent decades due to the extraordinary threats to architectural resources in the region. Large-scale internal and geo-political changes will need to transpire before these situations improve measurably, though there are some promising signs of long-term political stability in countries such as Kazakhstan that could create more favorable conditions for conservation. In addition to political stability, sustainable strategies for the protection of archaeological sites and for the care of ancient earthen architecture remain the greatest conservation-specific needs in the region. Very limited opportunities exist for advanced training in architectural conservation or site management in Central Asia, and political instability – particularly in Afghanistan – has also contributed to a paucity of qualified professional practitioners as the educated and well-trained are forced by strife to seek more secure lives elsewhere.

Effective urban conservation planning and master planning strategies would also greatly aid authorities' abilities to manage the inevitable change in the historic Central Asian cities, such as Samarkand, Kabul, Bukhara, Ashkabad, Herat and Tashkent. Too often approaches have consisted of hastily executed projects coordinated to commemorate anniversaries related to national figures or the founding of historic cities, rather than systematically planned and carefully completed conservation projects. In Afghanistan, some of the fiercest fighting occurred in the heart of its historic cities, with predictably destructive results. Risk preparedness strategies in this seismically active zone are another area with great potential benefits, as earthquakes affecting Tajikistan and Afghanistan in 2015 demonstrate. Seismic activity will continue to strike without warning, but preparation in the form of enforceable building codes and seismic strengthening of historic structures, including traditional residential buildings, would greatly aid architectural heritage conservation and the well-being of the local citizenry alike.

Looting, along with direct damage from warfare and related iconoclastic actions and the atmosphere of lawlessness that exists in conflict zones have proven devastating to the region's heritage resources. Ai Khanoum, the enormously significant fourth century BCE archaeological site in northern Afghanistan is sadly all but lost due to decades of uncontrolled looting, and of course the deliberate destruction of the seventh century CE Buddha statues at Bamiyan stands out as one of the worst cultural violations since World War II.

Beyond UNESCO, several conservation-focused organizations have maintained a steady presence in Central Asia, with generally positive results. The Aga Khan Historic Cities program has long been involved in the region, with a particularly successful string of community-oriented conservation projects in Kabul and Herat. These noteworthy efforts have focused on broader social benefits in the neighborhoods of the country's long-suffering cities – in particular Kabul – in addition to the conservation of their historic buildings. Among its crowning achievements is the revival of the sixteenth century garden and public park, Bagh-e Babur, which artfully combined cultural landscape and building restoration, urban design and community empowerment. Grenoble (France)-based CRATerre EAG, an organization that focuses on the conservation of earthen architecture, has undertaken projects and capacity building efforts at Merv and Old Nisa in Turkmenistan in sequential years, and in so doing has helped to identify common issues among the countries in Central Asia and means by which they may be addressed.[8]

The challenges facing architectural conservation in Central Asia are profound, but the consequences of further degradation to an unparalleled legacy of architecture and cultural development are greater. Perhaps more than any other region in Asia, the countries of Central Asia stand to benefit from an enhanced, collaborative approach among the six nations and a sustained level of engagement on the part of the broader international conservation community on their behalf. The increasingly dire circumstances of cultural heritage in Syria, Iraq and Yemen point to a worst-case scenario for further decline in Afghanistan or the potential failure of authoritarian or fragile governments in the former Soviet republics. With concerted effort to avoid these circumstances, this complex and rapidly changing region can position itself to regain the tremendous architectural and cultural achievements of its storied past.

Notes

1. In his book *Lost Enlightenment: Central Asia's Golden Age from the Arab Conquest to Tamerlane* historian S. Frederick Starr convincingly argues that the term "Silk Road" overly generalizes the nature of trade through Central Asia between 100 BCE and 1500 CE. Rather than an economy dominated by a single commodity shipped from China to points west, Starr notes that trade included a wide range of goods beyond silk, such as precious stones and manufactured goods, and that north/south exchange through Afghanistan to India was equally if not more important than the east/west routes. Accordingly, we will use the term "Silk Road" sparingly, and generally in reference to specific initiatives that carry the moniker. Instead, more general terms like "Asian trade routes" will be favored in order to more accurately reflect the nature of these crucial phenomena, and the role that Central Asia played therein. Reference: S. Frederick Starr. *Lost Enlightenment: Central Asia's Golden Age from the Arab Conquest to Tamerlane.* (Princeton: Princeton University Press, 2013), 43.
2. This term is attributable to the Uzbek scholar and archaeologist, Edvard Rtveladze, from his 2012 book *The Great Indian Road: From the History of the Most Important Trade Routes of Eurasia*.
3. In the twelfth century, during its time as a Seljuk capital, Merv's population has been estimated at 200,000. Starr, 425.
4. For information, see ICOMOS, Web. www.icomos.org/images/DOCUMENTS/Secretariat/Adresses/adresses-cn.pdf. Accessed June 14, 2016.
5. Laurent Lévi-Strauss and Roland Lin, "Safeguarding Silk Road Sites in Central Asia," in Neville Agnew (ed.), *Conservation of Ancient Sites on the Silk Road*. (Los Angeles: Getty Conservation Institute, 2010), 56–57.
6. UNESCO report, *Understanding World Heritage in Asia and the Pacific: The Second Cycle of Periodic Reporting 2010-2012.* (Paris: UNESCO, 2012), 45.
7. There are, sadly, a number of cultural sites on the list in continental Asia, specifically in Syria, Yemen, Palestine and Iraq. For details, see http://whc.unesco.org/en/danger/. Accessed June 14, 2016.
8. For information on CRATerre, see http://craterre.org/action:projets/?page=&perpage=&by=continent&continent=AS. Accessed June 14, 2016.

22

AFGHANISTAN

A global center of Buddhism and Zoroastrianism until 1,400 years ago when Islamic conquerors invaded from the west, Afghanistan remains today a vibrant and volatile crossroads of political and religious forces. The country's rich heritage, along with its beleaguered populace, has been subjected to the ravages of nearly four decades of strife, the result of ideological and military struggles between the former Soviet Union, the United States, religious fundamentalists, and the complex, heterogeneous ethnic makeup of the nation itself. The ensuing casualties from these conflicts cannot be overstated, from the much-publicized destruction of the Bamiyan Buddhas in March 2001 and the brazen looting of irreplaceable artifacts from the once-world-renowned National Museum in Kabul, to the systematic, decades-long pillaging of the fourth century BCE Greco-Bactrian site of Ai Khanoum.[1] Afghanistan today struggles mightily to support a heritage management infrastructure capable of protecting its priceless cultural assets.

The current state of professional practice in Afghanistan faces nearly every challenge that confronts the field of architectural conservation, including dispersed sites with sparse documentation, depleted professional capacity, narrow seasonal windows for fieldwork, deteriorated resources requiring all manner of conservation interventions, and a volatile security situation that places the physical safety of international and local teams in jeopardy.[2] Economic development, which is urgently needed in a country where nearly the entire economy relies upon international aid and ongoing military campaigns, has begun to bud, but in many cases opportunities have been positioned in conflict with conservation priorities. Urban development in the years since the Taliban's overthrow in December 2001 has generally not followed well-intended conservation plans or regulations for the country's unique historic cities instituted by international and local organizations. And, while large-scale expansion of a nascent mining sector holds much promise, early steps have discouragingly been presented as false dichotomies of conservation versus progress. Although some measures have been undertaken to re-establish national institutional capacity to manage the country's dispersed, varied cultural resources, the security situation remains fragile, political problems are entrenched, and the government's ability to protect highly vulnerable heritage sites across the entire country remains tenuous.

Millennia of cultural accomplishment and loss

Although the picture of present-day Afghanistan is blurred by images of war and ideological intolerance, the region historically has been a diverse melting pot of ideas and traditions, fueled by the rich Asian trade routes between the Indian subcontinent, the Iranian plateau, and the great civilizations of the Mediterranean and Far East. Through its large empires and dynastic capitals, the region spawned several sophisticated centers of art and learning, from the Buddhist center of Bamiyan, the madrassas of Herat, the intellectual court of Ghazni, to the gardens of Kabul, shrines of Kandahar and monasteries of Balkh. American archaeological expeditions led by Louis Dupree[3] in the 1960s and 1970s uncovered evidence of Paleolithic sites dating to 100,000 years before the present in Afghanistan's far northeast Badakhshan Province, demonstrating a deep human history within the country's boundaries.[4] Archaeological sites with Harappan-era (2600–1900 BCE) deposits, such as Shortugai and Mundigak, indicate early connections to the advanced civilizations of the Indus Valley (located mainly in today's India and Pakistan).

In 330–329 BCE Alexander of Macedon swept into Afghanistan, ultimately conquering the Zoroastrian center of Balkh and thus setting the stage for the later Seleucid and Greco-Bactrian kingdoms. Based at cities including Balkh and Ai Khanoum, the rulers of these dynasties maintained long-standing cultural and economic links to the West that influenced trade, the arts and religious practices across the region.[5] The formerly nomadic Kushans established an empire across Afghanistan that extended well into modern India and China between 100 BCE and 200 CE, fostering the spread of Buddhism and Zoroastrianism from their capital of Begram (in present day Parwan Province) and other major cities such as Purusapura (modern Peshawar, Pakistan) and Dilbarjin.[6] Sassanians from Iran replaced the Kushans by the third century CE, strengthening ties between Afghanistan, the Iranian plateau and Central Asia that had lasting architectural influences. The Arab invasions that swept east across Western Asia in the seventh century ended the Sassanian period, and established Islam as a dominant force in Afghanistan, a role it maintains to the present day.[7]

At the turn of the eleventh century, Sultan Mahmoud (971–1030 CE) established a great capital at Ghazni, from which he launched merciless raids into northern India, using the spoils of conquest to finance a spectacular period of architectural and intellectual flowering. Mahmoud's court served as patron to the great scholar Biruni, and his exploits funded the construction of a now-ruined, grandiose palace, Lashkari Bazar, and triumphal arch at Lashkar Gah (historically known as Bost, where the arch still stands).[8] The Ghorid and Kwarazim empires followed, but soon fell before the catastrophic Mongol invasions led by Chinggis Khan beginning in 1219 CE. The Mongol onslaught was followed by that of Timur (also known as Tamerlane), who launched his conquests from Balkh beginning in 1369 CE, and ultimately amassed one of the largest land empires in Asian history. Timurid successors developed Herat and Balkh, the former serving as a capital under Timur's son Shah Rukh and his queen Gawhar Shad, who were great patrons to the arts, literature and architecture. Between 1405 and 1457 CE the couple oversaw the construction of the Goharshad Mosque, which is located in today's Khorasan Province in northwest Iran and was named for the queen.[9] Babur (1483–1530 CE), Timur's direct descendant, established himself at Kabul before launching an invasion of India that ultimately led to the taking of Delhi in 1526, and thus the founding of the Mughal Empire that dominated much of South Asia for the next three centuries. Kabul remained linked to the Mughal Empire to the south while Herat, to its west, was under the influence of the Persian Safavids. Kandahar, in the south, alternated between the two rival empires until Ahmad Shah Durrani united the majority of modern Afghanistan from there in 1749. Known as Ahmad Shah Baba, he is considered the "father" of Afghanistan, and his turquoise-domed mausoleum remains a prominent building in Kandahar today.[10]

During the "Great Game" era of the nineteenth and early twentieth centuries, European empire builders viewed Afghanistan as a buffer zone between the British South Asian territories and that of the Russian czars. The Russian sphere of influence spread south and east during the 1860s through the 1880s, gradually absorbing all of the Central Asian khanates. The armies of Dost Mohammad Khan and his sons rebuffed British attempts to exert the same level of control in the First, Second and Third Anglo-Afghan Wars.[11] Although ultimately successful at keeping the British partly at bay, the wars resulted in the punitive destruction of the great citadel of Ghazni along with Kabul's ancient bazaar.

During most of the twentieth century, the country was a quasi-independent emirate and kingdom, though perpetually burdened by contentious and often violent internal leadership struggles. In 1922 the French signed an agreement with the then-new Afghan government establishing the *Délégation Archéologique Française en Afghanistan* (DAFA), which was granted exclusive rights to conduct archaeological excavations in the country, including an arrangement to share any finds between museums in Paris and Kabul.[12] Until its work was halted by the Soviet–Afghan conflict in 1982, the

FIGURE 22.1 The eleventh century triumphal arch at Lashkar Gah, the ancient city of Bost, remains despite several episodes of destruction over the centuries.

DAFA generated an enormous volume of scholarship concerning sites across the country, including the Greco-Buddhist sites at Hadda (first century BCE–first century CE, near Jalalabad), Kapisa (modern-day Begram, dating from the fifth century BCE, near Kabul), Mundigak (Harappan-era site, near Kandahar) and Ai Khanoum (Greco-Bactrian site on the Amu Darya River in northern Afghanistan). In the 1960s the French monopoly on archaeological work ceased, opening the door for various American, Japanese, German, Indian, Soviet and Italian archaeological missions. During this climate of tenuous stability, which lasted until 1979, the foreign archaeological teams worked in coordination with the National Museum in Kabul and the Afghan Institute of Archaeology (established in 1965), to expand the scholarly understanding of Afghanistan's history, and build the famed museum collections that would tragically come under siege in the decades that followed.[13]

A series of coups beginning in 1973 led to a Marxist rebellion in 1978, leaving Afghanistan vulnerable to Soviet occupation; in 1979 troops from the USSR entered Kabul. Afghan freedom fighters, known as the Mujahideen, operated with assistance from the United States, Saudi Arabia and Pakistan, and were ultimately able to drive out the Soviet forces after a decade of bitter struggle.[14] Tragically, the result of the Soviet withdrawal was yet more fighting by rival local groups resulting in another period of discord. This included numerous atrocities on the human scale, alongside cultural crimes such as the destruction of portions of Kabul's Old City and the serial looting of the National Museum. Taking advantage of the political vacuum, the Taliban, a militia of largely ethnic Pashtun Islamists, many of whom were former Mujahideen fighters, managed to assume control of the country in 1996. After seizing Kabul, the Taliban imposed a strict version of Islamic law in an effort to create their version of a pure Sharia state,[15] which banned representational imagery of all kinds, including sculpture and architectural ornament. Although in July 1999, Taliban leader Mullah Omar had issued a decree that appeared aimed at protecting Afghan cultural sites – including the famed 1,500-year-old Bamiyan Buddhas – the ruling militia's views soon changed.[16]

On February 27, 2001, the Taliban issued an edict that sealed the fate of the Buddhas, stating: "As ordered by the *ulema* (Islamic scholars) and the Supreme Court of the Islamic Emirate of Afghanistan all the statues must be destroyed so that no one can worship or respect them in the future."[17] With this, the monumental rock-cut Bamiyan Buddha statues, among the finest and most impressive examples of Gandharan-style Buddha images in Central Asia, became a prime target of Taliban extremists. Originally painted and gilded, and accompanied by numerous rock cut caves that were in turn covered with exquisite mural paintings, the 53 and 38 m tall Buddhas (174 ft and 125 ft, respectively) proved an all-too-tempting and symbolic target for the Taliban.

In one of the most barbaric acts of cultural assault since World War II, beginning on March 12, 2001 the statues were completely destroyed using anti-aircraft artillery, tank mines and finally explosive charges, despite the protests of Afghan and international heritage protection organizations alike. While the episode had its roots in the ancient tradition of iconoclasm, it was also part of a very modern rejection of the international community's concern over art objects at the perceived expense of the Afghan population itself. In the words of a Taliban envoy, they acted against an international community that "will give millions of dollars to save un-Islamic stone statues but not one cent to save the lives of Afghan men, women and children."[18] But despite the complexities of the circumstances that led to the destruction, the result is best summed up by a statement from then-UNESCO Director General Koichiro Matsuura issued the day after the action had been confirmed: "It is abominable to witness the cold and calculated destruction of cultural properties which were the heritage of the Afghan people, and, indeed, of the whole of humanity."[19]

In the last days before the destruction, UNESCO and numerous other governments, organizations and individuals mounted a massive campaign to stop this action, including assembling a delegation of fifteen Islamic scholars that were due to fly to Afghanistan on the day before the Buddhas were

FIGURE 22.2 The principal Bamiyan Buddha before (1963) and after (2009) destruction.

destroyed to make a last-minute appeal.[20] The ultimate failure of the international community to stave off the actions has led to some re-evaluation of the role of UNESCO and the United Nations in matters pertaining to cultural heritage in conflict. "One of the things, we should look into in the future is how to set up a new legal framework with credible punishment for … crimes against culture," commented former UNESCO Director General Matsuura, at the time. Then-UN Director-General Kofi Annan offered another view, ruling out punitive action, suggesting instead that the best way to prevent the destruction of old statues in the future was to launch a campaign to educate people to respect what was sacred to others.[21] (See also sidebar below on Bamiyan Buddhas.)

The fall of the Taliban at the hands of a US-led international coalition came in December of that year, leading to yet another epoch of war, chaos, neglect and looting of the nation's heritage assets. After thirteen years, 300,000 military and civilian casualties, and at least US$1 trillion spent by the American government on military operations and reconstruction efforts, the longest overseas campaign in US history officially concluded in 2014.[22] Over that period the international community invested heavily in the rebuilding of Afghanistan's institutions and professional capacity, not only in the field of architectural conservation, but also in the nation's government, infrastructure and political institutions.

To date, the potential and the promise of this period of rebuilding have been mixed. Transition from war to peacetime has critical implications for the Afghan economy: the World Bank estimates that 97 percent of the country's GDP is connected to the international military presence, which as of 2015 was coming to an end.[23] Economic development opportunities exist in Afghanistan, but will require sustained investment, a stable government and a secure environment to fully take root. The Afghan government estimates that its mineral wealth in the form of iron, copper and gold, along with oil and gas reserves, stands at US$1 trillion, representing a possible economic savior.[24] But, at least as currently imagined, extractive industries have been positioned in direct opposition to the country's architectural and heritage conservation goals. This conflict is playing out at some of its most vulnerable sites, such as Mes Aynak (Logar Province) and Hagjikak (Bamiyan Province), rich mining areas that each overlap important archaeological sites. At the same time, a pent-up desire to develop commercial and real estate opportunities, and the sudden availability of capital to do so, is resulting in the disappearance of remnant historic districts that managed to escape the wars, in places such as Herat, Kandahar and Kabul.[25]

Facing Afghanistan's rebuilding and recovery

Critics have noted a number of flaws in the international community's approach to the reconstruction of Afghan cultural heritage infrastructure, including the perceived prioritization of pre-Islamic heritage, which risks alienating the current, overwhelmingly Muslim population.[26] Accusations of organizational inefficiencies, including corruption, and a lack of overall coordination within what has become one of the largest international rebuilding efforts since World War II have been leveled by Afghan and foreign critics alike. The situation has led long-time practitioners in the field, such as the eminent Afghan archaeologist and current director of the DAFA, Zemaryalai Tarzi, to vent about the approach to the recovery effort: "All these endless discussions among experts are pitiful, yielding no positive results."[27]

Unchecked cultural vandalism and looting of Afghanistan's heritage were rampant problems years before the international community focused its attention on the Bamiyan destruction. In the decades following the departure of the DAFA in 1979, the hugely important archaeological site of Ai Khanoum has been almost completely destroyed by looters, reducing it to its current "lunarlike appearance."[28] Looting of archaeological sites throughout the country has been endemic, with some estimating that as many as 90 percent of sites across Afghanistan have been illegally excavated.[29] In the absence of any kind of conservation measures, large-scale sites have deteriorated irrevocably during the war years, including the Shahr-i-Mahmoud, the massive and architecturally influential eleventh century mud brick palace complex at Bost built by Mahmoud of Ghazni.[30] During the recent war years, much of the on-the-ground protection of Afghanistan's archaeological, architectural and movable cultural heritage fell to a small group of organized non-governmental organizations (NGOs), working alongside intrepid Afghan and foreign individuals who took great risks to try to save as much as possible. This period spawned a broad web of advocacy organizations, based in-country as well as abroad, that support various aspects of Afghanistan's cultural heritage.

FIGURE 22.3 The archaeological sites of Mes Aynak (Logar Province) among others nearby have been threatened in recent years due to mineral mining in the area.

The Society for the Preservation of Afghanistan's Cultural Heritage (SPACH) is one such early player. Founded in Islamabad, Pakistan in September 1994 by a group of concerned Afghani and foreign professionals including the American writer and heritage advocate Nancy Hatch Dupree, it was established in response to the desperate situation in Afghanistan and in an attempt to stop the destruction, plunder and illegal sales of Afghan artifacts. SPACH was involved in protecting the Bamiyan Buddhas at an earlier phase, when warlords were threatening to damage the statues, but perhaps its greatest moment came during an equally dire episode involving the National Museum in Kabul.[31] Established at its present location in 1931, the museum once possessed an enviable collection of artifacts that chronicled centuries of Afghanistan's diverse civilizations. During the war years that preceded the Taliban's rule, the facility suffered direct damage from heavy fighting, and its collection was thoroughly, and in some cases systematically, looted. These circumstances led dedicated Afghan and foreign professionals on the ground during the 1990s to undertake several emergency repair campaigns, in addition to removing and hiding portions of its collection for safekeeping. Ultimately over 70 percent of the museum's collection was looted and most likely illicitly sold to collectors. The Afghan Institute of Archaeology suffered a worse fate, with 100 percent of its artifacts stolen or destroyed.[32]

A hidden cache of these artifacts was recovered in 2003 and ultimately became a highly successful international traveling exhibit, entitled *Afghanistan: Hidden Treasures from the National Museum, Kabul*. A sixteen-city tour helped raise awareness of the collection's plight along with that of the country's cultural heritage, while generating much needed funding for the Ministry of Information and Culture's museums program. The National Museum's plight led to a partnership with the Oriental Institute in Chicago (USA) to aid in electronic cataloging, archival storage in preparation for a move to a new facility, and staff training, with the support of the Afghan Cultural Heritage Consulting Organization (ACHCO).[33] After an international competition, a Spanish firm was selected in 2012 to design a new National Museum, with financial commitments from the US and Afghan governments covering the cost of the new building, which will include flexible exhibition space and enhanced security as compared to the existing facility.[34]

Another focus of internationally supported NGOs in post-Taliban Afghanistan is the revival of traditional crafts industries, including jewelry making, miniature painting and calligraphy, along with architectural trades such as wood carving, stone masonry, tile making and plasterwork. The Turquoise Mountain Foundation, established in Kabul in 2006 by the British author and now-Member of Parliament, Rory Stewart, aims to train students (male and female alike) during three-year apprenticeship programs in marketable crafts and trade skills.[35] Housed in a series of rehabilitated traditional buildings in the Murad Khani neighborhood, the Foundation supports its activities by marketing students' products worldwide, generating as much as US$1.5 million in sales each year.[36] Attached to the German ICOMOS team at Bamiyan is a stone-carving workshop, which aims to revive the region's traditional stonemasonry skills that flourished for centuries in the valley, but have been threatened with extinction due to the decades of conflict and the iconoclastic views of the earlier regime.[37]

In a bid to reinforce a local professional capacity in the country that is severely depleted, nearly all internationally supported conservation projects include a training component for Afghan professionals. In an effort to "teach the teachers," the University of Arizona (USA) launched a program in 2013 to host three faculty members from Kabul University at its College of Architecture, Planning & Landscape Architecture in Tucson, with support from the US State Department and the US National Park Service.[38] The program aims to share the latest professional practices in architectural conservation and collections management, so that the Kabul University faculty can better prepare their students to undertake fieldwork and oversee conservation institutions in their home country.

Responsibility for managing architectural conservation policy and practice at the national level currently falls to the Ministry of Information and Culture, which also supports an Institute of Archaeology and Department for the Protection and Rehabilitation of Historical Monuments. In 2004 the transitional government adopted the national Law on the Protection of Historical and Cultural Properties, which establishes legal thresholds for protected objects (a minimum of 100 years of age), and empowers an Archaeological Committee with decision-making authority around designation and delineation of registered monuments. Owing to the epidemic of illegal looting, the legislation focuses principally on the treatment of movable objects, with provisions around the sale and transfer of antiquities, the management of archaeological excavations and museum collections.[39] Reconstructing Afghanistan's national heritage infrastructure remains a work in progress: the adoption of the Cultural Heritage Law in 2004 sets forth basic protections for historic buildings and archaeological sites, but does not address conservation practice or adherence to professional standards.[40]

Months after the fall of the Taliban, UNESCO began actively collaborating with the Ministry of Information and Culture to coordinate the work of various international conservation missions with the central government of Afghanistan. The move signaled a positive commitment on the part of the international community for supporting conservation projects in Afghanistan, and for helping to rebuild professional capacity in a country where the availability of domestic personnel and financial resources were severely constrained. In 2002 a working group set a series of priorities that constituted a roadmap for the next decade of international collaborations in the country: construction of a new National Museum in Kabul and reconstitution of its collection; identification of priority projects and potential World Heritage Sites; reassembly and updating of national inventories of sites and movable objects; support for a national theater program; stemming the tide of illegal antiquities trafficking; and establishment of an International Coordination Committee (ICC) to provide a forum for sharing effective strategies, engaging Afghan leaders and advocating for donor support.[41] Priority conservation projects that launched following the 2002 conference included stabilization of the twelfth century Minaret at Jam, urban conservation projects in Kabul and Herat, documentation and protection measures at Bamiyan, and a series of museum and collections-focused efforts in the central-eastern former imperial capital of Ghazni.[42]

The Italian Archaeological Mission in Afghanistan has a long history of research, excavation and collections management in the country, beginning in 1956 at Ghazni and continuing until the 1979 Soviet invasion. In 2002 when international teams began returning to Afghanistan after a more than two-decade absence, the Italians were at the fore. They participated in projects that included shoring up the foundations of the Minaret of Jam to protect the remote, vulnerable structure from seasonal flooding (work performed in 2005–2006), emergency structural measures to support the Fifth Minaret in the Musalla Complex in Herat, and the completion of the Museum of Islamic Art in Rawza (just outside of central Ghazni), which is housed in the rehabilitated Timurid-era Mausoleum of Abdul Razzaq.[43] The museum project originally began under the pre-war period of Afghan–Italian

FIGURE 22.4 The 65 m high (213 ft) Minaret at Jam (1194 CE) in Ghor Province east of Herat is a UNESCO World Heritage Site, and is a rare surviving structure of its era. The masonry foundation of the minaret is subject to periodic flooding by the adjacent Jam Rud and Hari Rud rivers, and the structure itself is leaning. UNESCO and the Ministry of Information and Culture have undertaken several campaigns to protect the foundation from erosion, to protect the site from looting, and to document the minaret and its context.

collaboration, but had to be suspended prior to completion due to the darkening political conditions. Despite a planned triumphant opening following years of work, a deteriorating security situation in the area led to its indefinite postponement. Underscoring the continued security volatility, in September 2014 a Taliban attack on the provincial governor's compound damaged another museum facility (the Museum of Pre-Islamic and Islamic Art in central Ghazni), killing or injuring dozens of persons while also destroying thousands of artifacts. Undeterred, the Italian team and their Afghan partners have vowed to rebuild the facility and restore the damaged artifacts.[44]

Of course, the nexus for recovery following ideologically driven destruction of cultural heritage remains the Bamiyan Valley. As of 2015, multiple efforts were under way to stabilize, interpret and protect the ruins of the Buddha statues, along with Islamic-era defensive fortifications and other threatened sites. In 2013 the government of Italy reaffirmed its involvement in heritage conservation in Afghanistan by committing to help fund conservation and interpretation of the Shahr-i-Gholghola and Shahr-i-Zohak, a pair of ruined fortresses dating to the twelfth through thirteenth centuries, a project that will help tell the story of the valley's medieval Islamic period.[45] The Italians joined efforts by Swiss, French, Japanese, Korean and German teams working in the valley, which together are supporting a broad range of architectural conservation programs. Efforts include capacity building, training, and the promotion of local and visitors' awareness of the valley's strikingly rich heritage. A major initiative involving UNESCO, the Ministry of Information and Culture and the government of the Republic of Korea includes the development of the Bamiyan Cultural Centre, a permanent facility with a mission to promote "cross cultural understanding and heritage safeguarding through education, training, research, lectures and performance events."[46] In 2015, the design jury and the president of Afghanistan endorsed a design by an Argentine-led firm, with construction on the ambitious facility slated to begin shortly thereafter.

FIGURE 22.5a, b and c A Museum of Pre-Islamic and Islamic Art in Ghazni was completed in 2013 (a) but was destroyed by a Taliban attack in 2014 (b, c). Despite a loss of life and much of the museum's holdings, internationally assisted efforts to conserve and display Afghanistan's earliest cultural heritage continue.

Reconstruction and commemoration in Bamiyan: controversy around the treatment of the Buddhas

The international response that followed the 2001 destruction of the Bamiyan Buddhas brought to the fore a vivid debate on the role of reconstruction, the application of the Venice Charter, and the decision making process between international conservation missions, UNESCO and host nations.[47] UNESCO and its Expert Working Group, which was assembled in 2002 to make recommendations on the conservation and development of the Bamiyan World Heritage Site, had determined in 2011 that fully reconstructing both Buddha statues was not feasible in terms of cost and current conservation tenets. The Afghan government, on the other hand, viewed reconstruction of at least the smaller (eastern) Buddha as both a symbol of defiance against the still-threatening Taliban, in addition to a major tourist draw for an area that expects to depend upon visitors for its economic development.

In December 2013 UNESCO asked the Afghan government to halt the ICOMOS Germany-led conservation project, which had been tasked with performing stabilization measures in the niches that once housed the huge statues. As part of an effort to structurally reinforce the cave wall, the conservators had begun to reconstruct the feet of the Buddha statue (a feature that had itself been rebuilt by a joint Afghan/Indian team in the 1970s). Although Afghan government officials had sanctioned the work, UNESCO officials in Paris and Kabul determined that it went beyond the scope of stabilization, instead approaching an unauthorized reconstruction of the lost statue.[48] Citing other examples of partially reconstructed buildings such as the Roman Forum as justification for the approach, along with the availability of some original material that could be used to reconstruct the statue, the German team argued they were facilitating future conservation measures, and acting in the interest of the local populace.[49] Afghan authorities confirmed that they remained interested in the reconstruction option, with the Ministry of Culture and Information having formally submitted a request to UNESCO to rebuild the eastern Buddha, and local government officials and the Bamiyan Tourism Association supportive of the approach.[50]

As of 2015 the debate remains unresolved, highlighting the complexity of defining appropriate means for the commemoration and recovery of lost heritage objects. Precedents exist elsewhere in the world for each end of the spectrum, including the rebuilt Stari Most (Old Bridge) in Mostar, Bosnia and Herzegovina and the ruins of the Genbaku Dome in Hiroshima – each representing different approaches to similar goals. Another argument posits that the Buddhas alone should not dominate the conversation around Bamiyan to the extent that they have, but instead should be part of a more holistic approach to recovery that involves multiple sites (such as the Shahr-i-Gholghola and Shahr-i-Zohak forts and the old Bazaar, the conservation of which is only beginning) along with broad-based economic development that includes but does not solely rely on tourism.

Conservation efforts at the urban scale

Since 2002, the Aga Khan Trust for Culture (AKTC) has remained active throughout the country, with significant projects executed in the Old Cities of Kabul and Herat. Kabul traces its roots to an early Buddhist center, described by Ptolemy in 150 BCE. The city re-emerged as an important center under the Mughals after Babur, the dynastic founder, launched his invasion of India from there in 1526 CE. Babur's architectural contributions to Kabul consist of his beloved gardens, in addition to his own mausoleum. This legacy was augmented by successive dynasties including that of Timur Shah Durrani, who moved his capital to Kabul from Kandahar in the late eighteenth century, thereby affirming its present status as the Afghan capital. Heavy fighting in the 1990s damaged or destroyed much of Kabul's old city, but the post-Taliban peace allowed for a sustained period of conservation planning, into which the AKTC stepped. The AKTC's goal involved developing conservation plans based on surveying and mapping of historic properties, along with consultation with hundreds of households on neighborhood priorities, including key historic buildings, infrastructure and the identification of community planning goals.[51]

Surveys of Kabul's Asheqan wa Arefan, Chindawol and Kuche Gharabat neighborhoods identified a range of conservation and rehabilitation issues including deficient infrastructure, deferred maintenance of historic properties, a lack of communal spaces, and limited professional capacity at the municipal government level. The findings led the AKTC team to help establish the Kabul Old City Commission within the city government to support and vet conservation initiatives, and to focus on rehabilitating key historic buildings that would benefit resident communities. Among the first projects undertaken was the Uzbekha Mosque, a nineteenth century courtyard building that featured decorative plaster finishes and finely carved timber structural members, which required on-site training to consolidate and conserve. This set the stage for the conservation of several other community mosques in the area, along with the revival of a ruined *madrasa* to serve as an early childhood education center, and the repair and re-commissioning of several *hammam* (public baths) to serve residents in an area that lacked washing facilities in homes. Neighborhood engagement continued until 2007 with the conservation of dozens of traditional homes, most dating from the early twentieth century. This approach both

FIGURE 22.6 Rehabilitation of the Bagh-e Babur garden and memorial garden in the capital city Kabul by the Aga Khan Trust for Culture was a project selected for its capacity to be expanded to include wider areas of its historic setting.

benefited the district's historic fabric while also generating a group of skilled traditional craftspeople that could be deployed into subsequent conservation projects. In parallel with the site-specific building work, infrastructure upgrades were undertaken to help manage household wastewater, to clear and re-pave streets and to provide access to communal neighborhood wells. The comprehensive approach aimed to incorporate individual conservation projects within a larger effort to improve overall living and sanitation conditions for all residents, in order to make the historic neighborhood more livable and beneficial for the community as a whole.[52]

Beginning in 2002 the AKTC began a comprehensive rehabilitation of the Bagh-e Babur, a traditional garden and the gravesite of the first Mughal emperor. Building on the experience gained by AKTC's Historic Cities Support Programme (HCSP) in developing Al Azhar Park in Cairo, Egypt, the team in Kabul sought to revitalize the city's largest green public open space, a walled area of over 11 ha (27 acres) as a historic site that also provides communal recreation facilities and gathering spaces to an otherwise congested urban environment. The gardens and structures of Bagh-e Babur had been in decline since the mid-nineteenth century, but the 1990s fighting that engulfed the surrounding area resulted in direct damage, looting of materials, and the peacetime need for the clearing of landmines and unexploded ordinance, waste and debris. Beginning with a survey undertaken during 2002–2003 with initial financial support from the German government, the team undertook reconstruction of the traditional mud wall that surrounded the garden. This phase was followed by work on the brick arcade and marble enclosure around the grave itself, and the small Shahjahan Mosque, which had been built as a tribute by Babur's successor.[53] The garden's restoration included re-establishing its axial water feature, along with a series of terraces and pools based on archaeological and photographic evidence, as well as planting thousands of fruit trees based on Babur's own memoirs, which enumerated the types of trees he valued. A later phase involved the adaptive reuse of a 1890s *haremserai* known as the "Queens Palace" to create a public events venue, the rental of which contributes to the cost of the garden's maintenance.

From its inception, the Bagh-e Babur project was conceived of as the cornerstone of a larger sustainable economic development effort that will help generate employment opportunities, and promote civic engagement, infrastructure investment and quality of life improvements for the residents of the surrounding neighborhoods.[54] Now managed by the independent Bagh-e Babur Trust, the garden has been visited by nearly three million Afghans since 2008, and the revenue generated from this and special events means that the operation is now self-sustaining. The AKTC has capitalized on the Bagh-e Babur project with other major investments in the conservation of significant public buildings and open spaces, including the Timur Shah Mausoleum and associated park, Zarnegar Park and Bagh-e Qazi located elsewhere in the Old Town.[55]

Building on its earlier conservation efforts in Kabul, the AKTC launched the Herat Old City Rehabilitation Initiative in 2005. A major cultural center under the Timurid Dynasty (fourteenth through sixteenth centuries CE), Herat became part of the Persianate Safavid Dynasty before incorporation into what would become modern Afghanistan under Dost Mohammed in 1863. Herat's Old City was principally residential before most of its residents fled the conflict of the 1970s and 1990s. Their subsequent return in the early 2000s placed major pressure on the remaining suitable building stock in the old town, which resulted in unregulated and problematically executed commercial construction throughout Old Herat. This has further exacerbated problems with deficient infrastructure and traffic congestion.[56]

A property survey taken in 2005 and 2006 enabled the detailed mapping of the fabric of Herat's entire Old City, while contributing to the identification of notable infrastructure needs, building conditions, and potential candidates for conservation projects. The effort identified critical deficiencies in public infrastructure including sewage and household water systems, as well as a shortage of communal schools and medical facilities. In response, the AKTC implemented the conservation of dozens of public and private buildings throughout the Old City, including the adaptive reuse of the twelfth century Malik and fourteenth century Chahar Suq cisterns as an events space and conservation workshop, respectively.[57] Between 2005 and 2010, support from the US Ambassador's Fund for Cultural Preservation enabled conservation of the part of the historic citadel of Qala Ikhtyaruddin that now houses an important regional museum established in collaboration with the German Archaeological

Institute. The citadel complex is now regularly used for public events, including conferences. The AKTC also helped establish a Commission for the Safeguarding and Development of the Old City of Herat, which helps to oversee future planning and conservation efforts, and reviews new development proposals in the Old City for their appropriateness per conservation objectives as well as monitoring the ongoing transformation of the urban fabric. Two public buildings in the old city that were restored under the AKTC's program in Herat received UNESCO's Asia-Pacific Awards for Cultural Heritage Conservation in 2008.[58]

Building on this work in Herat, ACHCO has since 2013 documented and undertaken critical conservation measures at the mausolea of Shahzada Abdullah and Shahzada Abdul Qasim, with funding from the US State Department.[59] Dating from the Timurid era, Shahzada Abdullah retains extensive mosaic faience decoration that has been documented in detail, cleaned and stabilized along with a range of structural repairs. An important aspect of the project is the training of young Afghan professionals in documentation and practical conservation skills, to enable them to contribute to future initiatives.

The long-term success of the Kabul and Herat projects will rely on the degree to which further fighting can be avoided in the war-weary country, and the level of sustained support the local governments and international players can bring to the recovery effort.

a

FIGURE 22.7a, b and c Numerous efforts to conserve parts of the Old City of Herat (a) have been attempted since the 1980s, such as restoration of its Ansari entrance portal (b). Some of the most successful are by the Aga Khan Trust for Culture that since 2005 has implemented strategic conservation and adaptive reuse initiatives at public and private buildings as well as support of traditional building craft workshops (c).

Safeguarding Afghanistan's urban heritage: perspectives from the field, by Jolyon Leslie

The cities and towns of Afghanistan have long been hubs of commercial, social and cultural activity, as well as sites on which political and military rivalries are played out. Traditional urban bazaars, community mosques and merchant homes serve as physical markers of the ebb and flow of their historical development. Most Afghan cities have witnessed repeated cycles of investment and destruction, as they are looted and laid waste by rivals, only to rise from the ashes under a new regime whose control is challenged in turn by others who demolish or transform the legacy of their predecessors. While the violent overthrow of rulers was somewhat less common, this process of urban transformation during the twentieth century became an important projection of an image of a modern Afghan state. It is on the urban landscape that similar visions of progress continue to be played out to this day, although the wholesale transformations that are now under way risk destroying important traces of history. The challenge for Afghans today is to find a balance between safeguarding what is left of their urban heritage and enabling appropriate processes of development.

Since 2003, Afghanistan's cities have seen significant increases in population and a surge in private investments. This recovery comes after a prolonged period of conflict that resulted in destruction in some cities and a general lack of development and stagnation. At the core of some cities that are now recovering – Kabul, Kandahar, Herat, Ghazni, Balkh, Kunduz among others – stand areas of historic fabric that provide evidence of their past, both above and below ground. These "old cities" generally comprise an area, once ringed with defensive walls, with distinct residential and commercial quarters, on whose bazaars many inhabitants depended for their livelihoods.

Despite the efforts at transformation by planners and their foreign advisers, Afghanistan was unique in how much of its urban heritage survived, albeit in a degraded state, until the early 1990s. Several old cities, including Herat and Kandahar, suffered direct damage during the 1980s, but the conflict largely deterred public or private investment, which spared the historic quarters from the kind of "redevelopment" that might have taken place in more peaceful circumstances.

Kabul was an exception, however, when between 1992 and 1994 it was the focus of intense inter-factional fighting that caused widespread damage across the city, and resulted in the looting by mujahideen fighters of the National Museum. As they battled for control of the strategically located old city, these fighters indiscriminately destroyed homes, bazaars, mosques and shrines. It took years for war-damaged historic neighborhoods to be de-mined and for the process of resettlement and reconstruction to begin. Those owners who did invest in repairs did so cautiously, using traditional forms and materials, but much of the old city remained in ruins.

Little changed when, in 1996, the Taliban occupied Kabul and urban residents found themselves in a state of suspended animation, in both political and economic terms. As had been the case during the mujahideen era, there were few public investments and, with many property owners in exile, the historic quarters continued to decay.

Following the flight in late 2001 of the Taliban from major cities, a gradual process of recovery began. Over time, with the return of refugees and in-migration from rural areas, urban populations grew significantly, creating an intense demand for land and housing, whose value soared. Almost without exception, Afghan cities have witnessed a dramatic urban sprawl, with much of the new development on the outskirts. Given the commercial potential of central districts, where the historic quarters are situated, developers have turned their attention to these areas. It is indeed ironic that, having in part survived a protracted conflict, these quarters have in recent years faced the very real threat of being destroyed by the availability of money.

In Kabul in 2003, a presidential decree prohibiting all new construction in the old city – ostensibly to safeguard the area – had little impact on the ground and developers continued to act with impunity, acquiring and demolishing historic property for "redevelopment," often in collusion with municipal officials. Parallel efforts to develop and enforce regulations aimed at protecting the historic fabric and ensuring appropriate processes of development fell victim to a turf-war between municipal and ministerial officials – a situation that has proved very useful and lucrative for property speculators.

A similar situation has played out in Herat, whose old city was until recently one of the best-preserved examples of historic urban fabric in the region. It was for this reason that in 2006 UNESCO agreed with Herat municipality and others on measures to safeguard the character of the historic fabric by restricting the height and volume of new structures and specifying external finishes. These guidelines have however rarely been enforced, and demolitions and inappropriate construction continue largely unchecked in the old city. As in Kabul, property adjoining roads seem to be the most sought-after by developers who generally construct multi-storey concrete "markets," often excavating two floors underground and thereby destroying any archaeological remains. In what was left of the old city of Kandahar, a similarly destructive process of commercialization has taken place, while the bulk of the historic part of Charikar was recently "redeveloped" with official sanction. Given the pace at which Afghan urban centers are growing, and the destructive nature of the transformations that are taking place, time is clearly running out for the surviving historic fabric.

The challenges in addressing this situation are multiple. The relevant legal provisions in the 2004 Afghan Cultural Property Law are vague and only state that "modification of the structure of a registered monument of historic and artistic value is prohibited, without the authorization of the Ministry of Information and Culture (which) ... makes proper arrangements for the protection of such monuments" (Article 12). As long as the law only applies to "registered monuments" – it has proved difficult to get areas of historic fabric designated as such – it is clearly not an effective deterrent to the kind of destruction that is taking place in Herat, Kabul and other cities.

Both the 2004 National Urban Strategy and the urban component of the 2006 Afghan National Development Strategy draw attention to the need for protection of urban heritage, but more work needs to be done on developing effective programs to address the legal, technical, economic and social issues in a coherent manner. Government entities that are responsible for safeguarding built heritage have limited resources and capacity, although they have facilitated externally funded urban conservation initiatives such as those implemented by the Aga Khan Trust for Culture and Turquoise Mountain organizations in Kabul and Herat. The modest investments made through these community-based NGO projects have resulted in the conservation of dozens of historic properties, training of craftspeople and improvements in living conditions in recent years. These achievements will however remain "islands" in a sea of uncontrolled construction without an effective legal and administrative framework in which to operate. And any laws and regulations will only be useful if they are enforced: presently government officials show very little willingness to stand up to powerful interests engaged in property speculation in these or other urban areas. Municipal officials can be forgiven for turning a blind eye to illegal demolition or construction in historic neighborhoods when the "permissions" obtained by developers bear the signature of senior civil servants in Kabul who publicly lament the loss of Afghanistan's built heritage. It is particularly ironic that this destruction is taking place during a period of prosperity for many Afghans, who arguably have the choices denied to previous generations.

What are these choices? Perhaps the most important is for Afghans to acknowledge that the ongoing process of urban transformation will, unless checked, irrevocably destroy an important part of their history. Despite the fact that the inhabitants of historic quarters are often marginal and poor, and therefore have few choices, many have a strong attachment and are protective of the environment in which they live. Their voice needs to be heard by the officials who presently make decisions on their behalf, and who in many cases seem set on a path of wholesale transformation. If they choose to adopt development approaches that are compatible with safeguarding, Afghan planners and urban managers can draw on the experience of cities elsewhere in the region that have grown and prospered while retaining their unique historic character in certain quarters. The choice facing Afghan political and professional leaders is between acting soon to protect their old cities or standing by as they disappear under characterless concrete. If the next generation of Afghans is to inherit a nation that is alive, today's citizens need to rise to the challenge and ensure that their culture, of which historic mosques and shrines, bazaars and merchant homes are an important component, remains alive.

Threats to rural cultural landscapes

Paradoxically, after the specter of political instability, the greatest threat to Afghanistan's historic cultural resources may be the way in which critically needed economic development is achieved, and the degree to which it follows existing laws meant to protect heritage sites. This tension has been acute at Mes Aynak, a remarkably rich archaeological area with findings dating from the Bronze Age to the early Islamic period, which also happens to be located atop one of the world's largest unexploited copper deposits, estimated to be worth US$100 billion.[60] First discovered in 1963 by a French mining survey, the site contains remnants of a Buddhist city, including rare residential areas in addition to temples and monasteries that had been abandoned in the tenth century. The political churn of the 1970s interrupted excavations at Mes Aynak, but the French returned in 2004 to find the site heavily looted and damaged by coalition aerial assaults due to its wartime use as a Taliban way station.[61]

In 2007 the Afghan government awarded a Chinese mining firm a thirty-year lease on the site for US$3 billion, which at the time represented the largest foreign investment in Afghan history. The mining operation announced its intention to begin work at the site immediately, declaring that copper extraction required the removal of the archaeological deposits in advance. This dictate triggered one of the largest rescue archaeology operations in the world, overseen by the French Archaeological Mission in Afghanistan (DAFA) and funded by contributions from China, the United States and US$8 million from the World Bank. The subsequent excavations have affirmed the wealth and scope of the archaeological site, while also raising important questions about the true cost of mineral extraction in Afghanistan. Estimates predict that copper mining at Mes Aynak could contribute up to US$40 billion to the legal Afghan economy, representing a profound windfall for a country that otherwise depends on development aid and military spending. However, scholars and organizations such as ARCH International (Alliance for the Restoration of Cultural Heritage) have questioned the zero-sum game narrative put forward by the mining interests to date, pointing out that it will take years for mining operations to ramp up, thus leaving time to develop a plan whereby mining can occur while the archaeological site is also responsibly researched, excavated and conserved. They also note that a greater level of transparency on the part of the mining interests and the Afghan government could reveal solutions whereby the mineral extraction – and its associated economic contribution – could move ahead, while the site could also be protected if not promoted as an economic engine in and of itself.[62] There remains hope that the window that has opened due to the mining concession's difficulty in getting their operation under way means that the mining vs. archaeology narrative need not be followed, and that the site may yet be treated in a sensitive manner that balances the economic and cultural priorities equally.

In addition to potentially damaging the archaeological site, the proposed mining at Mes Aynak opens other issues related to environmental justice, communal benefits of extraction industries, and the means by which the Afghan government will oversee development of its fledgling economy. Critics argue that risks to groundwater and other contamination have not been fully assessed, despite the site's proximity to Kabul (40 km/25 miles away) and the importance of the water supply from this area, along with the well-documented environmental risks associated with copper mining.[63] Preparation for mining operations included the forced relocation of six villages, which fueled local resentment of the project and invited attacks on the site itself. In 2015, deteriorating security conditions led the government to call in 1,500 Afghan troops to protect the mining facilities.[64]

In response to the international and local outcry, the Afghan Ministry of Mining has made overtures to protect the archaeological site and to appropriately assess and prepare for the environmental impacts of the mining operation, delaying the start of the work several times, and stating that mining will not commence without prior approval from the Ministry of Information and Culture.[65] But as of 2015 no comprehensive plan for reconciling the conflicts present in this great opportunity – or great tragedy – has been forthcoming. The issue raises great concern over the precedent it may set for future foreign investments in extractive industries. If mining is going to be a major component of the Afghan economy in the future, as geological resources predict it will, measures must be developed and followed so that economic development can occur while the country's cultural and environmental assets are also protected.

It is plausible to assert that the cultural heritage of Afghanistan, in particular its already-fragile historic architectural heritage, is under a level of assault unprecedented since World War II, and is more at risk than that of any other country in Central Asia.[66] The country's unrelenting succession of turbulent and destructive events going back to the 1970s, its currently depleted institutional capacity, the manner in which economic development is ramping up, the value and vulnerability of its cultural resources, and the international community's tendency to move on to the next crisis area make for a toxic blend of factors that will likely impede conservation efforts.

No good comes from acts of wanton destruction of cultural heritage that are motivated by intolerance. However, such action may present opportunities to test and refine certain conservation practices in the field, which may be instructive. The difficulties encountered by various international agencies working in Afghanistan, especially UNESCO, in the face of crises such as the campaign to protect the National Museum and the Bamiyan Buddhas, has led heritage protection groups to re-think

FIGURE 22.8 Citizens of Hagjikak village, Bamiyan Province, exemplifying traditional lifeways that are in the balance given the various societal changes facing Afghanistan today.

their policies and study ways of deterring the destruction of cultural properties. In 2003 UNESCO adopted its Declaration Concerning the Intentional Destruction of Cultural Heritage, which outlines steps that countries may take in order to prevent and/or respond to acts such as the destruction at Bamiyan. These include taking legislative action to create legally enforceable sanctions against individuals and/or states for such acts.[67] It remains unclear how effective such declarations may be in the face of determined ideologues, as episodes involving the willful destruction of ancient non-Islamic sites in Iraq and Syria by the so-called Islamic State since 2014 have demonstrated.

The protection of Afghanistan's diverse cultural heritage remains among the greatest challenges to the broader architectural conservation community in the region, and abroad. Furthermore, heritage conservation professionals are confronted with the difficulty of operating in a politically unstable country where memories of destruction are still fresh, and powerful pressures to develop the economy by any means necessary are at hand. At the same time, the goals of the wider architectural conservation community are no less than the rescue of a priceless collection of Asian cultural heritage, which remains on the brink of major loss, while also knitting together a fractious populace with the notion of a proud, heterogeneous cultural heritage that represents an opportunity for national rebirth. However, with several successful projects to point to in addition to the resiliency of the Afghan people and international conservation missions, there remains cause for hope. Undoubtedly, Afghanistan's full recovery is a fight worth fighting, as Nancy Hatch Dupree said regarding rebuilding the National Museum in Kabul: "It's not just talk, it takes a lot of hard work."[68]

Notes

1. Ai Khanoum, which scholars believe was founded by Alexander the Great in 327 BCE, is located on the Amu Darya (Oxus) River on the northern Afghan border with Tajikistan. The French archaeologist Paul Bernard of DAFA excavated the site from 1964 to 1978, uncovering a huge amount of information and artifacts from the Greco-Bactrian period. Owing to the site's prominence, it was systematically looted and utterly destroyed in the decades following the departure of DAFA. Items excavated by the French and subsequently stolen from museums in Afghanistan appear steadily in the illegal antiquities markets from Pakistan to Switzerland. Source: Osmund Bopearachchi. "Preserving Afghanistan's Cultural Heritage: What is to be Done?" in Neville Agnew and Janet Bridgeland (eds.), *Of the Past, for the Future: Integrating Archaeology and Conservation*. (Los Angeles: The Getty Conservation Institute, 2016), 270.
2. William C.S. Remsen and Laura A. Tedesco, "US Cultural Diplomacy, Cultural Heritage Preservation and Development at the National Museum of Afghanistan in Kabul," in Paul Basu and Wayne Modest (eds.), *Museums, Heritage and International Development*. (London: Routledge, 2015), 102.
3. Dr. Dupree was a research associate with the American Museum of Natural History from 1959 to 1971 and as director of the American Archeological Mission to Afghanistan led in-country expeditions. He was also an adviser to several European governments on Afghanistan, and consulted on Afghan affairs at the US State Department, the Peace Corps, the National Security Council, the Central Intelligence Agency, the Agency for International Development and the United Nations.
4. Nancy Hatch Dupree. *An Historical Guide to Afghanistan*. (Kabul: Afghan Tourist Organization, 1977), 19.
5. Dupree, 30.
6. The Kushans are credited with the development of the earliest representative forms of the Buddha, which were sanctioned under their greatest king, Kanishka, in the first and second centuries CE. Kanishka fostered the development of the Gandharan School of Art, which centered around Western-influenced representations of the Buddha from its base in Peshawar until the eleventh century. Source: Dupree, 33.
7. S. Frederick Starr. *Lost Enlightenment: Central Asia's Golden Age from the Arab Conquest to Tamerlane*. (Princeton: Princeton University Press, 2013), 53–54.
8. Starr, 340, 346. Biruni is the most accomplished of an impressive roster of intellectuals that enjoyed the patronage of the Ghaznid court. Others included the epic poet Abolquasem Ferdowsi, author of the *Shahnameh* (Book of Kings), and romantic poets Abul Qasim Unsuri, Abu Nazar Abdul Asjadi and Farukhi. Source: Starr, 352–354.
9. Shah Rukh died in 1447, while his queen Goharshad ruled for another ten years before her murder in 1457. Source: Dupree, 47. Under the rule of Shah Rukh, Herat flowered as a center of arts and science under the patronage of his sons Baisunghur and Ulughbeg, who encouraged and participated in schools of miniature painting, calligraphy, mathematics and astronomy. Ulughbeg's tomb in Ghazni and other buildings from the era of Timur and his successors proved highly influential to the next great builders to emerge from Afghanistan: the Mughals. Source: Starr, 488, 499.
10. Dupree, 39–49.
11. These conflicts were launched by the British in 1839, 1878 and 1919, respectively.
12. The French collections from this period are housed in the Musée Guimet in Paris, which served as a "sister" institution to the National Museum in Kabul under the DAFA agreement. Given the looting that occurred at Kabul, the Guimet has played an important role in maintaining the collection from the early twentieth century period of research, while helping to rebuild the Kabul institution in the twenty-first. Source: Pierre Cambon. "The Role of the Guimet Museum in the Study and the Preservation of Afghan Heritage," *Museum International* 55(3–4) (December 2003), 54.
13. United States Department of Defense: U.S. Central Command. "Rediscovering the Past: Two Centuries of Archaeology in Afghanistan." CENTCOM Historical/Cultural Advisory Group: Cultural Property Training Resource, Afghanistan. 2015. Web. www.cemml.colostate.edu/cultural/09476/afgh03enl.html. Accessed October 19, 2015.
14. Remsen and Tedesco, 101.
15. Sharia law incorporates both civil and criminal justice within a body of law based on the teachings of the Koran and the religion of Islam.
16. Luke Harding. "How the Buddha got his Wounds," *The Guardian* (UK), March 2, 2001. Web. www.theguardian.com/books/2001/mar/03/books.guardianreview2. Accessed August 4, 2013.
17. Translation of the Taliban's edict on Images, in Finbarr Barrt Flood. "Between Cult and Culture: Bamiyan, Islamic Iconoclasm, and the Museum," *The Art Bulletin* 84(4) (2002), 641–659.
18. Flood, 653.

19 UNESCO. "UNESCO Condemns the Taliban's Destruction of the Buddhas of Bamiyan." Press Release. March 12, 2001.
20 Transitional Islamic State of Afghanistan. World Heritage Nomination Form: Cultural Landscape and Archaeological Remains of the Bamiyan Valley. Web. www.whc.unesco.org/uploads/nominations/208rev.pdf. May 2003. Accessed October 10, 2015.
21 "U.N. Seeks Laws to Halt Cultural Vandals," March 14, 2001. Web. http://asia.cnn.com/2001/WORLD/asiapcf/central/03/13/afghanistan.buddhas/. Accessed September 19, 2015.
22 Geoff Dyer and Chloe Sorvino. "$1tn Cost of Longest US War Hastens Retreat from Military Intervention," *The Financial Times*. December 14, 2014. Web. www.ft.com/cms/s/2/14be0e0c-8255-11e4-ace7-00144feabdc0.html#slide0. Accessed September 19, 2015. Casualties statistics source: Mesrop Najarian. "War Casualties in Afghanistan, Pakistan Total 149,000, New Study Says," CNN. June 2, 2015. Web. www.cnn.com/2015/06/02/asia/afghanistan-pakistan-war-deaths-study/. Accessed September 19, 2015.
23 "Afghanistan's Economic Challenges," *The New York Times*. July 20, 2012. Web. http://www.nytimes.com/2012/07/21/opinion/afghanistans-economic-challenges.html?_r=0. Accessed October 10, 2015.
24 "Afghanistan Minerals Fully Mapped," BBC News. July 18, 2012. Web. http://www.bbc.com/news/science-environment-18882996. Accessed August 30, 2015.
25 See Jolyon Leslie sidebar for more on urban conservation in Afghanistan.
26 Constance Wyndham. "Reconstructing Afghan Identity: Nation-Building, International Relations and the Safeguarding of Afghanistan's Buddhist Heritage," in Paul Basu and Wayne Modest (eds.), *Museums, Heritage and International Development*. (London: Routledge, 2015), 140.
27 Frederic Bobin. "Disputes Damage Hopes of Rebuilding Afghanistan's Bamiyan Buddhas," *The Guardian* (UK). January 10, 2015. Web. www.theguardian.com/world/2015/jan/10/rebuild-bamiyan-buddhas-taliban-afghanistan. Accessed October 10, 2015.
28 Bopearachchi, 270.
29 Remsen and Tedesco, 97.
30 Lashkari Bazar was excavated by the DAFA from 1929 to 1952, revealing it to be among the most impressive and architecturally influential palace complexes in Central Asia. Features of Mahmud's palace, including the four-arched courtyard along with stucco and brick detailing, were repeated for centuries throughout Central Asia. Source: Starr, 346–348. Today, the ruins are subject to damage by locals who are displaced from their home villages by conflict, and have been "formally" resettled within the archaeological site by local officials who may not be acting in the best interests of the ancient buildings. Source: Leslie Jolyon, "A Short Walk in Helmand Province," *Minerva Magazine* 24(2) (March/April, 2013), 47.
31 Nancy Hatch Dupree. "Museum Under Siege," *Archaeology* Magazine. April 20, 1998. Web. www.archive.arcaheology.org/online/features/afghan/. Accessed October 10, 2015.
32 Remsen and Tedesco, 97.
33 The ACHCO is a non-profit cultural organization founded in 2011 by Afghan professionals to assist the Ministry of Information and Culture with its duties relative to museum collections and conservation projects. Source: Afghan Cultural Heritage Consulting Organization. "ACHCO Projects." 2013. Web. www.afghanculturalheritage.org. Accessed October 10, 2015.
34 Remsen and Tedesco, 109.
35 Turquoise Mountain Foundation. "About the Turquoise Mountain Foundation." 2015. Web. http://turquoisemountain.org/about. Accessed October 10, 2015. The Turquoise Mountain Foundation is named for the (perhaps mythical) Ghorid capital of Firozkoh, which was destroyed by Chingis Khan's son in the thirteenth century.
36 Rob Crilly. "Afghanistan Reclaims its Heritage with some British Help," *The Daily Telegraph* (UK). February 23, 2014. Web. www.telegraph.co.uk/news/worldnews/asia/afghanistan/10656960/Afghanistan-reclaims-its-heritage-with-some-British-help.html. Accessed October 10, 2015.
37 Emma Graham-Harrison. "Stone Carvers Defy Taliban to Return to Bamiyan Valley," *The Guardian* (UK). May 16, 2012. Web. www.theguardian.com/world/2012/may/16/stone-carvers-taliban-bamiyan. Accessed October 10, 2015.
38 Alexis Blue. "UA Helps Build Heritage Conservation Program in Afghanistan," University of Arizona College of Architecture, Planning & Landscape Architecture. May 21, 2013. Web. http://uanews.org/story/ua-helps-build-heritage-conservation-program-in-afghanistan. Accessed October 10, 2015.
39 Islamic State of Afghanistan, Ministry of Justice. "Law on the Protection of Historical and Cultural Properties." Unofficial translation by Khalil Rahman for UNESCO, edited by the Division of Cultural Heritage, UNESCO. May 21, 2004. Web. www.cemml.colostate.edu/cultural/09476/pdf/afghan-antiquities-law-2004.pdf. Accessed October 10, 2015.

40 UNESCO Asia Pacific Heritage Awards, 2008 Award for Excellent Project Profile: Herat Old City Conservation. Web. www.unescobkk.org/culture/world-heritage-and-immovable-heritage/asia-pacific-heritage-awards-for-culture-heritage-conservation/previous-heritage-awards-2000-2010/2008/award-winners/herat-old-city/. Accessed October 10, 2015.

41 UNESCO. "International Seminar on the Rehabilitation of Afghanistan's Cultural Heritage: Conclusions & Recommendations." Unpublished seminar report. June 11, 2002. Web. http://whc.unesco.org/archive/decrec02-annexes.htm. Accessed October 10, 2015.

42 Embassy of the Islamic Republic of Afghanistan, Canberra. "UNESCO in Afghanistan." 2015. Web. www.afghanembassy.net/cultural/unesco-in-afghanistan. Accessed October 10, 2015.

43 UNESCO Office in Kabul. "UNESCO and Italy Launch New Cooperation to Restore and Conserve Cultural Heritage in Bamiyan, Afghanistan," May 29, 2013. Web. http://whc.unesco.org/en/news/1013/. Accessed October 10, 2015.

44 Habib Khan Totakhil. "In Afghanistan, a Historic City Picks Up the Pieces," *Wall Street Journal.* September 15, 2014. Web. http://blogs.wsj.com/dispatch/2014/09/15/in-afghanistan-a-historic-city-picks-up-the-pieces/. Accessed October 10, 2015; and "Statement by the Director UNESCO Kabul Office Concerning the Destruction of Ancient Artifacts in Ghazni, Afghanistan."

45 UNESCO Office in Kabul. "Italy Grants US$1.2 Million for Heritage Preservation and Development in Afghanistan." March 14, 2013. Web. Accessed October 10, 2015.

46 UNESCO Office in Kabul. "UNESCO Announces the Bamiyan Cultural Centre Design Competition." November 11, 2014. Web. http://whc.unesco.org/en/news/1198/. Accessed October 10, 2015.

47 Article 9 of the Venice Charter (1964) stipulates that restoration is "based on respect for the original material and authentic documents" and "must stop at the point where conjecture begins." Sufficient concern exists that the amount of original material and information available to reconstruct the Buddhas is inadequate to complete the project consistent with the Venice Charter.

48 Alessandro Martini and Ermanno Rivetti. "UNESCO Stops Unauthorized Reconstruction of Bamiyan Buddhas," *The Art Newspaper.* February 6, 2014. Web. www.artsjournal.com/2014/02/unesco-stops-unauthorized-reconstruction-of-bamiyan-buddhas.html. Accessed October 10, 2015.

49 Estimates of available pieces of the original statues range from 10 percent to 30 percent.

50 Rod Nordland. "Countries Divided on Future of Ancient Buddhas," *The New York Times.* March 22, 2014. Web. www.nytimes.com/2014/03/23/world/asia/countries-divided-on-future-of-ancient-buddhas.html?_r=0. Accessed October 10, 2015.

51 Aga Khan Development Network. *Aga Khan Historic Cities Programme: Urban Conservation and Area Development in Afghanistan.* (Geneva: Aga Khan Trust for Culture, 2007), 6–7.

52 Ibid., 10–19.

53 Shah Jahan (1592–1666), his great-great grandson, also built the Taj Mahal.

54 Aga Khan Development Network, 26–40.

55 Aga Khan Trust for Culture. *Restoration Projects in Afghanistan: Project Brief.* (Geneva: Aga Khan Trust for Culture, 2012), 1–2. Bagh-e Babur visitation numbers are as of 2012.

56 Ibid., 59.

57 Ibid., 59–66.

58 UNESCO Bangkok. UNESCO Asia-Pacific Awards for Cultural Heritage Conservation, Project Profile: Herat Old City, 2008 Award of Excellence. Web. www.unescobkk.org/culture/heritage/wh/heritageawards/previous/2008/award-winners/2008ex1/. Accessed October 10, 2015.

59 ACHCO. "ACHCO Projects." November 2013. Web. www.afghanculturalheritage.org/7.html. Accessed October 10, 2015.

60 Archaeologists believe that the proximity of the settlement to the copper deposits is not a coincidence, but rather that Mes Aynak was a copper mining and production site in antiquity.

61 William Dalrymple. "Mes Aynak: Afghanistan's Buddhist Buried Treasure Faces Destruction," *The Guardian.* May 31, 2013. Web. www.theguardian.com/books/2013/may/31/mes-aynak-afghanistan-buddhist-treasure. Accessed October 10, 2015. Though the site had been looted consistently over the centuries, the period of relative lawlessness between ca. 1970 and 2001 invited systematic illegal excavations across Afghanistan, including Mes Aynak.

62 ARCH International. "Mes Aynak." 2015. Web. www.archinternational.org/mes_aynak.html. Accessed October 10, 2015.

63 Cheryl Benard and Eli Sugarman. "Afghanistan's Copper Conundrum," *Caucasus International* 2(3) (Autumn 2013), 151–158.

64 Ben Piven. "Chinese Firm, Taliban Battle over Afghanistan's Riches," *Al Jazeera America*. July 11, 2015. Web. http://america.aljazeera.com/articles/2015/7/11/chinese-company-taliban-battle-afghanistan.html. Accessed August 30, 2015.

65 Afghanistan Ministry of Mines and Petroleum. "Mes Aynak Archaeological Conservation Work to Continue." January 2, 2013. Web. http://mom.gov.af/en/news/16157. Accessed August 30, 2015.

66 Discouragingly, there is regional competition in this category, with other as-yet unresolved conflicts playing out in Iraq and Syria that may yet prove more dire than the current circumstances in Afghanistan.

67 UNESCO. "Declaration Concerning the International Destruction of Cultural Heritage." October 17, 2003. Web. http://portal.unesco.org/en/ev.php-URL_ID=17718&URL_DO=DO_TOPIC&URL_SECTION=201.html. Accessed October 10, 2015.

68 The Asia Society. "Preserving Afghanistan's Cultural Heritage: An Interview with Nancy Hatch Dupree." June 24, 2002. Web. www.asiasociety.org/preserving-afghanistans-cultural-heritage-interview-nancy-hatch-dupree. Accessed October 10, 2015.

Further reading

Afghan Cultural Heritage Organization. 2013. "ACHCO Projects." November. Web. www.afghanculturalheritage.org/7.html. Accessed October 10, 2015.

Afghanistan, Transitional Islamic State of. 2003. "World Heritage Nomination Form: Cultural Landscape and Archaeological Remains of the Bamiyan Valley." Web. www.whc.unesco.org/uploads/nominations/208rev.pdf. Accessed May 2003.

Afghanistan Embassy, Canberra. 2015. "UNESCO in Afghanistan." 2015. Web. http://www.afghanembassy.net/cultural/unesco-in-afghanistan. Accessed June 21, 2016.

Afghanistan Ministry of Justice 2014. "Law on the Protection of Historical and Cultural Properties." Unofficial translation by Khalil Rahman for UNESCO, edited by the Division of Cultural Heritage, UNESCO. May 21, 2004. Web. www.cemml.colostate.edu/cultural/09476/pdf/afghan-antiquities-law-2004.pdf. Accessed October 10, 2015.

Afghanistan Ministry of Mines and Petroleum. 2013. "Mes Aynak Archaeological Conservation Work to Continue." January 2, 2013. Web. http://mom.gov.af/en/news/16157. Accessed October 10, 2015.

Aga Khan Development Network. 2007. *Aga Khan Historic Cities Programme: Urban Conservation and Area Development in Afghanistan*. Geneva: Aga Khan Trust for Culture.

Aga Khan Trust for Culture. 2012. *Restoration Projects in Afghanistan: Project Brief*. Geneva: Aga Khan Trust for Culture.

ARCH International. "Mes Aynak". 2015. Web. www.archinternational.org/mes_aynak.html. Accessed October 10, 2015.

The Asia Society. 2002. "Preserving Afghanistan's Cultural Heritage: An Interview with Nancy Hatch Dupree." June 24, 2002. Web. www.asiasociety.org/preserving-afghanistans-cultural-heritage-interview-nancy-hatch-dupree. Accessed October 10, 2015.

Bechhoefer, William B. 1975. *Serai Lahori: Traditional Housing in the Old City of Kabul*. Baltimore: University of Maryland Press.

Benard, Cheryl and Eli Sugarman. 2013. "Afghanistan's Copper Conundrum," *Caucasus International* 2(3) (Autumn 2013), 151–158.

Blue, Alexis. 2013. "UA Helps Build Heritage Conservation Program in Afghanistan." University of Arizona College of Architecture, Planning & Landscape Architecture. May 21, 2013. Web. http://uanews.org/story/ua-helps-build-heritage-conservation-program-in-afghanistan. Accessed October 10, 2015.

Bobin, Frederic. 2015. "Disputes Damage Hopes of Rebuilding Afghanistan's Bamiyan Buddhas," *The Guardian* (UK). January 10, 2015. Web. http://www.theguardian.com/world/2015/jan/10/rebuild-bamiyan-buddhas-taliban-afghanistan. Accessed October 10, 2015.

CNN Asia. 2001. "U.N. seeks laws to halt cultural vandals," March 14, 2001. Web. http://asia.cnn.com/2001/WORLD/asiapcf/central/03/13/afghanistan.buddhas/. Accessed October 10, 2015.

Crilly, Rob. 2014. "Afghanistan Reclaims its Heritage with some British Help," *The Daily Telegraph* (UK). February 23, 2014. Web. www.telegraph.co.uk/news/worldnews/asia/afghanistan/10656960/Afghanistan-reclaims-its-heritage-with-some-British-help.html. Accessed October 10, 2015.

Dalrymple, William. 2013. "Mes Aynak: Afghanistan's Buddhist Buried Treasure Faces Destruction," *The Guardian*. May 31, 2013. Web. www.theguardian.com/books/2013/may/31/mes-aynak-afghanistan-buddhist-treasure. Accessed October 10, 2015.

Dupree, Nancy Hatch. 1977. *An Historical Guide to Afghanistan*. Kabul: Afghan Tourist Organization.

——. 1998. "Museum Under Siege," *Archaeology*. April 20, 1998. Web. www.archive.archaeology.org/online/features/afghan/. Accessed October 10, 2015.

Flood, Finbarr Barrt. 2002. "Between Cult and Culture: Bamiyan, Islamic Iconoclasm, and the Museum," *The Art Bulletin* 84(4): 641–659.

Graham-Harrison, Emma. 2012. "Stone Carvers Defy Taliban to Return to Bamiyan Valley," *The Guardian*. May 16, 2012. Web. www.theguardian.com/world/2012/may/16/stone-carvers-taliban-bamiyan. Accessed October 10, 2015.

Hallet, Stanley Ira and Rafi Samizay. 1980. *Traditional Architecture of Afghanistan*. New York: Garland STPM Press.

Harding, Luke. 2001. "How the Buddha Got his Wounds," *The Guardian*. March 2. Web. www.theguardian.com/books/2001/mar/03/books.guardianreview2. Accessed October 10, 2015.

Martini, Alessandro and Ermanno Rivetti. 2014. "UNESCO Stops Unauthorized Reconstruction of Bamiyan Buddhas," *The Art Newspaper*. February 6. Web. www.artsjournal.com/2014/02/unesco-stops-unauthorized-reconstruction-of-bamiyan-buddhas.html. Accessed October 10, 2015.

Nordland, Rod. 2014. "Countries Divided on Future of Ancient Buddhas," *The New York Times*. March 22, 2014. Web. www.nytimes.com/2014/03/23/world/asia/countries-divided-on-future-of-ancient-buddhas.html?_r=0. Accessed October 10, 2015.

Piven, Ben. 2015. "Chinese Firm, Taliban Battle over Afghanistan's Riches," *Al Jazeera America*. July 11. Web. http://america.aljazeera.com/articles/2015/7/11/chinese-company-taliban-battle-afghanistan.html. Accessed October 10, 2015.

Remsen, William C.S. and Laura A. Tedesco. 2015. "US Cultural Diplomacy, Cultural Heritage Preservation and Development at the National Museum of Afghanistan in Kabul," in Paul Basu and Wayne Modest (eds.), *Museums, Heritage and International Development*. London: Routledge.

Starr, S. Frederick. 2013. *Lost Enlightenment: Central Asia's Golden Age from the Arab Conquest to Tamerlane*. Princeton: Princeton University Press.

Totakhil, Habib Khan. 2014. "In Afghanistan, a Historic City Picks Up the Pieces," *Wall Street Journal*. September 15. Web. http://blogs.wsj.com/dispatch/2014/09/15/in-afghanistan-a-historic-city-picks-up-the-pieces/. Accessed October 10, 2016.

UNESCO. 2001. "UNESCO Condemns the Taliban's Destruction of the Buddhas of Bamiyan." Press Release. March 12.

———. 2002. International Seminar on the Rehabilitation of Afghanistan's Cultural Heritage: Conclusions & Recommendations. Unpublished seminar report. June 11. Web. http://whc.unesco.org/archive/decrec02-annexes.htm. Accessed October 10, 2016.

———. 2003. Declaration Concerning the International Destruction of Cultural Heritage. October 17. Web. http://portal.unesco.org/en/ev.php-URL_ID=17718&URL_DO=DO_TOPIC&URL_SECTION=201.html. Accessed October 10, 2015.

———. 2008. Asia Pacific Heritage Awards, 2008 Award for Excellent Project Profile: Herat Old City Conservation. Web. www.unescobkk.org/culture/world-heritage-and-immovable-heritage/asia-pacific-heritage-awards-for-culture-heritage-conservation/previous-heritage-awards-2000-2010/2008/award-winners/herat-old-city/. Accessed October 10, 2015.

UNESCO Bangkok. 2008. UNESCO Asia-Pacific Awards for Cultural Heritage Conservation, Project Profile: Herat Old City, 2008 Award of Excellence. Web. www.unescobkk.org/culture/heritage/wh/heritageawards/previous/2008/award-winners/2008ex1/. Accessed October 10, 2015.

UNESCO Kabul. 2013a. "Italy Grants US$1.2 Million for Heritage Preservation and Development in Afghanistan." March 14. Web. http://whc.unesco.org/en/news/. Accessed October 10, 2015.

———. 2013b. "UNESCO and Italy launch new cooperation to restore and conserve cultural heritage in Bamiyan, Afghanistan" May 29. Web. http://whc.unesco.org/en/news/1013/. Accessed October 10, 2015.

———. 2014. "UNESCO Announces the Bamiyan Cultural Centre Design Competition." November 11. Web. http://whc.unesco.org/en/news/1198/. Accessed October 10, 2015.

Wyndham, Constance. 2015. "Reconstructing Afghan Identity: Nation-Building, International Relations and the Safeguarding of Afghanistan's Buddhist Heritage," in Paul Basu and Wayne Modest (eds.), *Museums, Heritage and International Development*. London: Routledge.

23

KAZAKHSTAN, KYRGYZSTAN, TAJIKISTAN, TURKMENISTAN AND UZBEKISTAN

Situated in the midst of the great Asian land sea, and historically linked to the empires of East, West and South by the trade corridors commonly referred to as the Silk Road, the modern Central Asian republics have for millennia been a nexus of exchange, diversity, innovation and conflict.[1] Successive rulers have long grappled for this politically pivotal region, and in so doing left behind the prevailing ideas, religions, institutions and aesthetics of their respective cultures – be they Greek, Persian, Mongol, Turkish or Soviet. At the same time, the region supported numerous, highly sophisticated urban centers for centuries such as Nisa, Samarkand, Merv and Khiva. These cities cultivated and emanated their own influential ideas in science, religion and medicine far beyond their borders. The steady flow of commerce and people on the various trade routes nurtured this rich mélange, and created oases of wealth and architectural expression in these landlocked nations that today constitute many of the heritage sites and cities of the newly independent countries of Central Asia.

Cyrus the Great united the region under the Achaemenids in the sixth century BCE. His reign brought Central Asia into one of antiquity's great empires, connecting its population of Persianate people into a kingdom that stretched from eastern Greece to western China. The arrival of Alexander the Great's armies in what is now Tajikistan in the fourth century BCE cemented the connection between the Mediterranean and Central Asia and beyond, with his succeeding Selucid Empire maintaining long-term links between the Far East and Europe. Equally influential in forging these early routes of conquest and exchange were the Central Asian-based empires, including the Parthians, who competed with Rome itself from their capital at Nisa (in modern-day Turkmenistan), the Kushans in what is now Afghanistan, and the Sassanians based in today's northeastern Iran. Influential too were the nomadic groups of people that periodically threatened and overwhelmed, but also positively influenced the settled empires of Central Asia for more than three thousand years.[2] From the east, Han Dynasty merchants established trade routes into Central Asia by the second century BCE, creating the earliest link between China's markets and the Western world. Southern trade routes through what is now Afghanistan, across the Pamirs and Hindu Kush mountains to the riches of India were even older, facilitated by great cities such as the Kushan capital at Begram and the Zoroastrian center of Balkh. Trade between these regions – along with the exchange of ideas, technology, religion, goods and disease – flourished during the subsequent centuries, particularly during the period of Mongol rule from the thirteenth to the fifteenth centuries.[3]

Partly in response to the nineteenth century expansion of the British Empire northward from India into what is now Pakistan and Afghanistan, the Russian Empire gradually absorbed the areas that became the modern nations of Kazakhstan, Kyrgyzstan, Tajikistan, Turkmenistan and Uzbekistan.

These countries – which are predominantly Muslim yet as a whole multi-ethnic – owe their contemporary borders to their years under the Russian and later Soviet regimes. All five nations gained their independence in December 1991, following the collapse of the Soviet Union. Each entered the twenty-first century at various points in the process of establishing their individual identities and rekindling links to cultural pasts that had eroded or were actively suppressed during the Soviet period. Key regions such as the fertile Ferghana Valley were split between Uzbekistan, Tajikistan and Kyrgyzstan by a complex tangle of borders that have since been criticized as intentionally divisive.[4]

While the legendary ancient cities of Samarkand, Merv, Otrar and Bukhara have long been recognized as centers of cultural achievement, they – and the efforts to study and conserve them – remained largely hidden from the Western world during the Soviet era.[5] Today, the ramifications of this exclusionary legacy include a depleted professional infrastructure, and a paucity of available archival information from the extensive archaeological and conservation work that occurred during the Soviet period. As the international community has begun to engage in conservation efforts in Central Asia, it is also encountering challenges from three distinct sources: complications from specific Soviet-era conservation practices; issues arising from the political instability that followed independence; and environmental damage to the sites.

The transition to new statehood has not been universally smooth for the Central Asian nations: Tajikistan experienced a devastating five-year civil war, Kyrgyzstan had a series of political upheavals in the 2010s, and entrenched autocratic rulers govern Uzbekistan, Kazakhstan and Turkmenistan. Unsurprisingly, despite the promise of a new era of independence and international collaboration, conservation issues across each of the five Central Asian countries are numerous and complex, ranging from the political to legal to environmental, as each country has established its own heritage infrastructure.

Legislation and management structures at the government level were initially held over from the Soviet era in the Central Asian countries. In the late 1990s, however, most of the new nations began to revise their heritage management regulations and practices, while also updating inventories of archaeological and architectural sites, frequently in collaboration with international bodies. UNESCO,

FIGURE 23.1 The fortified city of Ancient Merv in Turkmenistan, which dates from the eleventh and twelfth centuries, has archaeological evidence dating to the third millennium BCE and reflects well the antiquity and richness of the architectural heritage of Central Asia.

active in the region since the post-independence era, has consistently encouraged a regional approach to nurturing a fully functioning cultural heritage sector in Central Asia, identifying common needs among the five nations and fostering a shared approach for addressing them. Based on coordinated efforts between local heritage management agencies, UNESCO and other international organizations such as ICCROM and Grenoble-based CRAterre-EAG, the focus to date has been on completing heritage inventories, strengthening conservation regulations, building regional professional capacity, and developing regional standards for dealing with typical conservation challenges, with a particular focus on ancient earthen architecture.[6]

As a result of these efforts, by the end of the 1990s Uzbekistan alone had listed over seven thousand properties on its state-level registry, including 2,500 architectural structures and over 2,700 archaeological sites. The nation had also identified and afforded special protection to ten historic cities and numerous historic districts (known as Architectural Reserves) among other significant clusters of buildings such as religious shrines, ruined trading outposts and remote defensive fortifications.[7]

The era during which the Central Asian republics were part of the USSR included systematic suppression of regional cultural expressions that were inconsistent with Soviet ideals. Such efforts, combined with severe pollution, disappearance of traditional maintenance regimes and poor water management, have contributed to a hostile environment for the region's characteristic mud brick buildings and decorative architectural ceramics. Many of the region's conservation challenges are connected to the properties of its most common traditional building material: dried mud brick. Without regular maintenance and replenishing of protective outer finishes, mud brick rapidly erodes, resulting in the literal melting of walls, towers and foundations. Airborne pollutants ranging from insecticides to industrial effluents compromise building materials and decorative finishes from the outside. High water tables attributable to over-irrigation, faulty plumbing and poor drainage create conditions for rising damp, which delivers salts present in sewage, fertilizers, hard cement and other sources into walls and foundations, causing major damage from within. The liberal use of modern concrete in repairs and replacements, along with ill-advised reconstruction campaigns not only introduces these corrosive salts into historic earthen structures, but also incompatible structural properties that can accelerate deterioration. Additionally, the earthquake-prone region has for centuries suffered from devastating tremors that have damaged or destroyed buildings. These seismic events have contributed to a cycle of inferior repairs to historic buildings, which has been reinforced by an endemic lack of local resources, diminished competency in traditional building practices, and a lack of appreciation for historic architecture.[8]

Conservation in Central Asia during the Soviet era

Throughout the Soviet era (1922–1991), conservation activity across Central Asia included numerous architectural and archaeological projects that greatly expanded the scholarly understanding of the region, but also left behind a number of problematic legacies. In many of the Central Asian cities, conservation of monuments frequently involved the destruction of the traditional, contextual built fabric, resulting in the isolation of individual mosques, palaces and mausoleums. Some of these monuments, notably the Bibi Khanum Mosque in Samarkand, were enthusiastically rebuilt, resulting in impressively restored interpretations of ancient architecture, but pushing the norms of conventional conservation practice. Frequently, in the early decades of the USSR, conservation plans were influenced by Soviet ideological motives, such as secularism and homogenization of cultural traditions, rather than universally accepted professional practice. These ideas often held that ancient buildings were a manifestation of the feudal, class-oriented societies, which was the very system that the Soviet Union was established to reject. As a result, many historically significant buildings – religious structures in particular – were physically razed, while others were culturally neutered in order to sever links to a non-socialist past.

By the 1960s, the situation began to change throughout the Soviet Union, as historic areas were increasingly recognized for their tourist potential and a global trend against colonialist practices became more prevalent. This shift resulted in new development plans for cities such as the largely intact, medieval trading city of Bukhara, which emphasized conservation of the traditional built environment, but often for the singular sake of enhancing the tourism economy. Rather than encouraging local residents to live among and care for their buildings, the government frequently resorted to relocating citizens from old town centers into new housing developments, draining populations in historic cities throughout Central Asia; this is very apparent in the former emirate of Khiva, which still suffers from the legacy of this misguided approach.

The collapse of the USSR essentially reversed this trend, as free market real estate speculation and an abandonment of the Soviet-era planning principles once again made historic city centers popular places in which to invest and build. In many cases, religious structures that had been de-consecrated and converted into secular uses were returned to their respective religious orders to be restored, both architecturally and spiritually, with magnificent results. While successful examples of these restorations exist, such as the early-twentieth century Russian Orthodox Saint Ascension Cathedral in Almaty, Kazakhstan (see below) and the fourteenth century Naqshbandiyya Sufi mausoleum of Baha al-Din Naqshband in Bukhara, the legacy of these trends will be difficult to overcome, and continues to inform many of the conservation policy decisions made by Central Asian countries presently and in the years to come.[9]

Kazakhstan

By far the largest of the central Asian republics in terms of area, Kazakhstan is contiguous with Russia and China, both of which have played influential roles over the centuries in the development of Kazakhstan's cultural heritage. Historically, the country has been split between a predominantly nomadic culture in the north and a string of ancient urban centers along its southern borders with Uzbekistan and Kyrgyzstan. Since independence, the Culture Committee within the Kazak Ministry of Culture oversees architectural conservation via the Law of the Republic of Kazakhstan on Protection and Use of Historical and Cultural Heritage (1992), with work carried out by the State Institute for Scientific Research and Planning on Monuments of Material Culture (known by the acronym NIPI PMK) and the Kazakhstan Restoration Agency (also called Kazrestoration).[10] Documentation of the country's extensive heritage inventory began during the Soviet period with the preparation of a National List of Monuments of History & Culture. Within a decade of independence this list included over 24,000 sites of both national and local importance, with most having local significance. In 2004 the Committee of Culture began excising sites that had been listed for their connection to the Soviet era in order to better reflect the emerging Kazakh national identity, and began recognizing historically significant religious and secular places that had been excluded under the previous regime.[11]

The Otrar Oasis in southern Kazakhstan illustrates several conservation challenges that confront heritage managers both in that country and in the surrounding region. A monumental ancient site associated with the great Asian trade routes that flourished from the first through eighteenth centuries CE, Otrar stands today largely abandoned and highly vulnerable.[12] The site is comprised of the remains of six medieval towns spread over an area of 100 ha, successively built and historically intertwined with sophisticated irrigation systems.[13] Archeological excavations in 1969 had exposed many building features and sub-grade deposits without adequate conservation measures, such as backfilling, thereby expediting the processes of decay and erosion.[14] Partly funded by the Japanese government in cooperation with UNESCO, the Otrar Project began in 2001 to address the rapidly deteriorating, exposed mud brick ruins common to these medieval-era sites. The multi-national team worked to confront the numerous challenges presented by the site by focusing on training Kazakh site managers with skills including the backfilling of exposed features, consolidation of mud brick walls, and raising national and regional awareness – particularly among local schoolchildren – of the significance of the heritage site through the production of a thirty-minute documentary film about the site that was broadcast on national television.[15]

Among Kazakhstan's more important architectural landmarks is the Mausoleum of Khoja Ahmed Yasavi (built 1389–1405), located in Turkestan (South Kazakhstan) that is an exceptional, highly intact example of Timurid architecture, exhibiting strong Persian characteristics, that would influence the later development of Samarkand's monumental buildings. In 2014 the building's visual context, which it had dominated for centuries relative to the surrounding town and landscape, was threatened by the

FIGURE 23.2 Architectural conservation at the Otrar Oasis, a large unspoiled cultural landscape of earthen architecture in southwest Kazakhstan, mainly entails consolidation and conservation of mud brick protective walls, fortifications and vernacular residential buildings.

FIGURE 23.3 The mausoleum of Khoja Ahmed Yasavi, Turkic poet and founder of the influential Tarīqah order, was begun by Tamerlane in the fourteenth century. Though never finished, it stands as one of the best-preserved of all Timurid constructions. Despite its importance it was threatened in 2013/14 with a proposed new mosque in its vicinity.

construction of a new mosque.[16] Though just outside the World Heritage Site's buffer zone, the proposed height of the new mosque would compete with the ancient mausoleum, underscoring the importance of management plans and contextual zoning around significant buildings in the region.

While the Soviet period introduced modern scholarship and archaeological research aimed at understanding the history of Central Asia and its peoples, its attendant political and cultural influences frequently resulted in the rupturing of traditional bonds between its people and their culturally significant sites. This dynamic played out across the region, affecting a wide range of cultures, from the nomadic people living in the central steppe to Russian Orthodox parishioners in the region's cities. Today, contemporary conservation efforts in the region are attempting to repair these cultural ruptures.

In the Mangystau region of southwestern Kazakhstan, nomadic and semi-nomadic cultures have left behind a distinctive built legacy in the central steppe, the largely treeless, semi-arid plains located on the eastern shore of the Caspian Sea. These limestone mausoleums, dedicated to ancestor worship, were mostly built in the eighteenth and nineteenth centuries. Changes in land management, subsistence practices and lifestyles of these groups during the Soviet era led to the abandonment and deterioration of the mausoleums in their often-remote sites. In the same region, necropolises dating from the eleventh century create a cultural landscape that reflects the transition from pre-Islamic to Islamic religious traditions, including Sufi sects.[17] Renewed attention spurred by international groups such as the World Monuments Fund, along with updated heritage inventories and newly secured protective status, have led to the restoration of a select few of these distinctive, yet modest structures.[18]

The collapse of the Soviet regime has also allowed for the revival of religious structures from the pre-Communist revolution period, which in many cases were demolished or insensitively repurposed for secular uses. The Saint Ascension Cathedral, built in 1907 in the center of Almaty, one of the region's largest cities, is a grand Russian Orthodox cathedral that had been de-consecrated during the Soviet period and converted to a radio communication facility and museum, among other uses. Following independence, conservation architects from NIPI PMK carried out a multi-phase restoration of the building, including its ornate interior detail and exuberant exterior finishes. Between 1994 and 2000 the team completed structural upgrades to the wood frame building – critical in this seismically volatile region – and a restoration of its traditional interior circulation features and places of worship. Incompatible and harmful cement plaster finishes from a 1970s-era restoration were removed and replaced with a historically compatible lime plaster substitute. Roof repairs were undertaken, along with a replacement of the original passive ventilation system and the original exterior polychromatic paint scheme based on painstaking archival research in Almaty and elsewhere in the former Soviet Union. Critical to the success of the project was the development and implementation of a building and site management plan and monitoring system, along with trained on-site maintenance and operations personnel, as well as an upgrade of the all-important fire suppression system for the wood structure. Funding for the project was generated by a combination of public and private contributions, and in 2004, UNESCO recognized the effort with an Award for Cultural Heritage Protection.[19]

FIGURE 23.4 The formerly de-consecrated Russian Orthodox Saint Ascension Cathedral in Almaty received a second major restoration in 2000 after some inexpert work done in the 1970s.

Kyrgyzstan

Mountainous Kyrgyzstan is home to a broad array of archaeological sites and cultural landscapes that represent the intermingling of religious traditions via ancient trade networks, and the harmonization of Islam with the religious practices of its indigenous nomadic and semi-nomadic peoples. Similar to efforts in neighboring Kazakhstan, conservation practice has in recent years focused on archaeological sites and ruined buildings associated with the Central Asian trade routes. The Ministry of Education, Science and Culture presently manages heritage policy, enabled by the Law on Protection and Use of Historical and Cultural Heritage (1999). Within the Ministry, the Republican Inspectorate for Registration of Historical and Cultural Heritage and the National Academy of Sciences support research and assessment efforts at historic sites in Kyrgyzstan.[20] One such area is the Chui River Valley, which contains sites representing a remarkable array of religious traditions that flourished in the region. Zoroastrian altars, Islamic towers, Buddhist temples and Nestorian (Christian) church sites dating from the seventh to the tenth centuries have been identified and documented in the valley. In 2003 a UNESCO-led team began preparing a master plan for their protection and management. Work to date has focused on issues of archaeological site documentation, conservation and research into the complex histories of these little-known sites.[21] In recognition of the remarkable archaeological and architectural remains representing cultures from China to India to Byzantium, and the need to further study and protect them, UNESCO added the Medieval Sites of the Upper Chui River Valley to the Tentative list of World Heritage Sites in 2009/10. A third to early second millennia BCE Saimaly-Tash petroglyph site, located among a series of alpine natural reserves located in the Western Tien Shan mountains, was also listed.[22]

Kyrgyzstan's Sulaiman-Too Sacred Mountain, inscribed on the World Heritage List in 2009, represents a distinctive Central Asian cultural landscape, consisting of a combination of culturally

FIGURE 23.5 The scenic historic city of Osh, Kyrgyzstan in the context of Sulaiman-Too Sacred Mountain. Both are subjects of efforts to prevent insensitive development.

significant natural features, pre-Islamic petroglyph sites, hermitages and mosques built into the rugged mountainside, all connected by a network of ancient footpaths. The majestic setting of the mountain rising above the surrounding Ferghana Valley, and set against the nearby city of Osh, also contributes to the cultural values of the site. Conservation of this complex, vast and interconnected composition relies heavily on a zoning and master planning effort for Osh, Kyrgyzstan's second-largest city, which is anticipated to include protection measures for the mountain and its associated buffer zone. The objective is to prevent inappropriate development on or around the lower slopes of Sulaiman-Too Sacred Mountain that would undermine the setting and overall composition of the landscape and mountain.[23]

Despite the promise of the above efforts, the cultural heritage framework in Kyrgyzstan remains underdeveloped, and quite lacking in the critical areas of professional capacity, up-to-date inventories, institutional support and public awareness. A series of political upheavals in 2005 and again in 2010, combined with ethnic conflict between the majority Kyrgyz people and minority Uzbeks, have largely inhibited the transition to a fully functioning independent nation state with government, local NGO and private-sector support for conservation efforts. Although these components exist, the development of a coordinated national policy for conservation management and heritage promotion remains incomplete.[24] While Kyrgyzstan has experienced a more difficult post-independence transition than some of its other Central Asian neighbors, its current situation illustrates the challenges they all face in emerging from seventy years of Soviet dominion, and in developing a new national identity along with associated heritage values.

Featuring heritage along Central Asia's ancient trade routes

Owing to the legacy of the great Asian trade networks, the nations of Central Asia, along with neighboring China, have emerged as regional leaders in the study, interpretation and management of culturally significant heritage routes. Borne out of ideas inherent in traditional built sites, intangible heritage and cultural landscapes, heritage routes are defined as "physical or perceived representations of frequent and repeated movement, linking places in time and space and generating an exchange of goods and ideas."[25] UNESCO has supported the study and nomination of heritage routes to the World Heritage List for several decades, beginning with the inclusion of Spain's Pilgrimage Route to Santiago de Compostela in 1993. Meanwhile, between 1988 and 1997, UNESCO sponsored an international project known as "Integral Study of the Silk Roads: Roads of Dialogue," which consisted of a series of multi-disciplinary seminars, meetings and research trips aimed at encouraging the study of topics related to the Central Asian trade routes. For its part, the Getty Conservation Institute organized and published the proceedings from conferences held in 1997 and 2010 on the conservation of ancient sites on the trade routes to Central Asia, with a particular focus on management of grotto and wall paintings. These developments, along with China's decision in 2008 to include a 4,500 km segment of the Silk Road stretching from Xi'an to Kashgar on its Tentative list of World Heritage Sites, have contributed much to the current level of discourse and interest in heritage routes in the region.

During the 1990s and early 2000s, leading international conservation bodies including UNESCO and ICOMOS organized conferences and adjusted their organizational framework in order to accommodate the codification and nomination of heritage routes around the globe. In 1994, ICOMOS established an International Scientific Committee on Cultural Routes (known as CIIC) in order to guide decision-making and set standards around the nomination of heritage routes to the World Heritage List. In 2003, the Operational Guidelines for the Implementation of the World Heritage Convention proposed amendments regarding heritage routes, identifying historic themes that should be present when nominating a heritage route, noting benchmarks for authenticity and characteristics that define a heritage route versus other types of resources (such as cultural landscapes). Through these actions, agreement has coalesced among conservation professionals around the typologies of heritage routes, which include religious roads (such as Santiago de Compostela), linear sites (including defensive fortifications such as China's Great Wall and the United Kingdom's Hadrian's Wall), transportation (such as the Darjeeling Himalayan Railway in India) and trade routes (notably, the Frankincense Trail in Oman). A framework for characterizing heritage routes also emerged from these efforts, including the idea that they are comprised of prominent "anchor" sites that are connected by "support" sites. Support sites could consist of topographical and landscape features, or minor structures. An important characteristic is that the anchor and support sites together constitute a whole that is greater than the sum of its parts, which in turn relates to significant themes such as the transmission of ideas, political movements, exchange of technologies and spread of religion, or other significant historical trends. Important, too, is the idea that the very nature of a historic route is dynamic, and is linked to context, experience and interpretation.

Encouraged by China's efforts to nominate its trade routes, in 2005 representatives from all five Central Asian countries jointly adopted an "Action Plan for the Implementation of the World Heritage Convention in Central Asia", which prioritized the nomination of trade route-related sites across the region. While China was the first country to make concrete moves towards formally designating its Silk Road sites on the World Heritage List, and has thus far led the way in management and documentation strategies for heritage routes in the region, other Central Asian nations are well positioned to follow suit in the years to come. There also exists great potential for incorporating the equally important trade routes that linked Central Asia to India through the modern states of Afghanistan and Pakistan. This trend could potentially result in the creation of a transnational series of heritage corridors that are truly representative of the breadth and diversity of the great Asian trade routes' historic significance.[26]

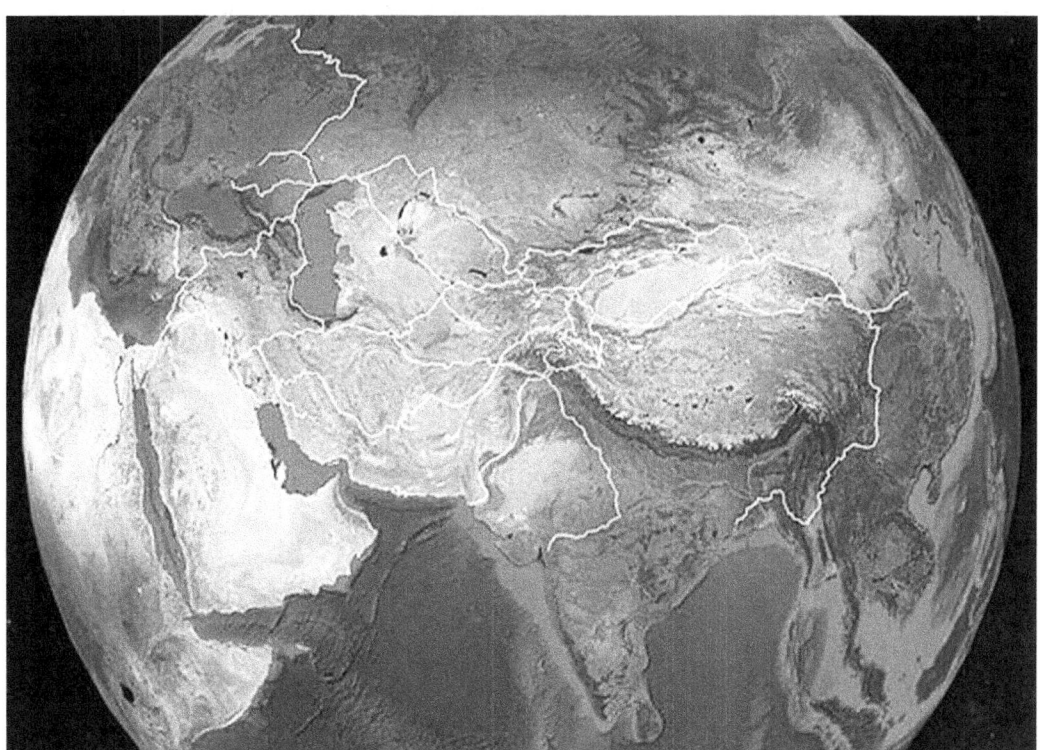

FIGURE 23.6 The ancient Silk Route system through Central Asia.

Tajikistan

Like its neighbor to the north, Tajikistan has not experienced a smooth transition from being a member of the USSR to independence, with its first five years consumed by a crippling civil war among rival clan groups. Nevertheless, the country has managed to establish and maintain a functioning conservation infrastructure at the national level, and has actively worked to nominate some of its wealth of diverse heritage sites to UNESCO's tentative list of World Heritage Sites. The Inspectorate for Heritage Protection – Historical and Cultural Reserves operating within the Ministry of Culture oversees national heritage policy and maintains the nation's List of Properties of National Significance. The Ministry of Culture and the Academy of Science – Institute of History, Archaeology and Ethnography are the principal state institutions responsible for heritage management and documentation, including maintenance of inventories, coordination with international parties, distribution of funds for conservation projects, researching sites' histories and establishing criteria for significance.[27] While these institutions are in place, consistent governmental support and funding remains a critical issue.

An overview of professional practice in Tajikistan reveals a troubling paradox that exists in many countries with nascent architectural conservation infrastructure: most significant heritage sites receive insufficient conservation attention, but those that do are frequently harmed by inappropriate or poorly executed interventions. The use of modern hard cement and reinforced concrete to repair earthen and masonry structures has proven to be particularly destructive, increasing ill effects of rising damp, inhibiting natural evaporation processes, and introducing soluble salts to centuries-old structures that can be highly damaging. One of the country's most prominent architectural sites, the 3,000-year-old Hissar, which served as an eastern capital of the Bukhara khanate until the late nineteenth century, offers one such example. Archaeological features exposed during the early Soviet era were left exposed and inadequately conserved for decades. Additionally, a 1980s Soviet-led restoration program relied heavily upon modern concrete to repair and consolidate a short section of the monumental masonry walls, towers and fortifications, thereby contributing to a rapid rate of deterioration that continues to vex conservators today.[28] A similar site of no less importance is Panjikent, where Soviet archaeologists began excavations in 1946, ultimately exposing the remains of a highly sophisticated pre-Islamic urban center dating to the fifth through eighth centuries CE. The ruins of this former capital of Sogdiana are comprised of multi-story mud brick and rammed earth bazaars, temples and residences, many of which feature vividly rendered wall paintings.[29] Archaeologists from the State Hermitage Museum in St. Petersburg remain active at the 13 ha site, approximately half of which has been excavated, most recently in collaboration with the History, Archaeology and Ethnography Institute of the Tajik Academy of Sciences.[30] The ambition and duration of the excavations have left the site's architectural and artistic remains highly vulnerable given the difficulty of conserving mud brick ruins, some standing up to 7 m (23 ft) high, along with the delicate wall paintings that remain in up to one-third of the residential buildings.[31] While some of the wall paintings have been conserved on-site or transferred to museums in Dushanbe and St. Petersburg, the protection and stabilization of the massive site itself remains a major task that is as yet not fully implemented.

FIGURE 23.7 The archaeological site of Sarazm in northwestern Tajikistan dates to the fourth through third millennia BCE. Modern wide-span steel frame shelters protect the site's most fragile archaeological remains.

The archaeological site of Sarazm contains deposits and fragmentary mud brick structures that chronicle evidence of proto-urban development, early pastoralism, agricultural practices, and early trade connections to points as far as the Indus Valley dating to the fourth through third millennia BCE. A locally based team of archaeologists and site managers at Sarazm has overseen conservation efforts in the 1990s and 2000s, including the backfilling of areas that had been excavated by the Soviets as early as the 1970s, and the construction of modern protective shelters over areas currently undergoing excavation. UNESCO and CRAterre-EAG assisted local site administrators in creating a management plan to ensure adequate site protection. This plan, along with the site's inclusion on the World Heritage List in 2010, means Sarazm should benefit from a level of protection superior to that of many other archaeological sites both in Tajikistan and elsewhere in the region.[32] However, like its counterparts, it struggles with a shortage of adequately trained staff and operational funding needed to carry out ongoing protection, maintenance and management of the large (approximately 50 ha), semi-rural site.[33]

Another site that benefits from the UNESCO-led Silk Road program has been Ajina-Tepa. This ruined mud brick monastery complex in the southwest of the country figured prominently in the spread of Buddhism into Central Asia during the seventh and eighth centuries CE. Between 1961 and 1975, Soviet teams conducted extensive excavations of the area, documenting the structures and unearthing an enormous statue of the Buddha in the reclining pose, which is now housed in the National Museum of Antiquities in Dushanbe. Following the conclusion of Soviet fieldwork the site was partially backfilled, yet erosion, unchecked vegetation growth and general lack of maintenance led to its inclusion on the ICOMOS list of Heritage at Risk in 2004. In response, UNESCO organized a multi-national collaboration between the National Research Institute for Cultural Property (NRICPT), Tokyo, and several Tajik governmental agencies, including the Ministry of Culture; the Institute of History, Archaeology and Ethnography; the Academy of Science; and the Institute of Innovation Technology and Communication.

The Ajina-Tepa collaboration focused on several critical issues: archaeological site conservation, management of mud brick architecture, enhancing local awareness of heritage resources, and professional capacity building. The team installed access control fencing in order to manage grazing animals and to deter a local tradition of quarrying the site for building materials. Site drainage was improved to direct water from adjacent agricultural activities away from its fragile mud brick foundations.

Using laboratory techniques and testing protocols developed at Otrar (Kazakhstan) and Chuy Valley (Kyrgyzstan), the conservation team instituted a program of materials testing and selective stabilization of the deteriorating mud brick structures. Structural buttressing constructed of mud brick – whose composition was deliberately differentiated from the ancient material – stabilized failing walls while functioning as a sacrificial wear coat for the unsheltered site.[34] Finally, the combined Japanese/Central Asian team completed a comprehensive survey of documentation from twentieth century field campaigns, some of which had to be translated from the original Russian, digitized and collated into a single archive.

Program work was carried out by collaborators from Saitama University and the National Research Institute for Cultural Property, Tokyo, who worked alongside staff from the Tajik Institute of History, Archaeology and Ethnography and students from the Institute of Innovation Technology and Communication in Dushanbe. This helped address the critical issue of local capacity development in conservation, site management and archaeological fieldwork.[35]

As of 2015, Tajikistan had more than a dozen sites on the tentative list for World Heritage designation, representing natural reserves, medieval Islamic mausoleums, Buddhist monasteries, and the archaeological remains of various temples, cities and citadels. This quantity represents a substantial effort on the part of the Tajik national committee to transcend the political strife that has marked their country's earliest years of independence and to take its place alongside the international conservation community.[36]

Turkmenistan

Home to ancient capitals since early antiquity, Turkmenistan possesses a wealth of archaeological sites, along with ruined and still-occupied cities that feature monumental mud brick fortifications dating to the peak years of the great Asian trade routes. Modern Turkmenistan includes portions of the Amu

Darya (Oxus River) valley, which from the Bronze Age (late third millennium BCE) has served as a cradle of early urban centers, including Gonur Depe and Anau, where archaeological evidence of the world's earliest cultivation of bread grains has been found.[37] Zoroastrianism, counted among the world's oldest and most-enduring faiths, is historically connected to Balkh (present day Afghanistan), but became firmly established in the early cities of the Margush (Margiana) in the Amu Darya valley.[38] Perhaps owing to the presence of some of the largest and best-preserved Central Asian cities – including the prominent, ruined capitals of Merv and Kunya Urgench – and its relative degree of political stability, the nation has benefitted from active international collaborations since independence. Members of several Turkmenistani organizations, such as the National Department for the Protection, Study and Restoration of the Historical and Cultural Monuments in Turkmenistan (DPM) within the Ministry of Culture, and the Academy of Sciences and State University, regularly collaborate with foreign teams from the USA, Japan and the United Kingdom in order to support local conservation projects.[39]

Nevertheless, as in its neighboring countries, the lack of ongoing conservation measures for archaeological excavations remains an issue of paramount importance. This phenomenon has imperiled several large-scale mud brick sites, such as the 2,000-year-old Parthian capital of Old Nisa, which was first excavated by Soviet teams beginning in the 1950s, and since 1990 by an Italian team from the University of Torino. In 2004 the World Monuments Fund placed Old Nisa on its Watch List, noting that while the decades of archaeological investigation had generated a great deal of information about the site, the absence of a comprehensive conservation plan had contributed to erosion of the fragile archaeological remains.[40] These conditions have been mitigated to an extent leading up to and immediately following the addition of the site to the World Heritage List in 2007, through improvements to drainage around the earthen building complexes, development of a visitor management strategy and technical conservation assistance by a pair of CRAterre missions in 2004 and 2005.[41] The older but no less significant site, Ulug Depe, which rose to prominence during the Iron Age, struggles with similar conditions: a lack of management and oversight has caused inadvertent damage to the delicate earthen remains due to visitor and local use of the area.[42]

Other prominent sites in Turkmenistan include the ancient city of Kunya-Urgench, which traces its origins to the Achaemenid Empire. It contains monumental mud brick and masonry buildings decorated with elaborate tilework dating from the eleventh through the sixteenth centuries, when it flourished as a trading center. These monuments include distinctive conically domed mausoleums, a mosque and a prominent minaret that are recognized as important stylistic influences in the wider region, reflected by later architectural expressions found from Iran to India. Listed as a World Heritage Site in 2005, Kunya-Urgench has well-established management plans and buffer zones that have effectively contributed to the protection of the abandoned city, which still plays host to religious pilgrims and tourists alike.[43] The site's high degree of material integrity is due in part to its remoteness, as modern materials that are more readily available in developed areas of Turkmenistan are frequently scarce in the country's thinly populated areas. The brick kilns of Kunya-Urgench still produce masonry units in the traditional style for use in conservation work at the site; bricks are even fired for use in conservation efforts in far-off Merv due to the high quality of the workmanship.[44]

While numerous significant sites dot the nation's largely arid landscape, ancient Merv crowns Turkmenistan's collection of heritage cities owing largely to its scale and relatively high degree of integrity. Inscribed to the World Heritage List in 1999, the State Historical and Cultural Park "Ancient Merv" is spread over more than 350 ha (865 acres). A series of fortified ruins reflect its days as the capital of the eleventh and twelfth century CE Seljuk Empire, along with archaeological deposits dating back to the third millennium BCE. The site represents a remarkably sophisticated level of urban development and monumental architecture that has earned it substantial local and international attention, both during the Soviet era and since Turkmenistan's independence. Safeguarded by the 1992 Law on the Protection of Turkmenistan Historical and Cultural Monuments, and administered by the National Department for the Protection, Study, and Restoration of Monuments within the federal Ministry of Culture, Merv (also known as Mary) contains standing mosques, mausoleums and towering citadel walls composed of mud brick. Much of the site is under threat, however, due to elevated groundwater conditions brought about by the construction of

FIGURE 23.8 In the ancient city of Kunya-Urgench, large-scale mud brick and fired masonry buildings decorated with brilliant blue tiles dating from the eleventh through sixteenth centuries were provided with buffer zones as part of planning associated with its listing on the UNESCO World Heritage List in 2005.

large-scale irrigation systems that have since the 1950s raised groundwater tables throughout the area, as well as an overall lack of maintenance during the Soviet years and beyond, which has led to a steady, relentless process of erosion.

Beginning in 2002 the World Monuments Fund, working in collaboration with University College, London, supported a program to consolidate several of the site's more vulnerable structures, to draft a site management plan, and to conduct training for local site managers responsible for overseeing Merv and other archaeological sites throughout Turkmenistan.[45] The success of this work and the regional prominence of Merv have led to the adoption of contemporary archaeological site conservation practices and mud brick building stabilization techniques both within Turkmenistan and beyond, an especially productive strategy given the similar conditions shared at hundreds of sites throughout the region.[46] Though the stabilization campaigns of the early 2000s have helped address critical conditions at a few select locations, the scope of the conservation challenge at Merv remains vast. Over 1,000 ha of archaeological deposits within the site and its buffer zone, 12 km of defensive walls, hundreds of exposed trenches from twentieth century excavations and numerous standing ruins are constantly assaulted by the corrosive powers of wind and water. The scale of the site and the urgency of its issues have led some to conclude that the most practical way to "save" Merv may be to carefully document it. In response, a second phase of the UCL project beginning in 2007 focused on 3D laser scanning and high definition photography of the most at-risk monuments in order to create a digital record of the resources before they are lost.[47]

Architectural reconstruction in the Central Asian context: room for debate

At the onset of most any discussion on architectural preservation in Central Asia the topic of conservation versus restoration versus reconstruction arises. The regional historic use of earthen architecture – be it layered rammed earthen protective walls or sun-baked and fired masonry units used in more elaborate buildings – carries with it the inherent problem of the material's durability. Earthen architecture of the kind used in Central Asia requires frequent maintenance without which deterioration begins within a few years, often in a progressive manner. There is irony here in that the finest works in the region from the standpoint of design, detailing and décor could be counted as among the best architecture of its time. American scholar on Central Asia and historian Frederick S. Starr has observed that: "If the buildings of Central Asia had been constructed of stone rather than mud brick its architectural legacy would have rivaled that of Western Europe or China."[48]

The combination of relatively short-lived building materials, destruction by natural processes and humans – especially as a result of conflict – and professional practice during the Soviet regime has left a legacy of mixed success in conservation projects throughout the region. Examples where varying levels of restoration versus reconstruction are found can be seen at the Tomb of Sanjar, rebuilt by Soviets at Merv and the complete reconstruction of the Bibi Khanoum Mosque in Samarkand.

The dilemma faced by the architects, engineers and their sponsors with such representative projects involves questions such as "How does one restore or conserve in ways that are more permanent, that comply with modern building standards, and that protect investments of expenditures in the restorations?" There may well have been the additional question of "Wouldn't a building restored completely to an earlier or its original appearance perform better as a work of architecture and be more desirable from the standpoint of didactic display?" If the first three concerns here are practical the latter two, by comparison, are philosophical. Debates on how and how far to restore the historic earthen architecture of Central Asia often center on the issue of preserving authenticity as promulgated in the Venice Charter of 1964, and criteria for UNESCO World Heritage Listing. "Over-restoration," especially that which entails conjecture and non-traditional materials, counters, in general, most doctrine and contemporary practice in architectural conservation as commonly experienced in Europe and the Americas. Hence we have a methodological difference in conservation practice between East, as in Uzbekistan, and West. (See also pages 51 and 81.)

The practical problems of restoring damaged or ruined structures throughout Central Asia are clear, since by now practically every possible approach has been tried. The fact is that the merits of the extensive restoration or reconstruction approach may well outweigh the conservation approach in many instances, which realistically begs the question of whether there should be an adjustment of international expectations and standards to accommodate the particular nature of built heritage in Central Asia. In the light of debate over somewhat similar issues in building conservation practices in China and Japan over the past two decades, the answer may well be "Yes."

Uzbekistan

Uzbekistan is distinguished in the region by the fact that many of its ancient cities, including Samarkand, Tashkent, Shakhrisyabz, Itchan Kala and Bukhara, remain major urban centers to this day. As a result, the country has been the primary hub of conservation activity in the region since the Soviet era, with several major efforts focused on its magnificent urban districts.[49]

Nevertheless, considerable tension exists within the prominent conservation initiatives in the historic cores of these cities, given their accumulated layers of cultural history, growing populations, and expanding modern urban features. Each of these places has stood as a major center of commerce and culture for successive dynasties over more than 2,500 years, and their complex, influential built heritage attests to the cycles of destruction and rebirth that came with each new dominant group. As a result, cities such as Samarkand still possess remarkable assemblages of Sogdian, Islamic, Timurid, Russian colonial, Soviet and modern architecture existing side by side within the densely packed city center. At Shakhrisyabz, a mid-sized city in southeast Uzbekistan, a largely intact Timurid-period (fourteenth through fifteenth centuries CE) historic core remains, consisting of palaces, *hammams* and mausoleums, including the tomb of Timur's eldest son, Jegangir.[50] At the other end of the spectrum, the capital Tashkent (a former hub for the Kokand khanate) was largely remade during the Soviet era, when Moscow decided that it would serve as the *de facto* first city of Central Asia and rebuilt it accordingly beginning in 1930.[51]

The khans of Khiva constructed imposing palaces and centers of learning at Itchan Kala beginning in the seventeenth century, after Chinggis Khan and the Turko-Mongol ruler Timur (also known as Tamerlane) had successively destroyed the important trading center. The walled city remains today within the modern city of Khiva, constituting Uzbekistan's first World Heritage Site.[52] The Historic Center of Bukhara was inscribed on the World Heritage List in 1993, in recognition of its collections of building complexes, including madrasas, minarets and monumental fortifications dating primarily from the sixteenth and seventeenth century CE reign of the Sheibanid Dynasty.[53] Together, these cities illustrate the challenges inherent in urban Central Asian architectural conservation. Today, zoning and other master planning tools are being used to manage levels of change, but in cases such as Khiva the legacy of Soviet-era tourism promotion efforts have had lasting negative effects on the populations since they are living in only minimally authentic tourist destinations, rather than actual functioning cities.

The Uzbek Law on the Preservation and Utilization of Objects of Cultural Heritage (2001) along with legislation for protecting archaeological sites (2009), govern architectural conservation policy and practice in the country. These are overseen at the national level by the Ministry of Culture and Sports, which is supported by an expert body known as the Principal Scientific Board for Preservation and Utilization of Cultural Monuments, along with regional authorities tasked with management of urban conservation programs, reconstruction and rehabilitation projects in Uzbekistan's historic cities. This framework supports a robust environment for architectural conservation practice in the country, which is enhanced by a network of traditional craftspeople with generations of expertise in traditional building materials and methods such as fired brick, plasterwork and architectural ceramics.

At Bukhara, conservation activity began under the Soviets in the 1920s, an era that established a tradition of large-scale restoration of its grand architectural monuments and building complexes, coupled with the removal of contextual, non-monumental buildings – an approach that remains

FIGURE 23.9a and b Traditional architecture in Bukhara as found in urban vernacular housing (a) and Madrasa Nadir Divangebi (b) preserved due to continuous use.

problematically common to this day. Beginning in the early 1970s the Soviet regime led a sustained, thorough urban conservation effort in the old town of Bukhara, and in its sister city Samarkand, largely for the purposes of tourism development. This program led to the retention, and in many cases the active restoration, of the city's historic core, with the majority of new development occurring outside of the city walls. A post-independence World Heritage designation and concurrent re-emergence on the international scene as an outstanding example of Central Asian architectural heritage have raised the international profile of the old city. Conservation efforts begun under the Soviet regime and continued by the Restoration Institute of Uzbekistan and its municipal partners earned recognition in the form of the Aga Khan Trust for Culture Award for Architecture (1995).[54] But, as with many urban conservation efforts in newly independent states, the ongoing work at Bukhara is challenged by the tension between the revitalization of the old city and a drive for economic development and infrastructure improvements.

In the fourteenth century CE, Timur designated Samarkand as the administrative and cultural capital of his vast empire. He expanded the city from its ancient Arab core of Afrasiab, and commissioned a number of influential monuments in a distinctive style based on other Islamic kingdoms from India to Persia. Among the most impressive of Samarkand's many majestic architectural spaces is the fifteenth to seventeenth century CE Registan Square. This collection of three domed *madrasas* arranged around a square, each exuberantly decorated in geometric glazed tile with facing *iwan* (vaulted halls), has been the subject of many conservation campaigns beginning in the 1920s.[55] National interest in the city's Timurid monuments, including Registan Square, Bibi Khanum mosque and Gur-i-Emir complex (Timur's mausoleum), surged after Uzbekistan gained independence in 1990, resulting in urban planning projects and extensive restorations that account for the present-day appearance of the buildings, along with many of their conservation issues.

Samarkand is organized into four distinctive areas: the archaeological zone, which encompasses the ruins of the city of Afrasiab, destroyed by Chinggis Khan in 1220 CE; the fourteenth and fifteenth century Timurid-era city; the nineteenth and early twentieth century Russian district; and the modern city, which surrounds the other three.[56] Administratively, the Samarkand State Historical Architectural Reserve encompasses the first three areas and is overseen by the Samarkand Regional State Inspection on Protection and Utilization of Cultural Heritage Objects. The Regional Inspection works in tandem with its national counterpart to manage planning and conservation decisions in the city of around 500,000 residents.

In the 1990s the Aga Khan Trust for Culture (AKTC) sponsored a long-term planning effort in the city that focused on transportation and infrastructure improvements. The latter included dredging the

The Aral Sea: at the intersection of ecological and cultural heritage conservation

The recent drying up of 90 percent (61,200 square kilometers or 20,000 square miles) of the Aral Sea, located on the border of Kazakhstan and Uzbekistan, marks one of the world's great environmental catastrophes. This calamity has also profoundly impacted the region's built heritage and the health of its inhabitants. Due to decades of water diversion for massive Soviet agricultural projects, the inland sea has all but vanished, increasing salinity in the soil and spreading thousands of tons of salt, pesticide and herbicide-laden dust from the former seabed over vast areas during annual dust storms. Damage to the environment and health of residents notwithstanding, the contaminated dust storms and increased groundwater salinity attack the mud-brick historic structures of the region from inside and out. As the saline groundwater is drawn up into porous building materials by natural capillary action, the water then evaporates, leaving the salts to crystallize. This salt crystallization mechanically damages mud brick walls and their surface finishes, which are also being further eroded by the contaminated dust deposited on their surfaces. By 2005 a US$85 million World Bank project had succeeded in restoring 230 square miles of the North Aral Sea by constructing a dam separating it from the rest of the lakebed and improving upstream irrigation infrastructure.[57] But large parts of the lake – including most of its eastern expanse – have likely been lost forever, illustrating how this especially poor environmental legacy of the Soviet Union affected everything, from wildlife to local economies to historic architecture.

city's system of canals to improve drainage, while also lowering the local water table to reduce damage to traditional buildings from capillary action and salt efflorescence. The problematic Soviet-era practice of clearing smaller, informal buildings that once surrounded the city's principal monuments – which created monuments isolated from the traditional urban context and activities – was addressed by planning efforts that encouraged compatible infill construction. Planners engaged the traditional network of mosque-based community support known as *mahalla* to drive local efforts in urban revitalization. Through these activities, community needs such as infrastructure replacement and the creation of craft and commercial centers in historic districts, were leveraged to secure support for conservation planning efforts.[58] Ambitious and well intentioned as these plans were, the sustainability of their impact suffered due to political and sectarian differences between the AKTC and the local government, along with continued development pressures in the historic city.

Issues that have threatened the historic city since its designation as a World Heritage Site in 2001 include large-scale road construction projects within the Architectural Reserve, inadequate documentation of the city's historic residential areas, the prevalence of incompatible new buildings in and around the Timurid-era city, and harmful reconstructions of the city's distinctive mausoleums and mosques. In response to concerns voiced by UNESCO regarding these issues, the Uzbek State Party developed a "Management Plan of the Conservation and Rehabilitation of the Historical Centre of Samarkand" in 2007, a well-received document that proposed to revise the approach to conservation in the ancient city. Under the plan, the city's Regional State Inspection committed to preserving the authenticity of heritage properties as much as feasible, seek to retain the built context of its monuments, and align city planning to international and national norms for heritage cities.[59] Balancing these objectives and carrying out their enforcement remain key challenges to the ongoing conservation of Samarkand, with observers noting that in 2013 authorities constructed a new road directly adjacent to the Registan, which included clearing a Timurid-era residential neighborhood, while increasing the amount of traffic directly adjacent to the fragile tile and mud brick structures.[60]

Extensive reconstructions are a legacy of the Soviet period of Uzbekistan's history, and in some cases the zeal with which projects are undertaken has contributed to poorly-executed craftsmanship, along with reconstructions that cross the line between restoration and conjecture. In some cases new materials – including glazed tile that is so characteristic of the region's architecture – have been replaced with new, substandard versions, and hard cement or concrete have been overused at the expense of traditional baked brick and lime mortar. The trio of madrasas that comprise the Registan Square were restored under a series of Soviet campaigns between 1920 and 1982 with varying levels of regard for the authenticity of the historic structures.[61] The Bibi Khanum mosque in Samarkand, constructed under the direct supervision of Timur between 1399 and 1404 and built to honor his wife, is one such example where modern brick, reinforced concrete and incompatible mortar were used to completely reconstruct large portions of an ancient building. Originally thought to feature multiple domes, imposing iwan and decorative tile façades, the mosque experienced a series of structural failures leading to a partial collapse in the centuries after its completion, culminating in an 1897 earthquake that toppled large portions of the mud brick building.

Despite the absence of complete historical records that described the lost portions of the building, a series of major projects were undertaken by Soviet and later Uzbek authorities, resulting in a near-total reconstruction of the building by the late 1990s. Critics of the effort point to poor craftsmanship, damage to original materials inflicted by the new elements, and the loss of authenticity such an extensive reconstruction entails.[62] Preparations for the 2007 events celebrating the 2,750th anniversary of Samarkand's founding included another flurry of speculative reconstructions at the Bibi Khanum mosque and mausoleum, including the addition of several walls separating the original complex from adjacent residential neighborhoods.[63] Similarly, skeptical conservationists in Samarkand and beyond have cited a desire to attract tourists and fuel the local construction industry – rather than internationally accepted conservation practices – as primary motivators for the reconstructions at Bibi Khanum and other sites in Uzbekistan's historic cities.[64]

Reconstruction campaigns tend to be linked to anniversary celebrations, which are geared toward celebrating the founding of a city or birth of a celebrated native son, and frequently include civic enhancement projects involving historic sites. Restorations of Timur-affiliated sites are particularly attractive to a national government invested in identifying itself with a famous conquering hero. In Bukhara, authorities have subjected several monuments to heavy-handed restorations in order to "improve" them ahead of the 2,500-year anniversary of the city's founding in the mid-1990s. For this, the prominent twelfth century Kalon minaret was heavily restored using concrete, thus robbing the structure of its original foundation system and patina.[65] While past efforts to conserve Uzbekistan's distinctive historic urban centers have been thoughtful and well intended, concern over development and implementation of management plans, restoration approaches to monuments, and the treatment of contextual urban fabric (such as historic residential districts) remains acute in Bukhara and other major centers.[66]

a

b

FIGURE 23.10a and b
Extensive reconstruction of the upper sections of the Bibi Khanum mosque and the twelfth century Kalon minaret in Bukhara with new materials including reinforced concrete have been met with criticism by international conservators concerned with the extent of their restorations and the retention of authenticity. Illustrated are its appearance as an open ruin in 1890 (a) and after restoration in the 1990s (b).

As the architectural heritage of Central Asia becomes increasingly well known globally in the post-Soviet era, many opportunities exist for capitalizing both on the international partnerships and on the local enthusiasm that accompanies newfound independence into best practices for conserving heritage resources. Examples of inspired conservation projects exist in each of the five countries, spurred by the motivation to establish new national identities, and to share the cultural contributions this distinctive region has ushered into the world. Also emerging in the post-Soviet era is an enhanced understanding of the characteristics that define these distinctively Central Asian heritage resources, including the materials, styles, historic connections and their meaning, along with a shared understanding of local threats. From the cultural landscapes and ancient traditions of Kyrgyzstan's Suleiman Too-Sacred Mountain to the diverse architectural traditions of the great Central Asian trading communities scattered across the region, opportunities exist for further documenting, studying, conserving and interpreting the region's unique heritage sites and sharing them with the local and international communities. In some cases, the international conservation community has stepped in to encourage positive solutions, such as the sponsorship of regional training missions, promotion of research into regional topics (such as the conservation of large-scale mud brick structures) and traditional aid projects, including the joint British/American assistance at Merv.

However, there remain significant conservation-specific challenges in the region, which sit alongside larger-scale macro problems facing Central Asia as a whole. In terms of the former, budgets for conservation projects and their publication are constrained; political and legal structures are weak; and professional training and capacity in conservation and heritage planning are underdeveloped. At a macro level, challenges include inefficient regional water management practices, political instability and environmental pollution and degradation, each of which inflict consequences across many aspects of life in the region, including architectural conservation.

Enhancing the local populations' appreciation of the value of their historic resources as objects beyond nationalistic symbols remains a critical task. Education and promotion of the use of locally available building materials in conservation projects, such as mud brick, should also be a priority in the region given the particular characteristics of traditional earthen architecture. Another need that must be met is development of appropriate and effective strategies for reinforcing historic buildings of all types against seismic activity, which remains a perpetual regional threat. Professional capacity building through ongoing international engagements will be important in the decades ahead, particularly in the fields of archaeological site conservation and traditional building trades. The ability to jointly develop and share the experience of trained professionals and contributions from the international community across the region is particularly promising, given the similarities between the types of heritage resources and common histories shared by the Central Asian nations.

Notes

1 In his book *Lost Enlightenment* historian S. Frederick Starr convincingly argues that the term "Silk Road" overly generalizes the nature of trade through Central Asia between 100 BCE and 1500 CE. Rather than an economy dominated by a single commodity shipped from China to points west, Starr notes that trade included a wide range of goods beyond silk, such as precious stones and manufactured goods, and that north/south exchange through Afghanistan to India was equally if not more important than the east/west routes. Accordingly, this chapter uses the term "Silk Road" sparingly, and generally in reference to specific initiatives that use this label. Instead, more general terms like "Asian trade routes" are favored in order to more accurately reflect the nature of these crucial phenomena, and the role that Central Asia played therein. Reference: S. Frederick Starr. *Lost Enlightenment: Central Asia's Golden Age from the Arab Conquest to Tamerlane.* (Princeton: Princeton University Press, 2013), 43.

2 Though Central Asian history is replete with instances of great urban centers falling under the assault of nomadic hordes, scholars also argue that over the long term the relationship between the settled and nomadic people of the region was symbiotic rather than exclusively adversarial. In addition to the fact that previously nomadic groups such as the Parthians, Turks and Kushans ultimately established city-based empires, long-standing arrangements concerning trade, transport and security formed mutually beneficial relationships over the centuries. Source: Starr, 54–58.

3 UNESCO, "The Silk Roads Project: Integral Study of the Silk Road – 1988–1997." UNESCO World Heritage Centre. Web. http://unesdoc.unesco.org/images/0015/001591/159189E.pdf. Accessed June 21, 2016.

4   Laurence Mitchell, *Kyrgyzstan*. (Guilford, CT: The Globe Pequot Press, 2012), 14.
5   Although Soviet archaeologists and conservators documented their work extensively, publications were not always forthcoming, and even less frequently translated or made available beyond the Soviet sphere.
6   CRAterre, *Central Asian Earth Programme: Building Capacity for Conservation, Preservation and Management of Immovable Cultural Heritage in Central Asia*. Program Brochure (2012). Web. http://craterre.org/terre.grenoble.archi.fr/documentation/downloads/central-asian-earth.pdf. Accessed July 4, 2014.
7   Boris Usmanov, "Revitalization of the Heritage of Uzbekistan," in Attilio Petruccioli (ed.), *Bukhara: The Myth and the Architecture*. (Cambridge: The Aga Khan Program for Islamic Architecture, 1999), 184–185.
8   Michael Barry Lane, "Site Management Summary: Samarkand and Bukhara, Uzbekistan." Paper delivered at *The Future of Asia's Past: Preservation of the Architectural Heritage of Asia* conference, Chiang Mai, Thailand, January 1995.
9   Mounira Azzout, "The Soviet Interpretation and Preservation of the Ancient Heritage of Uzbekistan: The Example of Bukhara," in Attilio Petruccioli (ed.), *Bukhara: The Myth and the Architecture*. (Cambridge: The Aga Khan Program for Islamic Architecture, 1999), 161.
10 UNESCO. "World Heritage List: Mausoleum of Khoja Ahmed Yasawi." UNESCO World Heritage Centre. Web. http://whc.unesco.org/en/list/1103. Accessed July 5, 2013.
11 Kazakh National Commission for UNESCO. "Application of the World Heritage Convention by the States Parties: Kazakhstan 2002 Report." Web. http://whc.unesco.org/archive/periodicreporting/apa/cycle01/section1/kz-summary.pdf. Accessed March 2, 2015.
12 Enrico Fodde, "Conserving Sites on the Central Asian Silk Roads: The Case of Otrar Tobe, Kazakhstan," *Conservation and Management of Archaeological Sites* 8(2) (2006), 77–87.
13 Michael Jansen, "Kazakhstan: The Oasis of Otrar." ICOMOS Heritage at Risk: 2002–2004. Web. www.international.icomos.org/risk/2002/kazakhstan2002.htm. Accessed July 4, 2014.
14 UNESCO Kazakhstan, "UNESCO/Japan Trust Fund Preservation and Restoration of Otrar Tobe, Kazakhstan." Web. www.unesco.kz/otrar_house. Accessed September 2, 2004.
15 Laurent Lévi-Strauss and Roland Lin, "Safeguarding Silk Road Sites in Central Asia," in Neville Agnew (ed.), *Conservation of Ancient Sites on the Silk Road*. (Los Angeles: Getty Conservation Institute, 2010), 56–57.
16 Khoja Ahmed Yasavi (1093–1166 CE) was a Turkic poet, founder of the Turkic Tarīqah (order) and pioneer of popular mysticism that rapidly spread over Turkic-speaking areas. Construction of his mausoleum was begun by Tamerlane in the fourteenth century and never completed, although it does stand as one of the best-preserved of all Timurid constructions.
17 World Monuments Fund, "Necropolises of Nomads in Mangystau." Web. www.wmf.org/project/necropolises-nomads-mangystau. Accessed July 4, 2014.
18 World Monuments Fund, "Vernacular Architecture of the Kazakh Steppe Sary-Arka." Web. www.wmf.org/project/vernacular-architecture-kazakh-steppe-sary-arka. Accessed July 4, 2013.
19 UNESCO. "Asia Conserved: Lessons Learned from the UNESCO Asia-Pacific Heritage Awards for Culture Heritage Protection (2000–2004)." Saint Ascension Cathedral, Almaty: 2004 Heritage Award of Distinction. (Bangkok: UNESCO Bangkok, 2007), 331–338.
20 Aida Abdykanova, "Kyrgyzstan: Cultural Heritage Management," in Claire Smith (ed.), *Encyclopedia of Global Archaeology*. (New York: Springer, 2014), 4336–4339.
21 Lévi-Strauss and Lin, 57–59.
22 UNESCO World Heritage Centre – List of Tentative Sites. "Silk Road Sites in Kyrgyzstan." Web. http://whc.unesco.org/en/tentativelists/5518/. Accessed July 5, 2013.
23 UNESCO World Heritage Centre. "Sulaiman-Too Sacred Mountain." Web. http://whc.unesco.org/en/list/1230. Accessed July 4, 2013.
24 UNESCO. *Periodical Report on Realisation of the Convention of World Heritage: Kyrgyz Republic*. (Paris: UNESCO 2002), 1–5.
25 Ron Van Ores. "Nomination of the Silk Road in China to UNESCO's World Heritage List: Proposals for a Strategic Approach and Reference Framework for Heritage Routes," in Neville Agnew (ed.), *Conservation of Ancient Sites on the Silk Road*. (Los Angeles: Getty Conservation Institute, 2010).
26 Jung Feng. "UNESCO's Efforts in Identifying the World Heritage Significance of the Silk Road," in 15th ICOMOS General Assembly and International Symposium: *Monuments and Sites in their Setting – Conserving Cultural Heritage in Changing Townscapes and Landscapes*, October 17–21, 2005, Xi'an, China.
27 Academy of Science, Republic of Tajikistan. *Sarazm: Management Plan (2006–2010)*. (Dushanbe: Academy of Science, 2005), 39.
28 Natalia Trekulova and Timur Turekulov. *ICOMOS Heritage at Risk 2004–05: Tajikistan – A View from Outside*. (Paris: ICOMOS, 2005) 239–242.

29 The Sogdians were key players in the trade route economies of pre-Islamic Central Asia, primarily based in Samarkand and Panjikent, but with a network of trading "colonies" extending from the Black Sea to Canton, and as far south as Sri Lanka. Source: Starr, 45.
30 Boris Marshak. "Panjikent: A Pre-Islamic Town in Central Asia," in Neville Agnew, Michael Taylor, Alejandro Alva Balderrama and Hugo Houben (eds.), *Adobe 90: 6th Conference on the Conservation of Earthen Architecture*. (Los Angeles: Getty Conservation Institute, 1990), 230–232.
31 State Hermitage Museum. "Penjikent Expedition." Web. www.hermitagemuseum.org/wps/portal/hermitage/research/archaeology-and-expeditions/expedition/pendzhikent/?lng=. Accessed August 12, 2015.
32 *Sarazm: Management Plan (2006–2010)*, 30–31.
33 UNESCO World Heritage Centre. "Proto-urban Site of Sarazm." Web. http://whc.unesco.org/en/list/1141. Accessed July 4, 2013.
34 Enrico Fodde, Kunio Watanabe and Yukiyasu Fujii. "Conservation and Documentation of the Buddhist Monastery of Ajina Tepa, Tajikistan: Heritage of the Silk Road," in Leslie Rainer et al. (eds.), *Terra 2008: The 10th International Conference on the Study and Conservation of Earthen Architectural Heritage*. (Los Angeles: Getty Publications, 2011), 171–176.
35 UNESCO/Japanese-Funds-in-Trust. *Preservation of the Buddhist Monastery of Ajina Tepa, Tajikistan: Report of the Archaeological Investigations of Ajina Tepa (2006–2008)*. (Tokyo: National Research Institute for Cultural Properties, 2012), 17–19.
36 UNESCO World Heritage Centre. "Tajikistan – List of Tentative World Heritage Sites." Web. http://whc.unesco.org/en/tentativelists/state=tj. Accessed July 7, 2013.
37 Starr, 34.
38 Gonordepe is the most extensive of these ruined centers, comprised of a vast (44 ha/109 acre) archaeological site consisting of two major palace complexes and a series of satellite settlements. The site was discovered by the Greek-Soviet archaeologist Victor Sarianidi in the late 1970s and has been under excavation since, revealing vast quantities of data about the Bactrian-Margina civilization, which developed along the Amu Darya beginning in the third millennium BCE. Source: C.C. Lamberg-Karlovsky. "The Oxus Civilization," *Cuadernos de Prehistoria y Arquelogia, Universidad de Autonoma de Madrid* (CuPAUAM), 39 (2013), 21–22.
39 UNESCO World Heritage Centre. "World Heritage Advisory Body Evaluation: Merv, Turkmenistan." Web. http://whc.unesco.org/archive/advisory_body_evaluation/886.pdf. Accessed September 2, 2004.
40 World Monuments Fund. "Past Watch Site: Old Nisa, Turkmenistan." Web. www.wmf.org/project/old-nisa. Accessed July 5, 2013.
41 CRAterre, "Project Sheet: Conservation of the Parthian Fortresses of Nisa." Web. http://craterre.org/action:projets/view/id/200b69f63f0923aa499c33c78cf02625?new_lang=en_GB. Accessed April 8, 2015.
42 World Monuments Fund. "World Monuments Fund 2012 Watch List: Ulug Depe." Web. www.wmf.org/project/ulug-depe. Accessed July 7, 2013.
43 UNESCO World Heritage Centre. "Kunya-Urgdench." Web. http://whc.unesco.org/en/list/1199. Accessed July 4, 2013.
44 Government of Turkmenistan. *Kunya-Urgench, Turkmenistan: Nomination of the Ancient Town of Kunya Urgench for Inclusion on the World Heritage List*. (Paris: UNESCO, 2004), 22–23.
45 Bairam Ali, "Ancient Merv Archaeological Site: Development of Long-Term Management Capacities in Turkmenistan." World Monuments Fund – Projects. Web. www.wmf.org/project/ancient-merv-archaeological-site. Accessed July 7, 2013.
46 Gaetano Palumbo et al. "Sustaining an Ancient Tradition: The World Monuments Fund and the Conservation of Earthen Architecture," in Leslie Rainer et al. (eds.), *Terra 2008: The 10th International Conference on the Study and Conservation of Earthen Architectural Heritage*. (Los Angeles: Getty Conservation Institute, 2008), 345–346.
47 CyArk. "Ancient Merv." Web. http://archive.cyark.org/ancient-merv-info. Accessed August 10, 2015.
48 Conversation with Frederick S. Starr, New Orleans, Louisiana, August 3, 2015.
49 Enrico Fodde, "Conservation and Conflict in the Central Asian Silk Roads," *Journal of Architectural Conservation* 16(1) (2010), 75–94.
50 UNESCO World Heritage Centre. "Historic Centre of Shakhrisyabz." Web. http://whc.unesco.org/en/list/885. Accessed July 5, 2013.
51 Paul Stronski. *Tashkent: Forging a Soviet City*. (Pittsburgh: University of Pittsburgh Press, 2010), 8.
52 UNESCO World Heritage Centre. "Itchan Kala." Web. http://whc.unesco.org/en/list/543/. Accessed July 5, 2013.
53 UNESCO World Heritage Centre. "The Historic Centre of Bukhara." Web. http://whc.unesco.org/en/list/602. Accessed July 5, 2013.

54 Selma Al-Radi. "Restoration of Bukhara Old City," in Cynthia Davidson and Ismail Serageldin (eds.), *Architecture Beyond Architecture*. (London: Academy Editions, 1995).
55 Yildirim Yavuz, *Registan Square and Tashkent Street, Samarkand, Uzbekistan*. 1992 Technical Review Summary for the Aga Khan Trust for Culture. Geneva: AKTC, 3.
56 UNESCO World Heritage Centre. "Samarkand – Crossroads of Cultures." Web. http://whc.unesco.org/en/list/603. Accessed July 5, 2013.
57 Pat Walters. "Aral Sea Recovery?" *National Geographic* (April 22, 2010). Web. http://news.nationalgeographic.com/news/2010/04/100402-aral-sea-story/. Accessed March 9, 2015.
58 Aga Khan Trust for Culture: Historic Cities Support Programme. *Planning for the Historic City of Samarkand*. (Geneva: AKTC, 1996), 44–54.
59 Ainura Tentieva and Nur Akin. *Report on the Reactive Monitoring Mission to Samarkand – Crossroads of Cultures World Heritage Site (Uzbekistan), 12–17 December 2007*. (Paris: UNESCO, 2007), 11.
60 Elena Paskaleva. "Samarqand Refashioned," *Silk Road Foundation Newsletter* 11 (2013), 143–144.
61 Ibid., 141.
62 Fodde, 80.
63 Paskaleva, 151.
64 Artur Samari, "Monumental Blunders in Uzbekistan," Institute for War and Peace Reporting. Web. http://iwpr.net/report-news/monumental-blunders-uzbekistan. Accessed August 13, 2013.
65 "Uzbekistan: Sloppy Work Risk in Bukhara Facelift," Institute for War and Peace Reporting. Web. http://iwpr.net/report-news/uzbekistan-sloppy-work-risk-bukhara-facelift. Accessed August 13, 2013.
66 UNESCO. "State of Conservation: Historic Urban Centre of Bukhara (Uzbekistan)." Web. www.whc.unesco.org/en/soc/3287. Accessed October 19, 2015.

Further reading

Abdykanova, Aida. 2014. "Kyrgyzstan: Cultural Heritage Management," in Claire Smith (ed.), *Encyclopedia of Global Archaeology*. New York: Springer.

Academy of Science, Republic of Tajikistan. 2005. *Sarazm: Management Plan (2006–2010)*. Dushanbe: Academy of Science.

Aga Khan Trust for Culture. 1996. "Planning for the Historic City of Samarkand." Historic Cities Support Programme. Geneva: AKTC.

Ali, Bairam. 2013. "Ancient Merv Archaeological Site: Development of Long-Term Management Capacities in Turkmenistan." World Monuments Fund – Projects. Web. www.wmf.org/project/ancient-merv-archaeological-site. Accessed July 7, 2013.

Al-Radi, Selma. 1995. "Restoration of Bukhara Old City," in Cynthia Davidson and Ismail Serageldin (eds.), *Architecture Beyond Architecture*. London: Academy Editions.

Azzout, Mounira. 1999. "The Soviet Interpretation and Preservation of the Ancient Heritage of Uzbekistan: The Example of Bukhara," in Attilio Petruccioli (ed.), *Bukhara: The Myth and the Architecture*. Cambridge: The Aga Khan Program for Islamic Architecture.

Beckwith, Christopher J. 2009. *Empires of the Silk Road*. Princeton: Princeton University Press.

Beeson, M. and R. Stubbs. 2012. "Introduction," in M. Beeson and R. Stubbs (eds.), *Routledge Handbook of Asian Regionalism*. London: Routledge, 1–7.

CRAterre. 2012. *Central Asian Earth Programme: Building Capacity for Conservation, Preservation and Management of Immovable Cultural Heritage in Central Asia*. Program Brochure. Web. http://craterre.org/terre.grenoble.archi.fr/documentation/downloads/central-asian-earth.pdf. Accessed July 4, 2014.

——. 2015. "Project Sheet: Conservation of the Parthian Fortresses of Nisa." Web. http://craterre.org/action:projets/view/id/200b69f63f0923aa499c33c78cf02625?new_lang=en_GB. Accessed July 4, 2014.

Feng, Jung. 2005. "UNESCO's Efforts in Identifying the World Heritage Significance of the Silk Road," paper presented at the 15th ICOMOS General Assembly and International Symposium: *Monuments and Sites in their Setting – Conserving Cultural Heritage in Changing Townscapes and Landscapes*, October 17–21, 2005, Xi'an, China. Paris: ICOMOS.

Fodde, Enrico. 2006. "Conserving Sites on the Central Asian Silk Roads: The Case of Otrar Tobe, Kazakhstan," *Conservation and Management of Archaeological Sites* 8(2): 77–87.

——. 2010. "Conservation and Conflict in the Central Asian Silk Roads," *Journal of Architectural Conservation* 16(1): 75–94.

Fodde, Enrico, Kunio Watanabe and Yukiyasu Fujii. 2011. "Conservation and Documentation of the Buddhist Monastery of Ajina Tepa, Tajikistan: Heritage of the Silk Road," in Leslie Rainer et al. (eds.), *Terra 2008: The 10th International Conference on the Study and Conservation of Earthen Architectural Heritage*. Los Angeles: Getty Publications.

Fong, Kecia L., et al. 2012. "Same but Different?: A Roundtable Discussion on the Philosophies, Methodologies, and Practicalities of Conserving Cultural Heritage in Asia," in Patrick Daly and Tim Winter (eds.), *Routledge Handbook of Heritage in Asia*. London: Routledge, 39–54.

Government of Turkmenistan. 2004. *Kunya-Urgench, Turkmenistan: Nomination of the Ancient Town of Kunya Urgench for Inclusion on the World Heritage List*. Paris: UNESCO.

Hiebert, Fredrik with Kakamurad Kurbansakhtov. 2003. *A Central Asian Village at the Dawn of Civilization, Excavations at Anau, Turkmenistan*. Philadelphia: University of Pennsylvania Press.

Institute for War and Peace Reporting. 2009. "Uzbekistan: Sloppy Work Risk in Bukhara Facelift." Web. http://iwpr.net/report-news/uzbekistan-sloppy-work-risk-bukhara-facelift. Accessed August 13, 2013.

Jansen, Michael. "Kazakhstan: The Oasis of Otrar." ICOMOS Heritage at Risk: 2002–2004. Web. www.international.icomos.org/risk/2002/kazakhstan2002.htm. Accessed July 4, 2014.

Khorosh, Yelena Khristoforovna. 2003. "Problems and Needs on Cultural Heritage Protection Activities in Kazakhstan," Asia/Pacific Cultural Centre for UNESCO. Web. www.nara.accu.or.jp/hp/English/topics/technological/kazakh.html. Accessed July 4, 2014.

Lane, Michael Barry. 1995. "Site Management Summary: Samarkand and Bukhara, Uzbekistan." Paper presented to the international conference *The Future of Asia's Past: Preservation of the Architectural Heritage of Asia*, Chiang Mai, January 11–14.

Mitchell, Laurence. 2012. *Kyrgyzstan*. Guilford, CT: The Globe Pequot Press.

Paskaleva, Elena. 2013. "Samarqand Refashioned." *Silk Road Foundation Newsletter* 11: 139–154. Web. www.silkroadfoundation.org/newsletter/vol11/SilkRoad_11_2013_paskaleva.pdf. Accessed June 21, 2016.

Petruccioli, Attilio (ed.). 1999. *Bukhara: The Myth and the Architecture*. Cambridge: The Aga Khan Program for Islamic Architecture.

Rainer, Leslie, et al. (eds.). 2008. *Terra 2008: The 10th International Conference on the Study and Conservation of Earthen Architectural Heritage*. Los Angeles: Getty Conservation Institute.

Samari, Artur. N.d. "Monumental Blunders in Uzbekistan," Institute for War and Peace Reporting. Web. http://iwpr.net/report-news/monumental-blunders-uzbekistan. Accessed August 13, 2013.

Stronski, Paul. 2010. *Tashkent: Forging a Soviet City*. Pittsburgh: University of Pittsburgh Press.

Trekulova, Natalia and Timur Turekulov. 2005. *ICOMOS Heritage at Risk 2004–05: Tajikistan – A View from Outside*. Paris: ICOMOS.

UNESCO. 2002. *Periodical Report on Realisation of the Convention of World Heritage: Kyrgyz Republic*. Paris: UNESCO.

UNESCO Bangkok. 2007. "Asia Conserved: Lessons Learned from the UNESCO Asia-Pacific Heritage Awards for Culture Heritage Protection (2000–2004)." Saint Ascension Cathedral, Almaty: 2004 Heritage Award of Distinction. Bangkok: UNESCO Bangkok.

UNESCO/Japanese-Funds-in-Trust. 2012. *Preservation of the Buddhist Monastery of Ajina Tepa, Tajikistan: Report of the Archaeological Investigations of Ajina Tepa (2006–2008)*. Tokyo: National Research Institute for Cultural Properties.

UNESCO Kazakh National Commission. 2002. "Application of the World Heritage Convention by the States Parties: Kazakhstan 2002 Report." Web. http://whc.unesco.org/archive/periodicreporting/apa/cycle01/section1/kz-summary.pdf. Accessed March 2, 2015.

UNESCO Kazakhstan. N.d. "UNESCO/Japan Trust Fund Preservation and Restoration of Otrar Tobe, Kazakhstan." Web. http://www.unesco.kz/otrar_house. Accessed September 2, 2004.

UNESCO World Heritage Centre. N.d. "The Historic Centre of Bukhara." Web. http://whc.unesco.org/en/list/602. Accessed July 5, 2013.

——. N.d. "Historic Centre of Shakhrisyabz." Web. http://whc.unesco.org/en/list/885. Accessed July 5, 2013.

——. N.d. "Itchan Kala." Web. http://whc.unesco.org/en/list/543/. Accessed July 5, 2013.

——. N.d. "Kunya-Urgdench." Web. http://whc.unesco.org/en/list/1199. Accessed July 5, 2013.

——. N.d. "Proto-urban Site of Sarazm." Web. http://whc.unesco.org/en/list/1141. Accessed July 5, 2013.

——. N.d. "Samarkand – Crossroads of Cultures." Web. http://whc.unesco.org/en/list/603. Accessed July 5, 2013.

——. N.d. "The Silk Roads Project: Integral Study of the Silk Road – 1988–1997." Web. http://unesdoc.unesco.org/images/0015/001591/159189E.pdf. Accessed July 5, 2013.

——. N.d. "Silk Road Sites in Kyrgyzstan." UNESCO World Heritage Centre – List of Tentative Sites. Web. http://whc.unesco.org/en/tentativelists/5518/. Accessed July 5, 2013.

——. N.d. "Sulaiman-Too Sacred Mountain." Web. http://whc.unesco.org/en/list/1230. Accessed July 5, 2013.

——. N.d. "Tajikistan – List of Tentative World Heritage Sites." UNESCO World Heritage Centre. Web. http://whc.unesco.org/en/tentativelists/state=tj. Accessed July 5, 2013.

——. N.d. "World Heritage Advisory Body Evaluation: Merv, Turkmenistan." Web. http://whc.unesco.org/archive/advisory_body_evaluation/886.pdf. Accessed September 2, 2004.

Usmanov, Boris. "Revitalization of the Heritage of Uzbekistan," in Attilio Petruccioli (ed.), *Bukhara: The Myth and the Architecture*. (Cambridge: The Aga Khan Program for Islamic Architecture, 1999).

Walters, Pat. 2010. "Aral Sea Recovery?" *National Geographic* (April 22, 2010). Web. http://news.nationalgeographic.com/news/2010/04/100402-aral-sea-story/. Accessed March 9, 2015.

World Monuments Fund. 2012. "World Monuments Fund 2012 Watch List: Ulug Depe." Web. www.wmf.org/project/ulug-depe. Accessed July 7, 2013.

———. N.d. "Necropolises of Nomads in Mangystau." Web. www.wmf.org/project/necropolises-nomads-mangystau. Accessed July 4, 2014.

———. N.d. "Past Watch Site: Old Nisa, Turkmenistan." World Monuments Fund. Web. www.wmf.org/project/old-nisa. Accessed July 5, 2013.

———. N.d. "Vernacular Architecture of the Kazakh Steppe Sary-Arka." Web. www.wmf.org/project/vernacular-architecture-kazakh-steppe-sary-arka. Accessed July 4, 2013.

Yavuz, Yildirim. 1992. *Registan Square and Tashkent Street, Samarkand, Uzbekistan*. 1992 Technical Review Summary for the Aga Khan Trust for Culture. Geneva: AKTC.

CONCLUSION TO PART V

Looking ahead, the architectural heritage of Central Asia faces many environmental, geopolitical and material challenges. The task of maintaining its numerous large-scale ancient mud brick structures, which together comprise the architectural landmarks of one of the world's great regional civilizations, remains daunting, and without simple solutions. Similarly, the conservation and protection of often-remote, vulnerable archaeological sites against looting and decay will require vigilance and creativity to achieve. Management and protection of contextual urban fabric, in addition to thoughtfully restored monuments and the rehabilitation of other historic buildings, along with complete national surveys of the built heritage of Central Asia are among other needs. Above all, regional stability will be required for many of the above-described issues to come to a successful conservation outcome.

The legacy of connection via the great Central Asian trade routes continues through multi-national efforts such as the UNESCO Silk Road Online Platform, involving a broad host of countries from the Republic of Korea to Germany. The online presence provides a clearinghouse of information and organizations concerned with various aspects of the Asian trade routes and their culture.[1] Although the impacts of tourism are relatively minor compared to the rest of Asia, particularly in war-weary Afghanistan, the UN has worked with the former Soviet states to strategize around development of a marketable, sustainable cultural tourism sector through its World Tourism Organization Silk Road Program. ICOMOS completed a Thematic Study in 2014 to assist in future World Heritage nominations and to inform a Roadmap for Development of heritage tourism that is coordinated and organized around cultural themes.[2] These efforts culminated in the 2014 listing of the Chang'an–Tian-shan corridor as a World Heritage Site, which includes supporting sites in China, Kazakhstan and Kyrgyzstan.[3]

Although there is not a regional body concerned with conservation and promotion of the shared heritage of Central Asia, UNESCO has organized several regional training workshops, more of which would be a welcome development in the region. Between 2007 and 2009 regional training entitled "Workshops in Persian, Mughal and Timurid Architecture" took place in Iran, Uzbekistan and India, involving professionals from each of those countries in addition to others in Central Asia.[4] Another project focused on the ancient Buddhist site of Ajina Tepa in Tajikistan whereby Japanese teams and UNESCO co-organized a program focused on archaeological site conservation strategies developed first in Kazakhstan and Kyrgyzstan prior to engagement with the Tajik team. The region would undoubtedly benefit from further such engagement. These could perhaps be under the aegis of a Central Asian cultural heritage partnership organization, as is elsewhere the case in Asia, that celebrates the country's millennia of storied cultural achievements, while also performing crucial tasks such as site monitoring, reporting and information sharing.

Notes

1. The UNESCO Silk Road Online Platform. Web. http://en.unesco.org/silkroad/unesco-silk-road-online-platform. Accessed June 21, 2016.
2. See the UNTWO Silk Road Programme publications list: http://silkroad.unwto.org/en/publications. Accessed June 21, 2016.
3. UNESCO World Heritage Centre. Web. http://whc.unesco.org/en/decisions/6110. Accessed June 21, 2016.
4. See, for example, UNESCO World Heritage Centre. Web. http://whc.unesco.org/en/events/451/ and http://whc.unesco.org/en/events/567/. Accessed June 21, 2016.

LOOKING FORWARD

This examination of the accomplishments in architectural conservation in the thirty countries that comprise Central, South, East and Southeast Asia offers a portrayal of how, why and when each nation became involved in conserving historic buildings and sites in a deliberate and organized way. Those issues have been addressed in this book, however broadly, and comparisons have been drawn at the close of each book section.

A remarkable conclusion from this exercise is that despite the great amount of change and diversity that can be found across Asia, one commonality is that all of its countries are significantly engaged in cultural heritage protection. The reasons range from pride, sentiment and respect for the past to the practicalities of conserving versus replacing, and the opportunities it affords for economic development. The social forces at work here include protection of cultural identity, expectations from tourism, public offering of amenities, jobs, local business interests, and perceived competition with similar places. Since cultural tourism is such a large and growing market in the region the stakes have increased over time and are expected to continue to do so.

The shared causes among professionals and others working in Conservation and Resource Management have engendered a spirit of collaboration and consultation that has benefited the field at large. The roles of local, national, regional and international government institutions have helped foster and harmonize goals and approaches. Sharing of information, technologies and economic assistance is commonplace in CRM, and reflects the concerns of professionals in the field as well as practical considerations. The new knowledge that is often developed and disseminated in relation to conservation practice presents opportunities for new research and understandings regarding the history of places and their importance to all who may be interested. Increased knowledge about the past has the tendency to generate respect for the work of others and to humanize, which in turn increases one's understanding and appreciation of the past. Such realizations shape the worldviews of people in their time and their ambitions. Preserved and effectively presented cultural heritage such as historic built environments inspires confidence, a sense of place and a sense of belonging and, as such, it also gives shape to the future.

Nonetheless change is ineluctable in both the object and its context, although the rate and nature of this change can and should be controlled. That is what cultural heritage management is: managing the process of change in the service of cultural values. Tourism management at Angkor, the Taj Mahal and Borobudur during peak visitation seasons may be examples of almost overwhelming pressures against limited capacity; the lost buildings of Old Karachi, Bangkok and Beijing offer another example of too little too late. The relentless pace of change in our world means we must move quickly and decisively before more of Asia's precious heritage is lost to us all.

Due to the enormity and depth of Asia's history, it is critical to realize that the *past* is always *present* and should be handled most carefully, and with deep understanding. For all of the accomplishments in cultural heritage management in Asia there remain numerous, powerful natural and human threats to its historic cultural resources, as the region's tumultuous history of human-created and natural ill effects have proven. Challenges ahead include meeting the following objectives:

- Continued efforts to plan for, mitigate and otherwise combat the natural forces that negatively affect physical cultural heritage
- Enhanced appreciation of the spiritual values of heritage sites imbued with religious or symbolic meaning, and the special design and construction features of traditional Asian architecture
- Ensuring that physical and intangible heritage of all kinds and scales is well understood, appreciated and preserved in an even-handed way
- Realizing the power and potential of grassroots participation and advocacy for heritage protection
- Appreciating the international peace, reconciliation and cooperation potential of joint international efforts at heritage protection
- Guarding against the overuse and commodification of heritage sites so as to avoid affecting their historic integrity, character and meaning for local populations
- Stemming uncontrolled development negatively affecting urban and rural cultural landscapes
- Guarding against detrimental human actions, be it poor planning, insensitive interventions during the conservation process, looting, vandalism, damage during conflict or the politicization of heritage
- Making more sites accessible both physically and economically to the greatest range of potential users
- Increasing government commitment where necessary toward the maintenance and sustainable development of heritage sites
- Teaching respect and appreciation for heritage and the importance of its conservation to all age levels
- Fostering ethical principles and responsible practice among cultural resources managers
- Ensuring the transfer of knowledge and know-how pertaining to heritage conservation across different generations
- Creating opportunities to link cultural heritage conservation with natural heritage conservation
- Better appreciating and prioritizing conservation of the ordinary, everyday vernacular
- Considering the inherent energy saving qualities of most historic buildings and the fact that their unnecessary replacement is wasteful of energy and resources
- Studying and valuing the lessons of the past in cultural resources management through the examples of experiences and best practices
- Appreciating the physical and environmental contexts of historic buildings both as individual structures and in their arrangement in groups
- Planning for growth and change that is congruent with the historic resources being conserved
- Recognizing that cultural resource management often requires many kinds of professional and vocational expertise that require shared philosophies, nomenclature and methodologies
- Investing in applicable building craft traditions, and supporting training for the sensitive treatment of heritage in the design professions of architecture, engineering, landscape architecture and interior design
- Applying the most current technologies and know-how to heritage conservation
- Using an anthropological and holistic approach to heritage conservation
- Recognizing the richness and values of "shared heritage" among constituencies of diverse backgrounds and locales.

Asia stands as one of the most culturally and geographically varied regions of the world. Asians and non-Asians alike share a profound appreciation for the special qualities of its environment, buildings, people and cultures. As the world develops to become more connected and more populated with increasing strains on its natural resources, the sustainable treatment of our historic built environments – be they charismatic monumental heritage or more commonplace structures – should be seen in yet new ways: as precious cultural resources that should be conserved with utmost care.

As among the world's growing economic leaders, Asia is well-poised to continue in its traditions and innovations in architectural conservation. Truly blessed with more similarities than differences, the countries of Asia are in a favorable position to combine efforts for heritage conservation and overcome residual conflicts in the region with this shared purpose.

GLOSSARY

Following is a glossary of key conservation and architectural terms used in this book. It begins with an annotated list of existing glossaries that have been assembled by state-specific organizations and institutions, along with information for finding those lists online. It also references more general conservation glossaries, such as that found in the initial volume in this series, John H. Stubbs, *Time Honored, A Global View of Architectural Conservation* (Wiley, 2009).

Country-specific glossaries (available online)

Bhutan

Corneille Jest. *Safeguarding the Cultural Heritage of Bhutan*. Paris: UNESCO (1992). Glossary begins on p. 81, available online: unesdoc.unesco.org/images/0009/000941/094150eo.pdf.

Cambodia

World Monuments Fund. *Preah Khan Conservation Project: Historic City of Angkor, Siem Reap, Cambodia. Report VIII, Field Campaign V, October 1996–September 1997*. New York: World Monuments Fund (1997). Glossary begins on p. 57, available online: www.wmf.org/sites/default/files/article/pdfs/Preah_Khan_Conservation_Project_Report_VIII.pdf.

China

ICOMOS China. *Principles for the Conservation of Heritage Sites in China (Revised 2015)*. Beijing: ICOMOS China (2015). Chinese–English Glossary found beginning on p. 106, available online: www.getty.edu/conservation/publications_resources/pdf_publications/china_principles_revised_2015.html

India

Archaeological Survey of India. *National Policy for Conservation of the Ancient Monuments, Archaeological Sites and Remains* (NPC-AMASR). New Delhi: Archaeological Survey of India (2014). Glossary found in Section 2 "Terms and Definitions," available online: http://asi.nic.in/national_consrv_policy_ancient_monu.asp

Japan

Mary N. Parent. *JAANUS: Online Dictionary of Japanese Architectural and Art Historical Terminology* (2001), available online: www.aisf.or.jp/~jaanus/

Nepal

Caterina Bonapace and Valerio Sestini. *Traditional Materials and Construction Technologies used in the Kathmandu Valley.* Paris: UNESCO (2003). Glossary begins on p. 163, available online: www.mbs-architecture.com/nepaltradbuildmat.pdf

Thailand

Pinraj Khanjanusthiti. *Buddhist Architecture: Meaning and Conservation in the Context of Thailand.* PhD thesis, University of York, Institute of Advanced Architectural Studies (1996). Glossary begins on p. 229, available online: www.etheses.whiterose.ac.uk/9785/1/297134.pdf

Singapore

Urban Redevelopment Authority. *Objectives, Principles and Standards for Preservation and Conservation in Singapore.* Singapore: URA (1993), available online: www.ura.gov.sg/uol/publications/technical/conservation-publications/objectives_principles_standards.aspx

Sri Lanka

Living Heritage Trust (Sri Lanka). *Glossary of Sri Lankan Terms* (2015), available online: http://livingheritage.org/glossary.htm

Taiwan

Academia Sinica Center for Digital Cultures. *Art & Architecture Thesaurus Taiwan* (2010), available online: http://aat.teldap.tw/index.php?_lang=en&_session=z8X56dE3KLvb9*10

Other general sources for useful conservation terminology in the Asian context (online)

Architecture of the Buddhist World. Kuala Lumpur: JF Publishing (2014), available online: http://architectureofbuddhism.com/books/buddhist-architecture-glossary/

Francois Le Blanc. *Cultural Heritage Conservation Terminology: Definitions of Terms from Various Sources.* Paris: ICOMOS (2011), available online: http://ip51.icomos.org/~fleblanc/documents/terminology/doc_terminology_e.html

William Chapman's *A Heritage of Ruins: The Ancient Sites of Southeast Asia and their Conservation* (University of Hawai'i Press, 2013), glossary beginning on p. 277, is an invaluable resource for architectural conservation terms applicable in Asia.

The Burra Charter: The Australia ICOMOS Charter for Places of Cultural Significance. Canberra: Australia ICOMOS (2013), available online: http://australia.icomos.org/wp-content/uploads/The-Burra-Charter-2013-Adopted-31.10.2013.pdf

The Metropolitan Museum of Art. *Art of the Islamic World: Glossary.* New York: Metropolitan Museum of Art (n.d.), available online: www.metmuseum.org/learn/educators/curriculum-resources/art-of-the-islamic-world/resources/glossary

John H. Stubbs's *Time Honored: A Global View of Architectural Conservation; Parameters, Theory and Evolution of an Ethos* (Wiley, 2009), glossary beginning on p. 375, for a list of terms used in international architectural conservation and their definitions.

Terms used in the text

adaptive reuse The act of sensitively changing a form or structure to serve a use different from its original design or purpose.

anastylosis Reassembling or rebuilding a structure using its own original materials; the practice may also include the judicious use of new materials to augment the old.

apsaras Sanskrit, also *apsarah*: plural *apsarasas* or *apsarasah*. The term refers to female divinities, celestial dancers who are the attendants of Kama, the god of love, in Indra's heaven.

authentic/authenticity Meaning real, not a replication; an object or material associated with an original design, fabrication, construction, building tradition or cultural practice. In the Asian context, *authentic* is not necessarily equivalent to *original*, as *authentic* practices or objects can be new or replacements that are nevertheless conceived according to long-standing traditions, practices or craftsmanship.

baray Khmer, an artificial reservoir used to store water, maintain water levels in its moats and canals, and likely also for agricultural irrigation.

bas-relief Sculpture in low-relief, with figures usually projecting only slightly from the background.

bodhisattva One whose essence is perfect knowledge. A bodhisattva is a being that has attained enlightenment but has postponed nirvana, or transcendence, in order to help others. In Mahayana Buddhism, many bodhisattvas are personifications of divine qualities such as compassion (*Avalokitesvara*) or wisdom (*Manjusri*) and are often depicted with multiple arms. In both Theravada and Mahayana Buddhism, the term applies as well to the earlier lives of the historical Buddha and to his former life as a prince.

boyuja Korean, "living national treasures," individuals who hold knowledge or skills essential for preserving Korean culture.

Brahma Sanskrit, creator of all things and principle deity (with Vishnu and Shiva) of Hinduism. Also appears in Buddhist art, especially of the Dvaravati period (Thailand, sixth–thirteenth centuries).

Buddha Sanskrit, meaning "enlightened one." The historical Buddha was called Siddhartha Gautama (in Pali, Siddhattha Gotama) and later received the epithet Sakyamuni (Sage of the Sakya Clan). The traditional dates for his life are from 563 BCE to 483 BCE.

candi/chandi Indonesian, a generic term used in Indonesia for all ancient temples, Hindu and Buddhist.

character An essential feature, look, feel or type as embodied in an object, building or place that makes it distinctive from other places and thus worthy of ongoing special care.

chedi Thai, a hemispherical monument, or stupa, for enshrining relics of the Buddha and his disciples.

compatibility Acceptability of the nature of one material, practice or design to an existing context, when also not harming or undermining the original.

conservation (cultural heritage) The practice of caring for a place, object, material or practice so as to maintain the characteristics for which it is deemed culturally significant.

conservation area An area, district or premises of special architectural, historic, traditional or aesthetic interest, the character or appearance of which it is desirable to preserve, enhance or restore.

consolidation Stabilizing building fabric or components by introducing new materials through injection or selective application in order to strengthen, repair or reconstitute an original material.

corbelled A construction technique that relies on overlapping, cantilevered units of stone, wood or masonry.

cornice A horizontal ornamental projection at floor and/or roof levels.

cultural heritage Traits, practices, crafts, traditions, aesthetics, objects or performance that are recognized as valuable based on their connection to the past or perpetuated human activity. Cultural heritage can be tangible (connected with a material object or place) or intangible (connected with an activity or knowledge).

cultural heritage, intangible Includes any form of expressions, languages, lingual utterances, sayings, musically produced tunes, notes, audible lyrics, songs, folk songs, oral traditions, poetry, music, dances as produced by the performing arts, theatrical plays, audible compositions of sounds and music, martial arts, that may have existed or exist in relation to the heritage of a country.

dzong The most prominent of Bhutan's architectural forms, a building complex that serves as a combined defensive fortification, administrative center and place of worship.

efflorescence The chemical function that results in salts migrating to the surface of a building material (stone, masonry) and resulting in staining or deterioration.

feng shui A central concept and series of applicable rules in Chinese spatial, social and ideological beliefs that governs the relationship buildings and temples have with the natural environment, in particular hills, bodies of water and the cardinal directions. Still widely in use today, the practice originated around 1000 BCE.

frieze A band of decoration on a building; in the Asian context, usually a relief carving or mural made by applying pigments onto wet lime plaster.

ger (or yurt) Mongolian, a mobile circular tent made of layers of canvas that are insulated with sections of felt and can be assembled and dismantled in a matter of a few hours, traditionally used by nomadic people. Groups of gers are known as *khoroos*.

gopura Sanskrit, a monumental, often richly decorated tower that functions as a temple entrance gate. Gopuram are associated with Hindu temples in southern India in particular, but also with the Khmer architecture of Southeast Asia.

gurdwara Punjabi, Sikh place of worship, ranging in scale from a single room to a large complex of buildings.

hammam Communal baths, found throughout the Islamic world.

hanok Korean urban residential district containing densely packed, one-storey courtyard homes on irregular lots separated by narrow lanes.

haveli South Asian residential building type, characterized by a courtyard, manifest as either large private residences (mansions) or townhouses.

heritage Cultural and natural elements, objects or places that are recognized as significant and are meant to be inherited/passed on from one generation to the next.

heritage management The process of maintaining and enhancing the significance of particular heritage, and making it available for groups of people to engage with it.

Hinayana Sanskrit, *Hinayana*, "Lesser Vehicle," refers to the oldest, traditional form of Buddhism. Linked to the present-day *Theravada* Buddhism practiced in Sri Lanka and mainland Southeast Asia. In contrast with *Mahayana* Buddhism ("Greater Vehicle"), which is practiced throughout the Asian Buddhist world.

hissar Persian, fortress.

hutong Chinese, residential courtyard housing typical to Beijing.

jiirnnoddharana Sanskrit, the Hindu concept of renewal that can be associated with temples or other significant buildings process; translates as "deliverance from decay" or "the raising up of what is old or decayed."

jiucheng gaizao Chinese, renewal of an old city. *Gaizao* can be translated as "renewal" when it refers to a general program to improve old areas of the city, or "redevelopment" when it refers to the actual replacement of old buildings and streets with new ones.

kampong Malay, village; in Brunei, the term refers to the distinctive residential enclaves constructed on stilts over waterways ("water villages").

klong Thai, canal or waterway.

kofun Japanese, key-shaped burial mounds found throughout Japan but especially near Osaka and Nara.

kund Hindi, a ceremonial pond or reservoir, also known as a tank.

kyaung Burmese, Buddhist monastery or school.

library Khmer, a pair of buildings located on either side of the main entrance to a temple. It is uncertain whether they actually served as libraries or depositories; they may have held sacred images and/or performed other functions.

LIDAR "Light detection and ranging." This laser-based technique determines the distance to an object by transmitting a laser beam. LIDAR is useful in creating building model and topographical maps. Its ability to map the ground in tree-covered areas, like the Angkor Park in Cambodia, has proven particularly effective for archaeologists in locating features that are otherwise unperceivable from the ground plane.

lilong Shanghainese, a community of traditional *li* (residences) in Shanghai organized around a lane; also known as *longtang*.

lingam Sanskrit, literally "sign" or "symbol," a phallic symbol of Shiva representing his role in creation. It is called a *mukhalingam* when a face is added to its surface. Of many different types, a *lingam* generally has three parts: a cubic lower element representing Brahma, and octagonal prism representing Vishnu, and a cylindrical section with a rounded top representing Shiva.

lintel A crossbeam resting on two posts and, in Southeast Asian architecture, usually featuring narrative scenes or decorative motifs. In Khmer temples the lintel is above the door or window opening and directly below the pediment.

longhouse A communal wooden thatched residential building with veranda, typical in Southeast Asian jungle locales to house numerous families. It is made from local materials (timber, bamboo, tree bark, rattan and palm leaves), and raised off the ground for air circulation and defense.

louvres A window shutter's operable wooden horizontal blades, which permit air circulation while also offering privacy.

lüli Chinese, urban residential quarter.

machiya Japanese, a traditional shophouse, comprised of a commercial space fronting the street, with residential quarters behind. Streetscapes of *machiya* are known as *machinami*.

madrasa Islamic religious school.

men Chinese, gate (e.g. Beijing's Tiananmen "The Gate of Heavenly Peace").

monuments Architectural works, sculpture, structures, artistic elements, archaeological sites, tombs, cave or rock art sites, landscapes, or other immovable heritage objects that bear cultural significance, and typically have been designated as such by a governing body or organization. Monuments can also constitute collections of the above, in addition to single objects. Designation as a monument generally indicates a level of formal protection, recognition, maintenance or care by the designating body.

national heritage Any heritage site, heritage object, underwater cultural heritage or any living person declared as a national heritage.

natural heritage Natural features or areas that possess ecological, aesthetic or physical characteristics that are valued scientifically and/or protected due to unique or threatened attributes.

niche A recessed part of a wall usually containing a sculpture and framed by a pair of pilasters.

pagoda Chinese, a multi-storey temple tower, or place for storing sacred objects or writings. Architecturally descended from a stupa, pagodas constitute an East and Southeast Asian adaptation of the earlier South Asian form.

pediment The triangular portion above a gate or window.

petroglyph An image or sculpture carved or etched into rock; typically associated with prehistoric cultures.

phnom Khmer, mountain; it can also apply to a temple, sanctuary, or other sacred site (e.g. Phnom Bakheng, a ninth century "temple mountain" located at Angkor).

photogrammetry Use of a photographic camera as an instrument for measuring distances as part of a survey or other documentation effort.

pilaster A column projecting slightly from a wall. In Southeast Asian temple architecture, it is usually found on either side of an open doorway.

pintu pagar Malaysian, swinging doors that aid air circulation and shade.

porte-cochère A covered porch associated with a building entrance; designed to offer protection for those dismounting or disembarking from a vehicle before entering a building.

prasada-purusa Sanskrit, a Hindu concept that maintains that temples and other prominent buildings are "living" things that experience the cycle of birth, adolescence, maturity, old age and death. The process is followed by *jiirnnoddharana* (see above).

preah Khmer, sacred or holy, often associated with the name of a temple building or complex (e.g., Preah Khan, a twelfth-century temple complex at Angkor).

preservation The process of maintaining, protecting, conserving, adapting or restoring the attributes of an object with cultural significance so as to retain or enhance its original characteristics. The term also applies to the field of architectural conservation in the USA.

preventative conservation Taking all necessary steps to prevent further deterioration to a historic building or object.

principles, conservation The guiding rules, standards of practice or underlying philosophy that underpin a conservation approach.

reassembly The practice of putting existing but dismembered architectural elements back together (similar to *anastylosis*, see above).

reconstruction Reconstitution of an architectural element, building, site or feature through the use of existing or new material (or a combination) based on documentation or other evidence.

rehabilitation The act of returning a building, site or district to a state of utility and contemporary standards through repair, alteration or adaptation while respecting significant cultural, architectural or artistic characteristics of the property.

repair To restore to an improved state or material condition by fixing, replacing or renewing deteriorated elements of a building, object or feature.

replacement The substitution of original damaged or lost building elements with new material that resembles or mimics the original.

reproduction Fabricating a duplicate and replacing a building or architectural feature that has been lost to achieve continuity or replace something that is no longer present.

resiliency A current design by-word referring to adaptability of existing systems, including extant buildings. The term appears to be replacing the term "sustainability" as a leading concept not only in architecture but in political economy as well. Referred to by other names such as "adaptability" and "design flexibility," resiliency has been a guiding precept in architectural heritage conservation for the last half century.

restoration Returning a building or object to its original state, sometimes by the removal of later additions or alterations and/or replacement of lost or deteriorated features.

sala Thai, an open-sided, covered meeting hall or shelter; from the Portuguese sala, or "room."

Sanskrit Meaning "pure," Sanskrit is an ancient South Asian language used in the sacred texts of Hinduism and Buddhism. It has influenced most modern languages of the Indian subcontinent as well as those of Southeast Asia.

saujana Indonesian, a concept advanced by the 2003 Indonesian Charter for Heritage Conservation that connotes the intertwined natural and cultural values present in Indonesia's heritage landscape.

shan Chinese, mountain or hill (e.g., the Tian Shan range of mountains on the border of China, Kyrgyzstan and Kazakhstan).

shikinen sengū Japanese, the practice of periodic, ritual reconstruction of a building.

shophouse A building that holds goods for sale on its street level and also houses the proprietor's family above or behind. Shophouses constitute a common urban architectural typology throughout East and Southeast Asia.

standards, conservation "Best practices," rules or methods to follow while in the process of conservation decision-making and work.

stele A Greek term for an inscribed stone panel or slab, the earliest method of recording important events.

stupa Sanskrit, a mound or dome-shaped structure used to shelter the relics of Buddha or especially revered monks. Known by several country/region specific terms, such as *chedi* (Thai), *zedi* (Burmese) or *dagoba* (Sinhalese).

subak A Balinese system whereby cooperatively managed water irrigation infrastructure that supports rice terraces are interwoven into places of worship and community gathering centers. The system is organized according to the Balinese *Tri Hita Karana* philosophy, which centers upon harmony among people, nature and God.

taq Kashmir's *taq* (timber laced masonry) and *dhajji dewari* (timber framed masonry infill) systems are traditional building practices that have evolved to withstand a certain amount of seismic movement.

thom Khmer, large or great (e.g., Angkor Thom, the twelfth century capital of the Khmer Empire).

torchis French, wood frame construction infilled by wattle and daub dried mud. Typical to the former French colonies of Southeast Asia.

uma lulik East Timor, sacred houses, buildings constructed of wood and thatch, often on stilts, used to house sacred items. They represent East Timor's most distinctive architecture.

varman Sanskrit, meaning "protected by"; the term was incorporated as a title into the names of various rulers, particularly Khmer (e.g. Jayavarman VII), Sailendra and Cham kings.

Vastushastras An ancient series of Sanskrit texts governing architectural, spatial, uses and organizational methodologies based on geometry, symmetry, orientation and linked to Hindu beliefs. Examples exist throughout South and Southeast Asia, including Angkor Wat and the Jaipur City Palace.

vat Lao and Khmer, temple or monastery (e.g., Vat Phou, the eleventh–thirteenth century Khmer temple complex in southern Laos). In Thai it is spelled "wat" taken from the Pali term *vatthuarama*. The term is pronounced "vat" in Lao, "wat" in Thai, and "vat" or "wat" in Khmer.

vernacular buildings Architecture or the design of objects that is comprised of local materials, and to serve purposes particular to a specific environment or locale; not linked to a larger prevailing style, but buildings that are rather simplified and suited to a singular place.

vihara Sanskrit/Pali, a Buddhist monastery complex.

wabi-sabi Japanese, an aesthetic concept that accepts impermanence, patina and imperfection as elements of beauty.

waqf An Islamic financial arrangement similar to a Western trust, a *waqf* (or *auqaf* in Pakistani Urdu) is a permanent, irrevocable religious endowment of specified non-perishable property (such as a building or land). The beneficiary may be either a person or an entity, and is often an institution such as a mosque or school.

xiang Chinese, lane.

xiao qu Chinese, small district.

Yingzao fashi Chinese, a Song dynasty manual of architectural building standards and methods.

yongxiang Chinese, a long palace corridor, which facilitates circulation.

zedi Burmese, a type of stupa consisting of a solid, hemispherical or gently tapering cone topped with a variety of metal and jewel finials. Traditionally, *zedi* contained relics of the Buddha.

zhonglou Chinese, bell tower.

GENERAL AND ADDITIONAL REFERENCES

General references on architectural conservation

Aplin, Graeme. 2002. *Heritage: Identification, Conservation, and Management.* New York: Oxford University Press.

Aramberri, Julio and Richard Butler (eds.). 2005. *Tourism Development: Issues for a Vulnerable Industry.* Ontario: Channel View.

Araoz, G. 2011. "Preserving Heritage Places Under a New Paradigm," *Journal of Cultural Heritage Management and Sustainable Development* 1(1): 55–60.

Ashurst, John. 2007. *Conservation of Ruins.* Oxford: Butterworth-Heinemann.

Asian Studies on the Pacific Coast (ASPAC). ca. 1972. *Proceedings of the Conference "Preservation of Cultural Heritage," May 31, 1971, Seoul.* Seoul: Hollym Publishers.

Askew, Marc. 2010. "The Magic List of Global Status: UNESCO, World Heritage and the Agendas of States," in Sophia Labadi and Colin Long (eds.), *Heritage and Globalisation*, 19–44.

Australia Heritage Commission. 1990. *What Do We Want to Pass on to Future Generations? An Overview of Criteria and Assessment Procedures for the Register of the National Estate.* April. Canberra: Australia Heritage Commission.

Avrami, E., R. Mason and M. de la Torre. 2000. *Values and Heritage Conservation – Research Report.* Los Angeles: Getty Conservation Institute.

Aygen, Zeynep. 2014. *International Heritage and Historic Building Conservation: Saving the World's Past.* New York: Routledge.

Bacon, Edmund N. 1975. *Design of Cities* (Revised edition). London: Thames and Hudson.

Bandarin, F. 2009. "Preface," in UNESCO, *World Heritage Papers 26: World Heritage Cultural Landscapes. A Handbook for Conservation and Management.* Paris: UNESCO, 3–4.

Basu, Dilip K. (ed.). 1985. *The Rise and Growth of the Colonial Port Cities in Asia.* Lanham, MD: University Press of America.

Basu, Paul and Wayne Modest (eds.). 2014. *Museums, Heritage and International Development.* London: Routledge.

Beeson, M. and R. Stubbs. 2012. "Introduction," in M. Beeson and R. Stubbs (eds.), *Routledge Handbook of Asian Regionalism.* London: Routledge, 1–7.

Benevolo, Leonardo. 1980. *The History of the City.* Translated by Geoffrey Culverwell. Cambridge, MA: MIT Press.

de Berval, Rene. 1951. *Hommage a l'Ecole Française d'Extrême-Orient.* Saigon: France-Asie.

Bharne, Vinyak (ed.). 2013. *The Emerging Asian City: Concomitant Urbanites and Urbanisms.* Abingdon, UK: Routledge.

Bigio, Anthony Gad, Maria Catalina Ochoa and Rana Amirtahmasebi. 2014. *Climate-resilient, Climate-friendly World Heritage Cities.* World Bank, Washington, DC: World Bank. https://openknowledge.worldbank.org/handle/10986/19288 License: CC BY 3.0 IGO.

Blust, Robert. 1996. "Beyond the Austronesian Homeland: The Austric Hypothesis and Its Implications for Archaeology," in Ward H. Goodenough (ed.), *Prehistoric Settlement of the Pacific.* Transactions of the American Philosophical Society 86. Philadelphia: American Philosophical Society, 117–140.

Bushell, Robyn and Russell Staiff. 2012. "Rethinking Relationships: World Heritage, Communities and Tourism," in Patrick Daly and Tim Winter (eds.), *Routledge Handbook of Heritage in Asia*, 247–265.

Byrne, Denis. 2004. "Chartering Heritage in Asia's Postmodern World," *Conservation: The Getty Conservation Institute Newsletter* 19(2): 16–19.

——. 2007. "Heritage Conservation as Social Action," in G. Fairclough et al. (eds.), *The Cultural Heritage Reader*, 149–173.

——. 2014. *Counterheritage: Critical Perspectives on Heritage Conservation in Asia*. New York: Routledge.

Campanella, Richard. (2014). "The Economics of Authenticity," in *Chronicle of the 2014 Preservation Matters III Symposium*. Co-sponsored by the Preservation Resource Center of New Orleans and Tulane School of Architecture Preservation Studies Program.

Carr, Gilly and Harold Mytum (eds.). 2012. *Cultural Heritage and Prisoners of War: Creativity Behind Barbed Wire*. London: Routledge.

Carroon, Jean. 2010. *Sustainable Preservation: Greening Existing Buildings*. Hoboken, NJ: John Wiley & Sons.

Chapagain, Neel Kamal. 2013a. "Introduction: Contexts and Concerns in Asian Heritage Management," in Kapila D. Silva and Neel Kamal Chapagain (eds.), *Asian Heritage Management*, 1–30.

——. 2013b. "Heritage Conservation in the Buddhist Context," in Kapila D. Silva and Neel Kamal Chapagain (eds.), *Asian Heritage Management*, 49–64.

Chape, S., et al. (eds.). 2008. *The World's Protected Areas: Status, Values, and Prospects in the Twenty-first Century*. Berkeley: University of California Press.

Charoenwongsa, Pisit. 1992. "When Should Laws and Ethics be Applied to the Management of the World's Cultural Heritage?" *SPAFA Journal* 2(2): 4–9.

Chaudhuri, K.N. 1990. *Asia before Europe: Economy and Civilisation of the Indian Ocean from the Rise of Islam to 1750*. Cambridge: Cambridge University Press.

Chen, Xiangming and Ahmed Kanna. 2012. *Rethinking Global Urbanism: Comparative Insights from Secondary Cities*. Routledge Advances in Geography. New York: Routledge.

Chhabra, D. 2010. *Sustainable Marketing of Cultural and Heritage Tourism*. London: Routledge.

Chihara, Dalgorö. 1996. *Hindu–Buddhist Architecture in Southeast Asia*. Leiden: Brill.

Ching, Francis D.K., Mark M. Jarzombek and Vikramaditya Prakash. 2007. *A Global History of Architecture*. Hoboken, NJ: John Wiley & Sons.

Chitty, Gill and David Baker (eds.). 1999. *Managing Historic Sites and Buildings: Reconciling Presentation and Preservation*. London: Routledge.

Choay, Françoise. 2001. *The Invention of the Historic Monument*. Cambridge: Cambridge University Press.

Cody, Jeffrey W. and Kecia L. Fong. 2012. "Beyond Band-Aids: The Need for Specialised Materials Conservation Expertise in Asia," in Patrick Daly and Tim Winter (eds.), *Routledge Handbook of Heritage in Asia*, 98–110.

Conti, Alessandro and Helen Glanville. 2007. *History of the Restoration and Conservation of Works of Art*. Oxford: Butterworth-Heinemann.

Corzo, Miguel Angel (ed.). 1995. *The Future of Asia's Past: Preservation of the Architectural Heritage of Asia: Summary of an International Conference Held in Chiang Mai, Thailand, January 11–14, 1995*. New York: Asia Society.

Costa, Frank, et al. (eds.). 1989. *Urbanization in Asia: Spatial Dimensions and Policy Issues*. Honolulu: University of Hawai'i Press.

Cotterell, Arthur. 2011. *Asia: A Concise History*. Singapore: John Wiley & Sons (Asia).

Cowherd, Robert A. 1998. "An 'Asian Values' of Conservation? Towards a Critical Practice." Paper presented to the symposium *Heritage and Habitat: The Context of Sustainable Development in Historic City Centers*, Darmstadt Technical University, Penang, April 14.

Crinson, Mark (ed.). 2005. *Urban Memory: History and Amnesia in the Modern City*. London: Routledge.

Crouch, Dora P. and June G. Johnson. 2001. *Traditions in Architecture: Africa, America, Asia and Oceania*. Oxford: Oxford University Press.

Daly, Patrick and Tim Winter (eds.). 2012. *Routledge Handbook of Heritage in Asia*. London: Routledge.

Demas, Margaret (ed.). 2003. *The GCI Project Bibliographies: Conservation and Management of Archaeological Sites*. Los Angeles: Getty Conservation Institute.

Denslagen, Wim and Niels Gutschow (eds.). 2005. *Architectural Imitations: Reproductions and Pastiches in East and West*. Maastricht: Shaker Publishing.

Dorfman, Eric (ed.). 2011. *Intangible Natural Heritage: New Perspectives on Natural Objects*. London: Routledge.

Dwyer, D.J. (ed.). 1972. *The City as a Centre of Change in Asia*. Hong Kong: Hong Kong University Press.

Earl, J. 2003. *Building Conservation Philosophy*. Shaftesbury, UK: Donhead Publishers.

Ecole française d'Extrême-Orient. 2002. *Chercheurs d'Asie: Repertoire biographique des membres scientifiques de l'Ecole française d'Extrême-Orient*. Paris: Ecole française d'Extrême-Orient.

Ekern, Stener, et al. (eds.). 2015. *World Heritage Management and Human Rights*. Abingdon, UK: Routledge.

Elwazani, Salim and Jamal Qawasmi (eds.). 2008. *Responsibilities and Opportunities in Architectural Conservation: Theory, Education and Practice*. Amman, Jordan: Center for Study of Architecture in Arab Region (CSAAR).

Engelhardt, Richard A. 2001. "Landscapes of Heaven Transposed to Earth: Achieving Ethos To Guide The Conservation of Cultural Landscapes in Asia and the Pacific." Unpublished Keynote Address to *Asian Places in the New Millennium*, 38th IFLA World Congress, June 26–29, 2001, Singapore.

———. 2002. "The Management of World Heritage Cities: Evolving Concepts, New Strategies," *Revista de cultura = Review of Culture* (4): 17–25.

Engelhardt, Richard A. and Montira Horayangura Unakul (eds.). 2007. *Asia Conserved: Lessons Learned from the UNESCO Asia-Pacific Heritage Awards for Culture Heritage Conservation (2000–2004)*. Bangkok: UNESCO.

Fairclough, G., R. Harrison, J.H. Jameson and J. Schofield (eds.). 2007. *The Cultural Heritage Reader*. London: Routledge.

Feilden, Bernard M. 1989. *Guidelines for Conservation: A Technical Manual*. New Delhi: The Indian National Trust for Art and Cultural Heritage.

———. 1994. *Conservation of Historic Buildings*. (3rd edition). London: Architectural Press.

Feilden, Bernard M. and Jukka Jokilehto. 1998. *Management Guidelines for World Cultural Heritage Sites*. (2nd edition). Rome: ICCROM.

Fisher, Robert E. 1993. *Buddhist Art and Architecture*. World of Art. London: Thames & Hudson.

Fong, Kecia L., et al. 2012. "Same but Different?: A Roundtable Discussion on the Philosophies, Methodologies, and Practicalities of Conserving Cultural Heritage in Asia," in Patrick Daly and Tim Winter (eds.), *Routledge Handbook of Heritage in Asia*, 39–54.

Forbes, Dean. 1996. *Asian Metropolis: Urbanisation and the Southeast Asian City*. Oxford: Oxford University Press.

Fowler, P.J. 2003. *World Heritage Cultural Landscapes 1992–2002*. World Heritage Papers 6. Paris: UNESCO.

Frampton, Kenneth. 1992. *Modern Architecture: A Critical History*. (3rd edition). New York: Oxford University Press.

Getty Conservation Institute. 2009. *Report on Experts Meeting on the Historic Urban Environment: Conservation Challenges and Priorities for Action. March 12–14, 2009*. Los Angeles: Getty Conservation Institute.

Getty Conservation Institute and Ministry of Culture (Mali). 2011. *Terra 2008: Proceedings of the 10th International Conference on the Study and Conservation of Earthen Architectural Heritage, Bamako, Mali, February 1–5, 2008 = Actes de la 10ème conférence international sur l'étude et la conservation su patrimoine bâti en terre, Bamako, Mali, 1–5 février 2008*. Los Angeles: Getty Conservation Institute.

Glendinning, Miles. 2013. *The Conservation Movement: A History of Architectural Preservation, Antiquity to Modernity*. Abingdon, UK: Routledge.

Global Heritage Fund. 2012. *Asia's Heritage in Peril*. Web. www.globalheritagefund.org/images/uploads/docs/GHFAsiaHeritageinPeril050112_lowres.pdf. Accessed June 20, 2016.

Grodach, Carl and Daniel Silver. 2013. *The Politics of Urban Cultural Policy: Global Perspectives*. London: Routledge.

Gugler, Josef (ed.). 2004. *World Cities beyond the West*. Cambridge: Cambridge University Press.

Hakim, B.S. 1991. "Urban Design in Traditional Islamic Culture: Recycling Its Successes," *Cities* (November): 274–277.

Hall, Kenneth R. (ed.). 2011. *The Growth of Non-Western Cities: Primary and Secondary Urban Networking, c. 900–1900*. New York: Lexington Books.

Hampton, Mark P. 2005. "Heritage, Local Communities and Economic Development," *Annals of Tourism Research* 32(3): 735–759.

Hardy, Mary, Claudia Cancino and Gail Ostergren (eds.). 2009. *Proceedings of the Getty Seismic Adobe Project 2006 Colloquium, April 11–13, 2006*. Los Angeles: Getty Conservation Institute.

Harrison, Rodney. *Heritage: Critical Approaches*. 2013. New York: Routledge.

Hashimota, Jun (ed.). 2009. *Ja 73: Renovation – Beyond Metabolism*. Tokyo: Shinkenchiku-sha Co.

Heng, Chye Kiang. 2000. "Preserving the Cultural Built Heritage of Cities." Paper presented to the World Bank Institute Training Programme, May 1–14, National University of Singapore.

Heritage Hong Kong. 2003. *Heritage Hong Kong 4(2). Quarterly Bulletin of the Antiquities and Monuments Office*. Hong Kong: Antiquities and Monuments Office.

Hewison, Robert. 1987. *The Heritage Industry: Britain in a Climate of Decline*. London: Methuen.

Hillenbrand, Robert. 1994. *Islamic Architecture*. Edinburgh: Edinburgh University Press.

———. 1999. *Islamic Art and Architecture*. London: Thames and Hudson.

Hodson, Mike and Simon Marvin. 2010. *World Cities and Climate Change: Producing Urban Ecological Security*. New York: McGraw-Hill.

Howe, R. and W.S. Logan. 2002. "Conclusion – Protecting Asia's Urban Heritage: The Way Forward," in W.S. Logan (ed.) *The Disappearing "Asian" City*, 245–256.

ICOM (International Council on Museums). 1997. *Cent Objets Disparus = One Hundred Missing Objects*. One Hundred Missing Objects Series. (2nd edition). Paris: ICOM and EFEO.

———. 2000. *Heritage at Risk*. Paris: ICOMOS.

———. 2010. *Guidance on Heritage Impact Assessments for Cultural World Heritage Properties*. Paris: ICOMOS. Web. www.international.icomos.org/world_heritage/WH_Committee_34th_session_Brasilia/ICOMOS_Heritage_Impact_Assessment_2010.pdf. Accessed June 20, 2016.

ICOMOS. 1965. *The Venice Charter*. Paris: International Committee on Monuments and Sites.

———. 1993. *Tourism at World Heritage Cultural Sites: The Site Manager's Handbook*. Paris: ICOMOS and Rome: ICCROM.

ICOMOS Canada. 1990. *Preserving Our Heritage: Catalogue of Charters and Other Guides. International Symposium on World Heritage Towns = La Conservation du Patrimoine: Recueil des chartes et autres guides. Colloque international des villes du patrimoine mondial*. Ottawa: ICOMOS Canada; Paris. In English and French. Quebec: Ville de Quebec.

ICOMOS Korea. 2007. *Heritage and Metropolis in Asia and the Pacific*: 2007 ICOMOS Asia and the Pacific Regional Meeting, May 29–June 1. Seoul: ICOMOS.

Imamuddin, Abu H. and Karen R. Longeteig (eds.). 1990. *Papers in Progress. Volume One. Architectural & Urban Conservation in the Islamic World*. A collection of papers based on a workshop sponsored by the Aga Khan Trust for Culture with the Institute of Architects Bangladesh, Bangladesh University of Engineering & Technology and the UNDP in April 1989. Geneva: The Aga Khan Trust for Culture.

Imon, Sharif Shams. 2013. "Issues of Sustainable Tourism at Heritage Sites in Asia," in Kapila D. Silva and Neel Kamal Chapagain (eds.) *Asian Heritage Management*, 253–270.

Isar, Yudhishthir Raj (ed.). 1986. *Why Preserve the Past? The Challenge to Our Cultural Heritage*. Washington, DC: Smithsonian Institution Press; Paris: UNESCO.

Jacobs, Jane. 1961. *The Death and Life of Great American Cities*. New York: Random.

Jodidio, Philip (ed.). 2011. *The Aga Khan Historic Cities Programme: Strategies for Urban Regeneration*. Munich: Prestel.

Jokilehto, Jukka. 2009. "Preservation Theory Unfolding," *Future Anterior* 3(9): 1–9.

———. 2009. "Conservation Principles in the International Context," in Alison Richmond and Alison Bracker (eds.), *Conservation Principles, Dilemmas and Uncomfortable Truths*. Oxford: Elsevier Butterworth-Heinemann, 73–83.

———. 2012. *A History of Architectural Conservation*. (2nd edition). Oxford: Routledge.

Jones, Gavin W. and Mike Douglass (eds.). 2008. *Mega-Urban Regions in Pacific Asia: Urban Dynamics in a Global Era*. Singapore: NUS Press.

Jones, Siân and Thomas Yarrow. 2013. "Crafting Authenticity: An Ethnography of Conservation Practice," *Journal of Material Culture* 18(1): 3–26.

Kalman, Harold. 2014. *Heritage Planning: Principles and Process*. New York: Routledge.

Kamalakar, Dr. G. and Dr. V. Pandit Rao (eds.). 1995. *Conservation, Preservation & Restoration: Traditions, Trends & Techniques*. Colloquium proceedings, January. Hyderabad: Birla Archaeological & Cultural Research Institute.

Kawakami, Kaori, et al. (eds.). 2012. *Understanding World Heritage in Asia and the Pacific: The Second Cycle of Periodic Reporting, 2010–2012*. Paris: UNESCO.

Kazimee, Bashir A. and Ayad B. Rahmani. 2003. *Place, Meaning and Form in the Architecture and Urban Structure of Eastern Islamic Cities*. Mellen Studies in Architecture, Volume 11. Lewiston, NY: The Edwin Mellen Press.

Keiner, Marco, Martina Koll-Schretzenmayr and Willy A. Schmid (eds.). 2005. *Managing Urban Futures*. Bodmin, UK: MPG Books.

Kila, Joris D. and James A. Zeidler (eds.). 2013. *Cultural Heritage in the Crosshairs: Protecting Cultural Property during Conflict*. Leiden: Brill.

Knapp, Ronald G. (ed.). 2003. *Asia's Old Dwellings: Tradition, Resilience, and Change*. London: Oxford University Press.

Kostof, Spiro. 1995. *History of Architecture: Settings and Rituals*. Revisions by Greg Castillo. New York: Oxford University Press.

Kuchitsu, Nobuaki and Yumi Isabelle Akieda (eds.). 2010. *Restoration and Conservation of Immovable Heritage Damaged by Natural Disasters: Expert Meeting on Cultural Heritage in Asia and the Pacific*. Bangkok/Ayutthaya, January 14–16, 2009. Tokyo: Japan Center for International Cooperation in Conservation, National Research Institute for Cultural Properties.

Labadi, Sophia. 2010. "World Heritage, Authenticity and Post-Authenticity: International and National Perspectives," in Sophia Labadi and Colin Long (eds.), *Heritage and Globalisation*, 66–84.

Labadi, Sophia and Colin Long (eds.). 2010. *Heritage and Globalisation*. Abingdon, UK: Routledge.

Lacoste, Anne and Fred Ritchin. 2010. *Felice Bento: A Photographer on the Eastern Road*. Los Angeles: J. Paul Getty Museum.

Larsen, Knut Einar, et al. (eds.). 1995. *Nara Conference on Authenticity in Relation to the World Heritage Convention*. Paris: ICOMOS; Rome: UNESCO; and Tokyo: ICCROM and Agency for Cultural Affairs.

Larsen, Knut Einar and Nils Marstein (eds.). 1993. *Proceedings, ICOMOS International Wood Committee (IIWC) 8th International Symposium*, November 23–25, 1992, Kathmandu, Patan and Bhaktapur, Nepal. Oslo: TAPIR Publishers.

———. 1994. *Conference on Authenticity in Relation to the World Heritage Convention. Preparatory Workshop*, Bergen, Norway, January 31–February 2, 1994.

Layton, R. and J. Thomas (eds.). 2001. *Destruction and Conservation of Cultural Property*. London: Routledge.

Leary, Michael E. and John McCarthy (eds.). 2014. *The Routledge Companion to Urban Regeneration*. London: Routledge.

Lewin, Seymour Z. "The Mechanism of Masonry Decay Through Crystallization," in Committee on Conservation of Historic Stone Buildings and Monuments, *Conservation of Historic Stone Buildings and Monuments*. Washington, DC: The National Academies Press, 120–144.

Licciardi, Guido and Rana Amirtahmesabi (eds.). 2012. *The Economics of Uniqueness: Investing in Historic City Cores and Cultural Heritage Assets for Sustainable Development*. Urban Development series. Washington, DC: The World Bank.

Logan, William (ed.). 2002. *The Disappearing "Asian" City: Protecting Asia's Urban Heritage in a Globalizing World*. Hong Kong: Oxford University Press.

Logan, William S. and K. Reeves (eds.). 2009. *Places of Pain and Shame: Dealing with "Difficult Heritage"*. London: Routledge.

Logan, William S. and K. Reeves. 2009. "Introduction: Remembering Places of Pain and Shame" in Logan and Reeves (eds.), *Places of Pain and Shame*, 1–14.

Long, Colin and Anita Smith. 2010. "Cultural Heritage and the Global Environment Crisis," in Sophia Labadi and Colin Long (eds.). *Heritage and Globalisation*, 173–191.

Lowenthal, David. 1998. *The Heritage Crusade and the Spoils of History*. Cambridge: Cambridge University Press.

Luján, Rodolfo. 1994. *Conservation of Mural Paintings and External Stuccoes, UNDP. April–May 1994*. Paris: UNESCO.

Luxen, J-L. 2004. "Reflections on the Use of Heritage Charters and Conventions," *Conservation: Getty Conservation Institute Newsletter*, 19(2): 4–9.

Macaulay, Rose. 1953. *Pleasure of Ruins*. Reprint. New York: Thames & Hudson.

MacLean, Margaret G.H. (ed.). 1993. *Cultural Heritage in Asia and the Pacific: Conservation and Policy: Proceedings of a Symposium Held in Honolulu, Hawaii, September 8–13, 1991*. Los Angeles: Getty Conservation Institute.

Marcotte, P. and L. Bourdeau. 2012. "Is the World Heritage Label Used as a Promotional Argument for Sustainable Tourism," *Journal of Cultural Heritage Management and Sustainable Development* 1(2): 80–91.

Mason, Randall (ed.). 1999. *Economics and Heritage Conservation: A Meeting Organized by the Getty Conservation Institute*. Los Angeles: Getty Conservation Institute.

Mason, Randall. 1999. "Economics and Heritage Conservation: Concepts, Values, and Agendas for Research," in Randall Mason (ed.), *Economics and Heritage Conservation*, 2–18.

———. 2007. "Assessing Values in Conservation Planning" in G. Fairclough et al. (eds.), *The Cultural Heritage Reader*, 99–124.

Massari, Giovanni. 1977. *Humidity in Monuments*. Rome: International Centre for the Study of the Preservation and Restoration of Cultural Property.

de Merode, E., R. Smeets and C. Westrikl (eds.). 2003. *Linking Universal and Local Values: Managing a Sustainable Future for World Heritage*. Proceedings of a conference organized by the Netherlands National Committee for UNESCO in collaboration with the Netherlands Ministry of Education, Culture and Science, May 22–24, 2003. Paris: UNESCO, 49–54.

Meskell, Lynn. 2010. "Conflict Heritage and Expert Failure," in Sophia Labadi and Colin Long (eds.), *Heritage and Globalisation*, 192–201.

Michell, George (ed.). 1988. *The Hindu Temple: An Introduction to its Meaning and Forms*. (2nd edition). Chicago: University of Chicago Press.

Michell, George. 2000. *Hindu Art and Architecture*. World of Art. London: Thames & Hudson.

Mieg, Harald A. and Klaus Töpfer (eds.). 2013. *Institutional and Social Innovation for Sustainable Urban Development*. Routledge Studies in Sustainable Development. London: Routledge.

Miura, Keiko. 2005. "Conservation of a 'Living Heritage Site': A Contradiction in Terms?" *Conservation and Management of Archaeological Sites* 7(1) (2005): 3–17.

Mumford, Lewis. 1968. *The City in History: Its Origins, Its Transformations and Its Prospects*. (2nd edition). New York: Harcourt, Brace.

Munjeri, Dawson. 2004. "Tangible and Intangible Heritage: From Difference to Convergence," *Museum International* 56 (1–2): 12–20.

Muramatsu, Shin and Yasushi Zenno. 2003. "How to Evaluate, Conserve and Revitalize Modern Architecture in Asia," in R. van Oers and S. Haraguchi (eds.), *Identification and Documentation of Modern Heritage*. Paris: UNESCO, 113–117.

Nakagawa, Shin (ed.). 2007. *Cultural Resources Management*. Bangkok: Urban Culture Research Center.

Nasution, Khoo Salma. 1997. *Heritage Habitat: A Source Book of the Urban Conservation Movement in Asia and the Pacific*. Penang: Asia & West Pacific Network for Urban Conservation.

Nishimura, Yukio. 2002. *Urban Conservation Planning*. Tokyo: University of Tokyo Press. (In Japanese).

Nugent, Ann. 1966. "Asia's French Connection: George Cœdès and the Cœdès Collection," *National Library of Australia News* 6(4) (January): 6–8.

Nuryanti, Wiendu (ed.). 1997. *Tourism and Cultural Management: Proceedings of the International Conference on Tourism and Heritage Management, October 28–30, 1996, Yogyakarta, Indonesia*. Yogyakarta: Gadjah Mada University Press.

Park, David, Kuenga Wangmo and Sharon Cather (eds.). 2013. *Art of Merit: Studies in Buddhist Art and Its Conservation: Proceedings of the Buddhist Art Forum 2012*. London: Archetype Publications.

Park, Hyung Yu. *Heritage Tourism*. 2013. London: Routledge.

Pearce, Douglas G., and Richard W. Butler (eds.). 2002. *Contemporary Issues in Tourism Development*. London: Routledge.

Perera, Nihal and Tang Wing-shing (eds.). 2013. *Transforming Asian Cities: Intellectual Impasse, Asianizing Space, and Emerging Trans-Localities*. London: Routledge.

Petzet, Michael. 1999. *Principles of Monuments Conservation/Principes de la Conservation des Monuments Historiques*. Translated from German into English by Margaret Thomas Will MA. Translated from German into French by Dr. Beatrice Hernad and Dr. Denis Andre Chevalley. Munich: ICOMOS Germany.

Poria, Y., A. Reichel and A. Biran. 2006. "Heritage Site Management: Motivations and Expectations," *Annals of Tourism Research* 33(1): 162–178.

Poulios, Ioannis. 2010. "Moving Beyond a Values-Based Approach to Heritage Conservation," *Conservation and Management of Archaeological Sites* 12(2): 170–185.

Prideaux, Bruce, Dallen Timothy and Kaye Chon. 2009. *Cultural and Heritage Tourism in Asia and the Pacific*. London: Routledge.

Prudon, Theodore H.M. 2008. *Preservation of Modern Architecture*. Hoboken, NJ: John Wiley & Sons.

Punja, Shobita and John Reeve (eds.). 2008. *Heritage Education in Asia*. In conjunction with the Asian Regional Cooperation Conference, New Delhi December 2–4, 2008. New Delhi: INTACH.

Qing, Chan. 2009. *The Way to Historic Environment Rebirth through Design*. Beijing: China Architecture and Building Press.

Robson, David. 1996. *Historical and Philosophical Issues in the Conservation of Cultural Heritage*. Los Angeles: Getty Conservation Institute.

Rössler, M. 2006. "World Heritage: Linking Nature and Culture," in *Conserving Cultural and Biological Diversity: The Role of Sacred Natural Sites and Cultural Landscapes*, UNESCO/IUCN International Symposium, United National University, Tokyo, May 30–June 2, 2005. Paris: UNESCO, 15–16.

Ruggles, D.F. 2009. "A Critical View of Landscape Preservation and the Role of Landscape Architects," *Preservation Education & Research* 2: 65–72.

Saito, Hidetoshi (ed.). 2002. *Public Systems for the Protection of Cultural Heritage: Organization, Human Resources and Financial Resources*. Proceedings of the Eleventh Seminar on the Conservation of Asian Cultural Heritage, November 11–16, 2002 in Tokyo. Tokyo: National Research Institute for Cultural Properties.

Schama, Simon. 1995. *Landscapes and Memory*. London: Harper Collins.

Schnapp, Alain. 1996. *The Discovery of the Past: The Origins of Archaeology*. London: British Museum Press.

Sharma, Kavita, Megha Agrawal and A.K. Jaiswal. 2011. "Biodeterioration of Ancient Monuments: Problems and Prospects," *Current Botany* 2(1): 23–24.

Shirley, Ian and Carol Neill (eds.). 2013. *Asian and Pacific Cities: Development Patterns*. New York: Routledge.

Silapacharanan, Siriwan and J. Campbell (eds.). 2006. *Research Conference Proceedings on Asian Approaches to Conservation*. Bangkok, Thailand. October 3–5, 2006. Bangkok: Faculty of Architecture, Chulalongkorn University.

Silva, Kapila D. 2010. "Tangible and Intangible Heritages: The Crisis of Official Definitions," *Housing and Building Research Journal*, 6(3): 12–18.

——. 2013. "Epilogue: Prospects for Asian Heritage Management," in Kapila D. Silva and Neel Kamal Chapagain (eds.), *Asian Heritage Management*, 345–356.

Silva, Kapila D. and Neel Kamal Chapagain (eds.). 2013. *Asian Heritage Management: Contexts, Concerns and Prospects*. New York: Routledge.

Sinha, A. 2010. "Conservation of Cultural Landscapes," *Journal of Landscape Architecture*, 28 (Summer): 24–31.

Smith, Laurajane. 2006. *The Uses of Heritage*. New York: Routledge.

Smith, Laurajane and Natsuko Akagawa (eds.). 2008. *Intangible Heritage*. London: Routledge.

Smith, Melanie and Greg Richards (eds.). 2013. *The Routledge Handbook of Cultural Tourism*. Abingdon, UK: Routledge.

Social Science Research Institute (ed.). 1976. *Asia Urbanizing: Population Growth & Concentration – & the Problems Thereof*. Tokyo: The Simul Press.

SPAFA 1988. *Consultative Workshop on Conservation of Ancient Cities and/or Settlements*. Bangkok: SPAFA.

——. 1989. *Principles and Methods of Preservation Applicable to the Ancient Cities of Asia*. Bangkok: SPAFA.

Staniforth, Sarah (ed.). 2013. *Historical Perspectives on Preventive Conservation*. Readings in Conservation. Los Angeles: Getty Conservation Institute.

Stanley-Price, Nicholas (ed.). 1999. *Conservation on Archaeological Excavations*. (2nd, revised edition). Rome: ICCROM.

Stanley-Price, Nicholas Stanley, et al. (eds.). 1996. *Historical and Philosophical Issues in the Conservation of Cultural Heritage*. Readings in Conservation. Los Angeles: The Getty Conservation Institute.

Stanley-Price, N. and J. Jing (eds.). 2011. *Conserving the Authentic: Essays in Honour of Jukka Jokilehto*. Rome: ICCROM, 127–136.

Starr, Fiona. 2012. *Corporate Responsibility for Cultural Heritage: Conservation, Sustainable Development, and Corporate Reputation*. London: Routledge.

Stovel, Herb. 1993. "Notes on Aspects of Authenticity, Reflections from the Bergen Meeting," in K.E. Larsen and N. Marstein (eds.), *Conference on Authenticity*, 121–125.

———. 1998. *Risk Preparedness: A Management Manual for World Cultural Heritage*. Rome: ICCROM.

Stovel, Herb, N. Stanley-Price and R. Killick (eds.). 2003. *Conservation of Living Religious Heritage: Papers from the ICCROM 2003 Forum on Living Religious Heritage: Conserving the Sacred*. Rome: ICCROM.

Stubbs, John H. 2009. *Time Honored: A Global View of Architectural Conservation*. Hoboken, NJ: Wiley.

Stubbs, John H. and Katherine L.R. McKee. 2007. "Applications of Remote Sensing to the Understanding and Management of Cultural Heritage Sites," in James Wiseman and Farouk El–Baz (eds.), *Remote Sensing in Archaeology*. London: Springer, 515–540.

Sullivan, Sharon. 1993. "Conservation Policy Delivery," in M. MacLean, *Cultural Heritage in Asia and the Pacific*, 15–26.

———. 2003. "Local Involvement and Traditional Practices in the World Heritage System," in E. de Merode et al. (eds.) *Linking Universal and Local Values*, 49–54.

Suntikul, Wantanee. 2013. "Commodification of Intangible Cultural Heritage in Asia," in Kapila D. Silva and Neel Kamal Chapagain (eds.), *Asian Heritage Management*, 236–252.

Swenson, Astrid and Peter Mandler (eds.). 2013. *From Plunder to Preservation: Britain and the Heritage of Empire c.1800–1940*. Oxford: Published for the British Academy by Oxford University Press.

Tadgett, Christopher. 2008. *The East: Buddhists, Hindus and the Sons of Heaven*. Abingdon, UK: Routledge.

Taylor, Ken. 2004. "Cultural Heritage Management: A Possible Role for Charters and Principles in Asia," *International Journal of Heritage Studies* 10(5), 417–433.

———. 2012. "Heritage Challenges in Asian Urban Cultural Landscape Settings," in Patrick Daly and Tim Winter (eds.), *Routledge Handbook of Heritage in Asia*, 266–280.

———. 2013. "The Challenges of the Cultural Landscape Construct and Associated Intangible Values in an Asian Context," in Kapila D. Silva and Neel Kamal Chapagain (eds.), *Asian Heritage Management*, 189–214.

Taylor, Ken and K. Altenburg. 2006. "Cultural Landscapes in Asia-Pacific: Potential for Filling World Heritage Gaps," *International Journal of Heritage Studies* 12(3): 267–282.

Taylor, Ken and Jane Lennon (eds.). 2012. *Managing Cultural Landscapes*. London: Routledge.

Taylor, Ken, Archer St. Clair and Nora J. Mitchell (eds.). 2015. *Conserving Cultural Landscapes: Challenges and New Directions*. New York: Routledge.

Thorsby, David. 2006. "The Value of Cultural Heritage: What Can Economics Tell Us?" Paper presented at Capturing the Public Value of Heritage, January 25–26, London.

Timothy, D.J. and G.P. Nyaupane (eds.). *Cultural Heritage and Tourism in the Developing World: A Regional Perspective*. New York: Routledge.

Tokyo National Research Institute of Cultural Properties. 1991. *Proceedings of the Second Seminar on the Conservation of Asian Cultural Heritage, November 18–21, 1991, Kyoto. Conservation in Museums*. Tokyo: Tokyo National Research Institute of Cultural Properties.

———. 1992. *Proceedings of the Third Seminar on the Conservation of Asian Cultural Heritage, November 22–24, 1992, Kyoto. Conservation of Wood and International Cooperation*. Tokyo: Tokyo National Research Institute of Cultural Properties.

———. 1993. *Proceedings of the Fourth Seminar on the Conservation of Asian Cultural Heritage, October 31–November 3, 1993, Nara. Traditional Material and Techniques in Conservation*. Tokyo: Tokyo National Research Institute of Cultural Properties.

———. 1995. *Proceedings of the Fifth Seminar on the Conservation of Asian Cultural Heritage, October 17–19, 1995, Nara. Technological Problems in the International Cooperation Activity for Conservation*. Tokyo: Tokyo National Research Institute of Cultural Properties.

———. 1996. *Proceedings of the Sixth Seminar on the Conservation of Asian Cultural Heritage, October 16–18, 1996, Nara. Conservation of Archaeological Objects*. Tokyo: Tokyo National Research Institute of Cultural Properties.

———. 1997. *Proceedings of the Seventh Seminar on the Conservation of Asian Cultural Heritage, October 13–18, 1997, Kyoto. The World Cultural Heritage in Asian Countries: Sustainable Development and Conservation*. Tokyo: Tokyo National Research Institute of Cultural Properties.

———. 1999a. *Proceedings of the Eighth Seminar on the Conservation of Asian Cultural Heritage, February 23–27, 1999. World Cultural Heritage in Asia: Conservation of Archaeological Sites and their Utilization*. Tokyo: Tokyo National Research Institute for Cultural Properties.

———. 1999b. *Proceedings of the Ninth Seminar on the Conservation of Asian Cultural Heritage, November 16–19, 1999, Tokyo. Conservation of Wall Paintings in Asia*. Tokyo: Tokyo National Research Institute of Cultural Properties.

Tom, Binumol. 2007. *Traditional Conservation of Timber Architecture: A Case Study of Thai Kottaram, Kerala.* Conservation Briefs. New Delhi: INTACH UK Trust.

———. 2013. "Jiirnnoddharana: The Hindu Philosophy of Conservation," in Kapila D. Silva and Neel Kamal Chapagain (eds.), *Asian Heritage Management*, 35–48.

Trechsel, Heinz R. (ed.). 1994. *Manual on Moisture Control in Buildings.* New York: American Society for Testing and Materials.

Tschudi-Madsen, Stephen. 1976. *Restoration and Anti-Restoration: A Study in English Restoration Philosophy.* (2nd edition). Oslo: Universitetsforlaget.

Ueno, Kunikazu. 2009. *Hội An Protocols for Best Conservation Practice in Asia: Professional Guidelines for Assuring and Preserving the Authenticity of Heritage Sites in the Context of the Cultures of Asia.* Bangkok: UNESCO.

UNESCO. 2000. *Conference Proceedings UNESCO Conference on Cultural Heritage Management and Tourism, 8–16 April 2000, Bakhtapur, Nepal.* Bangkok: UNESCO.

———. 2006. *Research Conference Proceedings on Asian Approaches to Conservation.* Asian Academy for Heritage Management and the Faculty of Architecture, Chulalonghorn University, Bangkok, Thailand, October 3–5, 2006. Paris: UNESCO; Rome: ICCROM.

———. 2007. *Research, Analysis and Preservation of Archeological Sites and Remains: Training Course on Cultural Heritage Protection in the Asia–Pacific Region, 2006:* September 11–October 11 2006, Nara, Japan. Nara: Cultural Heritage Protection Cooperation Office, Asia/Pacific Cultural Centre for UNESCO ACCU.

———. 2008a. *A Toolkit for Safeguarding Asian Cultural Heritage: Best Practices from the Office of the UNESCO Regional Advisor for Culture in Asia and the Pacific.* (CD–ROM). Bangkok: UNESCO.

———. 2008b. *Operational Guidelines for the Implementation of the World Heritage Convention,* Paris: UNESCO.

———. 2009. *Training Report on Cultural Heritage Protection: Training Course for Researchers in Charge of Cultural Heritage Protection in Asia and the Pacific, 2008. Uzbekistan: 16 July–18 August 2008.* Nara, Japan: Cultural Heritage Protection Cooperation Office, Asia/Pacific Cultural Centre for UNESCO ACCU.

———. 2012. *UNESCO World Heritage Atlas.* Paris: UNESCO.

U.S. National Park Service. 1996. "Approaches to Heritage: Hawaiian and Pacific Perspectives on Preservation," *Cultural Resource Management* 19(8). Web. http://crm.cr.nps.gov/issue.cfm?volume=19&number=08. www.nps.gov/history/CRMjournal/.../v19n8. Accessed June 21, 2016.

Valderrama, Fernando. 1995. *A History of UNESCO.* Paris: UNESCO.

Van Oers, Ron. 2007. "Towards New International Guidelines for the Conservation of Historic Urban Landscapes (HUL)," *City & Time*, 3(3): 43–51.

Vinas, S.M. 2005. *Contemporary Theory of Conservation.* Oxford: Elsevier Butterworth-Heinemann.

Vines, Elizabeth. 2005. *Streetwise Asia: A Practical Guide for the Conservation and Revitalisation of Heritage Cities and Towns in Asia.* Bangkok: UNESCO Bangkok/World Bank.

von Droste, Bernd, Mechtild Rössler, and Harald Plachter (eds.). 1995. *Cultural Landscapes of Universal Value.* Jena, Germany: Gustav Fischer Verlag.

Weber, Willi and Simos Yannas. 2014. *Lessons from Vernacular Architecture.* New York: Routledge.

Weiler, Katharina and Niels Gutchow (eds). 2017. *Authenticity in Architectural Heritage Conservation.* Switzerland: Springer International.

Weiss, Julian. 1989. *The Asian Century.* Oxford: Facts on File.

Wheeler, Sir Mortimer. 1965. *Splendors of the East: Temples, Tombs, Palaces and Fortresses of Asia.* New York: G.P. Putnam's Sons.

Winter, Tim. 2010. "Heritage Tourism: The Dawn of a New Era?" in Sophia Labadi and Colin Long (eds.), *Heritage and Globalisation*, 117–129.

———. 2013. "Heritage Conservation in an Age of Shifting Global Power." Paper presented at the Australia ICOMOS conference, Canberra, October 31 to November 3.

Winter, Tim and Patrick Daly. 2012. "Heritage in Asia: Converging Forces, Conflicting Values," in Patrick Daly and Tim Winter (eds.), *Routledge Handbook of Heritage in Asia*, 1–36.

Winter, Tim and William Logan. 2014. "Asian Cities: Cultural Heritage and the Interplay Between Nation Building and Internationalism," *Historic Environment* 26(3): 2–7.

Winter, Tim, Peggy Teo and T.C. Chang (eds). 2008. *Asia on Tour: Exploring the Rise of Asian Tourism.* London: Routledge.

Woodward, Christopher. 2001. *In Ruins: A Journey Through History, Art, and Literature.* New York: Vintage Books.

World Monuments Fund. 2015. *World Monuments; Fifty Irreplaceable Sites to Discover, Explore and Champion.* New York: Rizzoli.

Wright, Gwendolyn. 1991. *The Politics of Design in French Colonial Urbanism.* Chicago: University of Chicago Press.

Zhao, W. and J.R.B. Ritchie. 2007. "Tourism and Poverty Alleviation: An Integrative Research Framework," *Current Issues in Tourism* 10(2/3): 119–143.

Further readings by region

The following titles on architectural conservation in Asia follow the order of the contents of this book and offer readings supplementary to the books cited in each chapter's Further Reading and Notes. The majority of the following titles are in book form. It is assumed that readings contained within journals, conference proceedings, news outlets and solely electronically published material are better searched via the Worldwide Web.

Key Web-based sources for architectural conservation bibliographies include:
- Art and Archaeology Technical Abstracts (AATA), an online service of the Getty Conservation Institute in association with the International Institute for Conservation of Historic and Artistic Works, http://aata.getty.edu.
- The Bibliographic Database of the Conservation Information Network (BCIN), www.bcin.ca.
- International Council on Monuments and Sites (ICOMOS) Documentation Centre Catalogue, http://databases.unesco.org/icomos.

Part I – East Asia

Anon. *Yakushiji Temple*. 2008. Translated by Chiyoko Sudo. Nara: Yakushiji Temple.
Chung, Seung-Jin. 2005. "East Asian Values in Historic Conservation," *Journal of Architectural Conservation* 11(1) (March), 55–70.
Denslagen, Wim and Niels Gutschow (eds.). 2005. *Architectural Imitations: Reproductions and Pastiches in East and West*. Maastricht: Shaker Publishing.
Ebbe, Katrinka and Lee Joanna Harper (eds.). 1999. *Culture and Sustainable Development: East Asia and Pacific Working Group Proceedings*. In conjunction with the conference *Culture Counts: Financing, Resources and the Economics of Culture in Sustainable Development*. Florence, Italy, October 1999.
Enders, Siegfried and Niels Gutschow (eds.). 1999. *Hozon: Architectural and Urban Conservation in Japan*. Stuttgart: Edition Axel Menges.
Larsen, Knut Einar, et al. (eds). 1995. *Nara Conference on Authenticity in Relation to the World Heritage Convention*. Paris: ICOMOS; Rome: UNESCO; and Tokyo: ICCROM and Agency for Cultural Affairs.
Lee, Hye-Kyung and Lorraine Lim (eds.). 2014. *Cultural Policies in East Asia: Dynamics between the State, Arts and Creative Industries*. Basingstoke, UK: Palgrave Macmillan.
Reischauer, Edwin O. and John K. Fairbank. 1960. *East Asia: the Great Tradition in A History of East Asian Civilization*. Volume 1. Boston: Houghton Mifflin.
UNESCO. 2000. Proceedings of UNESCO conference: *China – Cultural Heritage Management and Urban Development: Challenge and Opportunity*, July 5–7, 2000, Beijing. Beijing: UNESCO.
Weatherford, Jack. 2004. *Genghis Khan and the Making of the Modern World*. New York: Crown Publishers.

Part II – Southeast Asia mainland countries

Alatas, Syed, et al. 2004. *Asia in Europe, Europe in Asia*. Singapore: Institute of Southeast Asian Studies.
Anderson, Benedict. 2002. *The Spectre of Comparisons: Nationalism, Southeast Asia and the World*. New York: Verso.
Bacus, Elisabeth A., Ian C. Glover and Vincent C. Pigott (eds.). 2006. *Uncovering Southeast Asia's Past*. Singapore: NUS Press.
Bacus, Elisabeth A., Ian C. Glover and Peter D. Sharrock (eds.). 2008. *Interpreting Southeast Asia's Past: Monument, Image and Text*. Singapore: NUS Press.
Ballio, G., G. Baronio and L. Binda. 2001. "First Results of the Characteristics of Bricks and Mortars from Mỹ Són Monuments." Paper presented to the UNESCO conference *Conserving the Past: An Asian Perspective of Authenticity*, Hội An, February 22, 2001.
Bishop, Ryan, et al. (eds.). 2003. *Postcolonial Urbanism: Southeast Asian Cities and Global Processes*. New York: Routledge.
Chapman, William. 2013. *A Heritage of Ruins: The Ancient Sites of Southeast Asia and Their Conservation*. Honolulu: University of Hawai'i Press.
Charoenwongsa, Pisit. 2006a. "Regional Site Management Planning and Training: the SPAFA Example in Southeast Asia," in Neville Agnew and Janet Bridgland (eds.), *Of the Past, for the Future: Integrating Archaeology and Conservation*. Proceedings of the Conservation Theme at the 5th World Archaeological Congress, Washington, DC, June 22–26, 2003. Getty Conservation Institute Symposium Proceedings Series. Los Angeles: The Getty Conservation Institute, 40–42.
——. 2006b. "Community-based Archeological Resource Management in Southeast Asia," in *Of the Past, for the Future*, 102–104.
Church, John Peter, (ed.). 2006. *A Short History of South–East Asia*. (4th edition). Hoboken, NJ: Wiley.

Clémentin-Ojha, Catherine and Pierre-Yves Manguin. 2007. *A Century in Asia: The History of the Ecole Française d'Extrême-Orient*. Translated by Helen Reid. Singapore: Editions Didier Millet; Paris: Ecole Française d'Extrême-Orient.

Cody, Jeffrey W. and Kecia L. Fong. 2009. "Sustaining Conservation Education in Southeast Asia," *Conservation: the GCI Newsletter* 24(1): 18–19.

Cœdès, George. 1966. *The Making of Southeast Asia*. Translated by H.M. Wright. London: Routledge & Kegan Paul.

——. 1968. *The Indianized States of Southeast Asia*. Edited by Walter F. Vella and translated by Susan Brown Cowing. Honolulu: East-West Center Press.

Dumarçay, Jacques 1987. *The House in South-East Asia*. Images of Asia. Singapore: Oxford University Press.

——. 1991. *The Palaces of South-East Asia: Architecture and Customs*. Translated and edited by Michael Smithies. Singapore: Oxford University Press.

——. 2003. *Architecture and its Models in South-East Asia*. Bangkok: Orchid Press.

Glover, Ian and Peter Bellwood. 2004. *Southeast Asia: From Prehistory to History*. London: Routledge-Curzon.

Hall, D.G.E. 1981. *A History of Southeast Asia*. (4th edition). London: Palgrave Macmillan.

Heidhues, Mary Somers. 2000. *Southeast Asia: A Concise History*. London: Thames & Hudson.

Higham, Charles. 1989. *The Archaeology of Mainland Southeast Asia*. Cambridge: Cambridge University Press.

Hitchcock, Michael, Victor T. King, and Michael Parnwell (eds.). 2009. *Tourism in Southeast Asia: Challenges and New Directions*. Honolulu: University of Hawai'i Press.

Hooker, M.B. 1997. *Islam in South-East Asia*. Leiden: Brill.

ICCROM. 2000. *A World Heritage Strategy for Southeast Asia*. Rome: ICCROM.

Klokke, Marijke J. and Veronique Degroot (eds.). 2008. *Unearthing Southeast Asia's Past*. Selected Papers from the 12th International Conference of the European Association of Southeast Asian Archaeologists, vol. 1. Singapore: NUS Press.

LeBar, Frank M., Gerald C. Hickey, and John K. Musgrave. 1984. *Ethnic Groups of Mainland Southeast Asia*. New Haven, CT: Yale University Press.

Lester, Robert C. 1973. *Theravada Buddhism in Southeast Asia*. Ann Arbor: University of Michigan Press.

Lieberman, Victor B. 2003. *Strange Parallels: Southeast Asia in Global Context, c. 800–1830*. Studies in Comparative World History. Cambridge: Cambridge University Press.

Logan, William S. and Marc Askew (eds.). 1994. *Cultural Identity and Urban Change in Southeast Asia: Interpretive Essays*. Geelong, Victoria: Deakin University Press.

MacKee, J. 2009. *Conserving Cultural Built Heritage in South and Southeast Asia: A Conceptual Framework for the Conservation of Non-Secular Built Heritage Based on the Philosophical and Cultural Experiences of the Region*. Saarbrücken: VDM Verlag Dr. Müller.

Madsen, Axel. 1989. *Silk Roads: The Asian Adventures of Clara and André Malraux*. New York: Pharos Books.

Malraux, André. 1935. *The Royal Way*. First published 1930 as *La Voie Royale*. Translated by Stuart Gilbert. New York: Knopf.

Miksic, John N., Geok Yian Goh and Sue O'Connor. 2011. *Rethinking Cultural Resource Management in Southeast Asia: Preservation, Development, and Neglect*. Anthem Southeast Asian Studies. London: Anthem Press.

Molyvann, Vann. 2008. *Cités du Sud-est Asiatique: Le Passe & Le Present*. Doctoral thesis, Architecture, Université de Paris, France.

Nagashima, Masayuki. 2002. *The Lost Heritage: The Reality of Artifact Smuggling in Southeast Asia*. Bangkok: Post Books.

Ooi, Keat Gin (ed.). 2004. *Southeast Asia: A Historical Encyclopedia from Angkor Wat to East Timor*. 3 volumes. Santa Barbara: ABC-CLIO.

O'Reilly, Dougald. 2007. *Early Civilizations of Southeast Asia*. Lanham, MD: AltaMira Press.

Owen, Norman G., David Chandler and William R. Roff (eds.). 2004. *The Emergence of Modern Southeast Asia: A New History*. Honolulu: University of Hawai'i Press.

Parmentier, Henri. ca. 1932. *Guide to Angkor*. Phnom Penh: E.K.L.I.P.

Posayananda, Vasu. 2002. "Limitation of Anastylosis Concept on Practical Conservation," in Fine Arts Department and National Research Institute of Cultural Properties, *Conservation of Monuments in Thailand (II)*.

Quang Nam Center for Conservation of Heritage and Management. 2001. *Conserving the Past: An Asian Perspective of Authenticity in the Consolidation, Restoration, and Reconstruction of Historic Monuments and Sites*. Hanoi: Quang Nam Center for Conservation of Heritage and Management.

Ricklefs, M.C., et al. 2010. *A New History of Southeast Asia*. New York: Palgrave Macmillan.

Rimmer, Peter J. and Howard Dick. 2009. *The City in Southeast Asia: Patterns, Processes and Policy*. Honolulu: University of Hawai'i Press.

SACH. 1998. *The Summer Palace*. (5th edition). Beijing: China Esperanto Press. (In Chinese and English.)

SarDesai, D.R. 2003. *Southeast Asia: Past and Present*. Boulder, CO: Westview Press.

Smithies, Michael. 1995. "Henri Mouhot," in Victor T. King (ed.), *Explorers of South-East Asia: Six Lives*. Kuala Lumpur: Oxford University Press.

Snodgrass, A. 1985. *The Symbolism of the Stupa*. Ithaca, NY: Southeast Asia Program, Cornell University.
Steinberg, David Joel (ed.). 1985. *In Search of Southeast Asia: A Modern History*. Honolulu: University of Hawai'i Press.
Strike, James. 2013. *Architecture in Conservation: Managing Development at Historic Sites*. Hoboken, NJ: Taylor and Francis. First published by Routledge in 1994.
Tarling, Nicholas. 2000a. *The Cambridge History of Southeast Asia: Volume I. From Early Times to c. 1800*. Cambridge: Cambridge University Press.
——. 2000b. *The Cambridge History of Southeast Asia: Volume 2. The Nineteenth and Twentieth Centuries*. Cambridge: Cambridge University Press.
Taylor, Ken. 2009. "Cultural Landscapes and Asia: Reconciling International and Southeast Asian Regional Values," *Landscape Research*, 34(1), 7–31.
Teo, Peggy, T.C. Chang and K.C. Ho (eds.). 2001. *Interconnected Worlds: Tourism in Southeast Asia*. Advances in Tourism Research. London: Pergamon.
Tuan, Tran Huu, Udomsak Seenprachawong and Stale Navrud. 2009. "Comparing Cultural Heritage Values in South East Asia: Possibilities and Difficulties in Cross-Country Transfers of Economic Values," *Journal of Cultural Heritage* 10(1): 9–21.
Tun Zaw. 2001. "Restoration of Historic Monuments and Sites" in Quang Nam Center, *Conserving the Past*.
Tunprawat, Tuncharawee. 2009. *Managing Living Heritage Sites in Mainland Southeast Asia*. PhD Thesis, Silpakorn University, Bankgok.
White, Stephen. 1986. *John Thomson: A Window to the Orient*. London: Thames and Hudson.
Winter, Tim. 2007. *Post-Conflict Heritage, Postcolonial Tourism: Culture, Politics and Development at Angkor*. London: Routledge.

Part III – Southeast Asia island countries

Cultural Heritage Centre for Asia and the Pacific. 2004. *Training Program for Heritage Managers in the Pacific – Conserving Pacific Places*. Produced in association with Australia ICOMOS and the Pacific Islands Museums Association. Melbourne: Deakin University.
Galván, Javier. 1998. *Pacific Islands: The Spanish Legacy*. Madrid: Ministerio de Educación y Cultura, Dirección General de Cooperación y Comunicación Cultural.
ICCROM. 1972. *Conservation in the Tropics: Proceedings of the Asia-Pacific Seminar on Conservation of Cultural Property Feb. 7–16, 1972, New Delhi*. Rome: International Centre for Conservation.
Jumsai, Sumet. 1997. *Naga: Cultural Origins in Siam and the West Pacific*. (3rd edition). Bangkok: Chalermnit Press.
Rodao, Florentino. 1998. *Pacific Islands: The Spanish Legacy*. Madrid: Lunwerg.
Van Dullemen, C.J. 2010. *Tropical Modernity: Life and Work of C.P. Wolff Schoenmaker*. Amsterdam: Martien de Vletter SUN.
World Monuments Fund and US/ICOMOS. 1992. *Trails to Tropical Treasures*. New York: World Monuments Fund.

Part IV – South Asia

Ameen, Farooq (ed.). 1997. *Contemporary Architecture and City Form: The South Asian Paradigm*. Mumbai: Marg Publications.
Chakrabarti, P.G. Dhar, Sanjay Srivastava and Shakya Binod. 2009. *Indigenous Knowledge for Disaster Risk Reduction in South Asia*. London: Macmillan Publishers.
Hammond, Norman. 1971. *South Asian Architecture*. Park Ridge, NJ: Noyes Press.
Larsen, Knut Einar and Nils Marstein (eds.). 1993. *Proceedings, ICOMOS International Wood Committee (IIWC) 8th International Symposium, 23–25 November 1992, Kathmandu, Patan and Bhaktapur, Nepal*. Oslo: TAPIR Publishers.
MacKee, J. 2009. *Conserving Cultural Built Heritage in South and Southeast Asia: A Conceptual Framework for the Conservation of Non-Secular Built Heritage Based on the Philosophical and Cultural Experiences of the Region*. Saarbrücken: VDM Verlag Dr. Müller.
Robson, David. 2002. *Geoffrey Bawa: The Complete Works*. London: Thames and Hudson.
——. 2008. *Beyond Bawa*. London: Thames and Hudson.
Silva, Roland. 2004. *Conservation Theory: National and International Contribution*. Colombo: ICOMOS Sri Lanka.
Volwahsen, Andreas. *Living Architecture: Islamic Indian*. New York: Grosset and Dunlap.

Part V – Central Asia

Golden, Peter B. 2011. *Central Asia in World History*. Oxford: Oxford University Press.

Knobloch, Edgar. 2001. *Monuments of Central Asia*. London: I.B. Tauris Publishers.

Levi, Scott C. and Ron Sela (eds.). 2010. *Islamic Central Asia: An Anthology of Historical Sources*. Bloomington: University of Indiana Press.

Mairs, Rachel. 2014. *The Hellenistic Far East*. Oakland: University of California Press.

Palumbo, Gaetano, Norma Barbacci and Mark Weber. 2008. "Sustaining an Ancient Tradition: The World Monuments Fund and the Conservation of Earthen Architecture." Paper presented at *Terra 2008: Proceedings of the 10th International Conference on the Study and Conservation of Earthen Architectural Heritage, Bamako, Mali, February 1–5, 2008 = Actes de la 10ème conférence international sur l'étude et la conservation su patrimoine bâti en terre, Bamako, Mali, 1–5 février 2008*. Los Angeles: Getty Conservation Institute, 344–351.

IMAGE CREDITS

The authors wish to thank the institutions and individuals who have kindly provided photographic or other material for use in *Architectural Conservation in Asia*. In all cases, every effort has been made to contact copyright holders but should there be any errors or omissions, the publisher would be pleased to insert the appropriate acknowledgements in reprints of this book.

Chapter 1 – Japan

1.3b, c; 1.6a, b; 1.7a, b, c; 1.8a, b	John H. Stubbs, author
1.1a	© National Land Image Information (Color Aerial Photographs), Ministry of Land, Infrastructure, Transport and Tourism, via Wikimedia Commons
1.1b	Courtesy and © World Monuments Fund
1.1c	By Jaycangel (Own work) [CC BY-SA 3.0 (http://creativecommons.org/licenses/by-sa/3.0)], via Wikimedia Commons
1.2	By Chris 73 (Own work) [CC BY-SA 3.0 (http://creativecommons.org/licenses/by-sa/3.0)], via Wikimedia Commons
1.3a	Shinto Online
1.4a, b	University of Hawai'i. Images from *Far East Quarterly*, London, 1860
1.5a	By Kanchi1979 (Own work) [CC BY-SA 4.0 (http://creativecommons.org/licenses/by-sa/4.0)], via Wikimedia Commons
1.5b	Jeffrey Friedl
1.9a, b, c	Courtesy Wesley Cheek

Chapter 2 – The People's Republic of China

2.9a, b; 2.15a, b; 2.16a, b; 2.18a, b	John H. Stubbs, author
2.1a	Image from *Madrolle's Guide Books: Northern China, The Valley of the Blue River, Korea*. Hachette & Company, 1912. Image from the Perry-Castañeda Library Map Collection, Courtesy of the University of Texas Libraries, The University of Texas at Austin via Wikimedia Commons.
2.1b, c	leilei-nancy blogspot

2.2a	www.travelchinaguide.com
2.2b	By Dennis Jarvis from Halifax Canada (China-7163) [CC BY-SA 2.0 (http://creativecommons.org/licenses/by-sa/2.0)], via Wikimedia Commons
2.3	www.chinareport.com
2.4a	By Yaohua 2000 [CC BY-SA 3.0 (http://creativecommons.org/licenses/by-sa/3.0)], via Wikimedia Commons
2.4b	Public Domain via Wikimedia Commons
2.5	By Dimitry B [CC BY-2.0 (http://creativecommons.org/licenses/by-/2.0)], via Wikimedia Commons
2.6	By Dr._Meierhofer [CC-BY-SA-3.0 http://creativecommons.org/licenses/by-sa/3.0/)], via Wikimedia Commons
2.7	By Gisling (Own work) [CC-BY-SA-3.0 http://creativecommons.org/licenses/by-sa/3.0/)], via Wikimedia Commons
2.8	Courtesy Australia ICOMOS
2.10a	Courtesy Atlim University, Kadriye Zaim library, Ankara, Turkey
2.10b	sinosploitation.blogspot
2.10c	The Telegraph
2.10d	Courtesy and © World Monuments Fund
2.11a	www.bricoleurbanism.org
2.11b	By Giorgio (own work) [CC BY SA 3.0] via Wikimedia Commons
2.12a–f	Courtesy Benjamin Clavan
2.13; 2.14	Courtesy Marilyn Novell
2.17a	By ralph repo [CC BY 2.0 (http://creativecommons.org/licenses/by/2.0)], via Wikimedia Commons. Herbert G. Ponting, photographer (1907)
2.17b	By Severin Stalder (Own work) [CC BY SA 3.0] via Wikimedia Commons
2.19a	By Anna Frodesiak (Own work) [Public domain], via Wikimedia Commons
2.19b	By Chi King, [CC BY 2.0 (http://creativecommons.org/licenses/by/2.0)], via Wikimedia Commons
2.19c	By Another Believer (Own work) [CC BY-SA 4.0 (http://creativecommons.org/licenses/by-sa/4.0)], via Wikimedia Commons

Chapter 3 – Taiwan

3.1a	By Taiwankengo (Own work) [CC BY-SA 3.0 (http://creativecommons.org/licenses/by-sa/3.0) via Wikimedia Commons
3.1b	www.tripadvisor.com
3.2	Public Domain via Wikimedia Commons
3.3	By Yeowatzup from Katlenburg-Lindau Germany [CC BY 2.0 (http://creativecommons.org/licenses/by/2.0)], via Wikimedia Commons
3.4a	By Alexander Synaptic from Changhua, Taiwan [CC BY-SA 2.0 (http://creativecommons.org/licenses/by-sa/2.0)], via Wikimedia Commons
3.4b	snipview.com
3.5a	By Zac Harper User: (WT-shared) Exactly~Divyn at wts wikivoyage (Own work) [Public domain], via Wikimedia Commons
3.5b	Taiwan Tourism Board

Chapter 4 – South and North Korea

4.1	By sellyourseoul [CC BY 2.0 (http://creativecommons.org/licenses/by/2.0)], via Wikimedia Commons
4.2	French Wikipedia. Source page: "fr:Image:Corée-Batiment palais Gyeongbokgung-Seoul-2005.jpg, photo by fr:Utilisateur:Mammique [CC BY-SA 3.0 (http://creativecommons.org/licenses/by-sa/3.0)],via Wikimedia Commons

Image credits **573**

4.3	By Kok Leng Yeo [CC BY 2.0 (http://creativecommons.org/licenses/by/2.0)], via Wikimedia Commons
4.4	© Robert Koehler
4.5a	qsl.net
4.5b	thecityfix.com
4.5c	By Daderot (Own work) [Public domain], via Wikimedia Commons
4.6a	By Mark Froelich [CC BY-SA 3.0 (http://creativecommons.org/licenses/by-sa/3.0)], via Wikimedia Commons
4.6b	Public Domain via Wikimedia Commons
4.7a, b	dezeen.com

Chapter 5 – Mongolia

5.3a, b; 5.5; 5.6a, b; 5.7b, c; 5.8a	Courtesy Alexandra Cleworth
5.1	By Torbenbrinker (Own work) [CC BY-SA 3.0 (http://creativecommons.org/licenses/by-sa/3.0)], via Wikimedia Commons
5.2	Mongolia expeditions, Panoramio image ID 48207584, licensed under the Creative Commons Attribution-Share Alike 3.0 Unported license
5.4	Courtesy whc.unesco.org
5.7a	Courtesy and © World Monuments Fund
5.7d	By Vadaro (Own work) [CC BY-SA 3.0 (http://creativecommons.org/licenses/by-sa/3.0)], via Wikimedia Commons
5.8b	By Ray Tsang via flickr
5.9	By Masha Svyatogor

Chapter 6 – Myanmar (Burma)

6.1; 6.2; 6.3; 6.4; 6.5a, b; 6.6a; 6.9	John H. Stubbs, author
6.5a, b	Courtesy Louis Freeman
6.6b	Wikimedia Commons. Source page: "Shwenandaw Monastery – Wikipedia, the free encyclopedia" http://en.wikipedia.org/wiki/Shwenandaw_Monastery [Creative Commons Attribution 2.0 Generic license]
6.7	Smile of Asia Travel Company
6.8a, b	Yangonite.com
6.8c	Jacques Maudy and Jimi Casaccia in *The Irrawaddy Magazine* online
6.8d	Wikimedia Commons. Source page: "Pegu Club – Wikipedia, the free encyclopedia" http://en.wikipedia.org/wiki/Pegu_Club [Creative Commons Attribution 3.0 Unported license]

Chapter 7 – Laos

7.3a, b; 7.4a, b; 7.5b, c; 7.6; 7.7	John H. Stubbs, author
7.1	By Tango 7174, licensed under the Creative Commons Attribution-Share Alike 4.0 International, 3.0 Unported, 2.5 Generic, 2.0 Generic and 1.0 Generic license.
7.2	By calflier001, licensed under the Creative Commons Attribution-Share Alike 2.0 Generic license.
7.5a	By Mattun211, made available under the Creative Commons CC0 1.0 Universal Public Domain Dedication.

Chapter 8 – Cambodia

8.2; 8.4a; 8.5; 8.7; 8.9b, c	John H. Stubbs, author
8.6c; 8.9a, b, c	Courtesy and © World Monuments Fund
8.1	By Mark Fischer (Angkor Wat Aerial View) [CC BY-SA 2.0 (http://creativecommons.org/licenses/by-sa/2.0)], via Wikimedia Commons
8.3	By Japanese pilgrim visiting Angkor (Shohohan Museum in Mito, Japan) [Public domain], via Wikimedia Commons
8.4b	madmonkeyhotel.com
8.6a	kitblog
8.6b	By Madelon van de Water (noledam) -Own work [GFDL (http://www.gnu.org/copyleft/fdl.html) or CC BY-SA 3.0 (http://creativecommons.org/licenses/by-sa/3.0)], via Wikimedia Commons licensed under the Creative Commons Attribution-Share Alike 3.0 Unported, 2.5 Generic, 2.0 Generic and 1.0 Generic license.
8.7	© Emiel van den Boomen
8.8	radioaustralia
8.10a	Public Domain
8.10b	© CALI, 2015.
8.10c	© Letellier, 2007.
8.11a, b	Courtesy Tess Davis

Chapter 9 – Thailand

9.1a, b, c; 9.5a; 9.8a, b	John H. Stubbs, author
9.2	asianitinerary.com
9.3	By Nicham (Own work) [CC BY-SA 3.0 (http://creativecommons.org/licenses/by-sa/3.0)], via Wikimedia Commons
9.4	By Tevaprapas Makklay Licensed under Public Domain via Wikimedia Commons
9.5b, c	Courtesy and © World Monuments Fund
9.6	By Sergey [CC BY-2.0 (http://creativecommons.org/licenses/by-/2.0)], via Wikimedia Commons
9.7	By Kaosaming. [CC SA 4.0, 3.0, 2.5, 2.0 and 1.0], via Wikimedia Commons.

Chapter 10 – Vietnam

10.1	By Dinkum (Own work) [CC0], via Wikimedia Commons
10.2	By Jorge Láscar from Australia (One Pillar Pagoda) [CC BY 2.0 (http://creativecommons.org/licenses/by/2.0)], via Wikimedia Commons
10.3	tripadvisor.com
10.4a	Eddie Adams, photographer/AP
10.4b	By Dennis Jarvis (http://www.flickr.com/photos/archer10/3442070161/) [CC BY-SA 2.0 (http://creativecommons.org/licenses/by-sa/2.0)], via Wikimedia Commons
10.4c	Public Domain via Wikimedia Commons, by Lu'u Ly
10.5a	© CEphoto, Uwe Aranas, via Wikimedia Commons
10.5b, c	Courtesy and © World Monuments Fund
10.6	milviatges.com
10.7a, b	slidesharecdn.com
10.7c	Mylittletrip-eklablog
10.8	Courtesy William Logan
10.9a, b	Courtesy Ken Taylor
10.10	By Francesco Paroni Sterbini (Own work) [CC BY 3.0 (http://creativecommons.org/licenses/by/3.0)], via Wikimedia Commons

Chapter 11 – Singapore

11.1a, b	Public Domain
11.1c	By Merlion444 (Own work) [Public domain or CC0], via Wikimedia Commons the Creative Commons CC0 1.0 Universal Public Domain Dedication.
11.2	By Sengkang (Own work) [Copyrighted free use], via Wikimedia Commons
11.3	By Sengkang (Own work) [Copyrighted free use], via Wikimedia Commons
11.4a	By Terence Ong [CC BY-SA 3.0 (http://creativecommons.org/licenses/by-sa/3.0)], via Wikimedia Commons
11.4b	By Lannuzel [CC BY-SA 3.0 (http://creativecommons.org/licenses/by-sa/3.0)], via Wikimedia Commons
11.5	By Erwin Soo [CC BY 2.0 (http://creativecommons.org/licenses/by/2.0)], via Wikimedia Commons
11.6	By chensiyuan, licensed under the Creative Commons Attribution-Share Alike 4.0 International, 3.0 Unported, 2.5 Generic, 2.0 Generic and 1.0 Generic license.
11.7	By William Cho [CC BY-SA 2.0 (http://creativecommons.org/licenses/by-sa/2.0)], via Wikimedia Commons

Chapter 12 – Malaysia

12.1	By Arne Müseler / www.arne-mueseler.de [CC BY-SA 3.0 de (http://creativecommons.org/licenses/by-sa/3.0/de/deed.en)], via Wikimedia Commons
12.2	*Straits Times*
12.3	From the Tropenmuseum, part of the National Museum of World Cultures [CC BY-SA 3.0 (http://creativecommons.org/licenses/by-sa/3.0)], via Wikimedia Commons
12.4a	Photograph ca. 1896 by Charles Hose. From Wellcome Library, London [CC 4.0] via Wikimedia Commons
12.4b	By Cerevisae [CC BY-SA 3.0 (http://creativecommons.org/ licenses/by-sa/3.0)], via Wikimedia Commons
12.5	backpackingmalaysia.com
12.6	Heritage Malaysia
12.7a	Matt Cope
12.7b	jacekphoto

Chapter 13 – Brunei

13.1	By audie from Canada [CC BY 2.0 (http://creativecommons.org/licenses/by-sa/2.0] the Creative Commons Attribution 2.0 Generic license, via Wikimedia Commons
13.2	borneobulletin.com.bn
13.3	By Hajotthu (Own work) [CC BY-SA 3.0 (http://creativecommons.org/-licenses/by-sa/3.0)], via Wikimedia Commons
13.4	rankly.com

Chapter 14 – Indonesia

14.1	From the Rijksmuseum – Public domain
14.2	Courtesy Leiden University Library
14.3a, c	From the Tropenmuseum, part of the National Museum of World Cultures [CC BY-SA 3.0 (http://creativecommons.org/licenses/by-sa/3.0)], via Wikimedia Commons
14.3b	Redrawn from a UNESCO report on Borobudur, August 31, 2004. No author noted for attribution. Licensed under the Creative Commons Attribution-Share Alike 3.0 Unported license, via Wikimedia Commons.

14.4a	From Collectie Muntz, Leiden University. Photo ca. 1890 by Kassian Cephas [CC BY-SA 4.0 (http://creativecommons.org/licenses/by-sa/4.0)], via Wikimedia Commons
14.4b	By Masgatotkaca (Own work) [CC-BY-SA-3.0 (http://creativecommons.org/licenses/by-sa/3.0/)], via Wikimedia Commons
14.5	timetravelturtle.com
14.6a	John H. Stubbs, author
14.6b	tripadvisor.com
14.7	agefotostock.com
14.8	tripfreakz
14.9	By David Stanley from Nanaimo, Canada (Market in Baucau) [CC BY 2.0 (http://creativecommons.org/licenses/by/2.0)], via Wikimedia Commons

Chapter 15 – The Philippines

15.1	By Jimaggro (Jim Colico) [CC BY-SA 4.0 (http://creativecommons.org/licenses/by-sa/4.0)], via Wikimedia Commons
15.2	Courtesy Bakás Pilipinas. Photographs by Roz Li and Anthony Mandling
15.3a	By John Tewell [Public domain], via Wikimedia Commons
15.3b	Wikipedia.org
15.3c	By Yeowatzup from Katlenburg-Lindau, Germany [CC BY 2.0 (http://creativecommons.org/licenses/by-sa/2.0] the Creative Commons Attribution 2.0 Generic license, via Wikimedia Commons
15.4	By Ramon F. Velasquez (Own work) [CC BY-SA 3.0 (http://creativecommons.org/licenses/by-sa/3.0)], via Wikimedia Commons
15.5	By Obra19 (Own work) [CC BY-SA 3.0 (http://creativecommons.org/licenses/by-sa/3.0)], via Wikimedia Commons
15.6	by Jose B. Calaba (Own work) [CC BY-SA 3.0 (http://creativecommons.org/licenses/by-sa/3.0)], via Wikimedia Commons
15.7	U.S. Strategic Bombing Survey – Public Domain, via Wikimedia Commons
15.8a	John H. Stubbs, author
15.8b	By fg2 (Own work) [Public domain], via Wikimedia Commons
15.8c	By PH1 David Maclean (Own work) [Public domain], via Wikimedia Commons

Chapter 16 – India

16.1	By Marc Hoffmann [CC BY-SA 2.0 (http://creativecommons.org/licenses/by-sa/2.0)], via Wikimedia Commons
16.2	By lotuspatch [CC BY-SA 2.0 (http://creativecommons.org/licenses/by-sa/2.0)], via Wikimedia Commons
16.3	By Soman [CC BY-3.0 (http://creativecommons.org/licenses/by-sa/3.0)], via Wikimedia Commons
16.4	www. southasiaarchive.com
16.5a	By Dhirad [CC BY-SA 3.0 (http://creativecommons.org/licenses/by-sa/3.0)], via Wikimedia Commons
16.5b, c	Courtesy and © World Monuments Fund
16.6a	tripadvisor
16.6b	By Yasnavi [CC BY-SA 3.0 (http://creativecommons.org/licenses/by-sa/3.0)], via Wikimedia Commons
16.6c	thehindu.com
16.7	By Ken Wieland [CC BY-SA 2.0 (http://creativecommons.org/licenses/by-sa/2.0)], via Wikimedia Commons
16.8	Courtesy INTACH

Image credits **577**

16.9a	By Dennis Jarvis [CC BY-SA 2.0 (http://creativecommons.org/licenses/by-sa/2.0)], via Wikimedia Commons
16.9b	By Koshy Koshy from Faridabad, Haryana, India [CC BY-SA 2.0 (http://creativecommons.org/licenses/by-sa/2.0)], via Wikimedia Commons
16.9c	By Singhsomendra [CC BY-SA 3.0 (http://creativecommons.org/licenses/by-sa/3.0)], via Wikimedia Commons
16.10	By Sonal Mahendru (Own work) [CC BY-SA 3.0 (http://creativecommons.org/licenses/by-sa/3.0)], via Wikimedia Commons
16.11	Courtesy INTACH
16.12	John H. Stubbs, author
16.13	By chenrezi, via flickr
16.14	By Atarax42, licensed under the Creative Commons Attribution-Share Alike 3.0 Unported, 2.5 Generic, 2.0 Generic and 1.0 Generic licenses.
16.15a	mygola.com
16.15b	By Bernard Gagnon, licensed under the Creative Commons Attribution-Share Alike 3.0 Unported, 2.5 Generic, 2.0 Generic and 1.0 Generic licenses.
16.16a	doubledolphinblogspot.in
16.16b	Courtesy and © World Monuments Fund
16.17a	By Serge Duchemin [CC BY-SA 1.0 (http://creativecommons.org/licenses/by-sa/1.0)], via Wikimedia Commons
16.17b	By Davi1974d [CC BY-SA 3.0 (http://creativecommons.org/licenses/by-sa/3.0)], via Wikimedia Commons

Chapter 17 – Sri Lanka and Maldives

17.1	By Sanjeewa Padmal Punchihewa, Public Domain via Wikimedia Commons
17.2	Public Domain
17.3	theluxurysrilanka.com
17.4a	By Cherubino (Own work) [CC BY-SA 3.0 (http://creativecommons.org/licenses/by-sa/3.0)], via Wikimedia Commons
17.4b	By Nota Bene (Own work) [GFDL (http://www.gnu.org/copyleft/fdl.html) or CC BY 3.0 (http://creativecommons.org/licenses/by/3.0)], via Wikimedia Commons
17.5a	By Ji-elle [CC BY-SA 3.0 (http://creativecommons.org/licenses/by-sa/3.0)], via Wikimedia Commons
17.5b	Licensed under Public domain via Wikimedia Commons by Løken
17.6a	Wikipedia.org [CC BY-SA 3.0 (http://creativecommons.org/licenses/by-sa/3.0)], via Wikimedia Commons
17.6b	www.cnn.com
17.6c	Courtesy and © World Monuments Fund
17.7a	By Urumashima, panoramio.com
17.7b	© Hirsch Bedner Associates

Chapter 18 – Pakistan

18.1	By Shah Zaman Baloch (Own work) [CC-BY-SA-3.0 (http://creativecommons.org/licenses/by-sa/3.0/)], via Wikimedia Commons
18.2a	historypak.com
18.2b	Alakazou1978 at English Wikipedia [CC-BY-SA-3.0 (http://creativecommons.org/licenses/by-sa/3.0/)], via Wikimedia Commons
18.2c	By Ibnazar [CC BY-SA 3.0 (http://creativecommons.org/licenses/by-sa/3.0)], via Wikimedia Commons
18.3	By Bilalhassan88 [CC-BY-SA-3.0 (http://creativecommons.org/licenses/by-sa/3.0/)], via Wikimedia Commons

18.4	No machine-readable author [CC-BY-SA-3.0 (http://creativecommons.org/licenses/by-sa/3.0/)], via Wikimedia Commons
18.5a	By Ilya Varmalov, flickr
18.5b	shughal.com
18.6	historyfiles.co.uk
18.7	By Saqib Qayyum [CC BY-SA 3.0 (http://creativecommons.org/licenses/by-sa/3.0)], via Wikimedia Commons
18.8	By Tmusky [CC BY-SA 3.0 (http://creativecommons.org/licenses/by-sa/3.0)], via Wikimedia Commons

Chapter 19 – Bangladesh

19.1	*The Daily Star*, Bangladesh
19.2	dhakainsider.com
19.3a, b, c	From "Vital Water Graphics 2", Grid Arendal, a centre collaborating with the UN Environmental Program. Cartographer and designer Philippe Rekacewicz, February 2008 (www.grida.no/graphicslib/detail/impact-of-sea-level-rise-in-bangladesh_e7fc)
19.4	By Ranadipam Basu • CC BY-SA 3.0Ranadipam Basu, [CC BY-SA 3.0 http://creativecommons.org/ licenses/by-sa/3.0)], via Wikimedia Commons
19.5a	By Karl Ernst Roehl (ke.roehl AT web.de) (http://www.wefer-roehl.de/photos/bangladesh.htm) [CC-BY-SA-3.0 (http://creativecommons.org/licenses/by-sa/3.0/)], via Wikimedia Commons
19.5b	© By Nahid Sultan and Saiful Aopu, photographers [CC BY-SA 3.0 (http://creativecommons.org/licenses/by-sa/3.0)], via Wikimedia Commons
19.6	By Shahnoor Habib Munmun (Own work) [CC BY 3.0 (http://creativecommons.org/licenses/by/3.0)], via Wikimedia Commons
19.7	By Man (originally posted to Flickr as [1]) [CC BY 2.0 (http://creativecommons.org/licenses/by/2.0)], via Wikimedia Commons

Chapter 20 – Bhutan

20.1	By Douglas J. McLaughlin (Photograph edited by Vassil) (Own work) [CC BY SA-3.0 (http://creativecommons.org/licenses/by-sa/3.0/)], via Wikimedia Commons
20.2	© Christopher J. Flynn [CC BY-SA 3.0 (http://creativecommons.org/licenses/by-sa/3.0)], via Wikimedia Commons
20.3a	By Olivier Lejade (Flickr: P1000481) [CC BY-SA 2.0 (http://creativecommons.org/licenses/by-sa/2.0)], via Wikimedia Commons
20.3b	By C.Michel (Own work) [CC BY SA-2.0 (http://creativecommons.org/licenses/by-sa/2.0/)], via Wikimedia Commons
20.4a, b, c	Courtesy and © World Monuments Fund
20.5a, b	© Helvetas Bhutan

Chapter 21 – Nepal

21.1	By Sd.shova (Own work) [CC BY-SA 4.0 (http://creativecommons.org/licenses/by-sa/4.0)], via Wikimedia Commons
21.2	By Miya.m (Own Work) [CC-BY-SA-3.0 (http://creativecommons.org/licenses/by-sa/3.0/)], via Wikimedia Commons
21.3	Courtesy Kathmandu Valley Preservation Trust
21.4a	Courtesy Mary Slusser
21.4b	Courtesy Mary Slusser
21.4c	angelfire.com
21.5	By Saroj Pandey [CC-BY-SA-3.0 (http://creativecommons.org/licenses/by-sa/3.0/)], via Wikimedia Commons

21.6a, b, c	By kathmandu-valley-temples [CC-BY-SA-3.0 (http://creativecommons.org/licenses/by-sa/3.0/)], via Wikimedia Commons
21.7a, b	By Punya [CC-BY-SA-3.0 (http://creativecommons.org/licenses/by-sa/3.0/)], via Wikimedia Commons
21.7c	By Hilmi Hacaloğlu [Public domain], via Wikimedia Commons

Chapter 22 – Afghanistan

22.1	Bernard Kane
22.2	By Buddha_Bamiyan_1963.jpg: UNESCO/A Lezine;Tsui at de.wikipedia. Later version(s) were uploaded by Liberal Freemason at de.wikipedia. Buddhas_of_Bamiyan4.jpg: Carl Montgomery derivative work: Zaccarias (Buddha_Bamiyan_1963.jpg Buddhas_of_Bamiyan4.jpg) [CC BY-SA 3.0 (http://creativecommons.org/licenses/by-sa/3.0)], from Wikimedia Commons
22.3	By Didier Tais [CC-BY-SA-3.0 (http://creativecommons.org/licenses/by-sa/3.0/)], via Wikimedia Commons
22.4	By David Adamec (Own work) Licensed under Public Domain via Wikimedia Commons
22.5a, b, c	Courtesy National Museum of Afghanistan
22.6	By Daniel Wilkinson (U.S. Department of State) – U.S Embassy Kabul Afghanistan. Licensed under Public Domain via Wikimedia Commons
22.7a	www.akdn.org
22.7b	By Sven Dirks, Wien (Own work) [CC BY-SA 4.0-3.0-2.5-2.0-1.0 (http://creativecommons.org/licenses/by-sa/4.0-3.0-2.5-2.0-1.0)], via Wikimedia Commons
22.7c	IMG 41970 © Aga Khan Trust for Culture – Aga Khan Historic Cities Programme, Nick Danziger, photographer
22.8	Courtesy and © World Monuments Fund

Chapter 23 – Kazakhstan, Kyrgyzstan, Tajikistan, Turkmenistan and Uzbekistan

23.1	Courtesy and © World Monuments Fund
23.2	seasontravel.kz
23.3	By Petar Milošević (Own work) [CC BY-SA 4.0 (http://creativecommons.org/licenses/by-sa/4.0)], via Wikimedia Commons
23.4	By Stomac (Own work) [CC BY 3.0 (http://creativecommons.org/licenses/by/3.0)], via Wikimedia Commons
23.5	No machine-readable author provided. Christian Gawron assumed (based on copyright claims) [CC-BY-SA-3.0 (http://creativecommons.org/licenses/by-sa/3.0/) or CC BY-SA 2.5-2.0-1.0], via Wikimedia Commons
23.6	By Erik Robson (Own work) [CC BY 3.0 (http://creativecommons.org/licenses/by/3.0)], via Wikimedia Commons
23.7	By Bertramz (Own work) [CC BY-SA 3.0 (http://creativecommons.org/licenses/by-sa/3.0)], via Wikimedia Commons
23.8	The original uploader was Atilin at French Wikipedia (transferred from fr.wikipedia to Commons) [CC-BY-SA-3.0 (http://creativecommons.org/licenses/by-sa/3.0/)], via Wikimedia Commons
23.9a	By Ziegler175 (Own work) [CC BY-SA 4.0 (http://creativecommons.org/licenses/by-sa/4.0)], via Wikimedia Commons from Wikimedia Commons
23.9b	By Jean-Pierre Dalbéra from Paris, France [CC BY 2.0 (http://creativecommons.org/licenses/by/2.0)], via Wikimedia Commons
23.10a	OrexCA.com, 1890 photograph by Paul Nadar
23.10b	By Fulvio Spada from Torino, Italy [CC BY SA 2.0 (http://creativecommons.org/licenses/by-sa/2.0)], via Wikimedia Commons

Full-page images

Page 66	Ornamented door, Yunnan. © CEphoto, Uwe Aranas, via Wikimedia Commons
Page 134	Danyang, Korea. By Steve46814 – Own work [CC BY-SA 3.0 (http://creativecommons.org/licenses/by-sa/3.0) or GFDL (http://www.gnu.org/copyleft/fdl.html)], via Wikimedia Commons
Page 188	Laotian corbel. By Hans A. Rosbach - Own work, CC BY-SA 3.0 via Wikimedia Commons
Page 200	Angkor Wat, Cambodia. By Phillip Maiwald (Nikopol) (Own work) [GFDL (http://www.gnu.org/copyleft/fdl.html) or CC BY-SA 3.0 (http://creativecommons.org/licenses/by-sa/3.0)], via Wikimedia Commons
Page 230	Wat Arun, Thailand. Diego Delso, Own work - CC BY-SA 3.0 (http://creativecommons.org/licenses/by-sa/3.0)], via Wikimedia Commons
Page 250	Temple of Literature, Hanoi, Vietnam. By Daderot (Own work) [CC0], via Wikimedia Commons
Page 274	Scaffolded wooden monastery tower, Mandalay, Burma. John H. Stubbs, Author
Page 277	Buddha, Borobodur. By Nappio – Own work, CC -BY-SA-3.0 (http://creativecommons.org/licenses/by-sa/3.0) or GFDL (http://www.gnu.org/copyleft/fdl.html)], via Wikimedia Commons
Page 310	Golden Mosque, Brunei. By Dcubillas - Own work, CC BY-SA 3.0 (http://creativecommons.org/licenses/by-sa/3.0) or GFDL (http://www.gnu.org/copyleft/fdl.html)], via Wikimedia Commons
Page 316	Stonework detail, Bali Tropenmuseum, part of the National Museum of World Cultures [CC BY- SA 3.0 (http://creativecommons.org/licenses/by-sa/3.0)], via Wikimedia Commons
Page 346	Modern Jakarta skyline. Kevin Aurell via Indonesian Wikipedia
Page 349	Stepwell, Abhaneri, India. By Arnie Papp (https://www.flickr.com/photos/apapp/11745536085/) [CC BY 2.0 (http://creativecommons.org/licenses/by/2.0)], via Wikimedia Commons
Page 398	Aerial view, Sigirya, Sri Lanka. By Parakrama, CC BY SA 3.0 (http://creativecommons.org/licenses/by-sa/3.0) via the English language Wikipedia
Page 480	Carved door, Patan, Nepal. By Jean-Pierre Dalbéra from Paris, France, CC BY 2.0 (http://creativecommons.org/licenses/by/2.0)], via Wikimedia Commons

INDEX

adaptation, adaptive re-use 16–17, 93–7, 147–8, 179, 182, 288, 291–2, 328, 412–23, 453, 458, 470–3, 488–95, 511–13

affluence: effect on conservation 18, 514; as a threat to conservation 84

Afghanistan: Ai Khanoum 497, 499, 502–3; Alliance for the Restoration of Cultural Heritage (ARCH) 516; Baghe-Babur/Shahjahan mosque 499, 510–11; Balkh 502, 514–15, 523, 534; Bamiyan Valley 502, 507–8, 517; Bamiyan Buddhas 499, 501–9, 516; Begram/Kapisa 502–3, 523; Ghazni 497, 502, 507, 514–15; Herat 497–9, 502, 505, 507, 511–15; Jam minaret 499, 507–8; Kabul 499, 502–5, 507, 510–11, 514–16; Kabul: decree forbidding new construction 514; Kandahar 502, 505, 514–15; Kunduz 514–15; Lashkar Gah 502–3, Law on the Protection of Historical and Cultural Properties (2004) 507, 515; legislation vaguely worded 514–5; Mahmoud of Ghazni 3, 429, 502; Mes Aynak 505–6, 515–6; Mundigak 502–3; National Development Strategy 515; National Urban Strategy 515; Qala Ikhtyaruddin citadel 511; Shahr-i-Gholghola, Shahr-i-Zohak 508–9; Shahr-i-Mahmoud 505; Shortugai 502

Afghanistani heritage organizations and initiatives: Afghan Cultural Heritage Consulting Organization 506; *Afghanistan: Hidden Treasures from the National Museum, Kabul* 506, 510–12; Archaeological Committee 507; Baghe-Babur Trust 511; Bamiyan Cultural Centre 508; Commission for the Safeguarding and Development of the Old City of Herat 512; *Délégation Archaeologique Française en Afghanistan* 498, 502, 505, 516; Department for the Protection and Rehabilitation of Historical Monuments 507; government agencies for heritage protection 503, 506–7; Institute of Archaeology 503, 506–7; Museum of Islamic Art 507; Museum of Pre-Islamic and Islamic Art 507–9; National Museum 401, 503, 506–7, 514–15; Society for the Preservation of Afghan Cultural Heritage 506; Turquoise Mountain 507, 515

Aga Khan Trust for Culture 7, 18, 22, 281, 297, 353–4, 373–5, 437, 515, 538; Aga Khan Award for Architecture 7, 458, 538; Aga Khan Cultural Service – Pakistan 354, 436; Aga Khan Development Network 7, 375; Aga Khan Herat Old City Rehabilitation Initiative 511–12; Aga Khan Historic Cities Programme 7, 439, 499, 511; Aga Khan Program for Islamic Architecture 7, 281

age threshold for heritage listing: Bangladesh 452; Cambodian elimination of 213; India 368, 371; Sri Lanka 404; Pakistan 432–3

Alexander the Great (of Macedon) 429, 502, 525

American Express Corporation 263, 375

anastylosis 204, 209–11, 240, 252, 260, 280, 319, 322

animals as a threat to heritage *see* environmental and natural threats

antiquarianism 71, 77, 112

apathy as a threat 28, 37, 51, 109, 123, 128, 223, 262, 337, 344, 369, 378, 412, 419, 452, 457

apprenticeship *see* education

APSARA Authority (Authority for Protection and Management of Angkor and the Region of Siem Reap): training programs 22, 171 *see also* Cambodia

archaeological site management, methods: Afghanistan 502–13, 515–17; Angkor concessions 215; Bhutan 475; Brunei 311–13; Central Asia 497–99; China 19; India 360–3, 369–70; Mongolia 158; Nepal 488; Philippines 336; SEAMEO SPAFA initiative 10; Soviet methodological shortfalls in Central Asia 498, 524–6, 531–41 *see also* country listings

archaeology of underwater sites *see* maritime and coastal heritage

architectural styles Art Deco style 359; Bauhaus style 94; Chinese Imperial style 162; Classical Revival style 285; Modern style, Modernism 8, 36, 56, 85, 251, 359; Peranakan Cina style 234, 280, 288, 300; Philippine Baroque 280, 336, 339; *see also* hybridized architecture

arson *see* fire, arson

Arts district, art galleries 148, 182, 383; in China 94–8; Kochi-Muziris Biennial 383; Mumbai Kala Ghoda district 377
ASEAN (Association of Southeast Asian Nations) 8, 172, 225, 281, 347; Cultural Heritage Fund 172
ASI (Archaeological Survey of India) *see* India
Asia, Central: Action Plan for the Implementation of the World Heritage Convention in Central Asia 531; regional overview 497–9; promising contemporary developments 541
Asia, East: regional overview 33–37; promising contemporary developments 167
Asia, South: regional overview 351–4; promising contemporary developments 494–5
Asia, Southeast: regional overview 169–72, 279–81; promising contemporary developments 275–6, 347–8
Asian Cultural Council 20
Asian Development Bank 8, 11, 240, 461
Asian Infrastructure Investment Bank 11, 167
ateliers *see* crafts training
Athens Charter *see* Charters, Conventions, Declarations and Principles
auction houses 172; art trafficking by 206–8
Australia 6, 20, 83, 149, 184, 214, 266, 354; Australian Heritage Commission 36, 83, 370; Darwin Military Museum 343
Austria 254, 488
authenticity 39, 69, 81, 171, 275, 363, 410; Asian vs. Western approaches to 23–5, 27, 42, 50, 81, 171; definition of 34–5, 43, 46; Nara Conference on, 81–2; *see also* Nara Document on Authenticity

Bacon, Edmund 86
Baig, Amita 370
Bangkok Charter *see* Charters, Conventions, Declarations and Principles
Bangladesh 19, 182, 352, 355, 362, 364, 431, 449–462; Ahsan Manzil palace 452, 457–8; Antiquities Act of 1968 452–3; Act No. XIV (1976) 452; Article 24, Constitution (1971) 452; Bagerhat 455, 460–462; Baro Bari 451; Chittagong Chummery House 452; Conservation and Rehabilitation of Historical and Cultural Heritage (National Building Code) (2012) 452–3; Dhaka/Dacca 450–3, 455, 457–8; Detailed Area Plan (Dhaka) 454; Gaur 450, 452; government agencies for heritage protection 452, 460, 462; Islam, Muzharul 459; Islam, Taimur 452; Jatiyo Sangsad Bhaban/National Assembly building 458–9; Lalbagh fort 451; Lalmai-Mainanati monuments 455; legislative weakness 451; Mahasthangarh, 460–2; National Museum 457–8, Old Dhaka 451, 453; Old Dhaka Protection Zone 454; Paharpur vihara 352, 450, 452, 460–1; Paharpur-Bagerhat International Safeguard campaign 461; Urban Study Group 451, 454, 462 *see also* Legislation – British Raj
Bartholomew, Peter 136–7
Bawa, Jeffrey 147
Belgium 266
Bell, Henry Charles Purvis 402, 416
Beyer, Henry Otley 336
Bhutan 5, 15, 352–4, 454, 467–76, 494; Bhutan 2020: A Vision for Peace, Prosperity and Happiness 475; Bhutan Trust Fund 353, 471; Cultural Trust Fund (Bhutan) 471; Drametse Lhakhang 473; Drapham Dzong 473; Five Year Master Plan 473, 475; Government agencies for heritage protection 471, 473; Heritage Sites Bill (2015) 473; King Jigme Singye Wangchuck 468; Namgyal, Ngawang 469; National Conservation Laboratory 471; National Forest Policy 473; National Museum/Paro Dzong 470; National survey 471, 475; Paro Taktsang/Tiger's Nest monastery 468; Phajoding 473; Punakha dzong 471–2; Semtokha Dzong 470; shortfalls in legislative coverage 473; Trashichho Dzong 470; Trashigang dzong 471, 473; National Conservation laboratory 471; Wangduechhoeling Palace 473
biodeterioration, biological growth as a threat to heritage 13, 258, 298, 319, 323, 366, 451–2, 460, 471; dégagement at Angkor 204, 211; honoring changes over time 80; *see also* environmental and natural threats
Boito, Camilo 236
Borneo *see* Malaysia
Bosnia and Herzegovina: Mostar, Stari Most/Old Bridge 509
Brearley Architects + Urbanists 97
brick 497–8; in Afghanistan 505, 511; in Bangladesh 452, 457–60; in India 357, 366, 380–1; in Laos 192, 204, 237; in Myanmar 158, 177, 179, 182; in Nepal 483, 488–9; in Pakistan 429, 439–41; in Soviet Central Asia 525–7, 532–41, 547; in Sri Lanka 409; in Vietnam 260
British Raj: British East India Company 283, 358, 361; Curzon, Lord George Nathaniel 176, 362–3, 450; "Great Game" era 523; Hastings, Warren 361; Lytton, Lord 361; *Preservation of National Monuments in India* 361; *see also* Colonial period, Britain, Legislation –British Raj
Bronze Age sites 158, 163, 251, 515, 534 *see also* Prehistoric sites, cultures
Brunei Darussalam 275, 279, 311–15; Abana Rocks Coral Reef Formation 313; Antiquities and Treasure Trove Enactment 311; Bandar Seri Begawan 311–13; Brunei Arts & Handicrafts Training Center 311; Bubungan Dua Belas/House of Twelve Roofs 311; Government agencies for heritage protection 311; Kampong Ayer/Water Village 280, 313–14, 348; Kota Batu 311, 313; National Archives 311; Omar Ali Saifuddin mosque 311; Tasek Merimbun Park 313 ; Serasa, The Industrial Heritage of Colliery 313–14
Brunelleschi, Filippo 219
Buddhist influences on conservation 4, 24, 35, 43, 101–2, 135, 318; Foundation for the Preservation of the Mahayana Tradition 155; Sangha craft training program 171, 192, 275; Sri Lankan Restoration Committees 403; Thai Department of Religious Affairs 238 *see also* religious merit
Buddhist temples, shrines *see* country site listings
buffer zones, preservation zones 353, 368–9, 377, 404, 432, 461; in Bagan 179; Bangladesh lack of 457; Indian "Eco Sensitive Zones" 368; Lao encroachment in 193; Laotian monastery zones 191, 193; in Lijiang 109; in Malaysia 300; in Macau 100; in Shanghai 93; Singapore lack of focus on 291; Sri Lankan "Sacred Areas" 404, 407, 409; Taj Trapezium Zone 366, 368
Burma: Archaeological Survey of Burma (Raj era) 176; *see also* legislation – British Raj, Myanmar
Burra Charter (The Australia ICOMOS Charter for Places of Cultural Significance) *see* Charters, Conventions, Declarations and Principles

calligraphy 130
Cambodia 1, 6, 10, 28, 169–71, 189–90, 201–226, 234–5, 244, 251–3, 255, 288, 318, 400; Ang Chan 204, 208–9; Angkor Archaeological Park 11, 12, 19, 24, 28, 58, 147, 169–72, 176, 193, 195, 201–225, 240, 251–2, 275–6, 280, 297, 318–19, 322, 370; Angkor Wat 2, 6, 7, 147, 201–2, 217–18; Churning of the Sea of Milk gallery 217–18; Banteay Chhmar 8, Banteay Srei 207, 211, 213; Baphuon 211; Bayon library 58, 147, 204, 222; Evans, Damian 216; Fletcher, Roland 216; Government agencies for heritage protection 213–15; Khmer empire, art 1, 3, 251; Molyvann, H.E. Vann 6, 147, 223–4; National Museum 204–6, 211; National Olympic Sports Stadium 223–4; Phnom Bakheng 208, 211, 217; Phnom Penh 13, 147, 169, 201–2, 207, 222; Planning: Implementation challenges 225; Preah Khan 19, 215, 217; Preah Vihear 225; Siem Reap 171, 209; Sihanouk, Prince Norodom 201, 212–4Ta Prohm 211; Ta Som 215, 217; Tourism Management Plan (Angkor) 12, 213; Tuol Sleng Genocide Museum 263–4; Yasodharapura 208; Zoning and Environmental Management Project (Siem Reap) 213–14 *see also* Legislation – Cambodia

Cambodian heritage organizations and initiatives: Angkor International Coordinating Committee 214, 217; Angkor National Museum 206; Angkor Zoning and Environmental Management Project 213–4; Applied Research Center for Archaeology and Fine Arts (ARCAFA) 21; APSARA Authority (Authority for Protection and Management of Angkor and the Region of Siem Reap) 6, 22, 171, 213–15; Center for Khmer Studies 172, 215, 223; *Conservation d'Angkor* 209, 214; German Apsara Conservation Project (GACP) 22, 214–15; Greater Angkor Project 208, 216–7; Japanese Team for Safeguarding Angkor (JSA) 22, 214; Royal Angkor Foundation 171, 214, 216

Canada 254, 266
Canning, Earl 361
capacity building 15–22, 170–2, 175, 195, 280, 353; in Afghanistan 507–8, 511; in Bangladesh 449, 461–2; in Cambodia 19–22, 172, 215–17in Central Asia 498–501, 526, 533–4; in India 363–370; in Indonesia 321; in Laos 172, 195; in Myanmar 184; in Nepal 485–488; in Pakistan 442–3; in Sri Lanka 405; in Thailand 172; in Vietnam 260–3; *see also* crafts training and education
cardinal direction, importance of *see* natural forces, harmony with
caves 2, 74, 136, 158, 163, 335–7, 352, 255, 357, 362, 366, 405–7 *see also* frescoes, petroglyphs, and country site listings
cement, hard *see* concrete, hard cement
cemeteries *see* tombs, mausolea
Central Asia *see* Asia, Central
Ceylon: Archaeological Survey of Ceylon (British Raj) 407, 416; Burrows, Stephen Montagu 402; Royal Asiatic Society, Ceylon branch 402; *see also* Sri Lanka
Chainani, Shyam 368
Chapagain, Neel Kamal 6
Chapman, William R. 18–22, 146–7, 203
Charters, Conventions, Declarations and Principles 25–6; Aotearoa Charter 26; Athens Charter 46, 69, 81, 83; ASEAN Declaration on Cultural Heritage 26; Bangkok Charter 171, 239; Burra Charter 25–6, 46, 69, 83, 371, 383, 484; China Principles 8, 19, 25–6, 36, 46, 68, 81–2, 84, 137, 171, 240; ICOMOS International Cultural Tourism Charter – Managing Tourism as Places of Heritage Significance 26; Ename charter for the Interpretation of. Cultural Heritage Sites26; Hague Convention 19, 212, 214, 225; Hội An Protocols for Best Conservation Practice in Asia 9, 25–6, 275; ICOMOS charter on the Interpretation and Presentation of Cultural Heritage Sites 26; Indonesian Charter for Heritage Conservation 26, 325, 327; INTACH Charter 23, 26, 55, 353, 355–6, 371–2, 389, 494; Kyoto Declaration on the Protection of Cultural Properties, Historical Areas and their Settings from Loss in Disasters, 26; Lahore Principles 353, 432–2; Lausanne charter 26; Manifesto of Eindhoven 8; Nara Document on Authenticity 19, 25–6, 36, 39, 46, 61, 69, 137, 171, 239, 491; Seoul Declaration on Tourism in Asia's Historic Towns and Areas 9, 26; Suzhou Declaration of International Co-operation for Safeguarding of Historic Cities 26; Taipei Declaration for Asian Industrial Heritage 26; UNESCO Charter on Built Vernacular Heritage 26; UNESCO Convention for the Safeguarding of the Intangible Cultural Heritage 15, 17, 26–7, 39, 146, 244, 268, 313; UNESCO Convention on the Means of Prohibiting and Preventing the Illicit Import, Export and Transfer of Ownership of Cultural Property 214–15; UNESCO Convention on the Protection of Underwater Cultural Heritage 171, 254, 275; UNESCO Declaration Concerning the Intentional Destruction of Cultural Heritage 515; UNESCO General Conference Recommendation on Historic Urban Landscape 268; Valletta Principles for Safeguarding and Management of Historic Cities, Towns and Urban Areas, 26; Venice charter 19, 25–6, 36, 42, 46, 69, 81, 83, 137, 213, 239, 371, 432, 484, 509, 536; Vienna Memorandum on World Heritage and Contemporary Architecture – Managing the Historic Urban Landscape 26; World Heritage Convention World Heritage Convention 11, 15, 25–6, 68, 139, 213–4, 352, 354, 399, 415, 481, 498; Xi'an Declaration on the Conservation of the Setting of Heritage Structures, Sites and Areas 9, 109, 137; Yamato Declaration on Integrated Approaches for Safeguarding Tangible and Intangible Cultural Heritage, 26

Cheek, Wesley 59–60
China 2, 3, 5, 6, 12–13, 15, 18–19, 27–8, 33–7, 67–113, 135, 137, 147, 169, 172, 189, 251, 253, 266, 268, 279, 400, 418, 427, 454, 470–1, 515, 526, 529–31; Anhui 111–12; Anyang 72; Bao'ensi/Temple of Gratitude 77; Beacon Tower 74; Beijing 34–5, 75–9, 84–95, 142, 149, 167; Bethanie Hall 93; Caochandi artist studios 149; Catholic Church of the Immaculate Conception 148; Central Museum 125; Central police Station Compound 96; Chang'an 41, 73; Chengde Mountain Resort and temples 83; Chengdu 110; Chinese Academy of Art 149; Chongqing 342; Foguang Temple 8; Forbidden City 2, 11, 35, 75, 77, 79, 85, 89–90; Grand Canal 2, 33, 73; Great Wall 2, 5, 10, 33, 72, 78, 105–7; Guangzhou/Canton 34, 342; Guia Hill 100–1; Gulou/Drum Tower 88; Hong Kong 13,

34, 84, 93–6; Hong Kong Arts Development Council 94; Hong Kong 93 Historic District; Hong Kong Jockey Club 94, 96; Huang He Lou/Yellow Crane Tower 81; Huaqing Hot Springs 74; Huang Yi 77; Hutong 36–7, 87, 142, 146; *Illustrated Principles for the Conservation of Heritage Sites in China* 83; Inner Mongolia 85, 101; International Arts Plaza 798 Art Zone/Dashanzi Art District 94–5; Jianfu Gong/Palace of Established Happiness 81, 89; Jockey Club Creative Arts Center 94, 96; Juanqinzhai/Studio of Exhaustion from Diligent Service 89–90; Kaifeng/Bianliang 74; Kashgar 15, 530; Kunming 3; Liang Sicheng 6, 23, 35, 79–80, 85; Liu Dunzhen 79; Lijiang 8, 11, 107–113; Long Museum West Bund 96; Lung, David 20, 93; Macau 84, 95, 98–100; Maosi Ecological Demonstration Primary School 149; Meridian Gate Exhibition 148; Mogao caves 2, 68, 74–5, 83, 85; Museum of Contemporary Art 149; M50 Creative Park/Chunming Slub Mill 95; Nanking 342; Nanjing 74; Nanjing Massacre Memorial 264; National inventory 55, 79; Ningbo History Museum 149; Ohel Rachel synagogue 93; Olympic National Stadium 149; Palace Museum 90, 125; Pingyao 85; PMQ Art Hub 96–7; Portuguese School 149; Provincial Museum of Honan 125; Pudong 91; Qufu, Temple of Confucius 35, 69–70; St. Paul's Church 98–9; Shanghai 28, 34, 37, 85, 91–3, 148, 341; Shanghai Bund 91–2; Shanghai Contemporary Art Museum/Power Station of Art 94, 96; Shanghai Sculpture Space/Redtown Culture & Art Community 95, 97; Shaxi 85, 107–113; Shikumen housing 92–3, 148; Shuxiang 83; Sichuan circular house 149; Suzhou Classical gardens 112; Suzhou River Warehouse 148; Temple of Heaven 75–78; Three Gorges Dam, 15; Today Art Museum 95; Tulou 34, 82, 85; Wanchai 93; Wang Qijun 110; West Lake Historic District 85; Whitfield barracks 148; Wuzhen 85; Xi'an: Qin Shihuangdi tomb/terra cotta warriors 34, 72, 75, 530; Xiannongtan/Temple of Agriculture 77, 88; Xidi 111–12; Xinjiang 33, 37, 85; Yau Ma Tei theater 93; Yihe Yuan/Summer Palace 68; Yuanming Yuan/Old Summer Palace 22, 35, 78, 95; Yuhu Primary School 148; Ye Rutang 110; *Yingzao fashi* 74, 79–80; Yuz Museum 96; Zhang Shule; 93 Zhi Qiqian 79; Zhonglu/Bell Tower 88; *Zhou Li* 72, 75 *see also* Legislation – China and Legislation – Taiwan

Chinese dynasties: Han 73, 523; Ming 75–8, 86, 105; Qin 2, 33; Qing 3, 75–7, 86, 112, 127, 153; Shang 72; Song 74, 416; Sui 33; Tang 74; Yin 125; Yuan 153; Zhou 72, 105, 125

Chinese heritage initiatives, organizations: Architectural Society of China 110; China Heritage Fund 81, 89; China Museums Association 94; Chinese Government Team for Safeguarding Angkor 214; Chinese Modern Architectural History Society 94; Dunhuang Research Academy 83; Friends of the Great Wall 107; Great Wall Society 107; Ju'er Hutong Project 88; Leadership Conference on Conservancy and Development 110; *One Belt, One Road* program 3, 167; Ruan Yisan Heritage Foundation 93; Shanghai Discovery and Documentation Society 93; Shaxi Rehabilitation Project 109; Society for the Study of Chinese Architecture 79–80; Yunnan Provincial Association of Cultural Exchanges with Foreign Countries 110

Chinese government agencies for heritage protection 25, 69, 83, 85, 88, 90, 93, 107, 110, 148, 161–2

Chinese Planning – China: Beijing General Development Plan 84, 86, 88; Chinese imperial planning 72–4, 77, 219; Lijiang Old Town Protection Plan 109; Master Plan, Great Wall 107; Mogao Master Plan, 83; Shang dynastic planning 72; Soviet-style planning in China 83, 86;

China Principles (Conservation and Management Principles of Cultural Heritage Sites in China) *see* Charters, Conventions, Declarations and Principles

Chisholm, Robert 357

Christianity, influences from 383, 399

Christian sites 2, 85, 339–40, 384, 529

church, cathedrals *see* country site listings

classification: Architectural Reserves (Uzbekistan) 525; Important Cultural Properties and National Cultural Treasures (Philippines) 344; only monumental sites (Afghanistan) 514; weak national protection (Pakistan) 356; in Singapore 289

Clément, Paul 20

Clavan, Benjamin 94–5

Cleworth, Alexandra 157–8

climate, climate change 13, 280–1, 353, 415, 454–6; Climate Adaptation Plan (Maldives) 415; Green Climate Trust Fund (S Korea) 141; Intergovernmental Panel on Climate Change 454; UN Conference on Climate Change 416; UN report, *Climate Change 2014: Impacts, Adaptation and Vulnerability* 454; *see also* environmental and natural threats

Cole, Major H.H. 361

Colonial period – British 2, 19, 91, 125, 170, 173, 176–82, 235, 279–80, 283, 292, 299, 317, 351, 355, 359–60, 372, 383, 402–4, 410, 415–6, 430–2, 435–6, 442, 449–52, 467, 469; architecture of 285; 384–5; influence on Indian conservation 360–3

Colonial period – Dutch 12, 19, 125, 176, 279, 297, 317, 329, 347, 383, 401, 410, 415–6; Dutch East India Company 127, 279, 318 Dutch East Indies: first survey of ancient structures 320

Colonial period – European 3, 6, 23, 28, 78, 169, 172, 190–1, 265, 280, 302, 344, 352–3, 355, 357, 359, 399, 401–4;

Colonial period – French 19, 91, 176, 189, 191, 194, 201, 222–3, 225, 235, 251–8, 260–1, 289, 360; architecture of 288–9

Colonial period – Italian 91

Colonial period – Japan 125, 128, 136

Colonial period, lack of: in Bhutan 475; in Thailand 231, 235

Colonial period – Portuguese 98, 297, 317, 327–8, 360, 383, 400–1, 410, 415–6

Colonial period – Spanish 125, 279, 329, 336; architecture of 339

Colonial period – USA 91, 279, 336, 338

color, importance of *see* natural forces, harmony with

Collins, Darryl 148

conjecture in restoration: in Ayutthaya 235; in Nepal 484; in Central Asia 498, 536; Restoration committees in Sri Lanka 403; in Samarkand 539

Conventions *see* Charters, Conventions, Declarations and Principles

community-based conservation *see* local involvement in conservation

concrete, hard cement 59, 147, 285, 439, 457; at Angkor 204; at Central Asian sites 525, 528, 532, 539; at Nagoya castle 501; problematic use of 171, 179, 194, 214, 313, 319, 373
Confucian beliefs, sites 4, 33, 35, 69–70, 72, 135, 169, 251
conservation science *see* research institutes, technology
conservation and construction handbooks, treatises 80; *Building Conservation in Nepal: A Handbook of Principles and Techniques* 483; *Conservation of Ancient Monuments* (Marshall) (India) 176, 351, 363–4; *Conservation Manual: A Handbook for the Use of Archaeological Officers and Others Entrusted with the Care of Ancient Monuments* (Marshall) (India) 176, 363–4, 371; *Guidelines for Conservation: A Technical Manual* (Feilden) 371; *Guidelines for Managing Post-Disaster Conservation of Heritage Buildings. Case Study: Padang* (Indonesia) 323; *Illustrated Principles for the Construction of Heritage Sites in China* 83; *Manasara* (India) 360; *Preservation of National Monuments in India* (Raj) 361; *Prima Carta del Restauro* (Boito) 236; *Secretary of the Interior's Standards for Rehabilitation* (USA) 83, 484; *Tantras, agamas, samhitas, vastushastras* (India) 360; *Yingzao fashi* (China) 74, 79–80; *Zhou Li* (China) 72, 75, 80
construction techniques, traditional 5, 14, 17, 28, 34–5, 39, 42, 45, 53, 55, 299, 352; being lost 136, 161, 451; importance to authenticity 20, 43, 81; incentivized 475; revival of 481–6, 506–7; *see also* craftsmen, master
contextual design 146–7
contextual heritage 147; unimportance of: to Indian planners 370; to Soviet planners 498, 537–40
contextual heritage: importance of 28, 104, 381–4; 389, 494
continuity of culture or use, importance of 5, 81, 113, 255, 473, 481, 537
copying as a learning method (linmo) 72
Correa, Charles 359
CRA-Terre EAG 499, 525, 533–4
crafts, crafts training 16–18, 22, 352, 270, 375, 436; in Afghanistan 506–7, 510–11, 513; in Bali 324; in Bhutan 468–73; at Borobodur 21; Brunei Arts & Handicrafts Training Center 311; caste, effect on 388; in China 89–90; in India 363, 370 Laotian Sangha program 171, 192, 275; Luang Prabang School of Fine Arts, 192; in Mongolia 161, 175; in Nepal 481–6; Turquoise Mountain Foundation 507; in Uzbekistan 537; in Vietnam 256, 258, 260, 268
craftsmen, master: Department of Court Craftsmen (Thailand) 237; Living National Treasure (*boyuja, Ingan munhwajae*) (South Korea) 140, 147; Living National Treasure (Japan) 36, 39, 46, 53, 371; *Raj mistris* (India) 353, 371; Shilpkars (India) 388; *Tambat* community (India) 371; *see also* Construction techniques, traditional
cultural continuity, importance of 3, 71, 158, 169, 406, 475
cultural discontinuity: in Laos 192; in Soviet Central Asia 525–7;
cultural landscapes 12, 107–12, 142, 154–7, 171, 189, 239–40, 340, 353, 357; Balinese *subak* system 280, 324; Bhutan-Swiss workshop 4473, 476; Japanese The Landscape Act 49; importance in India 381–4; in Kyrgyzstan 529–30; in Vietnam 256–8; *pungsu* 135–6; Xi'an Declaration 109, 137; Zenkoku Rekishiteki Fudo Hozon Renmei/Federation for the Preservation of Historic Landscapes 52 *see also* country site listings, gardens and parks, urban landscapes
cultural promotion as a means of defense (Bhutan) 475
CyArk 222
cyclones 450, 455

dams 3, 13, 68, 193, 455; Three Gorges 15, 105–7; Naranda Gedige 403 *see also* water as a threat
Davis, Tess 206–8
Declarations *see* Charters, Conventions, Declarations and Principles
de-listing 436
Democratic People's Republic of Korea *see* Korea, North
demolition, damage: legislative protection against: in India 362; in Pakistan 435; in Philippines 344
development pressures 12, 15, 36, 68, 84–105, 123, 136, 140, 171, 193, 231, 237, 242, 254, 261, 286–8, 304, in Bali 324; in India 377, 355; in Laos 191, 193, 198; in Macau 99–101; in Sri Lanka 410–2; *see also* urbanization
difficult legacies *see* Sites of Conscience
digital documentation *see* technology
disaster management *see* risk management
DOCOMOMO (International Working Party for the Documentation and Conservation of Buildings, Sites and Neighborhoods of the Modern Movement) 8; DOCOMOMO Japan 36, 56
Douglas, Lake 129–30
Dupree, Louis 502
Dupree, Nancy Hatch 506, 517
Dutch New Guinea *see* West Papua province, Indonesia

earthen structures/earthworks 2, 82, 357, 380–1, 455, 467; in Central Asia 498–9, 525–6, 530–1; in Pakistan 357, 428–41; restoration vs. reconstruction 536
earthquake *see* environmental and natural threats
earthquake-proof design 340
East Asia *see* Asia, East
East Timor/Timor-Leste 279, 327–8; Baucau 328–9, Dili 328; government agencies for heritage protection 328
Eastern vs. Western conservation approaches 19, 23–4, 27, 36, 69, 71, 158, 371; continuity of spirit 69; restoration vs. reconstruction 536; *see also* Authenticity
ecology, ecological conservation 4, 10–11, 105, 280, 473; environmental damage, Central Asia 515–17, 524
education, academic – Asia, Central: Kabul University (Afghanistan) 20, 507; State University (Turkmenistan) 534
education, academic – Asia, East 18–22; Academica Sinica (Taiwan) 20; Beijing University of Civil Engineering (China) 20; Chinese University of Hong Kong (China) 20; Hangzhou University (China) 20; Hong Kong Baptist University 20; Hong Kong University 20, 22; Hyupsung University (South Korea) 20; Korea National University of Cultural Heritage (South Korea) 20, 141; Kyoto University (Japan) 20; Kyushu University (Japan) 20; Mongolian University of Science and Technology 20; Peking University

(China) 19; Ritsumeikan University, Institute for Disaster Mitigation of Urban Cultural Heritage (Japan) 20, 53; Saitama University (Japan) 533; Seoul National University (South Korea) 21; Showa Women's University (Japan) 22; Sophia University (Japan) 20, 214–15; South East University (China) 20, 22; Tongji University (China) 10, 20; Tokyo Institute of Technology 22; Tokyo University (Japan) 47; Tokyo University of the Arts 9, 20, 53; Tsinghua University (China) 22, 83; Tsukuba University (Japan) 20, 53; University of Hong Kong 94; University of Science and Technology (Mongolia) 161; University of Tokyo 20, 53; Waseda University (Japan) 53; Xi'an University 20; Zhejiang University (China) 20

education, academic – Asia, South: Bangladesh University of Engineering and Technology 21; Beaconhouse National University (Pakistan) 21; Centre of Environmental Planning and Technology University (India) 21; Government College of Architecture (India) 21; Imperial University (Pakistan) 21; Indian Institute of Technology 21; Indus Valley School of Art and Architecture (Pakistan) 21; Institute of Archaeology (India) 20, 370; MBS School of Planning and Architecture (India) 21; National College of Arts (Pakistan) 21; National University of Science and Technology (Pakistan) 21; Peshawar University (Pakistan) 20, 429; Rajshahi University of Engineering and Technology (Bangladesh) 21; School of Planning and Architecture (India) 379; Sir J.J. School of Architecture (India) 20–1; Tribhuvan University (Nepal) 22; University of Baroda (India) 21; University of Engineering and Technology (Pakistan) 428; University of Gujrat (Pakistan) 21; University of Kelaniya (Sri Lanka) 22, 405, 413; University of Moratuwa (Sri Lanka) 22, 406; University of Peshawar (Pakistan) 442

education, academic – Asia, Southeast: Asian Academy for Heritage Management (Thailand) 20, 22; Burapha University (Thailand) 21; Chiang Mai University (Thailand) 20, 232–3; Chulalongkorn University, Department of Architecture and Institute of Thai Study (Thailand) 21–2, 244; Diponegoro University (Indonesia) 21; Gadja Mada University (Indonesia) 21–2; Hanoi Architectural University (Viet Nam) 21–2; Ho Chi Minh University (Vietnam) 21; Institut Teknologi Bandung (Indonesia) 21; Maldives National University 20; National University of Laos 21; National University of Singapore 21, 148; Padjadjaran University (Indonesia) 21; Royal University of Fine Arts (Cambodia) 20–23; Saint Louis University (Philippines) 21; Silpakorn University, (Thailand) 21–2, 244; Universitas Indonesia 21; Universiti Teknologi MARA (Malaysia) 21–2; University of Fine Arts (Cambodia) 215; University of Malaysia 21; University of the Philippines 21, 336; University of Phnom Penh (Cambodia) 21; University of Santo Tomas (Philippines) 21–2

education, academic – non-Asian: Architectural Association (UK) 20; Columbia University (USA) 20, Cornell University (USA) 20; Deakin University (Australia) 20, 22, 254; Ecole Nationale Supérieure d'Architecture-Belleville (France)20; Harvard University (USA) 7, 20; Massachusetts Institute of Technology (USA) 20; National University (Australia) 20, 22; Polytechnic University (Italy) 20, 260; University of Applied Arts (Austria) 370; University of Arizona (USA) 507; University of Bonn (Germany) 159; University of California, Berkeley (USA) 20; University of Hawai'i (USA) 20; University of Melbourne (Australia) 20, 22; University of Pennsylvania (USA) 20; University Polytechnic of Milan (Italy) 10; University of Sydney (Australia) 20, 208, 214; University of York (UK) 20

education, technical *see* research institutes

EFEO (École française d'Extrême-Orient) 6, 19, 170, 177, 190, 195–6, 209, 211–12, 214–16, 237–40, 252, 320; Colani, Madeleine 196

Egypt 208; Abu Simbel temples 58; Aswan High Dam, 105; pyramids 218

Ename Charter for the Interpretation of Cultural Heritage Sites *see* Charters, Conventions, Declarations and Principles

endangered sites, lists of: Global Heritage Fund list 184; ICOMOS Heritage@Risk 533; UNESCO Representative and Urgent Safeguarding list 56, 281; UNESCO World Heritage in Danger list 193, 331, 347, 379, 436, 461, 499; World Monuments Fund Watch List (*see* World Monuments Fund)

Engelhardt, Richard 22

environmental and natural threats 105, 172, 204, 305, 353, 498; Brundtland Report: *Our Common Future: Report on the UN World Commission on the Environment 288*; cyclones 450, 455; earthquake 11–14, 22, 36, 49, 53, 59–60, 107, 110, 171, 176, 185, 281, 318, 323, 330, 353, 427, 439, 470, 473, 482–3, 487–9, 499, 525, 528, 539; fire, arson 14, 36, 43, 143, 145, 179, 285, 471; tornados 458; tsunami 13, 36, 59–60, 281, 399, 401, 405, 410, 415; typhoon 56, 281, 341, 353, volcanoes 13, 33, 279, 281, 318, 330; Zoning and Environmental Management Project (Siem Reap) 213–14; *see also* climate change, water as a threat

epigraphy 6, 252, 361, 369, 407

erosion *see* water as a threat to built heritage

van Erp, Theodore 215, 280, 318

Espino, Nilson Ariel 306

Evans, Damian 216

explorers, exploration 203: de Almeida, Lorenzo 401; French Mekong Expedition 219; Delaporte, Louis 219; da Gama, Vasco 361; Ibn Battuta 416; Marco Polo 75, 125; Mekong Expedition 194; Magellan, Ferdinand 336; Magellan-Eclano Expedition 23; Stein, Marc Aurel 68

export controls *see* looting, legislation against

façadism 283

fantasy, historical 94, 100, 109

Feilden, Bernard 371

feng shui see natural forces

Fenollosa, Ernest Francisco 47

Finer, Jacques 109

fire, arson *see* environmental and natural threats

Fletcher, Roland 216

flooding *see* water as a threat

folkways, folk art 36, 47, 52, 130, 136, 140, 163, 324, 336; 369; as a tourist draw 128, 130, 330; China National Folk Culture Protection project 55

fortifications *see* military and defense sites

Foundations: American Express Corporation Foundation 240, 375; American Himalayan Foundation 354, 491; Bhutan Foundation 473; Calouste Gulbenkian Foundation 98; Hirayama Trust 9; Lerici Foundation/Fondazione Ing. Carlo Maurillo Lerici 10, 195, 260; Prince Claus Foundation 404; Royal Angkor Foundation 171; Toyota Foundation 22; *see also* country listings
France 172, 190–3, 214, 252, 254, 266, 484, 502–3, 508; CRA-Terre EAG 499, 525, 533–4; Duroiselle, Charles 176; Hanoi planning assistance 254, 262; Musée Guimet 204; *Patrimoine sans Frontières* 10, 18
frescoes, murals, wall paintings: in China 74–5; Getty Conservation Institute focus on 8, 530; in India 366, 380; in Laos 194; in Sri Lanka 402, 405–7; in Tajikistan 532

gardens and parks: Baghe Babur 510–12; as an expression of a time, place 129–30; in India 359, 369; in Papua province 2, 329; in Sri Lanka 401, 407; Suzhou classical garden 112; Thai network of, 233 *see also* Cultural landscapes and country site listings
genus loci (spirit of place) 71; versus architectural detail conservation 69
gentrification *see* urbanization
Genghis Khan/Chinggis Khan 160, 163, 502, 537
geomancy *see* natural forces
Geographic Positioning Systems (GPS) 107, 214, 373
ger/khoroos 34, 163–4
Germany 266, 484–6, 503; Bhaktapur Development Project of the Federal Republic of Germany 485; German Apsara Conservation Project (GACP) 22, 214–15; German Archaeological Institute 512; German Conservation, Restoration and Education Project 258; German World Heritage Foundation 159
Getty Conservation Institute 7, 19, 22, 36, 83, 172, 195, 370, 530
Global Heritage Fund 8, 11, 184, 195
global warming *see* climate change
globalization: as a catalyst for action 55; as an influence on cultural identity 2, 3, 11, 12, 24, 28, 266, 347, 467 *see also* explorers, exploration
governmental inaction or resistance to heritage conservation: in China 101–2, 105; in Malaysia 302; in Bangladesh 453
Great Britain *see* United Kingdom
Great Game 502
Greco-Bactrian sites 503
Greco-Buddhist sites 503
Groslier, Bernard-Philippe 212, 240
Gutschow, Niels 43

Hague Convention (Convention for the Protection of Cultural Property in the Event of Armed Conflict *see* Charters, Conventions, Declarations
handbooks *see* construction, conservation handbooks
Hanoks 36, 136, 142
Harappan civilization 357, 502
Haveli 358–9, 378
heritage, natural *see* cultural landscapes
"heritage diplomacy" 24
Heritage Routes, Walks: Ahmedabad: *Krantidarshan Padyatra* /Freedom Walk 378–9; Darjeeling Himalayan Railway 30; Frankincense Route, Oman 530; Great Wall 530; Hadrian's Wall (England) 530; Heritage Route, Delhi 375–6; ICOMOS International Scientific Committee on Cultural Routes (CIIC) 530; Royal Route, Lahore 437; Santiago de Compostela (Spain) 530; *see also* Silk Road
Hindu temples, shrines *see* country site listings
Hinduism, influences on conservation 204, 251, 357, 360, 366, 388, 403, 433; *Brithat Samhita* 360; Caste system 5, 388; *Jiirnoddharana* 351; *Shilpa Prakasha* 360
Hirayama Trust 9
Historic Districts 39, 91; *see also* country listings
Hội An Protocols for Best Conservation Practice in Asia *see* Charters, Conventions, Declarations and
hotels 78, 147–8, 183–4, 194, 263, 288, 324–5, 417; Aureum Palace (Myanmar) 178; Tea Factory Hotel (Sri Lanka) 413
Hungary 214; Royal Angkor Foundation 214, 216
Hutong 36–7, 87, 142, 146; Ju'er Hutong Project 88
hybridized architecture 2, 85, 92, 136, 201, 232–3, 280, 317, 328, 337–9; European/Asian 141, 235, 262, 301, 311, 410; Indo Saracenic 355, 357–8, 377, 458; pagoda form 27, 34, 74; Peranakan 234, 280, 288, 300; Philippine Baroque 280, 336, 339; Tibetan architecture in Mongolia 155–6

I Ching philosophy *see* Natural forces, harmony with
ICCROM (International Centre for the Restoration and Conservation of Cultural Property) 9, 26, 170–1, 176, 370, 455, 489; Asian Academy for Heritage Management 22; CollAsia program 9, TaNei Cultural Resource Management workshop 22, 217
ICOMOS (International Council on Museums and Sites) 7, 9–10, 18, 25–6, 33, 83, 170, 297, 351, 455, 489, 530; ICOMOS Australia 26; ICOMOS China 25–6, 69, 82–3, 109; ICOMOS Germany 507, 509; ICOMOS India 456; ICOMOS Indonesia 26, 325; ICOMOS Japan 26; ICOMOS Kazakhstan 498; ICOMOS Kyrgyzstan 498; ICOMOS New Zealand 26; ICOMOS Sri Lanka 404–5, 410–12; ICOMOS Tajikistan 498; International Conservation Center – Xi'an 9, 18; International Scientific Committee on Cultural Routes (CIIC) 531 *see also* Charters, Conventions, Declarations and Principles
iconoclasm, willful destruction 12, 47, 68, 79, 102, 105, 135–6, 153–4, 158, 192, 204, 207, 261, 264, 348, 409–10, 418, 431, 501, 503
IIC (International Institute for Conservation of Historic and Architectural Works) 9
immigration *see* population issues 12, 101–2, 123
India 3, 5, 6, 13, 18–9, 23, 58, 147, 172, 175, 190, 201, 214, 324, 352–4, 355–90, 399, 416, 427, 431, 451, 454–5, 462, 469, 497, 512–3, 523, 529, 531, 534; Agra, Taj Mahal 5, 7, 353, 357–9, 362, 364–5; 368, 372; Ajanta caves 2, 357, 362, 366–7; Ahmedabad 27, 364, 378; Archaeological Survey of India (ASI) 19, 176, 185, 195, 211–12, 214, 320–1, 352, 354, 355–7, 361–73, 419, 439, 452; Archaeological Survey of India (British Raj) 176, 451; Ashoka 357, 416, 481; Auliya shrine well 375–6; Babri Masjid 364; Baig, Amita 370; Basgo, Maitreya temples (Chamchung Lhaklang, Chamba Lhakhang, Serzang Lhakhang) 380–1 ; Bhimbetka caves 355; Bhirrana 357; Bikaner 358; Bishnupur

588 Index

temples 358; Bohd Gaya, Mahabodhi Temple 357; Chainani, Shyam 368; Chandigarh 359 ; Chandigarh Master Plan 359; Chhatrapati Shivaji (Victoria Terminus) 357, 359, 384, 455; Chittorgarh 358, 368 ; Chola empire 351, 416; *Conservation of Ancient Monuments* (Marshall) 176, 351, 363–4; *Conservation Manual: A Handbook for the Use of Archaeological Officers and Others Entrusted with the Care of Ancient Monuments* (Marshall) 176, 363–4, 371; Cunningham, Alexander 361; Darjeeling Himalayan Railway 384, 530 ; Dashavatara temples 357 ; Deccan Sultanates 358, 372; Delhi 353–4, 357–8, 364, 372, 376–8; Delhi Heritage Route 375–6, 381; Delhi Historic Zone 376; Delhi Master Plan 376; Dholavira 357; Elephanta cave 2, 357, 366–7, 455; Ellora cave 358; Fatehpur Sikri 359, 366; first archaeological inventory 361; Gandhi, Indira and Rajiv, 370; Goa 359, 368, 383–4, 455; Govardhan Hill 381–2; Government agencies for heritage protection 355, 369, 371–2, 376, 385, 389, Government agencies for heritage protection during Raj 361; Hampi 3, 358; Humayun's Tomb 354, 359, 373–6; Isa Khan tomb 372; Jaipur, Amber Fort 356, 358, 378; Jaisalmer, 11, 368, 385–7; Jama Masjid 359; Jayakar, Pupul 370; Jigyasu, Rohit 456; Jodhpur 358; Karnataka 358; Khajuraho temple 357–8 ; Kochi/Cochin, Paradisi synagogue 383–4; Kolkata/Calcutta 353, 359, 361, 450; Konarak/Odisha 358; Lothal 357; Lucknow 370; Madurai 358; Mahabalipuram 368, 455; Maharashtra 368; *Manasara* 360; Mauryan empire 357, 372, 429, 449, 481; Mughal empire 351, 355, 358–9, 372–3, 429–30, 450, 497, 502; Mumbai/Bombay 353, 359, 364, 368, 372, 377, 435; Mumbai Master Plan 359; Mutiny Memorial 372; National inventory 362; New Delhi 355, 359, 372; Nizamuddin Basti district 372–6; Osian, Jain temples 358; Puducherry/Pondicherry 148, 359; Qutub Minar 376; Rahman, Habib 359; Rajasthan 2, 357–9; Rakhigarhi 357; Red Fort 359; Varanasi/Banares 368–9; Sahni, Rai Bahadur Daya Ram 352, 363; Sanchi, Great Stupa 357; Shahjahanabad, Lutyens Bungalow zone 377; Shimla/Simla 359; Silva, Kapila D. 85; Singh, Martand 370; Sunder Nursery 375; *Tantras, agamas, samhitas* 360; Thakur, Nalini 379; Thanjavur/Tanjore 358; Thapar, B.K. 370; Thiruvanathapuram, Napier museum 357; Udaipur 358; *Vastushastras* 360; *see also* Legislation – British Raj and Legislation – India

Indian heritage organizations and initiatives: Asiatic Society 361, 452; Bombay Environmental Action Group 368; Braj Foundation 381; Centre for Action Research in Conservation of Heritage (ARCH) 385; Hazrat Nizamuddin Basti program 494; Heritage City Development and Augmentation (HRIDAY) 495; Indian National Trust for Art and Cultural Heritage (INTACH) 55, 353, 355–6, 366, 370–2, 376–7, 385, 387, 389, 494; Jaisalmer in Jeopardy 16, 385–7; Namgyal Institute for Research on Ladakhi Art and Culture (NIRLAC) 380; National Research Laboratory for the Conservation of Cultural Property 370, 419; Oval Cooperage Residents Association 377; Project Mausam 354; Sir Dorabji Tata Trust Fund 11, 373–4; Urban Design Research Institute (UDRI)(Mumbai) 377; Youth in INTACH programs 371

indigenous people, culture and sites, 34, 85, 102, 107–110, 123, 130, 146, 154, 172, 189, 231, 280, 299, 328–30, 330, 335–6, 357, 416, 449

Indochina, French Protectorate of, 1, 170, 237, 251–2; *see also* legislation – French Indochina

Indonesia 6, 8, 13–4, 21–3, 58, 170, 147, 251, 279, 288, 317–30, 401; Bali 280, 324–6; Banda Aceh 59, 323, 330; Borobodur 2, 5, 7, 12, 21, 24, 170, 176, 211, 238, 280–1, 285, 297, 317–23, 327, 347; government agencies for heritage protection 58, 321–3, 325; Government agencies for heritage protection (colonial) 280, 320; *Guidelines for Managing Post-Disaster Conservation of Heritage Buildings. Case Study: Padang* 323; Jakarta 279, 317–8, 455, 346; Kempers, A.J. Bernet 321; Prambanan 5, 280, 317, 319, 322–3; Semarang 317; Soekmono, R. 6, 280, 321; Surabaya 317; *subak* system 280, 324; Suleiman, Satyawati 321; Tanah Lot 325–6; Tjandi Djago, Tjandi Singosari 320; de Vink, J.J. 319; West Papua province/Irian Jaya 280, 329–30 *see also* Legislation – Indonesia/Dutch East Indies

Indonesian heritage organizations and initiatives: Badan Palestarian Pusaka Indonesia/Indonesia Heritage Trust (BPPI) 327; Centre for Borobudur Studies 281, 320; Indonesian Archeological Institute 319; Indonesian Disaster Fund 281, 323; Indonesian National Board for Disaster Management 281; National Research Center for Archaeology (NRCA) 321; "Save Borobudur" program 280, 319, 321, 347

Indonesian Charter for Heritage Conservation *see* Charters, Conventions, Declarations and Principles

industrialization 12, 28, 36, 127, 352, 450; in Brunei 313; in China 79; in India 364, 471; International Committee for the Conservation of Industrial Heritage 26; Meiji Industrial Revolution sites 264; repurposed industrial heritage 94–97, 148; Taipei declaration 26

INTACH (Indian National Trust for Art and Cultural Heritage) *see* Indian heritage initiatives

INTACH Charter (Charter for the Conservation of Unprotected Architectural Heritage and Sites in India) *see* Charters, Conventions, Declarations and Principles

intangible heritage 5, 7, 15, 24, 26, 36, 140, 159, 244, 254, 352, 256, 435–6; Bhutanese heritage villages 475; Chinese approach to 55, 79; Indian approach to 55; Japanese approach to 55, 498, 526; Music 55, 140, 146, 157, 244; National Intangible Heritage Center (S. Korea) 36, 141, 147; UNESCO convention concerning 15, 17, 26–7, 39, 146, 244, 268, 313; *see also* living heritage

International Court of Justice 225

International Fund for Monuments *see* World Monuments Fund

inventories, surveys 47, 56, 170, 353; *see also* country listings

Iraq 207, 499, 515

Iran 502, 523, 534

Irrawaddy River 169, 175, 179

Islamic influences on heritage: 7, 24, 311, 351, 353, 358, 431–2, 458; anti-Islamic sentiment 503–5, 508, 517; *auqaf/waqf* 303, 431, 453; Lahore Principles 353, 432–2; *mahalla* 539; *muhafazah* 431;

national approaches to non-Islamic heritage 418–9, 429; *sharia* 505
Islamic heritage *see* country site listings
Islamic State of Iraq and Syria (ISIS) 207, 515
isolation, effect on heritage: in Bhutan 467, 475; in Central Asian Soviet republics 525–6; in China 101–2; in Mongolia 159, 170–1; in Myanmar 174, 181–2
Italy 5, 58, 184, 190, 193, 260, 341, 484, 503, 508, 534; Italian Archaeological Mission in Afghanistan 507; Lerici Foundation/Fondazione Ing. Carlo Maurillo Lerici 10, 195, 260
IZIIS (Institute of Earthquake Engineering and Engineering Seismology) 176

Jackson, John Brinckerhoff 129
Jacobs, Jane 288
Jain civilization, building traditions 357, 366, 427, 450
Jain sites *see* country listings
Japan 3, 6, 12–20, 27, 33–7, 39–61, 74, 79, 135–7, 172, 214–15, 255, 268, 413, 460, 484, 503, 308, 526, 533–4; Akagawa, Natsuko 58; Asakusa Culture Center 149; Bato Hiroshige Museum 149; Chūta Itō 47–8; Fenollosa, Ernest Francisco 47; Fukuokua 56; Genbaku Dome 264, 509; Government agencies for heritage protection 52–3, 55, 58; Great Buddha hall 48; Hashima Island 264; Hirayana, Ikuo 9; Hiroshima 30, 56, 342–3, Hiroshima Peace Memorial Museum 343; Important Intangible Cultural Properties 55; Hōryū-ji temple 41–3, 47, 58; Hotel Okura 58; Ise shrines 35, 43–5; Ishinomaki 59; Kamakura 51; Kaminoyama Hachimangu 59–60; Kinkajui / Temple of the Golden Pavilion 41; Kiyoyoshi, Kigo 47; Kobe 49, 52, 342; *kofun* 41; *kumiodori* 55; Kyoto/Heian-kyo 39–41, 50–1, 56; Machiya 36, 39, 49–50; Marunouchi Building 56; Matsuura, Koichiro 504–5; Meiji Industrial Revolution sites 264; Meiji-Mura 56–7; Meiji period 6, 35, 47–52; Mount Funaoka Daitokuji temple 40; Murasaki shrine 59–60; Myonichikan 56; Nagasaki 50, 52, 342–3; Nagoya 50, 58, 352; Nara 34, 41, 50–1; National Register 49, 52; Ninomaru palace 42; Okakura, Tenshin 47; Osaka 41, 55, 56, 342; Osaka castle 42; Reikanji 40; Sekino, Masaru 43, 50; Sekino, Tadashi 47–8; Tōdaiji temple 2, 58; Tokaido highway 50; Tokyo 56, 342–3; Tsumaki, Yorinaka 48; Yakushiji 53–5; Yawatahama City, Hizuchi High School 56; Yusuhara Marche 149; *see also* legislation – Japan
Japanese heritage initiatives, organizations: Hirayama Trust 9; International Research Center for Intangible Cultural Heritage (IRCI) 55, 380; Japan Association for the Conservation of Architectural Monuments (JCAM) 53, 56, 58; Japan Consortium for International Cooperation in Cultural Heritage 37; Japan Foundation 20, 22, 36, 58; Japan International Cooperation Agency (JICA) 9, 18, 161, 254, 366; Japan National Trust for Culture and National Heritage Conservation 56; Japan Society for the Conservation of Cultural Property 56; Japanese Funds-in-Trust 36, 55, 258, 498, 526; Japanese Team for Safeguarding Angkor (JSA) 22, 214; Joint Council for the Conservation and Restoration of Ancient Japanese Art Works in Foreign Collections 9; Kamanza Cho-ie revitalization project 49; Kyo-machiya Council 49; Kyo-machiya Revitalization Project 49; Kyoto Center for Community Collaboration 49; Kyoto Mitate International 56; League of Historical Cities 10; Machiya Machiznakuri Fund 49; Nara National Cultural Properties Research Institute 19, 37, 58; National Research Institute for Cultural Properties 533; Nippon Institute of Technology 487; Tokyo Institute of Technology 22; Toyota Foundation 22; Zenkoku Machinami Hozon Renmei/Association for the Township Preservation 35, 52, 56; Zenkoku Rekishiteki Fudo Hozon Renmei/Federation for the Preservation of Historic Landscapes 52
Jayakar, Pupul 370
Jean-Julien, Olsen 218–222
Jewish heritage 93, 383–4 *see also* country site listings
JICA (Japan International Cooperation Agency) 9, 18, 161, 254, 366
Jigyasu, Rohit 456
Johnson, Samuel 361

Kathmandu Valley Preservation Trust *see* Nepal
Kazakhstan 58, 497–8, 523–41; Almaty 528; Government agencies for heritage protection 526, 528; Khoja Ahmed Yasavi mausoleum 526; Law of the Republic of Kazakhstan on Protection and Use of Historical and Cultural Heritage (1992) 526; Mangystau mausoleums, necropolis 527; Otrar 497, 524, 526, 533; St. Ascension Cathedral 526, 528
Khan, Louis I. 458–9
Korea (general) 3, 6, 12–13, 15, 18, 27, 79, 135–149, 167; Joseon dynasty 135
Korea, North (Democratic People's Republic of Korea) 5, 33–37, 135–142; Government agencies for heritage protection 138; Kaesong 139; Tomb of Tongmyong 139; *see also* Legislation – Korea, North and Legislation, Korean peninsula
Korea, South (Republic of Korea) 33, 37, 264, 508; Cheonggyecheon creek 144; Cheonwangmun 143; Chung, Seung-Jin 137; Daejon, missionary housing 141; Deoksugung Palace 135; Geukrakjeon temple 135; Go, Sangnyeol 146; Gookdo Theater 141; Government agencies for heritage protection 138, 140, 146, 149; Gyeongbokgung Palace 135, 137–8; Gyeongju 142; Hahoe 142; Hwaseong fortress 143; historic districts legally unprotected 140; Jeju island 149–50; Jeonju 36; Kilburn, David 136; Koguryo tombs 136; Korean architectural design 136; Namdaemun Gate 143, 145; ondol fireplaces 2, 136; *pungsu* 135–6; Seoul 142; Seoul Master Plan 136, 142; Supyo stone/Water Mark bridge 144; Yangdong 142; *see also* legislation – Korean peninsula
Kyrgyzstan 497–8, 523–41; Fergana valley 524, 530; Government agencies for heritage protection 529; Law on Protection and Use of Historical and Cultural Heritage (1999) 529; Osh 529–30; Preparing for a Master Plan 529; Saimaly-Tash petroglyphs 529; State Institute for Scientific Research and Planning on Monuments of Material Culture (NIPI PMK) 526, 528; Sulaiman-Too Sacred Mountain 498, 529, 541; Upper Chui River Valley, medieval sites 529, 533

laboratories *see* research institutes
Ladurie, Emanuel Le Roy 129
Lahore Principles *see* Charters, Conventions, Declarations and Principles

Laos 1, 3, 19, 169–71, 189–98, 201, 204, 207, 235, 244, 151–3; Champasak cultural landscape 189, 193; Champasak Heritage Management Plan 193; Government agencies for heritage protection 171, 191–2; Haw Pha Kaew temple 194; Hotel de la Paix/Ban Mano Prison 148; Luang Prabang 19, 147, 170, 172, 189–91, 193, 275; Luang Prabang Plan de Sauvegarde et Mis en Valeur 171, 191 Pakse 189; Plain of Jars 189, 196–7; Plain of Jars Master Plan 196; Savannakhet 189; Vientiane 190, 193–4; Wat Arun 230; Wat Phou 2, 10, 24, 169, 172, 189–95, 322, 347; Wat Si Muang 194; Wat Sis Saket 194; Wat Xieng Mouane 190, 192; Wat Xieng Thong 190

Laotian heritage programs: Luang Prabang School of Fine Arts, 192; Sangha craft training program 192, 275

layered significance 4–6, 17, 81, 91, 169, 204, 266–7, 321

Le Corbusier (Charles-Edouard Jeanneret-Gris) 359

legislation, heritage (general) 16, 35; Territorial dispute, Preah Vihear 225; U.S. v. 10th century Cambodian sandstone sculpture 206–8; Varanasi Development Authority, Public Interest Litigation against 369

legislation – Afghanistan: decree forbidding new construction in Kabul 514; Law on the Protection of Historical and Cultural Properties (2004) 507, 515; vague wording of 515

legislation – Bangladesh: Antiquities Act of 1968 452–3; Act No. XIV (1976) 452; Article 24, Constitution (1971) 452; Conservation and Rehabilitation of Historical and Cultural Heritage (National Building Code) (2012) 452–3; *see also* Legislation – British Raj

legislation – Bhutan: Heritage Sites Bill (2015) 473; National Forest Policy 473; shortfalls in coverage 473

legislation – British Raj – Ancient Monument Preservation Act (1904) 351, 362–3, 432, 452; Religious Endowments Act (Act XX) (1863) 361, 363; Treasure Trove Act (1874) 361

legislation – Brunei: Antiquities and Treasure Trove Enactment 311

legislation – Cambodia: Constitution (1993) 213, 223; International Court of Justice ruling on Preah Vihear 225; Law on the Protection of Cultural Heritage (1996) 213–14, 223; Royal decree on Siem Reap Angkor Region Identification and Management 213; Royal ordinances (1923, 1932) 213

legislation – China: Detailed Rules for the Implementation of the Law of the PRC on the Protection of Cultural Relics (1992) 80; Executive Regulation for the Implementation of the Conservation of Cultural Property 68; Law for the Preservation of Ancient Objects (1930) 79; Law for the Protection of Cultural Heritage 68, 80; Law of the Peoples' Republic of China for the Protection/Safeguarding of Cultural Property 68; Measures for the Protection of Ancient Sites (1909) 79; Protection and Management Regulations for Lijiang 109; Provision of Regulations on the Protection and Administration of Cultural Heritage (1960) 79

legislation – French Indochina: Legislation establishing "national domain" over art in Indochina 206, 213

legislation – India: Ancient and Historical Monuments and Archaeological Sites and Remains (Declaration of National Importance) Act (1951) 368; Ancient Monument and Archaeological Sites and Remains Act (AMASRA) (1958, amended 2010) 368, 372; Antiquities Act of 1947/Antiquities and Art Treasures Act (1972) 368; Constitution (1950) 368; Environmental Protection Act (1986) 368; National Policy for Conservation of Ancient Monuments, Archaeological Sites and Remains (2014) 356, 370; *see also* Legislation – British Raj

legislation – Indonesia/Dutch East Indies: Ordinance on Monuments (1931) 320

legislation – Japan: Ancient Capitals Preservation Law of 1966/Law for Special Measures for the Preservation of Historic Atmosphere (Ambiance) in Ancient Capitals 35, 51–2; The Landscape Act 49; Law for the Preservation of Ancient Sites/Shrines and Temples 47–8; Law for the Preservation of Historical Sites, Places of Beauty and Natural Monuments (1919) 48; Law for the Preservation of National Treasures (1929) 48–50; Law for the Protection of Traditional Techniques for Conservation of Cultural Properties 53; Law for the Protection of Cultural Properties (1950) 36, 50–2, 55; Law on the Promotion of International Cooperation for the Protection of Cultural Heritage Abroad 58; legal separation of church and state 51; Plan for the Preservation of Ancient Artifacts (1871) 35

legislation – Kazakhstan: Law of the Republic of Kazakhstan on Protection and Use of Historical and Cultural Heritage (1992) 526

legislation – Korea, North: Law on the Protection of Cultural Property (1994) and its Regulations (2009) 138

legislation – Korea, South: Cultural Heritage Protection Act (Munhwajae *Daehan Minguk Munhwa Jaecheong*) 140, 144; Cultural Properties Protection Act (1962) 36, 40; Korean 961 Law of 1962 (amended 1970) 55, 146; Traditional Building Preservation Act (1984) 140

legislation – Korea, pre-partition: Buddhist regulations about temple conservation 135; Preservation of Korean National Treasure, Historic Sites and Natural Monuments Act (1933) 138; Rules on Ancient Sites and Relics Preservation (1916) 137–8

legislation – Kyrgyzstan: Law on Protection and Use of Historical and Cultural Heritage (1999) 529

legislation – Macau: Chief Executive Order 248/2006

legislation – Malaysia 19; Antiquities Act (1976) 301; Control of Rent Act 301–4; National Heritage Act (2005) 304; Town and Country Planning Act of 1976 301

legislation – Maldives: Environmental Protection Act 415; Historical and Cultural Property Law of the Republic of Maldives (1978) 418; legislative weaknesses 418

legislation – Mongolia: Constitution 159; Ikh Zasag legal decrees (13th century) 154; Law of Protection of Historical and Cultural Values (modified 2001) 159; Rule of Preserving Ancient Monuments (1924) 155

legislation – Myanmar: Antiquities Preservation Act (1957) 176, 482

legislation – Nepal: Ancient Monuments Preservation Act 482

legislation – Pakistan: Antiquities Act of 1968 (amended) 432–3; National Charter for the Conservation and Preservation of Cultural Property 432; misc. regional legislations 432; *see also* Legislation – British Raj

legislation – Philippines: Cultural Properties Preservation and Protection Act (1966) 336; National Cultural Heritage Act of 2009 (RA10066) 344; Republic Act No. 7356 336

legislation – Singapore Control of Rent Act 286

legislation – Sri Lanka: Antiquities Ordinance of 1940 (amended 1998) 403–4, 410; Housing and Town Improvement Ordinance (1915) 404; Town and Country Planning Ordinance (1946, amended) 404, 409; Urban Development Act (1978) 404

legislation – Taiwan; Cultural Heritage Act (updated 2002) 126; Law for the Preservation of Ancient Objects (1909) 126; Measures for the Protection of Ancient Sites (1909) 126

legislation – Thailand: Act on Monuments, Antiquities, Objects of Art and National Museums 238; Conservation Act of 1934 238; Royal Proclamation of 1854 235

legislation – Turkmenistan: Law on the Protection of Turkmenistan Historical and Cultural Monuments 534; legislative weakness 534

legislation – Uzbekistan: legislative weakness 539; Uzbek Law on the Preservation and Utilization of Objects of Cultural Heritage (2001) 537; legal protection of archaeological sites (2009) 537

legislation – Vietnam: Decree on the Management, Classification and Methods to Organize the Protection and Restoration of Historical and Cultural Monuments (1957) 19; Ordinance on the Protection of Historical Cultural Relics and Scenic Sites (1984) 254; Law on Cultural Heritage (No. 28/2001/QH10of 29 June 2001) 254; legislation regarding maintenance of royal properties (medieval) 255

legislation against looting: during Raj 351, 362–3, 432, 452; in Brunei 311; in China 79; in Philippines 336; in Thailand 235; U.S. v. 10th century Cambodian sandstone sculpture 206–8

legislation, nongovernmental *see* Charters, Conventions, Declarations and Principles

legislation, religious: discriminatory legislation in Bangladesh 451; during the Raj 361; Japanese legal separation of church and state 51; Buddhist regulations about temple conservation (Korea) 135–6; in Pakistan 431–3; *sharia* 431

Lerici Foundation/Fondazione Ing. Carlo Maurillo Lerici 10, 195, 260

Leslie, Jolyon 514–5

Letellier, Robin 221

Liang Sicheng 6, 23, 35, 79–80, 85

LIDAR *see* Technology

Liles, Andrew M. 288–9

living cultural landscape: rice terraces, Cordilleras (Philippines) 340

living heritage 5, 9, 16, 27, 163–4, 281, 325, 351–2, 360, 363, 369, 371, 404–10, 495; Living National Treasure (*boyuja, Ingan munhwajae*) (South Korea) 140, 146; Living National Treasure (Japan) 371; Orchid Island (Taiwan) 130–1; *see also* craftsmen, master and intangible heritage

living vs. dead monuments 351, 363

local awareness/involvement in conservation 14–16, 24, 35–6, 52, 94, 110, 137, 140–2, 214–5, 242, 302–3, 339, 356–7, 412; Kamanza Cho-ie revitalization project 49; Kyoto Center for Community Collaboration 49; lack of local input 179, 322, 379, 515; Oval Cooperage Residents Association 377; Varanasi Development Authority lawsuit 369

local responsibility vs. national 149, 433, 368, 377, 538; devolved responsibility in Pakistan 427, 433, 436–7

Logan, Pamela 102

Logan, William S. 88, 261, 264–5

longhouses 280–299

looting 14, 35, 68, 138, 158, 172, 204, 206–8, 213, 240, 336, 362, 427–8, 441, 498–501, 505–8, 511, 514 *see also* legislation against looting

looting, colonial: 68, 78, 172, 361, 439

Lott, Nathan 454–6

Lujan, Rodolfo 22, 176

Lutyens, Edwin 357, 372

Macedonia: IZIIS (Institute of Earthquake Engineering and Engineering Seismology) 176

Macau 84, 98–103: Catholic Church of the Immaculate Conception 148; Chief Executive Order 248/2006; Guia lighthouse and fortress 100–1; St. Paul's church 98–9; Portuguese School 149; Sociedad de Turismo e Diversões de Macau, S.A. 98

maintenance, ritual *see* reconstruction

Malaysia 3, 8, 18–22, 175, 235, 244, 251, 279, 285, 297–307, 401; George Town 280–1, 297–8, 302–3, 305, 347; Government agencies for heritage protection 299, 304; Kuala Lumpur 279, 298, 302, 347; Melaka/Malacca 147, 280–1, 297–8, 302, 304–5, 317, 347; National Registry 304; Penang 147, 297–8, 304; Penang Master Planning 302; Sabah and Sarawak 299, 302; Terengganu 300

Malaysia: heritage organizations: Friends of the Heritage of Malaysia Trust 303; Heritage of Malaysia Trust 244, 281, 302–4, 347; state heritage societies 299, 303

Maldives 15, 351–4, 455–6, 495; Climate Adaptation Plan 415–6, 455; coral stone mosques 419, 455; Environmental Protection Act 415; Gayoom, Mahmoon Abudul 416; Government agencies for heritage protection 418; Historical and Cultural Property Law of the Republic of Maldives (1978) 418; legislative weakness 418–9; Nasheed, Mohamed 415, 418; National Center for Linguistics and Historical Research (NCLHR) 418; National Development Plans 418; National Museum 418; REVIVE 419; Shafeeq, Mohammed 417

Malraux, André 207, 213

Marchal, Henri 211, 280, 319

maritime and coastal heritage 22, 109, 275; Antiquities ordinance (Sri Lanka) 404; ASI Underwater Wing (India) 369; Coastal Regulation Zone Notification (India) 368; Hội An shipwreck 254; National Research Institute of Maritime Cultural Heritage (South Korea) 141; post-tsunami issues 410, 413; Southeast Asian Collaboration Programme on Underwater Archaeology 10; UNESCO Convention on the Protection of Underwater Cultural Heritage 171, 254, 275

Marrion Christopher 13
Marshall, Sir John 176, 351, 363
masonry, conservation of 240, 260, 434, 507 *see also* stone, masonry
mausoleums *see* tombs, mausoleums
Mehrotra, Rahul 382
Mekong River 169, 189–93, 201, 455
Menon, A.G. Krishna xi-xiii, 375, 389
merit *see* religious merit
Mesolithic culture 400; *see also* Pre-historic sites, cultures
metal, metalwork 79, 475
Mexico 208
Meydenbauer, Albrecht 219
Michell, George 388
migration *see* population issues
military and defense sites: Dutch barracks 383; in India 368; Korea 134; in Taiwan 125, 130; fortifications 2, 51, 75, 77, 82, 86, 136, 376–8, 385, 410, 413, 434, 436–7, 460–2, 470, 525, 537 *see also* country listings
mines, mining 13, 127, 161, 172, 234, 280, 313, 329, 362, 461, 501, 505; Chinkuashih mining town/ Gold Ecological Park 125, 127; Industrial Heritage of Colliery (Brunei) 313; Mes Aynak (Afghanistan) 505–6, 515–6
Modern style, Modernism 8, 36, 56, 85, 251, 359; DOCOMOMO 8; WMF/Knoll Modernism Prize 56
Molyvann H.E. Vann 6, 147, 223–4
monasteries, nunneries: in Japan 39; in Bhutan 471–5; in Mongolia 155–6; in Sri Lanka 399, 402–7; in Tajikistan 533; in Tibet; 101–2 *see also* country site listings
Mongolia 5, 33–7, 58, 153–164, 192; Altai petroglyphs 157; Amarbayasgalant Khiid 155, 158; Baldan Baraivan 155; Bogd Khans 153, 158, 160; Bogd Khan Palace Complex 153, 160–2; Chinggis/Genghis Khan 160, 163, 502, 537; Choibolsan, Khorloogiian 35, 153; Constitution 159; Erdene Zuu 155, 159; Gandantegchinlen Khiid monastery 155, 158; Gers 34, 163–4; Government agencies for heritage protection 159–60; Ikh Zasag legal decrees (13th century) 154; Institute of Archaeology 159; Kharkhorum 158–60; Law of Protection of Historical and Cultural Values (modified 2001) 159; National inventory 159; Kublai Khan 74–5, 153, 175; Orkhon valley 159; Rule of Preserving Ancient Monuments (1924) 155; Togchin temple 154; Tsedenbal, Yumjaagin 153; Ulaan Baator 153, 161–2
Mongolian historical organizations: Cultural Restoration Tourism project 155; Historical and Cultural Heritage Restoration Organization 155; Mongolian-Smithsonian Deer Stone Project 158
Mongols, Mongolian art and culture 3, 153, 524
monument-centrism: in Afghanistan 515; in Bangladesh 460; in India 356, 3790; in Nepal 488; during the Raj 353; in Soviet Central Asia 498
Morocco 207
mosaics 190, 512
Mosques *see* country site listings
Mouhot, Henri 209
mud structures *see* earthen structures
murals *see* frescoes, murals

Myanmar 3, 5, 15, 19, 169–85, 189, 195, 237, 275–6, 400; Antiquities Preservation Act (1957) 176, 482; Bagan/Pagan 170–1, 173–7, 179, 185, 275, 297; Bagan master plan proposal 177; Dhanyawadi 182; Golden Palace Museum 178; Government agencies for heritage protection 176–7, 184; Inwa/Ava 175; Lujan, Rodolfo 22, 176; Mandalay 169, 173, 175–6, 179; Mandalay Royal Palace 27, 179; Mrauk-U 182, 184, 347; Naypyidaw 181; Pagnin, Paolo 22; Pyu kingdom 169, 175; Shwedagon pagoda 174; Sri Ksetra 10, 175; Thant Myint-U 182, 184, 347; Thaton 175; Yangon/Rangoon 11, 169–71, 174, 181–3, 275; Yangon Heritage Trust 171, 179, 181–2, 185; Zan-ti group 177

Nara Document on Authenticity *see* Charters, Conventions, Declarations and Principles
nationalism, importance of heritage to: 6, 12, 28, 67, 91, 102, 130, 157, 161, 189, 193, 231, 254, 368, 462, 467, 538–9; in Thailand 169–70, 173, 235–6;
nationalism as a threat to heritage: Soviet sites in Kazakhstan 526
nationalization *see* ownership
natural forces, harmony with 26, 137; color, importance of 34, 53, 72, 130; cosmological considerations 137; Feng shui/pungsu 26, 34, 71–2, 136; Geomancy 72, 77, 139; I Ching 137; Yin and yang 73, 137
natural threats *see* environmental and natural threats
negative memories *see* Sites of Conscience
neglect as a threat to heritage 16, 106, 171, 179, 181, 204, 240, 258, 260, 385, 458, 473, 498; governmental purchase of neglected sites (India) 362
Neolithic sites Cekik (Bali) 325; Peinan (Taiwan) 125; *see also* Prehistoric sites, cultures
Nepal 3, 5, 13, 58, 351–4, 454, 456, 471, 481–91; Basantapur tower 483, 490; Bauddhanath 485; Bhaktapur 481, 485–6, 488; Bhairavnath temple 482; Bhaktapur Development Project of the Federal Republic of Germany 485; Bramayani shrine 483; *Building Conservation in Nepal: A Handbook of Principles and Techniques* (UNESCO) 483; Changu Narayan 485; Gokarna temple 484; Government agencies for heritage protection 481, 483, 488; Hanuman Dhoka Palace 483; Kanakmuni Buddha stupa 481; Kathmandu 481, 485; Kathmandu Durbar Square 486, 490; The Kathmandu Valley Masterplan 486; Keshab Naryan Chowk 488; Pashupatinath 485; Sulima temple 484–5; Swayambhunath 485, 488; Thubchen and Jamba Gompas 491
Nepalese heritage organizations and initiatives: American Himalayan Foundation 354, 491; Bhaktapur Development Project 485–6; Bramayani Conservation Project 483; Hanuman Dhoka Conservation Project 483, 494; JDR III Fund (Nepal) 483; Kathmandu Valley Preservation Trust 353, 481, 484–6, 488
Netherlands 8, 413, 484; Prince Claus Fund for Culture and Development 473; Prince Claus Foundation 404; *see also* Colonial period – Dutch
New Guinea *see* Indonesia, West Papua province
New Zealand 20
Nomadic culture in Central Asia: 497–8, 525–7, 529
North Korea *see* Korea, North

Norwegian Organization for Development Co-operation 460
nostalgia 4, 94, 382–3

van Oers, Ron 266
ordinary, the importance of 129–30
ownership issues 291, 302, 368, 404, 428, 433, 451, 473; Association of Heritage Building Owners (Sri Lanka) 410; development rights, transfer of (India) 379; government rights over privately-owned listed sites (India) 363; nationalization (Burma) 176; private ownership assistance 191, 281, 412, 434, 474; revitalizing Bukchon 142; *see also* real estate values as a threat

P&T Architects + Engineers Limited 97
paint, painted finishes 79, 158, 160, 258–9; at Basgo (India) 380–1; Bhutanese 470; Nepalese 481–6; Painting, Conservation & Research Center (Sri Lanka) 407; Qingming Shanghetu painting 74; *see also* frescoes, murals
Pakistan/West Pakistan 2–3, 19, 147, 351–2, 355, 357, 362, 264, 427–43, 451, 454–5, 462, 502–3, 506, 523, 531; Baltit Fort 442; Dani, A.H. 352, 429 ; Durrani, F.A. 429 ; Gilgit-Baltistan province 353, 436; Government agencies for heritage protection 431–5; Harappa 352, 357, 427, 429, 439; Hyderabad 435; Islamabad 15, 21, 450, 506; Jinnah, Muhammed Ali 428, 434; Karachi 353, 428, 434–6, 442–3, 454; Khan, Muhammed Ayub 431; Lahore 2, 28, 428–30, 439–43; Lahore Fort 353, 433, 436; Lari, Yasmeen 434; legislative weakness 427–8, 435–6; Mohenjo Daro 5, 23, 352, 357, 364, 427–9, 436, 439–41; Mohenjo Daro Master Plan 440; Mughal, Mohammed Rafique 427; Nankana Sahib, Janam Asthan 430; National Conservation Strategy 432; Northern Territories and Kashmir 439; Peshawar 503; Quaid-e-Azam/Flagstaff House Museum 434; Rawalpindi 428; Rehman Dheri 429; Sahr-i-Bahlol 429; Shalamar Gardens 436; Shahi Guzargah /Royal Route 437; Sheikhupura 429; Shikarpoor 441; Takhi-i-Bahi 429; Taxila 427, 429–30; Thatta 434–5; Uch 428
Pakistani Heritage organizations and initiatives; Aga Khan Cultural Service – Pakistan 354, 436; Endowment Fund Trust for Preservation of Heritage of the Sindh (Pakistan) 434; Evacuee Trust Properties Board 433; Heritage Foundation of Pakistan 353, 434, 443, 494; International Safeguarding Campaign for Mohenjo Daro 342, 400; National Fund for Cultural Heritage 434
Palacios, Genaro 340
Paleolithic sites 136, 429, 502 *see also* Pre-historic sites
parks *see* gardens and parks
Parmentier, Henri 240, 252
partition (Pakistan/Bangladesh) 352, 355, 364, 427, 431, 439, 449–51
partition (North/South Korea) 135, 137
Patina, importance of 80, 147, 321, 363 *see also* authenticity, *Wabi-sabi*
Pei, I.M. 147
People's Republic of China *see* China
petroglyphs: Altai 157–9; Saimaly-Tash 529–30
Philippines 8, 13, 21–2, 172, 244, 279–80, 335–44, 455; Banaue rice terraces 341; Batan Island 130–1; Baclayon church 337, 340; Burnham, Daniel 337; Cordilleras rice terraces 340; Corregidor 343; Cultural Properties Preservation and Protection Act (1966) 336; Gate of Santiago 338; Fox, Robert Bradley 336; Heritage Zone 353, 368; Intramuros 27, 280, 337–9, 343; Manila 279, 336–7, 342; National Cultural Heritage Act of 2009 (RA10066) 344; Philippine Baroque 280, 336, 339; Republic Act No. 7356 336; San Sebastián basilica 340; Santos, I.P.280 ; Tabon cave 335–6; Vigan 281, 339–40, 347; *see also* Legislation – Philippines
Philippines heritage organizations and initiatives: Bakás Pilipinas/Philippine Historic Preservation Society 337, 340; Church of San Agustin 339; Government agencies for heritage protection 336–7, 344, 337; Intramuros Administration 337–9; National Endowment Fund for Culture and the Arts 336; National Registry of Historic Structures 336; Philippine Historical Research and Markers Committee 336
physical balance, importance of *see* Natural forces, harmony with
Pichard, Pierre 177
Piranesi, Giovanni Batista 219
planning – Afghanistan: National Development Strategy 515; National Urban Strategy 515
planning – Bangladesh: Detailed Area Plan (Dhaka) 454
planning – Bhutan: *Bhutan 2020: A Vision for Peace, Prosperity and Happiness* 475; Five Year Master Plan 473, 475
planning – Cambodia: Implementation challenges 225; Tourism Management Plan (Angkor) 12, 213; Zoning and Environmental Management Project (Siem Reap) 213–14
planning – China: Beijing General Development Plan 84, 86, 88; Chinese imperial planning 72–4, 77, 219; Lijiang Old Town Protection Plan 109; Master Plan, Great Wall 107; Mogao Master Plan, 83; Shang dynastic planning 72; Soviet-style planning in China 83, 86
planning – India: Chandigarh Master Plan 359; Delhi Master Plan 376; Mumbai Master Plan 359
planning – Korea, South: Master Plan for Seoul 136, 142
planning – Kyrgyzstan: Preparing for a Master Plan 529
planning – Laos: Champasak Heritage Management Plan 193; Plan de Sauvegarde et Mis en Valeur (Luang Prabang) 171, 191; Master Plan, Plain of Jars 196
planning – Malaysia: Master Planning for Penang, Georgetown 302
planning – Maldives: Climate Adaptation Plan 415–6, 455; National Development Plans 418
planning – Myanmar: Bagan master plan proposal 177
planning – Nepal: The Kathmandu Valley Masterplan (Nepal) 486
planning – Pakistan: Mohenjo Daro Master Plan 440; National Conservation Strategy 432
planning – Singapore: Singapore River Master Plan 292; Tourism Product Development Plan (Singapore) 287
planning – Sri Lanka: Cultural Triangle of the South Plan 413–4; Dambulla Management Plan 406; Development Plan, Galle/ Galle Heritage Site Management Plan 412–3; in Kandy (Sri Lanka) 409–10; Sigirya Regional Plan 409

planning – Tajikistan: Management Plan for Sarazm 533
planning – Thailand: Fourth National Social and Economic Development Plan (Bangkok) 243; in Sukhothai 239
planning – Turkmenistan: Master Plan, Merv 535
planning – Vietnam: Hanoi master planning 252, 254–5, 261; Hanoi 2010: Heritage and Cultural Identity 263; Master Plan, Mỹ Sõn 260
planning – Uzbekistan: Master Plan 537–9
Pleistocene era 157 *see also* Pre-historic sites
Poland: Kwiatkowski, Kaźimierz 260; Polish Ateliers for Conservation of Cultural Properties (PKZ) 19, 253, 260
PKZ (Polish Ateliers for Conservation of Cultural Properties) *see* Poland
pollution 13, 86, 292, 364, 369, 525; *see also* transportation
population issues: population growth 105, 194, 262, 283, 292, 294, 317, 337, 352, 355, 409, 418, 428, 435, 439, 450–1, 536; forced resettlement 177, 239–40, 313, 379, 418, 431, 515, 526; immigration 12, 101–2, 123, 298, 330, 435; migration 13, 24, 28, 341, 352, 364, 433, 442, 455 *see also* urbanization
post-colonial issues 3, 12, 129, 170, 262, 297, 319, 321, 352, 359, 364, 370, 416
Prehistoric sites, cultures 158, 297, 320, 335
preservation zones *see* buffer zones, preservation zones
Principles *see* Charters, Conventions, Declarations and Principles
Prince Claus Foundation 404
Prince of Wales, HRH Charles 102
privatization *see* ownership
professional development *see* capacity building, education
prosperity as a threat to built heritage *see* Modernism
protection zone; *see* buffer zone

Qin dynasty 2, 33
Qing dynasty 3, 75–7, 86, 112, 127, 153
Queen Sirikit 246

railroad, tram heritage: in Burma 182; in China 86, 127; in India 384–5; in Taiwan 36, 125
Raj (British) *see* Colonial period, British
real estate values as a threat to heritage: 53, 142, 181, 224, 242, 262, 283, 286, 289, 291, 302, 325, 451, 526; effect of tax rates 16, 94, 126, 140–2
Reap, James 25–6
regional assistance and cooperation 3, 169, 275, 170; ASEAN 8, 172, 225, 244, 281, 315, 347; Cultural Property Specialists Dispatch Program (Japan Foundation) 36; Japan Consortium for International Cooperation in Cultural Heritage 37; SEAMEO-SPAFA 7, 10, 21, 172, 238, 244, 253, 275, 280–1, 321, 347; South Asian Association for Regional Cooperation (SAARC) 354; Yunnan Provincial Association of Cultural Exchanges with Foreign Countries 110 *see also* regional ICOMOS branches
reconstruction and restoration issues: Central Asian reconstruction vs. restoration 536; incompatible styles, materials in Laos 193, in Nepal 486, in South Asia in general 353; Insensitive design in Bagan (Myanmar) 174–84, in Vietnam 262; inappropriate restoration techniques in Bali 524, in Bangladesh 451, 457; in Nepal 488; in Soviet Central Asia 525, 532–3, 537–9; over-restoration in Lijiang (China) 107–8, in Soviet Central Asia 536; material substitution vs. authenticity 23, 42; ritual maintenance 23, 27, 34, 42–3, 50
regulations *see* legislation
religion as a threat to heritage: Japanese legal separation of church and state 47; non-Islamic sites in Afghanistan 505; differing treatment of religious sites in India 363; non-Islamic sites in Pakistan 429–31
religious intolerance *see* iconoclasm
religious legislation *see* legislation, religious
religious merit as a reason for conservation 4, 43, 101–2, 169–71, 175, 178, 231, 233–4, 351, 401, 431; *Brithat Samhita* 360; Buddhism 101–2, 176–8; *guthi* system 481 (Nepal); *jiimnoddharana* 351; *muhafazah* 351; Sangha program 192; *Shilpa Prakasha* 360; *waqf/auqaf* system 303, 431, 453
Republic of China *see* Taiwan
research institutes: Applied Research Center for Archaeology and Fine Arts (ARCAFA)(Cambodia) 21; Architectural Conservation laboratory, Hong Kong University 20; Centre for Action Research in Conservation of Heritage (ARCH) (India) 385; Center for Khmer Studies (Cambodia) 172, 215, 223; Centre for Borobudur Studies (Indonesia) 281, 320; Dunhuang Research Academy (China) 83; German Archaeological Institute 511; Getty Conservation Institute (GCI) 7, 19, 22, 36, 83, 172, 195, 370, 530; ICCROM, Ta Nei Cultural Resource Management Workshops 217; Institute of Archaeology (Mongolia) 159; IIC (International Institute for Conservation of Historic and Architectural Works) 9; Institute of Earthquake Engineering and Engineering Seismology(IZIIS) 176; Institute of Innovation Technology and Communication (Tajikistan) 533; International Research Centre for Intangible Heritage (IRCI) (Japan) 55; Namgyal Institute for Research on Ladakhi Art and Culture (NIRLAC) (India) 380; Nara National Cultural Properties Research Institute (Japan) 19, 37, 58; National Center for Linguistics and Historical Research (NCLHR) (Maldives) 418; National Research Center for Archaeology (NRCA)(Indonesia) 321; National Research Institute of Cultural Heritage (South Korea) 141; National Research Institute for Cultural Properties (Japan) 533; National Research Laboratory for the Conservation of Cultural Property (India) 370, 419; Nippon Institute of Technology (Japan) 487; Oriental Institute (USA) 506; Painting, Conservation & Research Center (Sri Lanka) 407; State Institute for Scientific Research and Planning on Monuments of Material Culture (NIPI PMK) (Kyrgyzstan) 526, 528; Tajik Academy of Sciences 532; Tokyo Institute of Technology (Japan) 22; Urban Design Research Institute (UDRI)(Mumbai) 377
revolution *see* war, civil strife
risk assessment, management 13–14, 195, 354, 499; *Guidelines for Managing Post-Disaster Conservation of Heritage Buildings. Case Study: Padang* 323; Hyogo Framework for Action 14; Sendai Framework for Disaster Risk Reduction 14; Indonesian National Board for Disaster Management 281; Ritsumeikan University, Institute for Disaster Mitigation of Urban Cultural Heritage (Japan) 20, 53

rising damp *see* water as a threat
rock art *see* petroglyphs, rock art
Ruskin, John 83
Russia 153, 502 colonial Russian architecture 536; *see also* USSR

Said, Edward 129
Sanday, John 177, 483–4, 491
Saudi Arabia: Mecca, al Masjid al Haram/Sacred Mosque 431; Medina, al Masjid an Nabawi/Prophet's Mosque 431
Schutz, Alfred 222
scientific issues *see* technology
scientific laboratories *see* research institutes
Scott, George Gilbert 93
SEAMEO-SPAFA (Southeast Asian Regional Centre for Archaeology and Fine Arts) 10, 21, 172, 238, 244, 253, 275, 280–1, 321, 347; capacity building, Wat Phou 195; training 280, 321
seascape *see* maritime and coastal heritage
Senegal, Gorée Island 264
sensitive or painful heritage *see* Sites of Conscience
Seoul Declaration on Tourism in Asia's Historic Towns and Areas *see* Charters, Conventions, Declarations and Principles
Sharia see Islamic influences on heritage, legislation, religious
Shinto beliefs, support for heritage conservation 4, 39, 47
shipwrecks *see* maritime and coastal heritage
shophouses *see* vernacular structures
Sikh religion 430–1, 436
Silk Road 3, 73, 107, 497, 530–1, 533; Center for the Study of the Silk Road/International Caravanserai of Culture 9; Hirayama Ikuo Silk Road Museum 9; One Belt, One Road program 3, 167; UNESCO Integral Study of the Silk Roads: Roads of Dialogue 529; UNESCO Silk Road Online Platform 547; World Tourism Organization Silk Road programme 533, 547
Silva, Kapila D. 85
Singapore 3, 8, 15, 27, 137, 147, 276, 279–80, 283–94, 298, 302, 315; Chinatown 286–90; Conservation District 292; Convent of the Holy Infant Jesus complex (CHIJMES) 148, 291; Fort Canning 287–8, 291; Geylang serai 287; Government agencies for heritage protection 283, 286–9, 291–2; Haw Par Villa 287–8; Istana 285; Little India 287–8; Kallang River basin 292; Kampong Glam 287–9; Lee, Kuan Yew 283, 285, 292; national inventory 289; National Monuments Fund 289; Raffles Hotel 147, 288; Raffles, Sir Thomas Stamford 283, 286, 292, 318; St. Andrew's cathedral 285; Singapore River Master Plan 292; Singapore River quays (Boat Quay, Clarke Quay, Robertson Quay) 16, 283, 287, 292–3; Sri Mariammam temple 285–6; Sultan mosque 289, 291; Tourism Product Development Plan 287; Urban Redevelopment Authority 280; *see also* Legislation – Singapore
Sites of Conscience, difficult legacies 18, 171, 181, 359, 384–5; Chinkuashi 128; Gorée Island 264; Hiroshima Hiroshima 30, 56, 342–3; Hōa Lō Prison 263; Nanjing Massacre Memorial 264; Robben Island 263; Tuol Sleng Genocide Museum 263

skills training *see* capacity building, crafts training
smuggling *see* looting
South Africa, Robben Island 263–4
South Asia *see* Asia, South
Southeast Asia *see* Asia, Southeast
South Korea *see* Korea, South
South Korean heritage initiatives, organizations: Cultural Heritage Conservation Science Center 141; National Intangible Heritage Center 36, 141, 147; National Research Institute of Cultural Heritage 141; National Research Institute of Maritime Cultural Heritage 141; National Trust of Korea 136, 141; Green Climate Trust Fund 141
Soviet era, Soviet cultural influences *see* USSR
Spain: Burgos cathedral 340; Santiago de Compostela pilgrimage route 530
sprawl *see* urbanization
Sri Lanka 2, 19, 27, 59, 175, 192, 352–4, 399–419, 427, 455, 471, 494–5; Antiquities Ordinance of 1940 (amended 1998) 403–4, 410; Anuradhapura 352, 399–403, 405; Colombo 354, 401, 404, 410; Cultural Triangle of the South Plan 413–4; Dambegoda Buddhas 403; Dambulla 2, 352, 399, 405–7; Dambulla Management Plan 406; Gal Vihara Buddhas 403; Galle 399, 401, 410–15, 494; Galle fort 148, 404, 412–14; Galle Heritage Site Management Plan 412–3; Gampola kingdom 401; Government agencies for heritage protection 402–4, 407, 412, 415; Housing and Town Improvement Ordinance (1915) 404; Jaffna Dutch fort 413; Kandy 399–402, 405, 409, 415; planning, Kandy 409–10; Kirivehera stupa 403; Maligawela Buddhas 403; Malwana fort 404; Mirisawetiya stupa 399, 402–3, 405; Nuwara Eliya 413; Painting, Conservation & Research Center 407; Paranavitana, P.L. 403; Paranavithana, Senarath 6, 352; Polonnaruwa kingdom 401; Sigirya 2, 399, 402, 405–9, 415; Sigirya Regional Plan 409; Silva, Roland 404–5; Sri Dalada Maligawa/Temple of the Tooth 401, 409–11; Town and Country Planning Ordinance (1946, amended) 404, 409; Urban Development Act (1978) 404; Yatala stupa 403; *see also* Ceylon
Sri Lankan heritage organizations and initiatives: Association of Heritage Building Owners (Kandy) 410; Central Cultural Fund (Sri Lanka) 405–7, 410, 415; Archaeological Impact Assessment survey 404, 412; Cultural Triangle Project 352–3, 404–7; Galle Heritage Foundation 412–3; Sigirya Heritage Foundation 409; Sri Lankan-Netherlands Cultural Cooperation Program 413
Stalinist era architecture *see* USSR
Starr, S. Frederick 536
Stevens, Frederick William 357
Stewart, Rory 507
stone, masonry, conservation of 81, 169, 475; lime mortar use 191, 371, 375, 387; problematic cleaning methods 171, 214, 365–6
Stone, Edward Durell 359
Stovel, Herb 22
Subak system 280, 324–5
Sufi religion 430, 526, 528; Dehlavi, Hazrat Amir Khusrau 375
surveys, heritage *see* inventories, surveys
sustainability of heritage sites 81, 113, 141, 264, 353, 407, 453, 539: Iroquois 7th generation rule 288; shophouse architecture 288–9; UNESCO

sustainability policy 264; *see also* Climate change and Cultural Heritage in South Asia, 454–6
Sweden 214
Switzerland 508; Helvetas 473, 476; Swiss Banteay Srei Conservation project 214; Swiss Federal Institute of Technology 109
synagogues: Ohel Rachel 93; Paradesi synagogue 383–4
Syria 172, 207, 499, 515

Taiwan 33–7, 123–32, 137, 167; Alishan Mountain and Old Mountain Line Railways 127; Chinkuashih 125; Cultural Heritage Act (updated 2002) 126; Fort Santo Domingo 127; Government agencies for heritage protection 125–6, 128, 130; Kinmen Island 125; Kishu An 124; Law for the Preservation of Ancient Objects (1909) 126; Lukang 128; Measures for the Protection of Ancient Sites (1909) 126; National Palace Museum 35–6, 125; Orchid Island 130–1; Peinan Culture Site 125; Tainan 125
Tajikistan 497–9, 523–41; Ajina Tepa 533; Government agencies for heritage protection 531–3; Hissar 532; Institute of Innovation Technology and Communication 533; List of Properties of National Significance 531; National Museum of Antiquities 533; Penjikent/ Sogdiana 497–8, 532; Sarazm 532–3; Sarazm Management Plan 533; Tajik Academy of Sciences 532
Taoism 137, 169, 279
Taylor, Ken 266–8
technology 18, 212; cameras, photogrammetry 161, 212, 219–20, 402, 535; Computer Aided Design (CAD) 217–8, 220; CyArk 222; digital documentation 18, 161, 171, 218–22, 373; Geographic Information Survey mapping (GIS) 214, 221, 260, 263; Greater Angkor Project (GAP) 217; global positioning system (GPS) 107, 214, 373; laser scanning 158, 535; LIDAR light detection and ranging technique 171, 216–7, 220; NASA radar imaging 171, 216
Thailand 3, 6, 8, 10, 16, 18, 20–1, 169–71, 189, 195, 201, 204, 225, 231–46, 251, 275, 400, 455; Act on Monuments, Antiquities, Objects of Art and National Museums 238; Amerinda Winitchai Hall 245; Asiatique development 148; Ayutthaya 15, 233, 235–6, 238, 240–1, 455; Bangkok 3, 169, 231, 234–5, 240–5; Bangkok Fourth National Social and Economic Development Plan 243; Chakri dynasty 6, 231, 235; Chiang Mai 147– 171, 231, 242; Chiang Rai 231, 242; Conservation Act of 1934 238; Government agencies for heritage protection 170, 237–8, 243–4; King Jayavarman II 201; King Jayavarman VII 201, 204; King Rama III/King Nangklao 235; King Rama IV/King Mongkut 235; King Rama V/King Chulalongkorn 235; King Rama VI/King Maha Vajiravudh 236–7; King Rama VII/King Prajadhipok 237; King Suryavarman I 202; Krung Rattanakosin 243; national identity, importance of 169–70, 173, 235–6; National Register 238; Old Customs House 242; Pattaya 231; Petchaburi 233; Phuket 231, 233–4; Prapaspipithapan Hall 235; Queen Sirikit 246; Royal Proclamation of 1854 235; Sukhothai 170, 233, 238–9, 400; planning in Sukhothai 239

Thai heritage organizations and initiatives: Antiquarian Society 236; Association of Siamese Architects 244; Krom Silpakorn 170, 237, 275, 455; Siam Society 8, 236, 244; Siamese Heritage Trust 244
Thapar, B.K. 370
theft *see* looting
Tibet 3, 37, 101–5, 153, 351, 470–1, 486; Alexander, André 102; Arniko highway 104; Drathang temple 102; Drongkher temple 102; Gongkar 102; Jokhang Temple monastery 102; Kham Aid Foundation 102; Lhasa 101–2; Norbulinka palace 102; Namseling Manor 102; Potala Palace 102–4; Shalu 102; Shalu Association 102; Tholing monastery 102–4; Tibet Heritage Fund 102; Vitali, Roberto 102; Yemar 102
Timor-Leste *see* East Timor
Timurid cultural influences 497, 511, 526, 536–8
tombs, mausolea *see* country listings
tourism: as an economic generator: 91, 99–100, 142, 178, 189, 214, 231, 238, 275, 283, 285–7, 313, 322, 409; eco-tourism (Borneo) 297–9; handicraft support by (Nepal) 481–5; importance of architecture to, 286–9; tourist pollution 13, 15, 196, 268, 275, 365, 409; facilitated by transit ease 6, 24, 239, 322, 352, 381–2, 454; monetizing sites 16, 128, 148, 157, 170–1, 178, 184, 366, 409, 413; Singaporean Tourism Task Force study 286–9
tourism campaigns, planning: Cultural Restoration Tourism project (Mongolia) 155; Indonesia Heritage decade/year 325; South Asia Tourism Infrastructure Development Project 462; Tourism Management Plan (Angkor, Cambodia) 12, 213; Tourism Development Strategy (Sri Lanka) 409; Tourism Product Development Plan (Singapore) 287; WTO Silk Road program 547; *Visit Malaysia* program 297; *Visit Myanmar* year 179; *see also* Seoul Declaration in Charters, Conventions, Declarations and Principles
townscapes support organizations: Association of Heritage Building Owners (Kandy, Sri Lanka) 410; Association for the Township Preservation/ Zenkoku Machinami Hozon Renmei (Japan) 35, 56
trade routes 2–3, 33, 167, 201, 279, 283, 337, 351, 354, 358, 385, 399–400, 416, 450, 526, 529–31, 533
traditional construction techniques *see* construction techniques, traditional
trafficking *see* looting
training *see* capacity building; crafts, crafts training; education
transportation as a threat to heritage 36, 68, 84, 184, 193, 231, 325, 353, 364, 412, 441; Beijing destruction 86; Hampi bridge 379; Karakoram highway 15; Mountain Railway (India) 384; Samarkand issues 539; Seoul-Pusan train route 142; Taj Mahal issues 364–6
tsunami 13, 36, 59–60, 281, 399, 401, 405, 410, 415 *see also* water as a threat
tube houses 288
Turkmenistan 497, 523–41; Amu Darya/Oxus River valley 534; Anau 534; Askabad 499; Gonur Depe 534; Government agencies for heritage protection 534; Kunya Urgench 534–5; Margush/Margiana 534; Merv 24, 497, 499, 523–4, 534, 541; Merv

Master Plan 535; Nisa 499, 523, 534; Ulug Depe 534
Tung, Anthony 85, 88
typhoon 56, 281, 341, 353; *see also* water as a threat

uma lulik 327–8
underwater heritage *see* maritime and coastal heritage
UNESCO (United Nations Educational, Scientific and Cultural Organization) 10, 12, 18–9, 22, 24, 85, 155, 170–1, 177–8, 184, 192–3, 204, 207–8, 214–16, 238, 253, 319, 354, 460, 469, 473, 486–8, 498–9, 503–8, 526, 529
UNESCO charters, conventions, declarations *see* Charters, Conventions, Declarations and Principles
UNESCO heritage organizations and initiatives relevant to the region: Action Plan for the Implementation of the World Heritage Convention in Central Asia 530–1; Asia/Pacific Award for Cultural Heritage Conservation 7, 16–17, 22, 142, 147–8, 232–3, 275, 381, 413, 511, 528; Asia/Pacific Cultural Centre 10; Asian Academy for Heritage Management 22; *Building Conservation in Nepal: A Handbook* 483; Funds in Trust 36, 55, 58, 498; Global Strategy for a Balanced, Credible and Representative World Heritage List 12; Intangible Cultural Heritage Register 10; Integral Study of the Silk Roads: Roads of Dialogue 529; International Assistance and Intangible Cultural Heritage Fund 56; International Safeguarding Campaign (for Mohenjo Daro) 352; 428; 439–41; Memories of the World Register/Memory of the World Programme 10; New Design in Heritage Contexts award 148–9; Organization of World Heritage Cities 10; Silk Road Online Platform 547; Sri Lankan Working Group 405; Training Workshops in Persian, Mughal and Timurid Architecture 547
UNESCO regional presence: UNESCO Bangkok 7, 196, 244, 275, 347, 413; UNESCO Jakarta 328; UNESCO Kathmandu 481; UNESCO Sri Lanka 407; UNESCO Tokyo 10; UNESCO Vietnam 269
unexploded ordnance, risk to heritage 170, 196, 511, 514
United Kingdom 502; English Heritage 244; National Trust 141, 244, 370; *see also* Colonial period – British and British Raj
UN (United Nations) 11, 60, 482; Brundtland Report: *Our Common Future: Report on the UN World Commission on the Environment 288;* Intergovernmental Panel on Climate Change 454; UN Conference on Climate Change 416; UN report, *Climate Change 2014: Impacts, Adaptation and Vulnerability* 454
USA (United States of America) 3, 83, 172, 190, 193, 253, 279, 354, 357, 484, 498, 515, 534, 541; Baltimore 148; Boston 148; Christie's 206; Cleveland Museum 206; Denver Museum 206; Metropolitan Museum of Art 206; National Park Service 507; New York City 94, 337, 377; Nimitz Museum (USA) 343; Pearl Harbor 342; San Antonio, Paseo del Rio 292; Sotheby's 206; World War II Museum (New Orleans USA) 343; *see also* Colonial period – USA; American heritage organizations and initiatives: Ambassador's Fund for Cultural Preservation 240; Ford Foundation 380; J. Paul Getty Trust 8; Getty Conservation Institute 7, 19, 22, 36, 83, 172, 195, 370, 530; Global Heritage Fund 8, 11, 184, 195; National Trust for Historic Preservation 370; *Secretary of the Interior's Standards for Rehabilitation* 83, 484; Smithsonian Institute 489
urban issues (general) 7, 12–3, 28, 172, 281, 289, 352, 355, 372, 428, 495; in China 79–80, 84–101, 109–110; in India 372; League of Historical Cities 10; in Sri Lanka 407–9; in Thailand 242–3; in Vietnam 171; Zenkoku Machinami Hozon Renmei/Association for the Township Preservation (Japan) 35, 52, 56
urban landscape: Historic Urban Landscape (HUL) approach 5, 85, 266–7, 381; Vienna memorandum 266–8
urban revitalization: Bukhara 538; Mumbai 377; Shaxi 109; Singapore Urban Redevelopment Authority 283, 288–9, 291–2; World Bank Lahore Urban Development project 436; Xintiandi project 92
urban-rural integration 110
USSR (Union of Soviet Socialist Republics) 3, 214, 498; communism 91, 153, 158; Siberia 158; Soviet architecture 536; Soviet era conservation methodology as a threat to heritage 498, 524–6, 531–41; Soviet era secularism as threat to heritage 525, 528; Soviet era isolation, effect on Central Asian heritage conservation 524, 531
Uzbekistan 497, 523–41; Babur 3, 429, 502, 510–12; Baha al-Din Naqshband mausoleum 526; Bibi Khanum mosque 498, 525, 536–9; Bukhara 497, 499, 524–5, 536–40; Government agencies for heritage protection 537–8; Gur-i-Emir 538; Khiva 523, 526, 537; International Caravanserai of Culture/Center for the tudy of the Silk Road 9; Itchan Kala 536–7; legal protection of archaeological sites (2009) 537; legislative weakness 539; Madrasa Nadir Divangebi 537; Master Plan 537–9; Restoration Institute of Uzbekistan 537; Samarkand 373, 498–9, 523–4, 526, 536–8; Shakhrisyabz 536; Tashkent 536; Uzbek Law on the Preservation and Utilization of Objects of Cultural Heritage (2001) 537

values-based approach for heritage conservation 17, 83; *see also* China Principles 8, 19, 25–6, 36, 46, 68, 81–2, 84, 137, 171, 240; *see also* cultural importance
vandalism: Ajanta, Ellora caves 362; Namdaemun Gate (South Korea) 143–5; Paharpur (Bangladesh) 460
Venice Charter (International Charter for the Conservation and Restoration of Monuments and Sites) *see* Charters, Conventions, Declarations and Principles
vernacular architecture: ger/khoroos 34, 163–4; hanoks 36, 136, 142; haveli 358–9, 378; hutong 36–7, 87, 142, 146; longhouses 280–299; shophouses 2, 109, 171, 190, 223, 261, 280, 285, 288–9; tube houses 262, 288; *uma lulik* 327–8
Vienna Memorandum on World Heritage and Contemporary Architecture – Managing the Historic Urban Landscape *see* Charters, Conventions, Declarations and Principles
Vietnam 1, 3, 6, 15, 19, 23, 58, 169–71, 189–90, 195, 201, 207, 244, 251, 270, 288, 400, 455; Bang An National Museum of Vietnamese History/Musée Albert Finot 252; Bao Đai 258; Dalat 148; Decree

on the Management, Classification and Methods to Organize the Protection and Restoration of Historical and Cultural Monuments (1957) 19; *Đổi mới* 262; Dourmer, Paul 261; German Conservation, Restoration and Education Project 258; Gia Long 258; Government agencies for heritage protection 254, 262; Hanoi 13, 169–71, 251, 253, 255–8, 261–3, 266, 288; Hanoi master planning 252, 254–5, 261; *Hanoi 2010: Heritage and Cultural Identity* 263; Hội An 18, 24, 171, 253–8, 260, 266–7, 455; Hue 170–1, 251, 253–4, 256–8, 260; Hue Conservation Center 256; Law on Cultural Heritage (No. 28/2001/QH10of 29 June 2001) 254; Le, Kha Phieu 254; legislation regarding maintenance of royal properties (medieval) 255; Maison Centrale/Hỏa Lò Prison 263, 265; Minh Mang tombs 254, 258; Museum of Cham Sculpture 253; Mỹ Sơn 8, 10, 24, 170, 252–3, 256–8, 260; Mỹ Sơn Master Plan 260; National Center for Monument Conservation 21; national inventory 254; Ordinance on the Protection of Historical Cultural Relics and Scenic Sites (1984) 254; Po Nagar 252; Saigon/Ho Chi Minh City 169, 251, 254–5; Temple of Literature 154, 263

Viollet-le-Duc, Eugène-Emmanuel 83

visitor issues *see* tourism

Vitruvius 219

volcanoes 13, 33, 279, 281, 318, 330 *see also* environmental and natural threats

wabi-sabi 34, 45 *see also* Patina, Authenticity

wall painting *see* frescos, murals, wall painting

war, conflict, invasion 2– 3, 12, 18, 27, 167, 190; American War/Vietnam War (1954–1975) 3, 19, 21, 170, 196–7, 201, 252, 254–5, 258, 260, 275; Anglo-Afghan wars 502; Bangladesh Liberation War 431, 450; Cambodian civil war (1975–1979) 170–1, 203; Communist Revolution (China) 34, 71, 78, 91; Cultural Revolution (China) 15, 37, 68, 78–80, 91, 101, 112, 123; First Indochina War (1946–1954) 19, 252; Indo-Pakistani Wars (1947, 1965, 1999) 431; Japanese occupation of Korean peninsula (1910–1945) 35, 135–6; Japanese occupation of Thailand (1940s) 238; Korean War (1950–1953) 3, 35, 135–6, 140; Mongol invasions (1200s) 74, 78, 358; Sepoy Mutiny/First War of Independence (1857) (India) 27, 359, 361; Soviet-Afghan conflict 129, 497–8; Sri Lankan civil war 352, 399, 409–10; *warchitecture* 197; World War II 3, 12, 34, 39, 49–51, 125, 128, 140, 171, 176, 180, 209, 231, 252, 254, 279–80, 285, 319, 330, 336–8, 342–3

Warrack, Simon 22

water as a threat 179, 318, 498; flooding 13, 353, 427, 434, 471; at Ayutthaya 240; in Bangladesh 449–53, 458, 462; at Borobodur 318–20; at Mỹ Sơn 260; at Mohenjo Daro 428–440; in Sri Lanka 401, 412

water, hydraulic management 169, 341, 381, 526; Angkor's hydrological system 2, 204–8; at Ayutthaya 14, 240–2; Jaisalmer sanitation 385; Herat sanitation 51; hydraulics at Shalamar Gardens 436–7; at Sigirya 2, 407–8; Balinese *Subak* system 280, 324–5; Thai water issues 240

water villages 311, 348

waterfront development: Asiatique, Bangkok 148; Bandar seri Begawan 280, 311, 348; Hongcun 112; Riverside quays, Singapore 292–3

weather as a threat to built heritage *see* environmental and natural threats

Western New Guinea/Papua *see* Indonesia

Winter, Tim 88

wood, woodcarvers 33, 35, 109, 113, 142, 169; in Afghanistan 507; in Bhutan 469–75; in Nepal 481–9; *shilpkars* in India 388

workshops *see* crafts, crafts training, capacity building

World Bank 10–11, 59, 85, 325, 436, 454–5, 473, 505, 515; International Development Agency (IDA) 10; International Bank for Reconstruction and Development (IBRD) 10, 11; Lahore Urban Development Project 436; Poverty Social Impact Analysis (Bhutan) 473; Punjab Municipal Services Improvement Project 436

World Heritage Convention 11, 15, 25–6, 68, 139, 213, 352, 354, 399, 415, 481, 498 *see also* UNESCO

World Heritage in Danger *see* endangered sites

World Heritage list 5, 11, 25, 27, 34, 39, 81, 98, 107, 112, 139, 154, 159, 191, 201, 213, 225, 239–40, 244, 258, 260, 302, 304, 329, 339, 354, 357, 364, 375, 384–5, 399, 407, 409–12, 430, 433–4, 436, 440, 455, 460, 483–4, 491, 508–9, 515, 529–30, 534, 537

World Heritage tentative list 5, 130–1, 139, 184, 196, 419, 451, 529, 530–1

WHITRAP (World Heritage Institute of Training) 10, 22, 37

World Heritage Convention (Convention concerning protection of the World Cultural and Natural World Heritage sites *see* Charters, Conventions, Declarations and Principles

World Monuments Fund 7, 11, 18–19, 49, 90, 102, 160, 162, 170–1, 214–16, 240, 254, 258–9, 263, 268, 303, 374–5, 380, 385, 387, 428, 473–4, 484, 489; Knoll Modernism Prize 56; Robert W. Wilson Challenge Grant 109; Watch List of Endangered Sites 49, 107, 109, 161, 240, 268, 303, 451, 473, 534

Wright, Frank Lloyd 56–7

WWF (World Wide Fund for Nature) 329

Xi'an Declaration on the Conservation of the Setting of Heritage Structures, Sites and Areas *see* Charters, Conventions, Declarations and Principles

Yemen 499

Yin and yang *see* Natural forces, harmony with

youth: INTACH First Student Heritage Club, 371

Zetter, R. 266

Zoroastrian civilization, sites 501, 529, 534

For Product Safety Concerns and Information please contact our EU
representative GPSR@taylorandfrancis.com
Taylor & Francis Verlag GmbH, Kaufingerstraße 24, 80331 München, Germany

www.ingramcontent.com/pod-product-compliance
Lightning Source LLC
Chambersburg PA
CBHW080849010526
44116CB00012B/2088